Occupational Outlook Handbook

1998-99 Edition

U.S. Department of Labor
Alexis M. Herman, Secretary

Bureau of Labor Statistics
Katharine G. Abraham, Commissioner

Bulletin 2500

A sampling of JIST's career-related materials are included in the back of this book. Please look there for ordering information and other details. Other JIST-published occupational reference books include:

- *The O*NET Dictionary of Occupational Titles* (new in 1998)
- *The Enhanced Guide for Occupational Exploration*
- *The Complete Guide for Occupational Exploration*
- *The Dictionary of Occupational Titles* (the new "classic" 1991 edition)
- *The Occupational Outlook Handbook*
- *The Young Person's Occupational Outlook Handbook*
- *The Enhanced Occupational Outlook Handbook*
- *Franchise Opportunities Handbook*
- *Luddens' Adult Guide to Colleges and Universities*
- *America's Top Jobs for People Without College Degrees*
- *America's Top Jobs for College Graduates*
- *America's Top 300 Jobs*
- *America's Top Resumes for America's Top Jobs*
- *Gallery of Best Resumes*

Software:
- JIST's Multimedia Occupational Outlook Handbook CD-ROM
- Young Person's Electronic Occupational Outlook Handbook
- JIST's Electronic Enhanced Dictionary of Occupational Titles
- JIST's Career Explorer CD-ROM
- Mike Farr's Get a Job Workshop on CD-ROM

Other Career Materials Published by JIST

Several pages at the back of this book present some of our many career-related products. Please look there for additional resource materials and for ordering information.

Additional Information on JIST

JIST has published information about careers and job search since the 1970s. Experienced career professionals think of us as the best source for information on occupations, including "hard core" occupational reference books. But that's not all we do! JIST sells hundreds of other books, videos, assessment devices, and software.

Quantity Discounts—Discounts are available for multiple copies of this and other books. Please call the JIST sales staff weekdays at 1-800-648-5478 for details.

Internet Site—Visit our web site at *www.jist.com* to find out about other JIST products, get free book chapters, and link to other career-related sites. You can also learn more about our authors and JIST training available to professionals. We even have damaged or discontinued books available at 50-90% off list price.

Free Professional/Institutional Catalog—JIST has the most comprehensive catalog of its kind, presenting hundreds of products on career, job search, self-help, and business topics published by JIST and other publishers. Please mail or fax your request on your organization's letterhead.

Occupational Outlook Handbook, 1998-99 Edition
© 1998
JIST Works, Inc.
720 North Park Avenue
Indianapolis, IN 46202-3431

Orders: 1-800-648-5478
Fax: 1-317-264-3709
E-mail: JISTWorks@aol.com
Internet site: www.JIST.com

Printed in the United States of America

ISBN 1-56370-464-1 Softcover   ISBN 1-56370-475-7 Hardcover

Published by JIST, this book is a complete reprint of the entire contents of the *Occupational Outlook Handbook,* as produced by our friends at the U.S. Department of Labor.

Message from the Secretary

Equipping every working American with the skills to find and hold a good job is one of the Department of Labor's primary goals. Rapid technological advances, growing foreign competition, and changing business practices are the challenges confronting the jobs of the future. These challenges will demand a highly skilled American workforce that can quickly adapt to a changing workplace.

The *Occupational Outlook Handbook*, the Government's premier career guidance publication, provides essential information about prospective changes in the world of work and the qualifications that will be needed by tomorrow's workers.

ALEXIS M. HERMAN

Foreword

For more than 50 years, the Bureau's *Occupational Outlook Handbook* has been a nationally recognized source of career information. Revised every two years, the *Handbook* describes what workers do on the job, working conditions, the training and education needed, earnings, and expected job prospects in a wide range of occupations. Employment in the approximately 250 occupations covered in the 1998-99 *Handbook* accounts for about 6 out of every 7 jobs in the economy. The occupational information presented in this new edition should provide valuable assistance to individuals making decisions about their future work lives.

KATHARINE G. ABRAHAM
Commissioner
Bureau of Labor Statistics

Acknowledgments

The *Handbook* was produced in the Bureau of Labor Statistics under the general guidance and direction of Neal H. Rosenthal, Associate Commissioner for Employment Projections. Mike Pilot, Chief, Division of Occupational Outlook, and Alan Eck, Manager, Occupational Outlook Studies, were responsible for planning and day-to-day direction.

Supervisors overseeing the research and preparation of material were Douglas Braddock, Chester C. Levine, and Jon Q. Sargent. Team leaders who monitored the work of occupational analysts and contributed material were Thomas A. Amirault, Theresa Cosca, and Kristina Shelley. Occupational analysts who contributed material were Megan Barkume, Verada P. Bluford, Hall Dillon, Geof Gradler, Jeffrey C. Gruenert, Jonathan Kelinson, R. Sean Kirby, Richard Melchionno, Mark Mittelhauser, Kurt Schrammel, Gary Steinberg, Michael Steinman, Carolyn M. Veneri, and Drew A. Warwick.

Word processing support was handled by Beverly A. Williams.

Note

A great many trade associations, professional societies, unions, industrial organizations, and government agencies provide career information that is valuable to counselors and jobseekers. For the convenience of *Handbook* users, some of these organizations and, in some cases, their homepage addresses on the Internet, are listed at the end of each occupational statement. Although these references were carefully compiled, the Bureau of Labor Statistics has neither authority nor facilities for investigating the organizations or the information or publications that may be sent in response to a request and cannot guarantee the accuracy of such information. The listing of an organization, therefore, does not constitute in any way an endorsement or recommendation by the Bureau either of the organization and its activities or of the information it may supply. Each organization has sole responsibility for whatever information it may issue.

The occupational information contained in the *Handbook* presents a general, composite description of jobs and cannot be expected to reflect work situations in specific establishments or localities. The *Handbook*, therefore, is not intended and should not be used as a guide for determining wages, hours, the right of a particular union to represent workers, appropriate bargaining units, or formal job evaluation systems. Nor should earnings data in the *Handbook* be used to compute future loss of earnings in adjudication proceedings involving work injuries or accidental deaths.

Material in this publication is in the public domain and, with appropriate credit, may be reproduced without permission. Comments about the contents of this publication and suggestions for improving it are welcome. Please address them to Chief, Division of Occupational Outlook, Bureau of Labor Statistics, U.S. Department of Labor, Washington, DC 20212.

Photograph Credits

The Bureau of Labor Statistics wishes to express its appreciation for the cooperation and assistance of the many government and private sources—listed below—that either contributed photographs or made their facilities available to photographers working under contract to the U.S. Department of Labor. Photographs may not be free of every possible safety or health hazard. Depiction of company or trade name in no way constitutes endorsement by the Department of Labor.

Allen-Mitchell Company, Machine Shop; Amaco Petroleum Products, Yorktown, Virginia Refinery; American Red Cross Blood Bank, Baltimore, Maryland; American University; Amtrak; Animal Disease Laboratory of the State of Illinois in Galesburg, Illinois; Appalachian Spring; Audio-Phone of Washington, DC; Baltimore Specialty Steels; Baltimore Homesteading Program; Brown's Arlington Honda; Burling and Northern Railroad, Galesburg, Illinois; Carlotta Joyner; City Paper of Washington, DC; Craddock-Terry, Inc., Farmville Plant; Cumberland Memorial Hospital; Dance Place, Washington, DC; Day's Inn, Keene, New Hampshire; D.C. Vending Company, Inc.; Department of State, Bureau of Diplomatic Security; District of Columbia Fire and Emergency Medical Service Department; D.L. Boyd, Hyattsville, Maryland; Dr. Bruce L. Lazerow, Sears Optical; Dr. David Walls-Kaufman, Capitol Hill Chiropractic Center; Dulles International Airport; Eddie Mercer, Inc.; Eric Margry Jewelry; Family Therapy Practice Center; Federal City Papers; Fern Hunt, Computing and Applied Mathematics Laboratory, NIST; Firefighting Department of Landover, Maryland; Fontana Affiliated Graphics, Inc.; General Accounting Office; George Hyman Construction Company; George Meany Labor Studies Center and Archives; George Washington University Hospital and Medical Library; Gerald A. Lipps, D.D.S., P.A.; Giant Food Stores; Gighi's African Fashions and Textile Gallery; Goddard Space Flight Center; H. & H. Bindery, Hyattsville, Maryland; H & R Block, Fort Washington Office; Herb Gordon Dodge, Silver Spring, Maryland; Howard University, Department of Geology; Hurly Company; Industrial Photo of Silver Spring; Institute of Textile Technology; Iona House; Johns Hopkins Hospital, Clinical Engineering Services; Jolles Brothers, Inc.; Joseph Passonneau, FAIA, ASCE; Karla Westjohn, Attorney; Kevin Hassett, State Farm Agent; Kim Roberts; La Parisien Furs, Washington, DC; La Pierre and Company Design Studio; Lee Lawrence; Legg, Mason, Wood, Walker, Inc.; Lewes-Cape May Ferry; Mar, Inc., Naval Engineering Group; Marc Rubenstein, Advanced Tool and Machine Service of Washington, DC; Maryann Honakar, D.D.S.; Medical Records Corporation; Mid-Town Pharmacy; Midway Marine of Galesburg, Illinois; Montgomery County Library, Chevy Chase Branch; National Court Reporters Association; National Weather Service Forecast Office; Northwestern Illinois Agricultural Research and Demonstration Center; Orthotic & Prosthetic Specialties, Inc. of Laurel, Maryland; Paris London Detective Agency; Parkview Elementary School, Washington, DC; Pastor Laureen E. Smith, Western Presbyterian Church; Pierce Associates, Alexandria, Virginia; Population Reference Bureau, Inc.; Port of Longview, Washington; Port of Portland, Oregon; Port of Seattle, Washington; Potomac Electric Power Company; Professor Therese Hein; Providence Opticians; Quad Cities Nuclear Power Plant; Rapp Funeral Home, Silver Spring, Maryland; Riggs National Bank of Washington, DC; Rock Terrace High School, Montgomery County, Maryland; Rolf Jensen Associates; SAIC; Sandy Springs School, Sandy Springs, Maryland; Seely Pine Furniture, Berkeley Springs, West Virginia; Sheraton Washington Hotel; Society for Technical Communication; Southern States Cooperative, Lothan, Maryland Grain Elevator; State Farm Insurance Agency; St. Martin's Catholic Church; Strasburger & Siegel, Inc.; Strauss Technical Photo; Suburban Dental Laboratories, Inc., Rockville, Maryland; Susan Pearcy, Visual Artist; Theophus Brooks Upholstery; Travel Bound; United Airlines, Dulles Airport Facility; University of Maryland, Electrical Engineering Department; Urban Institute of Washington, DC; U.S. Air Force; U.S. Army; U.S. Coast Guard; U.S. Marine Corps; U.S. Navy; U.S. Post Office; USG, Inc. Utilities of Lancaster, Pennsylvania; Violin House of Weaver, Bethesda, Maryland; Walter Reed Army Hospital, Washington, DC; Washington Area Metropolitan Transit Authority; Washington Park Zoo, Portland, Oregon; Washington Times; WETA; Whitman-Walker Clinic, Inc. of Washington, DC; Working Images Photographs, Martha Tabor; Wyatt Company.

Contents

Special Features

Occupational Coverage

Executive, Administrative, and Managerial Occupations

Professional and Technical Occupations

Air transportation-related occupations

Engineers and engineering technicians

Architects, surveyors, and drafters

Computer, mathematical, and operations research occupations

Scientists and science technicians
Life scientists

Physical scientists

Legal occupations

Social scientists

Social and recreation workers

Teachers, counselors, and library occupations

Additional Information About the 1996-2006 Projections

Readers interested in more information about projections and details on the labor force, economic growth, industry and occupational employment, or methods and assumptions should consult the November 1997 *Monthly Labor Review*; *Employment Outlook: 1996-2006*, BLS Bulletin 2502; or the Winter 1997-98 *Occupational Outlook Quarterly*. Information on the limitations inherent in economic projections also can be found in these publications.

For more information about employment change, job openings, earnings, unemployment rates, and training requirements by occupation, consult *Occupational Projections and Training Data, 1998 Edition*, BLS Bulletin 2501.

For occupational information from an industry perspective including some occupations and career paths that the *Occupational Outlook Handbook* does not cover, consult the *1998-99 Career Guide to Industries*, BLS Bulletin 2503.

Tomorrow's Jobs

Making informed career decisions requires reliable information about opportunities in the future. Opportunities result from the relationships between the population, labor force, and the demand for goods and services.

Population ultimately limits the size of the labor force—individuals working or looking for work—which constrains how much can be produced. Demand for various goods and services determines employment in the industries providing them. Occupational employment opportunities, in turn, result from skills needed within specific industries. Opportunities for registered nurses and other health-related specialists, for example, have surged in response to the rapid growth in demand for health services.

Examining the past and anticipating changes in these relationships are the foundation of the Occupational Outlook Program. This chapter presents highlights of Bureau of Labor Statistics projections of the labor force and occupational and industry employment that can help guide your career plans. Sources of detailed information about the projections appear on the preceding page.

The labor force will grow more slowly.

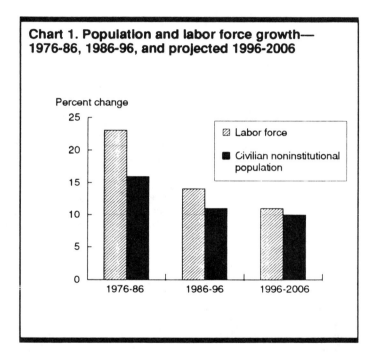

Chart 1. Population and labor force growth— 1976-86, 1986-96, and projected 1996-2006

The labor force will become increasingly diverse.

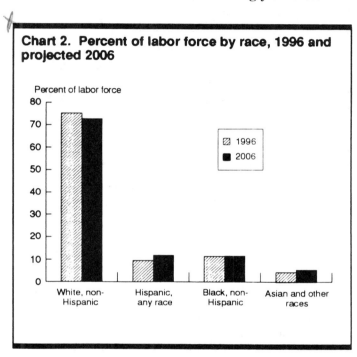

Chart 2. Percent of labor force by race, 1996 and projected 2006

- The Bureau of Labor Statistics (BLS) projects that the labor force will grow to 14.9 million between 1996 and 2006. This is 1.2 million less than the previous 10 years reflecting a slower growth in the civilian noninstitutional population 16 years of age and older. Growth was much faster from 1976 to 1986, when the baby boomers were entering the labor force.

- The labor force will grow 11 percent between 1996 and 2006, slightly slower than during the 1986-96 period but only half the rate of growth during the 1976-86 period.

- As a result of an increase in the percentage of the population working or looking for work, the labor force will continue to grow faster than the population rate.

- Between 1996 and 2006, employment will increase by 18.6 million or 14 percent. This is slower than during the 1986-96 period, when the economy added 21 million jobs.

- Wage and salary worker employment will account for 94 percent of this increase. In addition, the number of self-employed workers is expected to increase to 11.6 million in 2006, while the number of unpaid family workers will decline.

- The labor force growth of Hispanics, Asians and other races, will be faster than for blacks and white non-Hispanics. The projected labor force growth of these ethnic groups stems primarily from immigration.

- Despite relatively slow growth, white non-Hispanics will have the largest numerical growth between 1996 and 2006.

- Between 1996 and 2006, women's share of the labor force is projected to slowly increase from 46 to 47 percent, continuing a pattern since 1976. The participation rate for women will continue to increase for those 20- to 65-years old.

- The number of men in the labor force will grow at a slower rate than in the past, in part reflecting declining employment in well-paid production jobs in manufacturing, and a continued shift in demand for workers from the goods-producing sector to the service-producing sector. Participation rates for men will decline for all age groups below age 45 except for 16-19; the rates for those 16-19 will remain steady at 53 percent. Rates for age groups 45 and above will increase.

The labor force will become older.

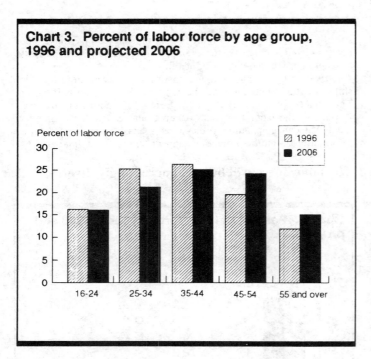

Chart 3. Percent of labor force by age group, 1996 and projected 2006

Percent of labor force

☑ 1996
■ 2006

16-24   25-34   35-44   45-54   55 and over

- Workers over age 45 will account for a larger share of the labor force as the baby-boom generation ages.
- Two age groups with large numbers of baby boomers will grow by more than 30 percent—people 45 to 54 and those 55 to 64. Only the trailing edge of the baby boomers, those born from 1962 to 1964, will be younger than 45 in 2006.
- The very large group of workers aged 35 to 44, which is about one-fourth of the labor force, will change hardly at all during the period. The 25- to 34-year old group will decline by 3.0 million, a result of falling birth rates in the late 1960's. Those 16 to 24 will increase by more than 3.0 million, making this group the largest it has been in 25 years.

Industry employment growth is projected to be highly concentrated in service-producing industries.

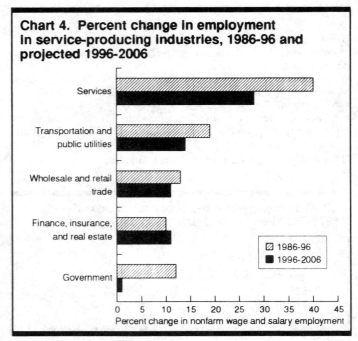

Chart 4. Percent change in employment in service-producing industries, 1986-96 and projected 1996-2006

Services

Transportation and public utilities

Wholesale and retail trade

Finance, insurance, and real estate

Government

☑ 1986-96
■ 1996-2006

0   5   10   15   20   25   30   35   40   45
Percent change in nonfarm wage and salary employment

- Employment in service-producing industries will increase faster than average, with growth near 30 percent. Service and retail trade industries will account for 14.8 million out of a total projected growth of 17.5 million wage and salary jobs.
- Business, health, and education services will account for 70 percent of the growth within the service industry.
- Health care services will increase 30 percent and account for 3.1 million new jobs, the largest numerical increase of any industry from 1996-2006. Factors contributing to continued growth in this industry include the aging population, which will continue to require more services, and the increased use of innovative medical technology for intensive diagnosis and treatment. Patients will increasingly be shifted out of hospitals and into outpatient facilities, nursing homes, and home health care in an attempt to contain costs.
- Educational services are projected to increase by 1.8 million jobs between 1996 and 2006. Most jobs will be for teachers, who are projected to account for 1.3 million jobs.
- Computer and data processing services will add over 1.3 million jobs from 1996-2006. The 108 percent increase is due to technological advancements and the need for higher skilled workers. The high percent increase makes this the fastest growing industry over the projection period.

Growth in goods-producing industries will be restrained by declines in manufacturing and mining.

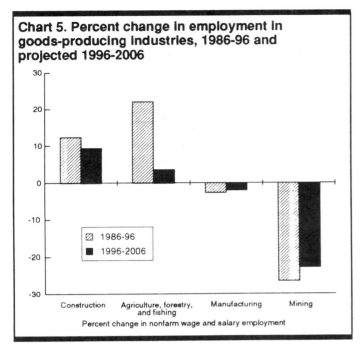

Chart 5. Percent change in employment in goods-producing industries, 1986-96 and projected 1996-2006

Percent change in nonfarm wage and salary employment

- Projected employment growth in the construction and agriculture industries will be offset by a decline in manufacturing and mining jobs. Manufacturing will account for 13 percent of total wage and salary worker employment in 2006, compared to 15 percent in 1996.

- Construction employment will grow one-fourth slower than during the previous 10-year period.

- Within the agriculture, forestry, and fishing industry, growth in agriculture services and forestry will more than offset the projected declines in crops, livestock, and livestock related products, and fishing, hunting, and trapping.

Replacement needs will account for three-fifths of the 50.6 million projected job openings between 1996 and 2006.

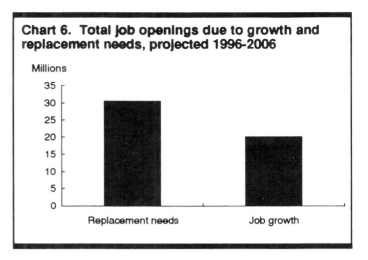

Chart 6. Total job openings due to growth and replacement needs, projected 1996-2006

- Job growth can be measured by percent change and numerical change. The fastest growing occupations do not necessarily provide the largest number of jobs. A larger occupation with slower growth may produce more openings than a smaller occupation with faster growth.

- Job opportunities are enhanced by additional openings resulting from the need to replace workers who leave the occupation. Some workers leave the occupation as they are promoted or change careers; others stop working to return to school, to assume household responsibilities, or retire.

- Replacement needs are greater in occupations with low pay and low training requirements with a high proportion of young and part-time workers.

Service and professional specialty occupations will provide about 2 out of every 5 job openings—primarily due to high replacement needs.

Of the 25 occupations with fast growth, high pay, and low unemployment that have the largest numerical growth, 18 require at least a bachelor's degree.

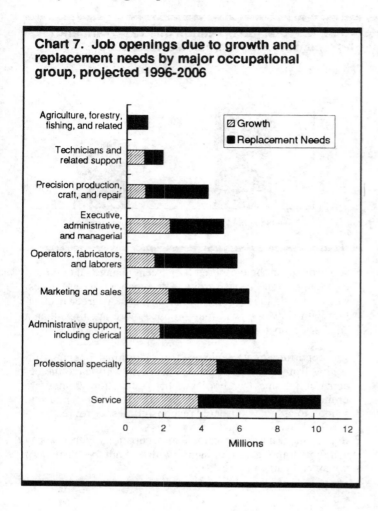

Chart 7. Job openings due to growth and replacement needs by major occupational group, projected 1996-2006

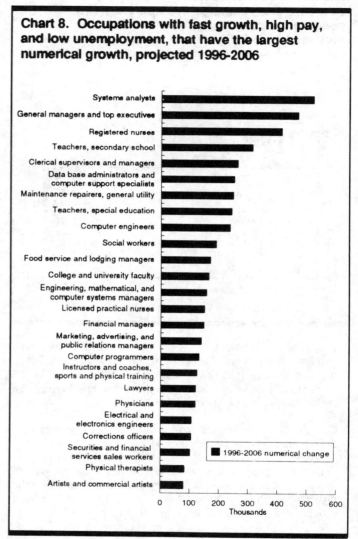

Chart 8. Occupations with fast growth, high pay, and low unemployment, that have the largest numerical growth, projected 1996-2006

- Employment in professional specialty occupations is projected to increase at a faster rate and have more job growth than any major occupational group.

- Within professional specialty occupations, computer related occupations and teachers will add 2.3 million new jobs, accounting for 15 percent of all new jobs from 1996 to 2006. Professional specialty occupations comprise the only group that will have a majority of job openings stemming from growth.

- Little or no change is expected in employment in agriculture, forestry, fishing, and related occupations. All job openings in this cluster will stem from replacement needs.

- Office automation will significantly affect many individual administrative and clerical support occupations. Overall, these occupations will increase more slowly than average, though some are projected to decline.

- Precision production, craft, and repair occupations and operators, fabricators, and laborers are projected to grow slower than average due to continuing advances in technology, changes in production methods, and overall decline in manufacturing jobs.

- These 25 occupations are somewhat concentrated, with 5 occupations in computer technology, 4 in health care, and 5 in education.

- The 25 occupations with fast growth, higher than average pay, and lower than average unemployment that have the largest numerical growth, will account for 5 million new jobs, or 27 percent of all job growth.

The fastest growing occupations reflect growth in computer technology and health care services.

Job growth varies widely by education and training requirements.

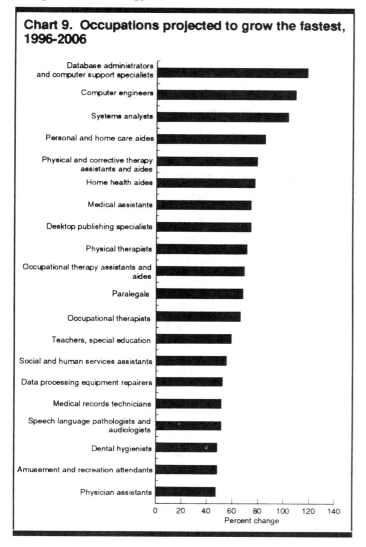

Chart 9. Occupations projected to grow the fastest, 1996-2006

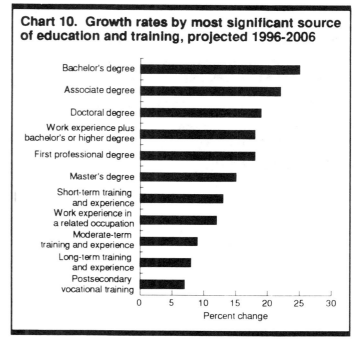

Chart 10. Growth rates by most significant source of education and training, projected 1996-2006

- Computer engineers and systems analysts jobs are expected to grow rapidly in order to satisfy expanding needs of scientific research and applications of computer technology. The three fastest growing occupations are in computer related fields.

- Many of the fastest growing occupations are concentrated in health services, which are expected to increase more than twice as fast as the whole economy. Personal and home care aides, and home health aides, will be in great demand to provide personal care for an increasing number of elderly people and for persons who are recovering from surgery and other serious health conditions. This is occurring, as hospitals and insurance companies require shorter stays for recovery to reduce costs.

- Five out of the 6 education and training categories projected to have the fastest growth require at least a bachelor's degree, and the sixth requires an associate's degree. All categories that do not require a college degree are projected to grow slower than average.

- Table 1 presents the fastest growing occupations and those having the largest numerical increase in employment over the 1996-2006 period, categorized by the level of education and training.

- Occupations usually requiring short-term on-the-job training accounted for 53.5 million jobs in 1996, more than any other education and training category. Occupations requiring a bachelor's degree or more education accounted for 22 percent of all jobs. Occupations in the four education categories not requiring postsecondary education accounted for about 70 percent of all jobs.

- Occupations that require a bachelor's degree are projected to grow the fastest, nearly twice as fast as the average for all occupations. All of the 20 occupations with the highest earnings require at least a bachelor's degree. Engineering and health occupations dominate this list.

- Education is essential in getting a high paying job. However, many occupations—for example, registered nurses, blue-collar worker supervisors, electrical and electronic technicians/technologists, automotive mechan-ics, and carpenters—do not require a college degree, yet offer higher than average earnings.

- Labor force groups with lower than average educational attainment in 1996, including Hispanics and blacks, will continue to have difficulty obtaining a share of the high paying jobs unless they raise their educational attainment. Although high paying jobs will be available without college training, most jobs that pay above average wages will require a college degree.

Jobs will be available for job seekers from every education and training background.

Declining occupational employment stems from declining industry employment and technological advancement.

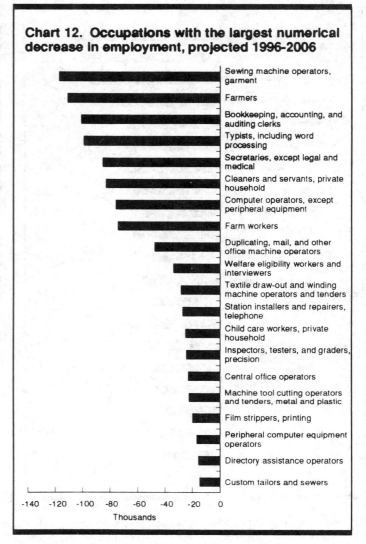

- Almost two-thirds of the projected growth will be in occupations that require less than a college degree. However, these positions generally offer the lowest pay and benefits.

- Jobs requiring the least education and training—those that can be learned on the job—will provide 2 of every 3 openings due to growth and replacement needs; 3 of every 4 openings will be in occupations that generally require less than a bachelor's degree.

- Manufacturing and agricultural related jobs, such as sewing machine operators and farmers, are examples of occupations that will lose employment due to declining employment in some goods-producing industries.

- Many declining occupations are affected by structural changes, as a result of factors including technological advances and organizational changes. For example, the use of typists and word processors will decline dramatically because of productivity improvements in office automation, and the increased use of word processing equipment by professional and managerial employees.

Table 1. Fastest growing occupations and occupations having the largest numerical increase in employment, projected 1996-2006, by level of education and training

Fastest growing occupations	Education/training category	Occupations having the largest numerical increase in employment
First-professional degree		
Chiropractors		Lawyers
Veterinarians and veterinary inspectors		Physicians
Physicians		Clergy
Lawyers		Veterinarians and veterinary inspectors
Clergy		Dentists
Doctoral degree		
Biological scientists		College and university faculty
Medical scientists		Biological scientists
College and university faculty		Medical scientists
Mathematicians and all other mathematical scientists		Mathematicians and all other mathematical scientists
Master's degree		
Speech-language pathologists and audiologists		Speech-language pathologists and audiologists
Counselors		Counselors
Curators, archivists, museum technicians		Psychologists
Psychologists		Librarians, professional
Operations research analysts		Operations research analysts
Work experience plus bachelor's or higher degree		
Engineering, science, and computer systems managers		General managers and top executives
Marketing, advertising, and public relations managers		Engineering, science, and computer systems managers
Artists and commercial artists		Financial managers
Management Analysts		Marketing, advertising, and public relations managers
Financial managers		Artists and commercial artists
Bachelor's degree		
Data base administrators and computer support specialists		Systems analysts
Computer engineers		Teachers, secondary school
Systems analysts		Data base administrators and computer support specialists
Physical therapists		Teachers, special education
Occupational therapists		Computer engineers
Associate degree		
Paralegals		Registered nurses
Health information technicians		Paralegals
Dental hygienists		Dental hygienists
Respiratory therapists		Radiologic technologists and technicians
Cardiology technologists		Health information technicians
Postsecondary vocational training		
Data processing equipment repairers		Licensed practical nurses
Emergency medical technicians		Automotive mechanics
Manicurists		Medical secretaries
Surgical technologists		Emergency medical technicians
Medical secretaries		Hairdressers, hairstylists, and cosmetologists
Work experience		
Food service and lodging managers		Clerical supervisors and managers
Teachers and instructors, vocational education and training		Marketing and sales worker supervisors
Lawn service managers		Food service and lodging managers
Instructors, adult education		Teachers and instructors, vocational education and training
Nursery and greenhouse managers		Instructors, adult (nonvocational) education
Long-term training and experience (more than 12 months of on-the-job training)		
Desktop publishing specialists		Cooks, restaurant
Flight attendants		Correction officers
Musicians		Musicians
Correction officers		Police patrol officers
Producers, directors, actors, and entertainers		Carpenters
Moderate-term training and experience (1 to 12 months of combined on-the-job experience and informal training)		
Physical and corrective therapy assistants and aides		Medical assistants
Medical assistants		Instructors and coaches, sports and physical training
Occupational therapy assistants and aides		Social and human services assistants
Social and human services assistants		Dental assistants
Instructors and coaches, sports and physical training		Physical and corrective therapy assistants
Short-term training and experience (up to 1 month of on-the-job experience)		
Personal and home care aides		Cashiers
Home health aides		Salespersons, retail
Amusement and recreation attendants		Truck drivers, light and heavy
Adjustment clerks		Home health aides
Bill and account collectors		Teacher aides and educational assistants

Sources of Career Information

This chapter identifies sources of information about occupations and career planning, counseling, training and education, and financial aid. The *Handbook* also includes a section on sources of additional information, which lists organizations you can contact for more information about particular occupations as well as the training and education that they require.

Career information

Listed below are several places to begin collecting information on careers and job opportunities.

Personal contacts. The people close to you—your family and friends—can be extremely helpful in providing career information. They may be able to answer your questions directly or put you in touch with someone else who can. This type of networking can lead to meeting someone who can answer your questions about a specific career or company, and who can provide inside information and other helpful hints. This is an effective way to learn the type of training necessary for a certain position, how someone in that position entered the field, the prospects for advancement, and what they like and dislike about the work.

Public libraries, career centers, and guidance offices. These institutions maintain a great deal of up-to-date career material. To begin your library search, look at the computer listings under "vocations" or "careers" and then under specific fields. Check the periodicals section, where you will find trade and professional magazines and journals about specific occupations and industries. Familiarize yourself with the concerns and activities of potential employers by skimming their annual reports and other information they distribute to the public. You can also find occupational information on video cassettes, in kits, and through computerized information systems. Don't forget the librarians; they can be a great source of information and can save you time by directing you to the information you need.

Check your school's career centers for programs such as individual counseling and testing, guest speakers, field trips, and career days. Also, read through any pamphlets that describe employment.

Always assess career guidance materials carefully. Information should be current. Beware of materials that seem to glamorize the occupation, overstate the earnings, or exaggerate the demand for workers.

Counselors. You may wish to seek help from a counselor. These professionals are trained to help you discover your strengths and weaknesses, guide you through an evaluation of your goals and values, and help you determine what you want in a career. The counselor will not tell you what to do, but will administer interest inventories and aptitude tests, interpret the results, and help you explore your options. Counselors also may discuss local job markets, and the entry requirements and costs of the schools, colleges, or training programs offering preparation for the kind of work that interests you. You can find counselors in:

- high school guidance offices
- college career planning and placement offices
- placement offices in private vocational/technical schools and institutions
- vocational rehabilitation agencies
- counseling services offered by community organizations
- private counseling agencies and private practices
- State employment service offices affiliated with the U.S. Employment Service

Before employing the services of a private counselor or agency, you may want to seek recommendations and check their credentials. The International Association of Counseling Services (IACS) accredits counseling services throughout the country. To receive a listing of accredited services for your region, send a self-addressed, stamped, business-size envelope to:

☛ IACS, 101 South Whiting St., Suite 211, Alexandria, VA 22304.

The *Directory of Counseling Services*, an IACS publication providing employment counseling and other assistance, may be available in your library or school career counseling center. A list of certified career counselors by State can be obtained from:

☛ The National Board of Certified Counselors, 3 Terrace Way, Suite D, Greensboro, NC 27403-3660. Phone: (910) 547-0607.

Internet networks and resources. The growth of on-line listings has made available a wide variety of resources at your fingertips—24 hours a day, 7 days a week. Many companies, professional societies, academic institutions, and government agencies maintain on-line resources or homepages with the latest information on their organization and it's activities.

Listings may include information such as government documents, schedules of events, job openings, and even networking contacts. Listings for academic institutions often provide links to career counseling and placement services through career resource centers, as well as information on financing your education. Colleges and universities also offer on-line guides to campus facilities and admission requirements and procedures.

The variety of career information available through the Internet provide much of the same information available through libraries, career centers, and guidance offices. However, no single network or resource will contain all desired information, so be prepared to search a variety of different places. As in a library search, look through various lists by field or discipline, or by using particular keywords.

Professional societies, trade associations, labor unions, business firms, and educational institutions. These organizations provide a variety of free or inexpensive career material. Many of these are in an additional information section of the *Handbook*. For information on occupations not covered in the *Handbook*, consult directories in your library's reference section for the names of potential sources. You may start with *The Guide to American Directories* or *The Directory of Directories*. Another useful resource is *The Encyclopedia of Associations*, an annual publication listing trade associations, professional societies, labor unions, and fraternal and patriotic organizations.

The National Technical Information Service Audiovisual Center, a central source for audiovisual material produced by the U.S. Government, sells material on jobs and careers. For a catalog, contact:

☞ NTIS Audiovisual Center, Springfield, VA 22161. Phone: (800) 553-6847.

For first-hand experience in an occupation, you may wish to work as an intern. Some internships offer academic credit or pay a stipend, and can lead to a full-time job after graduation. Check with guidance offices, college career resource centers, or directly with employers for opportunities.

Organizations for specific groups. The organizations listed below provide information on career planning, training, or job opportunities prepared for specific groups. Consult directories in your library's reference center or a career guidance office for information on additional organizations and associations geared towards specific groups.

Disabled:

☞ President's Committee on Employment of People with Disabilities, 1331 F St. NW., 3rd Floor, Washington, DC 20004. Phone: (202) 376-6200.

The blind: Information on the free national reference and referral service provided by the Federation of the Blind can be obtained by contacting:

☞ Job Opportunities for the Blind (JOB), National Federation of the Blind, 1800 Johnson St., Baltimore, MD 21230. Phone: (800) 638-7518, or (410) 659-9314 between the hours of 12:30 and 4:00 pm.

Older workers:

☞ National Association of Older Workers Employment Services, c/o National Council on the Aging, 409 3rd St. SW., Suite 200, Washington, DC 20024. Phone: (202) 479-1200.

☞ National Caucus/Center on Black Aged, Inc., 1424 K St. NW., Suite 500, Washington, DC 20005. Phone: (202) 637-8400.

Veterans: Contact the nearest regional office of the U.S. Department of Labor Veterans Employment and Training Service or:

☞ Veterans' Employment and Training Service (VETS), 200 Constitution Ave. NW., Room S-1315, Washington, DC 20210. Phone: (202) 219-9116.

Women:

☞ Department of Labor, Women's Bureau Clearinghouse, 200 Constitution Ave. NW., Washington, DC 20210. Phone: (800) 827-5335 Homepage: *http://www.dol.gov/dol/wb*

☞ Wider Opportunities for Women, 815 15th St. NW., Suite 916, Washington, DC 20005. Phone: (202) 638-3143.

Federal laws, executive orders, and selected Federal grant programs bar discrimination in employment based on race, color, religion, sex, national origin, age, and handicap. Information on how to file a charge of discrimination is available from U.S. Equal Employment Opportunity Commission offices around the country. Their addresses and telephone numbers are listed in telephone directories under U.S. Government, EEOC.

Education and training information

Colleges, schools, and training institutes readily reply to requests for information about their programs. When contacting these institutions, you may want to keep in mind the following items:

* admission requirements
* courses offered
* certificates or degrees awarded
* cost
* available financial aid
* location and size of school

Check with professional and trade associations for lists of schools that offer career preparation in a field you are interested in. High school guidance offices and libraries usually have copies of the directories listed below, as well as college catalogs that can provide more information on specific institutions. Helpful resources include the *Directory of Private Career Schools and Colleges of Technology*, put out by the Accrediting Commission of Career Schools and Colleges of Technology. Be sure to use the latest edition because these directories and catalogs are revised periodically.

Information about home or correspondence study programs appears in the *Directory of Accredited Institutions*. Send requests for the *Directory* and a list of other publications to:

☞ Distance Education and Training Council, 1601 18th St. NW., Washington, DC 20009. Phone: (202) 234-5100.

Local labor unions, school guidance counselors, and State employment offices provide information about apprenticeships. Send requests for copies of *The National Apprenticeship Program* to:

☞ Bureau of Apprenticeship and Training, U.S. Department of Labor, 200 Constitution Ave. NW., Room N-4649, Washington, DC 20210. Phone: (202) 219-5921.

Financial aid information

Information about financial aid is available from a variety of sources. Contact your high school guidance counselor and college financial aid officer for information concerning qualifications and applications for scholarships, fellowships, grants, loans, and work-study programs. Every State administers financial aid programs; contact State Departments of Education for information. Banks and credit unions will provide information about student loans. You also may want to consult the directories and guides for sources of student financial aid available in guidance offices and public libraries.

The Federal Government provides grants, loans, work-study programs, and other benefits to students. Information about programs administered by the U.S. Department of Education is presented in *The Student Guide to Federal Financial Aid Programs*, updated annually. To receive a copy, write to:

☞ Federal Student Aid Information Center, c/o Federal Student Aid Programs, P.O. Box 84, Washington, DC 20044-0084. Phone: toll-free, (800) 433-3243.

Meeting College Costs, an annual publication of the College Board, explains how student financial aid works and how to apply for it. The current edition is available to high school students through guidance counselors.

Need a Lift?, an annual publication of the American Legion, contains career and scholarship information. Copies cost $3 each, prepaid (including postage), and can be obtained from:

☛ American Legion, Attn: Emblem Sales, P.O. Box 1050, Indianapolis, IN 46206. For credit card orders only, call (888) 453-4466.

The Armed Forces have several educational assistance programs. These include the Reserve Officers' Training Corps (ROTC), the New G.I. bill, and tuition assistance. Information can be obtained from military recruiting centers, located in most cities.

State and local information

The *Handbook* provides information for the Nation as a whole. For help in locating State or local area information, you may contact the following:

State Occupational Information Coordinating Committee (SOICC). These committees may provide the information directly, or refer you to other sources. The addresses and telephone numbers of the directors of SOICC's are listed below.

State employment security agencies. These agencies develop detailed information about local labor markets, such as current and projected employment by occupation and industry, characteristics of the work force, and changes in State and local area economic activity. Addresses and telephone numbers of the directors of research and analysis in these agencies are listed below.

Most States have career information delivery systems (CIDS). Look for these systems in secondary schools, post-secondary institutions, libraries, job training sites, vocational rehabilitation centers, and employment service offices. The public can use the systems' computers, printed material, microfiche, and toll-free hotlines to obtain information on occupations, educational opportunities, student financial aid, apprenticeships, and military careers. Ask counselors and SOICC's for specific locations.

A computerized State Training Inventory (STI) developed by the National Occupational Information Coordinating Committee (NOICC) is also maintained by the SOICC's and available in every State. Education and training data are organized by occupation or training program title, type of institution, and geographic area. The database is compiled at the State level and includes more than 217,000 education and training programs offered by over 21,000 schools, colleges, and hospitals. If you are interested in STI, contact individual SOICC's for State-specific data.

State occupational projections are also available on the Internet at: http://www.udesc.state.ut.us/almis/stateproj/

Alabama
Chief, Labor Market Information, Department of Industrial Relations, 649 Monroe St., Room 422, Montgomery, AL 36130. Phone: (334) 242-8859.

Executive Director, Alabama Occupational Information Coordinating Committee, Alabama Center for Commerce, Room 424, 401 Adams Ave., P.O. Box 5690, Montgomery, AL 36103-5690. Phone: (334) 242-2990.

Alaska
Chief, Research and Analysis, Alaska Department of Labor, P.O. Box 25501, Juneau, AK 99802-5501. Phone: (907) 465-4500.

Executive Director, Alaska Occupational Information Coordinating Committee, Research and Analysis Section, P.O. Box 25501, Juneau, AK 99802-5501. Phone: (907) 465-4518.

American Samoa
Director, American Samoa Occupational Information Coordinating Council and Research, Department of Human Resources, American Samoa Government, Pago Pago, AS 96799. Phone: (684) 633-4485.

Arizona
Research Administrator, Department of Economic Security, P.O. Box 6123, Site Code 733A, Phoenix, AZ 85005. Phone: (602) 542-3871.

Executive Director, Arizona State Occupational Information Coordinating Council, P.O. Box 6123, Site Code 897J, 1789 West Jefferson St., First Floor North, Phoenix, AZ 85005-6123. Phone: (602) 542-3871.

Arkansas
LMI Director, Employment Security Department, P.O. Box 2981, Little Rock, AR 72203. Phone: (501) 682-3159.

Executive Director, Occupational Information Coordinating Council/ Employment Security Division, Employment and Training Services, P.O. Box 2981, Little Rock, AR 72203-2981. Phone: (501) 682-3159.

California
Chief, Labor Market Information Division, Employment Development Department, 7000 Franklin Blvd., Bldg. 1100, MIC 57, P.O. Box 826880, Sacramento, CA 94280-0001. Phone: (916) 262-2160.

Executive Director, California Occupational Information Coordinating Council, 1116 9th St. Lower Level, P.O. Box 944222, Sacramento, CA 94244-2220. Phone: (916) 323-6544.

Colorado
Director, LMI, Colorado Department of Labor, 1515 Arapahoe Ave., Tower 2, Suite 400, Denver, CO 80202-2117. Phone: (303) 620-4977.

Director, Colorado Occupational Information Coordinating Council, 1515 Arapahoe Street, Tower Two, level 3, Suite 300, Denver, CO 80202. Phone: (303) 620-4981.

Connecticut
Director of Research, Connecticut Labor Department, 200 Folly Brook Blvd., Wethersfield, CT 06109. Phone: (860) 566-2121.

Executive Director, Connecticut Occupational Information Coordinating Council, Connecticut Department of Labor, 200 Folly Brook Boulevard., Wethersfield CT 06109. Phone: (860) 566-7963.

Delaware
LMI Director, Department of Labor, 4425 N. Market Street, Wilmington, DE 19809-0965. Phone: (302) 761-8069.

Executive Director, Delaware OICC / Office of Occupational and Labor Market Information / DOL, University Office Plaza, P. O. Box 9965, Wilmington, DE 19809-0965. Phone: (302) 761-8050.

District of Columbia
Chief of Labor Market Information, Department of Employment Services, 500 C St. NW., Room 201, Washington, DC 20001. Phone: (202) 724-7214.

Executive Director, District of Columbia Occupational Information Coordinating Council, 500 C St. NW., Suite 200, Washington, DC 20001-2187. Phone: (202) 724-7205.

Florida
Chief, Bureau of LMI, Department of Labor and Employment Security, The Hartman Building, Suite 200, 2012 Capitol Circle SE., Tallahassee, FL 32399. Phone: (904) 488-6037.

Manager, Workplace Development Information Coordinating Committee, Bureau of Labor Market Information, Department of Labor and Employment Security, 2012 Capitol Circle SE., Hartman Bldg., Suite 200, Tallahassee, FL 32399-2151. Phone: (904) 488-1048.

Georgia
Director, Labor Information Systems, Department of Labor, 223 Courtlnad St. NE., Atlanta, GA 30303-1751. Phone: (404) 656-3177.

Executive Director, Georgia Occupational Information Coordinating Council, Department of Labor, 148 International Blvd., Sussex Place, Atlanta, GA 30303-1751. Phone: (404) 656-9639.

Guam
Executive Director, Guam OICC, Human Resource Development Agency, Guam ITC Bldg., Third Floor, P.O. Box 3358, Agana, GU 96910-2817. Phone: (671) 649-9759.

Hawaii
Chief, Research and Statistics Office, Department of Labor and Industrial Relations, 830 Punchbowl St., Rm 304, Honolulu, HI 96813. Phone: (808) 586-8999.

Executive Director, Hawaii State Occupational Information Coordinating Council, 830 Punchbowl St., Room 315, Honolulu, HI 96813-5080. Phone: (808) 586-8750.

Idaho
Director, Research and Analysis, Department of Employment, 317 Main St., Boise, ID 83735-0001. Phone: (208) 334-6169.

Director, Idaho Occupational Information Coordinating Council, Len B. Jordan Bldg., Room 301, 650 West State St., P.O. Box 83720, Boise, ID 83720-0095. Phone: (208) 334-3705.

Illinois
Economic Information and Analysis Manager, Department of Employment Security, 401 South State St., 2S, Chicago, IL 60605. Phone: (312) 793-2316.

Executive Director, Illinois Occupational Information Coordinating Council, 217 East Monroe, Suite 203, Springfield, IL 62706-1147. Phone: (217) 785-0789.

Indiana
Deputy Commissioner for Field Support and Business Development, Department of Workforce Development, 10 North Senate Ave., Indianapolis, IN 46204-2277. Phone: (317) 233-5724.

Director, Indiana Occupational Information Coordinating Committee/Workforce Development/Technical Education, Indiana Government Center South, 10 North Senate Ave., Second Floor, Indianapolis, IN 46204-2277. Phone: (317) 233-5099.

Iowa
Bureau Chief, Research and Information Services, Department of Workforce Development, 1000 East Grand Ave., Des Moines, IA 50319. Phone: (515) 281-8181.

Executive Director, Iowa Occupational Information Coordinating Council, Iowa Workforce Development, 200 East Grand Ave., Des Moines, IA 50319. Phone: (515) 242-5032.

Kansas
Chief, Labor Market Information Services, Department of Human Resources, 401 SW Topeka Avenue, Topeka, KS 66603-3182. Phone: (913) 296-5058.

Director, Kansas Occupational Information Coordinating Committee, 401 Topeka Ave., Topeka, KS 66603. Phone: (913) 296-3512.

Kentucky
Manager, LMI Branch, Department of Employment Services, 275 East Main St., Frankfort, KY 40621. Phone: (502) 564-7976.

Information Liaison/Manager, Kentucky Occupational Information Coordinating Council, 500 Mero Street, Room 2031, Frankfort, KY 40601. Phone: (502) 564-4258.

Louisiana
Director, Research and Statistics Division, Department of Employment and Training, P.O. Box 94094, Baton Rouge, LA 70804-9094. Phone: (504) 342-3141.

Director, Louisiana Occupational Information Coordinating Committee, P.O. Box 94094, Baton Rouge, LA 70804-9094. Phone: (504) 342-5149.

Maine
Director, Labor Market Information Services, Department of Labor/BES, 20 Union St., Augusta, ME 04330. Phone: (207) 287-2271.

SOICC Director, Maine Occupational Information Coordinating Committee, State House Station 71, Augusta, ME 04333. Phone: (207) 624-6200.

Maryland
Director, Office of Labor Market Analysis and Information, Department of Labor, Licensing, and Regulations, 1100 North Eutaw St., Room 601, Baltimore, MD 21201. Phone: (410) 767-2250.

Director, Maryland State Occupational Information Coordinating Council, State Department of Labor, Licensing & Regulation, 1100 North Eutaw St., Room 104, Baltimore, MD 21201-2298. Phone: (410) 626-2953.

Massachusetts
LMI and Research Director, Division of Employment and Training, Hurley Building, 5th Floor, 19 Staniford St., Boston, MA 02114. Phone: (617) 626-6556.

Director, Massachusetts Occupational Information Coordinating Council/Division of Employment Security, Charles F. Hurley Bldg., 2nd Floor, Government Center, Boston, MA 02114. Phone: (617) 727-5718.

Michigan
Deputy Director, Management and Financial Services, Employment Security Commission, 7310 Woodward Ave., Room 510, Detroit, MI 48202. Phone: (313) 876-5904.

Executive Coordinator, Michigan Occupational Information Coordinating Committee, Victor Office Center, 201 North Washington Square, 4th Floor Lansing, MI 48913. Phone: (517) 373-0363.

Minnesota
Director, Research and Statistical Services, Department of Economic Security, 390 North Robert St., 5th Floor, St. Paul, MN 55101. Phone: (612) 296-6546.

Director, Minnesota Occupational Information Coordinating Council/Department of Economic Security, 390 North Robert Street., St. Paul, MN 55101. Phone: (612) 296-2072.

Mississippi
Chief, Labor Market Information Department, Employment Security Commission, P.O. Box 1699, 1520 West Charles St., Jackson, MS 39215-1699. Phone: (601) 961-7424.

SOICC Director, Mississippi State Occupational Information Coordinating Committee, 301 West Pearl St., Jackson, MS 39203-3089. Phone: (601) 949-2240.

Missouri
Chief, Research and Analysis, Division of Employment Security, 421 East Dunkin St., P.O. Box 59, Jefferson City, MO 65104-0059. Phone: (573) 751-3595.

Director, Missouri Occupational Information Coordinating Committee, 400 Dix Rd., Jefferson City, MO 65109. Phone: (573) 751-3800.

Montana
Chief, Research and Analysis, Department of Labor and Industry, P.O. Box 1728, Helena, MT 59624. Phone: (406) 444-2430.

SOICC Director, Montana Occupational Information Coordinating Committee, P.O. Box 1728, 1301 Lockey St., Second Floor, Helena, MT 59624-1728. Phone: (406) 444-2741.

Nebraska
LMI Administrator, Department of Labor, 550 South 16th St., P.O. Box 94600, Lincoln, NE 68509-4600. Phone: (402) 471-9964.

Administrator, Nebraska Occupational Information Coordinating Committee, P.O. Box 94600, State House Station., Lincoln, NE 68509-4600. Phone: (402) 471-9953.

Nevada
Chief, Research and Analysis/LMI, Information, Development, and Processing Division, Employment Security Department, 500 East 3rd St., Carson City, NV 89713-0001. Phone: (702) 687-4550.

Manager, Nevada Occupational Information Coordinating Committee/ DETR, 500 East 3rd St., Carson City, NV 89713. Phone: (702) 687-4550.

New Hampshire
Director, Labor Market Information, Department of Employment Security, 32 South Main St., Concord, NH 03301. Phone: (603) 228-4123.

Director, New Hampshire Occupational Information Coordinating Committee, 64 Old Suncook Rd., Concord, NH 03301. Phone: (603) 228-3349.

New Jersey
Assistant Commissioner, Labor Research and Analysis, Department of Labor, CN056, Trenton, NJ 08625-0056. Phone: (609) 292-2643.

Staff Director, New Jersey Occupational Information Coordinating Committee, Labor Bldg., 5ᵗʰ Floor, CN057, Trenton, NJ 08625-0057. Phone: (609) 292-2682.

New Mexico
Chief, Economic Research and Analysis Bureau, Department of Labor, 401 Broadway Blvd. NE., P.O. Box 1928, Albuquerque, NM 87103. Phone: (505) 841-8645.

SOICC Director, New Mexico Occupational Information Coordinating Committee, 401 Broadway NE., Tiwa Bldg., P.O. Box 1928, Albuquerque, NM 87103. Phone: (505) 841-8455.

New York
Director, Division of Research and Statistics, New York State Department of Labor, State Office Building Campus, Room 401, Albany, NY 12240. Phone: (518) 457-6369.

Executive Director, New York State Occupational Information Coordinating Committee/DOL, Research and Statistics Division, State Campus, Bldg. 12, Room 488, Albany, NY 12240. Phone: (518) 457-3806.

North Carolina
Director, Labor Market Information, Employment Security Commission, P.O. Box 25903, Raleigh, NC 27611. Phone: (919) 733-2937.

Executive Director, North Carolina Occupational Information Coordinating Committee, 700 Wade Avenue, P.O. Box 25903, Raleigh, NC 27611. Phone: (919) 733-6700.

North Dakota
Director, Research and Statistics, Job Service North Dakota, P.O. Box 5507, Bismarck, ND 58506-5507. Phone: (701) 328-2868.

Program Administrator, North Dakota State Occupational Information Coordinating Committee, 1720 Burnt Boat Dr., P.O. Box 5507, Bismarck, ND 58506-5507. Phone: (701) 328-9734.

Northern Mariana Islands
Executive Director, Northern Mariana Islands Occupational Information Coordinating Committee, P.O. Box 149, Room N-1, Building N, Northern Mariana College, Saipan, CM 96950. Phone: (670) 234-7394.

Ohio
Administrator, Labor Market Information Division, Bureau of Employment Services, 78-80 Chestnut, 5ᵗʰ Floor, Columbus, OH 43215. Phone: (614) 752-9494.

Director, Ohio Occupational Information Coordinating Committee/Division of LMI, Ohio Bureau of Employment Services, 145 South Front St., Columbus, OH 43215. Phone: (614) 466-1109.

Oklahoma
Director, Research Division, Employment Security Commission, 305 Will Rogers Memorial Office Bldg., Oklahoma City, OK 73105. Phone: (405) 557-7265.

Executive Director, Oklahoma Occupational Information Coordinating Council, Department of Voc / Tech Education, 1500 W. 7th Ave., Stillwater, OK 74074-4364. Phone: (405) 743-5198.

Oregon
Adminstrator for Research, Tax and Analysis, Oregon Employment Department, 875 Union St. NE., Salem, OR 97311. Phone: (503) 378-8656.

SOICC Director, Oregon Occupational Information Coordinating Committee, 875 Union St. NE., Salem, OR 97311-0101. Phone: (503) 378-5747.

Pennsylvania
Director, Bureau of Research and Statistics, 300 Capitol Associates Building, 3rd Floor, 901 North Seventh St., Harrisburg, PA 17120-9969. Phone: (717) 787-3266.

Executive Director, Pennsylvania SOICC, Bureau of Research and Statistics, PA Department of Labor and Industry, 300 Capitol Associates Bldg., Harrisburg, PA 17120-0034. Phone: (717) 772-1330.

Puerto Rico
Director, Research and Statistics Division, Department of Labor and Human Resources, 505 Munoz Rivera Ave., 20th Floor, Hato Rey, PR 00918. Phone: (809) 754-5385.

Executive Director, Puerto Rico Occupational Information Coordinating Committee, P.O. Box 366212, San Juan, PR 00936-6212. Phone: (787) 723-7110.

Rhode Island
Labor Market Information Director, Department of Employment and Training, 101 Friendship St., Providence, RI 02903-3740. Phone: (401) 277-3730.

Director, Rhode Island Occupational Information Coordinating Committee, 101 Friendship St., Providence, RI 02903. Phone: (401) 272-0830.

South Carolina
Director, Labor Market Information, Employment Security Commission, P.O. Box 995, Columbia, SC 29202. Phone: (803) 737-2660.

Director, South Carolina Occupational Information Coordinating Committee, 1550 Gadsden St., P.O. Box 995, Columbia, SC 29202-0995. Phone: (803) 737-2733.

South Dakota
Director, Labor Information Center, Department of Labor, P.O. Box 4730, Aberdeen, SD 57402-4730. Phone: (605) 626-2314.

Director, South Dakota Occupational Information Coordinating Council, South Dakota Department of Labor, 420 South Roosevelt St., P.O. Box 4730, Aberdeen, SD 57402-4730. Phone: (605) 626-2314.

Tennessee
Director, Research and Statistics Division, Department of Employment Security, 500 James Robertson Pkwy., 11th Floor, Nashville, TN 37245-1000. Phone: (615) 741-2284.

Executive Director, Tennessee Occupational Information Coordinating Committee, 500 James Robertson Pkwy., 11th Floor-Volunteer Plaza, Nashville, TN 37245-1600. Phone: (615) 741-6451.

Texas
Director of Labor Market Information, Texas Workforce Commission, 101 East 15th St., Room 208T, Austin, TX 78778-0001. Phone: (512) 463-2616.

Director, Texas Occupational Information Coordinating Committee, Travis Bldg., Suite 205, 3520 Executive Center Dr., Austin, TX 78731. Phone: (512) 502-3750.

Utah
Director, Labor Market Information, Department of Employment Security, 140 East 300 South, P.O. Box 45249, Salt Lake City, UT 84145-0249. Phone: (801) 536-7860.

Director, Utah Occupational Information Coordinating Committee, c/o Utah Department of Employment Security, P.O. Box 45249, 140 East 300 South, Salt Lake City, UT 84147. Phone: (801) 536-7806.

Vermont
Director, Policy and Information, Department of Employment and Training, 5 Green Mountain Dr., P.O. Box 488, Montpelier, VT 05601-0488. Phone: (802) 828-4153.

Director, Vermont Occupational Information Coordinating Committee, 5 Green Mountain Dr., P.O. Box 488, Montpelier, VT 05601-0488. Phone: (802) 229-0311.

Virginia
Director, Economic Information Services Division, VA Employment Commission, 703 East Main St., Richmond, VA 23219. Phone: (804) 786-7496.

Acting Executive Director, Virginia Occupational Information Coordinating Committee/Virginia Employment Commission, 703 East Main St., P.O. Box 1358, Richmond, VA 23211. Phone: (804) 786-7496.

Virgin Islands
Chief, Bureau of Labor Statistics, Department of Labor, 53A and 54B Kronprindsens Gade, Charlotte Amalie, St. Thomas, VI 00802. Phone: (809) 776-3700.

Coordinator, Virgin Islands Occupational Information Coordinating Committee, P.O. Box 303359, St. Thomas, U.S. Virgin Islands 00803-3359. Phone: (809) 776-3700, extension 2136.

Washington
Director, Labor Market and Economic Analysis, P.O. Box 9046, Olympia, WA 98507-9046. Phone: (360) 438-4804.

Executive Director, Washington Occupational Information Coordinating Committee, c/o Employment Security Department, P.O. Box 9046, Olympia, WA 98507-9046. Phone: (360) 438-4803.

West Virginia

Assistant Director, Labor and Economic Research, JTP/ES Division, Bureau of Employment Programs, 112 California Ave., Charleston, WV 25305-0112. Phone: (304) 558-2660.

Executive Director, West Virginia Occupational Information Coordinating Committee, P O Box 487, Institute, WV 25112-0487. Phone: (304) 766-2687.

Wisconsin

Director, Department of Workforce Development, Jobs, Employment, and Training Services Division, 201 East Washington Ave., P.O. Box 7946, Madison, WI 53707-7946. Phone: (608) 266-5843.

A
(608

Wyoming

Manager, N
2760, Casper,

Acting Director, W
Post Office Box 276 Regional Information Coordinating Coun-
Phone: (307) 473-3809. WE/BWI, 201 East Washington
WI 53707-7944. Phone:

nding a Job
Evaluating a Job Offer

. Job

... great deal of time and effort to find a
...ers may walk right into an ideal employ-
... Do not be discouraged if you have to pursue
... Friends, neighbors, teachers, and counselors may
... available jobs in your field of interest. Read the clas-
...d ads. Consult State employment service offices and consider private employment agencies. You may also contact
employers directly.

Where To Learn About Job Openings

Parents, friends, acquaintances, and neighbors
School or college placement services
Classified ads
   —Local and out-of-town newspapers
   —Professional journals
   —Trade magazines
Employment agencies and career consultants
State employment service offices
Internet networks and resources
Civil service announcements (Federal, State, and local)
Labor unions
Professional associations (State and local chapters)
Libraries and community centers
Women's counseling and employment programs
Youth programs
Employers

Job Search Methods

Personal contacts. Your network of family, friends, and acquaintances may offer one of the most effective ways to find a
job. They may help you directly or put you in touch with
someone else who can. Such networking can lead to meeting
with someone who is hiring for their firm or who knows of
specific job openings.

Classified ads. The "Help Wanted" ads in newspapers list
hundreds of jobs. You should realize, however, that many
other job openings are not listed, and that the classified ads
sometimes do not give all important information. Many offer
little or no description of the job, working conditions, or pay.
Some ads do not identify the employer. They may simply
give a post office box for sending your resume. This makes
follow-up inquiries very difficult. Furthermore, some ads
offer out-of-town jobs; others advertise employment agencies
rather than actual employment openings.

Keep the following in mind when using classified ads:

- Do not rely solely on the classifieds to find a job; follow
  other leads as well.
- Answer ads promptly, since openings may be filled quickly,
  even before the ad stops appearing in the paper.

- Read the ads every day, particularly the Sunday edition,
  which usually includes the most listings.
- Beware of "no experience necessary" ads. These ads often
  signal low wages, poor working conditions, or commission
  work.
- Keep a record of all ads to which you have responded, including the specific skills, educational background, and personal qualifications required for the position.

Internet networks and resources. A variety of information is
available on the Internet including jobs and job search resources and techniques. Internet resources are available 7
days a week, 24 hours a day.

No single network or resource will contain all information
on employment or career opportunities, so be prepared to
search for what you need. Remember that job listings may be
posted by field or discipline, so begin your search using keywords.

When searching employment databases on the Internet, it is
sometimes possible to post your resume on-line or send it to
an employer via electronic mail. Some sources provide this
service free of charge; although be careful that you are not
going to incur any additional charges for postings or updates.

A good place to start your job search is *America's Job
Bank.* It can be found at: *http://www.ajb.dni.us/*

Public employment service. The State employment service,
sometimes called the Job Service, operates in coordination
with the U.S. Employment Service of the U.S. Department of
Labor. About 1,700 local offices help jobseekers find jobs
and help employers find qualified workers at no cost to themselves. To find the office nearest you, look in the State government telephone listings under "Job Service" or "Employment."

Job matching and referral. At the State employment service
office, an interviewer will determine if you are "job ready" or
if counseling and testing services would be helpful first. After
you are "job ready," you may examine available job listings
and select openings that interest you. A staff member can
then describe the job openings in detail and arrange for interviews with prospective employers. Employment counselors
can arrange for tests to assess your occupational aptitudes and
interests. They will also help you choose and prepare for a
career.

America's Job Bank, run by the U.S. Department of Labor's
Employment and Training Administration, provides information on preparing your resume and using the Internet for your
job search; trends in the U.S. job market and State occupational projections; and approximately 500,000 job openings
on any given day. A wide range of jobs are listed all over the
country, and most are full-time jobs in the private sector. Jobseekers can access these listings through the Internet; computers with access to the Internet are available to the public in

any local public employment service office, as well as in schools, libraries, and several hundred military installations.

Tips for Finding the Right Job, a U.S. Department of Labor pamphlet, offers advice on determining your job skills, organizing your job search, writing a resume, and making the most of an interview. *Job Search Guide: Strategies For Professionals*, another U.S. Department of Labor publication, discusses specific steps that jobseekers can follow to identify employment opportunities. This publication includes sections on such things as handling job loss, managing personal resources, assessing personal skills and interests, researching the job market, conducting the job search, and networking. Check with your State employment service office, or order a copy of these publications from the U.S. Government Printing Office's Superintendent of Documents. Phone: (202) 512-1800 for price and ordering information.

Services for special groups. By law, veterans are entitled to priority at State employment service centers. Veterans' employment representatives can inform you of available assistance and help you deal with any problems.

State service centers refer youths between 16 and 21 and economically disadvantaged applicants to opportunities available under the Job Training Partnership Act (JTPA) of 1982, which prepares persons facing barriers to employment for jobs.

Federal job information. Information on getting a job with the Federal Government is available from the Office of Personnel Management through a telephone based system. Consult your telephone directory under U.S. Government for a local number or call (912) 757-3000 (TDD 912 744-2299. Information also is available on the Internet: *http://www.usajobs.opm.gov*

Private employment agencies. These agencies can be helpful, but they are in business to make money. Most agencies operate on a commission basis, with the fee dependent upon a percentage of the salary paid to a successful applicant. You or the hiring company will have to pay a sizable fee. Find out the exact cost and who is responsible for paying it before using the service.

While employment agencies can help you save time and contact employers who otherwise might be difficult to locate, in cases where you are responsible for the fee, your costs may outweigh the benefits. Consider any guarantee they offer when determining the cost.

College career planning and placement offices. College placement offices facilitate matching job openings for their students and alumni. They set up appointments and use the facilities for interviews with recruiters. Placement offices usually list part-time, temporary, and summer jobs offered on campus. They also list jobs in regional business, nonprofit, and government organizations. Students can receive career counseling and testing, job search advice, and use of the career resource library. Here you may attend workshops on such topics as job search strategy, resume writing, letter writing, and effective interviewing; critique drafts of resumes and watch videotapes of mock interviews; explore files of resumes and references; and attend job fairs conducted by the office.

Community agencies. Many nonprofit organizations, including churches and synagogues, and vocational rehabilitation agencies, offer counseling, career development, and job placement services, generally targeted to a particular group, such as women, youth, minorities, ex-offenders, or older workers.

Employers. It is possible to apply directly to employers without a referral. You may locate a potential employer in the *Yellow Pages*, in directories of local chambers of commerce, and in other directories that provide information about employers. When you find an employer you are interested in, you can send a cover letter and resume even if you are not certain that an opening exists.

Applying for a Job

Resumes and application forms. Resumes and application forms are two ways to provide employers with written evidence of your qualifications and skills. Most information appears on both the resume and application form, but the way it is presented differs. Some employers prefer a resume while others require an application form. The accompanying box presents the basic information you should include in your resume.

There are many ways of organizing a resume. Depending on the job, you should choose the format that best highlights your skills, training, and experience. It may be helpful to look in a variety of books and publications in your local library or bookstore for different examples.

What Goes Into a Resume

- Name, address, and telephone number.
- Employment objective. State the type of work or specific
- job you are seeking.
- Education, including school name and address, dates of attendance, curriculum, and highest grade completed or degree awarded.
- Experience, paid or volunteer. Include the following for each job: Job title, name and location of employer, and dates of employment. Briefly describe your job duties.
- Special skills, proficiency in foreign languages, achievements, membership in organizations, and volunteer work.
- Note on your resume that "references available upon request."

In filling out an application form, make sure you fill it out completely and follow all instructions. Do not omit any information asked and make sure that all information provided is correct.

Cover letters. A cover letter is sent with a resume or application form, as a way to introduce yourself to employers. It should capture the employer's attention, follow a business letter format, and should usually include the following information:

- The name and address of the specific person to whom the letter is addressed.
- The reason for your interest in the company or position.
- Your main qualifications for the position (in brief).

• A request for an interview.
• Your home and work phone number.

Interviewing. An interview gives you the opportunity to showcase your qualifications to an employer, so it pays to be well prepared. The information in the accompanying box provides some helpful hints.

Job Interview Tips

Preparation:
Learn about the organization.
Have a specific job or jobs in mind.
Review your qualifications for the job.
Prepare answers to broad questions about yourself.
Review your resume.
Practice an interview with a friend or relative.
Arrive before the scheduled time of your interview.

Personal Appearance:
Be well groomed.
Dress appropriately.
Do not chew gum or smoke.

The Interview:
Relax and answer each question concisely.
Respond promptly.
Use good manners. Learn the name of your interviewer and shake hands as you meet.
Use proper English and avoid slang.
Be cooperative and enthusiastic.
Ask questions about the position and the organization.
Thank the interviewer, and follow up with a letter.

Test (if employer gives one):
Listen closely to instructions.
Read each question carefully.
Write legibly and clearly.
Budget your time wisely and don't dwell on one question

Information to Bring to an Interview:
Social Security number.
Driver's license number.
Resume. Although not all employers require applicants to bring a resume, you should be able to furnish the interviewer information about your education, training, and previous employment.
References. An employer usually requires three references. Get permission from people before using their names, and make sure they will give you a good reference. Try to avoid using relatives.

Evaluating a Job Offer

Once you receive a job offer, you are faced with a difficult decision and must evaluate the offer carefully. Fortunately, most organizations will not expect you to accept or reject an offer immediately.

There are many issues to consider when assessing a job offer. Will the organization be a good place to work? Will the job be interesting? How are opportunities for advancement?

Is the salary fair? Does the employer offer good benefits? If you have not already figured out exactly what you want, the following discussion may help you develop a set of criteria for judging job offers, whether you are starting a career, reenter-

ing the labor force after a long absence, or planning a career change.

The organization. Background information on an organization can help you decide whether it is a good place for you to work. Factors to consider include the organization's business or activity, financial condition, age, size, and location.

You can generally get background information on an organization, particularly a large organization, by telephoning its public relations office. A public company's annual report to the stockholders tells about its corporate philosophy, history, products or services, goals, and financial status. Most government agencies can furnish reports that describe their programs and missions. Press releases, company newsletters or magazines, and recruitment brochures also can be useful. Ask the organization for any other items that might interest a prospective employee.

If possible, speak to current or former employees of the organization. Background information on the organization also may be available on the Internet or at your public or school library. If you cannot get an annual report, check the library for reference directories that may provide basic facts about the company, such as earnings, products and services, and number of employees. Some directories widely available in libraries include the following:

• *Dun & Bradstreet's Million Dollar Directory*
• *Standard and Poor's Register of Corporations*
• *Directors and Executives*
• *Moody's Industrial Manual*
• *Thomas' Register of American Manufacturers*
• *Ward's Business Directory*

Stories about an organization in magazines and newspapers can tell a great deal about its successes, failures, and plans for the future. You can identify articles on a company by looking under its name in periodical or computerized indexes such as the following—however, it probably will not be useful to look back more than 2 or 3 years.

• *Business Periodicals Index*
• *Reader's Guide to Periodical Literature*
• *Newspaper Index*
• *Wall Street Journal Index*
• *New York Times Index*

The library also may have government publications that present projections of growth for the industry in which the organization is classified. Long-term projections of employment and output for more than 200 industries, covering the entire economy, are developed by the Bureau of Labor Statistics and revised every two years—see the November 1997 *Monthly Labor Review* for the most recent projections. The *U.S. Global Trade Outlook*, published annually by the U.S. Department of Commerce, presents detailed analyses of the globalization of U.S. industry and growth prospects for some industrial sectors. Trade magazines also have periodic articles on the trends for specific industries.

Career centers at colleges and universities often have information on employers that is not available in libraries. Ask a career center representative how to find out about a particular organization. The career center may have an entire file of information on the company.

Is the organization's business or activity in keeping with your own interests and beliefs?
It will be easier to apply yourself to the work if you are enthusiastic about what the organization does.

How will the size of the organization affect you?
Large firms generally offer a greater variety of training programs and career paths, more managerial levels for advancement, and better employee benefits than small firms. Large employers may also have more advanced technologies. However, jobs in large firms may tend to be highly specialized.

Jobs in small firms may offer broader authority and responsibility, a closer working relationship with top management, and a chance to clearly see your contribution to the success of the organization.

Should you work for a fledgling organization or one that is well established?
New businesses have a high failure rate, but for many people, the excitement of helping create a company and the potential for sharing in its success more than offset the risk of job loss. It may be as exciting and rewarding, however, to work for a young firm which already has a foothold on success.

Does it make any difference to you whether the company is private or public?
A privately owned company may be controlled by an individual or a family, which can mean that key jobs are reserved for relatives and friends. A publicly owned company is controlled by a board of directors responsible to the stockholders. Key jobs are open to anyone with talent.

Is the organization in an industry with favorable long-term prospects?
The most successful firms tend to be in industries that are growing rapidly.

The nature of the job. Even if everything else about the job is good, you will be unhappy if you dislike the day-to-day work. Determining in advance whether you will like the work may be difficult. However, the more you find out about it before accepting or rejecting the job offer, the more likely you are to make the right choice. Actually working in the industry and, if possible, for the company would provide considerable insight. You can gain work experience through part-time, temporary, or summer jobs, or through work-study programs while in school, all of which can lead to permanent job offers.

Where is the job located?
If it is in another section of the country, you need to consider the cost of living, the availability of housing and transportation, and the quality of educational and recreational facilities in the new location. Even if the place of work is in your area, consider the time and expense of commuting in your decision.

Does the work match your interests and make good use of your skills?
The duties and responsibilities of the job should be explained in enough detail to answer this question.

How important is the job in this company?
An explanation of where you fit in the organization and how you are supposed to contribute to its overall objectives should give you an idea of the job's importance.

Are you comfortable with the hours?
Most jobs involve regular hours—for example, 40 hours a week, during the day, Monday through Friday. Other jobs require night, weekend, or holiday work. In addition, some jobs routinely require overtime to meet deadlines or sales or production goals, or to better serve customers. Consider the effect of work hours on your personal life.

How long do most people who enter this job stay with the company?
High turnover can mean dissatisfaction with the nature of the work or something else about the job.

Opportunities offered by employers. A good job offers you opportunities to learn new skills, increase your earnings, and rise to positions of greater authority, responsibility, and prestige. A lack of opportunities can dampen interest in the work and result in frustration and boredom.

The company should have a training plan for you. What valuable new skills does the company plan to teach you?

The employer should give you some idea of promotion possibilities within the organization. What is the next step on the career ladder? If you have to wait for a job to become vacant before you can be promoted, how long does this usually take? Employers differ on their policies regarding promotion from within the organization. When opportunities for advancement do arise, will you compete with applicants from outside the company? Can you apply for jobs for which you qualify elsewhere within the organization, or is mobility within the firm limited?

Salaries and benefits. Wait for the employer to introduce these subjects. Some companies will not talk about pay until they have decided to hire you. In order to know if their offer is reasonable, you need a rough estimate of what the job should pay. You may have to go to several sources for this information. Try to find family, friends, or acquaintances who recently were hired in similar jobs. Ask your teachers and the staff in the college placement office about starting pay for graduates with your qualifications. Help-wanted ads in newspapers sometimes give salary ranges for similar positions.

If you are considering the salary and benefits for a job in another geographic area, make allowances for differences in the cost of living, which may be significantly higher in a large metropolitan area than in a smaller city, town, or rural area.

You also should learn the organization's policy regarding overtime. Depending on the job, you may or may not be exempt from laws requiring the employer to compensate you for overtime. Find out how many hours you will be expected to work each week and whether you receive overtime pay or compensatory time off for working more than the specified number of hours in a week.

Also take into account that the starting salary is just that, the start. Your salary should be reviewed on a regular basis—many organizations do it every year. How much can you expect to earn after 1, 2, or 3 or more years? An employer cannot be specific about the amount of pay if it includes commissions and bonuses.

Benefits can also add a lot to your base pay, but they vary widely. Find out exactly what the benefit package includes and how much of the costs you must bear.

Check the library or your school's career center for salary surveys such as those conducted by the National Association of Colleges and Employers or various professional associations.

Data on wages and benefits are also available from:

☛ Bureau of Labor Statistics, Office of Compensation and Working Conditions, 2 Massachusetts Ave. NE., Room 4160, Washington, DC 20212-0001. Phone: (202) 606-6225.

Data from the National Compensation Survey, which integrates data from three existing BLS programs—the Employment Cost Index, the Occupational Compensation Survey, and the Employee Benefits Survey—will become available between 1997 and the year 2000 from the BLS office above and from the Internet: *http://stats.bls.gov/comhome.htm*

Current Population Survey (CPS) data on median weekly earnings of full-time wage and salary workers, by detailed occupation, are available from:

☛ Bureau of Labor Statistics, Office of Employment and Unemployment Statistics, 2 Massachusetts Ave. NE., Room 4945, Washington, DC 20212-0001. Phone: (202) 606-6400.

CPS data can also be accessed at the following Internet address: *http://www.stats.bls.gov/cpsaatab.htm*

Occupational Information Included in the *Handbook*

The *Occupational Outlook Handbook* is best used as a reference; it is not meant to be read from cover to cover. Instead, start by looking at the table of contents, where related occupations are grouped in clusters, or look in the alphabetical index for specific occupations that interest you. This section is an overview of how the occupational descriptions, or statements, are organized. Two earlier chapters—Tomorrow's Jobs, and Sources of Career Information—highlight the forces that are likely to determine employment opportunities in industries and occupations through the year 2006, and tell you where to obtain additional information.

Unless otherwise noted, the source of employment and earnings data presented in the *Handbook* is the Bureau of Labor Statistics. Many *Handbook* statements cite earnings data from the Current Population Survey (CPS), while other statements include earnings data from outside sources. Since the characteristics of these data vary, it is difficult to compare earnings precisely among occupations.

For any occupation that sounds interesting, use the *Handbook* to find out what the work entails; what education and training is required; what the advancement possibilities, earnings, and job outlook are; and what related occupations are. Each occupational statement in the *Handbook* follows a standard format, making it easier for you to compare occupations. The following highlights information presented in each section of a *Handbook* statement, and gives some hints on how to interpret the information provided.

About those numbers at the beginning of each statement

The numbers in parentheses that appear just below the title of most occupational statements are from the *Dictionary of Occupational Titles* (D.O.T.), Fourth Edition, Revised 1991, a U.S. Department of Labor publication. D.O.T. numbers are used primarily by State employment service offices to classify applicants and job openings. They are included in the *Handbook* because some career information centers and libraries use them for filing occupational information.

An index at the back of this book beginning on page 496 cross-references the Revised Fourth Edition D.O.T. numbers to occupations covered in the *Handbook*. The D.O.T. is being replaced by O*NET, the Occupational Information Network. For more information about this electronic occupational information database, see the Note on page 496.

Significant Points
- Highlights key occupational characteristics.

Nature of the Work
- What workers do, the equipment they use, and how closely they are supervised.
- How the duties of workers vary by industry, establishment, and size of firm.
- How the responsibilities of entry-level workers differ from those of experienced, supervisory, or self-employed workers.

- How technological innovations are affecting what workers do and how they do it.
- Emerging specialties.

Working Conditions
- Typical hours worked.
- The workplace environment.
- Susceptibility to injury, illness, and job-related stress.
- Necessary protective clothing and safety equipment.
- Physical activities required.
- Extent of travel required.

Employment
- The number of jobs the occupation provided in 1996.
- Key industries employing workers in the occupation.
- Geographic distribution of jobs.
- The proportion of part-time (fewer than 35 hours a week) and self-employed workers in the occupation.

Training, Other Qualifications, and Advancement
- Most significant sources of training, typical length of training, and training preferred by employers.
- Whether workers acquire skills through previous work experience, informal on-the-job training, formal training (including apprenticeships), the Armed Forces, home study, or hobbies and other activities.
- Formal educational requirements—high school, postsecondary vocational or technical training, college, or graduate or professional education.
- Desirable skills, aptitudes, and personal characteristics.
- Certification, examination, or licensing required for entry into the field, advancement, or for independent practice.
- Continuing education or skill improvement requirements.
- Advancement opportunities.

Job Outlook
- Forces that will result in growth or decline in the number of jobs.
- Relative number of job openings an occupation provides. Occupations which are large and have high turnover rates generally provide the most job openings—reflecting the need to replace workers who transfer to other occupations or stop working.
- Degree of competition for jobs. Is there a surplus or shortage of jobseekers compared to the number of job openings available? Do opportunities vary by industry, size of firm, or geographic location? Even in overcrowded fields, job openings do exist, and good students or well-qualified individuals should not be deterred from undertaking training or seeking entry.
- Susceptibility to layoffs due to imports, slowdowns in economic activity, technological advancements, or budget cuts.

Key phrases in the *Handbook*

This box explains how to interpret the key phrases used to describe projected changes in employment. It also explains the terms used to describe the relationship between the number of job openings and the number of jobseekers. The descriptions of the relationship between the supply of and demand for workers in a particular occupation reflects the knowledge and judgment of economists in the Bureau's Office of Employment Projections.

Changing employment between 1996 and 2006

If the statement reads:	Employment is projected to:
Grow much faster than average	increase 36 percent or more
Grow faster than average	increase 21 to 35 percent
Grow about as fast as average	increase 10 to 20 percent
Grow more slowly than average, or little or no change	increase 0 to 9 percent
Decline	decrease 1 percent or more

Opportunities and competition for jobs

If the statement reads:	Job openings compared to jobseekers may be:
Very good to excellent opportunities	More numerous
Good or favorable opportunities	In rough balance
May face keen competition or can expect keen competition	Fewer

Earnings

- Typical earnings of workers in the occupation.
- If earnings tend to vary with experience, location, and tenure.
- Whether workers are compensated through annual salaries, hourly wages, commissions, piece rates, tips, or bonuses.
- Earnings of wage and salary workers compared to self-employed persons, who held about 8 percent of all jobs in 1996.
- Benefits, including health insurance, pensions, paid vacation and sick leave, family leave, child care or elder care, employee assistance programs, summers off, sabbaticals, tuition for dependents, discounted airfare or merchandise, stock options, profit sharing plans, savings plans, or expense accounts.

Related Occupations

- Occupations involving similar aptitudes, interests, education, and training.

Sources of Additional Information

- Listings of mailing addresses for associations, government agencies, unions, and other organizations which provide useful occupational information. In some cases, toll-free phone numbers, Internet homepage addresses, FAX numbers, and electronic mail addresses are provided.
- Free or relatively inexpensive publications offering more information, some of which may be available in libraries, school career centers, or guidance offices.

(For additional sources of information, read the earlier chapter, Sources of Career Information.)

Executive, Administrative, and Managerial Occupations

Accountants and Auditors

(D.O.T. 160 through .167-042, -054, .267-014)

Significant Points

- Most jobs require at least a bachelor's degree in accounting or a related field.

- Professional recognition through certification or licensure, a master's degree, familiarity with accounting and auditing computer software, or specialized expertise provide an advantage in the job market.

- Competition will remain keen for the most prestigious jobs—those with major accounting and business firms.

Nature of the Work

Accountants and auditors prepare, analyze, and verify financial reports and taxes, and monitor information systems that furnish this information to managers in business, industry, and government.

The major fields of accounting are public, management, and government accounting, and internal auditing. Public accountants have their own businesses or work for public accounting firms. They perform a broad range of accounting, auditing, tax, and consulting activities for their clients, who may be corporations, governments, nonprofit organizations, or individuals. Management accountants—also called industrial, corporate, or private accountants—record and analyze the financial information of the companies for which they work. Other responsibilities include budgeting, performance evaluation, cost management, and asset management. They are usually part of executive teams involved in strategic planning or new product development. Internal auditors verify the accuracy of their organization's records and check for mismanagement, waste, or fraud. Government accountants and auditors maintain and examine the records of government agencies, and audit private businesses and individuals whose activities are subject to government regulations or taxation.

Within each field, accountants often concentrate on one aspect of accounting. For example, many public accountants concentrate on tax matters, such as preparing individual income tax returns and advising companies of the tax advantages and disadvantages of certain business decisions. Others concentrate on consulting and offer advice on matters such as compensation or employee health care benefits; the design of accounting and data processing systems; and controls to safeguard assets. Some specialize in forensic accounting—investigating and interpreting bankruptcies and other complex financial transactions. Still others work primarily in auditing—examining a client's financial statements and reporting to investors and authorities that they have been prepared and reported correctly. However, accounting firms are performing less auditing relative to consulting services, which are more profitable.

Increasing numbers of accounting graduates are working in private corporations. Management accountants analyze and interpret the financial information corporate executives need to make sound business decisions. They also prepare financial reports for nonmanagement groups, including stockholders, creditors, regulatory agencies, and tax authorities. Within accounting departments, they may work in financial analysis, planning and budgeting, cost accounting, and other areas.

Internal auditing is increasingly important. As computer systems make information more timely, top management can base its decisions on actual data, rather than personal observation. Internal auditors examine and evaluate their firms' financial and information systems, management procedures, and internal controls to ensure that records are accurate and controls are adequate to protect against fraud and waste. They also review company operations—evaluating their efficiency, effectiveness, and compliance with corporate policies and procedures, laws, and government regulations. There are many types of highly specialized auditors, such as electronic data processing, environmental, engineering, legal, insurance premium, bank, and health care auditors.

Accountants employed by Federal, State, and local governments see that revenues are received and expenditures are made in accordance with laws and regulations. Many persons with an accounting background work for the Federal Government as Internal Revenue Service agents or in financial management, financial institution examination, and budget analysis and administration.

Computers are widely used in accounting and auditing. With the aid of special software packages, accountants summarize transactions in standard formats for financial records, or organize data in special formats for financial analysis. These accounting packages greatly reduce the amount of tedious manual work associated with data and records; some packages require few specialized computer skills, while others require formal training. Personal and laptop computers enable accountants and auditors in all fields to use their clients' computer system and to extract information from large mainframe computers. Internal auditors may recommend controls for their organization's computer system to ensure the reliability of the system and the integrity of the data. A growing number of accountants and auditors have extensive computer skills and specialize in correcting problems with software or developing software to meet unique data needs.

Working Conditions

Accountants and auditors work in a normal office setting. Self-employed accountants may be able to do part of their work at home.

Accountants with professional certification have an advantage in the job market.

Accountants and auditors employed by public accounting firms and government agencies may travel frequently to perform audits at clients' places of business, branches of their firm, or government facilities.

Most accountants and auditors generally work a standard 40-hour week, but many work longer, particularly if they are self-employed and free to take on the work of as many clients as they choose. Tax specialists often work long hours during the tax season.

Employment

Accountants and auditors held over 1 million jobs in 1996. They worked throughout private industry and government, but about one-third worked on salary for accounting, auditing, and bookkeeping firms, or were self-employed.

Many accountants and auditors were unlicensed management accountants, internal auditors, or government accountants and auditors. However, many are State-licensed Certified Public Accountants (CPA's), Public Accountants (PA's), Registered Public Accountants (RPA's), and Accounting Practitioners (AP's).

Most accountants and auditors work in urban areas, in which public accounting firms and central or regional offices of businesses are concentrated.

Many individuals with backgrounds in accounting and auditing are full-time college and university faculty; others teach part time while working as self-employed accountants, or as salaried accountants for private industry or government. (See the Handbook statement on college and university faculty.)

Training, Other Qualifications, and Advancement

Most accountant and internal auditor positions require at least a bachelor's degree in accounting or a related field. Based on recommendations made by the American Institute of Certified Public Accountants, a small number of States currently require CPA candidates to complete 150 semester hours of college coursework—an additional 30 hours beyond the usual 4-year bachelor's degree—and many more States are expected to introduce this requirement in the future. Most schools have altered their curricula accordingly, and prospective accounting majors should carefully research accounting curricula and the requirements for any States in which they hope to become licensed before enrolling. Some employers prefer applicants with a master's degree in accounting, or a master's degree in business administration with a concentration in accounting. Most employers also prefer applicants who are familiar with computers and their applications in accounting and internal auditing.

For beginning accounting and auditing positions in the Federal Government, 4 years of college (including 24 semester hours in accounting or auditing) or an equivalent combination of education and experience is required.

Previous experience in accounting or auditing can help an applicant get a job. Many colleges offer students an opportunity to gain experience through summer or part-time internship programs conducted by public accounting or business firms. Such training is advantageous in gaining permanent employment in the field.

Professional recognition through certification or licensure provides a distinct advantage in the job market. All CPA's must have a certificate and the partners in their firm must have a license issued by a State board of accountancy. The vast majority of States require CPA candidates to be college graduates, but a few States substitute a certain number of years of public accounting experience for the educational requirement. As indicated earlier, a growing number of States require 150 hours of coursework; the composition of the additional 30 hours is unspecified by most States.

All States use the four-part Uniform CPA Examination prepared by the American Institute of Certified Public Accountants. The 2-day CPA examination is rigorous, and only about one-quarter of those who take it each year pass each part they attempt. Candidates are not required to pass all four parts at once, although most States require candidates to pass at least two parts for partial credit. Many States require all sections of the test to be passed within a certain period of

time. Most States also require applicants for a CPA certificate to have some accounting experience.

The designations PA or RPA are also recognized by most States, and several States continue to issue these licenses. With the growth in the number of CPA's, however, the majority of States are phasing out non-CPA designations—PA, RPA, and AP—by not issuing any more new licenses. Accountants who hold PA or RPA designations have similar legal rights, duties, and obligations as CPA's, but their qualifications for licensure are less stringent. The AP designation requires less formal training and covers a more limited scope of practice than the CPA.

Nearly all States require CPA's and other public accountants to complete a certain number of hours of continuing professional education before their licenses can be renewed. The professional associations representing accountants sponsor numerous courses, seminars, group study programs, and other forms of continuing education.

Professional societies bestow other forms of credentials on a voluntary basis. Voluntary certification can attest to professional competence in a specialized field of accounting and auditing. It can also certify that a recognized level of professional competence has been achieved by accountants and auditors who acquired some skills on the job, without the formal education or public accounting work experience needed to meet the rigorous standards required to take the CPA examination. Employers are increasingly seeking applicants with these credentials.

The Institute of Management Accountants (IMA) confers the Certified Management Accountant (CMA) designation upon applicants who complete a bachelor's degree, although a minimum score on specified graduate school entrance exams can be substituted for a bachelor's degree; pass a four-part examination; agree to meet continuing education requirements; comply with standards of professional conduct; and have at least 2 years' work in management accounting. The CMA program is administered through the Institute of Certified Management Accountants, an affiliate of the IMA.

The Institute of Internal Auditors confers the designation Certified Internal Auditor (CIA) to graduates from accredited colleges and universities who have completed 2 years' work in internal auditing, and who have passed a four-part examination. The Information Systems Audit and Control Association confers the designation Certified Information Systems Auditor (CISA) upon candidates who pass an examination, and who have 5 years of experience in auditing electronic data processing systems. However, auditing or data processing experience and college education may be substituted for up to 3 years. The Accreditation Council for Accountancy and Taxation, a satellite organization of the National Society of Public Accountants, confers three designations—Accredited in Accountancy (AA), Accredited Tax Advisor (ATA), and Accredited Tax Preparer (ATP). Candidates for the AA must pass an exam, while candidates for the ATA and ATP must complete the required coursework and pass an exam. Other organizations, such as the National Association of Certified Fraud Examiners and the Bank Administration Institute, confer specialized auditing designations. It is not uncommon for a practitioner to hold multiple licenses and designations. For instance, an internal auditor might be a CPA, CIA, and CISA.

Persons planning a career in accounting should have an aptitude for mathematics; be able to analyze, compare, and interpret facts and figures quickly; and make sound judgments based on this knowledge. They must be able to clearly communicate the results of their work, orally and in writing, to clients and management.

Accountants and auditors must be good at working with people as well as with business systems and computers. Accuracy and the ability to handle responsibility with limited supervision are important. Perhaps most important, because millions of financial statement users rely on their services, accountants and auditors should have high standards of integrity.

Capable accountants and auditors should advance rapidly; those having inadequate academic preparation may be assigned routine jobs and find promotion difficult. Many graduates of junior colleges and business and correspondence schools, as well as bookkeepers and accounting clerks who meet the education and experience requirements set by their employers, can obtain junior accounting positions and advance to more responsible positions by demonstrating their accounting skills on the job.

Beginning public accountants usually start by assisting with work for several clients. They may advance to positions with more responsibility in 1 or 2 years, and to senior positions within another few years. Those who excel may become supervisors, managers, partners, open their own public accounting firms, or transfer to executive positions in management accounting or internal auditing in private firms.

Beginning management accountants often start as cost accountants, junior internal auditors, or as trainees for other accounting positions. As they rise through the organization, they may advance to accounting manager, chief cost accountant, budget director, or manager of internal auditing. Some become controllers, treasurers, financial vice presidents, chief financial officers, or corporation presidents. Many senior corporation executives have a background in accounting, internal auditing, or finance.

There is a large degree of mobility among public accountants, management accountants, and internal auditors. Practitioners often shift into management accounting or internal auditing from public accounting, or between internal auditing and management accounting. However, it is less common for accountants and auditors to move from either management accounting or internal auditing into public accounting.

Job Outlook

Accountants and auditors who have earned professional recognition through certification or licensure should have the best job prospects. For example, CPA's should continue to enjoy a wide range of job opportunities, especially as more States enact the 150-hour requirement, making it more difficult to obtain this certification. Similarly, CMA's should be in demand as their management advice is increasingly sought. Applicants with a master's degree in accounting, or a master's degree in business administration with a concentration in accounting, may also have an advantage in the job market. Familiarity with accounting and auditing computer software, or expertise in specialized areas such as international business, specific industries, or current legislation, may also be helpful in landing certain accounting and auditing jobs. In addition, employers increasingly seek well rounded applicants with strong interpersonal and communication skills. Regardless of one's qualifications, however, competition will remain keen for the most prestigious jobs—those with major accounting and business firms.

Employment of accountants and auditors is expected to grow about as fast as the average for all occupations through the year 2006. The need to replace accountants and auditors who retire or transfer to other occupations will produce thousands of additional job openings annually, reflecting the large size of this occupation.

As the economy grows, the number of business establishments increases, requiring more accountants and auditors to set up their books, prepare their taxes, and provide management advice. As these businesses grow, the volume and complexity of information developed by accountants and auditors on costs, expenditures, and taxes will increase as well. More complex requirements for accountants and auditors also arise from changes in legislation related to taxes, financial reporting standards, business investments, mergers, and other financial matters. In addition, businesses will increasingly need quick, accurate, and individually tailored financial information due to the demands of growing international competition.

The changing role of accountants and auditors also will spur job growth. Accountants will perform less auditing work due to potential liability and relatively low profits, and less tax work due to growing competition from tax preparation firms, but they will offer more management and consulting services in response to market demand. Accountants will continue to take on a greater advisory role as they develop more sophisticated and flexible accounting systems, and focus more on analyzing operations rather than just providing finan-

cial data. Internal auditors will be increasingly needed to discover and eliminate waste and fraud.

Earnings

According to a salary survey conducted by the National Association of Colleges and Employers, bachelor's degree candidates in accounting received starting offers averaging $29,400 a year in 1996; master's degree candidates in accounting, $33,000.

According to a survey of workplaces in 160 metropolitan areas, accountants with limited experience had median earnings of $26,000 in 1995, with the middle half earning between $23,300 and $29,400. The most experienced accountants had median earnings of $87,400, with the middle half earning between $77,600 and $98,000. Public accountants—employed by public accounting firms—with limited experience had median earnings of $29,400, with the middle half earning between $28,200 and $32,000. The most experienced public accountants had median earnings of $48,700, with the middle half earning between $44,500 and $54,000. Many owners and partners of firms earned considerably more.

According to a salary survey conducted by Robert Half International, a staffing services firm specializing in accounting and finance, accountants and auditors with up to 1 year of experience earned between $25,000 and $39,400 in 1997. Those with 1 to 3 years of experience earned between $27,000 and $46,600. Senior accountants and auditors earned between $34,300 and $57,800; managers earned between $40,000 and $81,900; and directors of accounting and auditing earned between $54,800 and $109,800 a year. The variation in salaries reflects differences in size of firm, location, level of education, and professional credentials.

In the Federal Government, the starting annual salary for junior accountants and auditors was about $19,500 in 1997. Candidates who had a superior academic record might start at $24,200, while applicants with a master's degree or 2 years of professional experience might begin at $29,600. Beginning salaries were slightly higher in selected areas where the prevailing local pay level was higher. Accountants employed by the Federal Government in nonsupervisory, supervisory, and managerial positions averaged about $54,000 a year in 1997; auditors averaged $57,900.

Related Occupations

Accountants and auditors design internal control systems and analyze financial data. Others for whom training in accounting is invaluable include appraisers, budget officers, loan officers, financial analysts and managers, bank officers, actuaries, underwriters, tax collectors and revenue agents, FBI special agents, securities sales representatives, and purchasing agents.

Sources of Additional Information

Information about careers in certified public accounting and about CPA standards and examinations may be obtained from:
☛ American Institute of Certified Public Accountants, Harborside Financial Center, 201 Plaza III, Jersey City, NJ 07311-3881.
Homepage: http://www.aicpa.org

Information on careers in management accounting and the CMA designation may be obtained from:
☛ Institute of Management Accountants, 10 Paragon Dr., Montvale, NJ . 7645-1760. Homepage: http://www.imanet.org

Information on the Accredited in Accountancy/Accredited Business Accountant, Accredited Tax Advisor, or Accredited Tax Preparer designations may be obtained from:
☛ National Society of Accountants and the Accreditation Council for Accountancy and Taxation, 1010 North Fairfax St., Alexandria, VA 22314. Homepage: http://www.nspa.org

Information on careers in internal auditing and the CIA designation may be obtained from:
☛ The Institute of Internal Auditors, 249 Maitland Ave., Altamonte Springs, FL 32701-4201. Homepage: http://www.theiia.org

Information on careers in information systems auditing and the CISA designation may be obtained from:

☛ The Information Systems Audit and Control Association, 3701 Algonquin Rd., Suite 1010, Rolling Meadows, IL 60008. Homepage: http://www.isaca.org

For information on accredited programs in accounting and business, contact:

☛ American Assembly of Collegiate Schools of Business, 605 Old Ballas Rd., Suite 220, St. Louis, MO 63141. Homepage: http://www.aacsb.edu

Administrative Services Managers

(D.O.T. 163.167-026; 169.167-034; 188.117-122, .167-106)

Significant Points

- Many advance to these jobs by acquiring work experience in various administrative positions.

- Keen competition is expected due to low turnover and an ample supply of competent, experienced workers seeking managerial jobs.

Nature of the Work

Administrative services managers are employed throughout the American economy, and their range of duties is broad. They coordinate and direct support services, which may include: secretarial and reception; administration; payroll; conference planning and travel; information and data processing; mail; facilities management; materials scheduling and distribution; printing and reproduction; records management; telecommunications management; personal property procurement, supply, and disposal; security; and parking.

In small organizations, a single administrative services manager may oversee all support services. In larger ones, however, first-line administrative services managers report to mid-level supervisors who, in turn, report to proprietors or top-level managers. The upper-level managers, with titles such as vice president of administrative services, are included in the *Handbook* statement on general managers and top executives.

First-line administrative services managers directly oversee a staff that performs various support services. Mid-level managers develop departmental plans, set goals and deadlines, develop procedures to improve productivity and customer service, and define the responsibilities of supervisory-level managers. They are often involved in the hiring and dismissal of employees, but generally have no role in the formulation of personnel policy.

As the size of the firm increases, administrative services managers are more likely to specialize in one or more support activities. For example, some administrative services managers work primarily as facilities managers, office managers, property managers, or unclaimed property officers. In many cases, the duties of these administrative services managers are quite similar to those of other managers and supervisors, some of whom are discussed in other *Handbook* statements.

Administrative services managers who specialize in facilities management or planning may oversee the purchase, sale, or lease of facilities; redesign work areas to be more efficient and user-friendly; ensure that facilities comply with government regulations; and supervise maintenance, grounds, and custodial staffs. In some firms, they are called facilities managers.

Some mid-level administrative services managers oversee first-line supervisors from various departments, including the clerical staff. In small firms, however, clerical supervisors, who are discussed in the *Handbook* statement on clerical supervisors and managers, perform this function.

Property management is divided into the following functions: Management and use of personal property such as office supplies, administrative services management, and real property management (a function of property and real estate managers, who are discussed elsewhere in the *Handbook*). Personal property managers acquire,

Some individuals start their own administrative management consulting firms.

distribute, and store supplies, and may sell or dispose of surplus property. Other property managers are engaged solely in surplus property disposal, which involves the resale of scraps, rejects, and surplus or unneeded supplies and machinery. This is an increasingly important source of revenue for many commercial organizations. In government, surplus property officers may receive surplus from various departments and agencies, and then sell or dispose of it to the public or other agencies.

Some administrative services managers oversee unclaimed property disposal. In government, this activity may entail auctioning off unclaimed liquid assets such as stocks, bonds, the contents of safe deposit boxes, or personal property such as motor vehicles, after attempts to locate their rightful owners have failed.

Working Conditions

Administrative services managers generally work in comfortable offices. In smaller organizations, they may work alongside the people they supervise and the office may be crowded and noisy.

The work of administrative services managers can be stressful, as they attempt to schedule work to meet deadlines. Although the 40-hour week is standard, uncompensated overtime is often required to resolve problems. Managers involved in personal property procurement, use, and disposal may travel extensively between their home office, branch offices, vendors' offices, and property sales sites. Facilities managers who are responsible for the design of work spaces may spend time at construction sites and may travel between different facilities while monitoring the work of maintenance, grounds, and custodial staffs.

Employment

Administrative services managers held about 291,000 jobs in 1996. Over half worked in service industries, including management, business, social, and health services organizations. Others were found in virtually every other industry.

Training, Other Qualifications, and Advancement

Many administrative services managers advance through the ranks in their organization, acquiring work experience in various administrative positions before assuming first-line supervisory duties. All managers who oversee departmental supervisors should be familiar with office procedures and equipment. Facilities managers may have a background in architecture, engineering, construction, interior design, or real estate, in addition to managerial experience. Managers of personal property acquisition and disposal need experience in purchasing and sales, and knowledge of a wide variety of supplies, machinery, and equipment. Managers concerned with supply, inventory, and distribution must be experienced in receiving, warehousing, packaging, shipping, transportation, and related operations. Managers of unclaimed property often have experience in insurance claims analysis and records management.

Educational requirements for these managers vary widely, depending on the size and complexity of the organization. In small organizations, experience may be the only requirement needed to enter a position as office manager. When an opening in administrative services management occurs, the office manager may be promoted to the position based on past performance. In large organizations, however, administrative services managers are normally hired from outside, and each position has formal requirements concerning education and experience. For first-line administrative services managers of secretarial, mail room, and related support activities, many employers prefer an associate degree in business or management, although a high school diploma may suffice when combined with appropriate experience. For managers of audiovisual, graphics, and other technical activities, postsecondary technical school training is preferred. For managers of highly complex services, a bachelor's degree in business, human resources, or finance is often required. The curriculum should include courses in office technology, accounting, business mathematics, computer applications, human resources, and business law. Similarly, facilities managers may need a bachelor's degree in engineering, architecture, or business administration, although some have an associate degree in a technical specialty. Some administrative services managers have advanced degrees. Whatever the manager's educational background, it must be accompanied by related work experience reflecting demonstrated ability.

Persons interested in becoming administrative services managers should have good communication skills and be able to establish effective working relationships with many different people, ranging from managers, supervisors, and professionals, to clerks and blue-collar workers. They should be analytical, detail oriented, flexible, and decisive. The ability to coordinate several activities at once and quickly analyze and resolve specific problems is important. Ability to work under pressure and cope with deadlines is also important.

Advancement in small organizations is normally achieved by moving to other management positions or to a larger organization. Advancement is easier in large firms employing several levels of administrative services managers. Attainment of the Certified Administrative Manager (CAM) designation, through work experience and successful completion of examinations offered by the Institute of Certified Professional Managers, can increase one's advancement potential. A bachelor's degree enhances a first-level manager's opportunities to advance to a mid-level management position, such as director of administrative services, and eventually to a top-level management position, such as executive vice president for administrative services. Those with the required capital and experience can establish their own management consulting firm.

Job Outlook
Employment of administrative services managers is expected to grow about as fast as the average for all occupations through the year 2006. Like other managerial occupations, this occupation is characterized by low turnover. These factors, coupled with the ample supply of competent, experienced workers seeking managerial jobs, should result in keen competition for administrative services management positions in the coming years.

Many firms are increasingly contracting out administrative services positions and otherwise streamlining these functions in an effort to cut costs. Corporate restructuring has reduced the number of administrative services manager positions in recent years, and this trend is expected to continue.

As it becomes more common for firms and governments at all levels to contract out administrative services, demand for administrative services managers will increase in the management services, management consulting, and facilities support services firms providing these services.

Earnings
Earnings of administrative services managers vary greatly depending on their employer, specialty, and geographic area in which they work. According to a 1996 survey conducted by the AMS Foundation, building services/facilities managers earned about $53,800 a year in 1996; office/administrative services managers earned about $41,400; and records managers about $37,900.

In the Federal Government, facilities managers in nonsupervisory, supervisory, and managerial positions averaged $49,140 a year in early 1997; miscellaneous administrative and program officers, $53,330; industrial property managers, $47,930; property disposal specialists, $43,460; administrative officers $49,070, and support services administrators, $39,700.

Related Occupations
Administrative services managers direct and coordinate support services and oversee the purchase, use, and disposal of personal property. Occupations with similar functions include administrative assistants, appraisers, buyers, clerical supervisors, contract specialists, cost estimators, procurement services managers, property and real estate managers, purchasing managers, and personnel managers.

Sources of Additional Information
For information about careers in facilities management, contact:
☛ International Facility Management Association, 1 East Greenway Plaza, Suite 1100, Houston, TX 77046-0194 Homepage: Http:// www.IFMA.org
For information about the certified administrative manager designation, contact:
☛ Institute of Certified Professional Managers, James Madison University, College of Business, Harrisonburg, VA 22807.
For information about compensation of administrative managers, contact:
☛ AMS Foundation, 350 W. Jackson Boulevard, Suite 360, Chicago, IL 60661.

Budget Analysts

(D.O.T. 161.117-010, .267-030)

Significant Points

- Federal, State, and local governments employ 1 out of 3 budget analysts.

- A bachelor's degree generally is the minimum educational requirement; however, some employers require a master's degree.

- Competition for jobs should remain keen because of the substantial number of qualified applicants; those with a master's degree should enjoy the best job prospects.

Nature of the Work
Budget analysts play a primary role in the development, analysis, and execution of budgets. Budgets are financial plans used to estimate future requirements and organize and allocate operating and capital resources effectively. The analysis of spending behavior and the planning of future operations are an integral part of the decision-making process in most corporations and government agencies.

Budget analysts work in private industry, nonprofit organizations, and the public sector. In private industry, a budget analyst examines, analyzes, and seeks new ways to improve efficiency and increase profits. Although analysts working in government generally are not concerned with profits, they too are interested in finding the most efficient distribution of funds and other resources among various departments and programs.

A major responsibility of budget analysts is to provide advice and technical assistance in the preparation of annual budgets. At the beginning of the budget cycle, managers and department heads submit proposed operating and financial plans to budget analysts for review. These plans outline expected programs, including proposed program increases and new initiatives; estimated costs and expenses; and capital expenditures needed to finance these programs.

Analysts begin by examining the budget estimates or proposals for completeness, accuracy, and conformance with established procedures, regulations, and organizational objectives. Sometimes they review financial requests by employing cost-benefit analysis, assessing program trade-offs, and exploring alternative funding methods. They also examine past and current budgets, and research economic and financial developments that affect the organization's spending. This process allows analysts to evaluate proposals in terms of the organization's priorities and financial resources.

After this review process, budget analysts consolidate the individual department budgets into operating and capital budget summaries. The analysts submit preliminary budgets to senior management, or sometimes, as is often the case in local and State governments, to appointed or elected officials, with comments and supporting statements that justify or deny funding requests. By reviewing different departments' operating plans, analysts gain insight into an organization's overall operations. This generally proves useful when they interpret and offer technical assistance to officials approving the budget. At this point in the budget process, budget analysts help the chief operating officer, agency head, or other top managers analyze the proposed plan and devise possible alternatives if the projected results are unsatisfactory. The final decision to approve the budget, however, is usually made by the organization head in a private firm or elected officials in government, such as the State legislative body.

Throughout the rest of the year, analysts periodically monitor the budget by reviewing reports and accounting records to determine if allocated funds have been spent as specified. If deviations appear between the approved budget and actual performance, budget analysts may write a report explaining the causes of the variations along with recommendations for new or revised budget procedures. They suggest reallocation of excess funds or recommend program cuts to avoid or alleviate deficits. They also inform program managers and others within their organization of the status and availability of funds in different budget accounts. Before any changes are made to an existing program or a new one is started, a budget analyst assesses its efficiency and effectiveness. Analysts also may project budget needs for long-range planning.

The budget analyst's role has broadened as limited funding has led to downsizing and restructuring throughout private industry and government. In addition to developing guidelines and policies governing the formulation and maintenance of the budget, analysts may measure organizational performance, assessing the effect of various programs and policies on the budget, and help draft budget-related legislation. Budget analysts sometimes conduct training sessions for company or government agency personnel on new budget procedures.

Working Conditions

Budget analysts work in a normal office setting, generally 40 hours per week. However, during the initial development and mid-year and final reviews of budgets, they often experience the pressure of deadlines and tight work schedules. The work during these periods can be extremely stressful, and analysts are usually required to work more than the routine 40 hours a week.

Budget analysts spend the majority of their time working independently, compiling and analyzing data and preparing budget pro-

Senior budget analysts are prime candidates for promotion to management positions.

posals. Nevertheless, their routine schedule can be interrupted by special budget requests, meetings, and training sessions. Others may travel to obtain budget details and explanations of various programs from coworkers, and to personally observe what funding is being used for in the field.

Employment

Budget analysts held about 66,000 jobs throughout private industry and government in 1996. Federal, State, and local governments are major employers, accounting for one-third of budget analyst jobs. The Department of Defense employed 7 of every 10 budget analysts working for the Federal Government. Other major employers of budget analysts are schools, hospitals, banks; and manufacturers of transportation equipment, chemicals and allied products, electrical and electronic machinery, and industrial machines.

Training, Other Qualifications, and Advancement

Private firms and government agencies generally require candidates for budget analyst positions to have at least a bachelor's degree. Within the Federal Government, a bachelor's degree in any field is sufficient background for an entry-level budget analyst position. State and local governments have varying requirements, but a bachelor's degree in one of many areas—accounting, finance, business or public administration, economics, political science, planning, statistics, or a social science such as sociology—may qualify one for entry into the occupation. Sometimes, a field closely related to the employing industry or organization within an industry, such as engineering, may be preferred. An increasing number of States and other employers require a candidate to possess a master's degree to ensure adequate analytical and communication skills. Some firms prefer candidates with business backgrounds because business courses emphasize quantitative analytical skills. Budget and financial experience can occasionally be substituted for formal education when applying for a budget analyst position.

Because developing a budget involves manipulating numbers and requires strong analytical skills, courses in statistics or accounting are helpful, regardless of the prospective budget analyst's major field of study. Financial analysis in most organizations is automated, and requires familiarity with word processing and the financial software packages used in budget analysis. Software packages commonly used by budget analysts include electronic spreadsheets and database and graphics software. Employers generally prefer job candidates who already possess these computer skills over those who need to be trained.

In addition to analytical and computer skills, those seeking a career as a budget analyst must also be able to work under strict time constraints. Strong oral and written communication skills are essential for analysts to prepare, present, and defend budget proposals to decision makers.

Entry-level budget analysts may receive some formal training when they begin their jobs. However, most employers feel that the best training is obtained by working through one complete budget cycle. During the cycle, analysts become familiar with all the steps involved in the budgeting process.

The Federal Government, on the other hand, offers extensive on-the-job and classroom training for entry-level analysts, who are initially called trainees. Analysts are encouraged to participate in the various classes offered throughout their careers.

Beginning analysts usually work under close supervision. Capable entry-level analysts can be promoted into intermediate level positions within 1 to 2 years, and then into senior positions within a few more years. Progressing to a higher level means added budgetary responsibility and can lead to a supervisory role.

In the Federal Government, for example, beginning budget analysts compare projected costs with prior expenditures; consolidate and enter data prepared by others; and assist higher grade analysts by doing research. As analysts progress, they begin to develop and formulate budget estimates and justification statements; perform in-depth analyses of budget requests; write statements supporting funding requests; advise program managers and others on the status and availability of funds in different budget activities; and present and defend budget proposals to senior managers.

Because of the importance and high visibility of their jobs, senior budget analysts are prime candidates for promotion to management positions in various parts of the organization.

Job Outlook

Despite the increase in demand for budget analysts, competition for jobs should remain keen because of the substantial number of qualified applicants. Job opportunities are generally best for candidates with a master's degree. In some cases, budget and financial experience can offset a lack of formal education. A working knowledge of computer financial software packages can also enhance one's employment prospects in this field.

Employment of budget analysts is expected to grow about as fast as the average for all occupations through the year 2006. In addition to employment growth, many job openings will result from the need to replace experienced budget analysts who transfer to other occupations or leave the labor force.

Planning and financial control demand more attention because of the growing complexity of business and the increasing specialization within organizations. Many companies will continue to rely heavily on budget analysts to examine, analyze, and develop budgets to determine capital requirements and to allocate labor and other resources efficiently among all parts of the organization. Managers will continue to use budgets as a vehicle to plan, coordinate, control, and evaluate activities within their organizations more effectively.

Expanding automation continues to make budget analysts more productive, allowing them to process more data in less time. Also, computers are increasingly used to organize, summarize, and disseminate data to top-level managers, thereby centralizing decision-making and reducing the need for middle managers in many organizations. However, any computer-induced effects on employment of budget analysts may be offset by growing demand for information and analysis. Easier manipulation of and accessibility to data provide management with more considerations on which to base decisions.

The financial work performed by budget analysts is an important function in every organization. Financial and budget reports must be completed during periods of economic growth and slowdowns.

Therefore, budget analysts generally are less subject to layoffs during economic downturns than many other workers.

Earnings

Salaries of budget analysts vary widely by experience, education, and employer. According to a survey conducted by Robert Half International, a staffing services firm specializing in accounting and finance, starting salaries of budget and other financial analysts in small firms ranged from $24,000 to $33,200 in 1997; in large organizations, from $28,000 to $38,700. In small firms, analysts with 1 to 3 years of experience earned from $28,000 to $43,100; in large companies, from $31,000 to $51,300. Senior analysts in small firms earned from $34,500 to $50,000; in large firms, from $39,000 to $60,600. Earnings of managers in this field ranged from $40,000 to $65,000 a year in small firms, while managers in large organizations earned between $47,000 and $83,800.

A survey of workplaces in 160 metropolitan areas reported that inexperienced budget analysts had median annual earnings of about $30,100 in 1995, with the middle half earning between $26,200 and $35,500 a year.

In the Federal Government, budget analysts generally started as trainees earning $19,500 or $24,200 a year in 1997. Candidates with a master's degree might begin at $29,600. Beginning salaries were slightly higher in selected areas where the prevailing local pay level was higher. The average annual salary for budget analysts employed by the Federal Government in nonsupervisory, supervisory, and managerial positions was $48,600 in 1997.

Related Occupations

Budget analysts review, analyze, and interpret financial data; make recommendations for the future; and assist in the implementation of new ideas. Workers who use these skills in other occupations include accountants and auditors, economists, financial analysts, financial managers, and loan officers.

Sources of Additional Information

Information about career opportunities as a budget analyst may be available from your State or local employment service.

Information on acquiring a job as a budget analyst with the Federal Government may be obtained from the Office of Personnel Management through a telephone-based system. Consult your telephone directory under U.S. Government for a local number, or call (912) 757-3000 (TDD 912 744-2299). That number is not toll-free and charges may result. Information also is available from their Internet site: http://www.usajobs.opm.gov

Construction and Building Inspectors

(D.O.T. 168.167-030, -034, -038, -046, and -050; .267-010, -102; 182.267; 850.387, .467)

Significant Points

- Over 50 percent are employed by local governments, primarily municipal or county building departments.
- Construction and building inspectors tend to be older, more experienced workers who have spent years working in other related occupations.

Nature of the Work

Construction and building inspectors examine the construction, alteration, or repair of buildings, highways and streets, sewer and water systems, dams, bridges, and other structures to ensure compliance with building codes and ordinances, zoning regulations, and contract specifications. Throughout the country, building codes and standards are the primary means by which building construction is regulated to assure the health and safety of the general public. Inspectors make an initial inspection during the first phase of construction, and follow-up inspections throughout the construction project to monitor compliance with regulations. However, no inspection is ever exactly the same. In areas where certain types of severe weather or natural disasters are more common, inspectors monitor compliance with additional safety regulations designed to protect structures and occupants in these events.

Building inspectors inspect the structural quality and general safety of buildings. Some specialize—for example, in structural steel or reinforced concrete structures. Before construction begins, *plan examiners* determine whether the plans for the building or other structure comply with building code regulations, and if they are suited to the engineering and environmental demands of the building site. Inspectors visit the work site before the foundation is poured to inspect the soil condition and positioning and depth of the footings. Later, they return to the site to inspect the foundation after it has been completed. The size and type of structure and the rate of completion determine the number of other site visits they must make. Upon completion of the entire project, they make a final comprehensive inspection.

In addition to structural characteristics, a primary concern of building inspectors is fire safety. They inspect structure's fire sprinklers, alarms, and smoke control systems, as well as fire doors and exits. Inspectors assess the type of construction, building contents, adequacy of fire protection equipment, and risks posed by adjoining buildings.

There are many types of inspections and inspectors. *Electrical inspectors* examine the installation of electrical systems and equipment to ensure they function properly and comply with electrical codes and standards. They visit work sites to inspect new and existing sound and security systems, wiring, lighting, motors, and generating equipment. They also inspect the installation of the electrical wiring for heating and air-conditioning systems, appliances, and other components.

Elevator inspectors examine lifting and conveying devices such as elevators, escalators, moving sidewalks, lifts and hoists, inclined railways, ski lifts, and amusement rides.

Mechanical inspectors inspect the installation of the mechanical components of commercial kitchen appliances, heating and air-conditioning equipment, gasoline and butane tanks, gas and oil piping, and gas-fired and oil-fired appliances. Some specialize in boilers or ventilating equipment as well.

Plumbing inspectors examine plumbing systems, including private disposal systems, water supply and distribution systems, plumbing fixtures and traps, and drain, waste, and vent lines.

Public works inspectors ensure that Federal, State, and local government construction of water and sewer systems, highways, streets, bridges, and dams conforms to detailed contract specifications. They inspect excavation and fill operations, the placement of forms for concrete, concrete mixing and pouring, asphalt paving, and grading operations. They record the work and materials used so contract payments can be calculated. Public works inspectors may specialize in highways, structural steel, reinforced concrete, or ditches. Others specialize in dredging operations required for bridges and dams or for harbors.

Home inspectors generally conduct inspections of newly built or previously owned homes. Increasingly, prospective home buyers hire home inspectors to inspect and report the condition of a home's major systems, components, and structure. They are typically hired either immediately prior to a purchase offer on a home, or as a contingency to a sales contract. In addition to structural quality, home inspectors must be able to inspect all home systems and features, from plumbing, electrical, and heating or cooling systems to roofing.

Specification inspectors are employed by the owner of a building or structure under construction to ensure work is done according to design specifications. They represent the owners' interests, not the general public. These inspectors may also be utilized by insurance companies or financial institutions.

Details concerning construction projects, building and occupancy permits, and other documentation are generally stored on computers so they can easily be retrieved and kept accurate and up to date. For example, inspectors may use laptop computers to record their findings while inspecting a site. Most inspectors use computers to help them monitor the status of construction inspection activities and keep track of issued permits.

Although inspections are primarily visual, most inspectors, except home inspectors, may use tape measures, survey instruments, metering devices, and test equipment such as concrete strength measurers. They keep a log of their work, take photographs, file reports, and, if necessary, act on their findings. For example, construction inspectors notify the construction contractor, superintendent, or supervisor when they discover a code or ordinance violation or something that does not comply with the contract specifications or approved plans. If the problem is not corrected within a reasonable or specified period of time, government inspectors have authority to issue a "stop-work" order.

Many inspectors also investigate construction or alterations being done without proper permits. Inspectors who are employees of municipalities enforce laws pertaining to the proper design, construction, and use of buildings. They direct violators of permit laws to obtain permits and submit to inspection.

Working Conditions
Construction and building inspectors usually work alone. However, several may be assigned to large, complex projects, particularly be-

Construction and building inspectors make follow-up inspections throughout each phase of a construction project to monitor compliance with regulations.

cause inspectors tend to specialize in different areas of construction. Though they spend considerable time inspecting construction work sites, inspectors may spend much of their time in a field office reviewing blueprints, answering letters or telephone calls, writing reports, and scheduling inspections.

Inspection sites are dirty and may be cluttered with tools, materials, or debris. Inspectors may have to climb ladders or many flights of stairs, or may have to crawl around in tight spaces. Although their work is not generally considered hazardous, inspectors, like other construction workers, wear hard hats and adhere to other safety requirements while at a construction site.

Inspectors normally work regular hours. However, if an accident occurs at a construction site, inspectors must respond immediately and may work additional hours to complete their report.

Employment

Construction and building inspectors held about 66,000 jobs in 1996. Over 50 percent worked for local governments, primarily municipal or county building departments. Employment of local government inspectors is concentrated in cities and in suburban areas undergoing rapid growth. Local governments employ large inspection staffs, including many plan examiners or inspectors who specialize in structural steel, reinforced concrete, boiler, electrical, and elevator inspection.

Another 19 percent of all construction and building inspectors worked for engineering and architectural services firms, conducting inspections for a fee or on a contract basis. Most of the remaining inspectors were employed by the Federal and State governments. Many construction inspectors employed by the Federal Government work for the U.S. Army Corps of Engineers. Other Federal employers include the Tennessee Valley Authority and the Departments of Agriculture, Housing and Urban Development, and Interior.

Training, Other Qualifications, and Advancement

Although requirements vary considerably depending upon where one is employed, individuals who want to become construction and building inspectors should have a thorough knowledge of construction materials and practices in either a general area, such as structural or heavy construction, or in a specialized area, such as electrical or plumbing systems, reinforced concrete, or structural steel. Construction or building inspectors need several years of experience as a manager, supervisor, or craft worker before becoming inspectors. Many previously worked as carpenters, electricians, plumbers, or pipefitters.

Because inspectors need to posses the right mix of technical knowledge, experience and education, employers prefer to hire inspectors who have formal training, as well as experience. Most require at least a high school diploma or equivalent even for those with considerable experience. More often, employers look for persons who have studied engineering or architecture, or who have a degree from a community or junior college, with courses in construction technology, drafting, mathematics, and building inspection. Many community colleges offer certificate or associate degree programs in building inspection technology. Courses in blueprint reading, algebra, geometry, and English are also useful.

Construction and building inspectors must be in good physical condition in order to walk and climb about construction sites. They must also have a driver's license. In addition, Federal, State, and many local governments may require that inspectors pass a civil service examination.

Construction and building inspectors usually receive much of their training on the job, although they must often learn building codes and standards on their own. Working with an experienced inspector, they learn about inspection techniques; codes, ordinances, and regulations; contract specifications; and record keeping and reporting duties. They may begin by inspecting less complex types of construction, such as residential buildings, and then progress to more difficult assignments. An engineering or architectural degree is often required for advancement to supervisory positions.

Because they advise builders and the general public on building codes, construction practices, and technical developments, construction and building inspectors must keep abreast of changes in these areas. Continuing education is imperative in this ever-changing field. Many employers provide formal training programs to broaden inspectors' knowledge of construction materials, practices, and techniques. Inspectors who work for small agencies or firms that do not conduct training programs can expand their knowledge and upgrade their skills by attending State-sponsored training programs, by taking college or correspondence courses, or by attending seminars sponsored by various related organizations such as model code organizations.

Most States and cities require some type of certification for employment and, even if not required, certification can enhance an inspector's opportunities for employment and advancement to more responsible positions. To become certified, inspectors with substantial experience and education must pass stringent examinations on code requirements, construction techniques, and materials. The three major model code organizations offer voluntary certification as do other professional membership associations. In most cases, there are no education or experience prerequisites, and certification consist of passing an examination in a designated field. Many categories of certification are awarded for inspectors and plan examiners in a variety of disciplines, including the designation "CBO," Certified Building Official.

Job Outlook

Employment of construction and building inspectors is expected to grow as fast as the average for all occupations through the year 2006. Growing concern for public safety and improvements in the quality of construction should continue to stimulate demand for construction and building inspectors. Despite the expected employment growth, most job openings will arise from the need to replace inspectors who transfer to other occupations or leave the labor force. Construction and building inspectors tend to be older, more experienced workers who have spent years working in other occupations.

Opportunities should be best for highly experienced supervisors and craft workers who have some college education, engineering or architectural training, or who are certified as inspectors or plan examiners. Thorough knowledge of construction practices and skills in areas such as reading and evaluating blueprints and plans are essential. However, inspectors are involved in all phases of construction, including maintenance and repair work, and are therefore less likely to lose jobs during recessionary periods when new construction slows. As the population grows and the volume of real estate transactions increases, greater emphasis on home inspections should result in rapid growth in employment of home inspectors. In addition, there should be good opportunities in engineering, architectural and management services firms due to the tendency of governments—particularly the Federal and State—to contract out inspection work, as well as expected growth in private inspection services.

Earnings

The median annual salary of construction and building inspectors was about $33,700 in 1996. The middle 50 percent earned between $26,500 and $45,800. The lowest 10 percent earned less than $21,600 and the highest 10 percent earned more than $55,800 a year. Generally, building inspectors, including plan examiners, earn the highest salaries. Salaries in large metropolitan areas are substantially higher than those in small local jurisdictions.

Related Occupations

Construction and building inspectors combine a knowledge of construction principles and law with an ability to coordinate data, diagnose problems, and communicate with people. Workers in other occupations using a similar combination of skills include engineers, drafters, estimators, industrial engineering technicians, surveyors, architects, and construction managers.

Sources of Additional Information

Information about certification and a career as a construction or building inspector is available from the following model code organizations:

☛ International Conference of Building Officials, 5360 Workman Mill Rd., Whittier, CA 90601-2298. Homepage: http://www.icbo.org

☛ Building Officials and Code Administrators International, Inc., 4051 West Flossmoor Rd., Country Club Hills, IL 60478. Homepage: http://www.bocai.org

☛ Southern Building Code Congress International, Inc., 900 Montclair Rd., Birmingham, AL 35213.

Information about a career as a home inspector is available from:

☛ American Society of Home Inspectors, Inc., 85 West Algonquin Rd., Arlington Heights, IL 60005. Homepage: http://www.ashi.com

For information about a career as a State or local government construction or building inspector, contact your State or local employment service.

Construction Managers

(D.O.T. 182.167-010, -018, -026, -030, and -034)

Significant Points

- Construction managers make decisions regarding daily construction activities at the job site.

- Good employment opportunities are expected because the increasing complexity of construction projects should increase demand for management level personnel.

- More and more employers—particularly, large construction firms—seek to hire individuals who combine industry work experience with a bachelor's degree in construction or building science or construction management.

Nature of the Work

Construction managers plan and direct construction projects. They may hold a variety of job titles, such as construction superintendent, general superintendent, project engineer, project manager, general construction manager, or executive construction manager. Construction managers may be owners or salaried employees of a construction management or contracting firm, or may work under contract or as a salaried employee of the owner, developer, contractor, or management firm overseeing the construction project. The *Handbook* uses the term "construction manager" to describe all salaried or self-employed managers of construction who oversee construction supervisors and workers.

In contrast with the *Handbook* definition, the term "construction manager" is used more narrowly within the construction industry to denote a management firm, or an individual employed by such a firm, involved in management oversight of a construction project. Under this narrower definition, construction managers generally act as representatives of the owner or developer with other participants throughout the life of a project. Although they generally play no direct role in the actual construction of a structure, they typically schedule and coordinate all design and construction processes including the selection, hiring, and oversight of specialty subcontractors.

Managers and other professionals who work in the construction industry, such as general managers, project engineers, cost estimators, and others, are increasingly referred to as *constructors*. This term refers to a broad group of professionals in construction who, through education and experience, are capable of managing, coordinating, and supervising the construction process from conceptual development through final construction on a timely and economical basis. Given designs for buildings, roads, bridges, or other projects, constructors oversee the organization, scheduling, and implementation of the project to execute those designs. They are responsible for coordinating and managing people, materials, and equipment; budgets, schedules, and contracts; and the safety of employees and the general public.

On large projects, construction managers may work for a *general contractor*—the firm with overall responsibility for all activities. There they oversee the completion of all construction in accordance with the engineer or architect's drawings and specifications and prevailing building codes. They arrange for *subcontractors* to perform specialized craft work or other specified construction work. On small projects, such as remodeling a home, a self-employed construction manager or skilled trades worker who directs and oversees employees is often referred to as the construction "contractor."

Large construction projects, such as an office building or industrial complex, are too complicated for one person to manage. These projects are divided into many segments: Site preparation, including land clearing and earth moving; sewage systems; landscaping and road construction; building construction, including excavation and laying foundations, erection of structural framework, floors, walls, and roofs; and building systems, including fire protection, electrical, plumbing, air-conditioning, and heating. Construction managers may work as part of a team or be in charge of one or more of these activities.

Construction managers evaluate various construction methods and determine the most cost-effective plan and schedule. They determine the appropriate construction methods and schedule all required construction site activities into logical, specific steps, budgeting the time required to meet established deadlines. This may require sophisticated estimating and scheduling techniques, and use of computers with specialized software. This also involves the selection and coordination of subcontractors hired to complete specific pieces of the project—which could include everything from structural metalworking and plumbing, to painting and carpet installation. Construction managers determine the labor requirements and, in some cases, supervise or monitor the hiring and dismissal of workers. They oversee the performance of all trade contractors and are responsible for ensuring all work is completed on schedule.

Managers direct and monitor the progress of construction activities, at times through other construction supervisors. This includes the delivery and use of materials, tools, and equipment; the quality of construction, worker productivity, and safety. They are responsible for obtaining all necessary permits and licenses and, depending upon the contractual arrangements, direct or monitor compliance with building and safety codes and other regulations. They may have several subordinates, such as assistant managers or superintendents, field engineers, or crew supervisors, reporting to them.

Construction managers regularly review engineering and architectural drawings and specifications to monitor progress and ensure

Duties of construction managers include tracking and controlling costs and budgeting the time required to meet established deadlines.

compliance with plans and specifications. They track and control construction costs to avoid cost overruns. Based upon direct observation and reports by subordinate supervisors, managers may prepare daily reports of progress and requirements for labor, material, and machinery and equipment at the construction site. They meet regularly with owners, subcontractors, architects, and other design professionals to monitor and coordinate all phases of the construction project.

Working Conditions

Construction managers work out of a main office from which the overall construction project is monitored or out of a field office at the construction site. Management decisions regarding daily construction activities are usually made at the job site. Managers usually travel when the construction site is in another State or when they are responsible for activities at two or more sites. Management of overseas construction projects usually entails temporary residence in another country.

Construction managers must be "on call" to deal with delays, bad weather, or emergencies at the site. Most work more than a standard 40-hour week because construction may proceed around-the-clock. This type of work schedule can go on for days, even weeks, to meet special project deadlines, especially if there are delays.

Although the work generally is not considered dangerous, construction managers must be careful while touring construction sites. Managers must be able to establish priorities and assign duties. They need to observe job conditions and to be alert to changes and potential problems, particularly involving safety on the job site and adherence to regulations.

Employment

Construction managers held about 249,000 jobs in 1996. Around 40,000 were self-employed. Over 85 percent were employed in the construction industry, primarily by specialty trade contractors—for example, plumbing, heating and air-conditioning, and electrical contractors—and general building contractors. Others were employed by engineering, architectural, surveying, and construction management services firms, as well as local governments, educational institutions, and real estate developers.

Training, Other Qualifications, and Advancement

Persons interested in becoming a construction manager need a solid background in building science, business, and management, as well as related work experience within the construction industry. They need to be able to understand contracts, plans, and specifications, and to be knowledgeable about construction methods, materials, and regulations. Familiarity with computers and software programs for job costing, scheduling, and estimating is increasingly important.

Traditionally, persons advanced to construction management positions after having substantial experience as construction craft workers—for example, as carpenters, masons, plumbers, or electricians—or after having worked as construction supervisors or as owners of independent specialty contracting firms overseeing workers in one or more construction trades. However, more and more employers—particularly, large construction firms—seek to hire individuals who combine industry work experience with a bachelor's degree in construction or building science or construction management.

Construction managers should be adaptable and be able to work effectively in a fast-paced environment. They should be decisive and able to work well under pressure, particularly when faced with unexpected occurrences or delays. The ability to coordinate several major activities at once, while analyzing and resolving specific problems, is essential, as is understanding engineering, architectural, and other construction drawings. Good oral and written communication skills are also important. Managers must be able to establish a good working relationship with many different people including owners, other managers, design professionals, supervisors, and craft workers.

Advancement opportunities for construction managers vary depending upon the size and type of company for which they work. Within large firms, managers may eventually become top-level managers or executives. Highly experienced individuals may become independent consultants; some serve as expert witnesses in court or as arbitrators in disputes. Those with the required capital may establish their own construction management services or general contracting firm.

In 1996, over 100 colleges and universities offered 4-year degree programs in construction management or construction science. These programs include courses in project control and development, site planning, design, construction methods, construction materials, value analysis, cost estimating, scheduling, contract administration, accounting, business and financial management, building codes and standards, inspection procedures, engineering and architectural sciences, mathematics, statistics, and information technology. Graduates from 4-year degree programs are usually hired as assistants to project managers, field engineers, schedulers, or cost estimators. An increasing number of graduates in related fields—engineering or architecture, for example—also enter construction management, often after having had substantial experience on construction projects or after completing graduate studies in construction management or building science.

Around 30 colleges and universities offer a master's degree program in construction management or construction science, and at least two offer a Ph.D. in the field. Master's degree recipients, especially those with work experience in construction, typically become construction managers in very large construction or construction management companies. Often, individuals who hold a bachelor's degree in an unrelated field seek a master's degree in order to work in the construction industry. Doctoral degree recipients generally become college professors or work in an area of research.

Many individuals also attend training and educational programs sponsored by industry associations, often in collaboration with postsecondary institutions. A number of 2-year colleges throughout the country offer construction management or construction technology programs.

Both the American Institute of Constructors (AIC) and the Construction Management Association of America (CMA) have established voluntary certification programs for construction professionals. Both programs' requirements combine written examinations with verification of professional experience. AIC awards the designations Associate Constructor (AC) and Certified Professional Constructor (CPC) to candidates who meet the requirements and pass appropriate construction examinations. CMA awards the designation Certified Construction Manager (CCM) to practitioners who meet the requirements, complete a professional construction management "capstone" course, and pass a technical examination. Although certification is not required to work in the construction industry, voluntary certification can be valuable because it provides evidence of competence and experience.

Job Outlook

Employment of construction managers is expected to increase as fast as the average for all occupations through the year 2006, as the level of construction activity and complexity of construction projects continues to grow. Prospects in construction management, engineering and architectural services, and construction contracting firms should be particularly favorable for persons with a bachelor's degree or higher in construction science, construction management, or construction engineering who have worked in construction. Employers prefer applicants with previous construction work experience who can combine a strong background in building technology with proven supervisory or managerial skills. In addition, many job openings should result annually from the need to replace workers who transfer to other occupations or leave the labor force.

The increasing complexity of construction projects should increase demand for management level personnel within the construction industry, as sophisticated technology and the proliferation of laws setting standards for buildings and construction materials, worker safety, energy efficiency, and environmental protection have further complicated the construction process. Advances in building materials and construction methods and the growing number of multipurpose buildings, electronically operated "smart" buildings, and energy-efficient structures will further add to the demand for more construction managers. However, employment of construction managers can be sensitive to the short-term nature of many construction projects and cyclical fluctuations in construction activity.

Earnings

Earnings of salaried construction managers and incomes of self-employed independent construction contractors vary depending upon the size and nature of the construction project, its geographic location, and economic conditions. According to a 1997 salary survey by the National Association of Colleges and Employers, bachelor's degree candidates with degrees in the field of construction management received offers averaging $28,060 a year. Bachelor's degree candidates with degrees in the field of construction science received offers averaging $31,949 a year. Based on the limited information available, the average salary for experienced construction managers in 1996 ranged from around $40,000 to $100,000 annually. Many salaried construction managers receive benefits such as bonuses, use of company motor vehicles, paid vacations, and life and health insurance.

Related Occupations

Construction managers participate in the conceptual development of a construction project and oversee its organization, scheduling, and implementation. Occupations in which similar functions are performed include architects, civil engineers, construction supervisors, cost engineers, cost estimators, developers, electrical engineers, industrial engineers, landscape architects, and mechanical engineers.

Sources of Information

For information about career opportunities in the construction industry contact:
☛ Associated Builders and Contractors, 1300 North 17th St., Rosslyn, VA 22209. Homepage: http://www.abc.org
☛ Associated General Contractors of America, 1957 E St. NW., Washington, DC 20006-5199. Homepage: http://www.agc.org

For information about constructor certification and professional career opportunities in the construction industry, contact:
☛ American Institute of Constructors, 466 94th Ave. North, St. Petersburg, FL 33702. E-mail address: aicnatl@aol.com Homepage: http://www.aicnet.org

For information about construction management and construction manager certification contact:
☛ Construction Management Association of America, 7918 Jones Branch Dr., Suite 540, McLean, VA 22102. Homepage: http://www.access.digex.net/~cmaa

Information on accredited construction science and management programs and accreditation requirements is available from:
☛ American Council for Construction Education, 1300 Hudson Lane, Suite 3, Monroe, LA 71201-6054. E-mail address: acce@iamerica.net

Cost Estimators

(D.O.T. 169.267-038; 221.362-018, and .367-014)

Significant Points

- Growth of the construction industry, where over 60 percent of all cost estimators are employed, will be the driving force behind the demand for these workers.

- Job prospects in construction should be best for those workers with a degree in construction management or

construction science, engineering, or architectural drafting, who have experience in various phases of construction or a specialty craft area.

Nature of the Work

Accurately predicting the cost of future projects is vital to the survival of any business. Cost estimators develop cost information for owners or managers to use in determining resource and material quantities, making bids for contracts, determining if a new product will be profitable, or determining which products are making a profit for a firm.

Regardless of the industry in which they work, estimators compile and analyze data on all the factors that can influence costs—such as materials, labor, location, and special machinery requirements, including computer hardware and software. Job duties vary widely depending upon the type and size of the project. Those with an engineering background who apply scientific principles and methods to undertake feasibility studies, value engineering, and life-cycle costing may be referred to as *cost engineers*.

The methods of, and motivations for estimating costs can vary greatly, depending on the industry. On a large construction project, for example, the estimating process begins with the decision to submit a bid. After reviewing the architect's drawings and specifications, the estimator visits the site of the proposed project. The estimator needs to gather information on access to the site and availability of electricity, water, and other services, as well as surface topography and drainage. The information developed during the site visit generally is recorded in a signed report that is made part of the final project estimate.

After the site visit is completed, the estimator determines the quantity of materials and labor the firm will have to furnish. This process, called the quantity survey or "takeoff," involves completing standard estimating forms, filling in dimensions, number of units, and other information. A cost estimator working for a general contractor, for example, will estimate the costs of all items the contractor must provide. Although subcontractors will estimate their costs as part of their own bidding process, the general contractor's cost estimator often analyzes bids made by subcontractors as well. Also during the takeoff process, the estimator must make decisions concerning equipment needs, sequence of operations, and crew size. Allowances for the waste of materials, inclement weather, shipping delays, and other factors that may increase costs must also be incorporated in the takeoff.

On completion of the quantity surveys, the chief estimator prepares a total project cost summary, including the costs of labor, equipment, materials, subcontracts, overhead, taxes, insurance, markup, and any other costs that may affect the project. The chief estimator then prepares the bid proposal for submission to the developer.

Construction cost estimators may also be employed by the project's architect or owner to estimate costs or track actual costs relative to bid specifications as the project develops. In large construction companies employing more than one estimator, it is common practice for estimators to specialize. For instance, one may estimate only electrical work and another may concentrate on excavation, concrete, and forms.

In manufacturing and other firms, cost estimators generally are assigned to the engineering, cost, or pricing departments. The estimators' goal in manufacturing is to accurately estimate the costs associated with making products. The job may begin when management requests an estimate of the costs associated with a major redesign of an existing product or the development of a new product or production process. When estimating the cost of developing a new product, for example, the estimator works with engineers, first reviewing blueprints or conceptual drawings to determine the machining operations, tools, gauges, and materials that would be required for the job. The estimator then prepares a parts list and determines whether it is more efficient to produce or to purchase the parts. To do this, the estimator must initiate inquiries for price information from potential suppliers. The next step is to determine the cost of manufacturing each component of the product. Some high technology products require a tremendous amount of computer programming during the design phase. The cost of software development is one of the fastest growing and most difficult activities to estimate. Some cost estimators now specialize in only estimating computer software development and related costs.

The cost estimator then prepares time-phase charts and learning curves. Time-phase charts indicate the time required for tool design and fabrication, tool "debugging"—finding and correcting all problems—manufacturing of parts, assembly, and testing. Learning curves graphically represent the rate at which performance improves with practice. These curves are commonly called "cost reduction" curves because many problems—such as engineering changes, rework, parts shortages, and lack of operator skills—diminish as the number of parts produced increases, resulting in lower unit costs.

Using all of this information, the estimator then calculates the standard labor hours necessary to produce a predetermined number of units. Standard labor hours are then converted to dollar values, to which are added factors for waste, overhead, and profit to yield the unit cost in dollars. The estimator then compares the cost of purchasing parts with the firm's cost of manufacturing them to determine which is cheaper.

Computers play an integral role in cost estimating today, because estimating may involve complex mathematical calculations and require advanced mathematical techniques. For example, to undertake a parametric analysis, a process used to estimate project costs on a per unit basis subject to the specific requirements of a project, cost estimators use a computer database containing information on costs and conditions of many other similar projects. Although computers cannot be used for the entire estimating process, they can relieve estimators of much of the drudgery associated with routine, repetitive, and time-consuming calculations. Computers are also used to produce all of the necessary documentation with the help of basic word-processing and spreadsheet software. This leaves estimators with more time to study and analyze projects and can lead to more accurate estimates.

Cost estimators compile and analyze data on all the factors that can influence costs.

Working Conditions

Although estimators spend most of their time in an office, construction estimators must make frequent visits to project work sites that are dirty and cluttered with debris. Likewise, estimators in manufacturing must spend time on the factory floor where it also can be noisy and dirty. In some industries, frequent travel between a firm's headquarters and its subsidiaries or subcontractors also may be required.

Although estimators normally work a 40-hour week, overtime is common. Cost estimators usually operate under pressure, especially when facing deadlines. Inaccurate estimating can cause a firm to lose out on a bid or lose money on a job that proves to be unprofitable.

Employment

Cost estimators held about 188,000 jobs in 1996, over 60 percent of which were in the construction industry. Another 26 percent were employed in manufacturing industries. The remainder worked for engineering and architectural services firms, business services firms, and throughout a wide range of other industries. Operations research, production control, cost, and price analysts who work for government agencies may also do significant amounts of cost estimating in the course of their regular duties. In addition, the duties of construction managers may also include estimating costs. (For more information, see the section on operations research analysts and construction managers elsewhere in the *Handbook*.)

Cost estimators work throughout the country, usually in or near major industrial, commercial, and government centers, and in cities and suburban areas undergoing rapid change or development.

Training, Other Qualifications, and Advancement

Entry requirements for cost estimators vary by industry. In the construction industry, employers increasingly prefer individuals with a degree in building construction, construction management, construction science, civil engineering, or architectural drafting. However, most construction estimators also have considerable construction experience. Applicants with a thorough knowledge of construction materials, costs, and procedures in areas ranging from heavy construction to electrical work, plumbing systems, or masonry work have a competitive edge.

In manufacturing industries, employers prefer to hire individuals with a degree in engineering, physical science, operations research, mathematics, or statistics, or in accounting, finance, business, economics, or a related subject. In most industries, great emphasis is placed on experience involving quantitative techniques.

Cost estimators should have an aptitude for mathematics, be able to quickly analyze, compare, and interpret detailed and sometimes poorly defined information, and be able to make sound and accurate judgments based on this knowledge. Assertiveness and self-confidence in presenting and supporting their conclusions are important, as are strong communications and interpersonal skills, because estimators may work as part of a project team alongside other managers as well as owners, engineers, and design professionals. Cost estimators also need to be at ease with computers and their application in the estimating process, including word-processing and spreadsheet packages used to produce necessary documentation. In some instances, familiarity with special estimation software or programming skills may be required.

Regardless of their background, estimators receive much training on the job; almost every company has its own way of handling estimates. Working with an experienced estimator, they become familiar with each step in the process. Those with no experience reading construction specifications or blueprints first learn that aspect of the work. They then may accompany an experienced estimator to the construction site or shop floor where they observe the work being done, take measurements, or perform other routine tasks. As they become more knowledgeable, estimators learn how to tabulate quantities and dimensions from drawings and how to select the appropriate material prices.

For most estimators, advancement takes the form of higher pay and prestige. Some move into management positions, such as project manager for a construction firm or manager of the industrial engineering department for a manufacturer. Others may go into business for themselves as consultants, providing estimating services for a fee to government or construction and manufacturing firms.

Many colleges and universities include cost estimating as part of bachelor and associate degree-level curriculums in civil engineering, industrial engineering, and construction management or construction engineering technology. In addition, cost estimating is a significant part of master's degree programs in construction science or construction management offered by many colleges and universities. Organizations representing cost estimators, such as American Association of Cost Engineers (AACE) International and the Society of Cost Estimating and Analysis, also sponsor educational and professional development programs. These programs help students, estimators-in-training, and experienced estimators stay abreast of changes affecting the profession. Specialized courses and programs in cost estimating techniques and procedures are also offered by many technical schools, community colleges, and universities.

Voluntary certification can be valuable to cost estimators, because it provides professional recognition of the estimator's competence and experience. In some instances, individual employers may even require professional certification for employment. Both AACE International and the Society of Cost Estimating and Analysis administer certification programs. To become certified, estimators generally must have between 3 and 7 years of estimating experience and must pass both a written and an oral examination. In addition, certification requirements may include publication of at least one article or paper in the field.

Job Outlook
Overall employment of cost estimators is expected to grow about as fast as average for all occupations through the year 2006. Given the fact that no new projects in construction, manufacturing, or other industries are undertaken without careful analysis and estimation of the costs involved, job opportunities should remain favorable. Even when construction and manufacturing activity decline, there should always remain a demand for cost estimators. In addition to openings created by growth, some job openings will also arise from the need to replace workers who transfer to other occupations or leave the labor force.

Growth of the construction industry, where over 60 percent of all cost estimators are employed, will be the driving force behind the demand for these workers. The fastest growing sectors of the construction industry are expected to be special trade contractors and those associated with heavy construction and spending on the Nation's infrastructure. Construction and repair of highways and streets, bridges, and construction of more subway systems, airports, water and sewage systems, and electric power plants and transmission lines will stimulate demand for many more cost estimators. Job prospects in construction should be best for those workers with a degree in construction management or construction science, engineering, or architectural drafting, who have experience in various phases of construction or a specialty craft area.

Employment of cost estimators in manufacturing should remain relatively stable as firms continue to use their services to identify and control their operating costs. Experienced estimators with degrees in engineering, science, mathematics, business administration, or economics and who have computer expertise should have the best job prospects in manufacturing.

Earnings
Salaries of cost estimators vary widely by experience, education, size of firm, and industry. According to limited available data, most starting salaries in the construction industry for cost estimators with limited training were between about $20,000 and $30,000 a year in 1996. College graduates with degrees in fields such as engineering or construction management that provide a strong background in cost estimating could start at a higher level. According to a 1997 salary survey by the National Association of Colleges and Employers, bachelor's degree candidates with degrees in construction science received offers averaging $31,949 a year.

Bachelor's degree candidates with degrees in construction management received offers averaging $28,060 a year. Highly experienced cost estimators earned $75,000 a year or more. Starting salaries and annual earnings in the manufacturing sector were usually somewhat higher.

Related Occupations
Other workers who quantitatively analyze information in a similar capacity include appraisers, cost accountants, auditors, budget analysts, cost engineers, economists, financial analysts, loan officers, operations research analysts, underwriters, and value engineers. In addition, the duties of production managers and construction managers may also involve analyzing costs.

Sources of Additional Information
Information about career opportunities, certification, educational programs, and cost estimating techniques may be obtained from:
☛ AACE International, 209 Prairie Ave., Suite 100, Morgantown, WV 26505. Homepage: http://www.aacei.org
☛ Professional Construction Estimators Association of America, P.O. Box 11626, Charlotte, NC 28220-1626.
☛ Society of Cost Estimating and Analysis, 101 S. Whiting St., Suite 201, Alexandria, VA 22304. Homepage: *http://www.erols.com/scea/*

Education Administrators

(D.O.T. 075.117-010, -018, -030; 090.117 except -034, .167; 091.107; 092.167; 094.117-010, .167-014; 096.167; 097.167; 099.117 except -022, .167-034; 100.117-010; 169.267-022; 239.137-010)

Significant Points

● Most jobs require experience in a related occupation, such as teacher or admissions counselor, and a master's or doctoral degree.

● Competition will be keen for jobs in higher education, but will be much less intense for jobs at the elementary and secondary school level.

Nature of the Work
Smooth operation of an educational institution requires competent administrators. Education administrators provide direction, leadership, and day-to-day management of educational activities in schools, colleges and universities, businesses, correctional institutions, museums, and job training and community service organizations. (College presidents and school superintendents are covered in the *Handbook* statement on general managers and top executives.) Education administrators set educational standards and goals and establish the policies and procedures to carry them out. They develop academic programs; monitor students' educational progress; train and motivate teachers and other staff; manage guidance and other student services; administer recordkeeping; prepare budgets; handle relations with parents, prospective and current students, employers, and the community; and perform many other duties.

Education administrators also supervise managers, support staff, teachers, counselors, librarians, coaches, and others. In an organization such as a small daycare center, one administrator may handle all these functions. In universities or large school systems, responsibilities are divided among many administrators, each with a specific function.

Those who manage elementary and secondary schools are called principals. They set the academic tone, hire teachers and other staff, help them improve their skills, and evaluate them. Principals confer with staff—advising, explaining, or answering procedural questions. They visit classrooms, observe teaching methods, review instructional objectives, and examine learning materials. They actively work with teachers to develop and maintain high curriculum standards, develop mission statements, and set performance goals and objectives. Principals must ensure they use clear, objective guidelines for teacher appraisals, since pay is often based on performance ratings.

Principals also meet and interact with other administrators, students, parents, and representatives of community organizations. Decision-making authority has shifted from school district central offices to individual schools. Thus, parents, teachers, and other members of the community play an important role in setting school policies and goals. Principals must pay attention to the concerns of these groups when making administrative decisions.

Budgets and reports on various subjects, including finances and attendance, are prepared by principals, who also oversee the requisitioning and allocation of supplies. As school budgets become tighter, many principals are more involved in public relations and fund raising to secure financial support for their schools from local businesses and the community.

Principals must take an active role to ensure that students meet national academic standards. Many principals develop school/ business partnerships and school-to-work transition programs for students. Increasingly, principals must be sensitive to the needs of the rising number of non-English speaking and culturally diverse students. Growing enrollments, which are leading to overcrowding at many existing schools, are also a cause for concern. When addressing problems of inadequate available resources, administrators serve as advocates to build new schools or repair existing ones.

Schools continue to be involved with students' emotional welfare as well as their academic achievement. As a result, principals face responsibilities outside the academic realm. For example, in response to the growing number of dual-income and single-parent families and teenage parents, schools have established before- and after-school child-care programs or family resource centers, which also may offer parenting classes and social service referrals. With the help of community organizations, some principals have established programs to combat the increase in crime, drug and alcohol abuse, and sexually transmitted disease among students.

Assistant principals aid the principal in the overall administration of the school. Some assistant principals hold this position for several years to prepare for advancement to principal; others are career assistant principals. Depending on the number of students, the number of assistant principals a school employs may vary. They are responsible for programming student classes, ordering textbooks and supplies, and coordinating transportation, custodial, cafeteria, and other support services. They usually handle discipline, attendance, social and recreational programs, and health and safety. They also may counsel students on personal, educational, or vocational matters. With site-based management, assistant principals play a greater role in developing curriculum, evaluating teachers, and school-community relations, responsibilities previously assumed solely by the principal.

Administrators in school district central offices manage public schools under their jurisdiction. This group includes those who direct subject area programs such as English, music, vocational education, special education, and mathematics. They plan, evaluate, standardize, and improve curriculums and teaching techniques, and help teachers improve their skills and learn about new methods and materials. They oversee career counseling programs, and testing which measures students' abilities and helps place them in appropriate classes. Central office administrators also include directors of programs such as guidance, school psychology, athletics, curriculum and instruction, and professional development. With site-based management, principals and assistant principals, along with teachers and other staff, have primary responsibility for many of these programs in their individual schools.

In colleges and universities, academic deans, deans of faculty, provosts, and university deans assist presidents and develop budgets and academic policies and programs. They direct and coordinate activities of deans of individual colleges and chairpersons of academic departments.

Education administrators provide day-to-day management of elementary and secondary schools and colleges and universities.

College or university department heads or chairpersons are in charge of departments such as English, biological science, or mathematics. In addition to teaching, they coordinate schedules of classes and teaching assignments; propose budgets; recruit, interview, and hire applicants for teaching positions; evaluate faculty members; encourage faculty development; and perform other administrative duties. In overseeing their departments, chairpersons must consider and balance the concerns of faculty, administrators, and students.

Higher education administrators also provide student services. Vice presidents of student affairs or student life, deans of students, and directors of student services may direct and coordinate admissions, foreign student services, health and counseling services, career services, financial aid, and housing and residential life, as well as social, recreational, and related programs. In small colleges, they may counsel students. Registrars are custodians of students' records. They register students, prepare student transcripts, evaluate academic records, assess and collect tuition and fees, plan and implement commencement, oversee the preparation of college catalogs and schedules of classes, and analyze enrollment and demographic statistics. Directors of admissions manage the process of recruiting, evaluating, and admitting students, and work closely with financial aid directors, who oversee scholarship, fellowship, and loan programs. Registrars and admissions officers must adapt to technological innovations in student information systems. For example, for those whose institutions present information—such as college catalogs and schedules—on the Internet, knowledge of on-line resources, imaging, and other computer skills is important. Directors of student activities plan and arrange social, cultural, and recreational activities, assist student-run organizations, and may orient new students. Athletic directors plan and direct intramural and intercollegiate athletic activities, including publicity for athletic events, preparation of budgets, and supervision of coaches.

Working Conditions

Education administrators hold management positions with significant responsibility. Coordinating and interacting with faculty, parents, and students can be fast-paced and stimulating, but also stressful and demanding. Some jobs include travel. Principals and assistant principals whose main duty often is discipline may find working with difficult students frustrating, but challenging. The number of school-age children is rising, and some school systems have hired assistant principals when a school's population increased significantly. In other school systems, principals may manage larger student bodies, which can also be stressful.

Most education administrators work more than 40 hours a week, including many nights and weekends when they oversee school activities. Many administrators work 10 or 11 months a year while others work year round.

Employment

Education administrators held about 386,000 jobs in 1996. About 9 out of 10 were in educational services—in elementary, secondary, and technical schools and colleges and universities. The rest worked in child daycare centers, religious organizations, job training centers, State departments of education, and businesses and other organizations that provide training for their employees.

Training, Other Qualifications, and Advancement

Most education administrators begin their careers in related occupations, and prepare for a job in education administration by completing a master's or doctoral degree. Because of the diversity of duties and levels of responsibility, their educational backgrounds and experience vary considerably. Principals, assistant principals, central office administrators, and academic deans usually have held teaching positions before moving into administration. Some teachers move directly into principal positions; others first become assistant principals, or gain experience in other central office administrative jobs at either the school or district level in positions such as department head, curriculum specialist, or subject matter advisor. In some cases, administrators move up from related staff jobs such as recruiter, guidance counselor, librarian, residence hall director, or financial aid or admissions counselor.

To be considered for education administrator positions, workers must first prove themselves in their current jobs. In evaluating candidates, supervisors look for determination, confidence, innovativeness, motivation, leadership, and managerial attributes, such as ability to make sound decisions and organize and coordinate work efficiently. Since much of an administrator's job involves interacting with others, from students to parents to teachers, they must have strong interpersonal skills and be effective communicators and motivators. Knowledge of management principles and practices, gained through work experience and formal education, is important.

In most public schools, principals, assistant principals, and school administrators in central offices need a master's degree in education administration or educational supervision. Some principals and central office administrators have a doctorate or specialized degree in education administration. Most States require principals to be licensed as school administrators. Requirements for licensure vary by State. National standards for school leaders, including principals and supervisors, were recently developed by the Interstate School Leaders Licensure Consortium. States may use these national standards as guidelines for licensure requirements, or for activities such as mentoring, professional development, or accreditation of training programs. In private schools, which are not subject to State certification requirements, some principals and assistant principals hold only a bachelor's degree; however, the majority have a master's or doctoral degree.

Academic deans and chairpersons usually have a doctorate in their specialty. Most have held a professorship in their department before advancing. Admissions, student affairs, and financial aid directors and registrars sometimes start in related staff jobs with bachelor's degrees—any field usually is acceptable—and obtain advanced degrees in college student affairs or higher education administration. A Ph.D. or Ed.D. usually is necessary for top student affairs positions. Computer literacy and a background in mathematics or statistics may be assets in admissions, records, and financial work.

Advanced degrees in higher education administration, educational supervision, and college student affairs are offered in many colleges and universities. The National Council for Accreditation of Teacher Education accredits programs. Education administration degree programs include courses in school management, school law, school finance and budgeting, curriculum development and evaluation, research design and data analysis, community relations, politics in education, counseling, and leadership. Educational supervision degree programs include courses in supervision of instruction and curriculum, human relations, curriculum development, research, and advanced pedagogy courses.

Education administrators advance by moving up an administrative ladder or transferring to larger schools or systems. They also may become superintendent of a school system or president of an educational institution.

Job Outlook

Substantial competition is expected for prestigious jobs as higher education administrators. Many faculty and other staff meet the education and experience requirements for these jobs, and seek promotion. However, the number of openings is relatively small; only the most highly qualified are selected. Candidates who have the most formal education and who are willing to relocate should have the best job prospects.

On the other hand, it is becoming more difficult to attract candidates for principal, vice principal, and administration jobs at the elementary and secondary school level—competition for these jobs is declining. Many teachers no longer have an incentive to move into these positions since the pay is not significantly higher and does not compensate for the added workload and responsibility of the position. Also, site-based management has given teachers more decision-making responsibility in recent years, possibly satisfying their desire to move into administration.

Employment of education administrators is expected to grow about as fast as the average for all occupations over the 1996-2006 period. However, most job openings will result from the need to replace administrators who retire or transfer to other occupations.

School enrollments at the elementary, secondary, and postsecondary level are all expected to grow over the projection period. Rather than opening new schools, many existing school populations will expand, spurring demand for assistant principals to help with the increased workload. Employment of education administrators will also grow as more services are provided to students and as efforts to improve the quality of education continue.

However, budget constraints are expected to moderate growth in this profession. At the postsecondary level, some institutions have been reducing administrative staffs to contain costs. Some colleges are consolidating administrative jobs and contracting with other providers for some administrative functions.

Earnings

Salaries of education administrators vary according to position, level of responsibility and experience, and the size and location of the institution. Generally, principals employed in public schools earn higher salaries than those in private schools.

According to a survey of public schools, conducted by the Educational Research Service, average salaries for principals and assistant principals in the 1996-97 school year were as follows:

Principals:

Elementary school	$62,900
Junior high/middle school	66,900
Senior high school	72,400

Assistant principals:

Elementary school	$52,300
Junior high/middle school	56,500
Senior high school	59,700
Directors, managers, coordinators, and supervisors of instructional services	70,800

In 1995-96, according to the College and University Personnel Association, median annual salaries for selected administrators in higher education were as follows:

Academic deans:

Medicine $201,200
Law 141,400
Engineering 112,800
Arts and sciences 82,500
Business 81,700
Education 80,000
Social sciences 61,800
Mathematics 59,900

Student services directors:

Admissions and registrar $50,700
Student financial aid 45,400
Student activities 34,500

Related Occupations

Education administrators apply organizational and leadership skills to provide services to individuals. Workers in related occupations include health services administrators, social service agency administrators, recreation and park managers, museum directors, library directors, and professional and membership organization executives. Since principals and assistant principals generally have extensive teaching experience, their backgrounds are similar to those of teachers and many school counselors.

Sources of Additional Information

For information on elementary and secondary school principals, assistant principals, and central office administrators, contact:

☛ American Federation of School Administrators, 1729 21st St. NW., Washington, DC 20009.

☛ American Association of School Administrators, 1801 North Moore St., Arlington, VA 22209.

For information on elementary school principals and assistant principals, contact:

☛ The National Association of Elementary School Principals, 1615 Duke St., Alexandria, VA 22314-3483.

For information on secondary school principals and assistant principals, contact:

☛ The National Association of Secondary School Principals, 1904 Association Dr., Reston, VA 20191.

For information on college student affairs administrators, contact:

☛ National Association of Student Personnel Administrators, 1875 Connecticut Ave. NW., Suite 418, Washington, DC 20009-5728.

For information on collegiate registrars and admissions officers, contact:

☛ American Association of Collegiate Registrars and Admissions Officers, One Dupont Circle NW., Suite 330, Washington, DC 20036-1171.

Employment Interviewers

(D.O.T. 166.267-010)

Significant Points

- Sales ability is required to succeed in personnel supply services firms, where most employment interviewers are found.

- Employment growth reflects expansion of personnel supply—particularly temporary help—firms.

Nature of the Work

Whether you are looking for a job or trying to fill one, you could find yourself turning to an employment interviewer for help. Sometimes called personnel consultants, human resources coordinators, personnel development specialists, or employment brokers, among other job titles, these workers help jobseekers find employment and help employers find qualified employees.

Working largely in private personnel supply firms or State employment security offices (also known as job or employment service centers), employment interviewers act as brokers, putting together the best combination of applicant and job. To accomplish this, they obtain information from employers as well as jobseekers.

A private industry employment interviewer is a salesperson. Counselors pool together a group of qualified applicants and try to sell them to many different companies. Often a consultant will call a company that has never been a client (cold-calling) with the aim of filling their employment needs.

Employers generally pay private (but not public) agencies to recruit workers. The employer places a "job order" with the agency describing the opening and listing requirements such as education, licenses or credentials, and experience. Employment interviewers often contact the employer to determine their exact personnel needs. Jobseekers are asked to fill out forms or present resumes that detail their education, experience, and other qualifications. They may be interviewed or tested and have their background, references, and credentials checked. The employment interviewer then reviews the job requirements and the jobseeker qualifications to determine the best possible match of position and applicant. Although computers are increasingly used to keep records and match employers with jobseekers, personal contact with an employment interviewer remains an essential part of an applicant's job search.

Maintaining good relations with employers is an important part of the employment interviewer's job because this helps assure a steady flow of job orders. Being prepared to fill an opening quickly with a qualified applicant impresses employers most and keeps them as clients.

Besides helping firms fill job openings, employment interviewers help individuals find jobs. The services they provide depend upon the company or type of agency they work for and the clientele it serves.

Employment interviewers in personnel supply firms who place permanent employees are generally called counselors. They usually place job applicants who have the right qualifications but lack knowledge of the job market for their desired position. Counselors in these firms offer tips on personal appearance, suggestions on presenting a positive image of oneself, background on the company with which an interview is scheduled, and recommendations about interviewing techniques. Many firms specialize in placing applicants in particular kinds of jobs—for example, secretarial, word processing, computer programming and computer systems analysis, engineering, accounting, law, or health. Counselors in such firms usually have 3 to 5 years of experience in the field into which they are placing applicants.

Some employment interviewers work in temporary help services companies. These companies send out their own employees to firms that need temporary help. Employment interviewers take job orders from client firms and match their requests against a list of available workers. Employment interviewers select the best qualified workers available and assign them to the firms requiring assistance. Sometimes employees placed with companies as temporaries are later hired as permanent employees.

Traditionally, firms that placed permanent employees usually dealt with highly skilled applicants, such as lawyers or accountants, and those placing temporary employees dealt with less skilled workers, such as secretaries or data entry operators. However, temporary help services increasingly place workers with a wide range of educational backgrounds and work experience; businesses are turning to temporary employees to fill all types of positions—from clerical to managerial, professional, and technical—to reduce costs of pay and benefits associated with hiring permanent employees.

Regular evaluation of employee job skills is an important part of the job for those interviewers working in temporary help services companies. Initially, interviewers evaluate or test new employees'

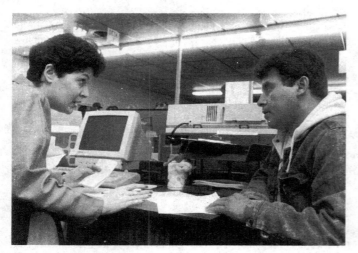

Employment interviewers need good interpersonal skills.

skills to determine their abilities and weaknesses. The results, which are kept on file, are referred to when filling job orders. In some cases, the temporary help company will train employees to improve their skills. Periodically, the interviewer may reevaluate or retest employees to identify any new skills they may have developed.

The duties of employment interviewers in job service centers differ somewhat because applicants may lack marketable skills. In these centers, jobseekers present resumes and fill out forms that ask about educational attainment, job history, skills, awards, certificates, and licenses. An employment interviewer reviews these forms and asks the applicant about the type of job sought and salary range desired. Applicants sometimes have exaggerated expectations. Employment interviewers must be tactful, but persuasive, if an applicant's job or salary requests are unreasonable.

Applicants may need help identifying the kind of work for which they are best suited. The employment interviewer evaluates the applicant's qualifications and either chooses an appropriate occupation or class of occupations, or refers the applicant for vocational testing.

After identifying an appropriate job type, the employment interviewer searches the file of job orders seeking a possible job match, and refers the applicant to the employer if a match is found. If no match is found, the interviewer shows the applicant how to use listings of available jobs.

Some applicants are high school dropouts or have poor English language skills, a history of drug or alcohol dependency, or a prison record, among other problems. The amount and nature of special help for such applicants vary from State to State. In some States, it is the employment interviewer's responsibility to counsel hard-to-place applicants and refer them elsewhere for literacy or language instruction, vocational training, transportation assistance, child care, and other services. In other States, specially trained counselors perform this task.

Working Conditions
Employment interviewers usually work in comfortable, well-lighted offices, often using a computer to match information about employers and jobseekers. Some interviewers, however, may spend much of their time out of the office interviewing. The work can prove hectic, especially in temporary help service companies which supply clients with immediate help for short periods of time. Some overtime may be required, and temporary workers may need their own transportation to make employer visits. The private placement industry is competitive, so counselors feel pressed to give their client companies the best service.

Employment
Employment interviewers held about 87,000 jobs in 1996. About 4 out of 5 worked in the private sector for personnel supply services,

generally for employment placement firms or temporary help services companies. About 1 out of 5 worked for State or local government. Others were employed by organizations that provide various services, such as job training and vocational rehabilitation.

Employees of career consulting or outplacement firms are not included in these estimates. Workers in these firms help clients market themselves; they do not act as job brokers, nor do they match individuals with particular vacancies.

Training, Other Qualifications, and Advancement
Although most public and private agencies prefer to hire college graduates for interviewer jobs, a degree is not always necessary. Hiring requirements in the private sector reflect a firm's management approach as well as the placements in which its interviewers specialize. Those that place highly trained individuals such as accountants, lawyers, engineers, physicians, or managers generally have some training or experience in the field in which they are placing workers. Thus, a bachelor's, master's, or even a doctoral degree may be a prerequisite for some interviewers. Even with the right education, however, sales ability is still required to succeed in the private sector.

Educational requirements play a lesser role for interviewers placing clerks or laborers—a high school diploma may be sufficient. In these positions, qualities such as energy level, telephone voice, and sales ability take precedence over educational attainment.

Entry-level employment interviewer positions in the public sector are generally filled by college graduates, even though the positions do not always require a bachelor's degree. Some States allow substitution of suitable work experience for college education. Suitable work experience is generally defined as public contact work or time spent at other jobs (including clerical jobs) in a job service office. In States that permit employment interviewers to engage in counseling, course work in counseling may be required.

Most States and many large city and county governments use some form of merit system for hiring interviewers. Applicants may take a written exam, undergo a preliminary interview, or submit records of their education and experience for evaluation. Those who meet the standards are placed on a list from which the top-ranked candidates are selected for later interviews and possible hiring.

Other desirable qualifications for employment interviewers include good communications skills, a desire to help people, office skills, and adaptability. A friendly, confidence-winning manner is an asset because personal interaction plays a large role in this occupation. Increasingly, employment interviewers use computers as a tool; thus, basic knowledge of computers is helpful.

Advancement as an employment interviewer in the public sector is often based on a system providing regular promotions and salary increases for those meeting established standards. Advancement to supervisory positions is highly competitive. In personnel supply firms, advancement often depends on one's success in placing workers and generally takes the form of greater responsibility and higher income. Successful individuals may form their own businesses.

Job Outlook
Employment in this occupation is expected to grow about as fast as the average for all occupations through the year 2006. The majority of new jobs will arise in personnel supply firms, especially those specializing in temporary help. Job growth is not anticipated in State job service offices because of budgetary problems and the growing use of computerized job matching and information systems, and as States increasingly contract out employment services to private firms. Other openings will stem from the need to replace experienced interviewers who transfer to other occupations, retire, or stop working for other reasons.

Rapid expansion of firms supplying temporary help will be responsible for much of the growth in this occupation. Businesses of all types are turning to temporary help services companies for additional workers for handling short-term assignments or one-time projects, for launching new programs, and to reduce costs of pay and benefits associated with hiring permanent employees.

Expansion of the personnel supply industry, in general, will also spur job growth. Job orders will increase as the economy expands and new businesses are formed; this is expected to heighten demand for employment interviewers. Firms that lack the time or resources to develop their own screening procedures will likely turn to personnel firms.

Employment opportunities should be better in private placement firms than in State job service centers. Entry to this occupation is relatively easy for college graduates, or people who have had some college courses, except in those positions specializing in placement of workers with highly specialized training, such as lawyers, doctors, and engineers.

Employment interviewers who place permanent workers may lose their jobs during recessions because employers reduce or eliminate hiring for permanent positions during downturns in the economy. State job service employment interviewers are less susceptible to layoffs than those who place permanent or temporary personnel in the private sector.

Earnings

Earnings in private firms vary, in part, because the basis for compensation varies. Workers in personnel supply firms tend to be paid on a commission basis; those in temporary help service companies receive a salary.

When workers are paid on a commission basis (or salary plus commission), total earnings depend on how much business they bring in. This is usually based on the type as well as the number of placements. Those who place more highly skilled or hard-to-find employees earn more. An interviewer or counselor working strictly on a commission basis often makes around 30 percent of what he or she bills the client, although this varies widely from firm to firm. Some work on a salary-plus-commission basis because they fill difficult or highly specialized positions requiring long periods of search. The salary, usually small by normal standards, guarantees these individuals security through slow times. The commission provides the incentive and opportunity for higher earnings.

Some personnel supply firms employ new workers for a 2- to 3-month probationary period during which they draw a regular salary. This gives new workers time to develop their skills and acquire some clients. At the end of the probationary period, the new employees are evaluated, and they are either let go or switched to a commission basis.

Related Occupations

Employment interviewers serve as intermediaries for jobseekers and employers. Workers in several other occupations do similar jobs.

Personnel officers screen and help hire new employees, but they concern themselves mainly with the hiring needs of the firm; they never represent individual jobseekers. Personnel officers may also have additional duties in areas such as payroll or benefits management.

Career counselors help students and alumni find jobs, but they primarily emphasize career counseling and decision making, not placement.

Counselors in community organizations and vocational rehabilitation facilities help clients find jobs, but they also assist with drug or alcohol dependencies, housing, transportation, child care, and other problems that stand in the way of finding and keeping a job.

Sources of Additional Information

For information on a career as an employment interviewer/counselor, contact:

☛ National Association of Personnel Services, 3133 Mt. Vernon Ave., Alexandria, VA 22305.

☛ National Association of Temporary Staffing Services, 119 S. Saint Asaph St., Alexandria, VA 22314. Homepage: http://www.natss.org

For information on a career as an employment interviewer in State employment security offices, contact offices of the State government for which you are interested in working.

Engineering, Science, and Computer Systems Managers

(D.O.T. 002.167-018; 003.167-034 and -070; 005.167-010 and -022; 007.167-014; 008.167-010; 010.161-010, -014, and .167-018; 011.161-010; 012.167-058 and -062; 018.167-022; 019.167-014; 022.161-010; 024.167-010; 029.167-014; 162.117-030; 169.167-030 and -082; and 189.117-014)

Significant Points

- The majority of growth in these managerial occupations is caused by the rapid expansion of employment in computer-related occupations.

- These managers need the specialized technical skills possessed by their staff to perform effectively.

Nature of the Work

Engineering, science, and computer systems managers plan, coordinate, and direct research, development, design, production, and computer-related activities. They supervise a staff which may include engineers, scientists, technicians, computer specialists, and information technology workers, along with support personnel.

Engineering, science, and computer systems managers determine scientific and technical goals within broad outlines provided by top management. These goals may include the redesigning of an aircraft, improvements in manufacturing processes, the development of a large computer program, or advances in scientific research. Managers make detailed plans for the accomplishment of these goals—for example, working with their staff, they may develop the overall concepts of new products or identify problems standing in the way of project completion. They determine the cost of and equipment and personnel needed for projects and programs. They hire and assign scientists, engineers, technicians, computer specialists, information technology workers, and support personnel to carry out specific parts of the projects. The managers supervise these employees' work, and review their designs, programs, and reports. They present ideas and projects to top management for approval or when seeking additional funds for development.

Managers coordinate the activities of their unit with other units or organizations. They confer with higher levels of management; with financial, industrial production, marketing, and other managers; and with contractors and equipment and materials suppliers. They also establish working and administrative procedures and policies.

Engineering managers supervise people who design and develop machinery, products, systems, and processes; or direct and coordinate production, operations, quality assurance, testing, or maintenance in industrial plants. Many are plant engineers, who direct and coordinate the design, installation, operation, and maintenance of equipment and machinery in industrial plants. Others manage research and development teams that produce new products and processes or improve existing ones.

Science managers oversee activities in agricultural science, chemistry, biology, geology, meteorology, or physics. They manage research and development projects and direct and coordinate experimentation, testing, quality control, and production in research institutes and industrial plants. Science managers are often involved in their own research in addition to managing the work of others.

Computer systems managers direct and plan programming, computer operations, and data processing, and coordinate the development of computer hardware, systems design, and software. Top-level managers direct all computer-related activities in an organization. They analyze the computer and data information requirements of their organization and assign, schedule, and review the work of systems analysts, computer programmers, and computer operators. They determine personnel and computer hardware requirements, evaluate equipment options, and make purchasing decisions.

Experience as an engineer, mathematician, scientist, or computer professional is the usual requirement for becoming an engineering, science, or computer systems manager.

Some engineering, science, and computer systems managers head a section of scientists, engineers, or computer professionals and support staff. Above them are heads of divisions composed of a number of sections. A few are directors of research or of large laboratories.

Working Conditions
Engineering, science, and computer systems managers spend most of their time in an office. Some managers, however, may also work in laboratories or industrial plants, where they are normally exposed to the same conditions as research scientists and may occasionally be exposed to the same conditions as production workers. Most managers work at least 40 hours a week and may work much longer on occasion if meeting project deadlines. Some may experience considerable pressure in meeting technical or scientific goals within a short time or a tight budget.

Employment
Engineering, science, and computer systems managers held about 343,000 jobs in 1996. Although these managers are found in almost all industries, about 38 percent are employed in manufacturing, especially in the industrial machinery and equipment, electrical and electronic equipment, instruments, chemicals, and transportation equipment industries. However, the two industries employing the greatest number of these managers were engineering and architectural services and computer and data processing services; each employed about 1 in 10 in 1996. The majority are most likely engineering managers, often managing industrial research, development, and design projects. Others work for government agencies, research and testing services, communications and utilities companies, financial and insurance firms, and management and public relations services companies.

Training, Other Qualifications, and Advancement
It is essential that engineering, science, and computer systems managers have a base of technical knowledge that allows them to understand and guide the work of their subordinates and to explain the work in non-technical terms to senior management and potential customers. Therefore, experience as an engineer, mathematician, scientist, or computer professional is usually required to become an engineering, science, or computer systems manager. Educational

requirements are consequently similar to those for scientists, engineers, and computer professionals.

Engineering managers first start as engineers. A bachelor's degree in engineering from an accredited engineering program is acceptable for beginning engineering jobs, but many engineers increase their chances for promotion to a managerial position by obtaining a master's degree in engineering, engineering management, or business administration. A degree in business administration or engineering management is especially useful for becoming a general manager, because these degree programs teach engineers about managing personnel and technical and financial resources.

Science managers usually start as a chemist, physicist, biologist, or other natural scientist. Most scientists engaged in basic research have a Ph.D. degree. Some in applied research and other activities may have lesser degrees. First-level science managers are usually specialists in the work they supervise. For example, the manager of a group of physicists doing optical research is almost always a physicist who is an expert in optics. Many scientific research firms are started and managed by scientists who obtain funding to build a staff and purchase technology to pursue their research agenda, with the goal of eventually developing a commercially successful product.

Most computer systems managers have been systems analysts, although some may have experience as computer engineers, programmers, operators, or other computer specialties. There is no universally accepted way of preparing for a job as a systems analyst. Many have degrees in computer or information science, computer information systems, or data processing and have experience as computer programmers. A bachelor's degree is usually required and a graduate degree is often preferred by employers. However, a few computer systems managers have associate degrees. A typical career advancement progression in a large organization would be from programmer to programmer/analyst, to systems analyst, and then to project leader or senior analyst. The first real managerial position might be as project manager, programming supervisor, systems supervisor, or software manager.

In addition to educational requirements, scientists, engineers, or computer specialists must demonstrate above-average technical skills to be considered for a promotion to manager. Superiors also look for leadership and communication skills, as well as managerial attributes such as the ability to make rational decisions, to manage time well, organize and coordinate work effectively, establish good working and personal relationships, and motivate others. Also, a successful manager must have the desire to perform management functions. Many scientists, engineers, and computer specialists want to be promoted but actually prefer doing technical work.

Some scientists and engineers become managers in marketing, personnel, purchasing, or other areas, or become general managers.

Job Outlook
Employment of engineering, science, and computer systems managers is expected to increase much faster than the average for all occupations through the year 2006. Underlying much of the growth of managers in science and engineering are competitive pressures and advancing technologies which force companies to update and improve products more frequently. Research and investment in plants and equipment to expand output of goods and services and to raise productivity will also add to employment requirements for science and engineering managers involved in research and development, design, and the operation and maintenance of production facilities.

Employment of computer systems managers will increase rapidly due to the fast-paced expansion of the computer and data processing services industry and the increased employment of computer systems analysts. Large computer centers are consolidating or closing as small computers become more powerful, resulting in fewer opportunities for computer systems managers at these centers. As the economy expands and as advances in technology lead to broader applications for computers, however, opportunities will increase and employment should grow rapidly.

Opportunities for those who wish to become engineering, science, and computer systems managers should be closely related to the growth of the occupations they supervise and the industries in which they are found. (See the statements on natural scientists, engineers, computer programmers, and computer scientists, computer engineers, and systems analysts elsewhere in the *Handbook*.) Because many engineers, natural scientists, and computer specialists are eligible for management and seek promotion, there may be substantial competition for these openings.

Many of the industries which employ engineers and scientists derive a large portion of their business from defense contracts. Because defense expenditures are being reduced, employment has declined and the job outlook for managers is not as favorable in these industries, compared to less defense-oriented industries.

Earnings

Earnings for engineering, science, and computer systems managers vary by specialty and level of management. According to 1996 data, science and engineering managers had average salaries that ranged from $41,000 to well over $100,000 for the most senior managers in large organizations. According to Robert Half International, computer systems managers earned salaries ranging from $33,000 to well over $100,000, depending on establishment size. Managers often earn about 15 to 25 percent more than those they directly supervise, although there are cases in which some employees are paid more than the manager who supervises them. This is especially true in research fields.

According to a survey of workplaces in 160 metropolitan areas, lower-level engineering managers had median annual earnings of $84,200 in 1995, with the middle half earning between $76,300 and $92,800. The highest-level engineering managers had median annual earnings of $117,000, with the middle half earning between $104,000 and $133,000. Beginning systems analysts managers had median annual earnings of $60,900, with the middle half earning between $55,100 and $67,000. The most senior systems analysts managers had median annual earnings of $84,200, with the middle half earning between $76,200 and $92,000.

In addition, engineering, science, and computer systems managers, especially those at higher levels, often are provided with more benefits (such as expense accounts, stock option plans, and bonuses) than non-managerial workers in their organizations.

Related Occupations

The work of engineering, science, and computer systems managers is closely related to that of engineers, natural scientists, computer personnel, and mathematicians. It is also related to the work of other managers, especially general managers and top executives.

Sources of Additional Information

For information about a career as an engineering, science, or computer systems manager, contact the sources of additional information for engineers, natural scientists, and computer occupations that are listed in statements on these occupations elsewhere in the *Handbook*.

Farmers and Farm Managers

(D.O.T. 180.117, .161, and .167-018, -026 through -046, -058, and -066; 401.161; 402.161; 403.161; 404.161; 405.161; 407.161; 410.161; 411.161; 412.161; 413.161; 421.161; and 446.161)

Significant Points

- Modern farming requires work experience, sometimes acquired through growing up on a farm, and formal education, preferably a bachelor's degree in agriculture or in business with a concentration in agriculture.

- Overall employment is projected to decline due to increasing productivity and consolidation in the highly efficient agricultural production industry.

Nature of the Work

American farmers and farm managers direct the activities of one of the world's largest and most productive agricultural sectors. They produce enough food and fiber to meet the needs of our Nation, and to export huge quantities to countries around the world.

Farmers may be farmer-owners or tenant farmers, who rent the use of land. Their specific tasks are determined by the type of farm they operate. On crop farms—farms growing grain, cotton and other fibers, fruit, and vegetables—farmers are responsible for planning, tilling, planting, fertilizing, cultivating, spraying, and harvesting. After the harvest, they make sure the crops are properly packaged, stored or marketed. On livestock, dairy, and poultry farms, farmers must feed, and plan and care for the animals and keep barns, pens, coops, and other farm buildings clean and in good condition. They also oversee breeding and marketing activities. On horticultural specialty farms, farmers oversee the production of ornamental plants, nursery products—such as flowers, bulbs, shrubbery, and sod—and fruits and vegetables grown in greenhouses. On aquaculture farms, farmers raise fish and shellfish in marine, brackish, or fresh water, usually in ponds, floating net pens, raceways, or recirculating systems. They stock, feed, protect, and otherwise manage aquatic life sold for consumption or used for recreational fishing.

Farmers must make many managerial decisions. Their farm output is strongly influenced by the weather, disease, fluctuations in prices of domestic and foreign farm products, and Federal farm programs. In a crop operation, farmers usually determine the best time to plant seed, apply fertilizer and chemicals, harvest, and market. They carefully plan the combination of crops they grow so if the price of one crop drops, they will have sufficient income from another to make up for the loss. Crop and livestock prices change frequently from one month to another. Farmers who plan ahead may be able to store their crops or keep their livestock to take advantage of better prices later in the year. Those who participate in the futures market—where contracts and options on futures contracts on commodities are traded through stock brokers—try to anticipate or track changes in the supply of and demand for agricultural commodities, and thus changes in the prices of farm products. By buying or selling futures contracts, or by pricing their products in advance of future sales, they attempt to either limit their risk or reap greater profits than would normally be realized. They may have to secure loans from credit agencies to finance the purchase of machinery, fertilizer, livestock, and feed. Farming operations have become more complex in recent years, so many farmers use computers to keep their extensive financial and inventory records. They also use computer databases and spreadsheets to manage breeding, dairy, and other farm operations.

Farmers perform tasks ranging from caring for livestock, to operating machinery and maintaining equipment and facilities. The size of the farm often determines which of these tasks farmers will handle themselves. Operators of large farms have employees who do much of the physical work that small-farm operators do themselves. Farmers are responsible for training workers in the use of equipment, and supervising them in the performance of their work. Although employment on most farms is limited to the farmer and one or two family workers or hired employees, some large farms have 100 or more full-time and seasonal workers. Some of these employees are in nonfarm occupations, working as truckdrivers, sales representatives, bookkeepers, and computer specialists.

Farm managers guide and assist farmers and ranchers in maximizing the financial returns to their land by managing the day-to-day activities. Their duties and responsibilities vary widely. For example, the owner of a very large livestock farm may employ a farm manager to oversee a single activity, such as feeding livestock. When managing a small crop farm for an absentee owner, on the other hand, a farm manager may assume responsibility for all functions, from selecting the

Modern farming requires increasingly complex scientific, business, and financial decisions.

crops to participating in planting and harvesting. Farm management firms and corporations involved in agriculture employ highly trained professional farm managers who may manage farm operations or oversee tenant operators of several farms. In these cases, farm managers may establish output goals; determine financial constraints; monitor production and marketing; hire, assign, and supervise workers; determine crop transportation and storage requirements; and oversee maintenance of the property and equipment.

Working Conditions
The work of farmers and farm managers is often strenuous, their work hours are frequently long, and their days off are sometimes infrequent. Of those who work full time, more than half work 60 or more hours a week. Nevertheless, to those who enter farming, these disadvantages are outweighed by the opportunities for living in a rural area, working outdoors, being self-employed, and making a living working the land.

Farmers and farm managers on crop farms usually work from sunrise to sunset during the planting and harvesting seasons. During the rest of the year they plan next season's crops, market their output, and repair machinery; some may earn additional income by working a second job off the farm.

On livestock producing farms, work goes on throughout the year. Animals must be fed and watered every day, unless they are grazing, and dairy cows must be milked two or three times a day. Farmers rarely get the chance to get away unless they hire an assistant or arrange for a temporary substitute.

Farm work can be hazardous. The proper operation of equipment and handling of chemicals is required to ensure a safe working environment.

On very large farms, farmers spend substantial time meeting with farm managers or farm supervisors in charge of various activities. Professional farm managers overseeing several farms may divide their time between traveling to meet farmers or landowners and planning the farm operations in their offices. As farming practices and agricultural technology become more sophisticated, farmers and farm managers are spending more time in offices and at computers, where they electronically manage many aspects of the business.

Employment
Farmers and farm managers held nearly 1.3 million jobs in 1996. About 85 percent were self-employed farmers. Most managed crop production activities while others managed livestock and dairy production. A relatively small number were involved in agricultural services, such as contract harvesting and farm labor contracting.

The soil, topography of the land, and the climate of an area generally determine the type of farming done. For example, wheat, corn, and other grains are most efficiently grown on large farms on level land where large, complex machinery can be used. Thus, these crops are prevalent on the prairies and plains of Iowa, Illinois, Indiana, Nebraska, Ohio, Kansas, and southern Minnesota and Wisconsin. Crops requiring longer growing seasons, such as cotton, tobacco, and peanuts, are grown chiefly in the South. Most of the country's fruits and vegetables come from California, Texas, and Florida. Many dairy herds are found in the areas with good pasture land, such as Wisconsin, New York, and Minnesota. However, in recent years dairy farming has expanded rapidly in California, Arizona, and Texas.

Training, Other Qualifications, and Advancement
Growing up on a family farm and participating in agricultural programs for young people sponsored by the National Future Farmers of America Organization or the 4-H youth educational programs are important sources of training for those interested in pursuing agriculture as a career. However, modern farming requires increasingly complex scientific, business, and financial decisions. Therefore, even people who were raised on farms must acquire the appropriate education. High school training should include courses in mathematics and the sciences. Completion of a 2-year and preferably a 4-year bachelor's degree program in a college of agriculture is becoming increasingly important.

Not all future farm managers grow up on farms. For these people, a bachelor's degree in business with a concentration in agriculture is important. In addition to formal education, they will need several years' work experience in the different aspects of farm operations in order to qualify for a farm manager position.

Students should select the college most appropriate to their specific interests and location. In the United States, all State university systems have one land-grant university with a school of agriculture. Common programs of study include agronomy, dairy science, agricultural economics and business, horticulture, crop and fruit science, and animal science. For students interested in aquaculture, formal programs are available, and include coursework in fisheries biology, fish culture, hatchery management and maintenance, and hydrology. Whatever one's interest, the college curriculum should include courses in agricultural production, finance, and economics.

Professional status can be enhanced through voluntary certification as an Accredited Farm Manager (AFM) by the American Society of Farm Managers and Rural Appraisers. Certification requires several years of farm management experience and the appropriate academic background—a bachelor's degree or preferably a master's degree in a field of agricultural science—and passing courses and examinations relating to business, financial, and legal aspects of farm management.

Farmers and farm managers need to keep abreast of continuing advances in farming methods both in the United States and abroad. They should be willing to try new processes and adapt to constantly changing technologies to produce their crops or raise their livestock more efficiently. Farmers must also have enough technical knowledge of crops, growing conditions, and plant and animal diseases to make decisions ensuring the successful operation of their farms. Knowledge of the relationship between farm operations—for example, the use of pesticides—and environmental conditions is essential. Mechanical aptitude and the ability to work with tools of all kinds are also valuable skills for the operator of a small farm, who often maintains and repairs machinery or farm structures.

Farmers and farm managers must have the managerial skills necessary to organize and operate a business. A basic knowledge of accounting and bookkeeping can be helpful in keeping financial records, and a knowledge of credit sources is essential. They must also be familiar with complex safety regulations and requirements of government agricultural support programs. Computer skills are increasingly important, especially on large farms, where computers are widely used for recordkeeping and business analysis. For example, some farmers use personal computers to get the latest information on prices of farm products and other agricultural news.

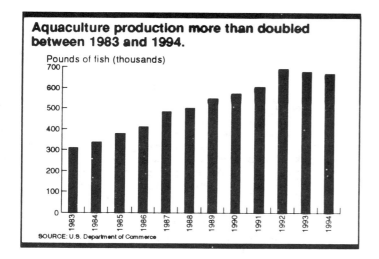

Aquaculture production more than doubled between 1983 and 1994.

Pounds of fish (thousands)

SOURCE: U.S. Department of Commerce

Job Outlook

Employment of farmers and farm managers is expected to continue to decline through the year 2006. The expanding world population is increasing the demand for food and fiber. In particular, improving economies and increasing personal income in developing nations have resulted in better diets and stronger demand for beef, poultry, pork, and feed grain. However, increasing productivity in the highly efficient agricultural production industry is expected to meet domestic and export requirements with fewer farmers and farm managers. The overwhelming majority of job openings will result from the need to replace farmers who retire or leave the occupation for economic or other reasons.

The long-term trend toward fewer and larger farms is expected to continue during the 1996-2006 period, as consolidation takes place in response to market pressures, further reducing the number of jobs for farmers and farm managers. Some farmers acquire farms by inheritance; however, purchasing a farm or additional land is expensive and requires substantial capital. In addition, sufficient funds are required to withstand the adverse effects of climate and price fluctuations upon farm output and income and to cover operating costs—livestock, feed, seed, and fuel. Also, the complexity of modern farming and keen competition among farmers leave little room for the marginally successful farmer.

Despite the projected decline in overall employment of farmers and farm managers, aquaculture should continue to provide new employment opportunities over the 1996-2006 period. Overfishing has resulted in reduced ocean catch, and the growing demand for certain seafood items—such as shrimp, salmon, and catfish—has spurred the growth of aquaculture farms. Aquaculture output increased strongly between 1983 and the mid-1990s, as indicated by the accompanying chart. Efforts to produce more farm-raised fish and shellfish should continue in response to demand.

Earnings

Farmers' incomes vary greatly from year to year, because prices of farm products fluctuate depending upon weather conditions and other factors that influence the amount and quality of farm output and the demand for those products. A farm that shows a large profit in one year may show a loss in the following year. Under the 1996 Farm Act, Federal Government subsidy payments, which have traditionally shielded some grain producers from the ups and downs of the market, are fixed regardless of yields or prices. Consequently, these farmers may experience more income variability from year to year than in the past. The Act also phases out price supports for dairy farmers, and may result in lower incomes for dairy producers. Many farmers—primarily operators of small farms—have income from off-farm business activities, often greater than that of their farm income.

Farm income also varies greatly depending upon the type and size of farm. For example, vegetable and cotton farms, and nurseries and greenhouses generally produce the highest income; fruit, nut, corn, and peanut farms produce more moderate income; and beef and hog farms generate relatively low income. Generally, large farms generate more income than small farms. Exceptions include some low volume specialty farms producing high value horticultural and fruit products.

Full-time, salaried farm managers, with the exception of horticultural managers, had median earnings of $485 a week in 1996. The middle half earned between $325 and $650 a week. The highest paid 10 percent earned about $760 a week in 1996, while the lowest paid 10 percent made less than $205 a week. Horticultural specialty farm managers generally earn considerably more.

Farmers and self-employed farm managers make their own provisions for benefits. As members of farm organizations, they may derive benefits such as group discounts on health and life insurance premiums. Salaried farm managers may receive housing and usual organizational benefits.

Related Occupations

Farmers and farm managers strive to improve the quality of agricultural products and the efficiency of farms. Workers with similar functions include agricultural engineers, animal breeders, animal scientists, county agricultural agents, dairy scientists, extension service specialists, feed and farm management advisors, horticulturists, plant breeders, and poultry scientists.

Sources of Additional Information

For general information about farming and agricultural occupations, contact:

☛ American Farm Bureau Federation, 225 Touhy Ave., Park Ridge, IL 60068. Homepage: http://www.fb.com

For information about certification as an accredited farm manager, contact:

☛ American Society of Farm Managers and Rural Appraisers, 950 South Cherry St., Suite 508, Denver, CO 80222.
Homepage: http://www.agriassociations.org

For general information about farm occupations, opportunities, and 4-H activities, contact your local county extension service office.

Financial Managers

(D.O.T. 160.167-058; 161.117-018; 169.167-086; 186.117-066, -070, -078, -086; .167-054, -086; 189.117-038)

Significant Points

- A bachelor's degree in finance or a related field is the minimum academic preparation, but many employers increasingly seek graduates with a master's degree and a strong analytical background.

- The need for skilled financial management will spur average employment growth; however, the number of applicants is expected to exceed the number of openings, resulting in competition for jobs.

Nature of the Work

Practically every firm has one or more financial managers. Among them are chief financial officers, vice presidents of finance, treasurers, controllers, credit managers, and cash managers; they prepare the financial reports required by the firm to conduct its operations and to ensure that the firm satisfies tax and regulatory requirements. Financial managers also oversee the flow of cash and financial instruments, monitor the extension of credit, assess the risk of transactions, raise capital, analyze investments, develop information to assess the present and future financial status of the firm, and communicate with stock holders and other investors.

In small firms, chief financial officers usually handle all financial management functions. In large firms, these officers oversee financial management departments and help top managers develop financial and economic policy, establish procedures, delegate authority, and oversee the implementation of these policies.

Highly trained and experienced financial managers head each financial department. Controllers direct the preparation of all financial reports—income statements, balance sheets, and special reports, such as depreciation schedules. They oversee the accounting, audit, or budget departments. Cash and credit managers monitor and control the flow of cash receipts and disbursements to meet the business and investment needs of the firm. For example, cash flow projections are needed to determine whether loans must be obtained to meet cash requirements, or whether surplus cash may be invested in interest-bearing instruments. Risk and insurance managers oversee programs to minimize risks and losses that may arise from financial transactions and business operations undertaken by the institution. Credit operations managers establish credit rating criteria, determine credit ceilings, and monitor their institution's extension of credit. Reserve officers review their institution's financial statements and direct the purchase and sale of bonds and other securities to maintain the asset-liability ratio required by law. Managers specializing in international finance develop financial and accounting systems for the banking transactions of multinational organizations. A working knowledge of the financial systems of foreign countries is essential.

Financial institutions—such as banks, savings and loan associations, credit unions, personal credit institutions, and finance companies—may serve as depositories for cash and financial instruments and offer loans, investment counseling, consumer credit, trust management, and other financial services. Some specialize in specific financial services. Financial managers in financial institutions include vice presidents, bank branch managers, savings and loan association managers, consumer credit managers, and credit union managers. These managers make decisions in accordance with policy set by the institution's board of directors and Federal and State laws and regulations.

Due to changing regulations and increased government scrutiny, financial managers in financial institutions must place greater emphasis on accurate reporting of financial data. They must have detailed knowledge of industries allied to banking—such as insurance, real estate, and securities—and a broad knowledge of business and industrial activities. With growing domestic and foreign competition, financial managers must keep abreast of an expanding and increasingly complex variety of financial products and services. Besides supervising financial services, financial managers in banks and other financial institutions may advise individuals and businesses on financial planning.

Working Conditions

Financial managers are provided with comfortable offices, often close to top managers and to departments which develop the financial data these managers need. Financial managers typically work 40 hours a week, but many work longer hours. They are often required to attend meetings of financial and economic associations, and may travel to visit subsidiary firms or meet customers.

Employment

Financial managers held about 800,000 jobs in 1996. Although these managers are found in virtually every industry, more than a third were employed by services industries, including business, health, social, and management services. Nearly 3 out of 10 were employed by financial institutions—banks, savings institutions, finance companies, credit unions, insurance companies, securities dealers, and real estate firms, for example.

Training, Other Qualifications, and Advancement

A bachelor's degree in finance, accounting, economics, or business administration is the minimum academic preparation for financial managers. However, many employers increasingly seek graduates with a master's degree, preferably in business administration, economics, finance, or risk management. These academic programs develop analytical skills, and provide knowledge of the latest financial analysis methods and information and technology management techniques, widely used in this field.

Experience may be more important than formal education for some financial manager positions—notably branch managers in banks. Banks typically fill branch manager positions by promoting experienced loan officers and other professionals who excel at their jobs.

Continuing education is vital for financial managers, reflecting the growing complexity of global trade, shifting Federal and State laws and regulations, and a proliferation of new, complex financial instruments. Firms often provide opportunities for workers to broaden their knowledge and skills, and encourage employees to take graduate courses at colleges and universities or attend conferences relating to their specialty. Financial management, banking, and credit union associations, often in cooperation with colleges and universities, sponsor numerous national or local training programs. Persons enrolled prepare extensively at home, then attend sessions on subjects such as accounting management, budget management, corporate cash management, financial analysis, international banking, and information systems. Many firms pay all or part of the costs for those who successfully complete courses. Although experience, ability, and leadership are emphasized for promotion, advancement may be accelerated by this type of special study.

In some cases, financial managers may also broaden their skills and exhibit their competency in specialized fields by attaining professional certification. For example, the Association for Investment Management and Research confers the Chartered Financial Analyst designation to investment professionals who have a bachelor's degree, pass three test levels, and meet work experience requirements. The National Association of Credit Management administers a three-part certification program for business credit professionals. Through a combination of experience and examinations, these financial managers pass through the level of Credit Business Associate, to Credit Business Fellow, to Certified Credit Executive. The Treasury Management Association confers the Certified Cash Manager credential on those who have 2 years of relevant experience and pass an exam, and the Certified Treasury Executive designation on those more senior in treasury management who meet experience and continuing education requirements.

Financial manager positions usually require substantial experience.

Persons interested in becoming financial managers should enjoy working independently, dealing with people, and analyzing detailed account information. The ability to communicate effectively, both orally and in writing, is also important. They also need tact, good judgment, and the ability to establish effective personal relationships to oversee staff.

Because financial management is critical for efficient business operations, well-trained, experienced financial managers who display a strong grasp of the operations of various departments within their organization are prime candidates for promotion to top management positions. Some financial managers transfer to closely related positions in other industries. Those with extensive experience and access to sufficient capital may start their own consulting firms.

Job Outlook

Like other managerial occupations, the number of applicants for financial management positions is expected to exceed the number of openings, resulting in competition for jobs. Those with lending experience, and familiarity with the latest lending regulations and financial products and services, should enjoy the best opportunities for branch management jobs in banks. Those with a graduate degree, a strong analytical background, and knowledge of various aspects of financial management, such as asset management and information and technology management, should enjoy the best opportunities for other financial management positions. Developing expertise in a rapidly growing industry, such as health care, could also be an advantage in the job market.

Employment of financial managers is expected to increase about as fast as the average for all occupations through the year 2006. The need for skilled financial management will increase due to the demands of global trade, the proliferation of complex financial instruments, and changing Federal and State laws and regulations. Many firms have reduced the ranks of middle managers in an effort to be more efficient and competitive, but much of the downsizing and restructuring is complete. The banking industry, on the other hand, is still undergoing mergers and consolidation, and may eliminate some financial management positions as a result.

Earnings

The median annual salary of financial managers was $40,700 in 1996. The lowest 10 percent earned $21,800 or less, while the top 10 percent earned over $81,100.

According to a 1997 survey by Robert Half International, a staffing services firm specializing in accounting and finance, salaries of assistant controllers range from $41,000 in the smallest firms, to $81,000 in the largest firms; controllers, $47,000 to $138,000; and chief financial officers/treasurers, $62,000 to $307,000.

The results of the Treasury Management Association's 1997 compensation survey are presented in table 1. The earnings listed in the table represent total compensation, including bonuses. The survey also found that financial managers with a master's degree in business administration average $10,900 more than managers with a bachelor's degree.

Table 1. Annual earnings for selected financial managers, 1997

Chief financial officer	$142,900
Vice president of finance	138,000
Treasurer	122,500
Assistant treasurer	88,400
Controller	85,100
Treasury manager	66,900
Assistant controller	56,200
Senior analyst	55,600
Cash manager	51,600
Analyst	40,500
Assistant cash manager	38,800

SOURCE: Treasury Management Association

Salary level depends upon the manager's experience and the size and location of the organization, and is likely to be higher in larger organizations and cities. Many financial managers in private industry receive additional compensation in the form of bonuses, which also vary substantially by the size of the firm.

Related Occupations

Financial managers combine formal education with experience in one or more areas of finance, such as asset management, lending, credit operations, securities investment, or insurance risk and loss control. Workers in other occupations requiring similar training and ability include accountants and auditors, budget officers, credit analysts, loan officers, insurance consultants, portfolio managers, pension consultants, real estate advisors, securities analysts and underwriters.

Sources of Additional Information

For information about financial management careers, contact:
☞ American Bankers Association, 1120 Connecticut Ave. NW., Washington, DC 20036.
☞ Financial Management Association, International, College of Business Administration, University of South Florida, Tampa, FL 33620-5500.

For information about financial careers in business credit management; the Credit Business Associate, Credit Business Fellow, and Certified Credit Executive programs; and institutions offering graduate courses in credit and financial management, contact:
☞ National Association of Credit Management (NACM), Credit Research Foundation, 8815 Centre Park Dr., Columbia, MD 21045-2117. E-mail address: nacm@nacm.org Homepage: http://www.nacm.org/

For information about careers in treasury management from entry level to chief financial officer, and the Certified Cash Manager and Certified Treasury Executive programs, contact:
☞ Treasury Management Association, 7315 Wisconsin Ave., Suite 600 West, Bethesda, MD 20814.

For information about the Chartered Financial Analyst program, contact:
☞ Association for Investment Management and Research, 5 Boar's Head Lane, P.O. Box 3668, Charlottesville, VA 22903. Homepage: http://www.aimr.com/

For information about financial management careers in the health care industry, contact:
☞ Healthcare Financial Management Association, Two Westbrook Corporate Center, Suite 700, Westchester, IL 60154.

State bankers' associations can furnish specific information about job opportunities in their respective States, or write directly to a particular bank to inquire about job openings. For the names and addresses of banks and savings and related institutions, as well as the names of their principal officers, consult the following directories.
☞ *The American Financial Directory* (Norcross, Ga., McFadden Business Publications).
☞ *The U.S. Savings and Loan Directory* (Chicago, Rand McNally & Co.).
☞ *Rand McNally Credit Union Directory* (Chicago, Rand McNally & Co.).
☞ *Polk's World Bank Directory* (Nashville, R.L. Polk & Co.).

Funeral Directors

(D.O.T. 187.167-030)

Significant Points

- Job opportunities should be excellent because the number of mortuary science graduates is expected to be insufficient to meet demand.

- Funeral directors must be licensed by the States who set the education and training requirements needed for entry.

Nature of the Work

Since the earliest of times, most peoples have held funeral ceremonies. The dead have ritually been interred in pyramids, cremated on burning pyres, and sunk beneath the oceans' waves. Even today, funeral practices and rites vary greatly among various cultures and religions. Among the many diverse groups in the United States, funeral practices generally share some common elements: Removal of the remains of the deceased to a mortuary, preparation of the remains, performance of a ceremony that honors the deceased and addresses the spiritual needs of the living as well as the dead, and the burial or destruction of the remains. To unburden themselves of arranging and directing these tasks, grieving families turn to funeral directors.

Funeral directors are also called morticians or undertakers. Although this career does not appeal to everyone, the men and women who work as funeral directors take great pride in their ability to provide efficient and appropriate services that give comfort to their customers.

Funeral directors interview the family to learn what they desire with regard to the nature of the funeral, the clergy members or other persons who will officiate, and the final disposition of the remains; sometimes the deceased leave detailed instructions for their own funerals. Together with the family, directors establish the location, dates, and times of wakes, memorial services, and burials. They also send a hearse to carry the body to the funeral home or mortuary.

Burial in a casket is the most common method of disposing of remains in this country, although entombments also occur. Cremation, which is the burning of the body in a special furnace, is increasingly selected because it can be more convenient and less costly. Cremations are appealing because the remains can be shipped easily, kept at home, buried, or scattered. Memorials can be held anywhere, and at any time, sometimes months later when all relatives and friends can get together. Even when remains are cremated, many people still want a funeral service.

A funeral service followed by cremation need not be any different from a funeral service followed by a burial. Usually cremated remains are placed in some type of permanent receptacle, referred to as an urn, before being committed to a final resting place. The urn may be buried, placed in an indoor or outdoor mausoleum or columbarium, or interred in a special urn garden that many cemeteries provide for cremated remains.

Directors arrange the details and handle the logistics of funerals. They prepare obituary notices and have them placed in newspapers, arrange for pallbearers and clergy, schedule with the cemetery the opening and closing of a grave, decorate and prepare the sites of all services, and provide for the transportation of the remains, mourners, and flowers between sites. They also direct preparation and shipment of remains for out-of-State burial.

Funeral services may take place in the home, a house of worship, or the funeral home and at the grave site or crematory. Services may be nonreligious, but often they reflect the religion of the family, so funeral directors must be familiar with the funeral and burial customs of many faiths, ethnic groups, and fraternal organizations. For example, members of some religions seldom have the bodies of the deceased embalmed or cremated.

Funeral directors also prearrange funerals. They are increasingly arranging funerals in advance of need to provide a peace of mind that the clients wishes will be taken care of in a way that is satisfying to the person and to those who will survive.

Most funeral directors are also trained, licensed, and practicing *embalmers*. Embalming is a sanitary, cosmetic, and preservative process through which the body is prepared for interment. If more than 24 hours or so elapses between death and interment, State laws usually require that remains be refrigerated or embalmed. The embalmer washes the body with germicidal soap and replaces the blood with embalming fluid to preserve the body. Embalmers may reshape and reconstruct disfigured or maimed bodies using materials, such as clay, cotton, plaster of Paris, and wax. They also may apply cosmetics to provide a natural appearance, and then dress the body and place it in a casket. Embalmers maintain records such as embalming reports, and itemized lists of clothing or valuables delivered with the body. In large funeral homes, an embalming staff of two or more embalmers, plus several apprentices, may be employed.

Funeral directors arrange the details of funerals and handle the logistics.

Funeral directors also handle the paper work involved with the person's death. They may help family members apply for veterans' burial benefits, notify the Social Security Administration of the death, apply on behalf of survivors for the transfer of any pensions, insurance policies, or annuities, and submit papers to State authorities so that a formal certificate of death may be issued and copies distributed to heirs.

Funeral directors are also responsible for the success and the profitability of their businesses. Directors keep records on expenses, purchases, and services rendered; prepare and send invoices for services; prepare and submit reports for unemployment insurance; prepare Federal, State, and local tax forms; and prepare itemized bills for customers. Directors also strive to foster a cooperative spirit and friendly attitude among employees and a compassionate demeanor toward the families. A growing number of funeral directors are also involved in helping individuals adapt to changes in their lives following a death through post-death counseling and support group activities.

Most funeral homes have a chapel, one or more viewing rooms, a casket-selection room, and a preparation room. An increasing number also have a crematory on the premises. Equipment may include a hearse, a flower car, limousines, and sometimes an ambulance. They usually stock a selection of caskets and urns for families to purchase or rent.

Working Conditions

Funeral directors often work long, irregular hours. Shift work is sometimes necessary because funeral home hours include evenings and weekends. In smaller funeral homes, working hours vary, but in larger homes employees generally work 8 hours a day, 5 or 6 days a week.

Funeral directors occasionally come into contact with the remains of persons who had contagious diseases, but the possibility of infection is remote if strict health regulations are followed.

To show proper respect and consideration for the families and the dead, funeral directors must dress appropriately. The profession usually requires short, neat hair cuts and trim beards if any, for men. Suits, ties, and dresses are customary for a conservative look.

Employment

Funeral directors held about 33,000 jobs in 1996. Almost 1 in 4 were self-employed. Nearly all worked in the funeral service and crematory industry, but a few worked for the Federal Government.

Training, Other Qualifications, and Advancement

Funeral directors must be licensed in all but one State, Colorado. Licensing laws vary from State to State, but most require applicants to be 21 years old, have a high school diploma, complete some college training in mortuary science, and serve an apprenticeship. After passing a State board licensing examination, new funeral directors may join the staff of a funeral home. Embalmers are required to be licensed in all States, and some States issue a single license for both funeral directors and embalmers. In States that have separate licensing and apprenticeship requirements for the two positions, most people in the field obtain both licenses. Persons interested in a career as a funeral director should contact their state board for specific state requirements.

College programs in mortuary science usually last from 2 to 4 years, depending on the school. There were 47 mortuary science programs accredited by the American Board of Funeral Service Education in 1996. Two-year programs are offered by a small number of community and junior colleges, and a few colleges and universities offer both 2- and 4-year programs. Mortuary science programs include courses in anatomy, physiology, embalming techniques, restorative art, business management, accounting and use of computers in funeral home management, and client services. They also include courses in the social sciences and legal, ethical, and regulatory subjects, such as psychology, grief counseling, oral and written communication, funeral service law, business law, and ethics.

The National Funeral Directors Association Educational Foundation offers a continuing education program designed for active practitioners in the field. It is a 3-week program in communications, counseling, and management. Over 25 States have continuing education requirements that funeral directors must meet before a license can be renewed.

Apprenticeships must be completed under an experienced and licensed funeral director or embalmer. Depending on State regulations, apprenticeships last from 1 to 2 years and may be served before, during, or after mortuary school. They provide practical experience in all facets of the funeral service from embalming to transporting remains.

State board licensing examinations vary, but they usually consist of written and oral parts and include a demonstration of practical skills. Persons who want to work in another State may have to pass the examination for that State, although many States will grant licenses to funeral directors from another State without further examination.

High school students can start preparing for a career as a funeral director by taking courses in biology and chemistry and participating in public speaking or debating clubs. Part-time or summer jobs in funeral homes consist mostly of maintenance and clean-up tasks, such as washing and polishing limousines and hearses, but these tasks can help students become familiar with the operation of funeral homes.

Important personal traits for funeral directors are composure, tact, and the ability to communicate easily with the public. They also should have the desire and ability to comfort people in their time of sorrow.

Advancement opportunities are best in large funeral homes at which directors may earn promotions to higher paying positions such as branch manager or general manager. Some directors eventually acquire enough money and experience to establish their own funeral businesses.

Job Outlook

Employment opportunities for funeral directors are expected to be excellent, because the number of graduates in mortuary science is likely to continue to be lower than the number of job openings in the field. Although funeral directors are highly attached to their jobs, more openings will occur because more funeral directors are 55 years old and over compared to workers in other areas.

Employment of funeral directors is expected to increase slower than the average for all occupations through the year 2006. Demand for funeral services will rise as the population grows, and with it the number of deaths. The population is projected to become older because the number of persons age 55 and over is expected to increase significantly faster than the population as a whole. However, employment growth will be slowed by the number of people going into the field; this type of work is not attractive to many people.

Earnings

Median weekly earnings of full-time salaried funeral directors were $590 in 1996. The middle 50 percent earned between $447 and $849. The lowest 10 percent earned less than $356 and the top 10 percent more than $1,072.

Salaries of funeral directors depend on the number of years of experience in funeral services, the number of services performed, the number of facilities operated, the area of the country, the size of the community, and the formal education of the funeral director. A 1995 survey conducted by the National Funeral Directors Association found that the median salary, including bonus, for funeral directors ranged from a low of $21,775 annually for those with less than 5 years in the funeral service business and who performed fewer than 100 services a year to a high of $106,200 for an owner/manager who operated more than three facilities. Those funeral directors who had bachelor degrees tended to earn more than those with just a high school education. Those who were located in large cities earned more than those in small towns and rural areas. Salaries were higher in New England than in the South.

Related Occupations

The job of a funeral director requires tact, discretion, and compassion when dealing with grieving people. Others who need these qualities include members of the clergy, social workers, psychologists, psychiatrists, and other health care professionals.

Sources of Additional Information

For a list of accredited mortuary science programs and information on the funeral service profession, write to:
☛ The National Funeral Directors Association, 11121 West Oklahoma Ave., Milwaukee, WI 53227-4096.

For information about college programs in mortuary science, scholarships, and funeral service as a career, contact:
☛ The American Board of Funeral Service Education, P.O. Box 1305, Brunswick, ME 04011.

For information on continuing education programs in funeral service, contact:
☛ The National Funeral Directors Association Educational Foundation, 11121 W. Oklahoma Ave., Milwaukee, WI 53227-4096.

For information on programs, publications, and statistics on cremations write to:
☛ The Cremation Association of North America, 401 N. Michigan, Chicago, IL 60611.

General Managers and Top Executives

(List of D.O.T. codes available upon request. See p. 496.)

Significant Points

- This group is among the highest paid workers in the Nation, but long hours and substantial travel often are required.

- Competition for top managerial jobs will be keen because of the large number of qualified applicants seeking jobs.

Nature of the Work

Chief executive officer, president, executive vice president, owner, partner, brokerage office manager, school superintendent, and police chief—each is a general manager or top executive—the individual who formulates the policies and directs the operations of businesses and corporations, nonprofit institutions, and government agencies. (The chief executives who formulate policy in government are discussed in detail in the *Handbook* statement on government chief executives and legislators.)

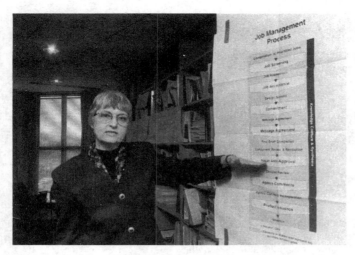

Top executives are generally provided with spacious offices and support staff.

The fundamental objective of private for-profit companies is to make a profit for their owners, or in corporations, to increase shareholder value. Nonprofit organizations and government agencies implement programs that further their policies within budgetary constraints. General managers and top executives set strategies and try to ensure that their organizations' objectives are met.

A corporation's general goals and policies are established by the chief executive officer in collaboration with other top executives, who are overseen by a board of directors. In a large corporation, the chief executive officer meets frequently with subordinate executives to ensure that operations are being carried out in accordance with these policies. Although the chief executive officer of a corporation retains overall accountability, a chief operating officer may be delegated the authority to oversee the executives who direct the activities of various departments and are responsible for implementing the organization's policies on a day-to-day basis. In publicly-held corporations, it is the board of directors that is ultimately accountable for the success or failure of the enterprise; the chief executive officer reports to the board. In nonprofit corporations, the board of trustees or board of directors fulfills the same role.

The scope of other high level executive's responsibilities depends upon the size of the organization. In large organizations, their duties are highly specialized. Managers of cost and profit centers are responsible for the overall performance of one aspect of the organization, such as manufacturing, marketing, sales, purchasing, finance, personnel, training, administrative services, electronic data processing, property management, transportation, or the legal services department. (Some of these and other managerial occupations are discussed elsewhere in this section of the *Handbook*.) In smaller firms, the chief executive or general manager might be responsible for all or a number of these functions.

Middle managers, in turn, direct their individual departments' activities within the framework of the organization's overall plan with the help of first-line managers and their staffs. First-line managers oversee and motivate the workers to achieve the departments' goals as rapidly and economically as possible. In smaller organizations, such as independent retail stores or small manufacturers, a partner, owner, or general manager may be responsible for all purchasing, hiring, training, quality control, and other day-to-day supervisory duties. (See the *Handbook* statement on retail managers.)

Working Conditions
Top executives are generally provided with spacious offices and secretarial and support staff. General managers in large firms or non-profit organizations are usually provided with comfortable offices close to the top executives to whom they report. Long hours, including evenings and weekends, are the rule for most top executives and general managers, though their schedules may be flexible.

Substantial travel often is required of managers and executives, who may travel between national, regional, and local offices, or overseas, to monitor operations and meet with customers, staff, and other executives. Many managers and executives attend meetings and conferences sponsored by associations. The conferences provide an opportunity to meet with prospective donors, customers, or government officials and contractors, and allow managers and executives to keep abreast of technological and managerial innovations.

In large organizations, frequent job transfers between local offices or subsidiaries are common. General managers and top executives are under intense pressure to earn ever higher profits, provide better service, or attain fundraising and charitable goals. Executives in charge of poorly performing organizations or departments generally find their jobs in jeopardy.

Employment
General managers and top executives held over 3.2 million jobs in 1996. They are found in every industry, but wholesale, retail, and services industries employ over 8 out of 10.

Training, Other Qualifications, and Advancement
The educational background of managers and top executives varies as widely as the nature of their responsibilities. Many general managers and top executives have a bachelor's degree or higher in liberal arts or business administration. Their major often is related to the departments they direct—for example, accounting for a manager of finance or computer science for a manager of information systems. Graduate and professional degrees are common. Many managers in administrative, marketing, financial, and manufacturing activities have a master's degree in business administration. Managers in highly technical manufacturing and research activities often have a master's degree in engineering or a doctoral degree in a scientific discipline. A law degree is mandatory for managers of legal departments; hospital administrators generally have a master's degree in health services administration or business administration. (For additional information, see the *Handbook* statement on health services managers.) College presidents and school superintendents generally have an advanced degree, the former, a doctorate in the field they originally taught, and the latter, often a masters degree in education administration. (See the *Handbook* statement on education administrators.) On the other hand, in industries such as retail trade or transportation, it is possible for individuals without a college degree to work their way up within the company and become managers.

In the public sector, many managers have liberal arts degrees in public administration or one of the social sciences. Park superintendents, for example, often have liberal arts degrees, while police chiefs are generally graduates of law enforcement academies and hold degrees in criminal justice or a related field.

Since many general manager and top executive positions are filled by promoting experienced, lower level managers when an opening occurs, many are promoted from within the organization. Some companies prefer that their top executives have specialized backgrounds and hire individuals who are managers in other organizations. Qualities critical for success include leadership, self-confidence, motivation, decisiveness, flexibility, the ability to communicate effectively, sound business judgment, and stamina.

Advancement may be accelerated by participation in company training programs to gain a broader knowledge of company policy and operations. Through attendance at national or local training programs sponsored by various industry and trade associations and by continuing their education, normally at company expense, managers can become familiar with the latest developments in management techniques and improve their chances of promotion. Every year, thousands of senior managers, who often have experience in a particular field, such as accounting or engineering, attend executive development programs to facilitate their promotion to general managers. Participation in conferences and seminars can expand knowledge of national and international issues influencing the organization and can help develop a network of useful contacts.

General managers and top executives must have highly developed personal skills. An analytical mind able to quickly assess large amounts of information and data is very important, as is the ability to consider and evaluate the interrelationships of numerous factors; they must also be able to communicate clearly and persuasively, and need highly developed interpersonal skills.

General managers may advance to top executive positions, such as executive vice president, in their own firm or they may take a corresponding position in another firm. They may even advance to peak corporate positions such as chief operating officer or chief executive officer. Chief executive officers often become members of the board of directors of one or more firms, typically as a director of their own firm and often as chair of its board of directors. Some general managers and top executives go on to establish their own firms or become independent consultants.

Job Outlook

Employment of general managers and top executives is expected to grow about as fast as the average for all occupations through the year 2006. Because this is a large occupation, many openings will occur each year as executives transfer to other positions, start their own businesses, or retire. Nonetheless, competition for top managerial jobs will be keen. Many executives who leave their jobs transfer to other executive or managerial positions, limiting openings for new entrants.

Projected employment growth of general managers and top executives varies widely among industries. For example, employment growth is expected to be faster than average in all services industries combined, but only about as fast as average in all finance, insurance, and real estate industry subgroups. Employment of general managers and top executives is projected to decline in manufacturing industries overall.

Experienced managers whose accomplishments reflect strong leadership qualities and the ability to improve the efficiency or competitive position of an organization will have the best opportunities. In an increasingly global economy, certain types of experience, such as international economics, marketing, information systems, and knowledge of several languages, may also help.

Earnings

General managers and top executives are among the highest paid workers in the Nation. However, salary levels vary substantially depending upon the level of managerial responsibility, length of service, and type, size, and location of the firm.

At the highest level, chief executive officers (CEOs) of medium and large corporations are extremely well paid. Salaries often are related to the size of the corporation—a top manager in a very large corporation can earn significantly more than a counterpart in a small firm. Total compensation often includes stock options, dividends, and other performance bonuses, in addition to salaries.

Salaries also vary substantially by type and level of responsibilities and by industry. According to a salary survey by Robert Half International, senior vice presidents/heads of lending in banks with $1 billion or more in assets earned about $200,000 to $215,000 in 1997. Executive Compensation Reports, a division of Harcourt Brace & Company, reports that the median salary for CEOs of public companies from the fiscal year 1995 Fortune 500 list was approximately $714,000, with three-quarters making less than about $900,000. In the nonprofit sector, three quarters of the CEOs make under $135,000 in 1996, according to a survey by Abbott, Langer, & Associates.

Company-paid insurance premiums and physical examinations, the use of executive dining rooms and company cars, and expense allowances are among benefits commonly enjoyed by general managers and top executives in private industry. CEOs often enjoy company-paid club memberships, a limousine with driver, and other amenities. CEOs of very large corporations may have the use of private aircraft.

Related Occupations

General managers and top executives plan, organize, direct, control, and coordinate the operations of an organization and its major departments or programs. The members of the board of directors and supervisory managers are also involved in these activities. Related occupations in government with similar functions are President, governor, mayor, commissioner, and legislator.

Sources of Additional Information

For a wide variety of information on general managers and top executives, including educational programs and job listings, contact:
☛ American Management Association, 1601 Broadway, New York, NY 10019-7420.
☛ National Management Association, 2210 Arbor Blvd., Dayton, OH 45439.

Government Chief Executives and Legislators

Significant Points

- Over 8 out of 10 government chief executives and legislators work in local government, while the rest work primarily in State governments.

- Many jobs at the local and even State level are part time and pay little.

- Few long-term career opportunities are available.

Nature of the Work

Chief executives and legislators at the Federal, State, and local level direct government activities and pass laws that affect each of us. Chief executives run the governmental bodies that formulate and enforce laws. These officials include the President and Vice President of the United States, State governors and lieutenant governors, county executives, town and township officials, mayors, and city, county, town, township, and special district managers. All except appointed government managers are elected by their constituents. Non-elected managers are hired by a local government council or commission.

Government chief executives, like their counterparts in the private sector, have overall responsibility for the performance of their organizations. Working in conjunction with legislators, they set goals and then organize programs to attain them. They appoint department heads who oversee the work of the civil servants who carry out programs and enforce laws enacted by their legislative bodies. They oversee budgets specifying how government resources will be used, and insure that resources are used properly and programs are carried out as planned.

Chief executives meet with legislators and constituents to discuss proposed programs and determine their level of support. They frequently confer with leaders of other governments to solve mutual problems. Chief executives nominate citizens to boards and commissions, solicit bids from and select contractors to do work for the government, encourage business investment and economic development in their jurisdictions, and seek Federal or State funds. Chief executives of large jurisdictions rely on a staff of aides and assistants, but those in small jurisdictions often must do much of the work themselves.

Legislators are the elected officials who pass or amend laws. They include U.S. Senators and Representatives, State senators and representatives, county legislators, and city and town council members.

Legislators may introduce bills in the legislative body and examine and vote on bills introduced by other legislators. In preparing legislation, they read staff reports and may work with constituents, representatives of interest groups, members of boards and commissions, the chief executive and department heads, and others with an interest in the legislation. They generally must approve budgets and the appointments of department heads and commission members submitted by the chief executive. In some jurisdictions, the legislative body appoints a city, town, or county manager. Many legisla-

Government chief executives have overall responsibility for the performance of their organizations.

tors, especially at the State and Federal levels, have a staff to perform research, prepare legislation, and help resolve constituents' problems.

Both chief executives and legislators perform many ceremonial duties such as opening new buildings, making proclamations, welcoming visitors, and leading celebrations.

Working Conditions
The working conditions of chief executives and legislators vary with the size and budget of the governmental unit. Time spent at work ranges from meeting once a month for a local council member to 60 or more hours per week for a U.S. Senator. U.S. Senators and Representatives, governors and lieutenant governors, and chief executives and legislators in large local jurisdictions usually work full time year round, as do county and city managers. Many State legislators work full time while legislatures are in session (usually for 2 to 6 months a year), and part time the rest of the year. Local elected officials in many jurisdictions work a schedule that is officially designated part time, but actually is the equivalent of a full-time schedule when unpaid duties are taken into account. In addition to their regular schedules, chief executives are on call at all hours to handle emergencies.

Some jobs require occasional out-of-town travel, but others involve long periods away from home to attend sessions of the legislature.

Employment
Chief executives and legislators held about 93,000 jobs in 1996. About 8 out of 10 worked in local government, while the rest worked primarily in State governments. Chief executives and legislators in the Federal Government include the 535 Senators and Representatives and the President and Vice President. State governors, legislators and other managers, as well as executives, managers, and council members for local governments made up the remainder.

Chief executives and legislators who do not hold full-time, year-round positions often work in a second occupation as well. This is commonly the one they held before being elected.

Training, Other Qualifications, and Advancement
Voters seek to elect the individual believed to be most qualified from among a number of candidates who meet the minimum age, residency, and citizenship requirements. Successful candidates usually have a strong record of accomplishment in paid and unpaid work in their district. Some have business, teaching, or legal experience, but others

come from a wide variety of occupations. In addition, many have experience as members of boards or commissions. Some candidates become well-known for their work with charities, political action groups, political campaigns, or with religious, fraternal, and social organizations.

Management-level work experience and public service help develop the planning, organizing, negotiating, motivating, fundraising, budgeting, public speaking, and problem-solving skills needed to run an effective political campaign. Candidates must make decisions quickly, sometimes on the basis of limited or contradictory information. They must inspire and motivate their constituents and their staff. They should appear sincere and candid, presenting their views thoughtfully and convincingly. Additionally, they must know how to hammer out compromises and satisfy the demands of constituents. National and Statewide campaigns require massive amounts of energy and stamina, as well as superior fund raising skills.

Town, city, and county managers are generally hired by a council or commission. Managers come from a variety of educational backgrounds. A master's degree in public administration, including courses such as public financial management and legal issues in public administration, is widely recommended. Virtually all town, city, and county managers have at least a bachelor's degree and the majority hold a master's degree. Working in management support positions in government is a prime source of the experience and personal contacts required in eventually securing a manager position.

Generally, a town, city, or county manager in a smaller jurisdiction is required to have expertise in a wide variety of areas. Those who work for larger jurisdictions specialize in financial, administrative, and personnel matters. For all managers, communication skills and the ability to get along with others are essential.

Advancement opportunities for elected public officials are not clearly defined. Because elected positions normally require a period of residency and local public support is critical, officials can usually advance to other offices only in the jurisdictions where they live. For example, council members may run for mayor or for a position in the State government, and State legislators may run for governor or for Congress. Many officials are not politically ambitious, however, and do not seek advancement. Others lose their bids for reelection or voluntarily leave the occupation. A lifetime career as a government chief executive or legislator is rare except for those who reach the national level.

Town, city, and county managers have a better defined career path. They generally obtain a master's degree in public administration, then gain experience as management analysts or assistants in government departments working for committees, councils or chief executives. They learn about planning, budgeting, civil engineering, and other aspects of running a government. With sufficient experience, they may be hired to manage a small government and often move on to manage progressively larger governments over time.

Job Outlook
Little, if any, growth is expected in the number of State or Federal Government chief executives and legislators through the year 2006. Few new governments at any level are likely to form, and the number of chief executives and legislators in existing governments rarely changes. Some increase will occur at the local level as counties, cities, and towns take on new responsibilities. New positions will develop as cities and counties turn to professional management to deal with growth, Federal regulations, and long-range planning, and volunteer positions are converted to paid positions.

Elections give newcomers the chance to unseat incumbents or to fill vacated positions. In many elections, there is substantial competition, although the level of competition varies from jurisdiction to jurisdiction and from year to year. Generally, there is less competition in small jurisdictions, which have part-time positions offering relatively low salaries and little or no staff to help with routine work, than in large jurisdictions, which have full-time positions offering higher salaries, more staff, and greater status.

Earnings
Earnings of public administrators vary widely, depending on the size of the government unit and on whether the job is part time, full time

and year round, or full time for only a few months a year. Salaries range from little or nothing for a small town council member to $200,000 a year for the President of the United States.

According to the International City/County Management Association, the average annual salary of chief elected county officials in 1996 was $25,600, while chief elected city officials was about $12,200. ICMA data indicate that the average salary for city managers was about $70,600 in 1996, while that of county managers was about $86,700.

According to the National Conference of State Legislatures, the salary for legislators in the 40 States that paid an annual salary ranged from about $10,000 to $47,000 per year. In 6 States, legislators received a daily salary plus an allowance for expenses while legislatures were in session. Two States paid no expenses and only nominal daily salaries, while 2 States paid no salary at all but did pay a daily expense allowance. Salaries and the expense allowance were generally higher in the larger States.

Data from *Book of the States, 1996-97* indicate that gubernatorial annual salaries ranged from $60,000 in Arkansas to $130,000 in New York. In addition to a salary, most governors received perquisites such as transportation and an official residence.

In 1997, U.S. Senators and Representatives earned $133,600, the Senate and House Majority and Minority leaders $148,400, and the Vice President $171,500.

Related Occupations
Related occupations include managerial positions that require a broad range of skills in addition to administrative expertise, such as corporate chief executives and board members, and high ranking officers in the military.

Sources of Additional Information
Information on appointed officials in local government can be obtained from:
☛ International City/County Management Association, 777 North Capitol St. NE., Suite 500, Washington, DC 20002.

Health Services Managers

(D.O.T. 072.117-010; 074.167-010, 075.117-014, -022, -026, -030 and -034, .167-010 and -014; 076.117-010; 077.117-010; 078.131-010, .161-010 and -014, .162-010; 079.117-010, .131-010, .151-010, and .167-014; 187.117-010, -058, -062, and .167-034, and -090; 188.117-082

Significant points
- Earnings of health services managers are high, but long weekly work hours are common.
- Most are employed by hospitals, but the fastest employment growth will be in home health care agencies, long-term care facilities, and practitioners' offices and clinics.

Nature of the Work
Health care is a business, albeit a special one. Like every other business, it needs good management to keep it running smoothly, especially during times of change. The term "health services manager" encompasses individuals in many different positions who plan, organize, coordinate, and supervise the delivery of health care. Health services managers include both generalists—administrators who manage or help to manage an entire facility or system—and health specialists—managers in charge of specific clinical departments or services found only in the health industry.

The structure and financing of health care is changing rapidly. Future health services managers must be prepared to deal with evolving integrated health care delivery systems, restructuring of work, technological innovations, and an increased focus on preventive care. They will be called upon to improve efficiency in all health care facilities, while continually improving quality of the health care

provided. Increasingly, health services managers work in organizations in which they must optimize efficiency of a variety of interrelated services, ranging from inpatient care to outpatient follow-up care, for example.

The top administrator or chief executive officer (CEO) and the assistant administrators without specific titles are health care generalists, who set the overall direction of the organization. They concentrate on such areas as community outreach, planning, marketing, human resources, finance, and complying with government regulations. Their range of knowledge is broad, including developments in the clinical departments as well as in the business arena. They often speak before civic groups, promote public participation in health programs, and coordinate the activities of the organization with those of government or community agencies. CEO's make long-term institutional plans by assessing the need for services, personnel, facilities, and equipment and recommending changes such as opening a home health service. CEO's need leadership ability, as well as technical skills, to provide quality health care while satisfying demand for financial viability, cost containment, and public and professional accountability.

Larger facilities typically have several assistant administrators to aid the top administrator and to handle day-to-day decisions. They may direct activities in clinical areas such as nursing, surgery, therapy, food service, and medical records; or the activities in nonhealth areas such as finance, housekeeping, human resources, and information management. (Because the nonhealth departments are not directly related to health care, these managers are not included in this statement. For information about them, see the statements on managerial occupations elsewhere in the *Handbook*). In smaller facilities, top administrators may handle more of the details of day-to-day operations. For example, many nursing home administrators directly manage personnel, finance, operations, admissions, and have a larger role in resident care.

Clinical managers have more narrowly defined responsibilities than generalists, and have training and/or experience in a specific clinical area. For example, directors of physical therapy are experienced physical therapists, and most health information administrators have a bachelor's degree in health information administration. These managers establish and implement policies, objectives, and procedures for their departments; evaluate personnel and work; develop reports and budgets; and coordinate activities with other managers.

In group practices, managers work closely with the physician owners. While an office manager may handle business affairs in small medical groups, leaving policy decisions to the physicians themselves, larger groups generally employ a full-time administrator to advise on business strategies and coordinate day-to-day business.

To make effective decisions, health services managers must be open to different opinions and good at analyzing contradictory information.

A small group of 10 or 15 physicians might employ a single administrator to oversee personnel matters, billing and collection, budgeting, planning, equipment outlays, and patient flow. A large practice of 40 or 50 physicians may have a chief administrator and several assistants, each responsible for different areas.

Health services managers in health maintenance organizations (HMO's) and other managed care settings perform functions similar to those in large group practices, except their staffs may be larger. Also, they may do more work in the areas of community outreach and preventive care than managers of a group practice. The size of the administrative staff in HMO's varies according to the size and type of HMO.

Some health services managers oversee the activities of a number of facilities in multifacility health organizations.

Working Conditions
Most health services managers work long hours. Facilities such as nursing homes and hospitals operate around the clock, and administrators and managers may be called at all hours to deal with problems. They may also travel to attend meetings or inspect satellite facilities.

Employment
Health services managers held about 329,000 jobs in 1996. Over one-half of all jobs were in hospitals. About 1 in 4 were in nursing and personal care facilities or offices and clinics of physicians. The remainder worked in home health agencies, medical and dental laboratories, offices of dentists and other practitioners, and other health and allied services.

Training, Other Qualifications, and Advancement
Health services managers must be familiar with management principles and practices. Some learn from work experience. However, formal education is usually necessary for advancement. Most CEO positions require a graduate degree in health services administration, nursing administration, public health, or business administration. For some generalist positions, employers seek applicants with clinical experience (as nurses or therapists, for example) as well as academic preparation in business or health services administration.

Bachelor's, master's, and doctoral degree programs in health administration are offered by colleges, universities, and schools of public health, medicine, allied health, public administration, and business administration. There are also some certificate or diploma programs, generally lasting less than 1 year, in health services administration and in medical office management. A master's degree—in health services administration, long term care administration, health sciences, public health, public administration, or business administration—is the standard credential for most generalist positions in this field. However, a bachelor's degree is adequate for some entry-level positions in smaller operations. A bachelor's degree is required to work in some settings, such as nursing homes, and for entry level positions at the departmental level within health care organizations. Physicians' offices and some other facilities may substitute on-the-job experience for formal education. For clinical department heads, a degree in the appropriate field and work experience may be sufficient, but a master's degree in health services administration usually is required to advance.

In 1997, 67 schools had accredited programs leading to the master's degree in health services administration, according to the Accrediting Commission on Education for Health Services Administration.

Some graduate programs seek students with undergraduate degrees in business or health administration; however, many programs prefer students with a liberal arts or health professions background. Competition for entry to these programs is keen, and applicants need above-average grades to gain admission. The programs generally last between 2 and 3 years. They may include up to 1 year of supervised administrative experience, and course work in areas such as hospital organization and management, marketing, accounting and budgeting, human resources administration, strategic planning, health economics, and health information systems. Some programs allow students to specialize in one type of facility—hospitals; nursing homes; mental health facilities; HMO's; or outpatient care facilities, including

medical groups. Other programs encourage a generalist approach to health administration education.

New graduates with master's degrees in health services administration may start as department managers or in staff positions. The level of the starting position varies with the experience of the applicant and size of the organization. Postgraduate residencies and fellowships are offered by hospitals and other health facilities; these are usually staff positions. Graduates from master's degree programs also take jobs in HMO's, large group medical practices, clinics, mental health facilities, and multifacility nursing home corporations.

Graduates with bachelor's degrees in health administration usually begin as administrative assistants or assistant department heads in larger hospitals, or as department heads or assistant administrators in small hospitals or nursing homes.

A Ph.D. degree may be required to teach, consult, or do research. Nursing service administrators are usually chosen from among supervisory registered nurses with administrative abilities and a graduate degree in nursing or health services administration.

Most States and the District of Columbia require nursing home administrators to have a bachelor's degree, pass a licensing examination, complete a State-approved training program, and pursue continuing education. A license is not required in other areas of health services management.

Health services managers are often responsible for millions of dollars of facilities and equipment and hundreds of employees. To make effective decisions, they need to be open to different opinions and good at analyzing contradictory information. They must understand finance and information systems, and be able to interpret data. Motivating others to implement their decisions requires strong leadership abilities. Tact, diplomacy, flexibility, and communication skills are essential because health services managers spend much of their time interacting with others.

Health services managers advance by moving into more responsible and higher paying positions, such as assistant or associate administrator, or by moving to larger facilities.

Job Outlook
Employment of health services managers is expected to grow faster than the average for all occupations through the year 2006 as health services continue to expand and diversify. Opportunities for health services managers should be closely related to growth in the industry in which they are employed. Opportunities will be good in home health care, long-term care and nontraditional health organizations such as managed care operations, particularly for health services managers with work experience in the health care field and strong business and management skills.

Hospitals will continue to employ the most managers, although the number of jobs will grow slowly compared to other areas. As hospitals continue to consolidate, centralize, and diversify functions, competition will increase at all job levels.

Employment will grow the fastest in home health agencies, offices of physicians and other health practitioners, and nursing and personal care facilities due to an increased number of elderly individuals who will need care. In addition, many services previously provided in hospitals will be shifted to these sectors, especially as medical technologies improve. Demand in medical group practice management will grow as medical group practices become larger and more complex. Health services managers will need to deal with the pressures of cost containment and financial accountability, as well as the increased focus on preventive and primary care. They will have more responsibility for improving the health of populations and communities.

Health services managers will also be employed by health care management companies who provide management services to hospitals and other organizations, as well as specific departments such as emergency, information management systems, managed care contract negotiations, and physician recruiting.

Earnings
Earnings of health services managers vary by type and size of the facility, as well as by level of responsibility. For example, the Medi-

cal Group Management Association reported that the median salary for administrators in small group practices—with fewer than 7 physicians—was about $56,000 in 1996; for those in larger group practices—with more than 7 physicians—$77,000.

According to a 1997 survey by *Modern Healthcare* magazine, half of all hospital CEO's earned total compensation of $190,500 or more. Salaries varied according to size of facility and geographic region. Clinical department heads' salaries varied also. Median total compensation in 1997 for heads of the following clinical departments were: Respiratory therapy, $54,500; home health care, $62,000; clinical laboratory, $63,700; radiology, $64,000; physical therapy, $64,900; ambulatory/outpatient services, $68,500; rehabilitation services, $70,400; and nursing services, $97,000.

According to the Buck Survey conducted by the American Health Care Association in 1996, nursing home administrators had median annual compensation of about $49,500. The middle 50 percent earned between $42,100 and $57,300. Assistant administrators earned about $32,000, with the middle 50 percent earning between $26,200 and $40,000.

Executives often receive bonuses based on performance outcomes such as cost-containment, quality assurance, and patient satisfaction.

Related Occupations

Health services managers have training or experience in both health and management. Other occupations requiring knowledge of both fields are public health directors, social welfare administrators, directors of voluntary health agencies and health professional associations, and underwriters in health insurance companies.

Sources of Additional Information

General information about health administration is available from:
☛ American College of Healthcare Executives, One North Franklin St., Suite 1700, Chicago, IL 60606. Homepage: http://www.ache.org

Information about undergraduate and graduate academic programs in this field is available from:
☛ Association of University Programs in Health Administration, 1911 North Fort Myer Dr., Suite 503, Arlington, VA 22209. Homepage: http://www.aupha.org

For a list of accredited graduate programs in health services administration, contact:
☛ Accrediting Commission on Education for Health Services Administration, 1911 North Fort Myer Dr., Suite 503, Arlington, VA 22209.

For information about career opportunities in long term care administration, contact:
☛ American College of Health Care Administrators, 325 S. Patrick St., Alexandria, VA 22314.

For information about career opportunities in medical group practices and ambulatory care management, contact:
☛ Medical Group Management Association, 104 Inverness Terrace East, Englewood, CO 80112.

Hotel Managers and Assistants

(D.O.T. 187.117-038, .137-018; .167-046, -078, -106, -122; and 320)

Significant Points

- Long hours and the stress of dealing with hotel patrons result in high turnover.

- College graduates with degrees in hotel or restaurant management should have good job opportunities.

Nature of the Work

A comfortable room, good food, and a helpful hotel staff can make being away from home an enjoyable experience for both vacationing families and business travelers. Hotel managers and assistant managers strive to ensure their guests will have a pleasant stay by providing many of the comforts of home, including cable television, fitness equipment, and voice mail. For business travelers, hotel managers

make available meeting rooms and various equipment, including slide projectors and fax machines.

Hotel managers are responsible for the efficient and profitable operation of their establishments. In a small hotel, motel, or inn with a limited staff, a single manager may direct all aspects of operations. However, large hotels may employ hundreds of workers, and the general manager may be aided by a number of assistant managers assigned to the various departments of the operation. Assistant managers must ensure that the day-to-day operations of their departments meet the standards set by the general manager.

Computers are used extensively by hotel managers and their assistants, to keep track of the guest's bill, reservations, room assignments, meetings, and special events; order food, beverages, and housekeeping and other supplies; and prepare reports for hotel owners and top-level managers. Managers work with computer specialists to ensure that the hotel's computer system functions properly. Should the hotel's computer system fail, managers must ensure that guests' needs continue to be met.

The *general manager* has overall responsibility for the operation of the hotel. Within guidelines established by the owners of the hotel or executives of the hotel chain, the general manager sets room rates, allocates funds to departments, approves expenditures, and establishes standards for service to guests, decor, housekeeping, food quality, and banquet operations. Managers who work for chains also may be assigned to organize and staff a newly built hotel, refurbish an older hotel, or reorganize a hotel or motel that is not operating successfully. In order to fill some low-paying service and clerical jobs in hotels, some managers attend career fairs. (For more information, see the statement on general managers and top executives elsewhere in the *Handbook.*)

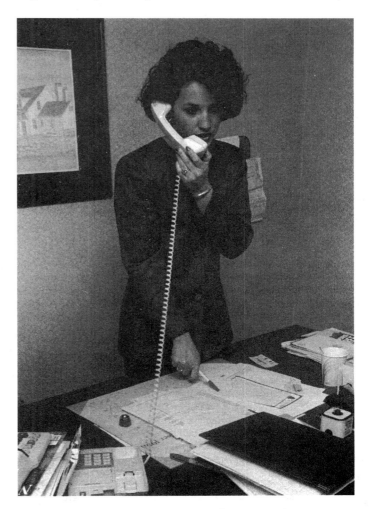

Hotel managers plan business, social, and recreational events.

Resident managers live in hotels and are on call 24 hours a day to resolve problems or emergencies. However, they typically work an 8-hour day, while overseeing the day-to-day operations of the hotel. In many hotels, the general manager also serves as the resident manager.

Executive housekeepers are responsible for ensuring guest rooms, meeting and banquet rooms, and public areas are clean, orderly, and well maintained. They train, schedule, and supervise the work of housekeepers; inspect rooms; and order cleaning supplies.

Front office managers coordinate reservations and room assignments as well as train and direct the hotel's front desk staff. They ensure guests are treated courteously, complaints and problems are resolved, and requests for special services are carried out. Front office managers often have authorization to adjust charges posted on a customer's bill.

Food and beverage managers direct the food service operations of hotels. They oversee the hotels' restaurants, cocktail lounges, and banquet facilities. They supervise and schedule food and beverage preparation and service workers, plan menus, estimate costs, and deal with food suppliers. (For more information, see the statement on restaurant and food service managers elsewhere in the *Handbook*.)

Convention services managers coordinate the activities of large hotels' various departments for meetings, conventions, and special events. They meet with representatives of groups or organizations to plan the number of rooms to reserve, the desired configuration of hotel meeting space, and any banquet services needed. During the meeting or event, they resolve unexpected problems and monitor activities to check that hotel operations conform to the expectations of the group.

Other assistant managers are responsible for personnel, accounting and office administration, marketing and sales, purchasing, security, maintenance, and recreational facilities. (For more information, see the *Handbook* statements on personnel, training, and labor relations specialists and managers; financial managers; and marketing, advertising, and public relations managers.)

Working Conditions

Because hotels are open around the clock, night and weekend work is common. Many hotel managers work considerably more than 40 hours per week. Managers who live in the hotel usually have regular work schedules, but they may be called to work at any time. Some employees of resort hotels are managers during the busy season and have other duties during the rest of the year.

Hotel managers sometimes experience the pressures of coordinating a wide range of functions. Conventions and large groups of tourists may present unusual problems. Dealing with irate patrons can be stressful. The job can be particularly hectic for front office managers around check-in and check-out time. Computer failures can further complicate an already busy time.

Employment

Hotel managers and assistant managers held about 175,000 jobs in 1996. A significant number of these jobs were held by self-employed managers—primarily owners of small hotels and motels. Some managers were employed by companies that manage hotels and motels under contract.

Training, Other Qualifications, and Advancement

Postsecondary training in hotel or restaurant management is preferred for most hotel management positions, although a college liberal arts degree may be sufficient when coupled with related hotel experience. In the past, many managers were promoted from the ranks of front desk clerks, housekeepers, waiters and chefs, and hotel sales workers. Although some employees still advance to hotel management positions without the benefit of education or training beyond high school, postsecondary education is preferred.

Restaurant management training or experience is also a good background for entering hotel management because the success of a hotel's food service and beverage operations is often of great importance to the profitability of the entire establishment.

Internships or part-time or summer work while in school is an asset to anyone seeking a career in hotel management. The experience gained and the contacts made with employers can greatly benefit students when they seek full-time employment after graduation. Most bachelor's degree programs include work-study opportunities. A bachelor's degree in hotel and restaurant administration provides particularly strong preparation for a career in hotel management. In 1996, over 160 colleges and universities offered bachelor's and graduate programs in this field. Over 800 community and junior colleges, technical institutes, vocational and trade schools, and other academic institutions also have programs leading to an associate degree or other formal recognition in hotel or restaurant management. For example, many colleges and universities have certification programs in executive housekeeping; these programs typically cover a wide variety of topics, including environmental and workplace safety as well as Federal, State, and local safety requirements. Graduates of hotel or restaurant management programs usually start as trainee assistant managers, or at least advance to such positions more quickly.

Hotel management programs include instruction in hotel administration, accounting, economics, marketing, housekeeping, food service management and catering, and hotel maintenance engineering. Computer training is an integral part of hotel management training due to the widespread use of computers in reservations, billing, and housekeeping management.

Hotel managers must be able to get along with all kinds of people, even in stressful situations. They must be able to solve problems and concentrate on details. Initiative, self-discipline, the ability to organize and direct the work of others, and effective communication skills are essential for managers at all levels.

Sometimes large hotels sponsor specialized on-the-job management training programs which allow trainees to rotate among various departments and gain a thorough knowledge of the hotel's operation. Other hotels may help finance formal training in hotel management for outstanding employees.

Most hotels promote employees who have proven their ability and completed formal education in hotel management. Newly built hotels, particularly those without well-established on-the-job training programs, often prefer experienced personnel for managerial positions. Large hotel and motel chains may offer better opportunities for advancement than small, independently owned establishments, but relocation every several years often is necessary for advancement. The large chains have more extensive career ladder programs and offer managers the opportunity to transfer to another hotel or motel in the chain or to the central office if an opening occurs. Career advancement can be accelerated by completion of certification programs offered by the associations listed below. These programs generally require a combination of course work, examinations, and experience.

Job Outlook

Employment of hotel managers is expected to grow about as fast as the average for all occupations through the year 2006. However, long hours and stressful working conditions result in high turnover in this field, with most job openings expected to occur as experienced managers transfer to other occupations, retire, or stop working for other reasons. Job opportunities in hotel management are expected to be good for persons with college degrees in hotel or restaurant management.

Business travel will continue to grow, and increased domestic and foreign tourism will also create demand for additional hotels and motels. However, manager jobs are not expected to grow as rapidly as the hotel industry due to consolidation, with chains and franchises acquiring independently owned establishments. In addition, front desk clerks are increasingly assuming some responsibilities previously reserved for managers. Also, to accommodate bargain-conscious guests, hotel chains are increasing the number of economy-class rooms. Economy hotels offer clean, comfortable rooms and front desk services without costly extras like restaurants and room service. Because there are not as many departments in each hotel, fewer managers are needed. Economy-class hotels have a general manager, and regional offices of the hotel management company employ department managers, such as executive housekeepers, to oversee several hotels.

Demand may also increase for suite hotels as some guests, especially business customers, are willing to pay higher prices for rooms with kitchens and suites that provide the space needed to conduct meetings. In addition to job growth in suite hotels and economy-class hotels, large full-service hotels—offering restaurants, fitness centers, large meeting rooms, and play areas for children, among other amenities—will continue to offer many trainee and managerial opportunities.

Earnings
Salaries of hotel managers vary greatly according to their responsibilities and the segment of the hotel industry in which they are employed. In 1996, annual salaries of assistant hotel managers averaged around $40,000, based on a hospitality industry survey conducted by Roth Young Personnel of Oklahoma City. Salaries of assistant managers also varied because of differences in duties and responsibilities. For example, food and beverage directors averaged $43,000, whereas front office managers averaged $28,000. The manager's level of experience is also an important factor.

In 1996, salaries of general managers averaged nearly $54,000, according to the Roth Young survey. Their salaries ranged from $39,000 to $81,000, depending on the size and type of establishment. Based on limited information, managers may earn bonuses up to 25 percent of their basic salary in some hotels. In addition, managers and their families may be furnished with lodging, meals, parking, laundry, and other services.

In addition to typical benefits, some hotels offer profit-sharing plans and educational assistance to their employees.

Related Occupations
Hotel managers and assistants are not the only workers concerned with organizing and directing a business where customer service is the cornerstone of their success. Other occupations sharing similar responsibilities include restaurant managers, apartment building managers, retail store managers, and office managers.

Sources of Additional Information
For information on careers and scholarships in hotel management, contact:
☛ The American Hotel and Motel Association (AH&MA), Information Center, 1201 New York Ave. NW., Washington, DC 20005-3931.

For information on educational programs, including correspondence courses, in hotel and restaurant management, write to:
☛ Council on Hotel, Restaurant, and Institutional Education, 1200 17th St. NW., Washington, DC 20036-3097.

Information on careers in housekeeping management may be obtained from:
☛ National Executive Housekeepers Association, Inc., 1001 Eastwind Dr., Suite 301, Westerville, OH 43081. Phone: (800) 200-6342.

General career information and a directory of accredited private trade and technical schools offering programs in hotel-motel management may be obtained from:
☛ Accrediting Commission of Career Schools and Colleges of Technology, 2101 Wilson Blvd., Suite 302, Arlington, VA 22201.

Human Resources Specialists and Managers

(D.O.T. 079.127; 099.167-010; 166.067, .117, .167 except -046, .257, .267-014 through -046; 169.107, .167-062, .207; 188.117-010, -086, .217)

Significant Points
- Employers generally seek college graduates for entry level jobs. Depending on the job duties, a strong background in human resources, business, technical, or liberal arts subjects is preferred.

- The job market is likely to remain competitive in view of the abundant supply of qualified college graduates and experienced workers.

Nature of the Work
Attracting the most qualified employees available and matching them to the jobs for which they are best suited is important for the success of any organization. However, many enterprises are too large to permit close contact between top management and employees. Human resources specialists and managers provide this link. These individuals recruit and interview employees, and advise on hiring decisions in accordance with policies and requirements that have been established in conjunction with top management. In an effort to improve morale and productivity and limit job turnover, they also help their firms effectively use employees' skills, provide training opportunities to enhance those skills, and boost employees' satisfaction with their jobs and working conditions. Although some jobs in the human resources field require only limited contact with people outside the office, most involve frequent contact. Dealing with people is an essential part of the job.

In a small organization, a human resources generalist may handle many, or all, aspects of human resources work, requiring a broad range of knowledge. The responsibilities of human resources generalists can vary widely, depending on their employer's needs. In a large corporation, the top human resources executive usually develops and coordinates personnel programs and policies. (Executives are included in the *Handbook* statement on general managers and top executives.) These policies are usually implemented by a director or manager of human resources and, in some cases, a director of industrial relations.

The director of human resources may oversee several departments, each headed by an experienced manager, who most likely specializes in one personnel activity such as employment, compensation, benefits, training and development, or employee relations.

Employment and placement managers oversee the hiring and separation of employees and supervise various workers, including equal employment opportunity specialists and recruitment specialists.

Recruiters maintain contacts within the community and may travel extensively, often to college campuses, to search for promising job applicants. Recruiters screen, interview, and test applicants. They may also check references and extend offers of employment to qualified candidates. These workers must be thoroughly familiar with the organization and its personnel policies to discuss wages, working conditions, and promotional opportunities with prospective employees. They must also keep informed about equal employment opportunity (EEO) and affirmative action guidelines and laws, such as the Americans With Disabilities Act.

EEO representatives or affirmative action coordinators handle this area in large organizations. They investigate and resolve EEO grievances, examine corporate practices for possible violations, and compile and submit EEO statistical reports.

Employer relations representatives—who usually work in government agencies—maintain working relationships with local employers and promote the use of public employment programs and services. Similarly, employment interviewers—whose many job titles include personnel consultants, personnel development specialists, and human resources coordinators—help match jobseekers with employers. (For more information, see the statement on employment interviewers elsewhere in the *Handbook*.)

Job analysts, sometimes called position classifiers, perform very exacting work. They collect and examine detailed information about job duties to prepare job descriptions. These descriptions explain the duties, training, and skills each job requires. Whenever a large organization introduces a new job or reviews existing jobs, it calls upon the expert knowledge of the job analyst.

Occupational analysts conduct research, generally in large firms. They are concerned with occupational classification systems and study the effects of industry and occupational trends upon worker relationships. They may serve as technical liaison between the firm and industry, government, and labor unions.

Establishing and maintaining a firm's pay system is the principal job of the compensation manager. Assisted by staff specialists, compensation managers devise ways to ensure fair and equitable pay rates. They may conduct surveys to see how their rates compare with others and to see that the firm's pay scale complies with changing laws and regulations. In addition, compensation managers often oversee their firm's performance evaluation system, and they may design reward systems such as pay-for-performance plans.

Employee benefits managers handle the company's employee benefits program, notably its health insurance and pension plans. Expertise in designing and administering benefits programs continues to gain importance as employer-provided benefits account for a growing proportion of overall compensation costs, and as benefit plans increase in number and complexity. For example, pension benefits might include savings and thrift, profit-sharing, and stock ownership plans; health benefits may include long-term catastrophic illness insurance and dental insurance. Familiarity with health benefits is a top priority at present, as more firms struggle to cope with the rising cost of health care for employees and retirees. In addition to health insurance and pension coverage, some firms offer their employees life and accidental death and dismemberment insurance, disability insurance, and relatively new benefits designed to meet the needs of a changing work force, such as parental leave, child care and elder care, long-term nursing home care insurance, employee assistance and wellness programs, and flexible benefits plans. Benefits managers must keep abreast of changing Federal and State regulations and legislation that may affect employee benefits.

Employee assistance plan managers—also called employee welfare managers—are responsible for a wide array of programs covering occupational safety and health standards and practices; health promotion and physical fitness, medical examinations, and minor health treatment, such as first aid; plant security; publications; food service and recreation activities; car pooling; employee suggestion systems; child care and elder care; and counseling services. Child care and elder care are increasingly important due to growth in the number of dual-income households and the elderly population. Counseling may help employees deal with emotional disorders, alcoholism, or marital, family, consumer, legal, and financial problems. Some employers offer career counseling as well. In large firms, some of these programs—such as security and safety—are in separate departments headed by other managers.

Training is supervised by training and development managers. Increasingly, management recognizes that training offers a way of developing skills, enhancing productivity and quality of work, and building loyalty to the firm. Training is widely accepted as a method of improving employee morale, but this is only one of the reasons for its growing importance. Other factors include the complexity of the work environment, the rapid pace of organizational and technological change, and the growing number of jobs in fields that constantly generate new knowledge. In addition, advances in learning theory have provided insights into how adults learn, and how training can be organized most effectively for them.

Training specialists plan, organize, and direct a wide range of training activities. Trainers conduct orientation sessions and arrange on-the-job training for new employees. They help rank-and-file workers maintain and improve their job skills, and possibly prepare for jobs requiring greater skill. They help supervisors improve their interpersonal skills in order to deal effectively with employees. They may set up individualized training plans to strengthen an employee's existing skills or to teach new ones. Training specialists in some companies set up programs to develop executive potential among employees in lower-level positions. In government-supported training programs, training specialists function as case managers. They first assess the training needs of clients, then guide them through the most appropriate training method. After training, clients may either be referred to employer relations representatives or receive job placement assistance.

Planning and program development is an important part of the training specialist's job. In order to identify and assess training needs within the firm, trainers may confer with managers and supervisors or

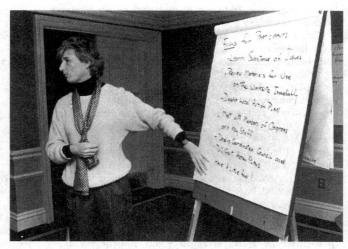

An interdisciplinary background is valuable for jobs in the human resources field.

conduct surveys. They also periodically evaluate training effectiveness.

Depending on the size, goals, and nature of the organization, trainers may differ considerably in their responsibilities and in the methods they use. Training methods include on-the-job training; schools in which shop conditions are duplicated for trainees prior to putting them on the shop floor; apprenticeship training; classroom training; programmed instruction, which may involve interactive videos, videodiscs, and other computer-aided instructional technologies; simulators; conferences; and workshops.

The director of industrial relations forms labor policy, oversees industrial labor relations, negotiates collective bargaining agreements, and coordinates grievance procedures to handle complaints resulting from disputes under the contract for firms with unionized employees. The director of industrial relations also advises and collaborates with the director of human resources, other managers, and members of their staff, because all aspects of personnel policy—such as wages, benefits, pensions, and work practices—may be involved in drawing up a new or revised contract.

Industrial labor relations programs are implemented by labor relations managers and their staff. When a collective bargaining agreement is up for negotiation, labor relations specialists prepare information for management to use during negotiation, which requires familiarity with economic and wage data as well as extensive knowledge of labor law and collective bargaining trends. The labor relations staff interprets and administers the contract with respect to grievances, wages and salaries, employee welfare, health care, pensions, union and management practices, and other contractual stipulations. As union membership is continuing to decline in most industries, industrial relations personnel are working more with employees who are not members of a labor union.

Dispute resolution—attaining tacit or contractual agreements—has become increasingly important as parties to a dispute attempt to avoid costly litigation, strikes, or other disruptions. Dispute resolution also has become more complex, involving employees, management, unions, other firms, and government agencies. Specialists involved in dispute resolution must be highly knowledgeable and experienced, and often report to the director of industrial relations. Conciliators, or mediators, advise and counsel labor and management to prevent and, when necessary, resolve disputes over labor agreements or other labor relations issues. Arbitrators, sometimes called umpires or referees, decide disputes that bind both labor and management to specific terms and conditions of labor contracts. Labor relations specialists who work for unions perform many of the same functions on behalf of the union and its members.

Other emerging specialists include international human resources managers, who handle human resources issues related to a company's foreign operations, and human resources information system specialists, who develop and apply computer programs to process personnel information, match jobseekers with job openings, and handle other personnel matters.

Working Conditions

Personnel work generally takes place in clean, pleasant, and comfortable office settings. Arbitrators and mediators may work out of their homes. Many human resources specialists and managers work a standard 35- to 40-hour week. However, longer hours might be necessary for some workers—for example, labor relations specialists and managers, arbitrators, and mediators—when contract agreements are being prepared and negotiated.

Although most human resources specialists and managers work in the office, some travel extensively. For example, recruiters regularly attend professional meetings and visit college campuses to interview prospective employees; arbitrators and mediators often must travel to the site chosen for negotiations.

Employment

Human resources specialists and managers held about 544,000 jobs in 1996. They were employed in virtually every industry. Specialists accounted for 3 out of 5 positions; managers, 2 out of 5. About 15,000 specialists were self-employed, working as consultants to public and private employers.

The private sector accounted for about 86 percent of salaried jobs. Among these salaried jobs, services industries—including business, health, social, management, and educational services—accounted for 4 out of 10 jobs; labor organizations, the largest employer among specific industries, accounted for 1 out of 10. Manufacturing industries accounted for 2 out of 10 jobs, while finance, insurance, and real estate firms accounted for about 1 out of 10.

Federal, State, and local governments employed about 14 percent of salaried human resources specialists and managers. They handled the recruitment, interviewing, job classification, training, salary administration, benefits, employee relations, and related matters of the Nation's public employees.

Training, Other Qualifications, and Advancement

Because of the diversity of duties and level of responsibility, the educational backgrounds of human resources specialists and managers vary considerably. In filling entry-level jobs, employers generally seek college graduates. Some employers prefer applicants who have majored in human resources, personnel administration, or industrial and labor relations; others look for college graduates with a technical or business background; and still others feel that a well-rounded liberal arts education is best.

Many colleges and universities have programs leading to a degree in personnel, human resources, or labor relations. Some offer degree programs in personnel administration or human resources management, training and development, or compensation and benefits. Depending on the school, courses leading to a career in human resources management may be found in departments of business administration, education, instructional technology, organizational development, human services, communication, or public administration, or within a separate human resources institution or department.

Because an interdisciplinary background is appropriate in this field, a combination of courses in the social sciences, business, and behavioral sciences is useful. Some jobs may require a more technical or specialized background in engineering, science, finance, or law, for example. Most prospective human resources specialists should take courses in compensation, recruitment, training and development, and performance appraisal, as well as courses in principles of management, organizational structure, and industrial psychology. Other relevant courses include business administration, public administration, psychology, sociology, political science, economics, and statistics. Courses in labor law, collective bargaining, labor eco-

nomics, labor history, and industrial psychology also provide a valuable background for the prospective labor relations specialist. As in many other fields, knowledge of computers and information systems is useful.

An advanced degree is increasingly important for some jobs. Many labor relations jobs require graduate study in industrial or labor relations. A strong background in industrial relations and law is highly desirable for contract negotiators, mediators, and arbitrators; in fact, many people in these specialties are lawyers. A background in law is also desirable for employee benefits managers and others who must interpret the growing number of laws and regulations. A master's degree in human resources, or labor relations- or in business administration with a concentration in human resources management is highly recommended for those seeking general and top management positions.

For many specialized jobs in the human resources field, previous experience is an asset; for more advanced positions including managers as well as arbitrators and mediators, it is essential. Many employers prefer entry-level workers who have gained some experience through an internship or work-study program while in school. Personnel administration and human resources development require the ability to work with individuals as well as a commitment to organizational goals. This field also demands other skills people may develop elsewhere—using computers, selling, teaching, supervising, and volunteering, among others. This field offers clerical workers opportunities for advancement to professional positions. Responsible positions are sometimes filled by experienced individuals from other fields, including business, government, education, social services administration, and the military.

The human resources field demands a range of personal qualities and skills. Human resources specialists and managers must speak and write effectively; work with or supervise people having various cultural backgrounds, levels of education, and experience; cope with conflicting points of view, and the unexpected and unusual; function under pressure; and demonstrate integrity, fair-mindedness, and a persuasive, congenial personality.

Entry-level workers often enter formal or on-the-job training programs in which they learn how to classify jobs, interview applicants, or administer employee benefits. They then are assigned to specific areas in the personnel department to gain experience. Later, they may advance to a managerial position, overseeing a major element of the personnel program—compensation or training, for example.

Exceptional human resources workers may be promoted to director of personnel or industrial relations, which can eventually lead to a top managerial or executive position. Others may join a consulting firm or open their own business. A Ph.D. is an asset for teaching, writing, or consulting work.

Most organizations specializing in human resources offer classes intended to enhance the marketable skills of their members. Some organizations offer certification programs, which are signs of competence and can enhance one's advancement opportunities. For example, the International Foundation of Employee Benefits Plans confers the Certified Employee Benefits Specialist certification to persons who complete a series of college-level courses and pass exams covering employee benefit plans. The Society for Human Resources Management has two levels of certification—Professional in Human Resources, and Senior Professional in Human Resources—both of which require experience and a comprehensive exam.

Job Outlook

The job market for human resources specialists and managers is likely to remain competitive through 2006, due to an abundant supply of qualified college graduates and experienced workers, despite large numbers of annual job openings that will stem from the need to replace workers who transfer to other jobs, retire, or stop working for other reasons coupled with projected average employment growth.

New jobs will stem from increasing efforts throughout industry to recruit and retain quality employees; employers are expected to devote greater resources to job-specific training programs in response to the increasing complexity of many jobs, the aging of the work force, and technological advances that can leave employees with obsolete skills. In addition, legislation and court rulings setting standards in occupational safety and health, equal employment opportunity, wages, and health, pension, family leave, and other benefits, will increase demand for experts in these areas. Rising health care costs, in particular, should spur demand for specialists to develop creative compensation and benefits packages that firms can offer prospective employees. Employment of labor relations staff, including arbitrators and mediators, should grow as firms become more involved in labor relations, and attempt to resolve potentially costly labor-management disputes out of court. Additional job growth may stem from increasing demand for specialists in international human resources management and human resources information systems.

Employment demand should be strong among firms involved in management, consulting, and personnel supply, as businesses increasingly contract out personnel functions or hire personnel specialists on a temporary basis to meet the increasing cost and complexity of training and development programs. Demand should also increase in firms that develop and administer complex employee benefits and compensation packages for other organizations.

Demand for human resources specialists and managers is also governed by the staffing needs of the firms for which they work. A rapidly expanding business is likely to hire additional human resources workers—either as permanent employees or consultants—while a business that has experienced a merger or a reduction in its work force will require fewer human resources workers. Also, as human resources management becomes increasingly important to the success of an organization, some small and medium-size businesses that do not have a human resources department may assign employees various human resources duties together with other unrelated responsibilities. In any particular firm, the size and the job duties of the human resources staff are determined by a variety of factors, including the firm's organizational philosophy and goals, the skills of its work force, the pace of technological change, government regulations, collective bargaining agreements, standards of professional practice, and labor market conditions.

Job growth could be limited by the widespread use of computerized human resources information systems that make workers more productive. Similar to other workers, employment of human resources specialists and managers, particularly in larger firms, may be adversely affected by corporate downsizing and restructuring.

Earnings

According to a salary survey conducted by the National Association of Colleges and Employers, bachelor's degree candidates majoring in human resources, including labor relations, received starting offers averaging $25,300 a year in 1996; master's degree candidates, $39,900.

According to a 1996 survey of compensation in the human resources field, conducted by Abbott, Langer, and Associates of Crete, Illinois, the median total cash compensation for selected personnel and labor relations occupations were:

Industrial/labor relations directors	$106,100
Divisional human resources directors	91,300
Compensation and benefits directors	90,500
Employee/community relations directors	87,500
Training and organizational directors	86,600
Benefits directors	80,500
Plant/location human resources managers	64,400
Recruitment and interviewing managers	63,800
Compensation supervisors	53,400
Training generalists	49,900
Employment interviewing supervisors	42,800
Safety specialists	42,500
Job evaluation specialists	39,600
Employee assistance/employee counseling specialists	39,000
Human resources information systems specialists	38,800
Benefits specialists	38,300
E.E.O./affirmative action specialists	38,200
Training material development specialists	37,200
Employee services/employee recreation specialists	35,000

According to a survey of workplaces in 160 metropolitan areas, personnel specialists with limited experience had median earnings of $25,700 a year in 1995, the middle half earned between $23,700 and $28,500 a year. Personnel supervisors/managers with limited experience had median earnings of $59,000 a year. The middle half earned between $54,000 and $65,200 a year.

In the Federal Government in 1997, persons with a bachelor's degree or 3 years' general experience in the personnel field generally started at $19,500 a year. Those with a superior academic record or an additional year of specialized experience started at $24,200 a year. Those with a master's degree may start at $29,600, and those with a doctorate in a personnel field may start at $35,800. Beginning salaries were slightly higher in areas where the prevailing local pay level was higher. There are no formal entry-level requirements for managerial positions. Applicants must possess a suitable combination of educational attainment, experience, and record of accomplishment.

Personnel specialists in the Federal Government averaged $52,900 a year in 1997; personnel managers, $55,400.

Related Occupations

All human resources occupations are closely related. Other workers with skills and expertise in interpersonal relations include employment, rehabilitation, and college career planning and placement counselors; lawyers; psychologists; sociologists; social workers; public relations specialists; and teachers. These occupations are described elsewhere in the *Handbook*.

Sources of Additional Information

For information about careers in employee training and development, contact:
☛ American Society for Training and Development, 1640 King St., Box 1443, Alexandria, VA 22313.

For information about careers and certification in employee compensation and benefits, contact:
☛ American Compensation Association, 14040 Northsight Blvd., Scottsdale, AZ 85260.

Information about careers and certification in employee benefits is available from:
☛ International Foundation of Employee Benefit Plans, 18700 W. Bluemound Rd., Brookfield, WI 53045.

For information about careers in arbitration and other aspects of dispute resolution, contact:
☛ American Arbitration Association, 140 West 51st St., New York, NY 10020. Phone: (800) 778-7879

For information about academic programs in industrial relations, write to:
☛ Industrial Relations Research Association, University of Wisconsin, 7226 Social Science Bldg., 1180 Observatory Dr., Madison, WI 53706.

Information about personnel careers in the health care industry is available from:
☛ American Society for Healthcare Human Resources Administration, One North Franklin, 31st Floor, Chicago, IL 60606.

Industrial Production Managers

(D.O.T. 180.167-054; 181.117-010; 182.167-022; 183.117-010, -014, .161-014, .167-010, -014, -018, -022, -026, -034, -038; 188.167-094; 189.117-042, .167-042, -046)

Significant Points

- The projected decline in employment reflects growing productivity and organizational restructuring.

- Applicants with college degrees in industrial engineering or business administration, and particularly those with MBA's and undergraduate engineering degrees, have the best job prospects.

Nature of the Work

Industrial production managers coordinate the resources and activities required to produce millions of goods every year in the United States. Although their duties vary from plant to plant, industrial production managers share many of the same major functions. These functions include responsibility for production scheduling, staffing, equipment, quality control, inventory control, and the coordination of production activities with those of other departments.

The primary mission of industrial production managers is planning the production schedule within budgetary limitations and time constraints. This entails analyzing the plant's personnel and capital resources to select the best way of meeting the production quota. Industrial production managers determine which machines will be used, whether overtime or extra shifts are necessary, and the sequence of production. They also monitor the production run to make sure that it stays on schedule and correct any problems that may arise.

Industrial production managers must also monitor product standards. When quality drops below the established standard, they must determine why standards aren't being maintained and how to improve the product. If the problem is poor work, the manager may implement better training programs, reorganize the manufacturing process, or institute employee suggestion or involvement programs. If the cause is substandard materials, the manager works with the purchasing department to improve the quality of the product's components.

Because the work of many departments is interrelated, managers work closely with heads of other departments such as sales, purchasing, and traffic to plan and implement company goals, policies, and procedures. For example, the production manager works with the purchasing department to ensure that plant inventories are maintained at their optimal level. This is vital to a firm's operation because maintaining the inventory of materials necessary for production ties up the firm's financial resources, yet insufficient quantities cause delays in production. A breakdown in communications between the production manager and the purchasing department can cause slowdowns and a failure to meet production schedules. Computers are coming to play a more important role not only in this coordination, but also in providing up-to-date data on inventory, work-in-progress, and quality standards.

Production managers usually report to the plant manager or the vice president for manufacturing, and may act as liaison between executives and first-line supervisors. (Information about these workers can be found in the statements on general managers and top executives, and blue-collar worker supervisors, elsewhere in the *Handbook*). In many plants, one production manager is responsible for all aspects of production. In large plants with several operations—aircraft assembly, for example—there are managers in charge of each operation, such as machining, assembly, or finishing.

Working Conditions

Most industrial production managers divide their time between the shop floor and their offices. While on the floor, they must follow established health and safety practices and wear the required protective clothing and equipment. The time in the office, which is often located on or near the production floor, is usually spent meeting with subordinates or other department managers, analyzing production data, and writing and reviewing reports.

Most industrial production managers work more than 40 hours a week, especially when production deadlines must be met. In facilities that operate around the clock, managers often work late shifts and may be called at any hour to deal with emergencies. This could mean going to the plant to resolve the problem, regardless of the hour, and staying until the situation is under control. Dealing with production workers as well as superiors when working under the pressure of production deadlines or emergency situations can be stressful. This stress has been compounded by restructuring that has eliminated levels of management and support staff, shifting more responsibilities to production managers.

Employment

Industrial production managers held about 207,000 jobs in 1996. Although employed throughout the manufacturing sector, about one half

Many industrial production managers have assumed additional responsibilities in recent years.

are employed in firms that produce industrial machinery and equipment, transportation equipment, electronic and electrical equipment, fabricated metal products, instruments and related products, and food products. Production managers work in all parts of the country, but jobs are most plentiful in areas where manufacturing is concentrated.

Training, Other Qualifications, and Advancement

Because of the diversity of manufacturing operations and job requirements, there is no standard preparation for this occupation. Many industrial production managers have a college degree in business administration or industrial engineering. Some have a master's degree in business administration (MBA). Others are former production line supervisors who have been promoted. Although many employers prefer candidates to have a degree in business or engineering, some companies hire liberal arts graduates.

As production operations become more sophisticated, an increasing number of employers are looking for candidates with MBA's. Combined with an undergraduate degree in engineering, this is considered particularly good preparation. Companies also are placing greater importance on a candidate's personality. Because the job requires the ability to compromise, persuade, and negotiate, successful production managers must be well-rounded and have excellent communication skills.

The few who enter the field directly from college or graduate school often are unfamiliar with the firm's production process. As a result, they may spend their first few months on the job in the company's training program. These programs familiarize trainees with the production line, company policies, and the requirements of the job. In larger companies, they may also include assignments to other departments, such as purchasing and accounting. A number of companies hire college graduates as blue-collar worker supervisors and later promote them.

Some industrial production managers have worked their way up the ranks, perhaps after having worked as blue-collar worker supervisors. These workers already have an intimate knowledge of the production process and the firm's organization. To be selected for promotion, they must have demonstrated leadership qualities and usually have taken company-sponsored courses in management skills and communication techniques.

In addition to formal training, industrial production managers must closely follow new production technologies and management practices. To do this, they belong to professional organizations and attend trade shows where new equipment is displayed; they also attend industry conferences and conventions where changes in production methods and technological advances are discussed.

Industrial production managers with a proven record of superior performance may advance to plant manager or vice president for manufacturing. Others transfer to jobs at larger firms with more responsibilities. Opportunities also exist as consultants. (For more information, see the statement on management analysts and consultants elsewhere in the *Handbook*.)

Job Outlook

Employment of industrial production managers is expected to decline slightly through the year 2006. However, a number of job openings will stem from the need to replace workers who transfer to other occupations or leave the labor force. Applicants with college degrees in industrial engineering or business administration, and particularly those with MBA's and undergraduate engineering degrees, will be in the best position to fill these openings. Employers also are likely to seek candidates who have excellent communication skills, and who are personable, flexible, and eager to participate in ongoing training.

Although manufacturing output is projected to rise, growing productivity among production managers and organizational restructuring will limit the demand for these workers. Productivity gains will result from the widening use of computers for scheduling, planning, and coordination. In addition, just-in-time manufacturing eases scheduling demands, and a growing emphasis on building quality inspection into the production process has redistributed some of the production manager's oversight responsibilities. Because production managers are so integral to the efficient operation of a plant, they have not been greatly affected by recent efforts to flatten management structures. Nevertheless, this trend has led production managers to assume more responsibilities and has discouraged the creation of more employment opportunities.

Earnings

Salaries of industrial production managers vary significantly by industry and plant size. According to Abbott, Langer, and Associates, the average salary for all production managers was $60,000 in 1996. In addition to salary, industrial production managers may receive bonuses based on job performance.

Related Occupations

Industrial production managers oversee production staff and equipment, insure that production goals and quality standards are being met, and implement company policies. Individuals with similar functions include materials, operations, purchasing, and traffic managers. Other occupations requiring similar training and skills are sales engineer, manufacturer's sales representative, and industrial engineer.

Sources of Additional Information

Information on industrial production management can be obtained from:

☛ National Management Association, 2210 Arbor Blvd., Dayton, OH 45439.
☛ American Management Association, 1601 Broadway, New York, NY 10019.

Inspectors and Compliance Officers, Except Construction

(List of D.O.T. codes available upon request. See p. 496.)

Significant Points

- Over 80 percent of the jobs are in Federal, State, and local government agencies that inspect and enforce rules on matters such as health, safety, food, licensing, or finance.

- Because responsibilities vary, ranging from those of aviation safety inspectors to food inspectors, for example, training requirements and working conditions vary greatly.

Nature of the Work

Inspectors and compliance officers enforce a wide range of laws, regulations, policies, or procedures. They inspect and enforce rules on matters such as health, safety, food, licensing, or finance. Inspectors' and compliance officers' duties vary widely.

Agricultural commodity graders apply quality standards to aid the buying and selling of commodities, and to insure that retailers and consumers know the quality of the products they purchase. Although this grading is not required by law, buyers may not be willing to purchase ungraded commodities. Graders usually specialize in an area such as eggs, meat, poultry, processed or fresh fruits and vegetables, grain, tobacco, cotton, or dairy products. They examine product samples to determine quality and grade, and issue official grading certificates. To maintain sanitation standards, graders may inspect the plant and equipment used in processing.

Attendance officers investigate continued absences of pupils from public schools.

Aviation safety inspectors ensure that Federal Aviation Administration (FAA) regulations that govern the quality, performance, and safety of aircraft equipment, aircraft operations, and personnel are adhered to. Aviation safety inspectors may inspect aircraft and equipment manufacturing, maintenance and repair, or flight procedures. They may work in the areas of flight operations, maintenance, or avionics, and usually specialize in either commercial or general aviation aircraft. They also examine and certify aircraft pilots, pilot examiners, flight instructors, repair stations, schools, and instructional materials.

Bank examiners investigate financial institutions to enforce Federal or State laws and regulations governing the institution's operations and solvency. Examiners schedule audits, determine actions protecting the institution's solvency and the interests of shareholders and depositors, and recommend acceptance or rejection of applications for mergers, acquisitions, or establishment of a new institution.

Consumer safety inspectors and *officers* inspect food, feeds, pesticides, weights and measures, biological products, cosmetics, drugs, medical equipment, and radiation emitting products. Some are proficient in several areas. Working individually or in teams under a senior inspector, they check on firms that produce, handle, store, or market the products they regulate. They ensure that standards are maintained and respond to consumer complaints by questioning employees, vendors, and others to obtain evidence. Inspectors look for inaccurate product labeling, and for decomposition or chemical or bacteriological contamination that could result in a product becoming harmful to health. They may use portable scales, cameras, ultraviolet lights, thermometers, chemical testing kits, radiation monitors, or other equipment to find violations. They may send product samples, collected as part of their examinations, to laboratories for analysis.

After completing their inspection, inspectors discuss their observations with plant managers or officials, and point out areas where corrective measures are needed. They write reports of their findings and, when necessary, compile evidence for use in court if legal action must be taken.

Customs inspectors enforce laws governing imports and exports. Stationed in the United States and overseas at airports, seaports, and border crossing points, they examine, count, weigh, gauge, measure, and sample commercial and noncommercial cargoes entering and leaving the United States, to determine admissibility and the amount of duties that must be paid. They insure that all cargo is properly described on accompanying importers' declarations to determine the proper duty and interdict contraband. They inspect baggage and articles carried by passengers and crew members to insure that all merchandise is declared, proper duties are paid, and contraband is not present. They also ensure that people, ships, planes, and anything used to import or export cargo comply with all appropriate entrance and clearance requirements.

Dealer compliance representatives inspect franchised establishments, such as motels and fast food restaurants, to ensure compliance with the franchiser's policies and procedures. They may suggest changes in financial or other operations which, if not followed, can result in loss of the franchise.

Environmental health inspectors, who work primarily for State and local governments, ensure that food, water, and air meet government standards. They check the cleanliness and safety of food and beverages produced in dairies and processing plants, or served in restaurants, hospitals, and other institutions. They often examine the handling, processing, and serving of food for compliance with sanitation rules and regulations, and oversee the treatment and disposal of sewage, refuse, and garbage. In addition, inspectors may visit pollution sources and test for pollutants by collecting air, water, or waste samples for analysis. They try to determine the nature and cause of pollution and initiate action to stop it.

In large local and State health or agriculture departments, environmental health inspectors may specialize in the areas of milk and dairy products, food sanitation, waste control, air pollution, water pollution, institutional sanitation, or occupational health. In rural areas and small towns, they may be responsible for a wide range of environmental health activities.

Equal opportunity representatives ascertain and correct unfair employment practices through consultation with and mediation between employers and minority groups.

Federal and State laws require *food inspectors* to inspect meat, poultry, their byproducts, and egg products to ensure they are safe for public consumption. Working onsite, frequently as part of a team, they inspect meat and poultry slaughtering, processing, and packaging operations, as well as egg products operations. They also check for correct product labeling and proper sanitation.

Immigration inspectors interview and examine people seeking entrance to the United States and its territories. They inspect passports to determine whether people are legally eligible to enter and verify their citizenship status and identity. Immigration inspectors also prepare reports, maintain records, and process applications and petitions for immigration or temporary residence in the United States.

Logging operations inspectors review contract logging operations. They prepare reports and issue remedial instructions for violations of contractual agreements and of fire and safety regulations.

Mine safety and health inspectors work to ensure the health and safety of miners. They visit mines and related facilities to obtain information on health and safety conditions and to enforce safety laws and regulations. They discuss their findings with the management of the mine and issue citations describing violations and hazards that must be corrected. Mine inspectors also investigate and report on mine accidents and may direct rescue and fire fighting operations when fires or explosions occur.

Inspectors and compliance officers work in a variety of settings and meet all kinds of people.

Motor vehicle inspectors verify the compliance of automobiles and trucks with State requirements for safe operation and emissions. They inspect truck cargoes to assure compliance with legal limitations on gross weight and hazardous cargoes.

Occupational safety and health inspectors visit places of employment to detect unsafe machinery and equipment, or unhealthy working conditions. They discuss their findings with the employer or plant manager and order that violations be promptly corrected in accordance with Federal, State, or local government safety standards and regulations. They interview supervisors and employees in response to complaints or accidents, and may order suspension of activity posing threats to workers.

Park rangers enforce laws and regulations in State and national parks. Their duties range from registering vehicles and visitors, collecting fees, and providing information regarding park use and points of interest, to patrolling areas to prevent fire, participating in first aid and rescue activities, and training and supervising other park workers. Some rangers specialize in snow safety and avalanche control. With increasing numbers of visitors to our national parks, some rangers specialize as law enforcement officers.

Postal inspectors observe the functioning of the postal system and enforce laws and regulations. As law enforcement agents, postal inspectors have statutory powers of arrest and the authority to carry firearms. They investigate criminal activities such as theft and misuse of the mail. In instances of suspected mismanagement or fraud, inspectors conduct management or financial audits. They also collaborate with other government agencies, such as the Internal Revenue Service, as members of special task forces.

Railroad inspectors verify the compliance of railroad systems and equipment with Federal safety regulations. They investigate accidents and review railroads' operating practices.

Revenue officers investigate and collect delinquent tax returns from individuals or businesses. They investigate leads from various sources. They attempt to resolve tax problems with taxpayers and recommend penalties, collection actions, and recommend criminal prosecutions when necessary.

Securities compliance examiners implement regulations concerning securities and real estate transactions. They investigate applications for registration of securities sales and complaints of irregular securities transactions, and recommend legal action when necessary.

Travel accommodations raters inspect hotels, motels, restaurants, campgrounds, and vacation resorts. They evaluate travel and tourist accommodations for travel guide publishers and organizations such as tourism promoters and automobile clubs.

Other inspectors and compliance officers include coroners, code inspectors, mortician investigators, and dealer-compliance representatives. Closely related work is done by construction and building inspectors. (Construction and building inspectors are discussed elsewhere in the *Handbook*.)

Working Conditions

Inspectors and compliance officers meet all kinds of people and work in a variety of environments. Their jobs often involve considerable field work, and some inspectors travel frequently. They are generally furnished with an automobile or are reimbursed for travel expenses.

Inspectors may experience unpleasant, stressful, and dangerous working conditions. For example, mine safety and health inspectors are exposed to the same hazards as miners. Some food inspectors examine and inspect the livestock slaughtering process in slaughterhouses and frequently come in contact with unpleasant conditions. Postal inspectors have to put up with the stress inherent in all law enforcement work, in addition to the danger inherent in making occasional arrests. Park rangers often work outdoors—in many cases, on rugged terrain—in very hot or bitterly cold weather for extended periods.

Many inspectors work long and often irregular hours. Even those inspectors not engaged in some form of law enforcement may find themselves in adversarial roles when the organization or individual being inspected objects to the inspection.

Employment

Inspectors and compliance officers held about 163,000 jobs in 1996. State governments employed 34 percent, the Federal Government—chiefly the Departments of Defense, Labor, Treasury, and Agriculture—employed 31 percent, and local governments employed 18 percent. The remaining 17 percent were employed throughout the private sector—primarily in education, hospitals, insurance companies, labor unions, and manufacturing firms.

Some consumer safety inspectors work for the U.S. Food and Drug Administration, but the majority of these inspectors work for State governments. Most food inspectors and agricultural commodity graders are employed by the U.S. Department of Agriculture. Many health inspectors work for State and local governments. Compliance inspectors are employed primarily by the Treasury and Labor departments on the Federal level, as well as by State and local governments. The Department of Defense employs the most quality assurance inspectors. The States and the Treasury Department employ internal revenue officers. Aviation safety inspectors work for the Federal Aviation Administration. The Environmental Protection Agency employs inspectors to verify compliance with pollution control and other laws. The U.S. Department of Labor and many State governments employ occupational safety and health inspectors, equal-opportunity officers, and mine safety and health inspectors. The U.S. Department of Interior employs park rangers. Department of the Treasury customs inspectors work in the United States and overseas at airports, seaports, and border crossing points.

Training, Other Qualifications, and Advancement

Because of the diversity of the functions they perform, qualifications for inspector and compliance officer jobs differ greatly. Requirements include a combination of education, experience, and often a passing grade on a written examination. Employers may require college training, including courses related to the job. The following examples illustrate the range of qualifications for various inspector jobs.

Postal inspectors must have a bachelor's degree and 1 year's work experience. It is desirable that they have one of several professional certifications, such as that of certified public accountant. They also must pass a background suitability investigation, meet certain health requirements, undergo a drug screening test, possess a valid State driver's license, and be a U.S. citizen between 21 and 36 years of age when hired.

Aviation safety inspectors working in operations must be pilots with varying certificates, ratings, and numbers of flight hours to their credit. In addition, FAA medical certificates are required. Some also are required to have an FAA flight instructor rating. Maintenance and avionics inspectors must have considerable experience in aviation maintenance and knowledge of industry standards and relevant Federal laws. Many aviation safety inspectors have had flight and maintenance training in the Armed Forces. No written examination is required.

Applicants for positions as mine safety and health inspectors generally must have experience in mine safety, management, or supervision. Some may possess a skill such as that of an electrician (for mine electrical inspectors). Applicants must meet strict medical requirements and be physically able to perform arduous duties efficiently. Many mine safety inspectors are former miners.

Applicants for internal revenue officer jobs must be a U.S. citizen and have a bachelor's degree or 3 years of experience in business, legal, financial, or investigative practices.

Park rangers need at least 2 years of college with at least 12 credits in science and criminal justice, although some start as part-time, seasonal workers with the U.S. Forest Service. Most positions require a bachelor's degree.

Environmental health inspectors, called sanitarians in many States, sometimes must have a bachelor's degree in environmental health or in the physical or biological sciences. In most States, they are licensed by examining boards.

All inspectors and compliance officers are trained in the applicable laws or inspection procedures through some combination of classroom and on-the-job training. In general, people who want to enter this occupation should be responsible and like detailed work. Inspectors and compliance officers should be neat and personable, and able to communicate well orally and in writing.

Federal Government inspectors and compliance officers whose job performance is satisfactory advance through their career ladder to a specified full performance level. For positions above this level (usually supervisory positions), advancement is competitive, based on agency needs and individual merit. Advancement opportunities in State and local governments and the private sector are often similar to those in the Federal Government.

Some civil service specifications, including those for mine inspectors, aviation safety inspectors, and agricultural commodity graders, rate applicants solely on their experience and education. Others require a written examination.

Job Outlook

Slower than average growth in employment of inspectors and compliance officers is expected through the year 2006, reflecting a balance of continuing public demand for a safe environment and quality products against the desire for smaller government and fewer regulations. Job openings will arise primarily from the need to replace those who transfer to other occupations, retire, or leave the labor force for other reasons. In private industry, employment growth will reflect industry growth, due to continuing self-enforcement of government and company regulations and policies, particularly among franchise operations in various industries.

Employment of inspectors and compliance officers is seldom affected by general economic fluctuations. Federal, State, and local governments—which employ most inspectors—provide workers with considerable job security.

Earnings

The median weekly salary of inspectors and compliance officers, except construction, was about $695 in 1996. The lowest 10 percent earned less than $381; the highest 10 percent earned over $1,215. In the Federal Government, the annual starting salaries for inspectors varied from $24,200 to $29,600 depending upon the nature of the inspection or compliance activity. Beginning salaries were slightly higher in selected areas where the prevailing local pay level was higher. The following tabulation presents 1997 average salaries for selected inspectors and compliance officers in the Federal Government in nonsupervisory, supervisory, and managerial positions.

Air safety investigators	$66,110
Highway safety inspectors	64,190
Mine safety and health inspectors	58,000
Railroad safety inspectors	55,910
Internal revenue agent	55,730
Equal employment opportunity officials	54,180
Environmental protection specialists	52,940
Safety and occupational health managers	50,070
Import specialists	49,370
Quality assurance inspectors	47,020
Customs inspectors	40,020
Securities compliance examiners	39,490
Agricultural commodity graders	39,080
Immigration inspectors	35,010
Consumer safety inspectors	34,360
Food inspectors	32,870
Environmental protection assistants	29,090

Most inspectors and compliance officers work for Federal, State, and local governments and in large private firms, all of which generally offer more generous benefits than do smaller firms.

Related Occupations

Inspectors and compliance officers are responsible for seeing that laws and regulations are obeyed. Construction and building inspectors, fire marshals, Federal, State, and local law enforcement professionals, corrections officers, and fish and game wardens also enforce laws and regulations.

Sources of Additional Information

Information on obtaining a job with the Federal Government may be obtained from the Office of Personnel Management through a telephone based system. Consult your telephone directory under U.S. Government for a local number or call (912) 757-3000 (TDD (912) 744-2299). The number is not toll free and charges may result. Information also is available from their internet site: http://www.usajobs.opm.gov

For information on a career as a specific type of Federal inspector or compliance officer, a Federal department or agency that employs them may also be contacted directly.

Information about State and local government jobs is available from State civil service commissions, usually located in each State capital, or from local government offices.

Information about jobs in private industry is available from the State Employment Service, which is listed under "Job Service" or "Employment" in the State government section of local telephone directories.

Insurance underwriters use computer software to evaluate a client's risk.

Insurance Underwriters

(D.O.T. 169.267-046)

Significant Points

- Most large insurance companies prefer college graduates who have a degree in business administration or finance, with courses or experience in accounting.

- Employment is projected to grow more slowly than average as insurance companies use "smart" underwriting software systems that automatically analyze and rate insurance applications, and as more businesses self-insure.

Nature of the Work

Insurance companies protect individuals and organizations from financial loss by assuming billions of dollars in risks each year. Underwriters identify and analyze the risk of loss from their policyholders, establish appropriate premium rates, and write policies that cover that risk. An insurance company may lose business to competitors if the underwriter appraises risks too conservatively, or it may have to pay more claims if the underwriting actions are too liberal.

Technology plays an increasingly important role in an underwriter's job. Underwriters use computer applications called "smart systems" to manage risks more efficiently and accurately. They enter into the computer various information relating to a person or organization whose application for insurance is pending. These systems automatically analyze and rate insurance applications, then recommend acceptance or denial of the risk, or they adjust the premium rate in accordance with the risk. Underwriters are then better equipped to make sound decisions in an effort to avoid excessive losses in the future.

With the aid of computers, underwriters analyze information in insurance applications, reports from loss control consultants, medical reports, and actuarial studies—reports that describe the probability of insured loss. They then decide whether to issue a policy and outline the terms of the contract, including the amount of the premium. Underwriters sometimes correspond with policyholders, agents, and managers about policy cancellations or other matters. On rare occasions, they accompany sales representatives on appointments with prospective clients. (Life insurance agents and brokers are increasingly called "life underwriters;" they are included in the section on insurance agents and brokers elsewhere in the *Handbook*.)

Most underwriters specialize in one of three major categories of insurance—life, property and casualty, or health. They further specialize in group or individual policies. Property and casualty underwriters often specialize by type of risk insured, such as fire, homeowners, automobile, marine, property, liability, or workers' compensation. In cases where casualty companies insure in a single "package" policy, covering various types of risks, the underwriter must be familiar with different lines of insurance. Some underwriters, called commercial account underwriters, handle business insurance exclusively. They often evaluate a firm's entire operation in appraising its application for insurance.

An increasing proportion of insurance sales, particularly in life and health insurance, are being made through group contracts. A standard group policy insures everyone in a specified group through a single contract at a standard premium rate. The group underwriter analyzes the overall composition of the group to assure that the total risk is not excessive. Another type of group policy provides members of a group—a labor union, for example—with individual policies reflecting their needs. These generally are casualty policies, such as those covering automobiles. The casualty underwriter analyzes the application of each group member and makes individual appraisals. Some group underwriters meet with union or employer representatives to discuss the types of policies available to their group.

Working Conditions

Underwriters have desk jobs that require no unusual physical activity. Their offices generally are comfortable and pleasant. Although overtime may be required, underwriters generally work from 35 to 40 hours a week. They occasionally attend meetings away from home for several days. Construction and marine underwriters often travel to inspect work sites and assess risks.

Employment

Insurance underwriters held about 95,000 jobs in 1996. The following tabulation shows the percent distribution of employment by industry in 1996.

Fire, marine, and casualty insurance carriers	37
Insurance agents, brokers, and service	33
Life insurance carriers	15
Pension funds and miscellaneous insurance carriers	4
Medical service and health insurance carriers	4
Other industries	7

Most underwriters worked for insurance companies, often called "carriers." Most of the remaining underwriters worked in independent insurance agencies (firms which represent one or more insurance companies) and brokers (firms which may deal with any insurance company and represent the interests of the buyers of insurance, known as "insureds.") A small number of underwriters worked in agencies owned and operated by banks, mortgage companies, and real estate firms.

Office underwriters in the life insurance industry are most likely to work in an insurance company's home office. In some large general agencies, underwriters help life insurance agents, or "producers," determine if the risk will be accepted or rejected by the home office. However, most local life insurance offices deal predominantly with sales, not underwriting. Property and casualty underwriters also work in home offices, but more work for agencies or regional branch offices, where they have the authority to underwrite risks and determine an appropriate rating without consulting the home office.

Training, Other Qualifications, and Advancement

For beginning underwriting jobs, most large insurance companies prefer college graduates who have a degree in business administration or finance, with courses or experience in accounting. However, a bachelor's degree in almost any field—plus courses in business law and accounting—provides a good general background and may be sufficient to qualify. Computer knowledge is essential.

Beginners typically start as underwriter trainees or assistant underwriters. They may help collect information on applicants and evaluate routine applications under the supervision of an experienced risk analyst. Property and casualty trainees may study claim files to become familiar with factors associated with certain types of losses. Many larger insurers offer a training program, lasting from a few months to a year, that combines study with work. As trainees gain experience, they are assigned policy applications that are more complex and cover greater risks. These require the use of computers for more efficient analysis and processing.

Continuing education is necessary for advancement. Insurance companies generally pay tuition for underwriting courses that their trainees successfully complete; some also offer salary incentives. Independent study programs for experienced property and casualty underwriters are also available. The Insurance Institute of America offers a program called "Introduction to Underwriting" for beginning underwriters, and the specialty designation, AU, or Associate Underwriting, the second formal step in developing a career in underwriting. To earn the AU designation, underwriters complete a series of courses and examinations; it usually takes about 2 years to earn the AU designation. The American Institute for Chartered Property Casualty Underwriters awards the designation, CPCU, or Chartered Property and Casualty Underwriter, the third and final stage of development for an underwriter. Earning the more advanced CPCU designation generally takes about 5 years, and requires passing 10 examinations covering personal and commercial insurance, risk management, business and insurance law, accounting, finance, management, economics, and ethics. Although CPCU's may be underwriters, the CPCU is intended for everyone working in all aspects of property and casualty insurance. The American Society of Chartered Life Underwriters provides the Chartered Life Underwriter (CLU) designation, intended for underwriters working in life insurance.

Underwriting can be a satisfying career for people who enjoy working with detail and analyzing information. In addition, underwriters must possess good judgment in order to make sound decisions. They must also be imaginative and aggressive, especially when they have to obtain information from many outside sources.

Experienced underwriters who complete courses of study may advance to senior underwriter or underwriting manager positions. Some underwriting managers are promoted to senior managerial jobs. Others are attracted to the earnings potential of sales and obtain State licensing to sell insurance and insurance products as agents or brokers.

Job Outlook

Employment of underwriters is expected to increase more slowly than the average for all occupations through the year 2006. Most job openings are expected to result from the need to replace underwriters who transfer to other occupations or stop working altogether.

A number of factors underlie the continuing need for underwriters. As people acquire assets and take on family responsibilities, the need for life, health, and property and casualty insurance grows. For example, concerns for financial security and liability contribute to demands for more insurance protection for homes, automobiles, pleasure craft, and other valuables. Expanding long-term healthcare and pension benefits for retirees—who are an increasing proportion of the population—also will increase underwriting opportunities. And, new or expanding businesses will need protection for new factories and equipment, and product liability, workers' compensation, and employee benefits insurance.

Employment of underwriters, however, is not expected to keep pace with growth in demand for insurance. Increased use of underwriting software systems will slow the demand for new underwriters. As more businesses self-insure—by setting a rate for their own company and paying premiums into a contingency fund—demand for some property and casualty underwriters will decline. Additionally, many property and casualty companies are foregoing personal lines of insurance—especially automobile and homeowners—and are concentrating on commercial lines of business.

Underwriters specializing in certain lines of insurance may find it difficult to transfer to another type of insurance if their jobs are threatened by corporate downsizing. Because insurance is usually regarded as a necessity, regardless of economic conditions, underwriters are unlikely to be laid off because of a recession.

Earnings

Median annual earnings of full-time wage and salary underwriters were about $31,400 in 1996. The middle 50 percent earned between $24,000 and $41,000 a year. The lowest 10 percent earned less than $18,400; the top 10 percent, more than $52,400.

In addition to typical benefits, almost all insurance companies provide employer-financed group life, health, and retirement plans.

Related Occupations

Underwriters make decisions on the basis of financial data. Other workers with the same type of responsibility include auditors, budget analysts, financial advisers, loan officers, credit managers, real estate appraisers, and risk managers.

Sources of Additional Information

General information about a career as an insurance underwriter is available from the home offices of many life insurance and property-liability insurance companies. Information about the insurance business in general and the underwriting function in particular also may be obtained from:

☛ The American Institute for Chartered Property and Casualty Underwriters, and the Insurance Institute of America, 720 Providence Rd., P.O. Box 3016, Malvern, PA 19355-0716.

Loan Officers and Counselors

(D.O.T. 186.167-078, .267-018, -022, -026)

Significant Points

- Loan officer positions generally require a bachelor's degree in finance, economics, or a related field; for commercial or mortgage loan officers, training or experience in sales is advantageous.

- Faster than average employment growth will stem from increases in the number and complexity of loans and in the importance of loan officers to the success of banks and other lending institutions.

Nature of the Work

Banks and other financial institutions need up-to-date information on companies and individuals applying for loans and credit. Customers and clients provide this information to the financial institution's loan officers, generally the first employees to be seen by them. Loan officers prepare, analyze, and verify loan applications, make decisions regarding the extension of credit, and help borrowers fill out loan applications. Loan counselors, also called loan collection officers, contact borrowers who have delinquent accounts and help them find a method of repayment to avoid a default on the loan.

Loan officers usually specialize in commercial, consumer, or mortgage loans. Commercial or business loans help companies pay for new equipment or expand operations. Consumer loans include home equity, automobile, and personal loans. Mortgage loans are made to purchase real estate or to refinance an existing mortgage.

Consumer loan officers attempt to lower their firm's risk by receiving collateral—property pledged as security for the payment of a loan. For example, when lending money for a college education, the bank may insist that the borrower offer his or her home as collateral. If the borrower were ever unable to repay the loan, the borrower would have to sell the home to raise the necessary money.

Commercial and mortgage loan officers behave as sales people who actively seek out potential customers. Commercial loan officers contact firms that may or may not have accounts with their bank. They find out if their potential client is planning any projects for which they may need a loan; if so, loan officers try to establish a relationship with the firm so that the firm will contact them when the loan is needed. Similarly, mortgage loan officers try to develop relationships with commercial or residential real estate agencies; when an individual or firm buys a property, the real estate agent might recommend contacting that loan officer for financing.

Banks and other lenders are offering a growing variety of loans. Loan officers must keep abreast of new types of loans and other financial products and services so they can meet their customers' needs.

Loan officers meet with customers to gather basic information about the loan request, and explain the different types of loans that are available to the applicant. Often customers will not fully understand the information requested, and will call the loan officer for clarification. Once the customer completes the financial forms, the loan officer begins to process them. The loan officer verifies that the customer has correctly identified the type and purpose of the loan. The loan officer then requests a credit report from one or more of the major credit reporting agencies. This information, along with comments from the loan officer, is included in a loan file, and is compared to the lending institution's requirements. Banks and other lenders have established requirements for the maximum percentage of income that can safely go to repay loans. At this point, the loan officer, in consultation with his or her manager, decides whether or not to grant the loan. A loan that would otherwise be denied may be approved if the customer can provide the lender appropriate collateral. The loan officer also informs the borrower if the loan is approved or denied.

Loan officers play a key role in the success of banks and other lending institutions.

Loan counselors contact holders of delinquent accounts in an effort to develop a repayment plan. If a repayment plan cannot be developed, the loan counselor initiates collateral liquidation, in which case the collateral used to secure the loan—a home or car, for example—is seized by the lender and sold to repay the loan.

Working Conditions

Commercial and mortgage loan officers frequently work away from their offices, relying on laptop computers, cellular phones, and pagers to keep in contact with their offices and clients. Mortgage loan officers frequently work out of their home or car, often visiting offices or homes of clients while completing the loan application. Commercial loan officers may travel to other cities to prepare complex loan agreements. Consumer loan officers and loan counselors are likely to spend most of their time in an office.

Most loan officers and counselors work a standard 40-hour week, but may work longer, particularly mortgage loan officers who are free to take on as many customers as they choose. Loan officers usually carry a heavy caseload and sometimes cannot accept new clients until they complete current cases. They are especially busy when interest rates are low, triggering a surge in loan applications.

Employment

Loan officers and counselors held about 209,000 jobs in 1996. About 3 out of 5 are employed by commercial banks, savings institutions, and credit unions. Others are employed by nonbank financial institutions, such as mortgage brokerage firms and personal credit firms. Loan officers are concentrated in urban and suburban areas. In rural areas, the loan application process is often handled by the branch or assistant manager.

Training, Other Qualifications, and Advancement

Loan officer positions generally require a bachelor's degree in finance, economics, or a related field. Most employers also prefer applicants who are familiar with computers and their applications in banking. For commercial or mortgage loan officer jobs, training or experience in sales is highly valued by potential employers. A small number of loan officers advance through the ranks in an organization, acquiring several years of work experience in various other occupations, such as teller or customer service representative.

Persons planning a career as a loan officer or counselor should be capable of developing effective working relationships with others, confident in their abilities, and highly motivated. Loan officers must be willing to attend community events as a representative of their employer.

The American Institute of Banking, which is affiliated with the American Bankers Association, offers courses through correspondence and in some colleges and universities for students and others interested in lending, as well as for experienced loan officers. Completion of these courses and programs enhances one's employment and advancement opportunities.

Capable loan officers and counselors may advance to larger branches of the firm or to a managerial position, while less capable workers and those having inadequate academic preparation may be assigned to smaller branches and find promotion difficult. Advancement from a loan officer position usually includes becoming a supervisor over other loan officers and clerical staff.

Job Outlook

While employment in banks—where most loan officers and counselors are found—is projected to decline, employment of loan officers and counselors is expected to grow faster than the average for all occupations through the year 2006. As the population and economy grow, applications for commercial, consumer, and mortgage loans will increase, spurring demand for loan officers and counselors. Growth in the variety and complexity of loans, and the importance of loan officers to the success of banks and other lending institutions, also should assure employment growth. Although increased demand will generate many new jobs, most openings will result from the need to replace workers who leave the occupation or retire. College graduates and those with banking, lending, or sales experience should have the best job prospects.

Loan officers and counselors are less likely to lose their jobs than other workers in banks and other lending institutions during economic downturns. Because loans are the major source of income for banks, loan officers are fundamental to the success of their organizations. Also, many loan officers are compensated in part on a commission basis. Loan counselors are likely to see an increase in the number of delinquent loans during difficult economic times.

Earnings

The form of compensation for loan officers varies, depending on the lending institution. Some banks offer salary plus commission as an incentive to increase the number of loans processed, while others pay only salaries.

According to a salary survey conducted by Robert Half International, a staffing services firm specializing in accounting and finance, residential real estate mortgage loan officers earned between $30,600 and $45,000 in 1997; commercial real estate mortgage loan officers, between $45,100 and $73,000; consumer loan officers, between $28,900 and $48,000; and commercial lenders, between $37,400 and $85,000. Smaller banks generally paid 15 percent less than larger banks. Loan officers who are paid on a commission basis generally earn more than those on salary only.

Banks and other lenders sometimes offer their loan officers free checking privileges and somewhat lower interest rates on personal loans.

Related Occupations

Loan officers help the public manage financial assets and secure loans. Occupations that involve similar functions include securities and financial services sales representatives, financial aid officers, real estate agents and brokers, and insurance agents and brokers.

Sources of Additional Information

Information about a career as a loan officer or counselor may be obtained from:
☛ American Bankers Association, 1120 Connecticut Ave. NW., Washington, DC 20036.

State bankers' associations can furnish specific information about job opportunities in their State. Or, contact individual banks to inquire about job openings, and for more details about the activities, responsibilities, and preferred qualifications of their loan officers. For the names and addresses of banks and savings and related institutions, as well as the names of their principal officers, consult one of the following directories.
☛ *The American Financial Directory* (Norcross, Ga., McFadden Business Publications).
☛ *Polk's World Bank Directory* (Nashville, R.L. Polk & Co.).
☛ *Rand McNally Bankers Directory* (Chicago, Rand McNally & Co.).
☛ *The U.S. Savings and Loan Directory* (Chicago, Rand McNally & Co.).
☛ *Rand McNally Credit Union Directory* (Chicago, Rand McNally & Co.).

Management Analysts and Consultants

(D.O.T. 100.117-014; 161.117-014, .167-010, -014, -018, and -022, .267 except -014 and -030; 169.167-074; 184.267; and 310.267-010)

Significant Points

- About 45 percent of these workers were self-employed, almost three times the average for other executive, administrative, and managerial occupations.

- A master's degree and at least five years' specialized experience generally are required for jobs in the private sector.

Nature of the Work

Management analysts and consultants analyze and suggest solutions to management problems. For example, a rapidly growing small company may need help in designing a better system of control over inventories and expenses and decides to engage a consultant who is an expert in just-in-time inventory management. In another case, a large company which realizes its corporate structure must be reorganized after acquiring a new division brings in management experts to restructure the company and eliminate duplicate and non-essential managerial positions. These are just some of the many organizational problems that management analysts, as they are called in government agencies, and consultants, as business firms refer to them, help solve.

The work of management analysts and consultants varies with each client or employer and from project to project. For example, some projects require a team of consultants, each specializing in one area; at other times, consultants work independently with the organization's managers. In general, analysts and consultants first collect, review, and analyze information. They then make recommendations to management and may assist in the implementation of their proposal.

Both public and private organizations use consultants for a variety of reasons. Some don't have the internal resources needed to handle a project, while others need a consultant's expertise to determine what resources will be required, and what problems may be encountered, if they pursue a particular opportunity.

Firms providing consulting services range in size from a single practitioner to large international organizations employing many thousands of consultants. Some analysts and consultants specialize in a specific industry while others specialize by type of business function, such as human resources or information systems. In government, management analysts tend to specialize by type of agency. Consulting services often are provided on a contract basis. To engage a consultant, a company first solicits proposals from a number of consulting firms specializing in the area in which it needs assistance. These proposals include the estimated cost and scope of the project, staffing requirements, references from a number of previous clients, and a completion deadline. The company then selects the best proposal for its needs.

Upon getting an assignment or contract, consultants or management analysts define the nature and extent of the problem. During this phase of the job, they analyze pertinent data such as annual reve-

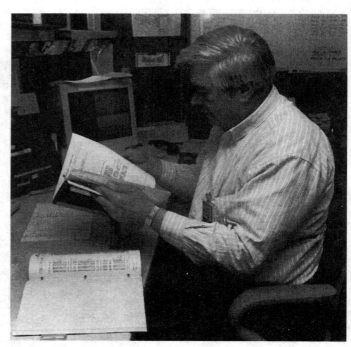

Management analysts and consultants advise managers on many types of issues.

nues, employment, or expenditures and interview managers and employees while observing their operations.

The analyst or consultant develops solutions to the problem. In the course of preparing their recommendations, they take into account the nature of the organization, the relationship it has with others in that industry, and its internal organization and culture. Insight into the problem may be gained by building and solving mathematical models.

Once they have decided on a course of action, consultants report their findings and recommendations to the client, often in writing. In addition, they generally make oral presentations regarding their findings. For some projects, this is all that is required. For others, consultants assist in the implementation of their suggestions.

Management analysts in government agencies use the same skills as their private-sector colleagues to advise managers on many types of issues, most of which are similar to the problems faced by private firms. For example, if an agency is planning to purchase personal computers, it must first determine which type to buy, given its budget and data processing needs. Management analysts would assess the various types of machines available by price range and determine which best meets their department's needs.

Working Conditions

Management analysts and consultants usually divide their time between their offices and their client's site. Although much of their time is spent indoors in clean, well-lighted offices, they may experience a great deal of stress as a result of trying to meet a client's demands, often on a tight schedule.

Typically, analysts and consultants work at least 40 hours a week. Uncompensated overtime is common, especially when project deadlines are near. Since they must spend a significant portion of their time with clients, they travel frequently.

Self-employed consultants can set their workload and hours and work at home. On the other hand, their livelihood depends on their ability to maintain and expand their client base. Salaried consultants also must impress potential clients to get and keep clients for their company.

Employment

Management analysts and consultants held about 244,000 jobs in 1996. Around 45 percent of these workers were self-employed. Most of the rest worked in financial and management consulting firms and for Federal, State, and local governments. The majority of those working for the Federal Government were found in the Department of Defense.

Management analysts and consultants are found throughout the country, but employment is concentrated in large metropolitan areas.

Training, Other Qualifications, and Advancement

Educational requirements for entry-level jobs in this field vary widely between private industry and government. Employers in private industry generally seek individuals with a master's degree in business administration or a related discipline and at least 5 years of experience in the field in which they hope to consult. Most government agencies hire people with a bachelor's degree and no work experience as entry-level management analysts.

Many fields of study provide a suitable educational background for this occupation because of the wide range of problem areas addressed by management analysts and consultants. These include most areas of business and management, as well as computer and information sciences and engineering.

Most entrants to this occupation have, in addition to the appropriate formal education, years of experience in management, human resources, inventory control, or other specialties . The value of this experience enables many to land consultant positions, since most prospective clients now demand experience in the area where they feel they need help.

Management analysts and consultants often work with little or no supervision, so they should be self-motivated and disciplined. Analytical skills, the ability to get along with a wide range of people,

strong oral and written communication skills, good judgment, the ability to manage time well, and creativity in developing solutions to problems are other desirable qualities for prospective management analysts and consultants.

Consulting teams are becoming more common. The team is responsible for the entire project and each consultant on the team is assigned to a particular area.

As consultants gain experience, they often become solely responsible for a specific project full-time, taking on more responsibility and managing their own hours. At the senior level, consultants may supervise lower-level workers and become increasingly involved in seeking out new business. Those with exceptional skills may eventually become a partner or principal in the firm. Others with entrepreneurial ambition may open their own firm.

Analysts and consultants routinely attend conferences to keep abreast of current developments in their field.

A high percentage of management consultants are self-employed, partly because business start-up costs are low. Self-employed consultants also can share office space, administrative help, and other resources with other self-employed consultants or small consulting firms—thus reducing overhead costs. Many such firms fail, however, because of an inability to acquire and maintain a profitable client base.

The Institute of Management Consultants (a division of the Council of Consulting Organizations, Inc.) offers the Certified Management Consultant (CMC) designation to those who pass an examination and meet minimum levels of education and experience. Certification is not mandatory for management consultants to practice, but it may give a job seeker a competitive advantage.

Job Outlook

Employment of management analysts and consultants is expected to grow faster than the average for all occupations through the year 2006 as industry and government increasingly rely on outside expertise to improve the performance of their organizations. Growth is expected in very large consulting firms, but also in smaller niche consulting firms whose consultants specialize in specific areas of expertise. For example, some consultants specialize in biotechnology, pharmacy, engineering, or telecommunications. Clients increasingly demand a team approach, which enables examination of a variety of different areas within the organization; this development may hinder individual practitioners.

Increased competition has forced American industry to take a closer look at its operations. As international and domestic markets become more competitive, firms must use resources more efficiently. Management consultants are being increasingly relied upon to help reduce costs, streamline operations, and develop marketing strategies. As businesses downsize, opportunities will be created for consultants to perform duties that were previously handled internally. Businesses attempting to expand, particularly into world markets, frequently need the skills of management consultants to help with organizational, administrative, and other issues. Continuing changes in the business environment also are expected to lead the demand for consultants to incorporate new technologies, and to adapt to a changing labor force. As businesses rely more on technology, there are increasing roles for consultants with a technical background, such as engineering or biotechnology, particularly when combined with an MBA.

Federal, State, and local agencies also are expected to expand their use of management analysts. Analysts' skills at identifying problems and implementing cost reduction measures are expected to become increasingly important.

Despite projected rapid employment growth, competition for jobs as management analysts and consultants is expected to be keen. Because management consultants can come from such diverse educational backgrounds, the pool of applicants from which employers can hire is quite large. Additionally, the independent and challenging nature of the work, combined with high earnings potential, make this occupation attractive to many. Job opportunities are expected to be best for those with a graduate degree, a talent for salesmanship and public relations, and industry expertise.

Because many small consulting firms fail each year for lack of managerial expertise and clients, those interested in opening their own firm must have good organizational and marketing skills and several years of consulting experience.

Earnings

Salaries for management analysts and consultants vary widely by experience, education, and employer. In 1996, those who were full-time wage and salary workers had median annual earnings of about $39,500. The middle 50 percent earned between $30,200 and $61,300, and the top 10 percent earned more than $81,500.

In 1996, according to the Association of Management Consulting Firms, earnings—including bonuses and/or profit sharing—for research associates in member firms averaged $32,400; for entry level consultants, $35,200; for management consultants, $50,500; for senior consultants, $74,300; for junior partners, $91,100; and for senior partners, $167,100.

The average annual salary for management analysts in the Federal Government in nonsupervisory, supervisory, and managerial positions was $55,240 in 1997.

Typical benefits for salaried analysts and consultants include health and life insurance, a retirement plan, vacation and sick leave, profit sharing, and bonuses for outstanding work. In addition, all travel expenses usually are reimbursed by the employer. Self-employed consultants have to maintain their own office and provide their own benefits.

Related Occupations

Management analysts and consultants collect, review, and analyze data; make recommendations; and assist in the implementation of their ideas. Others who use similar skills are managers, computer systems analysts, operations research analysts, economists, and financial analysts. Researchers prepare data and reports for consultants to use in their recommendations.

Sources of Additional Information

Information about career opportunities in management consulting is available from:
☛ The Association of Management Consulting Firms, 521 Fifth Ave., 35th Floor, New York, NY 10175-3598.

For information about a career as a State or local government management analyst, contact your State or local employment service.

Information on obtaining a management analyst position with the Federal Government may be obtained from the Office of Personnel Management through a telephone based system. Consult your telephone directory under U.S. Government for a local number or call (912) 757-3000 (TDD 912 744-2299). That number is not toll free and charges may result. Information also is available from their internet site: http:// www.usajobs.opm.gov

Marketing, Advertising, and Public Relations Managers

(D.O.T. 096.161-010; 141.137-010; 159.167-022; 163.117-014, -018, -022, -026, .167-010, -014, -018, -022, .267-010; 164.117-010, -014, -018, .167-010; 165.117-010, -014; 185.157-014, .167-042; 187.167-162, -170; 189.117-018)

Significant Points

- Employment is projected to increase rapidly, but competition is expected to be intense.

- Marketing, advertising, and public relations managers have high earnings, but substantial travel and long hours, including evenings and weekends, are common.

- A college degree with almost any major is suitable for entering this occupation, but most people enter these jobs

after acquiring experience in related, less responsible positions.

Nature of the Work

The objective of any firm is to market its products or services profitably. In small firms, all marketing responsibilities may be assumed by the owner or chief executive officer. In large firms, which may offer numerous products and services nationally or even worldwide, experienced marketing, advertising, and public relations managers coordinate these and related activities.

In large firms an executive vice president directs the overall marketing policy—including market research, marketing strategy, sales, advertising, promotion, pricing, product development, and public relations activities. (This occupation is included in the *Handbook* statement on general managers and top executives.) Middle and supervisory managers oversee and supervise staffs of professionals and technicians.

Marketing managers develop the firm's detailed marketing strategy. With the help of subordinates, including product development managers and market research managers, they determine the demand for products and services offered by the firm and its competitors and identify potential consumers—for example, business firms, wholesalers, retailers, government, or the general public. Mass markets are further categorized according to various factors such as region, age, income, and lifestyle. Marketing managers develop pricing strategy with an eye towards maximizing the firm's share of the market and its profits while ensuring that the firm's customers are satisfied. In collaboration with sales, product development, and other managers, they monitor trends that indicate the need for new products and services and oversee product development. Marketing managers work with advertising and promotion managers to best promote the firm's products and services and to attract potential users.

Sales managers direct the firm's sales program. They assign sales territories and goals and establish training programs for their sales representatives. Managers advise their sales representatives on ways to improve their sales performance. In large, multiproduct firms, they oversee regional and local sales managers and their staffs. Sales managers maintain contact with dealers and distributors. They analyze sales statistics gathered by their staffs to determine sales potential and inventory requirements and monitor the preferences of customers. Such information is vital to develop products and maximize profits.

Except in the largest firms, advertising and promotion staffs generally are small and serve as a liaison between the firm and the advertising or promotion agency to which many advertising or promotional functions are contracted out. Advertising managers oversee the account services, creative services, and media services departments. The account services department is managed by account executives, who assess the need for advertising and, in advertising agencies, maintain the accounts of clients. The creative services department develops the subject matter and presentation of advertising. This department is supervised by a creative director, who oversees the copy chief and art director and their staffs. The media services department is supervised by the media director, who oversees planning groups that select the communication media—for example, radio, television, newspapers, magazines, or outdoor signs—to disseminate the advertising.

Promotion managers supervise staffs of promotion specialists. They direct promotion programs combining advertising with purchase incentives to increase sales. In an effort to establish closer contact with purchasers—dealers, distributors, or consumers—promotion programs may involve direct mail, telemarketing, television or radio advertising, catalogs, exhibits, inserts in newspapers, in-store displays and product endorsements, and special events. Purchase incentives may include discounts, samples, gifts, rebates, coupons, sweepstakes, and contests.

Public relations managers supervise public relations specialists (see the *Handbook* statement on public relations specialists). These managers direct publicity programs to a targeted public. They use

Long hours, including evenings and weekends, are common for marketing, advertising, and public relations managers.

any necessary communication media in their effort to maintain the support of the specific group upon whom their organization's success depends, such as consumers, stockholders, or the general public. For example, public relations managers may clarify or justify the firm's point of view on health or environmental issues to community or special interest groups. They evaluate advertising and promotion programs for compatibility with public relations efforts, and, in effect, serve as the eyes and ears of top management. They observe social, economic, and political trends that might ultimately have an effect upon the firm, and make recommendations to enhance the firm's image based on those trends. Public relations managers may confer with labor relations managers to produce internal company communications—such as news about employee-management relations—and with financial managers to produce company reports. They assist company executives in drafting speeches, arranging interviews, and other forms of public contact; oversee company archives; and respond to information requests. In addition, some handle special events such as sponsorship of races, parties introducing new products, or other activities the firm supports in order to gain public attention through the press without advertising directly.

Working Conditions

Marketing, advertising, and public relations managers are provided with offices close to top managers. Long hours, including evenings and weekends, are common. Almost 45 percent of marketing, advertising, and public relations managers worked 50 hours or more a week, compared to 20 percent for all occupations. Working under pressure is unavoidable as schedules change, problems arise, and deadlines and goals must be met. Marketing, advertising, and public relations managers meet frequently with other managers; some meet with the public and government officials.

Substantial travel may be involved. For example, attendance at meetings sponsored by associations or industries is often mandatory. Sales managers travel to national, regional, and local offices and to various dealers and distributors. Advertising and promotion managers may travel to meet with clients or representatives of communications media. At times, public relations managers travel to meet with special interest groups or government officials. Job transfers between headquarters and regional offices are common—particularly among sales managers—and can disrupt family life.

Employment

Marketing, advertising, and public relations managers held about 482,000 jobs in 1996. They are found in virtually every industry. Industries employing them in significant numbers include motor vehicle dealers, printing and publishing, advertising, department stores, computer and data processing services, and management and public relations.

Training, Advancement, and Other Qualifications

A wide range of educational backgrounds are suitable for entry into marketing, advertising, and public relations managerial jobs, but many employers prefer a broad liberal arts background. A bachelor's degree in sociology, psychology, literature, or philosophy, among other subjects, is acceptable. However, requirements vary depending upon the particular job.

For marketing, sales, and promotion management positions, some employers prefer a bachelor's or master's degree in business administration with an emphasis on marketing. Courses in business law, economics, accounting, finance, mathematics, and statistics are also highly recommended. In highly technical industries, such as computer and electronics manufacturing, a bachelor's degree in engineering or science combined with a master's degree in business administration is preferred. For advertising management positions, some employers prefer a bachelor's degree in advertising or journalism. A course of study should include courses in marketing, consumer behavior, market research, sales, communications methods and technology, and visual arts—for example, art history and photography. For public relations management positions, some employers prefer a bachelor's or master's degree in public relations or journalism. The individual's curriculum should include courses in advertising, business administration, public affairs, political science, and creative and technical writing. For all these specialties, courses in management and completion of an internship while in school are highly recommended. Familiarity with word processing and data base applications also are important for many marketing, advertising, and public relations management positions. Today interactive marketing, product promotion, and advertising experience are increasingly important, and computer skills are very important.

Most marketing, advertising, and public relations management positions are filled by promoting experienced staff or related professional or technical personnel, for example, sales representatives, purchasing agents, buyers, product or brand specialists, advertising specialists, promotion specialists, and public relations specialists. In small firms, where the number of positions is limited, advancement to a management position generally comes slowly. In large firms, promotion may occur more quickly.

Although experience, ability, and leadership are emphasized for promotion, advancement can be accelerated by participation in management training programs conducted by many large firms. Many firms also provide their employees with continuing education opportunities, either in-house or at local colleges and universities, and encourage employee participation in seminars and conferences, often provided by professional societies. Often in collaboration with colleges and universities, numerous marketing and related associations sponsor national or local management training programs. Courses include brand and product management, international marketing, sales management evaluation, telemarketing and direct sales, promotion, marketing communication, market research, organizational communication, and data processing systems procedures and management. Many firms pay all or part of the cost for those who successfully complete courses.

Some associations (listed under sources of additional information) offer certification programs for marketing, advertising, and public relations managers. Certification is a sign of competence and achievement in this field that is particularly important in a competitive job market. While relatively few marketing, advertising, and public relations managers currently are certified, the number of managers who seek certification is expected to grow. For example, Sales and Marketing Executives International offers a management certification program based on education and job performance. The Public Relations Society of America offers an accreditation program for public relations practitioners based on years of experience and an examination. The International Association of Business Communicators offers an accreditation program for the manager or the person ready to move into communication management. The American Marketing Association is developing a certification program for marketing managers.

Persons interested in becoming marketing, advertising, and public relations managers should be mature, creative, highly motivated, resistant to stress, and flexible, yet decisive. The ability to communicate persuasively, both orally and in writing, with other managers, staff, and the public is vital. Marketing, advertising, and public relations managers also need tact, good judgment, and exceptional ability to establish and maintain effective personal relationships with supervisory and professional staff members and client firms.

Because of the importance and high visibility of their jobs, marketing, advertising, and public relations managers often are prime candidates for advancement. Well-trained, experienced, successful managers may be promoted to higher positions in their own or other firms. Some become top executives. Managers with extensive experience and sufficient capital may open their own businesses.

Job Outlook

Marketing, advertising, and public relations manager jobs are highly coveted and will be sought by other managers or highly experienced professional and technical personnel, resulting in substantial job competition. College graduates with extensive experience, a high level of creativity, and strong communication skills should have the best job opportunities. Those who have new media and interactive marketing skills will be particularly sought after.

Employment of marketing, advertising, and public relations managers is expected to increase faster than the average for all occupations through the year 2006. Increasingly intense domestic and global competition in products and services offered to consumers should require greater marketing, promotional, and public relations efforts by managers. Management and public relations firms may experience particularly rapid growth as businesses increasingly hire contractors for these services rather than support additional full-time staff.

Projected employment growth varies by industry. For example, employment of marketing, advertising, and public relations managers is expected to grow much faster than average in most business services industries, such as computer and data processing, and management and public relations firms, while average growth is projected in manufacturing industries overall. Many companies that eliminated in-house marketing and advertising departments during downsizing in recent years are now relying on firms which specialize in promotion, marketing, and advertising activities to provide these services.

Earnings

According to a National Association of Colleges and Employers survey, starting salaries for marketing majors graduating in 1997 averaged about $29,000; advertising majors, about $27,000.

The median annual salary of marketing, advertising, and public relations managers was $46,000 in 1996. The lowest 10 percent earned $23,000 or less, while the top 10 percent earned $97,000 or more. Many earn bonuses equal to 10 percent or more of their salaries. Surveys show that salary levels vary substantially depending upon the level of managerial responsibility, length of service, education, and the employer's size, location, and industry. For example, manufacturing firms generally pay marketing, advertising, and public relations managers higher salaries than nonmanufacturing firms. For sales managers, the size of their sales territory is another important-determinant of salary.

According to a 1996 survey by *Advertising Age Magazine*, the average annual salary of a vice president brand manager was $79,000; vice president product manager, $105,000; vice president advertising, $130,000; and vice president marketing, $133,000.

According to a 1996 survey by the Public Relations Society of America, senior public relations managers earned an average of $76,790.

Related Occupations

Marketing, advertising, and public relations managers direct the sale of products and services offered by their firms and the communication of information about their firms' activities. Other personnel involved with marketing, advertising, and public relations include art directors, commercial and graphic artists, copy chiefs, copywriters, editors, lobbyists, marketing research analysts, public relations specialists, promotion specialists, sales representatives, and technical writers. (Some of these occupations are discussed elsewhere in the *Handbook*.)

Sources of Additional Information

For information about careers in sales and marketing management, contact:
- American Marketing Association, 250 S. Wacker Dr., Chicago, IL 60606.
- Sales and Marketing Executives International, 458 Statler Office Tower, Cleveland, OH 44115.

For information about careers in advertising management, contact:
- American Advertising Federation, Education Services Department, 1101 Vermont Ave. NW., Suite 500, Washington, DC 20005.

Information about careers in promotion management is available from:
- Association of Promotion and Marketing Agencies Worldwide (APMA), 750 Summer St., Stamford, CT 06901.
- Promotion Marketing Association of America, Inc., 322 Eighth Ave., Suite 1201, New York, NY 10001.

Information about careers in public relations management is available from:
- Public Relations Society of America, 33 Irving Place, New York, NY 10003-2376.

Information on accreditation for business communicators is available from:
- International Association of Business Communicators, One Hallidie Plaza, Suite 600, San Francisco, CA 94102.

Property Managers

(D.O.T. 186.117-042, -046, -058, and -062, .167-018, -030, -038, -042, -046, -062, -066, and -090; 187.167-190; 191.117-046 and -050)

Significant Points

- Most persons enter the occupation as an on-site manager of an apartment complex, condominium, or community association, or as an assistant manager at a large property management company. Opportunities should be best for persons with college degrees in business administration and related fields.

- About 40 percent were self-employed, over twice the average for other executive, administrative, and managerial occupations.

Nature of the Work

Many people own real estate in the form of a home. To businesses and investors, however, properly managed real estate is a potential source of income and profits rather than simply a place for shelter. For this reason, property managers perform an important function in increasing and maintaining the value of real estate investments for investors. In general, property managers oversee the performance of income-producing commercial and residential properties or manage the communal property and services of condominium and community associations.

Most property managers work in the field of property management. When owners of apartments, office buildings, retail, or industrial properties lack the time or expertise needed for the day-to-day management of their real estate investments, they often hire a property manager, either directly or by contracting with a property management company.

Property managers handle the financial operations of the property, seeing to it that mortgages, taxes, insurance premiums, payroll, and maintenance bills are paid on time. They also supervise the preparation of financial statements and periodically report to the owners on the status of the property, occupancy rates, dates of lease expirations, and other matters.

If necessary, property managers negotiate contracts for janitorial, security, groundskeeping, trash removal, and other services. When contracts are awarded competitively, managers must solicit bids from several contractors and recommend to the owners which bid to accept. They monitor the performance of the contractors, and investigate and resolve complaints from residents and tenants when services are not properly provided. Managers also purchase supplies and equipment needed for the property, and make arrangements with specialists for any repairs that cannot be handled by the regular property maintenance staff.

On top of these duties, property managers must understand the provisions of legislation, such as the Americans With Disabilities Act and the Federal Fair Housing Amendment Act, as well as local fair housing laws, to be sure their renting and advertising practices are not discriminatory.

On-site property managers are responsible for the day-to-day operations for one piece of property, such as an office building, shopping center, or apartment complex. To insure the property is safe and being maintained properly, on-site managers routinely inspect the grounds, facilities, and equipment to determine what repairs are needed. They meet not only with current residents (when handling requests for repairs or trying to resolve complaints, for example), but also show vacant apartments or office space to prospective residents or tenants and explain the occupancy terms. On-site managers are also responsible for enforcing the terms of the rental or lease agreement, such as rent collection, parking and pet restrictions, and termination-of-lease procedures.

Other important duties of on-site managers include keeping accurate, up-to-date records of income and expenditures from property operations and the submission of regular expense reports to the property manager or owners.

The work of property managers who do not work on-site is similar to that of on-site managers, except that most of these managers are responsible for multiple properties and supervise on-site personnel. They act as a liaison between the on-site manager and the owner. They also market vacant space to prospective tenants through the use of a leasing agent, advertising, or by other means, and establish rental rates in accordance with prevailing local conditions.

Some property managers, termed real estate asset managers, act as the property owners' agent and adviser for the property. They plan and direct the purchase, development, and disposition of real estate on behalf of businesses and investors. These managers are involved in long-term strategic financial planning rather than the day-to-day operations of the property.

When looking to acquire property, real estate asset managers take several factors into consideration, such as property values, taxes, zoning, population growth, and traffic volume and patterns. Once a site is selected, they negotiate contracts for the purchase or lease of the property, securing the most beneficial terms.

Real estate asset managers periodically review their company's real estate holdings, identifying properties that are no longer commercially attractive. They then negotiate the sale or termination of the lease of properties selected for disposal.

The work of property managers employed by condominium and homeowner associations, often known as community association managers, is different than that of other property managers. Instead of renters, they interact on a daily basis with homeowners—members of the community association that employs the manager. Hired by

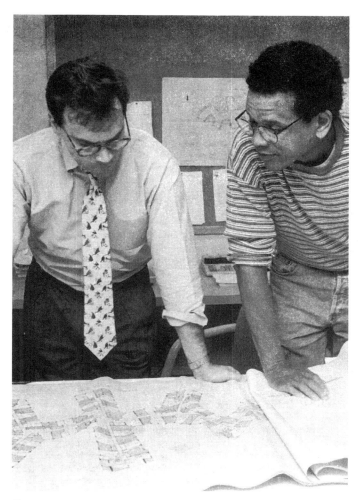

Property managers sometimes must work long hours in order to meet with key personnel.

the volunteer board of directors of the association, the community association manager administers daily affairs and oversees the maintenance of property and facilities that the homeowners own and use jointly through the association. Smaller community associations usually cannot afford professional management, but managers of larger condominiums or homeowner associations have many of the same responsibilities as the managers of large apartment complexes. Some homeowner associations encompass thousands of homes, and, in addition to administering the associations' financial records and budget, their managers are responsible for the operation of community pools, golf courses, community centers, and the maintenance of landscaping, parking areas, and streets. Other responsibilities usually include meeting with the elected boards of directors to discuss and solve legal and environmental issues and aiding in resolving disputes between neighbors.

Property managers who work for land development companies acquire land and plan the construction of shopping centers, houses and apartments, office buildings, or industrial parks. They negotiate with representatives of local government, other businesses, community and public interest groups, and public utilities to eliminate obstacles to the development of the land and gain support for the planned project. It sometimes takes years to win approval for a project, and in the process managers may have to modify the plans for the project many times. Once they are free to proceed with a project, managers negotiate short-term loans to finance the construction of the project, and later negotiate long-term permanent mortgage loans. They then contract with architectural firms to draw up detailed plans, and with construction companies to build the project.

Working Conditions

Offices of most property managers are clean, modern, and well-lighted. Many spend a major portion of their time away from their desks, however. On-site managers in particular may spend a large portion of their workday away from their office visiting the building engineer in the boiler room, showcasing apartments, checking on the janitorial and maintenance staff, or investigating problems reported by tenants. Property managers frequently visit the properties they oversee, sometimes on a daily basis when contractors are doing major repair or renovation work. Real estate asset managers may spend time away from home while traveling to company real estate holdings or searching for properties that might be acquired.

Property managers often must attend meetings in the evening with residents, property owners, community association boards of directors, or civic groups. Not surprisingly, many property managers put in long work weeks. Some apartment managers are required to live in the apartment complexes where they work so they are available to handle any emergency that occurs while they are off duty. They usually receive compensatory time off, however, for working at night or on weekends. Many apartment managers receive time off during the week so that they are available on weekends to show apartments to prospective residents.

Employment

Property managers held about 271,000 jobs in 1996. Most worked for real estate operators and lessors or for property management firms. Others worked for real estate development companies, government agencies that manage public buildings, and corporations with extensive holdings of commercial properties. About 4 out of 10 property managers were self-employed, and over a quarter worked part time.

Training, Other Qualifications and Advancement

Most employers prefer to hire college graduates for property management positions. Degrees in business administration, finance, real estate, public administration, or related fields are preferred, but persons with degrees in the liberal arts are often accepted. Good speaking, writing, and financial skills, as well as an ability to deal tactfully with people, are essential in all areas of property management.

Most persons enter property management as an on-site manager of an apartment complex, condominium, or community association, or as an assistant manager at a large property management company. As they acquire experience working under the direction of a property manager, they may advance to positions with greater responsibility at larger properties. Persons who excel as on-site managers often transfer to assistant property manager positions where they can acquire experience handling a broader range of property management responsibilities.

Previous employment as a real estate agent may be an asset to on-site managers because it provides experience useful in showing apartments or office space and dealing with people, as well as an understanding that an attractive, well-maintained property can command higher rental rates and result in lower turnover among tenants. In the past, many persons with backgrounds in building maintenance have advanced to on-site manager positions on the strength of their knowledge of building mechanical systems, but this is becoming less common as employers are placing greater emphasis on administrative, financial, and communication abilities for managerial jobs.

Although most persons who enter jobs as assistant property managers do so on the strength of on-site management experience, employers are increasingly hiring inexperienced college graduates with bachelor's or master's degrees in business administration, finance, or real estate for these jobs. Assistants work closely with a property manager and acquire experience performing a variety of management tasks, such as preparing the budget, analyzing insurance coverage and risk options, marketing the property to prospective tenants, and collecting overdue rent payments. In time, many assistants advance to property manager positions.

The responsibilities and compensation of property managers increase as they manage larger properties. Most property managers are responsible for several properties at a time, and as their careers advance they are gradually entrusted with properties that are larger or whose management is more complex. Many specialize in the management of one type of property, such as apartments, office buildings, condominiums, cooperatives, homeowner associations, or retail properties. Managers who excel at marketing properties to tenants may specialize in managing new properties, while those who are particularly knowledgeable about buildings and their mechanical systems might specialize in the management of older properties that require renovation or more frequent repairs. Some experienced property managers open their own property management firms.

Persons most commonly enter real estate asset manager jobs by transferring from positions as property managers or real estate brokers. Real estate asset managers must be good negotiators, adept at persuading and handling people, and good at analyzing data to assess the fair market value of property or its development potential. Resourcefulness and creativity in arranging financing are essential for managers who specialize in land development.

Attendance at short-term formal training programs conducted by various professional and trade associations active in the real estate field is often encouraged. Employers send managers to these programs to improve their management skills and expand their knowledge of specialized subjects, such as the operation and maintenance of building mechanical systems, enhancing property values, insurance and risk management, personnel management, business and real estate law, resident/tenant relations, communications, and accounting and financial concepts. Managers also participate in these programs to prepare themselves for positions of greater responsibility in property management. Completion of these programs, together with meeting job experience standards and achieving a satisfactory score on a written examination, leads to certification, or the formal award of a professional designation, by the sponsoring association. In addition to these qualifications, some associations require their members to adhere to a specific code of ethics. Some of the organizations that offer such programs are listed at the end of this statement.

Managers of public housing subsidized by the Federal Government are required to be certified, but many property managers who work with all types of property choose to earn a professional designation voluntarily because it represents formal industry recognition of their achievements and status in the occupation.

Job Outlook

Employment of property managers is projected to increase as fast as the average for all occupations through the year 2006. In addition to rising demand for these workers, many job openings are expected to occur as property managers transfer to other occupations or leave the labor force. Opportunities should be best for persons with college degrees in business administration, real estate, and related fields, as well as those who attain professional designations.

Growth in the demand for property managers will be evident in several areas. In commercial real estate, the demand for managers is expected to coincide with the projected expansion in wholesale and retail trade; finance, insurance, and real estate; and services. Some additional employment growth will come from adding on to existing buildings.

An increase in the Nation's stock of apartments and houses also should require more property managers. Developments of new homes are increasingly being organized with community or homeowner associations that provide community services and oversee jointly owned common areas, requiring professional management. To help properties become more profitable, more commercial and multi-unit residential property owners are expected to place their investments in the hands of professional managers.

Growth in demand should also arise as a result of the changing demographic composition of the population. The number of older people will increase during the projection period, creating a need for various types of suitable housing, such as assisted living arrangements and retirement communities. Accordingly, there will be a need for property managers to operate these facilities, especially those who have a background in the operation and administrative aspects of running a health unit.

Earnings

Median annual earnings of all property managers were $28,500 in 1996. The middle 50 percent earned between $19,000 and $39,800. Ten percent earned less than $12,000 and 10 percent earned more than $60,700 annually.

Community association managers received compensation comparable to on-site and property managers employed by other types of properties. Many resident apartment managers receive the use of an apartment as part of their compensation package. Property managers often are given the use of a company automobile, and managers employed in land development often receive a small percentage of ownership in projects they develop.

Related Occupations

Property managers plan, organize, staff, and manage the real estate operations of businesses. Workers who perform similar functions in other fields include restaurant and food service managers, hotel and resort managers, facilities managers, health services managers, education administrators, and city managers.

Sources of Additional Information

General information about careers in property management and programs leading to the award of a professional designation in the field is available from:

☞ Institute of Real Estate Management, 430 N. Michigan Ave., Chicago, IL 60611. Homepage: http://www.irem.org

For information on careers and certification programs in commercial property management, contact:

☞ Building Owners and Managers Association International, 1201 New York Ave. NW., Suite 300, Washington, DC 20005. Homepage: http://www.boma.org

☞ Building Owners and Managers Institute (BOMI) International, 1521 Ritchie Hwy., Arnold, MD 21012. Homepage: http://www.bomi-edu.org

For information on careers and certification programs in residential property management, contact:

☞ Community Associations Institute, 1630 Duke St., Alexandria, VA 22314. Homepage: http://www.caionline.org

☞ National Apartment Association, Education Department, 201 N. Union St., Suite 200, Alexandria, VA 22314.

☞ National Association of Home Builders, 1201 15th St. NW., Washington, DC 20005. Homepage: http://www.nahb.com/multi.html

☞ National Association of Residential Property Managers, 35 E. Wacker Dr., Suite 500, Chicago, IL 60601.

Purchasers and Buyers

(D.O.T. 162.117-014 and -018, .157-018, -022, -030, -034, and -038, .167 -022, and -030; 163.117-010; 169.167-054; 184.117-078; and 185.167-034)

Significant Points

● Computerization has reduced the demand for lower-level buyers.

● About one-half were employed in wholesale or retail trade.

Nature of the Work

Purchasers and buyers seek to obtain the highest quality merchandise at the lowest possible purchase cost for their employers. (In general, purchasers buy goods and services for the use of their company or organization whereas buyers buy items for resale.) They determine which commodities or services are best, choose the suppliers of the product or service, negotiate the lowest price, and award contracts that ensure the correct amount of the product or service is received at the appropriate time. In order to accomplish these tasks successfully, purchasers and buyers study sales records and inventory levels of current stock, identify foreign and domestic suppliers, and keep abreast of changes affecting both the supply of and demand for products and materials for which they are responsible.

Purchasers and buyers evaluate suppliers based upon price, quality, service support, availability, reliability, and selection. To assist them in their search, they review listings in catalogs, industry periodicals, directories, and trade journals, research the reputation and history of the suppliers, and advertise anticipated purchase actions in order to solicit bids. Also, meetings, trade shows, conferences, and visits to suppliers' plants and distribution centers provide opportunities for purchasers and buyers to examine products, assess a supplier's production and distribution capabilities, as well as discuss other technical and business considerations that influence the purchasing decision. Once all the necessary information on suppliers is gathered, orders are placed and contracts are awarded to those suppliers who meet the purchasers' needs. Other specific job duties and responsibilities vary by employer and by the type of commodities or services to be purchased.

Purchasing professionals employed by government agencies or manufacturing firms are usually called purchasing directors, managers, or agents; buyers or industrial buyers; or contract specialists. These workers acquire product materials, intermediate goods, machines, supplies, services, and other materials used in the production of a final product. Some purchasing managers specialize in negotiating and supervising supply contracts and are called contract or supply managers. Purchasing agents and managers obtain items ranging from raw materials, fabricated parts, machinery, and office supplies to construction services and airline tickets. The flow of work—or even the entire production process—can be slowed or halted if the right materials, supplies, or equipment are not on hand when needed. In order to be effective, purchasers and buyers must have a working technical knowledge of the goods or services to be purchased.

In large industrial organizations, a distinction often is drawn between the work of a buyer or purchasing agent and that of a purchasing manager. Purchasing agents and buyers typically focus on routine purchasing tasks, often specializing in a commodity or group of related commodities—for example, steel, lumber, cotton, fabricated metal products, or petroleum products. This usually requires the purchaser to track such things as market conditions, price trends, or futures markets. Purchasing managers usually handle the more complex or critical purchases and may supervise a group of purchasing agents handling other goods and services. Whether a person is titled purchasing agent, buyer, or manager depends more on specific industry and employer practices than on specific job duties.

Changing business practices have altered the traditional roles of purchasing professionals in many industries. For example, manufacturing companies increasingly involve purchasing professionals at most stages of product development because of their ability to forecast a part's or material's cost, availability, and suitability for its intended purpose. Furthermore, potential problems with the supply of materials may be avoided by consulting the purchasing department in the early stages of product design.

Another new practice is for businesses to enter into integrated supply contracts. These contracts increase the importance of supplier selection because agreements are larger in scope and longer in duration. A major responsibility of most purchasers is to work out problems that may occur with a supplier because the success of the relationship directly affects the buying firm's performance.

Purchasing professionals often work closely with other employees in their own organization when deciding on purchases, an arrangement sometimes called team buying. For example, they may discuss the design of custom-made products with company design engineers, quality problems in purchased goods with quality assurance engineers and production supervisors, or shipment problems with managers in the receiving department before submitting an order.

Contract specialists and managers in various levels of government award contracts for an array of items, including office and building supplies, services for the public, and construction projects. They typically use sealed bids, but sometimes use negotiated agreements for complex items. Increasingly, purchasing professionals in government are placing solicitations for and accepting bids through the internet. Government purchasing agents and managers must follow strict laws and regulations in their work. These legal requirements occasionally

Many employers prefer to hire purchasers and buyers who have a bachelor's degree.

are changed, so agents and contract specialists must stay informed about the latest regulations and their applications.

Other professionals, who buy finished goods for resale, are employed by wholesale and retail establishments where they commonly are referred to as "buyers" or "merchandise managers." Wholesale and retail buyers are an integral part of a complex system of distribution and merchandising that caters to the vast array of consumer needs and desires. Wholesale buyers purchase goods directly from manufacturers or from other wholesale firms for resale to retail firms, commercial establishments, institutions, and other organizations. In retail firms, buyers purchase goods from wholesale firms or directly from manufacturers for resale to the public. Buyers largely determine which products their establishment will sell. Therefore, it is essential that they have the ability to accurately predict what will appeal to consumers. They must constantly stay informed of the latest trends because failure to do so could jeopardize profits and the reputation of their company. Buyers also follow ads in newspapers and other media to check competitors' sales activities and watch general economic conditions to anticipate consumer buying patterns. Buyers working for large and medium-sized firms usually specialize in acquiring one or two lines of merchandise, whereas buyers working for small stores may purchase their complete inventory.

The use of private-label merchandise and the consolidation of buying departments have increased the responsibilities of retail buyers. Private-label merchandise, produced for a particular retailer, requires buyers to work closely with vendors to develop and obtain the desired product. The downsizing and consolidation of buying departments is also increasing the demands placed on buyers because, although the amount of work remains unchanged, there are fewer people needed to accomplish it. The result is an increase in the workloads and levels of responsibility.

Many merchandise managers assist in the planning and implementation of sales promotion programs. Working with merchandising executives, they determine the nature of the sale and purchase accordingly. They also work with advertising personnel to create the ad campaign. For example, they may determine the media in which the advertisement will be placed—newspapers, direct mail, television, or some combination of these. In addition, merchandising managers often visit the selling floor to ensure that the goods are properly

displayed. Often, assistant buyers are responsible for placing orders and checking shipments.

Computers are having a major effect on the jobs of purchasers and buyers. In manufacturing and service industries, computers handle most of the more routine tasks—enabling purchasing professionals to concentrate mainly on the analytical aspects of the job. Computers are used to obtain up-to-date product and price listings, to track inventory levels, process routine orders, and help determine when to make purchases. Computers also maintain bidders' lists, record the history of supplier performance, and issue purchase orders.

Computerized systems have dramatically simplified many of the routine buying functions and improved the efficiency of determining which products are selling. For example, cash registers connected to computers, known as point-of-sale terminals, allow organizations to maintain centralized, up-to-date sales and inventory records. This information can then be used to produce weekly sales reports that reflect the types of products in demand. Buyers also use computers to gain instant access to the specifications for thousands of commodities, inventory records, and their customers' purchase records. Some firms are linked with manufacturers or wholesalers by electronic purchasing systems. These systems speed selection and ordering and provide information on availability and shipment, allowing buyers to better concentrate on the selection of goods and suppliers.

Working Conditions

Most purchasers and buyers work in comfortable, well-lighted offices at stores, corporate headquarters, or production or service facilities. They frequently work more than a 40-hour week because of special sales, conferences, or production deadlines. Evening and weekend work is common. For those working in retail trade, this is especially true prior to holiday seasons. Consequently, many retail firms discourage the use of vacation time from late November until early January.

Buyers and merchandise managers often work under great pressure because wholesale and retail stores are so competitive; buyers need physical stamina to keep up with the fast-paced nature of their work.

Many purchasers and buyers spend at least several days a month traveling. Purchasers for worldwide manufacturing companies and large retailers, and buyers of high fashion, may travel outside the United States.

Employment

Purchasers and buyers held about 639,000 jobs in 1996. Purchasing agents and purchasing managers each accounted for slightly more than one-third of the total, while buyers accounted for the remainder.

About one-half of all purchasers and buyers worked in wholesale and retail trade establishments such as grocery or department stores, and another one-fourth worked in manufacturing. The remainder worked mostly in service establishments or different levels of government.

Training, Other Qualifications, and Advancement.

Qualified persons usually begin as trainees, purchasing clerks, expediters, junior buyers, or assistant buyers. Retail and wholesale firms prefer to hire applicants who are familiar with the merchandise they sell as well as with wholesaling and retailing practices. Some retail firms promote qualified employees to assistant buyer positions; others recruit and train college graduates as assistant buyers. Most employers use a combination of methods.

Educational requirements tend to vary with the size of the organization. Large stores and distributors, especially those in wholesale and retail trade, prefer applicants who have completed a bachelor's degree program with a business emphasis. Many manufacturing firms prefer applicants with a bachelor's or master's degree in business, economics, or technical training such as engineering or one of the applied sciences and tend to put a greater emphasis on formal training.

Regardless of academic preparation, new employees must learn the specifics of their employers' business. Training periods vary in length, with most lasting 1 to 5 years. In wholesale and retail establishments, most trainees begin by selling merchandise, supervising sales workers, checking invoices on material received, and keeping track of stock on hand, although widespread use of computers has simplified some of these tasks. As they progress, retail trainees are given more buying-related responsibilities. In manufacturing, new purchasing employees often are enrolled in company training programs and spend a considerable amount of time learning about company operations and purchasing practices. They work with experienced purchasers to learn about commodities, prices, suppliers, and markets. In addition, they may be assigned to the production planning department to learn about the material requirements system and the inventory system the company uses to keep production and replenishment functions working smoothly.

Because the procurement process is becoming more automated, it is extremely important for purchasers and buyers to be computer literate, including knowing how to use word processing and spreadsheet software. Other important qualities include the ability to analyze technical data in suppliers' proposals, good communicating, negotiating, and math skills, knowledge of supply chain management, and the ability to perform financial analyses.

Persons who wish to become wholesale or retail buyers should be good at planning and decision making and have an interest in merchandising. Anticipating consumer preferences and ensuring that goods are in stock when they are needed require resourcefulness, good judgment, and self-confidence. Buyers must be able to make decisions quickly and take risks. Marketing skills and the ability to identify products that will sell are also very important. Employers often look for leadership ability because buyers spend a large portion of their time supervising assistant buyers and dealing with manufacturers' representatives and store executives.

Experienced buyers may advance by moving to a department that manages a larger volume or by becoming a merchandise manager. Others may go to work in sales for a manufacturer or wholesaler.

An experienced purchasing agent or buyer may become an assistant purchasing manager in charge of a group of purchasing professionals before advancing to purchasing manager, supply manager, or director of materials management. At the top levels, duties may overlap into other management functions such as production, planning, and marketing.

Regardless of industry, continuing education is essential for advancement. Many purchasers participate in seminars offered by professional societies and take college courses in purchasing. Although no national standard exists, professional certification is becoming increasingly important.

In private industry, the recognized marks of experience and professional competence are the designations Accredited Purchasing Practitioner (A.P.P.) and Certified Purchasing Manager (C.P.M.), conferred by the National Association of Purchasing Management, and Certified Purchasing Professional (CPP), conferred by the American Purchasing Society. In Federal, State, and local government, the indications of professional competence are the designations Certified Professional Public Buyer (CPPB) and Certified Public Purchasing Officer (CPPO), conferred by the National Institute of Governmental Purchasing.

As more materials purchasing is conducted on a long-term basis, both private and public purchasing professionals are specializing in the contractual aspects of purchasing. The National Contract Management Association confers the designations Simplified Acquisition Specialists (SAS), Certified Associate Contract Manager (CACM), and Certified Professional Contract Manager (CPCM). These designations primarily apply to contract managers in the Federal Government and its suppliers.

Most designations are awarded only after work-related experience and education requirements are met, and written or oral exams are completed successfully.

Job Outlook

Employment of purchasers and buyers is expected to increase more slowly than the average for all occupations through the year 2006.

Demand for these workers will not keep pace with the rising level of economic activity because the increasing use of computers has allowed much of the paperwork typically involved in ordering and procuring supplies to be eliminated, reducing the demand for lower-level buyers who traditionally performed these duties. Also, limited sourcing and long-term contracting have allowed companies to negotiate with fewer suppliers less frequently. Consequently, most job openings will result from the need to replace workers who transfer to other occupations or leave the labor force.

In retail trade, mergers and acquisitions have forced the consolidation of buying departments, eliminating jobs. In addition, larger retail stores are removing their buying departments from geographic markets and centralizing them at their headquarters, eliminating more jobs.

The increased use of credit cards by some employees to purchase supplies without using the services of the procurement or purchasing office, combined with the growing number of buys being made electronically, will restrict demand of purchasing agents within governments and many manufacturing firms.

Persons who have a bachelor's degree in business should have the best chance of obtaining a buyer job in wholesale or retail trade or within government. A bachelor's degree, combined with industry experience and/or knowledge of a technical field, will be an advantage for those interested in working for a manufacturing or industrial company. A master's degree in business or public administration is usually required by government agencies and larger companies for top-level purchasing positions.

Earnings

Median annual earnings of purchasers and buyers were $33,200 in 1996. The middle 50 percent earned between $23,300 and $45,900. The lowest 10 percent earned less than $18,400 while the top 10 percent earned more than $63,000. Merchandise managers and purchasing managers generally earned higher salaries than buyers or agents. As a general rule, those with the most education in their field have the highest incomes.

The average annual salaries for purchasing agents and contract specialists in the Federal Government in early 1997 were about $28,700 and $51,110, respectively.

Purchasers and buyers receive the same benefits package as their coworkers, frequently including vacations, sick leave, life and health insurance, and pension plans. In addition to standard benefits, retail buyers often earn cash bonuses based on their performance and may receive discounts on merchandise bought from the employer.

Related Occupations

Workers in other occupations who need a knowledge of marketing and the ability to assess demand are retail sales workers, sales managers, marketing and advertising managers, manufacturers' and wholesale sales representatives, insurance sales agents, services sales representatives, and procurement services, materials, and traffic managers.

Sources of Additional Information

Further information about education, training, and/or certification for purchasing careers is available from:

☛ American Purchasing Society, 30 W. Downer Pl., Aurora, IL 60506. Homepage: http://www.american-purchasing.com

☛ National Association of Purchasing Management, Customer Service, 2055 East Centennial Circle, P.O. Box 22160, Tempe, AZ 85285. Homepage: http://www.napm.org

☛ National Institute of Governmental Purchasing, Inc., 11800 Sunrise Valley Dr., Suite 1050, Reston, VA 20191-5302. Homepage: http://www.nigp.org

☛ National Contract Management Association, 1912 Woodford Rd., Vienna, VA 22182. Homepage: http://www.ncmahq.org

☛ Federal Acquisition Institute (MVI), Office of Acquisition Policy, General Services Administration, 18th & F Streets NW., Room 4019, Washington, DC 20405. Homepage: http://www.gsa.gov/staff/v/mvi/key.htm

General information on buying careers in retail establishments is available from:

☛ National Retail Federation, 325 7th St. NW., Suite 1000, Washington, DC 20004. Homepage: http://www.nrf.com

Restaurant and Food Service Managers

(D.O.T. 185.137; 187.161-010 and .167-026, -106, -126, -206, and -210; 319.137-014, -018, and -030)

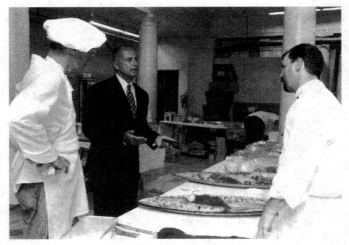

Restaurant and food service managers work long, irregular hours.

Significant Points

- While many jobs are filled by promoting experienced food and beverage preparation and service workers, job opportunities are expected to be best for those with bachelor's or associate degrees in restaurant and institutional food service management.

- Employment of wage and salary managers is expected to increase more rapidly than self-employed managers, as restaurants increasingly affiliate with national chains rather than being independently owned.

Nature of the Work

Food is consumed outside the home in a variety of settings. Eating places range from institutional cafeterias and fast food to elegant dining establishments. The cuisine, price, and setting where the meals are consumed vary, but managers of these dining facilities share many of the same responsibilities. Efficient and profitable operation of restaurants and institutional food service facilities requires managers and assistant managers to select and appropriately price menu items, use food and other supplies efficiently, and achieve consistent quality in food preparation and service. They also must attend to the various administrative aspects of the business, which includes recruiting, training, and supervising an adequate number of workers.

In most restaurants and institutional food service facilities, the manager is assisted by one or more assistant managers, depending on the size and operating hours of the establishment. In large establishments, as well as in many smaller ones, the management team consists of a *general manager*, one or more *assistant managers*, and an *executive chef*. The executive chef is responsible for the operation of the kitchen, while the assistant managers oversee service in the dining room and other areas of the operation. In smaller restaurants, the executive chef may be the general manager, and sometimes an owner. In fast-food restaurants and other food service facilities open for long hours, often 7 days a week, the manager is aided by several assistant managers, each of whom supervises a shift of workers. (For additional information, see the *Handbook* statements on general managers and top executives and chefs, cooks, and other kitchen workers.)

Many restaurants rarely change their menu, while others make frequent alterations. Institutional food service facilities and some restaurants offer a new menu every day. Managers or executive chefs select menu items, taking into account the likely number of customers, and the past popularity of dishes. Other issues taken into consideration when planning a menu include unserved food left over from prior meals that should not be wasted, the need for variety, and the availability of foods due to seasonality and other factors. Managers or executive chefs analyze the recipes of the dishes to determine food, labor, overhead costs and to assign prices to the various dishes. Menus must be developed far enough in advance that supplies can be ordered and received in time.

On a daily basis, managers estimate food consumption, place orders with suppliers, and schedule the delivery of fresh food and beverages. They receive and check the content of deliveries, evaluating the quality of meats, poultry, fish, fruits, vegetables, and baked goods. Managers meet with the sales representatives from restaurant suppliers to place orders replenishing stocks of tableware, linens, paper, cleaning supplies, cooking utensils, and furniture and fixtures. They also arrange for equipment maintenance and repairs, and for a variety of services such as waste removal and pest control.

Managers interview, hire, and, when necessary, fire employees. Many managers report difficulty in hiring experienced food and beverage preparation and service workers. Managers may attend career fairs or arrange for newspaper advertising to expand their pool of applicants. Managers explain the establishment's policies and practices to newly hired workers and oversee their training. Managers schedule the work hours of employees, making sure there are enough workers present to cover peak dining periods. If employees are unable to work, managers may have to fill in for them. Some managers regularly help with cooking, clearing of tables, or other tasks.

Restaurant and food service managers supervise the kitchen and the dining room. They oversee food preparation and cooking, examining the quality and portion sizes to ensure that dishes are prepared and garnished correctly and in a timely manner. They also investigate and resolve customers' complaints about food quality or service. They direct the cleaning of the kitchen and dining areas and the washing of tableware, kitchen utensils, and equipment to maintain company and government sanitation standards. They monitor the actions of their employees and patrons on a continual basis to ensure the health and safety standards and local liquor regulations are obeyed.

Managers have a variety of administrative responsibilities. In larger establishments, much of this work is delegated to a bookkeeper; in smaller establishments, including most fast-food restaurants, managers must keep records of the hours and wages of employees, prepare the payroll, and do paperwork to comply with licensing laws and reporting requirements of tax, wage and hour, unemployment compensation, and Social Security laws. They also maintain the records of supplies and equipment purchased, and ensure that accounts with suppliers are paid on a regular basis. In addition, some managers record the number, type, and cost of items sold to exclude dishes that are unpopular or less profitable.

Many managers are able to ease the burden of recordkeeping and paperwork through the use of computers. Point-of-service (POS) systems are used in many restaurants to increase employee productivity and allow managers to track the sales of specific menu items. Using a POS system, a server keys in the customer's order and the computer immediately sends the order to the kitchen so preparation can begin. The same system totals checks, acts as a cash register and credit card authorizer, and tracks daily sales. To minimize food costs and spoilage, many managers use inventory tracking software to compare the record of daily sales from the POS with a record of present inventory. In some establishments, when supplies needed for the preparation of popular menu items run low, additional inventory can be ordered directly from the supplier using the computer. Computers also allow restaurant and food service managers to more efficiently keep track of employee schedules and pay.

Managers are among the first to arrive and the last to leave. At the conclusion of each day, or sometimes each shift, managers tally the cash and charge receipts received and balance them against the record of sales. They are responsible for depositing the day's receipts at the bank, or securing it in a safe place. Managers are also responsible for locking up, checking that ovens, grills, and lights are off, and switching on alarm systems.

Working Conditions
Evenings and weekends are popular dining periods, making night and weekend work common. Many managers of institutional food service facilities work more conventional hours because factory and office cafeterias are generally open only on weekdays for breakfast and lunch. However, hours are unpredictable, as managers may have to fill in for absent workers on short notice. It is common for restaurant and food service managers to work 50 to 60 hours or more per week.

Managers often experience the pressure of simultaneously coordinating a wide range of activities. When problems occur, it is the responsibility of the manager to resolve them with minimal disruption to customers. The job can be hectic during peak dining hours, and dealing with irate customers or uncooperative employees can be stressful.

Employment
Restaurant and food service managers held about 493,000 jobs in 1996. Most managers were salaried workers, but many others were self-employed. Most worked in restaurants or for contract institutional food service companies, while a smaller number were employed by educational institutions, hospitals, nursing and personal care facilities, and civic, social, and fraternal organizations. Jobs are located throughout the country, with large cities and tourist areas providing more opportunities for more formal dining positions.

Training, Other Qualifications, and Advancement
Many restaurant and food service manager positions are filled by promoting experienced food and beverage preparation and service workers. Waiters, waitresses, chefs, and fast-food workers demonstrating potential for handling increased responsibility sometimes advance to assistant manager or management trainee jobs when openings occur. Executive chefs need extensive experience working as a chef, and general managers need experience working as assistant manager. However, most food service management companies and national or regional restaurant chains also recruit management trainees from 2- and 4-year college hospitality management programs. Food service and restaurant chains prefer to hire people with degrees in restaurant and institutional food service management, but they often hire graduates with degrees in other fields who have demonstrated interest and aptitude.

A bachelor's degree in restaurant and food service management provides a particularly strong preparation for a career in this occupation. In 1996, more than 160 colleges and universities offered 4-year programs in restaurant and hotel management or institutional food service management. For people not interested in pursing a 4-year degree, a good alternative are the more than 800 community and junior colleges, technical institutes, and other institutions that offer programs in these fields leading to an associate degree or other formal certification. Both 2- and 4-year programs provide instruction in subjects such as nutrition and food planning and preparation, as well as accounting, business law and management, and computer science. Some programs combine classroom and laboratory study with internships that provide on-the-job experience. In addition, many educational institutions offer culinary programs that provide food preparation training which can lead to a career as a cook or chef and provide a foundation for advancement to an executive chef position.

Most employers emphasize personal qualities. Restaurant and food service management can be demanding, so good health and stamina are important. Self-discipline, initiative, and leadership ability are essential. Managers must be able to solve problems and concentrate on details. They need good communication skills to deal with customers and suppliers, as well as to motivate and direct their subordinates. A neat and clean appearance is a must because they often are in close personal contact with the public.

Most restaurant chains and food service management companies have rigorous training programs for their management positions. Through a combination of classroom and on-the-job training, trainees receive instruction and gain work experience in all aspects of the operations of a restaurant or institutional food service facility—food preparation, nutrition, sanitation, security, company policies and procedures, personnel management, recordkeeping, and preparation of reports. Training on use of the restaurant's computer system is increasingly important as well. Often, supplies are ordered electronically and many restaurants use computers to track the popularity of menu items. Usually after 6 months or a year, trainees receive their first permanent assignment as an assistant manager.

A measure of professional achievement for restaurant and food service managers is to earn the designation of certified Foodservice Management Professional (FMP). Although not a requirement for employment or advancement in the occupation, voluntary certification provides recognition of professional competence, particularly for managers who acquired their skills largely on the job. The Educational Foundation of the National Restaurant Association awards the FMP designation to managers who achieve a qualifying score on a written examination, complete a series of courses that cover a range of food service management topics, and who meet standards of work experience in the field.

Willingness to relocate, usually to a big city, often is essential for advancement to positions with greater responsibility. Managers advance to larger establishments, or regional management positions within restaurant chains. Some eventually open their own eating and drinking establishments. Others transfer to hotel management positions, because their restaurant management experience provides a good background for food and beverage manager jobs at hotels and resorts.

Job Outlook
Job opportunities are expected to be best for those with a bachelor's or associate degree in restaurant and institutional food service management. Employment of restaurant and food service managers is expected to increase faster than the average for all occupations through the year 2006. In addition to employment growth, the need to replace managers who transfer to other occupations or stop working will create many job openings.

Projected employment growth varies by industry. Eating and drinking places will provide the most new jobs as the number of eating and drinking establishments increases and other industries continue to contract out their food services. Increases in population, personal incomes, and leisure time will continue to produce growth in the number of meals consumed outside the home. To meet the demand for prepared food, more restaurants will be built, and more managers will be employed to supervise them. In addition, the number of manager jobs will increase in eating and drinking places as schools, hospitals, and other businesses contract out more of their food services to institutional food service companies within the eating and drinking industry.

Employment of wage and salary managers in eating and drinking places is expected to increase more rapidly than self-employed managers. New restaurants are increasingly affiliated with national chains rather than being independently owned and operated. As this trend continues, fewer owners will manage restaurants themselves, and more restaurant managers will be employed to run the establishments.

Food service manager jobs are expected to increase in other industries, but growth will be slowed as contracting out becomes more common. Growth in the elderly population should result in more food service manager jobs in nursing homes and other health-care institutions, and residential-care and assisted-living facilities.

Employment in eating and drinking establishments is not very sensitive to changes in economic conditions, so restaurant and food service managers are rarely laid off during hard times. However, competition among restaurants is always intense, and many restaurants do not survive.

Earnings
Median earnings for restaurant and food service managers were about $460 a week in 1996. The middle 50 percent earned between about $320 and $630 a week. The lowest paid 10 percent earned $240 a week or less, while the highest paid 10 percent earned over $900 a week.

Earnings of restaurant and food service managers vary greatly according to their responsibilities and the type and size of establishment. Based on a survey conducted by the National Restaurant Association, the median base salary of restaurant managers was about $30,000 in 1995; managers of the largest restaurants and institutional food service facilities often had annual salaries in excess of $50,000. Besides a salary, most managers received an annual bonus or incentive payment based on their performance. In 1995, most bonuses ranged between $2,000 and $10,000.

Executive chefs had a median base salary of $38,000 in 1995. Annual bonus or incentive payments for most executive chefs averaged $3,000.

The median base salary of assistant managers was $23,000 in 1995, but ranged from $21,000 in fast-food restaurants to $27,000 in some of the largest restaurants and food service facilities. Annual bonus or incentive payments for most assistant managers ranged from $1,000 to $4,000.

Manager trainees had a median base salary of $21,000 in 1995, but earned $30,000 in some of the largest restaurants and food service facilities. Annual bonus or incentive payments of most trainees averaged $900.

In addition to typical benefits, most salaried restaurant and food service managers receive free meals and the opportunity for additional training depending on their length of service.

Related Occupations

Restaurant and food service managers direct the activities of businesses which provide a service to customers. Other managers in service-oriented businesses include hotel managers and assistants, health services administrators, retail store managers, and bank managers.

Sources of Additional Information

Information about job opportunities may be obtained from local employers and local offices of the State employment service.

Information about a career as a restaurant and food service manager, 2- and 4-year college programs in restaurant and food service management, and certification as a Foodservice Management Professional is available from:

☛ The Educational Foundation of the National Restaurant Association, Suite 1400, 250 South Wacker Dr., Chicago, IL 60606.

General information on hospitality careers may be obtained from:

☛ Council on Hotel, Restaurant, and Institutional Education, 1200 17th St. NW., Washington, DC 20036-3097.

For general career information and a directory of accredited private trade and technical schools offering programs in restaurant and food service management, write to:

☛ Accrediting Commission of Career Schools and Colleges of Technology, 2101 Wilson Blvd., Suite 302, Arlington, VA 22201.

Professional and Technical Occupations

Air Transportation Occupations

Aircraft Pilots

(D.O.T. 196, except .163 and .167-014 and 621.261-018)

Significant Points

- Competition is expected for jobs because aircraft pilots have very high earnings, especially those employed by airlines.

- Pilots usually start with smaller commuter and regional airlines to acquire the experience needed to qualify for higher paying jobs with national airlines.

- Most pilots have traditionally learned to fly in the military, but growing numbers are entering from civilian FAA certified pilot training schools.

Nature of the Work

Pilots are highly trained professionals who fly airplanes and helicopters to carry out a wide variety of tasks. Although most pilots transport passengers and cargo, others are involved in more unusual tasks, such as dusting crops, spreading seed for reforestation, testing aircraft, directing fire fighting efforts, tracking criminals, monitoring traffic, and rescuing and evacuating injured persons.

Except on small aircraft, two pilots usually make up the cockpit crew. Generally, the most experienced pilot, the *captain*, is in command and supervises all other crew members. The pilot and copilot split flying and other duties, such as communicating with air traffic controllers and monitoring the instruments. Some large aircraft still have a third pilot in the cockpit—the *flight engineer*—who assists the other pilots by monitoring and operating many of the instruments and systems, making minor inflight repairs, and watching for other aircraft. New technology can perform many flight tasks, however, and virtually all new aircraft now fly with only two pilots, who rely more heavily on computerized controls. Flight engineer jobs will be completely eliminated in the future.

Before departure, pilots plan their flights carefully. They thoroughly check their aircraft to make sure that the engines, controls, instruments, and other systems are functioning properly. They also make sure that baggage or cargo has been loaded correctly. They confer with flight dispatchers and aviation weather forecasters to find out about weather conditions enroute and at their destination. Based on this information, they choose a route, altitude, and speed that should provide the fastest, safest, and smoothest flight. When flying under instrument flight rules—procedures governing the operation of the aircraft when there is poor visibility—the pilot in command, or the company dispatcher, normally files an instrument flight plan with air traffic control so that the flight can be coordinated with other air traffic.

Takeoff and landing are the most difficult parts of the flight and require close coordination between the pilot and first officer. For example, as the plane accelerates for takeoff, the pilot concentrates on the runway while the first officer scans the instrument panel. To calculate the speed they must attain to become airborne, pilots consider the altitude of the airport, outside temperature, weight of the plane, and the speed and direction of the wind. The moment the plane reaches takeoff speed, the first officer informs the pilot, who then pulls back on the controls to raise the nose of the plane.

Unless the weather is bad, the actual flight is relatively easy. Airplane pilots, with the assistance of autopilot and the flight management computer, steer the plane along their planned route and are monitored by the air traffic control stations they pass along the way. They regularly scan the instrument panel to check their fuel supply, the condition of their engines, and the air-conditioning, hydraulic, and other systems. Pilots may request a change in altitude or route if circumstances dictate. For example, if the ride is rougher than expected, they may ask air traffic control if pilots flying at other altitudes have reported better conditions. If so, they may request a change. This procedure also may be used to find a stronger tailwind or a weaker headwind to save fuel and increase speed.

In contrast, helicopters are used for short trips at relatively low altitude, so pilots must be constantly on the lookout for trees, bridges, power lines, transmission towers, and other dangerous obstacles. Regardless of the type of aircraft, all pilots must monitor warning devices designed to help detect sudden shifts in wind conditions that can cause crashes.

If visibility is poor, pilots must rely completely on their instruments. Using the altimeter readings, they know how high above ground they are and whether or not they can fly safely over mountains and other obstacles. Special navigation radios give pilots precise information which, with the help of special maps, tell them their exact position. Other very sophisticated equipment provides directions to a point just above the end of a runway and enables pilots to land completely "blind."

Once on the ground, pilots must complete records on their flight for their organization and the Federal Aviation Administration (FAA).

The number of nonflying duties that pilots have depends on the employment setting. Airline pilots have the services of large support staffs, and consequently, perform few nonflying duties. Pilots employed by other organizations such as charter operators or businesses have many other duties. They may load the aircraft, handle all passenger luggage to ensure a balanced load, and supervise refueling; other nonflying responsibilities include keeping records, scheduling flights, arranging for major maintenance, and performing minor aircraft maintenance and repair work.

Some pilots are instructors. They teach their students the principles of flight in ground-school classes and demonstrate how to operate aircraft in dual-controlled planes and helicopters. A few specially trained pilots are "examiners" or "check pilots." They periodically fly with other pilots or pilot's license applicants to make sure that they are proficient.

Working Conditions

By law, airline pilots cannot fly more than 100 hours a month or more than 1,000 hours a year. Most airline pilots fly an average of 75 hours a month and work an additional 75 hours a month performing nonflying duties. Fifty percent of all pilots work more than 40 hours a week. Most spend a considerable amount of time away from home because the majority of flights involve overnight layovers. When pilots are away from home, the airlines provide hotel accommodations, transportation between the hotel and airport, and an allowance for meals and other expenses. Airlines operate flights at all hours of the day and night, so work schedules often are irregular. Flight assignments are based on seniority.

Those pilots not employed by the airlines often have irregular schedules as well; they may fly 30 hours one month and 90 hours the next. Because these pilots frequently have many nonflying responsibilities, they have much less free time than airline pilots. Except for business pilots, most do not remain away from home overnight. They may work odd hours. Flight instructors may have irregular and

Before departure, aircraft pilots plan their flights carefully.

seasonal work schedules depending on their students' available time and the weather and often give lessons at night or on weekends.

Airline pilots, especially those on international routes, often suffer jet lag—fatigue caused by many hours of flying through different time zones. The work of test pilots, who check the flight performance of new and experimental planes, may be dangerous. Pilots who are crop dusters may be exposed to toxic chemicals and seldom have the benefit of a regular landing strip. Helicopter pilots involved in police work may be subject to personal injury.

Although flying does not involve much physical effort, the mental stress of being responsible for a safe flight, no matter what the weather, can be tiring. Particularly during takeoff and landing, pilots must be alert and quick to react if something goes wrong.

Employment

Civilian pilots held about 110,000 jobs in 1996. Three-fifths worked for airlines. Many others worked as flight instructors at local airports or for large businesses that fly company cargo and executives in their own airplanes or helicopters. Some pilots flew small planes for air taxi companies, usually to or from lightly traveled airports not served by the airlines. Others worked for a variety of businesses performing tasks such as crop dusting, inspecting pipelines, or conducting sightseeing trips. Federal, State, and local governments also employed pilots. A few pilots were self-employed.

The employment of airplane pilots is not distributed like the population. Pilots are more concentrated in the States of California, Texas, Georgia, Washington, Nevada, Hawaii, and Alaska which have a higher amount of flying activity relative to their population.

Training, Other Qualifications, and Advancement

All pilots who are paid to transport passengers or cargo must have a commercial pilot's license with an instrument rating issued by the FAA. Helicopter pilots must hold a commercial pilot's certificate with a helicopter rating. To qualify for these licenses, applicants must be at least 18 years old and have at least 250 hours of flight experience. The time can be reduced through participation in certain flight school curricula approved by the FAA. They also must pass a strict physical examination to make sure that they are in good health and have 20/20 vision with or without glasses, good hearing, and no physical handicaps that could impair their performance. Applicants must pass a written test that includes questions on the principles of safe flight,

navigation techniques, and FAA regulations. They also must demonstrate their flying ability to FAA or designated examiners.

To fly in periods of low visibility, pilots must be rated by the FAA to fly by instruments. Pilots may qualify for this rating by having a total of 105 hours of flight experience, including 40 hours of experience in flying by instruments; they also must pass a written examination on procedures and FAA regulations covering instrument flying and demonstrate to an examiner their ability to fly by instruments.

Airline pilots must fulfill additional requirements. Those hired as flight engineers must pass FAA written and flight examinations to earn a flight engineer's license. Captains and first officers must have an airline transport pilot's license. Applicants for this license must be at least 23 years old and have a minimum of 1,500 hours of flying experience, including night and instrument flying. Usually they also have one or more advanced ratings, such as multi-engine aircraft or aircraft type ratings dependent upon the requirements of their particular flying jobs. Because pilots must be able to make quick decisions and accurate judgments under pressure, many airline companies reject applicants who do not pass required psychological and aptitude tests.

All licenses are valid as long as a pilot can pass the periodic physical examinations and tests of flying skills required by Government and company regulations.

The Armed Forces have always been an important source of trained pilots for civilian jobs. Military pilots gain valuable experience on jet aircraft and helicopters, and persons with this experience are generally preferred for civilian pilot jobs. This primarily reflects the extensive flying time military pilots receive. Persons without armed forces training also become pilots by attending flight schools. The FAA has certified about 600 civilian flying schools, including some colleges and universities that offer degree credit for pilot training. Over the projected period, Federal budget reductions are expected to reduce military pilot training. As a result, FAA certified schools will train a larger share of pilots than in the past.

Although some small airlines will hire high school graduates, most airlines require at least 2 years of college and prefer to hire college graduates; almost 90 percent of all pilots have completed some college. In fact, most entrants to this occupation have a college degree. If the number of college educated applicants continues to increases, employers may make a college degree an educational requirement.

Depending on the type of aircraft in use, new airline pilots start as first officers or flight engineers. Although some airlines favor applicants who already have a flight engineer's license, they may provide flight engineer training for those who have only the commercial license. Many pilots begin with smaller regional or commuter airlines where they obtain vital experience flying passengers on scheduled flights into busy airports in all weather conditions. These jobs are often a steppingstone to higher paying jobs with the bigger national airlines.

Initial training for pilots includes a week of company indoctrination, 3 to 6 weeks of ground school and simulator training, and 25 hours of initial operating experience, including a check-ride with an FAA aviation safety inspector. Once trained and "on the line" pilots are required to attend recurrent training and simulator checks periodically throughout their employment. Recurrent training is required twice a year.

Organizations other than airlines generally require less flying experience. However, a commercial pilot's license is a minimum requirement, and employers prefer applicants who have experience in the type of craft they will be flying. New employees usually start as first officers, or fly less sophisticated equipment. Test pilots often are required to have an engineering degree.

Advancement for all pilots generally is limited to other flying jobs. Many pilots start as flight instructors, building up their flying hours while they earn money teaching. As they become more experienced, these pilots occasionally fly charter planes or perhaps get jobs with small air transportation firms, such as air taxi companies.

Some advance to business flying jobs. A small number get flight engineer jobs with the airlines.

In the airlines, advancement usually depends on seniority provisions of union contracts. After 1 to 5 years, flight engineers advance according to seniority to first officer and, after 5 to 15 years, to captain. Seniority also determines which pilots get the more desirable routes. In a nonairline job, a first officer may advance to pilot and, in large companies, to chief pilot or director of aviation in charge of aircraft scheduling, maintenance, and flight procedures.

Job Outlook

Pilots are expected to face considerable competition for jobs through the year 2006 because the number of applicants for new positions is expected to exceed the number of job openings. Competition will be especially keen early in the projection period due to a temporary increase in the pool of qualified pilots seeking jobs. Mergers and bankruptcies during the recent restructuring of the industry caused a large number of airline pilots to lose their jobs. Also, Federal budget reductions resulted in many pilots leaving the Armed Forces. These and other qualified pilots seek jobs in this occupation because it offers very high earnings, glamour, prestige, and free or low cost travel benefits. As time passes, some pilots will fail to maintain their qualifications and the number of applicants competing for each opening should decline. Factors affecting demand, however, are not expected to ease that competition.

Relatively few jobs will be created from rising demand for pilots as employment is expected to increase about as fast as average for all occupations through the year 2006. The expected growth in airline passenger and cargo traffic will create a need for more airliners, pilots, and flight instructors. However, computerized flight management systems on new aircraft will eliminate the need for flight engineers on those planes, thus restricting the growth of pilot employment. In addition, the trend toward using larger planes in the airline industry will increase pilot productivity. Future business travel could also be adversely affected by advances in teleconferencing and facsimile mail and the elimination of many middle management positions in corporate downsizing. Employment of business pilots is expected to grow more slowly than in the past as more businesses opt to fly with regional and smaller airlines serving their area rather than buy and operate their own aircraft. On the other hand, helicopter pilots are expected to grow more rapidly as the demand expands for the type of services helicopters can offer.

Job openings resulting from the need to replace pilots who retire or leave the occupation traditionally have been very low. Aircraft pilots understandably have an extremely strong attachment to their occupation because it requires a substantial investment in specialized training that is not transferable to other fields and it generally offers very high earnings. However, many of the pilots who were hired in the late 1960's during the last major industry boom are approaching the age for mandatory retirement, so during the projected period, retirements of pilots are expected to increase and generate several thousand job openings each year.

Pilots who have logged the greatest number of flying hours in the more sophisticated equipment generally have the best prospects. This is the reason military pilots usually have an advantage over other applicants. Job seekers with the most FAA licenses will also have a competitive advantage. Opportunities for pilots in the regional commuter airlines and international service are expected to be more favorable as these segments are expected to grow faster than other segments of the industry.

Employment of pilots is sensitive to cyclical swings in the economy. During recessions, when a decline in the demand for air travel forces airlines to curtail the number of flights, airlines may temporarily furlough some pilots. Commercial and corporate flying, flight instruction, and testing of new aircraft also decline during recessions, adversely affecting pilots employed in those areas.

Earnings

Earnings of airline pilots are among the highest in the Nation. According to the Future Aviation Professionals of America (FAPA), the 1996 average starting salary for airline pilots ranged from about $15,000 at the smaller turboprop airlines to $26,2900 at the larger major airlines. Average earnings for experienced pilots with 6 years of experience ranged from $28,100 at the turboprop airlines to almost $76,8000 at the largest airlines. Some senior captains on the largest aircraft earned as much as $200,000 a year. Earnings depend on factors such as the type, size, and maximum speed of the plane, and the number of hours and miles flown. Extra pay may be given for night and international flights. Generally, pilots working outside the airlines earn lower salaries. Usually, pilots who fly jet aircraft earn higher salaries than non-jet pilots.

Data from the Future Aviation Professionals of America for 1996 show that commercial helicopter pilots averaged from $33,700 to $59,900 a year. Average pay for corporate helicopter pilots ranged from $47,900 to $72,500. Some helicopter pilots earned over $100,000 a year.

Airline pilots generally are eligible for life and health insurance plans financed by the airlines. They also receive retirement benefits and if they fail the FAA physical examination at some point in their careers, they get disability payments. In addition, pilots receive an expense allowance, or "per diem", for every hour they are away from home. Per diem can represent up to $500 each month in addition to their salary. Some airlines also provide allowances to pilots for purchasing and cleaning their uniforms. As an additional benefit, pilots and their immediate families usually are entitled to free or reduced fare transportation on their own and other airlines.

Most airline pilots are members of unions. Most airline pilots are members of the Airline Pilots Association, International, but those employed by one major airline are members of the Allied Pilots Association. Some flight engineers are members of the Flight Engineers' International Association.

Related Occupations

Although they are not in the cockpit, air traffic controllers and dispatchers also play an important role in making sure flights are safe and on schedule, and participate in many of the decisions pilots must make.

Sources of Additional Information

Information about job opportunities, salaries for a particular airline and the qualifications required may be obtained by writing to the personnel manager of the airline.

For information on airline pilots, contact:
☛ Airline Pilots Association, 1625 Massachusetts Ave. NW., Washington, DC 20036.
☛ Air Transport Association of America, 1301 Pennsylvania Ave. NW., Suite 1110, Washington, DC 20006.

For information on helicopter pilots, contact:
☛ Helicopter Association International, 1619 Duke St., Alexandria, VA 22314.

For a copy of *List of Certificated Pilot Schools*, write to:
☛ Superintendent of Documents, U.S. Government Printing Office, Washington, DC 20402.

For information about job opportunities in companies other than airlines, consult the classified section of aviation trade magazines and apply to companies that operate aircraft at local airports.

Air Traffic Controllers

(D.O.T. 193.162 except -022, .167-010)

Significant Points

- Nearly all air traffic controllers are employed and trained by the Federal Government.

- Keen competition is expected for the small number of job openings in this occupation.

Nature of the Work

The air traffic control system is a vast network of people and equipment that ensures the safe operation of commercial and private aircraft. Air traffic controllers coordinate the movement of air traffic to make certain that planes stay a safe distance apart. Their immediate concern is safety, but controllers also must direct planes efficiently to minimize delays. Some regulate airport traffic; others regulate flights between airports.

Although *airport tower or terminal controllers* watch over all planes traveling through the airport's airspace, their main responsibility is to organize the flow of aircraft in and out of the airport. Relying on radar and visual observation, they closely monitor each plane to ensure a safe distance between all aircraft and to guide pilots between the hangar or ramp and the end of the airport's airspace. In addition, controllers keep pilots informed about changes in weather conditions such as wind shear—a sudden change in the velocity or direction of the wind that can cause the pilot to lose control of the aircraft.

During arrival or departure, several controllers handle each plane. As a plane approaches an airport, the pilot radios ahead to inform the terminal of its presence. The controller in the radar room just beneath the control tower has a copy of the plane's flight plan and already has observed the plane on radar. If the way is clear, the controller directs the pilot to a runway; if the airport is busy, the plane is fitted into a traffic pattern with other aircraft waiting to land. As the plane nears the runway, the pilot is asked to contact the tower. There, another controller, who also is watching the plane on radar, monitors the aircraft the last mile or so to the runway, delaying any departures that would interfere with the plane's landing. Once the plane has landed, a ground controller in the tower directs it along the taxiways to its assigned gate. The ground controller usually works entirely by sight, but may use radar if visibility is very poor.

The procedure is reversed for departures. The ground controller directs the plane to the proper runway. The local controller then informs the pilot about conditions at the airport, such as the weather, speed and direction of wind, and visibility. The local controller also issues runway clearance for the pilot to take off. Once in the air, the plane is guided out of the airport's airspace by the departure controller.

After each plane departs, airport tower controllers notify *enroute controllers* who will next take charge. There are 21 enroute control centers located around the country, each employing 300 to 700 controllers, with more than 150 on duty during peak hours at the busier facilities. Airplanes generally fly along designated routes; each center is assigned a certain airspace containing many different routes. Enroute controllers work in teams of up to three members, depending on how heavy traffic is; each team is responsible for a section of the center's airspace. A team, for example, might be responsible for all planes that are between 30 to 100 miles north of an airport and flying at an altitude between 6,000 and 18,000 feet.

To prepare for planes about to enter the team's airspace, the radar associate controller organizes flight plans coming off a printer. If two planes are scheduled to enter the team's airspace at nearly the same time, location, and altitude, this controller may arrange with the preceding control unit for one plane to change its flight path. The previous unit may have been another team at the same or an adjacent center, or a departure controller at a neighboring terminal. As a plane approaches a team's airspace, the radar controller accepts responsibility for the plane from the previous controlling unit. The controller also delegates responsibility for the plane to the next controlling unit when the plane leaves the team's airspace.

The radar controller, who is the senior team member, observes the planes in the team's airspace on radar and communicates with the pilots when necessary. Radar controllers warn pilots about nearby planes, bad weather conditions, and other potential hazards. Two planes on a collision course will be directed around each other. If a pilot wants to change altitude in search of better flying conditions, the controller will check to determine that no other planes will be along the proposed path. As the flight progresses, the team responsible for the aircraft notifies the next team in charge. Through team coordination, the plane arrives safely at its destination.

Both airport tower and enroute controllers usually control several planes at a time and often have to make quick decisions about completely different activities. For example, a controller might direct a plane on its landing approach and at the same time provide pilots entering the airport's airspace with information about conditions at the airport. While instructing these pilots, the controller also would observe other planes in the vicinity, such as those in a holding pattern waiting for permission to land, to ensure that they remain well separated.

Currently, the Federal Aviation Administration (FAA) is in the midst of developing and implementing a new automated air traffic control system. As a result, more powerful computers will help controllers deal with the demands of increased air traffic. Some traditional air traffic controller tasks—like determining how far apart planes should be kept—will be done by computer. Present separation standards call for a 2,000 foot vertical spacing between two aircraft operating above 29,00 feet and flying the same ground track. With the aid of new technologies, the FAA will be able to reduce this vertical separation standard to 1,000 feet. Improved communication between computers on airplanes and those on the ground also is making the controller's job a little easier.

At present controllers sit at consoles with green-glowing screens that display radar images generated by a computer. In the future, controllers will work at a modern workstation computer that depicts air routes in full-color on a 20- by 20-inch screen. The controllers will select radio channels simply by touching on-screen buttons instead of turning dials or switching switches. However, the new automated air traffic control system will not be fully operational until after the year 2000.

The FAA is also moving toward implementing a system called "free flight" which would give pilots much more freedom in operating their aircraft. The change will require new concepts of shared responsibility between controllers and pilots. Air traffic controllers will still be central to the safe operation of the system, but their responsibilities will eventually shift from controlling to monitoring flights. At present, controllers assign routes, altitudes, and speeds. Under the new system, airlines and pilots would choose them. Controllers would intervene only to ensure that aircraft remained at safe distances from one another, to prevent congestion in terminal areas, to prevent entry into closed airspace, or to otherwise ensure safety. Today's practices often result in planes zigzagging from point to point along corridors rather than flying from city to city in a straight line. This results in lost time and fuel.

In addition to airport towers and enroute centers, air traffic controllers also work in flight service stations operated at over 100 locations. These *flight service specialists* provide pilots with information on the station's particular area, including terrain, preflight and inflight weather information, suggested routes, and other information important to the safety of a flight. Flight service station specialists

Air traffic controllers carefully monitor the movement of each plane.

help pilots in emergency situations and initiate and coordinate searches for missing or overdue aircraft. However, they are not involved in actively managing air traffic.

Working Conditions

Controllers work a basic 40-hour week; however, they may work additional hours for which they receive overtime pay or equal time off. Because most control towers and centers operate 24 hours a day, 7 days a week, controllers rotate night and weekend shifts.

During busy times, controllers must work rapidly and efficiently. This requires total concentration to keep track of several planes at the same time and make certain all pilots receive correct instructions. The mental stress of being responsible for the safety of several aircraft and their passengers can be exhausting for some persons.

Employment

Air traffic controllers held about 22,000 jobs in 1996. They were employed by the Federal Government at airports—in towers and flight service stations—and in enroute traffic control centers. The overwhelming majority worked for the FAA. About 17,500 controllers were actively working controlling air traffic; 3,600 worked at flight service stations and another 750 worked in administrative staff positions. Some professional controllers conduct research at the FAA's national experimental center in Atlantic City, New Jersey. Others serve as instructors at the FAA Academy in Oklahoma City, Oklahoma. A small number of civilian controllers worked for the Department of Defense. In addition to controllers employed by the Federal Government, some worked for private air traffic control companies providing service to non-FAA towers.

Training, Other Qualifications, and Advancement

Air traffic controller trainees are selected through the competitive Federal Civil Service system. Applicants must pass a written test that measures their ability to learn the controller's duties. Applicants with experience as a pilot, navigator, or military controller can improve their rating by scoring well on the occupational knowledge portion of the examination. Abstract reasoning and three-dimensional spatial visualization are among the aptitudes the exam measures. In addition, applicants generally must have 3 years of general work experience or 4 years of college, or a combination of both. Applicants also must survive a week screening at the FAA Academy in Oklahoma City which includes aptitude tests using computer simulators and physical and psychological examinations. Successful applicants receive drug screening tests. For airport tower and enroute center positions, applicants must be less than 31 years old. Those 31 years old and over are eligible for positions at flight service stations.

Controllers must be articulate, because directions to pilots must be given quickly and clearly. Intelligence and a good memory also are important because controllers constantly receive information that they must immediately grasp, interpret, and remember. Decisiveness is also required because controllers often have to make quick decisions. The ability to concentrate is crucial because controllers must make these decisions in the midst of noise and other distractions.

Trainees learn their craft through a combination of formal and on-the-job training. They receive 7 months of intensive training at the FAA academy, where they learn the fundamentals of the airway system, FAA regulations, controller equipment, aircraft performance characteristics, as well as more specialized tasks. To receive a job offer, trainees must successfully complete the training and pass a series of examinations, including a controller skills test that measures speed and accuracy in recognizing and correctly solving air traffic control problems. Based on aptitude and test scores, trainees are selected to work at either an enroute center or a tower.

After graduation, it takes several years of progressively more responsible work experience, interspersed with considerable classroom instruction and independent study, to become a fully qualified controller. This training includes instruction in the operation of the new, more automated air traffic control system—including the automated Microwave Landing System that enables pilots to receive instructions over automated data links—that is being installed in control sites across the country.

Controllers who fail to complete either the academy or the on-the-job portion of the training are usually dismissed. Controllers must pass a physical examination each year and a job performance examination twice each year. Failure to become certified in any position at a facility within a specified time may also result in dismissal. Controllers also are subject to drug screening as a condition of continuing employment.

At airports, new controllers begin by supplying pilots with basic flight data and airport information. They then advance to ground controller, then local controller, departure controller, and finally, arrival controller. At an enroute traffic control center, new controllers first deliver printed flight plans to teams, gradually advancing to radar associate controller and then radar controller.

Controllers can transfer to jobs at different locations or advance to supervisory positions, including management or staff jobs in air traffic control and top administrative jobs in the FAA. However, there are only limited opportunities for a controller to switch from a position in an enroute center to a tower.

Job Outlook

Competition for air traffic controller jobs is expected to remain extremely keen because the occupation attracts many more qualified applicants than the small number of job openings stemming from growth of the occupation and replacement needs. Turnover is very low; because of the relatively high pay and liberal retirement benefits, controllers have a very strong attachment to the occupation. Most of the current work force was hired as a result of the controller's strike during the 1980's, so the average age of current controllers is fairly young. Most controllers will not be eligible to retire until 2006 or later.

Employment of air traffic controllers is expected to show little or no change through the year 2006. Employment growth is not expected to keep pace with growth in the number of aircraft flying because of the implementation of a new air traffic control system over the next 10 years. This computerized system will assist the controller by automatically making many of the routine decisions. Automation will allow controllers to handle more traffic, thus increasing their productivity.

Air traffic controllers who continue to meet the proficiency and medical requirements enjoy more job security than most workers. The demand for air travel and the workloads of air traffic controllers decline during recessions, but controllers seldom are laid off.

Earnings

Air traffic controllers who started with the FAA in 1997 earned about $29,500,000 a year. Controllers at higher Federal pay grade levels earned 5 percent more than other Federal workers in an equivalent grade. A controller's pay is determined by both the worker's job responsibilities and the complexity of the particular facility. Earnings are higher at facilities where traffic patterns are more complex. In 1997, controllers averaged about $46,000 0 a year.

In 1997, the FAA is scheduled to implement a new more flexible pay classification. The system would feature 12 grade levels instead of the current 5 and pay would be based upon how many aircraft a controller works. The program will provide a 10 percent overall increase in base pay for about 2,200 personnel at seven of the FAA's busiest air traffic control facilities.

Depending on length of service, air traffic controllers receive 13 to 26 days of paid vacation and 13 days of paid sick leave each year, life insurance, and health benefits. In addition, controllers can retire at an earlier age and with fewer years of service than other Federal employees. Air traffic controllers are eligible to retire at age 50 with 20 years of service as an active air traffic controller or after 25 years of active service at any age. There is a mandatory retirement age of 56 for controllers who manage air traffic.

Related Occupations

Other occupations that involve the direction and control of traffic in air transportation are airline-radio operator and airplane dispatcher.

Sources of Additional Information
Information on obtaining a job as an air traffic controller with the Federal Government may be obtained from the Office of Personnel Management (OPM) through a telephone based system. Consult your telephone directory under U.S. Government for a local number or call 912-757-3000 (TDD 912-744-2299). That number is not toll free and charges may result. Information also is available from the OPM internet site: http://www.usajobs.opm.gov.

Engineers

Significant Points

- A bachelor's degree in engineering is almost always required for beginning engineering jobs. Good employment opportunities are expected for new graduates.

- Starting salaries are significantly higher than those of bachelor's degree graduates in other fields.

- Knowledge of technological advances must be acquired through continued study and education.

Nature of the Work
Engineers apply the theories and principles of science and mathematics to research and develop economical solutions to practical technical problems. Their work is the link between scientific discoveries and commercial applications. Engineers design products, the machinery to build those products, the factories in which those products are made, and the systems that ensure the quality of the product and efficiency of the workforce and manufacturing process. They design, plan, and supervise the construction of buildings, highways, and transit systems. They develop and implement improved ways to extract, process, and use raw materials, such as petroleum and natural gas. They develop new materials that both improve the performance of products, and make implementing advances in technology possible. They harness the power of the sun, the earth, atoms, and electricity for use in supplying the Nation's power needs, and create millions of products using power. Their knowledge is applied to improving many things, including the quality of health care, the safety of food products, and the efficient operation of financial systems.

Engineers consider many factors when developing a new product. For example, in developing an industrial robot, they determine precisely what function it needs to perform; design and test components; fit them together in an integrated plan; and evaluate the design's overall effectiveness, cost, reliability, and safety. This process applies to many different products, such as chemicals, computers, gas turbines, helicopters, and toys.

In addition to design and development, many engineers work in testing, production, or maintenance. They supervise production in factories, determine the causes of breakdowns, and test manufactured products to maintain quality. They also estimate the time and cost to complete projects. Some work in engineering management or in sales, where an engineering background enables them to discuss the technical aspects of a product and assist in planning its installation or use. (See the statements on engineering, science, and computer systems managers and manufacturers' and wholesale sales representatives elsewhere in the *Handbook*.)

Most engineers specialize in a particular area. More than 25 major specialties are recognized by professional societies, and within the major branches are numerous subdivisions. Structural, environmental, and transportation engineering, for example, are subdivisions of civil engineering. Engineers may also specialize in one industry, such as motor vehicles, or in one field of technology, such as jet engines or ceramic materials.

This section, which contains an overall discussion of engineering, is followed by separate sections on 10 engineering branches: Aerospace; chemical; civil; electrical and electronics; industrial; mechanical; metallurgical, ceramic, and materials; mining; nuclear; and petroleum engineering. Some branches of engineering not covered in detail here, but for which there are established college programs, include architectural engineering—the design of a building's internal support structure; biomedical engineering—the application of engineering to medical and physiological problems; environmental engineering—a growing discipline involved with identifying, solving, and alleviating environmental problems; and marine engineering—the design and installation of ship machinery and propulsion systems.

Engineers in each branch have a base of knowledge and training that can be applied in many fields. Electrical and electronics engineers, for example, work in the medical, computer, missile guidance, and power distribution fields. Because there are many separate problems to solve in a large engineering project, engineers in one field often work closely with specialists in other scientific, engineering, and business occupations.

Engineers use computers to produce and analyze designs; simulate and test how a machine, structure, or system operates; and generate blueprints for parts. Many engineers also use computers to monitor product quality and control process efficiency. They spend a great deal of time writing reports and consulting with other engineers, as complex projects often require an interdisciplinary team of engineers. Supervisory engineers are responsible for major components or entire projects.

Working Conditions
Most engineers work in office buildings, laboratories, or industrial plants. Others spend a considerable amount of time outdoors at construction sites, mines, and oil and gas exploration sites, where they monitor or direct operations or solve onsite problems. Some engineers travel extensively to plants or worksites.

Most engineers work a standard 40-hour week. At times, deadlines or design standards may bring extra pressure to a job. When this happens, engineers may work long hours and experience considerable stress.

Employment
In 1996, engineers held 1,382,000 jobs. Chart 1 shows the employment of the engineering disciplines covered in this statement. Forty-six percent of all wage and salary engineering jobs were located in manufacturing industries such as electrical and electronic equipment,

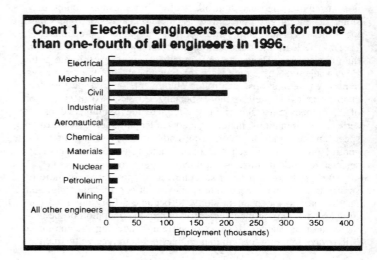

Chart 1. Electrical engineers accounted for more than one-fourth of all engineers in 1996.

industrial machinery, aircraft and parts, motor vehicles, chemicals, search and navigation equipment, fabricated metal products, and guided missiles and space vehicles. In 1996, 716,000 wage and salary jobs were in nonmanufacturing industries, primarily in engineering and architectural services, research and testing services, and business services, where firms designed construction projects or did other engineering work on a contract basis for organizations in other parts of the economy. Engineers also worked in the communications, utilities, and construction industries.

Federal, State, and local governments employed about 178,000 wage and salary engineers in 1996. Over half of these were in the Federal Government, mainly in the Departments of Defense, Transportation, Agriculture, Interior, and Energy, and in the National Aeronautics and Space Administration. Most engineers in State and local government agencies worked in highway and public works departments. In 1996, 46,000 engineers were self-employed, many as consultants.

Engineers are employed in every State, in small and large cities, and in rural areas. Some branches of engineering are concentrated in particular industries and geographic areas, as discussed in statements later in this chapter.

Training, Other Qualifications, and Advancement
A bachelor's degree in engineering is usually required for beginning engineering jobs. College graduates with a degree in a physical science or mathematics may occasionally qualify for some engineering jobs, especially in engineering specialties in high demand. Most engineering degrees are granted in electrical, mechanical, or civil engineering. However, engineers trained in one branch may work in related branches; for example, many aerospace engineers have training in mechanical engineering. This flexibility allows employers to meet staffing needs in new technologies and specialties in which engineers are in short supply. It also allows engineers to shift to fields with better employment prospects, or to ones that match their interests more closely.

In addition to the standard engineering degree, many colleges offer degrees in engineering technology, which are offered as either 2- or 4-year programs. These programs prepare students for practical design and production work rather than for jobs that require more theoretical, scientific and mathematical knowledge. Graduates of 4-year technology programs may get jobs similar to those obtained by graduates with a bachelor's degree in engineering. Some employers regard them as having skills between those of a technician and an engineer.

Graduate training is essential for engineering faculty positions, but is not required for the majority of entry-level engineering jobs. Many engineers obtain graduate degrees in engineering or business administration to learn new technology, broaden their education, and enhance promotion opportunities. Many high-level executives in government and industry began their careers as engineers.

About 320 colleges and universities offer bachelor's degree programs in engineering that are accredited by the Accreditation Board for Engineering and Technology (ABET), and about 250 colleges offer accredited bachelor's degree programs in engineering technology. ABET accreditation is based on an examination of an engineering program's faculty, curricular content, facilities, and admissions standards. Although most institutions offer programs in the major branches of engineering, only a few offer some of the smaller specialties. Also, programs of the same title may vary in content. For example, some emphasize industrial practices, preparing students for a job in industry, while others are more theoretical and are better for students preparing to take graduate work. Therefore, students should investigate curricula and check accreditations carefully before selecting a college. Admissions requirements for undergraduate engineering schools include a solid background in mathematics (algebra, geometry, trigonometry, and calculus), sciences (biology, chemistry, and physics), and courses in English, social studies, humanities, and computers.

Bachelor's degree programs in engineering are typically designed to last 4 years, but many students find that it takes between 4 and 5 years to complete their studies. In a typical 4-year college curriculum, the first 2 years are spent studying mathematics, basic sciences, introductory engineering, humanities, and social sciences. In the last 2 years, most courses are in engineering, usually with a concentration in one branch. For example, the last 2 years of an aerospace program might include courses such as fluid mechanics, heat transfer, applied aerodynamics, analytical mechanics, flight vehicle design, trajectory dynamics, and aerospace propulsion systems. Some programs offer a general engineering curriculum; students then specialize in graduate school or on the job.

Some engineering schools and 2-year colleges have agreements whereby the 2-year college provides the initial engineering education and the engineering school automatically admits students for their last 2 years. In addition, a few engineering schools have arrangements whereby a student spends 3 years in a liberal arts college studying pre-engineering subjects and 2 years in the engineering school, and receives a bachelor's degree from each. Some colleges and universities offer 5-year master's degree programs. Some 5- or even 6-year cooperative plans combine classroom study and practical work, permitting students to gain valuable experience and finance part of their education.

All 50 States and the District of Columbia require registration for engineers whose work may affect life, health, or property, or who offer their services to the public. Registration generally requires a degree from an ABET-accredited engineering program, 4 years of relevant work experience, and passing a State examination. Some States will not register people with degrees in engineering technology. Engineers may be registered in several states.

Engineers should be creative, inquisitive, analytical, and detail-oriented. They should be able to work as part of a team and be able to communicate well, both orally and in writing.

Beginning engineering graduates usually work under the supervision of experienced engineers and, in larger companies, may also receive formal classroom or seminar-type training. As they gain knowledge and experience, they are assigned more difficult projects with greater independence to develop designs, solve problems, and make decisions. Engineers may advance to become technical specialists or to supervise a staff or team of engineers and technicians. Some eventually become engineering managers or enter other managerial, management support, or sales jobs. (See the statements under executive, administrative, and managerial occupations; under sales occupations; and on computer scientists, computer engineers, and systems analysts elsewhere in the *Handbook*.)

Job Outlook
Employment opportunities in engineering are expected to be good through the year 2006 because employment is expected to increase about as fast as the average for all occupations while the number of degrees granted in engineering may not increase as rapidly as employment.

Competitive pressures and advancing technology will force companies to improve and update product designs more frequently, and to work to optimize their manufacturing processes. Employers will rely on engineers to further increase productivity as they increase investment in plant and equipment to expand output of goods and services. New computer systems have improved the design process, enabling engineers to produce and analyze design variations much more rapidly; these systems are increasingly used to monitor and control processes. Despite this widespread application, computer technology is not expected to limit employment opportunities. Finally, more engineers will be needed to improve or build new roads, bridges, water and pollution control systems, and other public facilities.

Many of the jobs in engineering are related to developing technologies used in national defense. Because defense expenditures, particularly expenditures for the purchase of aircraft, missiles, and other weapons systems, are expected to continue at low levels (compared with the cold war years), employment growth and job outlook for engineers working for defense contractors may not be strong through 2006.

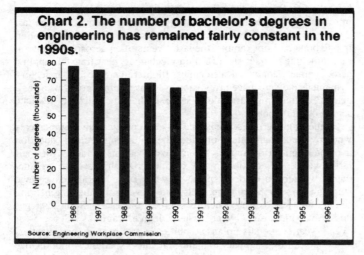

Chart 2. The number of bachelor's degrees in engineering has remained fairly constant in the 1990s.

Source: Engineering Workplace Commission

The number of bachelor's degrees awarded in engineering began declining in 1987, as shown in chart 2, and has stayed at about the same level in the 1990's. Although it is difficult to project engineering enrollments, the total number of students enrolled in colleges is expected to increase over the projection period, and it is likely that engineering enrollments and number of degrees awarded will follow. However, some engineering schools have restricted enrollments, especially in defense-related fields such as aerospace engineering, to accommodate the reduced opportunities in defense-related industries.

Only a relatively small proportion of engineers leave the profession each year. Despite this, most job openings will arise from replacement needs. A greater proportion of replacement openings is created by engineers who transfer to management, sales, or other professional specialty occupations than by those who leave the labor force.

Most industries are less likely to lay off engineers than other workers. Many engineers work on long-term research and development projects or in other activities which may continue even during recessions. In industries such as electronics and aerospace, however, large cutbacks in defense procurement expenditures, government research and development funds, and the increasing trend of contracting out engineering work to engineering services firms have resulted in significant layoffs for engineers.

It is important for engineers, like those working in other technical occupations, to continue their education throughout their careers because much of their value to their employer depends on their knowledge of the latest technology. Although the pace of technological change varies by engineering specialty and industry, advances in technology have affected every engineering discipline significantly. Engineers in high-technology areas, such as advanced electronics, may find that technical knowledge can become obsolete rapidly. Even those who continue their education are vulnerable if the particular technology or product in which they have specialized becomes obsolete. By keeping current in their field, engineers are able to deliver the best solutions and greatest value to their employers. Engineers who have not kept current in their field may find themselves passed over for promotions or vulnerable to layoffs, should they occur. On the other hand, it is often these high-technology areas that offer the greatest challenges, the most interesting work, and the highest salaries. Therefore, the choice of engineering specialty and employer involves an assessment not only of the potential rewards but also of the risk of technological obsolescence.

Earnings

Starting salaries for engineers with the bachelor's degree are significantly higher than starting salaries of bachelor's degree graduates in other fields. According to the National Association of Colleges and Employers, engineering graduates with a bachelor's degree averaged about $38,500 a year in private industry in 1997; those with a master's degree and no experience, $45,400 a year; and those with a

Ph.D., $59,200. Starting salaries for those with the bachelor's degree vary by branch, as shown in the following tabulation.

Aerospace	$37,957
Chemical	42,817
Civil	33,119
Electrical	39,513
Industrial	38,026
Mechanical	38,113
Metallurgical	38,550
Mining	36,724
Nuclear	37,194
Petroleum	43,674

A survey of workplaces in 160 metropolitan areas reported that beginning engineers had median annual earnings of about $34,400 in 1995, with the middle half earning between about $30,900 and $38,116 a year. Experienced midlevel engineers with no supervisory responsibilities had median annual earnings of about $59,100, with the middle half earning between about $54,000 and $65,000 a year. Median annual earnings for engineers at senior managerial levels were about $99,200. Median annual earnings for these and other levels of engineers are shown in the following tabulation.

Engineer I	$34,400
Engineer II	41,000
Engineer III	48,500
Engineer IV	59,100
Engineer V	71,400
Engineer VI	84,200
Engineer VII	99,200
Engineer VIII	117,000

The median annual salary for all engineers who worked full time was about $49,200 in 1996. Those with a bachelor's degree had median annual earnings of $49,800; master's degree, $56,700; and PhD, $64,700. Median annual salaries for some engineering specialties were:

Aerospace	$57,000
Chemical	52,600
Civil	46,000
Electrical	51,700
Industrial	43,700
Mechanical	49,700
Engineers, nec	49,700

The average annual salary for engineers in the Federal Government in nonsupervisory, supervisory, and managerial positions was $61,950 in 1997.

Related Occupations

Engineers apply the principles of physical science and mathematics in their work. Other workers who use scientific and mathematical principles include engineering, science, and computer systems managers; physical, life, and computer scientists; mathematicians; engineering and science technicians; and architects.

Sources of Additional Information

High school students interested in obtaining general information on a variety of engineering disciplines should contact the Junior Engineering Technical Society by sending a self-addressed business-size envelope with 6 first-class stamps affixed, to:
☛ JETS-Guidance, at 1420 King St., Suite 405, Alexandria, VA 22314-2794.
Homepage: http://www.asee.org/jets

High school students interested in obtaining information on ABET accredited engineering programs should contact:
☛ The Accreditation Board for Engineering and Technology, Inc., at 111 Market Place, Suite 1050, Baltimore, MD 21202-4012.
Homepage: http://www.abet.ba.md.us

Non-high school students and those wanting more detailed information should contact societies representing the individual branches of engineering. Each can provide information about careers in the particular branch.

Aeronautical and Aerospace Engineering, send $3 to:

☞ American Institute of Aeronautics and Astronautics, Inc., Suite 500, 1801 Alexander Bell Drive, Reston, VA 20191-4344.

Chemical Engineering

☞ American Institute of Chemical Engineers, 345 East 47th St., New York, NY 10017-2395.

☞ American Chemical Society, Department of Career Services, 1155 16th St. NW., Washington, DC 20036.

Civil Engineering

☞ American Society of Civil Engineers, 1801 Alexander Bell Drive, Reston, VA 20191-4400.

Electrical and Electronics Engineering

☞ Institute of Electrical and Electronics Engineers, 1828 L St. NW., Suite 1202, Washington, DC 20036.

Industrial Engineering

☞ Institute of Industrial Engineers, Inc., 25 Technology Park/Atlanta, Norcross, GA 30092. Homepage: http://www.iienet.org

Mechanical Engineering

☞ The American Society of Mechanical Engineers, 345 E. 47th St., New York, NY 10017.

☞ American Society of Heating, Refrigerating, and Air-Conditioning Engineers, Inc., 1791 Tullie Circle NE., Atlanta, GA 30329. Homepage://www.ashrae.org

Metallurgical, Ceramic, and Materials Engineering

☞ The Minerals, Metals, & Materials Society, 420 Commonwealth Dr., Warrendale, PA 15086-7514. Homepage: http://www.tms.org

☞ ASM International, Student Outreach Program, Materials Park, OH 44073-0002.

Mining Engineering

☞ The Society for Mining, Metallurgy, and Exploration, Inc., P.O. Box 625002, Littleton, CO 80162-5002.

Nuclear Engineering

☞ American Nuclear Society, 555 North Kensington Ave., LaGrange Park, IL 60525.

Petroleum Engineering

☞ Society of Petroleum Engineers, P.O. Box 833836, Richardson, TX 75083-3836.

Aerospace Engineers

(D.O.T. 002.061 and .167)

Nature of the Work

Aerospace engineers design, develop, and test missile, spacecraft, and commercial and military aircraft, and supervise manufacturing of these products. They develop new technologies for use in commercial aviation, defense systems, and space exploration, often specializing in areas like structural design, guidance, navigation and control, instrumentation and communication, or production methods. They also may specialize in a particular type of aerospace product, such as commercial transports, helicopters, spacecraft, or rockets. Aerospace engineers may be experts in aerodynamics, propulsion, thermodynamics, structures, celestial mechanics, acoustics, or guidance and control systems.

Employment

Aerospace engineers held about 53,000 jobs in 1996. More than two-fifths worked in the aircraft and parts and guided missile and space vehicle manufacturing industries. Federal Government agencies, primarily the Department of Defense and the National Aeronautics and Space Administration, provided more than 1 out of 7 jobs. Business services, engineering and architectural services, research and testing services, and electrical and electronics manufacturing firms accounted for most of the remaining jobs.

Prospective aerospace engineers are likely to face competition because the number of job opportunities is expected to be fewer than the pool of graduates.

California, Washington, Texas, and Florida—States with large aerospace manufacturers—have the most aerospace engineers.

Job Outlook

Those seeking employment as aerospace engineers are likely to face competition. The decline in Defense Department expenditures for military aircraft, missiles, and other aerospace systems has caused mergers and acquisitions among defense contractors. Federal Government funding for research and development of new systems has also declined. Growth in the civilian sector is projected to increase due to orders from domestic and foreign airlines that need more aircraft to accommodate increasing passenger traffic, and to replace the present fleet of airliners with quieter and more fuel-efficient aircraft. Consequently, employment of aerospace engineers is expected to grow more slowly than the average through the year 2006. Future growth of employment in this field could be moderate because a higher proportion of engineers in aerospace manufacturing may come from the materials, mechanical, or electrical engineering fields. Most job openings will result from the need to replace aerospace engineers who transfer to other occupations or leave the labor force.

(See introductory section of this chapter for information on training requirements, earnings, and sources of additional information.)

Chemical Engineers

(D.O.T. 008.061)

Nature of the Work

Chemical engineers apply the principles of chemistry and engineering to solve problems involving the production or use of chemicals. They design equipment and develop processes for large scale chemical manufacturing, plan and test methods of manufacturing the products and treating the by-products, and supervise production. Chemical engineers also work in industries other than chemical manufacturing such as electronics or photographic equipment. Because the knowledge and duties of chemical engineers cut across many fields, they apply principles of chemistry, physics, mathematics, and mechanical and electrical engineering in their work. They frequently specialize in a particular operation such as oxidation or polymerization. Others specialize in a particular area such as pollution control or the production of specific products such as automotive plastics or chlorine bleach. Chemical engineers are increasingly using computer technology to optimize all phases of production, and therefore need to understand how to apply computer skills to process analysis, computer control systems, and statistical quality control.

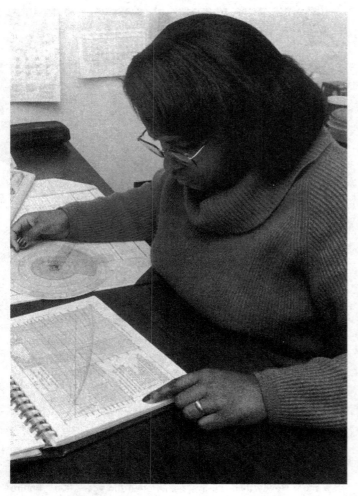

Two-thirds of chemical engineers are employed in the chemical, petroleum refining, paper, and other manufacturing industries.

Employment

Chemical engineers held over 49,000 jobs in 1996. Manufacturing industries employed two-thirds of all employees, primarily in the chemical, petroleum refining, paper, and related industries. Most of the rest worked for engineering services, research and testing services, or consulting firms that design chemical plants. Still others worked on a contract basis, for government agencies or as independent consultants.

Job Outlook

Although employment in the chemical manufacturing industry is projected to grow slowly through 2006, employment of chemical engineers should increase about as fast as the average for all occupations as chemical companies research and develop new chemicals and more efficient processes to increase output of existing chemicals. Much of the projected growth in employment, however, will be in nonmanufacturing industries, especially service industries. Chemical engineering graduates may face competition for jobs as the number of openings is projected to be lower than the number of graduates. Areas relating to the production of specialty chemicals, pharmaceuticals, and plastics materials may provide better opportunities than other portions of the chemical industry.

(See introductory part of this section for information on training requirements, earnings, and sources of additional information.)

Civil Engineers

(D.O.T. 005.061 except-042, .167-014 and -018; and 019.167-018)

Nature of the Work

Civil engineers work in the oldest branch of engineering, designing and supervising the construction of roads, buildings, airports, tunnels, bridges, and water supply and sewage systems. Major specialties within civil engineering are structural, water resources, environmental, construction, transportation, and geotechnical engineering.

Many civil engineers hold supervisory or administrative positions, ranging from supervisor of a construction site to city engineer. Others may work in design, construction, research, and teaching.

Employment

Civil engineers held about 196,000 jobs in 1996. Almost 47 percent were in firms providing engineering consulting services, primarily developing designs for new construction projects. Another 39 percent of the jobs were in Federal, State, and local government agencies. The construction industry, public utilities, transportation, and manufacturing industries accounted for most of the rest. About 13,000 civil engineers were self-employed, many as consultants.

Civil engineers usually work near major industrial and commercial centers, often at construction sites. Some projects are situated in remote areas or in foreign countries. In some jobs, civil engineers move from place to place to work on different projects.

Job Outlook

Employment of civil engineers is expected to increase about as fast as the average for all occupations through the year 2006. Graduates of civil engineering programs should find favorable opportunities. Spurred by general population growth and an expanding economy, more civil engineers will be needed to design and construct higher capacity transportation, water supply, and pollution control systems; large buildings and building complexes; and to repair or replace existing roads, bridges, and other public structures. Most job openings, however, will result from the need to replace civil engineers who transfer to other occupations or leave the labor force.

Because construction and related industries—including those providing design services—employ many civil engineers, employment opportunities will vary by geographic area and may decrease during economic slowdowns, when construction is often curtailed.

(See introductory part of this section for information on training requirements, earnings, and sources of additional information.)

Civil engineer makes a presentation on proposed highway routes.

Electrical and Electronics Engineers

(D.O.T. 003.061, .167 except -034 and -070, and .187)

Nature of the Work

Electrical and electronics engineers design, develop, test, and supervise the manufacture of electrical and electronic equipment. Electrical equipment includes power generating and transmission equipment used by electric utilities, and electric motors, machinery controls, and lighting and wiring in buildings, automobiles, and aircraft. Electronic equipment includes radar, computer hardware, and communications and video equipment.

The specialties of electrical and electronics engineers include several major areas—such as power generation, transmission, and distribution; communications; computer electronics; and electrical equipment manufacturing—or a subdivision of these areas—industrial robot control systems or aviation electronics, for example. Electrical and electronics engineers design new products, write performance requirements, and develop maintenance schedules. They also test equipment, solve operating problems, and estimate the time and cost of engineering projects. (See the statement on computer scientists, computer engineers, and systems analysts elsewhere in the *Handbook.*)

Employment

Electrical and electronics engineers held about 367,000 jobs in 1996, making it the largest branch of engineering. Most jobs were in engineering and business consulting firms, manufacturers of electrical and electronic equipment, industrial machinery manufacturers, professional and scientific instruments, and government agencies. Communications and utilities firms, manufacturers of aircraft and guided missiles, and computer and data processing services firms accounted for most of the remaining jobs.

Job Outlook

Job openings resulting from job growth and the need to replace electrical engineers who transfer to other occupations or leave the labor force should be sufficient to absorb the number of new graduates and other entrants, making for good employment opportunities through 2006. Employment of electrical and electronics engineers is expected to increase faster than the average for all occupations.

Electrical and electronics engineers comprise the largest branch of engineering.

The need for electronics manufacturers to invest heavily in research and development to remain competitive, will provide openings for graduates who have learned the latest technologies. Increased demand by businesses and government for improved computers and communications equipment is expected to account for much of the projected employment growth. Consumer demand for electrical and electronic goods should create additional jobs. Job growth is expected to be fastest in non-manufacturing industries, however, because firms are increasingly getting electronic engineering expertise from consulting and service companies.

Engineers who fail to keep up with the rapid changes in technology in some specialties risk technological obsolescence, which makes them more susceptible to layoffs or, at a minimum, more likely to be passed over for advancement. Opportunities for electronics engineers in defense-related firms may improve as the trend shifts to upgrading existing aircraft and weapons systems with improved navigation, control, guidance, and targeting systems.

(See introductory part of this section for information on training requirements, earnings, and sources of additional information.)

Industrial Engineers

(D.O.T. 005.167-026; 012.061 -018, .067, .167 except -022, -026, -034, -058, and -062, and .187)

Nature of the Work

Industrial engineers determine the most effective ways for an organization to use the basic factors of production—people, machines, materials, information, and energy—to make or process a product or produce a service. They are the bridge between management goals and operational performance. They are more concerned with increasing productivity through the management of people, methods of business organization, and technology than are engineers in other specialties, who generally work more with products or processes.

To solve organizational, production, and related problems most efficiently, industrial engineers carefully study the product and its requirements, use mathematical methods such as operations research to meet those requirements, and design manufacturing and information systems. They develop management control systems to aid in financial planning and cost analysis, design production planning and control systems to coordinate activities and control product quality, and design or improve systems for the physical distribution of goods and services. Industrial engineers determine which plant location has the best combination of raw materials availability, transportation, and costs. They also develop wage and salary administration systems and job evaluation programs. Many industrial engineers move into management positions because the work is closely related.

Employment

Industrial engineers held about 115,000 jobs in 1996. About 73 percent of these jobs were in manufacturing industries. Because their skills can be used in almost any type of organization, industrial engineers are more widely distributed among manufacturing industries than other engineers.

Their skills can be readily applied outside manufacturing as well. Some work in engineering and management services, utilities, and business services; others work for government agencies or as independent consultants.

Job Outlook

Employment of industrial engineers is expected to grow about as fast as the average for all occupations through the year 2006, making for favorable opportunities. Industrial growth, more complex business operations, and the greater use of automation in factories and in offices underlie the projected employment growth. Because the main function of an industrial engineer is to make a higher quality product as efficiently as possible, their services should be in demand in the

Industrial engineer conducts a time study in an apparel plant.

manufacturing sector as firms seek to reduce costs and increase productivity through scientific management and safety engineering. Most job openings, however, will result from the need to replace industrial engineers who transfer to other occupations or leave the labor force.

(See introductory part of this section for information on training requirements, earnings, and sources of additional information.)

Mechanical Engineers

(D.O.T. 007.061, .161-022, -034, and -038, and .267-010)

Nature of the Work

Mechanical engineers plan and design tools, engines, machines, and other mechanical equipment. They design and develop power-producing machines such as internal combustion engines, steam and gas turbines, and jet and rocket engines. They also design and develop power-using machines such as refrigeration and air-conditioning equipment, robots, machine tools, materials handling systems, and industrial production equipment.

The work of mechanical engineers varies by industry and function. Specialties include, among others, applied mechanics, design, energy systems, pressure vessels and piping, and heating, refrigeration, and air conditioning systems. Mechanical engineers design tools needed by other engineers for their work.

Mechanical engineering is the broadest engineering discipline, extending across many interdependent specialties. Mechanical engi-

Graduates of mechanical engineering programs should have favorable job opportunities.

neers may work in production operations, maintenance, or technical sales; many are administrators or managers.

Employment

Mechanical engineers held about 228,000 jobs in 1996. Almost 6 out of 10 jobs were in manufacturing—of these, most were in the machinery, transportation equipment, electrical equipment, instruments, and fabricated metal products industries. Business and engineering consulting services and Federal government agencies provided most of the remaining jobs.

Job Outlook

Employment of mechanical engineers is expected to grow about as fast as the average for all occupations through the year 2006. Graduates of mechanical engineering programs should have favorable job opportunities. Most of the expected job openings, resulting from both employment growth and the need to replace those who will leave the occupation, should be sufficient to absorb the supply of new graduates and other entrants.

Although overall employment in manufacturing is expected to decline, employment of mechanical engineers in manufacturing should increase as the demand for improved machinery and machine tools grows and industrial machinery and processes become increasingly complex. Employment of mechanical engineers in business and engineering services firms is expected to grow faster than average as other industries in the economy increasingly contract out to these firms to solve engineering problems.

(See introductory part of this section for information on training requirements, earnings, and sources of additional information.)

Metallurgical, Ceramic, and Materials Engineers

(D.O.T. 006.061; 011.061; and 019.061-014)

Nature of the Work

Metallurgical, ceramic, and materials engineers develop new types of metal alloys, ceramics, plastics, composites, and other materials, and adapt existing materials to new uses. Engineers manipulate the atomic and molecular structure of materials in controlled manufacturing environments, selecting materials with desirable mechanical, electrical, magnetic, chemical, and heat-transfer properties which meet special performance requirements. Examples are graphite golf club shafts that are light but stiff, ceramic tiles on the space shuttle that protect it from burning up during reentry into the atmosphere, and the alloy turbine blades in a jet engine.

Most metallurgical engineers work in one of the three main branches of metallurgy—extractive or chemical, physical, and mechanical or process. Extractive metallurgists are concerned with removing metals from ores and refining and alloying them to obtain useful metal. Physical metallurgists study the nature, structure, and physical properties of metals and their alloys, and methods of processing them into final products. Mechanical metallurgists develop and improve metalworking processes such as casting, forging, rolling, and drawing.

Ceramic engineers develop new ceramic materials and methods for making ceramic materials into useful products. Ceramics include all nonmetallic, inorganic materials which require high temperatures in their processing. Ceramic engineers work on products as diverse as glassware, semiconductors, automobile and aircraft engine components, fiber-optic phone lines, tile, and electric power line insulators.

Materials engineers evaluate technical requirements and material specifications to develop materials that can be used, for example, to reduce the weight, but not the strength of an object. Materials engineers also test and evaluate materials and develop new materials, such as the composite materials now being used in "stealth" aircraft.

Materials engineer measures the expansion characteristics of a material.

Employment

Metallurgical, ceramic, and materials engineers held about 18,000 jobs in 1996. One-fourth worked in metal-producing and processing industries. They also worked in aircraft manufacturing; research and testing services; Federal Government agencies; industries that manufacture machinery and electrical equipment; stone, clay, and glass products manufacturing; and engineering consulting firms.

Job Outlook

Individuals seeking employment as metallurgical, ceramic, and materials engineers should find good opportunities as the number of anticipated job openings should be sufficient to absorb the low number of new graduates relative to those in other engineering disciplines. Employment of metallurgical, ceramic, and materials engineers is expected to increase more slowly than the average for all occupations through the year 2006.

Many of the industries in which these engineers are concentrated, such as stone, clay, and glass products; primary metals; fabricated metal products; and transportation equipment industries, are expected to experience little if any employment growth through the year 2006. Anticipated employment growth in service industries, such as research and testing services and engineering and architectural services, however, should provide significant job openings as these firms are hired to develop improved materials for their industrial customers.

(See introductory part of this section for information on training requirements, earnings, and sources of additional information.)

Mining Engineers

(D.O.T. 010.061 except -018)

Nature of the Work

Mining engineers find, extract, and prepare coal, metals, and minerals for use by manufacturing industries and utilities. They design open pit and underground mines, supervise the construction of mine shafts and tunnels in underground operations, and devise methods for transporting minerals to processing plants. Mining engineers are responsible for the safe, economical, and environmentally sound operation of mines. Some mining engineers work with geologists and metallurgical engineers to locate and appraise new ore deposits. Others develop new mining equipment or direct mineral processing operations to separate minerals from the dirt, rock, and other materials with which they are mixed. Mining engineers frequently specialize in the mining of one mineral or metal, such as coal or gold. With increased emphasis on protecting the environment, many mining engineers work to solve problems related to land reclamation and water and air pollution.

Employment

Mining engineers held about 3,100 jobs in 1996. While two-thirds worked in the mining industry, other mining engineers worked in government agencies, manufacturing industries, or engineering consulting firms.

Mining engineers are usually employed at the location of mineral deposits, often near small communities, and sometimes outside the United States. Those in research and development, management, consulting, or sales, however, are often located in metropolitan areas.

Job Outlook

The mining industry traditionally has few openings. In fact, employment in the mining industry and of mining engineers is expected to decline through the year 2006. Therefore, graduates in mining engineering will face competition despite their low number.

Opportunities in the mining industry are closely related to the price of the metals and minerals they produce. If the price of these products is high, it makes it worthwhile for a mining company to invest the millions of dollars in material moving equipment and ore processing technology necessary to operate a mine. Although prices

Mining engineers design open pit as well as underground mines.

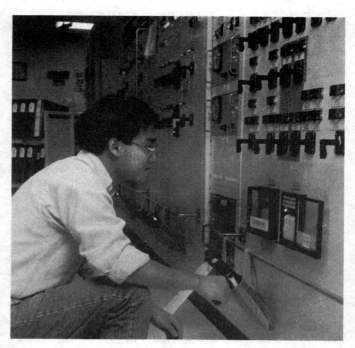

Nuclear engineer checks a control panel at a nuclear plant.

for mined products have been unstable, the increasing activity of auto manufacturing and expanded development and repair of the Nation's roadways will help provide demand for metals and minerals.

The long-term business environment for mining is generally perceived to be favorable, but because a mine takes years of research, planning, and development to become fully operational, it may not contribute to expansion in employment opportunities for mining engineers. Also, because mining operations around the world recruit graduates of U.S. mining engineering programs, opportunities may be better worldwide than within the United States.

(See introductory part of this section for information on training requirements, earnings, and sources of additional information.)

Nuclear Engineers

(D.O.T. 005.061-042; 015.061, .067, .137, and .167)

Nature of the Work

Nuclear engineers research and develop the processes, instruments, and systems used to derive benefits from nuclear energy and radiation. They design, develop, monitor, and operate nuclear power plants used to generate electricity and power Navy ships. They may work on the nuclear fuel cycle—the production, handling, and use of nuclear fuel and the safe disposal of waste produced by nuclear energy—or on fusion energy. Some specialize in the development of nuclear power sources for spacecraft; others develop industrial and medical uses for radioactive materials, such as equipment to diagnose and treat medical problems.

Employment

Nuclear engineers held about 14,000 jobs in 1996. About 20 percent each were in utilities, the Federal Government, and engineering consulting firms. Another 12 percent were in research and testing services. More than half of all federally employed nuclear engineers were civilian employees of the Navy, and most of the rest worked for the Nuclear Regulatory Commission, the Department of Energy, or the Tennessee Valley Authority. Most nonfederally employed nuclear engineers worked for public utilities or engineering consulting companies. Some worked for defense manufacturers or manufacturers of nuclear power equipment.

Job Outlook

Employment of nuclear engineers is expected to grow more slowly than the average for all occupations through the year 2006. Because this is a small occupation, it will translate into few growth-related opportunities. Most openings will arise as nuclear engineers transfer to other occupations or leave the labor force. However, good opportunities for nuclear engineers should still exist since the small number of nuclear engineering graduates is likely to be in balance with the number of job openings.

Due to public concerns over the cost and safety of nuclear power, there are only a small number of nuclear power plants under construction in the United States, and it is possible some older plants will shut down. Nevertheless, nuclear engineers will be needed to operate existing plants. In addition, nuclear engineers will be needed to work in defense-related areas, to develop nuclear medical technology, and to improve and enforce waste management and safety standards.

(See introductory part of this section for information on training requirements, earnings, and sources of additional information.)

Petroleum Engineers

(D.O.T. 010.061 except -014 and -026, .161-010, and .167-010 and -014)

Nature of the Work

Petroleum engineers search the world for underground reservoirs containing oil or natural gas. When one is discovered, petroleum engineers work with geologists and other specialists to understand the geologic formation and properties of the rock containing the reservoir, determine the drilling methods to be used, and monitor drilling and production operations. They design equipment and processes to achieve the maximum profitable recovery of oil and gas, sometimes using computer models to simulate reservoir performance using different recovery techniques.

Because only a small proportion of the oil and gas in a reservoir will flow out under natural forces, petroleum engineers develop and use various enhanced recovery methods. These include injecting water, chemicals, gases, or steam into an oil reservoir to force more of the oil out, and computer-controlled drilling or fracturing to connect a larger area of a reservoir to a single well. Since even the best

Petroleum engineer oversees drilling problems.

techniques in use today recover only a portion of the oil and gas in a reservoir, petroleum engineers research and develop technology and methods to increase this proportion and lower the cost of drilling and production operations.

Employment

Petroleum engineers held over 13,000 jobs in 1996, mostly in the petroleum industry and closely allied fields. Employers include major oil companies and hundreds of smaller, independent oil exploration, pro-duction, and service companies. Engineering consulting firms, government agencies, oil field services, and equipment suppliers also employ petroleum engineers. Others work as independent consultants.

Most petroleum engineers work where oil and gas are found. Large numbers are employed in Texas, Oklahoma, Louisiana, Colorado, and California, including offshore sites. Many American petroleum engineers also work overseas in oil-producing countries. Because petroleum engineers specialize in the discovery and production of oil and gas, relatively few are employed in the refining, transportation, and retail sectors of the oil and gas industry.

Job Outlook

Employment of petroleum engineers is expected to decline through the year 2006 unless oil and gas prices unexpectedly rise enough to encourage increased exploration for oil in this country. In spite of this, employment opportunities for petroleum engineers should be favorable because the number of degrees granted in petroleum engineering has traditionally been low. Therefore, new graduates are not likely to significantly exceed the number of job openings arising as petroleum engineers transfer to other occupations or leave the labor force. Also, petroleum engineers work around the globe, and many employers seek U.S.-trained petroleum engineers for jobs in other countries.

The price of oil has a major effect on the level of employment opportunities for petroleum engineers in the United States. A high price of oil and gas makes it profitable for oil exploration and production firms to seek oil and gas reservoirs, and they will hire petroleum engineers to do so. With low oil prices, however, it is cheaper to purchase needed oil from other countries, such as Saudi Arabia, which have vast oil reserves. Also, the best exploration opportunities are in other countries because many of the most likely petroleum-producing areas in the United States have already been explored. However, the implementation of new technologies that expand drilling possibilities and improve the performance of reservoirs in the U.S. and the Gulf of Mexico may create new opportunities.

(See introductory part of this section for information on training requirements, earnings, and sources of additional information.)

Engineering Technicians

(D.O.T. 002.261-014, .262-010; 003.161, .261-010, .362; 005.261; 006.261; 007.161-026 and -030, .167-010, .181 and .267-014; 008.261; 010.261-010 and -026; 011.261-010, -014, -018, and -022, .281, .361; 012.261-014, .267; 013.161; 017.261-010; 017.684; 019.161-014, .261-018, -022, -026, and -034, .267, .281; 194.381, .382-010; 199.261-014; 726.261-010 and -014; 806.281-014; 761.281-014; 828.261-018; and 869.261-026)

Significant Points

- About 43 percent of all engineering technicians employed in 1996 were electrical and electronic engineering technicians.

- Most employers prefer those with an associate's degree in engineering technology.

Nature of the Work

Engineering technicians use the principles and theories of science, engineering, and mathematics to solve technical problems in research and development, manufacturing, sales, construction, inspection, and maintenance. Their work is more limited in scope and more practically oriented than that of scientists and engineers. Many engineering technicians assist engineers and scientists, especially in research and development. Others work in quality control—inspecting products and processes, conducting tests, or collecting data. In manufacturing, they may assist in product design and development, process design, or production.

Engineering technicians who work in research and development, build or set up equipment, prepare and conduct experiments, calculate or record the results, and help engineers in other ways. Some make prototype versions of newly designed equipment. They also assist in design work, often using computer-aided design equipment.

Engineering technicians who work in manufacturing support the work of engineers. They may prepare specifications for materials, devise and run tests to ensure product quality, or study ways to improve manufacturing efficiency. They may also supervise production workers to make sure they follow prescribed procedures.

Most engineering technicians specialize in certain areas, learning skills and working in the same disciplines as engineers. Occupational titles, therefore, tend to follow the same structure as engineers. *Chemical engineering technicians* are usually employed in industries producing pharmaceuticals, chemicals, and petroleum products, among others. They work in laboratories as well as processing plants. They help develop new chemical products and processes, test processing equipment and instrumentation, monitor quality, and operate chemical manufacturing facilities.

Civil engineering technicians help civil engineers plan and build highways, buildings, bridges, dams, wastewater treatment systems, and other structures, and perform related surveys and studies. Some inspect water and wastewater treatment systems to ensure pollution control requirements are met. Others estimate construction costs and specify materials to be used. Some may even prepare drawings or perform land surveying duties. (Separate statements on cost estimators, drafters, and surveyors can be found elsewhere in the *Handbook*.)

Electrical and *electronics engineering technicians* help design, develop, test, and manufacture electrical and electronic equipment such as radios, radar, sonar, television, industrial and medical measuring or control devices, navigational equipment, and computers. They may work in product evaluation and testing, using measuring and diagnostic devices to adjust, test, and repair equipment. Workers who only repair electrical and electronic equipment are discussed in several other statements on mechanics, installers, and repairers found elsewhere in the *Handbook*. Many of these repairers are often referred to as electronics technicians.

Electrical and electronic engineering technology is also applied to a wide variety of systems such as communications and process controls. *Electromechanical engineering technicians* combine fundamental principles of mechanical engineering technology with knowledge of electrical and electronic circuits to design, develop, test, and manufacture electrical and computer controlled mechanical systems.

Industrial engineering technicians study the efficient use of personnel, materials, and machines in factories, stores, repair shops, and offices. They prepare layouts of machinery and equipment, plan the flow of work, make statistical studies, and analyze production costs.

Mechanical engineering technicians help engineers design, develop, test, and manufacture industrial machinery, mechanical parts, and other equipment. They may assist in the testing of a guided missile, or in the planning and design of an electric power generation plant. They make sketches and rough layouts, record data, make computations, analyze results, and write reports. When planning production, mechanical engineering technicians prepare layouts and drawings of the assembly process and of parts to be manufactured. They estimate labor costs, equipment life, and plant space. Some test and inspect machines and equipment in manufacturing departments or work with engineers to eliminate production problems.

Working Conditions
Most engineering technicians work 40 hours a week in a laboratory, office, manufacturing or industrial plant, or on a construction site. Some may be exposed to hazards from equipment, chemicals, or toxic materials.

Engineering technicians use computers to perform calculations and record the results of tests and experiments.

Employment
Engineering technicians held about 698,000 jobs in 1996. Almost 298,000 of these were electrical and electronics engineering technicians. About 33 of all engineering technicians worked in durable goods manufacturing, mainly in the electrical and electronic machinery and equipment, industrial machinery and equipment, instruments and related products, and transportation equipment industries. Another 25 percent worked in service industries, mostly in engineering or business services companies that do engineering work on contract for government, manufacturing, or other organizations.

In 1996, the Federal Government employed about 42,000 engineering technicians. The major employer was the Department of Defense, followed by the Departments of Transportation, Agriculture, and the Interior, the Tennessee Valley Authority, and the National Aeronautics and Space Administration. State governments employed about 37,000 and local governments about 27,000.

Training, Other Qualifications, and Advancement
Although it is possible to qualify for some engineering technician jobs with no formal training, most employers prefer to hire someone with at least a 2-year degree in engineering technology. Training is available at technical institutes, junior and community colleges, extension divisions of colleges and universities, public and private vocational-technical schools, and through some technical training programs in the Armed Forces. Persons with college courses in science, engineering, and mathematics may also qualify for some positions but may need additional specialized training and experience.

Prospective engineering technicians should take as many high school science and math courses as possible to prepare for postsecondary programs in engineering technology. Most 2-year associate programs accredited by the Accreditation Board for Engineering and Technology (ABET) require, at a minimum, college algebra and trigonometry, and one or two basic science courses. More math or science may be required depending on the area of specialty. The type of technical courses required also varies depending on the area of specialty. For example, prospective mechanical engineering technicians may take courses in fluid mechanics, thermodynamics, and mechanical design; electrical engineering technicians may take classes in electric circuits, microprocessors, and digital electronics; and those preparing to work in environmental engineering technology need courses in environmental regulations and safe handling of hazardous materials. Because many engineering technicians may become involved in design work, creativity is desirable. Good communication skills and the ability to work well with others is also important since they are often part of a team of engineers and other technicians.

Engineering technicians usually begin by performing routine duties under the close supervision of an experienced technician, technologist, engineer, or scientist. As they gain experience, they are given more difficult assignments with only general supervision. Some engineering technicians eventually become supervisors.

Many publicly and privately operated schools provide technical training; the type and quality of programs vary considerably. Therefore, prospective students should be careful in selecting a program. They should contact prospective employers regarding their preferences and ask schools to provide information about the kinds of jobs obtained by graduates, instructional facilities and equipment, and faculty qualifications. Graduates of ABET-accredited programs are generally recognized to have achieved an acceptable level of competence in the mathematics, science, and technical courses required for this occupation.

Technical institutes offer intensive technical training, but less theory and general education than junior and community colleges. Many offer 2-year associate degree programs, and are similar to or part of a community college or State university system. Other technical institutes are run by private, often for-profit, organizations, sometimes called proprietary schools. Their programs vary considerably in length and types of courses offered, although some are 2-year associate degree programs.

Junior and community colleges offer curriculums similar to those in technical institutes but may include more theory and liberal arts. Often there may be little or no difference between technical institute and community college programs, as both offer associate degrees. After completing the 2-year program, some graduates get jobs as engineering technicians, while others continue their education at 4-year colleges. However, there is a difference between an associate degree in pre-engineering and one in engineering technology. Students who enroll in a 2-year pre-engineering program may find it very difficult to find work as an engineering technician should they decide not to enter a 4-year engineering program, because pre-engineering programs usually focus less on hands-on applications and more on academic preparatory work. Conversely, graduates of 2-year engineering technology programs may not receive credit for many of the courses they have taken if they choose to transfer to a 4-year engineering program. Colleges with these 4-year programs usually do not offer engineering technician training, but college courses in science, engineering, and mathematics are useful for obtaining a job as an engineering technician. Many 4-year colleges offer bachelor's degrees in engineering technology, but graduates of these programs are often hired to work as technologists or applied engineers, not technicians.

Area vocational-technical schools include postsecondary public institutions that serve local students and emphasize training needed by local employers. Most require a high school diploma or its equivalent for admission.

Other training in technical areas may be obtained in the Armed Forces. Many military technical training programs are highly regarded by employers. However, skills acquired in military programs often are narrowly focused, so they are not necessarily transferrable to civilian industry, which often requires broader training. Therefore, some additional training may be needed, depending on the acquired skills and the kind of job.

The National Institute for Certification in Engineering Technologies (NICET) has established a voluntary certification program for engineering technicians. Although engineering technicians are not generally required to be certified by employers, certification may provide job seekers a competitive advantage. Certification is available at various levels, each level combining a written examination in one of over 30 specialty fields with a certain amount of job related experience.

Job Outlook

Overall, employment of engineering technicians is expected to increase as fast as the average for all occupations through the year 2006. However, the growing availability and use of advanced technologies, such as computer-aided design and drafting and computer simulation, will continue to increase productivity and impact employment growth. Opportunities should be best for individuals who have completed a 2-year program in engineering technology. As technology becomes more sophisticated, employers continue to look for technicians who are skilled in new technology and require a minimum of additional job training. In addition to growth, many job openings will be created to replace technicians who retire or leave the labor force for other reasons.

As production of technical products continues to grow, competitive pressures will force companies to improve and update manufacturing facilities and product designs more rapidly than in the past. Like engineers, employment of engineering technicians is influenced by local and national economic conditions. As a result, the employment outlook varies with area of specialization and industry. Employment of some types of engineering technicians, such as civil engineering and aeronautical engineering technicians, experience greater cyclical fluctuations than others. Technicians whose jobs are defense-related may experience fewer opportunities because of recent defense cutbacks. On the other hand, employment of the largest specialty group—electrical and electronics engineering technicians—is expected to grow slightly faster than the overall rate for all engineering technicians. Increasing demand for more sophisticated electrical and electronic products, as well as the expansion of these products and systems into all areas of industry and manufacturing processes, will contribute to stronger employment growth in this specialty area.

Earnings

According to a survey of workplaces in 160 metropolitan areas, engineering technicians at the most junior level had median earnings of about $20,200 in 1995, with the middle half earning between $17,700 and $22,800 a year. Engineering technicians with more experience and the ability to work with little supervision had median earnings of about $32,700, and those in supervisory or most senior level positions earned about $54,800.

In the Federal Government, engineering technicians started at about $15,500, $17,400, or $19,500 in early 1997, depending on their education and experience. Beginning salaries were slightly higher in selected areas of the country where the prevailing local pay level was higher. The average annual salary for engineering technicians in supervisory, nonsupervisory, and management positions in the Federal Government in 1997 was $42,710; for electronics technicians, $46,040; and for industrial engineering technicians, $43,510.

Related Occupations

Engineering technicians apply scientific and engineering principles usually acquired in postsecondary programs below the baccalaureate level. Similar occupations include science technicians, drafters, surveyors, broadcast technicians, and health technologists and technicians.

Sources of Additional Information

For a small fee, information on a variety of engineering technician and technology careers is available from:

☛ The Junior Engineering Technical Society (JETS), at 1420 King St., Suite 405, Alexandria, VA 22314-2794. Enclose $3.50 to obtain a full package of guidance materials and information. Brochures are available free on JETS homepage: http://www.asee.org/jets

Information on ABET-accredited engineering technology programs is available from:

☛ Accreditation Board for Engineering and Technology, Inc. 111 Market Place, Suite 1050, Baltimore, MD 21202. Homepage: htp://www.abet.ba.md.us

Architects, Surveyors, and Drafters

Architects

(D.O.T. 001.061-010 and .167-010)

Significant Points

• Nearly 30 percent—over three times the proportion for all professionals—are self-employed, practicing as partners in architecture firms or on their own.

• Licensure requirements include a professional degree in architecture, a period of practical training or internship, and passage of all sections of the Architect Registration Examination.

• Prospective architects may face competition, especially for jobs in the most prestigious firms; those who complete at least one summer internship while in school and know computer-aided design and drafting technology may have a distinct advantage in the job market.

Nature of the Work

Architects design buildings and other structures. The design of a building involves far more than its appearance. Buildings must also be functional, safe, and economical, and must suit the needs of the people who use them. Architects take all these things into consideration when they design buildings and other structures.

Architects provide a wide variety of professional services to individuals and organizations planning a construction project. They may be involved in all phases of development, from the initial discussion of general ideas with the client through the entire life of the facility. Their duties require a number of skills—design, engineering, managerial, communication, and supervisory.

The architect and client first discuss the purposes, requirements, and budget of a project. In some cases, architects provide various predesign services—conducting feasibility and environmental impact studies, selecting a site, or specifying the requirements the design must meet. For example, they may determine space requirements by researching the number and type of potential users of a building. The architect then prepares drawings and a report presenting ideas for the client to review.

After the initial proposals are discussed and accepted, architects develop final construction plans. These plans show the building's appearance and details for its construction. Accompanying these are drawings of the structural system; air-conditioning, heating, and ventilating systems; electrical systems; plumbing; and possibly site and landscape plans. They also specify the building materials and, in some cases, the interior furnishings. In developing designs, architects follow building codes, zoning laws, fire regulations, and other ordinances, such as those requiring easy access by disabled persons. Throughout the planning stage, they make necessary changes. Although they have traditionally used pencil and paper to produce design and construction drawings, architects are increasingly turning to computer-aided design and drafting (CADD) technology for these important tasks.

Architects may also assist the client in obtaining construction bids, selecting a contractor, and negotiating the construction contract. As construction proceeds, they may visit the building site to ensure the contractor is following the design, adhering to the schedule, using the specified materials, and meeting quality work standards. The job is not complete until all construction is finished, required tests are made, and construction costs are paid. Sometimes, architects also provide postconstruction services, such as facilities management. They advise on energy efficiency measures, evaluate how well the building design adapts to the needs of occupants, and make necessary improvements.

Architects design a wide variety of buildings, such as office and apartment buildings, schools, churches, factories, hospitals, houses, and airport terminals. They also design multibuilding complexes such as urban centers, college campuses, industrial parks, and entire communities. In addition to designing buildings, they may advise on the selection of building sites, prepare cost analysis and land-use studies, and do long-range planning for land development.

Architects sometimes specialize in one phase of work. Some specialize in the design of one type of building—for example, hospitals, schools, or housing. Others focus on planning and predesign services or construction management, and do little design work. They often work with engineers, urban planners, interior designers, landscape architects, and others.

During a training period leading up to licensure as architects, entry-level workers are called intern-architects. This training period gives them practical work experience while they prepare for the Architect Registration Examination (ARE). Typical duties may include preparing construction drawings on CADD, or assisting in the design of one part of a project.

Working Conditions

Architects generally work in a comfortable environment. Most of their time is spent in offices advising clients, developing reports and drawings, and working with other architects and engineers. However, they often visit construction sites to review the progress of projects.

Architects may occasionally be under great stress, working nights and weekends to meet deadlines. In 1996, about 2 out of 5 architects worked more than 40 hours a week, in contrast to 1 in 4 workers in all occupations combined.

Employment

Architects held about 94,000 jobs in 1996. The majority of jobs were in architecture firms—most of which employ fewer than 5 workers. A few worked for builders, real estate developers, and for government agencies responsible for housing, planning, or community development, such as the U.S. Departments of Defense and Interior, and the General Services Administration. Nearly 3 in 10 architects is self-employed, practicing as partners in architecture firms or on their own.

Training, Other Qualifications, and Advancement

All States and the District of Columbia require individuals to be licensed (registered) before they may call themselves architects or contract to provide architectural services. Many architecture school graduates work in the field even though they are not licensed. However, a licensed architect is required to take legal responsibility for all work. Licensure requirements include a professional degree in architecture, a period of practical training or internship, and passage of all sections of the ARE.

In many States, the professional degree in architecture must be from one of the 105 schools of architecture with programs accredited by the National Architectural Accrediting Board (NAAB). However, State architectural registration boards set their own standards, so graduation from a non NAAB-accredited program may meet the education requirement for licensure in some States. There are several types of professional degrees in architecture. The majority of all architecture degrees are from 5-year Bachelor of Architecture programs, intended for students entering from high school or with no previous architecture training. Some schools offer a 2-year Master of Architecture program for students with a preprofessional undergraduate degree in architecture or a related area, or a 3- or 4-year Master of Architecture program for students with a degree in another discipline.

Architects must be licensed before they may contract to provide architectural services.

In addition, there are many combinations and variations of these degree programs.

The choice of degree type depends upon each individual's preference and educational background. Prospective architecture students should carefully consider the available options before committing to a program. For example, although the 5-year Bachelor of Architecture program offers the fastest route to the professional degree, courses are specialized and, if the student does not complete the program, moving to a nonarchitecture program may be difficult. A typical program includes courses in architectural history and theory, building design, professional practice, math, physical sciences, and liberal arts. Central to most architecture programs is the design studio, where students put into practice the skills and concepts learned in the classroom. During the final semester of many programs, students devote their studio time to creating an architectural project from beginning to end, culminating in a 3-dimensional model of their design.

Many architecture schools also offer graduate education for those who already have a bachelor's or master's degree in architecture or other areas. Although graduate education beyond the professional degree is not required for practicing architects, it is normally required for research, teaching, and certain specialties.

Architects must be able to visually communicate their ideas to clients. Artistic and drawing ability is very helpful in doing this, but not essential. More important is a visual orientation and the ability to conceptualize and understand spatial relationships. Good communication skills, the ability to work independently or as part of a team, and creativity are important qualities for anyone interested in becoming an architect. Computer literacy is also required as most firms use computers for specifications writing, 2- and 3-dimensional drafting, and financial management. A knowledge of computer-aided design and drafting (CADD) is helpful and will become more important as architecture firms continue to adopt this technology.

All State architectural registration boards require a training period before candidates may sit for the ARE and become licensed. Many States have adopted the training standards established by the Intern Development Program, a branch of the American Institute of Architects and the National Council of Architectural Registration Boards. These standards stipulate broad and diversified training under the supervision of a licensed architect over a 3-year period. New graduates usually begin as intern-architects in architecture firms, where they assist in preparing architectural documents or drawings. They may also do research on building codes and materials, or write specifications for building materials, installation criteria, the quality of finishes, and other related details. Graduates with degrees in architecture also enter related fields such as graphic, interior, or industrial design; urban planning; real estate development; civil engineering; or construction management. In such cases, an architectural license, and thus the internship period, is not required.

After completing the internship period, intern-architects are eligible to sit for the ARE. The examination tests candidates on a broad body of architectural knowledge, and is given in sections throughout the year. Candidates who pass the ARE and meet all standards established by their State board are licensed to practice in that State.

After becoming licensed and gaining experience, architects take on increasingly responsible duties, eventually managing entire projects. In large firms, architects may advance to supervisory or managerial positions. Some architects become partners in established firms; others set up their own practice.

Several States require continuing education to maintain licensure, and many more States are expected to adopt mandatory continuing education. Requirements vary by State, but usually involve the completion of a certain number of credits every year or two through seminars, workshops, formal university classes, conferences, self-study courses, or other sources.

Job Outlook

Despite projected average employment growth coupled with job openings stemming from the need to replace architects who retire or leave the labor force for other reasons, prospective architects may face competition, especially if the number of architecture degrees awarded remain at, or above, current levels. Many individuals are attracted to this occupation, and the number of applicants often exceeds the number of available jobs, especially in the most prestigious firms. Prospective architects who complete at least one summer internship—either paid or unpaid—while in school and know CADD technology, may have a distinct advantage in getting an intern-architect position after graduation.

Because construction—particularly office and retail—is sensitive to cyclical changes in the economy, architects will face particularly strong competition for jobs or clients during recessions, and layoffs may occur. Those involved in the design of institutional buildings such as schools, hospitals, nursing homes, and correctional facilities, will be less affected by fluctuations in the economy.

Even in times of overall good job opportunities, however, there may be areas of the country with poor opportunities. Architects who are licensed to practice in one State must meet the licensing requirements of other States before practicing elsewhere. These requirements are becoming more standardized, however, facilitating movement to other States.

Employment of architects is strongly tied to the level of local construction, particularly nonresidential structures such as office buildings, shopping centers, schools, and healthcare facilities. The boom in nonresidential construction during the 1980s resulted in high vacancy rates and a slowdown in this type of construction during the first half of the 1990s. Although this sector of the construction industry is beginning to recover, slower labor force growth, rapid increases in telecommuting and flexiplace work, and the earlier overbuilding are expected to continue to suppress demand for new office space between 1996 and 2006. Nevertheless, employment of architects is expected to grow about as fast as the average for all occupations during this period.

As the stock of buildings ages, demand for remodeling and repair work should grow considerably. The needed renovation and rehabilitation of old buildings, particularly in urban areas where space for new buildings is becoming limited, is expected to provide many job opportunities for architects. In addition, demographic trends and changes in health care delivery are influencing the demand for certain institutional structures, and should also provide more jobs for architects in the future. For example, increases in the school-age population will result in new school construction and additions to existing schools. And, growth is expected in the number of adult care centers, assisted-living facilities, and community health clinics, all of which are preferable, less costly alternatives to hospitals and nursing homes.

Earnings

According to The American Institute of Architects, the median compensation, including bonuses, for intern-architects in architecture firms was $27,000 in 1996. Licensed architects with 3 to 5 of years experience had median earnings of $33,000; licensed architects with 8 to 10 years of experience, but who were not managers or principals of a firm, earned $45,000. Principals or partners of firms earned $75-100,000 in 1996, although partners in some large practices earned considerably more. Similar to other industries, small architecture firms (fewer than 5 employees) are less likely than larger firms to provide employee benefits.

Earnings of partners in established architecture firms may fluctuate due to changing business conditions. Some architects may have difficulty establishing their own practices, and may go through a period when their expenses are greater than their income, requiring substantial financial resources.

Related Occupations

Architects design and construct buildings and related structures. Others who engage in similar work are landscape architects, building contractors, civil engineers, urban planners, interior designers, industrial designers, and graphic designers.

Sources of Additional Information

Information about education and careers in architecture can be obtained from:

☛ Careers in Architecture Program, The American Institute of Architects, 1735 New York Ave. NW., Washington, DC 20006. Homepage: http://www.aiaonline.com

☛ Society of American Registered Architects, Nathan Kolodny Consultants, Suite 2A, 100 Pinewood Rd., Hartsdale, NY 10530.

Drafters

(D.O.T. 001.261; 002.261; 003.131, .261 except -010, .281; 005.281; 007.161-010, -014, and -018, .261, and .281; 010.281 except -022; 014.281; 017 except .261-010 and .684; 019.161-010, .261-014; and 726.364-014)

Significant Points

● Demand for particular drafting specializations varies geographically, depending on the needs of local industry.

● Little change in employment is expected through the year 2006.

● Opportunities should be best for individuals who have at least 2 years of training in a technically strong drafting program and who have considerable skill and experience using computer-aided drafting (CAD) systems.

Nature of the Work

Drafters prepare technical drawings and plans used by production and construction workers to build everything from manufactured products such as spacecraft or industrial machinery to structures such as office buildings or oil and gas pipelines. Their drawings provide visual guidelines, showing the technical details of the products and structures, specifying dimensions, materials to be used, and procedures and processes to be followed. Drafters fill in technical details, using drawings, rough sketches, specifications, codes, and calculations previously made by engineers, surveyors, architects, or scientists. For example, they use their knowledge of standardized building techniques to draw in the details of a structure. Some drafters employ a knowledge of engineering and manufacturing theory and standards to draw the parts of a machine in order to determine design elements such as the number and kind of fasteners needed to assemble it. To do this, they use technical handbooks, tables, calculators, and computers.

Traditionally, drafters sat at drawing boards and used compasses, dividers, protractors, triangles, and other drafting devices to prepare a drawing manually. Most drafters now use computer-aided drafting (CAD) systems to prepare drawings. These systems employ computer work stations which create a drawing on a video screen. The drawings are stored electronically so that revisions and/or duplications can be made easily. These systems also permit drafters to easily and quickly prepare variations of a design. Although this equipment has become easier to operate, CAD is only a tool. Persons who produce technical drawings using CAD still function as a drafter, and need most of the knowledge of traditional drafters—relating to drafting skills and standards—as well as CAD skills.

As CAD technology advances and the cost of the systems continues to fall, it is likely that almost all drafters will use CAD systems regularly in the future. However, manual drafting may still be used in certain applications, especially in specialty firms that produce many one-of-a-kind drawings with little repetition.

Drafting work has many specializations and titles may denote a particular discipline of design or drafting. *Architectural drafters* draw architectural and structural features of buildings and other structures. They may specialize by the type of structure, such as residential or commercial, or by material used, such as reinforced concrete, masonry, steel, or timber.

Aeronautical drafters prepare engineering drawings detailing plans and specifications used for the manufacture of aircraft, missiles, and parts.

Electrical drafters prepare wiring and layout diagrams used by workers who erect, install, and repair electrical equipment and wiring in communication centers, powerplants, electrical distribution systems, and buildings.

Electronic drafters draw wiring diagrams, circuit board assembly diagrams, schematics, and layout drawings used in the manufacture, installation, and repair of electronic devices and components.

Civil drafters prepare drawings and topographical and relief maps used in major construction or civil engineering projects such as highways, bridges, pipelines, flood control projects, and water and sewage systems.

Mechanical drafters prepare detail and assembly drawings of a wide variety of machinery and mechanical devices, indicating dimensions, fastening methods, and other requirements.

Process piping or *pipeline drafters* prepare drawings used for layout, construction, and operation of oil and gas fields, refineries, chemical plants, and process piping systems.

Working Conditions

Drafters usually work in comfortable offices furnished to accommodate their tasks. They may sit at adjustable drawing boards or drafting tables when doing manual drawings, although most drafters work at computer terminals much of the time. Like other workers who spend long periods of time in front of a computer terminals doing detailed work, drafters may be susceptible to eyestrain, back discomfort, and hand and wrist problems.

Though most work is done using computer-aided drafting systems, drafters may still prepare manual drawings using T-squares and triangles.

Employment

Drafters held about 310,000 jobs in 1996. Over 32 percent of all drafters worked in engineering and architectural services firms that design construction projects or do other engineering work on a contract basis for organizations in other parts of the economy. Another 29 percent worked in durable goods manufacturing industries, such as machinery, electrical equipment, and fabricated metals. The remainder were mostly employed in the construction, communications, utilities, and personnel supply services industries. About 5,000 were self-employed in 1996.

Training, Other Qualifications, and Advancement

Employers prefer applicants for drafting positions who have completed post-high school training in drafting, which is offered by technical institutes, junior and community colleges, and some colleges and universities. Employers are most interested in applicants who have well-developed drafting and mechanical drawing skills; a knowledge of standards, mathematics, science, and engineering technology; and a solid background in computer-aided drafting and design techniques. In addition, communication and problem-solving skills are required.

Individuals planning careers in drafting should take courses in math, science, computer technology, design or computer graphics, and any high school drafting courses available. Mechanical and visual aptitude are also important. Prospective drafters should be able to draw freehand, three-dimensional objects and do detailed work accurately and neatly. Artistic ability is helpful in some specialized fields, as is knowledge of manufacturing and construction methods. In addition, prospective drafters should have good interpersonal skills because they work closely with engineers, surveyors, architects, and other professionals.

Entry level or junior drafters usually do routine work under close supervision. After gaining experience, intermediate level drafters progress to more difficult work with less supervision. They may be required to exercise more judgment and perform calculations when preparing and modifying drawings. Drafters may eventually advance to senior drafter, designer, or supervisor. Many employers pay for continuing education, and with appropriate college degrees, drafters may go on to become engineering technicians, engineers, or architects.

Many types of publicly and privately operated schools provide some form of drafting training. The kind and quality of programs can vary considerably. Therefore, prospective students should be careful in selecting a program. They should contact prospective employers regarding their preferences and ask schools to provide information about the kinds of jobs obtained by graduates, type and condition of instructional facilities and equipment, and faculty qualifications.

Technical institutes offer intensive technical training but less of the general education than do junior and community colleges. Some award certificates or diplomas based on completion of a certain number of course hours. Many offer 2-year associate degree programs, which are similar to or part of the programs offered by community colleges or State university systems. Other technical institutes are run by private, often for-profit, organizations, sometimes called proprietary schools. Their programs vary considerably in both length and type of courses offered.

Junior and community colleges offer curriculums similar to those in technical institutes but include more courses on theory and liberal arts. Often there is little or no difference between technical institute and community college programs. However, courses taken at junior or community colleges are more likely to be accepted for credit at 4-year colleges than those at technical institutes. After completing a 2-year associate degree program, graduates may obtain jobs as drafters or continue their education in a related field at 4-year colleges. Four-year colleges usually do not offer drafting training, but college courses in engineering, architecture, and mathematics are useful for obtaining a job as a drafter.

Area vocational-technical schools are postsecondary public institutions that serve local students and emphasize training needed by local employers. Many offer introductory drafting instruction. Most require a high school diploma or its equivalent for admission.

Technical training obtained in the Armed Forces can also be applied in civilian drafting jobs. Some additional training may be necessary, depending on the technical area or military specialty, but often this can be gained on the job.

The American Design Drafting Association (ADDA) has established a certification program for drafters. Although drafters are not generally required to be certified by employers, certification demonstrates that nationally recognized standards have been met. Individuals who wish to become certified must pass the Drafter Certification Test, which is administered periodically at ADDA-authorized test sites. Applicants are tested on their knowledge and understanding of basic drafting concepts such as geometric construction, working drawings, and architectural terms and standards.

Job Outlook

Employment of drafters is expected to change little through the year 2006. Although industrial growth and increasingly complex design problems associated with new products and manufacturing will increase the demand for drafting services, greater use of CAD equipment by architects and engineers, as well as drafters, should offset this growth in demand. Many job openings, however, are expected to arise as drafters move to other occupations or leave the labor force.

Opportunities should be best for individuals who have at least 2 years of training in a technically strong drafting program and who have considerable skill and experience using CAD systems. CAD has become a powerful tool, simplifying many traditional drafting tasks. It has increased the complexity of drafting applications while enhancing the productivity of drafters. As technology continues to advance, employers will look for drafters who can combine a strong background in fundamental drafting principles with a higher level of technical sophistication and an ability to apply this knowledge to a broader range of responsibilities.

Demand for particular drafting specializations varies throughout the country because employment is generally contingent upon the needs of local industry. Employment of drafters remains highly concentrated in industries that are sensitive to cyclical changes in the economy, such as engineering and architectural services and durable goods manufacturing. During recessions, drafters may be laid off. A growing number of drafters should continue to be employed on a temporary or contract basis, as more companies turn to the personnel supply services industry to meet their changing needs.

Earnings

Median annual earnings of drafters who worked year round, full time were about $31,250 in 1996; the middle 50 percent earned between $23,400 and $41,500 annually. The top 10 percent earned more than $50,750, while the bottom 10 percent earned less than $19,000.

According to a survey of workplaces in 160 metropolitan areas, beginning drafters had median annual earnings of about $20,700 a year in 1995, with the middle half earning between about $18,600 and $22,400 a year. The most experienced drafters had median earnings of about $40,900 a year in 1996, with the middle half earning between about $36,100 and $45,800 a year.

Related Occupations

Other workers who prepare or analyze detailed drawings and make precise calculations and measurements include architects, landscape architects, designers, engineers, engineering technicians, science technicians, cartographers, and surveyors.

Sources of Additional Information

Information on schools offering programs in drafting and related areas is available from:
☛ Accrediting Commission of Career Schools and Colleges of Technology, 2101 Wilson Blvd., Suite 302, Arlington, VA 22201.

Landscape Architects

(D.O.T. 001.061-018)

Significant Points

- Nearly 30 percent—over three times the proportion for all professionals—are self-employed .

- A bachelor's degree in landscape architecture is the minimum requirement for entry-level jobs; many employers prefer to hire landscape architects who have completed at least one internship.

- Because many landscape architects work for small firms or are self-employed, benefits tend to be less generous than those provided to workers in large organizations.

Nature of the Work

Everyone enjoys attractively designed residential areas, public parks and playgrounds, college campuses, shopping centers, golf courses, parkways, and industrial parks. Landscape architects design these areas so that they are not only functional but beautiful and compatible with the natural environment as well. They may plan the location of buildings, roads, and walkways and the arrangement of flowers, shrubs, and trees. Historic preservation and natural resource conservation and reclamation are other important objectives to which landscape architects may apply their knowledge of the environment as well as their design and artistic talents.

Many types of organizations—from real estate development firms starting new projects to municipalities constructing airports or parks—hire landscape architects, who are often involved with the development of a site from its conception. Working with architects, surveyors, and engineers, landscape architects help determine the best arrangement of roads and buildings. They also collaborate with environmental scientists, foresters, and other professionals to find the best way to conserve or restore natural resources. Once these decisions are made, landscape architects create detailed plans indicating new topography, vegetation, walkways, and other landscaping details, such as fountains and decorative features.

In planning a site, landscape architects first consider the nature and purpose of the project and the funds available. They analyze the natural elements of the site, such as the climate, soil, slope of the land, drainage, and vegetation; observe where sunlight falls on the site at different times of the day and examine the site from various angles; and assess the effect of existing buildings, roads, walkways, and utilities on the project.

After studying and analyzing the site, they prepare a preliminary design. To account for the needs of the client as well as the conditions at the site, they may have to make many changes before a final design is approved. They must also take into account any local, State, or Federal regulations such as those protecting wetlands or historic resources. Computer-aided design (CAD) has become an essential tool for most landscape architects in preparing designs. Many landscape architects also use video simulation to help clients envision the proposed ideas and plans. For larger scale site planning, landscape architects also use geographic information systems technology, a computer mapping system.

Throughout all phases of the planning and design, landscape architects consult with other professionals involved in the project. Once the design is complete, they prepare a proposal for the client. They produce detailed plans of the site, including written reports, sketches, models, photographs, land-use studies, and cost estimates, and submit them for approval by the client and by regulatory agencies. If the plans are approved, landscape architects prepare working drawings showing all existing and proposed features. They also outline in detail the methods of construction and draw up a list of necessary materials.

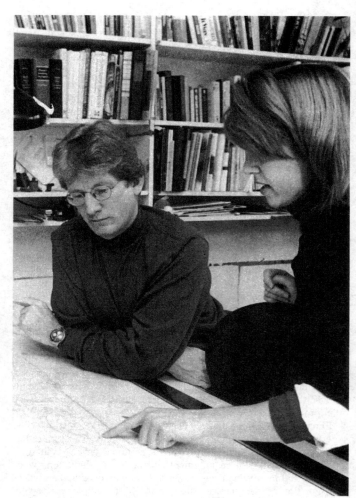

Two landscape architects discuss proposed changes to a client's plans.

Although many landscape architects supervise the installation of their design, some are involved in the construction of the site. However, this usually is done by the developer or landscape contractor.

Some landscape architects work on a wide variety of projects. Others specialize in a particular area, such as residential development, historic landscape restoration, waterfront improvement projects, parks and playgrounds, or shopping centers. Still others work in regional planning and resource management; feasibility, environmental impact, and cost studies; or site construction.

Although most landscape architects do at least some residential work, relatively few limit their practice to landscape design for individual homeowners because most residential landscape design projects are too small to provide suitable income compared with larger commercial or multiunit residential projects. Some nurseries offer residential landscape design services, but these services often are performed by lesser qualified landscape designers or others with training and experience in related areas.

Landscape architects who work for government agencies do site and landscape design for government buildings, parks, and other public lands, as well as park and recreation planning in national parks and forests. In addition, they may prepare environmental impact statements and studies on environmental issues such as public land-use planning. Some are involved in efforts to restore degraded land, such as mines or landfills.

Working Conditions

Landscape architects spend most of their time in offices creating plans and designs, preparing models and cost estimates, doing research, or attending meetings with clients and other professionals involved in a design or planning project. The remainder of their time is spent at the site. During the design and planning stage, landscape architects visit and analyze the site to verify that the design can be incorporated into the landscape. After the plans and specifications are completed, they may spend additional time at the site observing or supervising the construction. Those who work in large firms may spend considerably more time out of the office because of travel to sites outside the local area.

Salaried employees in both government and landscape architectural firms usually work regular hours; however, they may work overtime, sometimes 60 or more hours a week, to meet a project deadline. Hours of self-employed landscape architects may vary.

Employment
Landscape architects held about 17,000 jobs in 1996. About 2 out of 5 worked for firms that provide landscape architecture services. Most of the rest were employed by architectural firms. The Federal Government also employs these workers, primarily in the U.S. Departments of Agriculture, Defense, and Interior. About 3 of every 10 landscape architects was self-employed.

Employment of landscape architects is concentrated in urban and suburban areas throughout the country. Some landscape architects work in rural areas, particularly those in the Federal Government who plan and design parks and recreation areas.

Training, Other Qualifications, and Advancement
A bachelor's or master's degree in landscape architecture is usually necessary for entry into the profession. The bachelor's degree in landscape architecture takes 4 or 5 years to complete. There are two types of accredited master's degree programs. The master's degree as a first professional degree is a 3-year program designed for students with an undergraduate degree in another discipline; this is the most common type. The master's degree as the second professional degree is a 2-year program for students who have a bachelor's degree in landscape architecture and wish to teach or specialize in some aspect of landscape architecture, such as regional planning or golf course design.

In 1996, 54 colleges and universities offered 70 undergraduate and graduate programs in landscape architecture that were accredited by the Landscape Architecture Accreditation Board of the American Society of Landscape Architects.

College courses required in this field usually include technical subjects such as surveying, landscape design and construction, landscape ecology, site design, and urban and regional planning. Other courses include history of landscape architecture, plant and soil science, geology, professional practice, and general management. Many landscape architecture programs are adding courses which address environmental issues. In addition, most students at the undergraduate level take a year of prerequisite courses such as English, mathematics, and social and physical science. The design studio is an important aspect of many landscape architecture curriculums. Whenever possible, students are assigned real projects, providing them with valuable hands-on experience. While working on these projects, students may become more proficient in the use of technologies such as computer-aided design, geographic information systems, and video simulation.

In 1996, 45 States required landscape architects to be licensed or registered. Licensing is based on the Landscape Architect Registration Examination (L.A.R.E.), sponsored by the Council of Landscape Architectural Registration Boards and administered over a 3-day period. Admission to the exam usually requires a degree from an accredited school plus 1 to 4 years of work experience, although standards vary from State to State. Currently, 18 States require the passage of a State examination in addition to the L.A.R.E. to satisfy registration requirements. State examinations, which are usually 1 hour in length and completed at the end of the L.A.R.E., focus on laws, environmental regulations, plants, soils, climate, and any other characteristics unique to the State.

Because State requirements for licensure are not uniform, landscape architects may not find it easy to transfer their registration from one State to another. However, those who meet the national standards of graduating from an accredited program, serving 3 years of internship under the supervision of a registered landscape architect, and passing the L.A.R.E. can satisfy requirements in most States.

In the Federal Government, candidates for entry positions should have a bachelor's or master's degree in landscape architecture. The Federal Government does not require its landscape architects to be licensed.

Persons planning a career in landscape architecture should appreciate nature and enjoy working with their hands. Creative vision and artistic talent are desirable qualities, but they are not essential to success as a landscape architect. Good oral communication skills are important, because these workers must be able to convey their ideas to other professionals and clients and to make presentations before large groups. Strong writing skills are also valuable, as is knowledge of computer applications of all kinds, including word processing, desktop publishing, and spreadsheets. Landscape architects use these tools to develop presentations, proposals, reports, and land impact studies for clients, colleagues, and superiors. The ability to draft and design using CAD software is essential. Many employers recommend that prospective landscape architects complete at least one summer internship with a landscape architecture firm in order to gain an understanding of the day-to-day operations of a small business, including how to win clients, generate fees, and work within a budget.

In States where licensure is required, new hires may be called apprentices or intern landscape architects until they become licensed. Their duties vary depending on the type and size of employing firm. They may do project research or prepare working drawings, construction documents, or base maps of the area to be landscaped. Some are allowed to participate in the actual design of a project. However, interns must perform all work under the supervision of a licensed landscape architect. Additionally, all drawings and specifications must be signed and sealed by the licensed landscape architect, who takes legal responsibility for the work. After gaining experience and becoming licensed, landscape architects usually can carry a design through all stages of development. After several years, they may become project managers, taking on the responsibility for meeting schedules and budgets, in addition to overseeing the project design; and later, associates or partners, with a proprietary interest in the business.

Many landscape architects are self-employed because start-up costs, after an initial investment in CAD software, are relatively low. Self-discipline, business acumen, and good marketing skills are important qualities for those who choose to open their own business. Even with these qualities, however, some may struggle while building a client base.

Those with landscape architecture training also qualify for jobs closely related to landscape architecture, and may, after gaining some experience, become construction supervisors, land or environmental planners, or landscape consultants.

Job Outlook
Employment of landscape architects is expected to increase faster than the average for all occupations through the year 2006. The level of new construction plays an important role in determining demand for landscape architects. Overall, anticipated growth in construction is expected to increase demand for landscape architectural services over the long run. However, opportunities will vary from year to year and by geographic region, depending on local economic conditions. During a recession, when real estate sales and construction slow down, landscape architects may face layoffs and greater competition for jobs. The need to replace landscape architects who retire or leave the labor force for other reasons is expected to produce nearly as many job openings as new openings stemming from job growth.

An increasing proportion of office and other commercial and industrial development will occur outside cities. These projects are typically located on larger sites with more surrounding land which needs to be designed, in contrast to urban development, which often includes little or no surrounding land. Also, as the cost of land rises, the importance of good site planning and landscape design grows. Increasingly, new development is contingent upon compliance with environmental regulations and land use zoning, spurring demand for landscape architects to help plan sites and integrate man-made structures with the natural environment in the least disruptive way.

Increased development of open space into recreation areas, wildlife refuges, and parks will also require the skills of landscape architects. However, budget tightening in the Federal Government may restrict funding for such initiatives in the Forest Service and the National Park Service, agencies which traditionally employ many landscape architects.

In addition to the work related to new development and construction, landscape architects are expected to be involved in historic preservation, land reclamation, and refurbishment of existing sites, although these activities are expected to account for only a small proportion of new jobs.

New graduates can expect to face competition for jobs in the largest and most prestigious landscape architecture firms. The number of professional degrees awarded in landscape architecture has remained steady over the years, even during times of fluctuating demand due to economic conditions. Opportunities will be best for landscape architects who develop strong technical and communication skills and a knowledge of environmental codes and regulations. Those with additional training or experience in urban planning increase their opportunities for employment in landscape architecture firms that specialize in site planning as well as landscape design. Many employers prefer to hire entry-level landscape architects who have internship experience, which significantly reduces training time.

Earnings

Median annual earnings for all architects, including landscape architects, were about $39,500 in 1996. The middle 50 percent earned between $30,200 and $53,900; 10 percent earned less than $23,900; and 10 percent earned over $65,800. In 1997, the average annual salary for all landscape architects in the Federal Government in nonsupervisory, supervisory, and managerial positions was about $53,300.

Because many landscape architects work for small firms or are self-employed, benefits tend to be less generous than those provided to workers in large organizations.

Related Occupations

Landscape architects use their knowledge of design, construction, land-use planning, and environmental issues to develop a landscape project. Others whose work requires similar skills are architects, surveyors, civil engineers, soil conservationists, and urban and regional planners. Landscape architects also know how to grow and use plants in the landscape. Botanists, who study plants in general, and horticulturists, who study ornamental plants as well as fruit, vegetable, greenhouse, and nursery crops, do similar work.

Sources of Additional Information

Additional information, including a list of colleges and universities offering accredited programs in landscape architecture, is available from:

☛ American Society of Landscape Architects, Career Information, 4401 Connecticut Ave. NW., Suite 500, Washington, DC 20008.

General information on registration or licensing requirements is available from:

☛ Council of Landscape Architectural Registration Boards, 12700 Fair Lakes Circle, Suite 110, Fairfax, VA 22033. FAX (703) 818-1309. E-mail address: clarb2@aol.com

Surveyors and Mapping Scientists

(D.O.T. 018 except .167-022, and 024.061-014)

Significant Points

- One of the few professional occupations in which employment is expected to decline.

- More than 8 out of 10 are employed in engineering services and government.

- Skill in the use of new technologies enhances employment opportunities.

Nature of the Work

Measuring and mapping the earth's surface is the responsibility of several different types of workers. Traditional *land surveyors* establish official land, air space, and water boundaries. They write descriptions of land for deeds, leases, and other legal documents; define air space for airports; and measure construction and mineral sites. Other surveyors provide data relevant to the shape, contour, location, elevation, or dimension of land or land features. *Survey technicians* assist land surveyors by operating survey instruments and collecting information. *Mapping scientists* compile geographic information and prepare maps of large areas.

Land surveyors manage survey parties that measure distances, directions, and angles between points and elevations of points, lines, and contours on the earth's surface. They plan the fieldwork, select known survey reference points, and determine the precise location of important features in the survey area. Surveyors research legal records and look for evidence of previous boundaries. They record the results of the survey, verify the accuracy of data, and prepare plots, maps, and reports. Surveyors who establish boundaries must be licensed by the State in which they work.

The information needed by the land surveyor is gathered by a survey party. A typical survey party is made up of a party chief and several survey technicians and helpers. The party chief, who may be either a land surveyor or a senior survey technician, leads the day-to-day work activities. The party chief is assisted by survey technicians, who adjust and operate surveying instruments, such as the theodolite (used to measure horizontal and vertical angles) and electronic distance-measuring equipment. Survey technicians or assistants position and hold the vertical rods or targets that the theodolite operator sights on to measure angles, distances, or elevations. They may also hold measuring tapes, if electronic distance-measuring equipment is not used. Survey technicians compile notes, make sketches, and enter the data obtained from these instruments into computers. Survey parties may include laborers or helpers who perform less skilled duties, such as clearing brush from sight lines, driving stakes, or carrying equipment.

New technology is changing the nature of the work of surveyors and survey technicians. For larger projects, surveyors are increasingly using the Global Positioning System (GPS), a satellite system that precisely locates points on the earth using radio signals transmitted by satellites. To use this system, a surveyor places a satellite signal receiver—a small instrument mounted on a tripod—on a desired point. The receiver simultaneously collects information from several satellites to locate a precise position. The receiver can also be placed in a vehicle for uses such as tracing out road systems. Since receivers now come in different sizes and shapes and the cost of the receivers has fallen, much more surveying work is being done by GPS.

Mapping scientists measure, map, and chart the earth's surface, which involves everything from geographical research and data compilation to actual map production. They collect, analyze, and interpret both spatial data—such as latitude, longitude, elevation, and distance—and nonspatial data—such as population density, land use patterns, annual precipitation levels, and demographic characteristics. *Cartographers* prepare maps in both digital or graphic form, using information provided by geodetic surveys, aerial photographs, and satellite data. *Photogrammetrists* prepare detailed maps and drawings from aerial photographs, usually of areas that are inaccessible or difficult to survey by other methods. *Map editors* develop and verify map contents from aerial photographs and other reference sources.

Some surveyors perform specialized functions which are closer to those of a mapping scientist than a traditional surveyor. For example, *geodetic surveyors* use high-accuracy techniques, including satellite observations, to measure large areas of the earth's surface. *Geophysical prospecting surveyors* mark sites for subsurface exploration, usually petroleum related. *Marine surveyors* survey harbors, rivers, and other bodies of water to determine shorelines, topography of the bottom, water depth, and other features.

The work of surveyors and mapping scientists is changing due to advancements in technology. These advancements include not only the GPS, but also new earth resources data satellites, improved aerial photography, and geographic information systems (GIS)—which are computerized data banks of spatial data. From the older specialties of photogrammetrist and cartographer, a new type of mapping scientist is emerging. The *geographic information specialist* combines the functions of mapping science and surveying into a broader field concerned with the collection and analysis of geographic information.

Working Conditions

Surveyors usually work an 8-hour day, 5 days a week, and may spend a lot of time outdoors. Sometimes they work longer hours during the summer, when weather and light conditions are most suitable for fieldwork.

Land surveyors and technicians do active and sometimes strenuous work. They often stand for long periods, walk considerable distances, and climb hills with heavy packs of instruments and other equipment. They can also be exposed to all types of weather. Occasionally, they may commute long distances, stay overnight, or temporarily relocate near a survey site.

Although surveyors can spend considerable time inside, planning surveys, analyzing data, and preparing reports and maps, mapping scientists, on the other hand, spend virtually all their time in offices and seldom visit the sites they are mapping.

Employment

Surveyors and mapping scientists held about 101,000 jobs in 1996. Engineering and architectural services firms employed about three-fifths of these workers. Federal, State, and local governmental agencies employed an additional quarter. Major Federal Governmental employers are the U.S. Geological Survey, the Bureau of Land Management, the Army Corps of Engineers, the Forest Service, the National Oceanic and Atmospheric Administration, and the National Imagery and Mapping Agency (NIMA), formerly the Defense Mapping Agency. Most surveyors in State and local government work for highway departments and urban planning and redevelopment agencies. Construction firms, mining and oil and gas extraction companies, and public utilities also employ surveyors and mapping scientists. About 8,000 were self-employed in 1996.

Training, Other Qualifications, and Advancement

Most people prepare for a career as a licensed surveyor by combining postsecondary school courses in surveying with extensive on-the-job training. However, as technology advances, a 4-year degree is becoming more of a prerequisite. About 25 universities now offer 4-year programs leading to a B.S. degree in surveying. Junior and community colleges, technical institutes, and vocational schools offer 1-, 2-, and 3-year programs in both surveying and surveying technology.

All 50 States license land surveyors. For licensure, most State licensing boards require that individuals pass two written examinations, one prepared by the State and one given by the National Council of Examiners for Engineering and Surveying. In addition, they must meet varying standards of formal education and work experience in the field. In the past, many individuals started as members of survey crews and worked their way up to become licensed surveyors with little formal training in surveying. However, due to advancing technology and an increase in licensing standards, formal education requirements are increasing. At present, most States require some formal post-high school education coursework and 10 to 12 years of surveying experience to gain licensure. However, requirements vary among States. Generally, the quickest route to licensure is a combination of 4 years of college, 2 to 4 years of experience, and passing the licensing examinations. An increasing number of States require a

Members of a survey party take measurements and record the information obtained from surveying instruments.

bachelor's degree in surveying or in a closely related field, such as civil engineering or forestry (with courses in surveying) regardless of the number of years of experience.

High school students interested in surveying should take courses in algebra, geometry, trigonometry, drafting, mechanical drawing, and computer science. High school graduates with no formal training in surveying usually start as an apprentice. Beginners with postsecondary school training in surveying can generally start as technicians or assistants. With on-the-job experience and formal training in surveying—either in an institutional program or from a correspondence school—workers may advance to senior survey technician, then to party chief, and in some cases, to licensed surveyor (depending on State licensing requirements).

The American Congress on Surveying and Mapping has a voluntary certification program for survey technicians. Technicians are certified at four levels requiring progressive amounts of experience, in addition to passing written examinations. Although not required for State licensure, many employers require certification for promotion to positions with greater responsibilities.

Surveyors should have the ability to visualize objects, distances, sizes, and abstract forms. They must work with precision and accuracy because mistakes can be costly. Members of a survey party must be in good physical condition, because they work outdoors and often carry equipment over difficult terrain. They need good eyesight, coordination, and hearing to communicate verbally and via hand signals. Surveying is a cooperative process, so good interpersonal skills and the ability to work as part of a team are important. Leadership qualities are important for party chief and other supervisory positions.

Mapping scientists, such as cartographers and photogrammetrists, usually have a bachelor's degree in a field such as engineering, forestry, geography, or a physical science. Although it is possible to enter these positions through previous experience as a photogrammetric or cartographic technician, most cartographic and photogrammetric technicians now have had some specialized postsecondary school training. With the development of Geographic Information Systems, cartographers, photogrammetrists, and other mapping scientists need additional education and stronger technical skills, including more experience with computers than in the past.

The American Society for Photogrammetry and Remote Sensing has voluntary certification programs for photogrammetrists and mapping scientists. To qualify for these professional distinctions, individuals must meet work experience standards and pass an oral or written examination.

Job Outlook

Employment of surveyors and mapping scientists is expected to decline slightly through the year 2006, as the widespread availability and use of advanced technologies, such as the Global Positioning System, Geographic Information Systems, and remote sensing, are increasing both the accuracy and productivity of survey and mapping work. Job openings, however, will continue to result from the need to replace workers who transfer to other occupations or leave the labor force altogether.

As technologies become more complex, opportunities will be best for surveyors and mapping scientists who have at least a bachelor's degree and strong technical skills. Increasing demand for geographic data, as opposed to traditional surveying services, will mean better opportunities for mapping scientists involved in the development and use of geographic and land information systems. New technologies, such as GPS and GIS may also enhance employment opportunities for surveyors and survey technicians who have the educational background enabling them to use these systems, but upgraded licensing requirements will continue to limit opportunities for those with less education.

Even as demand is increasing in nontraditional areas such as urban planning and natural resource exploration and mapping, opportunities for surveyors and mapping scientists should remain concentrated in engineering, architectural, and surveying services firms. Growth in construction through the year 2006 should require surveyors to lay out streets, shopping centers, housing developments, factories, office buildings, and recreation areas. However, employment may fluctuate from year to year along with construction activity. In addition, employment of mapping scientists and surveyors by private firms and the Federal Government will continue to be affected by budget cutbacks and technological efficiency.

Earnings

The median weekly earnings for surveyors and mapping scientists were about $694 a week in 1996. The middle 50 percent earned between $547 and $849 a week; 10 percent earned less than $446 a week; 10 percent earned more than $1000 a week.

The median weekly earnings for survey technicians were about $461 a week in 1996. The middle 50 percent earned between $378 and $725 a week; 10 percent earned less than $294 a week; 10 percent earned more than $942 a week.

In 1997, the Federal Government hired high school graduates with little or no training or experience at salaries of about $14,240 annually for entry level jobs on survey crews. Those with 1 year of related postsecondary training earned about $15,540 a year. Those with an associate degree that included coursework in surveying generally started as instrument assistants with an annual salary of about $17,450. In 1997, entry level land surveyors or cartographers with the Federal Government earned about $19,520, $24,180 or $29,580 a year, depending on their qualifications. The average annual salary for Federal land surveyors in early 1997 was about $47,850; for cartographers, about $52,500; and for geodesists, about $62,760. The average annual salary for Federal surveying technicians was about $28,600; for cartographic technicians, about $34,840; and for geodetic technicians, about $45,050.

Related Occupations

Surveying is related to the work of civil engineers and architects, since an accurate survey is the first step in land development and construction projects. Mapping science and geodetic surveying are related to the work of geologists and geophysicists, who study the earth's internal composition, surface, and atmosphere. Mapping science is also related to the work of geographers and urban planners, who study and decide how the earth's surface is used.

Sources of Additional Information

Information about career opportunities, licensure requirements, and the survey technician certification program is available from:

☛ American Congress on Surveying and Mapping, 5410 Grosvenor Lane, Suite 100, Bethesda, MD 20814-2122.

General information on careers in photogrammetry is available from:

☛ American Society for Photogrammetry and Remote Sensing, 5410 Grosvenor Lane, Suite 210, Bethesda, MD 20814.

Computer, Mathematical, and Operations Research Occupations

Actuaries

(D.O.T. 020.167-010)

Significant Points

- A strong background in mathematics is essential for persons interested in a career as an actuary.

- Competition for jobs is expected due to relatively high earnings, the small size of the occupation, and downsizing and merger activity in the insurance industry.

Nature of the Work

Actuaries answer questions about future risk, make pricing decisions, and formulate investment strategies. Some design insurance, financial, and pension plans and ensure that these plans are maintained on a sound financial basis. Most actuaries specialize in life, health, or property and casualty insurance; others specialize in pension plans.

Actuaries assemble and analyze data to estimate probabilities of death, sickness, injury, disability, retirement income level, property loss, or return on investment. They use this information to estimate how much an insurance company will have to pay out in claims, or to make other business decisions. For example, actuaries may calculate the expected amount of claims due to automobile accidents, which can vary depending on the insured's age, sex, driving history, type of car, and other factors. Actuaries ensure that the price charged for such insurance, or premium, will enable the company to cover claims and expenses as they incur. Finally, this premium charged must be profitable and yet be competitive with other insurance companies. The actuary calculates premium rates and determines policy contract provisions for each type of insurance offered.

To perform their duties effectively, actuaries must keep informed about general economic and social trends and legislation, as well as developments in health, business, finance, and economics that may affect insurance or investment practices. Using their broad knowledge of business and mathematics, actuaries may work in investment, risk classification, or pension planning.

Actuaries in executive positions help determine company policy. In that role, they may be called upon to explain complex technical matters to other company executives, government officials, shareholders, policyholders, and the public in general. They may testify before public agencies on proposed legislation affecting their businesses or explain changes in contract provisions to customers. They also may help companies develop plans to enter new lines of business.

A small but growing group of actuaries work in the financial services industry, where they manage credit, prepayment, and other risks, and help price corporate securities offerings.

Consulting actuaries provide advice to various clients on a fee basis. Their clients include insurance companies, corporations, hospitals and other health care providers, labor unions, government agencies, and attorneys. Some consulting actuaries design pension and welfare plans, calculate future benefits, and determine the amount of employer contributions. Others provide advice to health care plans or financial services firms. Consultants may be called upon to testify in court regarding the value of potential lifetime earnings lost by a person who has been disabled or killed in an accident, the current value of future pension benefits in divorce cases, or the calculation of insurance rates. Pension actuaries enrolled under the provisions of the Employee Retirement Income Security Act of 1974 (ERISA) evaluate the pension plans covered by that act and report on their financial soundness to plan members, sponsors, and Federal regulators.

Working Conditions

Actuaries have desk jobs that require little physical activity, and their offices are generally comfortable and pleasant. They usually work at least 40 hours a week. Some actuaries, particularly consulting actuaries, often travel to meet with clients. Consulting actuaries may also be expected to work more than 40 hours per week.

Employment

Actuaries held about 16,000 jobs in 1996. Some were self-employed. In addition, some actuaries held faculty positions in colleges and universities. (See the statement on college and university faculty elsewhere in the *Handbook*.)

Almost one-half of the actuaries who were wage and salary workers were employed in the insurance industry. Most worked for life insurance companies; others worked for property, casualty, and health insurance companies, pension funds, and insurance agents and brokers. Most of the remaining actuaries worked for firms providing services, especially management and public relations, and actuarial

Using their broad knowledge of business and mathematics, actuaries may work in investment, risk classification, or pension planning.

consulting services. A relatively small number of actuaries worked for security and commodity brokers or government agencies. Some are employed developing computer software for actuarial calculations.

Training, Other Qualifications, and Advancement

A good educational background for a beginning job in a large life or casualty company is a bachelor's degree in mathematics, actuarial science, or statistics, or a business-related discipline, such as economics, finance, or accounting. Some companies hire applicants without specifying a major, provided the applicant has a working knowledge of mathematics, including calculus, probability, and statistics, and who has demonstrated this ability by passing at least the beginning actuarial exams required for professional designation. Courses in economics, accounting, computer science, and insurance are also useful. Companies increasingly prefer well-rounded individuals who, in addition to a strong technical background, have some training in liberal arts and business. Good communication and interpersonal skills are important, particularly for prospective consulting actuaries. About 55 colleges and universities offer an actuarial science program, and most colleges and universities offer a degree in mathematics or statistics.

A strong background in mathematics is essential for persons interested in a career as an actuary. It is an advantage to pass, while still in school, two or more of the examinations offered by professional actuarial societies. Two professional societies sponsor programs leading to full professional status in their specialty. The Society of Actuaries (SOA) administers a series of actuarial examinations for life and health insurance, pension, and finance and investment fields. The Casualty Actuarial Society (CAS) gives a series of examinations for the property and casualty field, which include fire, accident, medical malpractice, workers compensation, and personal injury liability. Because the first parts of the examination series of each society are jointly sponsored and cover the same material, students need not commit themselves to a specialty until they have taken the initial examinations. These examinations test an individual's competence in subjects such as linear algebra, probability, calculus, statistics, risk theory, and actuarial mathematics. The first few examinations help students evaluate their potential as actuaries. Those who pass one or more examination have better opportunities for employment and higher starting salaries than those who do not.

Actuaries are encouraged to complete the entire series of examinations as soon as possible, advancing first to the Associate level, and then to the Fellowship level. Completion of the examination process generally takes from 5 to 10 years. Examinations are given twice each year, in May and November. Although many companies allot time to their employees for study, extensive home study is required to pass the examinations; many actuaries study for months to prepare for each examination. Most reach Associateship within 4 to 6 years. Fellowship candidates usually have several years of experience. Most actuaries complete the Fellowship exams a few years after reaching Associateship. Both levels of examinations are extremely difficult.

Pension actuaries who verify the financial status of defined benefit pension plans to the Federal Government must be enrolled by the Joint Board for the Enrollment of Actuaries. To qualify for enrollment, applicants must meet certain experience and examination requirements, as stipulated by the Joint Board.

Beginning actuaries often rotate between jobs to learn various actuarial operations and phases of insurance work, such as marketing, underwriting, or product development. At first, they prepare data for actuarial projects or perform other simple tasks. As they gain experience, actuaries may supervise clerks, prepare correspondence and reports, and do research. They may move from one company to another in their early careers, as they move up to progressively more responsible positions.

Advancement depends largely on job performance and the number of actuarial examinations passed. Actuaries with a broad knowledge of the insurance, pension, investment, or employee benefits fields can advance to administrative and executive positions in their companies. Actuaries with supervisory ability may advance to management positions in other areas, such as underwriting, accounting, data processing, marketing, or advertising.

Job Outlook
Prospective actuaries who have passed the beginning actuarial exams will face competition for jobs, since the number of openings each year is limited by the relatively small size of the occupation.

Employment of actuaries is expected to grow more slowly than the average for all occupations through the year 2006, due to expected slower growth in the insurance industry. Anticipated downsizing and merger activity in the insurance industry is likely to have the greatest negative effect on those actuaries with the least experience. The expected growth in managed health plans in the health services industry should provide better prospects for actuaries, however.

Employment growth of consulting actuaries is expected to be faster than employment growth of actuaries in insurance carriers—traditionally the leading employer of actuaries. As many companies seek to boost profitability by streamlining operations, actuarial employment may be cut back by insurance carriers. Investment firms and large corporations may increasingly turn to consultants to provide actuarial services formerly performed in-house.

The liability of companies for damage resulting from their products has received much attention in recent years. Casualty actuaries will continue to be involved in the development of product liability insurance, medical malpractice and workers' compensation coverage, and self-insurance, which may involve internal reserve funds established by some large corporations. The growing need to evaluate catastrophic risks such as earthquakes and calculate prices for insuring facilities against such risks, which may involve huge losses, will be an increasing source of demand for property and casualty actuaries. So is planning for the systematic financing of environmental risks, such as toxic waste clean-up.

Earnings
In 1996, starting salaries for actuaries averaged about $37,600 for those with a bachelor's degree, according to the National Association of Colleges and Employers. New college graduates entering the actuarial field without having passed any actuarial exams averaged slightly lower salaries.

Insurance companies and consulting firms give merit increases to actuaries as they gain experience and pass examinations. Some companies also offer cash bonuses for each professional designation achieved. A 1996 salary survey of insurance and financial services companies, conducted by the Life Office Management Association, Inc., indicated that the average base salary for an entry-level actuary was about $36,500. Associate Actuaries, who direct and provide leadership in the design and pricing of products received a salary of about $78,600. Actuaries with additional experience earned an average of $93,500.

Actuaries typically receive other benefits including vacation and sick leave, health and life insurance, and pension plans.

Related Occupations
Actuaries determine the probability of income or loss from various risk factors. Other workers whose jobs involve related skills include accountants, economists, financial analysts, mathematicians, and statisticians.

Sources of Additional Information
For facts about actuarial careers, contact:
☛ American Academy of Actuaries, 1100 17th St. NW., 7th Floor, Washington, DC 20036.

For information about actuarial careers in life and health insurance, employee benefits and pensions, and finance and investments, contact:
☛ Society of Actuaries, 475 N. Martingale Rd., Suite 800, Schaumburg, IL 60173-2226.

For information about actuarial careers in property and casualty insurance, contact:
☛ Casualty Actuarial Society, 1100 N. Glebe Rd., Suite 600, Arlington, VA 22201.
Homepage: http://www.casact.org

Career information on actuaries specializing in pensions is available from:
☛ American Society of Pension Actuaries, 4350 N. Fairfax Dr., Suite 820, Arlington, VA 22203.

Computer Programmers

(D.O.T. 030.162-010, -018, -022, and .167-010)

Significant Points
- The level of education and quality of training required by employers has been rising due to the increasing complexity of programming tasks.
- A growing number of computer programmers are employed on a temporary or contract basis.

Nature of the Work
Computer programmers write, test, and maintain the detailed instructions—called "programs" or "software"—that list in a logical order the steps computers must execute to perform their functions. Programmers often are categorized as technicians, distinct from the higher level of theoretical expertise characteristic of computer scientists, computer engineers, and systems analysts. However, many technical innovations in programming—advanced computing technologies and sophisticated new languages and programming tools—have redefined the role of a programmer and elevated much of the programming work done today. It is becoming much more difficult to distinguish different computer specialists—including programmers—since job titles shift so rapidly, reflecting new areas of specialization or changes in technology. Job titles and descriptions also may vary depending on the organization. In this statement, "computer programmer" refers to individuals whose main job function is programming; this group has a wide range of responsibilities and educational backgrounds.

Computer programs tell the computer what to do, such as which information to identify and access, how to process it, and what equipment to use. Programs vary widely depending upon the type of information to be accessed or generated. For example, the instructions involved in updating financial records are very different from those required to duplicate conditions on board an aircraft for pilots training in a flight simulator. Although simple programs can be written in a few hours, programs that use complex mathematical formulas, whose solutions can only be approximated, or that draw data from many existing systems, require more than a year of work. In most cases, several programmers work together as a team under a senior programmer's supervision.

Programmers write specific programs by breaking down each step into a logical series of instructions the computer can follow. They then code these instructions in a conventional programming language, such as C and FORTRAN; an artificial intelligence language, such as LISP or Prolog; or one of the more advanced function-oriented or object-oriented languages, such as UML, Java, C++, Visual Basic, or Ada. Programmers usually know more than one programming language and since many languages are alike, they can often learn new languages relatively easily. In practice, programmers are often referred to by the language they know or the type of environment they generally work in such as mainframe programmer, object-oriented programmer, or Internet or World Wide Web programmer. In many large organizations, programmers follow descriptions that have been prepared by software engineers or systems analysts. These descriptions list the input required, the steps the

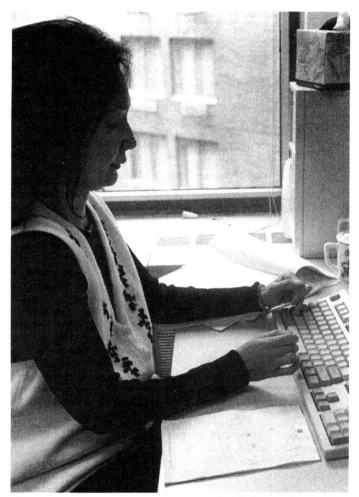

A programmer tests a program to ensure that the instructions are correct and it produces the desired information.

computer must follow to process data, and the desired arrangement of the output.

Many programmers are involved in updating, repairing, modifying and expanding existing programs. When making changes to a section of code, called a "routine," programmers need to make other users aware of the task the routine is to perform. They do this by inserting comments in the coded instructions so others can understand the program. Innovations such as Computer-Aided Software Engineering (CASE) tools enable a programmer to concentrate on writing the unique parts of the program because the tools automate various pieces of the program being built. CASE tools generate whole sections of code automatically, rather than line by line. This also yields more reliable and consistent programs and increases programmers' productivity by eliminating some of the routine steps.

Programmers test a program by running it to ensure the instructions are correct and it produces the desired information. If errors do occur, the programmer must make the appropriate change and re-check the program until it produces the correct results, a process called "debugging." Programmers working in a mainframe environment may still prepare instructions for a computer operator who will run the program. (The work of computer operators is described in the statement on computer operators elsewhere in the *Handbook*.) They may also contribute to a user's manual for the program.

Programmers often are grouped into two broad types: Applications programmers and systems programmers. *Applications programmers* usually are oriented toward business, engineering, or science. They write software to handle specific jobs within an organization, such as a program used in an inventory control system. They may also work alone to revise existing packaged software. *Systems programmers*, on the other hand, maintain and control the use of computer systems software. These workers make changes in the sets of instructions that determine how the network, workstations, and central processing unit of the system handles the various jobs they have been given and how they communicate with peripheral equipment, such as terminals, printers, and disk drives. Because of their knowledge of the entire computer system, systems programmers often help applications programmers determine the source of problems that may occur with their programs.

In some organizations, particularly smaller ones, workers more commonly referred to as *programmer-analysts* are responsible for both the systems analysis and the actual programming work. (A more detailed description of the work of programmer-analysts is presented in the statement on computer scientists, computer engineers, and systems analysts elsewhere in the *Handbook*.) Advanced programming languages and new object-oriented programming capabilities are increasing the efficiency and productivity of both programmers and users. The transition from a mainframe environment to a primarily PC-based environment has blurred the once rigid distinction between the programmer and the user. Increasingly, adept users are taking over many of the tasks previously performed by programmers. For example, the growing use of packaged software, like spreadsheet and data base management software packages, allows users to write simple programs to access data and perform calculations.

Programmers in software development companies may work directly with experts from various fields to create software—either programs designed for specific clients or packaged software for general use—ranging from games and educational software to programs for desktop publishing, financial planning, and spreadsheets. Much of this type of programming is in the preparation of packaged software, which comprises one of the most rapidly growing segments of the computer services industry.

Working Conditions

Programmers generally work in offices in comfortable surroundings. Although they usually work about 40 hours a week, programmers may work longer hours or weekends in order to meet deadlines or fix critical problems that occur during off hours. Given the technology available, telecommuting is becoming more common for a wider range of computer professionals—including computer programmers. Programmers can access a system directly, but from remote locations, to make corrections or fix problems.

Like other workers who spend long periods of time in front of a computer terminal typing at a keyboard, they are susceptible to eyestrain, back discomfort, and hand and wrist problems such as carpal tunnel syndrome or cumulative trauma disorder.

Employment

Computer programmers held about 568,000 jobs in 1996. Programmers are employed in almost every industry, but the largest concentration is in the computer and data processing services industry which includes firms that write and sell software. Large numbers of programmers can also be found working for firms that provide engineering and management services, manufacturers of computer and office equipment, financial institutions, insurance carriers, educational institutions, and government agencies.

A growing number of computer programmers are employed on a temporary or contract basis or work as independent consultants as companies demand expertise with newer programming languages or more specialized areas of application. Rather than hiring programmers as permanent employees and then laying them off after a job is completed, employers can contract with temporary help agencies, consulting firms, or directly with programmers themselves. A marketing firm, for example, may only require the services of several programmers to write and "debug" the software necessary to get a new database management system running. This practice also enables companies to bring in people with a specific set of skills, usually in one of the latest technologies as it applies to their business needs. Bringing in an independent contractor or consultant with a certain level of experience in a new or advanced programming language, for example, enables an establishment to complete a particular job without having to retrain existing workers. Such jobs may last anywhere from several weeks to a year or longer. There were 20,000 self-employed computer programmers in 1996 and this number is expected to increase.

Training, Other Qualifications, and Advancement

While there are many training paths available for programmers, mainly because employers' needs are so varied, the level of education and quality of training employers seek have been rising due to the growth in the number of qualified applicants and the increasing complexity of some programming tasks. Bachelor's degrees are now commonly required, although some programmers qualify with 2-year degrees or certificates. College graduates who are interested in changing careers or developing an area of expertise also may return to a two-year community college or technical school for additional training. In the absence of a degree, substantial specialized experience or expertise may be needed. Even with a degree, employers appear to be placing more emphasis on previous experience for all types of programmers.

Table 1. Percent distribution of highest level of school completed or degree received, computer programmers, 1996

	Percent
High school graduate or equivalent or less	10.0
Some college, no degree	20.9
Associate's degree	9.6
Bachelor's degree	45.2
Graduate degree	14.2

The majority of computer programmers—almost 60 percent—had a bachelor's degree or higher in 1996. (See table 1.) Of these, some hold a B.A. or B.S. in computer science, mathematics, or information systems while others have taken special courses in computer programming to supplement their study in fields such as accounting, inventory control, or other business areas. As the level of education and training required by employers continues to rise, this percentage should increase in the future.

Skills needed vary from job to job and the demand for various skills is generally driven by changes in technology. Employers using computers for scientific or engineering applications generally prefer college graduates who have degrees in computer or information science, mathematics, engineering, or the physical sciences. Graduate degrees in related fields may be required for some jobs. Employers who use computers for business applications prefer to hire people who have had college courses in management information systems (MIS) and business, and who possess strong programming skills. Although knowledge of traditional languages such as FORTRAN, COBOL, or C is still important, increasing emphasis is placed on more advanced object-oriented languages and tools such as CASE tools, C++, Visual C++, Ada, Smalltalk, Visual Basic, PowerBuilder, and Java as well as 4th and 5th generation languages, graphic user interface (GUI) and systems programming. General business skills and experience related to the operations of the firm are preferred by employers as well.

Most systems programmers hold a 4-year degree in computer science. Extensive knowledge of a variety of operating systems is essential. This includes being able to configure the operating system to work with different types of hardware, and adapting the operating system to best meet the needs of the particular organization. They must also be able to work with database systems such as DB2, Oracle, or Sybase, for example.

When hiring programmers, employers look for people with the necessary programming skills who can think logically and pay close attention to detail. The job calls for patience, persistence, and the ability to work on exacting analytical work, especially under pressure. Ingenuity and imagination are also particularly important when programmers design solutions and test their work for potential failures. The ability to work with abstract concepts and do technical analysis is especially important for systems programmers because they work with the software that controls the computer's operation. Since programmers are expected to work in teams and interact directly with users, employers want programmers who are able to communicate with non-technical personnel.

Beginning programmers may work alone on simple assignments after some initial instruction, or on a team with more experienced programmers. Either way, beginning programmers generally must work under close supervision. Because technology changes so rapidly, programmers must continuously update their training by taking courses sponsored by their employer or software vendors.

For skilled workers who keep up to date with the latest technology, the prospects for advancement are good. In large organizations, they may be promoted to lead programmer and be given supervisory responsibilities. Some applications programmers may move into systems programming after they gain experience and take courses in systems software. With general business experience, programmers may become programmer-analysts or systems analysts, or be promoted to a managerial position. Other programmers, with specialized knowledge and experience with a language or operating system, may work in research and development areas such as multimedia or Internet technology. As employers increasingly contract out programming jobs, more opportunities should arise for experienced programmers with expertise in a specific area to work as consultants.

Technical or professional certification is becoming more common as a way for employers to ensure a level of competency or quality in all areas. Many product vendors offer certification or may even require certification of technicians and professionals who work with their products. The number of voluntary certificate or certification programs is also growing and this type of certification is available through organizations such as the Institute for Certification of Computing Professionals (ICCP). ICCP confers the designation Certified Computing Professional (CCP) to those who have at least 4 years of experience or 2 years of experience and a college degree. To qualify, individuals must pass a core examination plus exams in two specialty areas, or an exam in one specialty area and two computing languages. Those with little or no experience may be tested for certification as an Associate Computer Professional (ACP). Certification is not mandatory, but it may give a job-seeker a competitive advantage.

Job Outlook

Employment of programmers is expected to grow faster than the average through the year 2006. Jobs for both systems and applications programmers should be plentiful in data processing service firms, software houses, and computer consulting businesses. These types of establishments are part of computer and data processing services, which is projected to be the fastest growing industry. As companies attempt to control costs and keep up with changing technology, they will maintain a need for programmers to assist in conversions to new languages and from one system to the next. In addition, numerous job openings for programmers will result from the need to replace programmers who move to other occupations or leave the labor force. Most programmers who leave transfer to other occupations, such as manager or systems analyst.

Despite numerous openings, however, the consolidation and centralization of systems and applications should continue to moderate growth, as will developments in packaged software, advanced programming languages and tools, and the growing ability of users to design, write, and implement more of their own programs to meet their changing needs. As the level of technological innovation and sophistication increases, programmers should continue to face increasing competition from programming businesses overseas where more of the routine work can be outsourced at a lower cost.

As programming tasks become more complex and increasingly sophisticated skills and experience are demanded by employers, graduates of 2-year programs, and people with less than a 2-year degree or its equivalent in work experience, should face stronger competition for programming jobs. Competition for entry-level positions, however, can even affect applicants with a bachelor's degree. Although demand fluctuates as employer's needs change with technology, prospects should be best for college graduates with knowledge of and experience working with a variety of programming languages and tools, particularly C++ and other object oriented languages—such as Smalltalk, Visual Basic, Ada, and Java—as well as newer, domain-specific languages that apply to computer networking, data base management, and Internet applications. In order to remain competitive, college graduates should keep up to date with the latest skills and technologies.

Many employers prefer to hire applicants with previous experience in the field. Employers are increasingly interested in programmers who can combine areas of technical expertise or who are adaptable and able to learn and incorporate new skills. Therefore, individuals who want to become programmers can enhance their chances of doing so by combining the appropriate formal training with practical work experience. Students should try to gain experience by participating in a college work-study program, or undertaking an internship. Students also can greatly improve their employment prospects by taking courses such as accounting, management, engineering, or science—allied fields in which applications programmers are in demand.

With the expansion of client/server environments, employers will continue to look for programmers with strong technical skills who understand their business and its programming needs. Businesses also look for programmers who develop a technical specialization in areas such as client/server programming, multimedia technology, graphic user interface (GUI), and 4th and 5th generation programming tools. Programmers will be creating and maintaining expert systems and embedding these technologies in more and more products. Other areas of progress include data communications and the business application of Internet technologies. Networking computers so they can communicate with each other is necessary to achieve the greater efficiency organizations require to remain competitive. Demand for programmers with strong object-oriented programming capabilities and experience should arise from the expansion of Intranets, extranets and World Wide Web applications.

Earnings

Median earnings of programmers who worked full time in 1996 were about $40,100 a year. The middle 50 percent earned between about $30,700 and $52,000 a year. The lowest 10 percent earned less than $22,700; the highest 10 percent earned more than $65,200. Starting salary offersfor graduates with a bachelor's degree in the area of computer programming averaged about $35,167 a year in private industry in 1997, according to the National Association of Colleges and Employers. Programmers working in the West and Northeast earned somewhat more than those working in the South and Midwest. On average, systems programmers earn more than applications programmers.

A survey of workplaces in 160 metropolitan areas reported that beginning programmers had median annual earnings of about $27,000 in 1995. Experienced mid-level programmers with some supervisory responsibilities had median annual earnings of about $40,000. Median annual earnings for programmers at the supervisory or team leader level were about $55,000.

According to Robert Half International Inc., starting salaries ranged from $32,500 to $39,000 for programmers and $47,500 to $60,000 for systems programmers in large establishments in 1997. Starting salaries for programmers in small establishments ranged from $28,000 to $37,000.

In the Federal Government, the entrance salary for programmers with a college degree or qualifying experience was about $19,520 a year in early 1997; for those with a superior academic record, $24,180.

Related Occupations

Programmers must pay great attention to detail as they write and "debug" programs. Other professional workers who must be detail-oriented include computer scientists, computer engineers, and systems analysts, statisticians, mathematicians, engineers, financial analysts, accountants, auditors, actuaries, and operations research analysts.

Sources of Additional Information

State employment service offices can provide information about job openings for computer programmers. Also check with your city's chamber of commerce for information on the area's largest employers.

For information about certification as a computing professional, contact:

☛ Institute for Certification of Computing Professionals (ICCP), 2200 East Devon Ave., Suite 268, Des Plaines, IL 60018. Homepage: http://www.iccp.org

Further information about computer careers is available from:

☛ The Association for Computing (ACM), 1515 Broadway, New York, NY 10036.

☛ IEEE Computer Society, Headquarters Office, 1730 Massachusetts Ave., NW., Washington, DC 20036-1992.

Computer Scientists, Computer Engineers, and Systems Analysts

(D.O.T. 030.062-010, .162-014, .167-014; 031; 032; 033; 039; and 109.067-010)

Significant Points

- Expected to be the top 3 fastest growing occupations and among the top 20 in the number of new jobs as computer applications continue to expand throughout the economy.

- A bachelor's degree is virtually a prerequisite for most employers. Relevant work experience also is very important. For some of the more complex jobs, persons with graduate degrees are preferred.

Nature of the Work

The rapid spread of computers has generated a need for highly trained workers to design and develop new hardware and software systems and to incorporate technological advances into new or existing systems. The *Handbook* refers to this group of professionals as computer scientists, computer engineers, and systems analysts, but in reality this group includes a wide range of professional computer-related occupations. Job titles used to describe this broad category of workers evolve rapidly, reflecting new areas of specialization or changes in technology as well as the preferences and practices of employers. Although many narrow specializations exist, the professional specialty group is commonly referred to as computer scientists, computer engineers, and systems analysts.

The title *computer scientist* can be applied to a wide range computer professionals who generally design computers and the software that runs them, develop information technologies, and develop and adapt principles for applying computers to new uses. Computer scientists perform many of the same duties as other computer professionals throughout a normal workday, but their jobs are distinguished by the higher level of theoretical expertise and innovation they apply to complex problems and the creation or application of new technology.

Computer scientists can work as theorists, researchers, or inventors. Those employed by academic institutions work in areas ranging from complexity theory, to hardware, to programming language design. Some work on multi-discipline projects, such as developing and advancing uses of virtual reality in robotics. Their counterparts in private industry work in areas such as applying theory, developing specialized languages or information technologies, or designing programming tools, knowledge-based systems, or even computer games.

Computer engineers also work with the hardware and software aspects of systems design and development. Whereas computer scientists emphasize the application of theory, computer engineers emphasize the building of prototypes, although there is much crossover. Computer engineers generally apply the theories and principles of science and mathematics to the design of hardware, software, networks, and processes to solve technical problems. They often work as part of a team that designs new computing devices or computer-related equipment, systems, or software. *Computer hardware engineers* generally design, develop, test, and supervise the manufacture of computer hardware—for example, chips or device controllers. *Software engineers*, on the other hand, are involved in the design and development of software systems for control and automation of manufacturing, business, and management processes. Software engineers or *software developers* also may design and develop both packaged and systems software or be involved in creating custom software applications for clients. These professionals also possess strong programming skills, but they are more concerned with analyzing and solving programming problems than with simply writing the code for the programs.

Far more numerous, *systems analysts* use their knowledge and skills to solve computer problems and enable computer technology to meet the individual needs of an organization. They study business, scientific, or engineering data processing problems and design new solutions using computers. This process may include planning and developing new computer systems or devising ways to apply existing systems' resources to additional operations. Systems analysts may design entirely new systems, including both hardware and software, or add a single new software application to harness more of the computer's power. They work to help an organization realize the maximum benefit from its investment in equipment, personnel, and business processes. Most systems analysts generally work with a specific type of system depending on the type of organization they work for—for example, business, accounting or financial systems, or scientific and engineering systems. Companies generally seek business systems analysts who specialize in the type of systems they use.

Analysts begin an assignment by discussing the systems problem with managers and users to determine its exact nature. Much time is devoted to clearly defining the goals of the system and understanding the individual steps used to achieve them so that the problem can be broken down into separate programmable procedures. Analysts then use techniques such as structured analysis, data modeling, information engineering, mathematical model building, sampling, and cost accounting to plan the system. Analysts must specify the inputs to be accessed by the system, design the processing steps, and format the output to meet the users' needs. Once the design has been developed, systems analysts prepare charts and diagrams that describe it in terms that managers and other users can understand. They may prepare cost-benefit and return-on-investment analyses to help management decide whether implementing the proposed system will be financially feasible.

When a system is accepted, analysts determine what computer hardware and software will be needed to set it up. They coordinate tests and observe initial use of the system to ensure it performs as planned. They prepare specifications, work diagrams, and structure charts for computer programmers to follow and then work with them to "debug," or eliminate errors from the system.

In some organizations a single worker called a *programmer-analyst* is responsible for both systems analysis and programming. (The work of computer programmers is described elsewhere in the *Handbook*.) As this becomes more commonplace, these analysts will increasingly work with Computer Aided Software Engineering (CASE) tools and object-oriented programming languages, as well as client/server applications development, and multimedia and Internet technology.

One obstacle associated with expanding computer use is the inability of different computer systems to communicate with each other. Because maintaining up-to-date information—accounting records, sales figures, or budget projections, for example—is important in modern organizations, systems analysts may be instructed to make the computer systems in each department compatible so that information can be shared. Many systems analysts are involved with "networking" or connecting all the computers in an individual office, department, or establishment. A primary goal of networking is to allow users to retrieve data from a mainframe computer or a server and use it on their machine. This connection also allows data to be entered into the mainframe from a personal computer. Analysts must design the hardware and software to allow free exchange of data, custom applications, and the computer power to process it all. They study the seemingly incompatible pieces and create ways to link them so users can access information from any part of the system. Networks come in many variations and network systems and data communications analysts design, test, and evaluate systems such as Local Area Networks (LAN), Wide Area Networks (WAN), Internet, and Intranet and other data communications systems. These analysts perform network modeling, analysis and planning, and even research and recommend necessary hardware and software.

Other computer professionals include *database administrators* and *computer support specialists*. Database administrators work with database management systems software, coordinating changes to, testing, and implementing computer databases. Since they also may be responsible for design implementation and system security, database administrators plan and coordinate security measures. Computer support specialists provide assistance and advice to users. They interpret problems and provide technical support for hardware, software, and systems. Support specialists may work within an organization or directly for a computer or software vendor. Increasingly, these technical professionals work for help-desk or support services firms, providing customer support on a contract basis to clients as more of this type of work is outsourced.

Many others specialize in analysis, application, or design of a particular system or piece of the system. Network or systems administrators, for example, may install, configure, and support an organizations systems or portion of a system. Telecommunications specialists generally are involved with the interfacing of computer and communications equipment. Computer security specialists are responsible for planning, coordinating, and implementing an organizations' information security measures. These and other growing specialty occupations reflect the increasing emphasis on client-server applications, the growth of the Internet, the expansion of World Wide Web applications and Intranets, and the demand for more end-user support. An example of this is the growing number of job titles relating to the Internet and World Wide Web such as Internet and Web developers, or Webmasters.

Working Conditions

Computer scientists, computer engineers, and systems analysts normally work in offices or laboratories in comfortable surroundings. They usually work about 40 hours a week—the same as many other professional or office workers. However, evening or weekend work may be necessary to meet deadlines or solve specific problems. Given the technology available today, telecommuting is becoming more common for computer professionals. More work, including technical support, can be done from remote locations using modems, laptops, electronic mail, and even through the Internet. It is now possible for technical personnel, such as computer support specialists, to tap into a customer's computer remotely to identify and fix problems.

Like other workers who spend long periods of time in front of a computer terminal typing on a keyboard, computer scientists, engineers, and systems analysts are susceptible to eye strain, back discomfort, and hand and wrist problems such as carpal tunnel syndrome or cumulative trauma disorder.

Systems analysts must specify the inputs to be accessed by the system, design the processing steps, and format the output to meet the user's needs.

Employment

Computer scientists, computer engineers, and systems analysts held about 933,000 jobs in 1996, including about 58,000 who were self-employed. About 216,000 were computer engineers, about 506,000 were computer systems analysts, and about 212,000 were database administrators, computer support specialists, and all other computer scientists.

Although they are employed in most industries, the greatest concentration is in the computer and data processing services industry. This industry includes firms providing nearly every service related to commercial computer use on a contract basis. Services include customized computer programming services and applications and systems software design; the design, development, and production of prepackaged computer software; systems integration, networking, and reengineering services; data processing and preparation services; information retrieval services including on-line data bases and Internet services; on-site computer facilities management; the development and management of data bases; and a variety of specialized consulting services. Many others work for government agencies, manufacturers of computer and related electronic equipment, insurance companies, financial institutions, and universities.

A growing number of computer professionals are employed on a temporary or contract basis—many of whom are self-employed, working independently as contractors or self-employed consultants. For example, a company installing a new computer system may need the services of several systems analysts just to get the system running. Because not all of them would be needed once the system is functioning, the company might contract directly with the systems analysts themselves or with a temporary help agency or consulting firm. Such jobs may last from several months up to 2 years or more. This growing practice enables companies to bring in people with the exact skills they need to complete a particular project, rather than having to spend time or money training or retraining existing workers. Often, experienced consultants then train a company's in-house staff as a project develops.

Training, Other Qualifications, and Advancement

While there is no universally accepted way to prepare for a job as a computer professional because employers' preferences depend on the work to be done, a bachelor's degree is virtually a prerequisite for most employers. Relevant work experience also is very important. For some of the more complex jobs, persons with graduate degrees are preferred.

Computer hardware engineers generally require a bachelor's degree in computer engineering or electrical engineering, whereas software engineers are more likely to need a degree in computer sci-

ence. For systems analyst or even database administrator positions, many employers seek applicants who have a bachelor's degree in computer science, information science, computer information systems, or data processing. Computer support specialists may also need a bachelor's degree in a computer-related field, as well as significant experience working with computers, including programming skills. Generally, a Ph.D., or at least a master's degree in computer science or engineering, is required for computer scientist jobs in research laboratories or academic institutions.

Many people develop advanced computer skills in other occupations in which they work extensively with computers, and then transfer into computer occupations. For example, an accountant may become a systems analyst or computer support specialist specializing in accounting systems development, or an individual may move into a systems analyst job after working as a computer programmer.

Regardless of college major, employers generally look for people who are familiar with programming languages and have broad knowledge of and experience with computer systems and technologies, strong problem-solving and analysis skills, and good interpersonal skills. Courses in computer programming or systems design offer good preparation for a job in this field. For jobs in a business environment, employers usually want systems analysts to have a background in business management or a closely related field, while a background in the physical sciences, applied mathematics, or engineering is preferred for work in scientifically oriented organizations. Since employers generally look for experience, entry-level employees enhance their employment opportunities by participating in internship or co-op programs offered through their schools. A related background in the industry in which the job is located, such as financial services, banking, or accounting, can also give an applicant an edge.

Computer scientists, computer engineers, and systems analysts must be able to think logically and have good communication skills. They often deal with a number of tasks simultaneously; the ability to concentrate and pay close attention to detail is important. Although many computer specialists sometimes work independently, they often work in teams on large projects. They must be able to communicate effectively with computer personnel, such as programmers and managers, as well as with users or other staff who may have no technical computer background.

Systems analysts may be promoted to senior or lead systems analysts with experience. Those who show leadership ability also can advance to management positions, such as manager of information systems or chief information officer.

Computer engineers and scientists employed in industry may eventually advance into managerial or project leadership positions. Those employed in academic institutions can become heads of research departments or published authorities in their field. Computer professionals with several years of experience and considerable expertise in a particular subject area or application may find lucrative opportunities as independent consultants or choose to start their own computer consulting firms.

Technological advances come so rapidly in the computer field that continuous study is necessary to keep skills up to date. Continuing education is usually offered by employers, hardware and software vendors, colleges and universities, or private training institutions. Additional training may come from professional development seminars offered by professional computing societies.

As technology becomes more sophisticated and complex, a higher level of skill and expertise is demanded by employers in all areas. Technical or professional certification is becoming a more common way to ensure employers of a level of competency or quality in a prospective employee. Many product vendors offer and may even require professionals who work with their products to be certified. Voluntary certification is also available through organizations such as the Institute for Certification of Computing Professionals (ICCP). ICCP offers the designation Certified Computing Professional (CCP) to those who have at least 4 years of work experience as a computer professional, or at least 2 years experience and a college degree. Candidates must pass a core examination testing general knowledge, plus exams in two specialty areas, or in one specialty area and two computer programming languages. The Quality Assurance Institute (QAI) awards the designation Certified Quality Analyst (CQA) to those who meet education and experience requirements, pass an exam, and endorse a code of ethics. Neither designation is mandatory, but professional certification may provide a job seeker a competitive advantage.

Job Outlook

Computer scientists, computer engineers, and systems analysts are expected to be the three fastest growing occupations through the year 2006. Employment of computing professionals is expected to increase much faster than average as technology becomes more sophisticated and organizations continue to adopt and integrate these technologies, making for plentiful job openings. Growth will be driven by very rapid growth in computer and data processing services, which is projected to be the fastest growing industry. In addition, thousands of job openings will result annually from the need to replace workers who move into managerial positions or other occupations or who leave the labor force.

Computer scientists, computer engineers, and systems analysts will need to continually upgrade their technical expertise and improve their ability to interact with users as the sophistication and complexity of technology advances. As more computing power is made available to the individual user and users develop more sophisticated knowledge of computers, they become more aware of the machine's potential and better able to suggest how computers could be used to increase their own productivity and that of the organization. Increasingly, users are able to design and implement more of their own applications and programs. The result is a growing demand for computer support specialists, help desk personnel, and technical consultants.

The demand for "networking" to facilitate the sharing of information, the expansion of client/server environments, and the need for specialists to use their knowledge and skills in a problem solving capacity will be a major factor in the rising demand for systems analysts. Falling prices of computer hardware and software should continue to induce more businesses to expand computerized operations and integrate new technologies. In order to maintain a competitive edge and operate more cost effectively, firms will continue to demand computer professionals who are knowledgeable about the latest technologies and able to apply them to meet the needs of businesses.

New growth areas generally arise from the development of new technologies. Therefore, it is important for computer professionals at all levels to keep their skills up to date. The expanding integration of Internet technologies by businesses, for example, has resulted in a rising demand for a variety of skilled professionals who can develop and support Internet, Intranet, and World Wide Web applications. Growth in these areas is also expected to create demand for computer scientists, computer engineers, and systems analysts knowledgeable about network, data and communications security.

Since employers look for the most qualified applicants possessing a high level of technical expertise, individuals with an advanced degree in computer science, management information systems (MIS), computer engineering, or an MBA with a concentration in information systems should enjoy very favorable employment prospects. College graduates with a bachelor's degree in computer science, computer engineering, information science, or information systems should also enjoy very favorable prospects, particularly if they have supplemented their formal education with some level of practical experience. College graduates with non-computer science majors who have had courses in computer programming, systems analysis, and other data processing areas, as well as training or experience in an applied field, should also be able to find jobs as computer professionals. Those who are familiar with client/server environments, CASE tools and object-oriented programming, Internet, Intranet, and multimedia technology will have an even greater advantage, as will individuals with significant networking, database, and systems experience. Employers will continue to seek computer professionals who can combine strong programming and traditional systems analysis skills with good interpersonal and business skills.

Earnings

Median annual earnings of computer systems analysts and scientists who worked full time in 1996 were about $46,300. The middle 50 percent earned between $34,000 and $59,900. The lowest 10 percent earned less than $24,800 and the highest tenth, more than $76,200. Computer scientists with advanced degrees generally earn more than systems analysts.

Starting salaries for computer scientists or computer engineers with a bachelor's degree can be significantly higher than starting salaries of bachelor's degree graduates in many other fields. According to the National Association of Colleges and Employers, starting salary offers for graduates with a bachelor's degree in computer engineering averaged about $39,722 a year in 1997; those with a master's degree, $44,734 a year; and those with a Ph.D., $63,367. Starting offers for graduates with a bachelor's degree in computer science averaged about $36,597 a year; in information sciences, about $35,407 a year; and in systems analysis, about $43,800 a year in 1997. Offers for those with the bachelor's degree vary by functional area for all types of employers, as shown in the following tabulation.

Computer programming	$35,167
Information systems	34,689
Systems analysis and design	36,261
Software design and development	39,190
Hardware design and development	41,237

Offers for graduates with a master's degree in computer science in 1997 averaged $45,853 a year; and those with a Ph.D. in computer and information sciences, $61,306.

According to Robert Half International Inc., starting salaries in 1997 for systems analysts employed by large establishments employing more than 50 staff members ranged from $46,000 to $57,500. Salaries for those employed in small establishments ranged from $38,000 to $48,000. Salaries for programmer-analysts ranged from $39,000 to $50,000 in large establishments and $33,500 to $43,000 in small establishments. Starting salaries ranged from $54,000 to $67,500 for data base administrators, from $36,000 to $55,000 for network administrators, from $25,000 to $36,500 for help desk support technicians, and from $49,000 to $67,500 for software development specialists.

In the Federal Government, the entrance salary for systems analysts who are recent college graduates with a bachelor's degree was about $19,520 a year in early 1997; for those with a superior academic record, $24,180. The average annual salary for computer engineers in the Federal Government in nonsupervisory, supervisory, and managerial positions was $62,900 in early 1997.

Related Occupations

Other workers who use research, logic, and creativity to solve business problems are computer programmers, financial analysts, urban planners, engineers, mathematicians, statisticians, operations research analysts, management analysts, and actuaries.

Sources of Additional Information

Further information about computer careers is available from:
☛ Association for Computing (ACM), 1515 Broadway, New York, NY 10036.
☛ IEEE Computer Society, Headquarters Office, 1730 Massachusetts Ave., NW., Washington, DC 20036-1992.

Information about the designation Certified Computing Professional is available from:
☛ Institute for Certification of Computing Professionals (ICCP), 2200 East Devon Ave., Suite 268, Des Plaines, IL 60018. Homepage: http://www.iccp.org

Information about the designation Certified Quality Analyst is available from:
☛ Quality Assurance Institute, 7575 Dr. Phillips Blvd., Suite 350, Orlando, FL 32819.

Mathematicians

(D.O.T. 020.067-014, .167-030; 199.267-014)

Significant Points

- Employment is expected to grow more slowly than the average as civilian and defense related research activities face limited expansion.

- Bachelor's degree holders with a strong background in computer science, electrical or mechanical engineering, or operations research should have good opportunities in related occupations.

Nature of the Work

Mathematics is one of the oldest and most fundamental sciences. Mathematicians create new mathematical theories and techniques involving the latest technology and solve economic, scientific, engineering, and business problems using mathematical knowledge and computational tools.

Mathematics falls into two broad classes: theoretical (pure) mathematics and applied mathematics. However, these classes are not sharply defined and often overlap.

Theoretical mathematicians advance mathematical knowledge by developing new principles and recognizing previously unknown relationships between existing principles of mathematics. Although they seek to increase basic knowledge without necessarily considering its practical use, such pure and abstract knowledge has been instrumental in producing or furthering many scientific and engineering achievements.

Applied mathematicians use theories and techniques, such as mathematical modeling and computational methods, to formulate and solve practical problems in business, government, engineering, and the physical, life, and social sciences. For example, they may analyze the most efficient way to schedule airline routes between cities, the effects of new drugs on disease, the aerodynamic characteristics of an experimental aircraft, or the distribution costs or manufacturing processes of businesses. Applied mathematicians working in industrial research and development may develop or enhance mathematical methods when confronted with difficult problems. Some mathematicians, called cryptanalysts, analyze and decipher encryption systems designed to transmit military, political, financial, or law enforcement-related information.

Mathematicians use computers extensively to analyze relationships among variables, solve complex problems, develop models, and process large amounts of data.

Much work in applied mathematics, however, is carried on by persons with titles other than mathematician. In fact, because mathematics is the foundation upon which so many other academic disciplines are built, the number of workers using mathematical techniques is many times greater than the number actually designated as mathematicians. Engineers, computer scientists, physicists, and economists are among those who use mathematics extensively but have job titles other than mathematician. Some workers, such as statisticians, actuaries, and operations research analysts, actually are specialists in a particular branch of mathematics. (See statements on actuaries, operations research analysts, and statisticians elsewhere in the *Handbook*.)

Working Conditions

Mathematicians working for government agencies or private firms usually have structured work schedules. They generally work as an integral part of a interdisciplinary team that may include engineers, computer scientists, physicists, technicians, and others. Deadlines, overtime work, special rush requests for information or analysis, and prolonged travel to attend seminars or conferences may be part of their jobs.

Mathematicians generally work as an integral part of a interdisciplinary team.

Employment

Mathematicians held about 16,000 jobs in 1996. In addition, about 20,000 persons held mathematics faculty positions in colleges and universities in 1995, according to the American Mathematical Society. (See the statement on college and university faculty elsewhere in the *Handbook*.)

Many nonfaculty mathematicians work for either Federal or State governments. The Department of Defense is the primary Federal employer of mathematicians, employing almost three-fourths of the mathematicians employed by the Federal Government. In the private sector, major employers include research and testing services, educational services, security and commodity exchanges, and management and public relations services. Within manufacturing, the drug industry is the key employer. Some mathematicians also work for banks, insurance companies, and public utilities.

Training, Other Qualifications, and Advancement

A bachelor's degree in mathematics is the minimum education needed for prospective mathematicians. In the Federal Government, entry-level job candidates usually must have a 4-year degree with a major in mathematics or a 4-year degree with the equivalent of a mathematics major—24 semester hours of mathematics courses.

In private industry, job candidates generally need a master's or a Ph.D. degree to obtain jobs as mathematicians. Most of the positions designated for mathematicians are in research and development laboratories as part of technical teams. These research scientists engage in either pure mathematical, or basic, research; or in applied research focusing on developing or improving specific products or processes. The majority of those with a bachelor's or master's degree in mathematics who work in private industry do so not as mathematicians, but in related fields such as computer science, where they have titles such as computer programmers, systems analysts, or systems engineers.

A bachelor's degree in mathematics is offered by most colleges and universities. Mathematics courses usually required for this degree are calculus, differential equations, and linear and abstract algebra. Additional courses might include probability theory and statistics, mathematical analysis, numerical analysis, topology, discrete mathematics, and mathematical logic. Many colleges and universities urge or even require students majoring in mathematics to take several courses in a field that uses or is closely related to mathematics, such as computer science, engineering, operations research, a physical science, statistics, or economics. A double major in mathematics and another discipline such as computer science, economics, or one of the sciences is particularly desirable to many employers. A prospective college mathematics major should take as many mathematics courses as possible while in high school.

In 1996, about 240 colleges and universities offered a master's degree as the highest degree in either pure or applied mathematics; 195 offered a Ph.D. in pure or applied mathematics. In graduate school, students conduct research and take advanced courses, usually specializing in a subfield of mathematics. Some areas of concentration are algebra, number theory, real or complex analysis, geometry, topology, logic, and applied mathematics.

For work in applied mathematics, training in the field in which the mathematics will be used is very important. Fields in which applied mathematics is used extensively include physics, actuarial science, engineering, and operations research; of increasing importance are computer and information science, business and industrial management, economics, statistics, chemistry, geology life sciences, and the behavioral sciences.

Mathematicians should have substantial knowledge of computer programming because most complex mathematical computation and much mathematical modeling is done by computer.

Mathematicians need good reasoning ability and persistence in order to identify, analyze, and apply basic principles to technical problems. Communication skills are also important, as mathematicians must be able to interact with others, including nonmathematicians, and discuss proposed solutions to problems.

Job Outlook

Employment of mathematicians is expected to increase more slowly than the average for all occupations through the year 2006. The number of jobs available for workers whose educational background is solely mathematics is not expected to increase significantly. Many firms engaged in civilian research and development that use mathematicians are not planning to expand their research departments much, and, in some cases, may reduce them. Expected reductions in defense-related research and development will also affect mathematicians' employment, especially in the Federal Government. Those whose educational background includes the study of a related discipline will have better job opportunities. However, as advancements in technology lead to expanding applications of mathematics, more workers with a knowledge of mathematics will be required. Many of these workers have job titles which reflect the end product of their work rather than the discipline of mathematics used in that work.

Bachelor's degree holders in mathematics are usually not qualified for most jobs as mathematicians. However, those with a strong background in computer science, electrical or mechanical engineering, or operations research should have good opportunities in industry. Bachelor's degree holders who meet State certification requirements may become high school mathematics teachers. (For additional information, see the statement on kindergarten, elementary, and secondary school teachers elsewhere in the *Handbook*.)

Holders of a master's degree in mathematics will face very strong competition for jobs in theoretical research. However, job opportunities in applied mathematics and related areas such as computer programming, operations research, and engineering design in industry and government will be more numerous.

Earnings

According to a 1997 survey by the National Association of Colleges and Employers, starting salary offers for mathematics graduates with a bachelor's degree averaged about $31,800 a year and for those with a master's degree, $38,300.

In the Federal Government in 1997, the average annual salary for mathematicians in supervisory, nonsupervisory, and managerial positions was $62,000; for mathematical statisticians, $65,660; and for cryptanalysts, $56,160.

Benefits for mathematicians tend to be similar to those offered to most professionals who work in office settings: Vacation and sick leave, health and life insurance, and a retirement plan, among others.

Related Occupations

Other occupations that require a degree in or extensive knowledge of mathematics include actuary, statistician, computer programmer, systems analyst, systems engineer, and operations research analyst. In addition, a strong background in mathematics facilitates employment in fields such as engineering, economics, finance, and physics.

Sources of Additional Information

For more information about the field of mathematics, including career opportunities and professional training, contact:
☛ American Mathematical Society, Department of Professional Programs and Services, P.O. Box 6248, Providence, RI 02940-6248.
☛ Mathematical Association of America, 1529 18th St. NW., Washington, DC 20036.

For a 1996 resource guide on careers in mathematical sciences contact:
☛ Conference Board of the Mathematical Sciences, 1529 18th St. NW., Washington, DC 20036.

For specific information on careers in applied mathematics, contact:
☛ Society for Industrial and Applied Mathematics, 3600 University City Science Center, Philadelphia, PA 19104-2688.

Information on obtaining a mathematician position with the Federal Government may be obtained from the Office of Personnel Management through a telephone based system. Consult your telephone directory under U.S. Government for a local number or call (912) 757-3000 (TDD 912 744-2299). That number is not toll free and charges may result. Information also is available from their internet site: http:// www.usajobs.opm.gov

Operations Research Analysts

(D.O.T. 020.067-018)

Significant Points

- Individuals with a master's or Ph.D. degree in management science or operations research should find good job prospects through the year 2006, despite projected slower than average employment growth.

- Skills acquired by operations research analysts are useful for higher-level management jobs.

Nature of the Work

Efficiently running a complex organization such as a manufacturing plant or an airline requires the precise coordination of materials, equipment, and people. Operations research analysts help organizations coordinate and operate in the most efficient manner by applying mathematical principles to organizational problems. Managers then evaluate alternatives and choose the course of action that best meets their goals.

Operations research analysts tackle a whole host of problems facing large business and government organizations, including strategy, forecasting, resource allocation, facilities layout, inventory control, personnel schedules, and distribution systems. Their methods generally use a mathematical model consisting of a set of equations that describe how things happen within the organization. Use of models enables the analyst to break down problems into their component parts, assign numerical values to different components, and determine the mathematical relationships between them. These values can be altered to examine what will happen to the system under different circumstances. The situation under consideration determines the mathematical method used. Some of the methods available include simulation, linear optimization, networks, waiting lines, and game theory.

Operations research analysts use computers extensively in their work. They are typically highly proficient in database collection and management, programming, and in the development and use of sophisticated software programs. Many of the models employed in operations research are so complicated that only a computer can solve them efficiently.

The type of problem they handle varies by industry. For example, a civilian analyst for the Armed Forces may coordinate flight and maintenance schedules to produce an optimal schedule for the safe deployment of troops and material. An analyst employed by a hospital concentrates on a different set of factors, such as scheduling admissions, managing patient flow, assigning shifts, monitoring use of pharmacy and laboratory services, and forecasting demand for hospital services.

The duties of the operations research analyst vary according to the structure and management philosophy of the employer or client. Some firms centralize operations research in one department, while others use operations research in all divisions. Firms may contract out operations research services to a consulting firm. Some operations research analysts specialize in one type of application, whereas others are generalists, especially at the beginning of their careers. In addition, economists, systems analysts, mathematicians, industrial engineers, and others may also apply operations research techniques to address problem areas within their respective fields.

The degree of supervision varies by organizational structure and experience. In some organizations, analysts have a great deal of professional autonomy, while in others, analysts are more closely supervised. Operations research analysts work closely with senior managers, who have a wide variety of support needs. Analysts must adapt their work to reflect these requirements.

Regardless of the industry or structure of the organization, operations research entails a similar set of procedures. Managers begin the process by describing the symptoms of a problem to the analyst, who then formally defines the problem. For example, an operations research analyst for an auto manufacturer may be asked to determine the best inventory level for each of the materials for a new production line or, more specifically, to determine how many windshields should be kept in inventory.

Analysts study the problem, then break it into its component parts. Then they gather information about each of these parts. Usually this involves consulting a wide variety of sources of information. To determine the most efficient amount of inventory to be kept on hand, for example, operations research analysts might talk with engineers about production levels, discuss purchasing arrangements with buyers, and examine data on storage costs provided by the accounting department.

With this information in hand, the analyst is ready to select the most appropriate analytical technique. There may be several techniques that could be used, but all techniques involve the construction of a mathematical model that explains the system and solves the problem. In almost all cases, the computer program used to solve the model must be modified repeatedly to reflect different solutions.

A model for airline flight scheduling, for example, might include variables for the cities to be connected, amount of fuel required to fly the routes, projected levels of passenger demand, varying ticket and fuel prices, pilot scheduling, and maintenance costs. The analyst then chooses values for these variables, enters them into a computer which is then programmed to solve the calculations, and runs the program to produce the best flight schedule consistent with various sets of assumptions.

At this point, the operations research analyst presents the final work to management along with recommendations based on the results of the analysis. Additional computer runs based on different assumptions may be needed to help in making the final decision between various options. Once a decision has been reached by management, the analyst may work with others in the organization to ensure the plan's successful implementation.

Operations research is performed by analysts who may hold a variety of job titles.

Working Conditions

Operations research analysts generally work regular hours in an office environment. Because they work on projects that are of immediate interest to management, analysts often are under pressure to meet deadlines and often work more than a 40-hour week.

Employment

Operations research analysts held about 50,000 jobs in 1996. They are employed in most industries. Major employers include telecommunication companies, air carriers, computer and data processing services, financial institutions, insurance carriers, engineering and management services firms, and the Federal Government. About 1 out of 5 analysts work for management, research, public relations, and testing agencies that do operations research consulting.

Most operations research analysts in the Federal Government work for the Armed Forces. In addition, many operations research analysts in private industry work directly or indirectly on national defense.

Training, Other Qualifications, and Advancement

Employers generally prefer applicants with at least a master's degree in operations research, industrial engineering, or management science, coupled with a bachelor's degree in computer science or one of the quantitative disciplines like economics, mathematics or statistics.

Employers often sponsor skills-improvement training for experienced workers, helping them keep up with new developments in operations research techniques as well as advances in computer science. Some analysts attend advanced university classes on these subjects at their employer's expense.

Operations research analysts must be able to think logically and work well with people, so employers prefer workers with good oral and written communication skills. The computer is the most important tool for quantitative analysis, and both training and experience in programming is a must.

Beginning analysts usually do routine work under the supervision of more experienced analysts. As they gain knowledge and experience, they are assigned more complex tasks, with greater autonomy to design models and solve problems. Operations research analysts advance by assuming positions as technical specialists or supervisors. The skills acquired by operations research analysts are useful for higher-level management jobs, and experienced analysts may leave the field to assume nontechnical managerial or administrative positions.

Job Outlook

Individuals seeking employment as operations research or management science analysts who hold master's or Ph.D. degrees in management science or operations research should find good opportunities through the year 2006 because the number of openings generated each year as a result of the slower than average employment growth expected and the need to replace those leaving the occupation is expected to exceed the number of persons graduating with these credentials. Graduates with only a bachelors degrees in operations research or management science should find opportunities as research assistants in a variety of related fields which allow them to use their quantitative abilities. Organizations are expected to use operations research and management science techniques to improve productivity and quality and to reduce costs. This reflects an acceptance of a systematic approach to decision making by top managers. This should result in a steady demand for workers knowledgeable in operations research techniques in the years ahead.

The importance of quantitative analysis in decision making ensures that training in operations research will continue to be valuable in obtaining employment. Employment opportunities will occur in the transportation, manufacturing, finance, and services sectors, where the use of quantitative analysis can achieve dramatic improvements in operating efficiency and profitability.

Earnings

In 1996, the median salary of operations and systems researchers and analysts was about $42,400 a year. The middle 50 percent earned between about $33,100 and $55,500; the lowest 10 percent were paid less than $24,300, while the highest 10 percent earned over $65,500 a year.

The average annual salary for operations research analysts in the Federal Government in nonsupervisory, supervisory, and managerial positions was $66,760 in 1997.

Related Occupations

Operations research analysts apply mathematical principles to large, complicated problems. Workers in other occupations that stress quantitative analysis include computer scientists, engineers, mathematicians, statisticians, and economists. Because its goal is improved organizational efficiency, operations research is closely allied to managerial occupations.

Sources of Additional Information

Information on career opportunities for operations research analysts is available from:
☛ The Institute for Operations Research and the Management Sciences, 901 Elkridge Landing Rd., Suite 400, Linthicum, MD 21090.

For information on careers in the Armed Forces and Department of Defense, contact:
☛ Military Operations Research Society, 101 South Whiting St., Suite 202, Alexandria, VA 22304.

Statisticians

(D.O.T. 020.067-022, .167-026)

Significant Points

- Many with bachelors and master's degrees in statistics enter jobs in which they do not have the title of statistician.

- In private industry and colleges and universities, many positions require a graduate degree, often a doctorate, in statistics.

Nature of the Work

Statistics is a science, applying mathematical tools, involved with the collection, analysis, interpretation, and presentation of numerical data. Many applications—including predicting population growth or economic conditions, providing quality control tests for manufactured products, and helping business managers and government officials make decisions—benefit from statistical techniques. Statisticians are the individuals who design surveys and experiments, collect data, and interpret the results. In doing so, they often apply their knowledge of statistical methods to a particular subject area, such as biology, economics, engineering, medicine, or psychology. Some statisticians develop new statistical methods.

Statisticians typically work with professionals in other fields to solve practical problems. For example, biostatisticians involved in clinical research have developed sequential procedures that minimize patients' exposure to harmful treatment and make beneficial treatments more rapidly accessible.

Often statisticians are able to obtain information about a group of people or things by surveying a small portion, called a sample, of the group. For example, to determine the size of the total audience for particular programs, television rating services ask only a few thousand families, rather than all viewers, which programs they watch. Statisticians decide where and how to gather the data, determine the type and size of the sample group, and develop the survey questionnaire or reporting form. They also prepare instructions for workers who will collect and tabulate the data. Finally, statisticians analyze,

Good communications skills are important for prospective statisticians.

interpret, and summarize the data, usually using sophisticated statistical computer software.

In manufacturing industries, statisticians play an important role in the area of quality improvement. For example, a statistician in an automobile manufacturing company might design experiments using statistical models to estimate the failure time of an engine exposed to extreme weather conditions and to identify factors that can lead to improved performance. In chemical companies, statisticians might design experiments to determine what combination of chemicals would produce the best product for a specific purpose.

Because statistics are used in so many areas, specialists in other fields who use statistics often have other designations. For example, a person using statistical methods on economic data may have the title of econometrician. (See the statement on economists and marketing research analysts elsewhere in the *Handbook*).

Working Conditions

Statisticians usually work regular hours in offices. Some statisticians travel to provide advice on research projects, supervise or set up surveys, or to gather statistical data. Some may have fairly repetitive tasks, while others may have a variety of tasks, such as designing experiments.

Employment

Statisticians held about 14,000 jobs in 1996. Over one-fourth of these jobs were in the Federal Government, where statisticians were concentrated in the Departments of Commerce, Agriculture, and Health and Human Services. Most of the remaining jobs were in private industry, especially in the biopharmaceutical industry. In addition, many statisticians work in academia. (See the statement on college and university faculty elsewhere in the *Handbook*.)

Training, Other Qualifications, and Advancement

A bachelor's degree with a major in statistics or mathematics is the minimum educational requirement for some beginning jobs in statistics. The training required for employment as an entry level statistician in the Federal Government is a college degree including at least 15 semester hours of statistics—or a combination of 15 hours of mathematics and statistics if at least 6 semester hours are in statistics. An additional 9 semester hours in another academic discipline, such as economics, physical or biological science, medicine, education, engineering, or social science, are also required. To qualify as a mathematical statistician in the Federal Government requires 24 semester hours of mathematics and statistics with a minimum of 6 semester hours in statistics and 12 semester hours in advanced mathematics, such as calculus, differential equations, or vector analysis. Research positions in institutions of higher education and many positions in private industry require a graduate degree, often a doctorate, in statistics.

About 80 colleges and universities offered bachelor's degrees in statistics in 1996. Many other schools also offered degrees in mathematics, operations research, and other fields which included a sufficient number of courses in statistics to qualify graduates for some beginning positions, particularly in the Federal Government. Required subjects for statistics majors include differential and integral calculus, statistical methods, mathematical modeling, and probability theory. Additional courses that undergraduates should take include linear algebra, design and analysis of experiments, applied multivariate analysis, and mathematical statistics. Because computers are used extensively for statistical applications, a strong background in computer science is highly recommended. For positions involving quality and productivity improvement, training in engineering or physical science is useful. A background in biological, chemical, or health science is important for positions involving the preparation and testing of pharmaceutical or agricultural products. For many jobs in market research, business analysis, and forecasting, courses in economics and business administration are helpful.

In 1996, approximately 110 universities offered a master's degree program in statistics, and 58 had statistics departments which offered

a doctoral degree program. Many other schools also offered graduate-level courses in applied statistics for students majoring in biology, business, economics, education, engineering, psychology, and other fields. Acceptance into graduate statistics programs does not require an undergraduate degree in statistics although a good mathematics background is essential.

Good communications skills are important for prospective statisticians, not only for those who plan to teach, but also to qualify for many positions in industry, where the need to explain technical processes to those who are not statisticians is common. A solid understanding of business and the economy is important for those who plan to work in private industry.

Beginning statisticians who have only the bachelor's degree often spend much of their time doing routine work supervised by an experienced statistician. With experience, they may advance to positions of greater technical and supervisory responsibility. However, opportunities for promotion are best for those with advanced degrees. Master's and Ph.D. degree holders enjoy greater independence in their work and are qualified to engage in research, to develop statistical methods, or, after a number of years of experience in a particular area, to become statistical consultants.

Job Outlook

Although employment of statisticians is expected to grow little through the year 2006, job opportunities should remain favorable for individuals with statistical training. Many individuals at the bachelor's degree level, and some at the master's degree level, will find positions in which they do not have the title of statistician. This is especially true for those involved in analyzing and interpreting data from other disciplines such as economics, biological science, psychology, or engineering.

Among graduates with a bachelor's degree in statistics, those with a strong background in mathematics, engineering, or computer science should have the best prospects of finding jobs related to their field of study. Federal Government agencies will need statisticians in fields such as demography, agriculture, consumer and producer surveys, Social Security, health care, education, energy conservation, and environmental quality. However, competition for entry level positions in the Federal Government is expected to be strong for those just meeting the minimum qualification standards for statisticians. Those who meet State certification requirements may become high school statistics teachers, a newly emerging field. (For additional information, see the statement on kindergarten, elementary, and secondary school teachers elsewhere in the *Handbook*.)

Private industry will continue to require statisticians, especially at the master's and Ph.D. degree levels, to monitor and improve productivity and quality in the manufacture of various products including pharmaceuticals, motor vehicles, chemicals, and food products. For example, pharmaceutical firms will need statisticians to assess the safety and effectiveness of the rapidly expanding number of drugs. To counter stiff competition, motor vehicle manufacturers will need statisticians to improve the quality of automobiles, trucks, and their components by developing and testing new designs. Some statisticians with a knowledge of engineering and the physical sciences will find jobs in research and development, working with teams of scientists and engineers to help improve design and production processes in order to ensure consistent quality of newly developed products. Business firms will rely more heavily on workers with a background in statistics to forecast sales, analyze business conditions, and help solve management problems. In addition, sophisticated statistical services will increasingly be contracted out to consulting firms.

Earnings

The average annual salary for statisticians in the Federal Government in nonsupervisory, supervisory, and managerial positions was $61,030 in 1997; mathematical statisticians averaged $65,660.

Statisticians who hold advanced degrees generally earn higher starting salaries.

Benefits for statisticians tend to resemble those offered most professionals: Vacation and sick leave, health and life insurance, and a retirement plan, among others.

Related Occupations
People in numerous occupations work with statistics. Among them are actuaries, mathematicians, operations research analysts, computer programmers, computer systems analysts, engineers, economists, financial analysts, information scientists, life scientists, physical scientists, and social scientists.

Sources of Additional Information
For information about career opportunities in statistics, contact:
☛ American Statistical Association, 1429 Duke St., Alexandria, VA 22314.

Information on obtaining a statistian position with the Federal Government may be obtained from the Office of Personnel Management through a telephone based system. Consult your telephone directory under U.S. Government for a local number or call (912) 757-3000 (TDD 912 744-2299). That number is not toll free and charges may result. Information also is available from their internet site: http:// www.usajobs.opm.gov

Life Scientists

Agricultural Scientists

(D.O.T. 040.061-010, -014, -018, -038, -042, and -058; 041.061-014, -018, -046, and -082; and 041.081)

Significant Points

- A large proportion, about 30 percent, work for Federal, State, and local governments.

- A bachelor's degree in agricultural science is sufficient for some jobs in applied research; a master's or doctoral degree is required for basic research.

- Those with advanced degrees have the best prospects; however, competition may be keen for some basic research jobs if Federal and State funding for these positions is cut.

Nature of the Work
The work agricultural scientists do plays an important part in maintaining and increasing the Nation's agricultural productivity. Agricultural scientists study farm crops and animals and develop ways of improving their quantity and quality. They look for ways to improve crop yield and quality with less labor, control pests and weeds more safely and effectively, and conserve soil and water. They research methods of converting raw agricultural commodities into attractive and healthy food products for consumers.

Agricultural science is closely related to biological science, and agricultural scientists use the principles of biology, chemistry, physics, mathematics, and other sciences to solve problems in agriculture. They often work with biological scientists on basic biological research and in applying to agriculture the advances in knowledge brought about by biotechnology.

Many agricultural scientists work in basic or applied research and development. Others manage or administer research and development programs or manage marketing or production operations in companies that produce food products or agricultural chemicals, supplies, and machinery. Some agricultural scientists are consultants to business firms, private clients, or to government.

Depending on the agricultural scientist's area of specialization, the nature of the work performed varies.

Food science. Food scientists or technologists are usually employed in the food processing industry, universities, or the Federal Government, and help meet consumer demand for food products that are healthful, safe, palatable, and convenient. To do this, they use their knowledge of chemistry, microbiology, and other sciences to develop new or better ways of preserving, processing, packaging, storing, and delivering foods. Some engage in basic research, discovering new food sources; analyzing food content to determine levels of vitamins, fat, sugar, or protein; or searching for substitutes for harmful or undesirable additives, such as nitrites. Many food technologists work in product development. Others enforce government regulations, inspecting food processing areas and ensuring that sanitation, safety, quality, and waste management standards are met.

Plant science. Agronomy, crop science, entomology, and plant breeding are included in plant science. Scientists in these disciplines study plants and their growth in soils, helping producers of food, feed, and fiber crops to continue to feed a growing population while conserving natural resources and maintaining the environment. Agronomists and crop scientists not only help increase productivity, but also study ways to improve the nutritional value of crops and the quality of seed. Some crop scientists study the breeding, physiology, and management of crops and use genetic engineering to develop crops resistant to pests and drought. Entomologists conduct research to develop new technologies to control or eliminate pests in infested areas and prevent the spread of harmful pests to new areas, and which are compatible with the environment. They also do research or engage in oversight activities aimed at halting the spread of insect-borne disease.

Soil science. These workers study the chemical, physical, biological, and mineralogical composition of soils as they relate to plant or crop growth. They study the responses of various soil types to fertilizers, tillage practices, and crop rotation. Many soil scientists who work for the Federal Government conduct soil surveys, classifying and mapping soils. They provide information and recommendations to farmers and other landowners regarding the best use of land and how to avoid or correct problems such as erosion. They may also consult with engineers and other technical personnel working on construction projects about the effects of, and solutions to, soil problems. Since soil science is closely related to environmental science, persons trained in soil science also apply their knowledge to ensure environmental quality and effective land use.

Animal science. Developing better, more efficient ways of producing and processing meat, poultry, eggs, and milk is the work of animal scientists. Dairy scientists, poultry scientists, animal breeders, and other related scientists study the genetics, nutrition, reproduction, growth, and development of domestic farm animals. Some animal scientists inspect and grade livestock food products, purchase livestock, or work in technical sales or marketing. As extension agents or consultants, animal scientists advise agricultural producers on how to upgrade animal housing facilities properly, lower mortality rates, or increase production of animal products, such as milk or eggs.

Working Conditions
Agricultural scientists involved in management or basic research tend to work regular hours in offices and laboratories. The working environment for those engaged in applied research or product development varies, depending on the discipline of agricultural science and the type of employer. For example, food scientists in private industry may work in test kitchens while investigating new processing techniques. Animal scientists working for Federal, State,

A soil scientist records the growth of grains in an agricultural research test plot.

or university research stations may spend part of their time at dairies, farrowing houses, feedlots, farm animal facilities, or outdoors conducting research associated with livestock. Soil and crop scientists also spend time outdoors conducting research on farms agricultural research stations. Entomologists work in laboratories, insectories, or agricultural research stations, and may also spend time outdoors studying or collecting insects in their natural habitat.

Employment
Agricultural scientists held about 24,000 jobs in 1996. In addition, several thousand persons held agricultural science faculty positions in colleges and universities. (See the statement on college and university faculty elsewhere in the *Handbook*.)

About 30 percent of all nonfaculty agricultural scientists work for Federal, State, or local governments. Nearly 1 out of 5 worked for the Federal Government in 1996, mostly in the Department of Agriculture. In addition, large numbers worked for State governments at State agricultural colleges or agricultural research stations. Some worked for agricultural service companies; others worked for commercial research and development laboratories, seed companies, pharmaceutical companies, wholesale distributors, and food products companies. About 2,000 agricultural scientists were self-employed in 1996, mainly as consultants.

Training, Other Qualifications, and Advancement
Training requirements for agricultural scientists depend on their specialty and the type of work they perform. A bachelor's degree in agricultural science is sufficient for some jobs in applied research or for assisting in basic research, but a master's or doctoral degree is required for basic research. A Ph.D. degree in agricultural science is usually needed for college teaching and for advancement to administrative research positions. Degrees in related sciences such as biology, chemistry, or physics or in related engineering specialties also may qualify persons for some agricultural science jobs.

All States have a land-grant college which offers agricultural science degrees. Many other colleges and universities also offer agricultural science degrees or some agricultural science courses. However, not every school offers all specialties. A typical undergraduate agricultural science curriculum includes communications, economics, business, and physical and life sciences courses, in addition to a wide variety of technical agricultural science courses. For prospective animal scientists, these technical agricultural science courses might include animal breeding, reproductive physiology, nutrition, and meats and muscle biology; students preparing as food scientists take courses such as food chemistry, food analysis, food microbiology, and food processing operations; and those preparing as crop or soil scientists take courses in plant pathology, soil chemistry, entomology, plant physiology, and biochemistry, among others. Advanced degree programs include classroom and fieldwork, laboratory research, and a thesis or dissertation based on independent research.

Agricultural scientists should be able to work independently or as part of a team and be able to communicate clearly and concisely, both orally and in writing. Most agricultural scientists also need an understanding of basic business principles.

The American Society of Agronomy offers certification in agronomy, crop science, soil science, soil classification, horticulture, plant pathology, and weed science. To become certified, applicants must meet certain examination, education, and professional work experience standards.

Agricultural scientists who have advanced degrees usually begin in research or teaching. With experience, they may advance to jobs such as supervisors of research programs or managers of other agriculture-related activities.

Job Outlook
Employment of agricultural scientists is expected to grow about as fast as the average for all occupations through the year 2006. Additionally, the need to replace agricultural scientists who retire or otherwise leave the occupation permanently will account for many more job openings than projected growth.

Past agricultural research has resulted in the development of higher-yielding crops, crops with better resistance to pests and plant pathogens, and chemically-based fertilizers and pesticides. Further research is necessary as insects and diseases continue to adapt to pesticides, and as soil fertility and water quality deteriorate. Agricultural scientists will be needed to balance increased agricultural output with protection and preservation of the soil, water, and ecosystems. They will practice "sustainable agriculture" by developing and implementing plans to manage pests, crops, soil fertility and erosion, and animal waste in ways that reduce the use of harmful chemicals and do little damage to the natural environment. Products developed using biotechnology methods will assist in these challenges. Also, an expanding population and a public increasingly focused on diet, health, and food safety, will result in growing opportunities for agricultural scientists to work in food science and technology.

Generally speaking, those with advanced degrees will be in the best position to enter jobs as agricultural scientists. However, competition may be keen for teaching positions in colleges or universities and for some basic research jobs, even for doctoral holders. Federal and State budget cuts may limit funding for these positions through the year 2006.

Bachelor's degree holders can work in some applied research and product development positions, but usually only in certain subfields, such as food science and technology. Also, the Federal Government hires bachelor's degree holders to work as soil scientists. Despite the more limited opportunities for those with only a bachelor's degree to obtain jobs as agricultural scientists, a bachelor's degree in agricultural science is useful for managerial jobs in businesses that deal with ranchers and farmers, such as feed, fertilizer, seed, and farm equipment manufacturers; retailers or wholesalers; and farm credit institutions. Four-year degrees may also help persons enter occupations such as farmer or farm or ranch manager, cooperative extension service agent, agricultural products inspector, or purchasing or sales agent for agricultural commodity or farm supply companies.

Earnings
According to the National Association of Colleges and Employers, beginning salary offers in 1997 for graduates with a bachelor's degree

in animal science averaged about $24,900 a year, and for graduates in plant science, $24,000.

The median salary for full-time food scientists or technologists was $55,200, according to a 1995 salary survey by the Institute of Food Technologists.

Average Federal salaries for employees in nonsupervisory, supervisory, and managerial positions in certain agricultural science specialties in 1997 were as follows: Animal science, $65,500; agronomy, $52,000; soil science, $49,400; horticulture, $50,400; and entomology, $62,200.

Related Occupations

The work of agricultural scientists is closely related to that of biologists and other natural scientists such as chemists, foresters, and conservation scientists. It is also related to agricultural production occupations such as farmer and farm manager and cooperative extension service agent. Certain specialties of agricultural science are also related to other occupations. For example, the work of animal scientists is related to that of veterinarians; horticulturists, to landscape architects; and soil scientists, to soil conservationists.

Sources of Additional Information

Information on careers in agricultural science is available from:
☛ American Society of Agronomy, Crop Science Society of America, Soil Science Society of America, 677 S. Segoe Rd., Madison, WI 53711-1086.
☛ Food and Agricultural Careers for Tomorrow, Purdue University, 1140 Agricultural Administration Bldg., West Lafayette, IN 47907-1140.

For information on careers in food technology, write to:
☛ Institute of Food Technologists, Suite 300, 221 N. LaSalle St., Chicago IL 60601.

For information on careers in entomology, contact:
☛ Entomological Society of America, 9301 Annapolis Rd., Lanham, MD 20706, Attn: Public Relations Coordinator.

Information on acquiring a job as an agricultural scientist with the Federal Government may be obtained from the Office of Personnel Management through a telephone-based system. Consult your telephone directory under U.S. Government for a local number, or call (912) 757-3000 (TDD 912-744-2299). That number is not toll-free and charges may result. Information also is available from their Internet site: http://www.usajobs.opm.gov

Biological and Medical Scientists

(D.O.T. 022.081-010; 041.061, except -014, -018, -046, and -082; 041.067-010; 041.261-010)

Significant Points

- For biological scientists, a Ph.D. degree is generally required for independent research; a master's degree is sufficient for some jobs in applied research or product development; a bachelor's degree is adequate for some nonresearch jobs.

- For medical scientists, the Ph.D. degree in a biological science is required; some need a medical degree.

- Doctoral degree holders face considerable competition for independent research positions; those with a bachelor's or master's degree in biological science can expect better opportunities for nonresearch positions.

Nature of the Work

Biological and medical scientists study living organisms and their relationship to their environment. Most specialize in some area of biology such as zoology (the study of animals) or microbiology (the study of microscopic organisms).

Many biological scientists and virtually all medical scientists work in research and development. Some conduct basic research to advance knowledge of living organisms, including viruses, bacteria, and other infectious agents. Past research has resulted in the development of vaccines, medicines, and treatments for cancer and other diseases. Basic biological and medical research continues to provide the building blocks necessary to develop solutions to human health problems and to preserve and repair the natural environment. Biological and medical scientists may work independently in private industry, university, or government laboratories, often exploring new areas of research or expanding on specialized research started in graduate school. Those who are not wage and salary workers in private industry typically submit grant proposals to obtain funding for their projects. Colleges and universities, private industry, and Federal Government agencies, such as the National Institutes of Health and the National Science Foundation, contribute to the support of scientists whose research proposals are determined to be financially feasible and have the potential to advance new ideas or processes.

Biological and medical scientists who work in applied research or product development use knowledge provided by basic research to develop new drugs and medical treatments, increase crop yields, and protect and clean up the environment. They usually have less autonomy than basic researchers to choose the emphasis of their research, relying instead on market-driven directions based on the firm's products and goals. Biological and medical scientists doing applied research and product development in private industry may be required to express their research plans or results to nonscientists who are in a position to veto or approve their ideas, and they must understand the business impact of their work. Scientists are increasingly working as part of teams, interacting with engineers, scientists of other disciplines, business managers, and technicians. They may also work with customers or suppliers, and manage budgets.

Biological and medical scientists who conduct research usually work in laboratories and use electron microscopes, computers, thermal cyclers, or a wide variety of other equipment. Some conduct experiments using laboratory animals or greenhouse plants. For some biological scientists, a good deal of research is performed outside of laboratories. For example, a botanist may do research in tropical rain forests to see what plants grow there, or an ecologist may study how a forest area recovers after a fire.

Some biological and medical scientists work in managerial or administrative positions, usually after spending some time doing research and learning about the firm, agency, or project. They may plan and administer programs for testing foods and drugs, for example, or direct activities at zoos or botanical gardens. Some biological scientists work as consultants to business firms or to government, while others test and inspect foods, drugs, and other products.

In the 1980s, swift advances in basic biological knowledge related to genetics and molecules spurred growth in the field of biotechnology. Biological and medical scientists using this technology manipulate the genetic material of animals or plants, attempting to make organisms more productive or resistant to disease. Research using biotechnology techniques, such as recombining DNA, has led to the discovery of important drugs, including human insulin and growth hormone. Many other substances not previously available in large quantities are starting to be produced by biotechnological means; some may be useful in treating cancer and other diseases. Today, many biological and medical scientists are involved in biotechnology, including those who work on the Human Genome project, isolating, identifying, and sequencing human genes. This work continues to lead to the discovery of the genes associated with specific diseases and inherited traits, such as certain types of cancer or obesity. These advances in biotechnology have opened up research opportunities in almost all areas of biology, including commercial applications in agriculture, environmental remediation, and the food and chemical industries.

Most biological scientists who come under the broad category of *biologist* are further classified by the type of organism they study or by the specific activity they perform, although recent advances in the understanding of basic life processes at the molecular and cellular levels have blurred some traditional classifications.

Aquatic biologists study plants and animals living in water. *Marine biologists* study salt water organisms and *limnologists* study fresh water organisms. Marine biologists are sometimes erroneously called oceanographers, but oceanography is the study of the physical characteristics of oceans and the ocean floor. (See the statement on geologists and geophysicists elsewhere in the *Handbook*.)

Biochemists study the chemical composition of living things. They try to understand the complex chemical combinations and reactions involved in metabolism, reproduction, growth, and heredity. Much of the work in biotechnology is done by biochemists and molecular biologists because this technology involves understanding the complex chemistry of life.

Botanists study plants and their environment. Some study all aspects of plant life; others specialize in areas such as identification and classification of plants, the structure and function of plant parts, the biochemistry of plant processes, the causes and cures of plant diseases, and the geological record of plants.

Microbiologists investigate the growth and characteristics of microscopic organisms such as bacteria, algae, or fungi. *Medical microbiologists* study the relationship between organisms and disease or the effect of antibiotics on microorganisms. Other microbiologists may specialize in environmental, food, agricultural, or industrial microbiology, virology (the study of viruses), or immunology (the study of mechanisms that fight infections). Many microbiologists use biotechnology to advance knowledge of cell reproduction and human disease.

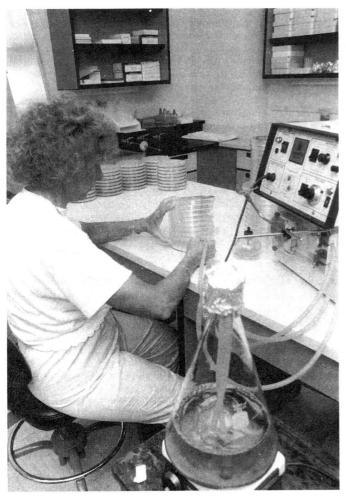

Many biological scientists and virtually all medical scientists work in research and development.

Physiologists study life functions of plants and animals, both in the whole organism and at the cellular or molecular level, under normal and abnormal conditions. Physiologists may specialize in functions such as growth, reproduction, photosynthesis, respiration, or movement, or in the physiology of a certain area or system of the organism.

Zoologists study animals—their origin, behavior, diseases, and life processes. Some experiment with live animals in controlled or natural surroundings while others dissect dead animals to study their structure. Zoologists are usually identified by the animal group studied—ornithologists (birds), mammalogists (mammals), herpetologists (reptiles), and ichthyologists (fish).

Ecologists study the relationship among organisms and between organisms and their environments and the effects of influences such as population size, pollutants, rainfall, temperature, and altitude.

Agricultural scientists, who may also be classified as biological scientists, are included in a separate statement elsewhere in the *Handbook*.

Biological scientists who do biomedical research are usually called *medical scientists*. Medical scientists working on basic research into normal biological systems often do so to understand the causes of and to discover treatment for disease and other health problems. Medical scientists may try to identify the kinds of changes in a cell, chromosome, or even gene that signal the development of medical problems, such as different types of cancer. After identifying structures of or changes in organisms that provide clues to health problems, medical scientists may then work on the treatment of problems. For example, a medical scientist involved in cancer research might try to formulate a combination of drugs which will lessen the effects of the disease. Medical scientists who have a medical degree might then administer the drugs to patients in clinical trials, monitor their reactions, and observe the results. (Medical scientists who do not have a medical degree normally collaborate with a medical doctor who deals directly with patients.) The medical scientist might then return to the laboratory to examine the results and, if necessary, adjust the dosage levels to reduce negative side effects or to try to induce even better results. In addition to using basic research to develop treatments for health problems, medical scientists attempt to discover ways to prevent health problems from developing, such as affirming the link between smoking and increased risk of lung cancer, or alcoholism and liver disease.

Working Conditions

Biological and medical scientists generally work regular hours in offices or laboratories and usually are not exposed to unsafe or unhealthy conditions. Those who work with dangerous organisms or toxic substances in the laboratory must follow strict safety procedures to avoid contamination. Medical scientists also spend time working in clinics and hospitals administering drugs and treatments to patients in clinical trials. Many biological scientists such as botanists, ecologists, and zoologists take field trips which involve strenuous physical activity and primitive living conditions.

Biological and medical scientists who depend on grant money to support their research may be under pressure to meet deadlines and conform to rigid grant-writing specifications when preparing proposals to seek new or extended funding.

Employment

Biological and medical scientists held about 118,000 jobs in 1996. Almost 1 in 4 biological scientists were employed by Federal, State, and local governments. Federal biological scientists worked mainly in the U.S. Departments of Agriculture, the Interior, and Defense, and in the National Institutes of Health. Most of the rest worked in the drug industry, which includes pharmaceutical and biotechnology establishments; hospitals; or research and testing laboratories. About 1 in 5 medical scientists worked in State government, with most of the remainder found in research and testing laboratories, educational institutions, the drug industry, and hospitals.

In addition, many biological and medical scientists held biology faculty positions in colleges and universities. (See the statement on college and university faculty elsewhere in the *Handbook*.)

Training, Other Qualifications, and Advancement
For biological scientists, the Ph.D. degree generally is required for independent research and for advancement to administrative positions. A master's degree is sufficient for some jobs in applied research or product development and for jobs in management, inspection, sales, and service. The bachelor's degree is adequate for some nonresearch jobs. Some graduates with a bachelor's degree start as biological scientists in testing and inspection, or get jobs related to biological science such as technical sales or service representatives. In some cases, graduates with a bachelor's degree are able to work in a laboratory environment on their own projects, but this is unusual. Some may work as research assistants. Others become biological technicians, medical laboratory technologists or, with courses in education, high school biology teachers. (See the statements on clinical laboratory technologists and technicians; science technicians; and kindergarten, elementary, and secondary school teachers elsewhere in the *Handbook*.) Many with a bachelor's degree in biology enter medical, dental, veterinary, or other health profession schools. Some enter a wide range of occupations with little or no connection to biology.

Most colleges and universities offer bachelor's degrees in biological science and many offer advanced degrees. Curriculums for advanced degrees often emphasize a subfield such as microbiology or botany, but not all universities offer all curriculums. Advanced degree programs include classroom and field work, laboratory research, and a thesis or dissertation. Biological scientists who have advanced degrees often take temporary postdoctoral research positions which provide specialized research experience. In private industry, some may become managers or administrators within biology; others leave biology for nontechnical managerial, administrative, or sales jobs.

Biological scientists should be able to work independently or as part of a team and be able to communicate clearly and concisely, both orally and in writing. Those in private industry, especially those who aspire to management or administrative positions, should possess strong business and communication skills and be familiar with regulatory issues and marketing and management techniques. Those doing field research in remote areas must have physical stamina.

The Ph.D. degree in a biological science is the minimum education required for prospective medical scientists because the work of medical scientists is almost entirely research oriented. A Ph.D. degree qualifies one to do research on basic life processes or on particular medical problems or diseases, and to analyze and interpret the results of experiments on patients. Medical scientists who administer drug or gene therapy to human patients, or who otherwise interact medically with patients—such as drawing blood, excising tissue, or performing other invasive procedures—must have a medical degree. It is particularly helpful for medical scientists to earn both Ph.D. and medical degrees.

In addition to the formal education, medical scientists are usually expected to spend several years in a postdoctoral position before they are offered permanent jobs. Postdoctoral work provides valuable laboratory experience, including experience in specific processes and techniques, such as gene splicing, which are transferable to other research projects. In some institutions, the postdoctoral position can lead to a permanent position.

Job Outlook
Despite prospects of faster-than-average job growth over the 1996-2006 period, biological and medical scientists can expect to face considerable competition for coveted basic research positions. Much research and development, including many areas of medical research, is funded by the Federal Government. Recent budget tightening has led to smaller increases in research and development expenditures, further limiting the dollar amount of each grant and slowing the growth of the number of grants awarded to researchers. At the same time, the number of newly trained scientists has continued to increase at a steady rate, so both new and established scientists have experienced greater difficulty winning and renewing research grants. If the number of advanced degrees awarded continues to grow unabated, this competitive scenario is likely to persist. Additionally, applied research positions in private industry may become more difficult if more scientists seek jobs in private industry than in the past due to the competitive job market for college and university faculty.

Opportunities for those with a bachelor's or master's degree in biological science are expected to be better. The number of science-related jobs in sales, marketing, and research management, for which non-Ph.D.'s generally qualify, are expected to be more plentiful than independent research positions. They may also fill positions as science or engineering technicians or health technologists and technicians. Some become high school biology teachers, while those with a doctorate in biological science may become college and university faculty. (See statements on science and engineering technicians, health technologists and technicians, secondary school teachers, and college and university faculty elsewhere in the *Handbook*.)

Biological and medical scientists enjoyed very rapid gains in employment between the mid-1980s and mid-1990s, in part reflecting increased staffing requirements in new biotechnology companies. Employment growth should slow as increases in the number of new biotechnology firms slows and existing firms merge or are absorbed into larger ones. However, much of the basic biological research done in recent years has resulted in new knowledge, including the isolation and identification of new genes. Biological and medical scientists will be needed to take this knowledge to the next stage, which is the understanding of how certain genes function within an entire organism so that gene therapies can be developed to treat diseases. Even pharmaceutical and other firms not solely engaged in biotechnology are expected to increasingly use biotechnology techniques, spurring employment increases for biological and medical scientists. In addition, efforts to discover new and improved ways to clean up and preserve the environment will continue to add to growth. More biological scientists will be needed to determine the environmental impact of industry and government actions and to prevent or correct environmental problems. Expected expansion in research related to health issues, such as AIDS, cancer, and Alzheimer's disease , should also result in growth.

Biological and medical scientists are less likely to lose their jobs during recessions than those in many other occupations because many are employed on long-term research projects. However, a recession could further influence the amount of money allocated to new research and development efforts, particularly in areas of risky or innovative research. A recession could also limit the possibility of extension or renewal of existing projects.

Earnings
According to the National Association of Colleges and Employers, beginning salary offers in private industry in 1997 averaged $25,400 a year for bachelor's degree recipients in biological science; about $26,900 for master's degree recipients; and about $52,400 for doctoral degree recipients.

Median annual earnings for biological and life scientists were about $36,300 in 1996; the middle 50 percent earned between $28,400 and $50,900. Ten percent earned less than $22,000, and 10 percent earned over $66,000. For medical scientists, median annual earnings were about $34,300; the middle 50 percent earned between $25,200 and $52,200. Ten percent earned less than $18,700, and 10 percent earned over $74,000.

In the Federal Government in 1997, general biological scientists in nonsupervisory, supervisory, and managerial positions earned an average salary of $52,100; microbiologists, $58,700; ecologists, $52,700; physiologists, $65,900; and geneticists, $62,700.

Related Occupations
Many other occupations deal with living organisms and require a level of training similar to that of biological and medical scientists. These include

the conservation occupations of forester, range manager, and soil conservationist; animal breeders, horticulturists, soil scientists, and most other agricultural scientists. Many health occupations are also related to those in the biological sciences, such as medical doctors, dentists, and veterinarians.

Sources of Additional Information

For information on careers in the biological sciences, contact:

☞ American Institute of Biological Sciences, Suite 200, 1444 I St. NW. Washington, DC 20005. Homepage: http://www.aibs.org

For information on careers in physiology, contact:

☞ American Physiological Society, Education Office, 9650 Rockville Pike, Bethesda, MD 20814. Homepage: http://www.faseb.org/aps

For information on careers in biotechnology, contact:

☞ Biotechnology Industry Organization, 1625 K St. NW., Suite 1100, Washington, DC 20006.

For information on careers in biochemistry, contact:

☞ American Society for Biochemistry and Molecular Biology, 9650 Rockville Pike, Bethesda, MD 20814.

For information on careers in biophysics, contact:

☞ Biophysical Society, 9650 Rockville Pike, Room 0512, Bethesda, MD 20814.

For information on careers in botany, contact:

☞ Botanical Society of America, Business Office, 1735 Neil Ave., Columbus, OH 43210-1293. Homepage: http://www.botany.org

For information on careers in microbiology, contact:

☞ American Society for Microbiology, Office of Education and Training—Career Information, 1325 Massachusetts Ave. NW., Washington, DC 20005. Homepage: http://www.asmusa.org

Information on acquiring a job as a biological or medical scientist with the Federal government may be obtained from the Office of Personnel Management through a telephone-based system. Consult your telephone directory under U.S. Government for a local number or call (912) 757-3000 (TDD 912 744-2299). That number is not toll-free and charges may result. Information also is available from their Internet site: http://www.usajobs.opm.gov

Foresters and Conservation Scientists

(D.O.T. 040.061-030, -046, -050, -054, and -062; .167-010; 049.127)

Significant Points

● About 2 out of 3 work for Federal, State, or local governments.

● A bachelor's degree in forestry, range management, or a related field is generally the minimum educational requirement.

● Projected average employment growth will stem from continuing emphasis on environmental protection and responsible land management.

Nature of the Work

Forests and rangelands serve a variety of needs: They supply wood products, livestock forage, minerals, and water; serve as sites for recreational activities; and provide habitats for wildlife. Foresters and conservation scientists manage, develop, use, and help protect these and other natural resources.

Foresters manage forested lands for a variety of purposes. Those working in private industry may procure timber from private landowners. To do this, foresters contact local forest owners and gain permission to take inventory of the type, amount, and location of all standing timber on the property, a process known as timber cruising. Foresters then appraise the timber's worth, negotiate the purchase of timber, and draw up a contract for procurement. Next, they subcontract with loggers or pulpwood cutters for tree removal, aid in road layout, and maintain close contact with the subcontractor's workers and the landowner to ensure that the work meets the landowner's requirements, as well as Federal, State, and local environmental specifications. Forestry consultants often act as agents for the forest owner, performing the above duties and negotiating timber sales with industrial procurement foresters.

Throughout the process, foresters consider the economics of the purchase as well as the environmental impact on natural resources, a function which has taken on added importance in recent years. To do this, they determine how best to conserve wildlife habitats, creek beds, water quality, and soil stability and how best to comply with environmental regulations. Foresters must balance the desire to conserve forested ecosystems for future generations with the need to use forest resources for recreational or economic purposes.

Through a process called regeneration, foresters also supervise the planting and growing of new trees. They choose and prepare the site, using controlled burning, bulldozers, or herbicides to clear weeds, brush, and logging debris. They advise on the type, number, and placement of trees to be planted. Foresters then monitor the seedlings to ensure healthy growth and to determine the best time for harvesting. If they detect signs of disease or harmful insects, they decide on the best course of treatment to prevent contamination or infestation of healthy trees.

Foresters who work for State and Federal governments manage public forests and parks and also work with private landowners to protect and manage forest land outside of the public domain. They may also design campgrounds and recreation areas.

Foresters use a number of tools to perform their jobs: Clinometers measure the heights, diameter tapes measure the diameter, and increment borers and bark gauges measure the growth of trees so that timber volumes can be computed and future growth estimated. Photogrammetry and remote sensing (aerial photographs and other imagery taken from airplanes and satellites) often are used for mapping large forest areas and for detecting widespread trends of forest and land use. Computers are used extensively, both in the office and in the field, for the storage, retrieval, and analysis of information required to manage the forest land and its resources.

Range managers, also called range *conservationists*, range *ecologists*, or range *scientists*, manage, improve, and protect rangelands to maximize their use without damaging the environment. Rangelands cover about 1 billion acres of the United States, mostly in the western States and Alaska. They contain many natural resources, including grass and shrubs for animal grazing, wildlife habitats, water from vast watersheds, recreation facilities, and valuable mineral and energy resources. Range managers help ranchers attain optimum livestock production by determining the number and kind of animals to graze, the grazing system to use, and the best season for grazing. At the same time, however, they maintain soil stability and vegetation for other uses such as wildlife habitats and outdoor recreation. They also plan and implement revegetation of disturbed sites.

Soil conservationists provide technical assistance to farmers, ranchers, State and local governments, and others concerned with the conservation of soil, water, and related natural resources. They develop programs designed to get the most productive use of land without damaging it. Conservationists visit areas with erosion problems, find the source of the problem, and help landowners and managers develop management practices to combat it.

Foresters and conservation scientists often specialize in one area such as forest resource management, urban forestry, wood technology, or forest economics.

Working Conditions

Working conditions vary considerably. Although some of the work is solitary, foresters and conservation scientists also deal regularly with landowners, loggers, forestry technicians and aides, farmers, ranchers, government officials, special interest groups, and the public in general. Some work regular hours in offices or labs. Others may split their time between field work and office work, while some—especially independent consultants or less experienced workers—spend the majority of their time outdoors overseeing or participating in hands-on work.

Some foresters and conservation scientists split their time between field work and office work.

The work can be physically demanding. Foresters and conservation scientists who work outdoors do so in all kinds of weather, sometimes in isolated areas. Some foresters may need to walk long distances through densely wooded land to carry out their work. Foresters also may work long hours fighting fires. Conservation scientists often are called in to prevent erosion after a forest fire, and they provide emergency help after floods, mudslides, and tropical storms.

Employment

Foresters and conservation scientists held about 37,000 jobs in 1996. Nearly 3 out of 10 salaried workers were in the Federal Government, mostly in the U.S. Department of Agriculture (USDA). Foresters were concentrated in the USDA's Forest Service; soil conservationists in the USDA's Natural Resource Conservation Service. Most range managers worked in the Department of the Interior's Bureau of Land Management or in the USDA's Natural Resource Conservation Service. Nearly another 3 out of 10 foresters and conservation scientists worked for State governments, and nearly 1 out of 10 worked for local governments. The remainder worked in private industry, mainly in the forestry industry, logging and lumber companies and sawmills, and research and testing services. Some were self-employed as consultants for private landowners, State and Federal governments, and forestry-related businesses.

Although foresters and conservation scientists work in every State, employment of foresters is concentrated in the western and southeastern States, where many national and private forests and parks, and most of the lumber and pulpwood-producing forests, are located. Range managers work almost entirely in the western States, where most of the rangeland is located. Soil conservationists, on the other hand, are employed in almost every county in the country.

Training, Other Qualifications, and Advancement

A bachelor's degree in forestry is the minimum educational requirement for professional careers in forestry. In the Federal Government, a combination of experience and appropriate education occasionally may substitute for a 4-year forestry degree, but job competition makes this difficult.

Fifteen States have mandatory licensing or voluntary registration requirements which a forester must meet in order to acquire the title "professional forester" and practice forestry in the State. Licensing or registration requirements vary by State, but usually entail completing a 4-year degree in forestry, a minimum period of training time, and passing an exam.

Foresters who wish to perform specialized research or teach should have an advanced degree, preferably a Ph.D.

Most land-grant colleges and universities offer bachelor's or higher degrees in forestry; 48 of these programs are accredited by the Society of American Foresters. Curriculums stress science, mathematics, communications skills, and computer science, as well as technical forestry subjects. Courses in forest economics and business administration supplement the student's scientific and technical knowledge. Forestry curricula increasingly include courses on best management practices, wetlands analysis, water and soil quality, and wildlife conservation, in response to the growing focus on protecting forested lands during timber harvesting operations. Prospective foresters should have a strong grasp on policy issues and on the increasingly numerous and complex environmental regulations which affect many forestry-related activities. Many colleges require students to complete a field session either in a camp operated by the college or in a cooperative work-study program with a Federal or State agency or private industry. All schools encourage students to take summer jobs that provide experience in forestry or conservation work.

A bachelor's degree in range management or range science is the usual minimum educational requirement for range managers; graduate degrees generally are required for teaching and research positions. In 1996, about 30 colleges and universities offered degrees in range management or range science or in a closely related discipline with a range management or range science option. A number of other schools offered some courses in range management or range science. Specialized range management courses combine plant, animal, and soil sciences with principles of ecology and resource management. Desirable electives include economics, forestry, hydrology, agronomy, wildlife, animal husbandry, computer science, and recreation.

Very few colleges and universities offer degrees in soil conservation. Most soil conservationists have degrees in environmental studies, agronomy, general agriculture, hydrology, or crop or soil science; a few have degrees in related fields such as wildlife biology, forestry, and range management. Programs of study generally include 30 semester hours in natural resources or agriculture, including at least 3 hours in soil science. The Soil and Water Conservation Society sponsors a certification program based on education, experience, and testing. Upon completion of the program, individuals are designated as Certified Professional Erosion and Sediment Control specialist.

In addition to meeting the demands of forestry and conservation research and analysis, foresters and conservation scientists generally must enjoy working outdoors, be physically hardy, and be willing to move to where the jobs are. They must also work well with people and have good communications skills.

Recent forestry and range management graduates usually work under the supervision of experienced foresters or range managers. After gaining experience, they may advance to more responsible positions. In the Federal Government, most entry-level foresters work in forest resource management. An experienced Federal forester may supervise a ranger district, and may advance to forest supervisor, regional forester, or to a top administrative position in the national headquarters. In private industry, foresters start by learning the practical and administrative aspects of the business and acquiring comprehensive technical training. They are then introduced to contract writing, timber harvesting, and decision making. Some foresters work their way up to top managerial positions within their companies. Foresters in management usually leave the field work behind, spending more of their time in an office, working with teams to develop management plans and supervising others. After gaining several years of experience, some foresters may become consulting foresters, working alone or with one or several partners. They contract with State or local governments, private landowners, private industry, or other forestry consulting groups.

Soil conservationists usually begin working within one county or conservation district and with experience may advance to the area, State, regional, or national level. Also, soil conservationists can transfer to related occupations such as farm or ranch management advisor or land appraiser.

Job Outlook

Employment of foresters and conservation scientists is expected to grow about as fast as the average for all occupations through the year 2006. Growth should be strongest in State and local governments, where demand will be spurred by a continuing emphasis on environmental protection and responsible land management. For example, the nationwide Stewardship Incentive Program, funded by the Federal Government, provides money to the States to encourage landowners to practice multiple-use forest management. Foresters will continue to be needed to help landowners manage their forested property. However, job opportunities are expected to be best for soil conservationists as government regulations, such as those regarding the management of stormwater and coastlines, has created demand for persons knowledgeable about erosion on farms and in cities and suburbs. Soil and water quality experts will also be needed as States attempt to improve water quality by preventing pollution by agricultural producers and industrial plants.

Fewer opportunities for foresters and conservation scientists are expected in the Federal Government, partly due to budgetary constraints. Also, Federal land management agencies, such as the Forest Service, are de-emphasizing their timber programs and increasingly focusing on wildlife, recreation, and sustaining ecosystems, thereby increasing demand for other life and social scientists relative to foresters. However, a large number of foresters is expected to retire or leave the Government for other reasons, resulting in some job openings between 1996 and 2006. In addition, the need for range and soil conservationists to provide technical assistance, through the Natural Resource Conservation Service, to owners of grazing land may lead to a small number of new jobs.

The recent reductions in timber harvesting on public lands, most of which are located in the Northwest and California, also will dampen job growth for private industry foresters in these regions. Opportunities will be better for foresters in the Southeast, where much forested land is privately owned. Rising demand for timber on private lands will increase the need for forest management plans which maximize production while sustaining the environment for future growth. Salaried foresters working for private industry—such as paper companies, sawmills, and pulp wood mills—and consulting foresters will be needed to provide technical assistance and management plans to landowners.

Research and testing firms have increased their hiring of foresters and conservation scientists in recent years in response to demand for professionals to prepare environmental impact statements and erosion and sediment control plans, monitor water quality near logging sites, and advise on tree harvesting practices required by Federal, State, or local regulations. Hiring in these firms should continue during the 1996-2006 period, though at a slower rate.

Earnings

In 1997, most graduates entering the Federal Government as foresters, range managers, or soil conservationists with a bachelor's degree started at $19,500 or $24,200 a year, depending on academic achievement. Those with a master's degree could start at $24,200 or $29,600. Holders of doctorates could start at $35,800 or, in research positions, at $42,900. Beginning salaries were slightly higher in selected areas where the prevailing local pay level was higher. In 1997, the average Federal salary for foresters in nonsupervisory, supervisory, and managerial positions was $47,600; for soil conservationists, $45,200; for rangeland managers, $43,100, and for forest products technologists, $62,000.

According to the National Association of Colleges and Employers, graduates with a bachelor's degree in natural resources received an average starting salary offer of $24,800 in 1997.

In private industry, starting salaries for students with a bachelor's degree were comparable to starting salaries in the Federal Government, but starting salaries in State and local governments were generally lower.

Foresters and conservation scientists who work for Federal, State, and local governments and large private firms generally receive more generous benefits than those working for smaller firms.

Related Occupations

Foresters and conservation scientists manage, develop, and protect natural resources. They are aided by range, soil conservation, and forestry technicians. Other workers with similar responsibilities include agricultural scientists, agricultural engineers, biological scientists, environmental scientists and engineers, farm and ranch managers, soil scientists, and wildlife managers.

Sources of Additional Information

For information about the forestry profession and lists of schools offering education in forestry, send a self-addressed, stamped business envelope to:
☛ Society of American Foresters, 5400 Grosvenor Ln., Bethesda, MD 20814. Homepage: http://www.safnet.org

For information about career opportunities in forestry in the Federal Government, contact:
☛ Chief, U.S. Forest Service, U.S. Department of Agriculture, P.O. Box 96090, SW., Washington, DC 20090-6090.

For information about a career in State forestry organizations, contact:
☛ National Association of State Foresters, 444 N. Capitol St. NW., Suite 540, Washington, DC 20001.

Information about a career as a range manager as well as a list of schools offering training is available from:
☛ Society for Range Management, 1839 York St., Denver, CO 80206.

Information about a career in conservation science is available from:
☛ Soil and Water Conservation Society, 7515 Northeast Ankeny Rd., RR #1, Ankeny, IA 50021-9764.

Physical Scientists

Chemists

(D.O.T. 022.061-010, -014, and .137-010)

Significant Points

● A bachelor's degree in chemistry or a related discipline is usually the minimum educational requirement; however, many research jobs require a Ph.D. degree.

● Job growth will be concentrated in drug manufacturing and research, development, and testing services firms.

Nature of the Work

Everything in our physical environment, whether naturally occurring or of human design, is composed of chemicals. Chemists search for and put to practical use new knowledge about chemicals. Chemical research has led to the discovery and development of new and improved synthetic fibers, paints, adhesives, drugs, cosmetics, electronic components, lubricants, and thousands of other products. Chemists also develop processes which save energy and reduce pollution, such as improved oil refining and petrochemical processing methods. Research on the chemistry of living things spurs advances in medicine, agriculture, food processing, and other fields.

Chemists can apply their knowledge of chemistry to various purposes. Many work in research and development (R&D). In basic research, chemists investigate the properties, composition, and structure of matter and the laws that govern the combination of elements and reactions of substances. In applied research and development, they create new products and processes or improve existing ones, often using knowledge gained from basic research. For example, synthetic rubber and plastics resulted from research on small molecules uniting to form large ones, a process called polymerization. R&D chemists use computers and a wide variety of sophisticated laboratory instrumentation. They also spend time documenting and analyzing the results of their work and writing formal reports.

Chemists also work in production and quality control in chemical manufacturing plants. They prepare instructions for plant workers which specify ingredients, mixing times, and temperatures for each stage in the process. They also monitor automated processes to ensure proper product yield, and they test samples of raw materials or finished products to ensure they meet industry and government standards, including the regulations governing pollution. Chemists also record and report on test results, and improve existing or develop new test methods.

Chemists often specialize in a subfield. *Analytical chemists* determine the structure, composition, and nature of substances by examining and identifying the various elements or compounds that make up a substance. They study the relations and interactions of the parts and develop analytical techniques. They also identify the presence and concentration of chemical pollutants in air, water, and soil. *Organic chemists* study the chemistry of the vast number of carbon compounds which make up all living things. Many commercial products, such as drugs, plastics, and elastomers (elastic substances similar to rubber), have been developed by organic chemists who synthesize elements or simple compounds to create new compounds or substances that have different properties and applications. *Inorganic chemists* study compounds consisting mainly of elements other than carbon, such as those in electronic components. *Physical chemists* study the physical characteristics of atoms and molecules and investigate how chemical reactions work. Their research may result in new and better energy sources.

Biochemists, whose work encompasses both biology and chemistry, are included under biological scientists elsewhere in the *Handbook*.

Chemical research and development continues to lead to new and improved consumer goods.

Working Conditions

Chemists usually work regular hours in offices and laboratories. Research chemists spend much time in laboratories, but also work in offices when they do theoretical research or plan, record, and report on their lab research. Although some laboratories are small, others are large and may incorporate prototype chemical manufacturing facilities as well as advanced equipment. Chemists may also do some of their work in a chemical plant or outdoors—while gathering water samples to test for pollutants, for example. Some chemists are exposed to health or safety hazards when handling certain chemicals, but there is little risk if proper procedures are followed.

Employment

Chemists held about 91,000 jobs in 1996. Nearly half of chemists are employed in manufacturing firms—mostly in the chemical manufacturing industry, which includes firms that produce plastics and synthetic materials, drugs, soaps and cleaners, paints, industrial organic chemicals, and other miscellaneous chemical products. Chemists also work for State and local governments, and for Federal agencies. Health and Human Services, which includes the Food and Drug Administration, the National Institutes of Health, and the Center for Disease Control, is the major Federal employer of chemists. The Departments of Defense and Agriculture, and the Environmental Protection Agency, also employ chemists. Other chemists work for research, development, and testing services. In addition, thousands of persons held chemistry faculty positions in colleges and universities. (See the statement on college and university faculty elsewhere in the *Handbook*.)

Chemists are employed in all parts of the country, but they are mainly concentrated in large industrial areas.

Training, Other Qualifications, and Advancement

A bachelor's degree in chemistry or a related discipline is usually the minimum educational requirement for entry-level chemist jobs. However, many research jobs require a Ph.D. degree.

Many colleges and universities offer a bachelor's degree program in chemistry, about 620 of which are approved by the American Chemical Society (ACS). Several hundred colleges and universities also offer advanced degree programs in chemistry; around 320 master's programs, and about 190 doctoral programs are ACS-approved.

Students planning careers as chemists should enjoy studying science and mathematics, and should like working with their hands building scientific apparatus and performing experiments. Perseverance, curiosity, and the ability to concentrate on detail and to work independently are essential. In addition to required courses in analytical, inorganic, organic, and physical chemistry, undergraduate chemistry majors usually study biological sciences, mathematics, and physics. Those who are interested in the environmental field should take courses in environmental studies and become familiar with current legislation and regulations. Computer courses are essential, as employers increasingly prefer job applicants who are able to apply computer skills to modeling and simulation tasks and operate computerized laboratory equipment.

Because research and development chemists are increasingly expected to work on interdisciplinary teams, some understanding of other disciplines, including business and marketing or economics, is desirable, along with leadership ability and good oral and written communication skills. Experience, either in academic laboratories or through internships or co-op programs in industry, also is useful. Some employers of research chemists, particularly in the pharmaceutical industry, prefer to hire individuals with several years of postdoctoral experience.

Graduate students typically specialize in a subfield of chemistry, such as analytical chemistry or polymer chemistry, depending on their interests and the kind of work they wish to do. For example, those interested in doing drug research in the pharmaceutical industry usually develop a strong background in synthetic organic chemistry.

However, students normally need not specialize at the undergraduate level. In fact, undergraduates who are broadly trained have more flexibility when job hunting or changing jobs than if they narrowly define their interests. Most employers provide new bachelor's degree chemists with additional training or education.

In government or industry, beginning chemists with a bachelor's degree work in quality control, analytical testing, or assist senior chemists in research and development laboratories. Many employers prefer chemists with a Ph.D. or at least a master's degree to lead basic and applied research. A Ph.D. is also often preferred for advancement to many administrative positions.

Job Outlook

Employment of chemists is expected to grow about as fast as the average for all occupations through the year 2006. Job growth will be concentrated in drug manufacturing and research, development, and testing services firms. The chemical industry, the major employer of chemists, should face continued demand for goods such as new and better pharmaceuticals and personal care products, as well as more specialty chemicals designed to address specific problems or applications. To meet these demands, chemical firms will continue to devote money to research and development—through in-house teams or outside contractors—spurring employment growth of chemists.

Within the chemical industry, job opportunities are expected to be most plentiful in pharmaceutical and biotechnology firms. Stronger competition among drug companies and an aging population are contributing to the need for innovative and improved drugs discovered through scientific research. Chemical firms that develop and manufacture personal products such as toiletries and cosmetics also must continually innovate and develop new and better products to remain competitive. Additionally, as the population grows and becomes better informed, the demand for different or improved grooming products—including vegetable-based products, products with milder formulas, treatments for aging skin, and products that have been developed using more benign chemical processes than in the past—will remain strong, spurring the need for chemists.

In the remaining segments of the chemical industry, employment growth is expected to be much slower than in drug manufacturing, and in some cases, may decline as companies downsize and turn to outside contractors to provide specialized services. Nevertheless, some job openings will result from the need to replace chemists who retire or otherwise leave the labor force. Quality control will continue to be an important issue in the chemical and other industries that use chemicals in their manufacturing processes. Chemists will also be needed to develop and improve the technologies and processes used to produce chemicals for all purposes, and to monitor and measure air and water pollutants to ensure compliance with local, State, and Federal environmental regulations.

Outside the chemical industry, firms that provide research, development, and testing services are expected to be the source of numerous job opportunities between 1996 and 2006. Chemical companies, including drug manufacturers, are increasingly turning to these services to perform specialized research and other work formerly done by in-house chemists. Chemists will also be needed to work in research and testing firms that focus on environmental testing and cleanup.

During periods of economic recession, layoffs of chemists may occur—especially in the industrial chemicals industry. This industry provides many of the raw materials to the auto manufacturing and construction industries, both of which are vulnerable to temporary slowdowns during recessions.

Earnings

A survey by the American Chemical Society reports that the median salary of all their members with a bachelor's degree was $49,400 a year in 1997; with a master's degree, $56,200; and with a Ph.D., $71,000. Median salaries were highest for those working in private industry; those in academia earned the least. According to an ACS survey of recent graduates, inexperienced chemistry graduates with a bachelor's degree earned a median starting salary of $25,000 in 1996; with a master's degree, $31,100; and with a Ph.D., $45,000. Among bachelor's degree graduates, those who had completed internships or had other work experience while in school commanded the highest starting salaries.

In 1997, chemists in nonsupervisory, supervisory, and managerial positions in the Federal Government earned an average salary of $60,000.

Related Occupations

The work of chemical engineers, agricultural scientists, biological scientists, and chemical technicians is closely related to the work done by chemists. The work of other physical and life science occupations, such as physicists and medical scientists, may also be similar to that of chemists.

Sources of Additional Information

General information on career opportunities and earnings for chemists is available from:
☛ American Chemical Society, Education Division, 1155 16th St. NW., Washington, DC 20036.

Information on acquiring a job as a chemist with the Federal Government may be obtained from the Office of Personnel Management through a telephone-based system. Consult your telephone directory under U.S. Government for a local number, or call (912) 757-3000 (TDD 912-744-2299). That number is not toll-free and charges may result. Information also is available from their Internet site: http://www.usajobs opm.gov

Geologists and Geophysicists

(D.O.T. 024.061 except -014, and .161)

Significant Points

- Work at remote field sites is common.

- A bachelor's degree in geology or geophysics is adequate for entry-level jobs; better jobs with good advancement potential usually require at least a master's degree; and a Ph.D. degree is required for most research positions in colleges and universities, and for some research jobs in government.

- Job opportunities are expected to be good in the petroleum and related industries, reflecting increasing demand for energy coupled with fewer degrees awarded in geology in recent years.

Nature of the Work

Geologists and geophysicists, also known as geological scientists or geoscientists, study the physical aspects and history of the Earth. They identify and examine rocks, study information collected by remote sensing instruments in satellites, conduct geological surveys, construct field maps, and use instruments to measure the Earth's gravity and magnetic field. They also analyze information collected through seismic studies, which involves bouncing energy waves off buried rock layers. Many geologists and geophysicists search for oil, natural gas, minerals, and groundwater.

Other geological scientists play an important role in preserving and cleaning up the environment. Their activities include designing and monitoring waste disposal sites, preserving water supplies, and reclaiming contaminated land and water to comply with Federal environmental regulations. They also help locate safe sites for hazardous waste facilities and landfills.

Geologists and geophysicists examine chemical and physical properties of specimens in laboratories. They study fossil remains of animal and plant life, or experiment with the flow of water and oil through rocks. Some geoscientists use two- or three-dimensional computer modeling to portray water layers and the flow of water or other fluids through rock cracks and porous materials. They use a variety of sophisticated laboratory instruments, including x-ray diffractometers, which determine the crystal structure of minerals, and petrographic microscopes, for the study of rock and sediment samples. Geoscientists also use seismographs, instruments which measure energy waves resulting from movements in the Earth's crust, to determine the locations and intensities of earthquakes.

Geoscientists working in metal mining or the oil and gas industry sometimes process and interpret the maps produced by remote sensing satellites to help identify potential new mineral, oil, or gas deposits. Seismic technology is also an important exploration tool. Seismic waves are used to develop three-dimensional computer models of underground or underwater rock formations. Seismic reflection technology may also reveal unusual underground features which sometimes indicate accumulations of natural gas or petroleum, facilitating exploration and reducing the risks associated with drilling in previously unexplored areas.

Geologists and geophysicists also apply geological knowledge to engineering problems in constructing large buildings, dams, tunnels, and highways. Some administer and manage research and exploration programs; others become general managers in petroleum and mining companies.

Geology and geophysics are closely related fields, but there are major differences. Geologists study the composition, structure, and history of the Earth's crust. They try to find out how rocks were formed and what has happened to them since formation. Geophysicists use the principles of physics, mathematics, and chemistry to study not only the Earth's surface, but its internal composition, ground and surface waters, atmosphere, oceans, and its magnetic, electrical, and gravitational forces. Both, however, commonly apply their skills and knowledge to the search for natural resources and to solve environmental problems.

There are numerous subdisciplines or specialties falling under the two major disciplines of geology and geophysics which further differentiate the type of work geoscientists do. For example, *petroleum geologists* explore for oil and gas deposits by studying and mapping the subsurface of the ocean or land. They use sophisticated geophysical instrumentation, well log data, and computers to collect information. *Mineralogists* analyze and classify minerals and precious stones according to composition and structure. *Paleontologists* study fossils found in geological formations to trace the evolution of plant and animal life and the geologic history of the Earth. *Stratigraphers* help to locate minerals by studying the distribution and arrangement of sedimentary rock layers and by examining the fossil and mineral content of such layers. Those who study marine geology are usually called *oceanographers* or *marine geologists*. They study and map the ocean floor, and collect information using remote sensing devices aboard surface ships or underwater research craft.

Geophysicists may specialize in areas such as geodesy, seismology, or marine geophysics, also known as physical oceanography. *Geodesists* study the size and shape of the Earth, its gravitational field, tides, polar motion, and rotation. *Seismologists* interpret data from seismographs and other geophysical instruments to detect earthquakes and locate earthquake-related faults. *Volcanologists*, *geochemists,* and *petrologists* study the chemical and physical evolution of rocks and minerals, particularly igneous and metamorphic rocks. *Geomagnetists* measure the Earth's magnetic field and use measurements taken over the past few centuries to devise theoretical models to explain its origin. *Paleomagnetists* interpret fossil magnetization in rocks and sediments from the continents and oceans, which record the spreading of the sea floor, the wandering of the continents, and the many reversals of polarity that the Earth's magnetic field has undergone through time. *Physical oceanographers* study the physical aspects of oceans such as currents and the interaction of the surface of the sea with the atmosphere. Other

Some geologists study fossil remains of plant and animal life to better understand the Earth's history.

geophysicists study atmospheric sciences and space physics. (See the statements on meteorologists and physicists and astronomers elsewhere in the *Handbook*.)

Hydrology is a discipline closely related to geology and geophysics. *Hydrologists* study the distribution, circulation, and physical properties of underground and surface waters. They study the form and intensity of precipitation, its rate of infiltration into the soil, movement through the Earth, and its return to the ocean and atmosphere. The work they do is particularly important in environmental preservation and remediation.

Working Conditions

Some geoscientists spend the majority of their time in an office, but many others divide their time between fieldwork and office or laboratory work. Geologists often travel to remote field sites by helicopter or four-wheel drive vehicles, and cover large areas on foot. Exploration geologists and geophysicists often work overseas or in isolated areas, leading to job relocation. Many exploration geologists travel to meet with prospective clients or investors. Marine geologists and oceanographers may spend considerable time at sea on academic research ships.

Geoscientists in positions funded by Federal Government agencies may be under pressure to design programs and write grant proposals in order to continue their data collection and research. Geoscientists in consulting jobs may face similar pressures to market their skills and write proposals to maintain steady work.

Employment

Geologists and geophysicists held about 47,000 jobs in 1996. Many more individuals held geology, geophysics, and oceanography faculty positions in colleges and universities, but they are considered college and university faculty. (See the statement on college and university faculty elsewhere in the *Handbook*.)

Among salaried geologists and geophysicists, nearly 4 in 10 were employed in engineering and management services, and 2 in 10 worked for oil and gas extraction companies or metal mining companies. About 1 geoscientist in 7 was self-employed; most were consultants to industry or government.

The Federal Government employed about 5,800 geologists, geophysicists, oceanographers, and hydrologists in 1996. Over half worked for the Department of the Interior, mostly within the U.S. Geological Survey (U.S.G.S.). Others worked for the Departments of Defense, Agriculture, Commerce, and Energy, and the Environmental Protection Agency. Over 3,000 worked for State agencies such as State geological surveys and State departments of conservation.

Training, Other Qualifications, and Advancement

A bachelor's degree in geology or geophysics is adequate for entry-level jobs, but better jobs with good advancement potential usually require at least a master's degree in geology or geophysics. Persons with degrees in physics, chemistry, mathematics, or computer science may also qualify for some geophysics or geology jobs if their coursework included study in geology. A Ph.D. degree is required for most research positions in colleges and universities, and is also important for work in Federal agencies and some State geological surveys involving basic research.

Hundreds of colleges and universities offer a bachelor's degree in geology; fewer schools offer programs in geophysics, oceanography, or other geosciences. Other programs offering related training for beginning geological scientists include geophysical technology, geophysical engineering, geophysical prospecting, engineering geology, petroleum geology, hydrology, and geochemistry. In addition, several hundred more universities award advanced degrees in geology or geophysics.

Traditional geoscience courses emphasizing classical geologic methods and topics (such as mineralogy, paleontology, stratigraphy, and structural geology) are important for all geoscientists. Those students interested in working in the environmental or regulatory fields, either in environmental consulting firms or Federal or State Government, should take courses in hydrology, hazardous waste management, environmental legislation, chemistry, fluid mechanics, and geologic logging. An understanding of environmental regulations and government permit issues is also valuable for those planning to work in mining and oil and gas extraction. Computer skills are becoming essential for prospective geoscientists; students who have some experience with computer modeling, data analysis and integration, digital mapping, remote sensing, and geographic information systems (GIS) will be the most prepared entering the job market. A knowledge of the Global Positioning System (GPS) is very helpful. Some employers seek applicants with field experience, so a summer internship may be beneficial to prospective geoscientists.

Geologists and geophysicists must be able to work as part of a team. Strong oral and written communication skills are important, as well as the ability to think independently and creatively. Those involved in fieldwork must have physical stamina.

Geologists and geophysicists often begin their careers in field exploration or as research assistants in laboratories or offices. They are given more difficult assignments as they gain experience. Eventually, they may be promoted to project leader, program manager, or another management and research position.

Job Outlook

Many jobs for geologists and geophysicists are in or related to the petroleum industry, especially the exploration for oil and gas. This industry is subject to cyclical fluctuations. During the 1980s and the early 1990s, low oil prices, higher production costs, improvements in energy efficiency, shrinking oil reserves, and restrictions on potential drilling sites caused exploration activities to be curtailed in the United States; this limited the number of job openings for geoscientists in the petroleum and related industries. As a result of generally poor job prospects, the number of graduates in geology and geophysics, especially in petroleum geology, dropped considerably during the last decade.

Recently, a growing worldwide demand for oil and gas, and new exploration and recovery techniques, have returned stability to the petroleum industry and increased the demand for geologists and geophysicists. Growing populations, stronger economies in the United States and abroad, and continuing industrialization of developing countries are driving the need for more energy. At the same time, the oil and gas and related industries—such as petroleum engineering services—are taking advantage of new technologies that lower costs and facilitate exploration and recovery of natural gas and oil, particularly in deep water and other previously inaccessible sites. Because of the lower number of degrees awarded in geology recently and the significant number of geoscientists who left the industry during earlier periods of downsizing, job opportunities in the petroleum and related industries are expected to be good. Employment prospects will be best for jobseekers who hold a master's degree and are familiar with advanced technologies, such as computer modeling and GPS, which are increasingly used to locate new oil and gas fields or pinpoint hidden deposits in existing fields. Because of the cyclical nature of the oil and gas industry, hiring on a contractual basis is common.

Employment of geologists and geophysicists is expected to grow about as fast as the average for all occupations through the year 2006, due in part to the generally improved outlook in the oil and gas industry. Geologists and geophysicists will also continue to be needed to work in areas of environmental protection and reclamation. Some will help clean up contaminated sites in the United States, and others will help private companies and government comply with numerous and complex environmental regulations. However, job opportunities in State and Federal Government and in environmental consulting firms are expected to be fewer in number than in the previous decade and, in some cases, may be limited to replacing retirees or those who leave geoscience jobs for other reasons. The U.S.G.S., the primary employer of geologists in the Federal Government, has recently faced cutbacks. Hiring should continue to be very limited in the U.S.G.S. and other agencies, as the Federal Government attempts to balance its budget during the 1996-2006 projection period. Oceanographers, whose work is often research-oriented and dependent on grants from Federal agencies, are expected to face strong competition. Budget constraints are expected to continue to limit hiring in State government as well.

Earnings

Surveys by the National Association of Colleges and Employers indicate that graduates with bachelor's degrees in geology and the geological sciences received an average starting salary offer of about $30,900 a year in 1997. However, starting salaries can vary widely depending on the employing industry. For example, according to a 1996 American Association of Petroleum Geologists survey, the average salary in the oil and gas industry for geoscientists with less than 2 years of experience was about $48,400.

The petroleum, mineral, and mining industries offer higher salaries, but less job security, than other industries. These industries are vulnerable to recessions and changes in oil and gas prices, among other factors, and usually release workers when exploration and drilling slow down.

In 1997, the Federal Government's average salary for geologists in managerial, supervisory, and nonsupervisory positions was $59,700; for geophysicists, $67,100; for hydrologists, $54,800; and for oceanographers, $62,700.

Related Occupations

Many geologists and geophysicists work in the petroleum and natural gas industry. This industry also employs many other workers in the scientific and technical aspects of petroleum and natural gas exploration and extraction, including engineering technicians, science technicians, petroleum engineers, and surveyors. Also, some life scientists, physicists, chemists, and meteorologists—as well as mathematicians, computer scientists, soil scientists, and mapping scientists—perform related work in both petroleum and natural gas exploration and extraction, and in environment-related activities.

Sources of Additional Information

Information on training and career opportunities for geologists is available from:

☛ American Geological Institute, 4220 King St., Alexandria, VA 22302-1502. Homepage: http://www.agiweb.org

☛ Geological Society of America, P.O. Box 9140, Boulder, CO 80301-9140. Homepage: http://www.geosociety.org

☛ American Association of Petroleum Geologists, Communications Department, P.O. Box 979, Tulsa, OK 74101.

Information on training and career opportunities for geophysicists is available from:

☛ American Geophysical Union, 2000 Florida Ave. NW., Washington, DC 20009.

A list of education and training programs in oceanography and related fields is available from:

☛ Marine Technology Society, 1828 L St. NW., Suite 906, Washington, DC 20036.

Information on acquiring a job as a geologist, geophysicist, hydrologist, or oceanographer with the Federal Government may be obtained from the Office of Personnel Management through a telephone-based system. Consult your telephone directory under U.S. Government for a local number or call (912) 757-3000 (TDD 912 744-2299). That number is not toll-free and charges may result. Information also is available from their Internet site: http://www.usajobs.opm.gov

Meteorologists

(D.O.T. 025.062-010)

Significant Points

- The Federal Government employs about 4 out of 10 meteorologists and is the largest employer of these workers.

- A bachelor's degree in meteorology, or in a closely related field with courses in meteorology, is the minimum educational requirement; a master's or Ph.D. degree is required for research positions.

- With slower-than-average employment growth expected through the year 2006, applicants may face competition if the number of degrees awarded in atmospheric science and meteorology remain near current levels.

Nature of the Work

Meteorology is the study of the atmosphere—the blanket of air covering the Earth. Meteorologists study the atmosphere's physical characteristics, motions, and processes, and the way it affects the rest of our environment. The best known application of this knowledge is in forecasting the weather. However, weather information and meteorological research are also applied in air-pollution control, agriculture, air and sea transportation, defense, and the study of trends in Earth's climate such as global warming or ozone depletion.

Meteorologists who forecast the weather, known professionally as *operational meteorologists*, are the largest group of specialists. They study information on air pressure, temperature, humidity, and wind velocity, and apply physical and mathematical relationships to make short- and long-range weather forecasts. Their data come from weather satellites, weather radar, and remote sensors and observers in many parts of the world. Meteorologists use sophisticated computer models of the world's atmosphere to make long-term, short-term, and local-area forecasts. These forecasts inform not only the general public, but also those who need accurate weather information for both economic and safety reasons, as in the shipping, air transportation, agriculture, fishing, and utilities industries.

The use of weather balloons, launched several times a day, to measure wind, temperature, and humidity in the upper atmosphere, is currently supplemented by sophisticated weather equipment that transmits data as frequently as every few minutes. Doppler radar, for example, can detect air flow patterns in violent storm systems—allowing forecasters to better predict tornadoes and other hazardous winds, as well as monitoring the storm's direction and intensity. Combined radar and satellite observations allow meteorologists to predict flash floods.

Some meteorologists work in research. *Physical meteorologists*, for example, study the atmosphere's chemical and physical properties; the transmission of light, sound, and radio waves; and the transfer of energy in the atmosphere. They also study factors affecting the formation of clouds, rain, snow, and other weather phenomena, such as severe storms. *Synoptic meteorologists* develop new tools for weather forecasting using computers and sophisticated mathematical models. *Climatologists* collect, analyze, and interpret past records of wind, rainfall, sunshine, and temperature in specific areas or regions. Their

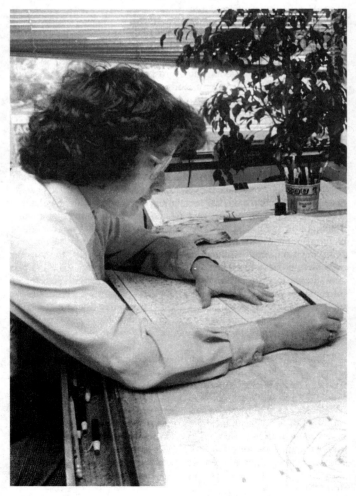

A meteorologist studies weather maps showing air pressure, temperature, and humidity of a specific region.

studies are used to design buildings, plan heating and cooling systems, and aid in effective land use and in agricultural production. Other research meteorologists examine the most effective ways to control or diminish air pollution.

Working Conditions

Most weather stations operate around the clock 7 days a week. Jobs in such facilities often involve night, weekend, and holiday work with rotating shifts. During times of weather emergencies, such as hurricanes, operational meteorologists may work overtime. Operational meteorologists are also often under pressure to meet forecast deadlines. Weather stations are found all over the country—at airports, in or near cities, and in isolated and remote areas. Some meteorologists also spend time observing weather conditions and collecting data from aircraft. Weather forecasters who work for radio or television stations broadcast their reports from station studios, and may work evenings and weekends. Meteorologists in smaller weather offices often work alone; in larger ones, they work as part of a team. Meteorologists not involved in forecasting work regular hours, usually in offices. Those who work for private consulting firms or for companies analyzing and monitoring emissions to improve air quality usually work with other scientists or engineers.

Employment

Meteorologists held about 7,300 jobs in 1996. The Federal Government is the largest employer of civilian meteorologists. The National Oceanic and Atmospheric Administration (NOAA) employed about 2,700 meteorologists; nearly 90 percent worked in the National Weather Service at stations throughout the Nation. The remainder of NOAA's meteorologists worked mainly in research or management. The Department of Defense employed about 280 civilian meteorologists. Others worked for private weather consulting services, research and testing services, and computer and data processing services.

Although hundreds of people teach meteorology and related courses in college and university departments of meteorology or atmospheric science, physics, earth science, and geophysics, these individuals are classified as college or university faculty, rather than meteorologists. (See the statement on college and university faculty elsewhere in the *Handbook*.)

In addition to civilian meteorologists, hundreds of members of the Armed Forces are involved in forecasting and other meteorological work. (See the statement on job opportunities in the Armed Forces elsewhere in the *Handbook*.)

Training, Other Qualifications, and Advancement

A bachelor's degree with a major in meteorology, or in a closely related field with courses in meteorology, is generally the minimum educational requirement for a beginning job as a meteorologist.

The preferred educational requirement for entry-level meteorologists in the Federal Government is a bachelor's degree—not necessarily in meteorology—with at least 24 semester hours of meteorology courses, including 6 hours in the analysis and prediction of weather systems and 2 hours of remote sensing of the atmosphere or instrumentation. Other required courses include differential and integral calculus, differential equations, 6 hours of college physics, and at least 9 hours of courses appropriate for a physical science major—such as statistics, computer science, chemistry, physical oceanography, or physical climatology. Sometimes, a combination of experience and education may be substituted for a degree.

Although positions in operational meteorology are available for those with only a bachelor's degree, obtaining a graduate degree enhances advancement potential. A master's degree is usually necessary for conducting research and development, and a Ph.D. is required for most basic research positions. Students who plan a career in research and development need not necessarily major in meteorology as an undergraduate. In fact, a bachelor's degree in mathematics, physics, or engineering provides excellent preparation for graduate study in meteorology.

Because meteorology is a small field, relatively few colleges and universities offer degrees in meteorology or atmospheric science, although many departments of physics, earth science, geography, and geophysics offer atmospheric science and related courses. Prospective students should make certain that courses required by the National Weather Service and other employers are offered at the college they are considering. Computer science courses, additional meteorology courses, a strong background in mathematics and physics, and good communication skills are important to prospective employers. Many programs combine the study of meteorology with another field, such as agriculture, engineering, or physics. For example, hydrometeorology is the blending of hydrology (the science of Earth's water) and meteorology, and is the field concerned with the effect of precipitation on the hydrologic cycle and the environment. Students who wish to become broadcast meteorologists for radio or television stations should develop excellent communication skills through courses in speech, journalism, and related fields. Those interested in air quality work should supplement their technical training with coursework in policy or government affairs.

Beginning meteorologists often do routine data collection, computation, or analysis, and some basic forecasting. Entry-level operational meteorologists in the Federal Government are usually placed in intern positions for training and experience. During this period, they learn about the Weather Service's forecasting equipment and procedures, and rotate to different offices to learn about various weather systems. After completing the training period, they are assigned a permanent duty station. Experienced meteorologists may advance to supervisory or administrative jobs, or may handle more complex forecasting jobs. After several years of experience, some meteorologists establish their own weather consulting services.

The American Meteorological Society offers professional certification of consulting meteorologists, administered by a Board of Certified Consulting Meteorologists. Applicants must meet formal education requirements (though not necessarily a college degree), pass an examination to demonstrate thorough meteorological knowledge, have a minimum of 5 years of experience or a combination of experience plus an advanced degree, and provide character references from fellow professionals.

Job Outlook

Prospective meteorologists may face competition if the number of degrees awarded in atmospheric science and meteorology remain near current levels, coupled with projected slower-than-average employment growth through the year 2006. The National Weather Service (NWS) recently completed an extensive modernization of its weather forecasting equipment and all hiring of meteorologists needed to staff the upgraded stations. The NWS has no plans to increase the number of weather stations or the number of meteorologists in existing stations for many years. Employment of meteorologists in other Federal agencies is expected to decline slightly as the Federal Government attempts to balance its budget.

On the other hand, private industry is expected to create a small number of new jobs for meteorologists over the 1996-2006 period. As research leads to continuing improvements in weather forecasting, the demand may grow for private weather consulting firms to provide more detailed information than has formerly been available, especially to weather-sensitive industries. Farmers, commodity investors, radio and television stations, and utilities, transportation, and construction firms can greatly benefit from additional weather information more closely targeted to their needs than the general information provided by the National Weather Service. Additionally, if research on seasonal and other long-range forecasting yields positive results, more meteorologists may be needed to interpret these forecasts and advise weather-sensitive industries. However, because many customers for private weather services are in industries sensitive to fluctuations in the economy, the sales and growth of private weather services depend on the health of the economy.

There will continue to be demand for meteorologists to analyze and monitor the dispersion of pollutants into the air to ensure compliance with Federal environmental regulations outlined in the Clean Air Act of 1990, but employment increases are expected to be small.

Earnings

The average salary for meteorologists in nonsupervisory, supervisory, and managerial positions employed by the Federal Government was about $57,000 in 1997. Meteorologists in the Federal Government with a bachelor's degree and no experience received a starting salary of $19,500 or $24,200 a year, depending on their college grades. Those with a master's degree could start at $24,200 or $29,600; those with the Ph.D. degree, at $35,800 or $42,900. Beginning salaries for all degree levels are slightly higher in selected areas of the country where the prevailing local pay level is higher.

Related Occupations

Workers in other occupations concerned with the physical environment include oceanographers, geologists and geophysicists, hydrologists, physicists, mathematicians, and civil, chemical, and environmental engineers.

Sources of Additional Information

Information about careers in meteorology is available from:

☞ American Meteorological Society, 45 Beacon St., Boston, MA 02108. Homepage: http://www.ametsoc.org/AMS

Information on acquiring a job as a meteorologist with the Federal Government may be obtained from the Office of Personnel Management through a telephone-based system. Consult your telephone directory under U.S. Government for a local number or call (912) 757-3000 (TDD 912 744-2299). That number is not toll-free and charges may result. Information also is available from their Internet site: http://www.usajobs.opm.gov

Physicists and Astronomers

D.O.T. 015.021-010; 021.067-010; 023.061-010, -014, and .067; 079.021-014)

Significant Points

- A doctoral degree is the usual educational requirement because most jobs are in basic research and development; a master's degree is sufficient for some jobs in applied research and development; a bachelor's degree is adequate for some nonresearch jobs.

- Ph.D.'s face competition for jobs as funding for research declines, and as the large pool of postdoctoral workers add to the supply of new graduates.

Nature of the Work

Physicists explore and identify basic principles governing the structure and behavior of matter, the generation and transfer of energy, and the interaction of matter and energy. Some physicists use these principles in theoretical areas, such as the nature of time and the origin of the universe; others apply their physics knowledge to practical areas such as the development of advanced materials, electronic and optical devices, and medical equipment.

Physicists design and perform experiments with lasers, cyclotrons, telescopes, mass spectrometers, and other equipment. Based on observations and analysis, they attempt to discover laws describing the forces of nature, such as gravity, electromagnetism, and nuclear interactions. They also find ways to apply physical laws and theories to problems in nuclear energy, electronics, optics, materials, commu-

nications, aerospace technology, navigation equipment, and medical instrumentation.

Astronomy is sometimes considered a subfield of physics. Astronomers use the principles of physics and mathematics to learn about the fundamental nature of the universe, including the sun, moon, planets, stars, and galaxies. They also apply their knowledge to problems in navigation and space flight, and to develop the instrumentation and techniques used to observe and collect astronomical data.

Most physicists work in research and development. Some do basic research to increase scientific knowledge. Physicists who conduct applied research build upon the discoveries made through basic research, and work to develop new devices, products, and processes. For instance, basic research in solid-state physics led to the development of transistors and then to the integrated circuits used in computers.

Physicists also design research equipment. This equipment often has additional unanticipated uses. For example, lasers are used in surgery; microwave devices are used for ovens; and measuring instruments can analyze blood or the chemical content of foods. A small number work in inspection, testing, quality control, and other production-related jobs in industry.

Much physics research is done in small or medium-size laboratories. However, experiments in plasma, nuclear, high energy, and some other areas of physics require extremely large, expensive equipment such as particle accelerators. Physicists in these subfields often work in large teams. Although physics research may require extensive experimentation in laboratories, research physicists still spend time in offices planning, recording, analyzing, and reporting on research.

Almost all astronomers do research. Some are theoreticians, working on the laws governing the structure and evolution of astronomical objects. Others analyze large quantities of data gathered by observatories and satellites, and write scientific papers or reports on their findings. Astronomers may spend only a few weeks each year making observations with optical telescopes, radio telescopes, and other instruments. For many years, satellites and other space-based instruments have provided tremendous amounts of astronomical data. New technology resulting in improvements in analytical techniques and instruments, such as computers and optical telescopes and mounts, is leading to a resurgence in ground-based research. A small number of astronomers work in museums housing planetariums. These astronomers develop and revise the programs presented to the public, and may also direct operations.

Physicists generally specialize in one of many subfields—elementary particle physics; nuclear physics; atomic and molecular physics; physics of condensed matter (solid-state physics); optics; acoustics; space physics; plasma physics; or the physics of fluids. Some specialize in a subdivision of one of these subfields; for example, within condensed matter physics, specialties include superconductivity, crystallography, and semiconductors. However, all physics involves the same fundamental principles, so specialties may overlap, and physicists may switch from one subfield to another. Also, growing numbers of physicists work in combined fields such as biophysics, chemical physics, and geophysics.

Working Conditions

Physicists often work regular hours in laboratories and offices. At times, however, those who are deeply involved in research may work long or irregular hours. Most do not encounter unusual hazards in their work. Some physicists temporarily work away from home at national or international facilities with unique equipment such as particle accelerators. Astronomers who make observations may spend long periods of time in observatories; this work usually involves travel to remote locations. Long hours, including routine night work, may create temporarily stressful conditions.

Physicists and astronomers whose work is dependent on grant money are often under pressure to write grant proposals to keep their work funded.

A large majority of physicists and astronomers have advanced degrees.

Employment

Physicists and astronomers held nearly 18,000 jobs in 1996. About 3 in 10 nonfaculty physicists and astronomers worked for commercial or noncommercial research, development, and testing laboratories. The Federal Government employed almost 2 in 10, mostly in the Department of Defense, but also in the Departments of Commerce, Health and Human Services, and Energy, and the National Aeronautics and Space Administration. Others worked in colleges and universities in nonfaculty positions, and for State governments, drug companies, and electronic equipment manufacturers.

Besides the jobs described above, many physicists held faculty positions in colleges and universities. (See the statement on college and university faculty elsewhere in the *Handbook.*)

Although physicists and astronomers are employed in all parts of the country, most work in areas in which universities, large research and development laboratories, or observatories are located.

Training, Other Qualifications, and Advancement

A doctoral degree is the usual educational requirement for physicists and astronomers, because most jobs are in basic research and development. Additional experience and training in a postdoctoral research assignment, although not required, is helpful in preparing physicists and astronomers for permanent research positions. Many physics and astronomy Ph.D. holders ultimately teach at the college or university level.

Master's degree holders usually do not qualify for basic research positions, but do qualify for many kinds of jobs requiring a physics background, including positions in applied research and development, and manufacturing. Physics departments in some colleges and universities are creating professional master's degree programs to specifically prepare students for physics-related research which does not require a Ph.D. degree in private industry. A master's degree may suffice for teaching jobs in 2-year colleges. Those having bachelor's degrees in physics are rarely qualified to fill positions as research or teaching physicists. They are, however, usually qualified to work in an engineering-related area or other scientific fields, to work as technicians, or to assist in setting up laboratories. Some may qualify for applied research jobs in private industry or nonresearch positions in the Federal Government. Some become science teachers in secondary schools. Astronomy bachelor's or master's degree holders often enter a field unrelated to astronomy, but they are also qualified to work in planetariums running science shows or to assist astronomers doing research. (See the statements on engineers, geologists and geophysicists, computer programmers, and computer scientists and systems analysts elsewhere in the *Handbook.*)

Over 500 colleges and universities offer a bachelor's degree in physics. The undergraduate program provides a broad background in the natural sciences and mathematics. Typical physics courses include mechanics, electromagnetism, optics, thermodynamics, atomic physics, and quantum mechanics.

About 180 colleges and universities have departments offering Ph.D. degrees in physics. Graduate students usually concentrate in a subfield of physics, such as elementary particles or condensed matter. Many begin studying for their doctorate immediately after receiving their bachelor's degree.

About 80 universities offer the master's or Ph.D. degree in astronomy, either through an astronomy, a physics, or combined physics/astronomy department. Applicants to astronomy doctoral programs face keen competition for available slots. Those planning a career in astronomy should have a very strong physics background. In fact, an undergraduate degree in either physics or astronomy is excellent preparation, followed by a Ph.D. in astronomy.

Mathematical ability, computer skills, an inquisitive mind, imagination, and the ability to work independently are important traits for anyone planning a career in physics or astronomy. Prospective physicists who hope to work in industrial laboratories applying physics knowledge to practical problems should broaden their educational background to include courses outside of physics, such as economics, computer technology, and business management. Good oral and written communication skills are also important because many physicists work as part of a team or have contact with clients or customers with non-physics backgrounds.

Most physics and astronomy Ph.D.'s begin their careers in a postdoctoral research position, where they may work with experienced physicists as they continue to learn about their specialty and develop ideas and results to be used in later work. The initial work may be under the close supervision of senior scientists. After some experience, they perform increasingly complex tasks and work more independently. Physicists who develop new products or processes sometimes form their own companies or join new firms to exploit their own ideas.

Job Outlook

Historically, many physicists and astronomers have been employed on research projects—often defense-related. Further reductions in defense-related research and a continued slowdown in the growth of civilian physics-related research will result in a small decline in employment of physicists and astronomers through the year 2006. The need to replace physicists and astronomers who retire will account for almost all expected job openings. Proposed employment cutbacks and overall budget tightening in the Federal Government will also affect employment of physicists, especially those dependent on Federal research grants. The Federal Government funds numerous noncommercial research and development facilities; the Government's plan to balance the Federal budget may limit funding and, consequently, the scope of research in these facilities.

The number of doctorates granted in physics has been much greater than the number of openings for physicists for several years, resulting in keen competition, particularly for research positions in colleges and universities and research and development centers. Competitive conditions may ease slightly when the number of degrees awarded begins to drop midway between 1996 and 2006, following recent declines in enrollment. However, job applicants should still expect to face competition from the large pool of postdoctoral workers who will add to the supply of new graduates. Also, more prospective researchers will likely compete for less grant money.

Although research and development budgets in private industry will continue to grow, many research laboratories in private industry are expected to reduce basic research, which includes much physics research, in favor of applied or manufacturing research and product and software development. Although many physicists and astronomers will be eligible for retirement over the next decade, it is possible not all of them will be replaced when they retire.

Opportunities may be more numerous for those with a master's degree, particularly graduates from programs preparing students for applied research and development, product design, and manufacturing positions in industry. Many of these positions, however, will have titles other than physicist, such as engineer or computer scientist.

Persons with only a bachelor's degree in physics or astronomy are not qualified to enter most physicist or astronomer jobs, but may qualify for a wide range of positions in engineering, technician, mathematics, and computer- and environment-related occupations. Those who meet State certification requirements may become high school physics teachers, an occupation reportedly in strong demand in many school districts. (See the statements on these occupations elsewhere in the *Handbook*.) Despite strong competition for traditional physics and astronomy research jobs, individuals with a physics degree at any level will find their skills useful for entry to many other occupations.

Earnings
According to a 1997 National Association of Colleges and Employers survey, the average starting salary offer to physics doctoral degree candidates was $34,700.

The American Institute of Physics reported a median salary of $65,000 in 1996 for its members with Ph.D.'s; with master's degrees, $55,000; and with bachelor's degrees, $50,000. Those working in temporary postdoctoral positions earned significantly less.

Average earnings for physicists in nonsupervisory, supervisory, and managerial positions in the Federal Government in 1997 were about $71,800 a year, and for astronomy and space scientists, $77,400.

Related Occupations
The work of physicists and astronomers relates closely to that of engineers, chemists, meteorologists, geophysicists, computer scientists, computer programmers, and mathematicians.

Sources of Additional Information
General information on career opportunities in physics is available from:
☛ American Institute of Physics, Career Planning and Placement, One Physics Ellipse, College Park, MD 20740-3843. Homepage: http://www.aip.org
☛ The American Physical Society, Education Department, One Physics Ellipse, College Park, MD 20740-3844. Homepage: http://www.aps.org
For a pamphlet containing information on careers in astronomy, send your request to:
☛ American Astronomical Society, Education Office, Adler Planetarium and Astronomy Museum, 1300 S. Lake Shore Dr., Chicago IL 60605. Homepage: http://www.aas.org

Science Technicians

(List of D.O.T. codes available on request. See p. 496.)

Significant Points
- Science technicians in production jobs often work in 8 hour shifts around the clock.

- Job opportunities are expected to be very good for qualified graduates of science technician training programs or applied science technology programs who are well-trained on equipment used in laboratories and production facilities.

Nature of the Work
Science technicians use the principles and theories of science and mathematics to solve problems in research and development and to help invent and improve products and processes. However, their jobs are more practically oriented than those of scientists. Technicians set up, operate, and maintain laboratory instruments, monitor experiments, make observations, calculate and record results, and often develop conclusions. Those who work in production monitor manufacturing processes and may be involved in quality control, testing products for proper proportions of ingredients, purity, or for strength and durability.

As laboratory instrumentation and procedures have become more complex in recent years, the role of science technicians in research and development has expanded. In addition to performing routine tasks, many technicians also develop and adapt laboratory procedures to achieve the best results, interpret data, and devise solutions to problems, under the direction of scientists. The increasing use of robotics to perform many routine tasks has freed technicians to operate more sophisticated laboratory equipment. Science technicians make extensive use of computers, computer-interfaced equipment, robotics, and high-technology industrial applications such as biological engineering.

Most science technicians specialize, learning skills and working in the same disciplines as scientists. Occupational titles, therefore, tend to follow the same structure as scientists. *Agricultural technicians* work with agricultural scientists in food, fiber, and animal research, production, and processing. Some conduct tests and experiments to improve the yield and quality of crops or to increase the resistance of plants and animals to disease, insects, or other hazards. Other agricultural technicians do animal breeding and nutrition work.

Biological technicians work with biologists studying living organisms. They may assist scientists who conduct medical research, helping to find a cure for cancer or AIDS, for example. Those who work in pharmaceutical companies help develop and manufacture medicinal and pharmaceutical preparations. Those working in the field of microbiology generally work as lab assistants, studying living organisms and infectious agents. Biological technicians also analyze organic substances such as blood, food, and drugs, and some examine evidence in criminal investigations. Biological technicians working in biotechnology labs use the knowledge and techniques gained from basic research by scientists, including gene splicing and recombinant DNA, and apply these techniques in product development.

Chemical technicians work with chemists and chemical engineers, developing and using chemicals and related products and equipment. Most do research and development, testing, or other laboratory work. For example, they might test packaging for design, integrity of materials, and environmental acceptability; assemble and operate new equipment to develop new products; monitor product quality; or develop new production techniques. Some chemical technicians collect and analyze samples of air and water to monitor pollution levels. Those who focus on basic research might produce compounds through complex organic synthesis. Chemical technicians within chemical plants are also referred to as *process technicians*. They may operate equipment, monitor plant processes and analyze plant materials.

Environmental technicians may perform laboratory and field tests to monitor environmental resources and determine the contaminants and sources of pollution. They may collect samples for testing or be involved in abating, controlling, or remediating sources of environmental pollutants. They may be responsible for waste management operations, control and management of hazardous materials inventory, or general activities involving regulatory compliance. There is a growing emphasis on pollution prevention activities.

Nuclear technicians operate nuclear test and research equipment, monitor radiation, and assist nuclear engineers and physicists in research. Some also operate remote control equipment to manipulate radioactive materials or materials to be exposed to radioactivity.

Petroleum technicians measure and record physical and geologic conditions in oil or gas wells using instruments lowered into wells or by analysis of the mud from wells. In oil and gas exploration, they collect and examine geological data or test geological samples to determine petroleum and mineral content. Some petroleum technicians, called scouts, collect information about oil and gas well drilling operations, geological and geophysical prospecting, and land or lease contracts.

Other science technicians collect weather information or assist oceanographers.

Working Conditions
Science technicians work under a wide variety of conditions. Most work indoors, usually in laboratories, and have regular hours. Some occasionally work irregular hours to monitor experiments that can't be completed during regular working hours. Production technicians often work in 8 hour shifts around the clock. Others, such as agricultural, petroleum, and environmental technicians, perform much of their work outdoors, sometimes in remote locations.

Some science technicians may be exposed to hazards from equipment, chemicals, or toxic materials. Chemical technicians sometimes work with toxic chemicals or radioactive isotopes; nuclear technicians may be exposed to radiation; and biological technicians sometimes work with disease-causing organisms or radioactive agents. However, there is little risk if proper safety procedures are followed.

Employment
Science technicians held about 228,000 jobs in 1996. Over 35 percent worked in manufacturing, mostly in the chemical industry, but

Job duties of science technicians include collecting and analyzing samples.

also in the food processing industry. About 16 percent worked in education services and another 15 percent worked in research and testing services. In 1996, the Federal Government employed about 16,000 science technicians, mostly in the Departments of Defense, Agriculture, and Interior.

Training, Other Qualifications, and Advancement
There are several ways to qualify for a job as a science technician. Most employers prefer applicants who have at least 2 years of specialized training or an associate degree in applied science or science related technology. Because employer's preferences vary, however, many science technicians may actually have a bachelor's degree in chemistry or biology, or have taken several science and math courses at 4-year colleges.

Many technical and community colleges offer associate degrees in a specific technology or a more general education in science and mathematics. A number of 2-year associate degree programs are designed to provide easy transfer to a 4-year college or university if desired. Technical institutes generally offer technician training, but provide less theory and general education than technical or community colleges. The length of programs at technical institutes varies, although 1-year certificate programs and 2-year associate degree programs are common. Some schools offer cooperative-education or internship programs, allowing students the opportunity to work at a local company or other workplace while attending classes in alternate terms. Participation in such programs can significantly enhance a student's employment prospects.

Persons interested in careers as science technicians should take as many high school science and math courses as possible. Science courses taken beyond high school, in an associate's or bachelor's program, should be laboratory oriented, with an emphasis on "bench" skills. Because computers and computer-interfaced equipment are often used in research and development laboratories, technicians should have strong computer skills. Communication skills are also important; technicians are often required to report their findings both verbally and in writing. Technicians should also be able to work well with others because teamwork is common.

Prospective science technicians may acquire good career preparation through 2-year formal training programs that combine the teaching of scientific principles and theory with practical hands-on application in a laboratory setting with up-to-date equipment. Graduates of 4-year bachelor's degree programs in science who have considerable experience in laboratory-based courses, have completed internships, or held summer jobs in laboratories, are also well-qualified for science technician positions and are preferred by some employers. However, those with a bachelor's degree who accept technician jobs generally cannot find employment that utilizes their advanced academic education.

Technicians usually begin work as trainees in routine positions under the direct supervision of a scientist or a more experienced technician. Job candidates whose training or educational background encompasses extensive hands-on experience with a variety of laboratory equipment, including computers and related equipment, usually require a much shorter period of on-the-job training. As they gain experience, technicians take on more responsibility and carry out assignments under only general supervision, and some eventually become supervisors.

Job Outlook
Employment of science technicians is expected to increase about as fast as the average for all occupations through the year 2006. Continued growth of scientific and medical research, and development and the production of technical products should stimulate demand for science technicians in all areas. In particular, the growing number of agricultural and medicinal products developed using biotechnology techniques will increase the need for biological technicians. Employment growth will also be fueled by demand for technicians to help regulate waste products, collect air, water, and soil samples to

measure levels of pollutants, monitor compliance with environmental regulations, and clean up contaminated sites. However, growth will be moderated somewhat by an expected slowdown in overall employment in the chemical industry.

Job opportunities are expected to be very good for qualified graduates of science technician training programs or applied science technology programs who are well-trained on equipment used in industrial and government laboratories and production facilities. As the instrumentation and techniques used in industrial research, development, and production become more complex, employers are seeking well trained individuals with highly developed technical and communication skills. In addition to opportunities created by growth, many job openings should arise from the need to replace technicians who retire or leave the labor force for other reasons.

Earnings
Median annual earnings of science technicians were about $27,000 in 1996; the middle 50 percent earned between $19,800 and $37,100. Ten percent earned less than $15,500, and 10 percent earned over $49,500. Median annual earnings were about $31,100 for chemical technicians and about $25,200 for biological technicians in 1996.

In the Federal Government in 1997, science technicians started at $15,500, $17,400, or $19,500, depending on education and experience. Beginning salaries were slightly higher in selected areas of the country where the prevailing local pay level was higher. The average annual salary for biological science technicians in nonsupervisory, supervisory, and managerial positions employed by the Federal Government in early 1997 was $28,500; for mathematical technicians, $34,870; for physical science technicians, $35,890; for geodetic technicians, $45,050; for hydrologic technicians, $33,230; and for meteorologic technicians, $41,460.

Related Occupations
Other technicians who apply scientific principles at a level usually taught in 2-year associate degree programs include engineering technicians, broadcast technicians, drafters, and health technologists and technicians. Some of the work of agricultural and biological technicians is related to that in agriculture and forestry occupations.

Sources of Additional Information
For information about a career as a chemical technician, contact:
☛ American Chemical Society, Education Division, Career Publications, 1155 16th St. NW., Washington, DC 20036. Homepage: http://www.acs.org

Legal Occupations

Lawyers and Judges

(D.O.T. 110; 111; 119.107, .117, .167-010, .267-014; 169.267-010)

Significant Points

- Formal educational requirements usually include a 4-year college degree, followed by 3 years in law school. After that, all States require applicants for admission to the bar to pass a written bar examination.

- Competition for admission to many law schools is intense, as the number of applicants greatly exceeds the number that may be admitted.

- Aspiring lawyers or judges should encounter keen competition for jobs.

Nature of the Work
Lawyers. Lawyers, also called *attorneys*, act as both advocates and advisors in our society. As advocates, they represent one of the parties in criminal and civil trials by presenting evidence in court supporting their client. As advisors, lawyers counsel their clients as to their legal rights and obligations, and suggest particular courses of action in business and personal matters. Whether acting as advocates or advisors, all attorneys interpret the law and apply it to specific situations.

Lawyers research the purposes behind laws and judicial decisions that have been applied to circumstances similar to those faced by their client. While all lawyers continue to use law libraries to prepare cases, some supplement their search of conventional printed sources with computer sources. Software can be used to search legal literature automatically, and to identify legal texts relevant to a specific case. In litigation involving many supporting documents, lawyers may use computers to organize and index material. Tax lawyers use computers for making tax computations and exploring alternative tax strategies for clients.

Lawyers increasingly use the Internet for research and to advertise their services. Ethical standards for advertising on the Internet are still evolving. Lawyers also use electronic filing, videoconferencing, and voice-recognition technology. Electronic filing promotes the sharing of information by providing all parties in a case access to a database

with all official filings, briefs, and other court documents; these technologies also save time and reduce legal costs.

Lawyers communicate the information obtained through research to others. They advise clients and draw up legal documents, such as wills and contracts. Lawyers may not disclose matters discussed in confidence with clients. They hold positions of great responsibility, and are obligated to adhere to a strict code of ethics.

The more detailed aspects of a lawyer's job depend upon his or her field of specialization and position. While all lawyers are licensed to represent parties in court, some appear in court more frequently than others; some lawyers specialize in trial work. Their ability to think quickly and speak with ease and authority as well as their familiarity with courtroom rules and strategy are particularly important in trial work. However, trial lawyers still spend most of their time outside the courtroom conducting research, interviewing clients and witnesses, and handling other details in preparation for trial.

Besides trials, lawyers may specialize in other areas, such as bankruptcy, probate, or international law. Environmental lawyers, for example, may represent public interest groups, waste disposal companies, or construction firms in their dealings with the Environmental Protection Agency (EPA) and other State and Federal agencies. They help clients prepare and file for licenses and applications for approval before certain activities may occur. They also represent clients' interests in administrative adjudications.

Some lawyers concentrate in the growing field of intellectual property. These lawyers help protect clients' claims to copyrights, art work under contract, product designs, and computer programs. Still other lawyers advise insurance companies about the legality of insurance transactions. They write insurance policies to conform with the law and to protect companies from unwarranted claims. They review claims filed against insurance companies and represent the companies in court.

The majority of lawyers are in private practice, where they concentrate on criminal or civil law. In criminal law, lawyers represent individuals who have been charged with crimes and argue their cases in courts of law. In civil law, attorneys assist clients with litigation, wills, trusts, contracts, mortgages, titles, and leases. Others handle only public interest cases—civil or criminal—which may have a potential impact extending well beyond the individual client.

Lawyers are sometimes employed full time by a single client. If the client is a corporation, the lawyer is known as "house counsel," and usually advises the company concerning legal issues related to its business activities. These issues might involve patents, government regulations, contracts with other companies, property interests, or collective bargaining agreements with unions.

A significant number of attorneys are employed at the various levels of government. Lawyers who work for State attorneys general, prosecutors, public defenders, and courts play a key role in the criminal justice system. At the Federal level, attorneys investigate cases for the Department of Justice or other agencies. Government lawyers also help develop programs, draft and interpret laws and legislation, establish enforcement procedures, and argue civil and criminal cases on behalf of the government.

Other lawyers work for legal aid societies—private, nonprofit organizations established to serve disadvantaged people. These lawyers generally handle civil, rather than criminal cases.

A relatively small number of trained attorneys work in law schools. Most are faculty members who specialize in one or more subjects, and others serve as administrators. Some work full time in nonacademic settings and teach part time. (For additional information, see the *Handbook* section on college and university faculty.) Some lawyers become judges.

Judges. Judges apply the law and oversee the legal process in courts according to local, State, and Federal statutes. They preside over cases concerning every aspect of society, from traffic offenses to disputes over management of professional sports, or from the rights of huge corporations to questions of disconnecting life support equipment for terminally ill persons. They must ensure trials and hearings are conducted fairly, and the court administers justice in a manner safeguarding the legal rights of all parties involved.

Judges preside over trials or hearings and listen as attorneys representing the parties present and argue their cases. They rule on the admissibility of evidence and methods of conducting testimony, and settle disputes between the opposing attorneys. They ensure rules and procedures are followed, and if unusual circumstances arise for which standard procedures have not been established, judges direct how the trial will proceed based on their knowledge of the law.

Judges often hold pretrial hearings for cases. They listen to allegations and, based on the evidence presented, determine whether there is enough merit for a trial to be held. In criminal cases, judges may decide that persons charged with crimes should be held in jail pending their trial, or may set conditions for release through the trial. In civil cases, judges may impose restrictions upon the parties until a trial is held.

When trials are held, juries are often selected to decide cases, including guilt or innocence in criminal cases, and the liability and the amount of compensation in civil cases. In these cases, judges instruct juries on applicable laws, direct them to deduce the facts from the evidence presented, and hear their verdict. However, judges decide cases when the law does not require a jury trial, or when the parties waive their right to a jury. In the absence of a jury, the judge determines guilt and imposes sentences in a criminal case; in civil cases, the judge rewards relief—such as compensation for damages—to the parties in the lawsuit (also called litigants).

Judges also work outside the courtroom "in chambers." In their private offices, judges read documents on pleadings and motions, research legal issues, write opinions, and oversee the court's operations. Running a court is like running a small business, and judges also manage their courts' administrative and clerical staff.

Judges' duties vary according to the extent of their jurisdictions and powers. *General trial court judges* of the Federal and State court systems have jurisdiction over any case in their system. They generally try civil cases transcending the jurisdiction of lower courts, and all cases involving felony offenses. Federal and State *appellate court judges*, although few in number, have the power to overrule decisions made by trial court or administrative law judges if they determine that legal errors were made in a case, or if legal precedent does not support the judgment of the lower court. They rule on fewer cases and rarely have direct contacts with litigants. Instead, they usually

Lawyers represent their clients in criminal and civil trials by presenting evidence in court.

base their decisions on lower court records and written and oral arguments by lawyers.

Many State court judges preside in courts in which jurisdiction is limited by law to certain types of cases. A variety of titles are assigned to these judges, but among the most common are *municipal court judge*, *county court judge*, *magistrate*, or *justice of the peace*. Traffic violations, misdemeanors, small claims cases, and pretrial hearings constitute the bulk of the work of these judges, but some States allow them to handle cases involving domestic relations, probate, contracts, and other selected areas of the law.

Administrative law judges, formerly called *hearing officers*, are employed by government agencies to make determinations for administrative agencies. They make decisions on a person's eligibility for various Social Security benefits or worker's compensation, protection of the environment, enforcement of health and safety regulations, employment discrimination, and compliance with economic regulatory requirements.

Working Conditions

Lawyers and judges do most of their work in offices, law libraries, and courtrooms. Lawyers sometimes meet in clients' homes or places of business and, when necessary, in hospitals or prisons. They may travel to attend meetings, gather evidence, and appear before courts, legislative bodies, and other authorities.

Salaried lawyers generally have structured work schedules. Lawyers in private practice may work irregular hours while conducting research, conferring with clients, or preparing briefs during nonoffice hours. Lawyers often work long hours, and about half regularly work 50 hours or more per week. They are under particularly heavy pressure, for example, when a case is being tried. Preparation for court includes keeping abreast of the latest laws and judicial decisions.

Although work is not generally seasonal, the work of tax lawyers and other specialists may be an exception. Because lawyers in private practice can often determine their own workload and when they will retire, many stay in practice well beyond the usual retirement age.

Many judges work a standard 40-hour week, but a third of all judges work over 50 hours per week. Some judges with limited jurisdiction are employed part time and divide their time between their judicial responsibilities and other careers.

Employment

Lawyers held about 622,000 jobs in 1996; judges, about 78,000. About 7 out of 10 lawyers practiced privately, either in law firms or in solo practices. Most of the remaining lawyers held positions in government, the greatest number at the local level. In the Federal

Government, lawyers work for many different agencies but are concentrated in the Departments of Justice, Treasury, and Defense. Other lawyers are employed as house counsel by public utilities, banks, insurance companies, real estate agencies, manufacturing firms, welfare and religious organizations, and other business firms and nonprofit organizations. Some salaried lawyers also have part-time independent practices; others work as lawyers part time while working full time in another occupation.

All judges, magistrates, and other judicial workers were employed by Federal, State, or local governments, with about 4 out of 10 holding positions in the Federal Government.

Law professors also hold law degrees, as well as other professionals such as politicians, managers, and administrators.

Training, Other Qualifications, and Advancement

Lawyers. To practice law in the courts of any State or other jurisdiction, a person must be licensed, or admitted to its bar, under rules established by the jurisdiction's highest court. All require that applicants for admission to the bar pass a written bar examination; most jurisdictions also require applicants to pass a separate written ethics examination. Lawyers who have been admitted to the bar in one jurisdiction may occasionally be admitted to the bar in another without taking an examination if they meet that jurisdiction's standards of good moral character, and have a specified period of legal experience. Federal courts and agencies set their own qualifications for those practicing before them.

To qualify for the bar examination in most States, an applicant must usually obtain a college degree and graduate from a law school accredited by the American Bar Association (ABA) or the proper State authorities. (ABA accreditation signifies that the law school—particularly its library and faculty—meets certain standards developed to promote quality legal education.) ABA currently accredits 179 law schools. Others are approved by State authorities only. With certain exceptions, graduates of schools not approved by the ABA are restricted to taking the bar examination and practicing in the State or other jurisdiction in which the school is located; most of these schools are in California. In 1997, seven States accepted the study of law in a law office or in combination with study in a law school; only California accepts the study of law by correspondence as qualifying for taking the bar examination. Several States require registration and approval of students by the State Board of Law Examiners, either before they enter law school or during the early years of legal study.

Although there is no nationwide bar examination, 47 States, the District of Columbia, Guam, the Northern Mariana Islands, and the Virgin Islands require the 6-hour Multistate Bar Examination (MBE) as part of the bar examination; the MBE is not required in Indiana, Louisiana, Washington, and Puerto Rico. The MBE covers issues of broad interest, and is sometimes given in addition to a locally prepared State bar examination. The 3-hour Multistate Essay Examination (MEE) is used as part of the State bar examination in a few States. States vary in their use of MBE and MEE scores.

Performance examinations to test practical skills of beginning lawyers are required by eight states. This program has been well received and more States are expected to require performance testing in the future. Requirements vary by State, although the test usually is taken at the same time as the bar exam, and is a one-time requirement.

The required college and law school education usually takes 7 years of full-time study after high school—4 years of undergraduate study followed by 3 years in law school. Although some law schools accept a very small number of students after 3 years of college, most require applicants to have a bachelor's degree. To meet the needs of students who can attend only part time, a number of law schools have night or part-time divisions which usually require 4 years of study; about 1 in 10 graduates from ABA-approved schools attends part time.

Although there is no recommended "prelaw" major, prospective lawyers should develop proficiency in writing and speaking, reading, researching, analyzing, and thinking logically—skills needed to succeed both in law school and in the profession. Whatever the major, a multidisciplinary background is recommended. Courses in English, foreign language, public speaking, government, philosophy, history, economics, mathematics, and computer science, among others, are useful.

Students interested in a particular aspect of law may find related courses helpful. For example, prospective patent lawyers need a strong background in engineering or science, and future tax lawyers must have extensive knowledge of accounting.

Acceptance by most law schools depends on the applicant's ability to demonstrate an aptitude for the study of law, usually through good undergraduate grades, the Law School Admission Test (LSAT), the quality of the applicant's undergraduate school, any prior work experience, and sometimes a personal interview. However, law schools vary in the weight they place on each of these and other factors.

All law schools approved by the ABA, except for those in Puerto Rico, require applicants to take the LSAT. Nearly all law schools require applicants to have certified transcripts sent to the Law School Data Assembly Service, which then sends applicants' LSAT scores and their standardized records of college grades to the law schools of their choice. Both this service and the LSAT are administered by the Law School Admission Council.

Competition for admission to many law schools is intense. Enrollments in these schools rose very rapidly during the 1970s, with applicants far outnumbering available seats. The number of applicants decreased markedly in the 1990s, easing competition slightly; however, the number of applicants to most law schools still greatly exceeds the number that can be admitted. Competition for admission to the more prestigious law schools is always keen.

During the first year or year and a half of law school, students generally study fundamental courses such as constitutional law, contracts, property law, torts, civil procedure, and legal writing. In the remaining time, they may elect specialized courses in fields such as tax, labor, or corporation law. Law students often acquire practical experience by participation in school sponsored legal clinic activities, in the school's moot court competitions in which students conduct appellate arguments, in practice trials under the supervision of experienced lawyers and judges, and through research and writing on legal issues for the school's law journal.

In 1997, law students in 48 States were required to pass the Multistate Professional Responsibility Examination (MPRE), which tests their knowledge of the ABA codes on professional responsibility and judicial conduct. In some States, the MPRE may be taken during law school, usually after completing a course on legal ethics.

A number of law schools have clinical programs in which students gain legal experience through practice trials and law school projects under the supervision of practicing lawyers and law school faculty. Law school clinical programs might include work in legal aid clinics, for example, or on the staff of legislative committees. Part-time or summer clerkships in law firms, government agencies, and corporate legal departments also provide valuable experience. Such training can provide references or lead directly to a job after graduation, and can help students decide what kind of practice best suits them. Clerkships may also be an important source of financial aid.

Graduates receive the degree of *juris doctor* (J.D.) as the first professional degree. Advanced law degrees may be desirable for those planning to specialize, do research, or teach. Some law students pursue joint degree programs, which generally require an additional semester or year. Joint degree programs are offered in a number of areas, including law and business administration or public administration.

After graduation, lawyers must keep informed about legal and nonlegal developments that affect their practice. Currently, 37 States and jurisdictions mandate Continuing Legal Education (CLE). Many law schools and State and local bar associations provide continuing education courses that help lawyers stay abreast of recent developments. Some States allow CLE credits to be obtained through participation in seminars on the Internet.

The practice of law involves a great deal of responsibility. Individuals planning careers in law should like to work with people, and be able to win the respect and confidence of their clients, associates, and the public. Perseverance and reasoning ability are essential to analyze complex cases and reach sound conclusions. Lawyers also need creativity when handling new and unique legal problems.

Most beginning lawyers start in salaried positions. Newly hired salaried attorneys usually start as associates and work with more experienced lawyers or judges. After several years of progressively more responsible salaried employment, some lawyers are admitted to partnership in their firm, or go into practice for themselves. Some lawyers, after several years of practice, become full-time law school faculty or administrators; a growing number have advanced degrees in other fields as well.

Some attorneys use their legal training in administrative or managerial positions in various departments of large corporations. A transfer from a corporation's legal department to another department often is viewed as a way to gain administrative experience and rise in the ranks of management.

Judges. Most judges have first been lawyers. Federal and State judges are generally required to be lawyers. About 40 States allow nonlawyers to hold limited jurisdiction judgeships, but opportunities are better with law experience. Federal administrative law judges must be lawyers and pass a competitive examination administered by the U.S. Office of Personnel Management. Some State administrative law judges and other hearing officials are not required to be lawyers, but law degrees are preferred for most positions.

Federal judges are appointed for life by the President, with the consent of the Senate. Federal administrative law judges are appointed by the various Federal agencies with virtually lifetime tenure. About half of all State judges are appointed, while the remainder are elected in partisan or nonpartisan State elections. Many State and local judges serve fixed renewable terms, which range from 4 or 6 years for some trial court judgeships, to as long as 14 years or life for other trial or appellate court judges. Judicial nominating commissions, composed of members of the bar and the public, are used to screen candidates for judgeships in many States, as well as for some Federal judgeships.

All States have some type of orientation for newly elected or appointed judges. The Federal Judicial Center, ABA, National Judicial College, and National Center for State Courts provide judicial education and training for judges and other judicial branch personnel. General and continuing education courses usually run from a couple of days to 3 weeks in length. Over half of the States, including Puerto Rico, require judges to enroll in continuing education courses while serving on the bench.

Job Outlook

Individuals interested in pursuing careers as lawyers or judges should encounter keen competition through the year 2006. The number of law school graduates is expected to continue to strain the economy's capacity to absorb them. As for judges, the prestige associated with serving on the bench should insure continued, intense competition for openings.

Lawyers. Employment of lawyers grew very rapidly from the early 1970s through the early 1990s, but has started to level off in the last several years. Employment is expected to grow about as fast as the average for all occupations through the year 2006. Continuing demand for lawyers will result from growth in the population and the general level of business activities. Demand will also be spurred by growth of legal action in such areas as health care, intellectual property, international law, elder law, sexual harassment, and the environment. The wider availability and affordability of legal clinics and prepaid legal service programs should result in increased use of legal services by middle-income people.

Employment growth should be slower than in the past. In an effort to reduce the money spent on legal fees, many businesses are turning to large accounting firms to provide employee benefit counseling, process documents, and handle other services previously performed by law firms. Also, mediation and dispute resolution are increasingly used as alternatives to litigation.

Competition for job openings should continue to be keen because of the large numbers graduating from law school each year. During the 1970s, the annual number of law school graduates more than doubled, outpacing the rapid growth of jobs. Growth in the yearly number of law school graduates slowed during the early to mid-1980s, but increased again in the late 1980s to early 1990s. Although graduates with superior academic records from well-regarded law schools will have more job opportunities, most graduates will encounter stiff competition for jobs. As in the past, some graduates may have to accept positions in areas outside their field of interest or for which they feel overqualified. They may choose to enter jobs for which legal training is an asset, but not normally a requirement—for example, administrative, managerial, and business positions in banks, insurance firms, real estate companies, government agencies, and other organizations.

Some recent law school graduates who are unable to find permanent positions are turning to the growing number of legal temporary staffing firms, which place attorneys in short-term jobs until they are able to secure full-time positions. This service allows companies to hire lawyers on an "as needed" basis and allows beginning lawyers to develop practical skills while looking for permanent positions.

Due to the competition for jobs, a law graduate's geographic mobility and work experience assume greater importance. The willingness to relocate may be an advantage in getting a job, but to be licensed in a new State, a lawyer may have to take an additional State bar examination. In addition, employers increasingly seek graduates who have advanced law degrees and experience in a specialty such as tax, patent, or admiralty law.

Employment growth for lawyers will continue to be concentrated in salaried jobs, as businesses and all levels of government employ a growing number of staff attorneys, and as employment in the legal services industry grows in larger law firms. Most salaried positions are in urban areas where government agencies, law firms, and big corporations are concentrated. The number of self-employed lawyers is expected to increase slowly, reflecting the difficulty of establishing a profitable new practice in the face of competition from larger, established law firms. Also, the growing complexity of law, which encourages specialization, along with the cost of maintaining up-to-date legal research materials, favor larger firms.

For lawyers who wish to work independently, establishing a new practice will probably be easiest in small towns and expanding suburban areas, as long as an active market for legal services exists. In such communities, competition from larger established law firms is likely to be less than in big cities, and new lawyers may find it easier to become known to potential clients.

Some lawyers are adversely affected by cyclical swings in the economy. During recessions, the demand declines for some discretionary legal services, such as planning estates, drafting wills, and handling real estate transactions. Also, corporations are less likely to litigate cases when declining sales and profits result in budgetary restrictions. Some corporations and law firms will not hire new attorneys until business improves or may cut staff to contain costs. Several factors, however, mitigate the overall impact of recessions on lawyers. During recessions, individuals and corporations face other legal problems, such as bankruptcies, foreclosures, and divorces requiring legal action.

Judges. Employment of judges is expected to grow more slowly than the average for all occupations. Contradictory social forces affect the demand for judges. Growing public concerns about crime, safety, and efficient administration of justice should spur demand; on the other hand, tight public funding should slow job growth.

Competition for judgeships should remain keen. Most job openings will arise as judges retire. Traditionally, many judges have held their positions until late in life. Now, early retirement is becoming more common, creating more job openings. However, becoming a judge will still be difficult. Besides competing with other qualified people, judicial candidates must gain political support in order to be elected or appointed.

Earnings
Median salaries of lawyers 6 months after graduation from law school in 1996 varied by type of work, as indicated by table 1.

Salaries of experienced attorneys also vary widely according to the type, size, and location of their employer. The median annual salary of all lawyers was about $60,000 in 1996. General attorneys in the Federal Government averaged around $72,700 a year in 1997; the relatively small number of patent attorneys in the Federal Government averaged around $81,600.

Table 1. Median salaries of lawyers 6 months after graduation, 1996

All graduates	$40,000

Type of work

Private practice	50,000
Business/industry	45,000
Academe	35,000
Judicial clerkship	35,000
Government	34,500
Public interest	30,000

SOURCE: National Association for Law Placement

Lawyers who practice alone usually earn less than those who are partners in law firms. Lawyers starting their own practice may need to work part time in other occupations to supplement their income until their practice is well-established.

According to the Administrative Office of the U.S. Courts, Federal district court judges had salaries of $133,600 in 1997, as did judges in the Court of Federal Claims; circuit court judges earned $141,700 a year. Federal judges with limited jurisdiction, such as magistrates and bankruptcy court judges, had salaries of $122,900. Full-time Federal administrative law judges had average salaries of $94,800. The Chief Justice of the United States Supreme Court earned $171,500, and the Associate Justices earned $164,100.

According to a survey by the National Center for State Courts, annual salaries of associate justices of States' highest courts averaged $101,800 in 1997, and ranged from about $68,900 to $133,600. Salaries of State intermediate appellate court judges averaged $91,000, and ranged from $79,400 to $124,200. Salaries of State judges with limited jurisdiction vary widely; some salaries are set locally.

Most salaried lawyers and judges are provided health and life insurance, and contributions are made on their behalf to retirement plans. Lawyers who practice independently are only covered if they arrange and pay for such benefits themselves.

Related Occupations
Legal training is useful in many other occupations. Some of these are arbitrator, mediator, journalist, patent agent, title examiner, legislative assistant, lobbyist, FBI special agent, political office holder, and corporate executive.

Sources of Additional Information
Information on law schools and law as a career may be obtained from:
☛ American Bar Association, 750 North Lake Shore Dr., Chicago, IL 60611.

Information on the LSAT, the Law School Data Assembly Service, applying to law school, and financial aid for law students may be obtained from:

☛ Law School Admission Council, P.O. Box 40, Newtown, PA 18940. Homepage: http://www.lsac.org

Information on acquiring a job as a lawyer with the Federal Government may be obtained from the Office of Personnel Management through a telephone-based system. Consult your telephone directory under U.S. Government for a local number or call (912) 757-3000 (TDD 912 744-2299). That number is not toll-free and charges may result. Information also is available from their Internet site: http://www.usajobs.opm.gov

The specific requirements for admission to the bar in a particular State or other jurisdiction may also be obtained at the State capital from the clerk of the Supreme Court or the administrator of the State Board of Bar Examiners.

Paralegals

(D.O.T. 119.267-022 and -026)

Significant Points

- Paralegals is expected to rank among the 20 fastest growing occupations in the economy as employers recognize that paralegals perform many legal tasks for lower salaries than lawyers.

- Competition for jobs should continue as the growing number of graduates from paralegal education programs keeps pace with employment growth.

Nature of the Work
Not all legal work requires a law degree. Lawyers are often assisted in their work by paralegals or legal assistants. Paralegals perform many of the same tasks as lawyers, except for those considered to be the practice of law.

Paralegals work for lawyers. Although the lawyers assume responsibility for the legal work, they often delegate many of their tasks to paralegals. Paralegals are prohibited from setting legal fees, giving legal advice, and presenting cases in court.

Paralegals generally do the preparatory work for lawyers involved in closings, hearings, trials, and corporate meetings. Paralegals investigate the facts of cases, ensuring all relevant information is uncovered. They conduct legal research to identify the appropriate laws, judicial decisions, legal articles, and other materials that are relevant to assigned cases. After organizing and analyzing the information, paralegals may prepare written reports that attorneys use in determining how cases should be handled. Should attorneys decide to file lawsuits on behalf of clients, paralegals may help prepare the legal arguments, draft pleadings and motions to be filed with the court, obtain affidavits, and assist attorneys during trials. Paralegals also organize and track files of all documents and correspondence important to cases, and make them available to attorneys.

Paralegals may work in all areas of the law, including litigation, bankruptcy, corporate law, criminal law, employee benefits, patent and copyright law, and real estate. They help draft contracts, mortgages, separation agreements, and trust instruments. They may also help prepare tax returns and plan estates. Some paralegals coordinate the activities of other law office employees, and keep the financial records for the office.

Paralegals who work for corporations help attorneys with employee contracts, shareholder agreements, stock option plans, and employee benefit plans. They may help prepare and file annual financial reports, maintain corporate minute books and resolutions, and help secure loans for the corporation. Paralegals may also review government regulations to ensure the corporation operates within the law.

The duties of paralegals who work in government vary depending on the agency in which they are employed. Generally, paralegals in government analyze legal material for internal use, maintain reference files, conduct research for attorneys, collect and analyze evidence for agency hearings, and prepare informative or explanatory material on the law, agency regulations, and agency policy for general use by the agency and the public.

Paralegals employed in community legal service projects help the poor, the aged, and others in need of legal assistance. They file forms, conduct research, and prepare documents. When authorized by law, they may represent clients at administrative hearings.

Some paralegals, usually those in small and medium-sized law firms, perform a variety of duties that require a general knowledge of the law. For example, they may research judicial decisions on improper police arrests or help prepare a mortgage contract.

Some paralegals employed by large law firms, government agencies, and corporations specialize in one aspect of the law, including real estate, estate planning, family law, labor law, litigation, and corporate law. Within specialties, functions often are broken down further so paralegals may deal with a specific area. For example, paralegals specializing in labor law may deal exclusively with employee benefits.

A growing number of paralegals use computers in their work. Computer software packages and on-line legal research are increasingly used to search legal literature stored in computer databases and on CD-ROM. The Internet is also used extensively for legal research. In litigation involving many supporting documents, paralegals may use computer databases to organize, index, and retrieve the material. Imaging software allows paralegals to scan documents directly into a database. Paralegals sometimes use billing programs to track hours billed to clients. They may also use computer software packages to perform tax computations and explore the consequences of possible tax strategies for clients.

Working Conditions
Paralegals do most of their work at desks in offices and law libraries. Occasionally, they travel to gather information and perform other duties.

Paralegals employed by corporations and government usually work a standard 40-hour week. Although most paralegals work year round, some are temporarily employed during busy times of the year, then released when the workload diminishes. Paralegals who work for law firms sometimes work very long hours when they are under

Paralegals conduct research to identify the appropriate laws and judicial decisions that are relevant to assigned cases.

pressure to meet deadlines. Some law firms reward such loyalty with bonuses and additional time off.

Paralegals handle many routine assignments, particularly when they are inexperienced. Paralegals usually assume more responsible and varied tasks as they gain experience. Furthermore, as new laws and judicial interpretations emerge, paralegals are exposed to new legal problems that make their work more interesting and challenging.

Employment
Paralegals held about 113,000 jobs in 1996. Private law firms employed the vast majority; most of the remainder worked for the various levels of government. Within the Federal Government, the Department of Justice is the largest employer, followed by the Departments of Treasury and Defense, and the Federal Deposit Insurance Corporation. Other employers include State and local governments, publicly funded legal service projects, banks, real estate development companies, and insurance companies. A small number of paralegals own their own businesses; as freelance legal assistants, they contract their services to attorneys or corporate legal departments.

Training, Other Qualifications, and Advancement
There are several ways to become a paralegal. Employers generally require formal paralegal training obtained through associate or bachelor's degree programs, or certificate programs. Increasingly employers prefer graduates of 4-year paralegal programs, or college graduates who have completed short-term paralegal certificate programs. However, the majority of paralegals hold associate degrees. Some employers prefer to train paralegals on the job, promoting experienced legal secretaries or hiring college graduates with no legal experience. Other entrants have experience in a technical field that is useful to law firms, such as a background in tax preparation for tax and estate practice or nursing or health administration for personal injury practice.

Over 800 formal paralegal training programs are offered by 4-year colleges and universities, law schools, community and junior colleges, business schools, and proprietary schools. There are currently 214 programs approved by the American Bar Association (ABA). Although this approval is neither required nor sought by many programs, graduation from an ABA-approved program can enhance one's employment opportunities. The requirements for admission to formal training programs vary widely. Some require some college courses or a bachelor's degree; others accept high school graduates or those with legal experience; and a few schools require standardized tests and personal interviews.

Paralegal programs include 2-year associate's degree programs, 4-year bachelor's degree programs, or certificate programs that take only a few months to complete. Many certificate programs only require a high school diploma or GED for admission. Programs typically include general courses on the law and legal research techniques, in addition to courses covering specialized areas of the law, such as real estate, estate planning and probate, litigation, family law, contracts, and criminal law. Many employers prefer applicants with specialized training. Programs increasingly include courses introducing students to the legal applications of computers. Many paralegal training programs include an internship in which students gain practical experience by working for several months in a law office, corporate legal department, or government agency. Experience gained in internships is an asset when seeking a job after graduation.

The quality of paralegal training programs varies; the better programs generally emphasize job placement. Prospective students should examine the experiences of recent graduates of programs in which they are considering enrolling.

Paralegals need not be certified, but the National Association of Legal Assistants has established standards for voluntary certification requiring various combinations of education and experience. Paralegals who meet these standards are eligible to take a 2-day examination, given 3 times each year at several regional testing centers. Those who pass this examination may use the designation Certified Legal Assistant (CLA). This designation is a sign of competence in the field and may enhance employment and advancement opportunities. The Paralegal Advanced Competency Exam, established in 1996 and administered through the National Federation of Paralegal Associations, offers professional recognition to paralegals with a bachelor's degree and at least 2 years of experience. Those who pass this examination may use the designation Registered Paralegal (RP).

Paralegals must be able to handle legal problems logically and communicate, both orally and in writing, their findings and opinions to their supervising attorney. They must understand legal terminology and have good research and investigative skills. Familiarity with the operation and applications of computers in legal research and litigation support is increasingly important. Paralegals must always stay abreast of new developments in the law that affect their area of practice. Paralegals can participate in continuing legal education seminars to maintain their legal knowledge.

Because paralegals often deal with the public, they must be courteous and uphold the high ethical standards of the legal profession. The National Association of Legal Assistants, the National Federation of Paralegal Associations, and a few States have established ethical guidelines paralegals must follow.

Paralegals are usually given more responsibilities and less supervision as they gain more work experience. In large law firms, corporate legal departments, and government agencies, experienced paralegals may supervise other paralegals and clerical staff, and delegate work assigned by the attorneys. Advancement opportunities include promotion to managerial and other law-related positions within the firm or corporate legal department. However, some paralegals find it easier to move to another law firm when seeking increased responsibility or advancement.

Job Outlook

Competition for jobs should continue as the growing number of graduates from paralegal education programs keeps pace with employment growth. Employment of paralegals is expected to grow much faster than average—ranking among the fastest growing occupations in the economy through the year 2006—as law firms and other employers with legal staffs increasingly hire paralegals to lower the cost, and increase the availability and efficiency, of legal services. While new jobs created by rapid employment growth will create most of the job openings for paralegals in the future, other job openings will arise as people leave the occupation.

Private law firms will continue to be the largest employers of paralegals as a growing population requires additional legal services, especially in areas such as intellectual property, health care law, international law, elder law, sexual harassment, and the environment. The growth of prepaid legal plans should also contribute to the demand for the services of law firms. A growing array of other organizations, such as corporate legal departments, insurance companies, real estate and title insurance firms, and banks will also hire paralegals.

Job opportunities for paralegals will expand even in the public sector. Community legal service programs—which provide assistance to the poor, aged, minorities, and middle-income families—operate on limited budgets. They will seek to employ additional paralegals in order to minimize expenses and serve the most people. Federal, State, and local government agencies, consumer organizations, and the courts should continue to hire paralegals in increasing numbers.

To a limited extent, paralegal jobs are affected by the business cycle. During recessions, demand declines for some discretionary legal

services, such as planning estates, drafting wills, and handling real estate transactions. Corporations are less inclined to initiate litigation when falling sales and profits lead to fiscal belt tightening. As a result, full-time paralegals employed in offices adversely affected by a recession may be laid off or have their work hours reduced. On the other hand, during recessions, corporations and individuals are more likely to face other legal problems, such as bankruptcies, foreclosures, and divorces, that require legal assistance. Paralegals, who provide many of the same legal services at a lower cost, may fare better than lawyers.

Earnings

Earnings of paralegals vary greatly. Salaries depend on education, training, experience, the type and size of employer, and the geographic location of the job. Generally, paralegals who work for large law firms or in large metropolitan areas earn more than those who work for smaller firms or in less populated regions.

According to the National Federation of Paralegal Associations, paralegals had an average annual salary of $32,900 in 1995. Starting salaries of paralegals with 1 year or less experience averaged $29,300. In addition to a salary, many paralegals received an annual bonus, which averaged about $1,900 in 1995.

The average annual salary of paralegal specialists who work for the Federal Government was about $44,400 in 1997.

Related Occupations

Several other occupations call for a specialized understanding of the law and the legal system, but do not require the extensive training of a lawyer. Some of these are abstractors, claim examiners, compliance and enforcement inspectors, occupational safety and health workers, patent agents, police officers, and title examiners.

Sources of Additional Information

General information on a career as a paralegal can be obtained from:

☛ Standing Committee on Legal Assistants, American Bar Association, 750 North Lake Shore Dr., Chicago, IL 60611.

For information on certification of paralegals, schools that offer training programs in a specific State, and standards and guidelines for paralegals, contact:

☛ National Association of Legal Assistants, Inc., 1516 South Boston St., Suite 200, Tulsa, OK 74119. Homepage: http://www.nala.org

Information on a career as a paralegal, schools that offer training programs, the Paralegal Advanced Competency Exam, and local paralegal associations can be obtained from:

☛ National Federation of Paralegal Associations, P.O. Box 33108, Kansas City, MO 64114.

Information on careers, training programs, and job postings for paralegals are available at the following Internet site: http://www.paralegals.org

Information on paralegal training programs, including the pamphlet "How to Choose a Paralegal Education Program," may be obtained from:

☛ American Association for Paralegal Education, P.O. Box 40244, Overland Park, KS 66204.

Information on acquiring a job as a paralegal specialist with the Federal Government may be obtained from the Office of Personnel Management through a telephone-based system. Consult your telephone directory under U.S. Government for a local number or call (912) 757-3000 (TDD 912 744-2299). That number is not toll-free and charges may result. Information also is available from their Internet site: http://www.usajobs.opm.gov

Social Scientists

Nature of the Work

Social scientists study all aspects of human society—from the optimal distribution of goods and services to human behavior and relationships between groups. Their research provides insights that help us understand the different ways in which individuals and groups make decisions, exercise power, and respond to change. Through their studies and analyses, social scientists suggest solutions to social, business, personal, governmental, and environmental problems.

Research is a basic activity for many social scientists. They use various methods to assemble facts and construct theories. Applied research usually is designed to produce information that will enable people to make better decisions or manage their affairs more effectively. Interviews and surveys are widely used to collect facts, opinions, or other information. Information collection takes many forms, however, including living and working among the population being studied; field investigations, including the analysis of historical records and documents; experiments with human or animal subjects in a laboratory; the administration of standardized tests and questionnaires; and the preparation and interpretation of maps and computer graphics.

The following paragraphs discuss the major specialties in social science. Specialists in one field, however, often find that their research overlaps work being conducted in another discipline.

Anthropologists study the origin and the physical, social, and cultural development and behavior of humans. They may study the way of life, archaeological remains, language, or physical characteristics of people in various parts of the world. Some compare the customs, values, and social patterns of different cultures. Anthropologists generally concentrate in sociocultural anthropology, archaeology, linguistics, or biological-physical anthropology. Sociocultural anthropologists study the customs, cultures, and social lives of groups in settings that vary from nonindustrialized societies to modern urban centers. Archaeologists recover and examine material evidence, such as tools and pottery remaining from past human cultures, in order to determine the history, customs, and living habits of earlier civilizations. Linguistic anthropologists study the role of language in various cultures. Biological-physical anthropologists study the evolution of the human body, look for the earliest evidences of human life, and analyze how culture and biology influence one another. Most anthropologists specialize in one particular region of the world.

Economists study the production, distribution, and consumption of goods and services. Most economists are concerned with the practical applications of economic policy in a particular area, such as finance, labor, agriculture, transportation, energy, or health. Others develop theories to explain economic phenomena such as unemployment or inflation. *Marketing research analysts* study local, regional, national, or world market conditions to determine potential sales of a product or service. They analyze data on past sales and trends to develop forecasts, and conduct extensive market surveys to test their conclusions.

Geographers analyze distributions of physical and cultural phenomena on local, regional, continental, and global scales. Economic geographers study the distribution of resources and economic activities. Political geographers are concerned with the relationship of geography to political phenomena, while cultural geographers study the geography of cultural phenomena. Physical geographers study the variations in climates, vegetation, soil, and land forms, and their implications for human activity. Urban and transportation geographers study cities and metropolitan areas, while regional geographers study the physical, economic, political, and cultural characteristics of regions, ranging in size from a congressional district to entire continents. Medical geographers study health care delivery systems, epidemiology (the study of the causes and control of epidemics), and the effect of the environment on health. (Some occupational classification systems include geographers under physical scientists rather than social scientists.)

Historians research, analyze, and interpret the past. They use many sources of information in their research, including government and institutional records, newspapers and other periodicals, photographs, interviews, films, and unpublished manuscripts such as personal diaries and letters. Historians usually specialize in a specific country or region; in a particular time period; or in a particular field, such as social, intellectual, political, or diplomatic history. Biographers collect detailed information on individuals. Genealogists trace family histories. Other historians help study and preserve archival materials, artifacts, and historic buildings and sites.

Political scientists study the origin, development, and operation of political systems and public policy. They conduct research on a wide range of subjects such as relations between the United States and other countries, the institutions and political life of nations, the politics of small towns or a major metropolis, or the decisions of the U.S. Supreme Court. Studying topics such as public opinion, political decisionmaking, ideology, and public policy, they analyze the structure and operation of governments as well as various political entities. Depending on the topic under study, a political scientist might conduct a public opinion survey, analyze election results, analyze public documents, or interview public officials.

Psychologists study human behavior and counsel or advise individuals or groups. Their research also assists business advertisers, politicians, and others interested in influencing or motivating people. While clinical psychology is the largest specialty, psychologists specialize in many other fields such as counseling, experimental, social, and industrial psychology.

Sociologists study human society and social behavior by examining the groups and social institutions that people form, as well as various social, religious, political, and business organizations. They also study the behavior and interaction of groups, trace their origin and growth, and analyze the influence of group activities on individual members. They are concerned with the characteristics of social groups, organizations, and institutions; the ways individuals are affected by each other and by the groups to which they belong; and the effect of social traits such as sex, age, or race on a person's daily life. The results of sociological research aid educators, lawmakers, administrators, and others interested in resolving social problems and formulating public policy.

Most sociologists work in one or more specialties, such as social organization, stratification, and mobility; racial and ethnic relations; education; family; social psychology; urban, rural, political, and comparative sociology; sex roles and relations; demography; gerontology; criminology; or sociological practice.

Urban and regional planners develop comprehensive plans and programs for the use of land. Planners prepare for situations that are likely to develop as a result of population growth or social and economic change.

Working Conditions

Most social scientists have regular hours. Generally working behind a desk, either alone or in collaboration with other social scientists, they read and write research reports. Many experience the pressures of writing and publishing articles, deadlines and tight schedules, and sometimes they must work overtime, for which they generally are not reimbursed. Social scientists often work as an integral part of a research team, where good communications skills are important. Travel may be necessary to collect information or attend meetings. Social scientists on foreign assignment must adjust to unfamiliar cultures, climates, and languages.

Some social scientists do fieldwork. For example, anthropologists, archaeologists, and geographers often travel to remote areas, live among the people they study, learn their languages, and stay for long periods at the site of their investigations. They may work under rugged conditions, and their work may involve strenuous physical exertion.

Social scientists employed by colleges and universities generally have flexible work schedules, often dividing their time among teaching, research and writing, consulting, or administrative responsibilities.

Employment

Social scientists held about 263,000 jobs in 1996. Over half of these social scientists are psychologists. Over one-quarter of all social scientists—overwhelmingly psychologists—are self-employed, involved in counseling, consulting, or research.

Salaried social scientists worked as researchers, administrators, and counselors for a wide range of employers, including Federal, State, and local governments, educational institutions, hospitals, research and testing services, and management and public relations firms. Other employers include social service agencies, international organizations, associations, museums, historical societies, and computer and data processing firms.

In addition, many individuals with training in a social science discipline teach in colleges and universities, and in secondary and elementary schools. (For more information, see the *Handbook* statements on college and university faculty, and kindergarten, elementary, and secondary school teachers.) The proportion of social scientists who teach varies by occupation—for example, the academic world generally is a more important source of jobs for graduates in history than for graduates in psychology.

Training, Other Qualifications, and Advancement

Educational attainment of social scientists is among the highest of all occupations. The Ph.D. or equivalent degree is a minimum requirement for most positions in colleges and universities and is important for advancement to many top level nonacademic research and administrative posts. Graduates with master's degrees in applied specialties generally have better professional opportunities outside of colleges and universities, although the situation varies by field. For example, job prospects for master's degree holders in urban or regional planning are brighter than for master's degree holders in history. Graduates with a master's degree in a social science qualify for teaching positions in junior colleges. Bachelor's degree holders have limited opportunities and in most social science occupations do not qualify for "professional" positions. The bachelor's degree does, however, provide a suitable background for many different kinds of entry-level jobs, such as research assistant, administrative aide, or management or sales trainee. With the addition of sufficient education courses, social science graduates also can qualify for teaching positions in secondary and elementary schools.

Training in statistics and mathematics is essential for many social scientists. Mathematical and quantitative research methods are increasingly used in economics, geography, political science, experimental psychology, and other fields. The ability to use computers for research purposes is mandatory in most disciplines.

Depending on their jobs, social scientists may need a wide range of personal characteristics. Because they constantly seek new information about people, things, and ideas, intellectual curiosity and creativity are fundamental personal traits. The ability to think logically and methodically is important to a political scientist comparing, for example, the merits of various forms of government. Similarly, the ability to analyze large amounts of data is important to an economist studying proposals to reduce Federal budget deficits. Objectivity, open-mindedness, and systematic work habits are important in all kinds of social science research. Perseverance is essential for an anthropologist, who might spend years accumulating artifacts from an ancient civilization. Emotional stability and sensitivity are vital to a psychologist working with mental patients.

Excellent written and oral communication skills are essential for all these professionals.

Job Outlook

Candidates seeking positions as social scientists can expect to encounter keen competition in many areas of social science. Many social science graduates, however, will find good employment opportunities in areas outside social science, often in jobs that are related to social science where their research, communication, and quantitative skills can be put to good use.

Prospects are best for those with advanced degrees, and generally are better in disciplines such as economics and psychology, which offer more opportunities in nonacademic settings. Government agencies, health and social service organizations, marketing, research and consulting firms, and a wide range of businesses seek social science graduates, although often in jobs with titles unrelated to their academic discipline. Social scientists will face stiff competition for academic positions. However, the growing importance and popularity of social science subjects in secondary schools is strengthening the demand for social science teachers at this level.

Overall employment of social scientists is expected to grow more slowly than the average for all occupations through the year 2006. The largest social science occupation, psychologists, is expected to grow more slowly than the average, although some growth is expected due to public concern for the development of human resources, including the growing elderly population and children in school. Employment of economists and marketing research analysts is expected to grow about as fast as the average for all occupations through the year 2006. Opportunities for economists should be best in private industry, especially in research, testing, and consulting firms, as more companies contract out for economic research. Demand for marketing research analysts should be strong due to an increasingly competitive global economy. Employment of urban and regional planners is expected to grow more slowly than the average for all occupations through the year 2006 because many work for local governments that will experience tight budget constraints in the years to come. Other social scientists, including sociologists, anthropologists, geographers, historians, and political scientists should experience slower than average growth.

Earnings

Median annual earnings of all social scientists were about $35,000 in 1996. The middle 50 percent earned between $24,400 and $47,800 annually. The lowest 10 percent earned under $18,000, while the highest 10 percent earned over $67,700.

According to a 1997 survey by the National Association of Colleges and Employers, people with a bachelor's degree in a social science field received starting offers averaging about $25,000 a year.

In the Federal Government, social scientists with a bachelor's degree and no experience could start at $19,500 or $24,200 a year in 1997, depending on their college records. Those with a master's degree could start at $29,600, and those having a Ph.D. degree could begin at $35,800, while some individuals with experience and an advanced degree could start at $42,900. Beginning salaries were slightly higher in selected areas of the country where the prevailing local pay level was higher. The average salary of social scientists working for the Federal Government was $48,190 in early 1997; in geography was $47,850; in history was $55,750; in sociology was $64,720; and in archeology was $43,450.

Related Occupations

A number of fields that require training and personal qualities similar to those of the various social science fields are covered elsewhere in the *Handbook*. These include lawyers; statisticians; mathematicians; computer programmers; computer scientists, computer engineers, and systems analysts; reporters and correspondents; social workers; college and university faculty; and counselors.

Sources of Additional Information

More detailed information about economists and marketing research analysts, psychologists, and urban and regional planners is presented in the *Handbook* statements that follow this introductory statement.

Anthropology

For information about careers in anthropology, contact:

☛ The American Anthropological Association, 4350 N. Fairfax Dr., Suite 640, Arlington, VA 22203.

Archaeology

For information about careers in archaeology, contact:

☛ Society for American Archaeology, 900 2nd St. NE., Suite 12, Washington, DC 20002.

☛ Archaeological Institute of America, 656 Beacon St., Boston, MA 02215.

Geography

For information about careers in geography, contact:

☛ Association of American Geographers, 1710 16th St. NW., Washington, DC 20009.

History

Information on careers for historians is available from:

☛ American Historical Association, 400 A St. SE., Washington, DC 20003.

☛ Organization of American Historians, 112 North Bryan St., Bloomington, IN 47408.

☛ American Association for State and Local History, 530 Church St., 6th Floor, Nashville, TN 37219.

Political Science

For information about careers in political science, contact:

☛ American Political Science Association, 1527 New Hampshire Ave. NW., Washington, DC 20036.

☛ National Association of Schools of Public Affairs and Administration, 1120 G St. NW., Suite 730, Washington, DC 20005.

Sociology

Information about careers in sociology is available from:

☛ American Sociological Association, 1722 N St. NW., Washington, DC 20036-2981.

For information about careers in demography, contact:

☛ Population Association of America, 721 Ellsworth Dr., Suite 303 Silver Spring, MD 20910.

Economists and Marketing Research Analysts

(D.O.T. 050.067)

Significant Points

● Demand for qualified marketing research analysts should be strong.

● Candidates who hold a master's degree in economics have much better employment prospects than bachelor's degree holders.

Nature of the Work

Economists. Economists study the ways society distributes scarce resources such as land, labor, raw materials, and machinery to produce goods and services. They conduct research, collect and analyze data, monitor economic trends, and develop forecasts. They research issues such as energy costs, inflation, interest rates, imports, or employment levels.

Most economists are concerned with practical applications of economic policy in a particular area. They use their understanding of economic relationships to advise businesses and other organizations, including insurance companies, banks, securities firms, industry and trade associations, labor unions, and government agencies. Economists use mathematical models to develop programs predicting answers to questions such as the nature and length of business cycles, the effects of a specific rate of inflation on the economy, or the effects of tax legislation on unemployment levels.

Economists devise methods and procedures for obtaining the data they need. For example, sampling techniques may be used to conduct a survey, and various mathematical modeling techniques may be used to develop forecasts. Preparing reports on the results of their research is an important part of the economist's job. Relevant data must be reviewed and analyzed, applicable tables and charts prepared, and the results presented in clear, concise language that can be understood by non-economists. Presenting economic and statistical concepts in a meaningful way is particularly important for economists whose research is directed toward making policies for an organization.

Economists who work for government agencies may assess economic conditions in the United States or abroad, in order to estimate the economic effects of specific changes in legislation or public policy. They may study areas such as how the dollar's fluctuation against foreign currencies affects import and export levels. The majority of government economists work in the area of agriculture, labor, or quantitative analysis; some economists work in almost every area of government. For example, some economists in the U.S. Department of Commerce study production, distribution, and consumption of commodities produced overseas, while economists employed with the Bureau of Labor Statistics analyze data on the domestic economy such as prices, wages, employment, productivity, and safety and health. An economist working in State or local government might analyze data on the growth of school-aged populations, prison growth, and employment and unemployment rates, in order to project spending needs for future years.

Marketing Research Analysts. Marketing research analysts are concerned with the potential sales of a product or service. They analyze statistical data on past sales to predict future sales. They gather data on competitors and analyze prices, sales, and methods of marketing and distribution. Like economists, marketing research analysts devise methods and procedures for obtaining the data they need. They often design telephone, personal, or mail interview surveys to assess consumer preferences. The surveys are usually conducted by trained interviewers under the marketing research analyst's direction. Once the data are compiled, marketing research analysts evaluate it. They then make recommendations to their client

Employment of economists and marketing research analysts is concentrated in large cities.

or employer based upon their findings. They provide a company's management with information needed to make decisions on the promotion, distribution, design, and pricing of company products or services, or to determine the advisability of adding new lines of merchandise, opening new branches, or otherwise diversifying the company's operations. Analysts may conduct opinion research to determine public attitudes on various issues. This can help political or business leaders and others assess public support for their electoral prospects or advertising policies.

Working Conditions
Economists and marketing research analysts have structured work schedules. They often work alone, writing reports, preparing statistical charts, and using computers, but they may also be an integral part of a research team. Most work under pressure of deadlines and tight schedules, and sometimes must work overtime. Their routine may be interrupted by special requests for data, as well as by the need to attend meetings or conferences; regular travel may be necessary to do this.

Employment
Economists and marketing research analysts held about 51,000 jobs in 1996. Private industry, particularly economic and marketing research firms, management consulting firms, banks, securities and commodities brokers, and computer and data processing companies, employed about 3 out of 4 salaried workers. The remainder, primarily economists, were employed by a wide range of government agencies, primarily in the State Government. The Departments of Labor, Agriculture, and Commerce are the largest Federal employers of economists. A number of economists and marketing research analysts combine a full-time job in government, academia, or business with part-time or consulting work in another setting.

Employment of economists and marketing research analysts is concentrated in large cities. Some economists work abroad for companies with major international operations, for U.S. Government agencies, and for international organizations like the World Bank and the United Nations.

Besides the jobs described above, many economists and marketing research analysts held economics and marketing faculty positions in colleges and universities. Economics and marketing faculty have flexible work schedules, and may divide their time among teaching, research, consulting, and administration. (See the statement on college and university faculty elsewhere in the *Handbook*.)

Training, Other Qualifications, and Advancement
Graduate training is required for most private sector economist and marketing research analyst jobs, and for advancement to more responsible positions. Economics includes many specialties at the graduate level, such as advanced economic theory, econometrics, international economics, and labor economics. Students should select graduate schools strong in specialties in which they are interested. Marketing research analysts may earn advanced degrees in economics, business administration, marketing, statistics, or some closely related discipline. Some schools help graduate students find internships or part-time employment in government agencies, economic consulting firms, financial institutions, or marketing research firms prior to graduation.

In the Federal Government, candidates for entry-level economist positions must have a bachelor's degree with a minimum of 21 semester hours of economics and 3 hours of statistics, accounting, or calculus. Competition is keen for those positions which require only a bachelor's degree, however, and additional education or superior academic performance is likely to be required to gain employment.

For a job as an instructor in many junior and some community colleges, a master's degree is the minimum requirement. In most colleges and universities, however, a Ph.D. is necessary for appointment as an instructor. A Ph.D. and extensive publications in academic journals are required for a professorship, tenure, and promotion.

Whether working in government, industry, research organizations, marketing, or consulting firms, economists and marketing research analysts who have a graduate degree usually qualify for more responsible research and administrative positions. A Ph.D. is necessary for top economist or marketing positions in many organizations. Many corporation and government executives have a strong background in economics or marketing.

A bachelor's degree with a major in economics or marketing is generally not sufficient to obtain positions as economist or marketing analyst, but is excellent preparation for many entry-level positions as a research assistant, administrative or management trainee, marketing interviewer, or any of a number of professional sales jobs.

Economics majors can choose from a variety of courses, ranging from those which are intensely mathematical such as microeconomics, macroeconomics, and econometrics, to more philosophical courses such as the history of economic thought.

In addition to courses in business, marketing, and consumer behavior, marketing majors should take other liberal arts and social science courses, including economics, psychology, English, and sociology. Because of the importance of quantitative skills to economists and marketing researchers, courses in mathematics, statistics, econometrics, sampling theory and survey design, and computer science are extremely helpful.

Aspiring economists and marketing research analysts should gain experience gathering and analyzing data, conducting interviews or surveys, and writing reports on their findings while in college. This experience can prove invaluable later in obtaining a full-time position in the field, since much of their work, in the beginning, may center around these duties. With experience, economists and marketing research analysts eventually are assigned their own research projects.

Those considering careers as economists or marketing research analysts should be able to work accurately because much time is spent on data analysis. Patience and persistence are necessary qualities since economists and marketing research analysts must spend long hours on independent study and problem solving. At the same time, they must work well with others, especially marketing research analysts, who often oversee interviews for a wide variety of individuals. Economists and marketing research analysts must be able to present their findings, both orally and in writing, in a clear, meaningful way.

Job Outlook
Employment of economists and marketing research analysts is expected to grow about as fast as the average for all occupations through the year 2006. Most job openings, however, are likely to result from the need to replace experienced workers who transfer to other occupations, retire, or leave the labor force for other reasons.

Opportunities for economists should be best in private industry, especially in research, testing, and consulting firms, as more companies contract out for economic research services. Competition, the growing complexity of the global economy, and increased reliance on quantitative methods for analyzing the current value of future funds, business trends, sales, and purchasing should spur demand for economists. The growing need for economic analyses in virtually every industry should result in additional jobs for economists. Employment of economists in the Federal Government should decline more slowly than the rate projected for the entire Federal workforce. Average employment growth is expected among economists in State and local government.

An advanced degree coupled with a strong background in economic theory, mathematics, statistics, and econometrics provides the basis for acquiring any specialty within the field. Those skilled in quantitative techniques and their application to economic modeling and forecasting, using computers, coupled with good communications skills, should have the best job opportunities.

Those who graduate with a bachelor's degree in economics through the year 2006 will face keen competition for the limited number of economist positions for which they qualify. They will qualify for a number of other positions, however, where they can take advantage of their economic knowledge in conducting research, developing surveys, or analyzing data. Many graduates with bachelor's degrees will find good jobs in industry and business as management or sales trainees, or administrative assistants. Economists with good quantitative skills are qualified for research assistant positions in a broad range of fields. Those who meet State certification requirements may become high school economics teachers. The demand for secondary school economics teachers is expected to grow as economics becomes an increasingly important and popular course. (See the statement on kindergarten, elementary, and secondary school teachers elsewhere in the *Handbook*.)

Candidates who hold a master's degree in economics have much better employment prospects than bachelor's degree holders. Many businesses, research and consulting firms, and government agencies seek master's degree holders who have strong computer and quantitative skills and can perform complex research, but do not command the higher salary of a Ph.D. Ph.D. degree holders are likely to face competition for teaching positions in colleges and universities.

Demand for qualified marketing research analysts should be strong due to an increasingly competitive economy. Marketing research provides organizations valuable feedback from purchasers, allowing companies to evaluate consumer satisfaction and more effectively plan for the future. As companies seek to expand their market and consumers become better informed, the need for marketing professionals is increasing. Opportunities for marketing research analysts with graduate degrees should be good in a wide range of employment settings, particularly in marketing research firms, as companies find it more profitable to contract out for marketing research services rather than support their own marketing department. Other organizations, including financial services organizations, health care institutions, advertising firms, manufacturing firms producing consumer goods, and insurance companies may offer job opportunities for marketing research analysts.

A strong background in marketing, mathematics, statistics, and econometrics provides the basis for acquiring any specialty within the field. Those skilled in quantitative techniques and their application to marketing research using computers should have the best job opportunities. Like economists, marketing research graduates with related work experience in a closely related business field or industry should have the best job opportunities.

Those with only a bachelor's degree but who have a strong background in mathematics, statistics, survey design, and computer science may be hired by private firms as research assistants or interviewers.

Earnings

According to a 1997 salary survey by the National Association of Colleges and Employers, persons with a bachelor's degree in economics received offers averaging $31,300 a year; for those with a bachelor's degrees in marketing, $27,900.

The median base salary of business economists in 1996 was $73,000, according to a survey by the National Association of Business Economists. The median entry-level salary was about $35,000, with most new entrants' possessing a masters degree. Ninety three percent of the respondents held advanced degrees. The highest salaries were reported by those who had a Ph.D., with a median salary of $85,000. Master's degree holders earned a median salary of $65,500, while bachelor's degree holders earned $60,000. The highest paid business economists were in the securities and investment industry, which reported a median income of $100,000, followed by banking and mining at $93,000 and the nondurable manufacturing industry at $87,000. The lowest paid were in government and nonprofit research.

The Federal Government recognizes education and experience in certifying applicants for entry level positions. The entrance salary for economists having a bachelor's degree was about $19,500 a year in 1997; however, those with superior academic records could begin at

$24,200. Those having a master's degree could qualify for positions at an annual salary of $29,600. Those with a Ph.D. could begin at $35,800, while some individuals with experience and an advanced degree could start at $42,900. Starting salaries were slightly higher in selected areas where the prevailing local pay was higher. The average annual salary for economists employed by the Federal Government was $63,870 a year in early 1997.

Related Occupations

Economists are concerned with understanding and interpreting financial matters, among other subjects. Other jobs in this area include financial managers, financial analysts, underwriters, actuaries, credit analysts, loan officers, and budget officers.

Marketing research analysts do research to find out how well products or services are received by the market. This may include the planning, implementation, and analysis of surveys to determine people's needs and preferences. Other jobs using these skills include psychologists, sociologists, and urban and regional planners.

Sources of Additional Information

For information on careers in economics and business, contact:
☛ National Association of Business Economists, 1233 20th St. NW., Suite 505, Washington, DC 20036.

For information about careers and salaries in marketing research, contact:
☛ Marketing Research Association, 2189 Silas Deane Hwy., Suite 5, Rocky Hill, CT 06067.
☛ Council of American Survey Research Organizations, 3 Upper Devon, Port Jefferson, NY 11777.

Information on obtaining a job with the Federal Government may be obtained from the Office of Personnel Management through a telephone based system. Consult your telephone directory under U.S. Government for a local number or call (912) 757-3000 (TDD 912 744-2299). That number is not toll free and charges may result. Information also is available from their internet site: http://www.usajobs.opm.gov

Psychologists

(D.O.T. 045.061, .067, .107-022, -026, -030, -034, and -046)

Significant Points

- Over 40 percent of all psychologists are self-employed, about 5 times the average for all professional workers.

- A doctoral degree generally is required for employment as a licensed clinical or counseling psychologist.

- Opportunities for employment in psychology for those with only a bachelor's degree are severely limited.

Nature of the Work

Psychologists study the human mind and human behavior. Research psychologists investigate the physical, cognitive, emotional, or social aspects of human behavior. Psychologists in applied fields provide mental health care in hospitals, clinics, schools, or private settings.

Like other social scientists, psychologists formulate hypotheses and collect data to test their validity. Research methods may vary depending on the topic under study. Psychologists sometimes gather information through controlled laboratory experiments, as well as through administering personality, performance, aptitude, and intelligence tests. Other methods include observation, interviews, questionnaires, clinical studies, and surveys.

Psychologists apply their knowledge to a wide range of endeavors, including health and human services, management, education, law, and sports. In addition to a variety of work settings, psychologists generally specialize in one of a number of different areas. *Clinical psychologists*—who constitute the largest specialty—generally work in counseling centers, independent or group practices, or in health maintenance organizations, hospitals, or clinics. They assist mentally or emotionally disturbed clients adjust to life and may help medical and surgical patients deal with their illnesses or injuries. Some work in physical rehabilitation settings, treating patients with spinal cord injuries, chronic pain or illness, stroke, arthritis, and neurologic conditions such as multiple sclerosis. Others help people deal with times of personal crisis, such as divorce or the death of a loved one. Clinical psychologists often interview patients and give diagnostic tests. They may provide individual, family, and group psychotherapy, and design and implement behavior modification programs. Some clinical psychologists collaborate with physicians and other specialists to develop and implement treatment and intervention programs that patients can understand and comply with. Other clinical psychologists work in universities and medical schools, where they train graduate students in the delivery of mental health and behavioral medicine services. Some administer community mental health programs.

Some areas of specialization within clinical psychology include health psychology, neuropsychology, and geropsychology. *Health psychologists* promote good health through health maintenance counseling programs that are designed to help people achieve goals such as to stop smoking or lose weight. *Neuropsychologists* study the relation between the brain and behavior. They often work in stroke and head injury programs. *Geropsychologists* deal with the special problems faced by the elderly. The emergence and growth of these specialties reflects the increasing participation of psychologists in providing direct services to special patient populations.

Cognitive psychologists deal with memory, thinking, and perceptions. Some conduct research related to computer programming and artificial intelligence.

Counseling psychologists use various techniques, including interviewing and testing, to advise people on how to deal with problems of everyday living. They work in settings such as university counseling centers, hospitals, and individual or group practices. (Also see the statements on counselors and social workers elsewhere in the *Handbook*.)

Developmental psychologists study the physiological development that takes place throughout life. Some specialize in behavior during infancy, childhood, and adolescence, changes that take place during maturity or old age, or developmental disabilities and their effects. Increasingly, research is developing ways to help elderly people stay as independent as possible.

Experimental or *research psychologists* work in university and private research centers, and in business, nonprofit, and governmental organizations. They study behavior processes with human beings and animals such as rats, monkeys, and pigeons. Prominent areas of study in experimental research include motivation, thinking, attention, learning and memory, sensory and perceptual processes, effects of substance abuse, and genetic and neurological factors affecting behavior.

Industrial-organizational psychologists (I/O) apply psychological principles and research methods to the workplace in the interest of improving productivity and the quality of worklife. They also are involved in research into management and marketing problems. They conduct applicant screening, training and development, counseling, and organizational development and analysis. An industrial psychologist might work with management to reorganize the work setting to improve productivity or quality of life in the workplace. They frequently act as consultants, brought in by management in order to solve a particular problem.

School psychologists work in elementary and secondary schools or school district offices with students, teachers, parents, and administrators to resolve students' learning and behavior problems. They collaborate with teachers, parents, and school personnel to improve classroom management strategies or parenting skills, counter substance abuse, work with students with disabilities or gifted and talented students, and improve teaching and learning strategies. They

Psychologists often must work evening and weekend hours to accommodate their clients.

may evaluate the effectiveness of academic programs, behavior management procedures, and other services provided in the school setting.

Social psychologists examine people's interactions with others and with the social environment. They work in organizational consultation, marketing research, systems design or other applied psychology fields. Prominent areas of study include group behavior, leadership, attitudes, and perception.

Working Conditions
A psychologist's specialty and place of employment determine working conditions. Clinical, school, and counseling psychologists in private practice have their own offices and set their own hours. However, they often must offer evening and weekend hours to accommodate their clients. Those employed in hospitals, nursing homes, and other health facilities may work shifts including evenings and weekends, while those who work in schools and clinics generally work regular hours. Psychologists employed as faculty by colleges and universities divide their time between teaching and research, and some have administrative responsibilities as well. Many have part-time consulting practices. Most psychologists in government and industry have structured schedules. Increasingly, psychologists work as part of a team and consult with other psychologists and professionals. Many experience pressures due to deadlines, tight schedules, and overtime work. Their routine may be interrupted frequently. Travel is required to attend conferences or conduct research.

Employment
Psychologists held about 143,000 jobs in 1996. Educational institutions employed nearly 4 out of 10 salaried psychologists in positions other than teaching, such as counseling, testing, research, and administration. Three out of 10 were employed in health services, primarily in hospitals, mental health clinics, rehabilitation centers, nursing homes, and other health facilities. Government agencies at the Federal, State, and local levels employed about 16 percent. Governments employ psychologists in hospitals, clinics, correctional facilities, and other settings. The Department of Veterans Affairs and the Department of Defense employ about 80 percent of the psychologists working for Federal agencies. Some psychologists work in social service organizations, research organizations, management consulting firms, marketing research firms, and other businesses.

After several years of experience, some psychologists—usually those with doctoral degrees—enter private practice or set up their own research or consulting firms. Over 40 percent of all psychologists are self-employed.

In addition to the jobs described above, many held positions as psychology faculty at colleges and universities, and as high school psychology teachers. (See the statements on college and university faculty and kindergarten, elementary, and secondary school teachers elsewhere in the *Handbook.*)

Training, Other Qualifications, and Advancement
A doctoral degree is generally required for employment as a licensed clinical or counseling psychologist. Psychologists with a Ph.D. qualify for a wide range of teaching, research, clinical, and counseling positions in universities, elementary and secondary schools, private industry, and government. Psychologists with a Psy.D.—Doctor of Psychology—generally work in clinical positions. Persons with a master's degree in psychology often work as school or industrial-organizational psychologists. Others work as psychological assistants, under the supervision of doctoral-level psychologists, and conduct research or psychological evaluations.

A bachelor's degree in psychology qualifies a person to assist psychologists and other professionals in community mental health centers, vocational rehabilitation offices, and correctional programs. They may work as research or administrative assistants or become sales or management trainees in business. Some work as technicians in related fields such as marketing research. However, without additional academic training, their opportunities in psychology are severely limited.

In the Federal Government, candidates having at least 24 semester hours in psychology and one course in statistics qualify for entry-level positions. Because this is one of the few areas in which one can work as a psychologist without an advanced degree, competition for these jobs is keen.

Clinical psychologists generally must have completed the Ph.D. or Psy.D. requirements and served an internship. Vocational and guidance counselors usually need 2 years of graduate study in counseling and 1 year of counseling experience. School psychology requires a master's degree followed by a 1-year internship.

Most students need at least 2 years of full-time graduate study to earn a master's degree in psychology. Requirements usually include practical experience in an applied setting and a master's thesis based on an original research project.

A doctoral degree usually requires 5 to 7 years of graduate study. The Ph.D. degree culminates in a dissertation based on original research. Courses in quantitative research methods, which include the use of computer-based analysis, are an integral part of graduate study and are necessary to complete the dissertation. The Psy.D. may be based on practical work and examinations rather than a dissertation. In clinical or counseling psychology, the requirements for the doctoral degree generally include a year or more of internship.

Competition for admission into graduate programs is keen. Some universities require an undergraduate major in psychology. Others prefer only course work in basic psychology with courses in the biological, physical, and social sciences, statistics, and mathematics.

Most colleges and universities offer a bachelor's degree in psychology. Over 650 departments offer either a master's or a full Ph.D. program. A smaller number of professional schools of psychology offer the Psy.D.

The American Psychological Association (APA) presently accredits doctoral training programs in clinical, counseling, and school psychology. The National Council for Accreditation of Teacher Education, with the assistance of the National Association of School Psychologists, also is involved in the accreditation of advanced degree programs in school psychology. The APA also accredits institutions that provide internships for doctoral students in school, clinical, and counseling psychology.

Psychologists in independent practice or those who offer any type of patient care, including clinical, counseling, and school psychologists, must meet certification or licensing requirements in all States and the District of Columbia. Licensing laws vary by State and by type of position. Clinical and counseling psychologists generally require a doctorate in psychology, completion of an approved internship, and 1 to 2 years of professional experience. In addition, all States require that applicants pass an examination. Most State boards administer a standardized test and many supplement that with additional oral or essay questions. Most States certify those with a master's degree as school psychologists after completion of an internship. Some States require continuing education for license renewal.

Most States require that licensed or certified psychologists limit their practice to areas in which they have developed professional competence through training and experience.

The American Board of Professional Psychology recognizes professional achievement by awarding certification, primarily in clinical psychology, clinical neuropsychology, counseling, forensic, industrial-organizational, and school psychology. Candidates for APA certification need a doctorate in psychology, 5 years of experience, professional endorsements, and a passing grade on an examination.

Aspiring psychologists who are interested in direct patient care must be emotionally stable, mature, and able to deal effectively with people. Sensitivity, compassion, and the ability to lead and inspire others are particularly important qualities for clinical work and counseling. Research psychologists should be able to do detailed work independently and as part of a team. Excellent communications skills are necessary to succeed in research. Patience and perseverance are vital qualities because results from psychological treatment of patients or from research usually take a long time.

Job Outlook
Employment of psychologists is expected to grow more slowly than the average for all occupations through the year 2006. Job opportunities in health care should increase slightly in health care provider networks, such as health maintenance and preferred provider organizations, and in nursing homes and alcohol and drug abuse programs. More job opportunities will arise in businesses, nonprofit organizations, and research and computer firms for psychologists working as consultants. Companies will use psychologists' expertise in survey design, analysis, and research to provide marketing evaluation and statistical analysis. The increase in employee assistance programs, which offer employees help with personal problems, should also spur job growth.

Opportunities for people holding doctorates from leading universities in areas with an applied emphasis, such as clinical, counseling, health, and educational psychology, should have particularly good prospects. Psychologists with extensive training in quantitative research methods and computer science may have a competitive edge over applicants without this background.

Graduates with a master's degree in psychology are qualified for positions in school and industrial-organizational psychology. Graduates of master's degree programs in school psychology should have the best job prospects, as schools are expected to increase student counseling and mental health services. Masters' degree holders with several years of industrial experience can obtain jobs in consulting and marketing research. Other master's degree holders may find jobs as psychological assistants in the community mental health field, which often requires direct supervision by a licensed psychologist. Still others may find jobs involving research and data collection and analysis in universities, government, or private companies.

Bachelor's degree holders can expect very few opportunities directly related to psychology. Some may find jobs as assistants in rehabilitation centers, or in other jobs involving data collection and analysis. Those who meet State certification requirements may become high school psychology teachers.

Earnings
According to a 1995 survey by the American Psychological Association, the median salary of psychologists with a doctoral degree and 5 to 9 years of experience was $55,000 in counseling psychology in individual private practice; $54,500 in private research organizations; $51,000 as clinical psychologists in public psychiatric hospitals; and

$59,000 in school psychology. The median annual salary of master's degree holders was $38,000 in counseling psychology; $43,000 in clinical psychology; $41,500 in research positions; $60,000 in school psychology, and $55,000 in industrial-organizational psychology. Some psychologists have much higher earnings, particularly those in private practice.

The Federal Government recognizes education and experience in certifying applicants for entry-level positions. In general, the starting salary for psychologists having a bachelor's degree was about $19,500 a year in 1997; those with superior academic records could begin at $24,200. Psychologists with a master's degree and 1 year of experience could start at $29,600. Psychologists having a Ph.D. or Psy.D. degree and 1 year of internship could start at $35,800, and some individuals with experience could start at $42,900. Beginning salaries were slightly higher in selected areas of the country where the prevailing local pay level was higher. The average salary for psychologists in the Federal Government in nonsupervisory, supervisory, and managerial positions was about $62,120 a year in 1997.

Related Occupations
Psychologists are trained to conduct research and teach, evaluate, counsel, and advise individuals and groups with special needs. Others who do this kind of work include marketing research analysts, advertising and public relations managers, clinical social workers, physicians, sociologists, clergy, special education teachers, and counselors.

Sources of Additional Information
For information on careers, educational requirements, financial assistance, and licensing in all fields of psychology, contact:
☛ American Psychological Association, Research Office and Education in Psychology and Accreditation Offices, 750 1st St. NE., Washington, DC 20002. Information is also available from their internet site: http://www.apa.org/

For information on careers, educational requirements, and licensing of school psychologists, contact:
☛ National Association of School Psychologists, 4030 East West Highway, Suite 402, Bethesda, MD 20814.

Information about State licensing requirements is available from:
☛ Association of State and Provincial Psychology Boards, P.O. Box 4389, Montgomery, AL 36103-4389.

Information on obtaining a job with the Federal Government may be obtained from the Office of Personnel Management through a telephone based system. Consult your telephone directory under U.S. Government for a local number or call (912) 757-3000 (TDD 912 744-2299). That number is not toll free and charges may result. Information also is available from their internet site: http://www.usajobs.opm.gov

Urban and Regional Planners

(D.O.T. 188.167-110 and 199.167-014)

Significant Points

- Most entry-level jobs require a master's degree in urban or regional planning or urban design, landscape architecture, or the equivalent in work experience.

- Most new jobs will arise in more affluent, rapidly growing communities.

Nature of the Work
Urban and regional planners are often referred to as community, county, or city planners because the majority are employed by local governments. They develop long and short-term land use plans to provide for growth and revitalization of urban, suburban, and rural communities, while helping local officials make decisions concerning social, economic, and environmental problems.

Planners promote the best use of a community's land and resources for residential, commercial, and recreational purposes. Planners may be involved in various other activities, including decisions on alternative public transportation system plans, resource development, and protection of ecologically sensitive regions. They address issues such as traffic congestion, air pollution, and the effect of growth and change on a community. They may formulate master plans relating to the construction of new school buildings, public housing, or other infrastructure. Some planners are involved in environmental issues ranging from pollution control to wetland preservation, forest conservation, or the location of new landfills. Planners also may be involved with drafting legislation on environmental, social, and economic issues, such as sheltering the homeless, planning a new park, or meeting the demand for new correctional facilities.

Planners examine proposed community facilities such as schools to be sure these facilities will meet the demands placed upon them over time by population growth. They keep abreast of the economic and legal issues involved in zoning codes, building codes, and environmental regulations. They ensure that builders and developers follow these codes and regulations. Planners also deal with land use issues created by population movements. For example, as suburban growth and economic development create more new jobs outside cities, the need for public transportation that enables urban workers get to jobs in the suburbs increases. In response, planners develop transportation models for possible implementation and explain their details to planning boards and the general public.

Before preparing plans for community development, planners report on the current use of land for residential, business, and community purposes. These reports include information on the location and capacity of streets, highways, water and sewer lines, schools, libraries, and cultural and recreational sites, and provide data on the types of industries in the community, characteristics of the population, and employment and economic trends. With this information, along with input from citizens' advisory committees, planners design the layout of buildings and other facilities such as subway lines and stations, and prepare reports showing how their programs can be carried out and what they will cost.

Planners use computers to record and analyze information, and to prepare reports and recommendations for government executives and others. Computer databases, spreadsheets, and analytical techniques are widely used to project program costs and forecast future trends in employment, housing, transportation, or population. Computerized geographic information systems enable planners to map land areas and overlay maps with geographic variables, such as population density, as well as to combine and manipulate geographic information to produce alternative plans for land use or development.

Urban and regional planners often confer with land developers, civic leaders, and public officials. They may function as mediators in community disputes and present alternatives that are acceptable to opposing parties. Planners may prepare material for community relations programs, speak at civic meetings, and appear before legislative committees and elected officials to explain and defend their proposals.

In large organizations, planners usually specialize in a single area such as transportation, demography, housing, historic preservation, urban design, environmental and regulatory issues, or economic development. In small organizations, planners must be generalists, available to do various kinds of planning.

Working Conditions
Urban and regional planners periodically travel to and personally inspect the features of land under consideration for development or regulation, including its current use and the types of structures on it. Some local government planners involved in site development inspections spend most of their time in the field. Although most planners have a scheduled 40-hour workweek, they frequently attend evening or weekend meetings or public hearings with citizens' groups. Planners may experience the pressure of deadlines and tight

Specializations most commonly offered by planning schools are environmental planning, land use and comprehensive planning, economic development, and housing. Other popular offerings include community development, transportation, and urban design. Graduate students spend considerable time in studios, workshops, and laboratory courses learning to analyze and solve planning problems. They are often required to work in a planning office part time or during the summer. Local government planning offices frequently offer students internships, providing experience that proves invaluable in obtaining a full-time planning position after graduation.

The American Institute of Certified Planners (AICP), a professional institute within the American Planning Association (APA), grants certification to individuals who have the appropriate combination of education and professional experience and who pass an examination. Certification may be helpful for promotion.

Planners must be able to think in terms of spatial relationships and visualize the effects of their plans and designs. Planners should be flexible and able to reconcile different viewpoints and to make constructive policy recommendations. The ability to communicate effectively, both orally and in writing, is necessary for anyone interested in this field.

After a few years of experience, planners may advance to assignments requiring a high degree of independent judgment, such as designing the physical layout of a large development or recommending policy and budget options. Some public sector planners are promoted to community planning director and spend a great deal of time meeting with officials, speaking to civic groups, and supervising a staff. Further advancement occurs through a transfer to a larger jurisdiction with more complex problems and greater responsibilities, or into related occupations, such as director of community or economic development.

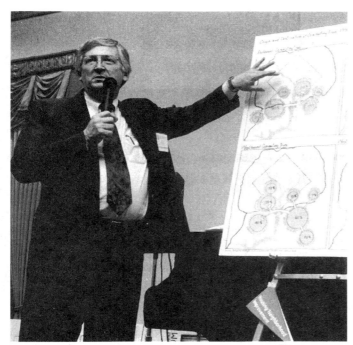

Most entry level jobs require a master's degree in urban or regional planning or urban design, or the equivalent in work experience.

work schedules, as well as political pressure generated by interest groups affected by their land use proposals.

Employment

Urban and regional planners held about 29,000 jobs in 1996, and about 2 out of 3 were employed by local governments. An increasing proportion of planners work in the private sector for companies involved with research and testing or management and public relations. Others are employed in State agencies dealing with housing, transportation, or environmental protection, and a small number work for the Federal Government.

Training, Other Qualifications, and Advancement

Employers prefer workers who have advanced training. Most entry-level jobs in Federal, State, and local government agencies require a master's degree in urban or regional planning or urban design, geography, or the equivalent in work experience. A bachelor's degree from an accredited planning program, coupled with a master's degree in architecture, landscape architecture, or civil engineering, is good preparation for entry-level planning jobs in areas such as urban design, traffic, or the environment. A master's degree from an accredited planning program provides the best training for a number of planning fields. Although graduates from one of the limited number of accredited bachelor's degree programs qualify for many beginning positions, their advancement opportunities are often limited unless they acquire an advanced degree. Courses in related disciplines such as architecture, law, earth sciences, demography, economics, finance, health administration, geographic information systems, and management are highly recommended. In addition, familiarity with computer models and statistical techniques is necessary.

In 1997, about 80 colleges and universities offered an accredited master's degree program, and about 10 offered an accredited bachelor's degree program in urban or regional planning. These programs are accredited by the Planning Accreditation Board, which consists of representatives of the American Institute of Certified Planners, the American Planning Association, and the Association of Collegiate Schools of Planning. Most graduate programs in planning require a minimum of 2 years.

Job Outlook

Employment of urban and regional planners is expected to grow more slowly than the average for all occupations through the year 2006. Factors contributing to the limited job growth expected in this sector include the need for governments to do more with less while still providing services such as regulation of commercial development, the environment, transportation, housing, and land use and development, and for the private sector to comply with such regulations. Non-governmental initiatives such as historic preservation and central city redevelopment will provide additional openings. Most job openings, however, are expected to arise from the need to replace experienced planners who transfer to other occupations, retire, or leave the labor force for other reasons.

Most planners work in local government, many of which have limited resources and many demands for services. When communities need to cut expenditures, planning services may be cut before more basic services such as police or education. The number of openings in private industry for consulting positions is expected to grow more rapidly than the number of openings in government.

Most new jobs for urban and regional planners will arise in more affluent, rapidly expanding communities. Local governments need planners to address an array of problems associated with population growth. For example, new housing developments require roads, sewer systems, fire stations, schools, libraries, and recreation facilities that must be planned while considering budgetary constraints. Small town chambers of commerce, economic development authorities and tourism bureaus may hire planners, preferring candidates with some background in marketing and public relations.

Earnings

Salaries of planners vary by educational attainment, type of employer, experience, size of community in which they work, and geographic location. According to a report by the American Planning Association (APA), in 1995, urban and regional planners with less than 5 years' experience earned median annual salaries of $30,000. Planners with between 5 and 10 years' experience earned median salaries of $39,900. Those with more than 10 years' experience earned median annual salaries of $55,000. The APA reports the median annual salary for all planners was $45,300. Salaries of community planners employed by the Federal Government in nonsupervisory, supervisory, and managerial positions averaged about $57,620 a year in early 1997.

Related Occupations

Urban and regional planners develop plans for the orderly growth of urban and rural communities. Others whose work is similar to the work of planners include architects, landscape architects, city managers, civil engineers, environmental engineers, directors of community or economic development, and geographers.

Sources of Additional Information

Information on careers, salaries, and certification in urban and regional planning is available from:
☛ American Planning Association, Education Division, 122 South Michigan Avenue, Suite 1600, Chicago, IL 60630-6107.

Social and Recreation Workers

Recreation Workers

(D.O.T. 153.137-010; 159.124-010; 187.167-238; 195.227-010, -014; 352.167-010)

Significant Points

- The recreation field has an unusually large number of part-time, seasonal, and volunteer jobs.

- Educational requirements range from a high school diploma, or sometimes less for many summer jobs, to a graduate degree in parks and recreation or leisure studies for some administrative positions.

- Competition will remain keen for full-time career positions; persons with experience gained in part-time or seasonal recreation jobs, together with formal recreation training, should have the best opportunities.

Nature of the Work

Many people spend much of their leisure time participating in a wide variety of organized recreation activities, such as aerobics, arts and crafts, water sports, tennis, camping and softball. Recreation programs, as diverse as the people they serve, are offered at local playgrounds and recreation areas, parks, community centers, health clubs, religious organizations, camps, theme parks, and most tourist attractions. Recreation workers plan, organize, and direct these activities.

Recreation workers organize and lead programs and watch over recreational facilities and equipment. They help people pursue their interest in crafts, art, or sports by leading activities. These activities enable people to share common interests in physical and mental activities for entertainment, physical fitness, and self-improvement. Recreation workers organize teams and leagues, and also teach the correct use of equipment and facilities.

In the workplace, recreation workers organize and direct leisure activities and athletic programs for all ages, such as bowling and softball leagues, social functions, travel programs, discount services, and, to an increasing extent, exercise and fitness programs. These activities are generally for adults.

Recreation workers hold a variety of positions at many different levels of responsibility. *Recreation leaders* are responsible for a recreation program's daily operation, and organize and direct participants. They may lead and give instruction in dance, drama, crafts, games, and sports; schedule use of facilities and keep records of equipment use; and ensure recreation facilities and equipment are used properly. Workers who provide instruction in specialties such as art, music, drama, swimming, or tennis may be called *activity specialists*. They conduct classes and coach teams in the activity in which they specialize.

Recreation supervisors plan, organize, and manage recreation activities to meet the needs of the population they serve, and supervise recreation leaders. A recreation supervisor serves as a liaison between the director of the park or recreation center and the recreation leaders. A recreation supervisor who has more specialized responsibilities may also direct special activities or events, and oversee a major activity, such as aquatics, gymnastics, or performing arts.

Directors of recreation and parks develop and manage comprehensive recreation programs in parks, playgrounds, and other settings. Directors usually serve as a technical advisor to State and local recreation and park commissions, and may be responsible for recreation and park budgets.

Camp counselors lead and instruct children and teenagers in outdoor-oriented forms of recreation, such as swimming, hiking, horseback riding, and camping. Activities are often intended to enhance campers' appreciation of nature and responsible use of the environment. In addition, counselors provide campers with specialized instruction in activities such as archery, boating, music, drama, gymnastics, tennis, and computers. In resident camps, counselors also provide guidance and supervise daily living and general socialization.

In a related occupation, *recreational therapists* help individuals recover or adjust to illness, disability, or specific social problems; this occupation is described elsewhere in the *Handbook*.

Recreation workers interact with young people.

Working Conditions

Recreation workers must work while others engage in leisure time activities. While most recreation workers put in about 40 hours a week, people entering this field, especially camp counselors, should expect some night and weekend work and irregular hours. About 3 out of 10 work part time, and many jobs are seasonal. The work setting for recreation workers may be anywhere from a cruise ship, to a woodland recreational park, to a playground in the center of a large urban community. Recreation workers often spend much of their time outdoors and may work under a variety of weather conditions. Recreation directors and supervisors may spend most of their time in an office planning programs and special events. Because full-time recreation workers spend more time acting as managers than hands-on activities leaders, they engage in less physical activity. However, as is the case for anyone engaged in physical activity, recreation workers risk suffering an injury, and the work can be physically challenging.

Employment

Recreation workers held about 233,000 jobs in 1996, and many additional workers held summer jobs in this occupation. Of those who held year-round jobs as recreation workers, about half worked in park and recreation departments of municipal and county governments. Nearly 2 out of 10 worked in membership organizations with a civic, social, fraternal, or religious orientation—the Boy Scouts, the YWCA, and Red Cross, for example. About 1 out of 10 were in programs run by social service organizations—senior centers and adult daycare programs, or residential care facilities such as halfway houses, group homes, and institutions for delinquent youth. Another 1 out 10 worked for nursing and other personal care facilities.

Other employers included commercial recreation stablishments, amusement parks, sports and entertainment centers, wilderness and survival enterprises, tourist attractions, vacation excursion companies, hotels and resorts, summer camps, health and athletic clubs, and apartment complexes.

The recreation field has an unusually large number of part-time, seasonal, and volunteer jobs. These jobs include summer camp counselors, lifeguards, craft specialists, and after-school and weekend recreation program leaders. Teachers and college students take many jobs as recreation workers when school is not in session.

Many unpaid volunteers assist paid recreation workers. The vast majority of volunteers serve as activity leaders at local day-camp programs, or in youth organizations, camps, nursing homes, hospitals, senior centers, YMCA's, and other settings. Some volunteers serve on local park and recreation boards and commissions. Volunteer experience, part-time work during school, or a summer job can lead to a full-time career as a recreation worker.

Training, Other Qualifications, and Advancement

Education needed for recreation worker jobs ranges from a high school diploma, or sometimes less for many summer jobs, to graduate education for some administrative positions in large public recreation systems. Full-time career professional positions usually require a college degree with a major in parks and recreation or leisure studies, but a bachelor's degree in any liberal arts field may be sufficient for some jobs in the private sector. In industrial recreation, or "employee services" as it is more commonly called, companies prefer to hire those with a bachelor's degree in recreation or leisure studies and a background in business administration.

Specialized training or experience in a particular field, such as art, music, drama, or athletics, is an asset for many jobs. Some jobs also require a certification. For example, when teaching or coaching water-related activities, a lifesaving certificate is a prerequisite. Graduates of associate degree programs in parks and recreation, social work, and other human services disciplines also enter some career recreation positions. Occasionally high school graduates are able to enter career positions, but this is not common. Some college students work part time as recreation workers while earning degrees.

A bachelor's degree and experience are preferred for most recreation supervisor jobs and required for most higher-level administrator jobs. However, increasing numbers of recreation workers who aspire to administrator positions are obtaining master's degrees in parks and recreation or related disciplines Also, many persons in other disciplines, including social work, forestry, and resource management, pursue graduate degrees in recreation.

Programs leading to an associate or bachelor's degree in parks and recreation, leisure studies, or related fields are offered at several hundred colleges and universities. Many also offer master's or doctoral degrees in this field.

In 1997, 93 bachelor's degree programs in parks and recreation were accredited by the National Recreation and Park Association (NRPA). Accredited programs provide broad exposure to the history, theory, and philosophy of park and recreation management. Courses offered include community organization, supervision and administration, recreational needs of special populations, such as older adults or the disabled, and supervised fieldwork. Students may specialize in areas such as therapeutic recreation, park management, outdoor recreation, industrial or commercial recreation, and camp management.

The American Camping Association offers workshops and courses for experienced camp directors at different times and locations throughout the year. Some national youth associations offer training courses for camp directors at the local and regional levels.

Persons planning recreation careers should be outgoing, good at motivating people, and sensitive to the needs of others. Good health and physical fitness are required. Activity planning calls for creativity and resourcefulness. Willingness to accept responsibility and the ability to exercise good judgment are important qualities since recreation personnel often work without close supervision. Part-time or summer recreation work experience while in high school or college may help students decide whether their interests really point to a human services career. Such experience also may increase their leadership skills and understanding of people.

Individuals contemplating careers in recreation at the supervisory or administrative level should develop managerial skills. College courses in management, business administration, accounting, and personnel management are likely to be useful.

Certification for this field is offered by the NRPA National Certification Board. The National Recreation and Parks Association, along with its State chapters, offers certification as a Certified Leisure Professional (CLP) for those with a college degree in recreation, and as a Certified Leisure Technician (CLT) for those with less than 4 years of college. Other NRPA certifications include Certified Leisure Provisional Professional (CLPP), Certified Playground Inspector (CPI), and Aquatic Facility Operations (AFO) Certification. Continuing education is necessary to remain certified.

Certification is not usually required for employment or advancement in this field, but it is an asset. Employers choosing among qualified job applicants may opt to hire the person with a demonstrated record of professional achievement represented by certification.

Job Outlook

Competition will remain keen for full-time career positions in recreation. All college graduates are eligible for recreation jobs, regardless of major. Also, many high school and junior college graduates are eligible, so the number of full-time career jobseekers often greatly exceed the number of job openings. Opportunities for staff positions should be best for persons with experience gained in part-time or seasonal recreation jobs, together with formal recreation training. Those with graduate degrees should have the best opportunities for supervisory or administrative positions.

Prospects are better for the large number of temporary seasonal jobs. These positions, typically filled by high school or college students, do not generally have formal education requirements and are open to anyone with the desired personal qualities. Employers compete for a share of the vacationing student labor force, and, while salaries in recreation are often lower than those in other fields, the nature of the work and the opportunity to work outdoors is attractive to many. Seasonal employment prospects should be good for applicants with specialized training and certification in an activity like swimming. These workers may obtain jobs as program directors.

Employment of recreation workers is expected to grow faster than the average for all occupations through the year 2006 as growing numbers of people possess both the time and the money to enjoy leisure services. Growth in these jobs will also stem from increased interest in fitness and health and the rising demand for recreational opportunities for older adults in senior centers and retirement communities. However, overall employment in local government—where half of all recreation workers are employed—is expected to grow more slowly than in other industries due to budget constraints, and some local park and recreation departments are expected to do less hiring for permanent, full-time positions than in the past. As a result, this sector's share of recreation worker employment will vary widely by region, since resources as well as priorities for public services differ from one community to another. Thus, hiring prospects for recreation workers will be much better in some park and recreation departments, but worse in others.

Recreation worker jobs should also increase in social services—more recreation workers will be needed to develop and lead activity programs in senior centers, halfway houses, children's homes, and daycare programs for the mentally retarded or developmentally disabled. Similarly, the increasing elderly population will spur job growth in nursing homes and other personal care facilities where recreation activities are becoming more important.

Recreation worker jobs in employee services and recreation will continue to increase as more businesses recognize the benefits to their employees of recreation programs and other services such as wellness programs and elder care. Job growth will also occur in the commercial recreation industry, composed of amusement parks, athletic clubs, camps, sports clinics, and swimming pools, for example.

Earnings

Median annual earnings of recreation workers who worked full time in 1996 were about $18,700, significantly lower than the median of $25,600 for workers in all occupations. The middle 50 percent earned between about $12,900 and $28,900, while the top 10 percent earned $37,500 or more. However, earnings of recreation directors and others in supervisory or managerial positions can be substantially higher.

Most public and private recreation agencies provide full-time recreation workers with typical benefits; part-time workers receive few, if any, benefits.

Related Occupations

Recreation workers must exhibit leadership and sensitivity in dealing with people. Other occupations that require similar personal qualities include recreational therapists, social workers, parole officers, human relations counselors, school counselors, clinical and counseling psychologists, and teachers.

Sources of Additional Information

For information on jobs in recreation, contact employers such as local government departments of parks and recreation, nursing and personal care facilities, and YMCA's.

Ordering information for materials describing careers and academic programs in recreation is available from:
☛ National Recreation and Park Association, Division of Professional Services, 2775 South Quincy St., Suite 300, Arlington, VA 22206. Homepage: http://www.nrpa.org

For information on careers in employee services and corporate recreation, contact:
☛ National Employee Services and Recreation Association, 2211 York Rd., Suite 207, Oakbrook, IL 60521.

For information on careers in camping and summer counselor opportunities, contact:
☛ American Camping Association, 5000 State Rd. 67 North, Martinsville, IN 46151.

Social and Human Service Assistants

(D.O.T. 195.367 except -026 and -030)

Significant Points

- Social and human service assistants ranks among the top 10 fastest growing occupations.

- Job opportunities should be excellent, particularly for applicants with appropriate postsecondary education, but pay is low.

Nature of the Work

Social and human service assistants is a generic term for people with various job titles, including social service assistant, case management aide, social work assistant, residential counselor, community support worker, alcohol or drug abuse counselor, mental health technician, child-care worker, community outreach worker, life skill counselor, and gerontology aide. They generally work under the direction of professionals from a wide variety of fields, such as nursing, psychiatry, psychology, rehabilitation, or social work. The amount of responsibility and supervision they are given varies a great deal. Some are on their own most of the time and have little direct supervision; others work under close direction.

Social and human service assistants provide direct and indirect client services. They assess clients' needs, establish their eligibility for benefits and services, and help clients obtain them. They examine financial documents such as rent receipts and tax returns to determine whether the client is eligible for food stamps, Medicaid, welfare, and other human service programs. They also arrange for transportation and escorts, if necessary, and provide emotional support. Social and human service assistants monitor and keep case records on clients and report progress to supervisors. Social and human service assistants also may transport or accompany clients to group meal sites, adult daycare programs, or doctors' offices; telephone or visit clients' homes to make sure services are being received; or help resolve disagreements, such as those between tenants and landlords. They may also help clients complete applications for financial assistance or assist with daily living needs.

Social and human service assistants play a variety of roles in community settings. They may organize and lead group activities, assist clients in need of counseling or crisis intervention, or administer a food bank or emergency fuel program. In halfway houses, group homes, and government-supported housing programs, they assist adult residents who need supervision in personal hygiene and daily living skills. They review clients' records, ensure they take correct doses of medication, talk with their families, and confer with medical personnel to gain better insight into clients' backgrounds and needs. They also provide emotional support and help clients become involved in community recreation programs and other activities.

In psychiatric hospitals, rehabilitation programs, and outpatient clinics, they may help clients master everyday living skills and teach them how to communicate more effectively and get along better with others. They support the client's participation in the treatment plan, such as individual or group counseling and occupational therapy.

Working Conditions

Working conditions of social and human service assistants vary. They work in offices, group homes, shelters, day programs, sheltered workshops, hospitals, clinics, and in the field visiting clients. Most work a regular 40-hour week, although some work may be in the evening and on weekends. Social and human service assistants in residential settings generally work in shifts because residents need supervision around the clock.

The work, while satisfying, can be emotionally draining. Understaffing and relatively low pay may add to the pressure. Turnover is

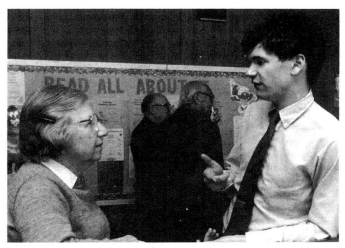

Human service assistants help the elderly.

reported to be high, especially among workers without academic preparation for this field.

Employment

Social and human service assistants held about 178,000 jobs in 1996. About 1 in 3 were employed by State and local governments, primarily in public welfare agencies and facilities for mentally disabled and developmentally delayed individuals. Another third worked in private social or human services agencies, offering a variety of services, including adult daycare, group meals, crisis intervention, counseling, and job training. Many social and human service assistants supervised residents of group homes and halfway houses. Social and human service assistants also held jobs in clinics, detoxification units, community mental health centers, psychiatric hospitals, day treatment programs, and sheltered workshops.

Training, Other Qualifications, and Advancement

While some employers hire high school graduates, most prefer applicants with some college preparation in human services, social work, or one of the social or behavioral sciences. Some prefer to hire persons with a 4-year college degree. The educational attainment of social and human service assistants often influences the kind of work they are assigned and the amount of responsibility entrusted to them. Workers with no more than a high school education are likely to receive on-the-job training to work in direct care services, while those with a college degree might be assigned to do supportive counseling, coordinate program activities, or manage a group home. Employers may also look for experience in other occupations, leadership experience in an organization, or human service volunteer exposure. Some enter the field on the basis of courses in human services, psychology, rehabilitation, social work, sociology, or special education. Most employers provide in-service training such as seminars and workshops.

Because so many human services jobs involve direct contact with people who are vulnerable to exploitation or mistreatment, employers try to select applicants with appropriate personal qualifications. Relevant academic preparation is generally required, and volunteer or work experience is preferred. A strong desire to help others, patience, and understanding are highly valued characteristics. Other important personal traits include communication skills, a strong sense of responsibility, and the ability to manage time effectively. Hiring requirements in group homes tend to be more stringent than in other settings. In some settings, applicants may need a valid driver's license and must meet the Criminal Offense Record Investigation (CORI) requirement. Special licensure or State certifications may also apply.

In 1996, about 380 certificate and associate degree programs in human services or mental health were offered at community and junior colleges, vocational-technical institutes, and other postsecondary institutions. In addition, approximately 400 programs offered a bachelor's degree in human services. Master's degree programs in human services administration are offered as well.

Generally, academic programs in this field educate students for specialized roles. Human services programs have a core curriculum that trains students in observation and recording, interviewing, communication techniques, behavior management, group dynamics, counseling, crisis intervention, case management, and referral. General education courses in liberal arts, sciences, and the humanities are also part of the curriculum. Many degree programs require completion of an internship.

Formal education is almost always necessary for advancement. In general, advancement requires a bachelor's or master's degree in counseling, rehabilitation, social work, or a related field.

Job Outlook

Opportunities for social and human service assistants are expected to be excellent, particularly for applicants with appropriate postsecondary education. The number of social and human service assistants is projected to grow much faster than the average for all occupations between 1996 and the year 2006—ranking among the most rapidly growing occupations. The need to replace workers who retire or stop working for other reasons will create additional job opportunities. These jobs are not attractive to everyone due to the emotionally draining work and relatively low pay, so qualified applicants should have little difficulty finding employment.

Opportunities are expected to be best in job training programs, residential settings, and private social service agencies, which include such services as adult daycare and meal delivery programs. Demand for these services will expand with the growing number of older people, who are more likely to need services. In addition, social and human service assistants will continue to be needed to provide services to the mentally disabled and developmentally delayed, those with substance-abuse problems, the homeless, and pregnant teenagers. Faced with rapid growth in the demand for services, but slower growth in resources to provide the services, employers are expected to rely increasingly on social and human service assistants rather than more highly trained workers, such as social workers, who command higher pay.

Job training programs are expected to require additional social and human service assistants as the economy grows and businesses change their mode of production, requiring workers to be retrained. Social and human service assistants help determine workers' eligibility for public assistance programs and help them obtain services while unemployed.

Residential settings should expand also as pressures to respond to the needs of the chronically mentally ill persist. For many years, chronic mental patients have been deinstitutionalized and left to their own devices. Now, more community-based programs, supported independent living sites, and group residences are expected to be established to house and assist the homeless and chronically mentally ill, and demand for social and human service assistants will increase accordingly.

The number of jobs for social and human service assistants will grow more rapidly than overall employment in State and local governments. State and local governments employ most of their social and human service assistants in corrections and public assistance departments. Corrections departments are growing faster than other areas of government, so social and human service assistants should find that their job opportunities increase along with other corrections jobs. Public assistance programs have been employing more social and human service assistants in an attempt to employ fewer social workers, who are more educated and higher paid.

Earnings

Based on limited information, starting salaries for social and human service assistants ranged from about $15,000 to $24,000 a year in 1997.

Experienced workers generally earned between $20,000 and $30,000 annually, depending on their education, experience, and employer.

Related Occupations

Workers in other occupations that require skills similar to those of social and human service assistants include social workers, religious workers, occupational therapy assistants, physical therapy assistants, psychiatric aides, and activity leaders.

Sources of Additional Information

Information on academic programs in human services may be found in most directories of 2- and 4-year colleges, available at libraries or career counseling centers.

For information on programs and careers in human services, contact:
- ☛ National Organization for Human Service Education, Brookdale Community College, Lyncroft, NJ 07738.
- ☛ Council for Standards in Human Service Education, Northern Essex Community College, Haverhill, MA 01830.

Information on job openings may be available from State employment service offices or directly from city, county, or State departments of health, mental health and mental retardation, and human resources.

Social Workers

(D.O.T. 189.267-010; 195.107, .137, .164, .167-010, -014, .267-018, -022, and .367-026)

Significant Points

- A bachelor's degree is the minimum requirement for many entry-level jobs; however, a master's degree in social work (MSW) is generally required for advancement.

- Employment is projected to grow faster than average.

- Competition for jobs is stronger in cities where training programs for social workers are prevalent; rural areas often find it difficult to attract and retain qualified staff.

Nature of the Work

Social work is a profession for those with a strong desire to help people. Social workers help people deal with their relationships with others; solve their personal, family, and community problems; and grow and develop as they learn to cope with or shape the social and environmental forces affecting daily life. Social workers often encounter clients facing a life-threatening disease or a social problem requiring a quick solution. These situations may include inadequate housing, unemployment, lack of job skills, financial distress, serious illness or disability, substance abuse, unwanted pregnancy, or antisocial behavior. They also assist families that have serious conflicts, including those involving child or spousal abuse.

Social workers practice in a variety of settings, including hospitals, from the obstetrics unit to the intensive care unit; in schools, helping children, teachers, and parents cope with problems; in mental health clinics and psychiatric hospitals; and in public agencies, from the employment office to the public welfare department. Through direct counseling, social workers help clients identify their concerns, consider solutions, and find resources. Often, they refer clients to specialists in various areas, including debt counseling, child care or elder care, public assistance or other benefits, or alcohol or drug rehabilitation programs. Social workers typically arrange for services in consultation with clients, following through to assure the services are helpful. They may review eligibility requirements, fill out forms and applications, arrange for services, visit clients on a regular basis, and provide support during crises.

Most social workers specialize—for example, in child welfare and family services, mental health, or school social work. Clinical social workers offer psychotherapy or counseling and a range of services in public agencies and clinics, and in private practice. Other social workers are employed in community organization, administration, or research.

Those specializing in child welfare or family services may counsel children and youths who have difficulty adjusting socially, advise parents on how to care for disabled children, or arrange for homemaker services during a parent's illness. If children have serious problems in school, child welfare workers may consult with parents, teachers, and counselors to identify underlying causes and develop plans for treatment. Some social workers assist single parents, arrange adoptions, and help find foster homes for neglected, abandoned, or abused children. Child welfare workers also work in residential institutions for children and adolescents.

Social workers in child or adult protective services investigate reports of abuse and neglect and intervene if necessary. They may institute legal action to remove children from homes and place them temporarily in an emergency shelter or with a foster family.

Mental health social workers provide services for persons with mental or emotional problems, such as individual and group therapy, outreach, crisis intervention, social rehabilitation, and training in skills of everyday living. They may also help plan for supportive services to ease patients' return to the community. (Counselors and psychologists, who may provide similar services, are discussed elsewhere in the *Handbook.*)

Health care social workers help patients and their families cope with chronic, acute, or terminal illnesses and handle problems that may stand in the way of recovery or rehabilitation. They may organize support groups for families of patients suffering from cancer, AIDS, Alzheimer's disease, or other illnesses. They also advise family caregivers, counsel patients, and help plan for their needs after discharge by arranging for at-home services—from meals-on-wheels to oxygen equipment. Some work on interdisciplinary teams that evaluate certain kinds of patients—geriatric or organ transplant patients, for example.

School social workers diagnose students' problems and arrange needed services, counsel children in trouble, and help integrate disabled students into the general school population. School social workers deal with problems such as student pregnancy, misbehavior in class, and excessive absences. They also advise teachers on how to deal with problem students.

Criminal justice social workers make recommendations to courts, prepare pre-sentencing assessments, and provide services for prison

Social workers often specialize in fields such as family services, mental health, or school social work.

inmates and their families. Probation and parole officers provide similar services to individuals sentenced by a court to parole or probation.

Occupational social workers generally work in a corporation's personnel department or health unit. Through employee assistance programs, they help workers cope with job-related pressures or personal problems that affect the quality of their work. They often offer direct counseling to employees whose performance is hindered by emotional or family problems or substance abuse. They also develop education programs and refer workers to specialized community programs.

Some social workers specialize in gerontological services. They run support groups for family caregivers or for the adult children of aging parents; advise elderly people or family members about the choices in such areas as housing, transportation, and long-term care; and coordinate and monitor services.

Social workers also focus on policy and planning. They help develop programs to address such issues as child abuse, homelessness, substance abuse, poverty, and violence. These workers research and analyze policies, programs, and regulations. They identify social problems and suggest legislative and other solutions. They may help raise funds or write grants to support these programs.

Working Conditions

Although some social workers work a standard 40-hour week, many work some evenings and weekends to meet with clients, attend community meetings, and handle emergencies. Some, particularly in voluntary nonprofit agencies, work part time. They may spend most of their time in an office or residential facility, but may also travel locally to visit clients or meet with service providers. Some have several offices within a local area.

The work, while satisfying, can be emotionally draining. Understaffing and large caseloads add to the pressure in some agencies.

Employment

Social workers held about 585,000 jobs in 1996. About 4 out of 10 jobs were in State, county, or municipal government agencies, primarily in departments of health and human resources, mental health, social services, child welfare, housing, education, and corrections. As government increasingly contracts out social services, many jobs are likely to shift from government to private organizations in the future. Most jobs in the private sector were in social service agencies, community and religious organizations, hospitals, nursing homes, or home health agencies.

Although most social workers are employed in cities or suburbs, some work in rural areas.

Training, Other Qualifications, and Advancement

A bachelor's degree is the minimum requirement for many entry-level jobs. Besides the bachelor's in social work (BSW), undergraduate majors in psychology, sociology, and related fields satisfy hiring requirements in some agencies, especially small community agencies. A master's degree in social work (MSW) is generally necessary for positions in health and mental health settings. Jobs in public agencies may also require an MSW. Supervisory, administrative, and staff training positions usually require at least an MSW. College and university teaching positions and most research appointments normally require a doctorate in social work.

In 1996, the Council on Social Work Education accredited over 430 BSW programs and over 130 MSW programs. There were 55 doctoral programs for Ph.D.'s in social work and DSW's (Doctor of Social Work). BSW programs prepare graduates for direct service positions such as case worker or group worker. They include courses in social work practice, social welfare policies, human behavior and the social environment, and social research methods. Accredited BSW programs require at least 400 hours of supervised field experience.

An MSW degree prepares graduates to perform assessments, manage cases, and supervise other workers. Master's programs usually last 2 years and include 900 hours of supervised field instruction, or internship. Entry into an MSW program does not require a bachelor's in social work, but courses in psychology, biology, sociology, economics, political science, history, social anthropology, urban studies, and social work are recommended. In addition, a second language can be very helpful. Some schools offer an accelerated MSW program for those with a BSW.

Since 1993, all States and the District of Columbia have had licensing, certification, or registration laws regarding social work practice and the use of professional titles. Standards for licensing vary by State. In addition, voluntary certification is offered by the National Association of Social Workers (NASW), which grants the title ACSW (Academy of Certified Social Worker) or ACBSW (Academy of Certified Baccalaureate Social Worker) to those who qualify. For clinical social workers, who are granted the title QCSW (Qualified Clinical Social Worker), professional credentials include listing in the *NASW Register of Clinical Social Workers*. Advanced credentials include the NASW Diplomate in Clinical Social Work, and School Social Work Specialist. An advanced credential is also offered by the *Directory of American Board of Examiners in Clinical Social Work*. Credentials are particularly important for those in private practice; some health insurance providers require them for reimbursement.

Social workers should be emotionally mature, objective, and sensitive to people and their problems. They must be able to handle responsibility, work independently, and maintain good working relationships with clients and coworkers. Volunteer or paid jobs as a social work aide offer ways of testing one's interest in this field.

Advancement to supervisor, program manager, assistant director, or executive director of a social service agency or department is possible but generally requires an MSW degree and related work experience. Although some social workers with a BSW may be promoted to these positions after gaining experience, some employers choose to hire managers directly from MSW programs that focus specifically on management. These graduates often have little work experience but have an understanding of management through their education and training. Other career options for social workers include teaching, research, and consulting. Some help formulate government policies by analyzing and advocating policy positions in government agencies, in research institutions, and on legislators' staffs.

Some social workers go into private practice. Most private practitioners are clinical social workers who provide psychotherapy, usually paid through health insurance. Private practitioners must have an MSW and a period of supervised work experience. A network of contacts for referrals is also essential.

Job Outlook

Employment of social workers is expected to increase faster than the average for all occupations through the year 2006. The number of older people, who are more likely to need social services, is increasing rapidly. In addition, growing concern about crime, juvenile delinquency, and services for the mentally ill, the mentally retarded, AIDS patients, and individuals and families in crisis will spur demand for social workers. Many job openings will also stem from the need to replace social workers who leave the occupation.

As hospitals increasingly emphasize early discharge of patients in an effort to control costs, more social workers will be needed to ensure that the necessary medical and social services are in place when individuals leave the hospital. Social worker employment in home health care services is growing, not only because hospitals are releasing patients earlier, but because a large and growing number of people have impairments or disabilities that make it difficult to live at home without some form of assistance.

Employment of social workers in private social service agencies will grow, but not as rapidly as demand for their services. Agencies will increasingly restructure services and hire more lower-paid human services workers instead of social workers. Employment in government may grow in response to increasing needs for public welfare and family services; however, many of these jobs will be contracted out to private agencies. Additionally, employment levels will depend on government funding for various social service programs.

Employment of school social workers is expected to grow, due to expanded efforts to respond to rising rates of teen pregnancy and to the adjustment problems of immigrants and children from single-parent families. Moreover, continued emphasis on integrating disabled children into the general school population will lead to more jobs. Availability of State and local funding will dictate the actual job growth in schools, however.

Opportunities for social workers in private practice will expand because of the anticipated availability of funding from health insurance and public-sector contracts. Also, with increasing affluence, people will be better able to pay for professional help to deal with personal problems. The growing popularity of employee assistance programs is also expected to spur demand for private practitioners, some of whom provide social work services to corporations on a contractual basis.

Competition for social worker jobs is stronger in cities where training programs for social workers are prevalent; rural areas often find it difficult to attract and retain qualified staff.

Earnings

Based on limited information, social workers with an MSW had median earnings of about $35,000 in 1997, while social workers with a BSW earned about $25,000.

According to a Hay Group survey of acute care hospitals, the median annual salary of full-time social workers with a master's degree was $35,000 in 1997. The middle 50 percent earned between $32,300 and $38,700.

The average annual salary for all social workers in the Federal Government in nonsupervisory, supervisory, and managerial positions was about $46,900 in 1997.

Related Occupations

Through direct counseling or referral to other services, social workers help people solve a range of personal problems. Workers in occupations with similar duties include the clergy, mental health counselors, counseling psychologists, and human services workers.

Sources of Additional Information

For information about career opportunities in social work, contact:

☛ National Association of Social Workers, Career Information, 750 First St. NE., Suite 700, Washington, DC 20002-4241.

☛ National Network For Social Work Managers, Inc., 1316 New Hampshire Ave. NW., Suite 602, Washington, DC 20036.

An annual *Directory of Accredited BSW and MSW Programs* is available for a nominal charge from:

☛ Council on Social Work Education, 1600 Duke St., Alexandria, VA 22314-3421.

Clergy

(D.O.T. 120.107-010)

Nature of the Work

Religious beliefs—be they Buddhist, Christian, Jewish, Moslem, or based on some other religion—are significant influences in the lives of millions of Americans, and prompt many believers to participate in organizations that reinforce their faith. Even within a single religion many sects may exist, with each group having unique traditions and responsibilities for its clergy. For example, Christianity has over 70 denominations, while Judaism has 4 major branches, as well as groups within each branch, with diverse customs.

Clergy are religious and spiritual leaders, and teachers and interpreters of their traditions and faith. They organize and lead regular religious services and officiate at special ceremonies, including confirmations, weddings, and funerals. They may lead worshipers in prayer, administer sacraments, deliver sermons, and read from sacred texts such as the Bible, Talmud, or Koran. When not conducting worship services, clergy organize, supervise, and lead religious education programs for their congregations. Clergy often visit the sick or bereaved to provide comfort, and counsel persons who are seeking religious or moral guidance, or who are troubled by family or personal problems. They also may work to expand the membership of their congregations and solicit donations to support its activities and facilities.

Clergy serving large congregations often share their duties with associates or have more junior members of the clergy to assist them. They often spend considerable time on administrative duties. They oversee the management of buildings, order supplies, contract for services and repairs when necessary, and supervise the work of paid staff and volunteers. Clergy also work with committees and officials, elected by the congregation, who guide the management of the congregation's finances and real estate.

Working Conditions

Members of the clergy typically work long and irregular hours. In 1996, about 1 in 4 full-time clergy worked 60 or more hours a week, compared to only 1 in 14 workers in all professional specialty occupations. Although many of their activities are sedentary and

intellectual in nature, they are frequently called upon at short notice to visit the sick, comfort the dying and their families, and provide counseling to those in need. Involvement in community, administrative, and educational activities may require clergy to work evenings, early mornings, holidays, and weekends.

Training and Other Qualifications

Educational requirements for entry into the clergy vary greatly. Similar to other professional occupations, about 3 out of 4 members of the clergy have completed at least a bachelor's degree. Many denominations require that clergy complete a bachelor's degree and a program of theological study; others will admit anyone who has been "called" to the vocation. Some sects do not allow women to become clergy. Those considering careers in the clergy should consult their religious leaders to verify specific entrance requirements.

Individuals considering a career in the clergy should realize they are choosing not only a career, but a way of life. In fact, a number of clergy remain in their chosen vocation throughout their lives; in 1996, 13 percent of clergy were 65 or older, compared to only 3 percent of workers in all professional specialty occupations. Religious leaders must exude confidence and motivation, while remaining tolerant and able to listen to the needs of others. They should be capable of making difficult decisions, working under pressure, and living up to the moral standards set by their faith and community.

The following statements provide more detailed information on Protestant ministers, Rabbis, and Roman Catholic priests.

Protestant Ministers

(D.O.T. 120.107-010)

Significant Points

- Entry requirements vary greatly; many denominations require a bachelor's degree followed by study at a theological school, while other denominations have no formal educational requirements.

- Competition for positions is expected because of the large number of qualified candidates; the degree of competition will vary among denominations and geographic regions.

Nature of the Work

Protestant ministers lead their congregations in worship services and administer the various rites of the church, such as baptism, confirmation, and Holy Communion. The services ministers conduct differ among the numerous Protestant denominations, and even among congregations within a denomination. In many denominations, ministers follow a traditional order of worship; in others, they adapt the services to the needs of youth and other groups within the congregation. Most services include Bible reading, hymn singing, prayers, and a sermon. In some denominations, Bible reading by a member of the congregation and individual testimonials may constitute a large part of the service. In addition to these duties, ministers officiate at weddings, funerals, and other occasions.

Each Protestant denomination has its own hierarchical structure. Some ministers are responsible only to the congregation they serve, while others are assigned duties by elder ministers, or by the bishops of the diocese they serve. In some denominations, ministers are reassigned to a new pastorate by a central governing body or diocese every few years.

Ministers serving small congregations generally work personally with parishioners. Those serving large congregations may share specific aspects of the ministry with one or more associates or assistants, such as a minister of education who assists in educational programs for different age groups, or a minister of music.

Protestant ministers lead their congregations in prayer and song.

Employment

According to the National Council of Churches, there were over 300,000 Protestant ministers in 1996, including those who served without a regular congregation or worked in closely related fields, such as chaplains in hospitals, the Armed Forces, universities, and correctional institutions. While there are many denominations, most ministers are employed by the five largest Protestant bodies—Baptist, Episcopalian, Lutheran, Methodist, and Presbyterian.

Although most ministers are located in urban areas, many serve two or more small congregations in less densely populated areas. Some small churches increasingly are employing part-time ministers who may be seminary students, retired ministers, or holders of secular jobs. Unpaid pastors serve other churches with meager funds. Some churches employ specially trained members of the laity to conduct nonliturgical functions.

Training and Other Qualifications

Educational requirements for entry into the Protestant ministry vary greatly. Many denominations require, or at least strongly prefer, a bachelor's degree followed by study at a theological school. However, some denominations have no formal educational requirements, and others ordain persons having various types of training in Bible colleges or institutes, or liberal arts colleges. Many denominations now allow women to be ordained, but others do not. Persons considering a career in the ministry should first verify the entrance requirements with their particular denomination.

In general, each large denomination has its own schools of theology that reflect its particular doctrine, interests, and needs. However, many of these schools are open to students from other denominations. Several interdenominational schools associated with universities give both undergraduate and graduate training covering a wide range of theological points of view.

In 1996, about 150 American Protestant theological schools were accredited by the Association of Theological Schools in the United States and Canada. These only admit students who have received a bachelor's degree or its equivalent in liberal arts from an accredited college. After college graduation, many denominations require a 3-year course of professional study in one of these accredited schools, or seminaries for the degree of Master of Divinity.

The standard curriculum for accredited theological schools consists of four major categories: Biblical, historical, theological, and practical. Courses of a practical nature include pastoral care, preaching, religious education, and administration. Many accredited schools require that students work under the supervision of a faculty member or experienced minister. Some institutions offer Doctor of Ministry degrees to students who have completed additional study, usually 2 or more years, and served at least 2 years as a minister. Scholarships and loans are often available for students of theological institutions.

Persons who have denominational qualifications for the ministry usually are ordained after graduation from a seminary or after serving a probationary pastoral period. Denominations that do not require seminary training ordain clergy at various appointed times. Some evangelical churches may ordain ministers with only a high school education.

Men and women entering the clergy often begin their careers as pastors of small congregations or as assistant pastors in large churches. Pastor positions in large metropolitan areas or in large congregations often require many years of experience.

Job Outlook

Competition is expected to continue for paid Protestant ministers through the year 2006, reflecting slow growth of church membership and the large number of qualified candidates. Graduates of theological schools should have the best prospects. The degree of competition for paid positions will vary among denominations and geographic regions. For example, relatively favorable prospects are expected for ministers in evangelical churches. Competition will still be keen for more responsible positions serving large, urban congregations. Ministers willing to work part time or for smaller, rural congregations should have better opportunities. Most job openings will stem from the need to replace ministers who retire, die, or leave the ministry.

Employment alternatives for newly ordained Protestant ministers who are unable to find positions in parishes include working in youth counseling, family relations, and welfare organizations; teaching in religious educational institutions; and serving as chaplains in the Armed Forces, hospitals, universities, and correctional institutions.

Earnings

Salaries of Protestant clergy vary substantially, depending on experience, denomination, size and wealth of congregation, and geographic location. Based on limited information, the estimated average annual income of Protestant ministers was about $30,000 in 1996. In large, wealthier denominations, ministers often earned significantly higher salaries. Ministers with modest salaries typically earn additional income from employment in secular occupations.

Sources of Additional Information

Persons who are interested in entering the Protestant ministry should seek the counsel of a minister or church guidance worker. Theological schools can supply information on admission requirements. Prospective ministers should also contact the ordination supervision body of their particular denomination for information on special requirements for ordination.

Rabbis

(D.O.T. 120.107-010)

Significant Points

- Ordination usually requires completion of a college degree followed by a 4- or 5-year program at a Jewish seminary.

- Graduates of Jewish seminaries have good job prospects, reflecting current unmet needs for rabbis and the need to replace the many rabbis approaching retirement age.

Nature of the Work

Rabbis serve either Orthodox, Conservative, Reform, or Reconstructionist Jewish congregations. Regardless of their particular point of view, all preserve the substance of Jewish religious worship. Congregations differ in the extent to which they follow the traditional form of worship—for example, in the wearing of head coverings, the use of Hebrew as the language of prayer, or the use of instrumental music or a choir. The format of the worship service and, therefore, the ritual that the rabbi uses may vary even among congregations belonging to the same branch of Judaism.

Rabbis are more independent than other clergy, because there is no formal hierarchy in Judaism. Rabbis are only responsible to the Board of Trustees of the congregation they serve. Those serving large congregations may spend considerable time in administrative duties, working with their staffs and committees. Large congregations frequently have associate or assistant rabbis, who often serve as educational directors.

Rabbis also may write for religious and lay publications, and teach in theological seminaries, colleges, and universities.

Employment

Based on information from organizations representing the 4 major branches of Judaism, there were approximately 1,800 Reform, 1,250 Conservative, 1,000 Orthodox, and 250 Reconstructionist rabbis in 1996. Although the majority served congregations, many rabbis functioned in other settings. Some taught in Jewish studies programs

Ordination as a rabbi requires many years of study.

at colleges and universities, while others served as chaplains in the military, hospitals, colleges, or one of the many Jewish community service agencies.

Although rabbis serve Jewish communities throughout the Nation, they are concentrated in major metropolitan areas with large Jewish populations.

Training and Other Qualifications

To become eligible for ordination as a rabbi, a student must complete a course of study in a seminary. Entrance requirements and the curriculum depend upon the branch of Judaism with which the seminary is associated. Most seminaries require applicants to be college graduates.

Jewish seminaries typically take 5 years for completion of studies, with an additional preparatory year required for students without sufficient grounding in Hebrew and Jewish studies. In addition to the core academic program, training generally includes field work and internships providing hands-on experience and, in some cases, study in Jerusalem. Seminary graduates are awarded the title Rabbi and the Master of Arts in Hebrew Letters degree; after more advanced study, some earn the Doctor of Hebrew Letters degree.

In general, the curriculums of Jewish theological seminaries provide students with a comprehensive knowledge of the Bible, Talmud, Rabbinic literature, Jewish history, theology, and courses in education, pastoral psychology, and public speaking. Students receive extensive practical training in dealing with social problems in the community. Training for alternatives to the pulpit, such as leadership in community services and religious education, is increasingly stressed. Some seminaries grant advanced academic degrees in such fields as Biblical and Talmudic research. All Jewish theological seminaries make scholarships and loans available.

About 35 seminaries educate and ordain Orthodox rabbis. The Rabbi Isaac Elchanan Theological Seminary and the Beth Medrash Govoha Seminary are representative of the two basic kinds of Orthodox seminaries. The former requires a bachelor's degree for entry and has a formal 4-year ordination program. The latter has no formal admission requirements but may require more years of study for ordination. The training is rigorous. When students have become sufficiently learned in the Talmud, the Bible, and other religious studies, they may be ordained with the approval of an authorized rabbi, acting either independently or as a representative of a rabbinical seminary.

Other major rabbinical seminaries include the Jewish Theological Seminary of America, which educates rabbis for the Conservative branch; the Hebrew Union College—Jewish Institute of Religion, which educates rabbis for the Reform branch; and the Reconstructionist Rabbinical College, which educates rabbis in the newest branch of Judaism.

Newly ordained rabbis usually begin as spiritual leaders of small congregations, assistants to experienced rabbis, directors of Hillel Foundations on college campuses, teachers in educational institutions, or chaplains in the Armed Forces. As a rule, experienced rabbis fill the pulpits of large and well-established Jewish congregations.

Job Outlook

Job opportunities for rabbis are expected to be favorable in the four major branches of Judaism through the year 2006, reflecting current unmet needs for rabbis together with the need to replace the many rabbis approaching retirement age. Rabbis willing to work in small communities should have particularly good prospects.

Graduates of Orthodox seminaries who seek pulpits should have good opportunities as growth in enrollments slows, and many graduates seek alternatives to the pulpit. Reconstructionist rabbis are expected to have very good employment opportunities as membership expands rapidly. Conservative and Reform rabbis are also expected to have good job opportunities serving congregations or in other settings.

Earnings

Based on limited information, annual average earnings of rabbis generally ranged from $45,000 to $75,000 in 1997, including benefits. Benefits may include housing, health insurance, and a retirement plan. Income varies widely, depending on the size and financial status of the congregation, as well as its denominational branch and geographic location. Rabbis may earn additional income from gifts or fees for officiating at ceremonies such as bar mitzvahs and weddings.

Sources of Additional Information

Persons who are interested in becoming rabbis should discuss their plans for a vocation with a practicing rabbi. Information on the work of rabbis and allied occupations can be obtained from:

☛ Rabbinical Council of America, 305 7th Ave., New York, NY 10001. (Orthodox)

☛ The Jewish Theological Seminary of America, 3080 Broadway, New York, NY 10027. (Conservative) Homepage: http://www.jtsa.edu

☛ Rabbinical Placement Commission, 192 Lexington Ave., New York, NY 10016. (Reform)

☛ Reconstructionist Rabbinical College, 1299 Church Rd., Wyncote, PA 19095.

Roman Catholic Priests

(D.O.T. 120.107-010)

Significant Points

- Preparation generally requires 8 years of study beyond high school, usually including a college degree followed by 4 years at a seminary.

- The shortage of Roman Catholic priests is expected to continue, resulting in a very favorable outlook.

Nature of the Work

Roman Catholic priests attend to the spiritual, pastoral, moral, and educational needs of the members of their church. A priest's day usually begins with morning meditation and mass and may end with an individual counseling session or an evening visit to a hospital or home.

Many priests direct and serve on church committees, work in civic and charitable organizations, and assist in community projects. Some counsel parishioners preparing for marriage or the birth of a child.

Priests in the Catholic church belong to one of two groups—diocesan or religious. Both types of priests have the same powers, acquired through ordination by a bishop. Their differences lie in their way of life, their type of work, and the church authority to whom they are responsible. *Diocesan priests* commit their lives to serving the people of a diocese, a church administrative region, and generally work in parishes assigned by the bishop of their diocese. Diocesan priests make promises of celibacy and obedience. *Religious priests* belong to a religious order, such as the Jesuits, Dominicans, or Franciscans. Religious priests are assigned duties by their superiors in their respective religious orders. Some religious priests specialize in teaching, while others serve as missionaries in foreign countries, where they may live under difficult and primitive conditions. Others live a communal life in monasteries, where they devote their lives to prayer, study, and assigned work. Religious priests take vows of chastity, poverty, and obedience.

Both religious and diocesan priests hold teaching and administrative posts in Catholic seminaries, colleges and universities, and high schools. Priests attached to religious orders staff a large proportion of the church's institutions of higher education and many high schools, whereas diocesan priests are usually concerned with the parochial schools attached to parish churches and with diocesan high schools. The members of religious orders do most of the missionary work conducted by the Catholic Church in this country and abroad.

Employment

According to the Official Catholic Directory, there were approximately 49,000 priests in 1996; about two-thirds were diocesan priests. There are priests in nearly every city and town and in many rural communities; however, the majority are in metropolitan areas, where most Catholics reside. Large numbers of priests are located in communities near Catholic schools, hospitals, social service agencies, and other institutions.

Training and Other Qualifications

Preparation for the priesthood generally requires 8 years of study beyond high school, usually including a college degree followed by 4 years at a seminary. There are 198 seminaries—72 for diocesan priests and 126 for religious priests. Priests commit themselves to celibacy, remaining unmarried. Only men are ordained as priests; women serve in other church positions that do not require priestly ordination.

Preparatory study for the priesthood may begin either in the first year of high school, at the college level, or in theological seminaries after college graduation. Today, most candidates for the priesthood take a 4-year degree program at a conventional college or university. After graduation from college, candidates generally receive 1 or 2 years of preparatory study (philosophy, religious studies, and prayer) before entering the seminary. Theology coursework in the seminary includes sacred scripture; dogmatic, moral, and pastoral theology; homiletics (art of preaching); church history; liturgy (sacraments); and canon (church) law. Fieldwork experience is usually required; in recent years, this aspect of a priest's training has been emphasized. Diocesan and religious priests attend different major seminaries, where slight variations in the training reflect the differences in their duties.

According to the U.S. Bishops Conference, 10 high school seminaries provided a college preparatory program in 1996. Programs emphasize English grammar, speech, literature, and social studies. Latin may be required, and modern languages are encouraged. In Hispanic communities, knowledge of Spanish is mandatory.

Young men are never denied entry into seminaries because of lack of funds. In seminaries for secular priests, scholarships or loans are available. Those in religious seminaries are financed by contributions of benefactors and the Catholic Church.

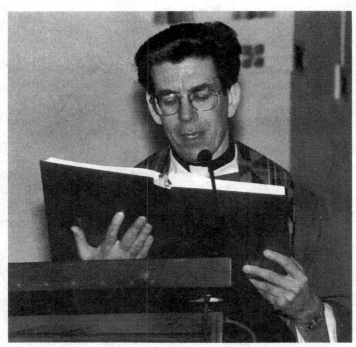

Some priests teach in Catholic high schools and colleges and universities.

Postgraduate work in theology is offered at a number of American Catholic universities or at ecclesiastical universities around the world, particularly in Rome. Also, many priests do graduate work in fields unrelated to theology. Priests are encouraged by the Catholic Church to continue their studies, at least informally, after ordination. In recent years, continuing education for ordained priests has stressed social sciences, such as sociology and psychology.

A newly ordained secular priest usually works as an assistant pastor. Newly ordained priests of religious orders are assigned to the specialized duties for which they are trained. Depending on the talents, interests, and experience of the individual, many opportunities for greater responsibility exist within the church.

Job Outlook
The shortage of Roman Catholic priests is expected to continue, resulting in a very favorable job outlook through the year 2006. Many priests will be needed in the years ahead to provide for the spiritual, educational, and social needs of the increasing number of Catholics. In recent years, the number of ordained priests has been insufficient to fill the needs of newly established parishes and other Catholic institutions, and to replace priests who retire, die, or leave the priesthood. This situation is likely to continue—even if the recent modest increase in seminary enrollments continues—as an increasing proportion of priests approach retirement age.

In response to the shortage of priests, certain traditional functions increasingly are being performed by permanent deacons and by teams of clergy and laity. Throughout most of the country, permanent deacons have been ordained to preach and perform liturgical functions such as baptisms, marriages, and funerals, and provide service to the community. Deacons are not authorized to celebrate Mass, nor administer the Sacraments of Reconciliation and the Anointing of the Sick. Teams of clergy and laity undertake some liturgical and nonliturgical functions such as hospital visits and religious teaching.

Earnings
Diocesan priests' salaries vary from diocese to diocese. Based on limited information, salaries averaged about $11,000 in 1996. In addition to a salary, diocesan priests receive a package of benefits which may include a car allowance, room and board in the parish rectory, health insurance, and a retirement plan.

Priests who do special work related to the church, such as teaching, usually receive a partial salary which is less than a lay person in the same position would receive. The difference between the usual salary for these jobs and the salary that the priest receives is called "contributed service." In some of these situations, housing and related expenses may be provided; in other cases, the priest must make his own arrangements. Some priests doing special work receive the same compensation that a lay person would receive.

Religious priests take a vow of poverty and are supported by their religious order. Any personal earnings are given to the order. Their vow of poverty is recognized by the Internal Revenue Service, which exempts them from paying Federal income tax.

Sources of Additional Information
Young men interested in entering the priesthood should seek the guidance and counsel of their parish priests and diocesan vocational office. For information regarding the different religious orders and the diocesan priesthood, as well as a list of the seminaries which prepare students for the priesthood, contact the diocesan director of vocations through the office of the local pastor or bishop.

Individuals seeking additional information about careers in the Catholic Ministry should contact their local diocese.

Teachers, Counselors, and Library Occupations

Adult Education Teachers

(D.O.T. 075.127-010; 090.222, .227-018; 097.221, .227; 099.223, .224-014, .227-014, -018, -026, -030, -038; 149.021; 150.027-014; 151.027-014; 152.021; 153.227-014; 159.227; 166.221, .227; 239.227; 375.227; 522.264; 621.221; 683.222; 689.324; 715.221; 740.221; 788.222; 789.222; 919.223; and 955.222)

Significant Points

- About half work part time; many also hold other jobs—often involving work related to the subject they teach.

- A graduate degree may be required to teach nonvocational courses, whereas practical experience is often all that is needed to teach vocational courses.

- Rising demand for adult education courses for career advancement, skills upgrading, or personal enrichment and enjoyment will spur faster-than-average employment growth; opportunities should be best for part-time positions.

Nature of the Work
Adult education teachers work in four main areas—adult vocational-technical education, adult remedial education, adult continuing education, and prebaccalaureate training. Adult vocational-technical education teachers provide instruction for occupations that do not require a college degree, such as welder, dental hygienist, automated systems manager, x-ray technician, auto mechanic, and cosmetologist. Other instructors help people update their job skills or adapt to technological advances. For example, an adult education teacher

may train students how to use new computer software programs. Adult remedial education teachers provide instruction in basic education courses for school dropouts or others who need to upgrade their skills to find a job. Adult continuing education teachers teach courses which students take for personal enrichment, such as cooking, dancing, writing, exercise and physical fitness, photography, and finance. Some adult education teachers in junior or community colleges prepare students for a 4-year degree program, teaching classes for credit that can be applied towards that degree.

Adult education teachers may lecture in classrooms or work in an industry or laboratory setting to give students hands-on experience. Increasingly, adult vocational-technical education teachers integrate academic and vocational curriculums so that students obtain a variety of skills that can be applied to the "real world." For example, an electronics student may be required to take courses in principles of mathematics and science in conjunction with hands-on electronics skills. Generally, teachers demonstrate techniques, have students apply them, and critique the students' work. For example, welding instructors show students various welding techniques, including the use of tools and equipment, watch them use the techniques, and have them repeat procedures until specific standards required by the trade are met.

Increasingly, minimum standards of proficiency are being established for students in various vocational-technical fields. Adult education teachers must be aware of new standards and develop lesson plans to ensure that students meet basic criteria. Also, adult education teachers and community colleges are assuming a greater role in students' transition from school to work, by helping establish internships and providing information about prospective employers.

Businesses also are increasingly providing their employees with work-related training to keep up with changing technology. Training is often provided through contractors, professional associations, or community colleges.

Adult education teachers who instruct in adult basic education programs may work with students who do not speak English; teach adults reading, writing, and mathematics up to the 8th-grade level; or teach adults through the 12th-grade level in preparation for the General Educational Development tests (GED). The GED offers the equivalent of a high school diploma. These teachers may refer students for counseling or job placement. Because many people who need adult basic education are reluctant to seek it, teachers also may recruit participants.

Adult education teachers also prepare lessons and assignments, grade papers and do related paperwork, attend faculty and professional meetings, and stay abreast of developments in their field. (For information on vocational education teachers in secondary schools, see the *Handbook* statement on kindergarten, elementary, and secondary school teachers.)

Working Conditions

Since adult education teachers work with adult students, they do not encounter some of the behavioral or social problems sometimes found when teaching younger students. The adults are there by choice, are highly motivated, and bring years of experience to the classroom— attributes that can make teaching these students rewarding and satisfying. However, teachers in adult basic education deal with students at different levels of development who may lack effective study skills and self-confidence, and who may require more attention and patience than other students.

About 1 out of 2 adult education teachers work part time. To accommodate students who may have job or family responsibilities, many institutions offer courses at night or on weekends, which range from 2- to 4-hour workshops and 1-day mini-sessions to semester-long courses. Some adult education teachers have several part-time teaching assignments or work a full-time job in addition to their part-time teaching job, leading to long hours and a hectic schedule.

Although most adult education teachers work in a classroom setting, some are consultants to a business and teach classes at the job site.

Adult education teachers may lecture in classrooms or work in an industry or laboratory setting to give students hands-on experience.

Employment

Adult education teachers held about 559,000 jobs in 1996. Many adult education teachers are self-employed.

Adult education teachers are employed by public school systems; community and junior colleges; universities; businesses that provide formal education and training for their employees; automotive repair, bartending, business, computer, electronics, medical technology, and similar schools and institutes; dance studios; health clubs; job training centers; community organizations; labor unions; and religious organizations.

Training, Other Qualifications, and Advancement

Training requirements vary by State and by subject. In general, teachers need work or other experience in their field, and a license or certificate in fields where these usually are required for full professional status. In some cases, particularly at educational institutions, a master's or doctoral degree is required to teach nonvocational courses which can be applied towards a 4-year degree program. Many vocational teachers in junior or community colleges do not have a master's or doctoral degree but draw on their work experience and knowledge, bringing practical experience to the classroom. For general adult education classes that are taken for interest or enjoyment, an acceptable portfolio of work is required. For example, to secure a job teaching a photography course, an applicant would need to show examples of previous work.

Most States and the District of Columbia require adult basic education teachers and adult literacy instructors to have a bachelor's degree from an approved teacher training program, and some require teacher certification.

Adult education teachers update their skills through continuing education to maintain certification—requirements vary among institutions. Teachers may take part in seminars, conferences, or graduate courses in adult education or training and development, or may return to work in business or industry for a limited time. Businesses are playing a growing role in adult education, forming consortiums with training institutions and junior colleges and providing input to curriculum development. Adult education teachers maintain an ongoing dialogue with businesses to determine the most current skills required in the workplace.

Adult education teachers should communicate and relate well with students, enjoy working with them, and be able to motivate them. Adult basic education instructors, in particular, must be patient, understanding, and supportive to make students comfortable, develop trust, and help them better understand concepts.

Some teachers advance to administrative positions in departments of education, colleges and universities, and corporate training departments. These positions often require advanced degrees, such as a doctorate in adult and continuing education. (See the statement on education administrators elsewhere in the *Handbook*.)

Job Outlook

Employment of adult education teachers is expected to grow faster than the average for all occupations through the year 2006 period as the demand for adult education programs continues to rise. Opportunities should be best for part-time positions, especially in fields such as computer technology, automotive mechanics, and medical technology, which offer very attractive, and often higher-paying, job opportunities outside of teaching.

An estimated 4 out of 10 adults participated in some form of adult education in 1995. Participation in continuing education grows as the educational attainment of the population increases. Both employers and employees are realizing that life-long learning is important for success. To keep abreast of changes in their fields and advances in technology, an increasing number of adults are taking courses—often subsidized or funded entirely by employers—for career advancement or to upgrade their skills. Also, an increasing number of adults are participating in classes for personal enrichment and enjoyment. Enrollment in adult basic education and literacy programs is increasing because of changes in immigration policy that require basic competency in English and civics. And, more employers are demanding higher levels of basic academic skills— reading, writing, and arithmetic—which is increasing enrollment in remedial education and GED preparation classes.

Employment growth of adult vocational-technical education teachers will result from the need to train young adults for entry-level jobs. Experienced workers who want to switch fields or whose jobs have been eliminated due to changing technology or business reorganization also require training. Businesses are finding it essential to provide training to their workers to remain productive and globally competitive. Cooperation between businesses and educational institutions continues to increase to insure that students are taught the skills employers desire. This should result in greater demand for adult education teachers, particularly at community and junior colleges. Since adult education programs receive State and Federal funding, employment growth may be affected by government budgets.

Additional job openings for adult education teachers will stem from the need to replace persons who leave the occupation. Many teach part time and move into and out of the occupation for other jobs, family responsibilities, or to retire.

Earnings

In 1996, salaried adult education teachers who usually worked full time had median earnings around $31,300 a year. The middle 50 percent earned between $19,200 and $44,800. The lowest 10 percent earned about $13,100, while the top 10 percent earned more than $56,600. Earnings varied widely by subject, academic credentials, experience, and region of the country. Part-time instructors generally are paid hourly wages and do not receive benefits or pay for preparation time outside of class.

Related Occupations

Adult education teaching requires a wide variety of skills and aptitudes, including the ability to influence, motivate, train, and teach; organizational, administrative, and communication skills; and creativity. Workers in other occupations that require these aptitudes include other teachers, counselors, school administrators, public relations specialists, employee development specialists, and social workers.

Sources of Additional Information

Information on adult basic education programs and teacher certification requirements is available from State departments of education and local school districts.

For information about adult vocational-technical education teaching positions, contact State departments of vocational-technical education.

For information on adult continuing education teaching positions, contact departments of local government, State adult education departments, schools, colleges and universities, religious organizations, and a wide range of businesses that provide formal training for their employees.

General information on adult education is available from:
- American Association for Adult and Continuing Education, 1200 19th St. NW., Suite 300, Washington, DC 20036.
- American Vocational Association, 1410 King St., Alexandria, VA 22314.
- ERIC Clearinghouse on Adult, Career, and Vocational Education, 1900 Kenny Rd., Columbus, OH 43210-1090.

Archivists and Curators

(D.O.T. 099.167-030; 101; 102 except .261-014 and .367-010; 109.067-014, .267-010, .281, .361, .364; 979.361)

Significant Points

- Employment generally requires graduate education and substantial work experience.
- Competition for jobs is expected to be keen as qualified applicants outnumber job openings.

Nature of the Work

Archivists, curators, museum and archives technicians, and conservators search for, acquire, appraise, analyze, describe, arrange, catalogue, restore, preserve, exhibit, maintain, and store items of lasting value so that they can be used by researchers or for exhibitions, publications, broadcasting, and other educational programs. Depending on the occupation, these items may consist of historical documents, audiovisual materials, institutional records, works of art, coins, stamps, minerals, clothing, maps, living and preserved plants and animals, buildings, computer records, or historic sites.

Archivists and curators plan and oversee the arrangement, cataloguing, and exhibition of collections and, along with technicians and conservators, maintain collections. Archivists and curators may coordinate educational and public outreach programs, such as tours, workshops, lectures, and classes, and may work with the boards of institutions to administer plans and policies. They also may conduct research on topics or items relevant to their collections. Although some duties of archivists and curators are similar, the types of items they deal with differ. Curators usually handle objects found in cultural, biological, or historical collections, such as sculptures, textiles, and paintings, while archivists mainly handle valuable records, documents, or objects that are retained because they originally accompanied and relate specifically to the document.

Archivists determine what portion of the vast amount of records maintained by various organizations, such as government agencies, corporations, or educational institutions, or by families and individuals, should be made part of permanent historical holdings, and which of these records should be put on exhibit. They maintain records in their original arrangement according to the creator's organizational scheme, and describe records to facilitate retrieval. Records may be saved on any medium, including paper, film, videotape, audiotape, electronic disk, or computer. They also may be copied onto some other format to protect the original from repeated handling, and to make them more accessible to researchers who use the records. As computers and various storage media evolve, archivists must keep abreast of technological advances in electronic information storage.

Archives may be part of a library, museum, or historical society, or may exist as a distinct archival unit within an organization or company. Archivists consider any medium containing recorded information as documents, including letters, books, and other paper documents, photographs, blueprints, audiovisual materials, and computer records. Any document which reflects organizational transactions, hierarchy, or procedures can be considered a record.

Archivists often specialize in an area of history or technology so they can better determine what records in that area qualify for retention and should become part of the archives. Archivists also may work with specialized forms of records, such as manuscripts, electronic records, photographs, cartographic records, motion pictures, and sound recordings.

Computers are increasingly used to generate and maintain archival records. Professional standards for use of computers in handling archival records are still evolving. However, use of computers is expected to transform many aspects of archival collections as computer capabilities, including multimedia and worldwide web use, expand and allow more records to be stored electronically.

Curators oversee collections in museums, zoos, aquariums, botanic gardens, nature centers, and historic sites. They acquire items through purchases, gifts, field exploration, intermuseum exchanges, or, in the case of some plants and animals, reproduction. Curators also plan and prepare exhibits. In natural history museums, curators collect and observe specimens in their natural habitat. Their work involves describing and classifying species, while specially trained collection managers and technicians provide hands-on care of natural history collections. Most curators use computer databases to catalogue and organize their collections. Many also use the Internet to make information available to other curators and the public. Increasingly, curators are expected to participate in grant writing and fund raising to support their projects.

Most curators specialize in a specific field, such as botany, art, paleontology, or history. Those working in large institutions may be highly specialized. A large natural history museum, for example, would employ specialists in birds, fishes, insects, and mollusks. Some curators maintain the collection, others do research, and others perform administrative tasks. Registrars, for example, keep track of and move objects in the collection. In small institutions, with only one or a few curators, one curator may be responsible for multiple tasks, from maintaining collections to directing the affairs of museums.

Conservators manage, care for, preserve, treat, and document works of art, artifacts, and specimens. This may require substantial historical, scientific, and archaeological research. They use x rays, chemical testing, microscopes, special lights, and other laboratory equipment and techniques to examine objects and determine their condition, the need for treatment or restoration, and the appropriate method for preservation. They then document their findings and treat items to minimize deterioration or restore items to their original state. Conservators usually specialize in a particular material or group of objects, such as documents and books, paintings, decorative arts, textiles, metals, or architectural material.

Museum directors formulate policies, plan budgets, and raise funds for their museums. They coordinate activities of their staff to establish and maintain collections. As their role has evolved, museum directors increasingly need business backgrounds in addition to an understanding and empathy for the subject matter of their collections.

Museum technicians assist curators and conservators by performing various preparatory and maintenance tasks on museum items. Some museum technicians may also assist curators with research. Archives technicians help archivists organize, maintain, and provide access to historical documentary materials.

Working Conditions

The working conditions of archivists and curators vary. Some spend most of their time working with the public, providing reference assistance and educational services. Others perform research or process records, which often means working alone or in offices with only a few people. Those who restore and install exhibits or work with bulky, heavy record containers may climb, stretch, or lift. Those in zoos, botanical gardens, and other outdoor museums or historic sites frequently walk great distances.

Curators who work in large institutions may travel extensively to evaluate potential additions to the collection, organize exhibitions,

Archivists and curators plan and oversee the arrangement, maintenance, and exhibition of museum collections.

and conduct research in their area of expertise. However, in small institutions, travel for curators is rare.

Employment

Archivists and curators held about 20,000 jobs in 1996. About a quarter were employed in museums, botanical gardens, and zoos, and approximately 2 in 10 worked in educational services, mainly in college and university libraries. About 4 in 10 worked in Federal, State, and local government. Most Federal archivists work for the National Archives and Records Administration; others manage military archives in the Department of Defense. Most Federal Government curators work at the Smithsonian Institution, in the military museums of the Department of Defense, and in archaeological and other museums managed by the Department of Interior. All State governments have archival or historical records sections employing archivists. State and local governments have numerous historical museums, parks, libraries, and zoos employing curators.

Some large corporations have archives or records centers, employing archivists to manage the growing volume of records created or maintained as required by law or necessary to the firms' operations. Religious and fraternal organizations, professional associations, conservation organizations, major private collectors, and research firms also employ archivists and curators.

Conservators may work under contract to treat particular items, rather than as a regular employee of a museum or other institution. These conservators may work on their own as private contractors, or as an employee of a conservation laboratory or regional conservation center which contracts their services to museums.

Training, Other Qualifications, and Advancement

Employment as an archivist, conservator, or curator generally requires graduate education and substantial work experience. Many archivists and curators work in archives or museums while completing their formal education, to gain the "hands-on" experience that many employers seek when hiring.

Employers generally look for archivists with undergraduate and graduate degrees in history or library science, with courses in archival science. Some positions may require knowledge of the discipline related to the collection, such as business or medicine. An increasing number of archivists have a double master's degree in history and library science. There are currently no programs offering a bachelor's or master's degree in archival science. However, approximately 65 colleges and universities offer courses or practical training in archival science as part of history, library science, or another discipline. The Academy of Certified Archivists offers voluntary certification for archivists. Certification requires the applicant to have experience in the field and to pass an examination offered by the Academy.

Archivists need research and analytical ability to understand the content of documents and the context in which they were created, and to decipher deteriorated or poor quality printed matter, handwritten manuscripts, or photographs and films. A background in preservation management is often required of archivists since they are responsible for taking proper care of their records. Archivists also must be able to organize large amounts of information and write clear instructions for its retrieval and use. In addition, computer skills and the ability to work with electronic records and databases are increasingly important.

Many archives are very small, including one-person shops, with limited promotion opportunities. Archivists typically advance by transferring to a larger unit with supervisory positions. A doctorate in history, library science, or a related field may be needed for some advanced positions, such as director of a State archives.

In most museums, a master's degree in an appropriate discipline of the museum's specialty—for example, art, history, or archaeology—or museum studies is required for employment as a curator. Many employers prefer a doctoral degree, particularly for curators in natural history or science museums. Earning two graduate degrees—in museum studies (museology) and a specialized subject—gives a candidate a distinct advantage in this competitive job market. In small museums, curatorial positions may be available to individuals with a bachelor's degree. For some positions, an internship of full-time museum work supplemented by courses in museum practices is needed.

Curatorial positions often require knowledge in a number of fields. For historic and artistic conservation, courses in chemistry, physics, and art are desirable. Since curators—particularly those in small museums—may have administrative and managerial responsibilities, courses in business administration, public relations, marketing, and fundraising also are recommended. Similar to archivists, curators need computer skills and the ability to work with electronic databases. Curators also need to be familiar with digital imaging, scanning technology, and copyright infringement, since many are responsible for posting information on the Internet.

Curators must be flexible because of their wide variety of duties. They need an aesthetic sense to design and present exhibits and, in small museums, manual dexterity to erect exhibits or restore objects. Leadership ability and business skills are important for museum directors, while marketing skills are valuable for increasing museum attendance and fundraising.

In large museums, curators may advance through several levels of responsibility, eventually to museum director. Curators in smaller museums often advance to larger ones. Individual research and publications are important for advancement in larger institutions.

Museum technicians generally need a bachelor's degree in an appropriate discipline of the museum's specialty, museum studies training, or previous museum work experience, particularly in exhibit design. Similarly, archives technicians generally need a bachelor's degree in library science or history, or relevant work experience. Technician positions often serve as a stepping stone for individuals interested in archival and curatorial work. With the exception of small museums, a master's degree is needed for advancement.

When hiring conservators, employers look for a master's degree in conservation, or in a closely related field, and substantial experience. There are only a few graduate programs in museum conservation techniques in the United States. Competition for entry to these programs is keen; to qualify, a student must have a background in chemistry, archaeology or studio art, and art history, as well as work experience. For some programs, knowledge of a foreign language is also helpful. Conservation apprenticeships or internships as an undergraduate can also enhance one's admission prospects. Graduate programs last 2 to 4 years; the latter years include internship training. A few individuals enter conservation through apprenticeships with museums, nonprofit organizations, and conservators in private practice. Apprenticeships should be supplemented with courses in chemistry, studio art, and history. Apprenticeship training, although accepted, generally is a more difficult route into the conservation profession.

Relatively few schools grant a bachelor's degree in museum studies. More common are undergraduate minors or tracks of study that are part of an undergraduate degree in a related field, such as art history, history, or archaeology. Students interested in further study may obtain a master's degree in museum studies. Colleges and universities throughout the country offer master's degrees in museum studies. However, many employers feel that, while museum studies are helpful, a thorough knowledge of the museum's specialty and museum work experience are more important.

Continuing education, which enables archivists, curators, conservators, and museum technicians to keep up with developments in the field, is available through meetings, conferences, and workshops sponsored by archival, historical, and museum associations. Some larger organizations, such as the National Archives, offer such training in-house.

Job Outlook

Competition for jobs as archivists and curators is expected to be keen as qualified applicants outnumber job openings. Graduates with highly specialized training, such as master's degrees in both library science and history, with a concentration in archives or records management, and extensive computer skills should have the best opportunities for jobs as archivists. A job as a curator is attractive to many people, and many applicants have the necessary training and subject knowledge; yet there are only a few openings. Consequently, candidates may have to work part time, as an intern, or even as a volunteer assistant curator or research associate after completing their formal education. Substantial work experience in collection management, exhibit design, or restoration, as well as database management skills, will be necessary for permanent status. Job opportunities for curators should be best in art and history museums, since these are the largest employers in the museum industry.

The job outlook for conservators may be more favorable, particularly for graduates of conservation programs. However, competition is stiff for the limited number of openings in these programs, and applicants need a technical background. Students who qualify and successfully complete the program, have knowledge of a foreign language, and are willing to relocate, will have an advantage over less qualified candidates in obtaining a position.

Employment of archivists and curators is expected to increase about as fast as the average for all occupations through the year 2006. Jobs are expected to grow as public and private organizations put more emphasis on establishing archives and organizing records and information, and as public interest in science, art, history, and technology increases. However, museums and other cultural institutions are often subject to funding cuts during recessions or periods of budget tightening, reducing demand for archivists and curators during these times. Although the rate of turnover among archivists and curators is relatively low, the need to replace workers who leave the occupation or stop working will create some additional job openings.

Earnings

Earnings of archivists and curators vary considerably by type and size of employer, and often by specialty. Average salaries in the Federal Government, for example, are generally higher than those in religious organizations. Salaries of curators in large, well-funded museums may be several times higher than those in small ones.

The average annual salary for all museum curators in the Federal Government in nonsupervisory, supervisory, and managerial positions was about $55,000 in 1997. Archivists averaged $53,600; museum specialists and technicians, $36,300; and archives technicians, $31,200.

According to a survey by the Association of Art Museum Directors, median salaries for selected workers in larger art museums in 1996 were as follows:

Director	$103,000
Curator	50,000
Senior conservator	48,500
Curatorial assistant	22,600

Related Occupations

Archivists' and curators' skills in preserving, organizing, and displaying objects or information of historical interest are shared by anthropologists, arborists, archaeologists, artifacts conservators, botanists, ethnologists, folklorists, genealogists, historians, horticulturists, information specialists, librarians, paintings restorers, records managers, and zoologists.

Sources of Additional Information

For information on archivists and on schools offering courses in archival studies, contact:

☛ Society of American Archivists, 600 South Federal St., Suite 504, Chicago, IL 60605.

For general information about careers as a curator and schools offering courses in museum studies, contact:

☛ American Association of Museums, 1575 I St. NW., Suite 400, Washington, DC 20005.

For information about conservation and preservation careers and education programs, contact:

☛ American Institute for Conservation of Historic and Artistic Works, 1717 K St. NW., Suite 301, Washington, DC 20006.

College and University Faculty

(D.O.T. 090.227-010)

Significant Points

- A Ph.D. is generally required for full-time positions in 4-year colleges and universities; in 2-year institutions, master's degree holders may qualify.

- Applicants for full-time college faculty positions face keen competition because many colleges and universities, in an effort to cut costs, will hire more part-time faculty.

- Job prospects will continue to be better in certain fields—computer science, engineering, and business, for example—that offer attractive nonacademic job opportunities and attract fewer applicants for academic positions.

Nature of the Work

College and university faculty teach and advise nearly 15 million full- and part-time college students and perform a significant part of our Nation's research. They also study and meet with colleagues to keep up with developments in their field and consult with government, business, nonprofit, and community organizations.

Faculty generally are organized into departments or divisions, based on subject or field. They usually teach several different courses in their department—algebra, calculus, and statistics, for example. They may instruct undergraduate or graduate students, or both. College and university faculty may give lectures to several hundred students in large halls, lead small seminars, or supervise students in laboratories. They prepare lectures, exercises, and laboratory experiments, grade exams and papers, and advise and work with students individually. In universities, they also counsel, advise, teach, and supervise graduate student teaching and research. College faculty work with an increasingly varied student population made up of growing shares of part-time, older, and culturally and racially diverse students.

Faculty keep abreast of developments in their field by reading current literature, talking with colleagues, and participating in professional conferences. They also do their own research to expand knowledge in their field. They experiment, collect and analyze data, and examine original documents, literature, and other source material. From this, they develop hypotheses, arrive at conclusions, and publish their findings in scholarly journals, books, and electronic media.

College and university faculty increasingly use technology in all areas of their work. In the classroom, they may use computers—including the Internet; electronic mail; software programs, such as statistical packages; and CD-ROMs—as teaching aids. Some professors teach "satellite" courses that are broadcast to students at off-campus sites through closed-circuit or cable television. Faculty also use computers to do their own research, participate in discussion groups in their field, or publicize their professional research papers.

Most faculty members serve on academic or administrative committees which deal with the policies of their institution, departmental matters, academic issues, curricula, budgets, equipment purchases, and hiring. Some work with student as well as community organizations. Department chairpersons are faculty members who usually teach some courses but generally have heavier administrative responsibilities.

The proportion of time spent on research, teaching, administrative, and other duties varies by individual circumstance and type of institution. Faculty members at universities generally spend a significant part of their time doing research; those in 4-year colleges, somewhat less; and those in 2-year colleges, relatively little. However, the teaching load usually is heavier in 2-year colleges and somewhat lower at 4-year institutions. Full professors at all types of institutions usually spend a larger portion of their time conducting research than assistant professors, instructors, and lecturers.

Working Conditions

College faculty generally have flexible schedules. They must be present for classes, usually 12 to 16 hours a week, and for faculty and committee meetings. Most establish regular office hours for student consultations, usually 3 to 6 hours per week. Otherwise, faculty are free to decide when and where they will work, and how much time to devote to course preparation, grading papers and exams, study, research, graduate student supervision, and other activities. Initial adjustment to these responsibilities can be challenging as new faculty adapt to switching roles from student to teacher. This adjustment may be even more difficult as class size grows in response to faculty and budget cutbacks, increasing an instructor's workload. Also, many institutions are increasing their reliance on part-time faculty, who generally have limited administrative and student advising duties, which leaves the declining number of full-time faculty with a heavier workload.

Some faculty members work staggered hours and teach classes at night and on weekends. This is particularly true for faculty who teach at 2-year community colleges or institutions with large enrollments of older students with full-time jobs or family responsibilities on weekdays. Most

College and university faculty teach, conduct research, and write scholarly papers.

faculty are employed on a 9-month contract, which allows them the time to teach, do research, travel, or pursue nonacademic interests during the summer and school holidays. Most colleges and universities have funds to support faculty research or other professional development needs, including travel to conferences and research sites.

Faculty may experience a conflict between their responsibilities to teach students and the pressure to do research and publish their findings. This may be a particular problem for young faculty seeking advancement in 4-year research universities. Increasing emphasis on undergraduate teaching performance in tenure decisions may alleviate some of this pressure, however.

Part-time faculty generally spend little time on campus, because they usually don't have an office. In addition, they may teach at more than one college, requiring travel between their various places of employment, earning the name "gypsy faculty." Part-time faculty are usually not eligible for tenure. Dealing with this lack of job security can be stressful.

Employment
College and university faculty held about 864,000 jobs in 1996, mostly in public institutions.

About 4 out of 10 college and university faculty worked part time in 1996. Some part-timers, known as "adjunct faculty," have primary jobs outside of academia—in government, private industry, or in non-profit research—and teach "on the side." Others seek full-time jobs but are unable to obtain them due to intense competition for available openings. Some work part time in more than one institution.

Training, Other Qualifications, and Advancement
Most college and university faculty are in four academic ranks: Professor, associate professor, assistant professor, and instructor. These positions are usually considered to be tenure-track positions. A small number of faculty, called lecturers, usually are not on the tenure track.

Most faculty members are hired as instructors or assistant professors. Four-year colleges and universities generally only consider doctoral degree holders for full-time, tenure-track positions, but may hire master's degree holders or doctoral candidates for certain disciplines, such as the arts, or for part-time and temporary jobs. In 2-year colleges, master's degree holders often qualify for full-time positions. However, with increasing competition for available jobs, institutions can be more selective in their hiring practices. Master's degree holders may find it increasingly difficult to obtain employment as they are passed over in favor of candidates holding a Ph.D.

Doctoral programs, including time spent completing a master's degree and a dissertation, take an average of 6 to 8 years of full-time study beyond the bachelor's degree. Some programs, such as the hu-

manities, take longer to complete; others, such as engineering, generally are shorter. Candidates usually specialize in a subfield of a discipline—for example, organic chemistry, counseling psychology, or European history—but also take courses covering the entire discipline. Programs include 20 or more increasingly specialized courses and seminars plus comprehensive examinations on all major areas of the field. Candidates also must complete a dissertation—a written report on original research in the candidate's major field of study. The dissertation sets forth an original hypothesis or proposes a model and tests it. Students in the natural sciences and engineering usually do laboratory work; in the humanities, they study original documents and other published material. The dissertation, done under the guidance of one or more faculty advisors, usually takes 1 or 2 years of full-time work.

In some fields, particularly the natural sciences, some students spend an additional 2 years on postdoctoral research and study before taking a faculty position. Some Ph.D.'s extend or take new postdoctoral appointments if they are unable to find a faculty job. Most of these appointments offer a nominal salary.

A major step in the traditional academic career is attaining tenure. New tenure-track faculty are usually hired as instructors or assistant professors, and must serve a certain period (usually 7 years) under term contracts. At the end of the contract period, their record of teaching, research, and overall contribution to the institution is reviewed; tenure is granted if the review is favorable. According to the American Association of University Professors, in 1995-96 about 65 percent of all full-time faculty held tenure while 88 percent were in tenure-track positions. Those denied tenure usually must leave the institution. Tenured professors cannot be fired without just cause and due process. Tenure protects the faculty's academic freedom—the ability to teach and conduct research without fear of being fired for advocating unpopular ideas. It also gives both faculty and institutions the stability needed for effective research and teaching, and provides financial security for faculty. Some institutions have adopted post-tenure review policies to encourage ongoing evaluation of tenured faculty.

The number of tenure-track positions is expected to decline as institutions rely more heavily on less costly part-time faculty who do not hold tenure-track positions. Consequently, increased reliance on part-time faculty is expected to shrink the total pool of faculty who hold tenure. Some institutions have placed "caps" on the percentage of faculty who can be tenured. Other institutions offer prospective faculty limited term contracts—typically 2-, 3-, or 5-year, full-time contracts—in an effort to adapt to changes in the budget and the size of the student body. These contracts may be terminated or extended at the end of the period. Institutions are not obligated to grant tenure to these contract holders.

Some faculty—based on teaching experience, research, publication, and service on campus committees and task forces—move into administrative and managerial positions, such as departmental chairperson, dean, and president. At 4-year institutions, such advancement requires a doctoral degree. At 2-year colleges, a doctorate is helpful but not generally required, except for advancement to some top administrative positions. (Deans and departmental chairpersons are covered in the *Handbook* statement on education administrators, while college presidents are included in the *Handbook* statement on general managers and top executives.)

College faculty should have inquiring and analytical minds, and a strong desire to pursue and disseminate knowledge. They must be able to communicate clearly and logically, both orally and in writing. They should be able to establish rapport with students and, as models for them, be dedicated to the principles of academic integrity and intellectual honesty. Additionally, they must be self-motivated and able to work in an environment where they receive little direct supervision.

Job Outlook
Employment of college and university faculty is expected to increase about as fast as the average for all occupations through the year 2006

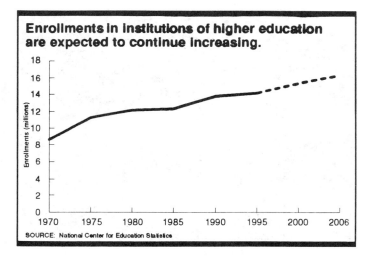

Enrollments in institutions of higher education are expected to continue increasing.

SOURCE: National Center for Education Statistics

as enrollments in higher education increase. Many additional openings will arise as faculty members retire. Faculty retirements should increase significantly from the late 1990s through 2006 as a large number of faculty who entered the profession during the 1950s and 1960s reach retirement age. Most faculty members likely to retire are full-time tenured professors. However, in an effort to cut costs, some institutions are expected to either leave these positions vacant or hire part-time, non-tenured faculty as replacements. Prospective job applicants should be prepared to face keen competition for available jobs as growing numbers of Ph.D. graduates, including foreign-born Ph.D.'s, vie for fewer full-time openings. As more and more Ph.D.'s compete for openings, master's degree holders may find competition for jobs even more intense.

Enrollments in institutions of higher education increased in the mid-1980s through the early 1990s despite a decline in the traditional college-age (18-24) population. This resulted from a higher proportion of 18- to 24-year-olds attending college, along with a growing number of part-time, female, and older students. Between 1996 and 2006, the traditional college-age population will begin to grow again, spurred by the leading edge of the baby-boom "echo" generation (children of the baby-boomers) reaching college age. College enrollment is projected to rise from 14 million in 1996 to 16 million in 2006, an increase of 14 percent (see accompanying chart).

In the past two decades, keen competition for faculty jobs forced some applicants to accept part-time or short-term academic appointments that offered little hope of tenure, and others to seek nonacademic positions. This trend of hiring adjunct or part-time faculty is likely to continue due to financial difficulties faced by colleges and universities. Many colleges, faced with reduced State funding for higher education, have increased the hiring of part-time faculty to save money on pay and benefits. Public 2-year colleges employ a significantly higher number of part-time faculty as a percentage of their total staff than public 4-year colleges and universities, but all institutions have increased their part-time hiring. With uncertainty over future funding, many colleges and universities are continuing to cut costs by eliminating some academic programs, increasing class size, and closely monitoring all expenses.

Once enrollments and retirements start increasing at a faster pace in the late 1990s, opportunities for college faculty may begin to improve somewhat. Growing numbers of students will necessitate hiring more faculty to teach. At the same time, many faculty will be retiring, opening up even more positions. Job prospects will continue to be better in certain fields—business, engineering, health science, and computer science, for example—that offer attractive nonacademic job opportunities and attract fewer applicants for academic positions.

Employment of college faculty is affected by the nonacademic job market. Excellent job prospects in a field—for example, computer

science from the late 1970s to the mid-1980s—cause more students to enroll, increasing faculty needs in that field. On the other hand, poor job prospects in a field, such as history in recent years, discourages students and reduces demand for faculty.

Earnings
Earnings vary according to faculty rank and type of institution, geographic area, and field. According to a 1995-96 survey by the American Association of University Professors, salaries for full-time faculty averaged $51,000. By rank, the average for professors was $65,400; associate professors, $48,300; assistant professors, $40,100; instructors, $30,800; and lecturers, $33,700. Faculty in 4-year institutions earn higher salaries, on the average, than those in 2-year schools. Average salaries for faculty in public institutions—$50,400—were lower in 1995-96 than those for private independent institutions—$57,500—but higher than those for religion-affiliated private institutions—$45,200. In fields with high-paying nonacademic alternatives—notably medicine and law but also engineering and business, among others—earnings exceed these averages. In others—such as the humanities and education—they are lower.

Most faculty members have significant earnings in addition to their base salary, from consulting, teaching additional courses, research, writing for publication, or other employment, both during the academic year and the summer.

Most college and university faculty enjoy some unique benefits, including access to campus facilities, tuition waivers for dependents, housing and travel allowances, and paid sabbatical leaves. Part-time faculty have fewer benefits than full-time faculty, and usually do not receive health insurance, retirement benefits, or sabbatical leave.

Related Occupations
College and university faculty function both as teachers and researchers. They communicate information and ideas. Related occupations include elementary and secondary school teachers, librarians, writers, consultants, lobbyists, trainers and employee development specialists, and policy analysts. Faculty research activities often are similar to those of scientists, as well as managers and administrators in industry, government, and nonprofit research organizations.

Sources of Additional Information
Professional societies generally provide information on academic and nonacademic employment opportunities in their fields. Names and addresses of these societies appear in statements elsewhere in the *Handbook*.

Special publications on higher education, available in libraries, such as *The Chronicle of Higher Education*, list specific employment opportunities for faculty.

Counselors

(D.O.T. 045.107-010, -014, -018, -038, -042 -050, -054, -058, .117; 090.107; 094.107-010; and 169.267-026)

Significant Points

● About 6 out of 10 counselors have a master's degree.

● Rapid job growth is expected among rehabilitation and mental health counselors; however, budgetary constraints may limit growth among school counselors, and employment counselors working in government.

Nature of the Work
Counselors assist people with personal, family, educational, mental health, and career decisions and problems. Their duties depend on the individuals they serve and the settings in which they work.

School and college counselors—who work at the elementary, middle, secondary, and postsecondary school levels—help students evaluate their abilities, interests, talents, and personality characteristics so that students can develop realistic academic and career goals. Counselors use interviews, counseling sessions, tests, or other methods when evaluating and advising students. They may operate career information centers and career education programs. High school counselors advise on college majors, admission requirements, entrance exams, and financial aid, and on trade, technical school, and apprenticeship programs. They help students develop jobfinding skills such as resume writing and interviewing techniques. College career planning and placement counselors assist alumni or students with career development and job hunting techniques.

Elementary school counselors observe younger children during classroom and play activities and confer with their teachers and parents to evaluate their strengths, problems, or special needs. They also help students develop good study habits. They do less vocational and academic counseling than secondary school counselors.

School counselors at all levels help students understand and deal with their social, behavioral, and personal problems. They emphasize preventive and developmental counseling to provide students with the life skills needed to deal with problems before they occur, and to enhance personal, social, and academic growth. Counselors provide special services, including alcohol and drug prevention programs, and classes that teach students to handle conflicts without resorting to violence. Counselors also try to identify cases involving domestic abuse and other family problems that can affect a student's development. Counselors work with students individually, in small groups, or with entire classes. They consult and work with parents, teachers, school administrators, school psychologists, school nurses, and social workers.

Rehabilitation counselors help people deal with the personal, social, and vocational effects of their disabilities. They may counsel people with disabilities resulting from birth defects, illness or disease, accidents, or the stress of daily life. They evaluate the strengths and limitations of individuals, provide personal and vocational counseling, and may arrange for medical care, vocational training, and job placement. Rehabilitation counselors interview individuals with disabilities and their families, evaluate school and medical reports, and confer and plan with physicians, psychologists, occupational therapists, and employers to determine the capabilities and skills of the individual. Conferring with the client, they develop a rehabilitation program, which may include training to help the person develop job skills. They also work toward increasing the client's capacity to live independently.

Employment counselors help individuals make wise career decisions. They explore and evaluate the client's education, training, work history, interests, skills, and personal traits, and may arrange for aptitude and achievement tests. They also work with individuals to develop jobseeking skills and assist clients in locating and applying for jobs.

Mental health counselors emphasize prevention and work with individuals and groups to promote optimum mental health. They help individuals deal with addictions and substance abuse, suicide, stress management, problems with self-esteem, issues associated with aging, job and career concerns, educational decisions, issues of mental and emotional health, and family, parenting, and marital problems. Mental health counselors work closely with other mental health specialists, including psychiatrists, psychologists, clinical social workers, psychiatric nurses, and school counselors. (Information on other mental health specialists appears in the *Handbook* statements on physicians, psychologists, registered nurses, and social workers.)

Other counseling specialties include marriage and family, multicultural, or gerontological counseling. A gerontological counselor provides services to elderly persons who face changing lifestyles due to health problems, and helps families cope with these changes. A multicultural counselor helps employers adjust to an increasingly diverse workforce.

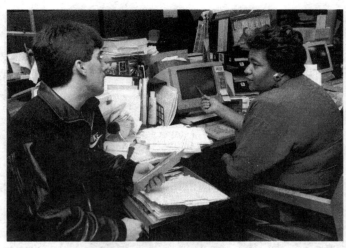

School counselors use interviews, counseling sessions, and tests to evaluate and advise students.

Working Conditions

Most school counselors work the traditional 9- to 10-month school year with a 2- to 3-month vacation, although an increasing number are employed on 10 1/2- or 11-month contracts. They generally have the same hours as teachers. College career planning and placement counselors may work long and irregular hours during recruiting periods.

Rehabilitation and employment counselors generally work a standard 40-hour week. Self-employed counselors and those working in mental health and community agencies often work evenings to counsel clients who work during the day.

Counselors must possess high physical and emotional energy to handle the array of problems they address. Dealing with these day-to-day problems can cause stress and emotional burnout.

Since privacy is essential for confidential and frank discussions with clients, counselors usually have private offices.

Employment

Counselors held about 175,000 jobs in 1996. (This employment estimate only includes vocational and educational counselors; employment data are not available for other counselors discussed in this statement, such as rehabilitation and mental health counselors.)

In addition to elementary and secondary schools and colleges and universities, counselors work in a wide variety of public and private establishments. These include health care facilities; job training, career development, and vocational rehabilitation centers; social agencies; correctional institutions; and residential care facilities, such as halfway houses for criminal offenders and group homes for children, the aged, and the disabled. Counselors also work in organizations engaged in community improvement and social change, as well as drug and alcohol rehabilitation programs and State and local government agencies. A growing number of counselors work in health maintenance organizations, insurance companies, group practice, and private practice. This growth has been spurred by laws allowing counselors to receive payments from insurance companies, and requiring employers to provide rehabilitation and counseling services to employees.

Training, Other Qualifications, and Advancement

Recent data indicate that 6 out of 10 counselors have a master's degree; fields of study include college student affairs, elementary or secondary school counseling, education, gerontological counseling, marriage and family counseling, substance abuse counseling, rehabilitation counseling, agency or community counseling, clinical mental health counseling, counseling psychology, career counseling, or a related field.

Graduate-level counselor education programs in colleges and universities usually are in departments of education or psychology.

Courses are grouped into eight core areas: Human growth and development; social and cultural foundations; helping relationships; groups; lifestyle and career development; appraisal; research and evaluation; and professional orientation. In an accredited program, 48 to 60 semester hours of graduate study, including a period of supervised clinical experience in counseling, are required for a master's degree. In 1996, 111 institutions offered programs in counselor education, including career, community, gerontological, mental health, school, student affairs, and marriage and family counseling, accredited by the Council for Accreditation of Counseling and Related Educational Programs (CACREP).

In 1997, 42 States and the District of Columbia had some form of counselor credentialing legislation, licensure, certification, or registry for practice outside schools. Requirements vary from State to State. In some States, credentialing is mandatory; in others, voluntary.

Many counselors elect to be nationally certified by the National Board for Certified Counselors (NBCC), which grants the general practice credential, "National Certified Counselor." To be certified, a counselor must hold a master's degree in counseling from a regionally accredited institution, have at least 2 years of supervised professional counseling experience, and pass NBCC's National Counselor Examination for Licensure and Certification. This national certification is voluntary and distinct from State certification. However, in some States those who pass the national exam are exempt from taking a State certification exam. NBCC also offers specialty certification in career, gerontological, school, clinical mental health, and addictions counseling. To maintain their certification, counselors must complete 100 hours of acceptable continuing education credit every 5 years.

All States require school counselors to hold State school counseling certification; however, certification requirements vary from State to State. Some States require public school counselors to have both counseling and teaching certificates. Depending on the State, a master's degree in counseling and 2 to 5 years of teaching experience may be required for a counseling certificate.

Vocational and related rehabilitation agencies generally require a master's degree in rehabilitation counseling, counseling and guidance, or counseling psychology for rehabilitation counselor jobs. Some, however, may accept applicants with a bachelor's degree in rehabilitation services, counseling, psychology, sociology, or related fields. A bachelor's degree may qualify a person to work as a counseling aide, rehabilitation aide, or social service worker. Experience in employment counseling, job development, psychology, education, or social work may be helpful.

The Council on Rehabilitation Education (CORE) accredits graduate programs in rehabilitation counseling. A minimum of 2 years of study—including 600 hours of supervised clinical internship experience—are required for the master's degree.

In most State vocational rehabilitation agencies, applicants must pass a written examination and be evaluated by a board of examiners to obtain licensure. In addition, many employers require rehabilitation counselors to be nationally certified. To become certified by the Commission on Rehabilitation Counselor Certification, counselors must graduate from an accredited educational program, complete an internship, and pass a written examination. They are then designated as "Certified Rehabilitation Counselors." To maintain their certification, counselors must complete 100 hours of acceptable continuing education credit every 5 years.

Some States require counselors in public employment offices to have a master's degree; others accept a bachelor's degree with appropriate counseling courses.

Clinical mental health counselors generally have a master's degree in mental health counseling, another area of counseling, or in psychology or social work. They are voluntarily certified by the National Board for Certified Counselors. Generally, to receive certification as a clinical mental health counselor, a counselor must have a master's degree in counseling, 2 years of post-master's experience, a period of supervised clinical experience, a taped sample of clinical work, and a passing grade on a written examination.

Some employers provide training for newly hired counselors. Many have work-study programs so that employed counselors can earn graduate degrees. Counselors must participate in graduate studies, workshops, institutes, and personal studies to maintain their certificates and licenses.

Persons interested in counseling should have a strong interest in helping others and the ability to inspire respect, trust, and confidence. They should be able to work independently or as part of a team. Counselors follow the code of ethics associated with their respective certifications and licenses.

Prospects for advancement vary by counseling field. School counselors may move to a larger school; become directors or supervisors of counseling, guidance, or pupil personnel services; or, usually with further graduate education, become counselor educators, counseling psychologists, or school administrators. (See the statements on psychologists and education administrators elsewhere in the *Handbook*.) Some counselors also may advance to work at the State department of education.

Rehabilitation, mental health, and employment counselors may become supervisors or administrators in their agencies. Some counselors move into research, consulting, or college teaching, or go into private or group practice.

Job Outlook

Overall employment of counselors is expected to grow about as fast as the average for all occupations through the year 2006. In addition, replacement needs should increase significantly as a large number of counselors reach retirement age.

Employment of school and vocational counselors is expected to grow as a result of increasing enrollments, particularly in secondary and postsecondary schools, State legislation requiring counselors in elementary schools, and the expanded responsibilities of counselors. Counselors are becoming more involved in crisis and preventive counseling, helping students deal with issues ranging from drug and alcohol abuse to death and suicide. Also, the growing diversity of student populations is presenting challenges to counselors in dealing with multicultural issues. Job growth among counselors, however, may be dampened by budgetary constraints. High student-to-counselor ratios in many schools could increase even more as student enrollments grow. When funding is tight, schools usually prefer to hire new teachers before adding counselors in an effort to keep classroom sizes at acceptable levels.

Rapid job growth is expected among rehabilitation and mental health counselors. Under managed care systems, insurance companies increasingly provide for reimbursement of counselors, enabling many counselors to move from schools and government agencies to private practice. Counselors are also forming group practices to receive expanded insurance coverage. The number of people who need rehabilitation services will rise as advances in medical technology continue to save lives that only a few years ago would have been lost. In addition, legislation requiring equal employment rights for people with disabilities will spur demand for counselors. Counselors not only will help individuals with disabilities with their transition into the work force, but also will help companies comply with the law. Employers are also increasingly offering employee assistance programs which provide mental health and alcohol and drug abuse services. A growing number of people are expected to use these services as the elderly population grows, and as society focuses on ways of developing mental well-being, such as controlling stress associated with job and family responsibilities.

As with other government jobs, the number of employment counselors, who work primarily for State and local government, could be limited by budgetary constraints. However, demand for government employment counseling may grow as new welfare laws require welfare recipients to find jobs. Opportunities for employment counselors working in private job training services should grow as counselors provide skill training and other services to laid-off workers, experienced workers seeking a new or second career, full-time homemakers seeking to enter or reenter the work force, and workers who want to upgrade their skills.

Earnings

Median earnings for full-time educational and vocational counselors were about $35,800 a year in 1996. The middle 50 percent earned between $25,600 and $48,500 a year. The bottom 10 percent earned less than $18,600 a year, while the top 10 percent earned over $60,100 a year.

According to the Educational Research Service, the average salary of public school counselors in the 1995-96 academic year was about $44,100. Many school counselors are compensated on the same pay scale as teachers. School counselors can earn additional income working summers in the school system or in other jobs.

Self-employed counselors who have well-established practices, as well as counselors employed in group practices, generally have the highest earnings, as do some counselors working for private firms, such as insurance companies and private rehabilitation companies.

Related Occupations

Counselors help people evaluate their interests, abilities, and disabilities, and deal with personal, social, academic, and career problems. Others who help people in similar ways include college and student affairs workers, teachers, personnel workers and managers, human services workers, social workers, psychologists, psychiatrists, psychiatric nurses, members of the clergy, occupational therapists, training and employee development specialists, and equal employment opportunity/affirmative action specialists.

Sources of Additional Information

For general information about counseling, as well as information on specialties such as school, college, mental health, rehabilitation, multicultural, career, marriage and family, and gerontological counseling, contact:

☛ American Counseling Association, 5999 Stevenson Ave., Alexandria, VA 22304.

For information on accredited counseling and related training programs, contact:

☛ Council for Accreditation of Counseling and Related Educational Programs, American Counseling Association, 5999 Stevenson Ave., Alexandria, VA 22304.

For information on national certification requirements for counselors, contact:

☛ National Board for Certified Counselors, 3 Terrace Way, Suite D, Greensboro, NC 27403. Homepage: http://www.nbcc.org/

For information on certification requirements for rehabilitation counselors and a list of accredited rehabilitation education programs, contact:

☛ Council on Rehabilitation Counselor Certification, 1835 Rohlwing Rd., Suite E, Rolling Meadows, IL 60008.

State departments of education can supply information on colleges and universities that offer approved guidance and counseling training for State certification and licensure requirements.

State employment service offices have information about job opportunities and entrance requirements for counselors.

Librarians

(D.O.T. 100 except .367-018; 109.267-014)

Significant Points

- A master's degree in library science is usually required; special librarians may need an additional graduate or professional degree.

- Slow employment growth, coupled with an increasing number of master of library science graduates, will result in more applicants competing for fewer jobs.

- Applicants for librarian jobs in large cities or suburban areas will face competition, while those willing to work in rural areas should have better job prospects.

Nature of the Work

The traditional concept of a library is being redefined, from a place to access paper records or books, to one which also houses the most advanced mediums, including CD-ROM, the Internet, virtual libraries, and remote access to a wide range of resources. Consequently, librarians are increasingly combining traditional duties with tasks involving quickly changing technology. Librarians assist people in finding information and using it effectively in their personal and professional lives. They must have knowledge of a wide variety of scholarly and public information sources, and follow trends related to publishing, computers, and the media to effectively oversee the selection and organization of library materials. Librarians manage staff and develop and direct information programs and systems for the public, to ensure information is organized to meet users' needs.

There are generally three aspects of library work—user services, technical services, and administrative services; most librarian positions incorporate all three aspects. Even librarians specializing in one of these areas may perform other responsibilities. Librarians in user services, such as reference and children's librarians, work with the public to help them find the information they need. This may involve analyzing users' needs to determine what information is appropriate, and searching for, acquiring, and providing information. It also includes an instructional role, such as showing users how to access information. For example, librarians commonly help users navigate the Internet, showing them how to most efficiently search for relevant information. Librarians in technical services, such as acquisitions and cataloguing, acquire and prepare materials for use and may not deal directly with the public. Librarians in administrative services oversee the management and planning of libraries, negotiate contracts for services, materials, and equipment, supervise library employees, perform public relations and fundraising duties, prepare budgets, and direct activities to ensure that everything functions properly.

In small libraries or information centers, librarians generally handle all aspects of the work. They read book reviews, publishers' announcements, and catalogues to keep up with current literature and other available resources, and select and purchase materials from publishers, wholesalers, and distributors. Librarians prepare new materials for use by classifying them by subject matter, and describe books and other library materials in a way users can easily find them. They supervise assistants who prepare cards, computer records, or other access tools that direct users to resources. In large libraries, librarians may specialize in a single area, such as acquisitions, cataloguing, bibliography, reference, special collections, or administration. Teamwork is increasingly important to ensure quality service to the public.

Librarians also compile lists of books, periodicals, articles, and audiovisual materials on particular subjects, analyze collections, and recommend materials to be acquired. They may collect and organize books, pamphlets, manuscripts, and other materials in a specific field, such as rare books, genealogy, or music. In addition, they coordinate programs such as storytelling for children, and literacy skills and book talks for adults; conduct classes on Internet use and other topics; publicize services; provide reference help; supervise staff; prepare budgets; write grants; and oversee other administrative matters.

Librarians may be classified according to the type of library in which they work—public libraries, school library media centers, academic libraries, and special libraries. They may work with specific groups, such as children, young adults, adults, or the disadvantaged. In school library media centers, librarians help teachers develop curricula, acquire materials for classroom instruction, and sometimes team teach.

Librarians may also work in information centers or libraries maintained by government agencies, corporations, law firms, advertising agencies, museums, professional associations, medical centers, hospitals, religious organizations, and research laboratories. They build and arrange the organization's information resources, usually limited to subjects of special interest to the organization. These special librarians can provide vital information services by preparing abstracts and indexes of current periodicals, organizing bibliographies, or analyzing background information and preparing reports on areas of particular interest. For instance, a special librarian working for a corporation may provide the sales department with information on competitors or new developments affecting their field.

Many libraries have access to remote databases, as well as maintaining their own computerized databases. The widespread use of automation in libraries makes database searching skills important to librarians. Librarians develop and index databases and act as trainers to help users develop searching skills to obtain the information they need. Some libraries are forming consortiums with other libraries through electronic mail (e-mail). This allows patrons to submit information requests to several libraries at once. Use of the Internet and other world-wide computer systems is also expanding the amount of available reference information. Librarians must be aware of how to use these resources to locate information.

Librarians with appropriate computer and information systems skills may work as automated systems librarians, planning and operating computer systems, and information science librarians, designing information storage and retrieval systems and developing procedures for collecting, organizing, interpreting, and classifying information. These librarians may analyze and plan for future information needs. (See statement on computer scientists and systems analysts elsewhere in the *Handbook*.) The increased use of automated information systems enables librarians to focus on administrative and budgeting responsibilities, grant writing, and specialized research requests, while delegating more technical and user services responsibilities to technicians. (See statement on library technicians elsewhere in the *Handbook*.)

Increasingly, librarians apply their information management and research skills to arenas outside of libraries—for example, database development, reference tool development, information systems, publishing, Internet coordination, marketing, and training of database users. Entrepreneurial librarians may start their own consulting practices, acting as free-lance librarians or information brokers and providing services to other libraries, businesses, or government agencies.

Working Conditions

Assisting users in obtaining information for their jobs, recreational purposes, and other needs can be challenging and satisfying; working

Librarians often help users search for relevant information on the Internet.

with users under deadlines may be demanding and stressful. Selecting and ordering new materials can be stimulating and rewarding. However, librarians also spend a significant portion of time at their desks or in front of computer terminals; extended work at video display terminals may cause eyestrain and headaches.

More than 3 out of 10 librarians work part time. Public and college librarians often work weekends and evenings, and may have to work some holidays. School librarians generally have the same workday schedule as classroom teachers and similar vacation schedules. Special librarians may work normal business hours, but in fast-paced industries, such as advertising or legal services, may work longer hours during peak times.

Employment

Librarians held about 154,000 jobs in 1996. Most were in school and academic libraries; others were in public and special libraries. A small number of librarians worked for hospitals and religious organizations. Others worked for governments at all levels.

Training, Other Qualifications, and Advancement

A master's degree in library science (MLS) is necessary for librarian positions in most public, academic, and special libraries, and in some school libraries. In the Federal Government, an MLS or the equivalent in education and experience is required. Many colleges and universities offer MLS programs, but employers often prefer graduates of the approximately 50 schools accredited by the American Library Association. Most MLS programs require a bachelor's degree; any liberal arts major is appropriate.

Most MLS programs take 1 year to complete; others take 2. A typical graduate program includes courses in the foundations of library and information science, including the history of books and printing, intellectual freedom and censorship, and the role of libraries and information in society. Other basic courses cover material selection and processing; the organization of information; reference tools and strategies; and user services. Courses are adapted to educate librarians to use new resources brought about by advancing technology such as on-line reference systems, Internet search methods, and automated circulation systems. Course options can include resources for children or young adults; classification, cataloguing, indexing, and abstracting; library administration; and library automation.

An MLS provides general preparation for library work, but some individuals specialize in a particular area such as reference, technical services, or children's services. A Ph.D. degree in library and information science is advantageous for a college teaching position, or a top administrative job in a college or university library or large library system.

In special libraries, an MLS is also usually required. In addition, most special librarians supplement their education with knowledge of the subject specialization, sometimes earning a master's, doctoral, or professional degree in the subject. Subject specialization include medicine, law, business, engineering, and the natural and social sciences. For example, a librarian working for a law firm may also be a licensed attorney, holding both library science and law degrees. In some jobs, knowledge of a foreign language is needed.

State certification requirements for public school librarians vary widely. Most States require that school librarians, often called library media specialists, be certified as teachers and have courses in library science. In some cases, an MLS, perhaps with a library media specialization, or a master's in education with a specialty in school library media or educational media, is needed. Some States require certification of public librarians employed in municipal, county, or regional library systems.

Librarians participate in continuing training once they are on the job, to keep abreast of new information systems brought about by changing technology.

Experienced librarians may advance to administrative positions, such as department head, library director, or chief information officer.

Job Outlook

Slow employment growth, coupled with an increasing number of MLS graduates will result in more applicants competing for fewer jobs. Applicants for librarian jobs in large cities or suburban areas, where most graduates prefer to work, will face competition; those willing to work in rural areas should have better job prospects.

Some job openings for librarians will stem from projected slower-than-average employment growth through the year 2006, reflecting budgetary constraints in school, public, and college and university libraries. Additional job openings will arise from replacement needs over the next decade, as many librarians reach retirement age. In an effort to reduce costs, however, libraries are reluctant to add new positions and may even reduce staff.

The increasing use of computerized information storage and retrieval systems may contribute to reduced demand for librarians. Computerized systems make cataloguing easier, and this task can now be handled by library technicians. In addition, many libraries are equipped for users to access library computers directly from their homes or offices. These systems allow users to bypass librarians and conduct research on their own. However, librarians are needed to manage staff, help users develop database searching techniques, address complicated reference requests, and define users' needs.

Opportunities will be best for librarians outside traditional settings. Nontraditional library settings include information brokers, private corporations, and consulting firms. Many companies are turning to librarians because of their research and organizational skills, and knowledge of computer databases and library automation systems. Librarians can review the vast amount of information that is available and analyze, evaluate, and organize it according to a company's specific needs. Librarians are also hired by organizations to set up information on the Internet. Librarians working in these settings may be classified as systems analysts, database specialists and trainers, webmasters or web developers, or LAN (local area network) coordinators.

Earnings

Salaries of librarians vary by the individual's qualifications and the type, size, and location of the library.

According to a survey by the American Library Association, the average salary of children's librarians in academic and public libraries was $34,600 in 1996; reference/information librarians averaged $35,800; and cataloguers and classifiers earned $36,600. Beginning librarians with a master's degree but no professional experience averaged $28,700 in 1996.

According to the Special Libraries Association, salaries for special librarians with 2 years or less of library experience averaged $33,100 in 1996, while those with 3 to 5 years of experience averaged $37,400. Salaries for special librarians with primarily administrative responsibilities averaged $58,400.

Salaries for medical librarians with 1 year or less experience averaged $25,900 in 1995, according to the Medical Library Association. The average salary for all medical librarians was $40,800.

The average annual salary for all librarians in the Federal Government in nonsupervisory, supervisory, and managerial positions was $50,400 in 1997.

Related Occupations

Librarians play an important role in the transfer of knowledge and ideas by providing people with access to the information they need and want. Jobs requiring similar analytical, organizational, and communicative skills include archivists, information scientists, museum curators, publishers' representatives, research analysts, information brokers, and records managers. The management aspect of a librarian's work is similar to the work of managers in a variety of business and government settings. School librarians have many duties similar to those of school teachers. Other jobs requiring the computer skills of some librarians include webmasters or web developers, database specialists, and systems analysts.

Sources of Additional Information

Information on librarianship, including information on scholarships or loans, is available from the American Library Association. For a listing of accredited library education programs, check their homepage:

☛ American Library Association, Office for Library Personnel Resources, 50 East Huron St., Chicago, IL 60611. Homepage: http://www.ala.org/

For information on a career as a special librarian, write to:

☛ Special Libraries Association, 1700 18th St. NW., Washington, DC 20009.

Material about a career in information science is available from:

☛ American Society for Information Science, 8720 Georgia Ave., Suite 501, Silver Spring, MD 20910.

Information on graduate schools of library and information science can be obtained from:

☛ Association for Library and Information Science Education, P.O. Box 7640, Arlington, VA 22207. Homepage: http://www.sils.umich.edu/ALISE/

For information on a career as a law librarian, scholarship information, and a list of ALA-accredited schools offering programs in law librarianship, contact:

☛ American Association of Law Libraries, 53 West Jackson Blvd., Suite 940, Chicago, IL 60604.

For information on employment opportunities as a health sciences librarian, scholarship information, credentialing information, and a list of MLA-accredited schools offering programs in health sciences librarianship, contact:

☛ Medical Library Association, 6 N. Michigan Ave., Suite 300, Chicago, IL 60602.

Information on acquiring a job as a librarian with the Federal Government may be obtained from the Office of Personnel Management through a telephone-based system. Consult your telephone directory under U.S. Government for a local number or call (912) 757-3000 (TDD 912 744-2299). That number is not toll-free and charges may result. Information also is available from their Internet site: http://www.usajobs.opm.gov

Information concerning requirements and application procedures for positions in the Library of Congress may be obtained directly from:

☛ Personnel Office, Library of Congress, 101 Independence Ave. SE., Washington, DC 20540.

State library agencies can furnish information on scholarships available through their offices, requirements for certification, and general information about career prospects in the State. Several of these agencies maintain job hotlines reporting openings for librarians.

State departments of education can furnish information on certification requirements and job opportunities for school librarians.

Many library science schools offer career placement services to their alumni and current students. Some allow non-affiliated students and jobseekers to use their services.

Library Technicians

(D.O.T. 100.367-018)

Significant Points

- Training ranges from on-the-job training to a bachelor's degree.

- Employment is expected to grow faster than average as libraries use technicians to perform some librarian duties in an effort to stretch shrinking budgets.

Nature of the Work

Library technicians, commonly called "paraprofessionals," help librarians acquire, prepare, and organize material, and assist users in finding materials and information. Technicians in small libraries handle a wide range of duties; those in large libraries usually specialize. As libraries increasingly use new technologies—such as CD-ROM, the Internet, virtual libraries, and automated databases—the duties of library technicians are expanding and evolving accordingly. Library technicians are assuming greater responsibilities, in some cases taking on tasks previously performed by librarians. (See the statement on librarians elsewhere in the *Handbook.*)

Depending on the employer, library technicians may have other titles, such as library technical assistants. Library technicians direct library users to standard references, organize and maintain periodicals, prepare volumes for binding, handle interlibrary loan requests, prepare invoices, perform routine cataloguing and coding of library materials, retrieve information from computer databases, and supervise other support staff.

The widespread use of computerized information storage and retrieval systems has resulted in technicians handling more technical and user services, such as entering catalogue information into the library's computer, that were once performed by librarians. Technicians may assist with customizing databases. In addition, technicians may instruct patrons how to use computer systems to access data. The increased use of automation has cut down on the amount of clerical work performed by library technicians. Many libraries now offer self-service registration and circulation with computers, decreasing the time library technicians spend manually recording and inputting records.

Some library technicians operate and maintain audiovisual equipment, such as projectors, tape recorders, and videocassette recorders, and assist library users with microfilm or microfiche readers. They may also design posters, bulletin boards, or displays.

Those in school libraries encourage and teach students to use the library and media center. They also help teachers obtain instructional materials and assist students with special assignments. Some work in special libraries maintained by government agencies, corporations, law firms, advertising agencies, museums, professional societies, medical centers, and research laboratories, where they conduct literature searches, compile bibliographies, and prepare abstracts, usually on subjects of particular interest to the organization.

Working Conditions

Technicians who work with library users answer questions and provide assistance. Those who prepare library materials sit at desks or computer terminals for long periods and may develop headaches or eyestrain from working with video display terminals. Some duties, like calculating circulation statistics, can be repetitive and boring. Others, such as performing computer searches using local and regional library networks and cooperatives, can be interesting and challenging.

Library technicians help librarians acquire, prepare, and organize material.

Library technicians in school libraries work regular school hours. Those in public libraries and college and university (academic) libraries may work weekends, evenings and some holidays. Library technicians in special libraries usually work normal business hours, although they are often called upon to work overtime.

Library technicians usually work under the supervision of a professional librarian, although they may work independently in certain situations.

Employment

Library technicians held about 78,000 jobs in 1996. Most worked in school, academic, or public libraries. Some worked in hospitals and religious organizations. The Federal Government, primarily the Department of Defense and the Library of Congress, and State and local governments also employed library technicians.

Training, Other Qualifications, and Advancement

Training requirements for library technicians vary widely, ranging from a high school diploma to specialized postsecondary training. Some employers hire individuals with work experience or other training; others train inexperienced workers on the job. Other employers require that technicians have an associate's or bachelor's degree. Given the rapid spread of automation in libraries, computer skills are needed for many jobs. Knowledge of databases, library automation systems, on-line library systems, on-line public access systems, and circulation systems is valuable.

Some 2-year colleges offer an associate of arts degree in library technology. Programs include both liberal arts and library-related study. Students learn about library and media organization and operation, and how to order, process, catalogue, locate, and circulate library materials and work with library automation. Libraries and associations offer continuing education courses to keep technicians abreast of new developments in the field.

Library technicians usually advance by assuming added responsibilities. For example, technicians may start at the circulation desk, checking books in and out. After gaining experience, they may be responsible for storing and verifying information. As they advance, they may become involved in budget and personnel matters in their department. Some library technicians advance to supervisory positions and are in charge of the day-to-day operation of their department.

Job Outlook

Employment of library technicians is expected to grow faster than the average for all occupations through the year 2006. Many additional job openings will result from the need to replace library technicians who transfer to other fields or leave the labor force. Similar to other fields, willingness to relocate enhances an aspiring library technician's job prospects.

The increasing use of library automation may spur job growth among library technicians. Computerized information systems have simplified certain tasks, such as descriptive cataloguing, which can now be handled by technicians instead of librarians. For instance, technicians can now easily retrieve information from a central database and store it in the library's own computer. Although budgetary constraints may dampen employment growth of library technicians in school, public, and college and university libraries, libraries may use technicians to perform some librarian duties in an effort to stretch shrinking budgets. Growth in the number of professionals and other workers who use special libraries should result in relatively fast employment growth among library technicians in those settings.

Earnings

Salaries for library technicians vary widely, depending on the type of library and geographic location. According to a salary survey by *Library Mosaics Magazine*, library technicians employed in 2-year colleges averaged $27,200 in 1996; in 4-year colleges or universities, $30,200; in special libraries, $24,100; and in public libraries,

$33,000. Salaries of library technicians in the Federal Government averaged $26,500 in 1997.

Related Occupations

Library technicians perform organizational and administrative duties. Workers in other occupations with similar duties include library clerks, information clerks, record clerks, medical record technicians, and title searchers. Library technicians also assist librarians. Other workers who assist professionals include museum technicians, teacher aides, legal assistants, and engineering and science technicians.

Sources of Additional Information

Information about a career as a library technician can be obtained from:
☛ Council on Library/Media Technology, P.O. Box 951, Oxon Hill, MD 20750.

For information on training programs for library/media technical assistants, write to:
☛ American Library Association, Office for Library Personnel Resources, 50 East Huron St., Chicago, IL 60611.

Information on acquiring a job as a library technician with the Federal Government may be obtained from the Office of Personnel Management through a telephone-based system. Consult your telephone directory under U.S. Government for a local number or call (912) 757-3000 (TDD 912 744-2299). That number is not toll-free and charges may result. Information also is available from their Internet site: http://www.usajobs.opm.gov

Information concerning requirements and application procedures for positions in the Library of Congress may be obtained directly from:
☛ Personnel Office, Library of Congress, Washington, DC 20540.

State library agencies can furnish information on requirements for technicians, and general information about career prospects in the State. Several of these agencies maintain job hotlines reporting openings for library technicians.

State departments of education can furnish information on requirements and job opportunities for school library technicians.

School Teachers—Kindergarten, Elementary, and Secondary

(D.O.T. 091.221, .227; 092.227-010, -014; 099.224-010, .227-022)

Significant Points

- Public school teachers must have a bachelor's degree, complete an approved teacher education program, and be licensed; some States require a master's degree.

- Many States offer alternative licensure programs to attract people into teaching and to fill certain jobs.

- Employment growth for secondary school teachers will be more rapid than for kindergarten and elementary school teachers due to student enrollments, but job outlook will vary by geographic area and by subject specialty.

Nature of the Work

Teachers act as facilitators or coaches, using interactive discussions and "hands-on" learning to help students learn and apply concepts in subjects such as science, mathematics, or English. As teachers move away from the traditional repetitive drill approaches and rote memorization, they are using more "props" or "manipulatives" to help children understand abstract concepts, solve problems, and develop critical thought processes. For example, they teach the concepts of numbers or adding and subtracting by playing board games. As children get older, they use more sophisticated materials such as tape recorders, science apparatus, cameras, or computers.

Many classes are becoming less structured, with students working in groups to discuss and solve problems together. Preparing students for the future workforce is the major stimulus generating the changes in education. To be prepared, students must be able to interact with others, adapt to new technology, and logically think through problems. Teachers provide the tools and environment for their students to develop these skills.

Kindergarten and elementary school teachers play a vital role in the development of children. What children learn and experience during their early years can shape their views of themselves and the world, and affect later success or failure in school, work, and their personal lives. Kindergarten and elementary school teachers introduce children to numbers, language, science, and social studies. They use games, music, artwork, films, slides, computers, and other tools to teach basic skills.

Most elementary school teachers instruct one class of children in several subjects. In some schools, two or more teachers work as a team and are jointly responsible for a group of students in at least one subject. In other schools, a teacher may teach one special subject—usually music, art, reading, science, arithmetic, or physical education—to a number of classes. A small but growing number of teachers instruct multilevel classrooms, with students at several different learning levels.

Secondary school teachers help students delve more deeply into subjects introduced in elementary school and expose them to more information about the world and themselves. Secondary school teachers specialize in a specific subject, such as English, Spanish, mathematics, history, or biology. They teach a variety of related courses—for example, American history, contemporary American problems, and world geography.

Special education teachers—who instruct elementary and secondary school students who have a variety of disabilities—are discussed separately in this section of the *Handbook*.

Teachers may use films, slides, overhead projectors, and the latest technology in teaching, including computers, telecommunication systems, and video discs. Use of computer resources, such as educational software and the Internet, exposes students to a vast range of experiences and promotes interactive learning. Through the Internet, American students can communicate with students in other countries to share personal experiences. Students also use the Internet for individual research projects and information gathering. Computers are used in other classroom activities as well, from helping students solve math problems to learning English as a second language. Teachers may also use computers to record grades and for other administrative and clerical duties. Teachers must continually update their skills to use the latest technology in the classroom.

Teachers often work with students from varied ethnic, racial, and religious backgrounds. With growing minority populations in many parts of the country, it is important for teachers to establish rapport with a diverse student population. Accordingly, some schools offer training to help teachers enhance their awareness and understanding of different cultures. Teachers may also include multicultural programming in their lesson plans to address the needs of all students, regardless of their cultural background.

Classroom presentations are designed by teachers to meet student needs and abilities. They also work with students individually. Teachers plan, evaluate, and assign lessons; prepare, administer, and grade tests; listen to oral presentations; and maintain classroom discipline. They observe and evaluate a student's performance and potential, and increasingly use new assessment methods. For example, teachers may examine a portfolio of a student's artwork or writing at the end of a learning period to judge the student's overall progress. They then provide additional assistance in areas where a student needs help. Teachers also grade papers, prepare report cards, and meet with parents and school staff to discuss a student's academic progress or personal problems.

In addition to classroom activities, teachers oversee study halls and homerooms and supervise extracurricular activities. They identify physical or mental problems and refer students to the proper resource or agency for diagnosis and treatment. Secondary school teachers occasionally assist students in choosing courses, colleges, and careers. Teachers also participate in education conferences and workshops.

In recent years, site-based management, which allows teachers and parents to participate actively in management decisions, has gained popularity. In many schools, teachers are increasingly involved in making decisions regarding the budget, personnel, textbook choices, curriculum design, and teaching methods.

Working Conditions

Seeing students develop new skills and gain an appreciation of knowledge and learning can be very rewarding. However, teaching may be frustrating when dealing with unmotivated and disrespectful students. Teachers may also experience stress when dealing with large classes, students from disadvantaged or multicultural backgrounds, and heavy workloads.

Teachers face isolation from their colleagues since they often work alone in a classroom of students. However, this autonomy provides teachers considerable freedom to choose their own teaching styles and methods.

Including school duties performed outside the classroom, many teachers work more than 40 hours a week. Most teachers work the traditional 10-month school year with a 2-month vacation during the summer. Those on the 10-month schedule may teach in summer sessions, take other jobs, travel, or pursue other personal interests. Many enroll in college courses or workshops to continue their education.

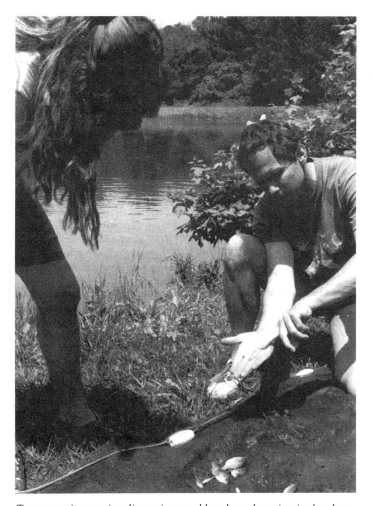

Teams use interactive discussions and hands-on learning in the classroom.

Teachers in districts with a year-round schedule typically work 8 weeks, are on vacation for 1 week, and have a 5-week midwinter break.

Most States have tenure laws that prevent teachers from being fired without just cause and due process. Teachers may obtain tenure after they have satisfactorily completed a probationary period of teaching, normally 3 years. Tenure does not absolutely guarantee a job, but it does provide some security.

Employment

Teachers held about 3.1 million jobs in 1996. Of those, about 1.7 million were kindergarten and elementary school teachers, and 1.4 million were secondary school teachers. Employment is distributed geographically, much the same as the population.

Training, Other Qualifications, and Advancement

All 50 States and the District of Columbia require public school teachers to be licensed. Licensure is not required for teachers in private schools. Usually licensure is granted by the State board of education or a licensure advisory committee. Teachers may be licensed to teach the early childhood grades (usually nursery school through grade 3); the elementary grades (grades 1 through 6 or 8); the middle grades (grades 5 through 8); a secondary education subject area (usually grades 7 through 12); or a special subject, such as reading or music (usually grades K through 12).

Requirements for regular licenses vary by State. However, all States require a bachelor's degree and completion of an approved teacher training program with a prescribed number of subject and education credits and supervised practice teaching. Some States require specific minimum grade point averages for teacher licensure. Some States require teachers to obtain a master's degree in education, which involves at least 1 year of additional coursework beyond the bachelor's degree with a specialization in a particular subject.

Almost all States require applicants for teacher licensure to be tested for competency in basic skills such as reading and writing, teaching skills, or subject matter proficiency. Most States require continuing education for renewal of the teacher's license. Many States have reciprocity agreements that make it easier for teachers licensed in one State to become licensed in another.

Increasingly, many States are moving towards implementing performance-based standards for licensure, which require passing a rigorous comprehensive teaching examination to obtain provisional licensure, and then demonstrating satisfactory teaching performance over an extended period of time to obtain full licensure.

Many States offer alternative teacher licensure programs for people who have bachelor's degrees in the subject they will teach, but lack the necessary education courses required for a regular license. Alternative licensure programs were originally designed to ease teacher shortages in certain subjects, such as mathematics and science. The programs have expanded to attract other people into teaching, including recent college graduates and midcareer changers. In some programs, individuals begin teaching quickly under provisional licensure. After working under the close supervision of experienced educators for 1 or 2 years while taking education courses outside school hours, they receive regular licensure if they have progressed satisfactorily. Under other programs, college graduates who do not meet licensure requirements take only those courses that they lack, and then become licensed. This may take 1 or 2 semesters of full-time study. States may issue emergency licenses to individuals who do not meet requirements for a regular license when schools cannot attract enough qualified teachers to fill positions. Teachers who need licensure may enter programs that grant a master's degree in education, as well as licensure.

In recent years, the National Board for Professional Teaching Standards began offering voluntary national certification for teachers. To become nationally certified, teachers must prove their aptitude by compiling a portfolio showing their work in the classroom, and by passing a written assessment and evaluation of their teaching knowledge. A teacher who is nationally certified may find it easier to obtain employment in another State. Certified teachers may also earn higher salaries, have more senior titles, and be eligible for more bonuses than non-certified teachers. While all States recognize national certification, however, many States have not established policies on specific benefits of holding national certification, such as salary differentials or reimbursement of certification fees.

The National Council for Accreditation of Teacher Education currently accredits over 500 teacher education programs across the United States. Generally, 4-year colleges require students to wait until their sophomore year before applying for admission to teacher education programs. Traditional education programs for kindergarten and elementary school teachers include courses—designed specifically for those preparing to teach—in mathematics, physical science, social science, music, art, and literature, as well as prescribed professional education courses, such as philosophy of education, psychology of learning, and teaching methods. Aspiring secondary school teachers either major in the subject they plan to teach while also taking education courses, or major in education and take subject courses. Teacher education programs are now required to include classes in the use of computers and other technologies to maintain accreditation. Most programs require students to perform student teaching.

Many States now offer professional development schools, which are partnerships between universities and elementary or secondary schools. Students enter these 1-year programs after completion of their bachelor's degree. Professional development schools merge theory with practice and allow the student to experience a year of teaching first-hand, with professional guidance.

In addition to being knowledgeable in their subject, the ability to communicate, inspire trust and confidence, and motivate students, as well as understand their educational and emotional needs, is essential for teachers. Teachers must be able to recognize and respond to individual differences in students, and employ different teaching methods that will result in high student achievement. They also should be organized, dependable, patient, and creative. Teachers must also be able to work cooperatively and communicate effectively with other teaching staff, support staff, parents, and other members of the community.

With additional preparation, teachers may move into positions as school librarians, reading specialists, curriculum specialists, or guidance counselors. Teachers may become administrators or supervisors, although the number of these positions is limited and competition for these desirable positions can be intense. In some systems, highly qualified, experienced teachers can become senior or mentor teachers, with higher pay and additional responsibilities. They guide and assist less experienced teachers while keeping most of their teaching responsibilities.

Job Outlook

The job market for teachers varies widely by geographic area and by subject specialty. Many inner cities—characterized by high crime rates, high poverty rates, and overcrowded conditions—and rural areas—characterized by their remote location and relatively low salaries—have difficulty attracting enough teachers, so job prospects should continue to be better in these areas than in suburban districts. Currently, many school districts have difficulty hiring qualified teachers in some subjects—mathematics, science (especially chemistry and physics), bilingual education, and computer science. Specialties that currently have an abundance of qualified teachers include general elementary education, English, art, physical education, and social studies. Teachers who are geographically mobile and who obtain licensure in more than one subject should have a distinct advantage in finding a job. With enrollments of minorities increasing, coupled with a shortage of minority teachers, efforts to recruit minority teachers should intensify. Also, the number of non-English speaking students has grown dramatically, especially in California and Florida which have large Spanish-speaking student populations, creating demand for bilingual teachers and those who speak English as a second language (ESL).

Overall employment of kindergarten, elementary, and secondary school teachers is expected to increase about as fast as the average for all occupations through the year 2006. The expected retirement of a large number of teachers currently in their 40s and 50s should open up many additional jobs. However, projected employment growth varies among individual teaching occupations.

Employment of secondary school teachers is expected to grow faster than the average for all occupations through the year 2006, while average employment growth is projected for kindergarten and elementary school teachers. Assuming relatively little change in average class size, employment growth of teachers depends on population growth rates and corresponding student enrollments. Enrollment of 14- to 17-year-olds is expected to grow through the year 2006 (see chart 1). Enrollment of 5- to 13-year olds also is projected to increase, but at a slower rate, through the year 2002, and then decline (see chart 2).

The number of teachers employed is also dependent on State and local expenditures for education. Pressures from taxpayers to limit spending could result in fewer teachers than projected; pressures to spend more to improve the quality of education could increase the teacher workforce.

The supply of teachers also is expected to increase in response to reports of improved job prospects, more teacher involvement in school policy, and greater public interest in education. In recent years, the total number of bachelor's and master's degrees granted in education has steadily increased. In addition, more teachers will be drawn from a reserve pool of career changers, substitute teachers, and teachers completing alternative certification programs, relocating to different schools, and reentering the workforce.

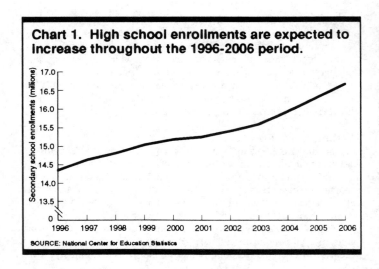

Chart 1. High school enrollments are expected to increase throughout the 1996-2006 period.

SOURCE: National Center for Education Statistics

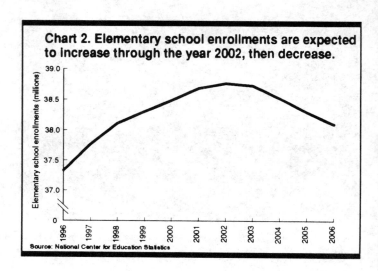

Chart 2. Elementary school enrollments are expected to increase through the year 2002, then decrease.

Source: National Center for Education Statistics

Earnings

According to the National Education Association, the estimated average salary of all public elementary and secondary school teachers in the 1995-96 school year was $37,900. Public secondary school teachers averaged about $38,600 a year, while public elementary school teachers averaged $37,300. Private school teachers generally earn less than public school teachers.

In 1996, over half of all public school teachers belonged to unions—mainly the American Federation of Teachers and the National Education Association—that bargain with school systems over wages, hours, and the terms and conditions of employment.

In some schools, teachers receive extra pay for coaching sports and working with students in extracurricular activities. Some teachers earn extra income during the summer working in the school system or in other jobs.

Related Occupations

Kindergarten, elementary, and secondary school teaching requires a wide variety of skills and aptitudes, including a talent for working with children; organizational, administrative, and recordkeeping abilities; research and communication skills; the power to influence, motivate, and train others; patience; and creativity. Workers in other occupations requiring some of these aptitudes include college and university faculty, counselors, education administrators, employment interviewers, librarians, preschool teachers, public relations specialists, sales representatives, social workers, and trainers and employee development specialists.

Sources of Additional Information

Information on licensure or certification requirements and approved teacher training institutions is available from local school systems and State departments of education.

Information on teachers' unions and education-related issues may be obtained from:

☛ American Federation of Teachers, 555 New Jersey Ave. NW., Washington, DC 20001.

☛ National Education Association, 1201 16th St. NW., Washington, DC 20036.

A list of institutions with accredited teacher education programs can be obtained from:

☛ National Council for Accreditation of Teacher Education, 2010 Massachusetts Ave. NW., Suite 500, Washington, DC 20036.

For information on voluntary national teacher certification requirements, contact:

☛ National Board for Professional Teaching Standards, 26555 Evergreen Rd., Suite 400, Southfield, MI 48076.

Special Education Teachers

(D.O.T. 094.107, .224, .227, .267; 099.227-042; 195.227-018)

Significant Points

● A bachelor's degree, completion of an approved teacher preparation program, and a license are required; many States require a master's degree.

● Many States offer alternative licensure programs to attract people into special education teaching jobs.

● Job openings arising from rapid employment growth and job turnover, coupled with a declining number of graduates from special education teaching programs, mean excellent job prospects; many school districts report shortages of qualified teachers.

Nature of the Work

Special education teachers work with children and youth who have a variety of disabilities. Most special education teachers instruct students at the elementary, middle, and secondary school level, although some teachers work with infants and toddlers. Special education teachers design and modify instruction to meet a student's special needs. Teachers also work with students who have other special instructional needs, including those who are gifted and talented.

The various types of disabilities delineated in Government special education programs include specific learning disabilities, mental retardation, speech or language impairment, serious emotional disturbance, visual and hearing impairment, orthopedic impairment, autism, traumatic brain injury, and multiple disabilities. Students are classified under one of the categories, and special education teachers are prepared to work with specific groups.

Special education teachers use various techniques to promote learning. Depending on the disability, teaching methods can include individualized instruction, problem-solving assignments, and group or individual work. Special education teachers are legally required to help develop an Individualized Education Program (IEP) for each special education student. The IEP sets personalized goals for each student and is tailored to a student's individual learning style and ability. This program includes a transition plan outlining specific steps to prepare special education students for middle school or high school, or in the case of older students, a job or postsecondary study. Teachers review the IEP with the student's parents, school administrators, and often the student's general education teacher. Teachers work closely with parents to inform them of their child's progress and suggest techniques to promote learning at home.

Teachers design curricula, assign work geared toward each student's ability, and grade papers and homework assignments. Special education teachers are involved in a student's behavioral as well as academic development. They help special education students develop emotionally, be comfortable in social situations, and be aware of socially acceptable behavior. Preparing special education students for daily life after graduation is an important aspect of the job. Teachers may help students with routine skills, such as balancing a check book, or provide them with career counseling.

As schools have become more inclusive, special education teachers and general education teachers increasingly work together in general education classrooms. Special education teachers help general educators adapt curriculum materials and teaching techniques to meet the needs of students with disabilities.

Special education teachers work in a variety of settings. Some have their own classrooms and teach classes comprised entirely of special education students; others work as special education resource teachers and offer individualized help to students in general education classrooms; and others teach along with general education teachers in classes composed of both general and special education students. Some teachers work in a resource room, where special education students work several hours a day, separate from their general education classroom. A significantly smaller proportion of special education teachers work in residential facilities or tutor students in homebound or hospital environments. Special education teachers who work with infants usually travel to the child's home to work with the child and his or her parents.

A large part of a special education teacher's job involves interacting with others. They communicate frequently with parents, social workers, school psychologists, occupational and physical therapists, school administrators, and other teachers.

Early identification of a child with special needs is another important part of a special education teacher's job. Early intervention is essential in educating these children.

Technology is playing an increasingly important role in special education. Special education teachers use specialized equipment such as computers with synthesized speech, interactive educational software programs, and audio tapes.

Working Conditions

Helping students with disabilities achieve goals, and making a difference in their lives can be highly rewarding. Special education teachers

Special education teachers design and modify instruction to meet a student's special needs.

enjoy the challenge of working with these students and the opportunity to establish meaningful relationships. However, the work can also be emotionally and physically draining. Special education teachers are under considerable stress due to heavy workloads and tedious administrative tasks. They must produce a substantial amount of paperwork documenting each student's progress. Exacerbating this stress is the threat of litigation by students' parents if correct procedures are not followed, or if the parent feels their child is not receiving an adequate education. Some special educators feel they are not adequately supported by school administrators, and feel isolated from general education teachers. The physical and emotional demands of the job result in a high "burnout" rate.

Many schools offer year-round education for special education students, but most special education teachers work the traditional 10-month school year with a 2-month vacation during the summer.

Employment

Special education teachers held about 407,000 jobs in 1996. The majority of special education teachers were employed in elementary, middle, and secondary public schools. The rest worked in separate educational facilities—public or private—residential facilities, or in homebound or hospital environments.

Training, Other Qualifications, and Advancement

All 50 States and the District of Columbia require special education teachers to be licensed. Special education licensure varies by State. In many States, special education teachers receive a general education credential to teach kindergarten through grade 12. These teachers train in a specialty, such as learning disabilities or behavioral disorders. Some States offer general special education licensure, others license several different specialties within special education, while others require teachers to first obtain general education licensure and then additional licensure in special education. Usually licensure is granted by the State board of education or a licensure advisory committee.

All States require a bachelor's degree and completion of an approved teacher preparation program with a prescribed number of subject and education credits and supervised practice teaching. Many States require special education teachers to obtain a master's degree in special education, involving at least one year of additional coursework, including a specialization, beyond the bachelor's degree.

Some States have reciprocity agreements allowing special education teachers to transfer their licensure from one State to another, but many still require special education teachers to pass licensure requirements for that State. National certification standards for special

education teachers are currently being developed by the National Board for Professional Teaching Standards.

About 700 colleges and universities across the United States offer programs in special education, including undergraduate, master's, and doctoral programs. Special education teachers usually undergo longer periods of training than general education teachers. Most bachelor's degree programs are 4-year programs including general and specialized courses in special education. However, an increasing number of institutions require a fifth year or other postbaccalaureate preparation. Courses include educational psychology, legal issues of special education, child growth and development, and knowledge and skills needed for teaching students with disabilities. Some programs require a specialization. Others offer generalized special education degrees, or study in several specialized areas. The last year of the program is usually spent student teaching in a classroom supervised by a certified teacher.

Alternative and emergency licensure is available in many States, due to the need to fill special education teaching positions. Alternative licensure is designed to bring college graduates and those changing careers into teaching more quickly. Requirements for alternative licensure may be less stringent than for regular licensure and vary by State. In some programs, individuals begin teaching quickly under provisional licensure. They can obtain regular licensure by teaching under the supervision of licensed teachers for a period of 1 to 2 years while taking education courses. Emergency licensure is enacted when States are having difficulty finding licensed special education teachers to fill positions.

Special education teachers must be patient, able to motivate students, understanding of their students' special needs, and accepting of differences in others. Teachers must be creative and apply different types of teaching methods to reach students who are having difficulty. Communication and cooperation are essential traits because special education teachers spend a great deal of time interacting with others, including students, parents, and school faculty and administrators.

Special education teachers can advance to become supervisors or administrators. They may also earn advanced degrees and become instructors in colleges that prepare others for special education teaching. In some school systems, highly experienced teachers can become mentor teachers to less experienced ones; they provide guidance to these teachers while maintaining a light teaching load.

Job Outlook

Special education teachers have excellent job prospects, as many school districts report shortages of qualified teachers. Job outlook varies by geographic area and specialty. Positions in rural areas and inner cities are more plentiful than job openings in suburban or wealthy urban areas. Also, job opportunities may be better in certain specialties—such as speech or language impairments, and learning

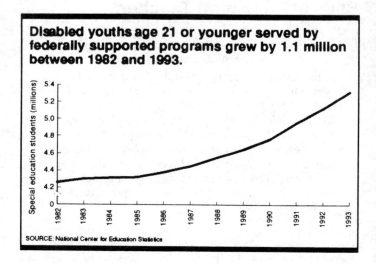

Disabled youths age 21 or younger served by federally supported programs grew by 1.1 million between 1982 and 1993.

SOURCE: National Center for Education Statistics

disabilities—due to the considerable shortages of teachers in these fields. Recent legislation encouraging early intervention and special education for infants, toddlers, and preschoolers has created a need for early childhood special education teachers. Special education teachers who are bilingual or have multicultural experience are also needed to work with an increasingly diverse student population.

Employment of special education teachers is expected to increase much faster than the average for all occupations through the year 2006, spurred by continued growth in the number of special education students needing services, legislation emphasizing training and employment for individuals with disabilities, growing public interest in individuals with special needs, and educational reform. The high "burnout" rate will lead to many additional job openings as special education teachers switch to general education or change careers altogether. Rapid employment growth and job turnover, coupled with a declining number of graduates from special education teaching programs, should result in a very favorable job market.

The number of students requiring special education services has been steadily increasing, as indicated by the accompanying chart. This trend is expected to continue due to legislation which expanded the age range of children receiving special education services to include those from birth to age 21; medical advances resulting in more survivors of accidents and illness; the postponement of childbirth by more women, resulting in a greater number of premature births and children born with birth defects; and growth in the general population.

The growing use of inclusive school settings, which integrate special education students into general education settings, will also lead to more reliance on special education teachers. The role of these teachers is expanding to include acting as a consultant to general education teachers, in addition to teaching special education students in resource rooms, general education classrooms, and separate classrooms made up entirely of special education students.

Earnings

Salaries of special education teachers follow the same scale as those for general education teachers. According to the National Education Association, the estimated average salary of all public elementary and secondary school teachers in the 1995-96 school year was $37,900. Public secondary school teachers averaged about $38,600 a year, while public elementary school teachers averaged $37,300. Private school teachers generally earn less than public school teachers.

In 1996, over half of all public school teachers belonged to unions—mainly the American Federation of Teachers and the National Education Association—that bargain with school systems over wages, hours, and the terms and conditions of employment.

In some schools, teachers receive extra pay for coaching sports and working with students in extracurricular activities. Some teachers earn extra income during the summer, working in the school system or in other jobs.

Related Occupations

Special education teachers work with students who have disabilities and special needs. Other occupations involved with the identification, evaluation, and development of students with disabilities include school psychologists, social workers, speech pathologists, rehabilitation counselors, adapted physical education teachers, special education technology specialists, and occupational, physical, creative arts, and recreational therapists.

Sources of Additional Information

For information on a career as a special education teacher, a list of accredited schools, financial aid information, and general information on special education-related personnel issues, contact:

☛ National Clearinghouse for Professions in Special Education, Council for Exceptional Children, 1920 Association Dr., Reston, VA 20191. Homepage: http://www.cec.sped.org

To learn more about the special education teacher certification and licensing requirements in your State, contact your State's department of education.

Health Diagnosing Occupations

Chiropractors

(D.O.T. 079.101-010)

Significant points

- Employment of chiropractors is expected to increase rapidly and job prospects should be good.

- Chiropractic treatment of back, neck, extremities, and other joint damage has become more accepted as a result of recent research and changing attitudes.

- In chiropractic, as in other types of independent practice, earnings are relatively low in the beginning, and increase as the practice grows.

Nature of the Work

Chiropractors, also known as doctors of chiropractic or chiropractic physicians, diagnose and treat patients whose health problems are associated with the body's muscular, nervous, and skeletal systems, especially the spine. Chiropractors believe interference with these systems impairs normal functions and lowers resistance to disease. They also hold that spinal or vertebral dysfunction alters many important body functions by affecting the nervous system, and that skeletal imbalance through joint or articular dysfunction, especially in the spine, can cause pain.

The chiropractic approach to health care is holistic, stressing the patient's overall well-being. It recognizes that many factors affect health, including exercise, diet, rest, environment, and heredity. Chiropractors use natural, drugless, nonsurgical health treatments, and rely on the body's inherent recuperative abilities. They also recommend lifestyle changes—in eating, exercise, and sleeping habits, for example—to their patients. When appropriate, chiropractors consult with and refer patients to other health practitioners.

Like other health practitioners, chiropractors follow a standard routine to secure the information needed for diagnosis and treatment: They take the patient's medical history, conduct physical, neurological, and orthopedic examinations, and may order laboratory tests. X rays and other diagnostic images are important tools because of the emphasis on the spine and its proper function. Chiropractors also employ a postural and spinal analysis common to chiropractic diagnosis.

In cases in which difficulties can be traced to involvement of musculoskeletal structures, chiropractors manually manipulate or adjust the spinal column. Many chiropractors also use water, light, massage, ultrasound, electric, and heat therapy and may apply supports such as straps, tapes, and braces. They may also counsel patients about wellness concepts such as nutrition, exercise, lifestyle changes, and stress management, but do not prescribe drugs or perform surgery.

Some chiropractors specialize in sports injuries, neurology, orthopedics, nutrition, internal disorders, or diagnostic imaging.

Many chiropractors are solo or group practitioners who also have the administrative responsibilities of running a practice. In larger offices, chiropractors delegate these tasks to office managers

Chiropractors need considerable hand dexterity to perform manipulations.

and chiropractic assistants. Chiropractors in private practice are responsible for developing a patient base, hiring employees, and keeping records.

Working Conditions

Chiropractors work in clean, comfortable offices. The average workweek is about 42 hours, although longer hours are not uncommon. Solo practitioners set their own hours, but may work evenings or weekends to accommodate patients.

Chiropractors who take x rays employ appropriate precautions against the dangers of repeated exposure to radiation.

Employment

Chiropractors held about 44,000 jobs in 1996. About 70 percent of active chiropractors are in solo practice. The remainder are in group practice or work for other chiropractors. A small number teach, conduct research at chiropractic institutions, or work in hospitals and clinics.

Many chiropractors are located in small communities. There are geographic imbalances in the distribution of chiropractors, in part because many establish practices close to chiropractic institutions.

Training, Other Qualifications, and Advancement

All States and the District of Columbia regulate the practice of chiropractic and grant licenses to chiropractors who meet educational requirements and pass a State board examination. Chiropractors can only practice in States where they are licensed. Some States have agreements that permit chiropractors licensed in one State to obtain a license in another without further examination.

Most State licensing boards require completion of a 4-year chiropractic college course following at least 2 years of undergraduate education, although a few States require a bachelor's degree. All State boards recognize academic training in chiropractic programs and institutions accredited by the Council on Chiropractic Education.

For licensure, most State boards recognize either all or part of the four-part test administered by the National Board of Chiropractic Examiners. State examinations may supplement the National Board tests, depending on State requirements.

To maintain licensure, almost all States require completion of a specified number of hours of continuing education each year. Continuing education programs are offered by accredited chiropractic programs and institutions, and chiropractic associations. Special councils within some chiropractic associations also offer programs leading to clinical specialty certification, called "diplomate" certification, in areas such as orthopedics, neurology, sports injuries, occupational and industrial health, nutrition, diagnostic imaging, thermography, and internal disorders.

In 1997, there were 16 chiropractic programs and institutions in the United States accredited by the Council on Chiropractic Education. All required applicants to have at least 60 semester hours of undergraduate study leading toward a bachelor's degree, including courses in English, the social sciences or humanities, organic and inorganic chemistry, biology, physics, and psychology. Many applicants have a bachelor's degree, which may eventually become the minimum entry requirement. Several chiropractic colleges offer prechiropractic study, as well as a bachelor's degree program.

During the first 2 years, most chiropractic programs emphasize classroom and laboratory work in basic science subjects such as anatomy, physiology, public health, microbiology, pathology, and biochemistry. The last 2 years stress courses in manipulation and spinal adjustments, and provide clinical experience in physical and laboratory diagnosis, neurology, orthopedics, geriatrics, physiotherapy, and nutrition. Chiropractic programs and institutions grant the degree of Doctor of Chiropractic (D.C.).

Chiropractic requires keen observation to detect physical abnormalities. It also takes considerable hand dexterity to perform manipulations, but not unusual strength or endurance. Chiropractors should be able to work independently and handle responsibility. As in other health-related occupations, empathy, understanding, and the desire to help others are good qualities for dealing effectively with patients.

Newly licensed chiropractors can set up a new practice, purchase an established one, or enter into partnership with an established practitioner. They may also take a salaried position with an established chiropractor, a group practice, or a health care facility.

Job Outlook

Job prospects are expected to be good for persons who enter the practice of chiropractic. Employment of chiropractors is expected to grow faster than the average for all occupations through the year 2006 as consumer demand for alternative medicine grows. Chiropractors emphasize the importance of healthy lifestyles and do not prescribe drugs or perform surgery. As a result, chiropractic care is appealing to many health-conscious Americans. Chiropractic treatment of back, neck, extremities, and other joint damage has become more accepted as a result of recent research and changing attitudes. The rapidly expanding older population, with their increased likelihood of mechanical and structural problems, will also increase demand.

Demand for chiropractic treatment is also related to the ability of patients to pay, either directly or through health insurance. Although more insurance plans now cover chiropractic services, details of such coverage vary among plans. Increasingly, chiropractors must educate communities about the benefits of chiropractic care, in order to establish a successful practice.

In this occupation, replacement needs arise almost entirely from re-tirements. Chiropractors generally remain in the occupation until they retire; few transfer to other occupations. Establishing a new practice will be easiest in areas with a low concentration of chiropractors.

Earnings
In 1995, median income for chiropractors was about $80,000, after expenses, according to the American Chiropractic Association. In chiropractic, as in other types of independent practice, earnings are relatively low in the beginning, and increase as the practice grows. In 1995, the lowest 10 percent of chiropractors had median net incomes of $30,000 or less, and the highest 10 percent earned $170,000 or more. Earnings are also influenced by the characteristics and qualifications of the practitioner, and geographic location. Self-employed chiropractors must provide for their own health insurance and retirement.

Related Occupations
Chiropractors treat and work to prevent bodily disorders and injuries. So do physicians, dentists, optometrists, podiatrists, veterinarians, occupational therapists, and physical therapists.

Sources of Additional Information
General information on chiropractic as a career is available from:
☛ American Chiropractic Association, 1701 Clarendon Blvd., Arlington, VA 22209.
☛ International Chiropractors Association, 1110 North Glebe Rd., Suite 1000, Arlington, VA 22201.
☛ World Chiropractic Alliance, 2950 N. Dobson Rd., Suite 1, Chandler, AZ 85224-1802.

For a list of chiropractic programs and institutions, as well as gen-eral information on chiropractic education, contact:
☛ Council on Chiropractic Education, 7975 North Hayden Rd., Suite A-210, Scottsdale, AZ 85258.

For information on State education and licensure requirements, contact:
☛ Federation of Chiropractic Licensing Boards, 901 54th Ave., Suite 101, Greeley, CO 80634.

For information on requirements for admission to a specific chi-ropractic college, as well as scholarship and loan information, contact the admissions office of the individual college.

Dentists

(D.O.T. 072, except .117)

Significant points

- Most dentists have at least 8 years of education beyond high school but they have very high earnings.

- Employment of dentists is expected to grow slower than the average as the middle-aged and elderly population re-quires more dental care, but young people are troubled less by tooth decay.

- If the number of dentists being trained increases signifi-cantly above present levels, job seekers may face competition.

Nature of the Work
Dentists diagnose, prevent, and treat problems of the teeth and tissues of the mouth. They remove decay, fill cavities, examine x rays, place protective plastic sealants on children's teeth, straighten teeth, and repair fractured teeth. They also perform corrective surgery of the gums and supporting bones to treat gum diseases. Dentists extract teeth and make molds and measurements for dentures to replace missing teeth. Dentists provide instruction in diet, brushing, flossing,

the use of fluorides, and other aspects of dental care, as well. They also administer anesthetics and write prescriptions for antibiotics and other medications.

Dentists use a variety of equipment, including x-ray machines, drills, and instruments such as mouth mirrors, probes, forceps, brushes, and scalpels.

Dentists in private practice oversee a variety of administrative tasks, including bookkeeping, and buying equipment and supplies. They may employ and supervise dental hygienists, dental assistants, dental laboratory technicians, and receptionists. (These occupations are described elsewhere in the *Handbook*.)

Most dentists are general practitioners, handling a wide variety of dental needs. Other dentists practice in one of eight specialty areas. Orthodontists, the largest group of specialists, straighten teeth. The next largest group, oral and maxillofacial surgeons, operate on the mouth and jaws. The remainder specialize in pediatric dentistry (dentistry for children); periodontics (treating the gums and the bone supporting the teeth); prosthodontics (making artificial teeth or den-tures); endodontics (root canal therapy); dental public health; and oral pathology (studying diseases of the mouth).

Working Conditions
Most dentists work 4 or 5 days a week. Some work evenings and weekends to meet their patients' needs. Most full-time dentists work about 40 hours a week, but others work more. Younger den-tists may work more hours as they establish their practice; older

Most dentists run their own practice and work alone or with a small staff.

dentists often work fewer hours. A considerable number continue in part-time practice well beyond the usual retirement age.

Most dentists are "solo practitioners," meaning they own their own businesses and work alone or with a small staff. Some dentists have partners, and a few work for other dentists as associate dentists.

Dentists wear masks, gloves, and safety glasses to protect themselves and their patients from infectious diseases, such as hepatitis.

Employment

Dentists held about 162,000 jobs in 1996. About 9 out of 10 dentists are in private practice. Others work in private and public hospitals and clinics, and in dental research.

Training, Other Qualifications, and Advancement

All 50 States and the District of Columbia require dentists to be licensed. To qualify for a license in most States, a candidate must graduate from a dental school accredited by the American Dental Association's Commission on Dental Accreditation, and pass written and practical examinations. Candidates may fulfill the written part of the State licensing by passing the National Board Dental Examinations. Individual States or regional testing agencies give the written and/or practical examinations.

Currently, about 17 States require dentists to obtain a specialty license before practicing as a specialist. Requirements include 2 to 4 years of post graduate education and, in some cases, completion of a special State examination. Most State licenses permit dentists to engage in both general and specialized practice. Dentists who want to teach or do research usually spend an additional 2 to 5 years in advanced dental training, in programs operated by dental schools or hospitals.

Dental schools require a minimum of 2 years of college-level predental education. However, most dental students have at least a bachelor's degree. Predental education emphasizes course work in the sciences.

All dental schools require applicants to take the Dental Admissions Test (DAT). They consider scores earned on the DAT, the applicants' overall grade point average (GPA), science course GPA, and information gathered through recommendations and interviews when selecting students.

Dental school generally lasts 4 academic years. Studies begin with classroom instruction and laboratory work in basic sciences including anatomy, microbiology, biochemistry, and physiology. Beginning courses in clinical sciences, including laboratory technique courses, are also provided at this time. During the last 2 years, students treat patients, usually in dental clinics, under the supervision of licensed dentists.

Most dental schools award the degree of Doctor of Dental Surgery (D.D.S.). The rest award an equivalent degree, Doctor of Dental Medicine (D.M.D.).

Dentistry requires diagnostic ability and manual skills. Dentists should have good visual memory, excellent judgment of space and shape, a high degree of manual dexterity, and scientific ability. Good business sense, self-discipline, and communication skills are helpful for success in private practice. High school students who want to become dentists should take courses in biology, chemistry, physics, health, and mathematics.

Some recent dental school graduates work for established dentists as associates for a year or two in order to gain experience and save money to equip an office of their own. Most dental school graduates, however, purchase an established practice or open a new practice immediately after graduation. Each year about one-fourth to one-third of new graduates enroll in postgraduate training programs to prepare for a dental specialty.

Job Outlook

Employment of dentists is expected to grow slower than the average for all occupations through the year 2006. While employment growth will provide some job opportunities, most jobs will result from the need to replace the large number of dentists projected to retire. Job prospects should be good if the number of dental school graduates does not grow significantly, thus keeping the supply of newly qualified dentists near current levels. There is cause for some concern about the outlook, however, because the number of first-year enrollees in dental school programs has increased over enrollment in the late 1980s. If the number of enrollees continues to increase, there will be a larger pool of dentists, and job seekers may face competition.

Demand for dental care should grow substantially through 2006. As members of the baby-boom generation advance into middle age, a large number will need maintenance on complicated dental work, such as bridges. In addition, elderly people are more likely to retain their teeth than their predecessors, so they will require much more care than in the past. The younger generation will continue to need preventive check-ups despite treatments such as fluoridation of the water supply, which decreases the incidence of tooth decay.

However, the employment of dentists is not expected to grow as rapidly as the demand for dental services. As their practices expand, dentists are likely to hire more dental hygienists and dental assistants to handle routine services they now perform themselves.

Earnings

According to the American Dental Association, median net income of dentists in private practice was about $120,000 a year in 1995. Median net income for those in specialty practice was about $175,000 a year, and for those in general practice, about $109,000 a year. Dentists in the beginning years of their practice often earn less, while those in mid-careers earn more.

A relatively large proportion of dentists are self-employed. Like other business owners, these dentists must provide their own health insurance, life insurance, and retirement benefits.

Related Occupations

Dentists examine, diagnose, prevent, and treat diseases and abnormalities. So do clinical psychologists, optometrists, physicians, chiropractors, veterinarians, and podiatrists.

Sources of Additional Information

For information on dentistry as a career and a list of accredited dental schools, contact:

☛ American Dental Association, Commission on Dental Accreditation, 211 E. Chicago Ave., Chicago, IL 60611.

☛ American Association of Dental Schools, 1625 Massachusetts Ave. NW., Washington, DC 20036. Homepage: http://www.ada.org

The American Dental Association will also furnish a list of State boards of dental examiners. Persons interested in practicing dentistry should obtain the requirements for licensure from the board of dental examiners of the State in which they plan to work.

Prospective dental students should contact the office of student financial aid at the schools to which they apply, for information on scholarships, grants, and loans, including Federal financial aid.

Optometrists

(D.O.T. 079.101-018)

Significant points

- All States and the District of Columbia require that optometrists be licensed. Applicants for a license must have a Doctor of Optometry degree from an accredited optometry school and pass both a written and a clinical State board examination.

- Although many optometrists practice alone, a growing number are in a partnership or group practice.

- Because optometrists generally remain in practice until they retire, the number of job openings arising from the need to replace optometrists who leave the occupation is low.

Nature of the Work

Over half the people in the United States wear glasses or contact lenses. Optometrists (doctors of optometry, also known as O.D.'s) provide most of the primary vision care people need.

Optometrists examine people's eyes to diagnose vision problems and eye diseases. They use instruments and observation to examine eye health and to test patients' visual acuity, depth and color perception, and their ability to focus and coordinate the eyes. They analyze test results and develop a treatment plan. Optometrists prescribe eyeglasses and contact lenses, and provide vision therapy and low vision rehabilitation. They use drugs for diagnosis of eye vision problems and prescribe drugs to treat some eye diseases. Optometrists often provide pre- and post-operative care to cataract and other eye surgery patients. They also diagnose conditions due to systemic diseases such as diabetes and high blood pressure, and refer patients to other health practitioners as needed.

Optometrists should not be confused with ophthalmologists or dispensing opticians. Ophthalmologists are physicians who perform eye surgery, and diagnose and treat eye diseases and injuries. Like optometrists, they also examine eyes and prescribe eyeglasses and contact lenses. Dispensing opticians fit and adjust eyeglasses and in some States may fit contact lenses according to prescriptions written by ophthalmologists or optometrists. (See statements on physicians and dispensing opticians elsewhere in the *Handbook.*)

Most optometrists are in general practice. Some specialize in work with the elderly, children, or partially sighted persons who need specialized visual devices to improve their vision. Others develop and implement ways to protect workers' eyes from on-the-job strain or injury. Some specialize in contact lenses, sports vision, or vision therapy. A few teach optometry, do research, or consult.

Most optometrists are private practitioners who also handle the business aspects of running an office, such as developing a patient base, hiring employees, keeping records, and ordering equipment and supplies. Optometrists who operate franchise optical stores may also have some of these duties.

Working Conditions

Optometrists work in places—usually their own offices—that are clean, well lighted, and comfortable. The work requires attention to detail and good manual dexterity. Most full-time optometrists work about 40 hours a week, but a substantial number work more than 50

An optometrist conducts an eye examination to diagnose vision problems and eye diseases.

hours a week. Many work Saturdays and evenings to suit the needs of patients, but emergency calls are rare.

Employment

Optometrists held about 41,000 jobs in 1996. The number of jobs is greater than the number of practicing optometrists because some optometrists hold two or more jobs. For example, an optometrist may have a private practice, but also work in another practice, clinic, or vision care center. According to the American Optometric Association, about two-thirds of practicing optometrists are in private practice.

Although many optometrists practice alone, a growing number are in a partnership or group practice. Some optometrists work as salaried employees of other optometrists or of ophthalmologists, hospitals, health maintenance organizations (HMO's), or retail optical stores. A small number of optometrists are consultants for industrial safety programs, insurance companies, manufacturers of ophthalmic products, HMO's, and others.

Training, Other Qualifications, and Advancement

All States and the District of Columbia require that optometrists be licensed. Applicants for a license must have a Doctor of Optometry degree from an accredited optometry school and pass both a written and a clinical State board examination. In many States, applicants can substitute the examinations of the National Board of Examiners in Optometry, usually taken during the student's academic career, for part or all of the written examination. Licenses are renewed every 1 to 3 years and in all States, continuing education credits are needed for renewal.

The Doctor of Optometry degree requires completion of a 4-year program at an accredited optometry school preceded by at least 3 years of preoptometric study at an accredited college or university (most optometry students hold a bachelor's degree). In 1997, 17 U.S. schools and colleges of optometry held an accredited status with the Council on Optometric Education of the American Optometric Association.

Requirements for admission to schools of optometry include courses in English, mathematics, physics, chemistry, and biology. A few schools require or recommend courses in psychology, history, sociology, speech, or business. Applicants must take the Optometry Admissions Test, which measures academic ability and scientific comprehension. Most applicants take the test after their sophomore or junior year. Competition for admission is keen.

Optometry programs include classroom and laboratory study of health and visual sciences, as well as clinical training in the diagnosis and treatment of eye disorders. Included are courses in pharmacology, optics, vision science, biochemistry, and systemic disease.

Business ability, self-discipline, and the ability to deal tactfully with patients are important for success.

Optometrists wishing to teach or do research may study for a master's or Ph.D. degree in visual science, physiological optics, neurophysiology, public health, health administration, health information and communication, or health education. One-year postgraduate clinical residency programs are available for optometrists who wish to specialize in family practice optometry, pediatric optometry, geriatric optometry, vision therapy, contact lenses, hospital based optometry, primary care optometry, or ocular disease.

Job Outlook

Employment of optometrists is expected to grow about as fast as the average for all occupations through the year 2006 in response to the vision care needs of a growing and aging population. As baby boomers age, they will be more likely to visit optometrists and ophthalmologists because of the onset of vision problems in middle age, including computer-related vision problems. The demand for optometric services will also increase because of growth in the oldest age group, with their increased likelihood of cataracts, glaucoma, diabetes, and hypertension. Employment of optometrists will also grow due to greater recognition of the importance of vision care, rising personal incomes, and growth in employee vision care plans.

Employment of optometrists would grow more rapidly were it not for anticipated productivity gains which will allow each optometrist to see more patients. These gains will result from greater use of optometric assistants and other support personnel, and the introduction of new equipment and procedures. New surgical procedures using lasers are available that can correct some vision problems, but they remain expensive.

In addition to growth, the need to replace optometrists who leave the occupation will create employment opportunities. Relatively few opportunities from this source are expected, however, because most optometrists continue to practice until they retire; few transfer to other occupations.

Earnings
According to the American Optometric Association, new optometry graduates in their first year of practice earned median net incomes of $57,500 in 1996. Overall, optometrists earned median net incomes of $80,000.

Incomes vary depending upon location, specialization, and other factors. Salaried optometrists tend to earn more initially than optometrists who set up their own independent practice. In the long run, those in private practice generally earn more.

Related Occupations
Workers in other occupations who apply scientific knowledge to prevent, diagnose, and treat disorders and injuries are chiropractors, dentists, physicians, podiatrists, veterinarians, speech-language pathologists, and audiologists.

Sources of Additional Information
For information on optometry as a career and a listing of accredited optometric educational institutions, as well as required preoptometry courses, contact:
☞ American Optometric Association, Educational Services, 243 North Lindbergh Blvd., St. Louis, MO 63141-7881. Homepage: http://www.aoanet.org/aoanet
☞ Association of Schools and Colleges of Optometry, 6110 Executive Blvd., Suite 510, Rockville, MD 20852. Homepage: http://www.opted.org

The Board of Optometry in each State can supply information on licensing requirements.

For information on specific admission requirements and sources of financial aid, contact the admissions officer of individual optometry schools.

Physicians

(D.O.T. 070 and 071)

Significant points

- Amid reports of an oversupply of physicians, opportunities will be best in primary care fields of general and family medicine, internal medicine, and general pediatrics.

- Physicians are much more likely to work as salaried employees of group medical practices, clinics, or health care networks than in the past.

- It takes many years of education and training to become a physician, but earnings are among the highest of any occupation.

Nature of the Work
Physicians serve a fundamental role in our society and have an effect upon all our lives. They diagnose illnesses and prescribe and administer treatment for people suffering from injury or disease. Physicians examine patients, obtain medical histories, and order, perform, and interpret diagnostic tests. They counsel patients on diet, hygiene, and preventive health care.

There are two types of physicians: The M.D.—Doctor of Medicine —and the D.O.—Doctor of Osteopathic Medicine. M.D.'s are also known as allopathic physicians. While M.D.'s and D.O.'s may use all accepted methods of treatment, including drugs and surgery, D.O.'s place special emphasis on the body's musculoskeletal system, preventive medicine, and holistic patient care.

About one third of M.D.'s are primary care physicians. They practice general and family medicine, general internal medicine, or general pediatrics and are usually the first health professionals patients consult. Primary care physicians tend to see the same patients on a regular basis for preventive care and to treat a variety of ailments. General and family practitioners emphasize comprehensive health care for patients of all ages and for the family as a group. Those in general internal medicine provide care mainly for adults who have a wide range of problems associated with the body's organs. General pediatricians focus on children's health. When appropriate, primary care physicians refer patients to specialists, who are experts in medical fields such as obstetrics and gynecology, cardiology, psychiatry, or surgery (See table 1). D.O.'s are more likely to be primary care providers than allopathic physicians, although they can be found in all specialties.

Table 1. Percent distribution of M.D.'s by specialty, 1995

	Percent
Total	100.0
Primary care	
General internal medicine	16.0
General and family medicine	10.5
General pediatrics	7.0
Medical specialties	
Allergy	.5
Cardiovascular diseases	2.6
Dermatology	1.2
Gastroenterology	1.3
Obstetrics and gynecology	5.2
Pediatric cardiology	.2
Pulmonary diseases	1.0
Surgical specialties	
Colon and rectal surgery	.1
General surgery	5.2
Neurological surgery	.7
Ophthalmology	2.4
Orthopedic surgery	3.1
Otalaryngology	1.3
Plastic surgery	.8
Thoracic surgery	.3
Urological surgery	1.4
Other specialties	
Aerospace medicine	.1
Anesthesiology	4.6
Child psychiatry	.8
Diagnostic radiology	2.7
Emergency medicine	2.7
Forensic pathology	.1
General preventive medicine	.2
Neurology	1.6
Nuclear medicine	.2
Occupational medicine	.4
Pathology	2.5
Physical medicine and rehabilitation	.8
Psychiatry	5.3
Public health	.2
Radiology	1.1
Radiation oncology	.5
Other specialty	1.0
Unspecified/unknown/inactive	14.4

SOURCE: American Medical Association

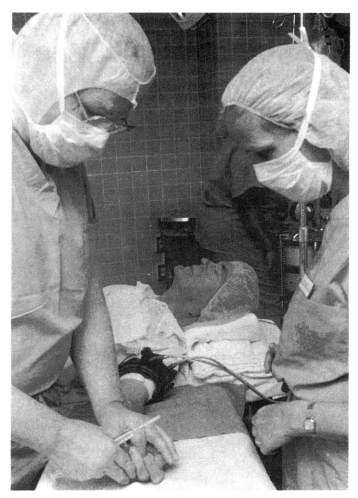

Prospective physicians must have a desire to serve patients, be self-motivated, and be able to survive the pressures and long hours of medical education and practice.

Working Conditions

Many physicians work long, irregular hours. About one-third of all full-time physicians worked 60 hours or more a week in 1996. They must travel frequently between office and hospital to care for their patients. Increasingly, physicians practice in groups or health care organizations that provide back-up coverage and allow for more time off. These physicians work as part of a team that coordinates care for a population of patients; they are less independent than solo practitioners of the past. Physicians who are on-call deal with many patients' concerns over the phone, and may make emergency visits to hospitals.

Employment

Physicians (M.D.'s and D.O.'s) held about 560,000 jobs in 1996. About 7 out of 10 were in office-based practice, including clinics and HMO's; about 2 out of 10 were employed by hospitals. Others practiced in the Federal Government, most in Department of Veterans Affairs hospitals and clinics or in the Public Health Service of the Department of Health and Human Services.

A growing number of physicians are partners or salaried employees of group practices. Organized as clinics or as groups of physicians, medical groups can afford expensive medical equipment and realize other business advantages. Also, hospitals are integrating physician practices into health care networks that provide a continuum of care both inside and outside of the hospital setting.

The Northeastern and Western States have the highest ratio of physicians to population; the South Central States, the lowest. D.O.'s are more likely than M.D.'s to practice in small cities and towns and in rural areas. M.D.'s tend to locate in urban areas, close to hospital and educational centers.

Osteopathic physicians locate chiefly in States that have osteopathic schools and hospitals. In 1997, about one-half of active D.O.'s practiced in six States: Pennsylvania, Michigan, Ohio, Florida, New Jersey, and Texas.

Training and Other Qualifications

It takes many years of education and training to become a physician: 4 years of undergraduate school, 4 years of medical school, and 3 to 8 years of internship and residency, depending on the specialty selected. A few medical schools offer a combined undergraduate and medical school program that lasts 6 years instead of the customary 8 years.

Premedical students must complete undergraduate work in physics, biology, mathematics, English, and inorganic and organic chemistry. Students also take courses in the humanities and the social sciences. Some students also volunteer at local hospitals or clinics to gain practical experience in the health professions.

The minimum educational requirement for entry to a medical or osteopathic school is 3 years of college; most applicants, however, have at least a bachelor's degree, and many have advanced degrees. There are 142 medical schools in the United States—125 teach allopathic medicine and award a Doctor of Medicine (M.D.); 17 teach osteopathic medicine and award the Doctor of Osteopathy (D.O.). Acceptance to medical school is very competitive. Applicants must submit transcripts, scores from the Medical College Admission Test, and letters of recommendation. Schools also consider character, personality, leadership qualities, and participation in extracurricular activities. Most schools require an interview with members of the admissions committee.

Students spend most of the first 2 years of medical school in laboratories and classrooms taking courses such as anatomy, biochemistry, physiology, pharmacology, psychology, microbiology, pathology, medical ethics, and laws governing medicine. They also learn to take medical histories, examine patients, and diagnose illness. During the last 2 years, students work with patients under the supervision of experienced physicians in hospitals and clinics to learn acute, chronic, preventive, and rehabilitative care. Through rotations in internal medicine, family practice, obstetrics and gynecology, pediatrics, psychiatry, and surgery, they gain experience in the diagnosis and treatment of illness.

Following medical school, almost all M.D.'s enter a residency—graduate medical education in a specialty that takes the form of paid on-the-job training, usually in a hospital. Most D.O.'s serve a 12-month rotating internship after graduation before entering a residency which may last 2 to 6 years. Physicians may benefit from residencies in managed care settings by gaining experience with this increasingly common type of medical practice.

All States, the District of Columbia, and U.S. territories license physicians. To be licensed, physicians must graduate from an accredited medical school, pass a licensing examination, and complete 1 to 7 years of graduate medical education. Although physicians licensed in one State can usually get a license to practice in another without further examination, some States limit reciprocity. Graduates of foreign medical schools can qualify for licensure after passing an examination and completing a U.S. residency.

M.D.'s and D.O.'s seeking board certification in a specialty may spend up to 7 years—depending on the specialty—in residency training. A final examination immediately after residency, or after 1 or 2 years of practice, is also necessary for board certification by the American Board of Medical Specialists (ABMS) or the American Osteopathic Association (AOA). There are 24 specialty boards, ranging from allergy and immunology to urology. For certification in a subspecialty, physicians usually need another 1 to 2 years of residency.

A physician's training is costly. While education costs have increased, student financial assistance has not. Over 80 percent of medical students borrow money to cover their expenses.

People who wish to become physicians must have a desire to serve patients, be self-motivated, and be able to survive the pressures and long hours of medical education and practice. Physicians must also have a good bedside manner, emotional stability, and the ability to make decisions in emergencies. Prospective physicians must be willing to study throughout their career to keep up with medical advances. They will also need to be flexible to respond to the changing demands of a rapidly evolving health care system.

Job Outlook

Employment of physicians will grow faster than the average for all occupations through the year 2006 due to continued expansion of the health care industries. The growing and aging population will drive overall growth in the number of physicians. In addition, new technologies permit more intensive care: Physicians can do more tests, perform more procedures, and treat conditions previously regarded as untreatable. Job prospects will be best for primary care physicians such as general and family practitioners, general pediatricians, and general internists; and for geriatric and preventive care specialists.

Because of efforts to control health care costs and increased reliance on utilization guidelines that often limit the use of specialty services, a lower percentage of specialists will be in demand. At the same time, the number of specialists continues to grow. Competition for jobs among specialists will be especially keen in large urban and suburban areas, and for those who work directly for hospitals, such as anesthesiologists and radiologists.

A number of prestigious organizations, including the National Academy of Sciences Institute of Medicine and the Pew Health Professions Commission, have found a current oversupply of physicians. They suggest that measures should be taken to reduce the number being trained through such means as a reduction in the number of residency slots. If successful, a reduction in the number of new physicians entering the workforce will help to alleviate the effects of any physician oversupply.

A physician oversupply may not substantially limit the ability of physicians to find employment. However, it could result in physicians working fewer hours, having lower earnings, and having to practice in underserved areas. Opportunities should be good in some rural and low income areas, because some physicians find these areas unattractive due to lower earnings potential, isolation from medical colleagues, or other reasons. It is also possible that physicians trained in specialties will provide primary care services as well as specialty care.

Unlike their predecessors, newly trained physicians face radically different choices of where and how to practice. New physicians are much less likely to enter solo practice and more likely to take salaried jobs in group medical practices, clinics, and health care networks.

Earnings

Physicians have among the highest earnings of any occupation. According to the American Medical Association, median income, after expenses, for allopathic physicians was about $160,000 in 1995. The middle 50 percent earned between $115,000 and $238,000. Self-employed physicians—those who own or are part owners of their medical practice—had higher median incomes than salaried physicians. Earnings vary according to number of years in practice; geographic region; hours worked; and skill, personality, and professional reputation. As shown in table 2, median income of allopathic physicians, after expenses, also varies by specialty.

Average salaries of medical residents ranged from $32,789 in 1996-97 for those in their first year of residency to $40,849 for those in their sixth year, according to the Association of American Medical Colleges.

Table 2. Median net income of M.D.'s after expenses, 1995

All physicians	$160,000
Radiology	230,000
Surgery	225,000
Anesthesiology	203,000
Obstetrics/gynecology	200,000
Pathology	185,000
Emergency medicine	170,000
General internal medicine	138,000
Pediatrics	129,000
Psychiatry	124,000
General/Family practice	124,000

SOURCE: American Medical Association

Related Occupations

Physicians work to prevent, diagnose, and treat diseases, disorders, and injuries. Professionals in other occupations that require similar kinds of skill and critical judgment include acupuncturists, audiologists, chiropractors, dentists, nurse practitioners, optometrists, physician assistants, podiatrists, speech pathologists, and veterinarians.

Sources of Additional Information

For a list of allopathic medical schools and residency programs, as well as general information on premedical education, financial aid, and medicine as a career, contact:

☛ American Medical Association, 515 N. State St., Chicago, IL 60610.
☛ Association of American Medical Colleges, Section for Student Services, 2450 N St. NW., Washington, DC 20037-1131. Homepage: http://www.aamc.org

For general information on osteopathic medicine as a career, contact:

☛ American Osteopathic Association, Department of Public Relations, 142 East Ontario St., Chicago, IL 60611. Homepage: http://www.am-osteo-assn.org
☛ American Association of Colleges of Osteopathic Medicine, 5550 Friendship Blvd., Suite 310, Chevy Chase, MD 20815-7321. Homepage: http://www.aacom.org

Information on Federal scholarships and loans is available from the directors of student financial aid at schools of allopathic and osteopathic medicine.

Information on licensing is available from State boards of examiners.

Podiatrists

(D.O.T. 079.101-022)

Significant points

- A limited number of job openings for podiatrists is expected because the occupation is small and most podiatrists remain in the occupation until they retire.

- Most podiatrists are solo practitioners, although more are entering partnerships and multi-specialty group practices.

- Podiatrists enjoy very high earnings.

Nature of the Work

The human foot is a complex structure. It contains 26 bones—plus muscles, nerves, ligaments, and blood vessels—and is designed for balance and mobility. The 52 bones in your feet make up about one fourth of all the bones in your body. Podiatrists, also known as doctors of podiatric medicine (DPM's), diagnose and treat disorders, diseases, and injuries of the foot and lower leg to keep this part of the body working properly.

Podiatrists treat corns, calluses, ingrown toenails, bunions, heel spurs, and arch problems; ankle and foot injuries, deformities and infections; and foot complaints associated with diseases such as diabetes. To treat these problems, podiatrists prescribe drugs, order physical therapy, set fractures, and perform surgery. They also fit corrective inserts called orthotics, design plaster casts and strappings to correct deformities, and design custom-made shoes. Podiatrists may use a force plate to help design the orthotics. Patients walk across a plate connected to a computer that "reads" the patients' feet. From the computer readout, podiatrists order the correct design.

To diagnose a foot problem, podiatrists order x rays and laboratory tests. The foot may be the first area to show signs of serious conditions such as arthritis, diabetes, and heart disease. For example, diabetics are prone to foot ulcers and infections due to poor circulation. Podiatrists consult with and refer patients to other health practitioners when they detect symptoms of these disorders.

Most podiatrists have a general practice. Some specialize in surgery, orthopedics, primary care, or public health. Besides these board-certified specialties, podiatrists may practice a subspecialty such as sports medicine, pediatrics, dermatology, radiology, geriatrics, or diabetic foot care. Podiatrists generally are in private practice, which means they run a small business. They may hire employees, order supplies, and keep records.

Working Conditions
Podiatrists usually work independently in their own offices. They may also spend time visiting patients in nursing homes or performing

A podiatrist examines a patient's feet to diagnose and treat disorders, diseases, and injuries of the foot and lower leg.

surgery at a hospital, but generally have fewer after-hours emergencies than other doctors. Those with private practices set their own hours, but to meet the needs of their patients, they may work evenings and weekends.

Employment
Podiatrists held about 11,000 jobs in 1996. Most podiatrists are solo practitioners, although more are entering partnerships and multispecialty group practices. Others are employed in hospitals, nursing homes, the U.S. Public Health Service, and the Department of Veterans Affairs.

Training, Other Qualifications, and Advancement
All States and the District of Columbia require a license for the practice of podiatric medicine. Each defines its own licensing requirements. Generally, the applicant must be a graduate of an accredited college of podiatric medicine and pass written and oral examinations. Some States permit applicants to substitute the examination of the National Board of Podiatric Examiners, given in the second and fourth years of podiatric medical college, for part or all of the written State examination. Most States also require completion of a postdoctoral residency program. Most States grant reciprocity to podiatrists who are licensed in another State. Most States require continuing education for licensure renewal.

Prerequisites for admission to a college of podiatric medicine include the completion of at least 90 semester hours of undergraduate study, an acceptable grade point average, and suitable scores on the Medical College Admission Test (MCAT). All require 8 semester hours each of biology, inorganic chemistry, organic chemistry, and physics, and 6 hours of English. The science courses should be those designed for pre-medical students. Potential podiatric medical students may also be evaluated on the basis of extracurricular and community activities, personal interviews, and letters of recommendation. Over 90 percent of podiatric students have at least a bachelor's degree.

Colleges of podiatric medicine offer a 4-year program whose core curriculum is similar to that in other schools of medicine. During the first 2 years, students receive classroom instruction in basic sciences, including anatomy, chemistry, pathology, and pharmacology. Third- and fourth-year students have clinical rotations in private practices, hospitals, and clinics. During these rotations, they learn how to take general and podiatric histories, perform routine physical examinations, interpret tests and findings, make diagnoses, and perform therapeutic procedures. Graduates receive the doctor of podiatric medicine (DPM) degree.

Most graduates complete a hospital residency program after receiving a DPM. Residency programs last from 1 to 3 years. Residents receive advanced training in podiatric medicine and surgery and serve clinical rotations in anesthesiology, internal medicine, pathology, radiology, emergency medicine, and orthopedic and general surgery. Residencies lasting more than 1 year provide more extensive training in specialty areas.

There are a number of certifying boards for the podiatric specialties of orthopedics, primary medicine, or surgery. Certification means that the DPM meets higher standards than those required for licensure. Each board requires advanced training, completion of written and oral examinations, and experience as a practicing podiatrist. Most managed care organizations prefer board-certified podiatrists.

People planning a career in podiatry should have scientific aptitude, manual dexterity, interpersonal skills, and good business sense.

Podiatrists may advance to become professors at colleges of podiatric medicine, department chiefs of hospitals, or general health administrators.

Job Outlook
Employment of podiatrists is expected to grow about as fast as the average for all occupations through the year 2006. More people will turn to podiatrists for foot care as the elderly population grows. The

elderly have more years of wear and tear on their feet and legs than most younger people, so they are more prone to foot ailments. Injuries sustained by an increasing number of men and women of all ages leading active lifestyles will also spur demand for podiatric care.

In addition to growth, the need to replace podiatrists who leave the occupation will create employment opportunities. Relatively few opportunities from this source are expected, however, because most podiatrists continue to practice until they retire; few transfer to other occupations. Even when combined, the number of job openings resulting from both growth and replacement needs is very low because the occupation is small.

Medicare and most private health insurance programs cover acute medical and surgical foot services, as well as diagnostic x rays and leg braces. Details of such coverage vary among plans. However, routine foot care—including the removal of corns and calluses—is ordinarily not covered, unless the patient has a systemic condition that has resulted in severe circulatory problems or areas of desensitization in the legs or feet. Like dental services, podiatric care is more dependent on disposable income than other medical services.

Employment of podiatrists would grow even faster were it not for continued emphasis on controlling the costs of specialty health care. Insurers will balance the cost of sending patients to podiatrists against the cost and availability of substitute practitioners, such as physicians and physical therapists. Opportunities will be better for board-certified podiatrists, because many managed care organizations require board-certification. Opportunities for newly trained podiatrists will be better in group medical practices, clinics, and health networks than in a traditional solo practice. Establishing a practice will be most difficult in the areas surrounding colleges of podiatric medicine because podiatrists are concentrated in these locations.

Earnings
According to a survey by *Podiatry Management*, median net income of podiatrists was about $91,400 in 1996. Earnings vary according to practice size and location, and years of experience.

According to a survey by the American Podiatric Medical Association, average net income for podiatrists in private practice was $108,156 in 1995. Those practicing for less than 2 years earned an average of $44,662; those practicing 16 to 30 years earned an average of $141,135.

Related Occupations
Workers in other occupations who apply scientific knowledge to prevent, diagnose, and treat disorders and injuries are chiropractors, dentists, optometrists, physicians, and veterinarians.

Sources of Additional Information
For information on podiatric medicine as a career, contact:
☛ American Podiatric Medical Association, 9312 Old Georgetown Rd., Bethesda, MD 20814-1621. Homepage: http://www.apma.org

Information on colleges of podiatric medicine, entrance requirements, curriculums, and student financial aid is available from:
☛ American Association of Colleges of Podiatric Medicine, 1350 Piccard Dr., Suite 322, Rockville, MD 20850-4307. Homepage: http://www.aacpm.org

Veterinarians
(D.O.T. 073.)

Significant Points
- Graduation from an accredited college of veterinary medicine and a license to practice are required.
- Competition for admission to veterinary school is keen.
- Job prospects may be better for those who specialize in farm animals than for small animal practitioners because fewer graduates have a desire to work in rural and isolated areas.

Nature of the Work
Veterinarians play a major role in the health care of pets, livestock, and zoo, sporting, and laboratory animals. Veterinarians also use their skills to protect humans against diseases carried by animals, and conduct clinical research on human and animal health problems.

Most veterinarians perform clinical work in private practices. About one-half of these veterinarians predominately or exclusively treat small animals. Small animal practitioners usually care for companion animals, such as dogs and cats, but also treat birds, reptiles, rabbits, and other animals that may be kept as pets. Some veterinarians work in mixed animal practices, where they see pigs, goats, sheep, and some nondomestic animals, in addition to companion animals. Veterinarians in clinical practice diagnose animal health problems, vaccinate against diseases such as distemper and rabies, medicate animals with infections or illnesses, treat and dress wounds, set fractures, perform surgery, and advise owners about feeding, behavior, and breeding.

A smaller number of private practice veterinarians work exclusively with large animals, focusing mostly on horses or cows, but may care for all kinds of food animals. These veterinarians usually drive to farms or ranches to provide veterinary services for herds or individual animals. Much of their work involves preventive care in order to maintain the health of food animals. They test for and vaccinate against diseases, and consult with farm or ranch owners and managers on production, feeding, and housing issues. They also treat and dress wounds, set fractures, perform surgery—including cesarean sections on birthing animals—and do artificial insemination. Veterinarians also euthanize animals when necessary.

Veterinarians who treat animals use surgical instruments; medical equipment, such as stethoscopes; and diagnostic equipment, such as radiology machines.

Veterinarians contribute to human as well as animal health. A number of veterinarians work with physicians and scientists as they research better ways to prevent and treat human health problems such as cancer, AIDS, and alcohol or drug abuse. Some test the effects of drug therapies, antibiotics, or new surgical techniques on animals. Veterinarians who are livestock inspectors check animals for transmissible diseases, advise owners on treatment, and may quarantine animals. Veterinarians who are meat, poultry, or egg product inspectors examine slaughtering and processing plants, check live animals and carcasses for disease, and enforce government regulations regarding food purity and sanitation. Some veterinarians care for zoo or aquarium animals, or for laboratory animals.

Working Conditions
Veterinarians often work long hours, with nearly half spending 50 or more hours on the job. Those in group practices may take turns being on call for evening, night, or weekend work, and solo practitioners may work extended and weekend hours responding to emergencies and squeezing in unexpected appointments.

Veterinarians in large animal practice also spend time driving between office and farm or ranch. They work outdoors in all kinds of weather, and may have to treat animals or perform surgery under less-than-sanitary conditions. When working with animals that are frightened or in pain, veterinarians risk being bitten, kicked, or scratched.

Employment
Veterinarians held about 58,000 jobs in 1996. About a third were self-employed, in solo or group practices. Most others were employees of a practice. The Federal Government employed about 2,000 civilian veterinarians, chiefly in the U.S. Department of Agriculture, and about 500 military veterinarians in the U.S. Army and U.S. Air Force. Other employers of veterinarians are State and local governments, colleges of veterinary medicine, medical schools, research laboratories, animal food companies, and pharmaceutical companies. A few veterinarians work for zoos. Most veterinarians caring for zoo animals are private practitioners who contract with zoos to provide services, usually on a part-time basis.

Self-employed veterinarians comprise about one-third of the profession and often work extended or weekend hours.

Although veterinarians are located in every State, in 1996 about 3 out of 10 establishments providing veterinary services were located in just four States: California, Florida, New York, and Texas.

Training, Other Qualifications, and Advancement

Prospective veterinarians must graduate from a 4-year program at an accredited college of veterinary medicine with a Doctor of Veterinary Medicine (D.V.M. or V.M.D.) degree and obtain a license to practice. There are 27 colleges in 26 States that meet accreditation standards set by the Council on Education of the American Veterinary Medical Association. The prerequisites for admission vary by veterinary medical college. Many do not actually require a bachelor's degree for entrance, but all require a significant number of credit hours at the undergraduate level, ranging from 45 to 90 semester hours. Preveterinary courses emphasize the sciences, and veterinary medical colleges typically require classes in organic and inorganic chemistry, physics, biochemistry, general biology, animal biology, animal nutrition, genetics, vertebrate embryology, cell or microbiology, zoology, and systemic physiology. Some programs require calculus; some require only statistics, college algebra and trigonometry, or precalculus; and others require no math at all. Most veterinary medical colleges also require some core courses, including English or literature, social science, and the humanities. Although a bachelor's degree is generally not required for entry to veterinary medical school, most of the students admitted have completed an undergraduate program.

Most veterinary medical colleges will only consider applicants who have a minimum grade point average (GPA). The required GPA varies by school from a low of 2.5 to a high of 3.2, based on a maximum GPA of 4.0. However, the average GPA of candidates at most schools is higher than these minimums. Those who receive offers of admission usually have a GPA of 3.0 or better.

In addition to satisfying preveterinary course requirements, applicants must also submit test scores from the Graduate Record Examination (GRE), the Veterinary College Admission Test (VCAT), or the Medical College Admission Test (MCAT), depending on the preference of each college.

Veterinary medical colleges also weigh heavily a candidate's veterinary and animal experience in the admissions process. Formal experience, such as work with veterinarians or scientists in clinics, agribusiness, research, or in some area of health science, is particularly advantageous. Less formal experience, such as working with animals on a farm, ranch, stable, or animal shelter, is also helpful. Students must demonstrate ambition and eagerness to work with animals.

Competition for admission to veterinary school is keen. The number of accredited veterinary colleges has remained at 27 since 1983, while the number of applicants has risen. About 1 in 3 applicants was accepted in 1996. Most veterinary medical colleges are public, State-supported institutions, and reserve the majority of their openings for in-State residents. Twenty States that do not have a veterinary medical college agree to pay a fee or subsidy to help cover the cost of veterinary education for a limited number of their residents at one or more out-of-State colleges. Nonresident students who are admitted under such a contract arrangement may have to pay out-of-State tuition, or they may have to repay their State of residency all or part of the subsidy that was provided to the contracting college. Residents of the remaining four States and the District of Columbia may apply to any of the 27 veterinary medical colleges as an "at-large" applicant. The number of positions available to "at-large" applicants is very limited at most schools, making admission difficult.

While in veterinary medical college, students receive additional academic instruction and are exposed to clinical procedures such as diagnosing and treating animal diseases and performing surgery. They also do laboratory work in anatomy, biochemistry, and other scientific and medical subjects. At most veterinary medical colleges, students who plan a career in research can earn both a D.V.M degree and a Doctor of Philosophy (Ph.D.) degree at the same time.

Veterinary graduates who plan to work with specific types of animals or specialize in a clinical area, such as pathology, surgery, radiology, or laboratory animal medicine, usually complete a 1-year internship. Interns receive only a small salary, but usually find that their internship experience leads to higher starting salaries relative to other starting veterinarians. Veterinarians who seek board certification in a specialty must also complete a 2- to 3-year residency program which provides intensive training in one of the following areas: Internal medicine, oncology, radiology, surgery, dermatology, anesthesiology, neurology, cardiology, ophthalmology, or exotic small animal medicine.

All States and the District of Columbia require that veterinarians be licensed before they can practice. The only exemptions are for veterinarians working for some Federal agencies and some State governments. Licensing is controlled by the States and is not strictly uniform, although all States require successful completion of the D.V.M. degree—or equivalent education—and passage of a national board examination. The Educational Commission for Foreign Veterinary Graduates (ECFVG) grants certification to individuals trained outside the U.S. who demonstrate that they meet specified English language and clinical proficiency requirements. ECFVG certification fulfills the educational requirement for licensure in all States except Nebraska.

Applicants for licensure satisfy the examination requirement by passing the National Board Examination (NBE) and the Clinical Competency Test (CCT). The NBE comprises 400 multiple choice questions covering all aspects of veterinary medicine and takes one day to complete. The CCT is a half-day examination consisting of 14 problems covering real-life situations in which the candidate is given a set of facts and must choose the correct course of action for the patient. Many States permit candidates to take the NBE in their third year of veterinary school, but those who pass must still graduate with the D.V.M. before they can be licensed.

The majority of States also require candidates to pass a State jurisprudence examination, covering State laws and regulations. Some States also do additional testing on clinical competency. There are very few reciprocal agreements between States, making it difficult for a veterinarian to practice in a new State without first taking another State examination.

Thirty-nine States have continuing education requirements for licensed veterinarians. Requirements differ by State, and may involve attending a class or otherwise demonstrating knowledge of recent medical and veterinary advances.

Most veterinarians begin as employees or partners in established practices. Despite the substantial financial investment in equipment, office space, and staff, many veterinarians with experience set up their own practice or purchase an established one.

Newly trained veterinarians may become U.S. Government meat and poultry inspectors, disease-control workers, epidemiologists, research assistants, or commissioned officers in the U.S. Public Health Service, U.S. Army, or U.S. Air Force. A State license may be required.

Prospective veterinarians must have good manual dexterity. They should have an affinity for animals and the ability to get along with animal owners. They must also be able to make decisions in emergencies.

Job Outlook

Employment of veterinarians is expected to grow faster than the average for all occupations through the year 2006. Job openings stemming from the need to replace veterinarians who retire or otherwise leave the labor force will be almost as numerous as new jobs resulting from employment growth over the 1996-2006 period.

Most veterinarians practice in animal hospitals or clinics, many of whom care primarily for companion animals. The number of pets is expected to increase more slowly during the projection period than in the previous decade, partly because the large baby-boom generation is aging and will acquire fewer dogs and cats. Slower pet population growth may curtail the demand for veterinarians who specialize in small animals. Nevertheless, new technologies and medical advancements will permit veterinarians to offer more and better care to animals. Pet owners are becoming more aware of the availability of advanced care. They may increasingly take advantage of nontraditional veterinary services such as preventive dental care, and more willingly pay for intensive care than in the past. Veterinarians who enter small animal practice may face competition. Large numbers of new graduates continue to be attracted to small animal medicine because they prefer to deal with pets, and live and work near or in populated areas. However, an oversupply does not necessarily limit the ability of veterinarians to find employment or set up and maintain a practice. It could result in more veterinarians taking positions requiring much evening or weekend work to accommodate the extended hours of operation which more practices are offering. Others could take salaried positions in retail stores offering limited veterinary services. Self-employed veterinarians may have to work harder and longer to build a sufficient clientele.

The number of jobs for large animal veterinarians is expected to grow slowly because productivity gains in the agricultural production industry mean demand for fewer veterinarians to treat food animals. Nevertheless, job prospects may be better for veterinarians who specialize in farm animals than for small animal practitioners because fewer veterinary medical college graduates have the desire to work in rural or isolated areas.

Continued support for public health and food safety, disease control programs, and biomedical research on human health problems will contribute to the demand for veterinarians, although such positions are relatively few in number. Also, anticipated budget tightening in the Federal Government may lead to lower funding levels for some programs, limiting job growth. Veterinarians with training in public health and epidemiology should have the best opportunities for a career in the Federal Government.

Earnings

Average starting salaries of 1995 veterinary medical college graduates varied by type of practice or employing industry, as indicated by table 1.

Table 1. Average starting salaries of veterinary medical college graduates, 1995

All graduates	$29,900
Type of practice	
Large animal, exclusive	39,500
Large animal, predominate	34,300
Mixed animal	31,900
Small animal, exclusive	31,900
Small animal, predominate	31,000
Equine	27,500
Industry	
Industry/commercial	44,500
Uniformed services	41,100
State/local government	40,000
Not-for-profit	36,000
Federal Government	32,800
University	19,700
Other public or corporate	34,000

SOURCE: American Veterinary Medical Association

The average income of veterinarians in private practice was $57,500 in 1995. New veterinary medical college graduates who enter the Federal Government usually start at $35,800. Beginning salaries were slightly higher in selected areas where the prevailing local pay level was higher. The average annual salary for veterinarians in the Federal Government in nonsupervisory, supervisory, and managerial positions was $57,600 in 1997.

Related Occupations

Veterinarians prevent, diagnose, and treat diseases, disorders, and injuries in animals. Those who do similar work for humans include chiropractors, dentists, optometrists, physicians, and podiatrists. Veterinarians also have extensive training in physical and life sciences, and some do scientific and medical research, closely paralleling occupations such as biological, medical, and animal scientists.

Animal trainers, animal breeders, and veterinary technicians work extensively with animals. Like veterinarians, they must have patience and feel comfortable with animals. However, the level of training required for these occupations is substantially less than that needed by veterinarians.

Sources of Additional Information

For more information on careers in veterinary medicine and a list of U.S. schools and colleges of veterinary medicine, send a letter-size, self-addressed, stamped envelope to:

☛ American Veterinary Medical Association, 1931 N. Meacham Rd., Suite 100, Schaumburg, IL 60173-4360.

For information on scholarships, grants, and loans, contact the financial aid officer at the veterinary schools to which you wish to apply.

For information on veterinary education, write to:

☛ Association of American Veterinary Medical Colleges, 1101 Vermont Ave. NW., Suite 710, Washington, DC 20005.

For information on the Federal agencies that employ veterinarians and a list of addresses for each agency, write to:

☛ National Association of Federal Veterinarians, 1101 Vermont Ave. NW., Suite 710, Washington, DC 20005.

Health Assessment and Treating Occupations

Dietitians and Nutritionists

(D.O.T. 077 except .117-010 and .124-010)

Significant points

- Employment of dietitians is expected to grow about as fast as the average for all occupations through the year 2006 due to increased emphasis on the prevention of disease by improved health habits.

- The basic educational requirement for dietitians and nutritionists is a bachelor's degree with a major in dietetics, foods and nutrition, food service systems management, or a related area.

Nature of the Work

Dietitians and nutritionists plan nutrition programs and supervise the preparation and serving of meals. They help prevent and treat illnesses by promoting healthy eating habits, scientifically evaluating clients' diets, and suggesting diet modifications, such as less salt for those with high blood pressure or reduced fat and sugar intake for those who are overweight.

Dietitians run food service systems for institutions such as hospitals and schools, promote sound eating habits through education, and conduct research. Major areas of practice are clinical, community, management, and consultant dietetics.

Clinical dietitians provide nutritional services for patients in institutions such as hospitals and nursing homes. They assess patients' nutritional needs, develop and implement nutrition programs, and evaluate and report the results. They also confer with doctors and other health care professionals in order to coordinate medical and nutritional needs. Some clinical dietitians specialize in the management of overweight patients, care of the critically ill, or care of renal (kidney) and diabetic patients. In addition, clinical dietitians in nursing homes or small hospitals may also manage the food service department.

Community dietitians counsel individuals and groups on nutritional practices designed to prevent disease and promote good health. Working in such places as public health clinics, home health agencies, and health maintenance organizations, they evaluate individual needs, develop nutritional care plans, and instruct individuals and their families. Dietitians working in home health agencies may provide instruction on grocery shopping and food preparation to the elderly, or patients with AIDS, cancer, or diabetes.

Popular interest in nutrition has led to opportunities in food manufacturing, advertising, and marketing, in which dietitians analyze foods, prepare literature for distribution, or report on issues such as the nutritional content of recipes, dietary fiber, or vitamin supplements.

Management dietitians oversee large-scale meal planning and preparation in such places as health care facilities, company cafeterias, prisons, and schools. They hire, train, and direct other dietitians and food service workers; budget for and purchase food, equipment, and supplies; enforce sanitary and safety regulations; and prepare records and reports.

Consultant dietitians work under contract with health care facilities or in their own private practice. They perform nutrition screening for their clients, and offer advice on diet-related concerns such as weight loss or cholesterol reduction. Some work for wellness programs, sports teams, supermarkets, and other nutrition-related businesses. They may consult with food service managers, providing expertise in sanitation, safety procedures, budgeting, and planning.

Working Conditions

Most dietitians work a regular 40-hour week, although some work weekends. Many dietitians work part time.

Dietitians and nutritionists spend much of their time in clean, well-lighted, and well-ventilated areas. However, some dietitians spend time in hot, steamy kitchens. Dietitians and nutritionists may be on their feet for most of the workday.

Employment

Dietitians and nutritionists held about 58,000 jobs in 1996. Over half were in hospitals, nursing homes, or offices and clinics of physicians.

State and local governments provided about 1 job in 6—mostly in health departments and other public health related areas. Other jobs were in restaurants, social service agencies, residential care facilities, diet workshops, physical fitness facilities, school systems, colleges and universities, and the Federal Government—mostly in the Department of Veterans Affairs. Others were employed by firms that provide food services on contract to such facilities as colleges and universities, airlines, and company cafeterias.

Some dietitians were self-employed, working as consultants to facilities such as hospitals and nursing homes, and seeing individual clients.

Training, Other Qualifications, and Advancement

The basic educational requirement for dietitians and nutritionists is a bachelor's degree with a major in dietetics, foods and nutrition, food service systems management, or a related area. Students take courses in foods, nutrition, institution management, chemistry, biology, microbiology, and physiology. Other suggested courses include business, mathematics, statistics, computer science, psychology, sociology, and economics.

Of the 40 States having laws governing dietetics, 27 require licensure, 12 require certification, and 1 requires registration. The Commission on Dietetic Registration of the American Dietetic Association (ADA)

Dietitians need a bachelor's degree in dietetics, foods and nutrition, food service systems management, or a related area.

awards the Registered Dietitian credential to those who pass a certification exam after completing their academic education and supervised experience.

As of 1997, there were 231 ADA-approved bachelor's degree programs. Supervised practice experience can be acquired in two ways. There are 49 ADA-accredited coordinated programs combining academic and supervised practice experience in a 4-year program. The second option requires completion of 900 hours of supervised practice experience, either in one of the 190 ADA-accredited internships or in one of the 64 ADA-approved preprofessional practice programs. Internships and preprofessional practice programs may be full-time programs lasting 9 to 12 months, or part-time programs lasting 2 years. Students interested in research, advanced clinical positions, or public health should get a graduate degree.

Recommended high school courses include biology, chemistry, mathematics, health, and home economics.

Experienced dietitians may advance to assistant, associate, or director of a dietetic department, or become self-employed. Some dietitians specialize in areas such as renal or pediatric dietetics. Others may leave the occupation to become sales representatives for equipment or food manufacturers.

Job Outlook

Employment of dietitians is expected to grow about as fast as the average for all occupations through the year 2006 due to increased emphasis on the prevention of disease by improved health habits. A growing and aging population will increase demand for meals and nutritional counseling in nursing homes, schools, prisons, community health programs, and home health care agencies. Public interest in nutrition and the emphasis on health education and prudent lifestyles will also spur demand. Besides employment growth, job openings will also result from the need to replace experienced workers who leave the occupation.

Employment of dietitians in hospitals is expected to decline because of anticipated slow growth in the number of inpatients, and as hospitals contract out food service operations. On the other hand, faster than average growth in employment is expected in nursing homes as the number of elderly people rises sharply, in contract providers of food services, in residential care facilities, in offices and clinics of physicians, and in other social services.

Employment growth for dietitians and nutritionists may be somewhat constrained by some employers substituting other workers such as nurses, health educators, food service managers, and dietetic technicians. Growth would be faster but there are limitations on insurance reimbursement for dietetic services.

Earnings

According to a Hay Group survey of acute care hospitals, the median annual base salary of full-time staff dietitians was $34,400 in January 1997. The middle 50 percent earned between $31,300 and $37,200.

According to the American Dietetic Association, median annual income for registered dietitians in 1995 varied by practice area as follows: clinical nutrition, $34,131; food and nutrition management, $42,964; community nutrition, $33,902; consultation and business, $43,374; and education and research, $42,784. Salaries also vary by years in practice, educational level, geographic region, and size of community.

Related Occupations

Dietitians and nutritionists apply the principles of nutrition in a variety of situations. Workers with duties similar to those of management dietitians include home economists and food service managers. Nurses and health educators often provide services related to those of community dietitians.

Sources of Additional Information

For a list of academic programs, scholarships, and other information about dietetics, contact:
☛ The American Dietetic Association, 216 West Jackson Blvd., Suite 800, Chicago, IL 60606-6995. Homepage: http://www.eatright.org

Occupational Therapists

(D.O.T. 076.121-010 and 076.167-010)

Significant points

- Occupational therapy offers good job opportunities and high pay.
- Occupational therapists will be among the fastest growing occupations, as rapid growth in the number of middle-aged and elderly individuals increases the demand for therapeutic services.
- Additional demand will result from medical advances that allow more patients with critical problems to survive and require rehabilitation.

Nature of the Work

Occupational therapists work with individuals who have conditions that are mentally, physically, developmentally, or emotionally disabling, and help them to develop, recover, or maintain daily living and work skills. They not only help clients improve basic motor functions and reasoning abilities, but also compensate for permanent loss of function. Their goal is to help clients have independent, productive, and satisfying lives.

Occupational therapists assist clients in performing activities of all types, ranging from using a computer, to caring for daily needs such as dressing, cooking, and eating. Physical exercises may be used to increase strength and dexterity, while paper and pencil exercises may be chosen to improve visual acuity and the ability to discern patterns. A client with short-term memory loss, for instance, might be encouraged to make lists to aid recall. One with coordination problems might be assigned exercises to improve hand-eye coordination. Occupational therapists also use computer programs to help clients improve decision making, abstract reasoning, problem solving, and perceptual skills, as well as memory, sequencing, and coordination—all of which are important for independent living.

For those with permanent functional disabilities, such as spinal cord injuries, cerebral palsy, or muscular dystrophy, therapists instruct in the use of adaptive equipment such as wheelchairs, splints, and aids for eating and dressing. They also design or make special equipment needed at home or at work. Therapists develop and teach clients with severe limitations to operate computer-aided adaptive equipment that helps them to communicate, and control other aspects of their environment.

An occupational therapist evaluates the range of motion in a patient's wrist and fingers.

Some occupational therapists, called industrial therapists, treat individuals whose ability to function in a work environment has been impaired. They arrange employment, plan work activities and evaluate the client's progress.

Occupational therapists may work exclusively with individuals in a particular age group, or with particular disabilities. In schools, for example, they evaluate children's abilities, recommend and provide therapy, modify classroom equipment, and in general, help children participate as fully as possible in school programs and activities.

Occupational therapists in mental health settings treat individuals who are mentally ill, mentally retarded, or emotionally disturbed. To treat these problems, therapists choose activities that help people learn to cope with daily life. Activities include time management skills, budgeting, shopping, homemaking, and use of public transportation. They may also work with individuals who are dealing with alcoholism, drug abuse, depression, eating disorders, or stress related disorders.

Recording a client's activities and progress is an important part of an occupational therapist's job. Accurate records are essential for evaluating clients, billing, and reporting to physicians and others.

Working Conditions

Occupational therapists in hospitals and other health care and community settings generally work a 40-hour week. Those in schools may also participate in meetings and other activities, during and after the school day. Almost one-third of occupational therapists work part-time. In large rehabilitation centers, therapists may work in spacious rooms equipped with machines, tools, and other devices generating noise. The job can be tiring, because therapists are on their feet much of the time. Those providing home health care may spend several hours a day driving from appointment to appointment. Therapists also face hazards, such as backstrain from lifting and moving clients and equipment.

Therapists are increasingly taking on supervisory roles. Due to rising health care costs, third party payers are beginning to encourage occupational therapy assistants and aides to take more hands-on responsibility. By having assistants and aides work more closely with clients under the guidance of a therapist, the cost of therapy should be more modest.

Employment

Occupational therapists held about 57,000 jobs in 1996. The largest number of jobs was in hospitals, including many in rehabilitation and psychiatric hospitals. Other major employers include offices and clinics of occupational therapists and other health practitioners, school systems, home health care services, nursing homes, community mental health centers, adult daycare programs, job training services, and residential care facilities.

A small number of occupational therapists are in private practice. Some are solo practitioners, while others are in group practices. They see clients referred by physicians or other health professionals, or provide contract or consulting services to nursing homes, schools, adult daycare programs, and home health agencies.

Training, Other Qualifications, and Advancement

A bachelor's degree in occupational therapy is the minimal requirement for entry into this field. All States, Puerto Rico, and the District of Columbia regulate occupational therapy. To obtain a license, applicants must graduate from an accredited educational program, and pass a national certification examination. Those who pass the test are awarded the title of registered occupational therapist.

In 1996, entry-level education was offered in 84 bachelor's degree programs; 15 post-bachelor's certificate programs for students with a degree other than occupational therapy; and 29 entry-level master's degree programs. Ten programs offered a combined bachelor's and master's degree. Most schools have full-time programs, although a growing number also offer weekend or part-time programs.

Occupational therapy coursework includes physical, biological, and behavioral sciences, and the application of occupational therapy theory and skills. Completion of 6 months of supervised fieldwork is also required.

Persons considering this profession should take high school courses in biology, chemistry, physics, health, art, and the social sciences. College admissions offices also look with favor on paid or volunteer experience in the health care field.

Occupational therapists need patience and strong interpersonal skills to inspire trust and respect in their clients. Ingenuity and imagination in adapting activities to individual needs are assets. Those working in home health care must be able to successfully adapt to a variety of settings.

Job Outlook

Job opportunities for occupational therapists are expected to continue to be good. Employment of occupational therapists is expected to increase much faster than the average for all occupations through the year 2006, due to anticipated growth in demand for rehabilitation and long-term care services. The baby-boom generation's move into middle age, a period during which the incidence of heart attack and stroke increases, will increase the demand for therapeutic services. Additional services will also be demanded by the population 75 years of age and above, a rapidly growing age group that suffers from a very high incidence of disabling conditions.

Medical advances are now making it possible for more patients with critical problems to survive. These patients, however, may need extensive therapy. Finally, additional therapists will be needed to help children with disabilities prepare to enter special education programs, as required by Federal legislation.

Due to industry growth and more intensive care, hospitals will continue to employ a large number of occupational therapists. Hospitals will also need occupational therapists to staff their growing home health-care and outpatient rehabilitation programs.

Fast employment growth in schools will result from expansion of the school-age population and extended services for disabled students. Employment of occupational therapists in the home health field is also expected to grow very fast. The rapidly growing number of people age 75 and older who are more likely to need home health care, and the greater use of at-home follow-up care, will encourage this growth.

Earnings

Median weekly earnings of full-time salaried occupational therapists were $780 in 1996. The middle 50 percent earned between $622 and $982. The lowest 10 percent earned less than $479; the top 10 percent earned more than $1,116.

According to a Hay Group survey of acute care hospitals, the median annual base salary of full-time occupational therapists was $42,700 in January 1997. The middle 50 percent earned between $39,100 and $46,100.

Related Occupations

Occupational therapists use specialized knowledge to help individuals perform daily living skills and achieve maximum independence. Other workers performing similar duties include orthotists, prosthetists, physical therapists, chiropractors, speech pathologists, audiologists, rehabilitation counselors, and recreational therapists.

Sources of Additional Information

For more information on occupational therapy as a career and a list of education programs, send a self-addressed label and $5.00 to:
☞ The American Occupational Therapy Association, 4720 Montgomery Ln., P.O. Box 31220, Bethesda, MD 20824-1220. Homepage: http://www.aota.org

Pharmacists

(D.O.T. 074.161-010 and -014)

Significant points

- Pharmacists are stepping beyond the traditional delivery of prescriptions to become more involved in drug therapy decision-making and patient counseling.

- Earnings are very high, but some pharmacists work long hours.

Nature of the Work

Pharmacists dispense drugs prescribed by physicians and other health practitioners and provide information to patients about medications and their use. They advise physicians and other health practitioners on the selection, dosages, interactions, and side effects of medications. Pharmacists must understand the use, composition, and effects of drugs. Compounding—the actual mixing of ingredients to form powders, tablets, capsules, ointments, and solutions—is only a small part of a pharmacist's practice, because most medicines are produced by pharmaceutical companies in a standard dosage and form.

Pharmacists in community (retail) pharmacies counsel patients, as well as answer questions about prescription drugs, such as possible adverse reactions and interactions. They provide information about over-the-counter drugs and make recommendations after asking a series of health questions, such as whether the customer is taking any other medications. They also give advice about durable medical equipment and home health care supplies. Those who own or manage community pharmacies may buy and sell nonhealth-related merchandise, hire and supervise personnel, and oversee the general operation of the pharmacy. Some community pharmacists offer specialized disease state management services for conditions such as diabetes, asthma, smoking cessation or high blood pressure.

Pharmacists in hospitals and clinics dispense medications and advise the medical staff on the selection and effects of drugs. They may make sterile solutions and buy medical supplies. They also assess, plan, and monitor drug regimens. They counsel patients on the use of drugs while in the hospital, and on their use at home when they are discharged. Pharmacists may also evaluate drug use patterns and outcomes in the hospital or in a patient population.

Pharmacists who work in home health care prepare infusions (solutions that are injected into patients) and other medications for use in the home, and monitor drug therapy.

Most pharmacists keep computerized records of patients' drug therapies to ensure that harmful drug interactions do not occur. They frequently teach pharmacy students serving as externs in preparation for graduation and licensure.

Some pharmacists specialize in specific areas, such as drugs for psychiatric disorders, intravenous nutrition support, oncology, nuclear pharmacy, or pharmacotherapy.

Working Conditions

Pharmacists usually work in clean, well-lighted, and well-ventilated areas. Many pharmacists spend most of their time on their feet. When working with sterile or potentially dangerous pharmaceutical products, pharmacists wear gloves and masks and work with special protective equipment. Many community and hospital pharmacies are open extended hours or around the clock, so pharmacists may work evenings, nights, weekends, and holidays. Consultant pharmacists may travel to nursing homes or other facilities to monitor people's drug therapy.

About 1 out of 5 pharmacists worked part time in 1996. Most full-time salaried pharmacists worked about 40 hours a week. Some, including most self-employed pharmacists, worked more than 50 hours a week.

A pharmacist discusses an over-the-counter medication with a customer.

Employment

Pharmacists held about 172,000 jobs in 1996. About 3 out of 5 worked in community pharmacies, either independently owned, part of a drug store chain, or part of a grocery store, department store, or mass merchandiser. Most community pharmacists were salaried employees, but some were self employed owners. About one-quarter worked in hospitals, and others worked in clinics, mail-order pharmacies, pharmaceutical wholesalers, home health care agencies, or the Federal Government.

Some pharmacists hold more than one job. They may work a standard week in their primary work setting, and also work part time elsewhere.

Training, Other Qualifications, and Advancement

A license to practice pharmacy is required in all States, the District of Columbia, and U.S. territories. To obtain a license, one must graduate from an accredited college of pharmacy, pass a State examination, and serve an internship under a licensed pharmacist. Most States grant a license without extensive reexamination to qualified pharmacists already licensed by another State—check with State boards of pharmacy for details. Many pharmacists are licensed to practice in more than one State. Most States require continuing education for license renewal.

At least 5 years of study beyond high school are required to graduate from programs accredited by the American Council on Pharmaceutical Education. A Bachelor of Science (B.S.) in Pharmacy, the degree received by most graduates, takes 5 years. A Doctor of Pharmacy (Pharm.D.) normally requires at least 6 years, during which an intervening bachelor's degree is usually not awarded. Those who already hold the bachelor's degree may enter Pharm.D. programs, but the combined period of study is usually longer than 6 years. In 1997, 79 colleges of pharmacy conferred degrees. The number of schools offering the Pharm.D. as the only professional degree increased to 41, and the number offering the B.S. in Pharmacy as the only professional degree continued to decline, reaching 4.

Requirements for admission to colleges of pharmacy vary. A few colleges admit students directly from high school. Most colleges of pharmacy, however, require 1 or 2 years of college-level prepharmacy education. Entry requirements usually include mathematics and basic sciences, such as chemistry, biology, and physics, as well as courses in the humanities and social sciences. Some colleges require the applicant to take the Pharmacy College Admissions Test.

All colleges of pharmacy offer courses in pharmacy practice, designed to teach students to dispense prescriptions, communicate with patients and other health professionals, and to strengthen their understanding of professional ethics and practice management responsibilities.

Pharmacists' training increasingly emphasizes direct patient care, as well as consultative services to other health professionals.

Recently, pharmacy schools voted to move toward offering the Pharm.D. as the only professional degree in pharmacy. However, some schools continue to offer the B.S. in Pharmacy. All accredited pharmacy schools are expected to graduate their last B.S. class by the year 2004. Either degree currently fulfills the requirements to take the licensure examination of a state board of pharmacy.

The bachelor's degree in pharmacy is generally acceptable for most positions in community pharmacies, at least in the forseeable future. A growing number of hospital employers prefer that a pharmacist have a Pharm.D. degree. A master's or Ph.D. degree in pharmacy or a related field usually is required to do research, and a Pharm.D. with additional residency or fellowship training, master's, or Ph.D. usually is necessary for faculty positions.

In 1996-97, 60 colleges of pharmacy awarded the Master of Science degree or the Ph.D. degree. Although a number of pharmacy graduates interested in further training pursue an advanced degree in pharmacy, there are other options. Some enter 1- or 2-year residency programs or fellowships. Pharmacy residencies are organized, directed, postgraduate training programs in pharmacy practice. Pharmacy fellowships are directed, highly individualized programs designed to prepare participants to work in research laboratories.

Areas of graduate study include pharmaceutics and pharmaceutical chemistry (physical and chemical properties of drugs and dosage forms), pharmacology (effects of drugs on the body), and pharmacy administration, including pharmacoeconomics and social-behavioral aspects of patient care.

Prospective pharmacists should have scientific aptitude, good communication skills, and a desire to help others. They must also be conscientious and pay close attention to detail, because the decisions they make affect human lives.

In community pharmacies, pharmacists usually begin at the staff level. After they gain experience and secure the necessary capital, many become owners or part owners of pharmacies. Pharmacists in chain drug stores may be promoted to pharmacy supervisor or manager at the store level and then at the district or regional level, and later to an executive position within the chain's headquarters.

Hospital pharmacists may advance to supervisory or administrative positions. Pharmacists in the pharmaceutical industry may advance in marketing, sales, research, quality control, production, packaging, and other areas.

Job Outlook

Employment of pharmacists is expected to grow as fast as the average for all occupations through the year 2006, due to the increased pharmaceutical needs of a larger and older population, and greater use of medication. Cost-conscious insurers and health systems will continue to emphasize the role of pharmacists in primary and preventive health services. They realize that the expense of using medication to treat diseases and conditions is often considerably less than the potential costs for patients whose conditions go untreated, and pharmacists can also play an important role in reducing the expenses resulting from unexpected complications due to allergic reactions or medication interactions.

The increased number of middle aged and elderly people will spur demand for pharmacists in all practice settings. The number of prescriptions influences the demand for pharmacists, and the middle aged and elderly population uses more prescription drugs, on average, than younger people.

Other factors likely to increase the demand for pharmacists through the year 2006 include the likelihood of scientific advances that will make more drug products available, new developments in administering medication, and increasingly sophisticated consumers seeking more information about drugs.

Employment in hospitals is expected to grow slowly, as hospitals reduce inpatient stays, downsize, and consolidate departments. Pharmacy services are shifting to long-term, ambulatory, and home care settings, where opportunities for pharmacists will be best. New opportunities for pharmacists are emerging in managed care organizations, where pharmacists analyze trends and patterns in medication use for their populations of patients. Fast growth is also expected for pharmacists employed in research, disease management, and pharmacoeconomics—determining the costs and benefits of different drug therapies.

Because of efforts to control prescription drug costs, retail pharmacies are taking steps to increase their prescription volume to make up for declining dispensing fees. Automation of drug dispensing and greater use of pharmacy technicians will help them dispense more prescriptions. The number of community pharmacists needed in the future will depend on the expansion rate of chain drug stores and the willingness of insurers to reimburse pharmacists for providing clinical services to patients taking prescription drugs. With its emphasis on cost control, managed care has encouraged the growth of lower-cost distributors of prescription drugs such as mail-order firms. Slower employment growth is expected in traditional chain and independent pharmacies.

Earnings

Median weekly earnings of full-time, salaried pharmacists were $992 in 1996. Half earned between $827 and $1,177. The lowest 10 percent earned less than $554 and the top 10 percent more than $1,422.

According to a survey by *Drug Topics* magazine, published by Medical Economics Inc., average base salaries of full-time, salaried pharmacists were $59,276 per year in 1996. Pharmacists working in chain drug stores had an average base salary of $61,735 per year, while pharmacists working in independent drug stores averaged $52,189, and hospital pharmacists averaged $61,317. Overall, salaries for pharmacists were highest in the West and second highest in the East. Many pharmacists also receive compensation in the form of bonuses, overtime, and profit-sharing.

Related Occupations

Persons in other professions who may work with pharmaceutical compounds are pharmaceutical chemists, pharmacologists, medical scientists, and biological technicians.

Sources of Additional Information

For information on pharmacy as a career, preprofessional and professional requirements, programs offered by all the colleges of pharmacy, and student financial aid, contact:

☛ American Association of Colleges of Pharmacy, 1426 Prince St., Alexandria, VA 22314.

Information on requirements for licensure in a particular State is available from the State board of pharmacy.

Information on specific college entrance requirements, curriculums, and financial aid is available from the dean of any college of pharmacy.

Physical Therapists

(D.O.T. 076.121-014)

Significant points

- Physical therapy offers very good job opportunities and high pay.
- Physical therapists will be among the fastest growing occupations, as growth in the number of individuals with disabilities or limited function increases the demand for physical therapy services.

Nature of the Work

Physical therapists provide services that help restore function, improve mobility, relieve pain, and prevent or limit permanent physical disabilities of patients suffering from injuries or disease. They restore, maintain, and promote overall fitness and health. Their patients include accident victims and individuals with disabling conditions such as low back pain, arthritis, heart disease, fractures, head injuries, and cerebral palsy.

Therapists examine patients' medical histories, then test and measure their strength, range of motion, balance and coordination, posture, muscle performance, respiration, and motor function. They also determine patients' ability to be independent and reintegrate into the community or workplace after injury or illness. Next, they develop treatment plans describing the treatment strategy, its purpose, and the anticipated outcome. After devising a treatment strategy, physical therapists often delegate specific procedures to physical therapist assistants and aides. (Physical therapist assistants and aides are discussed elsewhere in the *Handbook*.) Therapists are increasingly taking on supervisory roles.

Treatment often includes exercise for patients who have been immobilized and lack flexibility, strength, or endurance. They encourage patients to use their own muscles to further increase flexibility and range of motion before finally advancing to other exercises improving strength, balance, coordination, and endurance. Their goal is to improve how an individual functions at work and home.

Physical therapists also use electrical stimulation, hot packs or cold compresses, and ultrasound to relieve pain and reduce swelling. They may use traction or deep-tissue massage to relieve pain. Therapists also teach patients to use assistive and adaptive devices such as crutches, prostheses, and wheelchairs. They may show patients exercises to do at home to expedite their recovery.

As treatment continues, physical therapists document progress, conduct periodic examinations, and modify treatments when necessary. Such documentation is used to track the patient's progress, and identify areas requiring more or less attention.

Physical therapists often consult and practice with a variety of other professionals, such as physicians, dentists, nurses, educators, social workers, occupational therapists, speech-language pathologists, and audiologists.

Some physical therapists treat a wide range of ailments; others specialize in areas such as pediatrics, geriatrics, orthopedics, sports medicine, neurology, and cardiopulmonary physical therapy.

Working Conditions

Physical therapists practice in hospitals, clinics, and private offices that have specially equipped facilities or they treat patients in hospital rooms, homes, or schools.

Most physical therapists work a 40-hour week, which may include some evenings and weekends. The job can be physically demanding because therapists often have to stoop, kneel, crouch, lift, and stand for long periods of time. In addition, physical therapists move heavy equipment and lift patients or help them turn, stand, or walk.

Employment

Physical therapists held about 115,000 jobs in 1996; about 1 in 4 worked part time. Almost two-thirds were employed in either hospitals or offices of physical therapists. Other jobs were in home health agencies, outpatient rehabilitation centers, offices and clinics of physicians, and nursing homes. Some physical therapists are self-employed in private practices. They may provide services to individual patients or contract to provide services in hospitals, rehabilitation centers, nursing homes, home health agencies, adult daycare programs, and schools. They may be in solo practice or be part of a consulting group. Physical therapists also teach in academic institutions and conduct research.

Training, Other Qualifications, and Advancement

All States require physical therapists to pass a licensure exam after graduating from an accredited physical therapist educational program before they can practice.

Physical therapists help people rehabilitate their injuries.

According to the American Physical Therapy Association, there were 173 accredited physical therapist programs as of July, 1997. Of the accredited programs, 46 offered bachelor's degrees and 116 were master's degree programs. By the year 2001, all accredited physical therapy programs will be at the master's degree level and above. Currently, the bachelor's degree curriculum starts with basic science courses such as biology, chemistry, and physics, and then introduces specialized courses such as biomechanics, neuroanatomy, human growth and development, manifestations of disease, examination techniques, and therapeutic procedures. Besides classroom and laboratory instruction, students receive supervised clinical experience. Individuals who have a 4-year degree in another field and want to be a physical therapist, should enroll in a master's or a doctoral level physical therapist educational program.

Competition for entrance into physical therapist educational programs is very intense, so interested students should attain superior grades in high school and college, especially in science courses. Courses useful when applying to physical therapist educational programs include anatomy, biology, chemistry, social science, mathematics, and physics. Before granting admission, many professional education programs require experience as a volunteer in a physical therapy department of a hospital or clinic.

Physical therapists should have strong interpersonal skills to successfully educate patients about their physical therapy treatments. They should also be compassionate and posses a desire to help patients. Similar traits are also needed to interact with the patient's family.

Physical therapists are expected to continue professional development by participating in continuing education courses and workshops. A number of States require continuing education to maintain licensure.

Job Outlook

Anecdotal reports about shortages of physical therapists that existed in recent years are no longer common. The number of physical therapist educational programs has increased and more graduates have moved into the labor force. Nevertheless, job prospects are expected to continue to be very good.

Physical therapists are expected to be among the fastest growing occupations through the year 2006 as the demand for physical therapy services grows. The rapidly growing elderly population is particularly vulnerable to chronic and debilitating conditions that require therapeutic services. Also, the baby-boom generation is entering the prime age for heart attacks and strokes, increasing the demand for cardiac and physical rehabilitation. More young people will need physical therapy as technological advances save the lives of a larger proportion of newborns with severe birth defects. Future medical developments will also permit a higher percentage of trauma victims to survive, creating additional demand for rehabilitative care. Growth may also result from advances in medical technology which permit treatment of more disabling conditions.

Widespread interest in health promotion should also increase demand for physical therapy services. A growing number of employers are using physical therapists to evaluate worksites, develop exercise programs, and teach safe work habits to employees in the hope of reducing injuries.

Employment of physical therapits would grow even faster were it not for continued emphasis on controlling health care costs by limiting the use of therapeutic services in some instances.

Earnings
In 1996, median weekly earnings of salaried physical therapists who usually work full time were $757. The middle 50 percent earned between $577 and $1,055. The top 10 percent earned at least $1,294 and the bottom 10 percent earned less than $400.

According to the American Physical Therapy Association's survey of physical therapists practicing in hospital settings, the median annual base salary of full-time physical therapists was $48,000 in 1996. The middle 50 percent earned $42,000 and $57,000.

Related Occupations
Physical therapists rehabilitate persons with physical disabilities. Others who work in the rehabilitation field include occupational therapists, speech pathologists, audiologists, orthotists, prosthetists, and respiratory therapists.

Sources of Additional Information
Additional information on a career as a physical therapist and a list of accredited educational programs in physical therapy are available from:
☛ American Physical Therapy Association, 1111 North Fairfax St., Alexandria, VA 22314-1488. Homepage: http://www.apta.org/

Physician Assistants
(D.O.T. 079.364-018)

Significant points
- The typical physician assistant program lasts about 2 years and generally requires at least 2 years of college and some health care experience for admission.

- Earnings are high and job opportunities are expected to be excellent.

Nature of the Work
Physician assistants (PA's) provide health care services with supervision by physicians. They should not be confused with medical assistants, who perform routine clinical and clerical tasks (see separate statement elsewhere in the *Handbook*). PA's are formally trained to provide diagnostic, therapeutic, and preventive health care services under the direction of a physician. Working as members of the health care team, they take medical histories, examine patients, order and interpret laboratory tests and x rays, and make diagnoses. They also treat minor injuries by suturing, splinting, and casting. PA's record progress notes, instruct and counsel patients, and order or carry out therapy. In 39 States and the District of Columbia, physician assis-

tants may prescribe medications. PA's may also have managerial duties. Some order medical and laboratory supplies and equipment, while others supervise technicians and assistants.

Physician assistants always work under the supervision of a physician. The extent of supervision, however, depends upon State law. For example, a PA may provide care in rural or inner city clinics where a physician is present for only 1 or 2 days each week, conferring with the supervising physician and other medical professionals as needed or required by law. PA's may also make house calls or go to hospitals and nursing homes to check on patients and report back to the physician.

In some States, the duties of a physician assistant are determined by the supervising physician; in others, they are determined by the State's regulatory agency. Aspiring PA's should investigate the laws and regulations in the States where they wish to practice.

Many PA's work in primary care areas such as general internal medicine, pediatrics, and family practice. Others work in specialty areas, such as general and thoracic surgery, emergency medicine, orthopedics, and geriatrics. PA's specializing in surgery provide pre- and post-operative care and may work as first or second assistants during major surgery.

Working Conditions
Although PA's generally work in a comfortable, well-lighted environment, those in surgery often stand for long periods, and others do considerable walking. Schedules vary according to practice setting and often depend on the hours of the supervising physician. The workweek of PA's in physicians' offices may include weekends, night hours, or early morning hospital rounds to visit patients. They may also be on-call. PA's in clinics usually work a 5-day, 40-hour week.

Employment
Physician assistants held about 64,000 jobs in 1996. Sixty-six percent were in the offices and clinics of physicians, dentists, or other health practitioners. Almost 20 percent were in hospitals. The rest were mostly in public health clinics, nursing homes, prisons, home health care agencies, and the Department of Veterans Affairs.

According to the American Academy of Physician Assistants, about one-third of all PA's provide health care to communities having fewer than 50,000 residents where physicians may be in limited supply.

Training, Other Qualifications, and Advancement
Almost all States require that new PA's complete an accredited, formal education program. In 1997, there were 96 such educational programs for physician assistants; 53 of these programs offered a baccalaureate degree or a degree option. The rest offered either a

A physician assistant conducts a neurological examination on a patient.

certificate, an associate degree, or a master's degree. Most PA graduates have at least a bachelor's degree.

Admission requirements vary, but many programs require 2 years of college and some work experience in the health care field. Students should take courses in biology, English, chemistry, math, psychology, and social sciences. More than half of all applicants hold a bachelor's or master's degree. Many applicants are former emergency medical technicians, other allied health professionals, or nurses.

PA programs generally last 2 years. Most programs are in schools of allied health, academic health centers, medical schools, or 4-year colleges; a few are in community colleges, the military, or hospitals. Many accredited PA programs have clinical teaching affiliations with medical schools.

PA education includes classroom instruction in biochemistry, nutrition, human anatomy, physiology, microbiology, clinical pharmacology, clinical medicine, geriatric and home health care, disease prevention, and medical ethics. Students obtain supervised clinical training in several areas, including primary care medicine, inpatient medicine, surgery, obstetrics and gynecology, geriatrics, emergency medicine, psychiatry, and pediatrics. Sometimes, PA students serve one or more of these "rotations" under the supervision of a physician who is seeking to hire a PA. These rotations often lead to permanent employment.

As of 1997, 49 States and the District of Columbia had legislation governing the qualifications or practice of physician assistants. Mississippi did not. Forty-nine States required physician assistants to pass the Physician Assistants National Certifying Examination that is only open to graduates of an accredited educational program. Only those successfully completing the examination may use the credential "Physician Assistant-Certified (PA-C)." In order to remain certified, PA's must complete 100 hours of continuing medical education every 2 years. Every 6 years, they must pass a recertification examination or complete an alternate program combining learning experiences and a take-home examination.

Although they are not accredited, PA postgraduate residency training programs are available in gynecology, geriatrics, surgery, pediatrics, neonatology, and occupational medicine. Candidates must be graduates of an accredited program and be certified by the National Commission on Certification of Physician Assistants.

Physician assistants need leadership skills, self-confidence, and emotional stability. They must be willing to continue studying throughout their career to keep up with medical advances.

Some PA's pursue additional education in order to practice in a specialty area such as surgery, neonatology, or emergency medicine. Others, as they attain greater clinical knowledge and experience, advance to added responsibilities and higher earnings. However, by the very nature of the profession, individual PA's are usually supervised by physicians.

Job Outlook

Employment opportunities are expected to be excellent for physician assistants, particularly in areas or settings that have difficulty attracting physicians, such as rural and inner city clinics. Employment of PA's is expected to grow much faster than the average for all occupations through the year 2006 due to anticipated expansion of the health services industry and an emphasis on cost containment. Physicians and institutions are expected to employ more PA's to provide primary care and assist with medical and surgical procedures, because PA's are cost-effective and productive members of the health care team. Physician assistants can relieve physicians of routine duties and procedures. Telemedicine—using technology to facilitate interactive consultations between physicians and physician assistants—will also expand the use of physician assistants. Besides the traditional office-based setting, PA's should find a growing number of jobs in institutional settings such as hospitals, academic medical centers, public clinics, and prisons. Additional PA's may be needed to augment medical staffing in inpatient teaching hospital settings if the number

of physician residents is reduced. In addition, State-imposed legal limitations on the numbers of hours worked by physician residents are increasingly common and encourage hospitals to use PA's to supply some physician resident services. Opportunities will be best in States that allow PA's a wider scope of practice, such as the ability to prescribe medication.

Earnings

According to the American Academy of Physician Assistants, the median income for physician assistants in full time clinical practice in 1996 was $60,687; median income for first year graduates was $52,116. Income varies by specialty, practice setting, geographical location, and years of experience.

According to a Hay Group survey of HMO's, group practices, and hospital-based clinics, the median annual base salary of full-time physician assistants was $54,100 in May 1996. The middle 50 percent earned between $49,100 and $60,000.

The average annual salary for physician assistants employed by the Federal Government was $48,670 in early 1997.

Related Occupations

Other health workers who provide direct patient care that requires a similar level of skill and training include nurse practitioners, physical therapists, occupational therapists, clinical psychologists, speech-language pathologists, and audiologists.

Sources of Additional Information

For information on a career as a physician assistant, contact:
☞ American Academy of Physician Assistants Information Center, 950 North Washington St., Alexandria, VA 22314-1552. Homepage: http://www.aapa.org

For a list of accredited programs and a catalog of individual PA training programs, contact:
☞ Association of Physician Assistant Programs, 950 North Washington St., Alexandria, VA 22314-1552.

For eligibility requirements and a description of the Physician Assistant National Certifying Examination, write to:
☞ National Commission on Certification of Physician Assistants, Inc., 6849-B2 Peachtree Dunwoody Rd., Atlanta, GA 30328.

Recreational Therapists

(D.O.T. 076.124-014)

Significant Points

- Employment of recreational therapists is expected to increase rapidly as demand grows for physical and psychiatric rehabilitative services and for services for people with disabilities.

- Opportunities should generally be good for persons with a bachelor's degree in therapeutic recreation or in recreation with an option in therapeutic recreation.

Nature of the Work

Recreational therapists provide treatment services and recreation activities to individuals with illnesses or disabling conditions. They use a variety of techniques to treat or maintain the physical, mental, and emotional well-being of clients. Treatments may include the use of arts and crafts, animals, sports, games, dance and movement, drama, music, and community outings. Therapists help individuals reduce depression, stress, and anxiety. They help individuals recover their basic motor functioning and reasoning abilities, build confidence, and socialize more effectively to allow them to be more independent, as well as reduce or eliminate the effects of illness or disability. Their focus is to help integrate people with disabilities into the community by helping them use community resources and recreational activities. Recreational therapists should not be confused with recreation workers, who organize recreational activities primarily for enjoyment. (Recreation workers are discussed elsewhere in the *Handbook*.)

In acute health care settings, such as hospitals and rehabilitation centers, recreational therapists treat and rehabilitate individuals with specific health conditions, usually in conjunction or collaboration with physicians, nurses, psychologists, social workers, and physical and occupational therapists. In long-term care facilities and residential facilities, they use leisure activities—especially structured group programs—to maintain general health and well-being. They may also treat clients and provide interventions to prevent further medical problems and secondary complications related to illness and disabilities. In these settings they may be called activity directors or therapeutic recreation specialists.

Recreational therapists assess clients based on information from standardized assessments, observations, medical records, medical staff, family, and clients themselves. They then develop and carry out therapeutic interventions consistent with patient needs and interests. For instance, clients isolated from others may be encouraged to play games with others, a right-handed person with a right-side paralysis may be instructed in adaptation and compensatory strategies to use his or her non-affected left side to throw a ball or swing a racket. Recreational therapists may instruct patients in relaxation techniques to reduce stress and tension, in correct stretching and limbering exercises, in proper body mechanics for participation in recreation activities, in pacing and energy conservation techniques, and in individual as well as team activities.

Community based recreational therapists work in park and recreation departments, special education programs for school districts, or programs for older adults and people with disabilities. In these programs, therapists help clients develop leisure activities and provide them with opportunities for exercise, mental stimulation, creativity, and fun.

In schools, recreational therapists help counselors, parents, and special education teachers address the special needs of students. They are especially important in helping to ease the transition phase

Recreational therapists help individuals reduce depression, stress, and anxiety, and increase self-esteem and self-confidence.

into adult life for the disabled. The transition phase extends from age 14 until high school graduation. Recreational therapists provide assistance in teaching the student about recreational activities and how to use community resources. The primary responsibility for these therapists is to integrate students into the community.

Recreational therapists observe and record patients' participation, reactions, and progress. These records are used by the medical staff and others, to monitor progress, to justify changes or end treatment, and for billing.

Working Conditions

Recreational therapists provide services in special activity rooms, but also must plan events and keep records in offices. When working with clients during community integration programs, they may travel locally to instruct clients on the accessibility of public transportation and other public areas, such as parks, playgrounds, swimming pools, restaurants, and theaters.

Therapists often lift and carry equipment as well as lead recreational activities. Recreational therapists generally work a 40-hour week, which may include some evenings, weekends, and holidays.

Employment

Recreational therapists held about 38,000 jobs in 1996. About 42 percent of salaried jobs for therapists were in hospitals and 38 percent were in nursing homes. Others worked in residential facilities, community mental health centers, adult day care programs, correctional facilities, community programs for people with disabilities, and substance abuse centers. About 1 out of 4 therapists was self-employed, generally contracting with long-term care facilities or community agencies to develop and oversee programs.

Training, Other Qualifications, and Advancement

A bachelor's degree in therapeutic recreation (or in recreation with an option in therapeutic recreation) is the usual requirement for entry-level positions. Persons may qualify for paraprofessional positions with an associate degree in recreational therapy or a health care related field. An associates degree in recreational therapy; training in art, drama, or music therapy; or qualifying work experience may also be sufficient for activity director positions in nursing homes.

Most employers prefer to hire candidates who are certified therapeutic recreation specialists (CTRS). The National Council for Therapeutic Recreation Certification (NCTRC) certifies therapeutic recreation specialists. To become certified, specialists must have a bachelor's degree, pass a written certification examination, and complete an internship of at least 360 hours under the supervision of a certified therapeutic recreation specialist. A few colleges or agencies may require 600 hours of internship.

There are about 130 programs that prepare recreational therapists. Most offer bachelors degrees, although some offer associates, masters, or doctoral degrees. As of 1996, there were fewer than 50 recreation programs with options in therapeutic recreation that were accredited by the National Council on Accreditation.

In addition to therapeutic recreation course work in assessment, treatment and program planning, and intervention design and evaluation, students study human anatomy, physiology, abnormal psychology, medical and psychiatric terminology, characteristics of illnesses and disabilities, and the concepts of inclusion and normalization. Courses cover professional ethics, assessment and referral procedures, interdisciplinary teamwork, management, and the use of assistive devices and technology.

Recreational therapists should be comfortable working with persons who are ill or have disabilities. Therapists must be patient, tactful, and persuasive when working with people who have a variety of special needs. Ingenuity, a good sense of humor, and a strong imagination are needed to adapt activities to individual needs, and good physical coordination is necessary to demonstrate or participate in recreational events.

Therapists can advance to supervisory or administrative positions. Some teach, conduct research, or perform contract consulting work.

Job Outlook

Employment of recreational therapists is expected to grow faster than the average for all occupations through the year 2006, because of anticipated expansion in long-term care, physical and psychiatric rehabilitation, and services for people with disabilities. Job prospects are expected to be favorable for those with a strong health care background.

Health care facilities will provide a large number of recreational therapy jobs through the year 2006. A growing number of these will be in hospital-based adult day care and outpatient programs, or in units offering short-term mental health and alcohol or drug abuse services. Long-term rehabilitation, home-health care, transitional programs, and psychiatric facilities will provide additional jobs.

The rapidly growing number of older adults is expected to spur job growth for activity directors and recreational therapy paraprofessionals in nursing homes, assisted living facilities, adult day care programs, and social service agencies. Continued growth is expected in community residential facilities as well as day care programs for individuals with disabilities.

Earnings

According to a survey by the American Therapeutic Recreation Association, the average salary for recreational therapists was about $33,000 in 1996. The average annual salary for consultants, supervisors, administrators, and educators was about $42,000 in 1996. The average for all recreational therapists in the Federal Government in non-supervisory, supervisory, and managerial positions was about $39,400 in 1997.

Related Occupations

Recreational therapists design activities to help people with disabilities lead more fulfilling and independent lives. Other workers who have similar jobs are recreational therapy paraprofessionals, orientation therapists for persons who are blind or have visual impairments, art therapists, drama therapists, dance therapists, music therapists, occupational therapists, physical therapists, and rehabilitation counselors.

Sources of Additional Information

For information on how to order materials describing careers and academic programs in recreational therapy, write to:

☛ American Therapeutic Recreation Association, P.O. Box 15215, Hattiesburg, MS 39402-5215. Homepage: http://www.atra-tr.org.

☛ National Therapeutic Recreation Society, 22377 Belmont Ridge Rd., Ashburn, VA 20148 or by e-mail: NTRSNRPA@aol.com.

Certification information may be obtained from:

☛ National Council for Therapeutic Recreation Certification, P.O. Box 479, Thiells, NY 10984-0479.

Registered Nurses

(D.O.T. 075.124-010 and -014, .127-014, -026, -030 and -034, .137-010 and -014, .264-010 and -014, .364-010, .371-010, .374-014, -018, and -022)

Significant points

- The largest health care occupation, with over 1.9 million jobs.
- One of the five occupations projected to have the largest numbers of new jobs.
- Earnings are above average, particularly for advanced practice nurses who have additional education or training.

Nature of the Work

Registered nurses (R.N.'s) work to promote health, prevent disease, and help patients cope with illness. They are advocates and health educators for patients, families, and communities. When providing direct patient care, they observe, assess, and record symptoms, reactions, and progress; assist physicians during treatments and examinations; administer medications; and assist in convalescence and rehabilitation. R.N.'s also develop and manage nursing care plans; instruct patients and their families in proper care; and help individuals and groups take steps to improve or maintain their health. While State laws govern the tasks R.N.'s may perform, it is usually the work setting which determines their day-to-day job duties.

Hospital nurses form the largest group of nurses. Most are staff nurses, who provide bedside nursing care and carry out medical regimens. They may also supervise licensed practical nurses and aides. Hospital nurses usually are assigned to one area such as surgery, maternity, pediatrics, emergency room, intensive care, or treatment of cancer patients or may rotate among departments.

Office nurses assist physicians in private practice, clinics, surgicenters, emergency medical centers, and health maintenance organizations (HMO's). They prepare patients for and assist with examinations, administer injections and medications, dress wounds and incisions, assist with minor surgery, and maintain records. Some also perform routine laboratory and office work.

Home health nurses provide periodic services, prescribed by a physician, to patients at home. After assessing patients' home environments, they care for and instruct patients and their families. Home health nurses care for a broad range of patients, such as those recovering from illnesses and accidents, cancer, and child birth. They must be able to work independently and may supervise home health aides.

Nursing home nurses manage nursing care for residents with conditions ranging from a fracture to Alzheimer's disease. Although they generally spend most of their time on administrative and supervisory tasks, R.N.'s also assess residents' medical condition, develop treatment plans, supervise licensed practical nurses and nursing aides, and perform difficult procedures such as starting intravenous fluids. They also work in specialty-care departments, such as long-term rehabilitation units for strokes and head-injuries.

Public health nurses work in government and private agencies and clinics, schools, retirement communities and other community settings. They focus on populations, working with individuals, groups, and families to improve the overall health of communities. They also work as partners with communities to plan and implement programs. Public health nurses instruct individuals, families, and other groups in health education, disease prevention, nutrition, and child care. They arrange for immunizations, blood pressure testing, and other health screening. These nurses also work with community leaders, teachers, parents, and physicians in community health education.

Occupational health or *industrial nurses* provide nursing care at worksites to employees, customers, and others with minor injuries and illnesses. They provide emergency care, prepare accident reports, and arrange for further care if necessary. They also offer health counseling, assist with health examinations and inoculations, and assess work environments to identify potential health or safety problems.

Head nurses or *nurse supervisors* direct nursing activities. They plan work schedules and assign duties to nurses and aides, provide or arrange for training, and visit patients to observe nurses and to insure that care is proper. They may also insure that records are maintained and that equipment and supplies are ordered.

At the advanced level, *nurse practitioners* provide basic primary health care. They diagnose and treat common acute illnesses and injuries. Nurse practitioners can prescribe medications in most States. Other advanced practice nurses include *clinical nurse specialists, certified registered nurse anesthetists,* and *certified nurse-midwives.* Advanced practice nurses have met higher educational and clinical practice requirements beyond the basic nursing education and licensing required of all R.N.'s.

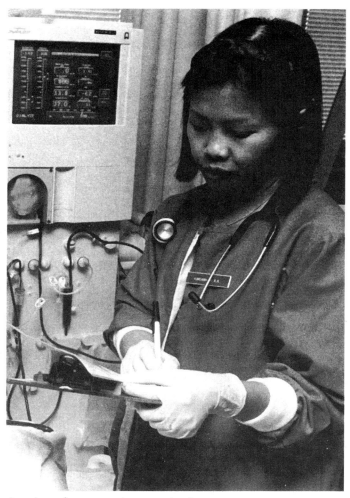

A *registered nurse monitors a patient's treatment.*

Working Conditions

Most nurses work in well-lighted, comfortable health care facilities. Home health and public health nurses travel to patients' homes and to schools, community centers, and other sites. Nurses may spend considerable time walking and standing. They need emotional stability to cope with human suffering, emergencies, and other stresses. Because patients in hospitals and nursing homes require 24-hour care, nurses in these institutions may work nights, weekends, and holidays. They may also be on-call. Office, occupational health, and public health nurses are more likely to work regular business hours. Almost 1 in 10 RN's held more than one job in 1996.

Nursing has its hazards, especially in hospitals, nursing homes, and clinics where nurses may care for individuals with infectious diseases such as hepatitis and AIDS. Nurses must observe rigid guidelines to guard against these and other dangers such as radiation, chemicals used for sterilization of instruments, and anesthetics. In addition, they face back injury when moving patients, shocks from electrical equipment, and hazards posed by compressed gases.

Employment

As the largest health care occupation, registered nurses held about 1,971,000 jobs in 1996. About 2 out of 3 jobs were in hospitals, in both inpatient and outpatient departments. Others were in offices and clinics of physicians, home health care agencies, nursing homes, temporary help agencies, schools, and government agencies. About 3 out of 10 R.N.'s worked part time.

Training, Other Qualifications, and Advancement

In all States, students must graduate from a nursing program and pass a national licensing examination to obtain a nursing license. Nurses may be licensed in more than one State, either by examination or endorsement of a license issued by another State. Licenses must be periodically renewed. Some States require continuing education for licensure renewal.

In 1996, there were over 1,500 entry level R.N. programs. There are three major educational paths to nursing: Associate degree (A.D.N.), diploma, and bachelor of science degree in nursing (B.S.N.). A.D.N. programs, offered by community and junior colleges, take about 2 years. About two-thirds of all R.N. graduates in 1995 were from A.D.N. programs. B.S.N. programs, offered by colleges and universities, take 4 or 5 years. Nearly one-third of all graduates in 1995 were from these programs. Diploma programs, given in hospitals, last 2 to 3 years. Only a small number of graduates come from these programs. Generally, licensed graduates of any of the three program types qualify for entry level positions as staff nurses.

There have been attempts to raise the educational requirements for an R.N. license to a bachelor's degree and, possibly, create new job titles. These changes, should they occur, will probably be made State by State, through legislation or regulation. Changes in licensure requirements would not affect currently licensed R.N.'s, who would be "grandfathered" in, no matter what their educational preparation. However, individuals considering nursing should carefully weigh the pros and cons of enrolling in a B.S.N. program, since their advancement opportunities are broader. In fact, some career paths are open only to nurses with bachelor's or advanced degrees. A bachelor's degree is generally necessary for administrative positions and is a prerequisite for admission to graduate nursing programs in research, consulting, teaching, or a clinical specialization.

Many A.D.N. and diploma-trained nurses enter bachelor's programs to prepare for a broader scope of nursing practice. They can often find a hospital position and then take advantage of tuition reimbursement programs to work toward a B.S.N. in their spare time.

Nursing education includes classroom instruction and supervised clinical experience in hospitals and other health facilities. Students take courses in anatomy, physiology, microbiology, chemistry, nutrition, psychology and other behavioral sciences, and nursing. Coursework also includes liberal arts classes.

Supervised clinical experience is provided in hospital departments such as pediatrics, psychiatry, maternity, and surgery. A growing number of programs include clinical experience in nursing homes, public health departments, home health agencies, and ambulatory clinics.

Nurses should be caring and sympathetic. They must be able to accept responsibility, direct or supervise others, follow orders precisely, and determine when consultation is required.

Experience and good performance can lead to promotion to more responsible positions. Nurses can advance, in management, to assistant head nurse or head nurse. From there, they can advance to assistant director, director, and vice president. Increasingly, management level nursing positions require a graduate degree in nursing or health services administration. They also require leadership, negotiation skills, and good judgment. Graduate programs preparing executive level nurses usually last 1 to 2 years.

Within patient care, nurses can advance to clinical nurse specialist, nurse practitioner, certified nurse-midwife, or certified registered nurse anesthetist. These positions require 1 or 2 years of graduate education, leading in most instances to a master's degree, or to a certificate.

Some nurses move into the business side of health care. Their nursing expertise and experience on a health care team equip them to manage ambulatory, acute, home health, and chronic care services. Some are employed by health care corporations in health planning and development, marketing, and quality assurance.

Job Outlook

Employment of registered nurses is expected to grow faster than the average for all occupations through the year 2006 and, because the occupation is large, many new jobs will result. As nursing school enrollments level off or decline, as they have on a cyclical basis in the past, the number of qualified applicants will fall, reducing reported competition for jobs. There will always be a need for traditional hospital nurses, but a large number of new nurses will be employed in home health, long-term, and ambulatory care.

Faster than average growth will be driven by technological advances in patient care, which permit a greater number of medical problems to be treated, and increasing emphasis on primary care. In addition, the number of older people, who are much more likely than younger people to need medical care, is projected to grow very rapidly. Many job openings also will result from the need to replace experienced nurses who leave the occupation, especially as the average age of the registered nurse population continues to rise.

Employment in hospitals, the largest sector, is expected to grow more slowly than in other health-care sectors. While the intensity of nursing care is likely to increase, requiring more nurses per patient, the number of inpatients (those who remain overnight) is not likely to increase much. Also, patients are being released earlier and more procedures are being done on an outpatient basis, both in and outside hospitals. Most rapid growth is expected in hospitals' outpatient facilities, such as same-day surgery, rehabilitation, and chemotherapy.

Employment in home health care is expected to grow the fastest. This is in response to a growing number of older persons with functional disabilities, consumer preference for care in the home, and technological advances which make it possible to bring increasingly complex treatments into the home. The type of care demanded will require nurses who are able to perform complex procedures.

Employment in nursing homes is expected to grow much faster than average due to increases in the number of people in their eighties and nineties, many of whom will require long-term care. In addition, the financial pressure on hospitals to release patients as soon as possible should produce more nursing home admissions. Growth in units to provide specialized long-term rehabilitation for stroke and head injury patients or to treat Alzheimer's victims will also increase employment.

An increasing proportion of sophisticated procedures, which once were performed only in hospitals, are being performed in physicians' offices and clinics, including HMO's, ambulatory surgicenters, and emergency medical centers. Accordingly, employment is expected to grow faster than average in these places as health care in general expands.

In evolving integrated health care networks, nurses may rotate among employment settings. Since jobs in traditional hospital nursing positions are no longer the only option, R.N.'s will need to be flexible. Opportunities will be best for nurses with advanced education and training, such as nurse practitioners.

Earnings

Median weekly earnings of full-time salaried registered nurses were $697 in 1996. The middle 50 percent earned between $571 and $868. The lowest 10 percent earned less than $415; the top 10 percent, more than $1,039.

According to a Hay Group survey of HMO's, group practices, and hospital-based clinics, the median annual base salary of full-time nurse practitioners was $66,800 in May 1996. The middle 50 percent earned between $54,200 and $69,200. Nurse midwives earned about $70,100, and the middle 50 percent earned between $59,300 and $75,700. According to the Hay Group's survey of acute care hospitals, the median annual base salary of full-time nurse anesthetists was $82,000 in January 1997. The middle 50 percent earned between $74,700 and $90,300.

According to the Buck Survey conducted by the American Health Care Association, staff R.N.'s in chain nursing homes had median hourly earnings of $15.85 in 1996. The middle 50 percent earned between $14.03 and $17.73.

Many employers offer flexible work schedules, child care, educational benefits, and bonuses.

Related Occupations

Workers in other health care occupations with responsibilities and duties related to those of registered nurses are occupational therapists, emergency medical technicians, physical therapists, physician assistants, and respiratory therapists.

Sources of Additional Information

The National League for Nursing (NLN) publishes a variety of nursing and nursing education materials, including a list of nursing programs and information on student financial aid. For a complete list of NLN publications, write for a career information brochure. Send your request to:

☛ Communications Department, National League for Nursing, 350 Hudson St., New York, NY 10014. FAX: (212) 989-2272.

For a list of B.S.N. and graduate programs, write to:

☛ American Association of Colleges of Nursing, 1 Dupont Circle NW., Suite 530, Washington, DC 20036. FAX: (202) 785-8320.

Information on registered nurses is also available from:

☛ American Nurses Association, 600 Maryland Ave. SW., Washington, DC 20024-2571.

Respiratory Therapists

(D.O.T. 076.361-014)

Significant points

● Hospitals will continue to employ more than 9 out of 10 respiratory therapists, but a growing number will work outside of hospitals under contract to home health agencies and nursing homes.

● Job opportunities will be best for therapists who work with newborns and infants.

Nature of the Work

You can live without water for a few days and without food for a few weeks. But without oxygen, you will suffer brain damage within a few minutes and die after about 9 minutes. Respiratory therapists, also known as respiratory care practitioners, evaluate, treat, and care for patients with breathing disorders.

In evaluating patients, therapists test the capacity of the lungs and analyze the oxygen and carbon dioxide concentration as well as the potential of hydrogen (pH), a measure of the acidity or alkalinity level of the blood. To measure lung capacity, therapists have patients breathe into an instrument that measures the volume and flow of oxygen during inhalation and exhalation. By comparing the reading with the norm for the patient's age, height, weight, and sex, respiratory therapists can determine whether lung deficiencies exist. To analyze oxygen, carbon dioxide, and pH levels, therapists draw an arterial blood sample, place it in a blood gas analyzer, and relay the results to a physician.

Respiratory therapists treat all types of patients, ranging from premature infants whose lungs are not fully developed, to elderly people whose lungs are diseased. They provide temporary relief to patients with chronic asthma or emphysema and emergency care for patients who suffered heart failure or a stroke, or are victims of drowning or shock. Respiratory therapists most commonly use oxygen or oxygen mixtures, chest physiotherapy, and aerosol medications. Therapists may place an oxygen mask or nasal cannula on a patient and set the oxygen flow at the level prescribed by a physician to increase a patient's concentration of oxygen. Therapists also connect patients who cannot breathe on their own to ventilators, which deliver pressurized oxygen into the lungs. They insert a tube into a patient's trachea, or windpipe; connect the tube to the ventilator; and set the rate, volume, and oxygen concentration of the oxygen mixture entering the patient's lungs. Therapists regularly check on patients and equipment. If the patient appears to be having difficulty or if the oxygen, carbon dioxide, or pH level of the blood is abnormal, they change the ventilator setting according to the doctor's order or check equipment for mechanical problems. In homecare, therapists teach patients and their families to use ventilators and other life support systems. They visit several times a month to inspect and clean equipment and ensure its proper use and make emergency visits if equipment problems arise.

Respiratory therapists perform chest physiotherapy on patients to remove mucus from their lungs to make it easier for them to breathe. For example, during surgery, anesthesia depresses respiration, so this treatment may be prescribed to help get the patient's lungs back to normal and prevent congestion. Chest physiotherapy also is used on patients suffering from lung diseases that cause mucus to collect in the lungs, such as cystic fibrosis. Therapists place patients in positions to help drain mucus, thump and vibrate patients' rib cages, and instruct them to cough.

Respiratory therapists also administer aerosols—generally liquid medications suspended in a gas that forms a mist which is inhaled—and teach patients how to inhale the aerosol properly to assure its effectiveness.

Therapists are increasingly working under the supervision of nurses and are being asked to perform tasks that fall outside of their traditional role. They are expanding into cardiopulmonary procedures like electrocardiograms and stress testing, but also perform other tasks like drawing blood samples from patients. They also keep records of the materials used and charges to patients. Some therapists teach or supervise other respiratory therapy personnel.

Working Conditions
Respiratory therapists generally work between 35 and 40 hours a week. Because hospitals operate around the clock, therapists may work evenings, nights, or weekends. They spend long periods standing and walking between patients' rooms. In an emergency, they work under a great deal of stress. Gases used by respiratory therapists are potentially hazardous because they are used and stored

Respiratory therapists connect patients who cannot breathe on their own to ventilators which deliver pressurized oxygen into the lungs.

under pressure. However, adherence to safety precautions and regular maintenance and testing of equipment minimize the risk of injury. As with many health occupations, respiratory therapists run a risk of catching infectious diseases, but careful adherence to proper procedures minimizes this risk, as well.

Employment
Respiratory therapists held about 82,000 jobs in 1996. About 9 out of 10 jobs were in hospital departments of respiratory care, anesthesiology, or pulmonary medicine. Home health agencies, respiratory therapy clinics, and nursing homes accounted for most of the remaining jobs.

Training, Other Qualifications, and Advancement
Formal training is necessary for entry to this field. Training is offered at the postsecondary level by hospitals, medical schools, colleges and universities, trade schools, vocational-technical institutes, and the Armed Forces. Some programs prepare graduates for jobs as respiratory therapists; other, shorter programs lead to jobs as respiratory therapy technicians. In 1996, 210 programs for respiratory therapists were accredited by the Commission on Accreditation of Allied Health Education Programs (CAAHEP) of the American Medical Association (AMA). Another 158 programs offered CAAHEP-accredited preparation for respiratory therapy technicians.

Formal training programs vary in length and in the credential or degree awarded. Most of the CAAHEP-accredited therapist programs last 2 years and lead to an associate degree. Some, however, are 4-year bachelor's degree programs. Technician programs last about 1 year and award certificates. Areas of study for respiratory therapy programs include human anatomy and physiology, chemistry, physics, microbiology, and mathematics. Technical courses deal with procedures, equipment, and clinical tests.

More and more therapists receive on-the-job training, allowing them to administer electrocardiograms and stress tests, as well as draw blood samples from patients.

Therapists should be sensitive to patients' physical and psychological needs. Respiratory care workers must pay attention to detail, follow instructions, and work as part of a team. Operating complicated respiratory therapy equipment requires mechanical ability and manual dexterity.

High school students interested in a career in respiratory care should take courses in health, biology, mathematics, chemistry, and physics. Respiratory care involves basic mathematical problem-solving and an understanding of chemical and physical principles. For example, respiratory care workers must be able to compute medication dosages and calculate gas concentrations.

Forty-seven States license respiratory care personnel. Only Nevada, Delaware, and Washington do not require licensure. The National Board for Respiratory Care offers voluntary certification and registration to graduates of CAAHEP-accredited programs. Two credentials are awarded to respiratory care practitioners who satisfy the requirements: Certified Respiratory Therapy Technician (CRTT) and Registered Respiratory Therapist (RRT). All graduates—those from 2- and 4-year programs in respiratory therapy, as well as those from 1-year technician programs—may take the CRTT examination first. CRTT's who meet education and experience requirements can take a separate examination, leading to the award of the RRT.

Individuals who have completed a 4-year program in a nonrespiratory field, but have college level courses in anatomy, physiology, chemistry, biology, microbiology, physics, and mathematics, can become a CRTT after graduating from an AMA accredited 1- or 2-year program. After they receive 2 years of clinical experience, they are eligible to take the registry exam to become an RRT.

Most employers require that applicants for entry-level or generalist positions hold the CRTT or are eligible to take the certification examination. Supervisory positions and those in intensive care specialties, usually require the RRT (or RRT eligibility).

Respiratory therapists advance in clinical practice by moving from care of "general" to "critical" patients, who have significant problems in other organ systems such as the heart or kidneys. Respiratory therapists, especially those with 4-year degrees, may also advance to supervisory or managerial positions in a respiratory therapy department. Respiratory therapists in home care and equipment rental firms may become branch manager.

Job Outlook
Job opportunities are expected to remain good. Employment of respiratory therapists is expected to increase much faster than the average for all occupations through the year 2006 because of substantial growth of the middle-aged and elderly population, a development that will heighten the incidence of cardiopulmonary disease.

Older Americans suffer most from respiratory ailments and cardiopulmonary diseases such as pneumonia, chronic bronchitis, emphysema, and heart disease. As their numbers increase, the need for respiratory therapists will increase as well. In addition, advances in treating victims of heart attacks, accident victims, and premature infants (many of who may be dependent on a ventilator during part of their treatment) will increase the demand for the services of respiratory care practitioners.

Opportunities are expected to be highly favorable for respiratory therapists with cardiopulmonary care skills and experience in working with infants.

Although hospitals will continue to employ the vast majority of therapists, a growing number of therapists can expect to work outside of hospitals under contract to home health agencies and nursing homes.

Earnings
Median weekly earnings for full time salaried respiratory therapists were $636 in 1996. The middle 50 percent earned between $506 and $767. The lowest 10 percent earned less than $367; the top 10 percent earned more than $978.

According to a Hay Group survey of acute care hospitals, the median annual base salary of full-time respiratory therapists was $32,500 in January 1997. The middle 50 percent earned between $29,300 and $35,000.

Related Occupations
Respiratory therapists, under the supervision of a physician, administer respiratory care and life support to patients with heart and lung difficulties. Other workers who care for, treat, or train people to improve their physical condition include dialysis technicians, registered nurses, occupational therapists, physical therapists, and radiation therapy technologists.

Sources of Additional Information
Information concerning a career in respiratory care is available from:
☛ American Association for Respiratory Care, 11030 Ables Ln., Dallas, TX 75229.

Information on gaining credentials as a respiratory therapy practitioner can be obtained from:
☛ The National Board for Respiratory Care, Inc., 8310 Nieman Rd., Lenexa, KS 66214.

For the current list of CAAHEP-accredited educational programs for respiratory therapy occupations, write to:
☛ Joint Review Committee for Respiratory Therapy Education, 1701 W. Euless Blvd., Suite 300, Euless, TX 76040.

Speech-Language Pathologists and Audiologists

(D.O.T. 076.101-010, .104-010, and .107-010)

Significant Points
- About half work in schools, and most others are employed by healthcare facilities.

- A master's degree in speech-language pathology or audiology is the standard credential.

- Projected much-faster-than-average employment growth reflects the increasing number of people who will need speech-language pathology and audiology services.

Nature of the Work
Speech-language pathologists assess, treat, and help to prevent speech, language, cognitive communication, voice, swallowing, fluency, and other related disorders; audiologists identify, assess, and manage auditory, balance, and other neural systems.

Speech-language pathologists work with people who cannot make speech sounds, or cannot make them clearly; those with speech rhythm and fluency problems, such as stuttering; people with voice quality problems, such as inappropriate pitch or harsh voice; those with problems understanding and producing language; and those with cognitive communication impairments, such as attention, memory, and problem solving disorders. They may also work with people who have oral motor problems causing eating and swallowing difficulties.

Speech and language problems can result from hearing loss, brain injury or deterioration, cerebral palsy, stroke, cleft palate, voice pathology, mental retardation, or emotional problems. Problems can be congenital, developmental, or acquired. Speech-language pathologists use written and oral tests, as well as special instruments, to diagnose the nature and extent of impairment and to record and analyze speech, language, and swallowing irregularities. Speech-language pathologists develop an individualized plan of care, tailored to each patient's needs. For individuals with little or no speech capability, speech-language pathologists select augmentative alternative communication methods, including automated devices and sign language, and teach their use. They teach these individuals how to make sounds, improve their voices, or increase their language skills to communicate more effectively. Speech-language pathologists help patients develop, or recover, reliable communication skills so patients can fulfill their educational, vocational, and social roles.

Most speech-language pathologists provide direct clinical services to individuals with communication disorders. In speech and language clinics, they may independently develop and carry out treatment programs. In medical facilities, they may work with physicians, social workers, psychologists, and other therapists to develop and execute treatment plans. Speech-language pathologists in schools develop individual or group programs, counsel parents, and may assist teachers with classroom activities.

Speech-language pathologists keep records on the initial evaluation, progress, and discharge of clients. This helps pinpoint problems, tracks client progress, and justifies the cost of treatment when applying for reimbursement. They counsel individuals and their families concerning communication disorders and how to cope with the stress and misunderstanding that often accompany them. They also work with family members to recognize and change behavior patterns that impede communication and treatment and show them communication-enhancing techniques to use at home.

Some speech-language pathologists conduct research on how people communicate. Others design and develop equipment or techniques for diagnosing and treating speech problems.

Audiologists work with people who have hearing, balance, and related problems. They use audiometers and other testing devices to measure the loudness at which a person begins to hear sounds, the ability to distinguish between sounds, and the nature and extent of hearing loss. Audiologists interpret these results and may coordinate them with medical, educational, and psychological information to make a diagnosis and determine a course of treatment.

Hearing disorders can result from trauma at birth, viral infections, genetic disorders, or exposure to loud noise. Treatment may include examining and cleaning the ear canal, fitting and dispensing a hearing aid or other assistive device, and audiologic rehabilitation (including auditory training or instruction in speech or lip reading). Audiologists may recommend, fit, and dispense personal or large area amplification systems, such as hearing aids and alerting devices. Audiologists provide fitting and tuning of cochlear implants and provide the necessary rehabilitation for adjustment to listening with implant amplification systems. They also test noise levels in workplaces and conduct hearing protection programs in industry, as well as in schools and communities.

Audiologists provide direct clinical services to individuals with hearing or balance disorders. In audiology (hearing) clinics, they may independently develop and carry out treatment programs. Audiologists, in a variety of settings, work as members of interdisciplinary professional teams in planning and implementing service delivery for children and adults, from birth to old age. Similar to speech-language pathologists, audiologists keep records on the initial evaluation, progress, and discharge of clients. These records help pinpoint problems, track client progress, and justify the cost of treatment, when applying for reimbursement.

Audiologists may conduct research on types of, and treatment for, hearing, balance, and related disorders. Others design and develop equipment or techniques for diagnosing and treating these disorders.

Working Conditions
Speech-language pathologists and audiologists usually work at a desk or table in clean comfortable surroundings. The job is not physically demanding but does require attention to detail and intense concentration. The emotional needs of clients and their families may be demanding. Most full-time speech-language pathologists and audiologists work about 40 hours per week; some work part-time. Those who work on a contract basis may spend a substantial amount of time traveling between facilities.

Employment
Speech-language pathologists and audiologists held about 87,000 jobs in 1996. About one-half provided services in preschools, elementary and secondary schools, or colleges and universities. More than 1 in 10 were in hospitals. Others were in offices of physicians; offices of speech-language pathologists and audiologists; speech, language, and hearing centers; home health care agencies; or other facilities. Some were in private practice, working either as solo practitioners or in a group practice. Some speech-language pathologists and audiologists contract to provide services in schools, hospitals, or nursing homes, or work as consultants to industry. Audiologists are more likely to be employed in independent healthcare offices, while speech-language pathologists are more likely to work in school settings.

Training, Other Qualifications, and Advancement
Of the States that regulate licensing (44 for speech-language pathologists and 47 for audiologists), almost all require a master's degree or equivalent. Other requirements are 300-375 hours of supervised clinical experience, a passing score on a national examination, and 9 months of postgraduate professional clinical experience. Thirty-four states have continuing education requirements for licensure renewal. Medicaid, medicare, and private health insurers generally require a practitioner to be licensed to qualify for reimbursement.

About 230 colleges and universities offer graduate programs in speech-language pathology. Courses cover anatomy and physiology of the areas of the body involved in speech, language, and hearing; the development of normal speech, language, and hearing; the nature of disorders; acoustics; and psychological aspects of communication. Graduate students also learn to evaluate and treat speech, language, and hearing disorders and receive supervised clinical training in communication disorders.

About 120 colleges and universities offer graduate programs in audiology in the United States. Course work includes anatomy; physiology; basic science; math; physics; genetics; normal and abnormal communication development; auditory, balance and neural systems assessment and treatment; audiologic rehabilitation; and ethics.

Audiologists use audiometers and other testing devices to measure the loudness at which a person begins to hear sounds.

Speech-language pathologists can acquire the Certificate of Clinical Competence in Speech-Language Pathology (CCC-SLP) offered by the American Speech-Language-Hearing Association, and audiologists can earn the Certificate of Clinical Competence in Audiology (CCC-A). To earn a CCC, a person must have a graduate degree and 375 hours of supervised clinical experience, complete a 36-week postgraduate clinical fellowship, and pass a written examination.

Speech-language pathologists and audiologists should be able to effectively communicate diagnostic test results, diagnoses, and proposed treatment in a manner easily understood by their clients. They must be able to approach problems objectively and provide support to clients and their families. Because a client's progress may be slow, patience, compassion, and good listening skills are necessary.

Speech-language pathologists and audiologists may work in a variety of settings, including schools, hospitals, health departments, clinics, and private practices. Some members of these professions also serve as clinical supervisors for student clinicians, professors in universities and colleges, or conduct research.

Job Outlook
Employment of speech-language pathologists and audiologists is expected to increase much faster than the average for all occupations through the year 2006. Employment in health and rehabilitation services will increase as a result of advances in medical technology and growth in the elderly population. Because hearing loss is strongly associated with aging, rapid growth in the population age 55 and over will cause the number of persons with hearing impairment to increase markedly. In addition, baby boomers are now entering middle age, when the possibility of neurological disorders and associated speech, language, and hearing impairments increases. Medical advances are also improving the survival rate of premature infants and trauma and stroke victims, who then need assessment and possible treatment.

Employment in schools will increase along with growth in elementary and secondary school enrollments, including enrollment of special education students. Federal law guarantees special education and related services to all eligible children with disabilities. Greater awareness of the importance of early identification and diagnosis of speech, language, and hearing disorders will also increase employment.

The number of speech-language pathologists and audiologists in private practice, though small, is likely to rise sharply due to the increasing use of contract services by managed care, hospitals, schools, and nursing homes. In addition to job openings stemming from rapid job growth over the 1996-2006 period, some openings for speech-language pathologists and audiologists will arise from the need to replace those who leave the occupation.

Earnings

Median weekly earnings of full-time salaried speech-language pathologists and audiologists were about $690 in 1996. The middle 50 percent earned between $560 and $880. The lowest 10 percent earned less than $440 and the top 10 percent more than $1,160.

According to a 1997 survey by the American Speech-Language-Hearing Association, the median annual salary for full-time certified speech-language pathologists was $44,000; for audiologists, $43,000. Certified speech-language pathologists with 1 to 3 years of experience earned a median annual salary of $38,000; licensed audiologists with 1 to 3 years of experience earned $32,000. Speech-language pathologists with 22 years' experience earned a median annual salary of $52,000, while audiologists with comparable experience earned about $55,000. Salaries also vary according to geographic location and type of employment facility.

Related Occupations

Speech-language pathologists specialize in the prevention, diagnosis, and treatment of speech and language problems. Workers in related occupations include occupational therapists, optometrists, physical therapists, psychologists, recreational therapists, and rehabilitation counselors.

Audiologists specialize in the prevention, diagnosis, and treatment of hearing problems. Workers in related occupations include neurologists, neonatologists, acoustical engineers, industrial hygienists, and other rehabilitation professionals.

Sources of Additional Information

State licensing boards in each State can provide information on licensure requirements. State departments of education can supply information on certification requirements for those who wish to work in public schools.

General information on careers in speech-language pathology and audiology is available from:

☛ American Speech-Language-Hearing Association, 10801 Rockville Pike, Rockville, MD 20852. Homepage: http://www.asha.org

Information on a career in audiology is also available from:

☛ American Academy of Audiology, 8201 Greensboro Dr., Suite 300, McLean, VA 22102.

Health Technologists and Technicians

Cardiovascular Technologists and Technicians

(D.O.T. 078.264-010, .362-018, -030, -050, -062, .364-014, and .367-010)

Significant points

- Employment will grow as fast as the average, but the number of job openings created will be low because the occupation is small.

- More than 9 out of 10 jobs are in hospitals, in both inpatient and outpatient settings.

Nature of the Work

Cardiovascular technologists and technicians assist physicians in diagnosing and treating cardiac (heart) and peripheral vascular (blood vessel) ailments.

Cardiovascular technicians who obtain electro (electrical)- cardio (heart)- grams (record), are known as *electrocardiograph* (abbreviated *EKG* or *ECG) technicians.* To take a "basic" EKG, which traces electrical impulses transmitted by the heart, technicians attach electrodes to the patient's chest, arms, and legs, and then manipulate switches on a electrocardiograph machine to obtain the reading. The test is done before most kinds of surgery and as part of a routine physical examination, especially for persons who have reached middle age or have a history of cardiovascular problems.

More skilled EKG technicians perform Holter monitor and stress testing. For a Holter monitoring, technicians place electrodes on the patient's chest and attach a portable EKG monitor to the patient's belt. Following 24-48 hours of normal routine for the patient, the technician removes a cassette tape from the monitor and places it in a scanner. After checking the quality of the recorded impulses on an electronic screen, the technician prints the information from the tape so it can be interpreted later. The printed output from the scanner is eventually used by a physician to diagnose heart ailments.

For a treadmill stress test, EKG technicians document the patient's medical history, explain the procedure, connect the patient to an EKG monitor, and obtain a baseline reading and resting blood pressure. Next, they monitor the heart's performance while the patient is walking on a treadmill, gradually increasing the treadmill's speed to observe the effect of increased exertion. Those cardiovascular technicians who perform EKG and stress tests are known as "noninvasive" technicians because the techniques they use do not equire the insertion of probes or other instruments into the patient's body.

Cardiovascular technologists who specialize in cardiac catheterization procedures are called *cardiology technologists.* They assist physicians with invasive procedures in which a small tube, or catheter, is wound through a patient's blood vessel from a spot on the patient's leg into the heart to determine if a blockage exists or for other diagnostic purposes. In balloon angioplasty, a procedure used to treat blockages of blood vessels, technologists assist physicians who insert a catheter with a balloon on the end to the point of the obstruction. Technologists may prepare patients for these procedures by positioning them on an examining table, then shaving, cleaning, and administering anesthesia to the top of the patient's leg near the groin. During the procedures, they monitor patients' blood pressure and heart rate using EKG equipment, and notify the physician if something appears wrong. Technologists may also prepare and monitor patients during open heart surgery and the implantation of pacemakers.

Cardiovascular technologists and technicians may also specialize in noninvasive peripheral vascular tests. Those who assist physicians in the diagnosis of disorders affecting circulation are known as *vascular technologists.* Vascular technologists use ultrasound instrumentation, such as doppler ultrasound, to noninvasively record information on the vessels such as blood pressure, limb volume changes, oxygen saturation, cerebral circulation, peripheral circulation, and abdominal circulation. Many of these tests are performed during or immediately after surgery. Technologists and technicians who use ultrasound on the heart are referred to as *echocardiographers.* They use ultrasound equipment that transmits sound waves, then collects the echoes to form an image on a screen.

Some cardiovascular technologists and technicians schedule appointments, type doctor's interpretations, maintain patient's files, and care for equipment.

Working Conditions

Technologists and technicians generally work a 5-day, 40-hour week, which may include weekends. Those in catheterization labs tend to work longer hours and may work evenings. They may also be on call during the night and on weekends.

Cardiovascular technologists and technicians spend a lot of time walking and standing. Those who work in catheterization labs may face stressful working conditions, because they are in close contact with patients who have serious heart ailments. Some patients, for

Cardiovascular technologists and technicians use computers to evaluate a patient's heart condition.

example, may encounter complications from time to time that have life or death implications.

Employment

Cardiovascular technologists and technicians held about 32,000 jobs in 1996. Most worked in hospital cardiology departments, while some worked in cardiologists' offices, cardiac rehabilitation centers, or ambulatory surgery centers. About one-half were EKG technicians.

Training, Other Qualifications, and Advancement

For basic EKG's, Holter monitoring, and stress testing, 1-year certificate programs exist, although most EKG technicians are still trained on the job by an EKG supervisor or a cardiologist. On-the-job training usually lasts about 8 to 16 weeks, applicants must be high school graduates. Most employers prefer to train people already in the health care field—nursing aides, for example. Some EKG technicians are students who are enrolled in 2-year programs to become technologists, but work part-time to gain experience and make contact with employers.

Although some cardiovascular technologists, vascular technologists, and echocardiographers are currently trained on the job, more are being trained in 2- to 4-year programs. Cardiology technologists complete a 2-year junior or community college program. One year is dedicated to core courses followed by a year of specialized instruction in either invasive, noninvasive, or noninvasive peripheral cardiology. Those who are qualified in a related allied health profession only need to complete the year of specialized instruction. Graduates from programs accredited by the Joint Review Committee on Education in Cardiovascular Technology are eligible to register as professional technologists with the American Registry of Diagnostic Medical Sonographers or Cardiovascular Credentialing International.

Cardiovascular technologists and technicians must be reliable, have mechanical aptitude, and be able to follow detailed instructions. A pleasant, relaxed manner for putting patients at ease is an asset.

Job Outlook

Employment of cardiovascular technologists and technicians is expected to grow more slowly than the average for all occupations through the year 2006, with technologists and technicians experiencing

different patterns of employment change. Employment of *cardiology technologists* is expected to grow faster than the average for all occupations. Growth will occur as the population ages, because older people have a higher incidence of heart problems. Likewise, employment of vascular technologists will grow faster than the average, as advances in vascular technology reduce the need for more costly and invasive procedures. In contrast, employment of *EKG technicians* is expected to decline as hospitals train registered nurses and others to perform basic EKG procedures. Individuals trained in Holter monitoring and stress testing are expected to have more favorable job prospects than those who can only perform a basic EKG.

Most job openings for cardiovascular technologists and technicians will arise from replacement needs as individuals transfer to other jobs or leave the labor force. Relatively few job openings due to both growth and replacement needs are expected, however, because the occupation is small.

Earnings

According to a Hay Group survey of acute care hospitals, the median annual base salary of full-time EKG technicians was $20,200 in January 1997. The middle 50 percent earned between $17,100 and $23,800 a year.

Based on limited information, the average salary for cardiovascular technologists was about $33,600 in 1996.

Related Occupations

Cardiovascular technologists and technicians operate sophisticated equipment that helps physicians and other health practitioners diagnose and treat patients. So do nuclear medicine technologists, radiologic technologists, diagnostic medical sonographers, electroencephalographic technologists, perfusionists, and respiratory therapists.

Sources of Additional Information

Local hospitals can supply information about employment opportunities.

For general information about a career in cardiovascular technology contact:
☛ Alliance of Cardiovascular Professionals, 910 Charles St., Fredericksburg, VA 22401.

For a list of accredited programs in cardiovascular technology, contact:
☛ Joint Review Committee on Education in Cardiovascular Technology, 3525 Ellicott Mills Dr., Suite N, Ellicott City, MD 21043-4547.

For information on vascular technology, contact:
☛ The Society of Vascular Technology, 4601 Presidents Dr., Suite 260, Lanham, MD 20706-4365.

For information on echocardiography, contact:
☛ American Society of Echocardiography, 4101 Lake Boone Trail, Suite 201, Raleigh, NC 27607.

For information regarding registration and certification contact:
☛ Cardiovascular Credentialing International, 4456 Corporation Lane, Suite 110, Virginia Beach, VA 23462.
☛ American Registry of Diagnostic Medical Sonographers, 600 Jefferson Plaza, Suite 360, Rockville, MD 20852-1150.

Clinical Laboratory Technologists and Technicians

(D.O.T. 078.221-010, .261-010, -014, -026, -030, and -038, .281-010, .381 -014, .687-010, and 559.361-010)

Significant points

- Medical and clinical laboratory technologists usually have a bachelor's degree with a major in medical technology or in one of the life sciences; medical and clinical laboratory technicians typically need either an associate's degree or a certificate.

• Competition for jobs has increased and individuals may now have to look longer to find employment than in the past.

Nature of the Work

Clinical laboratory testing plays a crucial role in the detection, diagnosis, and treatment of disease. Clinical laboratory technologists and technicians, also known as medical technologists and technicians, perform most of these tests.

Clinical laboratory personnel examine and analyze body fluids, tissues, and cells. They look for bacteria, parasites, or other micro-organisms; analyze the chemical content of fluids; match blood for transfusions, and test for drug levels in the blood to show how a patient is responding to treatment. They also prepare specimens for examination, count cells, and look for abnormal cells. They use automated equipment and instruments that perform a number of tests simultaneously, as well as microscopes, cell counters, and other kinds of sophisticated laboratory equipment to perform tests. Then they analyze the results and relay them to physicians.

The complexity of tests performed, the level of judgment needed, and the amount of responsibility workers assume depend largely on the amount of education and experience they have.

Medical and clinical laboratory technologists generally have a bachelor's degree in medical technology or in one of the life sciences, or have a combination of formal training and work experience. They perform complex chemical, biological, hematologic, immunologic, microscopic, and bacteriological tests. Technologists microscopically examine blood, tissue, and other body substances. They make cultures of body fluid or tissue samples to determine the presence of bacteria, fungi, parasites, or other micro-organisms. They analyze samples for chemical content or reaction and determine blood glucose or cholesterol levels. They also type and cross-match blood samples for transfusions.

Medical and clinical laboratory technologists may evaluate test results, develop and modify procedures, and establish and monitor programs to insure the accuracy of tests. Some medical and clinical laboratory technologists supervise medical and clinical laboratory technicians.

Technologists in small laboratories perform many types of tests, while those in large laboratories generally specialize. Technologists who prepare specimens and analyze the chemical and hormonal contents of body fluids are *clinical chemistry technologists*. Those who examine and identify bacteria and other micro-organisms are *microbiology technologists*. *Blood bank technologists* collect, type, and prepare blood and its components for transfusions. *Immunology technologists* examine elements and responses of the human immune system to foreign bodies. *Cytotechnologists*, prepare slides of body cells and microscopically examine these cells for abnormalities which may signal the beginning of a cancerous growth.

Medical and clinical laboratory technicians perform less complex tests and laboratory procedures than technologists. Technicians may prepare specimens and operate automatic analyzers, for example, or they may perform manual tests following detailed instructions. Like technologists, they may work in several areas of the clinical laboratory or specialize in just one. *Histology technicians* cut and stain tissue specimens for microscopic examination by pathologists, and *phlebotomists* draw and test blood. They usually work under the supervision of medical and clinical laboratory technologists or laboratory managers.

Working Conditions

Hours and other working conditions vary according to the size and type of employment setting. In large hospitals or in independent laboratories that operate continuously, personnel usually work the day, evening, or night shift, and may work weekends and holidays. Laboratory personnel in small facilities may work on rotating shifts rather than on a regular shift. In some facilities, laboratory personnel

A blood bank technologist collects, types, and prepares blood and its components for transfusions.

are on call, available in case of an emergency, several nights a week or on weekends.

Clinical laboratory personnel are trained to work with infectious specimens. When proper methods of infection control and sterilization are followed, few hazards exist.

Laboratories generally are well lighted and clean; however, specimens, solutions, and reagents used in the laboratory sometimes produce odors. Laboratory workers may spend a great deal of time on their feet.

Employment

Clinical laboratory technologists and technicians held about 285,000 jobs in 1996. More than half worked in hospitals. Most others worked in medical laboratories and offices and clinics of physicians. Some worked in blood banks, research and testing laboratories, and in the Federal Government—at Department of Veterans Affairs hospitals and U.S. Public Health Service facilities. About 1 laboratory worker in 6 worked part time.

Training, Other Qualifications, and Advancement

The usual requirement for an entry level position as a medical or clinical laboratory technologist is a bachelor's degree with a major in medical technology or in one of the life sciences. Universities and hospitals offer medical technology programs. It is also possible to qualify through a combination of on-the-job and specialized training.

Bachelor's degree programs in medical technology include courses in chemistry, biological sciences, microbiology, and mathematics, and specialized courses devoted to knowledge and skills used in the clinical laboratory. Many programs also offer or require courses in management, business, and computer applications.

Masters degrees in medical technology and related clinical laboratory sciences provide training for specialized areas of laboratory work or teaching, administration, or research.

The Clinical Laboratory Improvement Act (CLIA) requires technologists who perform certain highly complex tests to have at least an associate's degree.

Medical and clinical laboratory technicians generally have either an associate's degree from a community or junior college, or a certificate from a hospital, vocational or technical school, or from one of the Armed Forces. A few technicians learn on the job.

Nationally recognized accrediting agencies in the clinical laboratory science include the National Accrediting Agency for Clinical Laboratory Sciences, and the Accrediting Bureau of Health Education Schools (ABHES). National Accrediting Agency for Clinical Laboratory Sciences fully accredits 621, and approves 72 programs that provide education for medical and clinical laboratory technologists, cytotechnologists, histologic technicians, specialists in blood bank technology, and medical and clinical laboratory technicians. ABHES accredits training programs for medical and clinical laboratory technicians.

Some States require laboratory personnel to be licensed or registered. Information on licensure is available from State departments of health or boards of occupational licensing. Certification is a voluntary process by which a nongovernmental organization such as a professional society or certifying agency, grants recognition to an individual whose professional competence meets prescribed standards. Widely accepted by employers in the health industry, certification is a prerequisite for most jobs and often is necessary for advancement. Agencies that certify medical and clinical laboratory technologists and technicians include the Board of Registry of the American Society of Clinical Pathologists, the American Medical Technologists, the American Society for Clinical Laboratory Science, and the Credentialing Commission of the International Society for Clinical Laboratory Technology. These agencies have different requirements for certification and different organizational sponsors.

Clinical laboratory personnel need analytical judgment and the ability to work under pressure. Close attention to detail is essential because small differences or changes in test substances or numerical readouts can be crucial for patient care. Manual dexterity and normal color vision are highly desirable. With the widespread use of automated laboratory equipment, computer skills are important. In addition, technologists in particular are expected to be good at problem solving.

Technologists may advance to supervisory positions in laboratory work or become chief medical or clinical laboratory technologists or laboratory managers in hospitals. Manufacturers of home diagnostic testing kits and laboratory equipment and supplies seek experienced technologists to work in product development, marketing, and sales. Graduate education in medical technology, one of the biological sciences, chemistry, management, or education usually speeds advancement. A doctorate is sometimes needed to become a laboratory director. However, federal regulation allows directors of moderate complexity laboratories to have either a master's degree or a bachelor's degree combined with the appropriate amount of training and experience. Technicians can become technologists through additional education and experience.

Job Outlook

Employment of clinical laboratory workers is expected to grow about as fast as the average for all occupations through the year 2006 as the volume of laboratory tests increases with population growth and the development of new types of tests. Hospitals and independent laboratories have recently undergone considerable consolidation and restructuring that has boosted productivity and allowed the same number of personnel to perform more tests than previously possible. As a result, competition for jobs has increased and individuals may now have to look longer to find employment than in the past.

Technological advances will continue to have two opposing effects on employment through 2006. New, more powerful diagnostic tests will encourage more testing and spur employment. However, advances in laboratory automation and simpler tests, which make it possible for each worker to perform more tests, should slow growth. Research and development efforts are targeted at simplifying routine testing procedures so that nonlaboratory personnel, physicians and patients in particular, can perform tests now done in laboratories. Also, robots may prepare specimens, a job done now by technologists and technicians.

Although significant, growth will not be the only source of opportunities. As in most occupations, many openings will result from the need to replace workers who transfer to other occupations, retire, or stop working for some other reason.

Earnings

Median weekly earnings of full time, salaried clinical laboratory technologists and technicians were $520 in 1996. Half earned between $403 and $706. The lowest 10 percent earned less than $298 and the top 10 percent more than $852.

According to a Hay Group survey of acute care hospitals, the median annual base salary of full time laboratory technicians was $26,500 in January 1997. The middle 50 percent earned between $23,700 and $29,500. Full time salaried staff medical laboratory technologists earned about $35,100; the middle 50 percent earned between $32,500 and $37,900.

The average annual salary for medical technologists employed by the Federal Government was $40,680 in early 1997. Medical technicians earned an average of $26,130.

Related Occupations

Clinical laboratory technologists and technicians analyze body fluids, tissue, and other substances using a variety of tests. Similar or related procedures are performed by analytical, water purification, and other chemists; science technicians; crime laboratory analysts; food testers; and veterinary laboratory technicians.

Sources of Additional Information

Career and certification information is available from:

☛ American Society of Clinical Pathologists, Board of Registry, P.O. Box 12277, Chicago, IL 60612.

☛ American Medical Technologists, 710 Higgins Rd., Park Ridge, IL 60068.

☛ American Society of Cytopathology, 400 West 9th St., Suite 201, Wilmington, DE 19801.

☛ American Society for Clinical Laboratory Science, 7910 Woodmont Ave., Suite 530, Bethesda, MD 20814.

☛ International Society for Clinical Laboratory Technology, 917 Locust St., Suite 1100, St. Louis, MO 63101-1413.

For more career information, write to:

☛ American Association of Blood Banks, 8101 Glenbrook Rd., Bethesda, MD 20814-2749.

For a list of accredited and approved educational programs for clinical laboratory personnel, write to:

☛ National Accrediting Agency for Clinical Laboratory Sciences, 8410 W. Bryn Mawr Ave., Suite 670, Chicago, IL 60631.

For a list of training programs for medical and clinical laboratory technicians accredited by the Accrediting Bureau of Health Education Schools, write to:

☛ Secretary-ABHES, 2700 S. Quincy St., Suite 210, Arlington,, VA 22206.

For information about a career as a medical and clinical laboratory technician and schools offering training, contact:

☛ National Association of Health Career Schools, 750 First St. NE., Suite 940, Washington, DC 20002. FAX: (202) 842-1565 E-mail: NAHCS@aol.com

Dental Hygienists

(D.O.T. 078.361-010)

Significant points

- Dental hygienists are projected to be one of the 20 fastest growing occupations.

- Job opportunities should continue to be good if graduates of dental hygiene programs do not increase greatly in number.

- Part-time work and flexible schedules are common.

Nature of the Work

Dental hygienists clean teeth and provide other preventive dental care, as well as teach patients how to practice good oral hygiene. Hygienists examine patients' teeth and gums, recording the presence of diseases or abnormalities. They remove calculus, stains, and plaque from teeth; take and develop dental x rays; and apply cavity preventive agents such as fluorides and pit and fissure sealants. In some States, hygienists administer local anesthetics and anesthetic gas; place and carve filling materials, temporary fillings and periodontal dressings; remove sutures; and smooth and polish metal restorations.

Dental hygienists also help patients develop and maintain good oral health. For example, they may explain the relationship between diet and oral health, inform patients how to select toothbrushes, and show patients how to brush and floss their teeth.

Dental hygienists use hand and rotary instruments to clean teeth, x-ray machines to take dental pictures, syringes with needles to administer local anesthetics, and models of teeth to explain oral hygiene.

Working Conditions

Flexible scheduling is a distinctive feature of this job. Full-time, part-time, evening, and weekend work is widely available. Dentists frequently hire hygienists to work only 2 or 3 days a week, so hygienists may hold jobs in more than one dental office.

Dental hygienists work in clean, well-lighted offices. Important health safeguards include strict adherence to proper radiological procedures, and use of appropriate protective devices when administering anesthetic gas. Dental hygienists also wear safety glasses, surgical masks and gloves to protect themselves from infectious diseases, such as hepatitis.

Employment

Dental hygienists held about 133,000 jobs in 1996. Because multiple job holding is common in this field, the number of jobs greatly exceeds the number of hygienists. More than half of all dental hygienists worked part time—less than 35 hours a week.

A dental hygienist examines a patient's teeth and gums, noting the presence of diseases or abnormalities.

Almost all dental hygienists work in private dental offices. Some work in public health agencies, hospitals, and clinics.

Training, Other Qualifications, and Advancement

Dental hygienists must be licensed by the State in which they practice. To qualify for licensure, a candidate must graduate from an accredited dental hygiene school and pass both a written and clinical examination. The American Dental Association Joint Commission on National Dental Examinations administers the written examination that is accepted by all States and the District of Columbia. State or regional testing agencies administer the clinical examination. In addition, examinations on legal aspects of dental hygiene practice are required by most States. Alabama allows candidates to take its examination if they have been trained through a State-regulated on-the-job program in a dentist's office.

In 1997, 230 programs in dental hygiene were accredited by the Commission on Dental Accreditation. Although some programs lead to a bachelor's degree, most grant an associate degree. Twelve universities offer master's degree programs in dental hygiene or a related area.

An associate degree is sufficient for practice in a private dental office. A bachelor's or master's degree is usually required for research, teaching, or clinical practice in public or school health programs.

About half of the dental hygiene programs prefer applicants who have completed at least 1 year of college. Some of the bachelor's degree programs require applicants to have completed 2 years. However, requirements vary from school to school. These schools offer laboratory, clinical, and classroom instruction in subjects such as anatomy, physiology, chemistry, microbiology, pharmacology, nutrition, radiography, histology (the study of tissue structure), periodontology (the study of gum diseases), pathology, dental materials, clinical dental hygiene, and social and behavioral sciences.

Dental hygienists should work well with others and must have good manual dexterity because they use dental instruments with little room for error within a patient's mouth. Recommended high school courses for aspiring dental hygienists include biology, chemistry, and mathematics.

Job Outlook

Employment of dental hygienists is expected to grow much faster than the average for all occupations through the year 2006, in response to increasing demand for dental care and the greater substitution of hygienists for services previously performed by dentists. Job prospects are expected to remain very good unless the number of dental hygienist program graduates grows much faster than during the last decade, and results in a much larger pool of qualified applicants.

Demand will be stimulated by population growth, and greater retention of natural teeth by the larger number of middle-aged and elderly people. Also, dentists are likely to employ more hygienists for several reasons. Older dentists, who are less likely to employ dental hygienists, will leave and be replaced by recent graduates, who are more likely to do so. In addition, as dentists' workloads increase, they are expected to hire more hygienists to perform preventive dental care such as cleaning, so they may devote their own time to more profitable procedures.

Earnings

Earnings of dental hygienists are affected by geographic location, employment setting, and education and experience. Dental hygienists who work in private dental offices may be paid on an hourly, daily, salary, or commission basis.

According to the American Dental Association, experienced dental hygienists who worked 32 hours a week or more in a private practice averaged about $759 a week in 1995.

Benefits vary substantially by practice setting, and may be contingent upon full-time employment. Dental hygienists who work for school systems, public health agencies, the Federal Government, or State agencies usually have substantial benefits.

Related Occupations

Workers in other occupations supporting health practitioners in an office setting include dental assistants, ophthalmic medical assistants, podiatric medical assistants, office nurses, medical assistants, physician assistants, physical therapy assistants, and occupational therapy assistants.

Sources of Additional Information

For information on a career in dental hygiene and the educational requirements to enter this occupation, contact:
☛ Division of Professional Development, American Dental Hygienists' Association, 444 N. Michigan Ave., Suite 3400, Chicago, IL 60611. Homepage: http://www.adha.org

For information about accredited programs and educational requirements, contact:
☛ Commission on Dental Accreditation, American Dental Association, 211 E. Chicago Ave., Suite 1814, Chicago, IL 60611. Homepage: http://www.ada.org

The State Board of Dental Examiners in each State can supply information on licensing requirements.

Dispensing Opticians

(D.O.T. 299.361-010 and -014)

Significant points

- Although training requirements vary by State, most dispensing opticians receive their training on-the-job or through apprenticeships lasting 2 to 4 years.

- Employment of dispensing opticians is expected to increase as fast as the average for all occupations through the year 2006 as demand grows for corrective lenses.

Nature of Work

Dispensing opticians fit eyeglasses and contact lenses, following prescriptions written by ophthalmologists or optometrists. (The work of optometrists is described in a statement elsewhere in the *Handbook*. See the statement on physicians for information about ophthalmologists.)

Dispensing opticians help customers select appropriate frames, order the necessary ophthalmic laboratory work, and adjust the finished eyeglasses. In some States, they fit contact lenses under the supervision of an optometrist or ophthalmologist.

Dispensing opticians examine written prescriptions to determine lens specifications. They recommend eyeglass frames, lenses, and lens coatings after considering the prescription and the customer's occupation, habits, and facial features. Dispensing opticians measure clients' eyes, including the distance between the centers of the pupils and the distance between the eye surface and the lens. For customers without prescriptions, dispensing opticians may use a lensometer to record the present eyeglass prescription. They also may obtain a customer's previous record, or verify a prescription with the examining optometrist or ophthalmologist.

Dispensing opticians prepare work orders that give ophthalmic laboratory technicians information needed to grind and insert lenses into a frame. The work order includes lens prescriptions and information on lens size, material, color, and style. Some dispensing opticians grind and insert lenses themselves. After the glasses are made, dispensing opticians verify that the lenses have been ground to specifications. Then they may reshape or bend the frame, by hand or using pliers, so that the eyeglasses fit the customer properly and comfortably. Some also fix, adjust, and refit broken frames. They instruct clients about adapting to, wearing, or caring for eyeglasses.

Some dispensing opticians specialize in fitting contacts, artificial eyes, or cosmetic shells to cover blemished eyes. To fit contact lenses, dispensing opticians measure eye shape and size, select the type of contact lens material, and prepare work orders specifying the prescription and lens size. Fitting contact lenses requires considerable skill, care, and patience. Dispensing opticians observe customers' eyes, corneas, lids, and contact lenses with special instruments and microscopes. During several visits, opticians show customers how to insert, remove, and care for their contacts, and ensure the fit is correct.

Dispensing opticians keep records on customer prescriptions, work orders, and payments; track inventory and sales; and perform other administrative duties.

Working Conditions

Dispensing opticians work indoors in attractive, well lighted, and well ventilated surroundings. They may work in medical offices or small stores where customers are served one at a time, or in large stores where several dispensing opticians serve a number of customers at once. Opticians spend a lot of time with customers, most of it on their feet. If they also prepare lenses, they need to take precautions against the hazards associated with glass cutting, chemicals, and machinery.

Most dispensing opticians work a 40-hour week, although some work longer hours. Those in retail stores may work evenings and weekends. Some work part time.

Employment

Dispensing opticians held about 67,000 jobs in 1996. About half work for ophthalmologists or optometrists who sell glasses directly to patients. Many also work in retail optical stores that offer one-stop shopping. Customers may have their eyes examined, choose frames, and have glasses made on the spot. Some work in optical departments of drug and department stores.

Training, Other Qualifications, and Advancement

Employers generally hire individuals with no background in opticianry or those who have worked as ophthalmic laboratory technicians and then provide the required training. (See the statement on ophthalmic laboratory technicians elsewhere in the *Handbook*.) Training may be informal, on-the-job or formal apprenticeship. Some employers, however, seek people with postsecondary training in opticianry.

A dispensing optician adjusts finished eyeglasses to fit a customer.

Knowledge of physics, basic anatomy, algebra, geometry, and mechanical drawing is particularly valuable because training usually includes instruction in optical mathematics, optical physics, and the use of precision measuring instruments and other machinery and tools. Because dispensing opticians deal directly with the public, they should be tactful and pleasant and communicate well.

Large employers generally offer structured apprenticeship programs, and small employers provide more informal on-the-job training. In the 21 States that license dispensing opticians, individuals without postsecondary training work from 2 to 4 years as apprentices. Apprenticeship or formal training is offered in most of the other States as well.

Apprentices receive technical training and learn office management and sales. Under the supervision of an experienced optician, optometrist, or ophthalmologist, apprentices work directly with patients, fitting eyeglasses and contact lenses. In States requiring licensure, information about apprenticeships and licensing procedures is available from the State board of occupational licensing.

Formal opticianry training is offered in community colleges and a few colleges and universities. In 1997, there were 23 programs accredited by the Commission on Opticianry Accreditation that awarded 2-year associate degrees in ophthalmic dispensing or optometric technology. There are also shorter programs, including some under 1 year. Some States that license dispensing opticians allow graduates to take the licensure exam immediately upon graduation; others require a few months to a year of experience.

Dispensing opticians may apply to the American Board of Opticianry and the National Contact Lens Examiners for certification of their skills. Certification must be renewed every 3 years through continuing education.

Many experienced dispensing opticians open their own optical stores. Others become managers of optical stores or sales representatives for wholesalers or manufacturers of eyeglasses or lenses.

Job Outlook

Employment in this occupation is expected to increase as fast as the average for all occupations through the year 2006 as demand grows for corrective lenses. The number of middle-aged and elderly persons is projected to increase rapidly. Middle age is a time when many individuals use corrective lenses for the first time, and elderly persons require more vision care, on the whole, than others.

Fashion, too, influences demand. Frames come in a growing variety of styles and colors—encouraging people to buy more than one pair. Demand is also expected to grow in response to the availability of new technologies that improve the quality and look of corrective lenses, such as anti-reflective coatings and bifocal lenses without the line visible in old-style bifocals. Improvements in bifocal, extended wear, and disposable contact lenses will also spur demand.

Besides job openings expected due to employment growth, the need to replace those who leave the occupation will result in additional job openings. Nevertheless, the total number of job openings will be relatively small because the occupation is small. This occupation is vulnerable to changes in the business cycle because eyeglass purchases can often be deferred for a time. Employment of opticians often falls somewhat during downturns.

Earnings

According to survey results published in an April 1997 issue of *Eyecare Business* magazine, dispensing opticians earned an overall average salary of about $27,432. Owners, managers, and certified graduates of opticianry schools had higher earnings, as did dispensing opticians who worked in States that require licensure.

Related Occupations

Other workers who deal with customers and perform delicate work include jewelers, locksmiths, ophthalmic laboratory technicians, orthodontic technicians, dental laboratory technicians, prosthetics technicians, camera repairers, and watch repairers.

Sources of Additional Information

For general information about a career as a dispensing optician, contact:

☛ Opticians Association of America, 10341 Democracy Lane, Fairfax, VA 22030-2521.

For general information about a career as a dispensing optician and a list of accredited training programs, contact:

☛ Commission on Opticianry Accreditation, 10111 Martin Luther King, Jr. Hwy., Suite 100, Bowie, MD 20720-4299.

For general information on opticianry and a list of home-study programs, seminars, and review materials, contact:

☛ National Academy of Opticianry, 10111 Martin Luther King, Jr. Hwy., Suite 112, Bowie, MD 20720-4299.

Electroneurodiagnostic Technologists

(D.O.T. 078.362-022 and -042)

Significant points

- Although faster than average employment growth is expected, relatively few job openings will be created because the occupation is small.

- Most technologists learn on the job, but opportunities should be best for technologists with formal postsecondary training.

Nature of the Work

Electroneurodiagnostic technologists use instruments such as an electroencephalograph (EEG) machine, to record electrical impulses transmitted by the brain and the nervous system. They help physicians diagnose brain tumors, strokes, toxic/metabolic disorders, epilepsy and sleep disorders. They also measure the effects of infectious diseases on the brain, as well as determine whether individuals with mental or behavioral problems have an organic impairment such as Alzheimer's disease. Furthermore, they determine "cerebral" death, the absence of brain activity, and assess the probability of recovery from a coma.

Electroneurodiagnostic technologists who specialize in basic or "resting" EEG's, are called *EEG technologists*. The range of tests performed by electroneurodiagnostic technologists is broader than, but includes, those conducted by EEG technologists. Because it provides a more accurate description of work typically performed in the field, the title electroneurodiagnostic technologists generally has replaced that of EEG technologist.

Electroneurodiagnostic technologists take patients' medical histories and help them relax, then apply electrodes to designated spots on the patient's head. They must choose the most appropriate combination of instrument controls and electrodes to correct for mechanical or electrical interferences that come from somewhere other than the brain, such as eye movement or radiation from electrical sources.

Increasingly, technologists perform EEG's in the operating room, which requires that they understand anesthesia's effect on brain waves. For special procedure EEG's, technologists may secure electrodes to the chest, arm, leg, or spinal column to record activity from both the central and peripheral nervous systems.

In ambulatory monitoring, technologists monitor the brain, and sometimes the heart, while patients carry out normal activities over a 24-hour period. They then remove the small recorder carried by the patients and obtain a readout. Technologists review the readouts, selecting sections for the physician to examine.

Using "evoked potential" testing, technologists measure sensory and physical responses to specific stimuli. After the electrodes have been attached, they set the instrument for the type and intensity of the stimulus, increase the intensity until the patient reacts, and note the sensation level. The tests may take from 1 to 4 hours.

For nerve conduction tests, used to diagnose muscle and nerve problems, technologists place electrodes on the patient's skin over a nerve and over the muscle. Then they stimulate the nerve with an electrical current and record how long it takes the nerve impulse to reach the muscle.

Technologists who specialize in and administer sleep disorder studies are called *polysomnographic technologists.* The sleep studies are conducted in a clinic called a "sleep center." During the procedure, technologists monitor the patient's respiration and heart activity in addition to brain wave activity and must know the dynamics of the cardiopulmonary systems during each stage of sleep. They coordinate readings from several organ systems, separating them according to the stages of sleep, and relay them to the physician. For quantitative EEG's, technologists decide which sections of the EEG should be transformed into color-coded pictures of brain wave frequency and intensity, for interpretation by a physician. They may also write technical reports summarizing test results.

Technologists also look for changes in the patient's neurologic, cardiac, and respiratory status, which may indicate an emergency, such as a heart attack, and provide emergency care until help arrives.

Electroneurodiagnostic technologists may have supervisory or administrative responsibilities. They may manage an eletroneurodi-

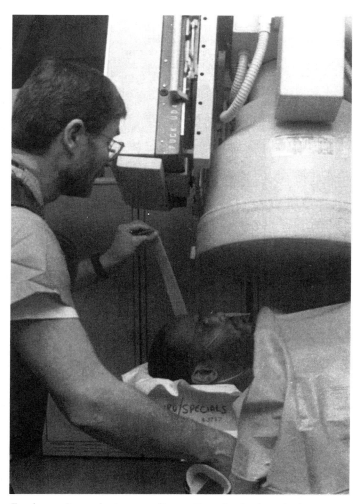

Employers favor electroneurodiagnostic technologists who have completed formal training.

agnostic laboratory, arrange work schedules, keep records, schedule appointments, order supplies, provide instruction to less experienced technologists, and may also be responsible for the equipment's upkeep.

Working Conditions

Electroneurodiagnostic technologists usually work in clean, well-lighted surroundings, and spend about half of their time on their feet. Bending and lifting are necessary because they may work with patients who are very ill and require assistance. Technologists employed in hospitals may do all their work in a single room, or may push equipment to a patient's bedside and obtain recordings there.

Most technologists work a standard workweek, although those in hospitals may be "on call" evenings, weekends, and holidays. Those performing sleep studies usually work evenings and nights.

Employment

Electroneurodiagnostic technologists held more than 6,400 jobs in 1996. Most worked in neurology laboratories of hospitals, while others worked in offices and clinics of neurologists and neurosurgeons, sleep centers, and psychiatric facilities.

Training, Other Qualifications, and Advancement

Although most electroneurodiagnostic technologists currently employed learned their skills on the job, employers are beginning to favor those who have completed formal training. Some hospitals require applicants for trainee positions to have postsecondary training while others only expect a high school diploma. Recommended high school and college subjects for prospective technologists include health, biology, anatomy and mathematics. Often, on-the-job trainees are transfers from other hospital jobs, such as licensed practical nurses.

Formal postsecondary training is offered in hospitals and community colleges. In 1996, the Joint Review Committee on Education in Electroneurodiagnostic Technology had approved 11 formal programs. Programs usually last from 1 to 2 years, and include laboratory experience as well as classroom instruction in human anatomy and physiology, neurology, neuroanatomy, neurophysiology, medical terminology, computer technology, electronics, and instrumentation. Graduates receive associate degrees or certificates.

The American Board of Registration of Electroencephalographic and Evoked Potential Technologists awards the credential "Registered EEG Technologist," "Registered Evoked Potential Technologist," and "Certificate in Neurophysiologic Intraoperative Monitoring" to qualified applicants. The Association of Polysomnographic Technologists registers polysomnographic technologists. Applicants interested in taking the registration exam must have worked in a sleep center for at least 1 year. Although not generally required for staff level jobs, registration indicates professional competence, and is usually necessary for supervisory or teaching jobs. In addition, the American Association of Electrodiagnostic Technologists provides certification in the field of nerve conduction studies for electroneurodiagnostic technologists.

Technologists should have manual dexterity, good vision, writing skills, an aptitude for working with electronic equipment, and the ability to work with patients as well as with other health personnel.

Experienced electroneurodiagnostic technologists can advance to chief or manager of a electroneurodiagnostic laboratory. Chief technologists are generally supervised by a physician—an electroencephalographer, neurologist, or neurosurgeon. Technologists may also teach or go into research.

Job Outlook

Job prospects for qualified applicants are expected to be good. Employment of electroneurodiagnostic technologists is expected to grow faster than the average for all occupations through the year 2006, reflecting the increased numbers of neurodiagnostic tests performed. There will be more testing as new procedures are developed and as the size of the population grows. A very low number of openings each year are expected, however, because the occupation is very small. Most jobs will be found in hospitals, but growth will be fastest in offices and clinics of neurologists.

Earnings

According to a Hay Group survey of acute care hospitals, the median annual base salary of full-time EEG technologists was $26,800 in January 1997. The middle 50 percent earned between $23,200 and $30,100.

Related Occupations

Other health personnel who operate medical equipment include radiologic technologists, nuclear medicine technologists, sonographers, perfusionists, and cardiovascular technologists.

Sources of Additional Information

Local hospitals can supply information about employment opportunities.

For general information about a career in electroneurodiagnostics, as well as a list of accredited training programs, contact:
☛ Executive Office, American Society of Electroneurodiagnostic Technologists, Inc., 204 W. 7ᵗʰ St., Carroll, IA 51401. Homepage: http://www.aset.org/

For information on work in sleep studies, contact:
☛ Association of Polysomnographic Technology, 2025 South Washington, Suite 300, Lansing, MI 48910-0817.

Information about specific accredited training programs is also available from:
☛ Joint Review Committee on Electroneurodiagnostic Technology, Route 1, Box 63A, Genoa, WI 54632.

Information on becoming a registered Electroneurodiagnostic technologist is available from:
☛ American Board of Registration of Electroencephalgraphic and Evoked Potential Technologists, P.O. Box 916633, Longwood, FL 32791-6633.

Information on certification in the field of nerve conduction studies is available from:
☛ American Association of Electrodiagnostic Technologists, 35 Hallett Lane, Chatham, MA 02633-2408.

Emergency Medical Technicians

(D.O.T. 079.364-026 and .374-010)

Significant Points

- Employment should grow rapidly as paid emergency medical technician positions replace unpaid volunteers.

- Competition is expected for the best paying jobs with rescue squads and police and fire departments.

- Depending on State requirements, as little as 110 to 120 hours of formal training is needed to qualify for jobs.

Nature of the Work

Automobile accident injuries, heart attacks, near drownings, unscheduled childbirths, poisonings, and gunshot wounds all demand urgent medical attention. Emergency medical technicians (EMT's) give immediate care and often transport the sick or injured to medical facilities.

Following instructions from a dispatcher, EMT's—who usually work in teams of two—drive specially equipped vehicles to the scene of emergencies. If necessary, they request additional help from police or fire department personnel. They determine the nature and extent of the patient's injuries or illness while also trying to determine whether the patient has epilepsy, diabetes, or other preexisting medical conditions. Following strict guidelines, EMT's employ procedures they are certified to use to give appropriate emergency care. All EMT's, including those with basic skills—the EMT-Basic—may open airways, restore breathing, control bleeding, treat for shock, administer oxygen, immobilize fractures, bandage wounds, assist in childbirth, manage emotionally disturbed patients, treat and assist heart attack victims, give

initial care to poison and burn victims, and use automated external defibrillators to assist in the care of patients experiencing cardiac arrest.

EMT-Intermediates have more advanced training that allows them to administer intravenous fluids; use manual defibrillators to give lifesaving shocks to a stopped heart, use advanced airway techniques and equipment to assist patient's experiencing respiratory emergencies, as well as use other intensive care procedures.

EMT-Paramedics provide the most extensive pre-hospital care. In addition to the procedures already described, paramedics may administer drugs orally and intravenously, interpret eletrocardiograms (EKG's), perform endotracheal intubations, and use monitors and other complex equipment.

When victims are trapped, as in the case of an automobile accident, cave-in, or building collapse, EMT's free them or provide emergency care while others free them. Some conditions are simple enough to be handled following general rules and guidelines. More complicated problems can only be carried out under the step-by-step direction of medical personnel by radio contact.

When transporting patients to a medical facility, EMT's may use special equipment such as backboards, to immobilize them before placing them on stretchers and securing them in the ambulance. While one EMT drives, the other monitors the patient's vital signs and gives additional care as needed. Some EMT's work for hospital trauma centers or jurisdictions which use helicopters to transport critically ill or injured patients.

At a medical facility, EMT's transfer patients to the emergency department, report to the staff their observations and the care they provided, and help provide emergency treatment.

In rural areas, some EMT-Paramedics are trained to treat patients with minor injuries on the scene of an accident or at their home without transporting them to a medical facility.

After each run, EMT's replace used supplies and check equipment. If patients have had a contagious disease, EMT's decontaminate the interior of the ambulance and report cases to the proper authorities.

Working Conditions

EMT's work both indoors and outdoors, in all types of weather. Much of their time is spent standing, kneeling, bending, and lifting. They may risk noise-induced hearing loss from ambulance sirens and

Emergency medical technicians often deal with life-or-death situations.

back injuries from lifting patients. EMT's may be exposed to diseases such as Hepatitis-B and AIDS, as well as violence from drug overdose victims or psychological emergencies. The work is not only physically strenuous, but stressful—not surprising in a job that involves life-or-death situations. Nonetheless, many people find the work exciting and challenging.

EMT's employed by fire departments often have about a 50-hour workweek. Those employed by hospitals frequently work between 45 and 60 hours a week, and those in private ambulance services, between 45 and 50 hours. Some EMT's, especially those in police and fire departments, are on call for extended periods. Because emergency services function 24 hours a day, EMT's have irregular working hours that add to job stress.

Employment

EMT's held about 150,000 jobs in 1996. About two-fifths were in private ambulance services; a third were in municipal fire, police, or rescue squad departments; and a quarter were in hospitals. In addition, there are many volunteer EMT's. Most paid EMT's work in metropolitan areas. In many smaller cities, towns, and rural areas, there are more volunteer positions than paid EMT jobs.

Training, Other Qualifications, and Advancement

Formal training is needed to become an EMT. Training is offered at three progressive levels— EMT-Basic, EMT-Intermediate, and EMT-paramedic—and fully qualified technicians complete all three programs. In some cases, First Responder training programs that provide emergency medical basics for firefighters, police officers, and others whose jobs make them likely to be the first persons to arrive at an incident scene may qualify individuals for entry-level jobs. However, continued employment requires completion of EMT training. EMT training is available in all 50 States and the District of Columbia, and is offered by police, fire, and health departments; in hospitals; and as nondegree courses in colleges and universities. In addition to EMT training, EMT's in fire and police departments must be qualified as firefighters or police officers.

The EMT-Basic is the minimum training needed to qualify for an emergency medical technician job. EMT-Basic training is 110 to 120 hours of classroom work plus 10 hours of internship in a hospital emergency room. The program provides instruction and practice in dealing with bleeding, fractures, airway obstruction, cardiac arrest, and emergency childbirth. Students learn to use and care for common emergency equipment, such as backboards, suction devices, splints, oxygen delivery systems, and stretchers. Graduates of approved EMT-Basic training programs who pass a written and practical examination administered by the State certifying agency or the National Registry of Emergency Medical Technicians earn the title of Registered EMT-Basic.

EMT-Intermediate training requirements vary from State to State, but typically include 35-55 hours of additional instruction beyond EMT-Basic and cover patient assessment as well as the use of advanced airway devices, and intravenous fluids. Prerequisites for taking the EMT-Intermediate examination include registration as an EMT-Basic, required classroom work, and a specified amount of clinical experience and field internship.

Most graduates of EMT-Intermediate programs continue their education and receive the EMT-Paramedic certification. EMT-Paramedic training programs generally last between 750 and 2,000 hours. Due to this strenuous training requirement, most EMT-Paramedics are in paid positions. Refresher courses and continuing education are available for EMT's at all levels.

In most State's, registration for EMT-Paramedics by the National Registry of Emergency Medical Technicians or a State emergency medical services agency requires current registration or State certification as an EMT-Basic, completion of an EMT-Paramedic training program and required clinical and field internships, as well as passing a written and practical examination. Although not a general requirement for employment, registration acknowledges an EMT's qualifications and makes higher paying jobs easier to obtain.

All 50 States possess a certification procedure. In 38 States and the District of Columbia, registration with the National Registry is required at some or all levels of certification. Other States require their own certification examination or provide the option of taking the National Registry examination.

To maintain their certification, all EMT's must reregister, usually every 2 years. In order to reregister, an individual must be working as an EMT and meet a continuing education requirement.

Applicants to an EMT training course generally must be at least 18 years old and have a valid driver's license. Recommended high school subjects for prospective EMT's are driver education, health, and science. First aid training in the Armed Forces is also good preparation.

EMT's should be emotionally stable, have good dexterity, agility, and physical coordination, and be able to lift and carry heavy loads. EMT's need good eyesight (corrective lenses may be used) with accurate color vision.

Advancement beyond the EMT-Paramedic level usually means leaving fieldwork. An EMT-Paramedic can become a supervisor, operations manager, administrative director, or executive director of emergency services. Some EMT's become EMT instructors, firefighters, dispatchers, or physicians assistants, while others move into sales or marketing of emergency medical equipment. Finally, some become EMT's to assess their interest in health care and then decide to return to school and become registered nurses, physicians, or other health workers.

Job Outlook

Competition for jobs will be keen in fire, police, and rescue squad departments because of attractive pay and benefits and good job security. Opportunities for EMT's are expected to be excellent in hospitals and private ambulance services, where pay and benefits usually are low.

Employment of EMT's is expected to grow much faster than average for all occupations through the year 2006. Much of this growth will occur as positions change from volunteer to paid positions. Also driving the growth will be an expanding population, particularly in older age groups that are the greatest users of emergency medical services. Additional job openings will occur as more States begin to allow EMT-Paramedics to perform primary care on the scene without transporting the patient to a medical facility.

Many job openings will occur because of this occupation's substantial replacement needs. Turnover is quite high, reflecting this occupation's stressful working conditions, limited advancement potential, and the modest pay and benefits in the private sector.

Earnings

Earnings of EMT's depend on the employment setting and geographic location as well as the individual's training and experience. According the 1996 *Journal of Emergency Medical Services* salary survey, average salaries were $25,051 for EMT- Basic, and $30,407 for EMT-Paramedic. EMT's working in fire departments command the highest salaries, as the accompanying table shows.

Table 1: Average annual salaries of emergency medical technicians, by type of employer, 1996

Employer	EMT-Basic	EMT-Paramedic
All employees	$25,051	$30,407
Fire Departments	29,859	32,483
Hospital based	18,686	28,373
Private ambulance services	18,617	23,995

Source: Journal of Emergency Medical Services

Those in emergency medical services who are part of fire or police departments receive the same benefits as firefighters or police officers.

Related Occupations

Other workers in occupations that require quick and level-headed reactions to life-or-death situations are police officers, firefighters, air traffic controllers, workers in other health occupations, and members of the Armed Forces.

Sources of Additional Information

Information concerning training courses, registration, and job opportunities for EMT's can be obtained by writing to the State Emergency Medical Service Director.

General information about EMT's is available from:

☛ National Association of Emergency Medical Technicians, 408 Monroe., Clinton, MS 39056.

☛ National Registry of Emergency Medical Technicians, P.O. Box 29233, Columbus, OH 43229.

Health Information Technicians

(D.O.T. 079.362-014, -018)

Significant points

- Health information technicians are projected to be one of the 20 fastest growing occupations.

- High school students can improve their chances of acceptance into a health information education program by taking courses in biology, chemistry, health, and especially computer training.

- Most technicians will be employed in hospitals, but job growth will be faster in offices and clinics of physicians, nursing homes, and home health agencies.

Nature of the Work

Every time health care personnel treat a patient, they record what they observed, and how the patient was treated medically. This record includes information the patient provides concerning their symptoms and medical history, the results of examinations, reports of x-rays and laboratory tests, diagnoses, and treatment plans. Health information technicians organize and evaluate these records for completeness and accuracy.

When assembling patients' health information, technicians, who may also be called medical record technicians, first make sure the medical chart is complete. They ensure all forms are present and properly identified and signed, and all necessary information is on a computer file. Sometimes, they talk to physicians or others to clarify diagnoses or get additional information.

Technicians assign a code to each diagnosis and procedure. They consult a classification manual and rely, also, on their knowledge of disease processes. Technicians then use a software program to assign the patient to one of several hundred "diagnosis-related groups," or DRG's. The DRG determines the amount the hospital will be reimbursed if the patient is covered by Medicare or other insurance programs using the DRG system. Technicians who specialize in coding are called health information coders, medical record coders, coder/abstractors, or coding specialists.

Technicians also use computer programs to tabulate and analyze data to help improve patient care or control costs, for use in legal actions, or in response to surveys. *Tumor registrars* compile and maintain records of patients who have cancer to provide information to physicians and for research studies.

Health information technicians' duties vary with the size of the facility. In large to medium facilities, technicians may specialize in one aspect of health information, or supervise health information clerks and transcribers while a *health information administrator* manages the department (see the statement on health services managers elsewhere in the *Handbook*). In small facilities, an accredited health information technician may manage the department.

Working Conditions

Health information technicians generally work a 40-hour week. Some overtime may be required. In hospitals where health information departments are open 18-24 hours a day, 7 days a week, they may work on day, evening, and night shifts.

Health information technicians work in pleasant and comfortable offices. This is one of the few health occupations in which there is little or no physical contact with patients. Accuracy is essential, therefore concentration and close attention to detail is required. Health information technicians who work at video display terminals for prolonged periods must guard against eyestrain and muscle pain.

Employment

Health information technicians held about 87,000 jobs in 1996. Less than one half of the jobs were in hospitals. Most of the rest were in nursing homes, medical group practices, clinics, and home health agencies. Insurance, accounting, and law firms that deal in health matters employ a small number of health information technicians to tabulate and analyze health information. Public health departments also hire technicians to supervise data collection from health care institutions and to assist in research.

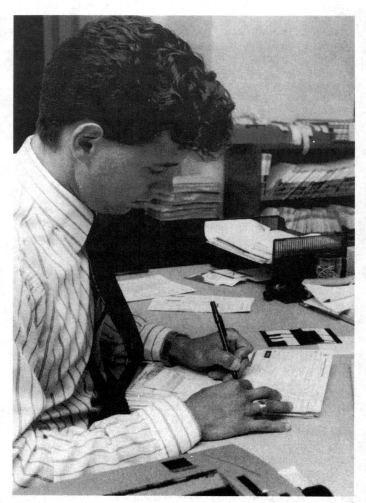

Health information technicians organize and evaluate medical records for completeness and accuracy.

Training, Other Qualifications, and Advancement

Health information technicians entering the field usually have an associate degree from a community or junior college. In addition to general education, coursework includes medical terminology, anatomy and physiology, legal aspects of health information, coding and abstraction of data, statistics, database management, quality assurance methods, and especially computer training. Applicants can improve their chances of admission into a program by taking biology, chemistry, health and computer courses in high school.

Technicians may also gain training through an Independent Study Program in Health Information Technology offered by the American Health Information Management Association (AHIMA). Hospitals sometimes advance promising health information clerks to jobs as health information technicians, although this practice may be less common in the future. Advancement generally requires 2-4 years of job experience and completion of the hospital's in-house training program.

Most employers prefer to hire Accredited Record Technicians (ART), who must pass a written examination offered by AHIMA. To take the examination, a person must graduate from a 2-year associate degree program accredited by the Commission on Accreditation of Allied Health Education Programs (CAAHEP) of the American Medical Association, or from the Independent Study Program in Health Information Technology that requires 30 semester hours of academic credit in prescribed areas. Technicians trained in non-CAAHEP accredited programs, or on the job, are not eligible to take the examination. In 1997, CAAHEP accredited 157 programs for health information technicians.

Experienced health information technicians generally advance in one of two ways—by specializing or managing. Many senior health information technicians specialize in coding, particularly Medicare coding, or in tumor registry.

In large health information departments, experienced technicians may advance to section supervisor, overseeing the work of the coding, correspondence, or discharge sections, for example. Senior technicians with ART credentials may become director or assistant director of a health information department in a small facility. However, in larger institutions, the director is a health information administrator, with a bachelor's degree in health information administration. (See the statement on health services managers elsewhere in the *Handbook*.)

Job Outlook

Job prospects for formally trained technicians should be very good. Employment of health information technicians is expected to grow much faster than the average for all occupations through the year 2006, due to rapid growth in the number of medical tests, treatments, and procedures which will be increasingly scrutinized by third-party payers, regulators, courts, and consumers.

Hospitals will continue to employ the most health information technicians, but growth will not be as fast as in other areas. Increasing demand for detailed records in offices and clinics of physicians should result in fast employment growth, especially in large group practices. Rapid growth is also expected in nursing homes and home health agencies.

Earnings

According to a 1996 survey by the American Health Information Management Association, the median annual salary for accredited health information technicians was $31,200 a year. The average annual salary for health information technicians employed by the Federal Government was $25,570 in early 1997.

Related Occupations

Health information technicians need a strong clinical background to analyze the contents of medical records. Other occupations requiring a knowledge of medical terminology, anatomy, and physiology without directly touching the patient, are medical secretaries, medical transcribers, medical writers, and medical illustrators.

Sources of Additional Information

Information on careers in health information technology, including the Independent Study Program, and a list of CAAHEP-accredited programs is available from:

☛ American Health Information Management Association, 919 N. Michigan Ave., Suite 1400, Chicago, IL 60611-1683. Homepage: http://www.ahima.org

Licensed Practical Nurses

(D.O.T. 079.374-014)

Significant points

- Training lasting about 1 year is available in about 1,100 State-approved programs, mostly in vocational or technical schools.

- Nursing homes will offer the most new jobs. Jobseekers in hospitals may face competition.

Nature of the Work

Licensed practical nurses (L.P.N.'s), or licensed vocational nurses as they are called in Texas and California, care for the sick, injured, convalescent, and disabled, under the direction of physicians and registered nurses. (The work of registered nurses is described elsewhere in the *Handbook*.)

Most L.P.N.'s provide basic bedside care. They take vital signs such as temperature, blood pressure, pulse, and respiration. They also treat bedsores, prepare and give injections and enemas, apply dressings, give alcohol rubs and massages, apply ice packs and hot water bottles, and insert catheters. L.P.N's observe patients and report adverse reactions to medications or treatments. They collect samples from patients for testing, perform routine laboratory tests, feed them and record food and liquid intake and output. They help patients with bathing, dressing, and personal hygiene, keep them comfortable, and care for their emotional needs. In States where the law allows, they may administer prescribed medicines or start intravenous fluids. Some L.P.N.'s help deliver, care for, and feed infants. Some experienced L.P.N.'s supervise nursing assistants and aides.

L.P.N.'s in nursing homes, in addition to providing routine bedside care, may also help evaluate residents' needs, develop care plans, and supervise the care provided by nursing aides. In doctors' offices and clinics, they may also make appointments, keep records, and perform

Most licensed practical nurses in hospitals and nursing homes work a 40-hour week, including nights, weekends, and holidays.

other clerical duties. L.P.N.'s who work in private homes may also prepare meals and teach family members simple nursing tasks.

Working Conditions

Most licensed practical nurses in hospitals and nursing homes work a 40-hour week, but because patients need round-the-clock care, some work nights, weekends, and holidays. They often stand for long periods and help patients move in bed, stand, or walk.

L.P.N.'s may face hazards from caustic chemicals, radiation, and infectious diseases such as AIDS and hepatitis and also are subject to back injuries when moving patients and shock from electrical equipment. They often are subject to stress from heavy workloads. In addition, the patients they care for may be confused, irrational, agitated, or uncooperative.

Employment

Licensed practical nurses held about 699,000 jobs in 1996. Thirty-two percent of L.P.N.'s worked in hospitals, 27 percent worked in nursing homes, and 13 percent in doctors' offices and clinics. Others worked for temporary help agencies, home health care services, or government agencies. Almost one-third worked part time.

Training, Other Qualifications, and Advancement

All States require L.P.N.'s to pass a licensing examination after completing a State-approved practical nursing program. A high school diploma is usually required for entry, but some programs accept people without a diploma.

In 1997, approximately 1,100 State-approved programs provided practical nursing training. Almost 6 out of 10 students were enrolled in technical or vocational schools, while 3 out of 10 were in community and junior colleges. Others were in high schools, hospitals, and colleges and universities.

Most practical nursing programs last about 1 year and include both classroom study and supervised clinical practice (patient care). Classroom study covers basic nursing concepts and patient-care related subjects, including anatomy, physiology, medical-surgical nursing, pediatrics, obstetrics, psychiatric nursing, administration of drugs, nutrition, and first aid. Clinical practice is usually in a hospital, but sometimes includes other settings.

L.P.N.'s should have a caring, sympathetic nature. They should be emotionally stable because work with the sick and injured can be stressful. As part of a health care team, they must be able to follow orders and work under close supervision.

Job Outlook

Employment of L.P.N.'s is expected to increase faster than the average for all occupations through the year 2006 in response to the long-term care needs of a rapidly growing population of very old people and to the general growth of health care. However, L.P.N.'s seeking positions in hospitals may face competition, as the number of hospital jobs for L.P.N.'s declines. The number of inpatients, with whom most L.P.N.'s work, is not expected to increase much. As in most other occupations, replacement needs will be the main source of job openings.

Employment in nursing homes is expected to grow much faster than the average. Nursing homes will offer the most new jobs for L.P.N.'s as the number of aged and disabled persons in need of long-term care rises rapidly. In addition to caring for the aged, nursing homes will be called on to care for the increasing number of patients who have been released from the hospital and have not yet recovered enough to return home.

Much faster than average growth is also expected in home health care services. This is in response to a growing number of older persons with functional disabilities, consumer preference for care in the home, and technological advances which make it possible to bring increasingly complex treatments into the home.

An increasing proportion of sophisticated procedures, which once were performed only in hospitals, are being performed in physicians'

offices and clinics, including health maintenance organizations, ambulatory surgicenters, and emergency medical centers, thanks largely to advances in technology. As a result, employment is projected to grow much faster than average in these places as health care in general expands.

Earnings

Median weekly earnings of full-time salaried licensed practical nurses were $468 in 1996. The middle 50 percent earned between $388 and $563. The lowest 10 percent earned less than $318; the top 10 percent, more than $673.

According to the Buck Survey conducted by the American Health Care Association, staff L.P.N.'s in chain nursing homes had median hourly earnings of $12.00 in 1996. The middle 50 percent earned between $10.60 and $13.50.

Related Occupations

L.P.N.'s work closely with people while helping them. So do emergency medical technicians, human service workers, and teacher aides.

Sources of Additional Information

For a list of State-approved training programs and information about practical nursing, write to:
☞ Communications Department, National League for Nursing, 350 Hudson St., New York, NY 10014. FAX (212) 989-2272.
☞ National Association for Practical Nurse Education and Service, Inc., 1400 Spring St., Suite 310, Silver Spring, MD 20910. FAX (301) 588-2839 E-mail address: napnes@aol.com

Nuclear Medicine Technologists

(D.O.T. 078.361-018)

Significant points

- Relatively few job openings will occur, because the occupation is small.

- Technologists trained in both nuclear medicine and radiologic technology will have the best prospects.

Nature of the Work

In nuclear medicine, radionuclides—unstable atoms that emit radiation spontaneously—are used to diagnose and treat disease. Radionuclides are purified and compounded like other drugs to form radiopharmaceuticals. Nuclear medicine technologists administer these radiopharmaceuticals to patients, then monitor the characteristics and functions of tissues or organs in which they localize. Abnormal areas show higher or lower concentrations of radioactivity than normal.

Nuclear medicine technologists operate cameras that detect and map the radioactive drug in the patient's body to create an image on photographic film. Radiologic technologists also operate diagnostic imaging equipment, but their equipment creates an image by projecting an x ray through the patient. (See the statement on radiologic technologists elsewhere in the *Handbook*.)

Nuclear medicine technologists explain test procedures to patients. They prepare a dosage of the radiopharmaceutical and administer it by mouth, injection, or other means. When preparing radiopharmaceuticals, technologists adhere to safety standards that keep the radiation dose to workers and patients as low as possible.

Technologists position patients and start a gamma scintillation camera, or scanner, which creates images of the distribution of a radiopharmaceutical as it localizes in and emits signals from the patient's body. Technologists produce the images on a computer screen or on film for a physician to interpret. Some nuclear medicine studies, such as cardiac function studies, are processed with the aid of a computer.

Some nuclear medicine studies, such as cardiac function studies, are conducted with the aid of a computer.

Nuclear medicine technologists also perform radioimmunoassay studies which assess the behavior of a radioactive substance inside the body. For example, technologists may add radioactive substances to blood or serum to determine levels of hormones or therapeutic drug content.

Technologists keep patient records and record the amount and type of radionuclides received, used, and disposed of.

Working Conditions
Nuclear medicine technologists generally work a 40-hour week. This may include evening or weekend hours in departments which operate on an extended schedule. Opportunities for part-time and shift work are also available. In addition, technologists in hospitals may have on call duty on a rotational basis.

Because technologists are on their feet much of the day, and may lift or turn disabled patients, physical stamina is important.

Although there is potential for radiation exposure in this field, it is kept to a minimum by the use of shielded syringes, gloves, and other protective devices. Technologists also wear badges that measure radiation levels. Because of safety programs, however, badge measurements rarely exceed established safety levels.

Employment
Nuclear medicine technologists held about 13,000 jobs in 1996. Almost 9 out of 10 jobs were in hospitals. The rest were in physicians' offices and clinics, including imaging centers.

Training, Other Qualifications, and Advancement
Nuclear medicine technology programs range in length from 1 to 4 years and lead to a certificate, associate's degree, or bachelor's degree. Generally, certificate programs are offered in hospitals; associate programs in community colleges; and bachelor's programs in 4-year colleges and in universities. Courses cover physical sciences, the biological effects of radiation exposure, radiation protection and procedures, the use of radiopharmaceuticals, imaging techniques, and computer applications.

One-year certificate programs are for health professionals, especially radiologic technologists and ultrasound technologists wishing to specialize in nuclear medicine. They also attract medical technologists, registered nurses, and others who wish to change fields or specialize. Others interested in the nuclear medicine technology field have three options: A 2-year certificate program, a 2-year associate program, or a 4-year bachelor's program.

The Joint Review Committee on Education Programs in Nuclear Medicine Technology accredits most formal training programs in nuclear medicine technology. In 1997, there were 104 accredited programs.

All nuclear medicine technologists must meet the minimum Federal standards on the administration of radioactive drugs and the operation of radiation detection equipment. In addition, about half of all States require technologists to be licensed. Technologists also may obtain voluntary professional certification or registration. Registration or certification is available from the American Registry of Radiologic Technologists and from the Nuclear Medicine Technology Certification Board. Most employers prefer to hire certified or registered technologists.

Technologists may advance to supervisor, then to chief technologist, and to department administrator or director. Some technologists specialize in a clinical area such as nuclear cardiology or computer analysis or leave patient care to take positions in research laboratories. Some become instructors or directors in nuclear medicine technology programs, a step that usually requires a bachelor's degree or a master's in nuclear medicine technology. Others leave the occupation to work as sales or training representatives for medical equipment and radiopharmaceutical manufacturing firms, or as radiation safety officers in regulatory agencies or hospitals.

Job Outlook
Employment of nuclear medicine technologists is expected to grow about as fast as the average for all occupations through the year 2006. The number of openings each year will be very low because the occupation is small. Growth will arise from an increase in the number of middle-aged and older persons who are the primary users of diagnostic procedures, including nuclear medicine tests. Nonetheless, job seekers will face more competition for jobs than in the recent past. In an attempt to employ fewer technologists and lower labor costs, hospitals have begun to merge nuclear medicine and radiologic technology departments. Consequently, opportunities will be best for technologists who can perform both nuclear medicine and radiologic procedures.

Technological innovations may increase the diagnostic uses of nuclear medicine. One example is the use of radiopharmaceuticals in combination with monoclonal antibodies to detect cancer at far earlier stages than is customary today, and without resorting to surgery. Another is the use of radionuclides to examine the heart's ability to pump blood. Wider use of nuclear medical imaging to observe metabolic and biochemical changes for neurology, cardiology, and oncology procedures, will also spur some demand for nuclear medicine technologists.

On the other hand, cost considerations will affect the speed with which new applications of nuclear medicine grow. Some promising nuclear medicine procedures, such as positron emission tomography, are extremely costly, and hospitals contemplating them will have to consider equipment costs, reimbursement policies, and the number of potential users.

Earnings
According to a Hay Group survey of acute care hospitals, the median annual base salary of full-time nuclear medicine technologists was $36,100 in January 1997. The middle 50 percent earned between $33,400 and $39,400.

Related Occupations
Nuclear medical technologists operate sophisticated equipment to help physicians and other health practitioners diagnose and treat patients. Radiologic technologists, diagnostic medical sonographers, cardiovascular technologists, electroneurodiagnostic technologists, clinical laboratory technologists, perfusionists, and respiratory therapists also perform similar functions.

Sources of Additional Information
Additional information on a career as a nuclear medicine technologist is available from:
☛ The Society of Nuclear Medicine-Technologist Section, 1850 Samuel Morse Dr., Reston, VA 22090.

For information on a career as a nuclear medicine technologist, enclose a stamped, self-addressed business size envelope with your request to:

☞ American Society of Radiologic Technologists, Customer Service Department, 15000 Central Ave., SE,. Albuquerque, NM 87123-3917, or call (800) 444-2778.

For a list of accredited programs in nuclear medicine technology, write to:

☞ Joint Review Committee on Educational Programs in Nuclear Medicine Technology, 350 South 400 East, Suite 200, Salt Lake City, UT 84111-2938.

Information on certification is available from:

☞ Nuclear Medicine Technology Certification Board, 2970 Clairmont Rd., Suite 610, Atlanta, GA 30329.

Radiologic Technologists

(D.O.T. 078.361-034, .362-026, -046, -054, -058, .364-010)

Significant points

- Job seekers may face competition for jobs as hospitals merge radiologic and nuclear medicine departments in an effort to cut costs; radiographers with cross training in nuclear medicine technology will have the best prospects.

- Sonographers should experience somewhat better job opportunities than other radiologic technologists, as ultrasound becomes an increasingly attractive alternative to radiologic procedures.

Nature of the Work

Perhaps the most familiar use of the x ray is the diagnosis of broken bones. However, medical uses of radiation go far beyond that. Radiation is used not only to produce images of the interior of the body, but to treat cancer as well. At the same time, the use of imaging techniques that do not involve x rays, such as ultrasound and magnetic resonance scans, is growing rapidly. The term "diagnostic imaging" embraces these procedures as well as the familiar x ray.

Radiographers produce x-ray films (radiographs) of parts of the human body for use in diagnosing medical problems. They prepare patients for radiologic examinations by explaining the procedure, removing articles such as jewelry, through which x rays cannot pass, and positioning patients so that the correct parts of the body can be radiographed. To prevent unnecessary radiation exposure, technologists surround the exposed area with radiation protection devices, such as lead shields, or limit the size of the x-ray beam. Radiographers position radiographic equipment at the correct angle and height over the appropriate area of a patient's body. Using instruments similar to a measuring tape, technologists may measure the thickness of the section to be radiographed and set controls on the machine to produce radiographs of the appropriate density, detail, and contrast. They place the x-ray film under the part of the patient's body to be examined and make the exposure. They then remove the film and develop it.

Experienced radiographers may perform more complex imaging tests. For fluoroscopies, radiographers prepare a solution of contrast medium for the patient to drink, allowing the radiologist, a physician who interprets x rays, to see soft tissues in the body. Some radiographers who operate computerized tomography scanners to produce cross sectional views of patients are called *CT technologists*. Others operate machines that use giant magnets and radiowaves rather than radiation to create an image and are called *magnetic resonance imaging (MRI) technologists*.

Radiation therapy technologists, also known as radiation therapists, prepare cancer patients for treatment and administer prescribed doses of ionizing radiation to specific body parts. They operate many kinds of equipment, including high-energy linear accelerators with electron capabilities. They position patients under the equipment with absolute accuracy in order to expose affected body parts to treatment while protecting the rest of the body from radiation.

They also check the patient's reactions for radiation side effects such as nausea, hair loss, and skin irritation. They give instructions and explanations to patients who are likely to be very ill. Radiation therapists, in contrast to other radiologic technologists, are likely to see the same patient a number of times during the course of treatment.

Sonographers, also known as ultrasound technologists, direct nonionizing, high frequency sound waves into areas of the patient's body; the equipment then collects reflected echoes to form an image. The image is viewed on a screen and may be recorded on videotape or photographed for interpretation and diagnosis by physicians. Sonographers explain the procedure, record additional medical history, and then position the patient for testing. Viewing the screen as the scan takes place, sonographers look for subtle differences between healthy and pathological areas, decide which images to include, and judge if the images are satisfactory for diagnostic purposes. Sonographers may specialize in neurosonography (the brain), vascular (blood flows), echocardiography (the heart), abdominal (the liver, kidneys, spleen, and pancreas), obstetrics/gynecology (the female reproductive system), and ophthalmology (the eye).

Radiologic technologists must follow physicians' instructions precisely and conform with regulations concerning use of radiation to ensure that they, patients, and coworkers are protected from over exposure.

In addition to preparing patients and operating equipment, radiologic technologists keep patient records and adjust and maintain equipment. They may also prepare work schedules, evaluate equipment purchases, or manage a radiology department.

Working Conditions

Most full-time radiologic technologists work about 40 hours a week; they may have evening, weekend, or on-call hours.

Technologists are on their feet for long periods and may lift or turn disabled patients. They work at radiologic machines but may also do some procedures at patients' bedsides. Some radiologic technologists travel to patients in large vans equipped with sophisticated diagnostic equipment.

Radiation therapists are prone to emotional "burn out" because they treat extremely ill and dying patients on a daily basis. Although potential radiation hazards exist in this occupation, they have been minimized by the use of lead aprons, gloves, and other shielding devices, as well as by instruments that monitor radiation exposure. Technologists wear badges that measure radiation levels in the radiation area, and detailed records are kept on their cumulative lifetime dose.

A radiologic technologist prepares a patient for a CT scan.

Employment

Radiologic technologists held about 174,000 jobs in 1996. Most technologists were radiographers. Some were sonographers and radiation therapists. About 1 radiologic technologist in 4 worked part time. More than half of jobs for technologists are in hospitals. Most of the rest are in physicians' offices and clinics, including diagnostic imaging centers.

Training, Other Qualifications, and Advancement

Preparation for this profession is offered in hospitals, colleges and universities, vocational-technical institutes, and the Armed Forces. Hospitals, which employ most radiologic technologists, prefer to hire those with formal training.

Formal training is offered in radiography, radiation therapy, and diagnostic medical sonography (ultrasound). Programs range in length from 1 to 4 years and lead to a certificate, associate's degree, or bachelor's degree. Two-year programs are most prevalent.

Some 1-year certificate programs are for individuals from other health occupations, such as medical technologists and registered nurses, who want to change fields or experienced radiographers who want to specialize in radiation therapy technology or sonography. A bachelor's or master's degree in one of the radiologic technologies is desirable for supervisory, administrative, or teaching positions.

The Joint Review Committee on Education in Radiologic Technology accredits most formal training programs for this field. They accredited 629 radiography programs and 97 radiation therapy programs in 1997. The Joint Review Committee on Education in Diagnostic Medical Sonography accredited 74 programs in sonography in 1997.

Radiography programs require, at a minimum, a high school diploma or the equivalent. High school courses in mathematics, physics, chemistry, and biology are helpful. The programs provide both classroom and clinical instruction in anatomy and physiology, patient care procedures, radiation physics, radiation protection, principles of imaging, medical terminology, positioning of patients, medical ethics, radiobiology, and pathology.

For training programs in radiation therapy and diagnostic medical sonography, applicants with a background in science, or experience in one of the health professions, generally are preferred. Some programs consider applicants with liberal arts backgrounds, however, as well as high school graduates with courses in math and science.

Radiographers and radiation therapists are covered by provisions of the Consumer-Patient Radiation Health and Safety Act of 1981, which aims to protect the public from the hazards of unnecessary exposure to medical and dental radiation by ensuring operators of radiologic equipment are properly trained. The act requires the Federal Government to set standards that the States, in turn, may use for accrediting training programs and certifying individuals who engage in medical or dental radiography. Because ultrasound does not use ionizing radiation, sonographers are excluded from this act.

In 1997, 36 States and Puerto Rico licensed radiologic technologists. No State requires that sonographers be licensed. Voluntary registration is offered by the American Registry of Radiologic Technologists (ARRT) in both radiography and radiation therapy. The American Registry of Diagnostic Medical Sonographers (ARDMS) certifies the competence of sonographers. To become registered, technologists must be graduates of an accredited program or meet other prerequisites and have passed an examination. Many employers prefer to hire registered technologists.

With experience and additional training, staff technologists may become specialists, performing CT scanning, ultrasound, angiography, and magnetic resonance imaging. Experienced technologists may also be promoted to supervisor, chief radiologic technologist, and—ultimately—department administrator or director. Depending on the institution, courses or a master's degree in business or health administration may be necessary for the director's position. Some technologists progress by becoming instructors or directors in radiologic technology programs; others take jobs as sales representatives or instructors with equipment manufacturers.

With additional education, available at major cancer centers, radiation therapy technologists can specialize as medical radiation dosimetrists. Dosimetrists work with health physicists and oncologists (physicians who specialize in the study and treatment of tumors) to develop treatment plans.

Radiographers and radiation therapists are required to fulfill 24 hours of continuing education every other year and provide documentation to prove that they are complying with these requirements. Sonographers must complete 30 hours of continuing education every 3 years.

Job Outlook

Jobseekers are likely to face competition from many other qualified applicants for most job openings through the year 2006. In an attempt to employ fewer technologists and lower labor costs, hospitals have begun to merge radiologic with nuclear medicine technology departments. Consequently, technologists who can perform both radiologic and nuclear medicine procedures will have the best job opportunities. The streamlining of these departments has led to slower job growth in hospitals at the same time that the number of qualified applicants entering the field has increased. The imbalance between job openings and jobseekers has caused competition for jobs to become intense. Though it is unclear how severe the imbalance will remain, it is expected to persist at some level through the year 2006.

Sonographers should experience somewhat better job opportunities than other radiologic technologist occupations. Ultrasound is becoming an increasingly attractive alternative to radiologic procedures. Ultrasound technology is expected to continue to evolve rapidly and spawn many new ultrasound procedures. Furthermore, because radiation is absent from ultrasound procedures, there are no known side effects to patients.

Employment of radiologic technologists is expected to grow faster than the average for all occupations through 2006, as the population grows and ages, increasing the demand for diagnostic imaging and therapeutic technology. For example, radiation therapy will continue to be used—alone or in combination with surgery or chemotherapy—to treat cancer. Although physicians are enthusiastic about the clinical benefits of new technologies, the extent to which they are adopted depends largely on cost and reimbursement considerations. Some promising new technologies may not come into widespread use because they are too expensive and third-party payers may not be willing to pay for their use.

Hospitals will remain the principal employer of radiologic technologists. However, employment is expected to grow most rapidly in offices and clinics of physicians, including diagnostic imaging centers. Health facilities such as these are expected to grow very rapidly through 2006 due to the strong shift toward outpatient care, encouraged by third-party payers and made possible by technological advances that permit more procedures to be performed outside the hospital. Some jobs will also come from the need to replace technologists who leave the occupation.

Earnings

In 1996, median weekly earnings for full-time salaried radiologic technologists were $559. Half earned between $478 and $672; 10 percent earned less than $317; and 10 percent earned more than $849.

According to a Hay Group Survey of acute care hospitals, the median annual base salary of full-time radiologic technologists was $28,800 in January 1997. The middle 50 percent earned between $26,600 and $31,800. Full-time radiation therapy technologists earned a median annual base salary of $37,300; and ultrasound technologists, $36,100.

Related Occupations

Radiologic technologists operate sophisticated equipment to help physicians, dentists, and other health practitioners diagnose and treat patients. Workers in related occupations include radiation dosimetrists, nuclear medicine technologists, cardiovascular technologists and technicians, perfusionists, respiratory therapists, clinical laboratory technologists, and electroneurodiagnostic technologists.

Sources of Additional Information

For career information, enclose a stamped, self-addressed business size envelope with your request to:

☛ American Society of Radiologic Technologists, 15000 Central Ave. SE., Albuquerque, NM 87123-3917.

☛ Society of Diagnostic Medical Sonographers, 12770 Coit Rd., Suite 708, Dallas, TX 75251.

☛ American Healthcare Radiology Administrators, 111 Boston Post Rd., Suite 105, P.O. Box 334, Sudbury, MA 01776.

For the current list of accredited education programs in radiography and radiation therapy technology, write to:

☛ Joint Review Committee on Education in Radiologic Technology, 20 N. Wacker Dr., Suite 600, Chicago, IL 60606-2901.

For a current list of accredited education programs in diagnostic medical sonography, write to:

☛ The Joint Review Committee on Education in Diagnostic Medical Sonography, 7108 S. Alton Way, Building C., Englewood, CO 80112.

Surgical Technologists

(D.O.T. 079.374-022)

Significant points

- Most educational programs for surgical technologists last approximately 1 year and result in a certificate.

- Increased demand for surgical technologists is expected as the number of surgical procedures grows.

Nature of the Work

Surgical technologists, also called surgical or operating room technicians, assist in operations under the supervision of surgeons, registered nurses, or other surgical personnel. Before an operation, surgical technologists help set up the operating room with surgical instruments and equipment, sterile linens, and sterile solutions. They assemble, adjust, and check nonsterile equipment to ensure that it is working properly. Technologists also prepare patients for surgery by washing, shaving, and disinfecting incision sites. They transport patients to the operating room, help position them on the operating table, and cover them with sterile surgical "drapes." Technologists also observe patients' vital signs, check charts, and help the surgical team scrub and put on gloves, gowns, and masks.

During surgery, technologists pass instruments and other sterile supplies to surgeons and surgeon assistants. They may hold retractors, cut sutures, and help count sponges, needles, supplies, and instruments. Surgical technologists help prepare, care for, and dispose of specimens taken for laboratory analysis and may help apply dressings. They may operate sterilizers, lights, or suction machines, and help operate diagnostic equipment. Technologists may also maintain supplies of fluids, such as plasma and blood.

After an operation, surgical technologists may help transfer patients to the recovery room and clean and restock the operating room.

Working Conditions

Surgical technologists work in clean, well-lighted, cool environments. They must stand for long periods and remain alert during operations. At times they may be exposed to communicable diseases and unpleasant sights, odors, and materials.

Most surgical technologists work a regular 40-hour week, although they may be on call or work nights, weekends and holidays on a rotating basis.

Employment

Surgical technologists held about 49,000 jobs in 1996. Most are employed by hospitals, mainly in operating and delivery rooms. Others are employed in clinics and surgical centers, and in the offices of physicians and dentists who perform outpatient surgery. A few,

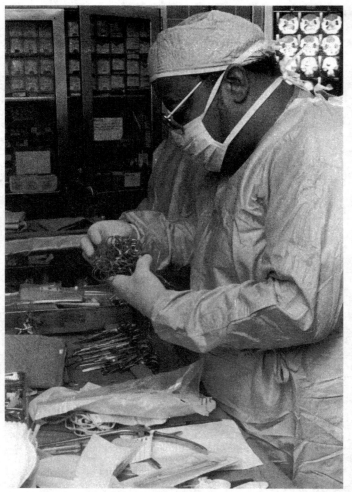

Surgical technologists spend much time cleaning medical instruments and setting up the operating room.

known as private scrubs, are employed directly by surgeons who have special surgical teams like those for liver transplants.

Training, Other Qualifications, and Advancement

Surgical technologists receive their training in formal programs offered by community and junior colleges, vocational schools, universities, hospitals, and the military. In 1997, the Commission on Accreditation of Allied Health Education Programs (CAAHEP) recognized 145 accredited programs. High school graduation normally is required for admission. Programs last 9 to 24 months and lead to a certificate, diploma, or associate degree. Shorter programs are designed for students who are already licensed practical nurses or military personnel.

Programs provide classroom education and supervised clinical experience. Students take courses in anatomy, physiology, microbiology, pharmacology, professional ethics, and medical terminology. Other studies cover the care and safety of patients during surgery, aseptic techniques, and surgical procedures. Students also learn to sterilize instruments; prevent and control infection; and handle special drugs, solutions, supplies, and equipment.

Technologists may obtain voluntary professional certification from the Liaison Council on Certification for the Surgical Technologist by graduating from a formal program and passing a national certification examination. They may then use the designation Certified Surgical Technologist, or CST. Continuing education or reexamination is required to maintain certification, which must be renewed every 6 years. Graduation from a CAAHEP-accredited program will be a prerequisite for certification by March 2000. Most employers prefer to hire certified technologists.

Surgical technologists need manual dexterity to handle instruments quickly. They also must be conscientious, orderly, and emotionally stable to handle the demands of the operating room environment. Technologists must respond quickly and know procedures well so that they may have instruments ready for surgeons without having to be told. They are expected to keep abreast of new developments in the field. Recommended high school courses include health, biology, chemistry, and mathematics.

Technologists advance by specializing in a particular area of surgery, such as neurosurgery or open heart surgery. They may also work as circulating technologists. A circulating technologist is the "unsterile" member of the surgical team who prepares patients; helps with anesthesia; gets, opens, and holds packages for the "sterile" persons during the procedure; interviews the patient before surgery; keeps a written account of the surgical procedure; and answers the surgeon's questions about the patient during the surgery. With additional training, some technologists advance to first assistants, who help with retracting, sponging, suturing, cauterizing bleeders, and closing and treating wounds. Some surgical technologists manage central supply departments in hospitals, or take positions with insurance companies, sterile supply services, and operating equipment firms.

Job Outlook

Employment of surgical technologists is expected to grow faster than the average for all occupations through the year 2006 as the volume of surgery increases. The number of surgical procedures is expected to rise as the population grows and ages. Older people require more surgical procedures. Technological advances, such as fiber optics and laser technology, will also permit new surgical procedures.

Hospitals will continue to be the primary employer of surgical technologists, although much faster employment growth is expected in offices and clinics of physicians, including ambulatory surgical centers.

Earnings

According to a 1996 membership survey conducted by the Association of Surgical Technologists, the average annual salary for surgical technologists, excluding overtime or on-call pay, was about $25,000. Beginning technologists earned about $20,900 a year, while the most experienced technologists earned about $28,000 a year.

Related Occupations

Other health occupations requiring approximately 1 year of training after high school include licensed practical nurses, respiratory therapy technicians, medical laboratory assistants, medical assistants, dental assistants, optometric assistants, and physical therapy aides.

Sources of Additional Information

For additional information on a career as a surgical technologist and a list of CAAHEP-accredited programs, contact:

☛ Association of Surgical Technologists, 7108-C South Alton Way, Englewood, CO 80112. Homepage: http://www.ast.org/

For information on certification, contact:

☛ Liaison Council on Certification for the Surgical Technologist, 7790 East Arapahoe Rd., Suite 240, Englewood, CO 80112-1274.

Communications Occupations

Broadcast Technicians

(D.O.T. 193.167-014, .262-018, and -038; 194.062, .122, .262-010, -014, -018, -022, .282, .362, and .382-014, -018, 962.167-010, and .382-010)

Significant Points

- Competition is expected for the better paying jobs at radio and television stations serving large cities.

- Beginners need formal training in broadcast technology to obtain their first job at a smaller station.

- Evening, weekend, and holiday work is common.

Nature of the Work

Broadcast technicians install, test, repair, set up, and operate the electronic equipment used to record and transmit radio and television programs. They work with television cameras, microphones, tape recorders, light and sound effects, transmitters, antennas, and other equipment. Some broadcast technicians develop movie sound tracks in motion picture production studios.

In the control room of a radio or television broadcasting studio, these technicians operate equipment that regulates the signal strength, clarity, and range of sounds and colors of recordings or broadcasts. They also operate control panels to select the source of the material. Technicians may switch from one camera or studio to another, from film to live programming, or from network to local programs. By means of hand signals and, in television, telephone headsets, they give technical directions to other studio personnel.

Broadcast technicians in small stations perform a variety of duties. In large stations and at the networks, technicians are more specialized, although job assignments may change from day to day. The terms "operator," "engineer," and "technician" often are used interchangeably to describe these jobs. *Transmitter operators* monitor and log outgoing signals and operate transmitters. *Maintenance technicians* set up, adjust, service, and repair electronic broadcasting equipment. *Audio control engineers* regulate sound pickup, transmission, and switching of television pictures while, *video control engineers* regulate their quality, brightness, and contrast. *Recording engineers* operate and maintain video and sound recording equipment. They may operate equipment designed to produce special effects, such as the illusions of a bolt of lightning or a police siren. *Field technicians* set up and operate broadcasting portable field transmission equipment outside the studio.

Television news coverage requires so much electronic equipment, and the technology is changing so fast, that many stations assign technicians exclusively to news. *Chief engineers, transmission engineers,* and *broadcast field supervisors* supervise the technicians who operate and maintain broadcasting equipment.

Technicians in the motion picture industry are called *sound mixers* or *rerecording mixers.* Mixers produce the sound track of a movie, using a process called dubbing. They sit at sound consoles facing the screen and fade in and fade out each sound and regulate its volume. Each technician is responsible for certain sounds. Technicians follow a script that tells at precisely what moment, as the film runs through the projector, each of the sounds must be faded in and out. All the sounds for each shot are thus blended on a master sound track.

Working Conditions

Broadcast technicians generally work indoors in pleasant surroundings. However, those who broadcast from disaster areas or crime scenes may work under unfavorable conditions. Technicians doing maintenance may climb poles or antenna towers, while those setting up equipment do heavy lifting.

Technicians in large stations and the networks usually work a 40-hour week, but may occasionally work overtime, under great pressure

Broadcast technicians must have manual dexterity and an aptitude for working with electrical, electronic, and mechanical systems and equipment.

to meet broadcast deadlines. Technicians in small stations routinely work more than 40 hours a week. Evening, weekend, and holiday work is usual, because most stations are on the air 18 to 24 hours a day, 7 days a week.

Those who work on motion pictures may be on a tight schedule to finish according to contract agreements.

Employment

Broadcast technicians held about 46,000 jobs in 1996. About 7 out of 10 broadcast technicians were in radio and television broadcasting. Almost 2 in 10 worked in the motion picture industry. About 8 percent worked for cable and other pay television services. A few were self employed. Television stations employ, on average, many more technicians than do radio stations. Some broadcast technicians are employed in other industries, producing employee communications, sales, and training programs. Technician jobs in television are located in virtually all cities, while jobs in radio are also found in many small towns. The highest paying and most specialized jobs are concentrated in New York City, Los Angeles, Chicago, and Washington, D.C.—the originating centers for most of network programs. Motion picture production jobs are concentrated in Los Angeles and New York City.

Training, Other Qualifications, and Advancement

The best way to prepare for a broadcast technician job in radio or television is to obtain technical school, community college, or college training in broadcast technology or in engineering or electronics.

This is particularly true for those who hope to advance to supervisory positions or jobs at large stations or the networks. On the other hand, there is no formal training for jobs in the motion picture industry. People are hired as apprentice editorial assistants and work their way up to more skilled jobs. Employers in the motion picture industry usually hire freelance technicians on a picture-by-picture basis. Reputation, determination, and luck are important in getting jobs.

Beginners learn skills on the job from experienced technicians and supervisors. They generally begin their careers in small stations and, once experienced, move on to larger ones. Large stations generally only hire technicians with experience. Many employers pay tuition and expenses for courses or seminars to help technicians keep abreast of developments in the field.

The Federal Communications Commission no longer requires the licensing of broadcast technicians, as the Telecommunications Act of 1996 eliminated this licensing requirement. Certification by the Society of Broadcast Engineers is a mark of competence and experience. The certificate is issued to experienced technicians who pass an examination. By offering the Radio Operator and the Television Operator levels of certification, the Society of Broadcast Engineers has filled the void left by the elimination of the FCC license.

Prospective technicians should take high school courses in math, physics, and electronics. Building electronic equipment from hobby kits and operating a "ham," or amateur radio, are good experience, as is work in college radio and television stations.

Broadcast technicians must have manual dexterity and an aptitude for working with electrical, electronic, and mechanical systems and equipment.

Experienced technicians may become supervisory technicians or chief engineers. A college degree in engineering is needed to become chief engineer at a large TV station.

Job Outlook

People seeking beginning jobs as radio and television broadcast technicians are expected to face strong competition in major metropolitan areas, where the number of qualified job seekers greatly exceeds the number of openings. There, stations seek highly experienced personnel. Prospects for entry level positions generally are better in small cities and towns for people with appropriate training.

The overall employment of broadcast technicians is expected to grow about as fast as the average through the year 2006. Growth in the number of new radio and television stations and an increase in the number of programming hours should require additional technicians. However, employment growth in radio and television broadcasting may be tempered somewhat because of laborsaving technical advances, such as computer-controlled programming and remote control of transmitters.

Employment in the cable industry should grow because of new products coming to market, such as cable modems, which deliver high speed Internet access to PCs, and digital set-top boxes, which transmit better sound and pictures, allowing cable operators to offer many more channels than in the past. These new products should cause traditional cable subscribers to sign up for additional services. Also, employment in the cable industry should grow, as today's young people establish their own households, for they are more accustomed to the idea of paying for TV than their parents.

Employment in the motion picture industry will grow faster than the average for all occupations. Job prospects are expected to remain competitive, because of the large number of people attracted to this relatively small field.

Virtually all job openings will result from the need to replace experienced technicians who leave the occupation. Turnover is relatively high for broadcast technicians. Many leave the occupation for electronic jobs in other areas, such as computer technology or commercial and industrial repair.

Earnings

Television stations usually pay higher salaries than radio stations; commercial broadcasting usually pays more than educational broadcasting; and stations in large markets pay more than those in small ones.

According to a survey conducted by the National Association of Broadcasters and the Broadcast Cable Financial Management Association, average earnings for technicians at radio stations were $30,251 a year in 1996. For chief engineer, average earnings were $46,602; and salaries ranged from $34,714 in the smallest markets to $46,602 in the largest markets. In television, average earnings for operator technicians were $24,260 a year and salaries ranged from $16,422 to $45,158; for technical directors, average earnings were $25,962 a year and the range was $18,444 to $44,531; for maintenance technicians, average earnings were $32,533 a year and the range was $24,210 to $50,235; and for chief engineers, the average earnings were $53,655 a year and salaries ranged from $38,178 in the smallest markets to $91,051 in the largest.

Earnings in the motion picture industry depend on skill and reputation and, based on limited information, range from $20,000 to $100,000 a year.

Related Occupations
Broadcast technicians need the electronics training and hand coordination necessary to operate technical equipment, and they generally complete specialized postsecondary programs. Others with similar jobs and training include drafters, engineering and science technicians, surveyors, air traffic controllers, radiologic technologists, respiratory therapy workers, cardiovascular technologists and technicians, electroneurodiagnostic technicians, and clinical laboratory technologists and technicians.

Sources of Additional Information
For information on careers for broadcast technicians, write to:
☛ National Association of Broadcasters Employment Clearinghouse, 1771 N St. NW., Washington, DC 20036.

For a list of schools that offer programs or courses in broadcasting, contact:
☛ Broadcast Education Association, National Association of Broadcasters, 1771 N St. NW., Washington, DC 20036.

For information on certification, contact:
☛ Society of Broadcast Engineers, 8445 Keystone Crossing, Suite 140, Indianapolis, IN 46240.

For information on careers in the motion picture and television industry, contact:
☛ Society of Motion Picture and Television Engineers (SMPTE), 595 W. Hartsdale Ave., White Plains, NY 10607.

Public Relations Specialists
(D.O.T. 165.017 and .167)

Significant Points
● Employment of public relations specialists is expected to increase rapidly, while keen competition is expected for entry-level jobs.

● Opportunities should be best for college graduates with degrees in journalism, public relations, advertising, or other communications-related fields.

● Public relations work experience in gained as an intern is an asset in competing for entry-level jobs.

Nature of the Work
An organization's reputation, profitability, and even its continued existence can depend on the degree to which its goals and policies are supported by its targeted "publics." Public relations specialists serve as advocates for businesses, governments, universities, hospitals, schools, and other organizations, and strive to build and maintain positive relationships with the public. As managers recognize the growing importance of good public relations to the success of their organizations, they increasingly rely on public relations specialists for advice on strategy and policy of such programs.

Public relations specialists handle such organizational functions as media, community, consumer, and governmental relations; political campaigns; interest-group representation; conflict mediation; or employee and investor relations. However, public relations is not only "telling the organization's story." Understanding the attitudes and concerns of consumers, employees, and various other groups is also a vital part of the job. To improve communications, public relations specialists establish and maintain cooperative relationships with representatives of community, consumer, employee, and public interest groups and those in print and broadcast journalism.

Public relations specialists put together information that keeps the general public, interest groups, and stockholders aware of an organization's policies, activities, and accomplishments. Their work keeps management aware of public attitudes and concerns of the many groups and organizations with which it must deal.

Public relations specialists prepare press releases and contact people in the media who might print or broadcast their material. Many radio or television special reports, newspaper stories, and magazine articles start at the desks of public relations specialists. Sometimes the subject is an organization and its policies towards its employees or its role in the community. Often the subject is a public issue, such as health, nutrition, energy, or the environment.

Public relations specialists also arrange and conduct programs for contact between organization representatives and the public. For example, they set up speaking engagements and often prepare the speeches for company officials. These specialists represent employers at community projects; make film, slide, or other visual presentations at meetings and school assemblies; and plan conventions. In addition, they are responsible for preparing annual reports and writing proposals for various projects.

In government, public relations specialists—who may be called press secretaries, information officers, public affairs specialists, or communications specialists—keep the public informed about the activities of government agencies and officials. For example, public affairs specialists in the Department of Energy keep the public informed about the proposed lease of offshore land for oil exploration. A press secretary for a member of Congress keeps constituents aware of their elected representative's accomplishments.

In large organizations, the key public relations executive, who is often a vice president, may develop overall plans and policies with other executives. In addition, public relations departments employ public relations specialists to write, do research, prepare materials, maintain contacts, and respond to inquiries.

People who handle publicity for an individual or who direct public relations for a small organization may deal with all aspects of the job. They contact people, plan and do research, and prepare material for distribution. They may also handle advertising or sales promotion work to support marketing.

Working Conditions
Some public relations specialists work a standard 35- to 40-hour week, but unpaid overtime is common. In addition, schedules often have to be rearranged to meet deadlines, deliver speeches, attend meetings and community activities, and travel out of town. Occasionally they have to be at the job or on call around the clock, especially if there is an emergency or crisis.

Employment
Public relations specialists held about 110,000 jobs in 1996. About two-thirds worked in services industries—management and public relations firms, educational institutions, membership organizations, health care organizations, social service agencies, and advertising agencies, for example. Others worked for a wide range of employers, including manufacturing firms, financial institutions, and government agencies. A few were self-employed.

Some experienced public relations specialists start their own consulting firms.

Public relations specialists are concentrated in large cities in which press services and other communications facilities are readily available, and many businesses and trade associations have their headquarters. Many public relations consulting firms, for example, are in New York, Los Angeles, Chicago, and Washington, DC. There is a trend, however, for public relations jobs to be dispersed throughout the Nation.

Training, Other Qualifications, and Advancement

Although there are no defined standards for entry into a public relations career, a college degree combined with public relations experience, usually gained through an internship, is considered excellent preparation for public relations work. The ability to write and speak well is essential. Many beginners have a college major in public relations, journalism, advertising, or communications. Some firms seek college graduates who have worked in electronic or print journalism. Other employers seek applicants with demonstrated communications skills and training or experience in a field related to the firm's business—science, engineering, sales, or finance, for example.

In 1996, well over 200 colleges and about 100 graduate schools offered degree programs or special curricula in public relations, usually in a journalism or communications department. In addition, many other colleges offered at least one course in this field. The Accrediting Council on Education in Journalism and Mass Communications is the only agency authorized to accredit schools or department in public relations. A commonly used public relations sequence includes the following courses: Public relations principles and techniques; public relations management and administration, including organizational development; writing, emphasizing news releases, proposals, annual reports, scripts, speeches, and related items; visual communications, including desktop publishing and computer graphics; and research, emphasizing social science research and survey design and implementation. Courses in advertising, journalism, business administration, political science, psychology, sociology, and creative writing also are helpful, as is familiarity with word processing and other computer applications. Specialties are offered in public relations for business, government, or nonprofit organizations.

Many colleges help students gain part-time internships in public relations that provide valuable experience and training. The Armed Forces can also be an excellent place to gain training and experience. Membership in local chapters of the Public Relations Student Society of America or the International Association of Business Communicators provides an opportunity for students to exchange views with public relations specialists and to make professional contacts who may help them find a full-time job in the field. A portfolio of published articles, television or radio programs, slide presentations, and other work is an asset in finding a job. Writing for a school publication or television or radio station provides valuable experience and material for one's portfolio.

Creativity, initiative, good judgment, and the ability to express thoughts clearly and simply are essential. Decision making, problem solving, and research skills are also important.

People who choose public relations as a career need an outgoing personality, self-confidence, an understanding of human psychology, and an enthusiasm for motivating people. They should be competitive, yet flexible and able to function as part of a team.

Some organizations, particularly those with large public relations staffs, have formal training programs for new employees. In smaller organizations, new employees work under the guidance of experienced staff members. Beginners often maintain files of material about company activities, scan newspapers and magazines for appropriate articles to clip, and assemble information for speeches and pamphlets. After gaining experience, they write news releases, speeches, and articles for publication, or design and carry out public relations programs. Public relations specialists in smaller firms generally get all-around experience, whereas those in larger firms tend to be more specialized.

The Public Relations Society of America accredits public relations specialists who have at least 5 years of experience in the field and have passed a comprehensive 6-hour examination (5 hours written, 1 hour oral). The International Association of Business Communicators also has an accreditation program for professionals in the communications field, including public relations specialists. Those who meet all the requirements of the program earn the designation, Accredited Business Communicator. Candidates must have at least 5 years of experience in a communication field and pass a written and oral examination. They also must submit a portfolio of work samples demonstrating involvement in a range of communication projects and a thorough understanding of communication planning. Employers consider professional recognition through accreditation a sign of competence in this field, and it may be especially helpful in a competitive job market.

Promotion to supervisory jobs may come as public relations specialists show they can handle more demanding managerial assignments. In public relations firms, a beginner may be hired as a research assistant or account assistant and be promoted to account executive, account supervisor, vice president, and eventually senior vice president. A similar career path is followed in corporate public relations, although the titles may differ. Some experienced public relations specialists start their own consulting firms. (For more information on public relations managers, see the *Handbook* statement on marketing, advertising, and public relations managers.)

Job Outlook

Keen competition for public relations jobs will likely continue among recent college graduates with a degree in communications—journalism, public relations, advertising, or a related field—as the number of applicants is expected to exceed the number of job openings. People without the appropriate educational background or work experience will face the toughest obstacles in finding a public relations job.

Employment of public relations specialists is expected to increase faster than the average for all occupations through the year 2006. Recognition of the need for good public relations in an increasingly competitive business environment should spur demand for public relations specialists in organizations of all sizes. Employment in public relations firms should grow as firms hire contractors to provide public relations services rather than support full-time staff. The vast majority of job opportunities should result from the need to replace public relations specialists who leave the occupation to take another job, retire, or for other reasons.

Earnings
Median annual earnings for salaried public relations specialists who usually worked full time were about $34,000 in 1996. The middle 50 percent earned between $25,000 and $54,000 annually; the lowest 10 percent earned less than $16,000, and the top 10 percent earned more than $75,000.

According to a 1995 salary survey conducted for the Public Relations Society of America, the overall median salary in public relations was $49,070. Salaries in public relations ranged from less than $15,000 to more than $150,000. There was little difference between the median salaries in public relations firms and corporations, $51,340 and $50,770, respectively. However, practitioners working for government, health-care, or non-profit organizations had a considerably lower median salary of $43,260.

Public affairs specialists in the Federal Government in nonsupervisory, supervisory, and managerial positions averaged about $52,540 a year in 1996.

Related Occupations
Public relations specialists create favorable attitudes among various organizations, special interest groups, and the public through effective communication. Other workers with similar jobs include fundraisers, lobbyists, promotion managers, advertising managers, and police officers involved in community relations.

Sources of Additional Information
A comprehensive directory of schools offering degree programs or a sequence of study in public relations, a brochure on careers in public relations, and a $5 brochure entitled *Where Shall I go to Study Advertising and Public Relations* are available from:
☛ Public Relations Society of America, Inc., 33 Irving Place, New York, NY 10003-2376.

Career information on public relations in hospitals and other health care settings is available from:
☛ The Society for Health Care Strategy and Market Development , One North Franklin St., Suite 3100S, Chicago, IL 60606.

For a list of schools with accredited programs in public relations in their journalism departments, send a stamped self-addressed envelope to:
☛ Accrediting Council on Education in Journalism and Mass Communications, University of Kansas School of Journalism, Stauffer Flint Hall, Lawrence, KS 66045.

For information on accreditation for public relations specialists contact:
☛ International Association of Business Communicators, One Hallidie Plaza, Suite 600, San Francisco, CA 94102.

Radio and Television Announcers and Newscasters

(D.O.T 131.067-010, .262-010; 159.147-010, -014, and -018)

Significant Points

- Competition for announcer and newscaster jobs will continue to be very keen.

- Jobs at small stations usually have low pay, but offer the best opportunities for beginners.

- Related unpaid work experience at a campus radio station or as an intern at a commercial station can be very helpful in breaking into the occupation.

Nature of the Work
Announcers and newscasters are well-known to radio and television audiences. Radio announcers, often called *disk jockeys*, select and introduce recorded music; present news, sports, weather, and commercials; interview guests; and report on community activities and other matters of interest to their audience. If a written script is required, they may do the research and writing. They often "ad-lib" much of the commentary. They also may operate the control board, sell commercial time to advertisers, and write commercial and news copy.

Some announcers at large stations usually specialize in sports or weather, or in general news, and may be called *newscasters* or *anchors*. Others are news analysts. In small stations, one announcer may do everything.

News anchors, or a pair of co-anchors, present news stories and introduce in-depth videotaped news or live transmissions from on-the-scene reporters. (See statement on reporters and correspondents elsewhere in the *Handbook*.) *Weathercasters*, also called weather reporters or meteorologists, report and forecast weather conditions. They gather information from national satellite weather services, wire services, and other local and regional weather bureaus. *Sportscasters* select, write, and deliver the sports news. This may include interviews with sports personalities and coverage of games played.

Broadcast news analysts, called *commentators*, present news stories and also interpret them and discuss how they may affect the Nation or listeners.

Show hosts interview guests about their lives, work, or topics of current interest.

Announcers frequently participate in community activities. Sports announcers, for example, may serve masters of ceremonies at sports club banquets or may be on hand to greet customers at openings of sporting goods stores.

Working Conditions
Announcers and newscasters usually work in well-lighted, air-conditioned, soundproof studios.

The broadcast day is long for radio and TV stations—some are on the air 24 hours a day—so announcers can expect to work unusual hours. Many present early morning shows, when most people are getting ready for work or commuting, or do late night newscasts.

They work within tight schedule constraints, which can be physically and mentally stressful. For many announcers, the intangible rewards—creative work, many personal contacts, and the satisfaction of becoming widely known—far outweigh the disadvantages of irregular and often unpredictable hours, work pressures, and disrupted personal lives.

Employment
Radio and television announcers and newscasters held about 52,000 jobs in 1996. Nearly all were staff announcers, but some were freelance announcers who sold their services for individual assignments to networks and stations, or to advertising agencies and other independent producers.

Training, Other Qualifications, and Advancement
Entry to this occupation is highly competitive. While formal training in broadcast journalism from a college or technical school (private broadcasting school) is valuable, station officials pay particular attention to taped auditions that show an applicant's delivery and—in television—appearance and style on commercials, news, and interviews. Those hired by television stations usually start out as production secretaries, production assistants, researchers, or reporters and are given a chance to move into announcing if they show an aptitude for "on-air" work. Newcomers to TV broadcasting also may begin as news camera operators. (See the statement on photographers and camera operators elsewhere in the *Handbook*.) A beginner's chance of landing an on-air newscasting job is remote, except possibly for a small radio station. In radio, newcomers generally start out taping interviews and operating equipment.

Many announcers present early morning shows, when many people are getting ready for work or commuting, or do late night newscasts.

Announcers usually begin at a station in a small community and, if qualified, may move to a better paying job in a large city. They also may advance by hosting a regular program as a disc jockey, sportscaster, or other specialist. In the national networks, competition for jobs is particularly intense, and employers look for college graduates with at least several years of successful announcing experience.

Announcers must have a pleasant and well-controlled voice, good timing, excellent pronunciation, and correct English usage. Television announcers need a neat, pleasing appearance as well. Knowledge of theater, sports, music, business, politics, and other subjects likely to be covered in broadcasts improves chances for success. Announcers also must be computer literate because stories are created and edited on the computer. In addition, they should be able to "ad-lib" all or part of a show and to work under tight deadlines. The most successful announcers attract a large audience by combining a pleasing personality and voice with an appealing style.

High school courses in English, public speaking, drama, foreign languages, and electronics are valuable, and hobbies such as sports and music are additional assets. Students may gain valuable experience at campus radio or TV facilities and at commercial stations serving as interns. For example, even answering the phone on the assignment desk gives the intern the experience of taking calls that may lead to a story. The intern learns what is potentially newsworthy and how to determine priorities. Interns are also favored applicants in the competition for jobs.

Persons considering enrolling in a broadcasting school should contact personnel managers of radio and television stations as well as broadcasting trade organizations to determine the school's reputation for producing suitably trained candidates.

As a result of the Telecommunications Act of 1996, the Federal Communications Commission (FCC) no longer requires anyone who works for a broadcasting station to have a license. Only the station is required to be licensed.

Job Outlook
Competition for jobs as announcers will be very keen because the broadcasting field typically attracts many more jobseekers than there are jobs. Small radio stations are more inclined to hire beginners, but the pay is low. Interns generally receive preference for available

positions. Because competition for ratings is so intense in major metropolitan areas, large stations will continue to seek announcers and newscasters who have proven that they can attract and retain a large audience.

Newscasters who are knowledgeable in such areas as business, consumer, and health news may have an advantage over others. While specialization is more common at larger stations and the networks, many smaller stations also encourage it

Employment of announcers is expected to decline slightly through the year 2006 due to the lack of growth of new radio and television stations. Openings in this relatively small field will arise from the need to replace those who transfer to other kinds of work or leave the labor force. Many announcers leave the field because they can not advance to better paying jobs.

Employment in this occupation is not significantly affected by downturns in the economy. If recessions cause advertising revenues to fall, stations tend to cut "behind-the-scenes" workers rather than announcers and broadcasters.

Earnings
Salaries in broadcasting vary widely. They are higher in television than in radio, higher in larger markets than in small ones, and higher in commercial than in public broadcasting.

According to a survey conducted by the National Association of Broadcasters and the Broadcast Cable Financial Management Association, the average salary for radio news announcers was $31,251 a year in 1996. Salaries ranged from $7,100 in the smallest markets to $102,676 in the largest markets. Sports announcers' average was $43,646, ranging from $10,608 in the smallest to $106,200 in the largest markets.

Among television announcers, news anchors' average salary was $65,520, ranging from $24,935 in the smallest to $199,741 in the largest markets. Weathercasters' average was $52,562, ranging from $25,638 to $103,919. Sportscasters' average was $48,704, ranging from $22,400 to $128,877.

Related Occupations
The success of announcers and news broadcasters depends upon how well they speak to their audiences. Others for whom oral communication skills are vital are interpreters, sales workers, public relations specialists, teachers, and actors.

Sources of Additional Information
For a list of schools that offer programs and courses in broadcasting, contact:
☛ Broadcast Education Association, 1771 N St. NW., Washington, DC 20036.
General information on the broadcasting industry is available from:
☛ National Association of Broadcasters, 1771 N St. NW., Washington, DC 20036.
For information on careers in broadcast news, scholarships, and internships, contact:
☛ Radio-Television News Directors Foundation, 1000 Connecticut Ave. NW., Washington, DC 20036.

Reporters and Correspondents

(D.O.T. 131.262-018)

Significant Points

- Employment is expected to decline and there should be keen competition for job openings.

- Less competition is expected for jobs with suburban and weekly newspapers.

- Jobs are often stressful due to irregular hours, frequent night and weekend work, and pressure to meet deadlines.

Nature of the Work

Reporters and correspondents play a key role in our society. They gather information and prepare stories that inform us about local, State, National, and international events; present points of view on current issues; and report on the actions of public officials, corporate executives, special interest groups, and others who exercise power. In covering a story, they investigate leads and news tips, look at documents, observe on-the-scene, and interview people. Reporters take notes and may also take photographs or shoot videos. At their office, they organize the material, determine their focus or emphasis, write their stories, and may also edit videos. Many enter information or write stories on portable computers, then submit them to their offices using a telephone modem. In some cases, newswriters write the story from information collected and submitted by the reporter.

Radio and television reporters often compose stories and report "live" from the scene. Later, they may tape a commentary in the studio.

General assignment reporters write up news as assigned, such as an accident, a political rally, the visit of a celebrity, or a company going out of business. Large newspapers and radio and television stations assign reporters to gather news about specific news categories such as crime or education. Some reporters specialize in fields such as health, politics, foreign affairs, sports, theater, consumer affairs, social events, science, business, and religion. Investigative reporters cover stories that take many days or weeks of information gathering.

News correspondents are stationed, and report on news occurring in large U.S. and foreign cities. Reporters on small publications cover all aspects of the news: They take photographs, write headlines, lay out pages, edit wire service copy, and write editorials. They also may solicit advertisements, sell subscriptions, and perform general office work.

Working Conditions

The work of reporters and correspondents is usually hectic. They are under great pressure to meet deadlines. Some reporters work in comfortable, private offices; others work in large rooms filled with the sound of keyboards and computer printers, as well as the voices of other reporters. Those reporting from the scene for radio and television may be distracted by curious onlookers, police, or other emergency workers. Covering wars, political uprisings, fires, floods, and similar events is often dangerous.

Working hours vary. Reporters on morning papers often work from late afternoon until midnight. Those on afternoon or evening papers generally work from early morning until early or mid-afternoon. Radio and television reporters are usually assigned to a day or evening shift. Magazine reporters generally work during the day. Reporters may have to change their work hours to meet a deadline, or to follow late-breaking developments. Their work demands long hours, irregular schedules, and some travel.

Employment

Reporters and correspondents held about 60,000 jobs in 1996. About 7 of every 10 worked for newspapers, either large city dailies or suburban and small town dailies or weeklies. Almost 2 in 10 worked in radio and television broadcasting, and others worked for magazines and wire services.

Training, Other Qualifications, and Advancement

Most employers prefer individuals with a bachelor's degree in journalism, but some hire graduates with other majors. They look for experience on school newspapers or broadcasting stations and internships with news organizations. Large city newspapers and stations may also prefer candidates with a degree in a subject-matter specialty such as economics, political science, or business. Large newspapers and broadcasters also require a minimum of 3 to 5 years experience as a reporter.

Bachelor's degree programs in journalism are available in over 410 colleges. About three-fourths of the courses in a typical cur-

Reporters and correspondents are under great pressure to meet deadlines.

riculum are in liberal arts; the remainder are in journalism. Journalism courses include introductory mass media, basic reporting and copy editing, history of journalism, and press law and ethics. Students planning a career in broadcasting take courses in radio and television newscasting and production. Those planning newspaper or magazine careers usually specialize in news-editorial journalism. Those planning careers in new media, such as online newspapers or magazines, require a merging of traditional and new journalism skills. To create a story for multimedia presentation, they need to know how to use computer software to combine online story text with graphics, audio and video elements, and even 3-D animation.

Many community and junior colleges offer journalism courses or programs; credits may be transferable to 4-year journalism programs.

A master's degree in journalism was offered by over 157 schools in 1996; about 32 schools offered a Ph.D. degree. Some graduate programs are intended primarily as preparation for news careers, while others prepare journalism teachers, researchers and theorists, and advertising and public relations workers.

High school courses in English, journalism, and social studies, provide a good foundation for college programs. Useful college liberal arts courses include English with an emphasis on writing, sociology, political science, economics, history, and psychology. Courses in computer science, business, and speech are useful as well. Fluency in a foreign language is necessary in some jobs.

Reporters need good word processing skills, and computer graphics and desktop publishing skills are useful. A knowledge of news photography is valuable for entry-level positions for combination reporter/camera operator or reporter/photographer.

Experience in a part-time or summer job or an internship with a news organization is important. The Dow Jones Newspaper Fund and newspapers, magazines, and broadcast news organizations offer summer reporting and editing internships. Work on high school and college newspapers and broadcasting stations, community papers, and Armed Forces publications also helps. In addition, more than 3,200 journalism scholarships, fellowships, and assistantships were awarded to college journalism students by universities, newspapers, foundations, and professional organizations in 1996.

Experience as a "stringer," a part-time reporter who is paid only for stories printed, is also helpful.

Reporters should be dedicated to providing accurate and impartial news. Accuracy is important both to serve the public and because untrue or libelous statements can lead to costly lawsuits. A "nose for news," persistence, initiative, poise, resourcefulness, a good memory, and the physical stamina are important, as well as the emotional stability to deal with pressing deadlines, irregular hours, and dangerous assignments. Broadcast reporters must be comfortable on camera. All reporters must be at ease in unfamiliar places and with a variety of people.

Most reporters start at small publications or broadcast stations as general assignment reporters or copy editors. Large publications and stations hire very few recent graduates; they generally require new reporters to have several years of experience.

Beginning reporters cover court proceedings and civic and club meetings, summarize speeches, and write obituaries. With experience, they report more difficult assignments, cover an assigned "beat," or specialize in a particular field.

Some reporters may advance by moving to larger papers or stations. A few experienced reporters become columnists, correspondents, writers, announcers, or public relations specialists. Others become editors in print journalism or program managers in broadcast journalism, who supervise reporters. Some eventually become broadcasting or publications industry managers.

Job Outlook

Competition will continue to be keen for reporting jobs on large metropolitan newspapers and broadcast stations and on national magazines. Small town and suburban newspapers will continue to offer better opportunities for beginners. Many openings arise on small publications as reporters become editors or reporters on larger publications or they leave the field. Talented writers who can handle highly specialized scientific or technical subjects have an advantage. Also, "stringers" and freelancers are being hired by more newspapers. In addition, online newspapers and magazines should continue to grow very fast and create numerous job opportunities.

Employment of reporters and correspondents is expected to decline through the year 2006—the result of mergers, consolidations and closures of newspapers, decreased circulations, increased expenses, and a decline in advertising profits. Some growth is expected in radio and television stations, and fast growth will occur in new online media areas.

Most job openings will arise from the need to replace reporters and correspondents who leave the occupation. Turnover is relatively high in this occupation—some may find the work too stressful and hectic, or may not like the lifestyle and transfer to other occupations where their skills are valuable. Journalism graduates have the background for work in such closely related fields as advertising and public relations, and many take jobs in these fields. Other graduates may accept sales, managerial, and other nonmedia positions, because of the difficulty related to finding media jobs.

The newspaper and broadcasting industries are sensitive to economic ups and downs. During recessions, few new reporters are hired and some reporters lose their jobs.

Earnings

The Newspaper Guild negotiates with individual newspapers on minimum salaries for both starting reporters, and those still on the job after 3 to 6 years. The median minimum salary for reporters was about $448 a week as of December 1, 1996. Of these contracts, 10 percent called for minimums of $342 or less; another 10 percent, $698 or more. The median minimum weekly salary for reporters after 3 to 6 years on the job was about $742 a week. Of these contracts, 10 percent called for top minimums of $484 or less; another 10 percent, $1,000 or more.

According to a survey conducted by the National Association of Broadcasters in 1996, annual average salaries of radio reporters ranged from $20,217 in the smallest stations, to $38,541 in the largest stations. For all stations, the median salary was $32,356. Salaries of television reporters ranged from $17,435 in the smallest stations, to $79,637 in the largest ones. For all stations, the median salary was $31,235.

Related Occupations

Reporters and correspondents must write clearly and effectively to succeed in their profession. Others for whom writing ability is es-

sential include technical writers, advertising copy writers, public relations workers, educational writers, fiction writers, biographers, screen writers, and editors.

Sources of Additional Information

Career information, including pamphlets entitled *Newspaper Career Guide*, and *Newspaper: What's In It For Me?* is available from:
☛ Newspaper Association of America, 1921 Gallows Rd., Suite 600, Vienna, VA 22182.

Information on careers in journalism, colleges and universities offering degree programs in journalism or communications, and journalism scholarships and internships may be obtained from:
☛ The Dow Jones Newspaper Fund, Inc., P.O. Box 300, Princeton, NJ 08543-0300.

Information on union wage rates for newspaper and magazine reporters is available from:
☛ The Newspaper Guild, Research and Information Department, 8611 Second Ave., Silver Spring, MD 20910.

For a list of schools with accredited programs in journalism, send a stamped, self-addressed envelope to:
☛ Accrediting Council on Education in Journalism and Mass Communications, University of Kansas School of Journalism, Stauffer-Flint Hall, Lawrence, KS 66045.

For general information about careers in journalism, contact:
☛ Association For Education in Journalism and Mass Communication, University of South Carolina, LeConte College, Room 121, Columbia, SC 29208-0251.

A pamphlet entitled Newspaper Careers and Challenges for the Next Century, can be obtained from:
☛ National Newspaper Association, 1525 Wilson Blvd., Suite 550, Arlington, VA 22209.

Names and locations of newspapers and a list of schools and departments of journalism are published in the *Editor and Publisher International Year Book*, available in most public libraries and newspaper offices.

Writers and Editors

(D.O.T. 052.067-010; 131 except .262-010 and -018; 132; and 203.362-026)

Significant Points

- Most jobs require a college degree in the liberal arts—communications, journalism, and English are preferred—or a technical subject for technical writing positions.

- Less competition is expected for lower paying jobs at small daily and weekly newspapers, trade publication, and radio and television broadcasting stations in small communities.

- Persons who fail to gain better paying jobs or earn enough as independent writers, are usually able to readily transfer to communications-related jobs in other occupations.

Nature of the Work

Writers and editors communicate through the written word. *Writers* develop original fiction and nonfiction for books, magazines and trade journals, newspapers, technical reports, company newsletters, radio and television broadcasts, movies, and advertisements. *Editors* select and prepare material for publication or broadcasting and supervise writers.

Writers first select a topic or are assigned one by an editor. They then gather information through personal observation, library research, and interviews. Writers select and organize the material and put it into words, effectively conveying it to the reader, and often revise or rewrite sections, searching for the best organization of the material or the right phrasing.

Newswriters prepare news items for newspapers or news broadcasts, based on information supplied by reporters or wire services.

Columnists analyze news and write commentaries, based on personal knowledge and experience. Editorial writers write comments to stimulate or mold public opinion, in accordance with their publication's viewpoint. Columnists and editorial writers are able to take sides on issues, be subjective, and express their opinions while other newswriters must be objective and neutral in their coverage. Reporters and correspondents, who may also write articles or copy for broadcast, are described elsewhere in this section of the *Handbook.*

Technical writers make scientific and technical information easily understandable to a nontechnical audience. They prepare operating and maintenance manuals, catalogs, parts lists, assembly instructions, sales promotion materials, and project proposals. They also plan and edit technical reports and oversee preparation of illustrations, photographs, diagrams, and charts.

Copy writers write advertising copy for use by publication or broadcast media, to promote the sale of goods and services.

Established writers may work on a freelance basis; they sell their work to publishers or publication units, manufacturing firms, and public relations and advertising departments or agencies. They sometimes contract to complete specific assignments such as writing about a new product or technique.

Editors frequently write and almost always review, rewrite, and edit the work of writers. However, their primary duties are to plan the contents of books, magazines, or newspapers and to supervise their preparation. They decide what will appeal to readers, assign topics to reporters and writers, and oversee the production of the publications. In small organizations, a single editor may do everything. In larger ones, an executive editor oversees associate or assistant editors who have responsibility for particular subjects, such as fiction, local news, international news, or sports, or who edit one or a few publications. Editors hire writers, reporters, or other employees; plan budgets; and negotiate contracts with freelance writers. In broadcasting companies, *program directors* have similar responsibilities.

Editors and program directors often have assistants, with the title of assistant editor, editorial assistant, copy editor, or production assistant. Many assistants hold entry-level jobs. They review copy for errors in grammar, punctuation, and spelling. They check manuscripts for readability, style, and agreement with editorial policy. They add and rearrange sentences to improve clarity or delete incorrect and unnecessary material. Editorial assistants do research for writers and verify facts, dates, and statistics. Assistants may also arrange page layouts of articles, photographs, and advertising. They may compose headlines, prepare copy for printing, and proofread printer's galleys. Some editorial assistants read and evaluate manuscripts submitted by freelance writers or answer letters about published or broadcast material. Production assistants on small papers or in radio stations clip stories that come over the wire services' printers, answer phones, and make photocopies. Most writers and editors use personal computers or word processors; many use desktop or electronic publishing systems.

Working Conditions
Some writers and editors work in comfortable, private offices; others work in noisy rooms filled with the sound of keyboards and computer printers as well as the voices of other writers tracking down information over the telephone. The search for information sometimes requires travel and visits to diverse workplaces, such as factories, offices, laboratories, the ballpark, or the theater, but many have to be content with telephone interviews and the library.

The workweek usually runs 35 to 40 hours. Those who prepare morning or weekend publications and broadcasts, work nights and/or weekends. Writers may work overtime to meet deadlines or to cover late-developing stories. They often face pressure to meet deadlines. On some jobs, deadlines are part of the daily routine.

Employment
Writers and editors held about 286,000 jobs in 1996. Nearly a third of salaried writers and editors work for newspapers, magazines, and

Nearly a third of salaried writers and editors work for newspapers, magazines, and book publishers.

book publishers. Substantial numbers also work in advertising agencies, in radio and television broadcasting, in public relations firms, and on journals and newsletters published by business and nonprofit organizations, such as professional associations, labor unions, and religious organizations. Others develop publications for government agencies or write for motion picture companies.

Many technical writers work for computer software firms or manufacturers of aircraft, chemicals, pharmaceuticals, and computers and other electronic equipment.

Jobs with major book publishers, magazines, broadcasting companies, advertising agencies and public relations firms, and the Federal Government are concentrated in New York, Chicago, Los Angeles, Boston, Philadelphia, San Francisco, and Washington, D.C. Jobs with newspapers; and professional, religious, business, technical, and trade union magazines or journals are more widely dispersed throughout the country. Technical writers are employed throughout the country, but the largest concentrations are in the Northeast, Texas, and California.

Thousands of other individuals work as freelancers, earning some income from their articles, books, and less commonly, television and movie scripts. Most support themselves primarily with income derived from other sources.

Training, Other Qualifications, and Advancement
A college degree generally is required for a position as a writer or editor. Although some employers look for a broad liberal arts background, most prefer to hire people with degrees in communications, journalism, or English.

Technical writing requires a degree in, or some knowledge about a specialized field—engineering, business, or one of the sciences, for example. In many cases, people with good writing skills can learn specialized knowledge on the job. Some transfer from jobs as technicians, scientists, or engineers. Others begin as research assistants, editorial assistants, or trainees in a technical information department, develop technical communication skills, and then assume writing duties.

Writers and editors must be able to express ideas clearly and logically and should love to write. Creativity, curiosity, a broad range of knowledge, self-motivation, and perseverance are also valuable. For some jobs, the ability to concentrate amid confusion, and to work under pressure is essential. Familiarity with electronic publishing, graphics, and video production equipment is increasingly needed. Online newspapers and magazines require knowledge of computer software used to combine online text with graphics, audio, video, and 3-D animation. Editors must have good judgment in deciding what material to accept and what to reject. They need tact and the ability to guide and encourage others in their work.

High school and college newspapers, literary magazines, and community newspapers and radio and television stations all provide valuable, but sometimes unpaid, practical writing experience. Many magazines, newspapers, and broadcast stations have internships for students. Interns write short pieces, conduct research and interviews, and learn about the publishing or broadcasting business.

In small firms, beginning writers and editors may not only work as editorial or production assistants, but also write or edit material right away. They often advance by moving to other firms. In larger firms, jobs usually are more formally structured. Beginners generally do research, fact checking, or copy editing. They take on full-scale writing or editing duties less rapidly than do the employees of small companies. Advancement comes as they are assigned more important articles.

Job Outlook

Through the year 2006, the outlook for most writing and editing jobs is expected to continue to be competitive, because so many people are attracted to the field. However, opportunities will be good for technical writers because of the more limited number of writers who can handle technical material. Online publications and services, which are relatively new, will continue to grow and require an increased number of writers and editors. Opportunities should be better on small daily and weekly newspapers, and in small radio and television stations, where the pay is low. Some small publications are hiring freelance copy editors as back-up for their staff editors, or for additional help with special projects. Persons preparing to be writers and editors should also have academic preparation in another field as well, either to qualify them as writers specializing in that field, or to enter that field if they are unable to get a job in writing.

Employment of writers and editors is expected to increase faster than the average for all occupations through the year 2006. Employment of salaried writers and editors by newspapers, periodicals, book publishers, and nonprofit organizations is expected to increase with growing demand for their publications. Growth of advertising and public relations agencies should also be a source of new jobs. Demand for technical writers is expected to increase because of the continuing expansion of scientific and technical information, and the continued need to communicate it. Many job openings will also occur as experienced workers transfer to other occupations or leave the labor force. Turnover is relatively high in this occupation—many freelancers leave because they can not earn enough money.

Earnings

In 1996, beginning salaries for writers and editorial assistants averaged $21,000 annually, according to the Dow Jones Newspaper Fund. According to the Newspaper Guild those who had at least 5 years experience averaged more than $30,000 and senior editors at the largest newspapers earned over $67,000 a year.

According to the 1996 Technical Communicator's Salary Survey, the median annual salary for technical writers was $44,000 annually.

The average annual salary for technical writers and editors in the Federal Government in nonsupervisory, supervisory, and managerial positions was about $47,440 in 1996; other writers and editors averaged about $46,590.

Related Occupations

Writers and editors communicate ideas and information. Other communications occupations include newspaper reporters and correspondents, radio and television announcers, advertising and public relations workers, and teachers.

Sources of Additional Information

For a guide to journalism careers and scholarships, contact:
☛ The Dow Jones Newspaper Fund, P.O. Box 300, Princeton, NJ 08540.

For information on college internships in magazine editing, contact:
☛ American Society of Magazine Editors, 919 3rd. Ave., New York, NY 10022.

For information on careers in technical writing, contact:
☛ Society for Technical Communication, Inc., 901 N. Stuart St., Suite 904, Arlington, VA 22203.

For information on union wage rates for newspaper and magazine editors, contact:
☛ The Newspaper Guild, Research and Information Department, 8611 Second Ave., Silver Spring, MD 20910.

For career information and a pamphlet entitled *Newspaper Careers and Challenges for the Next Century* contact:
☛ National Newspaper Association, 1525 Wilson Blvd., Suite 550, Arlington, VA 22209.

Visual Arts Occupations

Designers

(D.O.T. 141.051, .061, .067; 142 except .061-030, -054)

Significant Points

- Nearly 40 percent are self-employed, almost five times the proportion in all professional occupations.

- Creativity is crucial in all design occupations; formal education requirements range from a high school diploma for floral designers to a bachelor's degree for industrial designers.

- Despite projected faster than average employment growth, keen competition is expected for most jobs because many talented individuals are attracted to careers as designers.

Nature of the Work

Designers organize and design articles, products, and materials so they serve the purpose for which they were intended and are visually pleasing. Pleasant surroundings, beautiful clothes, and floral arrangements can boost our spirits, and products and packaging that are eye-catching are more likely to attract buyers than those that are not.

Many designers specialize in a particular area of design, such as automobiles, clothing, furniture, home appliances, industrial equipment, interiors of homes and office buildings, exhibits, movie and theater sets, packaging, or floral arrangements. Others work in more than one design field. The first step in developing a new design or altering an existing one is to determine the needs of the client. The designer then considers various factors, including the size, shape, weight, and color of the product; materials used; and the product functions. The ease of use, safety, and cost of the design are additional factors. Designers offer suggestions to their clients; some ideas are more practical, while others are more aesthetically appealing. The designer develops by hand, or with the aid of a computer, sketches of several design concepts they present for final selection to a client, an art or design director, a product development team, or producer of a play, film, or television production. The designer then makes a model, a prototype, or detailed plans drawn to scale. Designers in some specialties increasingly use computer-aided design (CAD) tools to create and better visualize a final product. Computers greatly reduce the cost and time necessary to create a model or prototype, which gives a real idea of what the product will look like. Industrial designers use computer-aided industrial design (CAID) to create designs and to communicate them to automated production tools.

Designers may supervise assistants who carry out their designs. Those who run their own businesses may also devote a considerable amount of time to developing new business contacts and to administrative tasks, such as reviewing catalogs and ordering samples.

Design encompasses a number of different fields. *Industrial designers* develop and design countless manufactured products including cars, home appliances, children's toys, computer equipment, and medical, office, or recreational equipment. They combine artistic talent with research on product use, marketing, materials, and production methods to create the most functional and appealing design and to make the product competitive with others in the marketplace.

Furniture designers design furniture for manufacture, according to knowledge of design trends, competitors' products, production costs, capability of production facilities, and characteristics of a company's market. They may also prepare detailed drawings of fixtures, forms, or tools required to be used in production of furniture, along with designing custom pieces or styles according to a specific period or country. They must be strongly involved with the fashion industry and aware of current trends and styles.

Interior designers plan the space and furnish the interiors of private homes, public buildings, and commercial establishments, such as offices, restaurants, hospitals, hotels, and theaters. They also may plan additions and renovations. With a client's tastes, needs, and budget in mind, they develop designs and prepare working drawings and specifications for interior construction, furnishings, lighting, and finishes. Increasingly, designers use computers to plan layouts that can be changed easily to include ideas received from the client. They also design lighting and architectural details such as crown molding, coordinate colors, and select furniture, floor coverings, and curtains. Interior designers must design space in accordance with Federal, State, and local laws, including building codes. Increasingly, they plan spaces that meet accessibility standards for the disabled and elderly.

Set designers design movie, television, and theater sets. They study scripts, confer with directors, and conduct research to determine appropriate architectural styles.

Fashion designers design clothing and accessories. Some high-fashion designers are self-employed and design for individual clients. They make fashion news by establishing the "line," colors, and kinds of materials that will be worn each season. Other high-fashion designers cater to specialty stores or high-fashion department stores. They design original garments, as well as follow the established fashion trends. Most fashion designers, however, work for apparel manufacturers, adapting men's, women's, and children's fashions for the mass market.

Textile designers design fabric for garments, upholstery, rugs, and other products, using their knowledge of textile materials and fashion trends. Computers are widely used in pattern design and grading; intelligent pattern engineering (IPE) systems enable even greater automation in generating patterns.

Floral designers cut and arrange live, dried, or artificial flowers and foliage into designs to express the sentiments of the customer. They trim flowers and arrange bouquets, sprays, wreaths, dish gardens, and terrariums. They usually work from a written order indicating the occasion, customer preference for color and type of flower, price, and the date, time, and place the floral arrangement or plant is to be delivered. The variety of duties performed by a floral designer depends on the size of the shop and number of designers employed. In a small operation, the floral designer may own the shop and do almost everything from growing flowers to keeping books.

Working Conditions

Working conditions and places of employment vary. Designers employed by manufacturing establishments or design firms generally work regular hours in well-lighted and comfortable settings. Self-employed designers tend to work longer hours—especially at first,

Creativity is crucial in all design occupations.

when they are trying to establish themselves and cannot afford to hire assistants or clerical help.

Designers frequently adjust their workday to suit their clients, meeting with them in the evenings, or on weekends when necessary. They may transact business in their own offices, clients' homes or offices, or may travel to other locations such as showrooms or manufacturing facilities.

Industrial designers usually work regular hours but occasionally work overtime to meet deadlines. In contrast, set designers, especially those in television broadcasting, often work long and irregular hours. The pace of television production is very fast, and set designers are often under pressure to make rapid changes in the sets. Fashion designers who work in the apparel industry usually have regular hours. During production deadlines or before fashion shows, however, they may be required to put in overtime. In addition, fashion designers may be required to travel to production sites overseas and across the United States. Interior designers generally work under deadlines and often work overtime to finish a job. Floral designers usually work regular hours in a pleasant work environment, except during holidays when overtime usually is required.

All designers face frustration at times, when their designs are rejected or when they cannot be as creative as they wish. Independent consultants, who are paid by the assignment, are under pressure to please clients and to find new ones to maintain their incomes.

Employment

Designers held about 342,000 jobs in 1996. Nearly 4 out of 10 were self-employed, compared to less than 1 out of 10 workers in all occupations.

Salaried designers work in a number of different industries, depending on their design specialty. Most industrial designers, for example, work for consulting firms or for large corporations. Interior designers usually work for design or architectural firms, department stores and home furnishing stores, or hotel and restaurant chains. Many do freelance work—full time, part time, or in addition to a salaried job in another occupation.

Set designers work for theater companies and film and television production companies. Fashion designers generally work for textile, apparel, and pattern manufacturers, or for fashion salons, high-fashion department stores, and specialty shops. Some work in the entertainment industry, designing costumes for theater, dance, television, and movies. Most floral designers work for retail flower shops, but a growing number work in floral departments of grocery stores.

Training, Other Qualifications, and Advancement

Creativity is crucial in all design occupations. People in this field must have a strong sense of color, an eye for detail, a sense of balance and proportion, and sensitivity to beauty. Sketching ability is especially important for fashion designers. A good portfolio—a collection of examples of a person's best work—is often the deciding factor in getting a job. However, formal preparation in design is important in all fields with the exception of floral design.

Educational requirements for entry-level positions vary. Some design occupations, notably industrial design, require a bachelor's degree. Interior designers also generally need a college education because few clients—especially commercial clients—are willing to entrust responsibility for designing living and working space to a designer with no formal credentials. Interior designers must also be knowledgeable about Federal, State, and local codes, and toxicity and flammability standards for furniture and furnishings.

Interior design is the only design field subject to government regulation. According to a 1997 survey from the American Society for Interior Designers, 22 States required interior designers to be licensed. Because licensing is not mandatory in all States, membership in a professional association is universally recognized as a mark of achievement for interior designers. Professional membership usually requires the completion of 3 or 4 years of postsecondary education in design, at least 2 years of practical experience in the field, and completion of the National Council for Interior Design qualification examination.

In fashion design, some formal career preparation, such as a 2- or 4-year degree, is usually needed to enter the field. Employers seek individuals who are knowledgeable in the areas of textiles, fabrics, and ornamentation, as well as trends in the fashion world. Similarly, furniture designers must keep abreast of trends in fashion and style, in addition to methods and tools used in furniture production. Several universities and schools of design offer degrees in furniture design.

In contrast to the other design occupations, a high school diploma ordinarily suffices for floral design jobs. Most floral designers learn their skills on the job. When they hire trainees, employers generally look for high school graduates who have a flair for color and a desire to learn. However, completion of formal training is an asset for floral designers, particularly for advancement to the chief floral designer level. Vocational and technical schools offer programs in floral design usually lasting less than a year, while 2- and 4-year programs in floriculture, horticulture, floral design, or ornamental horticulture are offered by community and junior colleges, and colleges and universities.

Formal training for some design professions is also available in 2- and 3-year professional schools which award certificates or associate degrees in design. Graduates of 2-year programs generally qualify as assistants to designers. The Bachelor of Fine Arts degree is granted at 4-year colleges and universities. The curriculum in these schools includes art and art history, principles of design, designing and sketching, and specialized studies for each of the individual design disciplines such as garment construction, textiles, mechanical and architectural drawing, computerized design, sculpture, architecture,

and basic engineering. A liberal arts education, with courses in merchandising, business administration, marketing, and psychology, along with training in art, is also a good background for most design fields. Persons with training or experience in architecture also qualify for some design occupations, particularly interior design.

Computer-aided design (CAD) courses are very useful. CAD is used in various areas of design, and many employers expect new designers to be familiar with the use of the computer as a design tool. For example, industrial designers extensively use computers in the aerospace, automotive, and electronics industries. Interior designers are using computers to create numerous versions of space designs. Images can be inserted, edited, or replaced—making it possible for a client to see and choose among several designs. In furniture design, a chair's basic shape and structure may be duplicated and updated by applying new upholstery styles and fabrics with the use of computers.

In 1997, the National Association of Schools of Art and Design accredited about 200 postsecondary institutions with programs in art and design; most of these schools award a degree in art. Some award degrees in industrial, interior, textile, graphic, or fashion design. Many schools do not allow formal entry into a bachelor's degree program until a student has successfully finished a year of basic art and design courses. Applicants may be required to submit sketches and other examples of their artistic ability.

The Foundation for Interior Design Education Research accredits interior design programs and schools. Currently, there are over 120 accredited programs in the United States and Canada, located in schools of art, architecture, and home economics.

Individuals in the design field must be creative, imaginative, persistent, and able to communicate their ideas both visually and verbally. Because tastes in style and fashion can change quickly, designers need to be open to new ideas and influences. Problem-solving skills and the ability to work independently are important traits. People in this field need self-discipline to start projects on their own, budget their time, and meet deadlines and production schedules. Business sense and sales ability are also important for those who are freelancers or run their own businesses.

Beginning designers usually receive on-the-job training, and normally need 1 to 3 years of training before they advance to higher-level positions. Experienced designers in large firms may advance to chief designer, design department head, or other supervisory positions. Some experienced designers open their own firms.

Job Outlook

Despite projected faster than average employment growth, designers in most fields—with the exception of floral and furniture design—are expected to face competition for available positions because many talented individuals are attracted to careers as designers. Individuals with little or no formal education in design who lack creativity and perseverance will find it very difficult to establish and maintain a career in design.

Finding a job as a floral designer should be relatively easy due to the relatively low pay and limited opportunities for advancement.

Overall, the employment of designers is expected to grow faster than the average for all occupations through the year 2006. Demand for industrial designers will stem from continued emphasis on product quality and safety; design of new products that are easy and comfortable to use; high-technology products in medicine, transportation, and other fields; and increasing global competition among businesses. Rising demand for professional design of private homes, office space, restaurants and other retail establishments, and institutions that care for the rapidly growing elderly population should spur employment growth among interior designers. Floral design should experience healthy growth with the addition of floral departments in many grocery and department stores. Demand for fashion, textile, and furniture designers should rise as consumers become more concerned with fashion and style. In addition to employment growth, many job openings will result from the need to replace designers who leave the field.

Earnings

Full-time designers in all specialties combined had median weekly earnings of about $590 in 1996. The middle 50 percent earned between $380 and $890 a week. The bottom 10 percent earned less than $280, while the top 10 percent earned over $1,300.

Earnings of floral designers were lower than most types of designers. According to a survey conducted by Floral Finance Inc., beginning floral designers had average earnings of $5.85 an hour in 1996. Designers with 1 to 3 years of experience earned $6.94, while designers with over 3 years of experience averaged $8.17. Managers had average earnings of $10.10 per hour in 1996.

According to the Industrial Designers Society of America, the average base salary for an entry-level industrial designer with 1 to 2 years of experience was about $27,000 in 1996. Staff designers with 5 years of experience earned $35,000, while senior designers with 8 years of experience earned $45,000. Industrial designers in managerial or executive positions earned substantially more—up to $140,000 annually.

Related Occupations

Workers in other occupations who design or arrange objects, materials, or interiors to improve their appearance and function include visual artists, architects, landscape architects, engineers, photographers, interior decorators, and merchandise displayers. Some computer-related occupations, including Internet page designer and webmaster, require design skills.

Sources of Additional Information

For a list of accredited schools of art and design, contact:

☛ National Association of Schools of Art and Design, 11250 Roger Bacon Dr., Suite 21, Reston, VA 20190.

For information on careers and a list of academic programs in industrial design, write to:

☛ Industrial Designers Society of America, 1142-E Walker Rd., Great Falls, VA 22066. Homepage: http://www.idsa.org

For information on degree, continuing education, and licensure programs in interior design, contact:

☛ American Society for Interior Designers, 608 Massachusetts Ave. NE., Washington, DC 20002-6006.

For a list of accredited programs in interior design, contact:

☛ Foundation for Interior Design Education Research, 60 Monroe Center NW., Grand Rapids, MI 49503. Homepage: http://www.fider.org

For information about careers in floral design, contact:

☛ Society of American Florists, 1601 Duke St., Alexandria, VA 22314.

For a list of schools with accredited programs in furniture design, contact:

☛ American Society of Furniture Designers, P.O. Box 2688, High Point, NC 27261.

Photographers and Camera Operators

(D.O.T. 143)

Significant Points

● Good business sense, imagination, creativity are essential.

● Only the most skilled, and those with the best business ability, can maintain a long-term career.

● A much higher proportion than average are self-employed.

Nature of the Work

By creatively using lighting, lenses, film, filters, and camera settings, photographers and camera operators produce pictures that record and event, capture a mood, or tell a story. Making commercial quality photographs and movies requires technical expertise and creativity. Producing a successful picture includes choosing and presenting a subject to achieve a particular effect and selecting equipment to accomplish the desired goal. For example, photographers and camera operators may enhance the subject's appearance with lighting or draw attention to a particular aspect of the subject by blurring the background.

Today, many cameras adjust settings like shutter speed and aperture automatically and also let the photographer to adjust these settings manually, thus allowing greater creative and technical control over the picture-taking process. In addition to automatic and manual cameras, photographers and camera operators use an array of film, lenses, and equipment—from filters, tripods, and flash attachments to specially constructed motorized vehicles and lighting equipment.

Photography increasingly involves the use of computer technology. A photographer using a traditional silver-halide film camera can take a picture and, once the film is processed and prints are made, use a scanner to transfer the images into digital form. Some photographers prefer to use digital cameras, which use electronic memory rather than a film negative to record an image. The electronic image can be transmitted instantly via a computer modem and telephone line or otherwise downloaded onto a personal computer. Then, using the computer and specialized software, the photographer can manipulate and enhance the scanned or digital image to create a desired effect. The images can be stored on a compact disk (CD) the same way as music. There are some photographers who use this technology to create electronic portfolios, as well.

Some photographers prefer to develop and print their own photographs, especially those who use black and white film or require special effects, but this requires a fully-equipped darkroom and the technical skill to operate it. Other photographers send their film to laboratories for processing. Color film, especially, requires expensive equipment and exacting conditions for correct processing and printing. (See the statement on photographic process workers elsewhere in the *Handbook*.)

Most photographers specialize in portrait, commercial, or news photography. Others specialize in areas such as aerial, police, medical, or scientific photography, which typically involves further specialization in fields like engineering, medicine, biology, or chemistry.

Portrait photographers take pictures of individuals or groups of people and often work in their own studios. Some specialize in weddings or school photographs. Portrait photographers who are business owners arrange for advertising; schedule appointments; set and adjust equipment; develop and retouch negatives; and mount and frame pictures. They also purchase supplies, keep records, bill customers, and may hire and train employees.

Commercial and industrial photographers take pictures of various subjects, such as manufactured articles, models, buildings, merchandise, landscapes, and groups of people. This photography is used in a wide variety of mediums, including reports, advertisements, and catalogs. Industrial photographers often take still or motion pictures of equipment and machinery, products, workers, and company officials. The pictures are then used for analyzing engineering projects, publicity, or as records of equipment development or deployment, such as the placement of an off-shore oil rig. Companies also use these photographs in publications to report to stockholders or to advertise company products or services. This photography frequently is done on location.

News photographers, also called photojournalists, photograph newsworthy people and places, as well as sporting, political, and community events, for newspapers, journals, magazines, or television. Some photojournalists are salaried staff, while others are work independently and are known as freelance photographers.

Self-employed photographers may license the use of their photographs through stock photo agencies. These agencies grant magazines and other customers the right to purchase the use of a photograph, and, in turn, pay the photographer on a commission basis. Stock photo agen-

Depending on their area of expertise, some photographers and camera operators work long and irregular hours.

cies require an application from the photographer and a sizable portfolio. Once accepted, a large number of new submissions are generally required from a photographer each year. Photographers frequently have their photos placed on CD's for this purpose.

Photography also is a fine art medium, and a small portion of photographers sell their photographs as artwork. In addition to technical proficiency, artistic photography requires an even greater emphasis on self expression and creativity.

Like photographers, camera operators work in a variety of settings. They generally use motion picture or video cameras to film a wide range of subjects, including commercial motion pictures, documentaries, music videos, news events, and training sessions. Some film private ceremonies and special events.

Many video camera operators are employed by independent television stations, local affiliates, or large cable and television networks. They often work in a broadcast studio or cover news events as part of a reporting team. Camera operators employed in the entertainment field use motion picture cameras to film movies, television programs, and commercials. Some camera operators specialize in filming cartoons or special effects for television and movies. Camera operators who work in the entertainment field often meet with directors, actors, and camera assistants to discuss ways of filming and improving scenes.

Working Conditions

Working conditions for photographers and camera operators vary considerably. Photographers employed in government, commercial studios, and advertising agencies usually work a 5-day, 40-hour week. News photographers and camera operators often work long, irregular hours and must be available to work on short notice.

Self-employment allows for greater autonomy, freedom of expression, and flexible scheduling. However, income can be uncertain and necessitates a continuous, time-consuming, and sometimes stressful search for new clients. Some self-employed photographers hire an assistant solely for the purpose of seeking additional business.

Portrait photographers often work in their own studios but may also travel to take photographs at schools and other places, as well as at weddings and other events. Press and commercial photographers and camera operators frequently travel locally, can stay overnight on

an assignment, or may travel to distant places for long periods of time. Their work may put them in uncomfortable, or even dangerous, surroundings. This is especially true for photojournalists covering natural disasters, civil unrest, or military conflicts.

Some photographers and camera operators must wait long hours in all kinds of weather for an event to take place and stand or walk for long periods while carrying heavy equipment. Photographers often work under severe time restrictions to meet deadlines and satisfy customers. While working on a motion picture production, camera operators are often required to work long and irregular hours. It may also be necessary for camera operators to work in helicopters or on the back of specially equipped vehicles in order to capture a scene or cover a news event.

Employment

Photographers and camera operators held about 154,000 jobs in 1996. About 4 out of 10 were self-employed, a much higher proportion than the average for all occupations. Some self-employed photographers contracted with advertising agencies, magazines, or others to do individual projects at a predetermined fee, while others operated portrait studios or provided photographs to stock photo agencies.

Most salaried photographers worked in portrait or commercial photography studios. Others were employed by newspapers, magazines, advertising agencies, and government agencies. Most camera operators were employed in television broadcasting or at motion picture studios; relatively few were self-employed. Most photographers and camera operators worked in metropolitan areas.

Training, Other Qualifications, and Advancement

Employers usually seek applicants with a good technical understanding of photography who are also imaginative and creative. Entry level positions in photojournalism, as well as in industrial, scientific, or technical photography, are likely to require a college degree in photography, with courses in the specific field being photographed, such as industrial products or botany. Camera operators generally acquire their skills through formal post-secondary training at colleges, photographic institutes, universities, or through on-the-job training. Those in entry-level jobs, including photography and cinematography assistants, learn to set up lights, cameras, and other equipment, and learn to load and unload film. They may receive routine assignments requiring camera adjustments or decisions on what subject matter to capture. With increased experience, they may advance to more demanding assignments. Photography assistants often learn to mix chemicals, develop film, print photographs, and the various other skills necessary to run a photography business.

Individuals interested in photography should subscribe to photographic newsletters and magazines, join camera clubs, and seek employment in camera stores or photo studios. Individuals also should decide on an area of interest and specialize in it. Completing a course of study at a private photographic institute, university, or community college provides many of the necessary skills to be a successful photographer. Summer or part-time work for a photographer, cable or television network, newspaper, or magazine is an excellent way to gain experience and eventual entry into this field.

Courses in photography are offered in many places, including universities, community and junior colleges, vocational-technical institutes, and private trade and technical schools. Courses in cinematography are most often offered by photography institutes and universities. Many photographers enhance their technical expertise by attending seminars.

Basic courses in photography cover equipment, processes, and techniques. Bachelors degree programs, especially those including business courses, provide a well-rounded education. Art schools offer useful training in design and composition, but may be weak in the commercial aspects of photography.

Photographers who wish to operate their own businesses need business skills as well as talent. These individuals must know how to submit bids; write contracts; hire models, if needed; get permission to take on-site photographs at locations normally not open to the public; obtain releases to use photographs of people; price photographs; know about copyright protection for their work; and keep financial records. Self-employed photographers should also develop individual styles of photography to differentiate themselves from the competition. Some photographers enter the field by submitting unsolicited photographs to magazines and art directors at advertising agencies.

Both photographers and camera operators need good eyesight, artistic ability, and manual dexterity. They should be patient, accurate, and enjoy working with details. In addition, photographers should be able to work alone or with others, as they frequently deal with clients, graphic designers, and advertising and publishing specialists. Camera operators should have good hand-eye coordination, communication skills, and, if needed, the ability to handhold a camera for extended periods of time.

Commercial photographers must be imaginative and original. Portrait photographers also need the ability to help people relax in front of the camera. Photojournalists must not only be good with a camera, but must also understand the story behind an event, so their pictures match the story. They must be decisive in recognizing a potentially good photograph and act quickly to capture it. This requires journalistic skills and explains why such employers increasingly look for individuals with a 4-year degree in photojournalism or journalism with an emphasis on photography.

Different types of filming environments require camera operators to have different strengths. For example, camera operators who want to work on music videos need a good sense of music and rhythm, while those who want to work in news teams must be able to set up quickly and capture the image on the first take whenever possible.

Camera operators are usually hired for a project based on recommendations from individuals such as producers, directors of photography, and camera assistants from previous projects, or through interviews with the producer.

As for career advancement, camera operators can become directors of photography for movie studios, advertising agencies, or television programs. Magazine and news photographers may become photography editors. A few photographers and camera operators become teachers and provide instruction in their own particular area of expertise.

Job Outlook

Photography, particularly commercial photography and photojournalism, is a highly competitive field, because there are more people who want to be photographers than there is employment to support them. Only the most skilled, those with the best business acumen, and those who have developed the best reputations in the industry are able to find salaried positions or attract enough work to support themselves as self-employed photographers. Many persons have full-time jobs in other fields and take photographs or videos of weddings and other events on weekends.

Employment of photographers is expected to increase as fast as the average for all occupations through the year 2006. The growing demand for visual images in education, communication, entertainment, marketing, research and development, and other areas should spur demand for photographers. Demand for portrait photographers should increase as the population grows. Also, as advances in telecommunications create new markets and products—electronic newspapers and magazines, for example, which rely heavily on images—the demand for pictures and images is expected to increase over the projection period.

Employment of camera operators is expected to grow as fast as the average for all occupations through the year 2006. Despite businesses making greater use of videos for training films, business meetings, sales campaigns, and public relations work, the growth in employment of camera operators will be restrained as their work and duties in motion pictures and film are expected to be slowly taken over by directors of photography or cinematographers. Expansion of

the entertainment industry will create some additional openings, but competition for these jobs will be keen for what generally is regarded as an exciting career field.

Earnings

The median annual earnings for salaried photographers and camera operators who worked full time were about $30,600 in 1996. The middle 50 percent earned between $21,000 and $46,500. The top 10 percent earned more than $75,100, while the lowest 10 percent earned less than $14,500.

Most salaried photographers work full time and earn more than the majority of self-employed photographers, many of whom work part time, but some self-employed photographers have high earnings. Earnings are affected by the number of hours worked, skills, marketing ability, and general business conditions. Because many camera operators who work in film or video do so as freelancers, earnings tend to fluctuate from year to year.

Unlike photojournalists and commercial photographers, very few artistic photographers are successful enough to support themselves solely through this specialty.

Related Occupations

Other jobs requiring visual arts talents include illustrators, visual artists, designers, painters, sculptors, and photo editors.

Sources of Additional Information

Career information on photography is available from:
☞ Professional Photographers of America, Inc., 57 Forsyth St., Suite 1600, Atlanta, GA 30303.
☞ Advertising Photographers of America, 7201 Melrose Ave., Los Angeles, CA 90046.
☞ American Society of Media Photographers, 14 Washington Rd., Suite 502, Princeton Junction, NJ 08550-1033.

General information on news photography careers is available from:
☞ National Press Photographers Association, 3200 Croasdaile Dr., Suite 306, Durham, NC 27705.

Visual Artists

(D.O.T. 102.261-014; 141.031-010, .061-010, -014, -018, -022, -026, -030, -034, .081-010; 142.061-030, -054; 144; 149.041, .051, .261; 970.131-014, .281-014, .361-018)

Significant Points

- Nearly 60 percent are self-employed—about seven times the proportion in all professional occupations.

- Artists usually develop their skills through a bachelor's degree program or other postsecondary training in art or design.

- Keen competition is expected for both salaried jobs and freelance work because the glamorous and exciting image of the graphic and fine arts fields attracts many talented people.

Nature of the Work

Visual artists communicate ideas, thoughts, and feelings through various methods and materials—including computers, oils, watercolors, acrylics, pastels, magic markers, pencils, pen and ink, silkscreen, plaster, or clay—or other media, such as photographs and sound. They create realistic and abstract works or images of objects, people, nature, topography, or events. (Designers, a closely related occupation, are discussed in a separate *Handbook* statement.)

Visual artists generally fall into one of two categories—graphic artists or graphic designers, and fine artists—depending not so much on the medium, but on the artist's purpose in creating a work of art. Graphic artists, many of who own their own studios, put their artistic skills and vision at the service of commercial clients, such as major corporations, retail stores, and advertising, design, or publishing firms. Fine artists, on the other hand, often create art to satisfy their own need for self-expression, and may display their work in museums, corporate collections, art galleries, and private homes. Some of their work may be done on request from clients, but not as exclusively as graphic artists.

Graphic artists, whether freelancers or employed by a firm, use a variety of print, electronic, and film media to create art that meets a client's needs. Most graphic artists use computer software to design new images; some of this work appears on the Internet and CD-ROM. As computer software becomes increasingly sophisticated, more artists are likely to become involved with this medium. Graphic artists may create promotional displays and marketing brochures for new products, visual designs of annual reports and other corporate literature, or distinctive logos for products or businesses. Artists may be responsible for the overall layout and design of magazines, newspapers, journals, and other publications, and may create graphics for television and computer-generated media. For example, many magazines and newspapers have a homepage on the Internet.

Fine artists may sell their works to stores, commercial art galleries, and museums, or directly to collectors. Commercial galleries may sell artists' works on consignment. The gallery and artist predetermine how much each earns from a sale. Only the most successful fine artists are able to support themselves solely through sale of their works; however, most fine artists hold other jobs as well. Those with teaching certification may teach art in elementary or secondary schools, while those with a master's or Ph.D. degree may teach in colleges or universities. Some fine artists work in arts administration in city, State, or Federal arts programs. Others may work as art critics, art consultants, or as directors or representatives in fine art galleries; give private art lessons; or work as curators setting up art exhibits in museums. Sometimes fine artists work in an unrelated field in order to support their careers.

Fine artists usually work independently, choosing whatever subject matter and medium suits them. Usually, they specialize in one or two forms of art. *Painters* generally work with two-dimensional art forms. Using techniques of shading, perspective, and color mixing, painters produce works depicting realistic scenes or may evoke different moods and emotions, depending on the artist's goals. Artists may combine mediums and include sound and motion in their works.

Sculptors design three-dimensional art works—either molding and joining materials such as clay, glass, wire, plastic, or metal, or cutting and carving forms from a block of plaster, wood, or stone. Some sculptors combine various materials such as concrete, metal, wood, plastic, and paper.

Printmakers create printed images from designs cut into wood, stone, or metal, or from computer-driven data. The designs may be engraved, as in the case of woodblocking; etched, as in the production of etchings; or derived from computers using advanced color printers.

Painting restorers preserve and restore damaged and faded paintings. They apply solvents and cleaning agents to clean the surfaces, reconstruct or retouch damaged areas, and apply preservatives to protect the paintings. This is very detailed work and is usually reserved for experts in the field.

Illustrators paint or draw pictures for books, magazines, and other publications; films; and paper products, including greeting cards, calendars, wrapping paper, and stationery. Many do a variety of illustrations, while others specialize in a particular style. Some illustrators draw "story boards" for television commercials, movies, and animated features. Storyboards present television commercials in a series of scenes similar to a comic strip, so an advertising agency and client (the company doing the advertising) can evaluate proposed commercials. Story boards may also serve as guides to placement of actors and cameras and to other details during the production of commercials. Some work is done electronically, using advanced computer

Many visual artists are self-employed.

software. This allows ideas to be electronically mailed between clients, or presented on the Internet.

Medical and *scientific illustrators* combine artistic skills with knowledge of the biological sciences. Medical illustrators draw illustrations of human anatomy and surgical procedures. Scientific illustrators draw illustrations of animals and plants. These illustrations are used in medical and scientific publications, and in audiovisual presentations for teaching purposes. Medical illustrators also work for lawyers, producing exhibits for court cases and doctors. *Fashion artists* draw illustrations of women's, men's, and children's clothing and accessories for newspapers, magazines, and other media.

Cartoonists draw political, advertising, social, and sports cartoons. Some cartoonists work with others who create the idea or story and write the captions. Most cartoonists, however, have humorous, critical, or dramatic talents in addition to drawing skills.

Animators work in the motion picture and television industries. They draw by hand and use computers to create the large series of pictures which, when transferred to film or tape, form the animated cartoons seen in movies and on television.

Art directors, also called visual journalists, read the material to be printed in periodicals, newspapers, and other printed media, and decide how to best present visually the information in an eye-catching and organized manner. They make decisions about which photographs or art work to use, and oversee production of the printed material. Art directors may also review graphics that will be shown on the Internet.

Working Conditions
Graphic and fine artists generally work in art and design studios located in office buildings or their own studios. While their surroundings are usually well lighted and ventilated, odors from glues, paint, ink, or other materials may be present. They may use computers for extended periods of time.

Graphic artists employed by publishing companies and art and design studios generally work a standard 40-hour week. During busy periods, they may work overtime to meet deadlines. Self-employed graphic artists can set their own hours, but may spend much time and effort selling their services to potential customers or clients and establishing a reputation.

Employment

Visual artists held about 276,000 jobs in 1996. Nearly 6 out of 10 were self-employed. Self-employed artists are either graphic artists who freelance, offering their services to advertising agencies, publishing firms, and other businesses, or fine artists who earn income when they sell a painting or other art work.

Of the artists who were not self-employed, many were graphic artists who worked for advertising agencies, design firms, commercial art and reproduction firms, or printing and publishing firms. Other artists were employed by the motion picture and television industries, wholesale and retail trade establishments, and public relations firms.

Training, Other Qualifications, and Advancement

In the fine arts field, formal training requirements do not exist, but it is very difficult to become skilled enough to make a living, without training. Many colleges and universities offer bachelor's and master's degree programs in fine arts; specialized art schools also offer postsecondary training in this field. In the graphic arts field, demonstrated artistic ability, appropriate training, or other qualifications are needed for success. Evidence of appropriate talent and skill, displayed in an artist's "portfolio," is an important factor used by art and design directors and others in deciding whether to hire or contract out work to an artist. The portfolio is a collection of hand-made, computer-generated, or printed examples of the artist's best work. Assembling a successful portfolio requires skills usually developed in a bachelor's degree program or other postsecondary training in art, design, or visual communications. Internships also provide excellent opportunities for artists to develop and enhance their portfolios. Formal educational programs in art and design also provide training in computer design techniques; computers are widely used in art and design, and knowledge and training in computer techniques are critical for many jobs in these fields.

Recent data from The American Institute of Graphic Arts indicate that over 9 out of 10 artists have a college degree; among this group, over 6 out of 10 majored in graphic design and nearly 2 out of 10 majored in fine arts. Nearly 2 out of 10 have a master's degree.

The appropriate training and education for prospective medical illustrators is more specific. Medical illustrators must not only demonstrate artistic ability, but must also have a detailed knowledge of living organisms, surgical and medical procedures, and human and sometimes animal anatomy. A 4-year bachelor's degree combining art and pre-medical courses is usually required, followed by a master's degree in medical illustration. This degree is offered in only a few accredited schools in the United States.

Persons hired in advertising agencies or graphic design studios often start with relatively routine work. While doing this work, however, they may observe and practice their skills on the side. Many graphic artists work part time as freelancers while continuing to hold a full-time job until they get established. Others have enough talent, perseverance, and confidence in their ability to start out freelancing full-time immediately after graduating from art school. Many freelance part time while still in school in order to develop experience and a portfolio of published work.

The freelance artist develops a set of clients who regularly contract for work. Some successful freelancers are widely recognized for their skill in specialties, such as children's book illustration, design, or magazine illustration. These artists may earn high incomes and can pick and choose the type of work they do.

Fine artists and illustrators advance as their work circulates, and as they establish a reputation for a particular style. The best artists and illustrators continually develop new ideas, and their work constantly evolves over time. Graphic artists may advance to assistant art director, art director, design director, and in some companies, creative director of an art or design department. Some artists may gain enough skill to succeed as a freelancer or may prefer to specialize in a particular area. Some graphic artists become webmasters, maintaining their company's Internet site. Others decide to open their own businesses.

Job Outlook

The glamorous and exciting image of graphic and fine arts fields attracts many talented people with a love for drawing and creative ability. As a result, the supply of aspiring artists will continue to exceed the number of job openings, resulting in keen competition for both salaried jobs and freelance work. Freelance work may be particularly hard to come by, especially at first, and many freelancers earn very little until they acquire experience and establish a good reputation. Fine artists, in particular, may find it difficult to earn a living solely by selling their art work. Nonetheless, graphic arts studios, galleries, and individual clients are always on the lookout for artists who display outstanding talent, creativity, and style. Talented artists who have developed a mastery of artistic techniques and skills, including computer skills, will have the best job prospects.

Employment of visual artists is expected to grow faster than the average for all occupations through the year 2006. Demand for graphic artists should remain strong as producers of information, goods, and services put increasing emphasis on visual appeal in product design, advertising, marketing, and television. The explosive growth of the Internet is expected to provide many additional opportunities for graphic artists. Employment growth for graphic artists, however, may be limited because some firms are turning to employees without formal artistic or design training to operate computer-aided design systems. Employment of fine artists is expected to grow because of population growth, rising incomes, and growth in the number of people who appreciate fine arts.

Demand for artists may also depend on the level of government funding for certain programs. For example, the National Endowment for the Arts offers a variety of grants to artists; however, competition is intense for most awards.

Earnings

Median earnings for salaried visual artists who usually work full time were about $27,100 a year in 1996. The middle 50 percent earned between $20,000 and $36,400 a year. The top 10 percent earned more than $43,000, and the bottom 10 percent earned less than $15,000.

The Society of Publication Designers estimates that entry-level graphic designers earned between $23,000 and $27,000 annually in 1997.

Earnings for self-employed visual artists vary widely. Those struggling to gain experience and a reputation may be forced to charge close to the minimum wage for their work. Well-established freelancers and fine artists may earn much more than salaried artists. Like other workers, self-employed artists must provide their own benefits.

Related Occupations

Many occupations in the advertising industry, such as account executive or creative director, are related to commercial and graphic art and design. Other workers who apply visual art skills include architects, display workers, landscape architects, photographers, and floral, industrial, and interior designers. Various printing occupations are also related to graphic art, as is the work of art and design teachers. In addition, several occupational options associated with the Internet have emerged—for example, webmaster and Internet page designer. These jobs often require artistic talent as well as computer skills.

Sources of Additional Information

Students interested in careers as illustrators should contact:
☛ The National Association of Schools of Art and Design, 11250 Roger Bacon Dr., Suite 21, Reston, VA 20190.

For information on careers in medical illustration, contact:

☛ The Association of Medical Illustrators, 1819 Peachtree St. NE., Suite 712, Atlanta, GA 30309-1848.

For a list of schools offering degree programs in graphic design, contact:

☛ The American Institute of Graphic Arts, 164 Fifth Ave., New York, NY 10010.

For information on magazine art and design occupations, contact:
☛ The Society of Publication Designers, 60 East 42nd St., Suite 721, New York, NY 10165-1416.

Performing Arts Occupations

Actors, Directors, and Producers

(D.O.T. 139.167; 150 except .027-014; 159.041, .044, .047, .067, .117, .167-010 through -022, .267, .341, .344-010, -014, .347 except -010, .367, .647 except -018; 184.117-010, .162, .167-014, -022, -034; 187.167-174, -178, -182; 961.364, .667-014; 962.162-010, .167-014)

Significant Points

- Aspiring actors face frequent rejections when auditioning for work and long periods of unemployment between jobs; competition for roles is extremely keen because the glamour associated with this profession attracts large numbers of individuals.

- While formal training is helpful, experience and talent are more critical for success.

Nature of the Work

Actors, directors, and producers include stage and screen actors; narrators; magicians; clowns; comedians; impersonators; acrobats; jugglers; equestrians; amusement park entertainers; stunt, rodeo, and aquatic performers; casting, stage, news, sports, and public service directors; production, stage, and artist and repertoire managers; and producers and their assistants. This *Handbook* statement focuses on actors, directors, and producers.

Actors, directors, and producers express ideas and create images, based on a script, in theaters, film, television, and radio. They "make the words come alive" for their audiences.

Actors entertain and communicate with people through their interpretation of dramatic roles. However, only a few actors ever achieve recognition as stars—whether on stage, in motion pictures, or on television. A somewhat larger number are well-known, experienced performers, who frequently are cast in supporting roles. Most actors struggle for a toehold in the profession and pick up parts wherever they can. Although actors often prefer a certain type of role, experience is so critical to success in this field that even established actors continue to accept small roles, including commercials and product endorsements. Other actors work as "extras," who have small parts with no lines to deliver; still others work for theater companies, teaching acting courses to the public.

Directors interpret plays or scripts. In addition, they audition and select cast members, conduct rehearsals, and direct the work of the cast and crew. Directors use their knowledge of acting, voice, and movement to achieve the best possible performance and usually approve the scenery, costumes, choreography, and music.

Producers are entrepreneurs. They select plays or scripts, arrange financing, and decide on the size and content of the production and its budget. They hire directors, principal members of the cast, and key production staff members, and negotiate contracts with artistic personnel, often in accordance with collective bargaining agreements. Producers also coordinate the activities of writers, directors, managers, and other personnel. Producers must have a working knowledge of new technologies as they relate to creating special effects.

Working Conditions

Acting demands patience and total commitment, because there are often rejections when auditioning for work and long periods of un-

The glamour associated with acting attracts many people.

employment between jobs. Actors typically work long, irregular hours, sometimes under adverse weather conditions that may exist "on location," and must travel when shows are "on the road." Coupled with the heat of stage or studio lights and heavy costumes, these factors require stamina. Evening work is a regular part of a stage actor's life as several performances are often held on one day. Flawless performances require tedious memorizing of lines and repetitive rehearsals. On television, actors must deliver a good performance with very little preparation.

Actors working on Broadway productions often work long hours during rehearsals. However, once the show opens, they have more regular hours, working about 30 hours a week.

Directors and producers often work under stress as they try to meet schedules, stay within budgets, and resolve personnel problems while putting together a production. Directors must be aware of union rules and how they effect production schedules. For example, actors must be paid a minimum salary and can work no more than a set number of hours, depending on their contract.

Employment

In 1996, actors, directors, and producers held an average of about 105,000 jobs in motion pictures, stage plays, television, and radio. Many others were between jobs, so that the total number of people actually employed as actors, directors, and producers over the year was higher. In winter, most employment opportunities on stage are in New York and other large cities, many of which have established professional regional theaters. In summer, stock companies in suburban and resort areas also provide employment. Cruise lines and amusement parks also provide opportunities. In addition, many cities have small nonprofit professional companies such as "little theaters," repertory companies, and dinner theaters, which provide opportunities for local amateur talent as well as for professional entertainers. Normally, casts are selected in New York City for shows that go on the road.

Employment in motion pictures and films for television is centered in Hollywood and New York City. However, studios are also located in Florida, Seattle, and other parts of the country. In addition, many films are shot on location and may employ local professionals and nonprofessionals as day players and extras if the union contract allows. In television, opportunities are at the network entertainment centers in New York, Los Angeles, and Atlanta, and at local television stations around the country.

Training, Other Qualifications, and Advancement

For experience, aspiring actors and directors should take part in high school and college plays, or work with little theaters and other acting groups. Most actors and directors try to work their way up to major productions, although few succeed, due to the intense competition.

Formal dramatic training or acting experience is generally necessary, although some people enter the field without it. Most people take college courses in theater, arts, drama, and dramatic literature. Many experienced actors get additional formal training to learn new skills and improve old ones. Training can be obtained at dramatic arts schools in New York and Los Angeles, and at colleges and universities throughout the country offering bachelor's or higher degrees in dramatic and theater arts. College drama curriculums usually include courses in liberal arts, stage speech and movement, directing, playwriting, play production, design, and history of the drama, as well as practical courses in acting.

The best way to start is to use local opportunities and build on them. Local and regional theater experience may help in obtaining work in New York or Los Angeles. Modeling experience may also be helpful. Actors need talent, creative ability, and training that will enable them to portray different characters. Training in singing and dancing is especially useful for stage work. Actors must have poise, stage presence, the capability to affect an audience, plus the ability to follow directions. Physical appearance is often a deciding factor in being selected for particular roles.

Many professional actors rely on agents or managers to find work, negotiate contracts, and plan their careers. Agents generally earn a percentage of an actor's contract. Other actors rely solely on attending open auditions for parts. Trade publications list the time, date, and location of these auditions—referred to as "cattle calls" in this industry.

To become a movie extra, one must usually be listed by a casting agency, such as Central Casting, a no-fee agency that supplies all extras to the major movie studios in Hollywood. Applicants are accepted only when the number of persons of a particular type on the list—for example, athletic young women, old men, or small children—is below the foreseeable need. In recent years, only a very small proportion of the applicants have succeeded in being listed.

There are no specific training requirements for directors and producers. However, talent, experience, and business acumen are very important. Directors and producers come from different backgrounds. Actors, writers, film editors, and business managers often enter these fields. Producers often start in the industry working behind the scenes with successful directors. Additionally, formal training in directing and producing is available at some colleges and universities.

As actors', directors', and producers' reputations grow, they are able to work on larger productions or in more prestigious theaters. Actors may also advance to lead or specialized roles. A few actors move into acting-related jobs, as drama coaches or directors of stage, television, radio, or motion picture productions. Some teach drama in colleges and universities. Many actors find that they must take a second job to support themselves.

The length of a performer's working life depends largely on training, skill, versatility, and perseverance. Some actors, directors, and producers continue working throughout their lives; however, many leave the occupation after a short time because they cannot find enough work to make a living.

Job Outlook

The glamour of actor, director, and producer jobs attracts a large number of people; this supply of potential workers, coupled with the lack of formal entry requirements, will continue to produce keen competition for these jobs. Only the most talented will find regular employment.

Employment of actors, directors, and producers is expected to grow faster than the average for all occupations through the year 2006. Rising foreign demand for American productions, combined with a growing domestic market—fueled by the growth of cable television, satellite television, home movie rentals, and television syndications—should stimulate demand for actors and other production personnel. Growth of opportunities in recorded media should be accompanied by increasing jobs in live productions. Growing numbers of people who enjoy live theatrical entertainment for excitement and aesthetics will attend stage productions. Touring productions of Broadway plays and other large shows are providing new opportunities for actors and directors. However, employment may be somewhat affected by government funding for the arts—a decline in funding could dampen future employment growth. Workers leaving the field will continue to create most job openings.

Earnings

Minimum salaries, hours of work, and other conditions of employment are covered in collective bargaining agreements between producers of shows and unions representing workers in this field. The Actors' Equity Association represents stage actors; the Screen Actors Guild and the Screen Extras Guild cover actors in motion pictures, including television, commercials, and films; and the American Federation of Television and Radio Artists (AFTRA) represents television and radio performers. Most stage directors belong to the Society of Stage Directors and Choreographers, and film and television directors belong to the Directors Guild of America. Of course, any actor or director may negotiate for a salary higher than the minimum.

According to Actors Equity Association, minimum weekly salary for actors in Broadway stage productions was $1,040 per week in 1997. Those in small "off-Broadway" theaters received minimums ranging from $400 to $625 a week, depending on the seating capacity of the theater. Smaller regional theaters pay $375-$600 per week. For shows on the road, actors receive about $100 per day more for living expenses. However, less than 15 percent of dues-paying members work during any given week. In 1996, less than half worked on a stage production. Average earnings for those able to find employment were $13,700 in 1996.

According to the Screen Actors Guild, motion picture and television actors with speaking parts earned a minimum daily rate of $559, or $1,942 for a 5-day week, in 1997. Actors also receive contributions to their health and pension plans and additional compensation for reruns and foreign telecasts.

Earnings from acting are low, because employment is so erratic. The Screen Actors Guild also reports that the average income its members earn from acting is less than $5,000 a year. Therefore, most actors must supplement their incomes by holding jobs in other fields.

Some well-known actors have salary rates well above the minimums, and the salaries of the few top stars are many times the figures cited, creating the false impression that all actors are highly paid.

Many actors who work more than a set number of weeks per year are covered by a union health, welfare, and pension fund, including hospitalization insurance, to which employers contribute. Under some employment conditions, Actors' Equity and AFTRA members have paid vacations and sick leave.

Earnings of stage directors vary greatly. According to the Society of Stage Directors and Choreographers, summer theaters offer compensation, including "royalties" (based on the number of performances), usually ranging from $2,500 to $8,000 for a 3- to 4-week run of a production. Directing a production at a dinner theater will usually pay less than a summer theater but has more potential for royalties. Regional theaters may hire directors for longer periods of time, increasing compensation accordingly. The highest paid directors work on Broadway productions, typically earning $80,000 plus royalties.

Producers seldom get a set fee; instead, they get a percentage of a show's earnings or ticket sales.

Related Occupations

People who work in occupations requiring acting skills include dancers, choreographers, disc jockeys, drama teachers or coaches, and radio and television announcers. Others working in occupations related to acting are playwrights, scriptwriters, stage managers, costume designers, makeup artists, hair stylists, lighting designers, and set designers. Workers in occupations involved with the business aspects of theater productions include managing directors, company managers, booking managers, publicists, and agents for actors, directors, and playwrights.

Sources of Additional Information

Information about opportunities in regional theaters may be obtained from:

☛ Theatre Communications Group, Inc., 355 Lexington Ave., New York, NY 10017.

A directory of theatrical programs may be purchased from:

☛ National Association of Schools of Theater, 11250 Roger Bacon Dr., Suite 21, Reston, VA 22090.

For general information on actors, directors, and producers, contact:

☛ Screen Actors Guild, 5757 Wilshire Blvd., Los Angeles CA 90036-3600.

☛ Association of Independent Video and Filmmakers, 304 Hudson Street, 6th Floor, New York, NY 10013.

☛ American Federation of Television and Radio Artists—Screen Actors Guild, 4340 East-West Hwy., Suite 204, Bethesda, MD 20814-4411.

Dancers and Choreographers

(D.O.T. 151.027-010 and .047-010)

Significant Points

- Due to the long hours and strenuous work, most dancers stop performing by their late thirties, but sometimes remain in the dance field as choreographers, dance teachers and coaches, or artistic directors.

- Most dancers begin their formal training between the ages of 5 to 15, and have their professional auditions by the age of 17 or 18; a college or graduate degree in dance is required to teach at the elementary/high school or college level.

- Dancers and choreographers face very keen competition for jobs; only the most talented find regular employment.

Nature of the Work

From ancient times to the present, dancers have expressed ideas, stories, rhythm, and sound with their bodies. A variety of dance forms exist, including classical ballet and modern dance, which allows more free movement and self-expression. Others perform in dance adaptations for musical shows, in folk, ethnic, tap, and jazz dances, and in other popular kinds of dancing. In addition to being an art form for its own sake, dance also complements opera, musical comedy, television, movies, music videos, and commercials. Therefore, many dancers sing and act, as well as dance.

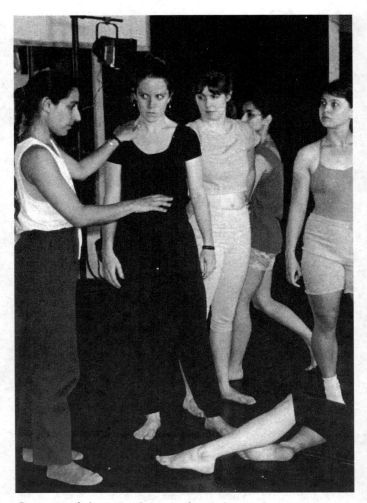

Dancers and choreographers spend many hours rehearsing.

Dancers most often perform as a group, although a few top artists dance solo. Many dancers combine stage work with teaching or choreographing.

Choreographers create original dances. They may also create new interpretations to traditional dances like the ballet, "Nutcracker." Few dance routines are written down. Instead, choreographers instruct performers at rehearsals to achieve the desired effect; they may also audition performers. Some choreographers use computers to develop dance routines for various productions.

Working Conditions

Dancing is strenuous. Rehearsals require very long hours and usually take place daily, including weekends and holidays. For shows on the road, weekend travel often is required. Most performances take place in the evening, while rehearsals and practice generally are scheduled during the day. Dancers must also work late hours. The work environment ranges from modern, temperature-controlled facilities to older, uncomfortable surroundings.

Due to the physical demands, most dancers stop performing by their late thirties, but they sometimes continue to work in the dance field as choreographers, dance teachers and coaches, or as artistic directors. Some celebrated dancers, however, continue performing beyond the age of 50.

Employment

Professional dancers and choreographers held an average of about 23,000 jobs at any one time in 1996. Many others were between engagements so that the total number of people employed as dancers over the course of the year was greater. Dancers work in a variety of settings, including eating and drinking establishments, theatrical and television productions, dance studios and schools, dance companies and bands, concert halls, and amusement parks.

In addition, there were many dance instructors in secondary schools, colleges and universities, and private studios. Many teachers also perform from time to time.

New York City is home to many of the major dance companies. Other cities with full-time professional dance companies include Atlanta, Boston, Chicago, Cincinnati, Cleveland, Columbus, Dallas, Houston, Miami, Milwaukee, Philadelphia, Pittsburgh, Salt Lake City, San Francisco, Seattle, and Washington, D.C.

Training, Other Qualifications, and Advancement

Training depends upon the type of dance. Early ballet training for women usually begins at 5 to 8 years of age and is often given by private teachers and independent ballet schools. Serious training traditionally begins between the ages of 10 and 12. Men often begin their training between the ages of 10 and 15. Students who demonstrate potential in the early teens receive more intensive and advanced professional training at regional ballet schools or schools conducted under the auspices of the major ballet companies. Leading dance school companies often have summer training programs from which they select candidates for admission to their regular full-time training program. Most dancers have their professional auditions by age 17 or 18; however, training and practice never end. Professional ballet dancers have 1 to 1 1/2 hours of lessons every day and spend many additional hours practicing and rehearsing.

Early and intensive training also is important for the modern dancer, but modern dance generally does not require as many years of training as ballet.

Because of the strenuous and time-consuming training required, a dancer's formal academic instruction may be minimal. However, a broad, general education including music, literature, history, and the visual arts is helpful in the interpretation of dramatic episodes, ideas, and feelings. Dancers sometimes conduct research to learn more about the part they are playing.

Many colleges and universities confer bachelor's or higher degrees in dance, generally through the departments of music, theater, or fine arts. Most programs concentrate on modern dance, but also offer courses in ballet and classical techniques, dance composition, dance history, dance criticism, and movement analysis.

A college education is not essential to obtaining employment as a professional dancer. In fact, ballet dancers who postpone their first audition until graduation may compete at a disadvantage with younger dancers. On the other hand, a college degree can help the dancer who retires at an early age, as often happens, and wishes to enter another field of work.

Completion of a college program in dance and education is essential to qualify for employment as a college or elementary/high school dance teacher. Colleges, as well as conservatories, generally require graduate degrees, but performance experience often may be substituted. However, a college background is not necessary for teaching dance or choreographing for local recreation programs. Studio schools usually require teachers to have experience as performers.

The dancer's life is one of rigorous practice and self-discipline; therefore, patience, perseverance, and a devotion to dance are essential. Good health and physical stamina are necessary in order to practice and perform and to follow the rugged schedule often required. Above all, one must have flexibility, agility, coordination, grace, a sense of rhythm, and a feeling for music, as well as a creative ability to express oneself through movement.

Dancers seldom perform unaccompanied, so they must be able to function as part of a team, highly motivated, and should be prepared to face the anxiety of intermittent employment and rejections when auditioning for work. For dancers, advancement takes the form of a growing reputation, more frequent work, bigger and better roles, and higher pay.

Choreographers typically are older dancers with years of experience in the theater. Through their performance as dancers, they develop reputations as skilled artists. Their reputation often leads to opportunities to choreograph productions.

Job Outlook

Dancers and choreographers face very keen competition for jobs. The number of applicants will continue to exceed the number of job openings, and only the most talented will find regular employment.

Employment of dancers and choreographers is expected to grow faster than the average for all occupations through the year 2006 due to the public's continued interest in this form of artistic expression. However, cuts in funding for the National Endowment for the Arts and related organizations could adversely affect employment in this field. Although jobs will arise each year due to increased demand, most job openings will occur as dancers and choreographers retire or leave the occupation for other reasons, and as dance companies search for and find outstanding talent.

National dance companies should continue to provide most jobs in this field. Opera companies and dance groups affiliated with colleges and universities and television and motion pictures will also offer some opportunities. Moreover, the growing popularity of dance in recent years has resulted in increased employment opportunities in teaching dance.

With innovations such as electronic sounds and music videos, choreography is becoming a more challenging field of endeavor, and will offer some employment opportunities for highly experienced, talented, and creative individuals.

Earnings

Earnings of many professional dancers are governed by union contracts. Dancers in the major opera ballet, classical ballet, and modern dance corps belong to the American Guild of Musical Artists, Inc., AFL-CIO; those on live or videotaped television belong to the American Federation of Television and Radio Artists; those who perform in films and on TV belong to the Screen Actors Guild; and those in musical comedies are members of the Actors' Equity Association. The unions and producers sign basic agreements specifying minimum salary rates, hours of work, benefits, and other conditions of employment. However, the contract each dancer signs with the producer of the show may be more favorable than the basic agreement.

For 1997-98, the minimum weekly salary for dancers in ballet and modern productions covered by the National Dance Basic Agreement was $693. According to the American Guild of Musical Artists, new first year dancers under the union agreement earned $543 per week. Dancers on tour received an additional allowance for room and board. The minimum performance rate for dancers in theatrical motion pictures was around $500 per day of filming. The normal workweek is 30 hours including rehearsals and matinee and evening performances, but may be longer. Extra compensation is paid for additional hours worked.

Earnings of choreographers vary greatly. Earnings from fees and performance royalties range from about $1,000 a week in small professional theaters, to over $30,000 for an 8- to 10-week rehearsal period for a Broadway production. In high budget films, choreographers make $3,400 for a 5-day week; in television, $8,000 to $12,500 for up to 14 work days.

Earnings from dancing are generally low because dancers' employment is irregular. They often must supplement their income by taking temporary jobs unrelated to dancing, or teach dance to students.

Dancers covered by union contracts are entitled to some paid sick leave, paid vacations, and various health and pension benefits, including extended sick pay and child birth provisions, provided by their unions. Employers contribute toward these benefits. Most other dancers do not receive any benefits.

Related Occupations

Other occupations require the dancer's knowledge of conveying ideas through physical motion. These include ice skaters, dance critics, dance instructors, and dance therapists. Athletes in most sports also need the same strength, flexibility, agility, and body control as dancers.

Sources of Additional Information

Directories of dance study and degree programs may be purchased from:

☞ National Association of Schools of Dance, 11250 Roger Bacon Dr., Suite 21, Reston, VA 20190.

☞ The National Dance Association, 1900 Association Dr., Reston, VA 20191.

Musicians

(D.O.T. 152 except .021)

Significant Points

- Musicians often must supplement their income with earnings from other sources because they can find only part-time or sporadic engagements.

- Aspiring musicians begin studying an instrument or training their voices at an early age; a bachelor's or higher degree in music or music education is required to teach at the elementary/secondary school or college level.

- Competition for jobs is keen because the glamour and potentially high earnings in this occupation attract many talented individuals.

Nature of the Work

Musicians may play musical instruments, sing, compose, arrange, or conduct groups in instrumental or vocal performances. Musicians may perform alone or as part of a group, before live audiences or on radio, or in recording studios, television, or movie productions. While most musicians play for live audiences, some prepare music exclusively for studios or computers.

Some specialize in a particular kind of music or performance. Instrumental musicians play a musical instrument in an orchestra, band, rock group, or jazz group. Some play any of a wide variety of string, brass, woodwind, or percussion instruments or electronic synthesizers; others learn several related instruments, such as the flute and clarinet, often improving their employment opportunities.

Singers interpret music using their knowledge of voice production, melody, and harmony. They sing character parts or perform in their own individual style. Singers are often classified according to their voice range—soprano, contralto, tenor, baritone, or bass—or by the type of music they sing, such as opera, rock, reggae, folk, rap, or country and western.

Composers create original music such as symphonies, operas, sonatas, or popular songs. They transcribe ideas into musical notation using harmony, rhythm, melody, and tonal structure. Many songwriters now compose and edit music using computers. Also, they may play the composition into the computer, which can record and play it back.

Arrangers transcribe and adapt musical composition to a particular style for orchestras, bands, choral groups, or individuals. Components of music—including tempo, volume, and the mix of instruments needed—are arranged to express the composer's message. While some arrangers write directly into a musical composition, others use computer software to make changes. Compositions created with computer software can also be mailed electronically or placed on an Internet site.

Conductors lead instrumental music groups, such as orchestras, dance bands, and various popular ensembles. Conductors audition and select musicians, choose the music to accommodate the talents and

Musicians begin studying at an early age.

abilities of the musicians, and direct rehearsals and performances, applying conducting techniques to achieve desired musical effects.

Choral directors lead choirs and glee clubs, sometimes working with a band or orchestra conductor. Directors audition and select singers and direct them at rehearsals and performances to achieve harmony, rhythm, tempo, shading, and other desired musical effects.

All musicians spend a considerable amount of time practicing, individually and with their band, orchestra, or other musical group.

Working Conditions

Musicians often perform at night and on weekends and spend considerable time in practice and rehearsal. Performances frequently require travel. Because many musicians find only part-time work or experience unemployment between engagements, they often supplement their income with other types of jobs. In fact, many decide they cannot support themselves as musicians and take permanent, full-time jobs in other occupations, while working only part time as musicians.

Most instrumental musicians come into contact with a variety of other people, including their colleagues, agents, employers, sponsors, and audiences. They usually work indoors, although some may perform outdoors for parades, concerts, and dances. Certain performances create noise and vibration. In some taverns and restaurants, smoke and odors may be present, and lighting and ventilation may be inadequate.

Employment

An average of about 274,000 musicians held jobs in 1996. Many were between engagements, so that the total number of people employed as musicians during the course of the year might have been greater. Many musicians were self-employed, and nearly 3 out of 5 musicians employed in 1996 worked part time.

Many work in cities in which entertainment and recording activities are concentrated, such as New York, Los Angeles, and Nashville. Classical musicians may perform with professional orchestras or in small chamber music groups like quartets or trios. Musicians may work in opera, musical comedy, and ballet productions. Many are organists who play in churches and synagogues—2 out of 3 musicians who are paid a wage or salary work in religious organizations. Musicians also perform in clubs and restaurants, and for weddings and other events. Well-known musicians and groups give their own concerts, appear "live" on radio and television, make recordings and music videos, or go on concert tours. The Armed Forces, too, offer careers in their bands and smaller musical groups.

Training, Other Qualifications, and Advancement

Aspiring musicians begin studying an instrument at an early age. They may gain valuable experience playing in a school or community band or orchestra, or with a group of friends. Singers usually start training when their voices mature. Participation in school musicals or in a choir often provides good early training and experience. Musicians need extensive and prolonged training to acquire the necessary skill, knowledge, and ability to interpret music. This training may be obtained through private study with an accomplished musician, in a college or university music program, in a music conservatory, or through practice with a group. For study in an institution, an audition frequently is necessary. Formal courses include musical theory, music interpretation, composition, conducting, and instrumental and voice instruction. Composers, conductors, and arrangers need advanced training in these subjects as well.

Many colleges, universities, and music conservatories grant bachelor's or higher degrees in music. A master's or doctoral degree is usually required to teach advanced courses in music in colleges and universities; a bachelor's degree may be sufficient to teach basic courses. A degree in music education qualifies graduates for a State certificate to teach music in an elementary or secondary school.

Those who perform popular music must have an understanding of and feeling for the style of music that interests them, but classical training can expand their employment opportunities, as well as their musical abilities. Although voice training is an asset for singers of popular music, many with untrained voices have successful careers. As a rule, musicians take lessons with private teachers when young, and seize every opportunity to make amateur or professional appearances.

Young persons who are considering careers in music should have musical talent, versatility, creative ability, and poise and stage presence to face large audiences. Since quality performance requires constant study and practice, self-discipline is vital. Moreover, musicians who play concert and nightclub engagements must have physical stamina because frequent travel and night performances are required. They must also be prepared to face the anxiety of intermittent employment and rejections when auditioning for work.

Advancement for musicians generally means becoming better known and performing for greater earnings with better known bands and orchestras. Successful musicians often rely on agents or managers to find them performing engagements, negotiate contracts, and plan their careers.

Job Outlook

Competition for musician jobs is keen, and talent alone is no guarantee of success. The glamour and potentially high earnings in this occupation attract many talented individuals. The ability to play several instruments and types of music enhances a musician's employment prospects.

Overall employment of musicians is expected to grow faster than the average for all occupations through the year 2006, reflecting the growing popularity of this form of entertainment. Almost all new wage and salary jobs for musicians will arise in religious organizations, bands, orchestras, and other entertainment groups. A decline in

employment is projected for salaried musicians in restaurants and bars, although they comprise a very small proportion of all wage and salary musicians. Bars, which regularly employ musicians, are expected to grow more slowly than eating establishments, where live entertainment is unusual, because consumption of alcoholic beverages outside the home is expected to continue to decline. Overall, most job openings for musicians will arise from the need to replace those who leave the field each year because they are unable to make a living solely as musicians.

Earnings

Earnings often depend on a performer's professional reputation, place of employment, and on the number of hours worked. The most successful musicians can earn far more than the minimum salaries indicated below.

According to the American Federation of Musicians, minimum salaries in major orchestras ranged from about $22,000 to $90,000 per year during the 1996-97 performing season. Each orchestra works out a separate contract with its local union. Top orchestras have a season ranging from 29 to 52 weeks, with most major orchestras working 52 weeks. In regional orchestras, minimum salaries are between $8,000 and $22,000 per year; the season lasts 7 to 48 weeks, with an average of 35 weeks. In contrast, community orchestras have more limited levels of funding and offer salaries that are much lower for seasons of shorter duration.

Musicians employed in motion picture or television recording and those employed by recording companies were paid a minimum ranging from about $120 to $250 per service (3 hours of work) in 1996.

Musicians employed by some symphony orchestras work under master wage agreements, which guarantee a season's work up to 52 weeks. Many other musicians may face relatively long periods of unemployment between jobs. Even when employed, however, many work part time. Thus, their earnings generally are lower than those in many other occupations. Moreover, since they may not work steadily for one employer, some performers cannot qualify for unemployment compensation, and few have typical benefits such as sick leave or vacations with pay. For these reasons, many musicians give private lessons or take jobs unrelated to music to supplement their earnings as performers.

Many musicians belong to a local of the American Federation of Musicians. Professional singers usually belong to a branch of the American Guild of Musical Artists.

Related Occupations

There are many music-related occupations. These include librettists, songwriters, and music therapists. A large number of music teachers work in elementary and secondary schools, music conservatories, and colleges and universities, or are self-employed. Many who teach music also perform.

Technical knowledge of musical instruments is required by instrument repairers, tuners, and copyists. In addition, there are a number of occupations in the business side of music such as booking agents, concert managers, music publishers, and music store owners and managers, as well as salespersons of records, sheet music, and musical instruments. Others whose work involves music include disc jockeys, music critics, sound and audio technicians, music librarians, and radio and television announcers.

Sources of Additional Information

For a directory of schools, colleges, and universities that offer accredited programs in music and music teacher education, contact:
☛ National Association of Schools of Music, 11250 Roger Bacon Dr., Suite 21, Reston, VA 22091.

Information on careers and employment opportunities for organists is available from:
☛ American Guild of Organists, 475 Riverside Dr., Suite 1260, New York, NY 10115.

For information on careers for bluegrass musicians, contact:
☛ International Bluegrass Music Association, 207 East 2nd St., Owensboro, KY 42303.

Marketing and Sales Occupations

Cashiers

(D.O.T. 209.567-014; 211.362-010, .367, .462, .467, .482-010; 249.467; and 294.567)

Significant Points

- Good employment opportunities are expected due to the large number who leave this occupation each year.
- The occupation offers plentiful opportunities for part-time work.

Nature of the Work

Supermarkets, department stores, gasoline service stations, movie theaters, restaurants, and many other businesses employ cashiers to register the sale of their merchandise. Most cashiers total bills, receive money, make change, fill out charge forms, and give receipts. Bank tellers, who perform similar duties but work in financial institutions, are discussed elsewhere in the *Handbook*.

Although specific job duties vary by employer, cashiers are usually assigned to a register at the beginning of their shifts and given drawers containing "banks" of money. They must count their banks to ensure that they contain the correct amount of money and that there are adequate supplies of change. At the end of their shifts, they once again count the drawers' contents and compare the totals with sales data. An occasional shortage of small amounts may be overlooked, but in many establishments, repeated shortages are grounds for dismissal.

In addition to counting the contents of their drawers at the end of their shifts, cashiers usually separate charge forms, return slips, coupons, and any other noncash items.

Cashiers also handle returns and exchanges and must ensure that merchandise is in good condition and determine where and when it was purchased and what type of payment was used.

After entering charges for all items and subtracting the value of any coupons or special discounts, cashiers total the bill and take payment. Acceptable forms of payment usually include cash, personal check, charge, and increasingly, debit cards. Cashiers must know the store's policies and procedures for accepting each type of payment the store accepts. For checks and charges, they may have to request additional identification from the customer or call in for an authorization. When the sale is complete, cashiers issue a receipt to the customer and return the appropriate change. They may also wrap or bag the purchase.

Cashiers traditionally have totaled customers' purchases using cash registers—manually entering the price of each product bought. However, most establishments are now using more sophisticated equipment, such as scanners and computers. In a store with scanners, a cashier passes a product's Universal Product Code over the scanning device, which transmits the code number to a computer. The computer identifies the item and its price. In other establishments, cashiers manually enter codes into computers, and descriptions of the items and their prices appear on the screen.

Depending on the type of establishment, cashiers may have other duties as well. In many supermarkets, for example, cashiers weigh produce and bulk food as well as return unwanted items to the shelves. In convenience stores, cashiers may be required to know how to use a variety of machines, other than cash registers, and how to furnish money orders. Operating ticket-dispensing machines and answering customers' questions are common duties for cashiers who work at movie theaters and ticket agencies. Counter and rental clerks, who perform many similar duties, are discussed elsewhere in the *Handbook*.

Some people find that work as a cashier is a good way to supplement their income.

Working Conditions

More than one half of all cashiers are on part-time schedules. Hours of work often vary depending on the needs of the employer. Generally, cashiers are expected to work weekends, evenings, and holidays to accommodate customers' needs. However, because of this, many employers offer flexible schedules. For example, full-time workers who work on weekends may receive time off during the week. Because the holiday season is the busiest time for most retailers, many employers restrict the use of vacation time from Thanksgiving through the beginning of January.

Most cashiers work indoors, usually standing in booths or behind counters. In addition, they are often unable to leave their workstations without supervisory approval because they are responsible for large sums of money. The work of cashiers can be very repetitious but improvements in workstation design are being made to combat problems caused by repetitive motion.

Employment

Cashiers held about 3,146,000 jobs in 1996. Although employed in nearly every industry, nearly one third of all jobs were in supermarkets and other food stores. Department stores, gasoline service stations, drug stores, and other retail establishments also employed large numbers of these workers. Because cashiers are needed in businesses and organizations of all types and sizes, job opportunities are found throughout the country.

Training, Other Qualifications, and Advancement

Cashier jobs tend to be entry-level positions requiring little or no previous work experience. Although there are no specific educational requirements, employers filling full-time jobs often prefer applicants with high school diplomas.

Nearly all cashiers are trained on the job. In small firms, beginners are often trained by an experienced worker. The first day is usually spent observing the operation and becoming familiar with the store's equipment, policies, and procedures. After this, trainees are assigned to a register—frequently under the supervision of a more experienced worker. In larger firms, before being placed at cash registers, trainees first spend several days in classes. Topics typically covered include a description of the industry and the company, instruction on the store's policies, procedures, and equipment operation, and security.

Training for experienced workers is not common, except when new equipment is introduced or when procedures change. In these cases, training is given on the job, by the employer or a representative of the equipment manufacturer.

Persons who want to become cashiers should be able to do repetitious work accurately. They also need basic arithmetic skills and good manual dexterity; and, because they deal constantly with the public, cashiers should be neat in appearance and able to deal tactfully and pleasantly with customers. In addition, some firms seek persons who have operated specialized equipment or who have business experience, such as typing, selling, or handling money.

Advancement opportunities for cashiers vary. For those working part time, promotion may be to a full-time position. Others advance to head cashier or cash office clerk. In addition, this job offers a good opportunity to learn an employer's business and can serve as a steppingstone to a more responsible position.

Job Outlook

As in the past, employment opportunities for cashiers are expected to continue to be good, because of the many job openings created each year due to the need to replace the large number of workers who transfer to other occupations or leave the labor force. Additional openings will be created by growth in employment of cashiers.

Cashier employment is expected to increase about as fast as the average for all occupations through the year 2006 due to expanding demand for goods and services by a growing population. Traditionally, workers under the age of 25 have filled many of the openings in this occupation—in 1996, about half of all cashiers were 24 years of age or younger. Recently, some establishments have begun hiring elderly and disabled persons as well to fill some of their job openings. Opportunities for part-time work are expected to continue to be excellent.

Earnings

Cashiers have earnings ranging from the minimum wage, to several times that amount. Wages tend to be higher in areas where there is intense competition for workers. In establishments covered by Federal law, those beginning at the minimum wage earned $5.15 an hour in 1997. In some States, the minimum wage in many establishments is governed by State law, and where State minimums are higher, the establishment must pay at least that amount.

In 1996, median weekly earnings for full-time cashiers were $247. The middle 50 percent earned between $198 and $328; 10 percent earned below $165; and 10 percent earned above $486.

Benefits for full-time cashiers tend to be better than for those working part time. Cashiers often receive health and life insurance and paid vacations. In addition, those working in retail establishments often receive discounts on purchases, and cashiers in restaurants may receive free or low-cost meals. Some employers also offer employee stock option plans.

Related Occupations

Cashiers accept payment for the purchase of goods and services. Other workers with similar duties include food counter clerks, bank tellers, counter and rental clerks, postal service clerks, and sales clerks, all of whom are discussed elsewhere in the *Handbook*.

Sources of Additional Information

General information on retailing is available from:
☛ National Retail Federation, 325 7th St. NW., Suite 1000, Washington, DC 20004. Homepage: http://www.nrf.com
☛ Food Marketing Institute, 800 Connecticut Ave. NW., Washington, DC 20006.

For information about employment opportunities as a cashier, contact:
☛ National Association of Convenience Stores, 1605 King St., Alexandria, VA 22314-2792.
☛ Service Station Dealers of America, 9420 Annapolis Rd., Suite 307, Lanham, MD 20706.
☛ International Mass Retail Association, 1700 N. Moore St., Suite 2250, Arlington, VA 22209-1998.

☛ United Food and Commercial Workers International Union, Education Office, 1775 K St. NW., Washington, DC 20006-1502.

Counter and Rental Clerks

(D.O.T. 216.482-030; 249.362-010; .366-010; 295.357-010, -014 and -018; .367-010, -014, and -026; .467; 299.367-018; 369.367-010 and -014; .467 -010; .477; and .677-010)

Significant Points

- Jobs are primarily entry level and require little or no experience and little formal education.
- Part-time employment opportunities are expected to be plentiful.

Nature of the Work

Whether renting video tapes or air compressors, dropping off clothes to be dry-cleaned or appliances to be serviced, we rely on counter and rental clerks to handle these transactions efficiently. Although specific duties vary by establishment, counter and rental clerks are responsible for answering questions involving product availability, cost, and rental provisions. Counter and rental clerks also take orders, calculate fees, receive payments, and accept returns. (Cashiers and retail sales workers, occupations with similar duties, are discussed elsewhere in the *Handbook*.)

Regardless of where they work, counter and rental clerks must be knowledgeable about the company's services, policies, and procedures. Depending on the type of establishment, counter and rental clerks use their special knowledge to give advice on a wide variety of products and services, which may range from hydraulic tools to shoe repair. For example, in the car rental industry, they inform customers about the features of the different types of automobiles available and daily and weekly rental costs, ensure that customers meet age and other requirements, and indicate when and in what condition cars must be returned. In dry-cleaning establishments, counter clerks inform customers when items will be ready.

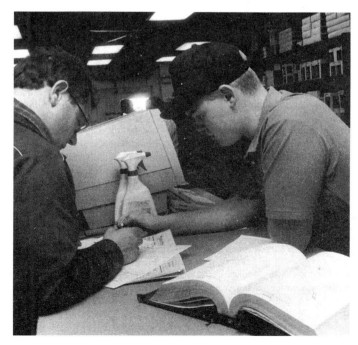

Training for counter and rental clerks is usually provided on the job.

When taking orders, counter and rental clerks use various types of equipment. In some establishments, they write out tickets and order forms. However, computers and bar code scanners are quickly becoming the norm. Most of these computer systems are user friendly and usually require very little data entry. Scanners "read" the product code and display a description of the item on a computer screen. Clerks must insure, however, that the data on the screen matches the actual product.

Working Conditions

Because firms employing counter and rental clerks generally operate at the convenience of customers, these workers often work night and weekend hours. However, because of this many, employers offer flexible schedules. Some counter and rental clerks work 40-hour weeks but over one-half are on part-time schedules—usually during rush periods, such as weekends, evenings, and holidays.

Working conditions are usually pleasant; most stores and service establishments are clean, well-lighted, and temperature controlled. However, clerks are on their feet much of the time and may be confined behind a small counter area. This job requires constant interaction with the public and can be taxing—especially during busy periods.

Employment

Counter and rental clerks held 374,000 jobs in 1996. About 1 of every 4 clerks worked for a video tape rental establishment. Other large employers included laundries or dry cleaners, automobile rental firms, equipment rental firms, and miscellaneous entertainment and recreation establishments.

Counter and rental clerks are employed throughout the country but are concentrated in metropolitan areas, where personal services and renting and leasing services are in greater demand.

Training, Other Qualifications, and Advancement

Counter and rental clerk jobs are primarily entry level and require little or no experience and little formal education. However, many employers prefer those with at least a high school diploma.

In most companies, counter and rental clerks are trained on the job, sometimes through the use of video tapes, brochures, and pamphlets. Clerks usually learn how to operate the equipment and become familiar with the establishment's policies and procedures, under the observation of a more experienced worker. However, some employers have formal classroom training programs, lasting from a few hours to a few weeks. Topics covered in this training usually include a description of the industry, the company and its policies and procedures, equipment operation, sales techniques, and customer service. Counter and rental clerks must also become familiar with the different products and services rented or provided by their company in order to give customers the best possible service.

Counter and rental clerks should enjoy working with people and have the ability to deal tactfully with difficult customers. In addition, good oral and written communication skills are essential.

Advancement opportunities depend on the size and type of company. Many establishments that employ counter or rental clerks tend to be small businesses, making advancement difficult. But in larger establishments with a corporate structure, jobs as counter and rental clerks offer good opportunities for workers to learn about their company's products and business practices. These jobs can be stepping-stones to more responsible positions, because it is common in many establishments to promote counter and rental clerks into assistant manager positions.

In certain industries, such as equipment repair, counter and rental jobs may be an additional or alternate source of income for workers who are unemployed or entering semi-retirement. For example, retired mechanics could prove invaluable at tool rental centers because of their relevant knowledge.

Job Outlook

Employment in this occupation is expected to increase faster than the average for all occupations through the year 2006, due to anticipated employment growth in the industries where they are concentrated—

business services, automotive rentals, and amusement and recreation services. Some openings due to growth are expected to meet consumers' anticipated increased acceptance of renting items instead of buying them. Despite this, most job openings will arise from the need to replace experienced workers who transfer to other occupations or leave the labor force. Part-time employment opportunities are expected to be plentiful.

Earnings

Counter and rental clerks typically start at the minimum wage, which, in establishments covered by Federal law, was $5.15 an hour in 1997. In areas where there is intense competition for workers, however, wages are often higher. In addition to wages, some counter and rental clerks receive commissions, based on the number of contracts they complete or services they sell.

Retail counter clerks earned a median weekly income of $303 in 1996. The middle 50 percent earned between $230 and $489 a week. The bottom 10 percent earned less than $184; the top 10 percent earned more than $631.

Full-time workers typically receive health and life insurance and paid vacation and sick leave. Benefits for counter and rental clerks who work part time tend to be significantly less than for those who work full time. Many companies offer discounts to both full- and part-time employees on the services they provide.

Related Occupations

Counter and rental clerks take orders and receive payment for services rendered. Other workers with similar duties include cashiers, retail sales workers, food counter clerks, postal service clerks, and bank tellers.

Sources of Additional Information

For general information on employment in the equipment rental industry contact:

☛ American Rental Association, 1900 19th St., Moline, IL 61265.

For more information about the work of counter clerks in dry cleaning and laundry establishments, contact:

☛ International Fabricare Institute, 12251 Tech Road, Silver Spring, MD 20904.

For general information on employment in the rent-to-own industry, contact:

☛ Association of Progressive Rental Organizations, 9015 Mountain Ridge Dr., Suite 220, Austin, TX 78759. Homepage: http://www.apro-rto.com

Insurance Agents and Brokers

(D.O.T. 169.167-050, 239.267-010, and 250.257-010)

Significant Points

- Employers prefer to hire college graduates and persons with proven sales ability or success in other occupations.

- Employment is projected to grow more slowly than average as the increasing use of computers allows agents to handle more sales.

- Many beginners find it difficult to establish a sufficiently large clientele in this highly competitive business; consequently, many eventually leave for other jobs.

Nature of the Work

Most people have their first contact with an insurance company through an insurance agent or broker. These professionals sell insurance policies to individuals and businesses to provide protection against financial loss. Insurance agents and brokers help individuals, families, and businesses select the policy that provides the best insurance protection for their lives and health, as well as for their automobiles, jewelry, personal valuables, furniture, household items, businesses, and other properties. Agents and brokers prepare reports, maintain records, and, in the event of a loss, help policyholders settle insurance claims. Some agents may help an employer provide employees the opportunity to buy insurance through payroll deductions. *Insurance agents* may work for one insurance company or as "independent agents" selling for several companies. *Insurance brokers* do not sell for a particular company, but place insurance policies for their clients with the company that offers the best rate and coverage.

Insurance agents sell one or more of several types of insurance—life, property and casualty, health, disability, and long-term care. Life insurance agents specialize in selling policies that pay beneficiaries when a policyholder dies. Depending on the policyholder's circumstances, a whole-life policy can be designed to provide retirement income, funds for the education of children, or other benefits. Life insurance agents and brokers are sometimes referred to as *life underwriters*. (See the statement on insurance underwriters elsewhere in the *Handbook*.)

Property and casualty insurance agents and brokers sell policies that protect individuals and businesses from financial loss as a result of automobile accidents, fire or theft, storms, and other events that can damage property. For businesses, property and casualty insurance can also cover injured workers' compensation, product liability claims, or medical malpractice claims. Many life and property and casualty insurance agents also sell health insurance policies covering the costs of medical care and loss of income due to illness or injury.

An increasing number of insurance agents and brokers offer comprehensive financial planning services to their clients such as retirement planning counseling. As a result, many insurance agents and brokers are involved in "cross-selling" or "total account development"—besides insurance, these agents may become licensed to sell mutual funds, annuities, and other securities. (See the statement on securities and financial services sales representatives elsewhere in the *Handbook*.)

Since insurance sales agents obtain many new accounts through referrals, it is important that agents maintain regular contact with their clients to ensure their financial needs are being met as personal and business needs change. Developing a satisfied clientele who will recommend an agent's services to other potential customers is a key to success in this field. Some insurance agents and brokers are also using the Internet to advertise and describe the financial products and services that they provide.

Insurance agents and brokers spend considerable time dealing with clients on the phone.

Working Conditions

Most insurance agents and brokers work in small offices, contacting clients and providing insurance policy information. However, most of their time is spent outside their offices, traveling locally to meet with clients and close sales. They generally arrange their own hours of work, and often schedule evening and weekend appointments for the convenience of clients. Although the majority of agents and brokers work no more than 40 hours a week, some work as much as 60 hours a week or even longer.

Employment

Insurance agents and brokers held about 409,000 jobs in 1996. About 3 out of 10 agents and brokers were self-employed. While most insurance agents specialize in life insurance, a growing number of "multiline agents" offer life, property/casualty, and health and disability policies. The following tabulation shows the percent distribution of wage and salary jobs by industry in 1996.

Insurance agents, brokers, and services	44
Life insurance carriers	35
Fire, marine, and casualty insurance carriers	12
Medical service and health insurance carriers	4
Pension funds and miscellaneous insurance carriers	1
Other industries	4

Agents and brokers are employed in cities and towns throughout the country, but most work in or near large population centers. Some insurance agents and brokers are employed in the headquarters of insurance companies, but the majority work out of local company offices or independent agencies.

Training, Other Qualifications, and Advancement

For jobs selling insurance, most companies and independent agencies prefer to hire college graduates—particularly those who have majored in business or economics. Some hire high school graduates with potential or proven sales ability or who have been successful in other types of work. In fact, most entrants to agent and broker jobs transfer from other occupations. As a result, agents and brokers tend to be older than the entrants in many other occupations.

College training may help agents or brokers grasp the technical aspects of insurance policies and the fundamentals and procedures of selling insurance. Many colleges and universities offer courses in insurance, and a few schools offer a bachelor's degree in insurance. College courses in finance, mathematics, accounting, economics, business law, government, and business administration enable insurance agents or brokers to understand how social, marketing, and economic conditions relate to the insurance industry. It is important for insurance agents and brokers to keep up to date with issues concerning clients. Changes in tax laws, government benefit programs, and other State and Federal regulations can affect the insurance needs of clients and how agents conduct business. Courses in psychology, sociology, and public speaking can prove useful in improving sales techniques. In addition, familiarity with computers and popular software packages is very important. The use of computers to provide instantaneous information on a wide variety of financial products has greatly improved agents' and brokers' efficiency and enabled them to devote more time to clients' needs.

Insurance agents and brokers must obtain a license in the States where they plan to sell insurance. By law in most States, licenses are issued only to applicants who complete specified courses and then pass State examinations covering insurance fundamentals and the State insurance laws. Agents and brokers who plan to sell mutual funds and other securities must also obtain a separate securities license. New agents usually receive training in a classroom setting at pre-licensing schools conducted by State insurance agents' associations or at the home or branch offices of the insurance company. Often they attend company-sponsored classes to prepare for examinations. Others study on their own and accompany experienced agents when they call on prospective clients.

As the diversity of financial products sold by insurance agents and brokers increases, employers are placing greater emphasis on continuing professional education. Agents and brokers can enhance their selling skills and broaden their knowledge of insurance and other financial services by taking courses at colleges and universities and attending institutes, conferences, and seminars sponsored by insurance organizations. Most States have mandatory continuing education requirements focusing on insurance laws, consumer protection, and the technical details of various insurance policies.

A number of organizations offer professional designation programs which certify expertise in specialties such as life, health, property, and casualty insurance, or financial consulting. Although voluntary, professional designation assures clients and employers that an agent has a thorough understanding of the relevant specialty. Many professional societies now require agents to commit to continuing education in order to retain their designation.

Insurance agents and brokers should be enthusiastic, outgoing, self-confident, disciplined, hard working, and able to communicate effectively. They should be able to inspire customer confidence. Because they usually work without supervision, agents and brokers must be able to plan their time well and have the initiative to locate new clients.

An insurance agent who shows sales ability and leadership may become a sales manager in a local office. A few advance to agency superintendent or executive positions. However, many who have built up a good clientele prefer to remain in sales work. Some, particularly in the property/casualty field, establish their own independent agencies or brokerage firms.

Job Outlook

Employment of insurance agents and brokers is expected to grow more slowly than the average for all occupations through the year 2006. Most job openings are expected to result from the need to replace agents and brokers who leave the occupation. Many beginners find it difficult to establish a sufficiently large clientele in this highly competitive business; consequently, many eventually leave for other jobs. Opportunities should be best for ambitious people who enjoy competitive sales work, and who have developed expertise and can advise people in a wide range of insurance and financial services.

Future demand for agents and brokers depends on the volume of sales of insurance and other financial products. The growing number of working women should increase insurance sales. Rising incomes as well as a concern for financial security should stimulate sales of mutual funds, variable annuities, and other financial products and services. Growing demand for long-term health care and pension benefits for retirees—an increasing proportion of the population—should spur insurance sales. Sales of property and casualty insurance should rise as more people seek coverage not only for their homes, cars, and valuables, but also for expensive, advanced technology products such as home computers. As new businesses emerge and existing firms expand coverage, sales of commercial insurance should increase. In addition, complex types of commercial coverage such as product liability, workers' compensation, employee benefits, and pollution liability insurance are increasingly in demand.

Employment of agents and brokers will not keep pace with the rising level of insurance sales, however. Using computers, agents can access an abundance of information on potential clients, allowing them to save time and money by carefully crafting individually tailored plans. Consequently, agents will be able to handle a greater volume of sales. Many companies and agencies are diversifying their marketing techniques to include some direct mail or telephone sales, as well as using the Internet to provide information on their product lines. These innovations reduce the time agents must spend developing sales leads, allowing them to concentrate on following up on potential clients. In some cases, clients can purchase certain policies without consultation from an agent. Also, customer service representatives are increasingly assuming some sales functions, such as expanding accounts and, occasionally, generating new accounts by offering additional financial products to interested clients. Trends toward multiline agents, group policies, and self-insurance, as more

businesses set rates for their own exposure to risks and pay premiums into a reserve fund, will also contribute to employment rising slower than the volume of insurance sales. In addition, large firms may increasingly hire risk managers to analyze their insurance needs and select the best policies.

Most individuals and businesses consider insurance a necessity, regardless of economic conditions. Therefore, agents are not likely to face unemployment because of a recession.

Earnings

The median annual earnings of salaried insurance sales workers was $31,500 in 1996. The middle 50 percent earned between $21,100 and $49,000 a year. The lowest 10 percent earned $15,000 or less, while the top 10 percent earned over $76,900.

Many independent agents are paid by commission only, whereas sales workers who are employees of an agency may be paid in one of three ways—salary only, salary plus commission, or salary plus bonus. Commissions, however, are the most common form of compensation, especially for experienced agents. The amount of the commission depends on the type and amount of insurance sold, and whether the transaction is a new policy or a renewal. Bonuses are usually awarded when agents meet their sales goals or when an agency's profit goals are met. Some agents involved with financial planning receive an hourly fee for their services rather than a commission.

Company-paid benefits to sales agents generally include continuing education, paid licensing training, group insurance plans, and office space and clerical support services. Some may pay for automobile and transportation expenses, attendance at conventions and meetings, promotion and marketing expenses, and retirement plans. Independent agents working for insurance agencies receive fewer benefits, but their commissions may be higher to help them pay for promotion and marketing expenses. They are typically responsible for their own travel and automobile expenses, life insurance, and retirement plans. In addition, all agents are legally responsible for any mistakes that they make, and independent agents must purchase their own insurance to cover damages from their errors and omissions.

Related Occupations

Other workers who sell financial products or services include real estate agents and brokers, securities and financial services sales representatives, financial advisors, estate planning specialists, and manufacturers' sales workers.

Sources of Additional Information

General occupational information about insurance agents and brokers is available from the home office of many life and casualty insurance companies. Information on State licensing requirements may be obtained from the department of insurance at any State capital.

For information about insurance sales careers, contact:

☛ Insurance Information Institute, 110 William Street, New York, NY 10038.

For information about insurance sales careers in independent agencies and brokerages, contact:

☛ Independent Insurance Agents of America, 127 S. Peyton St., Alexandria, VA 22314.

For information about life insurance sales careers, contact:

☛ National Association of Life Underwriters, 1922 F St. NW., Washington, DC 20006.

☛ National Association of Professional Insurance Agents, 400 N. Washington St., Alexandria, VA 22314.

For information regarding training for life insurance sales careers, contact:

☛ Life Underwriting Training Council, 7625 Wisconsin Ave., Bethesda, MD 20814.

For information about professional designation programs, contact:

☛ The American College, 270 Bryn Mawr Ave., Bryn Mawr, PA 19010-2195. Homepage: http://www.amercoll.edu

☛ Society of Certified Insurance Counselors, 3630 North Hills Dr., Austin, TX 78731. Phone: (800) 633-2165. Homepage: http://www.scic.com/alliance

☛ The American Institute for Chartered Property and Casualty Underwriters, and the Insurance Institute of America, 720 Providence Rd., P.O. Box 3016, Malvern, PA 19355.

Manufacturers' and Wholesale Sales Representatives

(List of D.O.T. codes available on request. See p. 496.)

Significant Points

- Although employers place an emphasis on a strong educational background, many individuals with previous sales experience who do not have a college degree still enter the occupation.

- Many jobs require a great deal of travel.

- Many are self-employed manufacturers' agents who work for a commission.

Nature of the Work

For both manufacturers and wholesalers, sales representatives are an important part of their company's success. Regardless of the type of product they sell, their primary duties are to interest wholesale and retail buyers and purchasing agents in their merchandise and ensure that any questions or concerns of current clients are addressed. They market their company's products to manufacturers, wholesale and retail establishments, government agencies, and other institutions. Sales representatives also provide advice to clients on how to increase sales. (Retail sales workers, who sell directly to consumers, are discussed elsewhere in the *Handbook*.)

Depending on where they work, sales representatives have different job titles. Many of those working directly for manufacturers are referred to as *manufacturers' representatives* and those employed by wholesalers generally are called *sales representatives*. In addition to those employed directly by firms, *manufacturers' agents* are self-employed sales workers who contract their services to all types of companies. Those selling technical products, for both manufacturers and wholesalers, are usually called *industrial sales workers* or *sales engineers*. Many of these titles, however, are used interchangeably.

Manufacturers' and wholesale sales representatives spend much of their time traveling to and visiting with prospective buyers and current clients. During a sales call, they discuss the customers' needs and suggest how their merchandise or services can meet those needs. They may show samples or catalogs that describe items their company stocks and inform customers about prices, availability, and how their products can save money and improve productivity. Because of the vast number of manufacturers and wholesalers selling similar products, they also try to emphasize the unique qualities of the products and services offered by their company. They also take orders and resolve any problems or complaints with the merchandise.

Depending on the products they sell, sales representatives may have additional duties. For example, sales engineers, who are among the most highly trained sales workers, typically sell products whose installation and optimal use require a great deal of technical expertise and support—products such as material handling equipment, numerical-control machinery, and computer systems. In addition to providing information on their firm's products, these workers help prospective and current buyers with technical problems by recommending improved materials and machinery for a firm's manufacturing process, drawing up plans of proposed machinery layouts and estimating cost savings from the use of their equipment. They present this information and negotiate the sale, a process that may take several months. During their presentation, they may use a portable computer so they can have instant access to technical, sales, and other information.

Increasingly, sales representatives who lack technical expertise work as a team with a technical expert. In this arrangement, the duties of a sales representative are to make the preliminary contact with customers, introduce the company's product, and close the sale. The technical expert will attend the sales presentation to explain and answer questions and concerns. In this way, the sales representative is able to spend more time maintaining and soliciting accounts and less time acquiring technical knowledge. After the sale, sales representatives may make frequent follow-up visits to ensure the equipment is functioning properly and may even help train customers' employees to operate and maintain new equipment.

Those selling consumer goods often suggest how and where their merchandise should be displayed. Working with retailers, they may help arrange promotional programs, store displays, and advertising.

Obtaining new accounts is an important part of the job. Sales representatives follow leads suggested by other clients, from advertisements in trade journals, and from participation in trade shows and conferences. At times, they make unannounced visits to potential clients. In addition, they may spend a lot of time meeting with and entertaining prospective clients during evenings and weekends.

Sales representatives also analyze sales statistics, prepare reports, and handle administrative duties, such as filing their expense account reports, scheduling appointments, and making travel plans. They study literature about new and existing products and monitor the sales, prices, and products of their competitors.

In addition to all these duties, manufacturers' agents who operate a sales agency must also manage their business. This requires organizational skills as well as knowledge of accounting, marketing, and administration.

Working Conditions

Some manufacturers' and wholesale sales representatives have large territories and do considerable traveling. Because a sales region may cover several States, they may be away from home for several days or weeks at a time. Others work near their "home base" and do most of their traveling by automobile. Due to the nature of the work and the amount of travel, sales representatives typically work more than 40 hours per week.

Although the hours are long and often irregular, most sales representatives have the freedom to determine their own schedule. As a result, they may be able to arrange their appointments so they can have time off when they want it.

Dealing with different types of people can be demanding but stimulating. In addition, sales representatives often face competition from representatives of other companies as well as from fellow workers. Companies may set goals or quotas that representatives are ex-

Manufacturers' and wholesale sales representatives keep in contact with their customers in order to provide the best service possible.

pected to meet. Because their earnings depend upon commissions, manufacturers' agents are also under the added pressure to maintain and expand their clientele.

Employment

Manufacturers' and wholesale sales representatives held about 1,557,000 jobs in 1996. Three of every 4 worked in wholesale trade—mostly for distributors of machinery and equipment, groceries and related products, and motor vehicles and parts. Others were employed in manufacturing and mining. Due to the diversity of products and services sold, employment opportunities are available in every part of the country.

In addition to those working directly for a firm, many sales representatives are self-employed manufacturers' agents who work for a straight commission based on the value of their sales. However, these workers generally gain experience and recognition with a manufacturer or wholesaler prior to going into business for themselves.

Training, Other Qualifications, and Advancement

The background needed for sales jobs varies by product line and market. As the number of college graduates has increased and the job requirements have become more technical and analytical, most firms have placed a greater emphasis on a strong educational background. Nevertheless, many employers still hire individuals with previous sales experience who do not have a college degree. In fact, for some consumer products, sales ability, personality, and familiarity with brands are as important as a degree. On the other hand, firms selling industrial products often require a degree in science or engineering in addition to some sales experience. In general, companies are looking for the best and brightest individuals who display the personality and desire necessary to sell.

Many companies have formal training programs for beginning sales representatives lasting up to 2 years. However, most businesses are accelerating these programs to reduce costs and expedite the return from training. In some programs, trainees rotate among jobs in plants and offices to learn all phases of production, installation, and distribution of the product. In others, trainees take formal classroom instruction at the plant, followed by on-the-job training under the supervision of a field sales manager.

In some firms, new workers are trained by accompanying more experienced workers on their sales calls. As these workers gain familiarity with the firm's products and clients, they are given increasing responsibility until they are eventually assigned their own territory. As businesses experience greater competition, increased pressure is placed upon sales representatives to produce faster.

These workers must stay abreast of new merchandise and the changing needs of their customers. They may attend trade shows where new products are displayed or conferences and conventions where they meet with other sales representatives and clients to discuss new product developments. In addition, many companies sponsor meetings of their entire sales force where presentations are made on sales performance, product development, and profitability.

Manufacturers' and wholesale sales representatives should be goal oriented, persuasive, and able to work both as part of a team and independently. A pleasant personality and appearance, the ability to communicate well with people, and problem-solving skills are important as well. In addition, patience and perseverance are needed because completing a sale can take several months. Because these workers may be on their feet for long periods and may have to carry heavy sample cases, some physical stamina is necessary. Sales representatives should also enjoy traveling because much of their time is spent visiting current and prospective clients.

Frequently, promotion takes the form of an assignment to a larger account or territory where commissions are likely to be greater. Experienced sales representatives may move into jobs as sales trainers—workers who train new employees on selling techniques and company policies and procedures. Those who have good sales records and leadership ability may advance to sales supervisor or district manager.

In addition to advancement opportunities within a firm, some go into business for themselves as manufacturers' agents. Others find opportunities in buying, purchasing, advertising, or marketing research.

Job Outlook

Overall, employment of manufacturers' and wholesale sales representatives is expected to grow about as fast as the average for all occupations through the year 2006 due to continued growth in the amount of goods provided that need to be sold. Many job openings will also result from the need to replace workers who transfer to other occupations or leave the labor force.

Unlike many other occupations, technology is not expected to have a dramatic effect on the demand for these workers because sales workers will still be needed to go to the prospective customer in order to demonstrate or illustrate the particulars about the good or service. Technology is expected, however, to make them more effective and productive because it allows them to provide accurate and current information to customers during sales presentations.

Within manufacturing, job opportunities as manufacturers' agents should be a little better than those for sales representatives. Manufacturers are expected to continue outsourcing their sales duties to these workers rather than using in-house or direct selling personnel because agents are more likely to work in a sales area or territory longer than representatives, creating a better working relationship and understanding how customers operate their businesses. Also, by using agents who usually lend their services to more than one company, companies can share costs with the other companies involved with that agent.

Those interested in this occupation should keep in mind that direct selling opportunities in manufacturing are likely to be best for products with strong demand. Furthermore, jobs will be most plentiful in small wholesale and manufacturing firms because a growing number of these companies will rely on wholesalers and manufacturers' agents to market their products as a way to control their costs and expand their customer base.

Employment opportunities and earnings may fluctuate from year to year because sales are affected by changing economic conditions, legislative issues, and consumer preferences. Prospects will be best for those with the appropriate knowledge or technical expertise as well as the personal traits necessary for successful selling.

Earnings

Compensation methods vary significantly by the type of firm and product sold. However, most employers use a combination of salary and commission or salary plus bonus. Commissions are usually based on the amount of sales, whereas bonuses may depend on individual performance, on the performance of all sales workers in the group or district, or on the company's performance.

Median annual earnings of full-time manufacturers' and wholesale sales representatives were about $36,100 in 1996. The middle 50 percent earned between $24,900 and $51,900 per year. The bottom 10 percent earned less than $16,700; the top 10 percent earned more than $75,000 per year. Earnings vary by experience and the type of goods or services sold.

In addition to their earnings, sales representatives are usually reimbursed for expenses such as transportation costs, meals, hotels, and entertaining customers. They often receive benefits such as health and life insurance, a pension plan, vacation and sick leave, personal use of a company car, and "frequent flyer" mileage. Some companies offer incentives such as free vacation trips or gifts for outstanding sales workers.

Unlike those working directly for a manufacturer or wholesaler, manufacturers' agents get paid strictly on commission. Depending on the type of product they are selling, their experience in the field, and the number of clients, their earnings can be significantly higher or lower than those working in direct sales. In addition, because manufacturers' agents are self-employed, they must pay their own travel and entertainment expenses as well as provide for their own benefits, which can be a significant cost.

Related Occupations

Manufacturers' and wholesale sales representatives must have sales ability and knowledge of the products they sell. Other occupations that require similar skills are retail, services, real estate, insurance, and securities sales workers, as well as wholesale and retail buyers.

Sources of Additional Information

Information on manufacturers' agents is available from:

☛ Manufacturers' Agents National Association, P.O. Box 3467, Laguna Hills, CA 92654-3467.

Career and certification information is available from:

☛ Sales and Marketing Executives International, Statler Office Tower, Suite 977, 1127 Euclid Ave., Cleveland OH, 44115. Homepage: http://www.smei.org

☛ Manufacturers' Representatives Educational Research Foundation, P.O. Box 247, Geneva, IL 60134.

Real Estate Agents, Brokers, and Appraisers

(D.O.T. 191.267-010 and 250.157-010, .357-010, -014, and -018)

Significant Points

- Real estate sales positions should continue to be relatively easy to obtain due to the thousands of people who leave this occupation each year.

- Real estate agents and brokers must be licensed in every State and in the District of Columbia.

Nature of the Work

The purchase or sale of a home or investment property is not only one of the most important financial events in peoples' lives, but one of the most complex transactions as well. As a result, people generally seek the help of real estate agents, brokers, and appraisers when trying to buy, sell, or establish a price for real estate.

Real estate agents and brokers have a thorough knowledge of the real estate market in their community. They know which neighborhoods will best fit their clients' needs and budgets. They are familiar with local zoning and tax laws, and know where to obtain financing. Agents and brokers also act as an intermediary in price negotiations between buyers and sellers. Real estate agents are generally independent sales workers who provide their services to a licensed broker on a contract basis. In return, the broker pays the agent a portion of the commission earned from property sold through the firm, by the agent.

Brokers are independent business people who, for a fee, sell real estate owned by others and rent and manage properties. In closing sales, brokers often provide buyers with information on loans to finance their purchase. They also arrange for title searches and for meetings between buyers and sellers when details of the transactions are agreed upon and the new owners take possession. A broker's knowledge, resourcefulness, and creativity in arranging financing that is most favorable to the prospective buyer often mean the difference between success and failure in closing a sale. In some cases, agents assume the responsibilities in closing sales, but in many areas, this is done by lawyers or lenders. Brokers also manage their own offices, advertise properties, and handle other business matters. Some combine other types of work, such as selling insurance or practicing law, with their real estate business.

Before showing properties to potential buyers, the broker or agent has an initial meeting with them to get a feeling for the type of home they would like and can afford. Often, an agent or broker uses a computer to generate lists of properties for sale, their location and description, and to identify available sources of financing. Traditionally, they then take the clients to see a number of homes that are likely to meet their needs and income. Increasingly, however, agents and brokers are able to use computers in their office to give clients a "virtual" tour of properties in which they are interested, allowing them to look at various types of images of the property, including interior and exterior images and floor plans.

Because buying real estate is such an important decision of a person's life, agents may have to meet several times with prospective buyers to discuss available properties. In answering questions, agents emphasize selling points likely to be most important to the buyer. To a young family looking at a house, for example, they may point out the convenient floor plan and the fact that quality schools and shopping centers are close by. To a potential investor seeking the tax advantages of owning a rental property, they may point out the proximity to the city and the ease of finding a renter. If bargaining over price becomes necessary, agents must carefully follow their client's instructions and may have to present counteroffers in order to get the best possible price.

Once the contract has been signed by both parties, the real estate broker or agent must see to it that all special terms of the contract are met before the closing date. For example, if the seller has agreed to a home inspection or a termite and radon inspection, the agent must make sure this is done. Also, if the seller has agreed to any repairs, the broker or agent must see they are made. Increasingly, brokers and agents handle environmental problems by making sure the property they are selling meets environmental regulations. For example, they may be responsible for dealing with problems such as lead paint on the walls. While many details are handled by loan officers, attorneys, or other persons, the agent must check to make sure that they also are completed.

There is more to an agent's and broker's job, however, than just making sales. Because they must have properties to sell, they may spend a significant amount of time obtaining "listings" (owner agreements to place properties for sale with the firm). When listing property for sale, agents and brokers compare the listed property with similar properties that have been sold recently to determine its competitive market price.

Most real estate agents and brokers sell residential property. A few, usually in large firms or small specialized firms, sell commercial, industrial, agricultural, or other types of real estate. Each specialty requires knowledge of that particular type of property and clientele. Selling or leasing business property, for example, requires an understanding of leasing practices, business trends, and location needs. Agents who sell or lease industrial properties must know about transportation, utilities, and labor supply. To sell residential properties, the agent or broker must know the location of schools, religious institutions, shopping facilities, and public transportation, and be familiar with tax rates and insurance coverage.

Because real estate transactions involve substantial financial commitments, parties to the transactions may seek the advice of real estate appraisers, who are objective experts and do not have a vested interest in the property. An appraisal is an unbiased estimate of the quality, value, and best use of a specific property. Appraisals may be used by prospective sellers to set a competitive price, by a lending institution to estimate the market value of a property as a condition for a mortgage loan, or by local governments to determine the assessed value of a property for tax purposes. Many real estate appraisers are independent fee appraisers or work for real estate appraisal firms, while others are employees of banks, savings and loan associations, mortgage companies, government agencies, or multiservice real estate companies.

During a property inspection, real estate appraisers investigate the quality of the construction, the overall condition of the property, and its functional design. They gather information on properties by taking measurements, interviewing persons familiar with the properties' history, and searching public records of sales, leases, assessments, and other transactions. Appraisers compare the subject property with similar properties for which recent sale prices or rental data are available, to arrive at an estimate of value. They may also estimate the current cost of reproducing any structures on the properties and how much the value of existing structures may have depreciated over time. Appraisers must consider the influence of the location of the properties, potential income, current market conditions, and real estate trends or impending changes that could influence the present and future value of the property. Depending on the purpose of the appraisal, they may estimate the market value of the property, the insurable value, the investment value, or other kinds of value. Appraisers must prepare formal written reports of their findings that meet the standards of The Appraisal Foundation.

Real estate appraisers often specialize in certain types of properties. Most appraise only homes, but others specialize in appraising apartment or office buildings, shopping centers, or a variety of other types of commercial, industrial, or agricultural properties. The amount of time necessary to do an appraisal varies by the type of property—for a residential property it may take a week, whereas for a commercial property, several months may be needed to complete the appraisal.

Working Conditions

Because of advances in telecommunications and the ability to retrieve data on properties over the Internet, a growing number of real estate agents, brokers, and appraisers work out of their homes instead of offices. Even with this convenience, much of their time is spent away from their desk—showing properties to customers, analyzing properties for sale, meeting with prospective clients, researching the state of the market, inspecting properties for appraisal, and performing a wide range of other duties.

Agents, brokers, and appraisers often work more than a standard 40-hour week; nearly 1 of every 4 worked 50 hours or more a week in 1996. They often work evenings and weekends to suit the needs of their clients.

Employment

Real estate agents, brokers, and appraisers held about 408,000 jobs in 1996. Many worked part time, combining their real estate activities with other careers. Most real estate agents and brokers were self-employed, working on a commission basis.

Most real estate and appraisal firms are relatively small; indeed, some are a one-person business. Some large real estate firms have several hundred real estate agents operating out of many branch offices. Many brokers have franchise agreements with national or regional real estate organizations. Under this type of arrangement, the

Employment of real estate appraisers is expected to grow about as fast as the average for all occupations through the year 2006.

broker pays a fee in exchange for the privilege of using the more widely known name of the parent organization. Although franchised brokers often receive help in training salespeople and in running their offices, they bear the ultimate responsibility for the success or failure of the firm.

Persons who are real estate agents, brokers, and appraisers are older, on average, than those in most other occupations. Historically, many homemakers and retired persons were attracted to real estate sales by the flexible and part-time work schedules characteristic of this field and may enter, leave, and later reenter the occupation, depending on the strength of the real estate market, family responsibilities, or other personal circumstances. Recently, however, the high startup costs associated with becoming an agent have made some look elsewhere when looking for part-time work. In addition to those entering or reentering the labor force, some transfer into real estate jobs from a wide range of occupations, including clerical and other sales jobs.

Real estate is sold and appraised in all areas, but employment is concentrated in large urban areas and in smaller, but rapidly growing communities.

Training, Other Qualifications, and Advancement

In every State and in the District of Columbia, real estate agents and brokers must be licensed. All States require prospective agents to be a high school graduate, be at least 18 years old, and pass a written test. The examination—more comprehensive for brokers than for agents—includes questions on basic real estate transactions and laws affecting the sale of property. Most States require candidates for the general sales license to complete between 30 and 90 hours of classroom instruction, whereas those seeking the broker's license are required to complete between 60 and 90 hours of formal training in addition to a specified amount of experience in selling real estate (generally 1 to 3 years). Some States waive the experience requirements for the broker's license for applicants who have a bachelor's degree in real estate. State licenses generally must be renewed every 1 or 2 years, usually without reexamination. Many States, however, require continuing education for license renewal. Prospective agents and brokers should contact the real estate licensing commission of the State(s) in which they wish to work to verify exact licensing requirements.

Federal law requires appraisers of most types of real estate (all property being financed by a Federally regulated lender) to be State licensed or certified. In some States, appraisers who are not involved with Federally regulated institutions do not have to be certified. State certification requirements for appraisers must meet Federal standards, but States are free to set more stringent requirements. Formal courses, appraisal experience, and a satisfactory score on an examination are needed to be certified. Requirements for licensure vary by State, but are somewhat less stringent than for certification. In some States, college education may be substituted for a portion of the experience requirement for licensure.

Individuals enter real estate appraisal from a variety of backgrounds. Traditionally, persons enter from real estate sales, management, and finance positions. However, as real estate transactions have become more complex, involving complicated legal requirements, many firms have turned to college graduates to fill positions. A large number of agents, brokers, and appraisers have some college training, and the number of college graduates selling real estate has risen substantially in recent years. College courses in real estate, finance and business administration, statistics, computer science, economics, and English are helpful. Because many workers start their own company, business courses such as marketing and accounting may be as important as those in real estate or finance.

However, personality traits are equally as important as academic background. Brokers look for applicants who possess a pleasant personality, honesty, and a neat appearance. Maturity, tact, and enthusiasm for the job are required in order to motivate prospective customers in this highly competitive field. Agents should also be well organized and detail oriented, as well as have a good memory for names, faces, and business details, such as taxes, zoning codes, and local land-use regulations. Appraisers should have good judgment, writing, and math skills.

Persons interested in beginning jobs as real estate agents often apply in their own communities, where their knowledge of local neighborhoods is an advantage. A beginner usually learns the practical aspects of the job, including the use of computers to locate or list available properties or identify sources of financing, under the direction of an experienced agent.

Many firms offer formal training programs for both beginners and experienced agents. Larger firms generally offer more extensive programs than smaller firms. Over 1,000 universities, colleges, and junior colleges offer courses in real estate. At some, a student can earn an associate or bachelor's degree with a major in real estate; several offer advanced degrees. Many local real estate associations that are members of the National Association of Realtors sponsor courses covering the fundamentals and legal aspects of the field. Advanced courses in appraisal, mortgage financing, property development and management, and other subjects are also available through various affiliates of the National Association of Realtors.

Many real estate appraisers voluntarily earn professional designations, representing formal recognition of their professional competence and achievements. A number of appraisal organizations have programs that, through a combination of experience, professional education, and examinations, lead to the award of such designations. These professional designations are desirable because requirements for them are more stringent than State standards.

Advancement opportunities for agents often take the form of higher commission rates and more and bigger sales, both of which increase earnings. This occurs as agents gain knowledge and expertise and become more efficient in closing a greater number of transactions. Experienced agents can advance in many large firms to sales or general manager. Persons who have received their broker's license may open their own offices. Others with experience and training in estimating property value may become real estate appraisers, and people familiar with operating and maintaining rental properties may become property managers. (See the statement on property managers elsewhere in the *Handbook*). Agents, brokers, and appraisers who gain general experience in real estate and a thorough knowledge of business conditions and property values in their localities, may enter mortgage financing or real estate investment counseling.

Job Outlook

Employment of real estate agents, brokers, and appraisers is expected to grow more slowly than the average for all occupations through the year 2006. However, a large number of job openings will arise due to replacement needs. Each year, thousands of jobs will become available as workers transfer to other occupations or leave the labor force. Because turnover is high, real estate sales positions should continue to be relatively easy to obtain. Not everyone is successful in this highly competitive field; many beginners become discouraged by their inability to get listings and to close a sufficient number of sales. Lacking financial sustenance and motivation, they subsequently leave the occupation. Well-trained, ambitious people who enjoy selling should have the best chance for success.

Increasing use of electronic information technology may increase the productivity of agents, brokers, and appraisers as the use of computers, faxes, modems, and databases becomes more commonplace. Some real estate companies are using computer generated images to show houses to customers without even leaving the office. These devices enable one agent to serve a greater number of customers. Use of this technology may eliminate some of the more marginal agents such as those practicing real estate part time or between jobs. These workers will not be able to compete as easily with full-time agents who have invested in this technology.

Another factor expected to impact the need for agents and brokers is the ability for prospective customers to search for properties that meet their criteria themselves by accessing certain real estate sites on the Internet. While they won't be able to conduct the entire real estate transaction on-line, it does allow the prospective homebuyer the convenience of looking at properties, as well as the ability to find out about issues such as financing, from their own home.

Computer technology has also impacted the need for appraisers. For example, the length of time needed to do a residential appraisal has declined as access to electronic databases has increased, streamlining their work process. Furthermore, specialized computer software programs have allowed lending institutions to derive property values without as much input from appraisers.

Employment growth in this field will stem primarily from increased demand for home purchases and rental units. Shifts in the age distribution of the population over the next decade will result in a growing number of persons in the prime working ages (25-54 years old) with careers and family responsibilities. This is the most geographically mobile group in our society, and the one that traditionally makes most of the home purchases. As their incomes rise, they also may be expected to invest in additional real estate.

Employment of real estate agents, brokers, and appraisers is sensitive to swings in the economy. During periods of declining economic activity and tight credit, the volume of sales and the resulting demand for sales workers may decline. During these periods, the earnings of agents, brokers, and appraisers decline, and many work fewer hours or leave the occupation.

Earnings

Commissions on sales are the main source of earnings of real estate agents and brokers—few receive a salary. The rate of commission varies according to the type of property and its value; the percentage paid on the sale of farm and commercial properties or unimproved land usually is higher than that paid for selling a home. Appraisers typically receive a flat fee.

Commissions may be divided among several agents and brokers. The broker and the agent in the firm who obtained the listing generally share their part of the commission when the property is sold; the broker and the agent in the firm who made the sale also generally share their part of the commission. Although an agent's share varies greatly from one firm to another, often it is about half of the total amount received by the firm. The agent who both lists and sells the property, maximizes his or her commission.

Real estate agents, brokers, and appraisers who usually worked full time had median annual earnings of $31,500 in 1996. The middle 50 percent earned between $20,500 and $49,700. The top 10 percent earned more than $75,400 and the lowest 10 percent earned less than $12,600.

Income usually increases as an agent gains experience, but individual ability, economic conditions, and the type and location of the property also affect earnings. Sales workers who are active in community organizations and local real estate associations can broaden their contacts and increase their earnings. A beginner's earnings are often irregular because a few weeks or even months may go by without a sale. Although some brokers allow an agent a drawing account against future earnings, this practice is not usual with new employees. The beginner, therefore, should have enough money to live on for about 6 months or until commissions increase.

Related Occupations

Selling expensive items such as homes requires maturity, tact, and a sense of responsibility. Other sales workers who find these character traits important in their work include motor vehicle sales workers, securities and financial services sales workers, insurance agents and brokers, and manufacturers' representatives. Other appraisers specialize in performing many types of appraisals besides real estate, including aircraft, antiques and fine arts, and business valuations.

Sources of Additional Information

Details on licensing requirements for real estate agents, brokers, and appraisers are available from most local real estate and appraiser organizations or from the State real estate commission or board.

For more information about opportunities in real estate, contact:
☞ National Association of Realtors, Realtor Information Center, 430 North Michigan Ave., Chicago, IL 60611.

Information on careers, and licensing and certification requirements, in real estate appraising is available from:
☞ The Appraisal Foundation, 1029 Vermont Avenue NW, Suite 900, Washington, DC 20005-3517.

Retail Sales Worker Supervisors and Managers

(D.O.T. 185.167-030, -038, and -046; 187.167-158; 291.157; 299.137-010 and -026)

Significant Points

- Candidates who have experience as a retail sales worker, cashier, or customer service worker should have the best opportunities.

- Work schedules may be irregular and often include evening and weekend work.

- Increasingly, a post-secondary degree is needed for advancement into upper management positions.

Nature of the Work

In every one of the thousands of retail stores across the country, there is at least one retail sales worker supervisor or manager. Because the retail trade industry provides goods and services directly to customers, the retail supervisor or manager is responsible for ensuring that customers receive satisfactory service and quality goods. They also answer customers' inquiries and handle complaints.

Retail supervisors and managers oversee the work of sales associates and cashiers, and customer service, stock, inventory, and grocery clerks. (Some of these occupations are discussed elsewhere in the *Handbook*.) They are responsible for interviewing, hiring, and training employees, as well as preparing work schedules and assigning workers to specific duties. (Managers in eating and drinking places are discussed in the *Handbook* statement on restaurant and food service managers.)

The responsibilities of retail sales worker supervisors and managers vary, depending on the size and type of establishment, as well as the level of management. As the size of retail stores and the types of goods and services increase, these workers increasingly specialize in one department or one aspect of merchandising. Larger organizations tend to have many layers of management. As in other industries, supervisory-level retail managers usually report to their mid-level counterparts who, in turn, report to top-level managers. Small stores, and stores that carry specialized merchandise, typically have fewer levels of management.

Supervisory-level retail managers, often referred to as department managers, provide day-to-day oversight of individual departments, such as shoes, cosmetics, or housewares in large department stores; produce and meat in grocery stores; and sales in automotive dealerships. Department managers commonly are found in large retail stores. These managers establish and implement policies, goals, objectives, and procedures for their specific departments; coordinate activities with other department heads; and strive for smooth operations within their departments. They supervise employees who price and ticket goods and place them on display; clean and organize shelves, displays, and inventory in stockrooms; and inspect merchandise to ensure that none is outdated. Department managers also review inventory and sales records, develop merchandising techniques, coordinate sales promotions, and may greet and assist customers and promote sales and good public relations.

In small or independent retail stores, retail sales worker supervisors and managers not only directly supervise sales associates, but are also responsible for the operation of the entire store. In these instances, they may be called store managers. Some are also store owners.

Advancement opportunities for retail sales worker supervisors and managers are often in the form of promotion to assistant store manager or store manager positions.

Working Conditions

Most retail sales worker supervisors and managers have offices within the stores. Although some time is spent in the office completing merchandise orders or arranging work schedules, a large portion of a their workday is spent on the sales floor.

Work hours of supervisors and managers vary greatly among retail establishments, with work schedules usually depending on consumers' needs. Most managers and supervisors work 40 hours or more a week. This is especially true during holidays, busy shopping hours and seasons, sales, and when inventory is taken. They are expected to work evenings and weekends but usually are compensated by getting a weekday off. Hours can change weekly, and managers sometimes may have to report to work on short notice, especially when employees are absent. Independent owners can often set their own schedules, but hours usually must be convenient to customers.

Employment

Retail sales worker supervisors and managers who work in retail trade held about 929,000 wage and salary jobs in 1996. In addition, there were thousands of self-employed retail sales managers, mainly store owners. Although managers are found throughout the retail trade industry, establishments that employ the most are grocery, department, and clothing and accessory stores.

Training, Other Qualifications, and Advancement

Knowledge of management principles and practices, often an essential requirement for a management position in retail trade, is usually acquired through work experience. Many supervisors and managers begin their careers on the sales floor as sales clerks, cashiers, or customer service workers. In these positions, they learn merchandising, customer service, and the basic policies and procedures of the store.

The educational background of retail sales worker supervisors and managers varies widely. Regardless of the education received, business courses, including accounting; administration; marketing; management; and sales; as well as courses in psychology; sociology; and communication; are helpful. Supervisors and managers increasingly must be computer literate since cash registers and inventory control systems have become computerized.

Most supervisors and managers who have post-secondary education hold associate or bachelor's degrees in liberal arts, social science, business, or management. To gain experience, many post-secondary students participate in internship programs that are usually planned between individual schools and retail firms.

Once on the job, the type and amount of training available for supervisors and managers varies from store to store. Many national chains have formal training programs for management trainees that include both classroom and in-store training. Training may last from 1 week to 1 year or more, as many retail organizations require their trainees to gain experience during all shopping seasons. Other retail organizations may not have formal training programs.

Ordinarily, classroom training includes such topics as interviewing and customer service skills, employee and inventory management, and scheduling. Management trainees may be placed in one specific department while training on the job, or they may be rotated through several departments to gain a well-rounded knowledge of the store's operation. Training programs for franchises are generally extensive, covering all functions of the company's operation, including promotion, marketing, management, finance, purchasing, product preparation, human resource management, and compensation. College graduates can usually enter management training programs directly.

Retail sales worker supervisors and managers must get along with all types of people. They need initiative, self-discipline, good judgment, and decisiveness. Patience and a mild temperament are necessary when dealing with demanding customers. They must also be able to motivate, organize, and direct the work of subordinates and communicate clearly and persuasively with customers and other managers.

Individuals who display leadership and team building skills, self-confidence, motivation, and decisiveness become candidates for promotion to assistant store manager or store manager. Increasingly, a post-secondary degree is needed for advancement, because it is viewed by employers as a sign of motivation and maturity—qualities deemed important for promotion to more responsible positions. In many retail establishments, managers are promoted from within the company. In small retail establishments, where the number of positions is limited, advancement to a higher management position may come slowly. Large establishments most often have extensive career ladder programs and may offer managers the opportunity to transfer to another store in the chain or to the central office if an opening occurs. Promotions may occur more quickly in large establishments, but relocation every several years may also be necessary for advancement. Within a central office, sales supervisors and managers can become marketing, advertising, or public relations managers. These managers coordinate marketing plans, monitor sales, and propose advertisements and promotions. Supervisors and managers can also become purchasers or buyers, who purchase goods and supplies for their organization or for resale. (Both occupations are covered in other *Handbook* statements.)

Some supervisors and managers, who have worked in the retail industry for a long time, decide to open their own stores. However, retail trade is highly competitive, and although many independent retail owners succeed, some fail to cover expenses and eventually go out of business. To prosper, retail owners usually need good business sense and strong customer service and public relations skills.

Job Outlook
Because most jobs for retail sales worker supervisors and managers do not require post-secondary education, competition is expected for jobs with the most attractive earnings and working conditions. Candidates who have retail experience will have the best opportunities.

Employment of wage and salary retail sales worker supervisors and managers is expected to grow more slowly than the average for all occupations through the year 2006. Growth in this occupation will be restrained as retail companies place more emphasis on sales staff employment levels and increase the number of responsibilities their retail sales worker supervisors and managers have. Furthermore, some companies have begun requiring their sales staff to report directly to upper management personnel, bypassing the department-level manager. However, many job openings are expected to occur as experienced supervisors and managers move into higher levels of management, transfer to other occupations, or leave the labor force.

Projected employment growth of retail managers will mirror, in part, the patterns of employment growth in the industries in which they are concentrated. For example, faster than average growth is expected

in grocery stores as they expand their selection of merchandise to accommodate customers' desires for one-stop shopping.

Unlike middle- and upper-level management positions, store-level retail supervisors and managers generally will not be affected by the restructuring and consolidating that is taking place at the corporate and headquarters level of many retail chain companies.

Earnings
Salaries of retail managers vary substantially, depending upon the level of responsibility; length of service; and type, size, and location of the firm.

Supervisors or managers of sales workers in the retail trade industry who usually worked full time had median annual earnings of $24,400 in 1996. The middle 50 percent earned between $16,900 and $34,400. The top 10 percent earned more than $50,400, and the lowest 10 percent earned less than $12,900.

According to a survey sponsored by the National Association of Convenience Stores, the average total compensation for assistant store managers in the U.S. and Canada ranged between $12,400 and $15,800 a year in 1996, depending on where the organization is located. Store managers received between $24,400 and $31,200 on average.

Compensation systems vary by type of establishment and merchandise sold. Many managers receive a commission, or a combination of salary and commission. Under a commission system, retail managers receive a percentage of department or store sales. These systems offer managers the opportunity to significantly increase their earnings, but they may find that their earnings depend on their ability to sell their product and the condition of the economy. Those managers who sell large amounts of merchandise often are rewarded with bonuses and awards and receive recognition throughout the store or chain.

Retail managers receive typical benefits and, in some cases, stock options. In addition, retail managers generally are able to buy their store's merchandise at a discount.

Related Occupations
Retail supervisors and managers serve customers, supervise workers, and direct and coordinate the operations of an establishment. Others with similar responsibilities include managers in wholesale trade, hotels, banks, and hospitals.

Sources of Additional Information
Information on employment opportunities for retail managers may be obtained from the employment offices of various retail establishments or State employment service offices.

General information on management careers in retail establishments is available from:

☛ National Retail Federation, 325 7th St. NW., Suite 1000, Washington, DC 20004. Homepage: http://www.nrf.com

☛ International Mass Retail Association, 1700 N. Moore St., Suite 2250, Arlington, VA 22209-1998. Homepage: http://www.imra.org

Information on management careers in grocery stores, and schools offering related programs, is available from:

☛ Food Marketing Institute, 800 Connecticut Ave. NW., Publications Dept., Washington, DC 20006-2701.

Information about management careers and training programs in the motor vehicle dealers industry is available from:

☛ National Automobile Dealers Association, Communications/Public Relations Dept., 8400 Westpark Dr., McLean, VA 22102-3591.

Information about management careers in convenience stores is available from:

☛ National Association of Convenience Stores, 1605 King St., Alexandria, VA 22314-2792.

Information about management careers in service stations is available from:

☛ Service Station Dealers of America, 9420 Annapolis Rd., Suite 307, Lanham, MD 20706.

Retail Sales Workers

(List of D.O.T. codes available on request. See page 496.)

Significant Points

- Good employment opportunities are expected due to the need to replace the large number who leave the occupation each year.

- Most salespersons can expect to work some evening and weekend hours, and longer than normal hours may be scheduled during Christmas and other peak retail periods. Plentiful opportunities for part time work exist.

Nature of the Work

Whether selling shoes, computer equipment, or automobiles, retail sales workers assist customers in finding what they are looking for and try to interest them in the merchandise. This may be done by describing a product's features, demonstrating its use, or showing various models and colors. For some sales jobs, particularly those selling expensive and complex items, special knowledge or skills are needed. For example, workers who sell automobiles must be able to explain to customers the features of various models, the meaning of manufacturers' specifications, and the types of options and financing that are available.

Consumers, who spend millions of dollars a day on merchandise, often form their impressions of a store by evaluating its sales force. Therefore, retailers are increasingly stressing the importance of providing courteous and efficient service, in order to remain competitive. When a customer wants an item that is not on the sales floor, for example, the sales worker may check the stockroom or place a special order or call another store to locate the item.

In addition to selling, most retail sales workers, especially those who work in department and apparel stores, make out sales checks; receive cash, check, and charge payments; bag or package purchases; and give change and receipts. Depending on the hours they work, retail sales workers may have to open or close cash registers. This may include counting the money; separating charge slips, coupons, and exchange vouchers; and making deposits at the cash office. Sales workers are often held responsible for the contents of their registers, and repeated shortages are cause for dismissal in many organizations. (Cashiers, who have similar job duties, are discussed elsewhere in the *Handbook*.)

Sales workers may also handle returns and exchanges of merchandise, perform gift wrapping services, and keep their work areas neat. In addition, they may help stock shelves or racks, arrange for mailing or delivery of purchases, mark price tags, take inventory, and prepare displays.

Frequently, sales workers must be aware of, not only the promotions their store is sponsoring, but also those that are being sponsored by competitors. Also, salespersons must often recognize possible security risks and know how to handle such situations.

Although most sales workers have many duties and responsibilities, in jobs selling standardized articles, such hardware, linens, and housewares, they often do little more than take payments and wrap purchases.

Working Conditions

Most sales workers in retail trade work in clean, comfortable, well-lighted stores. However, they often stand for long periods and may need supervisory approval to leave the sales floor.

The Monday through Friday, 9 to 5 work week is the exception, rather than the rule, in retail trade. Most salespersons can expect to work some evening and weekend hours, and longer than normal hours may be scheduled during Christmas and other peak retail periods. In addition, most retailers restrict the use of vacation time from Thanksgiving until early January.

Retail sales workers must be able to communicate clearly with customers.

This job can be rewarding for those who enjoy working with people. Patience is required, however, when the work is repetitious and the customers demanding.

Employment

Retail sales workers held about 4,522,000 jobs in 1996. They worked in stores ranging from small specialty shops employing several workers, to giant department stores with hundreds of salespersons. In addition, some were self-employed representatives of direct sales companies and mail-order houses. The largest employers of retail sales workers, however, are department stores, clothing and accessories stores, furniture and home furnishing stores, and motor vehicle dealers.

This occupation offers many opportunities for part-time work and is especially appealing to students, retirees, and others looking to supplement their income. However, most of those selling "big ticket" items, such as cars, furniture, and electronic equipment, work full time and have substantial experience.

Because retail stores are found in every city and town, employment is distributed geographically in much the same way as the population.

Training, Other Qualifications, and Advancement

There usually are no formal education requirements for this type of work, although a high school diploma or equivalent is increasingly preferred. Employers look for persons who enjoy working with people and have the tact and patience to deal with difficult customers. Among other desirable characteristics are an interest in sales work, a neat appearance, and the ability to communicate clearly and effectively. The ability to speak more than one language may be helpful for employment in stores in communities where people from various cultures tend to live and shop. Before hiring a sales worker, some employers may conduct a background check, especially for a job selling high-priced items.

In most small stores, an experienced employee, or the proprietor, instructs newly-hired sales personnel in making out sales checks and operating cash registers. In large stores, training programs are more formal and usually conducted over several days. Topics usually discussed are customer service, security, the store's policies and procedures, and how to work a cash register. Depending on the type of product they are selling, they may be given additional specialized training by manufacturers' representatives. For example, those working in cosmetics receive instruction on the types of products available and for whom the cosmetics would be most beneficial. Likewise, sales workers employed by motor vehicle dealers may be required to participate in training programs, designed to provide information on the technical details of standard and optional equipment available on new models. Because providing the best service to customers is a high priority for many employers, employees are often given periodic training to update and refine their skills.

As salespersons gain experience and seniority, they usually move to positions of greater responsibility and may be given their choice of departments. This often means moving to areas with potentially higher earnings and commissions. The highest earnings potential is usually found in selling big-ticket items. This type of position often requires the most knowledge of the product and the greatest talent for persuasion.

Traditionally, capable sales workers without college degrees could advance to management positions; but today, large retail businesses generally prefer to hire college graduates as management trainees, making a college education increasingly important. Despite this trend, capable employees without college degrees should still be able to advance to administrative or supervisory positions in large establishments.

Opportunities for advancement vary in small stores. In some establishments, advancement is limited, because one person, often the owner, does most of the managerial work. In others, however, some sales workers are promoted to assistant managers.

Retail selling experience may be an asset when applying for sales positions with larger retailers or in other industries, such as financial services, wholesale trade, or manufacturing.

Job Outlook

As in the past, employment opportunities for retail sales workers are expected to continue to be good because of the many job openings created each year due to the need to replace the large number of workers who transfer to other occupations or leave the labor force. Additional openings will be created by growth in employment of retail sales workers, which is expected to increase about as fast as the average for all occupations through the year 2006 due to anticipated growth in retail sales created by a growing population. There will continue to be many opportunities for part-time workers, and demand will be strong for temporary workers during peak selling periods, such as the Christmas season.

During economic downturns, sales volumes and the resulting demand for sales workers generally decline. Purchases of costly items, such as cars, appliances, and furniture, tend to be postponed during difficult economic times. In areas of high unemployment, sales of many types of goods decline. However, because turnover of sales workers is usually very high, employers often can control employment simply by not replacing all those who leave.

Earnings

The starting wage for many retail sales positions is the Federal minimum wage, which was $5.15 an hour in 1997. In some areas where employers are having difficulty attracting and retaining workers, wages are higher than the established minimum. The following

tabulation shows 1996 median weekly earnings by class of sales worker:

Motor vehicle and boats	$593
Radio, television, hi-fi, and appliances	423
Parts	409
Furniture and home furnishings	403
Hardware and building supplies	372
Street and door-to-door sales workers	372
Shoes	328
Apparel	265

Compensation systems vary by type of establishment and merchandise sold. Sales workers receive either hourly wages, commissions, or a combination of wages and commissions. Under a commission system, salespersons receive a percentage of the sales that they make. This system offers sales workers the opportunity to significantly increase their earnings, but they may find their earnings depend on their ability to sell their product and the ups and downs of the economy. Employers may use incentive programs such as awards, banquets, and profit-sharing plans to promote teamwork among the sales staff.

Benefits may be limited in smaller stores, but in large establishments benefits are usually comparable to those offered by other employers. In addition, nearly all sales workers are able to buy their store's merchandise at a discount, with the savings depending upon on the type of merchandise.

Related Occupations

Sales workers use sales techniques, coupled with their knowledge of merchandise, to assist customers and encourage purchases. These skills are used by people in a number of other occupations, including manufacturers' and wholesale trade sales representatives, service sales representatives, securities and financial services sales representatives, counter and rental clerks, real estate sales agents, purchasers and buyers, insurance agents and brokers, and cashiers.

Sources of Additional Information

Information on careers in retail sales may be obtained from the personnel offices of local stores, or from State merchants' associations.

General information about retailing is available from:

☛ National Retail Federation, 325 7th St. NW., Suite 1000, Washington, DC 20004. Homepage: http://www.nrf.com

☛ International Mass Retail Association, 1700 N. Moore St., Suite 2250, Arlington, VA 22209-1998.

Information about retail sales employment opportunities is available from:

☛ United Food and Commercial Workers International Union, Education Office, 1775 K St. NW., Washington, DC 20006-1502.

Information about training for a career in automobile sales is available from:

☛ National Automobile Dealers Association, Communications/Public Relations Dept., 8400 Westpark Dr., McLean, VA 22102-3591.

Securities and Financial Services Sales Representatives

(D.O.T. 162.167-034 and -038; 250.257-014, -018, and -022.)

Significant Points

- A college degree and sales ability are among the most important qualifications.

- Employment is expected to grow much faster than average as investment increases.

• Many beginning securities sales representatives leave the occupation because they are unable to establish a sufficient clientele; once established, however, these workers have a very strong attachment to their occupation because of high earnings and the considerable investment in training.

Nature of the Work

Most investors, whether they are individuals with a few hundred dollars to invest or large institutions with millions, use *securities sales representatives* when buying or selling stocks, bonds, shares in mutual funds, insurance annuities, or other financial products. Securities sales representatives often are called stock brokers, registered representatives, or account executives.

When an investor wishes to buy or sell securities, sales representatives may relay the order through their firms' offices to the floor of a securities exchange, such as the New York Stock Exchange. There, securities sales representatives known as brokers' floor representatives buy and sell securities. If a security is not traded on an exchange, the sales representative sends the order to the firm's trading department, where it is traded directly with a dealer in an over-the-counter market, such as the NASDAQ computerized trading system. After the transaction has been completed, the sales representative notifies the customer of the final price.

Securities sales representatives also provide many related services for their customers. They may explain the meaning of stock market terms and trading practices; offer financial counseling; devise an individual client financial portfolio, including securities, life insurance, corporate and municipal bonds, mutual funds, certificates of deposit, annuities, and other investments; and offer advice on the purchase or sale of particular securities.

Not all customers have the same investment goals. Some individuals prefer long-term investments for capital growth or to provide income over the years; others might want to invest in speculative securities that they hope will rise in price quickly. Securities sales representatives furnish information about advantages and disadvantages of an investment based on each person's objectives. They also supply the latest price quotations on any security in which an investor is interested, as well as information on the activities and financial positions of the corporations issuing these securities.

Most securities sales representatives serve individual investors, but others specialize in institutional investors. In institutional investing, most sales representatives concentrate on a specific financial product, such as stocks, bonds, options, annuities, or commodity futures. Some handle the sale of new issues, such as corporate securities issued to finance plant expansion.

The most important part of a sales representative's job is finding clients and building a customer base. Thus, beginning securities sales representatives spend much of their time searching for customers—relying heavily on telephone solicitation. They may meet some clients through business and social contacts. Many sales representatives find it useful to get additional exposure by teaching adult education investment courses or by giving lectures at libraries or social clubs. Brokerage firms may give sales representatives lists of people with whom the firm has done business in the past. Sometimes sales representatives inherit the clients of representatives who have retired.

Financial services sales representatives sell banking and related services. They contact potential customers to explain their services and to ascertain customers' banking and other financial needs. They may discuss services such as deposit accounts, lines of credit, sales or inventory financing, certificates of deposit, cash management, or investment services. They may solicit businesses to participate in consumer credit card programs. At most small and medium-size banks, branch managers and commercial loan officers are responsible for marketing the bank's financial services. As banks offer more and increasingly complex financial services—for example, securities brokerage and financial planning—the job of financial services sales representative is assuming greater importance.

Financial planners, using their knowledge of tax and investment strategies, securities, insurance, pension plans, and real estate, develop and implement financial plans for individuals and businesses. They interview clients to determine their assets, liabilities, cash flow, insurance coverage, tax status, and financial objectives. Then they analyze this information and develop a financial plan tailored to each client's needs.

Working Conditions

Securities sales representatives usually work in offices, where there is much activity. They have access to "quote boards" or computer terminals that continually provide information on the prices of securities. When sales activity increases, due perhaps to unanticipated changes in the economy, the pace can become very hectic.

Established securities sales representatives usually work the same hours as others in the business community. Beginners who are seeking customers may work much longer hours, however. Most securities sales representatives accommodate customers by meeting with them in the evenings or on weekends.

Financial services sales representatives normally work in a comfortable, less stressful office environment. They generally work 40 hours a week. They may spend considerable time outside the office meeting with present and prospective clients, attending civic functions, and participating in trade association meetings. Some financial services sales representatives work exclusively inside banks, providing service to "walk-in" customers.

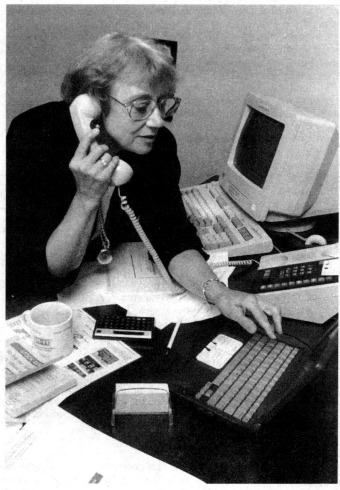

Securities sales representatives need good sales ability and communication skills.

Employment

Securities and financial services sales representatives held 263,000 jobs in 1996; securities sales representatives accounted for 8 out of 10. In addition, a substantial number of people in other occupations sold securities. These include partners and branch office managers in securities firms, as well as insurance agents and brokers offering securities to their customers.

Securities sales representatives are employed by brokerage and investment firms in all parts of the country. Many of these firms are very small. Most sales representatives, however, work for a small number of large firms with main offices in large cities, especially New York.

Financial services sales representatives are employed by banks, savings and loan associations, and other credit institutions.

Training, Other Qualifications, and Advancement

Because securities sales representatives must be well informed about economic conditions and trends, a college education is increasingly important, especially in the larger securities firms. In fact, the overwhelming majority of workers in this occupation are college graduates. Although employers seldom require specialized academic training, courses in business administration, economics, and finance are helpful.

Many employers consider personal qualities and skills more important than academic training. Employers seek applicants who have good sales ability and communication skills, are well groomed, and have a strong desire to succeed. Self-confidence and an ability to handle frequent rejections also are important ingredients for success.

Because maturity and the ability to work independently also are important, many employers prefer to hire those who have achieved success in other jobs. Some firms prefer candidates with sales experience, particularly those who have worked on commission in areas such as real estate or insurance. Therefore, most entrants to this occupation transfer from other jobs. Some begin working as securities sales representatives following retirement from other fields.

Securities sales representatives must meet State licensing requirements, which generally include passing an examination and, in some cases, furnishing a personal bond. In addition, sales representatives must register as representatives of their firm, according to regulations of the securities exchanges where they do business or the National Association of Securities Dealers, Inc. (NASD). Before beginners can qualify as registered representatives, they must pass the General Securities Registered Representative Examination, administered by the NASD, and be an employee of a registered firm for at least 4 months. Most States require a second examination—the Uniform Securities Agents State Law Examination. These tests measure the prospective representative's knowledge of the securities business, customer protection requirements, and recordkeeping procedures. Many take correspondence courses in preparation for the securities examinations.

Most employers provide on-the-job training to help securities sales representatives meet the requirements for registration. In most firms, this training period takes about 4 months. Trainees in large firms may receive classroom instruction in securities analysis, effective speaking, and the finer points of selling; take courses offered by business schools and associations; and undergo a period of on-the-job training lasting up to 2 years. Many firms like to rotate their trainees among various departments in the firm, to give them a broad perspective of the securities business. In small firms, sales representatives often receive training in outside institutions and on the job.

Securities sales representatives must understand the basic characteristics of a wide variety of financial products offered by brokerage firms. Representatives periodically take training, through their firms or outside institutions, to keep abreast of new financial products as they are introduced on the market and to improve their sales techniques. Training in the use of computers is important, as the securities sales business is highly automated.

The principal form of advancement for securities sales representatives is an increase in the number and size of the accounts they handle. Although beginners usually service the accounts of individual investors, eventually they may handle very large institutional accounts, such as those of banks and pension funds. Some experienced sales representatives become branch office managers and supervise other sales representatives while continuing to provide services for their own customers. A few representatives advance to top management positions or become partners in their firms.

Banks and other credit institutions prefer to hire college graduates for financial services sales jobs. A business administration degree with a specialization in finance or a liberal arts degree including courses in accounting, economics, and marketing serves as excellent preparation for this job.

Financial services sales representatives learn through on-the-job training under the supervision of bank officers. Outstanding performance can lead to promotion to managerial positions.

Job Outlook

Due to the highly competitive nature of securities sales work, many beginners leave the occupation because they are unable to establish a sufficient clientele. Once established, however, securities sales representatives have a very strong attachment to their occupation because of high earnings and the considerable investment in training.

The demand for securities sales representatives fluctuates, as the economy expands and contracts. Thus, in an economic downturn, the number of persons seeking jobs usually exceeds the number of openings—sometimes by a great deal. Even during periods of rapid economic expansion, competition for securities sales training positions—particularly in larger firms—is keen, because of potentially high earnings.

Job opportunities for both securities and financial services sales representatives should be best for mature individuals with successful work experience. Opportunities for inexperienced sales representatives should be best in smaller firms.

Employment of securities sales representatives is expected to grow much faster than the average for all occupations through the year 2006, as economic growth, rising personal incomes, and greater inherited wealth increase the funds available for investment. As banks offer increasingly complex financial services, employment of financial services sales representatives should grow rapidly, even as overall employment in banking declines and more people conduct their banking from home via personal computer.

More individual investors are expected to purchase common stocks, mutual funds, and other financial products after seeking advice from securities sales representatives regarding the increasing array of investment alternatives. Deregulation has enabled brokerage firms to sell certificates of deposit, offer checking and deposit services through cash management accounts, and sell insurance products, such as annuities and life insurance. Growth in the number and size of institutional investors will be strong, as more people enroll in pension plans, set up individual retirement accounts, establish trust funds, and contribute to the endowment funds of colleges and other nonprofit institutions. Additional representatives also will be needed to sell securities issued by new and expanding corporations, by State and local governments financing public improvements, and by foreign governments, whose securities have become attractive to U.S. investors, as international trade expands.

Investors increasingly rely on the growing number of financial planners to assist them in selecting the proper options among a wide variety of financial alternatives. In addition, demand should increase as banks and credit institutions expand the range of financial services they offer and issue more loans for personal and commercial use.

Earnings

In 1996, median annual earnings of securities and financial services sales representatives were $38,800; the middle 50 percent earned between $24,300 and $73,500. Ten percent earned less than $18,100 and 10 percent earned more than $98,400. On average, financial services sales representatives earn considerably less than securities sales representatives.

Trainees usually are paid an hourly wage or salary, until they meet licensing and registration requirements. After candidates are licensed and registered, their earnings depend on commissions from the sale or purchase of stocks and bonds, life insurance, or other securities for customers. Commission earnings are likely to be high when there is much buying and selling and low when there is a slump in market activity. Most firms provide sales representatives with a steady income by paying a "draw against commission"—a minimum salary based on commissions which they can be expected to earn. Securities sales representatives who can provide their clients with the most complete financial services should enjoy the greatest income stability.

Financial services sales representatives usually are paid a salary; some receive a bonus, if they meet certain established goals.

Related Occupations
Similar sales jobs requiring specialized knowledge include insurance agents and real estate agents.

Sources of Additional Information
Information about job opportunities as a securities sales representative may be obtained from the personnel departments of individual securities firms.

For information about job opportunities for financial services sales representatives in various States, contact State bankers' associations or write directly to a particular bank.

Services Sales Representatives

(D.O.T. 165.157; 236.252; 250.357-022; 251.157, .257, .357; 252.257, .357; 253; 254; 259 except .257-014; 269.357-018; 273.357-014; 279.357-042; and 293 except .137-010 and .357-018)

Significant Points
- A significant part of earnings may be in the form of commissions, which can vary considerably depending on performance.
- Considerable travel may be required.

Nature of the Work
Services sales representatives sell a wide variety of services. For example, sales representatives for data processing services firms sell complex services such as inventory control, payroll processing, sales analysis, and financial reporting systems. Hotel sales representatives contact government, business, and social groups to solicit convention and conference business. Sales representatives for temporary help services firms locate and acquire clients who will hire the firm's employees. Telephone services sales representatives visit commercial customers to review their telephone systems, analyze their communications needs, and recommend services, such as installation of additional equipment. Other representatives sell automotive leasing, public utility, burial, shipping, protective, and management consulting services. (Information on other sales workers, including insurance agents and brokers, real estate agents and brokers, securities and financial services sales representatives, retail sales workers, manufacturers' and wholesale sales representatives, and travel agents, appears in other *Handbook* statements.)

Services sales representatives act as industry experts, consultants, and problem solvers when selling their firm's services. The sales representative, in some cases, creates demand for his or her firm's services. A prospective client who is asked to consider buying a particular service may never have used, or even been aware of a need for, that service. For example, wholesalers might be persuaded to order a list of credit ratings for checking their customers' credit prior to making sales, because the list could be used to solicit new business.

There are several different categories of services sales jobs. *Outside sales representatives* call on clients and prospects at their homes or offices. They may have an appointment, or they may practice "cold calling," arriving without an appointment. *Inside sales representatives* work on their employer's premises, assisting individuals

Skill, knowledge, and personality are important for the necessary rapport between services sales representatives and their clients.

interested in the company's services. *Telemarketing sales representatives* sell over the telephone. They make large numbers of calls to prospects, attempting to sell the company's service themselves, or to arrange an appointment between the prospect and an outside sales representative. Some sales representatives deal exclusively with one, or a few, major clients.

Despite the diversity of services sold, the jobs of all services sales representatives have much in common. All sales representatives follow similar procedures and must fully understand and be able to discuss the services their company offers. Many sales representatives develop lists of prospective clients through telephone and business directories, asking business associates and customers for leads, and calling on new businesses as they cover their assigned territory. Some services sales representatives acquire clients through inquiries about their company's services.

Regardless of how they first meet the client, all services sales representatives must explain how the offered services meet the client's needs. This often involves demonstrations of the company's services. They answer questions about the nature and cost of the services and try to overcome objections in order to persuade potential customers to purchase the services. If they fail to make a sale on the first visit, they may follow up with more visits, letters, or phone calls. After closing a sale, services sales representatives generally follow up to see that the purchase meets the customer's needs, and to determine if additional services can be sold. Good customer service is becoming increasingly important and can give a company a competitive advantage.

Because services sales representatives obtain many of their new accounts through referrals, their success hinges on developing a satisfied clientele who will continue to use the services and recommend them to other potential customers. Like other types of sales jobs, a services sales representative's reputation is crucial to his or her success.

Services sales work varies with the kind of service sold. Selling highly technical services, such as communications systems or computer consulting services, involves complex and lengthy sales negotiations. In addition, sales of such complex services may require extensive after-sale support. In these situations, sales representatives may operate as part of a team of sales representatives and experts from other departments. Sales representatives receive valuable technical assistance from these experts. For example, those who sell data processing services might work with a systems engineer or computer scientist, and those who sell telephone services might receive technical assistance from a communications consultant. Teams enhance customer service and build strong long-term relationships with customers, resulting in increased sales.

Because of the length of time between the initial contact with a customer and the actual sale, representatives who sell complex technical services generally work with several customers simultaneously. Sales representatives must be well organized and efficient in managing their work. Selling less complex services, such as linen supply or pest control services, generally involves simpler and shorter sales negotiations.

A sales representative's job may also vary with the size of the employer. Those working for large companies are generally more specialized and are assigned a specific territory, a specific line of services, and their own accounts. In smaller companies, sales representatives may have broader responsibilities—administrative, marketing, or public relations, for example—in addition to their sales duties.

A sales representative often services a specific territory. A representative for a company offering services widely used by the general public, such as lawn care, generally has numerous clients in a relatively small territory. On the other hand, a sales representative for a more specialized organization, such as a standardized testing service, may need to service several States to acquire an adequate customer base.

Working Conditions
Working conditions for sales representatives vary. Outside sales representatives responsible for a large territory may spend a great deal of time traveling, sometimes for weeks at a time. Representatives with smaller territories may seldom, or never, travel overnight. Outside sales representatives may spend part of their time in an office keeping records, preparing various documents, and setting up appointments with customers. Increasingly, sales representatives may share office space with others rather than have their own permanently assigned space. Inside sales representatives and telemarketers spend all their time in their offices, which can range from bright and cheerful customer showrooms to cramped and noisy rooms. Many outside sales representatives have the flexibility to set their own schedules as long as they meet their company's goals.

Selling is stressful work. Companies generally set sales quotas and have contests with prizes for those who make the most sales. There often is considerable pressure on the sales representative to meet monthly sales quotas. Many sales representatives work more than 40 hours per week.

Employment
Services sales representatives held over 694,000 wage and salary jobs in 1996. Over half were in firms providing business services, including computer and data processing; personnel supply; advertising; mailing, reproduction, and stenographic services; and equipment rental and leasing. Other sales representatives worked for firms offering a wide range of other services, as the following tabulation shows.

Total (percent)	100
Business services	59
Computer and data processing	10
Personnel supply	10
Advertising	7
Mailing, reproduction, and stenographic	3
Miscellaneous equipment rental and leasing	3
Miscellaneous business services	26
Engineering and management services	11
Personal services	5
Amusement and recreation services	5
Automotive repair services	4
Membership organizations	3
Hotels and other lodging places	2
Motion pictures	2
Health services	2
Social services	2
All other services	5

Training, Other Qualifications, and Advancement
Some employers require services sales representatives to have a college degree, but requirements vary depending on the industry a company represents. Employers who market advertising services seek individuals with a college degree in advertising, marketing or business administration. Companies marketing educational services prefer individuals

with a degree in education, marketing or a related field. Many hotels seek graduates from college hotel or tourism administration programs. Companies selling computer, communications, engineering and other highly technical services generally require a bachelor's degree appropriate to their field. Certification and licensing is also becoming more common for technical sales representatives.

Employers may hire sales representatives with only a high school diploma if they have a proven sales record. This is particularly true for those who sell nontechnical services, such as linen supply, pest control, cleaning services, or funeral services. Applicants enhance their chances of being hired into these positions if they have taken some college courses.

Many firms conduct intensive training programs for their sales representatives, including the history of the business, origin, development, and uses of the service, effective prospecting methods, presentation of the service, answering customer objections, creating customer demand, closing a sale, using the company's computer system, entering an order, company policies, communications technology, and the use of technical support personnel. Sales representatives may also attend seminars on a wide range of subjects given by outside or in-house training institutions. These sessions acquaint them with new services and products, and help them maintain and update their sales techniques, and may include motivational or sensitivity training to make sales representatives more effective in dealing with people.

Large companies often hire sales representatives directly out of college and closely monitor their progress while training them. In general, smaller companies prefer to hire individuals with a proven sales record because they cannot afford the expense of providing formal training programs.

In order to be successful, sales representatives should be persuasive and have a pleasant, outgoing, and enthusiastic disposition. Sales representatives must be highly motivated, energetic, well organized, and efficient. Good grooming and a neat appearance are essential, as are self-confidence, reliability, and the ability to communicate effectively both orally, and in writing. Sales representatives should be self-starters who have the ability to work under pressure to meet sales goals. They must also have a thorough knowledge of the service they are selling, and be able to anticipate and respond to their clients' questions and objections in a professional manner.

Sales representatives with good sales records and leadership ability may advance to supervisory and managerial positions. Frequent contact with business people in other firms provides sales workers with leads about job openings, enhancing advancement opportunities.

Job Outlook
Employment of services sales representatives, as a group, is expected to grow much faster than the average for all occupations through the year 2006, in response to growth of the services industries employing them. However, the projected growth of particular services industries varies. For example, the continued growth in factory and office automation should lead to much faster than average employment growth for computer and data processing services sales representatives. Growth will be tempered in some industries by the expanded use of various technologies, such as voice and electronic mail, cellular telephones, and laptop computers that increase sales workers' productivity.

In addition to the jobs generated by this growth, openings will occur each year because of the need to replace sales workers who transfer to other occupations or leave the labor force. Each year, many sales representatives discover they are unable to earn enough money and leave the occupation. Turnover is generally higher among representatives who sell nontechnical services, because they have invested less time and effort in specialized training. As a result of this turnover, job opportunities should be good, especially for those with a college degree or a proven sales record.

With improved technology, companies are finding it harder to justify the expense of travel, on-site presentations, waiting, and the preparation that supports those activities. Therefore, many companies are putting more emphasis on in-house sales by phone and other methods, and less emphasis on the use of outside sales staff. In addition, temporary or contract sales people are used more frequently for outside sales.

Earnings

In 1996, the median annual income for full-time advertising sales representatives was $26,000, while representatives selling other business services earned $30,264. Earnings of representatives who sold technical services were generally higher than earnings of those who sold nontechnical services.

Earnings of experienced sales representatives depend on performance. Successful sales representatives who establish a strong customer base can earn more than managers in their firm. According to Dartnell Corporation's 1996 Sales Compensation Survey, entry-level sales representatives received $36,000 in average total cash compensation, intermediate-level sales representatives earned $46,000, and senior sales representatives received $63,000.

Sales representatives are paid in a variety of ways. Some receive a straight salary; others are paid solely on a commission basis—a percentage of the dollar value of their sales. Most firms use a combination of salary and commissions. Some services sales representatives receive a base salary, plus incentive pay that can add 25 to 75 percent to the sales representative's base salary. In addition to the same benefits package received by other employees of the firm, outside sales representatives have expense accounts to cover meals and travel, and some drive a company car. Many employers offer bonuses, including vacation trips and prizes, for sales that exceed company quotas.

Because sales are affected by changing economic conditions and consumer and business expectations, earnings may vary greatly from year to year.

Related Occupations

Services sales representatives must have sales ability and knowledge of the service they sell. Workers in other occupations requiring these skills include real estate agents, insurance agents, securities and financial services sales representatives, retail sales workers, manufacturers' and wholesale sales representatives, and travel agents.

Sources of Additional Information

For details about employment opportunities for services sales representatives, contact:

Sales and Marketing Executives International, 6600 Hidden Lake Trail, Brecksville, OH 44141.

Travel Agents

(D.O.T. 252.152-010)

Significant Points

- Training at a postsecondary vocational school or college or university is increasingly important for getting a job.

- Projected faster-than-average employment growth reflects expected increases in spending on pleasure and business travel.

Nature of the Work

Constantly changing air fares and schedules, thousands of available vacation packages and business/pleasure trips, and the vast amount of travel information advertised on the Internet, makes travel planning frustrating and time-consuming. Many people who travel turn to travel agents, who assess their needs and make the best possible travel arrangements for them. Also, many major cruise lines, resorts, and specialty travel groups use travel agents to promote travel packages to the millions of people who travel every year.

Depending on the needs of the client, travel agents give advice on destinations, make arrangements for transportation, hotel accommodations, car rentals, tours, and recreation, or plan the right vacation package or business/pleasure trip. They may also advise on weather conditions, restaurants, and tourist attractions and recreation. For international travel, agents also provide information on customs

regulations, required papers (passports, visas, and certificates of vaccination), and currency exchange rates.

Travel agents consult a variety of published and computer-based sources for information on departure and arrival times, fares, and hotel ratings and accommodations. They may visit hotels, resorts, and restaurants to judge, firsthand, their comfort, cleanliness, and quality of food and service so they can base recommendations on their own travel experiences or those of colleagues or clients.

Travel agents also promote their services, using telemarketing, direct mail, and the Internet. They make presentations to social and special interest groups, arrange advertising displays, and suggest company-sponsored trips to business managers.

Depending on the size of the travel agency, an agent may specialize by type of travel, such as leisure or business, or destination, such as Europe or Africa.

Working Conditions

Travel agents spend most of their time behind a desk conferring with clients, completing paperwork, contacting airlines and hotels for travel arrangements, and promoting group tours. They may be under a great deal of pressure at times, such as during vacation seasons. Many agents, especially those who are self-employed, frequently work long hours. With advanced computer systems and telecommunication networks, some travel agents are able to work at home. These agents make travel arrangements for their clients, and promote travel offered by the travel agency and organizations they represent.

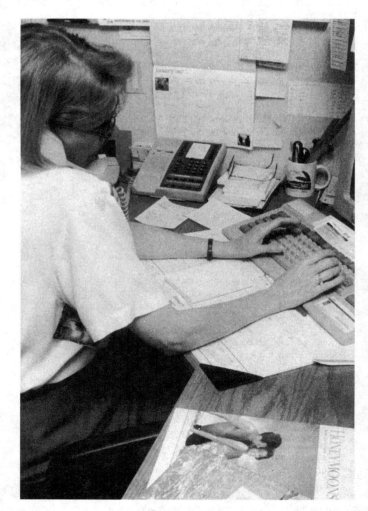

Travel agents use computers to book travel arrangements quickly.

Employment

Travel agents held about 142,000 jobs in 1996 and are found in every part of the country. More than 9 out of 10 salaried agents worked for travel agencies; some worked for membership organizations.

Training, Other Qualifications, and Advancement

The minimum requirement for those interested in becoming a travel agent is a high school diploma or equivalent. With technology and computerization having a profound effect on the work of travel agents, formal or specialized training is becoming increasingly important. Many vocational schools offer 6- to 12-week full-time travel agent programs, as well as evening and weekend programs. Travel courses are also offered in public adult education programs and in community and 4-year colleges. A few colleges offer bachelor's or master's degrees in travel and tourism. Although few college courses relate directly to the travel industry, a college education is sometimes desired by employers to establish a background in areas such as computer science, geography, communication, foreign languages, and world history. Courses in accounting and business management also are important, especially for those who expect to manage or start their own travel agencies. Travel agents must be well-organized, accurate, and meticulous to compile information from various sources, and plan and organize their clients' travel itineraries. Other desirable qualifications include good writing, computer, and sales skills.

The American Society of Travel Agents (ASTA) offers a correspondence course that provides a basic understanding of the travel industry. Travel agencies also provide on-the-job training for their employees, a significant part of which consists of computer instruction. Computer skills are required by all employers to operate airline and centralized reservation systems.

Experienced travel agents can take advanced self or group study courses from the Institute of Certified Travel Agents (ICTA), that lead to the designation of Certified Travel Counselor (CTC). The ICTA also offers marketing and sales skills development programs and destination specialist programs, which provide a detailed knowledge of the geographic areas of North America, Western Europe, the Caribbean, and the Pacific Rim.

Travel experience is an asset since personal knowledge about a city or foreign country often helps to influence clients' travel plans, as is experience as an airline reservation agent. Patience and the ability to gain the confidence of clients are also useful qualities.

Some employees start as reservation clerks or receptionists in travel agencies. With experience and some formal training, they can take on greater responsibilities and eventually assume travel agent duties. In agencies with many offices, travel agents may advance to office manager or to other managerial positions.

Those who start their own agencies generally have experience in an established agency. They must generally gain formal supplier or corporation approval before they can receive commissions. Suppliers or corporations are organizations of airlines, ship lines, or rail lines. The Airlines Reporting Corporation and the International Airlines Travel Agency Network, for example, are the approving bodies for airlines. To gain approval, an agency must be financially sound and employ at least one experienced manager/travel agent.

There are no Federal licensing requirements for travel agents. However, nine States require some form of registration or certification of retail sellers of travel services: California, Florida, Hawaii, Illinois, Iowa, Ohio, Oregon, Rhode Island, and Washington. More information may be obtained by contacting the Office of the Attorney General or Department of Commerce for each State.

Job Outlook

Employment of travel agents is expected to grow faster than the average for all occupations through the year 2006. Many job openings will arise as new agencies open and existing agencies expand, but most openings will occur as experienced agents transfer to other occupations or leave the labor force.

Spending on travel is expected to increase significantly over the next decade. With rising household incomes, smaller families, and an increasing number of older people who are more likely to travel, more people are expected to travel on vacation—and to do so more frequently—than in the past. In fact, many people take more than one vacation a year. Business-related travel should also grow as business activity expands. Employment of managerial, professional, and sales workers—those who do most business travel—is projected to grow at least as fast as the average for all occupations.

Charter flights and larger, more efficient planes have brought air transportation within the budgets of more people. The easing of Government regulation of air fares and routes has fostered greater competition among airlines, resulting in more affordable service. In addition, American travel agents organize tours for the growing number of foreign visitors. Also, travel agents are often able to offer various travel packages at a substantial discount. Although most travel agencies now have automated reservation systems, this has not weakened demand for travel agents.

Some developments, however, may reduce job opportunities for travel agents in the future. The Internet allows people to access travel information from their personal computers and make their own travel arrangements. Suppliers of travel services are increasingly able to make their services available through other means, such as electronic ticketing machines and remote ticket printers. Also, airline companies have put a cap on the amount of commissions they will pay to travel agencies. The full effect of these practices, though, has yet to be determined as many consumers prefer to use a professional travel agent to ensure reliability and save time and, in some cases, money.

The travel industry generally is sensitive to economic downturns and international political crises, when travel plans are likely to be deferred. Therefore, the number of job opportunities fluctuates.

Earnings

Experience, sales ability, and the size and location of the agency determine the salary of a travel agent. According to a Louis Harris survey, conducted for *Travel Weekly,* 1996 median annual earnings of travel agents on straight salary with less than 1 year experience were $16,400; from 1 to 3 years, $20,400; from 3 to 5 years, $22,300; from 5 to 10 years, $26,300; and more than 10 years, $32,600. Salaried agents usually have standard benefits, such as medical insurance coverage and paid vacations, that self-employed agents must provide for themselves. Among agencies, those focusing on corporate sales pay higher salaries and provide more extensive benefits, on average, than those who focus on leisure sales.

Earnings of travel agents who own their agencies depend mainly on commissions from airlines and other carriers, cruise lines, tour operators, and lodging places. Commissions for domestic travel arrangements, cruises, hotels, sightseeing tours, and car rentals are about 7-10 percent of the total sale; and for international travel, about 10 percent. They may also charge clients a service fee for the time and expense involved in planning a trip.

During the first year of business or while awaiting corporation approval, self-employed travel agents generally have low earnings. Their income usually is limited to commissions from hotels, cruises, and tour operators and to nominal fees for making complicated arrangements. Even established agents have lower profits during economic downturns.

When they travel for personal reasons, agents usually get reduced rates for transportation and accommodations.

Related Occupations

Travel agents organize and schedule business, educational, or recreational travel or activities. Other workers with similar responsibilities include tour guides, meeting planners, airline reservation agents, rental car agents, and travel counselors.

Sources of Additional Information

For further information on training opportunities, contact:
☛ American Society of Travel Agents, Education Department, 1101 King St., Alexandria, VA 22314.
Homepage: http://www.astanet.com/ www/astanet/whatis/becomeag.html

For information on certification qualifications, contact:
☛ The Institute of Certified Travel Agents, 148 Linden St., P.O. Box 812059, Wellesley, MA 02181-0012. Phone: (800) 542-4282.

Administrative Support Occupations, Including Clerical

Adjusters, Investigators, and Collectors

(D.O.T. 168.267-014 and -038; 191.167-022; 195.267-010; 203.382-014; 205.367-018, -034 and -046; 209.382-014 and .687-018; 219.362-042, and -050, .367-014, and .482-014; 241.217, .267-014, -018, -030, and -034, .357, .362, .367-010, -014, -022, and -034, and .387; and 249.367-030)

Significant Points

- A high school education is sufficient to qualify for most positions, but a bachelor's degree is preferred for most claim representative positions.

- Projected employment change varies widely by occupation—for example, adjustment clerks are expected to grow much faster than average as businesses emphasize good customer relations, while policy processing clerks decline as their duties are increasingly computerized and assumed by other workers.

Nature of the Work

Organizations must deal smoothly and efficiently with a variety of problems to maintain good relations with their customers. Handling complaints, interpreting and explaining policies or regulations, resolving billing disputes, collecting delinquent accounts, and determining eligibility for governmental assistance are just a few examples. Organizations like insurance companies, department stores, banks, and government social services agencies employ adjusters, investigators, and collectors to act as intermediaries with the public in these situations. The following is a discussion of occupations that comprise this group of workers.

Claim Representatives. Claim representatives at insurance companies investigate claims, negotiate settlements, and authorize payments to claimants. When a policyholder files a claim for damage or a loss, the *claim adjuster*, *claim examiner*, or *claim investigator* must initially determine whether the customer's insurance policy covers the loss and the amount of the loss covered.

Minor claims filed by automobile or homeowner policyholders are frequently handled by "inside adjusters" or "telephone adjusters." These workers contact claimants by telephone or by mail to get information on repair costs, medical expenses, or other details the company requires. Many companies centralize this operation in a drive-in claims center, where the cost of repair is determined and a check is issued immediately.

More complex cases are referred to an "independent adjuster" or "insurance company adjuster." Claim adjusters plan and schedule the work required to process a claim. They investigate claims by interviewing the claimant and witnesses, consulting police and hospital records, and inspecting property damage to determine the extent of the company's liability. They make photographs, take written or taped statements, and maintain computer files of information obtained from witnesses, and then prepare reports of their findings. When the policyholder's claim is legitimate, the claim adjuster negotiates with the claimant and settles the claim. When claims are contested, adjusters may testify in court.

Some adjusters work with multiple lines of insurance. Others specialize in claims associated with fire damage, marine loss, automotive damage, product liability, or workers' compensation. Material damage adjusters inspect automobile damage and use the latest computerized estimating equipment to prepare estimates of the damage.

In life and health insurance companies, the counterpart of the claim adjuster is the claim examiner. In property and casualty insurance companies, the claim examiner may supervise claim adjusters. In both cases, they investigate questionable claims or authorize payment for those exceeding a designated amount. Larger claims are referred to senior examiners. Examiners may check claim applications for completeness and accuracy, interview medical specialists, consult policy files to verify information on a claim, or calculate benefit payments. They also maintain records of settled claims and prepare reports to be submitted to their company's data processing department.

Claim representatives are making greater use of computers to keep records of clients and actions taken in various claims. Most have computer terminals on their desks, and many use portable laptop computers to enter or access information when they are on assignment outside the office.

Insurance Processing Clerks. *Policy processing clerks* use computers to process new insurance policies, modifications to existing policies, and claims. They begin the new policy process by reviewing the insurance application to ensure that all the questions have been answered. After an application has been reviewed by underwriters and the company determines that it will issue a policy, a policy processing clerk prepares the necessary forms and informs the insurance sales agent of an application's processing status. Policy processing clerks also update existing policies—such as a change in beneficiary, amount of coverage, or type of insurance—and recalculate premiums. They mail correspondence notices regarding changes to the sales agent and to the policyholder. Policy processing clerks maintain computer files for each policyholder, including policies that are to be reinstated or canceled.

Claim clerks, also called *claim interviewers*, obtain information from policyholders regarding claims. Claims may concern various types of loss, such as fire damage, personal injury, or an automobile accident. They prepare reports and review insurance claim forms and related documents for completeness. They call or write the insured or other party involved for missing information to update claim files. They may transmit routine claims for payment or advise the claim supervisor if further investigation is needed.

Like policy processing clerks, claim clerks use computers extensively in their work. Most spend a large part of their time creating and updating records at a personal computer or terminal.

Adjustment Clerks. Adjustment clerks investigate and resolve customers' complaints about merchandise, service, billing, or credit rating. They may work for banks, department stores, utility companies, and other large organizations selling products and services to the public. Sometimes they are referred to as *customer service representatives*, *customer complaint clerks*, or *adjustment correspondents*.

Adjustment clerks examine all pertinent information to determine if a customer's complaint is valid. In a department store, this may mean checking sales slips or warranties, as well as the merchandise in question. In a bank, it could mean reviewing records and videotapes of automated teller machine transactions. In a utility company, they review meter books, microfilm, computer printouts, and machine accounting records. Regardless of the setting, these clerks get information—in person, by telephone, or through written correspondence—from all parties involved.

After an investigation and evaluation of the facts, adjustment clerks report their findings, adjustments, and recommendations. These may include exchanging merchandise, refunding money, crediting customers' accounts, or adjusting customers' bills. Adjustment clerks ensure that the appropriate changes are set in motion and follow up on the recommendations to ensure customer satisfaction. To prevent similar complaints in the future, they may recommend to management improvements in product, packaging, shipping methods, service, or billing methods and procedures. Adjustment clerks keep records of all relevant matters, using them to prepare reports for their supervisors.

Adjustment clerks also respond to inquiries from customers. Clerks frequently can answer these inquiries with a form letter, but other times they must compose a letter themselves. Upon request, adjustment clerks issue duplicate or additional credit cards for banks and department stores.

Bill and Account Collectors. Bill and account collectors, sometimes called *collection correspondents*, are responsible for ensuring customers pay their overdue accounts. Some are employed by third-party collection agencies, while others, known as "in-house collectors," work directly for the original creditors, like department stores, hospitals, or banks.

Many companies automatically notify customers by mail if their account is overdue. When customers do not respond, collectors are called on to locate and notify them of the delinquent account, usually over the telephone, sometimes by letter. When customers move without leaving a forwarding address, collectors may check with the post office, telephone companies, credit bureaus, or former neighbors to obtain their new address. This is called "skip-tracing."

Once collectors find the debtor, they inform them of the overdue account and solicit payment. If necessary, they review the terms of the sale, service, or credit contract with the customer. Collectors may attempt to learn the cause of the delay in payment. Where feasible, they offer the customer advice and counsel on how to pay off the debts, such as by taking out a bill consolidation loan. However, the collector's objective is always to ensure that the customer first pays the debt in question.

If customers agree to pay, collectors note that for the record and check later to verify that the payment was indeed made. Collectors may have authority to grant an extension of time if customers ask for one. If customers fail to respond at all, collectors prepare a statement to that effect for the credit department of the establishment. In more extreme cases, collectors may initiate repossession proceedings or service disconnections, or hand the account over to an attorney for legal action.

Most collectors handle other administrative functions for the accounts assigned to them. This may include recording changes of addresses, and purging the records of the deceased. Bill and account collectors keep records of the amounts collected and the status of the accounts. Some fill out daily reports to keep their supervisors apprised of their progress. In some organizations, inside collectors receive payments and post the amounts to the customers' account. In most operations, however, the posting and receiving are done by other clerical workers. Collectors employed by collection agencies do not receive payments; rather, their primary responsibility is to get customers to pay their obligation.

Collectors use computers and a variety of automated systems to keep track of overdue accounts. Typically, collectors work at video display terminals that are linked to computers. In sophisticated predicted dialer systems, the computer dials the telephone automatically and the collector speaks only when a connection has been made. Such systems eliminate time spent calling busy or nonanswering numbers. Many collectors use regular telephones; some wear headsets like those used by telephone operators. Occasionally, supervisors may listen in on collectors' conversations with customers to evaluate their job performance.

Welfare Eligibility Workers and Interviewers. Welfare eligibility workers and interviewers—sometimes referred to as intake workers, eligibility determination workers, eligibility specialists, family investment counselors, or income maintenance specialists—determine who can receive welfare and other types of social assistance. They interview and investigate applicants and recipients; based on the personal and financial information they obtain and the rules and regulations of each program, they initiate procedures to grant, modify,

deny, or terminate individuals' eligibility for various aid programs. This information is recorded and evaluated to determine the amounts of the grants.

Welfare eligibility workers and interviewers work with various public assistance programs. The best-known are Aid to Families with Dependent Children, Medicaid, Food Stamps, and the Work Incentive Program. Depending on local circumstances, there may be other programs, such as those for public housing, refugee assistance, and fuel assistance.

Many welfare eligibility workers and interviewers specialize in an area such as housing, but most are responsible for several areas. They may assist social workers by informing them of pertinent information they have gathered during their interviews with applicants. In some areas, particularly rural ones, eligibility workers may also perform other welfare duties.

These workers often provide information to applicants and current recipients. For example, they may explain and interpret eligibility rules and regulations or identify other resources available in the community for financial or social welfare assistance. More experienced workers may help train new workers. In addition, they may be assigned to special units whose responsibility is to detect fraud.

An increasing number of jurisdictions are using computers to increase worker productivity and to reduce the incidence of welfare fraud. In these settings, welfare eligibility workers and interviewers sit in front of computer terminals when they interview applicants and recipients. Welfare eligibility workers then enter the information provided. In the most advanced systems, the computer terminal prompts them with a variety of questions to ask during an interview.

Although these workers usually interview applicants and recipients who visit their offices, they may make occasional home visits, especially if the applicant or recipient is elderly or disabled. They may also check with employers or other references to verify answers and get further information.

The authority of welfare eligibility workers and interviewers varies from one jurisdiction to another. In some places, these workers are authorized to decide on an applicant's eligibility, subject to review by their supervisor. In other places, however, they can only make recommendations to their supervisors, who in turn make the ultimate decision.

Because most companies provide 24-hour claim service to their policyholders, some adjusters, investigators, and collectors work evenings and weekends.

Working Conditions

Most claim examiners have desk jobs that require no unusual physical activity. They typically work a standard 5-day, 40-hour week. Claim examiners may work longer hours during peak periods or when quarterly and annual statements are prepared. Sometimes they travel to obtain information by personal interview.

Many claim adjusters work outside the office, visiting and inspecting damaged buildings, for example. Occasionally, experienced adjusters are away from home for days when they travel to the scene of a disaster—such as a tornado, hurricane, or flood—to work with local adjusters and government officials. Some adjusters are on "emergency call" in the case of such incidents. Material damage adjusters work at local claim centers where policyholders take their cars for estimates of damage.

Adjusters generally have the flexibility to arrange their work schedule to accommodate evening and weekend appointments with clients. Some report to the office every morning to get their assignments while others simply call from home and spend their days traveling to claim sites. This enables some adjusters to work independently.

Most insurance processing clerks work 40 hours a week in an office. Much of the work is routine and requires remaining at work stations for extended periods of time. Because most insurance information is stored in computers, many of these workers sit at video display terminals and enter or access information while the customer is on the phone. Because most companies provide 24-hour claim service to their policyholders, some claim clerks work evenings and weekends. Many claim clerks work part time.

Adjustment clerks, bill and account collectors, and welfare eligibility workers and interviewers work in offices, usually during regular business hours. Some work part time. Many bill and account collectors work as temporaries for collection agencies. From their offices, they deal with customers, clients, or applicants, either by telephone or in person. Dealing with upset or angry clients is often part of the daily routine in these jobs, making the work stressful at times.

Some welfare eligibility workers and interviewers may be hired on a seasonal basis to help administer a specific program. For example, some States hire these workers for the winter to help run emergency fuel-assistance programs.

Employment

Adjusters, investigators, and collectors held about 1.3 million jobs in 1996. The following tabulation shows the percent distribution of employment by detailed occupation in 1996.

Adjustment clerks	30
Bill and account collectors	20
Insurance policy processing clerks	14
Insurance adjusters, examiners, and investigators	12
Insurance claims clerks	9
Welfare eligibility workers and interviewers	8
Claims examiners, property and casualty insurance	4
All other adjusters and investigators	3

Insurance companies employ the vast majority of claim adjusters, examiners, investigators, property and casualty insurance claim examiners, policy processing clerks, and claim clerks. The remainder are employed by real estate firms and government agencies.

Nearly 2 out of 10 adjustment clerks are employed by department stores, grocery stores, or catalog and mail order houses. Manufacturing firms, banks and other financial institutions, and telephone companies are other major employers of these workers.

About 1 in 6 bill and account collectors works for a credit reporting and collection agency. Many others work in banks, department stores, and other institutions that extend credit.

Around 9 of every 10 welfare eligibility workers and interviewers work for State or local government agencies. In many States, these workers are employed exclusively by the State government. In the remainder, they are employed by the county or municipal government. Most of those not employed by government work for private social service agencies.

Training, Other Qualifications, and Advancement

Training and entry requirements vary widely for adjuster, investigator, and collector jobs. A high school education is sufficient to qualify for most insurance processing clerk , adjustment clerk, and bill and account collector positions, while a bachelor's degree is preferred for most claim representative positions. While some college education is preferred for positions as adjuster or welfare eligibility worker or interviewer, many people qualify for these positions on the strength of related prior work experience. Because a significant and growing proportion of adjusters, investigators, and collectors use computers, word processing skills are recommended. Employers view experience with computers as an asset.

Claim Representatives. Most companies prefer to hire college graduates for claim representative positions. Entry-level workers may be hired without college coursework if they have specialized experience. For example, people with knowledge of automobile mechanics or body repair may qualify as material damage adjusters and those with extensive clerical experience might be hired as inside adjusters. Both adjusters and examiners should be observant and enjoy working with details.

No specific college major is recommended as the best preparation for these occupations. Although courses in insurance, economics, or other business subjects are helpful, a degree in almost any field is adequate. An adjuster who has a business or an accounting background might specialize in claims of financial loss due to strikes, breakdowns in equipment, or damage to merchandise. College training in engineering is helpful in adjusting industrial claims, such as damage from fires and other accidents. A legal background is most helpful to those handling workers' compensation and product liability cases. Knowledge of computer applications is extremely important.

Many States require adjusters to be licensed. Applicants usually must comply with one or more of the following: Pass a licensing examination covering the fundamentals of adjusting; complete an approved course in insurance or loss adjusting; furnish character references; be at least 20 or 21 years of age and a resident of the State; and file a surety bond.

Because they often work closely with claimants, witnesses, and other insurance professionals, claim representatives must be able to communicate effectively with others. Some companies require applicants to pass a battery of written aptitude tests designed to measure communication, analytical, and general mathematical skills. Examiners must understand Federal and State insurance laws and regulations.

Some large insurance companies provide on-the-job training and home-study courses for entry-level claim adjusters and examiners. For example, material damage adjusters would learn about automobile body construction, analysis of collision data, and repair cost estimation, including computerized estimating equipment. They also learn how to deal with customers.

Workers may receive their training through courses offered by the Insurance Institute of America, a nonprofit organization offering educational programs and professional certification to persons in the property-liability insurance industry. The Insurance Institute of America offers an Associate in Claims designation upon successful completion of 4 essay examinations. Adjusters can prepare for the examination by independent home study or through company or public classes. The Institute also offers a certificate upon successful completion of the Introduction to Claims program and an examination.

The International Claim Association offers a program on life and health insurance claim administration. Completion of the 6-examination program leads to the professional designation, Associate, Life and Health Claims.

The Life Office Management Association (LOMA) offers a comprehensive 10-course life and health insurance educational program that leads to the professional designation, Fellow, Life Management

Institute (FLMI). LOMA also offers the Master Fellow Program that is designed specifically to meet the continuing education needs of life and health insurance professionals. Students can prepare for FLMI exams through independent home study or through insurance company or FLMI Society classes.

Beginning adjusters and examiners work on small claims under the supervision of an experienced worker. As they learn more about claim investigation and settlement, they are assigned larger, more complex claims. Trainees are promoted as they demonstrate competence in handling assignments and as they progress in their coursework. Because of the complexity of insurance regulations and claim procedures, workers who lack formal academic training tend to advance more slowly than those with additional education. Employees who demonstrate competence in claim work or administrative skills may be promoted to department supervisor in a field office or to a managerial position in the home office. Other claim examiners are promoted to investigators, whose role is to detect fraud.

Insurance Processing Clerks. High school graduation is considered adequate preparation for most insurance processing clerk positions. Courses in typing and word processing, and business arithmetic are desirable. Employers view favorably previous office experience and familiarity with computers. Most new workers begin as file clerks and move into insurance processing positions as they demonstrate their ability. However, people with considerable clerical experience may begin processing insurance policies immediately.

A few experienced insurance processing clerks may be promoted to a clerical supervisor position. Advancement to a claim representative or an underwriting technician position is possible for clerks who demonstrate potential, have college coursework, or have taken specialized courses in insurance. Many companies offer home-study courses for their employees so they can acquire the knowledge necessary to advance.

Adjustment Clerks. Many employers do not require any formal education for adjustment clerk positions. Instead, they look for people who can read and write well and who possess good communication and interpersonal skills. Word processing ability is also viewed favorably.

Adjustment clerk is an entry level position in some, but not all, organizations. Depending on their assignment, new adjustment clerks may receive training on the job from a supervisor or an experienced coworker, or they may enter a formal training course offered by the organization. Training covers such topics as how to use computers, what standard forms to use, whom to contact in other departments of the organization, and how to deal with customers. Some employers provide more advanced training for experienced adjustment clerks. This training may be offered in-house or from trade associations or local colleges.

Bill and Account Collectors. While high school graduation sometimes is required by employers when they hire bill and account collectors, formal education beyond high school is not stressed. Previous work experience as a collector is particularly valuable. Experience in the field of telemarketing or as a telephone operator also is helpful, as is knowledge of the billing process. Employers seek individuals who speak well and who are persistent and detail-oriented.

Employers normally provide training to new bill and account collectors. This training, which may last up to a couple of months, is usually conducted in a classroom or on the job. Although not required by law, many employers also require their collectors to get certified through the American Collectors Association (ACA). ACA seminars concentrate on current State and Federal compliance laws. Since most States recognize these credentials, ACA-certified collectors have greater career mobility. In training seminars, employers use videotapes, computer programs, role-playing, and hands-on experience. Novice collectors learn about skip-tracing, billing procedures, and most importantly, communications and negotiating. Learning to use the firm's computer and telephone systems is also an integral part of their training.

Successful bill and account collectors may become supervisors. Some even start their own collection agencies.

Welfare Eligibility Workers and Interviewers. Hiring requirements for welfare eligibility workers and interviewers vary widely. Depending on the jurisdiction, applicants may need a high school diploma, associate degree, or bachelor's degree. Work experience in a closely related field—such as employment interviewing, social work, or insurance claims—may also qualify one for this job. In parts of the country with a high concentration of non-English speaking people, fluency in a foreign language may be an advantage.

Because they deal with people who are in difficult economic circumstances, welfare eligibility workers and interviewers should be compassionate and empathetic. Attention to detail is important because there are many procedures and regulations that must be observed.

After they are hired, eligibility workers are given training, sometimes in a formal classroom setting, other times in a more informal manner. They are taught the policies, procedures, and program regulations that they are expected to use to determine eligibility. If a formal training program is selected, it generally is followed by on-the-job training provided by the supervisor.

Advancement to the job of social worker is possible, although additional formal education, such as a bachelor's or master's degree, usually is needed.

Job Outlook
Overall employment of adjusters, investigators, and collectors is expected to grow faster than the average for all occupations over the 1996-2006 period. Most job openings, however, will result from the need to replace workers who transfer to other occupations or leave the labor force.

Growth rates will vary considerably by occupation. Employment of insurance claim examiners is expected to grow faster than the average as the increasing volume of insurance results in more insurance claims. As people accumulate assets and take on family responsibilities, the need for insurance—including life, health, home, and automobile—will increase. Also, new or expanding businesses will need protection for new plants and equipment and for insurance covering their employees' health and safety. Opportunities should be particularly good for claim representatives who specialize in complex business insurance such as marine cargo, workers' compensation, and product and pollution liability.

Employment of adjustment clerks is expected to grow much faster than average as business establishments place an increased emphasis on maintaining good customer relations. An important aspect of good customer service is resolving customers' complaints in a friendly and timely fashion. Because much of their work involves direct communication with customers, demand for adjustment clerks is expected to keep pace with growth in the number of customers.

Bill and account collector jobs also are expected to grow much faster than average as the level of consumer debt rises. As the economy expands, firms will strive to increase the efficiency of their debt collection to keep losses at a minimum. Contrary to the pattern in most occupations, employment of bill and account collectors tends to rise during recessions, reflecting the difficulty that many people have in meeting their financial obligations.

Overall employment of insurance claims and policy processing occupations is expected to grow about as fast as the average for all occupations. Within this group, employment of adjusters and claim clerks will increase faster than average because their work requires much interpersonal contact, which cannot be automated. However, employment of policy processing clerks will decline as their duties are increasingly computerized and assumed by other workers.

Employment of welfare eligibility workers and interviewers is expected to decline as many people move from welfare to work, and as State and local governments attempt to curb the growth in their expenditures for public assistance.

Earnings

Earnings of adjusters, investigators, and collectors vary significantly. For adjusters and investigators, the median weekly earnings in 1996 were $440. The middle 50 percent earned between about $340 and $590 a week. Adjusters are also furnished a company car or are reimbursed for use of their own vehicle for business purposes.

Specific information on earnings of insurance processing clerks is not available. However, median weekly earnings for records clerks, a category that includes policy processing clerks, were $390 in 1996. Interviewers, whose work is similar to that of claim clerks, also had median weekly earnings of $390.

Median weekly earnings of full-time bill and account collectors were $410 in 1996; the middle 50 percent earned between $330 and $510 a week. Ten percent earned less than $280 and 10 percent earned more than $660. Some bill and account collectors receive a base salary and work on commission beyond that.

Median weekly earnings of full-time welfare eligibility workers and interviewers were about $450 in 1996; the middle 50 percent earned between $360 and $590 a week. The lowest 10 percent earned less than $290 and the top 10 percent earned more than $670.

Welfare eligibility workers and interviewers are twice as likely to belong to unions than workers in all occupations. In 1996, about 26 percent of all welfare eligibility workers and interviewers were union members, compared to 13 for all occupations. The two principal unions representing these workers are the American Federation of State, County, and Municipal Employees, and the Service Employees International Union.

Related Occupations

Insurance adjusters and examiners investigate, analyze, and determine the validity of their firm's liability concerning personal, casualty, or property loss or damages, and settle with claimants. Workers in other occupations that require similar skills include cost estimators, budget analysts, and private investigators.

The work of insurance processing clerks and adjustment clerks is similar to that of other workers who compile, review, or maintain records—including title searchers and coding, contract, auditing, and reservation clerks.

The work of bill and account collectors is related to that of customer service representatives, telemarketers, telephone interviewers, and other workers who deal with the public over the telephone.

The work of welfare eligibility workers is similar to that of social and human service assistants, financial aid counselors, loan and credit counselors, probation officers, and other workers who interview customers or clients.

Sources of Additional Information

General information about a career as a claim representative or an insurance processing clerk is available from the home offices of many life and property and liability insurance companies.

Information about career opportunities in these occupations may be obtained from:
☛ Insurance Information Institute, 110 William St., New York, NY 10038.
☛ Alliance of American Insurers, 1501 Woodfield Rd., Suite 400 West, Schaumburg, IL 60173-4980.

Information about licensing requirements for claim adjusters may be obtained from the department of insurance in each State.

For information about the designation, Associate in Claims (AIC), or the Introduction to Claims program, contact:
☛ Insurance Institute of America, 720 Providence Rd., P.O. Box 3016, Malvern, PA 19355-0716.

Information on the Associate, Life and Health Claims, and the Fellow, Life Management Institute designations can be obtained from:
☛ Life Office Management Association, 2300 Windy Ridge Pkwy., Atlanta, GA 30327-4308.

Career information on bill and account collectors is available from:
☛ American Collectors Association, Inc., P.O. Box 39106, Minneapolis, MN 55439-0106. Homepage: http//www.collector.com/ consumer/careers.html

Employment information on welfare eligibility workers and interviewers is available at social service offices of municipal, county, and State governments.

Bank Tellers

(D.O.T. 211.362 except -010; 211.382-010; 219.462-010)

Significant Points

- Little or no change in employment is expected as banking technology spreads and consolidation among banks forces changes in the operations, duties, and staffing of branch offices; applicants for part-time jobs should fare better than applicants for full-time jobs.

- Many job openings will arise from replacement needs in this large occupation because turnover is high—characteristic of occupations that generally require little formal education and offer relatively low pay.

Nature of the Work

Bank tellers interact with the majority of bank customers. Tellers generally handle a wide range of banking transactions, such as cashing checks, accepting deposits and loan payments, and processing withdrawals. They sell savings bonds; accept payment for customers' utility bills; receive deposits for special accounts; keep records and perform the necessary paperwork for customer loans; process the proliferating variety of certificates of deposit and money market accounts; and sell travelers' checks. Some tellers specialize in handling foreign currencies or commercial or business accounts.

Before cashing a check, the teller must verify the date, bank name, and identity of the person to receive payment, and see that the document is legal tender, that written and numerical amounts agree, and that the account has sufficient funds to cover the check. The teller must carefully count out the cash to avoid errors. Sometimes a customer withdraws money in the form of a cashier's check, which the teller prepares and verifies. When accepting a deposit, the teller checks the accuracy of the deposit slip and processes the transaction. Tellers may use machines to calculate and record transactions and to prepare documents, such as receipts and drafts. In some banks, they type or write deposit receipts and passbook entries by hand, but this is uncommon. In most banks, tellers use computer terminals to record deposits and withdrawals. Some banks use very sophisticated computer systems that give tellers quick access to detailed information on customer accounts. Tellers may use this information to tailor their services to fit the customer's needs or recommend an appropriate bank product or service.

Often, the duties of tellers begin before the bank opens and end after the bank closes. They begin the day by receiving and counting an amount of working cash for their drawer; this amount is verified by a supervisor, usually the head teller. Tellers use this cash for payments during the day and are responsible for its safe and accurate handling. After banking hours, tellers count cash on hand, list the currency-received tickets on a balance sheet, and balance the day's accounts. They sort checks and deposit slips. Tellers also spend time learning about the bank's products and services and changes in the bank's procedures. Some tellers spend time refreshing and upgrading their skills.

Tellers may process numerous mail transactions. Some tellers replenish cash drawers and corroborate deposits and payments to automated teller machines (ATMs).

Head tellers are responsible for the teller line. Their duties include preparing work schedules, accessing the vault, ensuring the correct cash balance in the vault, and taking responsibility for shipments of cash to and from the Federal Reserve.

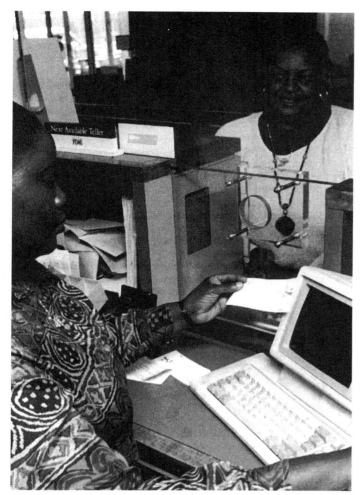

Many bank tellers work part time.

Because their banks offer more and increasingly complex financial services, tellers in most large banks are trained to act as customer service representatives, in addition to their other duties. These tellers can briefly explain to customers the various types of accounts and financial services offered by their bank and refer interested customers to customer service representatives or bank managers. (New accounts clerks, who also may act as customer service representatives, are discussed in the *Handbook* statement on interviewing and new accounts clerks. Bank managers are covered in the *Handbook* statement on financial managers.)

Working Conditions

Tellers generally work during the day, Monday through Friday; some evening and weekend work may be required. The job offers ample opportunity to work part time with flexible hours; in some banks, 90 percent of tellers work part time. Banks often hire part-time, or "peak-time," tellers for busy banking periods such as lunch hours and weekend mornings. Increasing numbers of tellers work outside the traditional bank setting. Instead, they work in shopping malls, grocery stores, or other large retail establishments. Continual communication with customers, repetitive tasks, long periods of standing, working in a fairly small area, and a high level of attention to security also characterize the job.

Small banks are able to provide more personal service to their customers than larger institutions. Small banks generally are not as busy, and tellers typically recognize their customers and often know their names. Full-time employment of tellers is also much more common in small banks, increasing familiarity between customers and tellers. As in most occupations, full-time tellers command the

full range of employee benefits and generally exhibit lower turnover than part-time workers.

Employment

Bank tellers held about 545,000 jobs in 1996; about 1 out of 4 worked part time. The overwhelming majority, 95 percent, worked in commercial banks, savings institutions, or credit unions. The rest worked in personal, business, or Federal credit institutions; mortgage banks; security and commodity brokerages; and holding and other investment offices.

Training, Other Qualifications, and Advancement

When hiring tellers, banks seek applicants who enjoy public contact and have good numerical, clerical, and communication skills. Tellers must feel comfortable handling large amounts of cash and working with computers and video terminals, since their work is dependent on this technology. In some metropolitan areas, employers seek multilingual tellers.

Although tellers work independently, their recordkeeping is closely supervised. Accuracy and attention to detail are vital. Tellers should be courteous, attentive, and patient in dealing with the public, because customers often judge a bank by the way they are treated at the teller window. Maturity, tact, and the ability to quickly explain bank procedures and services are important in helping customers complete transactions or make financial decisions.

Many entrants transfer from other occupations; virtually all have at least a high school education. In general, banks prefer applicants who have had high school courses in mathematics, accounting, bookkeeping, economics, and public speaking. Previous cash handling experience is also important to employers. New tellers at larger banks receive at least 1 week of formal classroom training. Formal training is followed by several weeks of on-the-job training, where tellers observe experienced workers before doing the work themselves. Smaller banks rely primarily upon on-the-job training. In addition to instruction in basic duties, many banks now include extensive training in the bank's products and services—so tellers can refer customers to appropriate products—communication and sales skills, and instruction on equipment, such as ATMs and on-line video terminals.

In large banks, beginners usually start for a few days as limited-transaction tellers, cashing checks and processing simple transactions, before becoming full-service tellers. Often, banks simultaneously train tellers for other clerical duties as well.

Advancement opportunities are good for well-trained, motivated employees. Experienced tellers may advance to head teller, customer service representative, or new accounts clerk. Outstanding tellers who have had some college or specialized training offered by the banking industry may be promoted to a managerial position. Banks encourage this upward mobility, by providing access to education and other sources of additional training.

Tellers can prepare for better jobs by taking courses offered or accredited by the American Institute of Banking (an educational affiliate of the American Bankers Association) or the Institute of Financial Education. These organizations have several hundred chapters in cities across the country and numerous study groups in small communities, and they offer correspondence courses. They also work closely with local colleges and universities in preparing courses of study. Most banks use the facilities of these organizations, which assist local banks in conducting cooperative training programs or developing independent training programs. In addition, many banks refund college tuition fees to their employees, upon successful completion of their courses. Although most courses are meant for employed tellers, some community colleges offer preemployment training programs. These programs can help prepare applicants for a job in banking, and can give them an advantage over other job-seekers.

Job Outlook

Little or no change in employment of bank tellers is expected through the year 2006. Nevertheless, many job openings will arise from replacement needs because turnover is high—characteristic of occupations that generally require little formal education and offer relatively low pay—and the occupation is large. Applicants for part-time jobs should fare better than applicants for full-time jobs.

Banks are expected to decline in number and increase in size as interstate banking grows. As banks become larger, the operations, duties and responsibilities, and staffing of branch offices will change. To cut costs, banks are likely to increasingly shift from employing full-time tellers to part-time tellers. Banks also have branches inside supermarkets and department stores; instead of tellers, many have ATMs and more highly trained customer service representatives, who can perform the standard duties of tellers, as well as open new accounts and arrange for customers to receive other services or products the bank provides.

Banks also are increasingly using technology to cut costs. For example, some banks have introduced branches that consist entirely of ATMs and kiosks. Kiosks use ATM technology and video screens and cameras to allow customers at several remote locations to conduct transactions with tellers at a central location. Some banks also allow banking by computer and by telephone.

Earnings
In 1996, median annual earnings of full-time tellers were $16,300. The lowest 10 percent earned less than $11,900 while the top 10 percent earned more than $24,800. Some banks offer incentives, whereby tellers earn supplemental rewards for inducing customers to use other financial products and services offered by the bank. In general, greater responsibilities result in a higher salary. Experience, length of service, and, especially, the location and size of the bank also are important.

Part-time tellers generally do not receive typical benefits, such as life and health insurance.

Related Occupations
Tellers combine customer service and a knowledge of bank procedures with quickness and accuracy to process money, checks, and other financial items for customers. Other workers with similar duties include new accounts clerks, cashiers, toll collectors, post office clerks, auction clerks, and ticket sellers.

Sources of Additional Information
General information about tellers and other banking occupations, training opportunities, and the banking industry is available from:
☛ American Bankers Association, 1120 Connecticut Ave. NW., Washington, DC 20036.

State bankers' associations can furnish specific information about job opportunities in their State. Or contact individual banks to inquire about job openings and for more details about the activities, responsibilities, and preferred qualifications of tellers. For the names and addresses of banks and savings and related institutions, as well as the names of their principal officers, consult one of the following directories.
☛ *The American Financial Directory* (Norcross, Ga., McFadden Business Publications).
☛ *Polk's World Bank Directory* (Nashville, R.L. Polk & Co.).
☛ *Rand McNally Bankers Directory* (Chicago, Rand McNally & Co.).
☛ *The U.S. Savings and Loan Directory* (Chicago, Rand McNally & Co.).
☛ *Rand McNally Credit Union Directory* (Chicago, Rand McNally & Co.).

Clerical Supervisors and Managers

(List of D.O.T. codes available on request. See page 496.)

Significant Points

- Most jobs are filled by promoting individuals from within the organization, very often from the ranks of clerks they subsequently supervise.

- While office automation will cause employment in some clerical occupations to slow or even decline, supervisors will be more likely to retain their jobs because of their relatively higher skills and longer tenure.

Nature of the Work
All organizations need timely and effective clerical and administrative support to operate efficiently. Coordinating this support is the responsibility of clerical supervisors and managers. They can be found in nearly every sector of the economy, working in fields as varied as office management, or, customer services.

Although some functions may vary considerably, many duties are common to all clerical supervisors and managers. Supervisors perform administrative tasks to ensure that their staffs can work efficiently. For example, equipment and machinery used in their departments must be in good working order. If the computer system goes down or a photocopier malfunctions, they must try to correct the problem or alert repair personnel. They also request new equipment or supplies for their department when necessary.

Planning and supervising the work of their staff is another key function of this job. To do this effectively, the supervisor must know the strengths and weaknesses of each member of the staff, as well as the required level of quality and time allotted to each job. They must make allowances for unexpected absences and other disruptions, and adjust assignments or perform the work themselves if the situation requires it.

After allocating work assignments and issuing deadlines, clerical supervisors oversee the work to ensure that it is proceeding on schedule and meets established quality standards. This may involve reviewing each person's work on a computer, as in the case of accounting clerks, or, in the case of cashiers, listening to how they deal with customers. When supervising long-term projects, the supervisor may establish regular meetings with staff members to discuss their progress.

Clerical supervisors also evaluate each worker's performance. If a worker has done a good job, the supervisor records it in the employee's personnel file and may recommend a promotion or other award. Alternatively, if a worker is performing poorly, the supervisor discusses the problem with the employee to determine the cause and helps the worker improve his or her performance. This might entail sending the employee to a training course or arranging personal counseling. If the situation does not improve, the supervisor may recommend a transfer, demotion, or dismissal.

Clerical supervisors and managers generally interview and evaluate prospective clerical employees. When new workers arrive on the job, supervisors greet them and provide orientation to acquaint them with the organization and its operating routines. Some may be actively involved in recruiting new workers by performing functions such as making presentations at high schools and business colleges. They may also serve as the primary liaisons between their offices and the general public through direct contact and helping to prepare promotional information.

Supervisors also help train new employees in organization and office procedures. They may teach them how to use the telephone system and operate office equipment. Because much clerical work is computerized, they must also teach new employees to use the organization's computer system. When new office equipment or updated computer software is introduced, supervisors retrain experienced employees in using it efficiently. If this is not possible, they may arrange for special outside training for their employees.

Clerical supervisors often act as liaisons between the clerical staff and the professional, technical, and managerial staff. This may involve implementing new company policies or restructuring the workflow in their departments. They must also keep their superiors informed of their progress, and abreast of any potential problems. Often this communication takes the form of research projects and progress reports. Because they have access to information such as their department's performance records, they may compile and present these data for use in planning or designing new policies.

Clerical supervisors serve as liaisons between clerks and professionals, technicians, and managers.

Clerical supervisors may be called upon to resolve interpersonal conflicts among the staff. In organizations covered by union contracts, supervisors must know the provisions of labor-management agreements and run their departments accordingly. They may meet with union representatives to discuss work problems or grievances.

Working Conditions
Clerical supervisors and managers are employed in a wide variety of work settings, but most work in offices that are clean, well-lit, and generally comfortable.

Most work a standard 40-hour week. Because some organizations operate around the clock, however, clerical supervisors may have to work nights, weekends, and holidays. In some cases, supervisors rotate among the three shifts. In others, shifts are assigned on the basis of seniority.

Employment
Clerical supervisors and managers held nearly 1.4 million jobs in 1996. Although jobs for clerical supervisors are found in practically every industry, the largest number are found in organizations with a large clerical work force, such as government agencies, retail establishments, wholesalers, business service firms, banks, and insurance companies. Due to the need in most organizations for continuity of supervision, few clerical supervisors and managers work on a temporary or part-time basis.

Training, Other Qualifications, and Advancement
Most firms fill clerical supervisory and managerial positions by promoting individuals within their organization from the clerical ranks. To be eligible for promotion to a supervisory position, clerical or administrative support workers must prove they are capable of handling additional responsibilities. When evaluating candidates, superiors look for strong teamwork skills, determination, loyalty, poise, and confidence. They also look for more specific supervisory attributes, such as the ability to organize and coordinate work efficiently, set priorities, and motivate others. Increasingly, supervisors need a broad base of office skills coupled with personal flexibility to adapt to changes in organizational structure and move among departments when necessary.

In addition, supervisors must pay close attention to detail in order to identify and correct errors made by subordinates. Good working knowledge of the organization's computer system is also an advantage. Many employers require postsecondary training—in some cases, an associate's or even a bachelor's degree.

A clerk with potential supervisory abilities may be given occasional supervisory assignments. To prepare for full-time supervisory duties, he or she may attend in-house training or take courses in time

management or interpersonal relations, for example, at a local community college or vocational school.

Some clerical supervisors are hired from outside the organization for positions with more managerial duties. These positions may serve as entry-level training for potential higher-level managers. New college graduates may rotate through departments of an organization at this level to learn the work of the entire organization.

Job Outlook
Like other supervisory occupations, applicants for clerical supervisor or manager jobs will encounter competition because the number of applicants is expected to exceed the number of job openings. Employment of clerical supervisors and managers is expected to grow about as fast as the average for all occupations through the year 2006. Most job openings, however, will stem from the need to replace workers who transfer to other occupations or leave this large occupation for other reasons.

Employment of clerical supervisors is affected by the demand for clerical workers, which is determined by the volume of clerical work and the development of office automation. More managers will be needed to coordinate the increasing amount of clerical work. With the spread of office automation, however, this work can be accomplished with fewer clerical workers. As office automation causes employment in some clerical occupations to slow or even decline, supervisors may have smaller staffs and perform more professional tasks. In other cases, fewer supervisors will be needed. In most cases though, the relatively higher skills and longer tenure of clerical supervisors and managers places them among the clerical workers most likely to retain their jobs.

Earnings
Median annual earnings of full-time clerical supervisors were about $28,900 in 1996; the middle 50 percent earned between $21,500 and $38,900 a year. The lowest paid 10 percent earned less than $16,300, while the highest paid 10 percent earned more than $50,600. Employers in major metropolitan areas tend to pay higher salaries than those in rural areas.

Clerical supervisors generally receive typical benefits. Some clerical supervisors in the private sector may receive additional compensation in the form of bonuses and stock options.

Related Occupations
Clerical supervisors and managers must understand and sometimes perform the work of the people whom they oversee, including accounting clerks, cashiers, bank tellers, and telephone operators. Their supervisory and administrative duties are similar to those of other managers.

Sources of Additional Information
State employment service offices can provide information about earnings, hours, and employment opportunities in this and other clerical jobs.

Computer Operators

(D.O.T. 213.362, .382, and .582)

Significant Points

- Employment is expected to decline sharply.

- A high school diploma is the minimum requirement, although previous experience and familiarity with operating systems have become increasingly important.

Nature of the Work
Computer operators oversee the operation of computer hardware systems, ensuring that these machines are used as efficiently as possible. They may work with mainframes, minicomputers, or even

networks of personal computers. Computer operators must anticipate problems and take preventive action as well as solve problems that occur during operations.

The duties of computer operators vary with the size of the installation, the type of equipment used, and the policies of the employer. Generally, operators control the console of either a mainframe digital computer or a group of minicomputers. Working from operating instructions prepared by programmers, users, or operations managers, computer operators set controls on the computer and on peripheral devices required to run a particular job. In certain establishments, some operators may only operate separate peripheral equipment or prepare printouts or other output for distribution to computer users. These types of computer operators generally do not run control consoles.

Computer operators load the equipment with tapes, disks, and paper as needed. While the computer is running—which may be 24 hours a day for large computers—computer operators monitor the control console and respond to operating and computer messages. Messages indicate the individual specifications of each job being run. If an error message occurs, operators must locate and solve the problem or terminate the program. Operators also maintain log books or operating records listing each job that is run and events such as machine malfunctions that occur during their shift. In addition, computer operators may supervise and train new employees. They also may help programmers and systems analysts test and debug new programs. (Detailed descriptions of these occupations are presented elsewhere in the *Handbook*.)

As the trend toward networking computers accelerates, a growing number of computer operators are working on personal computers (PCs) and minicomputers. In many offices, factories, and other work settings, PCs and minicomputers are connected in networks, often referred to as local area networks or multi-user systems. While some of these computers are operated by users in the area, many require the services of full-time operators. The tasks performed are very similar to those performed on the larger computers.

As organizations continue to look for opportunities to increase productivity, automation is expanding into more areas of computer operations. Sophisticated software coupled with robotics, enable the computer to perform many routine tasks formerly done by computer operators. Scheduling, loading and downloading programs, mounting tapes, rerouting messages, and running periodic reports can be done without the intervention of an operator; these improvements will change what computer operators do in the future. As technology advances, many computer operators will essentially monitor an automated system. These operators may then be responsible for ensuring that the automated equipment and operating systems perform correctly. For others, changes resulting from new technology may shift their responsibilities to areas such as network operations, user support, or database maintenance.

Working Conditions
Computer operating personnel generally work in well-lighted, well-ventilated, comfortable rooms. Because many organizations use their computers 24 hours a day, 7 days a week, computer operators may be required to work evening or night shifts and weekends. Shift assignments generally are made on the basis of seniority. However, increasingly automated operations will lessen the need for shift work because many companies let the computer take over all operations during less desirable working hours. In addition, advances in telecommuting technologies—such as faxes, modems, and e-mail—and data center automation—such as automated tape libraries—even enable some operators to monitor batch processes, check systems performance, and record problems for the next shift.

Since computer operators generally spend a lot of time in front of a computer monitor, as well as performing repetitive tasks such as loading and unloading printers, they may be susceptible to eyestrain, back discomfort, and hand and wrist problems.

Employment
In 1996, computer operators held about 291,000 jobs. Although jobs for computer operators are found in almost every industry, the ma-

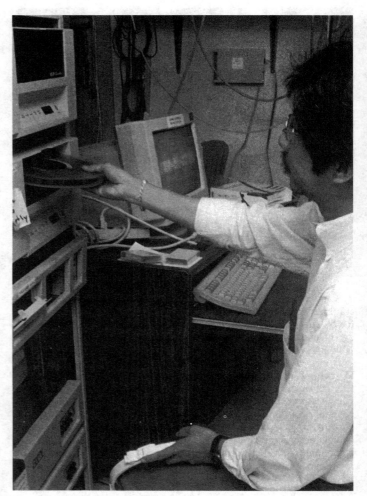

In addition to loading the equipment with tapes, disks, and paper, computer operators monitor the control console and respond to operating and computer messages.

jority are found in organizations that have data processing needs requiring large computer installations such as wholesale trade establishments, manufacturing companies, data processing service firms, financial institutions, and government agencies. A growing number are employed by service firms in the computer and data processing services industry, as more companies contract out the operation of their data processing centers.

Less than 1 out of 5 computer operators works part time.

Training, Other Qualifications, and Advancement
Previous work experience is the key to obtaining an operator job in many large establishments. Employers generally look for specific, hands-on experience with the type of equipment and related operating systems they use. Additionally, formal computer-related training, perhaps through a community college or technical school, is recommended. As computer technology changes and data processing centers become more automated, more employers will require candidates to have formal training, as well as experience, for the remaining operator jobs.

In the past, a high school diploma, previous experience with an operating system, and familiarity with the latest technologies have been the minimum requirements for employment. However, employers increasingly require some post secondary education or training as technologies advance. Completion of vocational training is an asset. Related training can also be obtained through the Armed Forces and from some computer manufacturers. Workers usually receive on-the-job training in order to become acquainted with their employer's equipment and routines. The length of training varies with the job and the experience of the worker.

Because computer technology changes so rapidly, operators must be adaptable and willing to learn. Greater analytical and technical expertise are also needed to deal with the unique or higher level problems the computer is not programmed to handle, particularly by operators who work in automated data centers. Operators must be able to communicate well in order to work effectively with programmers or users, as well as with other operators. Computer operators also must be able to work independently because they may have little or no supervision.

Computer operators generally advance from operating peripheral equipment to responsibilities such as controlling the console. A few computer operators may advance to supervisory jobs, although most management positions within data processing or computer operations centers require more formal education such as a bachelor's degree or higher. Through on-the-job experience and additional formal education, some computer operators may advance to jobs in areas such as network operations or support. As they gain experience in programming, some operators may advance to jobs as programmers or analysts. A move into these types of jobs is becoming much more difficult as employers increasingly require candidates for more skilled computer professional jobs to possess at least a bachelor's degree.

Job Outlook
Employment of computer operators is expected to decline sharply through the year 2006. Experienced operators are expected to compete for the small number of openings that will arise each year to replace workers who transfer to other occupations or leave the labor force. Opportunities will be best for operators who are familiar with a variety of operating systems and who keep up to date with the latest technology.

Advances in technology have reduced both the size and cost of computer equipment while increasing the capacity for data storage and processing automation. These improvements in technology have fueled an expansion in the use of sophisticated computer hardware and software in practically every industry in such areas as factory and office automation, telecommunications, medicine, education, and administration. The expanding use of software that automates computer operations gives companies the option of making systems user-friendly, greatly reducing the need for operators. These new technologies will require operators to monitor a greater number of operations at the same time and be capable of solving a broader range of problems that may arise. The result is that fewer and fewer operators will be needed to perform more highly skilled work.

Computer operators who are displaced by automation may be reassigned to support staffs that maintain personal computer networks or assist other members of the organization. Operators who keep up with changing technology, by updating their skills and enhancing their training, should have the best prospects of moving into other areas such as network administration or technical support. Others may be retrained to perform different job duties, such as supervising an operations center, maintaining automation packages, or analyzing computer operations to recommend ways to increase productivity. In the future, operators who wish to work in the computer field will need to know more about programming, automation software, graphics interface, client/server environments, and open systems in order to take advantage of changing opportunities.

Earnings
In 1996, full-time computer operators had median earnings of about $22,400 a year. The middle 50 percent earned between $16,600 and $30,900. The lowest 10 percent earned less than $13,800 and the top 10 percent earned more than $41,400.

According to Robert Half International Inc., the average starting salaries for console operators in large establishments ranged from $24,750 to $32,750 and from $22,000 to $29,000 in small ones in 1997. Salaries generally are higher in large organizations than in small ones.

In the Federal Government, computer operators with a high school diploma started at about $15,540 a year in 1997; those with 1 year of college started at $17,450. Applicants with operations experience started at higher salaries. The average annual salary for all computer operators employed by the Federal Government in non supervisory, supervisory, and managerial positions was about $31,400 in early 1997.

Related Occupations
Other occupations involving work with computers include computer scientists, engineers, and systems analysts, programmers, and computer service technicians. Other occupations in which workers operate electronic office equipment include data entry keyers, secretaries, typists and word processors, and typesetters and compositors.

Sources of Additional Information
For information about work opportunities in computer operations, contact firms that use computers such as banks, manufacturing and insurance firms, colleges and universities, and data processing service organizations. The local office of the State employment service can supply information about employment and training opportunities.

Court Reporters, Medical Transcriptionists, and Stenographers
(D.O.T. 202.362, .382-010, and 203.582-058)

Significant Points

- A high school diploma is sufficient for stenographers; employers prefer medical transcriptionists who have completed a vocational school or community college program; and court reporters generally complete a 2- or 4-year postsecondary school program.

- Overall employment is projected to grow more slowly than average, as growth among medical transcriptionists is offset by the decline among stenographers. Certified medical transcriptionists and court reporters should have the best prospects.

- Court reporters generally earn higher salaries than stenographers or medical transcriptionists.

Nature of the Work
Court reporters and stenographers take verbatim reports of speeches, conversations, legal proceedings, meetings, or other events when written accounts of spoken words are necessary for correspondence, records, or legal proof. Medical transcriptionists translate and edit recorded dictation by physicians and other healthcare providers regarding patient assessment and treatment.

Court reporters document all statements made in an official proceeding using a stenotype machine, and present their record as the official transcript. Because there is only one person creating an official transcript, accuracy is vitally important.

Although many court reporters record official proceedings in the courtroom, most court reporters work outside the courtroom. Freelance reporters take depositions for attorneys in offices, and document proceedings of meetings, conventions, and other private activities. Others capture the proceedings in the U.S. Congress, State and local governing bodies, and government agencies at all levels.

Court reporters use stenotype machines, which allow them to press more than one key at a time to record combinations of letters representing sounds, words, or phrases. The symbols are then recorded on computer disks. The disks are loaded into a computer that translates and displays the symbols in English—this is called computer-aided transcription. Stenotype machines that link directly to the computer are used for real-time captioning. That is, as the reporter keys in the symbols, they are instantly transcribed by the computer. This is used for closed captioning for the deaf or hearing-impaired on television, or in courts, classrooms, or meetings. Court reporters who specialize in captioning live television programming are commonly known as *stenocaptioners*, and work for television networks or cable stations captioning news, emergency broadcasts, sporting events, and other programming.

Using a transcribing machine with headset and foot pedal, *medical transcriptionists* listen to recordings by physicians and other healthcare professionals dictating a variety of medical reports such as emergency room visits, diagnostic imaging studies, operations, chart reviews, and final summaries. To understand and accurately transcribe dictated reports into a format that is clear and comprehensible for the reader, the medical transcriptionist must understand the language of medicine, anatomy and physiology, diagnostic procedures, and treatment, and must be able to translate medical jargon and abbreviations into their expanded forms. Editing as necessary for grammar and clarity, the medical transcriptionist transcribes the dictated reports and returns them in either printed or electronic form to the dictator for review and signature, or correction. These reports eventually become a part of the patient's permanent file. (Medical secretaries, who are discussed in the *Handbook* statement on secretaries, may also transcribe as part of their jobs.)

Stenographers take dictation and then transcribe their notes on a word processor or onto a computer diskette. They may take dictation using either shorthand or a stenotype machine, which prints shorthand symbols. General stenographers, including most beginners, take routine dictation and perform other office tasks such as typing, filing, answering telephones, and operating office machines. Experienced and highly skilled stenographers take more difficult dictation. For example, they attend staff meetings and provide word-for-word records or summary reports of the proceedings to the participants. They also supervise other stenographers, typists, and clerical workers. Some experienced stenographers take dictation in foreign languages; others work as public stenographers serving traveling business people and others. Technical stenographers must know the medical, legal, engineering, or scientific terminology used in a particular profession.

Working Conditions

Court reporters work in the offices of attorneys, courtrooms, legislatures, and conventions. Transcriptionists work in hospitals, doctors' offices, or medical transcription services. An increasing number of court reporters and medical transcriptionists work from home-based offices as subcontractors for law firms, hospitals, and transcription services. Stenographers usually work in clean, well-lighted offices. Sitting in the same position for long periods can be tiring, and workers can suffer wrist, back, neck, or eye problems due to strain, and risk repetitive motion injuries such as carpal tunnel syndrome. The pressure to be accurate and fast can also be stressful.

Many court reporters, medical transcriptionists, and stenographers work a standard 40-hour week, although about 1 in 4 works part time. A substantial number of court reporters and medical transcriptionists, however, are self-employed, which may result in irregular working hours.

Employment

Court reporters medical transcriptionists, and stenographers held 98,000 jobs in 1996. More than 1 in 4 were self-employed. Of those who worked for a wage or salary, about one-third worked for State and local governments, a reflection of the large number of court reporters working in courts, legislatures, and various agencies. About one-fourth worked for hospitals and physicians' offices. Other stenographers and court reporters worked for colleges and universities, secretarial and court reporting services, temporary help supply services, and law firms.

Training, Other Qualifications, and Advancement

Court reporters generally complete a 2- or 4-year training program, offered by about 300 postsecondary vocational and technical schools

Court reporters, medical transcriptionists, and stenographers take verbatim reports of speeches, legal proceedings, or meetings.

and colleges. About 110 programs have been approved by the National Court Reporters Association (NCRA), all of which teach computer-aided transcription and real-time reporting. NCRA-approved programs require students to capture 225 words per minute. Court reporters in the Federal Government generally must capture at least 205 words a minute.

Some States require court reporters to be notary publics, or to be a Certified Court Reporter (CCR); reporters must pass a State certification test administered by a board of examiners to earn this designation. The National Court Reporters Association confers the designation, Registered Professional Reporter (RPR), upon those who pass a two-part examination and participate in continuing education programs. Although voluntary, the RPR designation is recognized as a mark of distinction in this field.

For medical transcriptionist jobs, understanding medical terminology is essential. Good English grammar and punctuation skills are required, as well as familiarity with personal computers and word processing software. Good listening skills are also necessary, because some doctors and health care professionals speak English as a second language.

Employers prefer to hire transcriptionists who have completed postsecondary training in medical transcription, offered by many vocational schools and community colleges. Completion of a 2-year associate's degree program—including coursework in anatomy, medical terminology, medicolegal issues, and English grammar and punctuation—is highly recommended. Many of these programs include supervised on-the-job experience. The American Association for Medical Transcription awards the voluntary designation, Certified Medical Transcriptionist (CMT), to those who earn passing scores on written and practical examinations. As in many other fields, certification is recognized as a sign of competence in medical transcription. To retain this credential, CMT's must obtain at least 30 continuing education credits every 3 years.

Stenographic skills are taught in high schools, vocational schools, community colleges, and proprietary business schools. For stenographer jobs, employers prefer to hire high school graduates, and seldom have a preference among the many different shorthand methods. Although requirements vary in private firms, applicants with the best speed and accuracy usually receive first consideration in hiring. To qualify for jobs in the Federal Government, stenographers must be able to take dictation at a minimum of 80 words per minute and type at least 40 words per minute. Workers must achieve higher rates to advance to more responsible positions.

Stenographers can advance to more responsible secretarial positions, especially if they develop their interpersonal and communication skills. Some stenographers complete the necessary education to become court reporters.

Job Outlook
Overall employment of court reporters, medical transcriptionists, and stenographers is projected to grow more slowly than the average for all occupations. Employment growth among medical transcriptionists should be offset by the decline among stenographers, and the number of court reporters should remain fairly stable.

Demand for medical transcriptionists is expected to increase with growth in the need for health care and the industries that provide it. Growing numbers of medical transcriptionists will be needed to amend patients' records, edit for grammar, and discover discrepancies in medical records. Those who earn an associate's degree or American Association for Medical Transcription certification, should have favorable job prospects.

Employment of court reporters should be stable. The growing number of conventions, conferences, depositions, seminars, and similar meetings in which proceedings are recorded should create demand for court reporters. Although many of these events are videotaped, a written transcript must still be created for legal purposes or if the proceedings are to be published. Also, the trend to provide instantaneous written captions for the deaf and hearing impaired should strengthen demand for stenocaptioners. In addition, demand should grow for court reporters willing to freelance or take depositions for court reporting service bureaus. However, budget constraints should limit the ability of Federal, State, and local courts to expand, even in the face of rising numbers of criminal court cases and civil lawsuits. Competition for entry-level jobs is increasing, as more workers are attracted to the occupation. Opportunities should be best for those who earn National Court Reporters Association certification.

The widespread use of dictation machines has greatly reduced the need for office stenographers. The traditional "steno pool" is almost a thing of the past. Audio recording equipment and the use of personal computers by managers and other professionals should continue to greatly decrease the demand for these workers.

Earnings
Court reporters, medical transcriptionists, and stenographers had median earnings of about $410 a week in 1996. The middle 50 percent earned between $340 and $550; the lowest paid 10 percent earned less than $280; and the highest paid 10 percent earned over $840 a week.

Court reporters generally earn higher salaries than stenographers or medical transcriptionists, and many supplement their income by doing additional freelance work. According to a National Court Reporters Association survey of its members, average earnings for court reporters were about $1,080 per week in 1995. According to a 1996 survey by the American Association for Medical Transcription, over 4 out of 10 members earned less than $25,000 a year, more than 3 out of 10 earned between $25,000 and $35,000, and over 2 out of 10 earned over $35,000. Regardless of specialty, earnings depend on education, experience, and geographic location.

Related Occupations
A number of other workers type, record information, and process paperwork. Among these are bookkeepers, receptionists, secretaries, personnel clerks, administrative assistants, and medical assistants.

Sources of Additional Information
For information about careers, training, and certification in court reporting, contact:
☛ National Court Reporters Association, 8224 Old Courthouse Rd., Vienna, VA 22182. Homepage: http://www.verbatimreporters.com

For information on a career as a medical transcriptionist, visit AAMT's Internet site or send a self-addressed, stamped envelope to:

☛ American Association for Medical Transcription, P.O. Box 576187, Modesto, CA 95357. Homepage: http://www.aamt.org/aamt

For information about job openings for stenographers, contact State employment service offices.

General Office Clerks
(D.O.T. 209.362-030, .562-010; 219.362-010, -022, -026; 243.362-014; 245.362-014, .367-010, -014, -018; 249.367-010, -014; 375.362-010)

Significant Points
- Most general office clerk jobs are entry level administrative support positions, although previous office or business experience may be required.
- The number of job openings is large due to the size of this occupation and high turnover.

Nature of the Work
The duties of general office clerks are too varied and diverse for them to be classified in any specific administrative support occupation. Rather than performing a single specialized task, the duties of a general office clerk change with the needs of their employer. Some may spend their days filing or typing; others enter data at a computer terminal. They also may operate photocopiers, fax machines, or other office equipment; prepare mailings; proofread copy; and answer telephones and deliver messages.

Duties vary significantly depending upon the office in which a clerk works. A general office clerk in a doctor's office may not perform the same tasks as a clerk in a large financial institution or in the office of an auto parts wholesaler. Although they all may sort checks, keep payroll records, take inventory, or access information, they may also perform duties unique to their employer, such as organizing medications, making transparencies for a presentation, or filling orders received by fax machine.

Duties also vary by level of experience. Inexperienced employees may make photocopies, stuff envelopes, or record inquiries. Experienced clerks might maintain financial or other records, verify statistical reports for accuracy and completeness, handle and adjust customer complaints, make travel arrangements, take inventory of equipment and supplies, answer questions on departmental services and functions, or help prepare invoices or budgetary requests. In addition, senior general office clerks may be expected to oversee and direct the work of lower level clerks.

Working Conditions
For the most part, working conditions for general office clerks are the same as those for other office employees within the same company. Those on a full-time schedule usually work a standard 40-hour week. Some may work shifts or overtime during busy periods and about 1 in 3 works part time. In addition, many general office clerks work as temporaries.

Employment
General office clerks held about 3,111,000 jobs in 1996. Most are employed in relatively small businesses. Although they work in every sector of the economy, almost 60 percent worked in the services or wholesale and retail trade industries.

Training, Other Qualifications, and Advancement
Most general office clerk jobs are entry level administrative support positions, although previous office or business experience may be required. Employers usually require a high school diploma, and some require typing, basic computer skills, and other general office skills. Familiarity with computer word processing software and applications is becoming increasingly important.

In addition to other clerical duties, general office clerks operate photocopiers and other office equipment.

Training for this occupation is available through business education programs offered in high schools, community and junior colleges, and postsecondary vocational schools. Courses in word-processing, computer applications, and office practices are particularly helpful.

Because general office clerks usually work with other office staff, they should be cooperative and be able to work as part of a team. They should have good communication skills and pay close attention to details. They must also be willing to change with the needs of the work environment or take on additional responsibilities.

General office clerks who exhibit strong communication, interpersonal, and analytical skills may be promoted to supervisory positions. Others may move into different, more senior clerical or administrative jobs, such as receptionist, secretary, or administrative assistant. After gaining some work experience or specialized skills, many workers often transfer to jobs with higher pay or greater advancement potential. Advancement to professional occupations within an establishment usually requires more formal education, including a college degree.

Job Outlook

Employment of general office clerks is expected to grow more slowly than the average for all occupations through the year 2006. Nonetheless, good job opportunities should continue to exist. Due to the large size and the high turnover associated with these positions, the occupation will continue to produce a large number of job openings.

Increasing use of computers and expanding office automation mean a wider variety of duties can be performed by fewer office workers. As more small businesses consolidate their clerical staffs and job responsibilities become more diverse, it is common to find a single general office clerk in charge of all clerical work. However, as duties expand, employers will seek workers with more advanced computer skills and a broader range of office experience.

Job seekers who have computer word-processing skills and other secretarial skills, and knowledge of the operation of basic office machinery, such as fax machines and copiers, should have the best opportunities. Because they must be so versatile, general office clerks find work in virtually every kind of industry. In addition, they should find many opportunities for part-time or temporary work, especially during peak business periods in industries where these jobs are concentrated.

Earnings

Median annual earnings of full-time general office clerks were about $19,300 in 1996; the middle 50 percent earned between $15,300 and $26,200 annually. Ten percent earned less than $12,400, and 10 percent more than $34,600.

According to a survey of workplaces in 160 metropolitan areas, beginning general office clerks had median annual earnings of about $14,200 in 1995, with the middle half earning about $12,500 to $16,400 a year. The most experienced general office clerks had median annual earnings of about $25,300, with the middle half earning between about $21,800 and $29,000 a year. General office clerks' salaries varied by industry.

In early 1997, the Federal Government paid general office clerks a starting salary of between $16,710 and $21,720 a year, depending on education and experience. General office clerks employed by the Federal Government earned an average annual salary of about $26,350.

Related Occupations

General office clerk usually is an entry-level office job. Since the duties of general office clerks may include a combination of bookkeeping, typing, office machine operation, and filing, a variety of other administrative support workers perform similar duties. Entry-level jobs in other settings include cashier, medical assistant, teacher aide, and food and beverage service worker.

Sources of Additional Information

State employment service offices and agencies specializing in placing administrative support personnel can provide information about job openings for general office clerks.

Information Clerks

Significant Points

- Expected faster than average employment growth and relatively high turnover should create numerous job openings for most types of information clerks.

- A high school diploma or its equivalent is the most common educational requirement for most information clerk jobs.

Nature of the Work

Information clerks gather information from, and provide information to the public. They are found in a variety of organizations and have many different job titles and responsibilities. *Hotel and motel desk clerks* are a guest's first contact for check-in, check-out, and other services within hotels, motels, and resorts. *Interviewing* and *new account clerks*, found most often in medical facilities, research firms, and financial institutions, assist the public in completing forms, applications or questionnaires. *Receptionists* are often a visitor's or caller's first contact within an organization, providing information and routing calls. *Reservation and transportation ticket agents*, as well as *travel clerks*, assist the public in making travel plans, reservations, and purchasing tickets for a variety of transportation services.

Although their day-to-day duties vary widely, most information clerks greet customers, guests, or other visitors. Others answer telephones or elicit information from the public. Most information clerks use general office equipment such as multiline telephones, fax machines, and personal computers. This section, which contains an overall discussion of information clerks, is followed by separate sections providing more information on the four types of clerks identified above.

Working Conditions

Information clerks who greet customers and visitors usually work in highly visible areas, designed and furnished to make a good impression. Most work stations are clean, well lighted, and relatively quiet, and overall working conditions are usually pleasant. Reservation agents and interviewing clerks who do much of their work over the telephone, generally work away from the public, often in large centralized reservation or phone centers. Because a number of agents or clerks may share the same work space, it may be crowded and noisy. Occasionally, interviewing clerks may conduct surveys on the street or in shopping malls, or go door to door. Both hotel desk clerks and ticket agents may be on their feet most of the time, and ticket agents may have to lift heavy baggage. In addition, prolonged exposure to a video display terminal may lead to eye strain.

Although most information clerks work a standard 40-hour week, about 3 out of 10 work part time. Some high school and college students work part time as information clerks, after school or during vacations. Some jobs—such as those in the transportation industry, hospitals, and hotels, in particular—may require working evenings, late night shifts, weekends, and holidays. In many cases, employees with the least seniority are assigned the least desirable shifts. Interviewing clerks conducting surveys or other research may mainly work evenings or weekends.

The work performed by information clerks may be repetitive and stressful. Many receptionists spend all day answering continuously ringing telephones while performing additional clerical or secretarial tasks. Many reservation agents and travel clerks work under stringent time constraints or have quotas on the number of calls answered or reservations made. The current technology enables management to electronically monitor their use of computer systems, monitor or tape record their telephone calls, or limit the time spent on each call.

The work of hotel and motel desk clerks and transportation ticket agents also can be stressful when trying to serve the needs of difficult or angry customers. When flights are canceled, reservations mishandled, or guests are dissatisfied, these clerks must act as a buffer between the establishment and its customers.

Employment

Information clerks held almost 1.6 million jobs in 1996. The following tabulation shows 1996 employment for the individual occupations.

Receptionists 1,074,000
Interviewing and new account clerks... 208,000
Reservation and transportation ticket agents and travel clerks............. 166,000
Hotel and motel desk clerks.. 144,000

Although information clerks are found in a variety of industries throughout the economy, employment is concentrated in hotels and motels, the health services industry, banks and savings institutions, the transportation industry, and firms providing business or real estate services.

Training, Other Qualifications, and Advancement

Although hiring requirements for information clerk jobs vary from industry to industry, a high school diploma or its equivalent is the most common educational requirement. However, good interpersonal skills and familiarity or experience with computers are often more important to employers. For airline reservation and ticket agent jobs, some college education may be preferred.

Because many information clerks deal directly with the public, good grooming habits and a pleasant personality are imperative, as are good problem-solving and interpersonal skills. A clear speaking voice and fluency in the English language are essential because these employees frequently use the telephone or public address systems. Coursework useful to persons wanting to enter these occupations include basic math, English, geography, U.S. history, psychology, communications, and public speaking. Good spelling, typing ability, and computer literacy are often needed, particularly because most work involves considerable computer use. It also is increasingly helpful for those wishing to enter the lodging or travel industries to fluently speak a foreign language.

With the exception of airline reservation and transportation ticket agents, orientation and training for information clerks generally takes place on the job. For example, orientation for hotel and motel desk clerks usually includes an explanation of the job duties and information about the establishment, such as room locations and available services. New employees learn job tasks through on-the-job training under the guidance of a supervisor or an experienced clerk. They often need additional training in how to use the computerized reservation, room assignment, and billing systems and equipment.

Receptionists generally receive on-the-job training. However, employers often look for applicants who already possess certain skills, such as prior computer and word processing experience. Some employers may prefer previous experience, some formal education, or training with office equipment or procedures. On the job, they learn how to operate the telephone system, computers, and the proper procedures for greeting visitors, and distributing mail, fax, and parcel deliveries.

Most airline reservation and ticket agents learn their skills through formal company training programs. They spend some time in a classroom setting, learning company and industry policies, computer systems, and ticketing procedures. They learn to use the airline's computer system to obtain information on schedules, seat availability, and fares; to reserve space for passengers; and to plan passenger itineraries. They must learn airport and airline code designations, regulations, and safety procedures, and may be tested on this knowledge. After completing classroom instruction, new agents work on the job with supervisors or experienced agents for a period of time. During this period, monitoring of telephone conversations may serve as a training device to improve the quality of customer service. Agents are expected to provide good service while limiting the time spent on each call without being discourteous to customers.

In contrast, automobile clubs, bus lines, and railroads tend to train their ticket agents or travel clerks on the job, through short in-house classes that can last several days. Most information clerks continue to receive instruction on new procedures and company policies after their initial training ends.

Advancement for information clerks generally comes about either by transfer to a different, more responsible occupation or by promotion to a supervisory position. The more skills, experience, and additional training an employee possesses, the better their advancement opportunities. Receptionists, interviewers, and new accounts clerks with word processing or other clerical skills may advance to a better paying job as a secretary or administrative assistant. Within the airline industry, a ticket agent may advance to lead worker on the shift.

Additional training is helpful in preparing information clerks for promotion. In the lodging industry, clerks can improve their chances for advancement by taking home or group study courses in lodging management, such as those sponsored by the Educational Institute of the American Hotel and Motel Association. In some industries—such as lodging, banking, or the airline industry—workers commonly are promoted through the ranks. Positions such as airline reservation agent or hotel and motel desk clerk offer good opportunities for qualified workers to get started in the business. In many industries, a college degree may be required for advancement to management ranks.

Job Outlook

Overall employment of information clerks is expected to increase faster than the average for all occupations through the year 2006. In addition to the many openings occurring as businesses and organizations expand, numerous job openings for information clerks will result from the need to replace experienced workers who transfer to other occupations or leave the labor force. Replacement needs reflect the relatively high turnover among these jobs. Many young people work as information clerks for a few years before switching to other, better paying jobs. This work is well suited to flexible work schedules, and many opportunities for part-time work will continue to be available, particularly as organizations look to cut labor costs by hiring more part-time or temporary workers.

Economic growth and general business expansion are expected to stimulate faster than average growth in the large number of receptionist jobs. Hotel and motel desk clerks are also expected to grow faster than the average as the composition of the lodging industry changes and services provided by these workers expand. Employment in other information clerk jobs, however, is projected to range from a decline to average growth, reflecting the impact of new technology and trends in the industries where their employment is concentrated.

Earnings

In 1996, median weekly earnings of full-time information clerks were about $345. The middle 50 percent earned between $279 and $447. The bottom 10 percent earned less than $213, while the top 10 percent earned more than $576. Earnings vary widely by occupation and experience. Weekly earnings ranged from less than $185 for the lowest paid hotel clerks, to over $710 for the highest paid reservation agents. Salaries of reservation and ticket agents tend to be significantly higher than for other information clerks, while hotel and motel desk clerks tend to earn quite a bit less, as the following tabulation of median weekly earnings shows.

Reservation and transportation ticket agents and travel clerks	$421
Interviewing clerks	356
Receptionists	333
Hotel and motel desk clerks	267

Earnings of hotel and motel desk clerks also vary considerably depending on the location, size, and type of establishment in which they work. Large luxury hotels and those located in metropolitan and resort areas generally pay clerks more than less exclusive or "budget" establishments and those located in less populated areas.

In early 1997, the Federal Government commonly paid beginning receptionists with a high school diploma or 6 months of experience, salaries ranging from $18,980 to $19,240 a year. The average annual salary for all receptionists employed by the Federal Government was about $21,240 in 1997.

In addition to their hourly wage, full-time information clerks who work evenings, nights, weekends, or holidays may receive shift differential pay. Some employers offer educational assistance to their employees. Reservation and transportation ticket agents and travel clerks receive free or reduced rate travel on their company's carriers for themselves and their immediate family and, in some companies, for friends. Relatively few information clerks belong to unions. However, unions representing these workers include the Transportation Communications International Union, the Amalgamated Transit Union, and the Hotel Employees and Restaurant Employees International Union.

Related Occupations

A number of other workers deal with the public, receive and provide information, or direct people to others who can assist them. Among these are dispatchers, security guards, bank tellers, guides, telephone operators, record clerks, counter and rental clerks, survey workers, and ushers and lobby attendants.

Hotel and Motel Desk Clerks

(D.O.T. 238.367-038)

Nature of the Work

Hotel and motel desk clerks perform a variety of services for guests of hotels, motels, and other lodging establishments. They register arriving guests and assign them rooms, and check guests out at the end of their stay. Clerks must consider their guests' preferences while trying to maximize the establishment's revenues. They keep records of room assignments and other registration information on computers, and when guests check out, they prepare and explain the bill of charges, as well as process payments.

Front desk clerks are always in the public eye and, through their attitude and behavior, greatly influence the public's impressions of the establishment. They answer questions about services, checkout times, the local community, and other matters of public interest. Should guests report problems with their rooms, clerks contact members of the housekeeping or maintenance staff to correct them.

In some smaller hotels and motels, clerks may have a variety of additional responsibilities usually performed by specialized employees in most larger establishments. These clerks may also perform the work of a bookkeeper, advance reservation agent, cashier, laundry attendant, and telephone switchboard operator.

Employment

Hotel and motel desk clerks held about 144,000 jobs in 1996. This occupation is well suited to flexible work schedules, with over 1 in 4 desk clerks working part time. Because hotels and motels are found in all parts of the country, so are these jobs.

Job Outlook

Employment of hotel and motel desk clerks is expected to grow faster than the average for all occupations through the year 2006 as more hotels, motels, and other lodging establishments are built, and as occupancy rates rise. Job opportunities for hotel and motel desk clerks should be good because turnover is very high. Each year, thousands of workers transfer to other occupations offering better pay and advancement opportunities, or simply leave the workforce altogether. Opportunities for part-time work should continue to be plentiful, because the front desk must be staffed 24 hours a day, 7 days a week.

Employment of hotel and motel desk clerks should be favorably affected by an increase in business and leisure travel. Shifts in travel preference away from long vacations and toward long weekends and other, more frequent short trips also should increase demand. The expansion of smaller, budget hotels and less construction of larger, luxury establishments reflects a change in the composition of the

Hotel desk clerks register arriving guests and keep records of room assignments.

hotel and motel industry. As employment shifts from luxury hotels and the broad services they provide to more "no-frills" operations, the proportion of hotel desk clerks should increase in relation to staff such as waiters, waitresses, and recreation workers. Often the hotel desk clerk is responsible for all front office operations, information, and services in a no-frills establishment.

However, the growing effort to cut labor costs while moving towards more efficient service is expected to slow the growth somewhat of desk clerk employment. The role of the front desk is changing as some of the more traditional duties are replaced by technology. New technologies automating check-in and check-out procedures now allow guests to bypass the front desk in many larger establishments, reducing staffing needs. The expansion of automating technologies, such as interactive television and computer systems to dispense information, should further impact employment in the future as such services become more widespread.

Employment of desk clerks is also sensitive to cyclical swings in the economy. During recessions, vacation and business travel declines and hotels and motels need fewer clerks.

Sources of Additional Information

Information on working conditions, training requirements, and earnings appears in the *Information clerks* introduction to this section.

Information on careers in the lodging industry, as well as information about professional development and training programs, may be obtained from:
☛ The Educational Institute of the American Hotel and Motel Association, P.O. Box 531126, Orlando, FL 32853-1126. Homepage: http://www.ei-ahma.org

---

Interviewing and New Accounts Clerks

(D.O.T. 205.362-018, -026, -030, .367-014, -026, -042, -054, and -058)

Nature of the Work

Interviewing and new accounts clerks obtain information that organizations need to enable individuals to open bank accounts, gain admission to medical facilities, participate in consumer surveys, and complete various other forms. By mail, telephone, or in person, they solicit and verify information, create files, and perform various processing tasks. The specific duties and job titles of these workers depend upon the type of employer.

Many *interviewing clerks* work in hospitals, doctors' offices, and other health care facilities, where they are also known as *admitting interviewers*. They interview patients to obtain all preliminary information required for admission, such as the patient's name, address, age, medical history, present medications, previous hospitalizations, religion, persons to notify in case of emergency, attending physician, and the party responsible for payment. They may assign patients to rooms and summon escorts to conduct patients to the rooms; sometimes they may escort patients themselves. Using the facility's computer system, they prepare admitting and discharge records and route them to appropriate departments. They may also bill patients, receive payments, and answer the telephone. In an outpatient setting, they also schedule appointments, keep track of cancellations, and provide general information about care.

Interviewing clerks also work for research firms conducting market research surveys and polls. Market research is not limited to the consumer market, but also includes executive, medical, and industrial research. No selling is involved. Often reading from a prepared script, interviewers ask a carefully worded series of questions, record the responses, and forward the results to management. They may ask individuals questions on such topics as their occupation and earnings, political preferences, buying habits, or customer satisfaction.

New accounts clerks, more commonly referred to as *customer service representatives*, work for financial institutions such as commercial banks, credit unions, and savings and loan associations. They interview people who want to open a checking or savings ac-

Hospital admitting interviewers obtain all preliminary information about a patient and prepare admitting and discharge records.

count and record the data directly into a computer. They must be familiar with the products and services of the bank for which they work, because it is their job to explain the increasing array of available financial services. They help people fill out enrollment forms for special services, such as automated teller machine (ATM) cards. They may also answer telephone inquiries concerning bank services or procedures for opening or closing accounts. (Bank tellers, who also may perform customer service representative duties, are discussed elsewhere in the *Handbook*.)

Employment

Interviewing and new accounts clerks held about 208,000 jobs in 1996. More than 50 percent were employed by commercial banks and other depository institutions. Most of the rest worked in hospitals and other health-care facilities, while a small number of clerks worked for research and testing service firms in the business services industry. Around 3 of every 10 interviewing clerks worked part time.

Job Outlook

Employment of interviewing and new accounts clerks is expected to increase about as fast as the average for all occupations through the year 2006; however, growth rates will vary by industry. Opportunities will be best for applicants with a broad range of job skills.

Employment of interviewing clerks in the health services industry, for example, is expected to grow as fast as the average as hospitals and health-care facilities consolidate their staffs and the duties of admitting interviewers expand. Much faster than average employment growth of interviewing clerks will occur in personnel supply services, as more organizations contract out for the services of these types of clerks rather than support a full-time staff. On the other hand, little change in employment is expected for new accounts clerks, reflecting the general lack of employment growth among commercial banks and savings and loan institutions as banking technology and consolidation decrease the role of branch offices.

Sources of Additional Information

Information on working conditions, training requirements, and earnings appears in the *Information clerks* introduction to this section.

State employment service offices can provide information about employment opportunities.

A brochure on careers in banking, including information on new accounts clerks, referred to as customer service representatives in the brochure, is available from:
☛ American Bankers Association, 1120 Connecticut Ave. NW., Washington, DC 20036.

Receptionists

(D.O.T. 203.362-014; 205.367-038; 237.267, .367-010, -018, -022, -026, -038, -042, -046, and -050; 238.367-022 and -034; 249.262 and .367-082)

Nature of the Work

All organizations want to make a good first impression, and this is often the responsibility of the receptionist, who may be the first representative of the organization a visitor encounters. Receptionists answer questions from the public and provide information about the organization. In addition to traditional duties such as answering telephones, routing calls, and greeting visitors, a receptionist may serve a security function within an organization, such as monitoring the access of visitors.

The day-to-day duties of a receptionist can vary depending upon the type of establishment in which they work. Receptionists in hospitals and doctors' offices may obtain personal and financial information and direct patients to the proper waiting rooms. At beauty or hair salons, they arrange appointments, direct customers to the hairstylist, and also may serve as cashier. In factories, large corporations, and government offices, they may provide identification cards and arrange for escorts to take visitors to the proper office. Those working for bus and train companies respond to inquiries about departures, arrivals, stops, and related matters.

Increasingly, receptionists use multiline telephone systems, personal computers, and fax machines. Despite the widespread use of automated answering systems or voice mail, many receptionists take messages and inform other employees of a visitors' arrival or cancellation of an appointment. When they are not busy with callers, most are expected to perform a variety of secretarial duties including opening and sorting mail, collecting and distributing parcels, making fax transmittals and deliveries, updating appointment calendars, preparing travel vouchers, and doing simple bookkeeping, word processing, and filing.

Employment

Receptionists held about 1,074,000 jobs in 1996, accounting for over two-thirds of all information clerk jobs. More than two-thirds of all receptionists worked in services industries, and almost half of these were located in the health services industry—doctors' and dentists' offices, hospitals, nursing homes, urgent care centers, surgical centers, and clinics. Manufacturing, wholesale and retail trade, government, and real estate industries also employed large numbers of receptionists. About 3 of every 10 receptionists worked part time.

Job Outlook

Employment of receptionists is expected to grow faster than the average for all occupations through the year 2006, because so many receptionists work for firms in services industries—including physician's offices, law firms, temporary help agencies, and consulting firms—that are expected to experience significant growth. Job openings should be plentiful due to the large size and high rate of turnover associated with this occupation. In addition to openings from growth, thousands of openings are expected each year from the need to replace receptionists who transfer to other occupations, seeking better pay or career advancement, or who leave the labor force altogether. Opportunities should be best for persons with a wide range of clerical skills and experience.

The demand for receptionists may be tempered somewhat by the increasing use of voice mail and other telephone automation. Where several receptionists may have been required to answer the company's telephones in the past, voice mail now makes it possible for one person to do the job of many. However, many receptionists also perform secretarial duties and often employers look to hire receptionists with good word processing and computer skills, coupled with strong interpersonal and communications skills. Because establishments need someone to perform their duties even during economic downturns, receptionists are less subject to layoffs during recessions than other clerical workers.

Receptionists greet visitors and provide information about the organization.

Sources of Additional Information

Information on working conditions, training requirements, and earnings appears in the *Information clerks* introduction to this section.

State employment offices can provide information on job openings for receptionists.

Reservation and Transportation Ticket Agents and Travel Clerks

(D.O.T. 214.362-030; 238.167, .362, .367-010, -014, -018, -026, -030; and 248.382)

Nature of the Work

Each year, millions of Americans travel by plane, train, ship, bus, and automobile. When they make reservations for travel or accommodations, purchase tickets, or check their luggage, they deal with reservation and transportation ticket agents and travel clerks.

Most *reservation agents* work for large hotel chains or airlines, helping people plan trips and make reservations. They usually work in large reservation centers answering telephone inquiries and offering suggestions on travel arrangements such as routes, time schedules, rates, and types of accommodation. They quote fares and room rates, make and confirm transportation and hotel reservations, and sell tickets. Agents use computerized systems to quickly obtain information needed to make, change, or cancel reservations for customers.

Transportation ticket agents are sometimes known as passenger service agents, passenger-booking clerks, reservation clerks, airport service agents, ticket clerks, or ticket sellers. They work in airports, train, and bus stations selling tickets, assigning seats to passengers, and checking baggage. In addition, they may answer inquiries and give directions, examine passports and visas, or check in animals. Other ticket agents, more commonly known as *gate* or *station agents*, work in airport terminals assisting passengers when boarding airplanes. These workers direct passengers to the correct boarding area, check tickets and seat assignments, make boarding announcements, and provide special assistance to young, elderly, or disabled passengers when they board or disembark.

Passenger rate clerks generally work for bus companies. They sell tickets for regular bus routes and arrange nonscheduled or chartered trips. They plan travel routes, compute rates, and keep customers informed of appropriate details. They also may arrange travel accommodations.

Most *travel clerks* are employed by membership organizations such as automobile clubs. These workers, sometimes called *member services counselors* or *travel counselors*, plan trips, calculate mileage, and offer travel suggestions for club members. They highlight the best

Job duties of transportation ticket agents include assigning seats, examining passports, and checking in baggage.

route from the point of origin to the destination, as well as the return. They also may prepare an itinerary indicating points of interest, restaurants, overnight accommodations, and availability of emergency services during the trip. In some cases, they may make rental car, hotel, or restaurant reservations for club members.

Employment

Reservation and transportation ticket agents and travel clerks held about 166,000 jobs in 1996. About 7 of every 10 workers are employed by the airlines. Others work for membership organizations such as automobile clubs, hotels and other lodging places, railroad companies, bus lines, and other companies that provide transportation services.

Although agents and clerks are found throughout the country, most work at large metropolitan airports, downtown ticket offices, large reservation centers, and train or bus stations. The remainder work in smaller communities served only by intercity bus or railroad lines.

Job Outlook

Employment of reservation and transportation ticket agents and travel clerks is expected to decline slightly through the year 2006. The work of these occupations is being significantly affected by technology. Automated reservations and ticketing, as well as "ticketless" travel, is reducing the need for some of these positions. Most train stations and airports have satellite ticket printer locations or "kiosks," enabling passengers to make reservations and purchase tickets themselves. It is also possible for passengers to check flight times and fares, make reservations, and purchase tickets on the Internet. Nevertheless, all travel-related passenger services can never be fully automated for safety and security reasons; therefore, job openings will become available as workers transfer to other occupations, retire, or leave the labor force altogether.

Applicants for reservation and transportation ticket agent jobs are likely to encounter considerable competition because the supply of qualified applicants exceeds the expected number of job openings. Entry requirements for these jobs are minimal, and many people seeking to get into the airline industry or travel business often start out in these types of positions. These jobs provide excellent travel benefits and many people view airline and travel-related jobs as glamorous.

Employment of reservation and transportation ticket agents and travel clerks is sensitive to cyclical swings in the economy. During recessions, discretionary passenger travel declines and transportation service companies are less likely to hire new workers and even may resort to layoffs.

Sources of Additional Information

Information on working conditions, training requirements, and earnings appears in the *Information clerks* introduction to this section.

For information about job opportunities as reservation and transportation ticket agents and travel clerks, write the personnel manager of individual transportation companies. Addresses of airlines are available from:
☛ Air Transport Association of America, 1301 Pennsylvania Ave. NW., Suite 1100, Washington, DC 20004-1707.

Loan Clerks and Credit Authorizers, Checkers, and Clerks

(D.O.T. 205.367-022; 209.362-018; 219.362-038, .367-046; 237.367-014; 241.367-018, -026, -030; 249.362-014, -018, -022, .367-022)

Significant Points

- No specific training is needed for most entry-level positions; however, loan closers and interviewers are often required to have previous work experience in financial institutions, and some knowledge of underwriting.

- Little change is expected in employment. The interpersonal nature of the work should ensure that computers do not significantly affect future employment levels.

Nature of the Work

Loan clerks and credit authorizers, checkers, and clerks review credit history and obtain the information needed to determine the creditworthiness of loan and credit card applicants. Credit clerks contact applicants, credit bureaus, and other sources for information, and verify the completeness of loan applications. Credit checkers in credit bureaus secure, update, and verify information for credit reports. These workers are often called credit investigators or reporters.

Loan clerks, often called loan processing clerks, prepare loan applications for underwriters. They review loan applications, contact credit bureaus and reporting agencies for applicant records, and contact employers, banks, and references to verify personal and financial information. Clerks order appraisals from appraisal companies and secure tax forms, bank statements, and any required government forms from applicants. If any information in the loan package is inaccurate or incomplete, clerks contact the proper source for further information. Mortgage loans are the primary type of loans handled by loan processors. Closing clerks obtain and prepare documents needed for real estate settlements. The closing clerks check to see that all documents are complete, accurate, and correctly signed, including deeds of trust, hazard insurance papers, and title commitments—and that all loan conditions required for settlement have been met.

Credit authorizers approve charges against customers' existing accounts. Most charges are approved automatically by computer. However, when accounts are past due, overextended, invalid, or show a change of address, sales persons refer transactions to credit authorizers located in a central office. Authorizers evaluate the customers' computerized credit records and payment histories and quickly decide whether or not to approve new charges. Authorizers may enter address changes and credit extensions into computer credit files.

Loan interviewers help potential borrowers fill out the loan application. Interviewers investigate the applicant's background and references, verify information on the application, and forward any findings, reports, or documents to the appraisal department. Interviewers inform the applicant whether the loan has been accepted or denied.

Working Conditions

Loan clerks and credit authorizers, checkers, and clerks usually work a 35- to 40-hour week. However, during particularly busy periods, they may work overtime. For credit clerks handling residential real estate, the busy periods are spring and summer and at the end of the month. For credit authorizers, busy periods are during the holiday shopping seasons and on store sale days. In fact, temporary workers

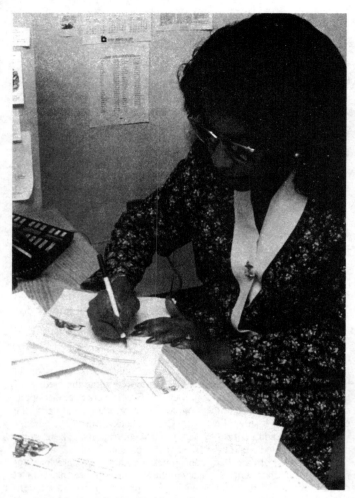

Credit clerks must be good with numbers.

are often hired as credit authorizers during peak workloads. In retail establishments, authorizers may work nights and weekends during store hours.

Some clerks may sit for long periods in front of video display terminals, which may cause eyestrain and headaches.

Employment

Loan clerks and credit authorizers, checkers, and clerks held about 252,000 jobs in 1996. About 8 out of 10 were employed by commercial banks and other depository institutions, and mortgage banks and other nondepository institutions. Other clerks were employed by insurance and real estate firms, credit reporting and collection agencies, and wholesale and retail trade establishments.

Training, Other Qualifications, and Advancement

No specific training is needed for most entry-level positions. However, loan closers and interviewers are often required to have previous work experience, preferably in financial institutions, and some knowledge of underwriting.

New employees are generally trained on the job, working under the close supervision of more experienced employees, although some firms offer formal training. Some credit workers also take courses in credit offered by banking and credit associations, public and private vocational schools, and colleges and universities. Workers at these positions typically advance to team leader of a small group of clerks, loan or credit department supervisor, underwriter, or loan officer.

Because positions in these fields involve much telephone contact, good communication skills are a necessity. Good organizational skills and the ability to pay attention to detail are also important.

Many clerks use computers to enter and retrieve data, so some computer skills and good typing speed are required.

Job Outlook

Little change is expected in the employment of loan clerks and credit authorizers, checkers, and clerks over the 1996-2006 period. Employment in the banking industry, where most of these workers are found, is projected to decline slightly. However, demand for real estate, retail sales, and other transactions requiring credit will grow, and the interpersonal nature of loan clerking and the judgment required of credit authorizers should ensure that computers do not significantly affect future employment levels. Many job openings will arise from replacement needs as loan clerks and credit authorizers, checkers, and clerks leave the occupation for various reasons.

Job outlook in this occupation is affected by changes in the economy. During periods when credit or loans are restricted, the number of job openings for loan clerks and credit authorizers, checkers, and clerks may be limited, and layoffs may occur.

Earnings

According to a 1996 survey of mortgage banking companies conducted by Carl D. Jacobs & Associates, the average salary for loan processors was $24,700, and the average salary for loan closers was $24,000.

In addition to standard benefits, workers in retail establishments usually receive a discount on store purchases.

Related Occupations

Occupations with duties similar to those of loan clerks and credit authorizers, checkers, and clerks include claim examiners and adjusters, customer-complaint clerks, procurement clerks, probate clerks, and collection clerks.

Sources of Additional Information

Information about local job opportunities for loan clerks and credit authorizers, checkers and clerks may be obtained from banks and credit institutions, retail stores, and credit reporting agencies.

Mail Clerks and Messengers

(D.O.T. 209.587-018 and .687-026; 222.367-022, .387-038, .567-018, and .587-030 and -032; 230.647-010 and .663-010; 239.567, .677, and .687; and 243.367-010)

Significant Points

- Automated mail systems and other computerized innovations are expected to limit employment growth.

- This is a first job for many because there are no formal qualifications or training requirements.

Nature of the Work

Mail clerks and messengers help businesses, institutions, and government agencies run efficiently by moving and distributing information, documents, and small packages.

Most large organizations employ *mail clerks* to handle their internal mail. Internal mail goes back and forth among people, offices, or departments within a firm or institution. It ranges from memos to key personnel to bulletins on job issues to all employees. Mail clerks sort internal mail and deliver it to their fellow employees, often using carts to carry the mail between offices.

Mail clerks also handle external mail, serving as the link between the U.S. Postal Service and individual offices and workers. They sort incoming mail and deliver mail within large office buildings. They also prepare outgoing mail—which may range from advertising flyers, to customers' orders, to legal documents—for delivery to the post office. To facilitate delivery of outgoing mail, mail clerks often determine if the mail is to be sent registered, certified, special delivery, or first, second, third, or fourth class, and may group mailings by ZIP code. When necessary, they contact delivery services to send important letters or parcels. In larger organizations, or organizations with a large volume of outgoing mail, mail clerks often operate machines which collate, fold, and insert material to be mailed into envelopes. They also operate machines which affix postage. In addition, mail clerks increasingly use computers to keep records of incoming and outgoing items.

Messengers, also called couriers, pick up and deliver letters, important business documents, or packages which need to be sent or received in a hurry from within a local area. By sending an item by messenger, the sender ensures that it reaches its destination the same day or even within the hour. Messengers also deliver items which the sender is unwilling to entrust to other means of delivery, such as important legal or financial documents. Some messengers pick up and deliver important packages, such as medical samples to be tested.

Messengers receive their instructions either by reporting to their office in person, by telephone, or by two-way radio. They then pick up the item and carry it to its destination. After a delivery, they check with their office and receive instructions about the next delivery. Consequently, most messengers spend much of their time outdoors or in their vehicle. Messengers usually maintain records of deliveries and often obtain signatures from the persons receiving the items.

Most messengers deliver items within a limited geographic area, such as a city or metropolitan area. Items which need to go longer distances usually are sent by mail or by an overnight delivery service. Some messengers carry items only for their employer, which typically might be a law firm, bank, or financial institution. Other messengers may act as part of an organization's internal mail system and mainly carry items between an organization's buildings or entirely within one building. Many messengers work for messenger or courier services; for a fee they pick up items from anyone and deliver them to specified destinations within a local area.

Messengers reach their destination by several methods. Many drive vans or cars or ride motorcycles. A few travel by foot, especially in urban areas or when making deliveries nearby. In congested urban areas, messengers often use bicycles, because this is the fastest way to travel in heavy traffic. Bicycle messengers usually are employed by messenger or courier services. Although fax machines and computerized electronic mail (e-mail) can deliver information faster than messengers, for many types of business transactions an electronic copy cannot substitute for the original document.

Working Conditions
Working conditions for mail clerks are much different from the working conditions for most messengers. Most mail clerks work regular hours, spending much of their time in mailrooms, which are usually located in office buildings. Most of the rest of their time is spent making mail deliveries throughout an office building. Although mailrooms are usually clean and well lighted, there may be noise from mail-handling machines. While sorting and delivering mail and operating machinery, mail clerks spend most of their time on their feet, which can be tiring and physically demanding. They are sometimes required to lift heavy objects or operate a motor vehicle to make deliveries and pick-ups.

Messengers work in a less structured environment than mail clerks because they spend most of their time alone making deliveries and usually are not closely supervised. Although many messengers work full time during regular business hours, some messengers work nights and weekends.

Messengers who deliver by bicycle must be physically fit and are exposed to all weather conditions as well as the many hazards connected with heavy traffic. The pressure to make as many deliveries as possible to increase earnings can be stressful and may lead to unsafe driving or bicycling practices.

Employment
Messengers and mail clerks together held about 268,000 jobs in 1996; about 130,000 were mail clerks and 138,000 were messengers.

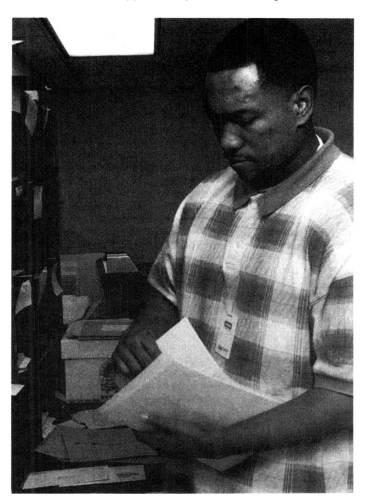

Employment of mail clerks and messengers is expected to grow slowly through the year 2006.

About 14 percent of messengers worked for law firms, another 13 percent worked for hospitals and medical and dental laboratories, and 11 percent for air carriers. Financial institutions, such as commercial banks, saving institutions, and credit unions, employed 7 percent. The rest were employed in a wide variety of other industries. Technically, many messengers are self-employed independent contractors because they provide their vehicles and, to a certain extent, set their own schedules, but in many respects they are like employees because they usually work for one company.

In 1996, about 14 percent of all mail clerks worked in Federal, State, and local governments, and both the insurance industry and personnel supply industry employed 10 percent. Others were employed in a wide range of industries.

Training, Other Qualifications, and Advancement
There are no formal qualifications or training required to be a mail clerk or messenger, although some employers prefer high school graduates. This is a first job for many.

Mail clerks must be careful and dependable workers. They must be able to do routine work and work well with their hands. They are usually trained on the job. If they operate computers and mail-handling machinery to help prepare mailings, training may be provided by another employee or by a representative of the machinery manufacturer. Mail clerks are sometimes required to have a driver's license if they make deliveries to other buildings.

Messengers who work as independent contractors for a messenger or delivery service may be required to have a valid drivers license, a registered and inspected vehicle, a good driving record, and insurance coverage. Many messengers who are employees, not independent contractors, are also required to provide and maintain their own vehicle. A good knowledge of the geographic area in which they travel as well as a good sense of direction are also important.

Some mail clerks, depending on the size of the operation, advance to positions as clerical staff supervisors or office managers. Other mail clerks transfer to related jobs with the U.S. Postal Service, if they pass the competitive entrance examination. (Information on postal clerk and mail carrier careers appears elsewhere in the *Handbook*.) Messengers, especially those who work for messenger or courier services, have limited advancement opportunities.

Job Outlook

Favorable employment opportunities are expected for mail clerks and messengers due to the need to replace the large number of workers who leave the occupation each year. Mail clerk and messenger jobs are attractive to many persons seeking their first job or a short-term source of income because the limited formal education and training requirements allow easy entry. This is especially true for messengers, many of whom work in this occupation a relatively short time.

Employment of mail clerks and messengers is expected to grow more slowly than the average for all occupations through the year 2006 despite an increasing volume of internal mail, parcels, business documents, promotional materials, and other written information that must be handled and delivered as the economy expands.

Businesses' growing reliance on directly mailing advertising and promotional materials to prospective customers will result in increasing amounts of mail to be handled. However, increasing automation of mail-handling will enable mail clerks to handle a growing volume of mail.

Employment of messengers will be impacted as new electronic information-handling technology comes into more widespread use. Fax machines, for example, allow copies of documents to be immediately sent across town or across the country and have become standard office equipment. The transmission of information through telephone lines between computers (e-mail) will also reduce the demand for messengers as more computers are connected to networks. However, messengers will still be needed to transport materials which cannot be sent electronically, such as legal documents, blueprints and other oversized materials, large multipage documents, and securities. Also, messengers will still be required by medical and dental laboratories to pick up and deliver medical samples, specimens, and other materials.

Earnings

Median weekly earnings of full-time mail clerks were about $339 in 1996; the middle 50 percent earned between $279 and $468 a week. Median weekly earnings of full-time messengers were about $360. The middle 50 percent of messengers earned between $275 and $561 a week. Messengers occasionally receive tips from clients, but this is not a significant part of their earnings.

Messengers are compensated in one of three ways—salary, commission, or a combination of both. The commission usually is based on the fee charged to the customer and is usually considerably higher for those who strictly work by commission than for those messengers whose earnings are based on a combination of salary and commission. Other factors like the number of deliveries made and the distance traveled may also be taken into consideration when determining earnings. The more deliveries they make and the faster they travel, the more they earn. Some messengers work as independent contractors and therefore seldom receive paid vacations, sick leave, health insurance, or other benefits from the messenger or delivery company. They must provide their own transportation and must pay fuel and maintenance costs. Messengers working for employers other than messenger and courier services usually are paid by the hour and receive the benefits offered to all employees.

Mail clerks are usually paid by the hour and benefits often include health and life insurance, sick leave, vacation pay, and pension plan.

Related Occupations

Messengers and mail clerks sort and deliver letters, parcels, and other items. They also keep accurate records of their work. Others who do similar work are postal clerks and mail carriers; route drivers; traffic, shipping, and receiving clerks; and parcel post clerks.

Sources of Additional Information

Information about job opportunities may be obtained from local employers and local offices of the State employment service. Persons interested in mail clerk and messenger jobs may also contact messenger and courier services, mail order firms, banks, printing and publishing firms, utility companies, retail stores, or other large firms.

For information on training and certification programs in mail systems management, contact:
☛ Mail Systems Management Association, J.A.F. Building, P.O. Box 2155, New York, NY 10116-2155.

Material Recording, Scheduling, Dispatching, and Distributing Occupations

Significant Points

* Slower than average growth is expected as additional automation increases worker productivity.

* Many of the occupations in this group are entry level and do not require more than a high school degree.

Nature of the Work

Workers in this group are responsible for a variety of communications, recordkeeping, and scheduling operations in business and government. Typically, they coordinate, expedite, and track orders for personnel, materials, and equipment.

Dispatchers receive requests for service and initiate action to provide that service. Duties vary, depending on the needs of the employer. Police, fire, and ambulance dispatchers, also called public safety dispatchers, handle calls from people reporting crimes, fires, and medical emergencies; truck, bus, and train dispatchers schedule and coordinate the movement of these vehicles to ensure they arrive on schedule; taxicab dispatchers relay requests for cabs to individual drivers; tow truck dispatchers take calls for emergency road service; and utility company dispatchers handle calls related to utility and telephone service.

Stock clerks receive, unpack, and store materials and equipment, and issue and maintain inventories. Inventories may be merchandise in wholesale and retail establishments, or equipment, supplies, or materials in other kinds of organizations. In small firms, they may perform all of the above tasks, as well as those usually handled by shipping and receiving clerks. In large establishments, they may be responsible only for one task.

Traffic, shipping, and receiving clerks track all incoming and outgoing shipments of goods transferred between businesses, suppliers, and customers. Traffic clerks record destination, weight, and charge of all incoming and outgoing shipments. Shipping clerks assemble, address, stamp, and ship merchandise or materials. Receiving clerks unpack, verify, and record incoming merchandise. In a small company, one clerk may perform all of these tasks. More detail on these occupations is available in the following statements.

Other administrative support occupations in this group include *production, planning, and expediting clerks*—who coordinate and expedite the flow of work and material according to production schedules; *procurement clerks*—who draw up purchase orders to obtain merchandise or material; *weighers, measurers, checkers, and samplers*—who weigh, measure, and check materials; and *utility meter readers*—who read electric, gas, water, or steam meters and record the quantity used.

Working Conditions

Working conditions vary considerably by occupation and employment setting. Meter readers, for example, spend a good portion of their workday traveling around communities and neighborhoods taking readings, either directly or with remote reading equipment. The work of dispatchers can be very hectic when a large number of calls come in at the same time. The job of public safety dispatcher is particularly stressful, because slow or improper response to a call can result in serious injury or further harm. Also, callers who are anxious or afraid may become excited and be unable to provide needed information; some may become abusive. Despite provocations, dispatchers must remain calm, objective, and in control of the situation.

Dispatchers work in surroundings that are typical of office jobs. They sit for long periods, using telephones, computers, and two-way radios. Much of their time is spent at video display terminals, viewing monitors and observing traffic patterns. As a result of working for long stretches with computers and other electronic equipment, dispatchers can experience significant eyestrain and back discomfort. Generally, dispatchers work a 40-hour week; however, rotating shifts and compressed work schedules are common. Alternative work schedules are necessary to accommodate evening, weekend, and holiday work, as well as 24-hours-per-day, seven-days-per-week operations.

Traffic, shipping, receiving, and stock clerks work in a wide variety of businesses, institutions, and industries. Some work in warehouses, stock rooms, or in shipping and receiving rooms that may not be temperature controlled. Others may spend time in cold storage rooms or outside on loading platforms, where they are exposed to the weather. Most jobs involve frequent standing, bending, walking, and stretching. Some lifting and carrying of smaller items may be involved. Although automation, robotics, and pneumatic devices have lessened the physical demands in this occupation, their use remains somewhat limited. Work still can be strenuous, even though mechanical material-handling equipment is employed to move heavy items. The typical workweek is Monday through Friday; however, evening and weekend hours are standard for some jobs, such as stock clerks who work in retail trade, and may be required in others when large shipments are involved or when inventory is taken.

Employment

In 1996, material recording, scheduling, dispatching, and distributing workers held about 3,633,000 jobs. Employment was distributed among the occupations in this group as follows:

Total	3,633,000
Stock clerks	1,844,000
Traffic, shipping, and receiving clerks	759,000
Production, planning, and expediting clerks	239,000
Dispatchers	234,000
Order fillers, wholesale and retail sales	227,000
Procurement clerks	56,000
Meter readers, utilities	55,000
Weighers, measurers, checkers, and samplers	47,000
All other	170,000

Almost 3 out of 4 material recording, scheduling, dispatching, and distributing jobs were in manufacturing or wholesale and retail trade. Although these workers are found throughout the country, most work near population centers where retail stores, warehouses, factories, and large communications centers are concentrated.

Training, Other Qualifications, and Advancement

Many of the occupations in this group are entry-level, and do not require more than a high school degree. Employers, however, increasingly prefer to hire those with some familiarity with computers and other high technology office and business equipment. Those who have taken business courses or have previous business, dispatching, or specific job-related experience may be preferred. Also, good oral and written communications skills are becoming essential. This is true, in part, because the nature of the work is to communicate effectively with other people. Typing, filing, recordkeeping, and other clerical skills are important functions of these occupations. In larger, more automated facilities, these tasks may be accomplished electronically.

Traffic, shipping, and receiving clerks and stock clerks who handle jewelry, liquor, or drugs may be bonded. Police, fire, and ambulance dispatching jobs generally are governed by State or local government civil service regulations. Candidates for these positions may have to pass written, oral, and performance tests. Also, they may be asked to attend certification training classes and attain the proper certification in order to qualify for advancement.

Trainees usually develop the necessary skills on the job. This informal training lasts from several days to a few months, depending on the complexity of the job. Dispatchers usually require the most extensive training. Working with an experienced dispatcher, they monitor calls and learn how to operate a variety of communications equipment, including telephones, radios, and wireless appliances. As trainees gain confidence, they begin to handle calls themselves. Many public safety dispatchers also participate in structured training programs sponsored by their employer. Some employers offer a course designed by the Associated Public Safety Communications Officers (APCO). This course covers topics such as interpersonal communications; overview of the police, fire, and rescue functions; modern public safety telecommunications systems; basic radio broadcasting; local, State, and national crime information computer systems; and telephone complaint/report processing procedures. Other employers develop in-house programs based on their own needs. Emergency medical dispatchers often receive special training or have special skills. Increasingly, public safety dispatchers receive training in stress and crisis management, as well as family counseling. Employers are recognizing the toll this work has on daily living and the potential impact stress has on the job, on the work environment, and in the home.

Although there are no mandatory licensing or certification requirements, some States require that public safety dispatchers possess a certificate to work on a State network, such as the Police Information Network. Certification programs are offered by both APCO and the International Municipal Signal Association. Many dispatchers participate in these programs in order to improve their prospects for career advancement.

Stock clerks and traffic, shipping, and receiving clerks usually learn the job by doing simple tasks under close supervision. They learn how to count and mark stock, and then start keeping records and taking inventory. Stock clerks whose sole responsibility is to bring merchandise to the sales floor and stock shelves and racks need little or no training. Traffic, shipping, and receiving clerks start out by checking items to be shipped and then attaching labels and making sure the addresses are correct. Training in the use of automated equipment is usually done informally, on the job. As these occupations become more automated, however, workers in these jobs may need longer training in order to master the use of the equipment.

Communications skills and the ability to work under pressure are important personal qualities for dispatchers. Residency in the city or county of employment frequently is required for public safety dispatchers. Dispatchers in transportation industries must be able to deal with sudden influxes of shipments and disruptions of shipping schedules caused by bad weather, road construction, or accidents. Strength, stamina, good eyesight, and an ability to work at repetitive tasks, sometimes under pressure, are important characteristics for stock clerks and traffic, shipping, and receiving clerks.

Advancement opportunities vary with the place of employment. Dispatchers who work for private firms, which are usually small, will find few opportunities for advancement. Public safety dispatchers, on the other hand, may become a shift or divisional supervisor or chief of communications, or move to higher paying administrative jobs. Some go on to become police officers or firefighters. In large firms, stock clerks can advance to invoice clerk, stock control clerk, or procurement clerk. Traffic, shipping, and receiving clerks are promoted to head clerk, and those with a broad understanding of shipping and receiving may enter a related field such as industrial traffic management. With additional training, some stock clerks and traffic, shipping, and receiving clerks advance to jobs as warehouse manager or purchasing agent.

Job Outlook

Overall employment of material recording, scheduling, dispatching, and distributing workers is expected to grow more slowly than the average for all occupations through the year 2006. However, employment growth among the individual occupations in this group is expected to vary. Employment of stock clerks, for example, will be affected by increased automation. New technologies will enable clerks to handle more stock, thus holding down employment growth. The effect of automation also will tend to restrict potential employment growth of employment of traffic, shipping, and receiving clerks. Automation in warehouses and stockrooms plus other productivity improvements will enable these clerks to handle materials more efficiently and more accurately than before. Employment of public safety dispatchers is expected to grow more slowly than the average as governments endeavor to combine dispatching services across governmental units and across governmental jurisdictions.

Because employment in material recording, scheduling, dispatching, and distributing occupations is substantial, workers who leave the labor force or transfer to other occupations are expected to create many job openings each year.

Earnings

Median weekly earnings of workers in all material recording, scheduling, dispatching, and distributing occupations were $412 in 1996. The middle 50 percent earned between $303 and $567. The lowest 10 percent earned $241or less; the top 10 percent earned over $746.

Earnings vary somewhat by occupation and industry. Dispatchers earn slightly more than the average for these occupations, and stock clerks and traffic, shipping, and receiving clerks generally earn less. Median weekly earnings of dispatchers were $471in 1996, whereas the median weekly earnings of traffic, shipping, and receiving clerks and stock clerks were $367 and $429, respectively, in 1996.

Workers in material recording, scheduling, dispatching, and distributing occupations usually receive the same benefits as most other workers. If uniforms are required, employers usually either provide the uniforms, or an allowance to purchase them.

Dispatchers

(D.O.T. 184.167-010, -262; 215.167, .367-018, .563; 221.362-014, .367-070, -082; 239.167-014; .367-014, -022, -030; 248.367-026; 249.167-014, .367 -070; 372.167-010; 379.162; .362-010, and -018; 579.137-030; 910.167-014, .367-018; 911.167; 913.167-010; .367; 914.167-014; 919.162; 932.167; 939.362-010; 952.167-010; 953.167; 954.367; 955.167; and 959.167)

Nature of the Work

The work of dispatchers varies greatly depending on the industry in which they work. Regardless of where they work, however, all dispatchers are assigned a specific territory and have responsibility for all communications within this area. Dispatchers keep records, logs, and schedules of the calls they receive, the transportation vehicles they monitor and control, and the actions they take. They maintain information on each call and then prepare a detailed report on all activities occurring during the shift. Many dispatchers employ computer-aided, or computer-assisted, dispatch systems to accomplish these tasks. The cost of these systems, however, still limits their widespread use.

Many police, ambulance, taxicab, and tow truck dispatchers work as part of teams, especially in large communications centers or companies. One person usually handles all dispatching calls to the response units or company's drivers, while the other members of the team generally receive the incoming calls and deal with the public.

Police, fire, and ambulance dispatchers, also called public safety dispatchers, monitor the location of emergency services personnel from any one or all of the jurisdiction's emergency services departments. They dispatch the appropriate type and number of units in response to calls for assistance. Dispatchers, or call takers, often are the first people the public talks to when they call for emergency assistance. If certified for emergency medical services, then the dispatcher may provide medical instruction to those on the scene until the medical staff arrives. Commonly, they constitute the communications workforce on a shift. A dispatcher is a person in an assignment position, while the call takers are people receiving calls and transferring information to the dispatchers. During the course of the shift, personnel will rotate such that the assignment responsibility of the dispatcher will be shared with those in the call taker role.

Dispatchers work in a variety of settings; they may work in a police station, a fire station, a hospital, or a centralized city communications center. In many cities, the police department serves as the communications center. In these situations, all 911 emergency calls go to the police department, where a dispatcher handles the police calls and screens the others before transferring them to the appropriate service.

When handling calls, dispatchers carefully question each caller to determine the type, seriousness, and location of the emergency. This information is posted either electronically by computer, or, with decreasing frequency, by hand, and communicated immediately to uniformed or supervisory personnel. They quickly decide on the priority of the incident, the kind and number of units needed, and the location of the closest and most suitable ones available. Typically, there is a team of call takers who answer calls and relay the information to the dispatchers. Responsibility then shifts to the dispatchers who send response units to the scene and monitor the activity of the public safety personnel answering the dispatch.

When appropriate, dispatchers stay in close contact with other service providers—for example, a police dispatcher would monitor the response of the fire department when there is a major fire. In a medical emergency, dispatchers not only keep in close touch with the dispatched units, but also with the caller. They may give extensive pre-arrival first aid instructions while the caller is waiting for the

Dispatchers ensure the smooth flow of transportation vehicles.

ambulance. They continuously give updates on the patient's condition to the ambulance personnel, and often serve as a link between the medical staff in a hospital and the emergency medical technicians in the ambulance. (The work of emergency medical technicians is described elsewhere in the *Handbook*.)

Truck dispatchers, who work for local and long distance trucking companies, coordinate the movement of trucks and freight between cities. They direct the pickup and delivery activities of drivers. They receive customers' requests for pickup and delivery of freight; consolidate freight orders into truckloads for specific destinations; assign drivers and trucks; and draw up routes and pickup and delivery schedules. *Bus dispatchers* make sure local and long distance buses stay on schedule. They handle all problems that may disrupt service and dispatch other buses, or arrange for repairs to restore service and schedules. *Train dispatchers* are responsible for the timely and efficient movement of trains according to train orders and schedules. They must be aware of track switch positions, track maintenance areas, and the location of other trains running on the track. *Taxicab dispatchers,* or starters, dispatch taxis in response to requests for service and keep logs on all road service calls. *Tow truck dispatchers* take calls for emergency road service. They relay the problem to a nearby service station or a tow truck service and see to it that the emergency road service is completed. *Gas and water service dispatchers* monitor gas lines and water mains and send out service trucks and crews to take care of emergencies. Other dispatchers coordinate deliveries, service calls, and related activities for a variety of firms.

Employment

Dispatchers held 234,000 jobs in 1996. Almost two-fifths were police, fire, and ambulance dispatchers, almost all of whom worked for State and local governments—primarily for local police and fire departments. Most of the remaining dispatchers worked for local and long distance trucking companies and bus lines; telephone, electric, and gas utility companies; wholesale and retail establishments; railroads; and companies providing business services.

Although dispatching jobs are found throughout the country, most dispatchers work in urban areas where large communications centers and businesses are located.

Job Outlook

Overall employment of dispatchers is expected to grow about as fast as the average for all occupations through the year 2006. Most job openings will result from the need to replace those who transfer to other occupations or leave the labor force.

Employment of police, fire, and ambulance dispatchers is expected to grow more slowly than the average for all occupations. Intense competition for available resources among governmental units should limit the ability of many growing communities to keep pace with rapidly growing emergency services needs. To balance the increased demand for emergency services, many districts are seeking to consolidate their communications centers into a shared, areawide facility, thus further restricting opportunities in this industry.

Population growth and economic expansion are expected to lead to overall employment growth of dispatchers not involved in public safety. Although the overall increase will be about average, not all specialties will be affected in the same way. For example, employment of taxicab, train, and truck dispatchers is sensitive to economic conditions. When economic activity falls, demand for transportation services declines. They may experience layoffs or a shortened workweek, and jobseekers may have some difficulty finding entry-level jobs. Employment of tow truck dispatchers, on the other hand, is seldom affected by general economic conditions because of the emergency nature of their business.

Related Occupations

Other occupations that involve directing and controlling the movement of vehicles, freight, and personnel, as well as information and message distribution, are airline dispatchers, air traffic controllers, radio and television transmitter operators, telephone operators, customer service representatives, and transportation agents.

Sources of Additional Information

For further information on training for police, fire, and emergency dispatchers contact:

☛ National Academy of Emergency Medical Dispatch, 139 East South Temple, Suite 530, Salt Lake City, UT 84111.

☛ Associated Public Safety Communications Officers, 2040 S. Ridgewood, South Daytona, FL 32119-2257.

☛ International Municipal Signal Association, 165 East Union St., P.O. Box 539, Newark, NY 14513-1526.

☛ American Society for Testing and Materials, 100 Barr Harbor Drive, West Conshohocken, PA 19428.

For general information on dispatchers contact:

☛ Service Employees International Union, AFL-CIO; CLC, 1313 L St. NW., Washington, DC 20005-4100.

☛ American Train Dispatchers Association, 1370 Ontario St., Cleveland, OH 44113.

Information on job opportunities for police, fire, and emergency dispatchers is available from the personnel offices of State and local governments or police departments. Information about work opportunities for other types of dispatchers is available from local employers and State employment service offices. (Information on training and earnings is in the introduction to material recording, scheduling, dispatching, and distributing occupations.)

Stock Clerks

(D.O.T. 219.367-018, .387-026 and -030; 221.587-018 and -022; 222.167, .367-014, -026, -038, -042, -050, and -062, .387-018, -026, -030, -034, -042, -058, and -062, .487, .587-022 and -054, .684, .687-038 and -046; 229.367, .587-014; 249.367-058; 299.367-014, .677-014; 339.687; 381.687-010; and 969.367)

Nature of the Work

Stock clerks receive, unpack, check, store, and track merchandise or materials. They keep records of items entering or leaving the stock room and inspect damaged or spoiled goods. They sort, organize, and mark items with identifying codes, such as prices or stock or inventory control codes, so that inventories can be located quickly and easily. In many firms, stock clerks use hand-held scanners connected to computers to keep inventories up to date. In retail stores, stock clerks bring merchandise to the sales floor and stock shelves and racks. In stockrooms and warehouses, they store materials in bins, on floors, or on shelves. In larger establishments, where they may be responsible for only one specific task, they may be known as inventory clerk, stock-control clerk, merchandise distributor, order filler, property custodian, or storekeeper. In smaller firms, they may also be responsible for tasks usually handled by shipping and receiving clerks.

Employment

Stock clerks held about 1,844,000 jobs in 1996, with almost 80 percent working in wholesale or retail trade. The greatest numbers were employed in grocery and department stores, respectively. Jobs for stock clerks are found in all parts of the country, but most work in large urban areas that have many large suburban shopping centers, warehouses, and factories.

Job Outlook

Job prospects for stock clerks should be favorable even though employment is expected to grow more slowly than the average for all occupations through the year 2006. This occupation is very large, and many job openings will occur each year to replace those who transfer to other jobs or leave the labor force. Many jobs are entry-level, and many vacancies tend to occur naturally through normal career progression.

The growing use of computers for inventory control and the installation of new, automated equipment are expected to slow growth in demand for stock clerks somewhat. This is especially true in manufacturing and wholesale trade, industries whose operations are automated most easily. In addition to computerized inventory control systems, firms in these industries are expected to rely more on sophisticated conveyor belts and automatic high stackers to store and

Stock clerks maintain inventories of parts or merchandise in warehouses and stores.

retrieve goods. Also, expanded use of battery-powered, driverless automatically guided vehicles can be expected.

Employment of stock clerks who work in grocery, general merchandise, department, apparel, and accessories stores is expected to be somewhat less affected by automation because much of their work is done manually on the sales floor and is difficult to automate. In addition, the ever-increasing role of large retail outlets and warehouses, as well as catalogue, mail, telephone, and Internet shopping services in the Nation's economy should bolster employment of stock clerks in these sectors of retail trade.

Related Occupations
Other workers who also handle, move, organize, and store materials include shipping and receiving clerks, distributing clerks, routing clerks, stock supervisors, and cargo checkers.

Sources of Additional Information
State employment service offices can provide information about job openings for stock clerks. Also, see clerical and sales occupations elsewhere in the *Handbook* for sources of additional information.

General information about stock clerks can be obtained by contacting:
☞ National Retail Federation, 325 Seventh Street, NW., Suite 1000, Washington, DC 20004. Homepage: http://www.nrf.com

(Information on training and earnings is in the introduction to material recording, scheduling, dispatching, and distributing occupations.)

Traffic, Shipping, and Receiving Clerks

(D.O.T. 209.367-042; 214.587-014; 219.367-022 and -030; 221.367-022; 222.367-066, .387-014, -022, -050, and -054, .485, .567-010 and -014, .587-018, -034, and -058, .687-022 and -030; 248.362-010, .367-014 and -022; 919.687-010; and 976.687-018)

Nature of the Work
Traffic, shipping, and receiving clerks keep records of all goods shipped and received. Their duties depend on the size of the establishment and the level of automation employed. Larger companies typically are better able to finance the purchase of computers and other equipment to handle some or all of a clerk's responsibilities. In smaller companies, an individual clerk may be responsible for maintaining records, preparing shipments, and accepting deliveries.

Traffic clerks maintain records on the destination, weight, and charges on all incoming and outgoing freight. They verify rate charges by comparing the classification of materials with rate charts. In many companies, this work may be automated. Information either is scanned, or is hand-entered into a computer for use by accounting or other departments within the company. Also, they keep a file of claims for overcharges and for damage to goods in transit.

Shipping clerks are record keepers responsible for all outgoing shipments. They prepare shipping documents and mailing labels, and make sure orders have been filled correctly. Also, they record items taken from inventory and note when orders were filled. Sometimes they fill the order themselves, obtaining merchandise from the stockroom, noting when inventories run low, and wrapping it or packing it in shipping containers. They also address and label packages, look up and compute freight or postal rates, and record the weight and cost of each shipment. Shipping clerks also may prepare invoices and furnish information about shipments to other parts of the company, such as the accounting department. Once a shipment is checked and ready to go, shipping clerks may move the goods from the plant—sometimes by forklift truck—to the shipping dock and direct its loading.

Receiving clerks perform tasks similar to those of shipping clerks. They determine whether orders have been filled correctly by verifying incoming shipments against the original order and the accompanying bill of lading or invoice. They make a record of the shipment and the condition of its contents. In many firms, receiving clerks record the information by using hand-held scanners to read bar codes on incoming products or by hand-entering this information into computers. These data then can be transferred to the appropriate departments. The shipment is checked for any discrepancies in quantity, price, and discounts. Receiving clerks may route or move shipments to the proper department, warehouse section, or stockroom. They may also arrange for adjustments with shippers whenever merchandise is lost or damaged. Receiving clerks in small businesses also may perform some stock clerk duties. In larger establishments, receiving clerks may control all receiving-platform operations, such as truck scheduling, recording of shipments, and handling of damaged goods.

Employment
Traffic, shipping, and receiving clerks held about 759,000 jobs in 1996. Nearly 7 out of 8 were employed in manufacturing or by wholesale or retail establishments. Although jobs for traffic, ship-

Traffic, shipping, and receiving clerks record the flow of goods through loading docks and warehouses.

ping, and receiving clerks are found throughout the country, most clerks work in urban areas, where shipping depots in factories and wholesale establishments generally are located. Many traffic, shipping, and receiving clerks work for the U.S. Postal Service. For information on these workers, see the statement on postal clerks and mail carriers elsewhere in the *Handbook*.

Job Outlook

Employment of traffic, shipping, and receiving clerks is expected to increase about as fast as the average for all occupations through the year 2006. Employment growth will continue to be affected by automation, as all but the smallest firms move to hold down labor costs by using computers to store and retrieve shipping and receiving records.

Methods of material handling have changed significantly in recent years. Large warehouses are increasingly automated, using equipment such as computerized conveyor systems, robots, computer-directed trucks, and automatic data storage and retrieval systems. Automation, coupled with the growing use of hand-held scanners and personal computers in shipping and receiving departments, has increased the productivity of these workers.

Despite automation, job openings will continue to arise due to increasing economic and trade activity, and because certain tasks cannot be automated. For example, someone needs to check shipments before they go out and when they arrive to ensure everything is in order. However, most job openings will occur because of the need to replace traffic, shipping, and receiving clerks who leave the occupation. Because this is an entry-level occupation, many vacancies are created by normal career progression.

Related Occupations

Traffic, shipping, and receiving clerks record, check, and often store the materials that a company receives. They also process and pack goods for shipment. Other workers who perform similar duties are stock clerks, material clerks, distributing clerks, routing clerks, express clerks, expediters, and order fillers.

Sources of Additional Information

General information about traffic, shipping, and receiving clerks can be obtained by contacting:
☛ National Retail Federation, 325 Seventh St. NW., Suite 1000, Washington, DC 20004. Homepage: http://www.nrf.com

(Information on training and earnings is in the introduction to material recording, scheduling, dispatching, and distributing occupations.)

Postal Clerks and Mail Carriers

(D.O.T. 209.687-014; 222.387-050; .587-018 and -034; and .687-022; 230.363-010, .367-010; 239.367-018; and 243.367-014)

Significant Points

- Those seeking a job in the Postal Service can expect to encounter keen competition because of the large number of qualified applicants.

- Jobs as postal clerks and mail carriers offer attractive salaries, a good pension plan, and job security.

- Few people under the age of 25 are hired as career postal clerks or mail carriers.

Nature of the Work

Each day, the U.S. Postal Service receives, sorts, and delivers millions of letters, bills, advertisements, and packages. To do this, it employs about 856,000 workers. Almost 3 out of 4 of these workers are either mail handlers or clerks, who sort mail and serve customers in post offices, or mail carriers, who deliver the mail.

Clerks and carriers are distinguished by the type of work they do. Clerks are usually classified by the mail processing function they per-

form, whereas carriers are classified by their type of route—city or rural.

Postal clerks at local post offices—sometimes called window or counter clerks—sort local mail for delivery to individual customers; sell stamps, money orders, postal stationary, and mailing envelopes and boxes; weigh packages to determine postage; and check that packages are in satisfactory condition for mailing. These clerks also register, certify, and insure mail and answer questions about postage rates, post office boxes, mailing restrictions, and other postal matters. They also may help customers file claims for damaged packages.

About 350 mail processing centers throughout the country service post offices in surrounding areas and are staffed primarily by clerks and mail handlers. Mail handlers unload the sacks of incoming mail; separate letters, parcel post, magazines, and newspapers; and transport these to the proper sorting and processing area. In addition, they may load mail into automated letter sorting machines, perform postage canceling operations, and rewrap packages damaged in processing.

After letters have been put through stamp-canceling machines, they are taken to other workrooms to be sorted according to destination. A growing proportion of clerks operate optical character readers (OCR's) and bar code sorters. Optical character readers "read" the ZIP code and spray a bar code onto the mail. Bar code sorters then scan the code and sort the mail. Because this is significantly faster than older sorting methods, it is becoming the standard sorting technology in mail processing centers.

Other clerks, who operate older electronic letter-sorting machines, push keys corresponding to the ZIP code of the local post office to which each letter will be delivered; the machine then drops the letters into the proper slots. This older, less automated method of letter sorting is being phased out. Still other clerks sort odd-sized letters, magazines, and newspapers by hand. Finally, the mail is sent to local post offices for sorting according to delivery route and delivered.

Once the mail has been processed and sorted, it is ready to be delivered by mail carriers. Duties of city and rural carriers are very similar. Most travel established routes delivering and collecting mail. Mail carriers start work at the post office early in the morning, where they spend a few hours arranging their mail in delivery sequence and taking care of other details. Recently, automated equipment has reduced the time needed to sort the mail, allowing mail carriers to spend more time delivering mail.

Carriers cover their routes on foot, by vehicle, or a combination of both. On foot, they carry a heavy load of mail in a satchel or push it in a cart. In some urban and most rural areas, they use a car or small truck. Although the Postal Service may provide vehicles to city carriers, most rural carriers use their own automobiles. Deliveries are made house-to-house, to roadside mailboxes, and to large buildings, such as offices or apartments, which generally have all the mailboxes on the first floor.

Besides delivering and collecting mail, carriers collect money for postage-due and c.o.d. (cash on delivery) fees and obtain signed receipts for registered, certified, and insured mail. If a customer is not home, the carrier leaves a notice that tells where special mail is being held.

After completing their routes, carriers return to the post office with mail gathered from street collection boxes, homes, and businesses. They turn in the mail receipts and money collected during the day and may separate letters and parcels for further processing by clerks.

The duties of some city carriers may be very specialized; some deliver only parcel post while others collect mail from street boxes and receiving boxes in office buildings. In contrast, rural carriers provide a wider range of postal services—in addition to delivering and picking up mail, they sell stamps and money orders and accept parcels, letters, and items to be registered, certified, or insured.

All carriers answer customers' questions about postal regulations and services and provide change-of-address cards and other postal forms when requested. In addition to their regularly scheduled duties, carriers often participate in neighborhood service programs in which they check on elderly or shut-in patrons or notify the police of any suspicious activities along their routes.

Although sorting work has become increasingly automated, postal clerks still need to manually route irregular sized parcels and letters.

Postal clerks and mail carriers are classified as casual, part-time flexible, part-time regular, or full time. Casual workers, hired for 90 days at a time, help process and deliver mail during peak mailing or vacation periods. Part-time flexible workers do not have a regular work schedule or weekly guarantee of hours; they replace absent workers and help with extra work as the need arises. Part-time regulars have a set work schedule of fewer than 40 hours per week. Full-time postal employees work a 40-hour week over a 5-day period.

Working Conditions

Window clerks usually work in clean, well ventilated, and well lit buildings. They have a wide variety of duties, frequent contact with the public, and rarely work at night. However, they may have to deal with upset customers and stand for long periods of time, and they are held accountable for the assigned stock of stamps and postal funds. Depending on the size of the post office in which they work, they may also be required to perform some sorting as well.

The working conditions of other postal clerks can vary. In small post offices, mail handlers use handtrucks to move heavy mail sacks from one part of the building to another and clerks may sort mail by hand. In large post offices and mail processing centers, chutes and conveyors move the mail, and much of the sorting is done by machines. Despite the use of automated equipment, the work of mail handlers and postal clerks can be physically demanding. These workers are usually on their feet, reaching for sacks and trays of mail or placing packages and bundles into sacks and trays.

Mail handlers and distribution clerks may become wearied with the routine of moving and sorting mail. Many work at night or on weekends because most large post offices process mail around the clock, and the largest volume of mail is sorted during the evening and night shifts. Workers may experience stress as they process and deliver ever larger quantities of mail under tight production deadlines and quotas.

Most carriers begin work early in the morning, in some cases as early as 4 a.m., if they have routes in a business district. A carrier's schedule has its advantages, however. Carriers who begin work early in the morning are through by early afternoon, and they spend most of the day on their own, relatively free from direct supervision. Overtime hours may be required during peak delivery times, such as before holidays.

Carriers spend most of their time outdoors, and deliver mail in all kinds of weather. Even those who drive often must walk when making deliveries and must lift heavy sacks of parcel post items when loading their vehicles. In addition, carriers always must be cautious of potential hazards on their routes. Wet roads and sidewalks can be treacherous, and each year numerous carriers are bitten by dogs.

Employment

The U.S. Postal Service employed 297,000 clerks and mail handlers and 332,000 mail carriers in 1996. About 90 percent of them worked full time. Most postal clerks provided window service and sorted mail at local post offices, although some worked at mail processing centers. Although most mail carriers worked in cities and suburban communities, 48,000 were rural carriers.

Training, Other Qualifications, and Advancement

Postal clerks and mail carriers must be U.S. citizens or have been granted permanent resident-alien status in the United States. They must be at least 18 years old (or 16, if they have a high school diploma). Qualification is based on a written examination that measures speed and accuracy at checking names and numbers and the ability to memorize mail distribution procedures. Applicants must pass a physical examination and drug test as well, and may be asked to show that they can lift and handle mail sacks weighing up to 70 pounds. Applicants for jobs as postal clerks operating electronic sorting machines must pass a special examination that includes a machine aptitude test. Applicants for mail carrier positions must have a driver's license, a good driving record, and receive a passing grade on a road test.

Applicants should apply at the post office or mail processing center where they wish to work in order to determine when an exam will be given. Applicants' names are listed in order of their examination scores. Five points are added to the score of an honorably discharged veteran, and 10 points to the score of a veteran wounded in combat or disabled. When a vacancy occurs, the appointing officer chooses one of the top three applicants; the rest of the names remain on the list to be considered for future openings until their eligibility expires, usually 2 years from the examination date.

Relatively few people under the age of 25 are hired as career postal clerks or mail carriers, a result of keen competition for these jobs and the customary waiting period of 1-2 years or more after passing the examination. It is not surprising, therefore, that most entrants transfer from other occupations.

New postal clerks and mail carriers are trained on the job by experienced workers. Many post offices offer classroom instruction. Workers receive additional instruction when new equipment or procedures are introduced. They usually are trained by another postal employee or, sometimes, a training specialist hired under contract by the Postal Service.

Window clerks and mail carriers must be courteous and tactful when dealing with the public, especially when answering questions or receiving complaints. A good memory, good coordination, and the ability to read rapidly and accurately are also important. Mail handlers and distribution clerks work closely with other clerks, frequently under the tension and strain of meeting dispatch transportation deadlines.

Postal clerks and mail carriers often begin on a part-time flexible basis and become regular or full time in order of seniority as vacancies occur. Full-time clerks may bid for preferred assignments such as the day shift or a higher level nonsupervisory position as expediter or window service technician. Carriers can look forward to obtaining preferred routes as their seniority increases, or to higher level jobs such as carrier technician. Both clerks and carriers can advance to supervisory positions.

Job Outlook

Those seeking a job in the Postal Service can expect to encounter keen competition—the number of applicants for postal clerk and mail carrier positions is expected to continue to far exceed the number of openings. Job opportunities will vary by occupation and duties performed.

Overall employment of postal clerks is expected to increase more slowly than the average through the year 2006. Despite efforts by the U.S. Postal Service to provide higher levels of customer service at their window and counter operations, the demand for window clerks will be moderated by the increased sales of stamps and other postal products by grocery stores and other retail outlets, as well as the use of electronic communications technologies and private delivery companies. As for other postal clerks, more mail will be moved using automated materials handling equipment and sorted using optical character readers, bar code sorters, and other automated sorting equipment. Despite the increase in the use of productivity increasing machinery, the expected increase in mail volume will require some additional clerks.

Conflicting factors also are expected to influence demand for mail carriers. Despite competition from alternative delivery systems and new forms of electronic communication, the volume of mail handled by the U.S. Postal Service is expected to continue to grow. Population growth and the formation of new households will stimulate demand for mail delivery. However, increased use of the "ZIP + 4" system, which sorts mail to the carrier route, and other automated sorting equipment should decrease the amount of time carriers spend sorting their mail, allowing them more time to handle longer routes. In addition, the Postal Service is moving toward more centralized mail delivery, such as the use of more cluster boxes, to cut down on the number of door-to-door deliveries. These trends are expected to increase carrier productivity. Employment of mail carriers is expected to increase about as fast as average for all occupations through the year 2006.

Jobs will become available because of the need to replace postal clerks and mail carriers who retire or stop working for other reasons. However, the factors that make entry to these occupations highly competitive—attractive salaries, a good pension plan, job security, and modest educational requirements—contribute to a high degree of job attachment. Accordingly, replacement needs produce relatively fewer job openings than in other occupations of this size. In contrast to the typical pattern, postal workers generally remain in their jobs until they retire; relatively few transfer to other occupations.

Although the volume of mail to be processed and delivered rises and falls with the level of business activity, as well as with the season of the year, full-time postal clerks and mail carriers have never been laid off. When mail volume is high, full-time clerks and carriers work overtime, part-time clerks and carriers work additional hours, and casual clerks and carriers may be hired. When mail volume is low, overtime is curtailed, part-timers work fewer hours, and casual workers are discharged.

Earnings
In 1996, base pay for beginning full-time postal clerks who operate scanning and sorting machines was $24,599 a year, rising to a maximum of $35,683 after 14 years of service. Entry-level pay for window clerks and clerks in retail outlets was $26,063 a year in 1996 whereas those with 14 years of service earned $36,551 a year. Entry-level pay for full-time regular mail handling clerks ranged from $21,676 to $22,944 a year in 1996.

Experienced, full-time, city delivery mail carriers earn, on average, $34,135 a year. Postal clerks and carriers working part-time flexible schedules begin at $12.82 an hour and, based on the number of years of service, increase to a maximum of $18.07 an hour. Rural delivery carriers had average base salaries of $35,000 in 1996. Their earnings are determined through an evaluation of the amount of work required to service their routes. Carriers with heavier workloads generally earn more than those with lighter workloads. Rural carriers also receive an equipment maintenance allowance when required to use their own vehicles. In 1996, this was approximately 36.5 cents per mile.

Postal workers enjoy a variety of employer-provided benefits. These include health and life insurance, vacation and sick leave, and a pension plan.

In addition to their hourly wage and benefits package, some postal workers receive a uniform allowance. This group includes those workers who are in the public view for 4 or more hours each day and various maintenance workers. The amount of the allowance depends on the job performed—some workers are only required to wear a partial uniform, and their allowance is lower. In 1996, for example, the allowance for a letter carrier was $277 per year, compared to $119 for a window clerk.

Most of these workers belong to one of four unions: American Postal Workers Union, AFL-CIO; National Association of Letter Carriers, AFL-CIO; National Postal Mail Handlers Union, AFL-CIO; and National Rural Letter Carriers Association.

Related Occupations
Other workers whose duties are related to those of postal clerks include mail clerks, file clerks, routing clerks, sorters, material moving equipment operators, clerk typists, cashiers, data entry operators, and ticket sellers. Others with duties related to those of mail carriers include messengers, merchandise deliverers, and delivery-route truckdrivers.

Sources of Additional Information
Local post offices and State employment service offices can supply details about entrance examinations and specific employment opportunities for postal clerks and mail carriers.

Record Clerks

Significant Points
- Most record clerk jobs require only a high school diploma, but earnings are low.
- Turnover in this very large occupation will result in numerous job opportunities.
- Little or no change is expected in employment of record clerks, reflecting the spread of computers and other office automation; however, job growth is projected for some record clerks, including billing clerks, brokerage clerks, and library assistants.

Nature of the Work
Organizations of all kinds—businesses, government agencies, unions, health care facilities, and colleges and universities—must keep accurate records. Maintaining and updating records, ranging from payrolls to information on the shipment of goods to bank statements, is the job of record clerks. (Additional information about specific record clerk occupations is provided in separate statements that follow this introductory statement.)

Record clerks perform a wide variety of recordkeeping duties. Billing clerks and billing machine operators prepare bills and invoices. Bookkeeping, accounting, and auditing clerks maintain financial data in computer and paper files. Brokerage clerks prepare and maintain the records generated when stocks, bonds, and other types of investments are traded. Statement clerks prepare monthly statements for bank customers. File clerks store and retrieve various kinds of office information for use by staff members. Library assistants and bookmobile drivers assist library patrons. Order clerks process incoming orders for goods and services. Payroll and timekeeping clerks compute wages for payroll records. Personnel clerks maintain employee records.

Record clerks' duties may vary with the size of the firm. In a small business, one bookkeeping clerk may handle all financial records and transactions, as well as payroll and personnel duties. On the other hand, a large firm may employ specialized accounting clerks to work on different aspects of the balance sheet, as well as specialized payroll and personnel clerks. However, it is increasingly common for clerical staff in firms of all sizes to perform a broader variety of tasks than in the past. This is especially true for clerical occupations involving accounting work. As the growing use of computers enables bookkeeping, accounting, and auditing clerks to become more productive, these workers may assume billing, payroll, and timekeeping duties.

Many record clerks use financial software to enter and manipulate data. In these cases, computer programs can automatically perform calculations on data that previously had to be calculated manually. Computers also enable clerks to access data within files more quickly than the former method of leafing through stacks of paper. Despite increased automation, however, workers still keep backup paper records for research, auditing, and reference purposes.

Interaction with the public and coworkers is a basic part of the job for many record clerks. Payroll clerks, for example, answer employees' questions concerning benefits; bookmobile drivers help patients in nursing homes and hospitals select books; and order clerks call customers to verify special mailing instructions.

Other record clerks include *advertising clerks*—who receive orders for classified advertising for newspapers or magazines, prepare copy according to customer specifications, and verify conformance of published ads to specifications for billing purposes—and *correspondence clerks*—who reply to customers regarding damage claims, delinquent accounts, incorrect billings, complaints of unsatisfactory service, and requests for merchandise exchanges and/or returns.

Working Conditions

With the exception of library assistants and bookmobile drivers, record clerks typically are employed in an office environment. Most work alongside their organization's other clerical workers, but some record clerks work in centralized units away from the front office. Clerks who review detailed data may have to sit for extended periods of time. Although they do not do heavy lifting, file clerks and library assistants spend a lot of time on their feet and frequently stoop, bend, and reach. Bookmobile drivers must maneuver large vehicles in all kinds of traffic and weather conditions, and may also be responsible for the maintenance of the bookmobile.

As the majority of record clerks use computers as part of their daily routine, these workers may experience eye and muscle strain, backaches, headaches, and repetitive motion injuries.

Most record clerks work regular business hours. Library assistants may work evenings and weekends, but those employed in school libraries generally work only during the school year. Accounting clerks may work longer hours to meet deadlines at the end of the fiscal year, during tax time, or when monthly and yearly accounting audits are performed. Billing, bookkeeping, and accounting clerks in hotels, restaurants, and stores may work overtime during peak holiday and vacation seasons. Similarly, order clerks in retail establishments typically work overtime during these seasons, when sales volume is high. Brokerage clerks may also have to work overtime, if there is a high volume of activity in the stock or bond markets.

Employment

Record clerks held about 3.9 million jobs in 1996. The following tabulation shows employment in individual clerical occupations.

Bookkeeping, accounting, and auditing clerks	2,250,000
Billing clerks and billing machine operators	437,000
Order clerks	329,000
File clerks	293,000
Payroll and timekeeping clerks	161,000
Library assistants and bookmobile drivers	125,000
Personnel clerks, except payroll and timekeeping	124,000
Brokerage and statement clerks	102,000
Correspondence clerks	31,000
Advertising clerks	18,000

These workers are employed in virtually every industry. The largest number of record clerks work for firms providing health, business, and other types of services. Many also work in trade; finance, insurance, and real estate; manufacturing; and government.

Training, Other Qualifications, and Advancement

Most record clerk jobs are entry-level, with most employers requiring applicants to have at least a high school diploma or its equivalent. A higher level of education is usually favored over a high school diploma, but is not generally required. However, in some cases, more extensive education is mandatory. For example, brokerage firms increasingly seek college graduates for brokerage clerk jobs; and order clerks in high-technology firms often need to understand scientific and mechanical processes, which may require some college education. Regardless of the type of work, most employers prefer workers who are computer-literate. Knowledge of word processing and spreadsheet software is especially valuable, as are experience working in an office and good interpersonal skills.

High schools, business schools, and community colleges teach those office skills needed by record clerks. Business education programs typically include courses in typing (keyboarding), word processing, shorthand, business communications, records management, and office systems and procedures. Technical training needed for some specialized order clerk positions can be obtained in technical institutes and in 2- and 4-year colleges.

Some entrants into the record clerk field are college graduates with degrees in business, finance, or liberal arts. Although a degree is rarely required, many graduates accept entry-level clerical positions to get into a particular company or to enter the finance or accounting field, with the hope of being promoted to professional or managerial jobs. Some companies, such as brokerage and accounting firms, have a set plan of advancement that tracks college graduates from entry-level clerk jobs into managerial positions. Workers with college degrees are likely to start at higher salaries and advance more easily than those without degrees.

Once hired, record clerks generally receive on-the-job training. Under the guidance of a supervisor or other senior worker, new employees learn company procedures. Some formal classroom training may also be necessary, such as training in specific computer software.

Record clerks must be careful, orderly, and detail-oriented, in order to avoid making errors and to be able to recognize errors made by others. These workers must also be honest, discreet, and trustworthy, because they frequently come in contact with confidential material. Additionally, payroll clerks, billing clerks, and bookkeeping, accounting, and auditing clerks should have a strong aptitude for numbers. Because statement clerks have access to individuals' financial information, these workers must be bonded. Many bookmobile drivers are now required to have a commercial driver's license.

Records clerks usually advance by taking on more duties in the same occupation for higher pay. Others advance transferring to closely related occupations. For example, some order clerks use their experience to move into sales positions. Others move into another clerical job, such as secretary, or advance to supervisory positions. With appropriate experience and education, some clerks may become accountants, personnel specialists, securities sales representatives, or librarians.

Job Outlook

Turnover in this very large occupation places it among those occupations providing the most job openings. Opportunities will be plentiful for full-time, part-time, and seasonal employment, as record clerks transfer to other occupations or leave the labor force.

Little or no change is expected in employment of record clerks through the year 2006. Despite continued growth in the volume of business transactions, fewer record clerks will be needed, because of rising productivity stemming from the spread of office automation. Many record clerk jobs have already become heavily automated. Productivity has increased significantly, as workers use personal computers instead of more time-consuming equipment such as typewriters, adding machines, and calculators. The growing use of bar code readers, point-of-sale terminals, and optical scanners by other employees also reduces much of the data entry handled by record clerks. Additionally, managers and professionals now do much of their own clerical work, using computers to access, create, and store data directly into their computer systems. The growing use of local area networks is also facilitating electronic data interchange—the sending of data from computer to computer—abolishing the need for clerks to reenter the data. To further eliminate duplicate functions, many large companies are consolidating their clerical operations in a central office where accounting, billing, personnel, and payroll functions are performed for all offices, main and satellite, within the organization.

Despite the spread of automation, job growth is projected for some record clerks, including billing clerks, brokerage clerks, and library assistants and bookmobile drivers. (See the separate statements on these and other record clerks that follow this introductory statement.)

Earnings
Salaries of record clerks vary considerably. The region of the country, size of city, and type and size of establishment all influence salary levels. The level of industry or technical expertise required and the complexity and uniqueness of a clerk's responsibilities may also affect earnings. Median earnings of full-time record clerks in 1996 are shown in the following tabulation.

Order clerks	$23,700
Payroll and timekeeping clerks	23,100
Personnel clerks	23,100
Bookkeeping, accounting, and auditing clerks	20,700
Billing clerks	20,600
Billing machine operators	20,500
Library clerks	19,200
File clerks	17,100

In the Federal Government in 1997, record clerks with a high school diploma or clerical experience typically started at $17,400 a year. Beginning salaries were slightly higher in areas where the prevailing local pay level was higher. In 1997, the average salary for all personnel clerks employed by the Federal Government was $27,600.

Related Occupations
Today, most record clerks enter data into a computer system and perform basic analysis of the data. Other clerical workers who enter and manipulate data include bank tellers, statistical clerks, receiving clerks, medical record clerks, hotel and motel clerks, credit clerks, and reservation and transportation ticket agents.

Sources of Additional Information
State employment service offices can provide information about job openings for record clerks.

Billing Clerks and Billing Machine Operators

(D.O.T. 184.387-010; 210.382-022, -026, -066; 211.482-014, -018; 214.267-010, .362-010, -014, -022, -026, -038, -042, .382-014, -018, -030, .387-010, -014, -018, .462-010, .467-010, -014; 214.482-010, -014, -018, -022, .587-010; 216.382-022, -034, -050, -054; 217.382-010; 241.267-026; and 249.367-034)

Nature of the Work
Billing clerks keep the records, calculate the charges, and maintain the files of payments made for goods or services. Billing machine operators run the machines that generate the bills, statements, and invoices.

Billing clerks review purchase orders, bills of lading, sales tickets, hospital records, or charge slips to calculate the total amount due from a customer. In accounting, law, consulting, and similar firms, billing clerks calculate client fees based on the actual time required to perform the task. They keep track of the accumulated hours and dollar amounts to charge to each job, the type of job performed for a

customer, and the percentage of work completed. In hospitals, calculating the charges for an individual's hospital stay may require a letter to an insurance company, whereas a clerk computing trucking rates for machine parts may consult a rate book. After billing clerks review all necessary information, they compute the charges using calculators or computers. They then prepare the itemized statements, bills, or invoices—depending on the organization's needs—used for billing and recordkeeping purposes. In one organization, the clerk might prepare a simple bill that only contains the amount due and the date and type of service; in another, the clerk would produce a detailed invoice that includes the codes for all goods and services provided. This latter form might list the items sold, credit terms, date of shipment or dates services were provided, a salesperson's or doctor's identification, if necessary, and the sales total.

Once all the information has been entered, billing machine operators then run off the bill that will be sent to the customer. In a growing number of firms, billing machines are being replaced by computers and specialized billing software that allow clerks to calculate charges and prepare bills in one step. Computer packages prompt clerks to enter data from hand-written forms and manipulate the necessary entries of quantities, labor, and rates to be charged. Billing clerks verify the entry of information and check for errors before the bill is printed by the computer. After the bills are printed, billing clerks check them again for accuracy.

Employment
In 1996, billing clerks held about 335,000 jobs, and billing machine operators held about 102,000. About 1 of every 10 billing clerks and billing machine operators were employed by banks and other finan-

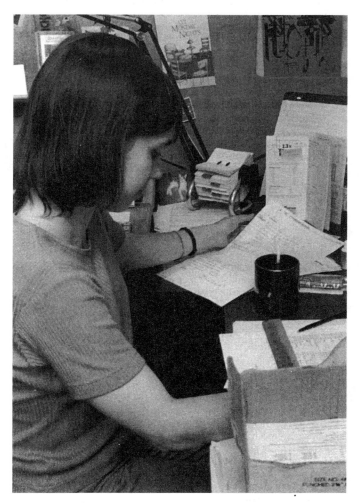

A high school diploma is sufficient for a job as a billing clerk.

cial institutions, insurance companies, and other organizations providing business and health services. About 2 of every 10 employees was found in wholesale and retail establishments, and a significant number worked in manufacturing, transportation, communications, and utilities. Approximately 2 in 10 billing clerks and billing machine operators worked part time in 1996.

Job Outlook

Job openings for persons seeking work as billing clerks or billing machine operators are expected to be numerous through the year 2006. Despite the lack of employment growth, many job openings will occur as these workers transfer to other occupations or leave the labor force. Turnover in this occupation is relatively high, characteristic of an entry-level occupation requiring only a high school diploma.

Employment of billing clerks is expected to grow about as fast as the average for all occupations through the year 2006. A growing economy and a greater demand for billing services will result in more business transactions; rising worker productivity stemming from the increasing use of computers to manage account information will not keep employment from rising. More complex billing applications will increasingly require workers with greater technical expertise.

Employment of billing machine operators, on the other hand, is expected to decline through the year 2006 as billing machines are replaced by more advanced machines and computers which enable billing clerks to perform the jobs formerly done by billing machine operators. In some organizations, productivity gains from billing software will increasingly allow accounting clerks to take over the responsibilities of billing clerks and billing machine operators.

(See the introductory statement on record clerks for information on working conditions, training requirements, and earnings.)

Bookkeeping, Accounting, and Auditing Clerks

(D.O.T. 209.687-010; 210.362-010, .367-010, -014, .382-010, -014, -030, -038, -042, -046, -050, -054, -062; 216.362-014, -022, -026, -034, -038, -042, .382-022, -026, -058, .482-010, -026, .587-010; 219.362-066, .367-042, .387-018, .487-010, and .587-010)

Nature of the Work

Bookkeeping, accounting, and auditing clerks are an organization's financial recordkeepers. They compute, classify, record, and verify numerical data in order to develop and maintain financial records.

In smaller establishments, bookkeeping clerks handle all aspects of financial transactions. They record debits and credits, compare current and past balance sheets, summarize details of separate ledgers, and prepare reports for supervisors and managers. They may also prepare bank deposits by compiling data from cashiers, verifying and balancing receipts, and sending the cash, checks, or other forms of payment to the bank.

In larger offices and accounting departments, accounting clerks are more specialized. Their title may reflect the type of accounting they do, such as accounts payable clerk or accounts receivable clerk. Entry-level accounting clerks post details of transactions, total accounts, and compute interest charges. They may also monitor loans and accounts payable and receivable to ensure that payments are up to date. More advanced clerks may total, balance, and reconcile billing vouchers; ensure completeness and accuracy of data on accounts; and code documents according to company procedures. They post transactions in journals and on computer files, and update these files when needed. They also review computer printouts against manually maintained journals, and make necessary corrections. Senior workers review invoices and statements to make sure all information is accurate and complete, and may reconcile computer reports with operating reports.

Bookkeeping, accounting, and auditing clerks hold over 2 million jobs.

Auditing clerks verify records of transactions posted by other workers. They check figures, postings, and documents for correct entry, mathematical accuracy, and proper codes. They also correct or note errors for accountants or other workers to adjust.

As organizations computerize their financial records, more bookkeeping, accounting, and auditing clerks are using specialized accounting software on personal computers. They increasingly post charges to accounts on computer spreadsheets and data bases; manual posting to general ledgers is becoming a thing of the past. Information is entered into the computer from receipts or bills and then is stored either electronically or as computer printouts, or both. The increased use of computers has also allowed bookkeeping, accounting, and auditing clerks to take on additional responsibilities, such as payroll, timekeeping, and billing.

Employment

Bookkeeping, accounting, and auditing clerks held over 2.2 million jobs in 1996. About 25 percent were in wholesale and retail trade, and 34 percent were in organizations providing business, health, educational, and social services. Approximately 30 percent of bookkeeping, accounting, and auditing clerks worked part time in 1996.

Job Outlook

Virtually all job openings for bookkeeping, accounting, and auditing clerks through the year 2006 will stem from replacement needs. Each year, several hundred thousand jobs will become available as these clerks transfer to other occupations or leave the labor force. Turnover is lower than among other record clerks, but the large size of the occupation ensures plentiful job openings, including many opportunities for temporary and part-time work.

Employment of bookkeeping, accounting, and auditing clerks is expected to decline through 2006. A growing economy should result in more financial transactions and other activities and, therefore, more demand for accounting services. However, the continuing spread of office automation should result in increasing worker productivity. Organizations of all sizes are likely to continue the consolidation of various recordkeeping functions, thus reducing the demand for these clerks.

(See the introductory statement on record clerks for information on working conditions, training requirements, and earnings.)

Brokerage Clerks and Statement Clerks

(D.O.T. 214.362-046; 216.362-046, .382-046, .482-034; 219.362-018, -054, .482-010)

Nature of the Work

Brokerage clerks and statement clerks work behind the scenes to produce records associated with financial transactions.

Brokerage clerks, who work in the operations areas of securities firms, perform many duties to facilitate the sale and purchase of stocks, bonds, commodities, and other kinds of investments. These clerks produce the necessary records of all transactions that occur in their area of the business.

Job titles depend upon the type of work performed. Purchase-and-sale clerks match orders to buy with orders to sell. They balance and verify stock trades by comparing the records of the selling firm to those of the buying firm. Dividend clerks ensure timely payments of stock or cash dividends to clients of a particular brokerage firm. Transfer clerks execute customer requests for changes to security registration and examine stock certificates for adherence to banking regulations. Receive-and-deliver clerks facilitate the receipt and delivery of securities among firms and institutions. Margin clerks post accounts and monitor activity in customers' accounts. Their job is to ensure that customers make their payments and stay within legal boundaries concerning stock purchases.

A significant and growing number of brokerage clerks use custom-designed software programs to process transactions, allowing transactions to be processed more quickly than if they were done manually. Currently, only a few customized accounts are handled manually.

Statement clerks assemble, verify, and send individual and commercial bank statements every month.

In most banks, statement clerks, sometimes called statement operators, run sophisticated, high-speed machines. These machines fold the computer-printed statement, collate it if it is more than one page, insert the statement and cancelled checks into an envelope, seal it, and weigh it for postage. Statement clerks load the machine with the statements, cancelled checks, and envelopes. They then monitor the equipment and correct minor problems. For serious problems, they call repair personnel.

In banks that do not have such machines, statement clerks perform all operations manually. They may also be responsible for verifying signatures and checking for missing information on checks, placing cancelled checks into trays, and retrieving them to send with the statements.

In a growing number of banks, only the statement is printed and sent to the account holder. The cancelled checks are not returned; this is known as check truncation.

Statement clerks are employed primarily by large banks. In smaller banks, their function is usually handled by a teller or a bookkeeping clerk who performs other duties during the rest of the month. Some small banks send their statement information to larger banks for processing, printing, and mailing.

Employment

Brokerage clerks held about 76,000 jobs in 1996, and statement clerks held about 25,000 jobs. Brokerage clerks worked in firms involved in the sales of securities and commodities. Almost all statement clerks were employed by banking institutions.

Job Outlook

Employment of brokerage clerks is expected to grow about as fast as the average for all occupations through the year 2006. Employment of statement clerks is projected to decline. Nevertheless, some jobs will become available each year to replace brokerage and statement clerks who transfer to other occupations or leave the labor force.

Similar to other record clerks, employment will be adversely affected by automation and changes in business practices. For example, computers now calculate the dividends due on stocks, something done for decades by brokerage clerks with adding machines and calculators. However, brokerage clerks are still needed to enter data into the computer and to process information. In the past, the record of security ownership was a piece of paper—a stock certificate. Today, most securities are stored in computer form and traded using electronic data interchange. Although less paper changes hands, clerks continue to enter and verify all transactions.

Automated statement processing will grow as the increased volume of transactions justifies the cost of the necessary equipment, and this will dampen demand for statement clerks. In addition, the further spread of check truncation is expected to hold down employment of statement clerks. The use of automatic teller machines and other electronic money transfers should increase as well, resulting in significantly fewer checks being written and processed.

(See introductory statement on record clerks for information on working conditions, training requirements, and earnings.)

File Clerks

(D.O.T. 206.362-010, .367-014, -018; .387-010, -014, -022, -034)

Nature of the Work

File clerks classify, store, retrieve, and update information generated by their employers. They are employed by all kinds of organizations, including businesses, nonprofit organizations, and government agencies.

File clerks, also called records and information clerks or record center clerks, examine incoming material and code it numerically, alphabetically, or by subject matter. They then store forms, letters, receipts, or reports in paper form or enter necessary information into other storage devices. Some clerks operate mechanized files that rotate to bring the needed records to them. Others film documents that are then stored on microforms (microfilm or microfiche). A growing number of file clerks use imaging systems that scan paper files or film and store the material on optical disks.

Records must be current to be useful. File clerks ensure that new information is added to the files in a timely manner and may destroy outdated file materials or transfer them to inactive storage. They also check files at regular intervals to make sure that all items are correctly sequenced and placed. Whenever records cannot be located,

Brokerage clerks process stock transactions.

Many file clerks work for temporary help firms.

the file clerk searches for the missing material. As an organization's needs for information change, file clerks implement changes to the filing system established by supervisory personnel.

When records are requested, file clerks locate them and give them to the borrower. The document may be a sheet of paper stored in a drawer in a file cabinet or an image on microform. In the first example, the clerk manually retrieves the document and hands or forwards it to the borrower. In the latter example, the clerk retrieves the microform and displays it on a microform reader. If necessary, file clerks make copies of records and distribute them. They keep track of materials removed from the files and ensure that those given out are returned.

A growing number of file clerks are using computerized filing and retrieval systems. There are a variety of computerized storage systems—data may be stored on a mainframe computer, magnetic tape, CD-ROM, or even floppy disk, depending on their needs. To retrieve a document, the clerk enters the document's identification code, obtains the location, and pulls the document. Even when files are stored electronically, backup paper or electronic copies generally are also kept. Accessing files in a computer data base is much quicker than locating and physically retrieving paper files.

In small offices, file clerks often have additional responsibilities. These may include data entry, word processing, sorting mail, and operating copying machines.

Employment

File clerks held about 293,000 jobs in 1996. Many other clerical workers also perform filing in connection with their work. While file clerk jobs are found in nearly every sector of the economy, about 90 percent of file clerks are employed in services, government, finance, insurance, and real estate. More than 1 out of every 4 is employed in temporary services firms, and about 1 out of 3 worked part time in 1996.

Job Outlook

Employment of file clerks is expected to grow more slowly than the average for all occupations through the year 2006, reflecting productivity gains stemming from office automation and the restructuring of work as professionals and managers increasingly use personal computers. Despite the projected slow growth in employment, job opportunities for file clerks should be plentiful because a large number of workers will be needed to replace workers who leave the occupa-

tion each year. Turnover is the highest among all record clerk occupations. This reflects the lack of formal training requirements, limited advancement potential, and relatively low pay.

Jobseekers who have typing (keyboarding) and other secretarial skills and are familiar with a wide range of office machines, especially personal computers, should have better opportunities than less experienced applicants. File clerks should find many opportunities for temporary or part-time work, especially during peak business periods.

(See introductory statement on record clerks for information on working conditions, training requirements, and earnings.)

Library Assistants and Bookmobile Drivers

(D.O.T. 209.387-026; 222.587-014; 249.363-010, .365-010, .367-046, .687 -014)

Nature of the Work

Library assistants and bookmobile drivers keep library resources in order and make them readily available to a variety of users. They work under the direction of librarians, and in some cases, library technicians.

Library assistants—sometimes referred to as library media assistants, library aides, or circulation assistants—register patrons so they can borrow materials from the library. They record the borrower's name and address from an application and then issue a library card. Most library assistants enter and update patrons' records using computer databases.

At the circulation desk, assistants lend and collect books, periodicals, video tapes, and other materials. When an item is borrowed, assistants stamp the due date on the material and record the patron's identification from his or her library card. They inspect returned materials for damage, check the due dates, and compute any fines that may be owed. They review records to compile a list of overdue materials and send out notices. They also answer patrons' questions in person and on the telephone and refer those they cannot answer to a librarian.

Throughout the library, assistants sort returned books, periodicals, and other items and return them to their designated shelves, files, or storage areas. They locate materials to be loaned, either to a patron or another library. Many card catalogues are computerized, so library assistants must be familiar with the computer system for their particular library. If any materials have been damaged, these workers repair them, if possible. For example, they use tape or paste to repair torn pages or book covers and other specialized processes to repair more valuable materials.

Some library assistants specialize in helping patrons with vision problems. Sometimes referred to as library, talking-books, or braille-and-talking-books clerks, they review the borrower's list of desired reading material. They locate those materials or closely related substitutes from the library collection of large type or braille volumes, tape cassettes, and open-reel talking books. They complete the necessary paperwork and give or mail them to the borrower.

To extend library services to a vast audience, many libraries operate bookmobiles. Bookmobile drivers drive trucks stocked with books, or drive light trucks that pull book trailers to designated sites on a regular schedule. Bookmobiles serve community organizations such as shopping centers, apartment complexes, schools, and nursing homes. They may also be used to extend library service to patrons living in remote areas. Depending on local conditions, they may drive alone or may be accompanied by a library technician.

When working alone, the drivers perform many of the same functions as a library assistant in a main or branch library. They answer patrons' questions, receive and check out books, collect fines, maintain the book collection, shelve materials, and occasionally operate audiovisual equipment to show slides or films. They participate and may assist in planning programs sponsored by the library such as reader advisory programs, used book sales, or outreach programs.

Library assistants register patrons so they can borrow materials from the library.

Bookmobile drivers keep track of their mileage, the materials lent out, and the amount of fines collected. In some areas, they are responsible for the maintenance of the vehicle and any photocopiers or other equipment in it. They record statistics on circulation and the number of people visiting the bookmobile. Drivers may also record requests for special items from the main library and arrange for the materials to be mailed or delivered to a patron during the next scheduled visit. Many bookmobiles are equipped with personal computers and CD-ROM systems linked to the main library system; this allows bookmobile drivers to reserve or locate books immediately. Some bookmobiles now offer Internet access to users.

Because bookmobile drivers may be the only link some people have to the library, much of their work is helping the public. They may assist handicapped or elderly patrons to the bookmobile, or shovel snow to assure their safety. They may enter hospitals or nursing homes to deliver books directly to patrons who are bedridden.

The schedules of bookmobile drivers depend on the size of the area being served. Some of these workers go out on their routes every working day, while others do so only on certain days of the week. On the other days, they perform library assistant duties at the library. Some now work evenings and weekends to give patrons as much access to the library as possible.

Employment

Library assistants and bookmobile drivers held about 125,000 jobs in 1996. Over one-half of these workers were employed by local government in public libraries; most of the remaining worked in school libraries. Opportunities for flexible schedules are abundant; over one-half of these workers were on part-time schedules.

Job Outlook

Opportunities should be good for persons interested in jobs as library assistants or bookmobile drivers through the year 2006. Turnover of these workers is quite high, reflecting the limited investment in training and subsequent weak attachment to this occupation. This work is attractive to retirees, students, and others who want a part-time schedule, and there is a lot of movement into and out of the occupation. Many openings will become available each year to replace workers who transfer to another occupation or leave the labor force. Some positions become available as library assistants move

within the organization. Library assistants can be promoted to library technicians, and eventually supervisory positions in public service or technical service areas. Advancement opportunities are greater in larger libraries and may be more limited in smaller ones.

Employment is expected to grow about as fast as the average for all occupations through the year 2006. The vast majority of library assistants and bookmobile drivers work in public or school libraries. Efforts to contain costs in local governments and academic institutions of all types, may result in more hiring of library support staff than librarians. Because most are employed by public institutions, library assistants and bookmobile drivers are not directly affected by the ups and downs of the business cycle. Some of these workers may lose their jobs, however, if there are cuts in government budgets.

Sources of Additional Information

Information about a career as a library assistant can be obtained from:
☛ Council on Library/Media Technology, P.O. Box 951, Oxon Hill, MD 20750.

Public libraries and libraries in academic institutions can provide information about job openings for library assistants and bookmobile drivers.

Specific information on bookmobile drivers is available from:
☛ The State Library of Ohio, Field Operations Department, 65 South Front St., Columbus, OH 43215.

(See the introductory part of this section for information on working conditions, training requirements, and earnings.)

Order Clerks

(D.O.T. 209.387-018; 245.367-026; 249.367-042, -054; 295.367-018; and 659.462-010)

Nature of the Work

Order clerks receive and process incoming orders for such items as spare parts for machines, consumer appliances, gas and electric power connections, film rentals, and articles of clothing. They are sometimes called order-entry clerks, customer service representatives, sales representatives, order processors, or order takers.

Orders for materials, merchandise, or services can come from within an organization or from outside of it. In large companies with many work sites, such as automobile manufacturers, parts and equipment need to be ordered from the company's warehouses. Inside order clerks receive orders from other workers employed by the same company or from salespersons in the field. Many other order clerks, however, receive orders from other companies or from individuals. Order clerks in wholesale businesses, for instance, receive orders for merchandise from retail establishments that the retailer in turn sells to the public. An increasing number of order clerks work in catalog sales, receiving orders from individual customers either by phone, fax, or mail. Order clerks dealing primarily with the public sometimes are referred to as outside order clerks.

Today, most order clerks sit at computers and receive orders directly by telephone, entering the required information as the customer places the order. Some orders are received through the computer system; they are sent directly from the customer's terminal to the order clerk's terminal.

The computer provides the order clerk with ready access to information such as stock numbers, prices, and inventory. Orders frequently depend on which products are in stock and which products are most appropriate for the customer's needs. Some order clerks, especially those in industrial settings, must be able to give price estimates for entire jobs, not just single parts. Others must be able to take special orders or give expected arrival dates.

Although the large majority of orders are now placed by phone, some order clerks also receive orders by mail and increasingly by fax machine. These clerks review the hand-written or typed orders for completeness and clarity. They extract the checks or money orders, sort them, and send them for processing. The clerk may complete missing information or contact the customer for the information.

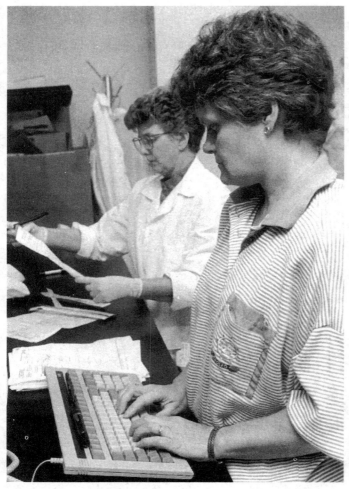

Most order clerks work for wholesale and retail establishments and manufacturing firms.

Similarly, if customers need additional information, such as prices, shipping dates, or anticipated delays, the order clerk contacts them. These orders may be processed by order clerks in small establishments or, in large organizations, entered into the computer system by data-entry clerks.

After an order has been verified and entered, the customer's final cost is calculated. The clerk then routes the order to the proper department—such as the warehouse—that actually sends out or delivers the item in question.

In organizations with computer systems, inventory records are adjusted automatically as sales are made. In less automated organizations, order clerks adjust inventory records. For example, after processing an order for bolts, the clerk verifies that the bolts were sent and subtracts the order from the inventory control form. Clerks may also notify other departments when inventories are low or when orders would deplete supplies.

Some order clerks must establish priorities in filling orders. For example, an order clerk in a blood bank may receive a request from a hospital for a certain type of blood. The clerk must first find out if the request is routine or an emergency, and then take appropriate action.

Employment
Order clerks held about 329,000 jobs in 1996. Most worked for wholesale and retail establishments and manufacturing firms.

Job Outlook
Job openings for order clerks should be plentiful through the year 2006 due to sizable replacement needs. Numerous jobs will become

available each year to replace order clerks who transfer to other occupations or leave the labor force. Many of these openings will be for seasonal work, especially in catalogue companies that cater to holiday gift buyers.

Employment of order clerks is expected to grow more slowly than average through the year 2006 as office automation continues to increase worker productivity. As the economy grows, more orders for goods and services will be placed. How this growing business activity relates to employment of order clerks depends in large measure on the setting. Demand for outside order clerks who deal mainly with the public should remain fairly strong. The greater use of toll-free numbers that makes "home shopping" easier and more convenient will stimulate demand for these workers. However, productivity gains from the increasing use of automation will absorb some of the growth in the volume of orders. The increased presence of mail order companies on the Internet will also affect employment of order clerks. Orders placed over the Internet are entered into the computer system by the customer; thus, the order clerk is not involved in placing the order.

Demand for inside order clerks will be much weaker, however. The spread of electronic data interchange, a system that enables computers to communicate directly with each other, allows orders between establishments to be placed with little human intervention. Although currently limited to large organizations, it is expected that orders will increase between computers of different companies and from home computers.

Other types of automation should also depress the demand for order clerks. Sophisticated inventory control and automatic billing systems allow companies to track their inventory and accounts with much less help from order clerks. A large and increasing number of companies are using fax machines to receive orders. Increasingly, data-entry keyers enter the information from faxed or mailed orders. Some companies use automated menus that can be accessed with a touch-tone phone to receive orders, and others use answering machines. Interactive voice recognition equipment is expected to be available by the year 2006, further reducing the demand for order clerks.

(See introductory statement on record clerks for information on working conditions, training requirements, and earnings.)

Payroll and Timekeeping Clerks

(D.O.T. 215.362-018, .367-022, .382-014, .482-010)

Nature of the Work
Payroll and timekeeping clerks perform a vital function—ensuring that employees are paid on time and that their paychecks are correct. They adjust monetary errors or incorrect amounts of vacation time, research these records, and perform other clerical tasks.

Timekeeping clerks distribute and collect timecards each pay period. These workers review employee workcharts, timesheets, and timecards to ensure that information is properly recorded, and that the records have the signatures of authorizing officials. For example, they may recalculate total hours on a timesheet that has many complex entries. In companies that bill for the time spent by staff, such as law or accounting firms, timekeeping clerks make sure the hours recorded are charged to the correct job so the client can be properly billed. They review computer reports listing timecards that cannot be processed because of errors and contact the employee or the employee's supervisor to resolve the problem. Timekeeping clerks also keep informed of new payroll policies and inform managers and other employees of procedural changes.

In the payroll department, payroll clerks, also called payroll technicians, screen the timecards for calculating, coding, or other errors. Then they compute pay by subtracting allotments like retirement, Federal and State taxes, insurance, or savings from gross earnings. Increasingly, computers perform these calculations and alert payroll clerks to problems or errors in the data. For small organizations or for new employees whose records are not yet entered into a computer

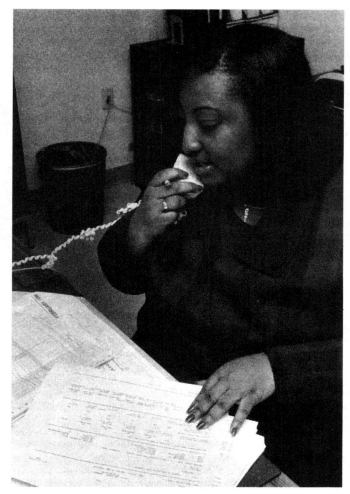

Payroll and timekeeping clerks process timecards.

system, clerks may perform all the necessary calculations. In some small offices, payroll is processed by clerks or other employees in the accounting department.

Payroll clerks also maintain paper backup files for research and reference. They record changes in employee addresses; close out files when workers retire, resign, or transfer; and advise employees on income tax withholding and other mandatory deductions. They also issue and record adjustments to pay because of previous errors or retroactive increases. Payroll clerks must follow changes in tax and deduction laws, so they have to be aware of the most current revisions. They prepare and mail earnings and tax withholding statements in early January for employees' use in preparing their income tax returns.

In small offices, payroll and timekeeping duties are more likely to be included in the duties of a general office clerk, secretary, or accounting clerk. Larger organizations employ specialized payroll and timekeeping clerks to perform these functions.

Employment

Payroll and timekeeping clerks held about 161,000 jobs in 1996. About 35 percent of all payroll and timekeeping clerks worked in business, health, education, and social services; about 25 percent worked in manufacturing; and more than 10 percent were in wholesale and retail trade or in government. About 14 percent of all payroll and timekeeping clerks worked part time in 1996.

Job Outlook

Numerous job openings for persons seeking work as payroll and timekeeping clerks should be available through the year 2006. Many jobs will open up each year as these workers transfer to other occu-

pations—many payroll clerks use this position as a steppingstone to higher-level accounting jobs—or leave the labor force.

Employment of payroll and timekeeping clerks is expected to decline through the year 2006 as continuing automation of the payroll and timekeeping function makes these workers more productive. The technology having the greatest effect on employment is the expanding use of automated timeclocks to calculate employees' hours and balances. These automated timeclocks allow large organizations to centralize their timekeeping duties in one location. At individual sites, employee hours are increasingly tracked by computer and verified by managers. Then, this information is compiled and sent to a central office to be processed by payroll clerks. This eliminates the need to have payroll clerks at every site. Also, timekeeping duties are more commonly being distributed to secretaries, general office clerks, or accounting clerks, or are being contracted out to organizations that specialize in these services.

(See introductory statement on record clerks for information on working conditions, training requirements, and earnings.)

Personnel Clerks

(D.O.T. 205.362-010, -014, -022, .367-062, .567-010; 209.362-026; 241.267-010; 249.367-090)

Nature of the Work

Personnel clerks maintain the personnel records of the organization's employees. These records include information such as name, address, job title, earnings, benefits such as health and life insurance, and tax withholding. On a daily basis, they record and answer questions about employees' absences and supervisory reports on job performance. When an employee receives a promotion or switches health insurance plans, the personnel clerk updates the appropriate form. Personnel clerks may also prepare reports for managers elsewhere in the organization. For example, they might compile a list of employees eligible for an award.

In smaller organizations, some personnel clerks perform a variety of other clerical duties. They answer telephone or letter inquiries from the public, send out announcements of job openings or job examinations, and issue application forms. When credit bureaus and finance companies request confirmation of a person's employment, the personnel clerk provides authorized information from the employee's personnel records. Payroll departments and insurance companies may also be contacted to verify changes to records.

Some personnel clerks are also involved in hiring. They screen job applicants to obtain information such as education and work experience; administer aptitude, personality, and interest tests; explain the organization's employment policies and refer qualified applicants to the employing official; and request references from present or past employers. Personnel clerks inform job applicants, by telephone or letter, of their acceptance or rejection for employment.

Other personnel clerks are known as assignment clerks. Their role is to notify a firm's existing employees of position vacancies and to identify and assign qualified applicants. They keep track of vacancies throughout the organization and complete and distribute vacancy advertisement forms. The clerks review applications in response to the advertisement and verify the information using personnel records. After the selection is made, they notify all the applicants of their acceptance or rejection.

In some job settings, personnel clerks have more specific job titles. Identification clerks are responsible for security matters at defense installations. They compile and record personal data about vendors, contractors, and civilian and military personnel and their dependents. Their job duties include interviewing applicants, corresponding with law enforcement authorities, and preparing badges, passes, and identification cards.

Employment

Personnel clerks held about 124,000 jobs in 1996. Although these workers are found in most industries, about 1 in every 4 works for a

Personnel clerks often screen applications for employment.

government agency. Colleges and universities, hospitals, department stores, and banks also employ large numbers of personnel clerks.

Job Outlook

Replacement needs will account for most job openings for personnel clerks through the year 2006. Jobs will open up as clerks advance within the personnel department, take a job unrelated to personnel administration, or leave the labor force.

Little or no change is expected in employment of personnel clerks through the year 2006. Contributing to the lack of employment growth is the increased use of computers. The growing use of computers and electronic data interchange in personnel or human resource departments means that a lot of data entry work done by personnel clerks can be eliminated as employees themselves enter the data and send it to the personnel office. This is most feasible in large organizations with multiple personnel offices. In addition, as professionals in personnel offices increasingly use computers and other automated office equipment, there could be less work for personnel clerks.

(See introductory statement on record clerks for information on working conditions, training requirements, and earnings.)

Secretaries

(D.O.T. 201 and 219.362-074)

Significant Points

- Training ranges from high school vocational education programs, to 1- to 2-year programs in secretarial science offered by business schools, vocational-technical institutes, and community colleges.

- Increasing office automation will ensure little or no change in overall employment of secretaries; growth in the health and legal services industries, however, will spur employment growth among medical and legal secretaries.

- Job openings should be plentiful, especially for well qualified and experienced secretaries, primarily due to the need to replace workers who leave this very large occupation.

Nature of the Work

Secretarial work continues to evolve along with new office automation and organizational restructuring. In many cases, secretaries have assumed new responsibilities and learned to operate new office technologies. In the midst of these changes, though, their core responsibilities remain much as they were. Most organizations still employ secretaries to perform and coordinate office activities and to ensure information gets disseminated to staff and clients. Managers, professionals, and other support staff still rely on them to keep administrative operations under control.

Secretaries are responsible for a variety of administrative and clerical duties necessary to run and maintain organizations efficiently. Secretaries are often the information clearinghouse for the office. They schedule appointments, provide information to callers, organize and maintain paper and electronic files, manage projects, and produce correspondence for themselves and others. They may also type letters, handle travel arrangements, or contact clients. In addition, secretaries operate office equipment such as facsimile machines, photocopiers, and telephone systems.

Secretaries increasingly use personal computers to run spreadsheet, word processing, database management, desktop publishing, and graphics programs—tasks previously handled by managers and other professionals. Because they are often relieved from dictation and typing, they can support several members of the professional staff. Secretaries often work in groups of three or four so that they can work more flexibly and share their expertise.

Executive secretaries or administrative assistants perform fewer clerical tasks than lowerlevel secretaries. In addition to receiving visitors, arranging conference calls, and scheduling meetings, they may handle more complex responsibilities such as conducting research, preparing statistical reports, training employees, and supervising other clerical staff.

Some secretaries do highly specialized work requiring knowledge of technical terminology and procedures. Further specialization is common among legal secretaries, for example. They prepare correspondence and legal papers such as summonses, complaints, motions, responses, and subpoenas under the supervision of an attorney. They also may review legal journals and assist in other ways with legal research, such as verifying quotes and citations in legal briefs. Medical secretaries are another type of specialized secretary. These workers transcribe dictation, prepare correspondence, and assist physicians or medical scientists with reports, speeches, articles, and conference proceedings. They also record simple medical histories, arrange for patients to be hospitalized, and order supplies. Most medical secretaries need to be familiar with insurance rules, billing practices, and hospital or laboratory procedures. Other technical secretaries assist engineers or scientists. They may prepare correspondence, maintain the technical library, and gather and edit materials for scientific papers.

Working Conditions

Secretaries usually work in offices with other professionals in schools, hospitals, or in legal and medical offices. Their jobs often involve sitting for long periods. If they spend a lot of time typing, particularly at a video display terminal, they may encounter problems of eyestrain, stress, and repetitive motion, such as carpal tunnel syndrome.

Office work can lend itself to alternative or flexible working arrangements, like telecommuting or flex time, and 1 secretary in 5 works part time. In addition, a significant number of secretaries work in temporary positions. A few participate in job sharing arrangements in which two people divide responsibility for a single job. The majority of secretaries, however, are full-time employees who work a standard 40-hour week. Legal secretaries frequently work overtime.

Employment

Secretaries held about 3.4 million jobs in 1996, ranking this among the largest occupations in the U.S. economy. The following tabulation shows the distribution of employment by secretarial specialty.

Secretaries are employed throughout government and private industry.

Secretaries, total	3,403,000
Legal secretaries	284,000
Medical secretaries	239,000
Secretaries, except legal and medical	2,881,000

Secretaries are employed in organizations of every description. About 6 out of 10 secretaries are employed in firms providing services, ranging from education and health, to legal and business services. Others work for firms engaging in manufacturing, construction, wholesale and retail trade, transportation, and communications. Banks, insurance companies, investment firms, and real estate firms are important employers, as are Federal, State, and local government agencies.

Training, Other Qualifications, and Advancement
High school graduates who have basic office skills may qualify for entry-level secretarial positions. Secretaries should be proficient in keyboarding and good at spelling, punctuation, grammar, and oral communication. Shorthand is necessary for some positions. Knowledge of software applications, such as word processing, spreadsheet, and database management, is becoming essential to most employers. Because secretaries must be tactful in their dealings with many different people, employers also look for good interpersonal skills. Discretion, good judgment, organizational ability, and initiative are especially important for higherlevel secretarial positions.

As office automation continues to evolve, retraining and continuing education will remain an integral part of secretarial jobs. Continuing changes in the office environment have increased the demand for secretaries who are adaptable and versatile. Secretaries may have to attend classes to learn how to operate new office technologies such as information storage systems, scanners, the Internet, or new updated software packages.

Secretaries acquire their skills in various ways. Secretarial training ranges from high school vocational education programs that teach office skills and keyboarding, to 1- to 2-year programs in office administration offered by business schools, vocational-technical institutes, and community colleges. Many temporary help agencies provide formal training in computer and office skills. These skills are most often acquired, however, through on-the-job instruction by other employees or by equipment and software vendors. Specialized training programs are available for students planning to become medical or legal secretaries or administrative technology specialists.

Testing and certification for entry-level office skills is available through the Office Proficiency Assessment and Certification program offered by Professional Secretaries International—The Association for Office Professionals (PSI). As secretaries gain experience, they can earn the designation, Certified Professional Secretary (CPS), by meeting certain experience requirements and passing a 1-day examination given by the Institute for Certifying Secretaries, a department of PSI. This designation is recognized by many employers as the mark of excellence for seniorlevel office professionals. Similarly, those without experience who want to be certified as a legal support professional may be certified as an Accredited Legal Secretary (ALS) by the Certifying Board of the National Association of Legal Secretaries. This organization also administers an examination to certify a legal secretary with 3 years of experience as a Professional Legal Secretary (PLS). Legal Secretaries International confers the designation, Board Certified Civil Trial Legal Secretary, in specialized areas such as litigation and probate, to those who have 5 years of law-related experience and who pass the examination.

Secretaries generally advance to a more responsible secretarial position by promotion. Qualified secretaries who broaden their knowledge of the company's operations and enhance their skills may be promoted to other positions such as senior or executive secretary, clerical supervisor, or office manager.

Secretaries with word processing experience can advance to jobs as word processing trainers, supervisors, or managers within their own firms or in a secretarial or word processing service bureau. Their experience as a secretary can lead to jobs such as instructor or sales representative with manufacturers of software or computer equipment. With additional training, many legal secretaries become paralegals.

Job Outlook
Job openings should be plentiful, especially for well qualified and experienced secretaries, primarily due to the need to replace workers who transfer to other occupations or leave this very large occupation for other reasons each year. Projected employment growth for secretaries over the 1996-2006 period will vary by occupational specialty. Growth in health services industries will spur faster than average employment growth for medical secretaries; expansion of the legal services industry will contribute to average employment growth among legal secretaries. Employment of secretaries who do not specialize in legal or medical work—about 7 out of 8—is expected to decline due to the widespread application of new office automation. Despite this projected decline, rapidly growing industries—such as personnel supply, computer and data processing, and management and public relations— will generate some new job opportunities.

Secretaries have become more productive with the help of personal computers, electronic mail, scanners, facsimile machines, and voice message systems. The use of automated equipment is also changing the workflow in many offices. Due to corporate restructuring, administrative duties are being reassigned, as are the functions of entire departments. In some cases, such traditional secretarial duties as typing or keyboarding, filing, copying, and accounting are being assigned to workers in other units or departments. In some law offices and physicians' offices, for example, paralegals and medical assistants are assuming some tasks formerly done by secretaries. Professionals and managers increasingly do their own word processing rather than submit the work to secretaries and other support staff. In addition, there is a trend in many offices for groups of professionals and managers to "share" secretaries. The traditional arrangement of one secretary per manager is becoming less prevalent; instead, secretaries increasingly support systems or units. This approach often means secretaries assume added responsibilities and are seen as valuable members of a team, but it also contributes to the decline in employment projected for most secretaries.

Developments in office technology are certain to continue, and they will bring about further changes in the secretary's work environment. However, many secretarial job duties are of a personal, interactive nature and, therefore, not easily automated. Duties such as planning conferences, working with clients, and transmitting staff instructions require tact and communication skills. Because automated equipment cannot substitute for these personal skills, secretaries will continue to play a key role in the office activities of most organizations.

Earnings

Based on a survey of 160 metropolitan areas, the average annual salary for secretaries with limited experience was $19,700 in 1995. Salaries vary a great deal, however, reflecting differences in skill, experience, and level of responsibility, with averages ranging up to $40,600.

Salaries in different parts of the country also vary; earnings are generally lowest in southern cities, and highest in northern and western cities. In addition, salaries vary by industry; salaries of secretaries tend to be highest in transportation, legal services, and public utilities, and lowest in retail trade and finance, insurance, and real estate. Certification in this field generally is rewarded by a higher salary.

The starting salary for inexperienced secretaries in the Federal Government was $17,400 a year in 1997. Beginning salaries were slightly higher in selected areas where the prevailing local pay level was higher. All secretaries employed by the Federal Government averaged about $27,900 a year in 1997.

Related Occupations

A number of other workers type, record information, and process paperwork. Among these are bookkeepers, receptionists, stenographers, personnel clerks, typists and word processors, paralegals, medical assistants, and medical record technicians. A growing number of secretaries share in managerial and human resource responsibilities. Occupations requiring these skills include clerical supervisor, systems manager, office manager, and human resource specialist.

Sources of Additional Information

For information on the Certified Professional Secretary designation, contact:
☛ Professional Secretaries International, P.O. Box 20404, Kansas City, MO 64195-0404. Homepage: http://www.gvi.net/psi

Information on the Accredited Legal Secretary and Certified Professional Legal Secretary designations is available from:
☛ National Association of Legal Secretaries, 2448 East 81st St., Suite 3400, Tulsa, OK 74137-4238. Homepage: http://www.nals.org

Information on the Board Certified Civil Trial Legal Secretary designation can be obtained from:
☛ Legal Secretaries International Inc., 8902 Sunnywood Dr., Houston, TX 77088-3729. Homepage: http://www.compassnet.com/legalsec

State employment offices can provide information about job openings for secretaries.

Teacher Aides

(D.O.T. 099.327; 219.467; 249.367-074, -086)

Significant Points

- Half of all teacher aides work part time.

- Educational requirements range from a high school diploma to some college training.

- Strong demand for aides to assist and monitor students, to provide teachers with clerical assistance, and to help teachers meet the education needs of a growing special education population will contribute to much faster than average employment growth.

Nature of the Work

Teacher aides, also called instructional aides or paraeducators, provide instructional and clerical support for classroom teachers, allow-

ing teachers more time for lesson planning and teaching. Teacher aides tutor and assist children in learning class material using the teacher's lesson plans, providing students with individualized attention. Aides also assist and supervise students in the cafeteria, schoolyard, school discipline center, or on field trips. They record grades, set up equipment, and help prepare materials for instruction.

In large school districts, some teacher aides are hired to perform exclusively non-instructional or clerical tasks, such as monitoring nonacademic settings. Playground and lunchroom attendants are examples of such aides. Most teacher aides, however, perform a combination of instructional and clerical duties. They generally instruct children, under the direction and guidance of teachers. They work with students individually or in small groups—listening while students read, reviewing or reinforcing class work, or helping them find information for reports. At the secondary school level, teacher aides often specialize in a certain subject, such as math or science. Aides often take charge of special projects and prepare equipment or exhibits, such as for a science demonstration. Some aides work in computer laboratories, assisting students using computers and educational software programs.

In addition to instructing, assisting, and supervising students, teacher aides grade tests and papers, check homework, keep health and attendance records, type, file, and duplicate materials. They also may stock supplies, operate audiovisual equipment, and keep classroom equipment in order.

Many teacher aides work extensively with special education students. Schools are becoming more inclusive, integrating special education students into general education classrooms. As a result, teacher aides in general education and special education classrooms increas-

Teacher aides work with students individually or in small groups.

ingly assist students with disabilities. Aides may attend to a student's physical needs, including feeding, teaching good grooming habits, or assisting students riding the school bus. They also may provide personal attention to students with other special needs, such as those whose families live in poverty, or students who speak English as a second language or need remedial education. Aides help assess a student's progress by observing performance and recording relevant data.

Working Conditions

Half of all teacher aides work part time. Most aides who provide educational instruction work the traditional 9- to 10-month school year, usually in a classroom setting. Aides also may work outdoors supervising recess when weather allows, and spend much of their time standing, walking, or kneeling.

Seeing students develop and gain appreciation of the joy of learning can be very rewarding. However, working closely with students can be both physically and emotionally tiring. Teacher aides who work with special education students may perform more strenuous tasks, including lifting, as they help students with their daily routine. Those who perform clerical work may feel overwhelmed by tedious administrative duties, such as making copies or typing.

Employment

Teacher aides held about 981,000 jobs in 1996. About 9 out of 10 worked in elementary and secondary schools, mostly in the lower grades. A significant number assisted special education teachers in working with children who have disabilities. Most of the others worked in child daycare centers and religious organizations.

Training, Other Qualifications, and Advancement

Educational requirements for teacher aides range from a high school diploma to some college training. Aides with instructional responsibilities usually require more training than those who don't perform teaching tasks. Increasingly, employers prefer aides who have some college training. Some teacher aides are aspiring teachers who are working towards their degree while gaining experience. Many schools require previous experience in working with children. Schools may also require a valid driver's license, and perform a background check on applicants.

A number of 2-year and community colleges offer associate degree programs that prepare graduates to work as teacher aides. However, most teacher aides receive on-the-job training. Those who tutor and review lessons with students must have a thorough understanding of class materials and instructional methods, and should be familiar with the organization and operation of a school. Aides also must know how to operate audiovisual equipment, keep records, and prepare instructional materials, as well as have adequate computer skills.

Teacher aides should enjoy working with children from a wide range of cultural backgrounds, and be able to handle classroom situations with fairness and patience. Aides also must demonstrate initiative and a willingness to follow a teacher's directions. They must have good oral and writing skills and be able to communicate effectively with students and teachers. Teacher aides who speak a second language, especially Spanish, are in great demand to communicate with growing numbers of students and parents whose primary language is not English.

About half of all States have established guidelines or minimum educational standards for the hiring and training of teacher aides, and an increasing number of States are in the process of implementing them. Although requirements vary by State, most require an individual to have at least a high school diploma or general equivalency degree (G.E.D.), or some college training.

Advancement for teacher aides, usually in the form of higher earnings or increased responsibility, comes primarily with experience or additional education. Some school districts provide time away from the job or tuition reimbursement so that teacher aides can earn their bachelor's degrees and pursue licensed teaching positions. In return for tuition reimbursement, aides are often required to commit to teaching a certain length of time for the school district.

Job Outlook

Employment of teacher aides is expected to grow much faster than the average for all occupations through the year 2006. Student enrollments at the elementary and secondary level are expected to rise, spurring strong demand for teacher aides to assist and monitor students and provide teachers with clerical assistance. Teacher aides will also be required to help teachers meet the educational needs of a growing special education population, particularly as these students are increasingly assimilated into general education classrooms. Education reform and the rising number of students who speak English as a second language will continue to contribute to the demand for teacher aides. In addition to jobs stemming from employment growth, numerous job openings will arise as workers transfer to other occupations, leave the labor force to assume family responsibilities, return to school, or leave for other reasons—characteristic of occupations that require limited formal education and offer relatively low pay.

The number of special education programs is growing in response to increasing enrollments of students with disabilities. Federal legislation mandates appropriate education for all children, and emphasizes placing disabled children into regular school settings, when possible. Children with special needs require much personal attention, and special education teachers, as well as general education teachers with special education students, rely heavily on teacher aides. At the secondary school level, teacher aides work with special education students as job coaches, and help students make the transition from school to work.

School reforms which call for more individual instruction should further enhance employment opportunities for teacher aides. Schools are hiring more teacher aides to provide students with the personal instruction and remedial education they need.

Teacher aide employment is sensitive to changes in State and local expenditures for education. Pressures on education budgets are greater in some States and localities than in others. A number of teacher aide positions, such as those in Head Start classrooms, are financed through Federal Government programs, which also may be affected by budget constraints.

Earnings

According to a survey of salaries in public schools, conducted by the Educational Research Service, aides involved in teaching activities averaged $9.04 an hour in 1995-96; those performing only nonteaching activities averaged $8.52 an hour. Earnings varied by region, work experience, and academic qualifications. About 3 out of 10 teacher aides belonged to unions in 1996—mainly the American Federation of Teachers and the National Education Association—which bargain with school systems over wages, hours, and the terms and conditions of employment.

Related Occupations

Teacher aides who instruct children have duties similar to those of preschool, elementary, and secondary school teachers and school librarians. However, teacher aides do not have the same level of responsibility or training. The support activities of teacher aides and their educational backgrounds are similar to those of child-care workers, family daycare providers, library technicians, and library assistants.

Sources of Additional Information

For information on teacher aides, including training and unionization, and on a wide range of education-related subjects, contact:

☛ American Federation of Teachers, Organizing Department, 555 New Jersey Ave. NW., Washington, DC 20001.

For information on a career as a teacher aide, contact:

☛ National Resource Center for Paraprofessionals in Education and Related Services, 25 West 43rd St., Room 620, New York, NY 10036.

School superintendents and State departments of education can provide details about employment requirements.

Telephone Operators

(D.O.T. 235.222-010, .462-010, .562-014, .662-014, -018, -022, and -026)

Significant Points

- Employment of telephone operators is projected to continue to decline, and few job opportunities are expected.

- Limited job opportunities are expected for switchboard or PBX operators, whose employment is not expected to decline.

- Customer service is now the primary function of operators, not switching calls, so familiarity with computers is essential and fluency in a foreign language is an asset.

Nature of the Work

Although most telephone numbers are dialed directly, a few still require the assistance of a telephone operator. Telephone company central office operators help customers with person-to-person or collect calls, or with special billing requests, such as charging a call to a third number or giving customers credit or a refund for a wrong number or a bad connection. Operators are also called upon to handle emergency calls and assist children or people with physical limitations.

Technological innovations have changed the responsibilities of central office operators. Electronic switching systems have eliminated the need for manual switching, and new systems automatically record information about the length and cost of calls into a computer that processes the billing statements. Now in most places, it is also possible to call other countries, person-to-person, or collect without the help of an operator. The task of responding to "intercept" calls (vacant, changed, or disconnected numbers) also is automated, and a computerized recording explains the reason for the interception and gives the new number. The monitoring and computing of charges on calls from pay telephones also is an automated function formerly performed by operators.

Directory assistance operators answer inquiries by accessing computerized alphabetical and geographical directories. They generally no longer read numbers; numbers are read by a computerized recording.

Many organizations, such as hotels and medical centers, employ operators to run private branch exchange (PBX) switchboards. These switchboard, or PBX operators, connect interoffice or house calls, answer and relay outside calls, connect outgoing calls, supply information to

Telephone operators should be pleasant, courteous, and patient.

callers, and record charges. Many also act as receptionists or information clerks, relaying messages or announcing visitors. (Receptionists are described elsewhere in this section of the *Handbook*.)

Operators also work in other settings. Telephone-answering-service operators manage switchboards to provide answering service for clients. Communication-center operators handle airport authority communication systems. For example, they use the public address system to page passengers or visitors. They also monitor electronic equipment alarms.

Private-branch-exchange service advisors, sometimes called customer instructors or telephone usage counselors, train switchboard operators. Service advisors monitor conversations between operators and customers to observe the operator's behavior, technical accuracy, and adherence to company policies.

Working Conditions

The hours of PBX or switchboard operators are generally the same as those of other clerical workers in the firm. In some organizations, they work 40 hours a week during regular business hours. Operators in hotels, hospitals, and other places in which telephone service is needed on a 24-hour basis, even work shifts on holidays and weekends. Telephone company operators generally work 32 1/2 to 37 1/2 hours a week. They also may work day, evening, or night shifts, including weekends and holidays.

Some operators work split shifts. That is, they are on duty during the peak calling periods in the late morning and early evening and have time off in between. Telephone companies normally assign shifts by seniority, allowing the most experienced workers to choose when they will work. These operators, like all telephone company employees, may be on call 24-hours a day. In general, though, they work overtime only during emergencies.

Telephone company operators work at video display terminals in pleasant, well-lighted, air-conditioned surroundings. But if the work site is not well designed, these operators may experience eyestrain and back discomfort.

The job of a telephone operator requires little physical exertion; during peak calling periods, however, the pace at the switchboard may be hectic. Telephone companies continually strive to increase operator efficiency, and this can create a tense work environment. An operator's work is generally quite repetitive and, in telephone companies, closely supervised. Computerized pacing and monitoring by supervisors, combined with the rapid pace, may cause stress. Operators must sit for long periods and usually need supervisory approval to leave their work stations.

Employment

Telephone operators held about 319,000 jobs in 1996. About 3 out of 4 worked as PBX operators in hotels, hospitals, department stores, or other organizations. The remainder worked in telephone companies. Roughly one-fifth of all operators worked part time, although relatively few of those employed by telephone companies were part-timers.

Training, Other Qualifications, and Advancement

New operators are taught how to use the equipment on the job. Because of technological developments, telephone operators should be computer literate. In telephone companies, classroom instruction lasts up to 3 weeks and is followed by on-the-job training. Classroom instruction covers time zones and geography, so central office operators understand rates and know where major cities are located. Tapes are used to familiarize trainees with the dial tone, busy signal, and other telephone sounds, and to improve diction and courtesy by giving them an opportunity to hear their own voices. Close supervision continues after training is completed.

PBX operators who handle routine calls usually have a somewhat shorter training period than telephone company operators. These workers are usually trained informally by experienced personnel, although in some organizations they may be trained by a telephone company instructor.

Telephone operators should be pleasant, courteous, and patient. A clear, pleasing voice and good hearing are important. In addition to being a good listener, prospective operators should have good reading, spelling, and arithmetic skills. Good eye-hand coordination and manual dexterity are useful, as is an ability to work well under pressure. Many employers require operators to pass a physical examination. Some employers require a high school diploma. High school courses in speech, office practices, and business math provide a helpful background; fluency in a foreign language is also looked upon favorably.

After 1 or 2 years of experience, telephone company operators may be promoted to service assistant, aiding the supervisor by monitoring telephone conversations. Direct promotion to supervisor may also be possible in some companies. Some operators advance to other clerical jobs or to telephone craft jobs, such as installer or repairer. Large firms may promote PBX operators to more responsible clerical positions; however, many small businesses have limited advancement opportunities.

Job Outlook
Job opportunities for telephone operators are expected to be extremely limited over the next decade. Overall employment is expected to decline, but variations in growth will occur among different groups of operators. Employment of operators in telephone companies is expected to decline sharply through the year 2006 as automation continues to increase these workers' productivity, and deregulation increases competition for phone services from other industries. Voice recognition technology, which gives computers the capacity to understand speech and to talk back, has replaced many directory assistance operators and central office operators. Many telephone companies do not plan to replace operators who leave, and many are being laid off. However, some job opportunities may become available as more independent phone companies enter the market. With the passing of the Telecommunications Act of 1996, which virtually eliminated the barriers for entering the telephone industry, it will be easier for the independent companies to enter into competition with existing companies.

In contrast, the number of switchboard or PBX operators is expected to grow more slowly than the average for all workers. As older switchboards requiring operators to make connections are replaced by those routing calls automatically, fewer operators will be needed. In addition, voice message systems have proliferated as computers became smaller, cheaper, and more powerful. These systems record, store, play, and forward telephone messages—work currently performed by PBX operators. When callers need to speak to an operator, they may be helped by receptionists who have been trained to make telephone connections. However, many firms may still keep switchboard operators for the "personal touch," which is somewhat limit the effects of new technology.

Earnings
Telephone operators who worked full time, earned a median weekly salary of $371 in 1996. The middle 50 percent earned between $288 and $516. The bottom 10 percent earned less than $220; the top 10 percent earned more than $603 a week.

According to a 1995 survey of workplaces in 160 metropolitan areas, switchboard operators had median weekly earnings of $336. The middle 50 percent earned between $292 and $390 a week.

Telephone company operators generally earn more than switchboard operators. Most telephone company operators are members of the Communications Workers of America (CWA), or the International Brotherhood of Electrical Workers (IBEW). According to the CWA, telephone operators started at an average of $244 a week in 1996, and averaged $638 a week after 5 years on the job. According to IBEW, operators averaged $12.70 an hour in 1996. For these operators, union contracts govern wage rates, wage increases, and the time required to advance from one step to the next (it normally takes 4 years to rise from the lowest paying, nonsupervisory operator position to the highest). Contracts also call for extra pay for work beyond

the normal 6 1/2 to 7 1/2 hours a day or 5 days a week, for Sunday and holiday work, and for a pay differential for nightwork and split shifts. Many contracts provide for a 1-week vacation with 6 months of service; 2 weeks for 1 to 6 years; 3 weeks for 7 to 14 years; 4 weeks for 15 to 24 years; and 5 weeks for 25 years and over. Holidays range from 9 to 11 days a year.

Related Occupations
Other workers who provide information to the general public include customer service representatives, dispatchers, hotel clerks, information clerks, police aides, receptionists, reservation agents, and travel clerks.

Sources of Additional Information
For more details about employment opportunities, contact a telephone company. For general information on the telephone industry and career opportunities contact:
☛ United States Telephone Association, 1401 H St. NW., Suite 600, Washington, DC 20005-2136.
☛ Communications Workers of America, Department of Apprenticeships, Benefits, and Employment, 501 3rd St. NW., Washington, DC 20001.
☛ International Brotherhood of Electrical Workers, Telecommunications Department, 1125 15th. St. NW., Room 807, Washington, DC 20005.

Typists, Word Processors, and Data Entry Keyers

(D.O.T. 203.362-010, -022, .382-018, -026, .582-014, -038, -042, -046, -054, -062, -066, -078; 208.382-010; and 209.382-010)

Significant Points
● For many people, a job as a typist, word processor, or data entry keyer is their first job after graduating from high school or after a period of full-time family responsibilities, serving as a steppingstone to higher paying jobs.

● Workers acquire their skills through high schools, community colleges, business schools, or self-teaching aids such as books, audio or video tapes, and personal computers.

● Employment is projected to decline due to the proliferation of personal computers and other technologies; job prospects will be brightest for those with expertise in computer equipment and software packages.

Nature of the Work
The information that many of today's organizations need to process is growing rapidly. Typists, word processors, and data entry keyers help insure this work is handled smoothly and efficiently.

Typists and word processors usually set up and enter reports, letters, mailing labels, and other text material. Typists make neat, typed copies of materials written by other clerical, professional, or managerial workers. They may begin as entry-level workers by typing headings on form letters, addressing envelopes, or preparing standard forms on typewriters or computers. As they gain experience, they may begin work requiring a higher degree of accuracy and independent judgment. Senior typists may work with highly technical material, plan and type complicated statistical tables, combine and rearrange materials from different sources, or prepare master copies to be reproduced on photocopiers.

Although it is becoming less common, some centralized word processing teams handle the transcription and typing for several departments. Regardless of how work is organized, though, most keyboarding is now done on word processing equipment. Word processors use this equipment to record, edit, store, and revise letters, memos, reports, statistical tables, forms, and other printed materials.

Persons with expertise in computer equipment and software packages have the best prospects for typist, word processor, and data entry keyer jobs.

Word processing equipment—usually a personal computer or part of a larger computer system—normally includes a keyboard, video display terminal, and printer, and may have "add-on" capabilities such as optical character recognition readers.

Typists and word processors often perform other office tasks as well. They answer telephones, file, and operate copiers, calculators, and other office machines. Job titles of typists vary by duties performed and by work setting. For example, clerk typists combine typing with filing, sorting mail, answering telephones, and other general office work. Notereaders transcribe stenotyped notes of court proceedings into standard formats.

Data entry keyers usually fill forms that appear on a computer screen or enter lists of items or numbers. They may also manipulate existing data, edit current information, or proofread new entries to a database. Some examples of data sources include customers' personal information, medical records, and membership lists. Usually this information is used internally by a company, and may be reformatted before use by other departments or by customers.

Keyers can enter data on a variety of typewriter-like equipment. Many keyers use a machine that converts the information they type to magnetic impulses on tapes or disks for entry into a computer system. Others prepare materials for printing or publication by using data entry composing machines. Some keyers operate on-line terminals or personal computers. Data entry keyers increasingly work with nonkeyboard forms of data entry such as scanners and electronically transmitted files. When working with these new optical character recognition systems, data entry keyers often enter only those data which cannot be recognized by machines. In some offices, keyers also operate computer peripheral equipment such as printers and tape readers, act as tape librarians, and perform other clerical duties.

Working Conditions

Typists, word processors, and data entry keyers usually work in clean offices. They sit for long periods and sometimes must contend with high noise levels caused by various office machines. These workers are susceptible to repetitive strain injuries, such as carpal tunnel syndrome and neck, back, and eye strain. To help prevent these from occurring, some offices have scheduled exercise breaks, installed ergonomically designed keyboards, and workstations that allow workers to stand or sit as they wish. They generally work a standard 40-hour week.

Employment

Typists, word processors, and data entry keyers held about 1.1 million jobs in 1996, and were employed in every sector of the economy. Some workers telecommute by working from their homes via personal computers linked by telephone lines to those in the main office. This enables them to type material at home, and almost instantly produce printed copy in their offices.

About 3 out of 10 typists, word processors, and data entry keyers held jobs in firms providing business services, including temporary help, word processing, and computer and data processing. Nearly 2 out of 10 worked in Federal, State, and local government agencies.

Training, Other Qualifications, and Advancement

Employers generally hire high school graduates who can meet their requirements for keyboarding speed. Increasingly, employers also expect applicants to have word processing or data entry training or experience. Spelling, punctuation, and grammar skills are also important, as is familiarity with standard office equipment and procedures.

Students acquire skills in keyboarding and in the use of word processing, spreadsheet, and database management computer software packages through high schools, community colleges, business schools, temporary help agencies, or self-teaching aids such as books, audio or video tapes, and personal computers.

For many people, a job as a typist, word processor, or data entry keyer is their first job after graduating from high school or after a period of full-time family responsibilities. This work frequently serves as a steppingstone to higher paying jobs with more responsibilities. Large companies and government agencies generally have training programs to help clerical employees upgrade their skills and advance to other positions. It is common for typists, word processors, and data entry keyers to transfer to other clerical jobs, such as secretary, statistical clerk, or court reporter, or to be promoted to a supervisory job in a word processing or data entry center.

Job Outlook

Although the volume of information and business transactions is expected to grow rapidly, employment of typists, word processors, and data entry keyers is projected to decline through the year 2006, largely due to productivity gains and organizational restructuring brought about by new technologies. In particular, the proliferation of personal computers has enabled other workers to perform work formerly done by typists, word processors, and data entry keyers. Most professionals and managers now use desktop personal computers or work stations to enter data and do their own word processing.

As technologies are improved and more widely used, demand for typists, word processors, and data entry keyers will continue to decline. For example, bar code scanners, which are now common in large retail establishments, should continue to spread to smaller establishments; increasingly sophisticated optical character recognition readers, which scan documents and enter their text and data into a computer, are being used in more workplaces; and improved voice recognition technologies, enabling people to enter text and data by simply speaking to a computer, should also be more widely used.

In addition to these technologies designed to make traditional data entry more productive, others are being implemented, aiming to make data entry unnecessary. Data are being captured at the point of origin and entered into the system without human intervention. An example of this in the banking industry is automatic teller machines. As telecommunications technology improves, many organizations will take advantage of computer networks that allow more data to be transmitted electronically, thereby avoiding the reentry of data.

Employment of typists, word processors, and data entry keyers will also be influenced by international and service sector outsourcing. Some large data entry and processing firms employ workers in nations with low wages to enter data. As international trade barriers continue to fall and telecommunications technology improves, this transfer will continue to have a negative effect on employment of data entry keyers in the United States. Employment is also being redistributed among industries within the United States. As organizations have demanded more flexibility from workers, they have reduced permanent in-house staff in favor of using temporary help and staffing services firms.

Despite declining employment, the need to replace typists, word processors, and data entry keyers who transfer to other occupations or leave this large occupation for other reasons each year will produce numerous job openings. Job prospects will be brightest for those with the best technical skills—in particular, expertise in computer equipment and software packages. Applicants for these positions, however, must be willing to continuously upgrade their skills.

Earnings
Based on a survey of 160 metropolitan areas, word processors with limited experience averaged $20,000 a year in 1995; relatively inexperienced data entry keyers averaged $18,100.

The salaries of these workers vary by industry; they tend to be highest in transportation and public utilities, and lowest in retail trade and finance, insurance, and real estate. Similarly, their salaries tend to vary by region, with salaries in the West being the highest. Regardless of industry or region, typists generally receive higher salaries if they have word processing experience.

In the Federal Government, clerk-typists and data entry keyers without work experience started at about $15,500 a year in 1997. Beginning salaries were slightly higher in selected areas where the prevailing local pay level was higher. The average annual salary for all clerk-typists in the Federal Government was about $21,500 in 1997.

Related Occupations
Typists, word processors, and data entry keyers must transcribe information quickly. Other workers who deliver information in a timely manner are stenographers, dispatchers, and telephone operators. They must also be comfortable working with office automation, and in this regard they are similar to court reporters, medical transcriptionists, secretaries, and computer and peripheral equipment operators.

Sources of Additional Information
For information about job opportunities in data entry, contact the nearest office of the State employment service.

Service Occupations

Food Preparation and Beverage Service Occupations

Chefs, Cooks, and Other Kitchen Workers

(D.O.T. 311.674-014; 313 except .131; 315.361, .371, and .381; 316.661 and .684-014; 317; 318.687; and 319.484)

Significant Points

- About 40 percent of cooks and 60 percent of other kitchen and food preparation workers were on part-time schedules, approximately two and three times the proportion for all workers throughout the economy.

- Many young people work in these occupations—over 20 percent of food preparation workers are 16-19 years old.

- Job openings are expected to be plentiful through the year 2006, reflecting substantial turnover—characteristic of occupations attractive to people seeking a short-term source of income rather than a career.

Nature of the Work

A reputation for serving good food is essential to any restaurant or hotel, whether it prides itself on exotic cuisine or hamburgers. Chefs, cooks, and other kitchen workers are largely responsible for the reputation a restaurant acquires. Some restaurants offer a varied menu featuring meals that are time-consuming and difficult to prepare, requiring highly skilled employees. Other restaurants emphasize fast service, offering hamburgers and other food that can be prepared in advance or in a few minutes by a fast-food or short-order cook, with limited cooking skills.

Chefs and *cooks* are responsible for preparing meals that are pleasing to the palate and the eye. Chefs are the most highly skilled and trained of all kitchen workers. Although the terms chef and cook are still used interchangeably, cooks are less skilled. Due to their skillful preparation of traditional dishes and refreshing twists in creating new ones, many chefs have earned fame for both themselves and the establishments where they work. (For information on *executive chefs*, see the *Handbook* statement on restaurant and food service managers.)

Institutional chefs and *cooks* work in the kitchens of schools, industrial cafeterias, hospitals, and other institutions. For each meal, they prepare a small selection, but large quantity, of entrees, vegetables, and desserts. *Restaurant chefs* and *cooks* generally prepare a wide selection of dishes for each meal, cooking most orders individually. Whether in institutions or restaurants, chefs and cooks measure, mix, and cook ingredients according to recipes. In the course of their work they use a variety of pots, pans, cutlery, and other equipment, including ovens, broilers, grills, slicers, grinders, and blenders. They are often responsible for directing the work of other kitchen workers, estimating food requirements, and ordering food supplies. Some chefs and cooks also assist in planning meals and developing menus.

Bread and *pastry bakers*, called pastry chefs in some kitchens, produce baked goods for restaurants, institutions, and retail bakery shops. Unlike bakers who work in large, automated industrial bakeries, bread and pastry bakers need only to supply the customers who visit their establishment. They bake small quantities of breads, rolls, pastries, pies, and cakes, doing most of the work by hand. They measure and mix ingredients, shape and bake the dough, and apply fillings and decorations.

Short-order cooks prepare foods to order in restaurants and coffee shops that emphasize fast service. They grill and garnish hamburgers, prepare sandwiches, fry eggs, and cook french fries, often working on several orders at the same time. Prior to busy periods, short-order cooks slice meats and cheeses and prepare coleslaw or potato salad. During slow periods, they may clean the grill, food preparation surfaces, counters, and floors.

Specialty fast-food cooks prepare a limited selection of menu items in fast-food restaurants. They cook and package batches of food, such as hamburgers and fried chicken, which are prepared to order or kept warm until sold.

Some workers are employed in coffee houses which may also serve pastries or other snacks. These workers operate specialized equipment such as cappuccino and expresso machines. Some food products are made on the premises, while others are delivered daily.

Other kitchen workers, under the direction of chefs and cooks, perform tasks requiring less skill. They weigh and measure ingredients, fetch pots and pans, and stir and strain soups and sauces. These workers also clean, peel, and slice potatoes, other vegetables, and fruits and make salads. They may cut and grind meats, poultry, and seafood in preparation for cooking. And their responsibilities also include cleaning work areas, equipment, utensils, dishes, and silverware.

The number and types of workers employed in kitchens depends on the type of establishment. For example, fast-food outlets offer only a few items, which are prepared by fast-food cooks. Small, full-service restaurants offering casual dining often feature a limited number of easy-to-prepare items, supplemented by short-order specialties and ready-made desserts. Typically, one cook prepares all the food with the help of a short-order cook and one or two other kitchen workers.

Large eating places tend to have varied menus and employ kitchen workers who prepare much more of the food they serve from scratch. Kitchen staffs often include several chefs and cooks, sometimes called assistant or apprentice chefs and cooks; a bread and pastry baker; and many less-skilled kitchen workers. Each chef or cook usually has a special assignment and often a special job title—vegetable, fry, or sauce cook, for example. Executive chefs coordinate the

Job openings for chefs, cooks, and other kitchen workers are expected to be plentiful.

312

work of the kitchen staff and often direct the preparation of certain foods. They decide the size of servings, sometimes plan menus, and buy food supplies. They often adjust their menu in response to changes in dietary standards or food consumption.

Working Conditions

Many restaurant and institutional kitchens have modern equipment, convenient work areas, and air-conditioning; but in older and smaller eating places, the kitchens often are not as well equipped. Working conditions depend on the type and quantity of food being prepared and the local laws governing food service operations. Workers generally must withstand the pressure and strain of working in close quarters, standing for hours at a time, lifting heavy pots and kettles, and working near hot ovens and grills. Job hazards include slips and falls, cuts, and burns, but injuries are seldom serious.

Work hours in restaurants may include early mornings, late evenings, holidays, and weekends, while hours in factory and school cafeterias may be more regular. Over 4 out of 10 cooks and 6 out of 10 other kitchen and food preparation workers were on part-time schedules, compared to 1 out of 4 workers throughout the economy. The wide range in dining hours creates work opportunities attractive to homemakers, students, and other individuals seeking supplemental income. For example, well over 20 percent of food preparation workers are 16-19 years old. Kitchen workers employed by public and private schools may work during the school year only, usually for 9 or 10 months. Similarly, establishments at vacation resorts generally only offer seasonal employment.

Employment

Chefs, cooks, and other kitchen workers held more than 3.4 million jobs in 1996. Short-order and fast-food cooks held 804,000 of the jobs; restaurant cooks, 727,000; institutional cooks, 435,000; bread and pastry bakers, 182,000; and other kitchen workers, 1,252,000.

About three-fifths of all chefs, cooks, and other kitchen workers were employed in restaurants and other retail eating and drinking places. One-fifth worked in institutions such as schools, universities, hospitals, and nursing homes. The remainder were employed by grocery stores, hotels, and many other organizations.

Training, Other Qualifications, and Advancement

Most kitchen workers start as fast-food or short-order cooks, or in another low-skilled kitchen position. These positions require little education or training and most skills are learned on the job. After acquiring some basic food handling, preparation, and cooking skills, these workers may be able to advance to an assistant cook or short-order cook position. To achieve the level of skill required of an executive chef or cook in a fine restaurant, many years of training and experience are necessary. Although a high school diploma is not required for beginning jobs, it is recommended for those planning a career as a cook or chef. High school or vocational school courses in business arithmetic and business administration are particularly helpful. Large corporations in the food service and entertainment industries also offer paid internships and summer jobs, which can provide valuable experience.

Many school districts, in cooperation with State departments of education, provide on-the-job training and sometimes summer workshops for cafeteria kitchen workers with aspirations of becoming cooks. Employees who have participated in these training programs are often selected for jobs as cooks.

An increasing number of chefs and cooks obtain their training through high school, post-high school vocational programs, or 2- or 4-year colleges. Chefs and cooks also may be trained in apprenticeship programs offered by professional culinary institutes, industry associations, and trade unions. An example is the 3-year apprenticeship program administered by local chapters of the American Culinary Federation in cooperation with local employers and junior colleges or vocational education institutions. In addition, some large hotels and restaurants operate their own training programs for cooks and chefs.

People who have had courses in commercial food preparation may be able to start in a cook or chef job without having to spend time in a lower-skilled kitchen job. Their education may give them an advantage, when looking for jobs in better restaurants and hotels, where hiring standards often are high. Although some vocational programs in high schools offer this kind of training, employers usually prefer training given by trade schools, vocational centers, colleges, professional associations, or trade unions. Postsecondary courses range from a few months to 2 years or more, and are open in some cases only to high school graduates. The Armed Forces are also a good source of training and experience.

Although curricula may vary, students usually spend most of their time learning to prepare food through actual practice. They learn to bake, broil, and otherwise prepare food, and to use and care for kitchen equipment. Training programs often include courses in menu planning, determination of portion size, food cost control, purchasing food supplies in quantity, selection and storage of food, and use of leftover food to minimize waste. Students also learn hotel and restaurant sanitation and public health rules for handling food. Training in supervisory and management skills sometimes is emphasized in courses offered by private vocational schools, professional associations, and university programs.

Culinary courses are offered by 700 schools across the Nation. The American Culinary Federation accredited about 100 programs in 1996. Accreditation is an indication that a culinary program meets recognized standards regarding course content, facilities, and quality of instruction. The American Culinary Federation has been accrediting culinary programs for a relatively short time; many programs have yet to seek accreditation.

Certification provides valuable formal recognition of the skills of a chef or cook. The American Culinary Federation certifies chefs and cooks at the levels of cook, working chef, executive chef, and master chef. It also certifies pastry professionals and culinary educators. Certification standards are based primarily on experience and formal training.

Important qualifications for chefs, cooks, and other kitchen workers include the ability to work as part of a team, possessing a keen sense of taste and smell, and personal cleanliness. Most States require health certificates indicating workers are free from communicable diseases.

Advancement opportunities for chefs and cooks are better than for most other food and beverage preparation and service occupations. Many acquire high-paying positions and new cooking skills by moving from one job to another. Besides culinary skills, advancement also depends on ability to supervise less-skilled workers and limit food costs, by minimizing waste and accurately anticipating the amount of perishable supplies needed. Some cooks and chefs gradually advance to executive chef positions or supervisory or management positions, particularly in hotels, clubs, or larger, more elegant restaurants. Some eventually go into business as caterers or restaurant owners, while others become instructors in vocational programs in high schools, community colleges, or other academic institutions.

Job Outlook

Job openings for chefs, cooks, and other kitchen workers are expected to be plentiful through the year 2006. While job growth will create new positions, the overwhelming majority of job openings will stem from replacement needs. There is substantial turnover in many of these jobs because of the minimal educational and training requirements. The occupation also offers many part-time positions, attractive to people seeking a short-term source of income rather than a career. Many workers who leave these jobs transfer to other occupations, while others stop working to assume household responsibilities or to attend school full time.

Overall employment of chefs, cooks, and other kitchen workers is expected to increase about as fast as the average for all occupations through the year 2006. Employment growth will be spurred by increases in population, household income, and leisure time that will allow people to dine out and take vacations more often. In addition, as the number of two-income households grows, more families may find dining out a convenience.

Projected employment varies by specialty, however. As the number of families grows and as the more affluent, 55-and-older population increases rapidly, demand will grow for restaurants that offer table service and more varied menus—requiring more higher-skilled cooks and chefs. The popularity of fresh baked breads and pastries should ensure continued rapid growth in the employment of bakers. Employment of short-order and specialty fast-food cooks, most of whom work in fast-food restaurants, is also expected to increase in response to growth of the 16-24 year-old population and the continuing fast-pace lifestyle of many Americans. Employment of institutional and cafeteria chefs and cooks, on the other hand, will grow more slowly than other types of cooks. Their employment will not keep pace with the rapid growth in the educational and health services industries—where their employment is concentrated. Many high schools and hospitals are trying to make "institutional food" more attractive to students, staff, visitors, and patients. While some establishments employ more highly trained chefs and cooks to prepare more appealing meals, many contract out their food services. Many of the contracted companies emphasize fast food and employ short-order and fast-food cooks, instead of institutional and cafeteria cooks.

Earnings

Wages of chefs, cooks, and other kitchen workers depend greatly on the part of the country and the type of establishment in which they are employed. Wages generally are highest in elegant restaurants and hotels, where many executive chefs earn over $38,000 annually, according to a survey conducted by the National Restaurant Association. Median hourly earnings of cooks were less than $7.00 in 1995, with most earning between $6.00 and $8.00. Assistant cooks had median hourly earnings of $6.25, with most earning between $5.50 and $7.00.

The same survey indicated that short-order cooks had median hourly earnings of $6.50 in 1995; most earned between $5.50 and $7.25. Median hourly earnings of bread and pastry bakers were $6.50; most earned between $6.00 and $7.75. Salad preparation workers generally earned less, with median hourly earnings of $5.50; most earned between $5.25 and $6.50.

Some employers provide employees with uniforms and free meals, but Federal law permits employers to deduct from their employees' wages the cost or fair value of any meals or lodging provided, and some employers do so. Chefs, cooks, and other kitchen workers who work full time often receive typical benefits, but part-time workers generally do not.

In some large hotels and restaurants, kitchen workers belong to unions. The principal unions are the Hotel Employees and Restaurant Employees International Union and the Service Employees International Union.

Related Occupations

Workers who perform tasks similar to those of chefs, cooks, and other kitchen workers include butchers and meat cutters, cannery workers, and industrial bakers.

Sources of Additional Information

Information about job opportunities may be obtained from local employers and local offices of the State employment service.

Career information about chefs, cooks, and other kitchen workers, as well as a directory of 2- and 4-year colleges that offer courses or programs that prepare persons for food service careers, is available from:
☛ The National Restaurant Association, 1200 17th St. NW., Washington, DC 20036-3097.

For information on the American Culinary Federation's apprenticeship and certification programs for cooks, as well as a list of accredited culinary programs, send a self addressed, stamped envelope to:
☛ American Culinary Federation, P.O. Box 3466, St. Augustine, FL 32085.

For general information on hospitality careers, write to:
☛ Council on Hotel, Restaurant, and Institutional Education, 1200 17th St. NW., Washington, DC 20036-3097.

For general career information and a directory of accredited private career and technical schools offering programs in the culinary arts, write to:
☛ Accrediting Commission of Career Schools and Colleges of Technology, 2101 Wilson Blvd., Suite 302, Arlington, VA 22201.

Food and Beverage Service Workers

(D.O.T. 310.137-010 and .357; 311.472, .477, .674-010, and -018, and .677; 312; 319.474, .677-014, and .687; 350.677-010, -026, -030; and 352.677-018)

Significant Points

- Most jobs are part time and many opportunities exist for young people— 2 out of 3 food counter and fountain workers are 16-19 years old.

- Job openings are expected to be abundant through the year 2006, reflecting substantial turnover—characteristic of occupations attractive to people seeking a short-term source of income rather than a career.

- Tips comprise a major portion of earnings; consequently, keen competition is expected for bartender, waiter and waitress, and other jobs in popular restaurants and fine dining establishments, where potential earnings from tips are greatest.

Nature of the Work

Whether they work in small, informal diners or large, elegant restaurants, all food and beverage service workers deal with customers. The quality of service they deliver determines in part whether or not the patron will return.

Waiters and *waitresses* take customers' orders, serve food and beverages, prepare itemized checks, and sometimes accept payments. The manner in which they perform their tasks varies considerably, depending on the establishment where they work. In coffee shops, they are expected to provide fast and efficient, yet courteous, service. In fine restaurants, where gourmet meals are accompanied by attentive formal service, waiters and waitresses serve meals at a more leisurely pace and offer more personal service to patrons. For example, servers may recommend a certain wine as a complement to a particular entree, explain how various items on the menu are prepared, or complete preparations on a salad or other special dishes at table side. Additionally, waiters and waitresses may check the identification of patrons to ensure they meet the minimum age requirement for the purchase of alcohol and tobacco products.

Depending on the type of restaurant, waiters and waitresses may perform additional duties generally associated with other food and beverage service occupations. These tasks may include escorting guests to tables, serving customers seated at counters, setting up and clearing tables, or cashiering. However, formal restaurants frequently hire staff to perform these duties, allowing their waiters and waitresses to concentrate on customer service.

Bartenders fill the drink orders that waiters and waitresses take from customers seated in the restaurant or lounge, as well as orders from customers seated at the bar. They prepare standard mixed drinks and, occasionally, are asked to mix drinks to suit a customer's taste. Most bartenders know dozens of drink recipes and are able to mix drinks accurately, quickly, and without waste, even during the busiest periods. Besides mixing and serving drinks, bartenders collect payment, operate the cash register, clean up after customers leave, and, on occasion, serve food items to customers seated at the bar. Bartenders check identification of customers seated at the bar, to ensure they meet the minimum age requirement for the purchase of alcohol and tobacco products.

Bartenders at service bars have little contact with customers, as they work at small bars in restaurants, hotels, and clubs where drinks are served only by waiters and waitresses. However, the majority of bartenders who work in eating and drinking establishments directly serve patrons and interact with them.

Some establishments, especially larger ones, use automatic equipment to mix drinks of varying complexity, at the push of a button. However, bartenders still must be efficient and knowledgeable, in case the device malfunctions or a customer requests a drink not handled by the equipment. Additionally, most customers frequent drinking establishments for the friendly atmosphere and would rather have their drinks prepared by a bartender than a lifeless machine.

Bartenders usually are responsible for ordering and maintaining an inventory of liquor, mixes, and other bar supplies. They often form attractive displays out of bottles and glassware and wash the glassware and utensils after each use.

Hosts and *hostesses* try to evoke a good impression of the restaurant, by warmly welcoming guests. They may courteously direct patrons to where coats and other personal items may be left and indicate where patrons can wait until their table is ready. Hosts and hostesses assign guests to tables suitable for the size of their group, escort patrons to their seats, and provide menus.

Hosts and hostesses are restaurants' personal representatives. They try to insure that service is prompt and courteous and that the meal meets expectations. Hosts and hostesses schedule dining reservations, arrange parties, and organize any special services that are required. In some restaurants, they also act as cashiers.

Dining room attendants and *bartender helpers* assist waiters, waitresses, and bartenders by keeping serving areas stocked with supplies, cleaning tables, and removing dirty dishes to the kitchen. They replenish the supply of clean linens, dishes, silverware, and glasses in the restaurant dining room, and keep the bar stocked with glasses, liquor, ice, and drink garnishes. Bartender helpers also keep bar equipment clean and wash glasses. Dining room attendants set tables with clean tablecloths, napkins, silverware, glasses, and dishes and serve ice water, rolls, and butter. At the conclusion of meals, they remove dirty dishes and soiled linens from tables. Cafeteria attendants stock serving tables with food, trays, dishes, and silverware and may carry trays to dining tables for patrons.

Counter attendants take orders and serve food at counters. In cafeterias, they serve food displayed on counters and steam tables, as requested by patrons; carve meat; dish out vegetables; ladle sauces and soups; and fill beverage glasses. In lunchrooms and coffee shops, counter attendants take orders from customers seated at the counter, transmit the orders to the kitchen, and pick up and serve the food, when it is ready. They also fill cups with coffee, soda, and other beverages and prepare fountain specialties, such as milkshakes and ice cream sundaes. Counter attendants prepare some short-order items, such as sandwiches and salads, and wrap or place orders in containers for carry out. They also clean counters, write itemized checks, and accept payment.

Fast-food workers take orders from customers at counters or drive-through windows at fast-food restaurants. They get the ordered beverage and food items, serve them to customer, and accept payment. Many fast-food workers also cook and package food, make coffee, and fill beverage cups using drink-dispensing machines.

Working Conditions

Food and beverage service workers are on their feet most of the time and often carry heavy trays of food, dishes, and glassware. During busy dining periods, they are under pressure to serve customers quickly and efficiently. The work is relatively safe, but care must be taken to avoid slips, falls, and burns.

Part-time work is more common among food and beverage service workers than in almost any other occupation. Workers on part-time schedules include half of all bartenders, 2 out of 3 waiters and waitresses, and 8 out of 10 food counter and fountain workers, compared to 1 out of 4 workers throughout the economy. The wide range in dining hours creates work opportunities attractive to homemakers, students, and other individuals seeking supplemental income. For example, 2 out of 3 food counter and fountain workers are 16-19

The abundance of part-time food and beverage service jobs is attractive to homemakers, students, and others seeking supplemental income.

years old. Many food and beverage service workers are expected to work evenings, weekends, and holidays. Some work split shifts—that is, they work for several hours during the middle of the day, take a few hours off in the afternoon, and then return to their jobs for the evening hours.

Employment

Food and beverage service workers held 4.8 million jobs in 1996. Waiters and waitresses held 2 million of these jobs; counter attendants and fast-food workers, 1.7 million; dining room and cafeteria attendants and bartender helpers, 439,000; bartenders, 390,000; and hosts and hostesses, 260,000.

Restaurants, coffee shops, bars, and other retail eating and drinking places employed the overwhelming majority of food and beverage service workers. Others worked in hotels and other lodging places, bowling alleys, casinos, and country clubs and other membership organizations.

Jobs are located throughout the country but are typically plentiful in large cities and tourist areas. Vacation resorts offer seasonal employment, and some workers alternate between summer and winter resorts, instead of remaining in one area the entire year.

Training, Other Qualifications, and Advancement

There are no specific educational requirements for food and beverage service jobs. Although many employers prefer to hire high school graduates for waiter and waitress, bartender, and host and hostess positions, completion of high school is generally not required for fast-food workers, counter attendants, and dining room attendants and bartender helpers. For many people, a job as a food and beverage service worker serves as a source of immediate income, rather than a career. Many entrants to these jobs are in their late teens or early twenties and have a high school education or less. Usually, they have little or no work experience. Many are full-time students or homemakers. Food and beverage service jobs are a major source of part-time employment for high school and college students.

Because maintaining a restaurant's "image" is important to its success, employers emphasize personal qualities. Food and beverage service workers are in close contact with the public, so these workers should be well-spoken and have a neat, clean appearance. They should enjoy dealing with all kinds of people, and possess a pleasant disposition.. State laws often require that food and beverage service workers obtain health certificates showing that they are free of communicable diseases.

Waiters and waitresses need a good memory to avoid confusing customers' orders and to recall faces, names, and preferences of frequent patrons. These workers should also be good at arithmetic, so they can total bills without the assistance of a calculator or cash register if necessary. In restaurants specializing in foreign foods, knowledge of a foreign language is helpful. Prior experience waiting on tables is preferred by restaurants and hotels that have rigid table service standards. Jobs at these establishments often have higher earnings, but may also have higher educational requirements than less demanding establishments.

Generally, bartenders must be at least 21 years of age, but usually employers prefer to hire people who are 25 or older. Batenders should be familiar with State and local laws concerning the sale of alcoholic beverages.

Most food and beverage service workers pick up their skills on the job by observing and working with more experienced workers. Some employers, particularly those in fast-food restaurants, use self-instruction programs with audiovisual presentations and instructional booklets to teach new employees food preparation and service skills. Some public and private vocational schools, restaurant associations, and large restaurant chains provide classroom training in a generalized food service curriculum.

Some bartenders acquire their skills by attending a bartending or vocational and technical school. These programs often include instruction on State and local laws and regulations, cocktail recipes, attire and conduct, and stocking a bar. Some of these schools help their graduates find jobs.

Due to the relatively small size of most food-serving establishments, opportunities for promotion are limited. After gaining some experience, some dining room and cafeteria attendants and bartender helpers are able to advance to waiter, waitress, or bartender jobs. For waiters, waitresses, and bartenders, advancement usually is limited to finding a job in a more expensive restaurant or bar where prospects for tip earnings are better. Some bartenders open their own businesses. Some hosts and hostesses and waiters and waitresses advance to supervisory jobs, such as maitre d'hotel, dining room supervisor, or restaurant manager. In larger restaurant chains, food and beverage service workers who excel at their work are often invited to enter the company's formal management training program. (For more information, see the *Handbook* statement on restaurant and food service managers.)

Job Outlook

Job openings for food and beverage service workers are expected to be abundant through the year 2006. However, keen competition is expected for bartender, waiter and waitress, and other food and beverage service jobs in popular restaurants and fine dining establishments, where potential earnings from tips are greatest.

While employment growth will produce many new jobs, the overwhelming majority of openings will arise from the need to replace the high proportion of workers who leave this very large occupation each year. There is substantial movement into and out of the occupation because education and training requirements are minimal; and the predominance of part-time jobs is attractive to people seeking a short-term source of income rather than a career. Many of these workers move to other occupations, while others stop working to assume household responsibilities or to attend school.

Employment of food and beverage service occupations is expected to grow about as fast as the average for all occupations through the year 2006. Employment growth will stem from increases in population, personal incomes, and leisure time. Since it is common for both husband and wife to be in the work force, families may increasingly find dining out a convenience.

Growth of the different types of food and beverage service jobs will vary. As the number of families grow, and as the more affluent,

55-and-older population increases rapidly, demand will grow for restaurants that offer table service and more varied menus—spurring demand for waiters and waitresses and hosts and hostesses. Employment of fast-food workers is also expected to increase in response to growth of the 16-24 year-old population and the continuing fast-pace lifestyle of many Americans. However, little change is expected in the employment of dining room attendants as waiters and waitresses increasingly assume their duties. Employment of bartenders is expected to decline as drinking of alcoholic beverages outside the home—particularly cocktails—continues to drop.

Earnings

Food and beverage service workers derive their earnings from a combination of hourly wages and customer tips. Earnings varies greatly, depending on the type of job and establishment. For example, fast-food workers and hosts and hostesses generally do not receive tips, so their wage rates may be higher than those of waiters and waitresses and bartenders, who may earn more from tips than from wages. In some restaurants, these workers contribute a portion of their tips to a tip pool, which is distributed among the establishment's other food and beverage service workers and kitchen staff. Tip pools allow workers who normally do not receive tips, such as dining room attendants, to share in the rewards for a well-served meal.

In 1996, median weekly earnings (including reported tips) of full-time waiters and waitresses were about $270. The middle 50 percent earned between $200 and $350; the top 10 percent earned at least $470 a week. For most waiters and waitresses, higher earnings are primarily the result of receiving more in tips rather than higher hourly wages. Tips generally average between 10 and 20 percent of guests' checks, so waiters and waitresses working in busy, expensive restaurants earn the most.

Full-time bartenders had median weekly earnings (including tips) of about $310 in 1996. The middle 50 percent earned from $230 and $400; the top 10 percent earned at least $520 a week. Like waiters and waitresses, bartenders employed in public bars may receive more than half of their earnings as tips. Service bartenders are often paid higher hourly wages, to offset their lower tip earnings.

Median weekly earnings (including tips) of full-time dining room attendants and bartender helpers were about $260 in 1996. The middle 50 percent earned between $200 and $320; the top 10 percent earned over $410 a week. Most received over half of their earnings as wages; the rest of their income was their share of the proceeds from tip pools.

Full-time counter attendants and fast-food workers had median weekly earnings (including any tips) of about $220 in 1996. The middle 50 percent earned between $190 and $270, while the highest 10 percent earned over $360 a week. Although some counter attendants receive part of their earnings as tips, fast-food workers generally do not.

In establishments covered by Federal law, workers beginning at the minimum wage earn $5.15 an hour. Employers are also permitted to deduct from wages the cost, or fair value, of any meals or lodging provided. However, many employers provide free meals and furnish uniforms. Food and beverage service workers who work full time often receive typical benefits, while part-time workers generally do not.

In some large restaurants and hotels, food and beverage service workers belong to unions—principally the Hotel Employees and Restaurant Employees International Union and the Service Employees International Union.

Related Occupations

Other workers whose jobs involve serving customers and helping them enjoy themselves include flight attendants, butlers, and tour busdrivers.

Sources of Additional Information

Information about job opportunities may be obtained from local employers and local offices of the State employment service.

A guide to careers in restaurants, a list of 2- and 4-year colleges that have food service programs, and information on scholarships to those programs is available from:

☛ National Restaurant Association, 1200 17th St. NW., Washington, DC 20036-3097.

For general information on hospitality careers, write to:

☛ Council on Hotel, Restaurant, and Institutional Education, 1200 17th St. NW., Washington, DC 20036-3097.

For general career information and a directory of private career colleges and schools that offer training for bartender and other food and beverage service jobs, write to:

☛ Accrediting Commission of Career Schools and Colleges of Technology, 2101 Wilson Blvd., Suite 302, Arlington, VA 22201.

Health Service Occupations

Dental Assistants

(D.O.T. 079.361-018)

Significant points

- Rapid employment growth and above average job turnover should result in good job opportunities.
- Population growth and greater retention of natural teeth by middle-aged and older people will fuel demand for dental services, and create opportunities for dental assistants.
- Dentists are expected to hire more assistants to perform routine tasks, so they may devote their own time to more profitable procedures.

Nature of the Work

Dental assistants perform a variety of patient care, office, and laboratory duties. They work at chairside as dentists examine and treat patients. They make patients as comfortable as possible in the dental chair, prepare them for treatment, and obtain dental records. Assistants hand instruments and materials to dentists, and keep patients' mouths dry and clear by using suction or other devices. Assistants also sterilize and disinfect instruments and equipment; prepare tray setups for dental procedures; provide postoperative instruction; and instruct patients in oral health care. Some dental assistants prepare materials for making impressions and restorations, expose radiographs, and process dental x-ray film as directed by a dentist. They may also remove sutures, apply anesthetics and cavity preventive agents to teeth and gums, remove excess cement used in the filling process, and place rubber dams on the teeth to isolate them for individual treatment.

Those with laboratory duties make casts of the teeth and mouth from impressions taken by dentists, clean and polish removable appliances, and make temporary crowns. Dental assistants with office duties schedule and confirm appointments, receive patients, keep treatment records, send bills, receive payments, and order dental supplies and materials.

Dental assistants should not be confused with dental hygienists, who are licensed to perform different clinical tasks. (See the statement on dental hygienists elsewhere in the *Handbook*.)

Working Conditions

Dental assistants work in a well-lighted, clean environment. Their work area is usually near the dental chair, so they can arrange instruments, materials, and medication, and hand them to the dentist when needed. Dental assistants wear gloves and masks to protect themselves from infectious diseases, such as hepatitis. Handling radiographic equipment poses dangers, but they can be minimized with safety procedures.

Most dental assistants have a 32- to 40-hour workweek, which may include work on Saturdays or evenings.

Employment

Dental assistants held about 202,000 jobs in 1996. More than 1 out of 3 worked part time, sometimes in more than one dental office.

Almost all dental assistants work in private dental offices. Some work in dental schools, private and government hospitals, State and local public health departments, or in clinics.

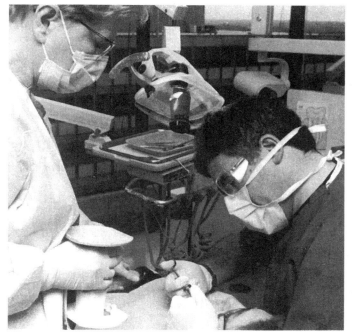

Dental assistants work at chairside as dentists examine and treat patients.

Training, Other Qualifications, and Advancement

Most assistants learn their skills on the job, though many are trained in dental assisting programs offered by community and junior colleges, trade schools, and technical institutes. Some assistants are trained in Armed Forces schools. Assistants must be a dentist's "third hand"; therefore, dentists look for people who are reliable, can work well with others, and have good manual dexterity. High school students interested in careers as dental assistants should take courses in biology, chemistry, health, and office practices.

The American Dental Association's Commission on Dental Accreditation approved 240 training programs in 1996. Programs include classroom, laboratory, and preclinical instruction in dental assisting skills and related theory. In addition, students gain practical experience in dental schools, clinics, or dental offices. Most programs take 1 year or less to complete and lead to a certificate or diploma. Two-year programs offered in community and junior colleges lead to an associate degree. All programs require a high school diploma or its equivalent, and some require a typing or science course for admission. Some private vocational schools offer 4- to 6-month courses in dental assisting, but these are not accredited by the Commission on Dental Accreditation.

Certification is available through the Dental Assisting National Board. Certification is an acknowledgment of an assistant's qualifications and professional competence, but is not usually required for employment. In several States that have adopted standards for dental assistants who perform radiologic procedures, completion of the certification examination meets those standards. Candidates may qualify to take the certification examination by graduating from an accredited training program, or by having 2 years of full-time experience as a dental assistant. In addition, applicants must have current certification in cardiopulmonary resuscitation.

Without further education, advancement opportunities are limited. Some dental assistants working the front office become office managers. Others, working chairside, go back to school to become dental hygienists.

Job Outlook

Job prospects for dental assistants should be good. Employment is expected to grow much faster than the average for all occupations through the year 2006. Also, the proportion of workers leaving and who must be replaced is above average. Many opportunities are for entry-level positions offering on-the-job training.

Population growth and greater retention of natural teeth by middle-aged and older people will fuel demand for dental services. Also, dentists are likely to employ more assistants, for several reasons. Older dentists, who are less likely to employ assistants, will leave and be replaced by recent graduates, who are more likely to use one, or even two. In addition, as dentists' workloads increase, they are expected to hire more assistants to perform routine tasks, so they may devote their own time to more profitable procedures.

Most job openings for dental assistants will arise from the need to replace assistants leaving the occupation. For many, this entry-level occupation provides basic training and experience and serves as a stepping-stone to more highly skilled and higher paying jobs. Other assistants leave the job to take on family responsibilities, return to school, or for other reasons.

Earnings

In 1996, median weekly earnings for dental assistants working full time were $361. The middle 50 percent earned between $284 and $452 a week. The lowest 10 percent earned less than $212; the top 10 percent, more than $516.

According to the American Dental Association, experienced dental assistants who worked 32 hours a week or more in a private practice averaged $406 a week in 1995.

Related Occupations

Workers in other occupations supporting health practitioners include medical assistants, physical therapy assistants, occupational therapy assistants, pharmacy technicians and assistants, and veterinary technicians.

Sources of Additional Information

Information about career opportunities, scholarships, accredited dental assistant programs, and requirements for certification is available from:
☛ Commission on Dental Accreditation, American Dental Association, 211 E. Chicago Ave., Suite 1814, Chicago, IL 60611. Homepage: http://www.ada.org
☛ Dental Assisting National Board, Inc., 216 E. Ontario St., Chicago, IL 60611.

For information about a career as a dental assistant and schools offering training, contact:
☛ National Association of Health Career Schools, 750 First St. NE., Suite 940, Washington, DC 20002. FAX: (202) 842-1565 E-mail: NAHCS@aol.com

Medical Assistants

(D.O.T. 078.361-038; 079.362-010, .364-010 and -014, and .374-018; and 355.667-010)

Significant points

- Medical assistants is expected to be one of the 10 fastest growing occupations through the year 2006.
- Job prospects should be best for medical assistants with formal training or experience.

Nature of the Work

Medical assistants perform routine administrative and clinical tasks to keep the offices and clinics of physicians, podiatrists, chiropractors, and optometrists running smoothly. Medical assistants should not be confused with physician assistants who examine, diagnose, and treat patients, under the direct supervision of a physician. (Physician assistants are discussed elsewhere in the *Handbook*.)

The duties of medical assistants vary from office to office, depending on office location, size, and specialty. In small practices, medical assistants are usually "generalists," handling both administrative and clinical duties and reporting directly to an office manager, physician, or other health practitioner. Those in large practices tend to specialize in a particular area under the supervision of department administrators.

Medical assistants perform many administrative duties. They answer telephones, greet patients, update and file patient medical records, fill out insurance forms, handle correspondence, schedule appointments, arrange for hospital admission and laboratory services, and handle billing and bookkeeping.

Clinical duties vary according to State law and include taking medical histories and recording vital signs, explaining treatment procedures to patients, preparing patients for examination, and assisting the physician during the examination. Medical assistants collect and prepare laboratory specimens or perform basic laboratory tests on the premises, dispose of contaminated supplies, and sterilize medical instruments. They instruct patients about medication and special diets, prepare and administer medications as directed by a physician, authorize drug refills as directed, telephone prescriptions to a pharmacy, draw blood, prepare patients for x rays, take electrocardiograms, remove sutures, and change dressings.

Medical assistants may also arrange examining room instruments and equipment, purchase and maintain supplies and equipment, and keep waiting and examining rooms neat and clean.

Assistants who specialize have additional duties. *Podiatric medical assistants* make castings of feet, expose and develop x rays, and assist podiatrists in surgery. *Ophthalmic medical assistants* help ophthalmologists provide medical eye care. They administer diagnostic tests, measure and record vision, and test the functioning of eyes and eye muscles. They also show patients how to use eye dressings, protective shields, and safety glasses, and how to insert, remove, and care for contact lenses. Under the direction of the physician, they may administer medications, including eye drops. They also maintain optical and surgical instruments and assist the ophthalmologist in surgery.

Employment of medical assistants is projected to grow much faster than average.

Working Conditions

Medical assistants work in well-lighted, clean environments. They constantly interact with other people, and may have to handle several responsibilities at once.

Most full-time medical assistants work a regular 40-hour week. Some work part-time, evenings or weekends.

Employment

Medical assistants held about 225,000 jobs in 1996. Seven in 10 jobs were in physicians' offices, and over 1 in 10 were in offices of other health practitioners such as chiropractors, optometrists, and podiatrists. The rest were in hospitals, nursing homes, and other health care facilities.

Training, Other Qualifications, and Advancement

Most employers prefer to hire graduates of formal programs in medical assisting. Formal programs in medical assisting are offered in vocational-technical high schools, postsecondary vocational schools, community and junior colleges, and in colleges and universities. Postsecondary programs usually last either 1 year, resulting in a certificate or diploma, or 2 years, resulting in an associate degree. Courses cover anatomy, physiology, and medical terminology as well as typing, transcription, recordkeeping, accounting, and insurance processing. Students learn laboratory techniques, clinical and diagnostic procedures, pharmaceutical principles, medication administration, and first aid. They study office practices, patient relations, medical law, and ethics. Accredited programs include an internship that provides practical experience in physicians' offices, hospitals, or other health care facilities.

Although formal training in medical assisting is available, such training—while generally preferred—is not always required. Some medical assistants are trained on the job, although this is less common than in the past. Applicants usually need a high school diploma or the equivalent. Recommended high school courses include mathematics, health, biology, typing, bookkeeping, computers, and office skills. Volunteer experience in the health care field is also helpful.

Two agencies recognized by the U.S. Department of Education accredit programs in medical assisting: the Commission on Accreditation of Allied Health Education Programs (CAAHEP) and the Accrediting Bureau of Health Education Schools (ABHES). In 1997, there were about 350 medical assisting programs accredited by CAAHEP and over 150 accredited by ABHES. The Committee on Accreditation for Ophthalmic Medical Personnel accredited 18 programs in ophthalmic medical assisting.

Although there is no licensing for medical assistants, some States require them to take a test or a short course before they can take x rays or perform other specific clinical tasks. Employers prefer to hire experienced workers or certified applicants who have passed a national examination, indicating that the medical assistant meets certain standards of competence. The American Association of Medical Assistants awards the Certified Medical Assistant credential; the American Medical Technologists awards the Registered Medical Assistant credential; the American Society of Podiatric Medical Assistants awards the Podiatric Medical Assistant Certified credential; and the Joint Commission on Allied Health Personnel in Ophthalmology awards the Ophthalmic Medical Assistant credential at three levels: Certified Ophthalmic Assistant, Certified Ophthalmic Technician, and Certified Ophthalmic Medical Technologist.

Because medical assistants deal with the public, they must be neat and well-groomed and have a courteous, pleasant manner. Medical assistants must be able to put patients at ease and explain physicians' instructions. They must respect the confidential nature of medical information. Clinical duties require a reasonable level of manual dexterity and visual acuity.

Medical assistants may be able to advance to office manager. They may qualify for a wide variety of administrative support occupations, or may teach medical assisting. Some, with additional education, enter other health occupations such as nursing and medical technology.

Job Outlook

Employment of medical assistants is expected to grow much faster than the average for all occupations through the year 2006 as the health services industry expands due to technological advances in medicine, and a growing and aging population. It is one of the fastest growing occupations.

Employment growth will be driven by the increase in the number of group practices, clinics, and other health care facilities that need a high proportion of support personnel, particularly the flexible medical assistant who can handle both administrative and clinical duties. Medical assistants primarily work in outpatient settings, where much faster than average growth is expected.

In view of the preference of many health care employers for trained personnel, job prospects should be best for medical assistants with formal training or experience, particularly those with certification.

Earnings

The earnings of medical assistants vary widely, depending on experience, skill level, and location. According to the *1997 Staff Salary Survey* published by the Health Care Group®, average hourly wages for medical assistants with less than 2 years of experience ranged from $8.07 to $10.90 in 1996. Average hourly wages for medical assistants with more than 5 years of experience ranged from $10.38 to $13.46. Wages were higher in the Northeast and West and lower in the Midwest and South.

Related Occupations

Workers in other medical support occupations include medical secretaries, hospital admitting clerks, pharmacy helpers, medical record clerks, dental assistants, occupational therapy aides, and physical therapy aides.

Sources of Additional Information

Information about career opportunities, CAAHEP-accredited educational programs in medical assisting, and the Certified Medical Assistant exam is available from:
☞ The American Association of Medical Assistants, 20 North Wacker Dr., Suite 1575, Chicago, IL 60606-2903.

Information about career opportunities and the Registered Medical Assistant certification exam is available from:
☞ Registered Medical Assistants of American Medical Technologists, 710 Higgins Rd., Park Ridge, IL 60068-5765.

For a list of ABHES-accredited educational programs in medical assisting, write:
☞ Accrediting Bureau of Health Education Schools, 2700 South Quincy St., Suite 210, Arlington, VA 22206.

For information about a career as a medical assistant and schools offering training, contact:
☞ National Association of Health Career Schools, 750 First St. NE., Suite 940, Washington, DC 20002. FAX: (202) 842-1565 E-mail: NAHCS@aol.com

Information about career opportunities, training programs, and the Certified Ophthalmic Assistant exam is available from:
☞ Joint Commission on Allied Health Personnel in Ophthalmology, 2025 Woodlane Dr., St. Paul, MN 55125-2995.

Information about careers for podiatric assistants is available from:
☞ American Society of Podiatric Medical Assistants, 2124 S. Austin Blvd., Cicero, IL 60650.

Nursing Aides and Psychiatric Aides

(D.O.T. 354.374-010, .377-010, and .677-010; 355.377-014 and -018, .674-014 and -018, and .677-014)

Significant points

- Job prospects for nursing aides will be good because of fast growth and high turnover in this large occupation.

- Minimum education or training is generally required for entry level jobs, but earnings are low.

Nature of the Work

Nursing aides and psychiatric aides help care for physically or mentally ill, injured, disabled, or infirm individuals confined to hospitals, nursing or residential care facilities, and mental health settings. (Homemaker-home health aides, whose duties are similar but who work in clients' homes, are discussed elsewhere in the *Handbook*.)

Nursing aides, also known as nursing assistants, geriatric aides, unlicensed assistive personnel, or hospital attendants, perform routine tasks under the supervision of nursing and medical staff. They answer patients' call bells, deliver messages, serve meals, make beds, and help patients eat, dress, and bathe. Aides may also provide skin care to patients, take temperatures, pulse, respiration, and blood pressure, and help patients get in and out of bed and walk. They may also escort patients to operating and examining rooms, keep patients' rooms neat, set up equipment, or store and move supplies. Aides observe patients' physical, mental, and emotional conditions and report any change to the nursing or medical staff.

Nursing aides employed in nursing homes are often the principal caregivers, having far more contact with residents than other members of the staff. Since some residents may stay in a nursing home for months or even years, aides develop ongoing relationships with them and interact with them in a positive, caring way.

Psychiatric aides are also known as mental health assistants and psychiatric nursing assistants. They care for mentally impaired or emotionally disturbed individuals. They work under a team that may include psychiatrists, psychologists, psychiatric nurses, social workers, and therapists. In addition to helping patients dress, bathe, groom, and eat, psychiatric aides socialize with them and lead them in educational and recreational activities. Psychiatric aides may play games such as cards with the patients, watch television with them, or participate in group activities such as sports or field trips. They observe patients and report any physical or behavioral signs which might be important for the professional staff to know. They accompany patients to and from wards for examination and treatment. Because they have the closest contact with patients, psychiatric aides have a great deal of influence on patients' outlook and treatment.

Working Conditions

Most full-time aides work about 40 hours a week, but because patients need care 24 hours a day, some aides work evenings, nights, weekends, and holidays. Many work part-time. Aides spend many hours standing and walking, and they often face heavy workloads. Because they may have to move patients in and out of bed or help them stand or walk, aides must guard against back injury. Nursing aides may also face hazards from minor infections and major diseases such as AIDS and hepatitis, but can avoid infections by following proper procedures.

Nursing aides often have unpleasant duties; they empty bed pans and change soiled bed linens. The patients they care for may be disoriented, irritable, or uncooperative. Psychiatric aides must be prepared to care for patients whose illness may cause violent behavior. While their work can be emotionally demanding, many aides gain satisfaction from assisting those in need.

Employment

Nursing aides held about 1,312,000 jobs in 1996, and psychiatric aides held about 103,000 jobs. About one-half of all nursing aides worked in nursing homes, and about one-fourth worked in hospitals. Others worked in residential care facilities, such as halfway houses and homes for the aged or disabled, or in private households. Most psychiatric aides worked in psychiatric units of general hospitals, psychiatric hospitals, State and county mental institutions, homes for mentally retarded and psychiatric patients, and community mental health centers.

Training, Other Qualifications, and Advancement

In many cases, neither a high school diploma nor previous work experience is necessary for a job as a nursing or psychiatric aide. A few

Nursing aides help patients walk and get in and out of bed.

employers, however, require some training or experience. Hospitals may require experience as a nursing aide or home health aide. Nursing homes often hire inexperienced workers who must complete a minimum of 75 hours of mandatory training and pass a competency evaluation program within 4 months of employment. Aides who complete the program are placed on the State registry of nursing aides. Some States require psychiatric aides to complete a formal training program.

These occupations can offer individuals an entry into the world of work. The flexibility of night and weekend hours also provides high school and college students a chance to work during the school year.

Nursing aide training is offered in high schools, vocational-technical centers, some nursing homes, and community colleges. Courses cover body mechanics, nutrition, anatomy and physiology, infection control, communication skills, and resident rights. Personal care skills such as how to help patients bathe, eat, and groom are also taught.

Some facilities, other than nursing homes, provide classroom instruction for newly hired aides, while others rely exclusively on informal on-the-job instruction from a licensed nurse or an experienced aide. Such training may last several days to a few months. From time to time, aides may also attend lectures, workshops, and in-service training.

Applicants should be healthy, tactful, patient, understanding, emotionally stable, dependable, and have a desire to help people. They should also be able to work as part of a team, have good communication skills, and be willing to perform repetitive, routine tasks.

Opportunities for advancement within these occupations are limited. To enter other health occupations, aides generally need additional formal training. Some employers and unions provide opportunities by simplifying the educational paths to advancement. Experience as an aide can also help individuals decide whether to pursue a career in the health care field.

Job Outlook

Job prospects for nursing aides should be good through the year 2006. Numerous openings will arise from a combination of fast growth and high turnover for this large occupation. Employment of nursing aides is expected to grow faster than the average for all occupations in response to an emphasis on rehabilitation and the long-term care needs of a rapidly aging population. Employment will increase as a result of the expansion of nursing homes and other long-term care facilities for people with chronic illnesses and disabling conditions, many of whom are elderly. Financial pressure on hospitals to release patients as soon as possible should produce more nursing home admissions. Modern medical technology will also increase the employment of nursing aides. This technology, while saving and extending more lives, increases the need for long-term care provided by aides. As a result, nursing and personal care facilities are expected to grow very rapidly and to provide most of the new jobs for nursing aides.

Employment of psychiatric aides is expected to grow slower than the average for all occupations. Employment will rise in response to the sharp increase in the number of older persons—many of whom will require mental health services. Employment of aides in outpatient community mental health centers is likely to grow because of increasing public acceptance of formal treatment for drug abuse and alcoholism, and a lessening of the stigma attached to those receiving mental health care. However, employment in hospitals—where one-half of psychiatric aides work—is likely to decline due to attempts to contain costs by limiting inpatient psychiatric treatment.

Replacement needs will constitute the major source of openings for aides. Turnover is high, a reflection of modest entry requirements, low pay, and lack of advancement opportunities.

Earnings
Median weekly earnings of full-time salaried nursing aides and psychiatric aides were $292 in 1996. The middle 50 percent earned between $233 and $372. The lowest 10 percent earned less than $189; the top 10 percent, more than $507.

According to the Buck Survey conducted by the American Health Care Association, nursing aides in chain nursing homes had median hourly earnings of about $6.60 in 1996. The middle 50 percent earned between $5.95 and $7.50.

Aides in hospitals generally receive at least 1 week's paid vacation after 1 year of service. Paid holidays and sick leave, hospital and medical benefits, extra pay for late-shift work, and pension plans also are available to many hospital and some nursing home employees.

Related Occupations
Nursing aides and psychiatric aides help people who need routine care or treatment. So do homemaker-home health aides, child-care workers, companions, occupational therapy aides, and physical therapy aides.

Sources of Additional Information
For information about a career as a nursing aide and schools offering training, contact:
☛ National Association of Health Career Schools, 750 First St. NE., Suite 940, Washington, DC 20002. FAX: (202) 842-1565
E-mail: NAHCS@aol.com

Information about employment opportunities may be obtained from local hospitals, nursing homes, psychiatric facilities, State boards of nursing and local offices of the State employment service.

Occupational Therapy Assistants and Aides

(D.O.T. 076.364-010 and 355.377-010)

Significant points

- Occupational therapy assistants and aides are projected to be among the 10 fastest growing occupations, but only a small number of job openings will result, because the occupation is small.

- Occupational therapy assistants need an associate's degree or certificate from an accredited community college or technical school; occupational therapy aides usually receive most of their training on the job.

Nature of the Work
Occupational therapy assistants and aides work under the direction of occupational therapists to provide rehabilitative services to persons with mental, physical, emotional, or developmental impairments. The ultimate goal is to improve clients' quality of life by helping them compensate for limitations. For example, they help injured workers re-enter the labor force by improving their motor skills, or help persons with learning disabilities increase their independence by teaching them to prepare meals or use public transportation.

Occupational therapy assistants help clients with rehabilitative activities and exercises outlined in a treatment plan developed in collaboration with the occupational therapist. The activities range from teaching the proper method of moving from a bed into a wheelchair, to the best way to stretch and limber the muscles of the hand. Assistants monitor the individual to ensure activities are performed correctly and to provide encouragement. They also record their observations of client's progress for use by the occupational therapist. If the treatment is not having the intended effect, or the client is not improving as expected, the treatment program may be altered to obtain better results. They also document billing of the client's health insurance provider.

Occupational therapy aides typically prepare materials and assemble equipment used during treatment, and are responsible for a

Occupational therapy assistants and aides improve quality of life by helping patients overcome limitations.

range of clerical tasks. Their duties may include scheduling appointments, answering the telephone, restocking or ordering depleted supplies, and filling out insurance forms or other paperwork. Aides are not licensed, so by law they are not allowed to perform as wide a range of tasks as occupational therapy assistants.

Working Conditions

Occupational therapy assistants and aides usually work during the day, but may occasionally work evenings or weekends in order to accommodate the client's schedule. They should be in good physical shape because they are on their feet for long periods of time and may be asked to help lift and move clients or equipment.

Employment

Occupational therapy assistants and aides held 16,000 jobs in 1996. Over one-third worked in hospitals, and about one-fourth worked in nursing and personal care facilities. The rest primarily worked in offices and clinics of occupational therapists and other health practitioners. A small number of assistants and aides worked in residential care facilities, outpatient rehabilitation centers, and home health care services.

Training, Other Qualifications, and Advancement

Occupational therapy assistants need an associate's degree or certificate from an accredited community college or technical school. There were 117 accredited occupational therapy assistant programs in the United States in 1996. The first year of study typically involves an introduction to healthcare, basic medical terminology, anatomy, and physiology. In the second year, courses are more rigorous and usually include occupational therapy courses in areas such as mental health, gerontology, and pediatrics. Students must also complete supervised fieldwork in a clinic or community setting. Applicants to occupational therapy assistant programs can improve their chances of admission by taking high school courses in biology and health, and by performing volunteer work in nursing homes, occupational or physical therapist's offices, or elsewhere in the healthcare field.

Occupational therapy assistants are regulated in most States, and must pass a national certification examination after they graduate. Those who pass the test are awarded the title of certified occupational therapy assistant.

Occupational therapy aides usually receive most of their training on the job. Qualified applicants must have a high school diploma, strong interpersonal skills, and a desire to help people in need. Applicants may increase their chances of getting a job by volunteering their services, thus displaying initiative and their aptitude to the employer.

Assistants and aides must be responsible, patient, and willing to take directions and work as part of a team. Furthermore, they should be caring and want to help people who are not able to help themselves.

Job Outlook

Opportunities for job seekers should be favorable. Employment of occupational therapy assistants and aides is expected to grow much faster than the average for all occupations through 2006. Although the occupation is expected to be one of the fastest growing in the economy, only a small number of job openings will result, because the occupation is small.

Growth will result from an aging population, including the "baby-boom" cohort, which will need more occupational therapy services. Demand will also result from advances in medicine that allow more people with critical problems to survive, who then need rehabilitative therapy. Furthermore, employers seeking to reduce health care costs are expected to hire more occupational therapy assistants and aides for tasks currently performed by more highly paid occupational therapists.

Earnings

According to a membership survey of the American Occupational Therapy Association, mean annual income for new full-time occupational therapy assistants was about $27,442 in 1995. Based on limited information, occupational therapy aides usually start between $6.50 and $7.50 an hour.

Related Occupations

Occupational therapy assistants and aides work under the direction of occupational therapists. Other occupations in the healthcare field that work under the supervision of professionals include dental assistants, medical assistants, optometric assistants, pharmacy assistants, and physical therapy assistants and aides.

Sources of Additional Information

Information on a career as an occupational therapy assistant and a list of accredited programs can be obtained by sending a self-addressed label and $5.00 to:

☛ The American Occupational Therapy Association, 4720 Montgomery Lane., P.O. Box 31220, Bethesda, MD 20824-1220. Homepage: http://www.aota.org

Physical Therapy Assistants and Aides

(D.O.T. 076.224-010 and 355.354-010)

Significant points

- Physical therapist assistants and aides are projected to be among the fastest growing occupations in the economy, as growth in the number of individuals with disabilities or limited function increases the demand for support personnel for physical therapy services.

- Most licensed physical therapist assistants have an associate's degree, but aides usually learn skills on the job.

Nature of the Work

Physical therapist assistants and aides perform physical therapy procedures and related tasks selected and delegated by a supervising physical therapist. They assist the physical therapist in providing services that help improve mobility, relieve pain, and prevent or limit permanent physical disabilities of patients suffering from injuries or disease. Their patients include accident victims and individuals with disabling conditions such as low back pain, arthritis, heart disease, fractures, head injuries, and cerebral palsy.

Physical therapist assistants perform a wide variety of tasks. Treatment procedures delegated to physical therapist assistants may involve exercises, massages, electrical stimulation, paraffin baths, hot/cold packs, traction, and ultrasound. Assistants record the patient's progress during treatment and report the outcome of each treatment to the physical therapist.

Physical therapist aides help make therapy sessions productive, under the direct supervision of a physical therapist or physical therapist assistant. They are usually responsible for keeping the treatment area clean and organized, and preparing for each patient's therapy. When patients need assistance to, or from the treatment area, aides may push them in a wheelchair, or provide them with a shoulder to lean on. Aides may inform the therapist or assistant if patients are experiencing difficulty with the treatment. Because they are not licensed, aides perform a smaller range of tasks than physical therapist assistants.

The duties of assistants and aides include some clerical tasks, such as ordering depleted supplies, maintaining patient records, answering the phones, and filling out insurance forms and other paperwork. Records kept by the assistant or aide keep the therapist informed about patients' progress and any problems that may develop during treatment. The extent to which an aide, or even an assistant, performs clerical tasks depends on the size and location of the facility.

Working Conditions

The hours and days that physical therapist assistants and aides work vary depending on the facility, and whether they are full or part-time employees. Many outpatient physical therapy offices and clinics

Physical and corrective therapy assistants and aides receive on-the-job training.

have evening and weekend hours to help coincide with patients' personal schedules.

Physical therapist assistants and aides need to have a moderate degree of strength due to the physical exertion required in assisting patients with their treatment. For example, constant kneeling, stooping and standing for long periods of time are all part of the job. In some cases, assistants and aides may need to help lift patients.

Employment

Physical therapist assistants and aides held 84,000 jobs in 1996. They work alongside physical therapists in a variety of settings. Two-thirds of all assistants and aides work in hospitals or offices of physical therapists. Others work in outpatient rehabilitation centers, nursing homes, offices and clinics of physicians, and in patients' homes. In sports physical therapy, they may work part of the time on the sidelines of sporting events.

Training, Other Qualifications, and Advancement

Physical therapist assistants typically have earned an associate's degree from an accredited physical therapist assistant program. As of January 1997, 44 States and Puerto Rico regulated assistants. Other requirements include certification in CPR and First Aid, and a minimum number of hours of clinical experience.

According to the American Physical Therapy Association , there were 225 accredited physical therapist assistant programs in the United States as of July, 1997. Accredited physical therapist assistant programs are designed to last two years, or four semesters, and culminate in an associate's degree. Admission into physical therapist assistant programs is competitive and it is not unusual for colleges to have long waiting lists of prospective candidates. The programs are divided into academic study and "hands on" clinical experience. Academic coursework includes algebra, anatomy and physiology, biology, chemistry, and psychology. Before students begin their clinical field experience, many programs require that they complete a semester of anatomy and physiology and have certifications in CPR and First Aid. Both educators and prospective employers view clinical experience as an integral part of ensuring that students understand the responsibilities of a physical therapist assistant.

Employers typically require physical therapist aides to have a high school diploma, strong interpersonal skills, and a desire to assist people in need. Most employers provide clinical on-the-job training.

Job Outlook

Physical therapist assistants and aides are expected to be among the fastest growing occupations through the year 2006. Demand for physical therapist assistants and aides will continue to rise with growth in the number of individuals with disabilities or limited function. The rapidly growing elderly population is particularly vulnerable to chronic and debilitating conditions that require therapeutic services. Also, the baby-boom generation is entering the prime age for heart attacks and strokes, increasing the demand for cardiac and physical rehabilitation. Older patients often need more assistance in their treatment, making the roles of assistants and aides vital.

Licensed physical therapist assistants can enhance the cost-effective provision of physical therapy services. After a patient is evaluated and a treatment plan is designed by the physical therapist, the physical therapist assistant can provide many aspects of treatment, as prescribed by the therapist.

Earnings

According to the limited information available, starting salaries for physical therapist assistants average about $24,000 a year in 1996. Starting salaries of assistants working in hospitals tended to be lower than those in private practice. The American Physical Therapy Association reports that experienced assistants working in private practice earned an average of about $30,000 in 1996.

In 1996, median annual earnings of full-time salaried health aides, including physical therapist aides, were $16,000. The middle 50 percent earned between $13,000 and $21,000. The top 10 percent earned at least $28,000, and the bottom 10 percent earned less than $10,000.

Related Occupations

Physical therapist assistants and aides work under the supervision of physical therapists. Other occupations in the healthcare field that work under the supervision of professionals include dental, medical, occupational therapy, optometric, recreational therapy, and pharmacy assistants.

Sources of Additional Information

Information on a career as a physical therapist assistant or aide, and a list of schools offering accredited programs can be obtained from:
☛ The American Physical Therapy Association, 1111 North Fairfax Street, Alexandria, VA 22314-1488. Homepage: http://www.apta.org

Personal, Buildings, and Grounds Service Occupations

Barbers and Cosmetologists

(D.O.T. 330; 331; 332; 333; 339.361, .371)

Significant Points

- The proportion who are self-employed is very high, as is the proportion who work part time.
- All barbers and cosmetologists must be licensed.
- Cosmetologists will account for virtually all employment growth; employment of barbers is expected to decline.

Nature of the Work

Looking your best has never been easy. It requires the perfect hairstyle, exquisite nails, a neatly trimmed beard, or the proper make-up to accent your coloring. More and more, it also requires the services of barbers and cosmetologists. As people increasingly demand styles that are better suited to their individual characteristics, they must choose from a vast array of cosmetic products and rely on these workers to help them make sense of the different options. Although tastes and fashions change from year to year, the basic job of barbers and cosmetologists has remained the same—helping people to look their best.

Barbers cut, trim, shampoo, and style hair. Many people still go to a barber for just a haircut, but an increasing number seek more personalized hairstyling services, such as perms or coloring. In addition to these services, barbers may fit hairpieces, provide hair and scalp treatments, shave male customers, or give facial massages. Barbers in most States are licensed to perform all the duties of cosmetologists except skin care and nail treatment, but a growing number of barbers are trained to perform these services as well.

Cosmetologists primarily shampoo, cut, and style hair, but they also perform a number of other services. These workers, who are often called hairstylists, may advise patrons on how to care for their hair, straighten or permanent wave a customer's hair, or lighten or darken hair color. In addition, most cosmetologists are trained to give manicures, pedicures, and scalp and facial treatments; provide makeup analysis for women; and clean and style wigs and hairpieces. Cosmetologists generally are licensed to provide all of the services that barbers do except shaving men.

A growing number of workers in cosmetology offer specialized services. The largest and fastest growing of these is manicurists, who work exclusively on nails and provide manicures, pedicures, and nail extensions to clients. Another group of specialists are estheticians, who cleanse and beautify the skin by giving facials, full-body treatments, head and neck massages, and offer hair-removal through waxing. Electrologists, on the other hand, use an electrolysis machine to remove hair. Finally, shampooers specialize in shampooing and conditioning patrons' hair in some larger salons.

In addition to their work with customers, barbers and cosmetologists are expected to keep their work area clean and their hairdressing implements sanitized. They may make appointments and keep records of hair color and permanent wave formulas used by their regular patrons. A growing number also actively sell hair products and other cosmetic supplies. Barbers and cosmetologists who operate their own salons have managerial duties that include hiring, supervising, and firing workers, as well as keeping records and ordering supplies.

Working Conditions

Barbers and cosmetologists generally work in clean, pleasant surroundings with good lighting and ventilation. Good health and stamina are important because these workers usually have to be on their feet for most of their shift. Prolonged exposure to some hair and nail chemicals may be hazardous and cause irritation, so special care must be taken when working with these chemicals.

Most full-time barbers and cosmetologists work 40 hours a week, but longer hours are common in this occupation, especially among self-employed workers. Work schedules may include evenings and weekends, when beauty and barber shops and salons are busiest. Although weekends and lunch periods are generally very busy, barbers and cosmetologists are able to take breaks during less popular times. Nearly half of all cosmetologists are part-time workers, double the rate for barbers and for all other workers in the economy.

Employment

Barbers and cosmetologists held 701,000 jobs in 1996. Employment in these occupations is distributed as follows:

Hairdressers, hairstylists, and cosmetologists	586,000
Barbers	59,000
Manicurists	43,000
Shampooers	13,000

Most of these workers are employed in beauty salons, barber shops, or department stores, and a few are employed by hospitals, hotels, and prisons. Nearly every town has a barber shop or beauty salon, but employment in this occupation is concentrated in the most populous cities and States. Hairstylists usually work in cities and suburbs, where the greatest demand for their services exists. Stylists who set fashion trends with their hairstyles usually work in New York City, Los Angeles, and other centers of fashion and the performing arts.

Approximately 3 of every 4 barbers and 2 in 5 cosmetologists are self-employed. Many self-employed barbers and cosmetologists own the salon in which they work, but a growing share of these workers leases the booth or chair where they work from the salon's owner.

Training, Other Qualifications, and Advancement

Although all States require barbers and cosmetologists to be licensed, the qualifications necessary to obtain a license vary. Generally, a

Barbers and cosmetologists must be licensed to work in barber and beauty shops.

person must have graduated from a State-licensed barber or cosmetology school, pass a physical examination, and be at least 16 years old. Some States require graduation from high school while others require as little as an eighth grade education. In a few States, completion of an apprenticeship can substitute for graduation from a school, but very few barbers or cosmetologists learn their skills in this way. Applicants for a license usually are required to pass a written test and demonstrate an ability to perform basic barbering or cosmetology services.

Some States have reciprocity agreements that allow licensed barbers and cosmetologists to practice in a different State without additional formal training. Other States do not recognize training or licenses obtained in another State; consequently, persons who wish to become a barber or a cosmetologist should review the laws of the State in which they want to work before entering a training program.

Public and private vocational schools offer daytime or evening classes in barbering and cosmetology. Full-time programs in barbering and cosmetology usually last 6 to 12 months, but training for manicurists, estheticians, and electrologists requires significantly less time. An apprenticeship program can last from 1 to 2 years. Formal training programs include classroom study, demonstrations, and practical work. Students study the basic services—haircutting, shaving, facial massaging, and hair and scalp treatments—and, under supervision, practice on customers in school "clinics." Most schools also teach unisex hairstyling and chemical styling. Students attend lectures on barber services, the use and care of instruments, sanitation and hygiene, basic anatomy, and recognition of certain skin ailments. Instruction also is provided in sales and general business practices. There are also advanced courses for experienced barbers in hairstyling, coloring, and the sale and service of hairpieces. Most schools teach hairstyling of men's as well as women's hair.

After graduating from a training program, students can take the State licensing examination. The examination consists of a written test and, in some cases, a practical test of cosmetology skills. A few States include an oral examination in which the applicant is asked to explain the procedures he or she is following while taking the practical test. In many States, cosmetology training may be credited towards a barbering license, and vice versa. A few States have even combined the two licenses into one hair styling license. In most States, a separate examination is given for people who want only a manicurist, esthetician, or electrolysis license.

For many cosmetologists, formal training and a license are only the first steps in a career that requires years of continuing education. Because hairstyles are constantly changing, barbers and cosmetologists must keep abreast of the latest fashions and beauty techniques. They do this by attending training in salons, at cosmetology schools, or at product shows. These shows offer workshops and demonstrations of the latest techniques and expose cosmetologists to a wide range of products that they can recommend to clients, an important skill as retail sales become a more important part of the beauty salon industry.

Successful barbers or cosmetologists usually have finger dexterity and a sense of form and artistry. They should enjoy dealing with the public and be willing and able to follow patrons' instructions. Some cosmetology schools consider "people" skills to be such an integral part of the job that they require coursework in this area. Business skills are important for those who plan to operate their own salons, and the ability to be an effective salesperson is becoming vital for nearly all barbers and cosmetologists.

During their first months on the job, new workers are given relatively simple tasks or are assigned the simpler hairstyling patterns. Once they have demonstrated their skills, they are gradually permitted to perform the more complicated tasks such as giving shaves, coloring hair, or applying a permanent. As they continue to work in the field, more training is generally required to learn the techniques used in each salon and to build on the basics learned in cosmetology school.

Advancement usually takes the form of higher earnings as barbers and cosmetologists gain experience and build a steady clientele. Some barbers and cosmetologists manage large salons or open their own after several years of experience. Others teach in barber or cos-

metology schools. Other options include becoming sales representatives for cosmetics firms, opening businesses as beauty or fashion consultants, or working as examiners for State licensing boards.

Job Outlook

Overall employment of barbers and cosmetologists is expected to grow about as fast as the average for all occupations through the year 2006. Increasing population, incomes, and demand for cosmetology services will stimulate job growth. In addition, numerous job openings will stem from rapid turnover in salons and the large size of the occupation. The extent of competition for jobs and customers may be greater at the higher paying, prestigious salons, however, as applicants vie with a large pool of licensed and experienced cosmetologists. The number of part-time and self-employed, booth-renting cosmetologists should continue to grow, creating a dynamic labor market with many opportunities for people to enter the field, particularly workers who are licensed to provide a broad range of cosmetology services.

Different employment trends are expected among barbers and cosmetologists. Cosmetologists will account for virtually all of the employment growth, reflecting the continuing shift in consumer preferences to more personalized services in unisex establishments. Demand for manicurists and for cosmetologists who are trained in nail care will be particularly strong. In addition, cosmetologists who are trained to provide specialized services such as skin care and manicurists who learn new skills like air brushing should be able to attract more clients. Employment of barbers is expected to decline slightly, but in spite of this decline, a couple of thousand job openings will arise annually for new barber licensees as older barbers retire.

Earnings

Barbers and cosmetologists receive income either from commissions or wages and tips. Their median weekly income in 1996 was $290, significantly lower than the $490 for all workers. A number of factors determine the total income for barbers and cosmetologists, including the size and location of the shop, the number of hours worked, customers' tipping habits, and the competition from other barber shops and salons. A cosmetologist's or barber's initiative and ability to attract and hold regular customers are also key factors in determining their earnings. Earnings for entry-level workers are generally lower, ranging from the minimum wage to considerably more in prestigious or exceptionally busy salons.

Related Occupations

Other workers whose main activity consists of improving a patron's personal appearance include beauty consultants and make-up and wig specialists. Other related workers are employed in the cosmetology industry as instructors, beauty supply distributors, and salon managers.

Sources of Additional Information

A list of licensed training schools and licensing requirements for cosmetologists can be obtained from:

☛ National Accrediting Commission of Cosmetology Arts and Sciences, 901 North Stuart St., Suite 900, Arlington, VA 22203-1816.

Information about a career in cosmetology is available from:

☛ National Cosmetology Association, 3510 Olive St., St. Louis, MO 63017.

For details on State licensing requirements and approved barber or cosmetology schools, contact the State board of barber examiners or the State board of cosmetology in your State capital.

Flight Attendants

(D.O.T. 352.367-010)

Significant Points

- Job duties are learned through extensive formal training after being are hired.

- The opportunity for travel attracts many to this career, but this occupation requires working nights, weekends, and holidays and frequently being away from home.

Nature of the Work

Major airlines are required by law to provide flight attendants for the safety of the flying public. Although the primary job of the flight attendants is to ensure that safety regulations are adhered to, they also try to make flights comfortable and enjoyable for passengers.

At least 1 hour before each flight, flight attendants are briefed by the captain, the pilot in command, on such things as emergency evaluation procedures, crew coordination, length of flights, expected weather conditions and special passenger problems. Flight attendants check that first aid kits and other emergency equipment are aboard and in working order and that the passenger cabin is in order, with adequate supplies of food, beverages, and blankets. As passengers board the plane, flight attendants greet them, check their tickets, and instruct them on where to store coats and carry-on items.

Before the plane takes off, flight attendants instruct all passengers in the use of emergency equipment and check to see that seat belts are fastened, seat backs are forward, and all carry on items are properly stowed. In the air, helping passengers in the event of an emergency is the most important responsibility of a flight attendant. Safety-related tips may range from reassuring passengers during occasional encounters with strong turbulence to directing passengers in evacuating a plane following an emergency landing. They also may answer questions about the flight; distribute reading material, pillows, and blankets; and help small children, elderly or disabled persons, and any others needing assistance. They may administer first aid to passengers who become ill. Flight attendants may serve alcoholic beverages and other refreshments and, on many flights, heat and distribute precooked meals or snacks. After the plane has landed, flight attendants take inventory of alcoholic beverages, monies collected, and headsets and may report on medical problems of passengers, and cabin equipment conditions or incidents.

Lead or first flight attendants, sometimes known as pursers, oversee the work of the other attendants aboard the aircraft, while performing most of the same duties.

Working Conditions

Since airlines operate around the clock year round, flight attendants may work at night and on holidays and weekends. They usually fly 75 to 85 hours a month and, in addition generally spend about 75 to 85 hours a month on the ground preparing planes for flights, writing reports following completed flights, and waiting for planes to arrive. Because of variations in scheduling and limitations on flying time, many flight attendants have 11 or more days off each month. They may be away from their home base at least one-third of the time. During this period, the airlines provide assigned hotel accommodations and an allowance for meal expenses.

The combination of free time and discount air fares provides flight attendants the opportunity to travel and see new places. However, the work can be strenuous and trying. Short flights require speedy service if meals are served and a turbulent flight can make serving drinks and meals difficult. Flight attendants stand during much of the flight and must remain pleasant and efficient regardless of how tired they are or how demanding passengers may be. Flight attendants are susceptible to injuries because of the job demands in a moving aircraft. Back injuries and mishaps opening overhead compartments are common. In addition, medical problems can occur from working in a pressurized environment and breathing recycled air, irregular sleeping and eating pattens; and dealing with stressful passengers.

Employment

Flight attendants held about 132,000 jobs in 1996. Commercial airlines employed the vast majority of all flight attendants, most of whom live in major cities at the airlines' home bases. A small number of flight attendants worked for large companies that operated company aircraft for business purposes.

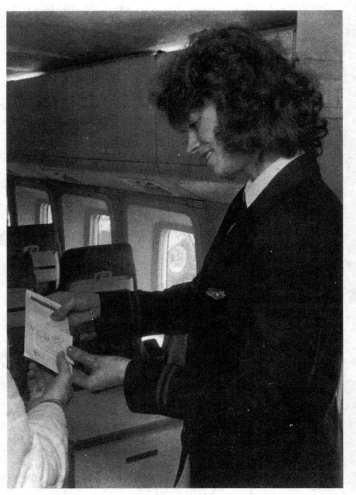

As passengers board the plane, flight attendants greet them, check their tickets, and direct them where to store carry-on items.

Training, Other Qualifications, and Advancement

Airlines prefer to hire poised, tactful, and resourceful people who can interact comfortably with strangers and remain calm under duress. Applicants usually must be at least 19 to 21 years old. Flight attendants must have excellent health and the ability to speak clearly. In addition, there are height requirements and applicants should not have visible tatoos.

Applicants must be high school graduates. Those having several years of college or experience in dealing with the public are preferred. More and more flight attendants being hired are college graduates. Highly desirable areas of concentration include such people oriented disciplines as psychology and education. Flight attendants for international airlines generally must speak an appropriate foreign language fluently. Some of the major airlines prefer candidates who can speak two major foreign languages for their international flights.

Most large airlines require that newly hired flight attendants complete 4 to 6 weeks of intensive training in the airlines' flight training centers. Airlines that do not operate training centers generally send new employees to the center of another airline. Transportation to the training centers and an allowance for board, room, and school supplies may be provided. Trainees learn emergency procedures such as evacuating an airplane, operating emergency systems and equipment, administering first aid, and water survival tactics. In addition, trainees are instructed to deal with hijacking and terrorist situations. Flight attendants also are taught flight regulations and duties, company operations and policies, and receive instruction on personal grooming and weight control. Trainees for the international routes get additional instruction in passport and customs regulations. Towards the end of their training, students go on practice flights. Additionally, flight attendants must annually receive recurrent 12 to 14 hours of training in emergency procedures and passenger relations.

After completing initial training, flight attendants are assigned to one of their airline's bases. New flight attendants are placed on "reserve status" and are called on either to staff extra flights or fill in for crew members who are sick or on vacation or rerouted. Reserve flight attendants on duty must be available on short notice, and usually remain on reserve for at least 1 year. However, at some cities, it may take 5 to 10 years or longer to advance from reserve status. Flight attendants who no longer are on reserve bid monthly for regular assignments. Because assignments are based on seniority, usually only the most experienced attendants get their choices of base and flights. Advancement takes longer today than in the past because experienced flight attendants are remaining in this career for more years than they used to.

Some flight attendants transfer within the airline to become supervisors, or may take on additional duties such as recruiting and instructing.

Job Outlook

Opportunities should be favorable for persons seeking flight attendant jobs as the number of applicants is expected to be roughly in balance with the number of job openings. Those with at least 2 years of college and experience in dealing with the public should have the best chance of being hired.

As airline restrictions on employment have been abolished, turnover—which traditionally was very high—has declined. Therefore, the majority of job openings through the year 2006 should be due to replacement needs. Many flight attendants are attracted to the occupation by the glamour of the airline industry and the opportunity to travel, but some eventually leave in search of jobs that offer higher earnings and require fewer nights be spent away from their families. Several thousand job openings will arise each year as a result of the need to replace flight attendants who transfer to another occupation or who leave the labor force.

Employment of flight attendants is expected to grow faster than the average for all occupations through the year 2006. Growth in population and income is expected to increase the number of airline passengers. Airlines enlarge their capacity by increasing the number and size of planes in operation. Since Federal Aviation Administration safety rules require one attendant for every 50 seats, more flight attendants will be needed.

Employment of flight attendants is sensitive to cyclical swings in the economy. During recessions, when the demand for air travel declines, many flight attendants are put on part-time status or laid off. Until demand increases, few flight new attendants are hired.

Earnings

Beginning flight attendants had median earnings of about $12,800 a year in 1996, according to data from the Association of Flight Attendants. Flight attendants with 6 years of flying experience had median annual earnings of about $19,000, while some senior flight attendants earned as much as $40,000 a year. Flight attendants receive extra compensation for night and international flights and for increased hours. In addition, flight attendants and their immediate families are entitled to free fares on their own airline and reduced fares on most other airlines.

Many flight attendants belong to the Association of Flight Attendants. Others may be members of the Transport Workers Union of America, the International Brotherhood of Teamsters, or other unions.

Flight attendants are required to buy uniforms and wear them while on duty. Uniform replacement items are usually paid for by the company. The airlines generally provide a small allowance to cover cleaning and upkeep of the uniforms.

Related Occupations

Other jobs that involve helping people as a safety professional while requiring the ability to be pleasant even under trying circumstances

include emergency medical technician, firefighter, maritime crew, and camp counselor.

Sources of Additional Information

Information about job opportunities in a particular airline and the qualifications required may be obtained by writing to the personnel manager of the company.

Homemaker-Home Health Aides

(D.O.T. 309.354-010 and 354.377-014)

Significant points

- Numerous job openings will result due to very fast employment growth and very high turnover.

- Education required for entry-level jobs is generally minimal, but earnings are low.

Nature of the Work

Homemaker-home health aides help elderly, disabled, and ill persons live in their own homes instead of in a health facility. Most work with elderly or disabled clients who need more extensive care than family or friends can provide. Some homemaker-home health aides work with families in which a parent is incapacitated and small children need care. Others help discharged hospital patients who have relatively short-term needs. These workers are sometimes called home care aides and personal care attendants.

Homemaker-home health aides provide housekeeping services, personal care, and emotional support for their clients. They clean clients' houses, do laundry, and change bed linens. Aides may also plan meals (including special diets), shop for food, and cook.

Home health aides provide personal care services, also known as "hands on" care, because they physically touch the patient. These aides help clients move from bed, bathe, dress, and groom. They also check pulse, temperature, and respiration; help with simple prescribed exercises; and assist with medication routines. Occasionally, they change nonsterile dressings, use special equipment such as a hydraulic lift, give massages and alcohol rubs, or assist with braces and artificial limbs. Some accompany clients outside the home, serving as guide, companion, and aide.

Homemaker-home health aides also provide instruction and psychological support. For example, they may assist in toilet training a severely mentally handicapped child, or just listen to clients talk

Homemaker-home health aides provide housekeeping services, personal care, and emotional support for their clients.

about their problems. Aides keep records of services performed and of clients' condition and progress.

In home care agencies, homemaker-home health aides are supervised by a registered nurse, a physical therapist, or a social worker, who assigns them specific duties. Aides report changes in the client's condition to the supervisor or case manager. Homemaker-home health aides also participate in case reviews, consulting with the team caring for the client—registered nurses, therapists, and other health professionals.

Working Conditions

The homemaker-home health aide's daily routine may vary. Aides may go to the same home every day for months or even years. However, most aides work with a number of different clients, each job lasting a few hours, days, or weeks. Aides often visit four or five clients on the same day.

Surroundings differ from case to case. Some homes are neat and pleasant, while others are untidy or depressing. Some clients are angry, abusive, depressed, or otherwise difficult; others are pleasant and cooperative.

Homemaker-home health aides generally work on their own, with periodic visits by their supervisor. They receive detailed instructions explaining when to visit clients and what services to perform. Many aides work part time, and weekend hours are common.

Most aides generally travel by public transportation, but some need a car. Either way, they are responsible for getting to the client's home. Aides may spend a good portion of the working day traveling from one client to another; motor vehicle accidents are always a danger. They are particularly susceptible to injuries resulting from all types of overexertion when assisting patients, and falls inside and outside their homes. Mechanical lifting devices that are available in institutional settings are seldom available in patients' homes.

Employment

Homemaker-home health aides held about 697,000 jobs in 1996. Most aides are employed by homemaker-home health agencies, home health agencies, visiting nurse associations, residential care facilities with home health departments, hospitals, public health and welfare departments, community volunteer agencies, and temporary help firms. Self-employed aides have no agency affiliation or supervision, and accept clients, set fees, and arrange work schedules on their own.

Training, Other Qualifications, and Advancement

In some States, this occupation is open to individuals with no formal training. On-the-job training is generally provided. Other States may require formal training, depending on Federal or State law.

The Federal Goverment has enacted guidelines for home health aides whose employers receive reimbursement from Medicare. Federal law requires home health aides to pass a competency test covering 12 areas: Communication skills; observation, reporting, and documentation of patient status and the care or services furnished; reading and recording vital signs; basic infection control procedures; basic elements of body function and changes; maintenance of a clean, safe, and healthy environment; recognition of, and procedures for emergencies; the physical, emotional, and developmental characteristics of the patients served; personal hygiene and grooming; safe transfer techniques; normal range of motion and positioning; and basic nutrition.

A home health aide may also take training before taking the competency test. Federal law suggests at least 75 hours of classroom and practical training supervised by a registered nurse. Training and testing programs may be offered by the employing agency, but must meet the standards of the Health Care Financing Administration. Training programs vary depending upon State regulations.

The National Association for Home Care offers a National Homemaker-Home Health Aide certification. The certification is a voluntary demonstration that the individual has met industry standards.

Successful homemaker-home health aides like to help people and do not mind hard work. They should be responsible, compassionate, emotionally stable, and cheerful. Aides should also be tactful, honest, and discreet because they work in private homes.

Homemaker-home health aides must be in good health. A physical examination including State regulated tests such as those for tuberculosis may be required.

Advancement is limited. In some agencies, workers start out performing homemaker duties, such as cleaning. With experience and training, they may take on personal care duties. The most experienced aides assist with medical equipment such as ventilators, which help patients breathe.

Job Outlook

A large number of job openings is expected for homemaker-home health aides, due to very rapid growth and very high turnover. Homemaker-home health aides is expected to be one of the fastest growing occupations through the year 2006.

The number of people in their seventies and older is projected to rise substantially. This age group is characterized by mounting health problems requiring some assistance. Also, there will be an increasing reliance on home care for patients of all ages. This trend reflects several developments: Efforts to contain costs by moving patients out of hospitals and nursing facilities as quickly as possible, the realization that treatment can be more effective in familiar surroundings rather than clinical surroundings, and the development and improvement of medical technologies for in-home treatment.

In addition to jobs created by the increase in demand for these workers, replacement needs are expected to produce numerous openings. Turnover is high, a reflection of the relatively low skill requirements, low pay, and high emotional demands of the work. For these same reasons, many people are unwilling to perform this kind of work. Therefore, persons who are interested in this work and suited for it should have excellent job opportunities, particularly those with experience or training as homemaker-home health aides or nursing aides.

Earnings

Earnings for homemaker-home health aides vary considerably. According to a National Association for Home Care survey, the starting average hourly wage for homemakers who worked primarily in Medicare-certified agencies ranged from $5.25 to $6.95 in October 1996. Home health aides' average starting hourly wage ranged from $5.96 to $8.29. Wages were somewhat higher in the Northeast and West and somewhat lower in the Midwest and South. Some aides are paid on a salary or per-visit basis.

Most employers give slight pay increases with experience and added responsibility. Aides are usually paid only for the time worked in the home. They normally are not paid for travel time between jobs. Most employers hire only "on-call" hourly workers and provide no benefits.

Related Occupations

Homemaker-home health aide is a service occupation combining duties of health workers and social service workers. Workers in related occupations that involve personal contact to help or instruct others include attendants in children's institutions, childcare attendants in schools, child monitors, companions, nursery school attendants, occupational therapy aides, nursing aides, physical therapy aides, playroom attendants, and psychiatric aides.

Sources of Additional Information

General information about training and referrals to State and local agencies about opportunities for homemaker-home health aides, a list of relevant publications, and information on national certification are available from:

☛ National Association for Home Care, 228 7th St., SE., Washington, DC 20003.

For information about a career as a home health aide and schools offering training, contact:

☛ National Association of Health Career Schools, 750 First St. NE., Suite 940, Washington, DC 20002. FAX: (202) 842-1565 E-mail: NAHCS@aol.com

Janitors and Cleaners and Cleaning Supervisors

(D.O.T. 321.137-010, -014; 323.137-010, .687; 350.137-026; 358.687-010; 381.137-010, .687 except -010; 382.664-010; 389.667-010, .683-010, .687-014; 739.687-198; 891.687-010 and -018; and 952.687-010)

Significant Points

- Job openings should be plentiful because limited training requirements coupled with low pay and numerous part-time and temporary jobs contribute to high turnover in this very large occupation.

Nature of the Work

Janitors and cleaners—also called building custodians, executive housekeepers, or maids—keep office buildings, hospitals, stores, apartment houses, hotels, and other types of buildings clean and in good condition. Some only do cleaning, while others have a wide range of duties. They may fix leaky faucets, empty trash cans, do painting and carpentry, replenish bathroom supplies, mow lawns, and see that heating and air-conditioning equipment works properly. On a typical day, janitors may wet- or dry-mop floors, clean bathrooms, vacuum carpets, dust furniture, make minor repairs, and exterminate insects and rodents. In hospitals, where they are mostly known as maids or housekeepers, they may also wash bed frames, brush mattresses, make beds, and disinfect and sterilize equipment and supplies using germicides and sterilizing equipment. In hotels, aside from cleaning and maintaining the premises, they may deliver ironing boards, cribs, and rollaway beds to guests' rooms.

Janitors and cleaners use various equipment, tools, and cleaning materials. For one job, they may need a mop and bucket; for another, an electric polishing machine and a special cleaning solution. Improved building materials, chemical cleaners, and power equipment have made many tasks easier and less time-consuming, but janitors must learn proper use of equipment and cleaners to avoid harming floors, fixtures, and themselves.

Cleaning supervisors coordinate, schedule, and supervise the activities of janitors and cleaners. They assign tasks and inspect building areas to see that work has been done properly, issue supplies and equipment, inventory stocks to ensure an adequate amount of supplies is present, screen and hire job applicants, and recommend promotions, transfers, or dismissals. They also train new and experienced employees. Supervisors may prepare reports concerning room occupancy, hours worked, and department expenses. Some also perform cleaning duties.

Working Conditions

Because most office buildings are cleaned while they are empty, many cleaners work evening hours. Some, however, such as school and hospital custodians, work in the daytime. When there is a need for 24-hour maintenance, janitors may be assigned to shifts. Most full-time janitors, cleaners, and cleaning supervisors work about 40 hours a week. Part-time cleaners usually work in the evenings and on weekends.

Janitors, cleaners, and cleaning supervisors in large office and residential buildings often work in teams. These teams consist of workers who specialize in vacuuming, trash pickup, and restroom cleaning, among other things. Supervisors conduct inspections to ensure the building is cleaned properly and the team is functioning efficiently.

Janitors and cleaners usually work inside heated, well-lighted buildings. However, they sometimes work outdoors sweeping walkways, mowing lawns, or shoveling snow. Working with machines can be noisy, and some tasks, such as cleaning bathrooms and trash rooms, can be dirty and unpleasant. Janitors may suffer cuts, bruises, and burns from machines, handtools, and chemicals. They spend most of their time on their feet, sometimes lifting or pushing heavy furniture or equipment. Many tasks, such as dusting or sweeping,

There will be numerous opportunities for janitors and cleaners and cleaning supervisors, who hold over 3 million jobs.

require constant bending, stooping, and stretching. As a result, janitors may also suffer back injuries and sprains.

Employment

Janitors and cleaners, including cleaning supervisors, held over 3.2 million jobs in 1996. About a third worked part time (more than 35 hours a week).

About 19 out of 20 jobs are held by janitors and cleaners. They worked in every type of establishment. About 24 percent worked for firms supplying building maintenance services on a contract basis; 16 percent, in educational institutions; and 14 percent, in hotels. Other employers included hospitals, restaurants, religious institutions, manufacturing firms, government agencies, and operators of apartment buildings, office buildings, and other types of real estate.

Cleaning supervisors held about 1 job in 20. About 37 percent were employed in hotels; 20 percent, in firms supplying building maintenance services on a contract basis; 15 percent, in hospitals; and 12 percent, in nursing and personal care facilities. Other employers included educational institutions, residential care establishments, and amusement and recreation facilities.

Although cleaning jobs can be found in all cities and towns, most are located in highly populated areas where there are many office buildings, schools, apartment houses, and hospitals.

Training, Other Qualifications, and Advancement

No special education is required for most cleaning jobs, but beginners should know simple arithmetic and be able to follow instructions. High school shop courses are helpful for jobs involving repair work.

Most janitors and cleaners learn their skills on the job. Usually, beginners work with an experienced cleaner, doing routine cleaning. They are given more complicated work as they gain experience.

In some cities, programs run by unions, government agencies, or employers teach janitorial skills. Students learn how to clean buildings thoroughly and efficiently, how to select and safely use various cleansing agents, and how to operate and maintain machines, such as wet and dry vacuums, buffers, and polishers. Students learn to plan their work, to follow safety and health regulations, to interact positively with people in the buildings they clean, and to work without supervision. Instruction in minor electrical, plumbing, and other repairs may also be given. Those who come in contact with the public should have good communication skills. Employers usually look for dependable, hard-working individuals who are in good health, follow directions well, and get along with other people.

Janitors and cleaners usually find work by answering newspaper advertisements, applying directly to organizations where they would like to work, contacting local labor unions, or contacting State employment service offices.

Advancement opportunities for janitorial workers are usually limited in organizations where they are the only maintenance worker. Where there is a large maintenance staff, however, janitors can be promoted to supervisor and to area supervisor or manager. A high school diploma improves the chances for advancement. Some janitors set up their own maintenance business.

Supervisors usually move up through the ranks. In many establishments, they are required to take some in-service training to perfect housekeeping techniques and procedures, and to enhance supervisory skills.

A small number of cleaning supervisors and managers are members of the International Executive Housekeepers Association (IEHA). IEHA offers two kinds of certification programs to cleaning supervisors and managers—Certified Executive Housekeeper (CEH) and Registered Executive Housekeeper (REH). The CEH designation is offered to those with a high school education, while the REH designation is offered to those who have a 4-year college degree. Both designations are earned by attending courses and passing exams, and must be renewed every 2 years to ensure that workers keep abreast of new cleaning methods. Those with the REH designation typically oversee the cleaning services of hotels, hospitals, casinos, and other large institutions which rely on well-trained experts for their cleaning needs.

Job Outlook

Job openings should be plentiful for janitors and cleaners because limited formal education and training requirements coupled with low pay and numerous part-time and temporary jobs contribute to high turnover in this very large occupation.

While the need to replace workers who transfer to other occupations or leave the labor force will create most job openings, some opportunities will also stem from job growth. Employment of janitors, cleaners, and cleaning supervisors is expected to grow slower than the average for all occupations through the year 2006. To clean the increasing number of office complexes, apartment houses, schools, factories, hospitals, and other buildings, more workers will be assigned to specialized teams with more efficient cleaning equipment and supplies. As many firms reduce costs by hiring independent contractors, businesses providing janitorial and cleaning services on a contract basis are expected to be one of the fastest growing employers of janitors, cleaners, and cleaning supervisors.

Earnings

Median earnings for janitors and cleaners who usually worked full time were only about $300 a week in 1996, compared to $490 for workers in all occupations combined. Among janitors and cleaners, the middle 50 percent earned between $240 and $420. Ten percent earned less than $190, and 10 percent earned more than $560. Maids and housekeepers had median earnings of $270 a week in 1996, with the middle 50 percent earning between $210 and $320. Ten percent

earned less than $180 and 10 percent earned more than $410. Cleaning supervisors had median earnings of $400 a week in 1996; the middle 50 percent earned between $300 and $570. Ten percent earned less than $230 and 10 percent earned more than $760.

According to a 1997 International Executive Housekeepers Association membership survey, certified directors or managers of housekeeping who had completed some college averaged about $37,000 a year. Those who worked in industrial plants, manufacturing plants, and hospitals had higher paying jobs than those who worked in government, hotels, or as contract cleaners.

Related Occupations

Private household workers have job duties similar to janitors and cleaners. Workers who specialize in one of the many job functions of janitors and cleaners include refuse collectors, floor waxers, street sweepers, window cleaners, gardeners, boiler tenders, pest controllers, and general maintenance repairers.

Sources of Additional Information

Information about janitorial jobs may be obtained from a local State employment service office.

For information on certification in executive housekeeping, contact:
☛ International Executive Housekeepers Association, Inc., 1001 Eastwind Dr., Suite 301, Westerville, OH 43081-3361. Homepage: http://www.ieha.org

Landscaping, Groundskeeping, Nursery, Greenhouse, and Lawn Service Occupations

(D.O.T. 182.167-014; 405.687-014; 406.381-010, .683-010, .684-010, -014, -018, .687-010; 408.161-010, .662-010, .684-010, -014, -018, and .687-014)

Significant Points

- There usually are no minimum educational requirements for entry-level jobs; most workers learn through short-term on-the-job training.

- Applicants should find excellent job opportunities, reflecting significant turnover; however, earnings for laborer jobs are low.

Nature of the Work

Attractively designed, healthy, and well-maintained lawns, gardens, and grounds create a positive first impression, establish a peaceful mood, and increase property values. Workers in landscaping, groundskeeping, nursery, greenhouse, and lawn service occupations are responsible for the variety of tasks necessary to achieve a pleasant and functional outdoor environment. They also care for indoor gardens and plantings in commercial and public facilities, such as malls, hotels, and botanical gardens.

Nursery and greenhouse workers help to cultivate the plants used to beautify landscapes. They prepare nursery acreage or greenhouse beds for planting; water, weed, and spray trees, shrubs, and plants; cut, roll, and stack sod; stake trees; tie, wrap, and pack flowers, plants, shrubs, and trees to fill orders; and dig up and/or move field-grown and containerized shrubs and trees. Nursery and greenhouse managers make decisions about the type and quantity of horticultural plants to be grown; select and purchase seed, fertilizers, and disease control chemicals; hire laborers and direct and coordinate their activities; manage recordkeeping, accounting, and marketing activities; and generally oversee operations.

Landscape contractors usually follow the designs developed by a landscape architect. They coordinate and oversee the installation of trees, flowers, shrubs, sod, benches, and other ornamental features. They also implement construction plans at the site, which may involve grading the property, installing lighting or sprinkler systems, and building walkways, terraces, patios, decks, and fountains. They must determine the type and amount of labor, equipment, and materials needed to complete a project, and inspect work at various stages of completion. Some work exclusively on large properties, such as office buildings and shopping malls, while others also provide these services to residential customers.

Landscaping laborers physically install and maintain landscaped areas. In addition to initially transporting and planting new vegetation, they also transplant, mulch, fertilize, water, and prune flowering plants, trees, and shrubs, and mow and water lawns. Supervisors generally perform the same work, but are also responsible for directing the landscaping crew's activities, adhering to schedules, and keeping track of labor costs. Some landscaping laborers, called pruners, specialize in pruning, trimming, and shaping ornamental trees and shrubs. Others, called lawn service workers, specialize in maintaining lawns and shrubs for a fee. A growing number of residential and commercial clients, such as managers of office buildings, shopping malls, multiunit residential buildings, and hotels and motels favor this full-service landscape maintenance. These workers perform a range of duties on a regular basis during the growing season, including mowing, edging, trimming, fertilizing, dethatching, and mulching. Those working for chemical lawn service firms are more specialized. They inspect lawns for problems and apply fertilizers, herbicides, pesticides, and other chemicals to stimulate growth and prevent or control weed, disease, or insect infestation, as well as practice integrated pest management techniques. Lawn service managers oversee operations, negotiate fees, schedule jobs, and hire and train new workers.

Groundskeeping laborers, also called groundskeepers or grounds maintenance personnel, maintain a variety of facilities including athletic fields, golf courses, cemeteries, university campuses, and parks. Many of their duties are similar to those of landscaping laborers. But, they also rake and mulch leaves, clear snow from walkways and parking lots, employ irrigation methods to adjust the amount of water consumption and prevent waste, and apply pesticides. They see to the proper upkeep and repair of sidewalks, parking lots, groundskeeping equipment, pools, fountains, fences, planters, and benches. Grounds managers may participate in many of the same tasks as maintenance personnel but typically have more extensive knowledge in horticulture, turf management, ornamental plants, landscape design and construction, pest management, irrigation, and erosion control. In addition, grounds managers have supervisory responsibilities and must manage and train personnel, draw up work contracts, allocate labor and financial resources efficiently, and engage in public relations activities.

Groundskeepers who care for athletic fields keep natural and artificial turf fields in top condition and mark out boundaries and paint turf with team logos and names before events. Groundskeepers must make sure the underlying soil on natural turf fields has the proper composition to allow proper drainage and support the appropriate grasses used on the field. They regularly mow, water, fertilize, and aerate the fields. In addition, groundskeepers apply chemicals and fungicides to control weeds, kill pests, and prevent diseases. Groundskeepers also vacuum and disinfect synthetic turf after use in order to prevent growth of harmful bacteria. They periodically remove the turf and replace the cushioning pad.

Workers who maintain golf courses work under the direction of golf course superintendents and are called greenskeepers. Greenskeepers do many of the same things other groundskeepers do. In addition, greenskeepers periodically relocate the holes on putting greens to eliminate uneven wear of the turf and add interest and challenge to the game. Greenskeepers also keep canopies, benches, ball washers, and tee markers repaired and freshly painted.

Some groundskeepers specialize in caring for cemetery and memorial gardens grounds. They dig graves to specified depth, generally using a back-hoe. They may place concrete slabs on the bottom and around the sides of the grave to line it for greater support. When readying a site for the burial ceremony, they position the casket-lowering device over the grave, cover the immediate area with an artificial grass carpet, erect a canopy, and arrange folding chairs to accommodate mourners. They regularly mow grass, apply fertilizers and other chemicals, prune shrubs and trees, plant flowers, and re-

Because most of the work is outdoors, many jobs for landscaping, groundskeeping, nursery, greenhouse, and lawn service workers are seasonal.

move debris from graves. They also must periodically build the ground up around new gravesites to compensate for settling.

Groundskeepers in parks and recreation facilities care for lawns, trees, and shrubs, maintain athletic fields and playgrounds, clean buildings, and keep parking lots, picnic areas, and other public spaces free of litter. They may also remove snow and ice from roads and walkways, erect and dismantle snow fences, and maintain swimming pools. These workers inspect buildings and equipment, make needed repairs, and keep everything freshly painted.

Landscaping, groundskeeping, and lawn service workers use handtools such as shovels, rakes, pruning saws, saws, hedge and brush trimmers, and axes, as well as power lawnmowers, chain saws, snow blowers, and electric clippers. Some use equipment such as tractors and twin-axle vehicles. Park, school, cemetery, and golf course groundskeepers may use sod cutters to harvest sod that will be replanted elsewhere. Athletic turf groundskeepers use vacuums and other devices to remove water from athletic fields. In addition, some workers in large operations use spraying and dusting equipment. Landscape contractors and those in managerial positions increasingly use computers to develop plans and blueprints, to estimate and track project costs, and to maintain payroll and personnel information.

Working Conditions
Many of the jobs for landscaping, groundskeeping, and nursery workers are seasonal, mainly in the spring and summer, when most cleanup, planting, and mowing and trimming is necessary . The work, most of which is performed outdoors in all kinds of weather, can be repetitive and physically demanding, involving much bending, lifting, and shoveling. Landscaping and groundskeeping workers may be under pressure to get the job completed, especially when preparing for scheduled events, such as athletic competitions or burials.

Those who work with pesticides, fertilizers, and other chemicals, as well as potentially dangerous equipment and tools such as power lawnmowers, chain saws, and power clippers, must exercise safety precautions.

Employment
Landscaping, groundskeeping, nursery, greenhouse, and lawn service workers held about 925,000 jobs in 1996. The following tabulation shows employment by detailed occupation:

Gardening and nursery workers and landscaping and groundskeeping
  laborers....................817,000
Lawn service managers 55,000
Pruners 26,000
Sprayers/applicators 18,000
Nursery and greenhouse managers 10,000

About 30 percent worked for lawn and garden service companies, 8 percent worked for firms operating and building real estate, 7 percent for amusement and recreation facilities such as golf courses and race tracks, 3 percent for hotels, and 2 percent for retail nurseries. Others were employed by local governments, installing and maintaining landscapes for parks, schools, hospitals, and other public facilities.

Almost 1 of every 4 landscapers, groundskeepers, and nursery workers was self-employed, providing landscape maintenance directly to customers on a contract basis. About 1 of every 4 worked part time, many of whom were school age and most likely working their way through school.

Training, Other Qualifications, and Advancement

There usually are no minimum educational requirements for entry-level laborer positions in landscaping, groundskeeping, nursery, greenhouse, and lawn service occupations. In 1996, 2 in 5 workers did not have a high school diploma, although this diploma is necessary for some jobs. Short-term on-the-job training usually is sufficient to teach new hires how to operate equipment such as mowers, trimmers, leaf blowers, and small tractors, and follow correct safety procedures. Entry-level workers must be able to follow directions and learn proper planting procedures. If driving is an essential part of a job, employers look for applicants with a good driving record and some experience driving a truck. Workers who deal directly with customers must get along well with people. Employers also look for responsible, self-motivated individuals, since many gardeners and groundskeepers work with little supervision.

Laborers who demonstrate a willingness to work hard and quickly, have good communication skills, and take an interest in the business may advance to crew leader or other supervisory positions. Advancement or entry into positions as grounds managers or landscape contractors usually require some formal education beyond high school, and several years of progressively responsible experience. Prospective grounds managers or landscape contractors should be knowledgeable about turf care, horticulture, ornamental plants, soils, and erosion prevention and irrigation techniques. They must be familiar with all landscaping and grounds maintenance equipment, and know how and when to mix and apply fertilizers and pesticides. Some are responsible for designing and developing installation and maintenance plans for landscapes and proper grounds management. They also estimate and track project costs, and handle personnel issues. Those in managerial positions must also be aware of local or Federal environmental regulations and building codes. Several years of hands-on experience plus a 4-year bachelor's degree, a 2-year associate's degree, or a 1-year vocational-technical degree in grounds management or landscape design or a closely related "green" discipline, usually provide a good background for those who wish to deal with the full range of landscaping responsibilities. Some schools offer cooperative education programs in which students work alternate semesters or quarters for a lawn care or landscape contractor.

Most States require certification for workers who apply pesticides. Certification requirements vary, but usually include passing a test on the proper and safe use and disposal of insecticides, herbicides, and fungicides. Some States require that landscape contractors be licensed.

The Professional Grounds Management Society (PGMS) offers certification to grounds managers who have a combination of 8 years of experience and formal education beyond high school, and pass an examination covering subjects such as equipment management, personnel management, environmental issues, turf care, ornamentals, and circulatory systems. The PGMS also offers certification to groundskeepers who have a high school diploma or equivalent, plus two years of experience in the grounds maintenance field.

The Associated Landscape Contractors of America (ALCA) offers the designations, Certified Landscape Professional or Certified Landscape Technician, to those who meet established education and experience standards and pass an ALCA examination. The hands-on test for technicians covers areas such as maintenance equipment operation and the installation of plants by reading a plan. A written safety test is also administered.

Some workers in landscaping, groundskeeping, nursery, greenhouse, and lawn service occupations open their own business after several years of experience.

Job Outlook

Those interested in landscaping, groundskeeping, nursery, greenhouse, and lawn service occupations should find excellent job opportunities in the future. Because of high turnover, a large number of job openings are expected to result from the need to replace workers who transfer to other occupations or leave the labor force. These occupations attract many part-time workers and people who underestimate the amount of hard physical labor or are not committed to this work. Some take landscaping, groundskeeping, or nursery jobs to earn money for school or only until they find a better-paying job. Because wages for beginners are low and the work is physically demanding, many employers have difficulty attracting enough workers to fill all openings.

Employment of landscaping, groundskeeping, nursery, greenhouse, and lawn service workers is expected to grow about as fast as the average for all occupations through the year 2006 in response to increasing demand for landscaping, groundskeeping, and related services. Expected growth in the construction of commercial and industrial buildings, shopping malls, homes, highways, and recreational facilities, though slower than occurred from the early 1980s through the mid-1990s, should contribute to demand for these workers. Developers will continue to use landscaping services, both interior and exterior, to attract prospective buyers and tenants.

The upkeep and renovation of existing landscapes and grounds is a growing source of demand for landscaping, groundskeeping, and lawn service workers. Owners of many existing buildings and facilities, including colleges and universities, recognize the importance of curb appeal and are expected to use these services more extensively to maintain and upgrade their properties. In recent years, the large number of baby boomers, wishing to conserve leisure time by contracting out for basic yard services, spurred employment growth in landscaping and lawn service occupations. Homeowners are expected to continue using such services to maintain the beauty and value of their property. As the "echo" boom generation (children of baby boomers) comes of age, the demand for parks, athletic fields, and recreational facilities also can be expected to add to the demand for landscaping, groundskeeping, and lawn service workers. The need for nursery and greenhouse laborers and managers will grow due to the continued popularity of home gardening, as well as the need to cultivate and provide the vegetation used by landscaping services.

Job opportunities for nonseasonal work are more numerous in regions with temperate climates where landscaping and lawn services are required all year. However, opportunities may vary depending on local economic conditions. During economic downturns, many individuals turn to landscaping as a second source of income or a new career. At the same time, demand for landscaping services often slows as corporations, governments, and homeowners reduce spending on all nonessential expenditures, increasing the level of competition for available jobs.

Earnings

Landscapers and groundskeepers had median weekly earnings of about $300 in 1996; the middle 50 percent earned between $220 and $410; the lowest 10 percent earned less than $180, and the top 10 percent earned more than $560.

According to a salary survey conducted by *Grounds Maintenance Magazine* (Intertec Publishing Corporation) of its readership, institutional grounds managers had median earnings of about $38,900 in 1996; lawn-care operators, $32,500; landscape contractors, $37,300; and golf-course superintendents, $38,600.

Related Occupations

Landscaping, groundskeeping, nursery, greenhouse, and lawn service workers perform most of their work outdoors and have some knowledge of plants and soils. Others whose jobs may be performed outdoors and are otherwise related are botanists, construction workers, landscape architects, farmers, horticultural workers, tree surgeon helpers, forest conservation workers, and soil conservation technicians.

Sources of Additional Information

For career and certification information, contact:
- ☞ Associated Landscape Contractors of America, Inc., 12200 Sunrise Valley Dr., Suite 150, Reston, VA 20191.
- ☞ Professional Grounds Management Society, 120 Cockeysville Rd., Suite 104, Hunt Valley, MD 21031.

Preschool Teachers and Child-Care Workers

(D.O.T. 092.227-018; 355.674-010; 359.677-010, -018, -026)

Significant Points

- About 40 percent of preschool teachers and child-care workers—4 times the proportion for all workers—are self-employed; most are family daycare providers.

- Turnover is high due to stressful conditions and low pay and benefits.

- While training requirements vary from a high school diploma to a college degree, a high school diploma and little or no experience is usually adequate.

Nature of the Work

Preschool teachers and child-care workers nurture and teach preschool children—age 5 or younger—in child care centers, nursery schools, preschools, public schools, and family child care homes. These workers play an important role in a child's development by caring for the child when the parents are at work or away for other reasons. Some parents enroll their children in nursery schools or child-care centers primarily to provide them with the opportunity to interact with other children. In addition to attending to children's basic needs, these workers organize activities that stimulate the children's physical, emotional, intellectual, and social growth. They help children explore their interests, develop their talents and independence, build self-esteem, and learn how to behave with others.

Preschool teachers and child-care workers spend most of their day working with children. However, they do maintain contact with parents or guardians, through daily informal meetings or scheduled conferences, to discuss each child's progress and needs. Many preschool teachers and child-care workers keep records of each child's progress and suggest ways parents can increase their child's learning and development at home. Some preschools and child care centers actively recruit parent volunteers to work with the children and participate in administrative decisions and program planning.

Most preschool teachers and child-care workers perform a combination of basic care and teaching duties. Through many basic care activities, preschool teachers and child-care workers provide opportunities for children to learn. For example, a worker who shows a child how to tie a shoe teaches the child and also provides for that child's basic care needs. Through their experiences in preschool and child-care programs, children learn about trust and gain a sense of security.

Children at this age learn mainly through play. Recognizing the importance of play, preschool teachers and child-care workers build their program around it. They capitalize on children's play to further language development (storytelling and acting games), improve social skills (working together to build a neighborhood in a sandbox), and introduce scientific and mathematical concepts (balancing and counting blocks when building a bridge or mixing colors when painting). (A statement on teacher aides—who assist classroom teachers—appears elsewhere in the *Handbook*.)

Thus, a less structured approach is used to teach preschool children, including small group lessons, one-on-one instruction, and learning through creative activities, such as art, dance, and music. Interaction with peers is an important part of a child's early development. Preschool children are given an opportunity to engage in conversation and discussions, and learn to play and work cooperatively with their classmates. Preschool teachers and child-care workers play a vital role in preparing children to build the skills they will need in elementary school.

Preschool teachers and child-care workers greet children as they arrive, help them remove outer garments, and select an activity of interest. When caring for infants, they feed and change them. To ensure a well-balanced program, preschool teachers and child-care workers prepare daily and long-term schedules of activities. Each day's activities balance individual and group play and quiet and active time. Children are given some freedom to participate in activities in which they are interested.

Helping to keep children healthy is an important part of the job. Preschool teachers and child-care workers serve nutritious meals and snacks and teach good eating habits and personal hygiene. They see to it that children have proper rest periods. They spot children who may not feel well or show signs of emotional or developmental problems and discuss these matters with their supervisor and the child's parents. In some cases, preschool teachers and child-care workers help parents identify programs that will provide basic health services.

Early identification of children with special needs, such as those with behavioral, emotional, physical, or learning disabilities, is important to improve their future learning ability. Special education teachers often work with these preschool children to provide the individual attention they need. (Special education teachers are covered in a separate statement in the *Handbook*.)

Working Conditions

Preschool facilities include private homes, schools, religious institutions, workplaces where employers provide care for employees' children, or private buildings. Individuals who provide care in their own homes are generally called family child care providers. (Child-care workers who work in the child's home are covered in the statement on private household workers found elsewhere in the *Handbook*.)

Watching children grow, enjoy learning, and gain new skills can be very rewarding. While working with children, preschool teachers and child-care workers often improve the child's communication, learning, and other personal skills. Also, the work is never routine; each day is marked by new activities and challenges. However, child care can be physically and emotionally taxing, as workers constantly stand, walk, bend, stoop, and lift to attend to each child's interests and problems.

Preschool teachers and child-care workers attend to children's basic needs and organize activities that stimulate development.

To ensure that children receive proper supervision, State regulations require certain ratios of workers to children. The ratio varies with the age of the children. Child development experts generally recommend that a single caregiver be responsible for no more than 3 or 4 infants (less than 1 year old), 5 or 6 toddlers (1 to 2 years old), or 10 preschool-age children (between 2 and 5 years old).

The working hours of preschool teachers and child-care workers vary widely. Child care centers are generally open year round with long hours so that parents can drop off and pick up their children before and after work. Some centers employ full-time and part-time staff with staggered shifts to cover the entire day. Some workers are unable to take regular breaks during the day due to limited staffing. Public and many private preschool programs operate during the typical 9- or 10-month school year, employing both full-time and part-time workers. Many preschool teachers may work extra unpaid hours each week on curriculum planning, parent meetings, and occasional fundraising activities. Family daycare providers have flexible hours and daily routines, but may work long or unusual hours to fit parents' work schedules.

Turnover in this occupation is high. Many preschool teachers and child-care workers suffer burnout due to long hours, low pay and benefits, and stressful conditions.

Employment

Preschool teachers and child-care workers held about 1.2 million jobs in 1996. Many worked part time. About 4 out of 10 preschool teachers and child-care workers are self-employed, most of whom are family daycare providers.

Over 50 percent of all salaried preschool teachers and child-care workers are found in child care centers and preschools, and more than 15 percent work for a religious institution. The rest work in other community organizations and in government. Some child care programs are for-profit centers; some are affiliated with a local or national chain. Religious institutions, community agencies, school systems, and State and local governments operate nonprofit programs. A growing number of business firms operate on-site child care centers for the children of their employees.

Training, Other Qualifications, and Advancement

The training and qualifications required of preschool teachers and child-care workers vary widely. Each State has its own licensing requirements that regulate caregiver training, ranging from a high school diploma, to community college courses, to a college degree in child development or early childhood education. Some States require continuing education for workers in this field. However, most State requirements are minimal. Formal education requirements in some private preschools and child care centers are often lower than in public programs since they are not bound by State requirements. Often, child-care workers can obtain employment with a high school diploma and little or no experience.

Some States prefer preschool teachers and child-care workers to have a Child Development Associate (CDA) credential, which is offered by the Council for Early Childhood Professional Recognition. The CDA credential is recognized as a qualification for teachers and directors in 46 States and the District of Columbia. To be eligible, applicants must have 120 hours of training, a high school diploma, and 480 hours of experience. If applicants lack the required experience, they may participate in a 1-year child development training program. Those who meet eligibility requirements must also demonstrate their knowledge and skills to a team of child-care professionals from the Council for Early Childhood Professional Recognition. Applicants whose skills meet certain nationally recognized standards receive the CDA credential.

Some employers may not require a CDA credential, but may require secondary or postsecondary courses in child development and early childhood education, and possibly work experience in a child-care setting. Other schools require their own specialized training. For example, Montessori preschool teachers must complete an additional year of training after receiving their bachelor's degree in early childhood education or a related field. Public schools typically require a bachelor's degree and State teacher certification. Teacher training programs include a variety of liberal arts courses, courses in child development, student teaching, and prescribed professional courses, including instruction in teaching gifted, disadvantaged, and other children with special needs.

Preschool teachers and child-care workers must be enthusiastic and constantly alert, anticipate and prevent problems, deal with disruptive children, and provide fair but firm discipline. They must communicate effectively with the children and their parents, as well as other teachers and child-care workers. Workers should be mature, patient, understanding, and articulate, and have energy and physical stamina. Skills in music, art, drama, and storytelling are also important. Those who work for themselves must have business sense and management abilities.

Opportunities for advancement are limited in this occupation. However, as preschool teachers and child-care workers gain experience, some may advance to supervisory or administrative positions in large child-care centers or preschools. Often these positions require additional training, such as a bachelor's or master's degree. Other workers move on to work in resource and referral agencies, consulting with parents on available child services. Some workers become involved in policy or advocacy work related to child care and early childhood education. With a bachelor's degree, preschool teachers may become certified to teach in public schools at the kindergarten, elementary, and secondary school levels. Some workers set up their own child-care businesses.

Job Outlook

Employment of preschool teachers and child-care workers is projected to increase faster than the average for all occupations through the year 2006. In addition, many preschool teachers and child-care workers leave the occupation each year for other—often better paying—jobs, family responsibilities, or other reasons. High turnover, combined with rapid job growth, is expected to create many openings for preschool teachers and child-care workers. Qualified persons who are interested in this work should have little trouble finding and keeping a job.

Although the number of children under 5 years of age is expected to decline slightly through the year 2006, the proportion of youngsters in child care and preschool should increase, keeping demand high for preschool teachers and child-care workers. Women between the ages of 20 and 44 have been joining the labor force in growing numbers. Moreover, women are returning to work sooner after childbirth. As more mothers of preschool and school-age children enter the work force, the need for child care will grow. Many parents will continue to turn to formal child-care arrangements because they find it too difficult to set up a satisfactory arrangement with a relative, babysitter, or live-in worker, or because they prefer a more structured learning and social environment. Additionally, many employers are increasing child-care benefits to their employees in the form of direct child-care assistance—such as vouchers and subsidies for community child care centers—more flexible work schedules, and on-site child care facilities, thus making child care more affordable and convenient for many parents.

Recently enacted welfare reform legislation requiring more mothers of young children to work may also spur demand for child-care workers as parents seek suitable child care for children previously cared for at home. These women may turn to lower-cost child care, such as family child care homes, rather than child care centers or nursery schools.

Earnings

Pay depends on the employer and educational attainment of the worker. Although the pay is generally very low, more education means higher earnings in some cases.

In 1996, median weekly earnings of full-time, salaried child-care workers were $250. The middle 50 percent of child-care workers earned between $190 and $310. The top 10 percent earned at least $390; the bottom 10 percent earned less than $140.

Preschool teachers in public schools who have State teacher certification generally have salaries and benefits comparable to kindergarten and elementary school teachers. According to the National Education Association, public elementary school teachers earned an estimated average salary of $37,300 in the 1995-96 school year. (A statement on kindergarten, elementary, and secondary school teachers is found elsewhere in the *Handbook*.) Preschool teachers in privately funded child care centers generally earn much lower salaries than other comparably educated workers.

Earnings of self-employed child-care workers vary depending on the hours worked, number and ages of the children, and the location.

Benefits vary, but are minimal for most preschool and child-care workers. Many employers offer free or discounted child care to employees. Some offer a full benefits package, including health insurance and paid vacations, but others offer no benefits at all. Some employers offer seminars and workshops to help workers improve upon or learn new skills. A few are willing to cover the cost of courses taken at community colleges or technical schools. Nonprofit and religiously-affiliated centers often pay higher wages and offer more generous benefits than independent for-profit centers.

Related Occupations

Child-care work requires patience; creativity; an ability to nurture, motivate, teach, and influence children; and leadership, organizational, and administrative abilities. Others who work with children and need these aptitudes include teacher aides, children's tutors, kindergarten and elementary school teachers, early childhood program directors, and child psychologists.

Sources of Additional Information

For information on careers in educating children and issues affecting preschool teachers and child-care workers, contact:
☛ National Association for the Education of Young Children, 1509 16th St. NW., Washington, DC 20036.
☛ Association for Childhood Education International, 11501 Georgia Ave., Suite 315, Wheaton, MD 20902-1924.

For eligibility requirements and a description of the Child Development Associate credential, write to:
☛ Council for Early Childhood Professional Recognition, 2460 16th St. NW., Washington, DC 20009.

For information on salaries and efforts to improve compensation in child care, contact:
☛ National Center for the Early Childhood Work Force, 733 15th St. NW., Suite 1037, Washington, DC 20005.

State Departments of Human Services or Social Services can supply State regulations and training requirements for child-care workers.

Private Household Workers

(D.O.T. 301 except .687-018; 302; 305; 309 except .354-010 and .677-014)

Significant Points

- Demand will far outstrip the supply of workers willing to provide private household services because the work is hard, low paying, with few benefits and advancement opportunities.

- Persons who are interested in and suited for this work should have no trouble finding and keeping jobs.

Nature of the Work

Private household workers clean homes, care for children, plan and cook meals, do laundry, administer the household, and perform numerous other duties. They are employed by many types of households of various income levels. Although wealthy families may employ a large staff, it is much more common for one worker to be employed in a household where both parents work. Many workers are employed in households having one parent. A number of household workers work part time for two or more employers.

Most household workers are *general houseworkers* and usually the only worker employed in the home. They dust and polish furniture; sweep, mop, and wax floors; vacuum; and clean ovens, refrig-

erators, and bathrooms. They may also wash dishes, polish silver, and change and make beds. Some wash, fold, and iron clothes; a few wash windows. Other duties may include looking after a child or an elderly person, cooking, feeding pets, answering the telephone and doorbell, and calling and waiting for repair workers. General houseworkers may also take clothes and laundry to the cleaners, buy groceries, and do many other errands.

Household workers whose primary responsibility is taking care of children are called *child-care workers*. Those employed on an hourly basis are usually called baby-sitters. Child-care workers bathe, dress, and feed children; supervise their play, wash their clothes, and clean their rooms. They may also put them to sleep and waken them, read to them, involve them in educational games, take them for doctors' visits, and discipline them. Those who are in charge of infants, sometimes called *infant nurses*, also prepare bottles and change diapers.

Nannies generally take care of children from birth to age 10 or 12, tending to the child's early education, nutrition, health, and other needs. They may also perform the duties of a general housekeeper, including general cleaning and laundry duties. *Governesses* look after children in addition to other household duties. They may help them with schoolwork, teach them a foreign language, and guide them in their general upbringing. (Child-care workers who work outside the child's home are covered in the statement on child-care workers elsewhere in the *Handbook*.)

Those who assist elderly, handicapped, or convalescent people are called *companions* or *personal attendants*. Depending on the employer's needs, a companion or attendant might help with bathing and dressing, preparing and serving meals, and keeping the house tidy. They also may read to their employers, write letters for them, play cards or games, and go with them on walks and outings. Companions may also accompany their employers to medical appointments and handle their social and business affairs.

Households with a large staff may include a household manager, housekeeper or butler, cook, caretaker, and launderer. *Household managers, housekeepers* and *butlers* hire, supervise, and coordinate the household staff to keep the household running smoothly. Butlers also receive and announce guests, answer telephones, deliver messages, serve food and drinks, chauffeur, or act as a personal attendant. *Cooks* plan and prepare meals, clean the kitchen, order groceries and supplies, and may also serve meals. *Caretakers* do heavy housework and general home maintenance. They wash windows, wax floors, and hang draperies. They maintain heating and other equipment and do light carpentry, painting, and odd jobs. They may also mow the lawn and do some gardening if the household does not have a gardener.

Working Conditions

Private household workers usually work in pleasant and comfortable homes or apartments. Most are dayworkers who live in their own homes and travel to work. Some live in the home of their employer,

Many private household workers supervise children.

generally with their own room and bath. Live-ins usually work longer hours. However, if they work evenings or weekends, they may get other time off. Live-ins may feel isolated from family and friends. On the other hand, they often become part of their employer's family, and may derive satisfaction from caring for them. Being a general houseworker can also be isolating, since work is usually done alone.

Housekeeping is hard work. Both dayworkers and live-ins are on their feet most of the day and do much walking, lifting, bending, stooping, and reaching. In addition, some employers may be very demanding.

Employment

Private household workers held about 802,000 jobs in 1996. About 63 percent were general houseworkers, mostly dayworkers; 34 percent were child-care workers, including baby sitters; and less than 3 percent were housekeepers, butlers, cooks, and launderers. Most jobs are in big cities and their affluent suburbs. Some are on large estates or in resorts away from cities.

Training, Other Qualifications, and Advancement

Private household workers generally do not need any special training. Individuals who cannot find other work because of limited language or other skills often turn to this work. Most jobs require the ability to clean well, cook, or take care of children. These skills are generally learned by young people while helping with housework at home. Some training takes place on the job. Employers show the household workers what they want done and how. For child-care workers and companions, general education and the ability to get along with the person they will care for are most important.

Home economics courses in high schools and vocational and adult education schools offer training in cooking and child care. Courses in child development, first aid, and nursing in postsecondary schools are highly recommended.

Special schools for butlers, nannies, and governesses teach household administration, early childhood education, nutrition, child care, and bookkeeping. These schools may offer certifications in household management—for example, Certified Household Manager, Certified Professional Nanny, or Certified Professional Governess—and assist in job placement. However, most private household workers get jobs through employment agencies and recommendations from previous employers.

Private household workers must be able to work well with others and be honest, discreet, dependable, courteous, and neat. They also need physical stamina.

There are very few opportunities for advancement within this occupation. Few large households exist with big staffs where general houseworkers can advance to cook, executive housekeeper, butler, or governess, and these jobs may require specialized training. Advancement usually consists of better pay and working conditions. Workers may move to similar jobs in hotels, hospitals, and restaurants, where the pay and fringe benefits are usually better. Others transfer into better-paying, unrelated jobs.

Job Outlook

Job opportunities for people wishing to become private household workers are expected to be excellent through 2006, as the demand for these services continues to far outpace the supply of workers willing to provide them. Those with formal training or excellent recommendations from previous employers should be particularly sought after.

For many years, demand for household help has outstripped the supply of workers willing to take domestic jobs. The imbalance is expected to persist, and possibly worsen. Demand is expected to grow as more women join the labor force and need help running their households. Demand for companions and personal attendants is also expected to rise due to projected rapid growth in the elderly population.

The supply situation is not likely to improve. The physical demands of the work, low status, low pay, few fringe benefits, and limited advancement potential deter many prospective household workers. Due to the limited supply of household workers, many employers have turned to domestic cleaning firms, child-care centers, and temporary help firms to meet their needs for household help. This trend is expected to continue. (See the statements on janitors and cleaners, preschool teachers and child-care workers, and homemaker-home health aides elsewhere in the *Handbook*.)

Although employment of private household workers is expected to decline through 2006, many jobs will be available because of the need to replace the large number of workers who leave these occupations every year. Persons who are interested in and suited for this work should have no trouble finding and keeping jobs.

Earnings

Earnings of private household workers depend on the type of work, the number of hours, household and staff size, geographic location, training, and experience.

Most private household workers are employed part time, or less than 35 hours a week. Some work only 2 or 3 days a week, while others may work half a day 4 or 5 days a week. Earnings vary from about $10 an hour or more in a big city to less than the Federal minimum wage—$5.15 an hour—in some rural areas (some domestic workers are not covered by minimum wage laws). In addition, dayworkers often get carfare and a free meal. Live-in domestics usually earn more than dayworkers and also get free room and board. However, they often work longer hours. Baby-sitters usually have the lowest earnings.

The following tabulation presents 1996 median earnings for full-time private household workers.

Cleaners and servants	$11,600
Cooks	11,100
Child-care workers	10,500
Housekeepers and butlers	7,500

Some full-time live-in housekeepers, cooks, butlers, nannies, and governesses earn considerably more. Based on limited information, experienced and highly recommended workers employed by wealthy families in major metropolitan areas may earn $800 to $1,200 a week. Private household workers who live with their employers may be given room and board, medical benefits, a car, vacation days, and education benefits. However, most private household workers receive very limited or no benefits.

Related Occupations

Other workers with similar duties are building custodians, hotel and restaurant cleaners, child-care workers in daycare centers, home-health aides, cooks, kitchen workers, waiters and waitresses, and bartenders.

Sources of Additional Information

Information about job opportunities for private household workers is available from local private employment agencies and State employment service offices.

For information about careers and schools offering training for nannies, contact:
☛ American Council of Nanny Schools, Delta College, University Center, MI 48710.

Veterinary Assistants and Nonfarm Animal Caretakers

(D.O.T. 410.674-010, -022; 412.674-010, -014; 418.381-010, .674-010, 677-010; and 449.674-010)

Significant Points

- People who love animals get satisfaction in this occupation, but the work can be unpleasant and physically and emotionally demanding.

- Most animal caretakers are trained on the job, but advancement depends on experience and/or formal training.

- Job outlook is generally good; however, competition will be keen for animal caretaker jobs in zoos.

Nature of the Work

Many people like animals. But, as pet owners can attest, taking care of them is hard work. Animal caretakers, sometimes called animal attendants or animal keepers, feed, water, groom, bathe, and exercise animals and clean, disinfect, and repair their cages. They also play with the animals, provide companionship, and observe behavioral changes that could indicate illness or injury.

Kennels, animal shelters, animal hospitals and clinics, stables, laboratories, aquariums, and zoological parks all house animals and employ caretakers. Job titles and duties vary by employment setting.

Kennel staff usually care for small companion animals like dogs and cats while their owners are working or traveling out of town. Beginning attendants perform basic tasks, such as cleaning cages and dog runs, filling food and water dishes, and exercising animals. Experienced attendants may provide basic animal health care, bathe and groom animals, and clean their ears. Caretakers who work in kennels also sell pet food and supplies, assist in obedience training, help with breeding, or prepare animals for shipping.

Animal caretakers who specialize in grooming, or maintaining a pet's—usually a dog's or cat's—appearance are called groomers. Some groomers work in kennels and others operate their own grooming business. Groomers answer telephones, schedule appointments, discuss with clients how they want their pets to look, and collect information on the pet's disposition and veterinarian. Grooming the pet involves several steps: An initial brush-out is followed by a first clipping of hair or fur using electric clippers, combs, and grooming shears; the groomer then cuts the nails, cleans the ears, bathes, and blow-dries the animal, and ends with a final clipping and styling.

Animal caretakers in animal shelters perform a variety of duties and work with a wide variety of animals. In addition to attending to the basic needs of the animals, caretakers must also keep records of the animals received and discharged and any tests or treatments done. Some vaccinate newly admitted animals under the direction of a veterinarian, and euthanize (put to death) seriously ill, severely injured, or unwanted animals. Caretakers in animal shelters also interact with the public, answering telephone inquiries, screening applicants for animal adoption, or educating visitors on neutering and other animal health issues.

Workers in stables saddle and unsaddle horses, give them rubdowns, and walk them through a cool-off after a ride. They also feed, groom, and exercise the horses, clean out stalls and replenish bedding, polish saddles, clean and organize the tack (harness, saddle, and bridle) room, and store supplies and feed. Experienced staff may help train horses.

Animal caretakers in animal hospitals or clinics are called veterinary assistants. Veterinarians rely on caretakers to keep a constant eye on the condition of animals under their charge. Caretakers watch as animals recover from surgery, check whether dressings are still on correctly, observe the animals' overall attitude, and notify a doctor if anything seems out of the ordinary. While among the animals, caretakers clean constantly to maintain sanitary conditions in the hospital.

Laboratory animal caretakers work in research facilities and assist with the care of a wide variety of animals, including mice, rats, sheep, pigs, cattle, dogs, cats, monkeys, birds, fish, and frogs. They feed and water the animals, clean cages and change bedding, and examine the animals for signs of illness, disease, or injury. They may administer medications orally or topically according to instructions, prepare samples for laboratory examination, sterilize laboratory equipment, and record information regarding genealogy, diet, weight, medications, and food intake. They work with scientists, physicians, veterinarians, and laboratory technicians.

In zoos, caretakers called keepers prepare the diets and clean the enclosures of animals, and sometimes assist in raising their wards. They watch for any signs of illness or injury, monitor eating patterns or any changes in behavior, and record their observations. Keepers

Animal caretakers in zoos work with exotic species, while other non-farm animal caretakers generally care for companion or laboratory animals.

also may answer questions and assure that the visiting public behaves responsibly toward the exhibited animals. Depending on the zoo, keepers may be assigned to work with a broad group of animals such as mammals, birds, or reptiles, or they may work with a limited collection of animals such as primates, large cats, or small mammals.

Working Conditions

People who love animals get satisfaction from working with and helping animals. However, some of the work may be unpleasant and physically and emotionally demanding. Caretakers have to clean animal cages and lift, hold, or restrain animals, risking exposure to bites or scratches. Their work often involves kneeling, crawling, repeated bending, and lifting heavy supplies like bales of hay or bags of feed. Animal caretakers must take precautions when treating animals with germicides or insecticides. The work setting can be noisy. Animal caretakers who witness abused animals or assist in the euthanizing of unwanted, aged, or hopelessly injured animals may experience emotional stress.

Caretakers may work outdoors in all kinds of weather. Hours are irregular. Animals have to be fed every day, so caretakers must work weekend and holiday shifts. In some animal hospitals, research facilities, and animal shelters an attendant is on duty 24 hours a day, which means night shifts. Most full-time caretakers work about 40 hours a week; some work 50 hours a week or more. Caretakers of show and sports animals travel to competitions.

Employment

Animal caretakers held about 163,000 jobs in 1996. About 33,000 of the total worked as veterinary assistants in veterinary services. The remainder worked primarily in boarding kennels, but also in animal shelters, stables, grooming shops, zoos, and local, State, and Federal agencies. In 1996, 2 out of every 10 caretakers was self-employed, and 4 in 10 worked part time.

Training, Other Qualifications, and Advancement

Most animal caretakers are trained on the job. Employers generally prefer to hire people with some experience with animals. Some training programs are available for specific types of animal caretakers, but formal training is usually not necessary for entry-level positions.

Most pet groomers learn their trade by completing an informal apprenticeship, usually lasting 6 to 10 weeks, under the guidance of an experienced groomer. Prospective groomers may also attend one of the 50 State-licensed grooming schools throughout the country, with programs varying in length from 4 to 18 weeks. The National Dog Groomers Association of America certifies groomers who pass a written and practical skills examination. Beginning groomers often start by taking on one duty, such as bathing and drying the pet. They eventually assume responsibility for the entire grooming process, from the initial brush-out to the final clipping. Groomers who work in large retail establishments or kennels may, with experience, move into supervisory or managerial positions. Experienced groomers often choose to open their own shops.

Beginning animal caretakers in kennels learn on the job, and usually start by cleaning cages and feeding and watering animals. Kennel caretakers may be promoted to kennel supervisor, assistant manager, and manager, and those with enough capital and experience may open up their own kennels. The American Boarding Kennels Association (ABKA) offers a 3-stage, home-study program for individuals interested in pet care. The first two study programs address basic and advanced principles of animal care, while the third program focuses on in-depth animal care and good business procedures. Those who complete the third program and pass oral and written examinations administered by the ABKA become Certified Kennel Operators (CKO).

There are no formal educational requirements for animal caretakers in veterinary facilities. They are trained on the job, usually under the guidance of a veterinarian or veterinary technician. They start by performing tasks related to basic animal health care, such as keeping cages and examination areas sanitary. They also help veterinarians prepare for surgery, sterilize surgical equipment, observe recovering animals, and give medications and basic medical treatment under the directions of a veterinarian or veterinary technician. Highly motivated veterinary assistants may become veterinary technicians, with additional training from one of approximately 65 accredited veterinary technology programs.

Employers of entry-level laboratory animal caretakers generally require a high school diploma or General Educational Development (GED) test. A few colleges and vocational schools offer programs in laboratory animal science which provide training for technician positions, but such training is not strictly necessary. New animal caretakers working in laboratories begin by providing basic care to laboratory animals. With additional training and experience, they may advance to more technical positions in laboratory animal care, such as research assistant, mid-level technician, or senior-level technologist. The American Association for Laboratory Animal Science (AALAS) offers certification for three levels of technician competence. Those who wish to become certified as Assistant Laboratory Animal Technicians (ALAT) must satisfy education and experience requirements before taking an examination administered by AALAS.

Some zoological parks may require their caretakers to have a bachelor's degree in biology, animal science, or a related field. Most require experience with animals, preferably as a volunteer or paid keeper in a zoo. Zoo keepers may advance to senior keeper, assistant head keeper, head keeper, and assistant curator, but few openings occur, especially for the higher-level positions.

Animal caretakers in animal shelters are not required to have any specialized training, but training programs and workshops are increasingly available through the Humane Society of the United States and the National Animal Control Association. Workshop topics include cruelty investigations, appropriate methods of euthanasia for shelter animals, and techniques for preventing problems with wildlife. With experience and additional training, caretakers in animal shelters may become an adoption coordinator, animal control officer, emergency rescue driver, assistant shelter manager, or shelter director.

Job Outlook

Employment opportunities for animal caretakers generally are expected to be good. The outlook for caretakers in zoos, however, is not favorable; jobseekers will face keen competition because of expected slow growth in zoo capacity, low turnover, and the fact that the occupation attracts many candidates.

Employment is expected to grow faster than the average for all occupations through the year 2006. The growth of the pet population, which drives employment of animal caretakers in kennels, grooming shops, animal shelters, and veterinary clinics and hospitals, is expected to slow. Nevertheless, pets remain popular and pet owners—including a large number of baby boomers whose disposable income is expected to increase as they age—may increasingly take advantage of grooming services, daily and overnight boarding services, and veterinary services, spurring employment growth for animal caretakers and veterinary assistants. Demand for animal caretakers in animal shelters is expected to remain steady. Communities are increasingly recognizing the connection between animal abuse and abuse toward humans, and should continue to commit funds to animal shelters, many of which are working hand-in-hand with social service agencies and law enforcement teams.

Despite growth in demand for animal caretakers, the overwhelming majority of jobs will result from the need to replace workers leaving the field. Many animal caretaker jobs that require little or no training have work schedules which tend to be flexible; therefore, it is ideal for people seeking their first job and for students and others looking for temporary or part-time work. Because turnover is quite high, largely due to the hard physical labor, the overall availability of jobs should be very good. Much of the work of animal caretakers is seasonal, particularly during vacation periods.

Earnings

Animal caretakers who worked full time earned a median weekly salary of $290 in 1996. The middle 50 percent earned between $220 and $380. The bottom 10 percent earned less than $170; the top 10 percent earned more than $500 a week. According to a salary survey by the National Animal Control Association, nonsupervisory animal caretakers working in animal care and control agencies earned a yearly average of about $17,100 in 1996.

Related Occupations

Others who work extensively with animals include animal breeders, animal trainers, livestock farm workers, ranchers, veterinarians, veterinary technicians and technologists, and wildlife biologists and zoologists.

Sources of Additional Information

For more information on jobs in animal caretaking and control, and the animal shelter and control personnel training program, write to:
☛ The Humane Society of the United States, 2100 L St. NW, Washington, DC 20037-1598.
☛ National Animal Control Association, P.O. Box 480851, Kansas City, MO 64148-0851.

To obtain a listing of State-licensed grooming schools, send a stamped, self-addressed envelope to:
☛ National Dog Groomers Association of America, Box 101, Clark, PA 16113.

For information on training and certification of kennel staff and owners, contact:
☛ American Boarding Kennels Association, 4575 Galley Rd., Suite 400A, Colorado Springs, CO 80915. Homepage: http://www.abka.com

For information on laboratory animal technicians and certification, contact:
☛ American Association for Laboratory Animal Science, 70 Timber Creek Dr., Cordova, TN 38018-4233. FAX (901) 753-0046
E-mail address: info@aalas.org

Protective Service Occupations

Correctional Officers

(D.O.T. 372.367-014, .567-014, .667-018, and .677; and 375.367-010)

Significant Points

- Job opportunities are expected to be plentiful due to much faster than average employment growth coupled with high turnover.
- Most jobs are in large regional jails or prisons located in rural areas.
- The work can be stressful because of concerns about personal safety.

Nature of the Work

Correctional officers are responsible for overseeing individuals who have been arrested, are awaiting trial or other hearing, or who have been convicted of a crime and sentenced to serve time in a jail, reformatory, or penitentiary. They maintain security and observe inmate conduct and behavior to prevent disturbances and escapes.

Correctional officers' duties differ with the setting in which they are performed. The majority of the approximately 3,300 jails in the United States are operated by county governments, with about three-quarters of all jails under the jurisdiction of an elected sheriff. Duty in jails differs from that in prisons in a number of important ways. For instance, the jail population changes constantly. The American jail system processes more than 22 million people a year, with about half a million inmates in jail at any given time. Approximately one million inmates are incarcerated in Federal and State prisons. The prison population by contrast is far more stable.

Many correctional officers are employed by police and sheriffs departments in county and municipal jails or precinct station houses. These officers often have no law enforcement responsibilities outside the jail. (See the statement on Police, Detectives, and Special Agents elsewhere in the *Handbook*.) Others are employed by large regional jails or State and Federal prisons where job duties are specialized. A relatively small number supervise aliens being held by the Immigration and Naturalization Service before being released or deported. Regardless of the setting, correctional officers maintain order within the institution, enforce rules and regulations, and may supplement whatever counseling inmates receive.

To make sure inmates are orderly and obey rules, correctional officers monitor inmates' activities, including working, exercising, eating, and showering. They assign and supervise inmates' work assignments. Sometimes it is necessary for them to search inmates and their living quarters for weapons or drugs, to settle disputes between inmates, and to enforce discipline. Correctional officers cannot show favoritism and must report any inmate who violates the rules. A few officers in prison settings hold security positions in towers, where they are equipped with high-powered rifles. In both jail and prison facilities with direct supervision cell blocks, officers are unarmed—they are locked in a cell-block alone, or with another officer, among the 50 to 100 inmates who reside there. The officers enforce regulations primarily through their interpersonal communications skills, although they may have inmates who do not obey their orders transferred to facilities with less desirable living arrangements and fewer privileges.

Correctional officers periodically inspect the facilities. They may, for example, check cells and other areas of the institution for unsanitary conditions, weapons, drugs, fire hazards, and any evidence of infractions of rules. In addition, they routinely inspect locks, window bars, grille doors, and gates for signs of tampering.

Correctional officers report orally and in writing on inmate conduct and on the quality and quantity of work done by inmates. Officers also report disturbances, violations of rules, and any unusual occurrences. They usually keep a daily record of their activities. In the most high security facilities where the most dangerous inmates are housed, correctional officers can monitor the activities of prisoners from a centralized control center with the aid of closed circuit television cameras and a computer tracking system. In such an environment, the inmates may not see anyone but officers for days or weeks at a time and only rarely leave their cells.

Depending on the offender's security classification within the institution, correctional officers may have to escort inmates to and from cells and other areas and accompany them to see authorized visitors. Officers may also escort prisoners between the institution and courtrooms, medical facilities, and other destinations. Officers inspect mail and visitors for prohibited items. Should the situation arise, they assist the responsible law enforcement authorities by helping to investigate crimes committed within their institution or by helping search for escaped inmates.

Correctional sergeants directly supervise correctional officers. They usually are responsible for maintaining security and directing the activities of a group of inmates during an assigned shift or in an assigned area.

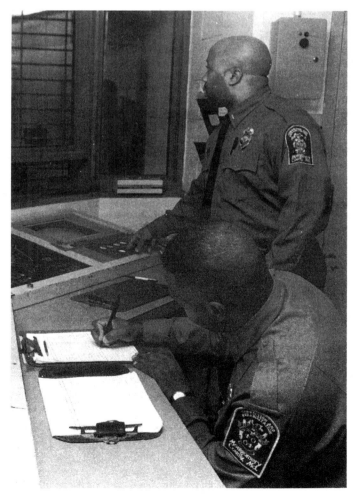

Correctional officers maintain order within the institution and enforce rules and regulations.

Working Conditions

Correctional officers may work indoors or outdoors, depending on their specific duties. Some correctional institutions are well lighted, temperature controlled, and ventilated, but many others are overcrowded, hot, and noisy. Outdoors, weather conditions may be disagreeable, for example when standing watch on a guard tower in cold weather. Working in a correctional institution can be stressful and hazardous; correctional officers occasionally are injured in confrontations with inmates who may feel that they have little to lose from violent behavior.

Correctional officers usually work an 8-hour day, 5 days a week, on rotating shifts. Prison security must be provided around the clock, which often means that junior officers work weekends, holidays, and nights. In addition, officers may be required to work paid overtime.

Employment

Correctional officers held about 320,000 jobs in 1996. Six of every 10 worked at State correctional institutions such as prisons, prison camps, and reformatories. Most of the remainder worked at city and county jails or other institutions run by local governments. About 11,000 correctional officers worked at Federal correctional institutions, and about 5,100 worked in privately owned and managed prisons.

Most correctional officers work in relatively large institutions located in rural areas, although a significant number work in jails and other smaller facilities located in law enforcement agencies throughout the country.

Training, Other Qualifications, and Advancement

Most institutions require that correctional officers be at least 18 or 21 years of age, have a high school education or its equivalent, have no felony convictions, and be a United States citizen. In addition, correctional institutions increasingly seek correctional officers with postsecondary education, particularly in psychology, criminal justice, police science, criminology, and related fields.

Correctional officers must be in good health. The Federal System and many States require candidates to meet formal standards of physical fitness, eyesight, and hearing. Strength, good judgment, and the ability to think and act quickly are indispensable. The Federal System and some States screen applicants for drug abuse and require candidates to pass a written or oral examination, along with a background check.

Federal, State, and some local departments of corrections provide training for correctional officers based on guidelines established by the American Correctional Association, the American Jail Association, and other professional organizations. Some States have regional training academies which are available to local agencies. All States and local departments of correction provide on-the-job training at the conclusion of formal instruction. Officer trainees receive several weeks or months of training in an actual job setting under the supervision of an experienced officer. Entry requirements and on-the-job training vary widely from agency to agency.

Academy trainees generally receive instruction on institutional policies, regulations, and operations, as well as custody and security procedures, among other subjects. New Federal correctional officers must undergo 200 hours of formal training within the first year of employment. They must complete 120 hours of specialized correctional instruction at the Federal Bureau of Prisons residential training center at Glynco, Georgia, within the first 60 days after appointment. Experienced officers receive inservice training to keep abreast of new ideas and procedures.

Correctional officers have the opportunity to join prison tactical response teams, which are trained to respond to riots, hostage situations, forced cell moves, and other potentially dangerous confrontations. Team members often receive monthly training and practice with weapons, chemical agents, forced entry methods, and other tactics.

With education, experience, and training, qualified officers may advance to correctional sergeant or other supervisory or administrative positions. Many correctional institutions require experience as a correctional officer for other corrections positions. Ambitious correctional officers can be promoted all the way up to warden. Officers sometimes transfer to related areas, such as parole officer.

Job Outlook

Job opportunities for correctional officers are expected to be favorable through the year 2006. The need to replace correctional officers who transfer to other occupations or leave the labor force, coupled with rising employment demand, will generate many thousands of job openings each year. In addition, some local and a few State correctional agencies have traditionally experienced difficulty in attracting qualified applicants, largely due to relatively low salaries and the concentration of jobs in rural locations. This situation is expected to continue.

Employment of correctional officers is expected to increase faster than the average for all occupations through the year 2006 as additional officers are hired to supervise and control a growing inmate population. Increasing public concern about the spread of crime and illegal drugs—resulting in more police making more arrests and getting more convictions—and the adoption of mandatory sentencing guidelines calling for longer sentences and reduced parole for inmates will spur demand for correctional officers. Expansion and new construction of correctional facilities also are expected to create many new jobs for correctional officers, although State and local government budgetary constraints could affect the rate at which new facilities are built and staffed. Some employment opportunities also may arise in the private sector as public authorities opt to contract with private companies to provide and staff corrections facilities.

Layoffs of correctional officers are rare because security must be maintained in correctional institutions at all times.

Earnings

According to a 1996 survey in *Corrections Compendium,* a national journal for corrections professionals, Federal and State correctional officers' annual salaries averaged about $26,100 and ranged from a low of $17,300 in South Carolina to a high of $41,700 in Rhode Island.

At the Federal level, the starting salary was about $20,200 to $22,600 a year in 1996; supervisory correctional officers started at about $28,300 a year. Starting salaries were slightly higher in selected areas where prevailing local pay levels were higher. The annual average salary for correctional officers employed by the Federal Government was $33,540 in early 1997.

Correctional officers employed in the public sector usually are provided uniforms or a clothing allowance to purchase their own uniforms. Most are provided or can participate in hospitalization or major medical insurance plans; many officers can get disability and life insurance at group rates. They also receive vacation and sick leave and pension benefits. Officers employed by the Federal Government and most State governments are covered by civil service systems or merit boards. Their retirement coverage entitles them to retire at age 50 after 20 years of service or at any age with 25 years of service. In the Federal system and some States, many correctional officers are represented by labor unions.

Related Occupations

A number of related careers are open to high school graduates who are interested in protective services and the field of security. Bodyguards escort people and protect them from injury or invasion of privacy. House or store detectives patrol business establishments to protect against theft and vandalism and to enforce standards of good behavior. Security guards protect government, commercial, and industrial property against theft, vandalism, illegal entry, and fire. Police officers and deputy sheriffs maintain law and order, prevent crime, and arrest offenders. Probation and parole officers monitor and counsel offenders and evaluate their progress in becoming productive members of society. Some of these related occupations are discussed elsewhere in the *Handbook*.

Sources of Additional Information

Information about entrance requirements, training, and career opportunities for correctional officers on the State and local levels may be obtained from State departments of corrections, or nearby correctional institutions and facilities including police department and county sheriff offices.

Information on entrance requirements, training, and career opportunities for correctional officers on the Federal level may be obtained by calling the Federal Bureau of Prisons. Regional recruitment offices have toll-free telephone numbers listed in local phone directories. In addition, information on obtaining a job with the Federal Government may be obtained from the Office of Personnel Management through a telephone based system. Consult your telephone directory under U.S. Government for a local number or call (912) 757-3000 (TDD (912) 744-2299). The number is not toll free and charges may result. Information also is available from their internet site: http:// www.usajobs.opm.gov

Firefighting Occupations

(D.O.T. 169.167-022; 373 except .117; 379.687-010; 452.134, .167, .364-014, .367-010, -014, .687-014)

Significant Points

- Keen competition for positions is expected. Firefighting attracts many people because a high school education is usually sufficient, and earnings are above average.

- Work hours are longer and vary more widely than hours of most other workers.

- Firefighting is very hazardous.

Nature of the Work

Firefighters respond to a variety of emergency situations in which life, property, or the environment are at risk. They are frequently the first emergency response team at the scene of an accident, fire, flood, earthquake, or act of terrorism. Every year, fires and other emergency conditions take thousands of lives and destroy property worth billions of dollars. Firefighters help protect the public against these dangers. This statement only provides information about career firefighters; it does not cover volunteer firefighters, who perform the same duties, and who may comprise the majority of firefighters in a residential area.

Most calls to which firefighters respond involve medical emergencies, and many fire departments provide ambulance service for victims. Firefighters receive training in emergency medical procedures, and many fire departments require them to be certified as emergency medical technicians. (For more information on this occupation, see the *Handbook* statement on emergency medical technicians.)

During duty hours, firefighters must be prepared to respond immediately to a fire or any other emergency situation that arises. Each situation a firefighter encounters is unique. Because firefighting is dangerous and complex, it requires organization and teamwork. At every emergency scene, firefighters perform specific duties assigned by a superior officer. They may connect hose lines to hydrants, operate a pump or other equipment, or position ladders. They may rescue victims and administer emergency medical aid, ventilate smoke-filled areas, and salvage the contents of buildings. Their duties may change several times while the company is in action. Sometimes they remain at the site of a disaster for several days or more, rescuing survivors and assisting with medical emergencies.

The job of firefighter has become more complicated in recent years due to the use of increasingly sophisticated equipment and the need to assume a wider range of responsibilities. These responsibilities include emergency medical treatment, assisting in the recovery from natural disasters such as earthquakes and tornadoes, and the control, prevention and cleanup of oil spills and other hazardous materials incidents.

Firefighters are primarily involved with protecting business and residential structures, but they also work at airports on crash and rescue crews, at chemical plants, by waterfronts, and in forests and wilderness areas. In forests, air patrols locate fires and report their findings to headquarters by telephone or radio. Fire rangers patrol areas of the forest to locate and report fires and hazardous conditions and to ensure travelers and campers comply with fire regulations. When fires break out, firefighters use hand tools and water hoses to battle the blaze. Some specialized firefighters parachute from airplanes when necessary to reach inaccessible areas.

Most fire departments have a fire prevention division, usually headed by a fire marshal. Fire inspectors conduct inspections of structures to prevent fires and ensure fire code compliance. These firefighters may also work with developers and planners to check and approve plans for new buildings. Fire prevention personnel often speak on these subjects before public assemblies and civic organizations. Some firefighters become fire investigators, who determine the origin and causes of fires. They collect evidence, interview witnesses, and prepare reports on fires in cases where the cause may be arson or criminal negligence. Some investigators have police powers and may arrest suspects. They may also be called upon to testify in court.

Between alarms, firefighters participate in educational activities. In addition to taking classes themselves, they sometimes give lectures or demonstrations on safety issues to the local community. They may also clean and maintain equipment, conduct practice drills and fire inspections, and participate in physical fitness activities. They prepare written reports on fire incidents and review fire science literature to keep abreast of technological developments and changing administrative practices and policies.

Working Conditions

Firefighters spend much of their time at fire stations, which usually have features common to a residential facility. When an alarm comes in, firefighters must respond rapidly, regardless of the weather or hour. They may spend long periods on their feet, sometimes in adverse weather, tending to fires, medical emergencies, hazardous materials incidents, and other emergencies.

Firefighting is a very hazardous occupation. It involves risk of death or injury from sudden cave-ins of floors or toppling walls, and from exposure to flames and smoke. Strong winds and falling trees and branches can make fighting forest fires particularly dangerous. Firefighters may also come in contact with poisonous, flammable, or explosive gases and chemicals, or radioactive or other hazardous materials that may have immediate or long-term effects on their health. For these reasons, they must wear appropriate protective gear, which can be very heavy.

Firefighting can be very stressful but rewarding.

Work hours of firefighters are longer and vary more widely than hours of most other workers. Many work more than 50 hours a week. During some weeks, they may work significantly longer hours. In some cities, they are on duty for 24 hours, then off for 48 hours, and receive an extra day off at intervals. In other cities, they work a day shift of 10 hours for 3 or 4 days, a night shift of 14 hours for 3 or 4 nights, have 3 or 4 days off, and then repeat the cycle. In addition, firefighters often work extra hours at fires and other emergencies and are regularly assigned to work on holidays. Fire lieutenants and fire captains often work the same hours as the firefighters they supervise. Duty hours include time when firefighters study, train, and perform fire prevention duties.

Employment

Firefighters held about 293,000 jobs in 1996. More than nine of every 10 worked in municipal or county fire departments. Some very large cities have several thousand firefighters, while many small towns have only a few. Most of the remainder worked in fire departments on Federal and State installations, including airports. Private firefighting companies employ a small number of firefighters.

Training, Other Qualifications, and Advancement

Applicants for municipal firefighting jobs may have to pass a written test; tests of strength, physical stamina, coordination, and agility; and a medical examination, including a drug screening. Workers also may be monitored on a random basis for drug use after accepting employment. Examinations are generally open to persons who are at least 18 years of age and have a high school education or the equivalent. Those who receive the highest scores in all phases of testing have the best chances for appointment. The completion of community college courses in fire science may improve an applicant's chances for appointment. In recent years, an increasing proportion of entrants to this occupation have some postsecondary education.

As a rule, beginners in large fire departments are trained for several weeks at the department's training center. Through classroom instruction and practical training, the recruits study firefighting techniques, fire prevention, hazardous materials, local building codes, and emergency medical procedures, including first aid and cardiopulmonary resuscitation. They also learn how to use axes, saws, fire extinguishers, ladders, and other firefighting and rescue equipment. After successfully completing this training, they are assigned to a fire company, where they undergo a period of probation.

A number of fire departments have accredited apprenticeship programs lasting up to 5 years. These programs combine formal, technical instruction with on-the-job training under the supervision of experienced firefighters. Technical instruction covers subjects such as firefighting techniques and equipment, chemical hazards associated with various combustible building materials, emergency medical procedures, and fire prevention and safety.

Most experienced firefighters continue studying to improve their job performance and prepare for promotion examinations. Today, firefighters need more training to operate increasingly sophisticated equipment, and to deal safely with the greater hazards associated with fighting fires in larger, more complex structures. To progress to higher-level positions, they must acquire expertise in the most advanced firefighting equipment and techniques and in building construction, emergency medical technology, writing, public speaking, management and budgeting procedures, and labor relations. Fire departments frequently conduct training programs, and some firefighters attend training sessions sponsored by the National Fire Academy. These training sessions cover various topics, including executive development, anti-arson techniques, disaster preparedness, hazardous materials control, and public fire safety and education. Some States also have extensive firefighter training and certification programs.

Many colleges and universities offer courses leading to 2- or 4-year degrees in fire engineering or fire science. Many fire departments offer firefighters incentives such as tuition reimbursement or higher pay for completing advanced training.

Among the personal qualities firefighters need are mental alertness, self-discipline, courage, mechanical aptitude, endurance, strength, and a sense of public service. Initiative and good judgment are extremely important because firefighters independently make quick decisions in emergencies. Because members of a crew live and work closely together under conditions of stress and danger for extended periods, they should be dependable and able to get along well with others in a group. Leadership qualities are necessary for officers, who must establish and maintain discipline and efficiency, as well as direct the activities of firefighters in their companies.

Opportunities for promotion are good in most fire departments. As firefighters gain expertise, they may advance to a higher rank. The line of promotion is usually to engineer, lieutenant, captain, battalion chief, assistant chief, deputy chief, and finally to chief. Advancement generally depends upon scores on a written examination, job performance, interviews, and seniority. Increasingly, fire departments are using assessment centers—which simulate a variety of actual job performance tasks—to screen for the best candidates for promotion. Many fire departments now require a bachelor's degree, preferably in fire science, public administration, or a related field, for promotion to positions higher than battalion chief. Some departments also require a master's degree for the chief, as well as for executive fire officer certification from the National Fire Academy, and for State chief officer certification.

Job Outlook

Firefighters are expected to face keen competition for available job openings. Firefighting attracts many people because a high school education is usually sufficient, earnings are relatively high, and a pension is guaranteed upon retirement. In addition, the work is frequently exciting and challenging and affords an opportunity to perform a valuable public service. Consequently, the number of qualified applicants in most areas generally exceeds the number of job openings, even though the written examination and physical requirements eliminate many applicants. This situation is expected to persist through the year 2006.

Employment of firefighters is expected to increase more slowly than the average for all occupations through the year 2006, as fire departments continue to compete with other public service providers for funding. Most growth in employment will be due to an expected increase in number of paid firefighter positions versus volunteer firefighters, because the increased level of specialized training required in this occupation makes it more difficult for volunteer firefighters to remain qualified. Little employment growth is expected in large, urban fire departments. A small number of local governments are expected to contract with private companies for firefighting services.

In response to the expanding role of firefighters, some municipalities have combined fire prevention, public fire education, safety, and emergency medical services into a single organization commonly referred to as a public safety organization. Some local and regional fire departments are being consolidated into county-wide establishments in order to cut overhead, take advantage of economies of scale, reduce administrative staffs, and establish consistent training standards and work procedures.

Turnover of firefighter jobs is unusually low, particularly for a hazardous occupation that requires a relatively limited investment in formal education. Nevertheless, most job openings are expected to result from the need to replace those who retire, stop working for other reasons, or transfer to other occupations.

Layoffs of firefighters are not common. Fire protection is an essential service, and citizens are likely to exert considerable pressure on city officials to expand or at least preserve the level of fire-protection coverage. Even when budget cuts do occur, local fire departments usually cut expenses by postponing equipment purchases or not hiring new firefighters, rather than by laying off staff.

Earnings

Median weekly earnings for firefighting occupations were around $658 in 1996. The middle 50 percent earned between $513 and $832 weekly. The lowest 10 percent earned less than $387, while the highest 10 percent earned more than $979. The average annual salary for all firefighters in the Federal Government in nonsupervisory, supervisory, and managerial positions was about $28,800 in 1996. Fire lieutenants and fire captains may earn considerably more.

Firefighters who average 53 or more hours a week during their work period, which ranges from 7 to 28 days, are required to be paid overtime. Firefighters often earn overtime for working extra shifts to maintain minimum staffing levels, or for special emergencies.

Firefighters receive benefits usually including medical and liability insurance, vacation and sick leave, and some paid holidays. Almost all fire departments provide protective clothing (helmets, boots, and coats) and breathing apparatus, and many also provide dress uniforms. Firefighters are generally covered by pension plans often providing retirement at half pay after 25 years of service or if disabled in the line of duty.

Many career firefighters and company officers are unionized, and belong to the International Association of Firefighters. Many chief officers belong to the International Association of Fire Chiefs.

Related Occupations
An occupation closely related to fire protection is fire-protection engineer, in which the engineer identifies fire hazards in homes and workplaces, and designs prevention programs and automatic fire detection and extinguishing systems. Other occupations in which workers respond to emergencies include police officers and emergency medical technicians.

Sources of Additional Information
Information about a career as a firefighter may be obtained from local fire departments and:
☛ International Association of Firefighters, 1750 New York Ave. NW., Washington, DC 20006.
☛ U.S. Fire Administration, 16825 South Seton Ave., Emmitsburg, MD 21727.

Information about firefighter professional qualifications and a list of colleges and universities offering 2- or 4-year degree programs in fire science or fire prevention may be obtained from:
☛ National Fire Protection Association, 1 Batterymarch Park, Quincy, MA 02269.
☛ National Fire Academy, Degrees at a Distance Program, 16825 South Seton Ave., Emmitsburg, MD 21727.

Guards

(D.O.T. 372.563, .567-010, .667-010, -014, -030 through -038; 376.667-010; 379.667-010)

Significant Points

- Job opportunities are expected to be favorable through the year 2006. High turnover and this occupation's large size ranks it among those providing the greatest number of job openings in the economy.

- Many employers of unarmed guards do not have any specific educational requirements.

- Employers generally will not hire applicants that have been convicted of a serious crime.

Nature of the Work
Guards, also called security officers, patrol and inspect property to protect against fire, theft, vandalism, and illegal entry. Their duties vary with the size, type, and location of their employer. (Correctional officers—guards who work in prisons and other correctional institutions—and police, detectives, and special agents are discussed separately in this section of the *Handbook*.)

In office buildings, banks, hospitals, and department stores, guards protect people, records, merchandise, money, and equipment. In department stores, they often work with undercover detectives to watch for theft by customers or store employees.

At air, sea, and rail terminals, and other transportation facilities, guards protect people, merchandise being shipped, property, and equipment. They screen passengers and visitors for weapons, explosives, and other contraband, ensure nothing is stolen while being loaded or unloaded, and watch for fires and prowlers. They may direct traffic.

Guards who work in public buildings, such as museums or art galleries, protect paintings and exhibits by inspecting the people and packages entering and leaving the building. They answer routine questions from visitors and sometimes guide tours.

In factories, laboratories, government buildings, data processing centers, and military bases in which valuable property or information—such as information on new products, computer codes, or defense secrets—must be protected, guards check the credentials of persons and vehicles entering and leaving the premises. University, park, or recreation guards perform similar duties and also may issue parking permits and direct traffic. Golf course patrollers prevent unauthorized persons from using the facility and help keep play running smoothly.

At social affairs, sports events, conventions, and other public gatherings, guards provide information, assist in crowd control, and watch for persons who may cause trouble. Some guards patrol places of entertainment, such as nightclubs, to preserve order among customers and to protect property.

Armored car guards protect money and valuables during transit. Bodyguards protect individuals from bodily injury, kidnapping, or invasion of privacy.

In a large organization, a security officer is often in charge of the guard force; in a small organization, a single worker may be responsible for all security measures. Patrolling is usually done on foot, but if the property is large, guards may make their rounds by car or motor scooter. As more businesses purchase advanced electronic security systems to protect their property, more guards are being assigned to stations where they monitor perimeter security, environmental functions, communications, and other systems. In many cases, these guards maintain radio contact with other guards patrolling on foot or in motor vehicles. Some guards use computers to store information on matters relevant to security—for example, visitors or suspicious occurrences—during their hours on duty.

As they make their rounds, guards check all doors and windows, see that no unauthorized persons remain after working hours, and ensure that fire extinguishers, alarms, sprinkler systems, furnaces, and various electrical and plumbing systems are working properly.

Guards who carry weapons must be licensed by the appropriate government authority, and some receive further certification as special police officers, which allows them to make limited types of arrests while on duty. Unarmed guards may carry a flashlight, whistle, two-way radio, and a watch clock—a device that indicates the time at which they reach various checkpoints.

Working Conditions
Most guards spend considerable time on their feet patrolling buildings, industrial plants, and grounds. Indoors, they may be stationed at a guard desk to monitor electronic security and surveillance devices, or to check the credentials of persons entering or leaving the premises. They also may be stationed at a gate, or may patrol grounds in all weather.

Because some guards work alone, especially at night, there may be no one nearby to help if an accident or injury occurs. Many guards use a portable radio or telephone that allows them to be in constant contact with a central station outside the guarded area. If they fail to transmit an expected signal, the central station investigates. Guard work is usually routine, but guards must be constantly alert for threats to themselves and the property they are protecting.

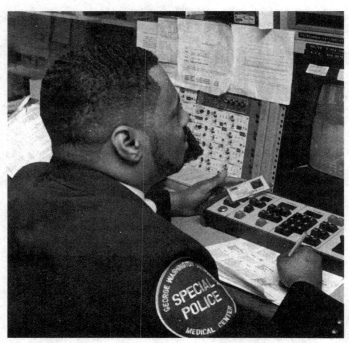

Although guard jobs are found throughout the country, most are located in metropolitan areas.

Guards who work during the day may have a great deal of contact with other employees and members of the public.

Many guards work alone at night; the usual shift lasts 8 hours. Some employers have three shifts, and guards rotate to divide daytime, weekend, and holiday work equally. Guards usually eat on the job instead of taking a regular break away from the site.

Employment

Guards held about 955,000 jobs in 1996. Industrial security firms and guard agencies employed 59 percent of all guards. These organizations provide security services on contract, assigning their guards to buildings and other sites as needed. The remainder were in-house guards, employed in many settings including banks, building management companies, hotels, hospitals, retail stores, restaurants, bars, schools, and government.

Guard jobs are found throughout the country, mostly in metropolitan areas.

Training, Other Qualifications, and Advancement

Most States require that guards be licensed. To be licensed as a guard, individuals must generally be 18 years old, pass a background examination, and complete classroom training in such subjects as property rights, emergency procedures, and detention of suspected criminals.

Many employers of unarmed guards do not have any specific educational requirements. For armed guards, employers generally prefer individuals who are high school graduates. Some jobs require a driver's license. For positions as armed guards, employers often seek people who have had experience in the military or in law enforcement. Most persons entering guard jobs have prior work experience, although it is usually unrelated. Because of limited formal training requirements and flexible hours, this occupation attracts some persons seeking a second job.

Applicants are expected to have good character references, no serious police record, good health—especially hearing and vision—and good personal habits such as neatness and dependability. They should be mentally alert, emotionally stable, and physically fit in order to cope with emergencies. Guards who have frequent contact with the public should be friendly and personable. Some employers require applicants to take a polygraph examination or a psychological

profile. Many employers require applicants and experienced workers to submit to drug screening tests as a condition of employment.

Candidates for guard jobs in the Federal Government must have some experience as a guard and pass a written examination in order to be certified by the General Services Administration. Armed Forces experience is an asset. For most Federal guard positions, applicants must qualify in the use of firearms.

The amount of training guards receive varies. Training requirements are higher for armed guards, because their employers are legally responsible for any use of force. Armed guards receive formal training in areas such as weapons retention and laws covering the use of force.

Many employers give newly hired guards instruction before they start the job and also provide several weeks of on-the-job training. An increasing number of States are making ongoing training a legal requirement for retention of certification. Guards may receive training in protection, public relations, report writing, crisis deterrence, first aid, as well as specialized training relevant to their particular assignment.

Guards employed at establishments placing a heavy emphasis on security usually receive extensive formal training. For example, guards at nuclear power plants undergo several months of training before being placed on duty under close supervision. They are taught to use firearms, administer first aid, operate alarm systems and electronic security equipment, and spot and deal with security problems. Guards authorized to carry firearms may be periodically tested in their use. Some guards are likewise periodically tested for health, strength and endurance.

Although guards in small companies receive periodic salary increases, advancement is limited. However, most large organizations use a military type of ranking that offers the possibility of advancement in position and salary. Guards with talent and some college education may advance to jobs that involve administrative and management duties. Guards with management skills may open their own contract security guard agencies.

Job Outlook

Job opportunities for persons seeking work as guards are expected to be favorable through the year 2006. High turnover and this occupation's large size rank it among those providing the greatest number of job openings in the economy. Many opportunities are expected for persons seeking full-time employment, as well as for those seeking part-time or second jobs at night or on weekends. However, some competition is expected for higher paying, high security positions. Compared to unarmed security guards, armed guards and special police enjoy higher earnings and benefits, greater job security, more advancement potential, and are usually given more training and responsibility.

Employment of guards is expected to grow faster than the average for all occupations through the year 2006. Increased concern about crime, vandalism, and terrorism will heighten the need for security in and around homes, plants, stores, offices, and recreation areas. Demand for guards will also grow as private security firms increasingly perform duties—such as monitoring crowds at airports and providing security in courts—formerly handled by government police officers and marshals. Because engaging the services of a security guard firm is easier and less costly than assuming direct responsibility for hiring, training, and managing a security guard force, job growth is expected to be concentrated among contract security guard agencies.

Guards employed by industrial security and guard agencies are occasionally laid off when the firm at which they work does not renew its contract with their agency. Most are able to find employment with other agencies, however, and may continue to work at the same location for the firm that won the contract. Guards employed directly by the firm at which they work are seldom laid off because a plant or factory must still be protected even when economic conditions force it to close temporarily.

Earnings

Median annual earnings of guards who worked full time in 1996 were about $17,300. The middle 50 percent earned between $10,300 and

$25,100. The lowest 10 percent earned less than $10,300 and the highest tenth earned more than $35,600. Guards generally earn slightly more in urban areas.

According to a survey of workplaces in 160 metropolitan areas, guards with the least responsibility and training had median hourly earnings of $6.50 in 1995. The middle half earned between $5.50 and $7.92 an hour. Guards with more specialized training and experience had median hourly earnings of $11.73.

Depending on their experience, newly hired guards in the Federal Government earned $15,500 or $17,500 a year in 1997. Beginning salaries were slightly higher in selected areas where the prevailing local pay level was higher. Guards employed by the Federal Government averaged about $22,900 a year in 1997. These workers usually receive overtime pay as well as a wage differential for the second and third shifts.

Related Occupations

Guards protect property, maintain security, and enforce regulations for entry and conduct in the establishments at which they work. Related security and protective service occupations include bailiffs, correction officers, house or store detectives, and private investigators.

Sources of Additional Information

Further information about work opportunities for guards is available from local detective and guard firms and the nearest State employment service office.

Information about licensing requirements for guards may be obtained from the State licensing commission or the State police department. In States where local jurisdictions establish licensing requirements, contact a local government authority such as the sheriff, county executive, or city manager.

Police, Detectives, and Special Agents

(D.O.T. 168.167-010; 372.167-018, .267, .363 and .367-010; 375.133, .137 except -022 and -038, .163, .167 except -018, -026, and -054, .263, .264, .267, .363 through .384; 376.167 and .667-018; 377; and 379.167 and .263-014)

Significant Points

- Police work can be dangerous and stressful.

- The number of qualified candidates exceeds the number of job openings in Federal law enforcement agencies and in most State, local, and special police departments.

- Opportunities will be best in those urban communities whose departments offer relatively low salaries and where the crime rate is relatively high.

Nature of the Work

The safety and well being of our Nation's citizens greatly depends on the police officers, detectives, and special agents responsible for enforcing statutes, laws, and regulations. Duties vary widely by the size and type of organization but in most jurisdictions, whether on or off duty, law enforcement officers are expected to exercise their authority whenever necessary. And, regardless of where they work or what they do, police, detectives, and special agents must spend considerable time writing reports and maintaining records that are needed when legal actions require them to testify in court.

Police officers who work in small communities and rural areas have general law enforcement duties. In the course of a day's work, they may direct traffic at the scene of a fire, investigate a burglary, or give first aid to an accident victim. In large police departments, by contrast, officers usually are assigned to a specific type of duty. Most officers are detailed to patrol a designated area to prevent crime. Pa-

trols generally cover an area such as business districts or outlying residential neighborhoods. Officers may work alone, but in large agencies they usually patrol with a partner. They attempt to become thoroughly familiar with conditions throughout their patrol area and, while on patrol, remain alert for anything unusual. Suspicious circumstances, such as open windows or lights in vacant buildings, as well as hazards to public safety are noted. They identify, pursue, and arrest suspected criminals, resolve problems within the community, and enforce traffic laws. Officers are becoming more involved in community policing—building partnerships with the citizens of local neighborhoods and mobilizing the public to help the police fight crime.

Some police officers specialize and become experts in chemical and microscopic analysis, firearms identification, handwriting and fingerprint identification. Others may work with special units such as mounted and motorcycle patrol, harbor patrol, canine corps, special weapons and tactics or emergency response teams, or task forces formed to combat specific types of crime.

Detectives and special agents are plainclothes investigators who gather facts and collect evidence for criminal cases. They conduct interviews, examine records, observe the activities of suspects, and participate in raids or arrests.

Some local departments provide security officers, sometimes called bailiffs, to maintain order in courtrooms.

Sheriffs and deputy sheriffs enforce the law on the county level. In metropolitan areas where there are also regular police departments, the sheriffs' department may perform specialized duties such as serving legal documents or operating the jail. A sheriffs' duties resemble those of a local or county police chief, but the department is generally on a smaller scale. Most sheriffs' departments employ fewer than 25 sworn officers, and many employ fewer than 10.

State police officers (sometimes called State troopers or highway patrol officers) patrol highways and enforce motor vehicle laws and regulations. They issue traffic citations to motorists who violate the law. At the scene of an accident, they may direct traffic, give first aid, and call for emergency equipment. They also write reports that may be used to determine the cause of the accident. In addition, State police officers may provide services to motorists on the highways, such as calling for road service for drivers with mechanical trouble.

State police also enforce criminal laws. They are frequently called upon to render assistance to officers of other law enforcement agencies. In rural areas that do not have a police force or a local deputy from the sheriff's department, the State police are the primary law enforcement agency, investigating any crimes that occur, such as burglary or assault.

The Federal government maintains a high profile in many areas of law enforcement. *Federal Bureau of Investigation (FBI) special agents* are the Government's principal investigators, responsible for investigating violations of more than 260 statutes. Agents may conduct surveillance, monitor court-authorized wiretaps, examine business records to investigate white-collar crime, track the interstate movement of stolen property, collect evidence of espionage activities, or participate in sensitive undercover assignments. *Drug Enforcement Administration (DEA) special agents* specialize in enforcement of drug laws and regulations. Agents may conduct complex criminal investigations, carry out surveillance of criminals, and infiltrate illicit drug organizations using undercover techniques. *U.S. marshals and deputy marshals* provide security for Federal courts, including judges, witnesses, and prisoners, and apprehend fugitives. *U.S. Border Patrol special agents* are responsible for protecting more than 8,000 miles of international land and water boundaries. Their primary mission is to detect and prevent the smuggling and unlawful entry of undocumented aliens into the United States and to apprehend those persons found in violation of the immigration laws. *Immigration and Naturalization Service (INS) agents* facilitate the entry of legal visitors and immigrants to the United States and detain and deport those arriving illegally.

Special agents employed by the U.S. Department of the Treasury work for the Bureau of Alcohol, Tobacco, and Firearms, the U.S. Customs Service, the Internal Revenue Service, and U.S. Secret Service. *Bureau of Alcohol, Tobacco, and Firearms special agents* investigate violations of Federal firearms and explosives laws, as well as Federal alcohol and tobacco regulations. *Customs agents* inspect cargo, collect appropriate duties or fees, and intercept contraband while ensuring that all goods entering the United States comply with United States laws and regulations. *Internal Revenue Service special agents* collect evidence against individuals and companies that are evading the payment of Federal taxes. *U.S. Secret Service special agents* protect the President, Vice President, and their immediate families, Presidential candidates, ex-Presidents, and foreign dignitaries visiting the United States. Secret Service agents also investigate counterfeiting, the forgery of Government checks or bonds, and the fraudulent use of credit cards.

Various other Federal agencies employ police and special agents with sworn arrest powers and the authority to carry firearms. These agencies include the U.S. Forest Service under the Department of Agriculture, the National Park Service under the Department of the Interior, and Federal Air Marshals under the Department of Transportation. Other police agencies generally evolved from the need for security for the agency's property and personnel. The largest such agency is the General Services Administration's Federal Protective Service, which provides security for Federal buildings and property nationwide.

Working Conditions

Police work can be very dangerous and stressful. In addition to the obvious dangers of confrontations with criminals, the need to be constantly alert and ready to deal appropriately with any situation can be very stressful. Police, detectives, and special agents usually work a 40-hour week, but paid overtime work is common. Shift work is necessary because police protection must be provided around the clock. Junior officers frequently must work weekends, holidays, and nights. Police officers, detectives, and special agents are subject to call at any time their services are needed and may work long hours during investigations. All law enforcement officers are required to file reports of their activities, often involving long hours of paperwork. In most jurisdictions, whether on or off duty, officers are expected to be armed and to exercise their arrest authority whenever necessary.

The jobs of some Federal agents such as U.S. Secret Service and DEA special agents require extensive travel, often on very short notice.

Competition is expected to remain keen for higher paying jobs with police departments in more affluent areas and State and Federal agencies.

They frequently relocate a number of times over the course of their career. Some police, detectives, and special agents with agencies such as the U.S. Border Patrol must work outdoors for long periods in all kinds of weather.

Employment

Police, detectives, and special agents held about 704,000 jobs in 1996. About 63 percent of police detectives and investigators were employed by local governments, primarily in cities with more than 25,000 inhabitants. Some cities have very large police forces, while hundreds of small communities employ fewer than 25 officers each. State police agencies employed about 10 percent of all police, detectives, and investigators; various Federal agencies employed the other 27 percent.

Training, Other Qualifications, and Advancement

Civil service regulations govern the appointment of police and detectives in practically all State and large city agencies and in many smaller ones. Candidates must be U.S. citizens, usually at least 20 years of age, and must meet rigorous physical and personal qualifications. Eligibility for appointment generally depends on performance in competitive written examinations as well as on education and experience. Physical examinations often include tests of vision, hearing, strength, and agility.

Because personal characteristics such as honesty, judgment, integrity, and a sense of responsibility are especially important in law enforcement work, candidates are interviewed by senior officers, and their character traits and background are investigated. In some agencies, candidates are interviewed by a psychiatrist or a psychologist, or given a personality test. Most applicants are subjected to lie detector examinations or drug testing. Some agencies subject sworn personnel to random drug testing as a condition of continuing employment. Although police, detectives, and special agents work independently, they must perform their duties in accordance with the law and departmental rules. They should enjoy working with people and meeting the public.

In larger police departments, where the majority of law enforcement jobs are found, applicants usually must have at least a high school education. Federal agencies generally require a college degree. A few police departments accept applicants as recruits who have less than a high school education, but the number is declining.

The Federal agency with the largest number of special agents is the FBI. To be considered for appointment as an FBI special agent, an applicant either must be a graduate of an accredited law school; be a college graduate with a major in accounting; or be a college graduate with either fluency in a foreign language or 3 years of full-time work experience. All new agents undergo 16 weeks of training at the FBI academy on the U.S. Marine Corps base in Quantico, Virginia.

Applicants for special agent jobs with the U.S. Department of Treasury's Secret Service and the Bureau of Alcohol, Tobacco, and Firearms must have a bachelor's degree or a minimum of 3 years' work experience which demonstrates the ability to deal effectively with individuals or groups, among other things. Prospective special agents undergo 8 weeks of training at the Federal Law Enforcement Training Center in Glynco, Georgia, and another 8-11 weeks of specialized training with their particular agencies.

Applicants for special agent jobs with the U.S. Drug Enforcement Administration (DEA) must have a college degree and either 1 year of experience conducting criminal investigations, 1 year of graduate school, or have achieved at least a 2.95 grade point average while in college. DEA special agents undergo 14 weeks of specialized training at the FBI Academy in Quantico, Virginia.

Police departments are encouraging applicants to take postsecondary school training in law enforcement. Many entry level applicants to police jobs have completed some formal postsecondary education and a significant number are college graduates. In 1993, the most recent year for which data are available, 12 percent of local police departments required new officer recruits to have at least some college education. Many junior colleges, colleges, and universities offer programs in law enforcement or administration of justice. Other courses helpful in preparing for a career in law enforcement include accounting, finance, electrical engineering or computer science, and foreign languages. Physical education and sports are helpful in developing the courage, competitiveness, stamina, and agility needed for law enforcement work. Knowledge of a foreign language is an asset in many agencies.

Some large cities hire high school graduates who are still in their teens as police cadets or trainees. They do clerical work and attend classes, and can be appointed to the regular force at the conclusion of their training, usually in 1 to 2 years, upon reaching the minimum age requirement.

Before their first assignments, officers usually go through a period of training. In State and large local departments, recruits get training in their agency's police academy, often for 12 to 14 weeks. In small agencies, recruits often attend a regional or State academy. Training includes classroom instruction in constitutional law and civil rights, State laws and local ordinances, and accident investigation. Recruits also receive training and supervised experience in patrol, traffic control, use of firearms, self-defense, first aid, and handling emergencies.

Police officers usually become eligible for promotion after a probationary period ranging from 6 months to 3 years. In a large department, promotion may enable an officer to become a detective or specialize in one type of police work such as laboratory analysis of evidence or working with juveniles. Promotions to corporal, sergeant, lieutenant, and captain usually are made according to a candidate's position on a promotion list, as determined by scores on a written examination and on-the-job performance.

Continuing training helps police officers, detectives, and special agents improve their job performance. Through police department academies, regional centers for public safety employees established by the States, and Federal agency training centers, instructors provide annual training in defensive tactics, firearms, use-of-force policies, sensitivity and communications skills, crowd-control techniques, legal developments that affect their work, and advances in law enforcement equipment. Many agencies pay all or part of the tuition for officers to work toward degrees in criminal justice, police science, administration of justice, or public administration, and pay higher salaries to those who earn such a degree.

Job Outlook

The opportunity for public service through law enforcement work is attractive to many. The job is challenging and involves much personal responsibility. Furthermore, in many agencies, law enforcement officers may retire with a pension after 20 or 25 years of service, allowing them to pursue a second career while still in their 40s. Because of relatively attractive salaries and benefits, the number of qualified candidates exceeds the number of job openings in Federal law enforcement agencies and in most State, local, and special police departments—resulting in increased hiring standards and selectivity by employers. Competition is expected to remain keen for the higher paying jobs with State and Federal agencies and police departments in more affluent areas. Persons having college training in police science, military experience, or both should have the best opportunities. Opportunities will be best in those urban communities whose departments offer relatively low salaries and where the crime rate is relatively high.

Employment of police officers, detectives, and special agents is expected to increase about as fast as the average for all occupations through the year 2006. A more security-conscious society and concern about drug-related crimes should contribute to the increasing demand for police services. At the local and State levels, growth is likely to continue as long as crime remains a serious concern. However, employment growth at the Federal level will be tempered by continuing budgetary constraints faced by law enforcement agencies. Turnover in police, detective, and special agent positions is among the lowest of all occupations; nevertheless, the need to replace workers who retire, transfer to other occupations, or stop working for other reasons will be the source of most job openings.

The level of government spending determines the level of employment for police officers, detectives, and special agents. The number of job opportunities, therefore, can vary from year to year and from place to place. Layoffs, on the other hand, are rare because retirements enable most staffing cuts to be handled through attrition. Trained law enforcement officers who lose their jobs because of budget cuts usually have little difficulty finding jobs with other agencies.

Earnings

In 1996, the median salary of nonsupervisory police officers and detectives was about $34,700 a year. The middle 50 percent earned between about $25,700 and $45,300; the lowest 10 percent were paid less than $19,200, while the highest 10 percent earned over $58,500 a year.

Police officers and detectives in supervisory positions had a median salary of about $41,200 a year, also in 1996. The middle 50 percent earned between about $29,200 and $38,400; the lowest 10 percent were paid less than $22,500, while the highest 10 percent earned over $64,500 annually.

Sheriffs and other law enforcement officers had a median annual salary of about $26,700 in 1996. The middle 50 percent earned between about $20,300 and $37,800; the lowest 10 percent were paid less than $15,900, while the highest 10 percent earned over $48,400.

Federal law provides special salary rates to Federal employees who serve in law enforcement. Additionally, Federal special agents receive availability pay or administratively uncontrolled overtime (AUO)—equal to 25 percent of the agent's grade and step—awarded because of the large amount of overtime that these agents are expected to work. For example, in 1996 FBI agents started at a base salary of $33,800 a year, earning $42,250 a year with availability pay. Other Justice and Treasury Department special agents started at about $25,000 or $30,700 a year, earning $31,300 or $38,400 per year including availability pay, depending on their qualifications. Salaries of Federal special agents progress to $55,600 including availability pay, while supervisory agents started at $66,100 including availability pay. Salaries were slightly higher in selected areas where the prevailing local pay level was higher. Because Federal agents may be eligible for a special law enforcement benefits package, applicants should ask their recruiter for more information.

Total earnings for local, State, and special police and detectives frequently exceed the stated salary due to payments for overtime, which can be significant. In addition to the common benefits—paid vacation, sick leave, and medical and life insurance—most police and sheriffs' departments provide officers with special allowances for uniforms. In addition, because police officers generally are covered by liberal pension plans, many retire at half-pay after 20 or 25 years of service.

Related Occupations

Police, detectives, and special agents maintain law and order. Workers in related occupations include correctional officers, guards, fire marshals, and inspectors.

Sources of Additional Information

Information about entrance requirements may be obtained from Federal, State, and local law enforcement agencies.

Further information about qualifications for employment as an FBI Special Agent is available from the nearest State FBI office; the address and phone number are listed in the local telephone directory.

Further information about qualifications for employment as a DEA Special Agent is available from the nearest DEA office, or call 1-800 DEA-4288.

Information about career opportunities, qualifications, and training to become a deputy marshal is available from:
☛ United States Marshals Service, Employment and Compensation Division, Field Staffing Branch, 600 Army Navy Dr., Arlington, VA 22202.

An overview of career opportunities, qualifications, and training for U.S. Secret Service Special Agents is available from:
☛ U.S. Secret Service, Personnel Division, Room 912, 1800 G St. NW., Washington, DC 20223.

Private Detectives and Investigators

(D.O.T. 189.167-054; 343.367-014; 376.137, .267; 367; and .667-014)

Significant Points

- Work hours are often irregular.
- No formal education requirements exist for applicants, although almost all have experience in other occupations, often law enforcement or the military.
- A license is required in most areas.

Nature of the Work

Private detectives and investigators assist attorneys, businesses, and the public with a variety of problems. Their services include protecting businesses and their employees, customers, and guests from theft, vandalism, and disorder as well as gathering evidence for a trials, tracing debtors, or conducting background investigations. While detectives concentrate on providing protection and investigators specialize in gathering information, many do some of each.

Private detectives and investigators' duties range from locating missing persons to exposing fraudulent workers' compensation claims. Some specialize in one field, such as finance, where they might use accounting skills to investigate the financial standing of a company or locate funds stolen by an embezzler. Others specialize in locating missing persons, investigating infidelity, or conducting background investigations, including financial profiles and asset searches; others do executive protection and bodyguard work.

Most detectives and investigators are trained to perform physical surveillance, often for long periods of time, in a car or van. They may observe a site, such as the home of a subject, from an inconspicuous location. The surveillance continues using still and video cameras, binoculars, and a citizen's band radio or a car phone, until the desired evidence is obtained. They perform on-line computer database searches, or work with someone who does. Computers allow detectives and investigators to obtain massive amounts of information in a short period of time from the dozens of on-line data bases containing probate records, motor-vehicle registrations, credit reports, association membership lists, and other information.

Private detectives and investigators obtain information by interviewing witnesses and assembling evidence and reports for litigation or criminal trials. They get cases from clients or are assigned to cases by the manager of the firm they work for. Many spend considerable time conducting surveillance, seeking to observe inconsistencies in a subject's behavior. For example, a person who has recently filed a workers' compensation claim stating that an injury has made walking difficult should not be able to jog or mow the lawn. If such behavior is observed, the investigator takes video or still photographs to document the activity and reports back to the supervisor or client.

Some investigations involve verification of facts, such as an individual's place of employment or income. This might involve a phone call or a visit to the workplace. In other investigations, especially in missing persons cases and background checks, the investigator interviews people to gather as much information as possible about an individual.

Legal investigators specialize in cases involving the courts and are normally employed by law firms or lawyers. They frequently assist in preparing criminal defenses, locate witnesses, interview police, gather and review evidence, take photographs, and testify in court. To assist attorneys in the preparation of civil litigation, they interview prospective witnesses, collect information on the parties to the litigation, and search out testimonial, documentary, or physical evidence.

Corporate investigators work for companies other than investigative firms—often large corporations. They conduct internal or external investigations. External investigations may consist of undercover operations aimed at preventing criminal schemes, thefts of company assets, or fraudulent deliveries of products by suppliers. In internal investigations, they may investigate drug use in the workplace, insure that expense accounts are not abused, and determine if employees are stealing merchandise or information.

Detectives and investigators who specialize in finance may be hired to develop confidential financial profiles of individuals or companies who may be parties to large financial transactions and often work with investment bankers and accountants. They also may search for assets after fraud or theft, to recover damages awarded by a court.

Private detectives and investigators who work for retail stores or malls are responsible for loss control and asset protection. *Store detectives* safeguard the assets of retail stores by apprehending anyone attempting to steal merchandise or destroy store property. They detect theft by shoplifters, vendor representatives, delivery personnel, and even store employees. Store detectives also conduct periodic inspections of stock areas, dressing rooms, and rest rooms, and sometimes assist in the opening and closing of the store. They may prepare loss prevention and security reports for management and testify in court against persons they apprehend.

Working Conditions

Private detectives and investigators often work irregular hours because of the need to conduct surveillance and contact people who may not be available during normal working hours. Early morning, evening, weekend, and holiday work is common.

Many detectives and investigators spend much time away from their offices conducting interviews or doing surveillance, but some work in their office most of the day conducting computer searches and making phone calls. Some split their time between office and field. Those who have their own agencies and employ other investigators may work primarily in an office and have normal business hours.

When working a case away from the office, the environment might range from plush boardrooms to seedy bars. Store and hotel detectives work mostly in the businesses that they protect. Investigators generally work alone, but sometimes work with others during surveillance or when following a subject.

Much of the work detectives and investigators do can be confrontational because the person being observed or interviewed may not want to be. As a result, the job can be stressful and sometimes dan-

Private detectives and investigators interview witnesses and assemble evidence and reports for litigation or criminal trials.

gerous. Some detectives and investigators carry handguns. In most cases, a weapon is not necessary because the purpose of their work is the gathering of information and not law enforcement or apprehension of criminals. Owners of investigative agencies have the added stress of having to deal with demanding and sometimes distraught clients.

Employment

Private detectives and investigators held about 58,000 jobs in 1996. About 17 percent were self-employed. About 36 percent of wage and salary workers worked for detective agencies and about 42 percent were employed as store detectives in department or clothing and accessories stores. Others worked for hotels and other lodging places, legal services firms, and in other industries.

Training, Other Qualifications, and Advancement

There are no formal education requirements for most private detective and investigator jobs, although most employers prefer high school graduates; many private detectives have college degrees. Almost all private detectives and investigators have previous experience in other occupations. Some work initially for insurance or collections companies or in the security industry. Many investigators enter the field after serving in military or law enforcement jobs.

Retired law enforcement officers, military investigators, and government agents frequently become private detectives and investigators as a second career. Others enter from such diverse fields as finance, accounting, investigative reporting, insurance, and law. These individuals often can apply their prior work experience in a related investigation specialty. A few enter the occupation directly after graduation from college, generally with majors in such fields as criminal justice or police science.

The majority of the States and the District of Colombia require private detectives and investigators be licensed by the State or local authorities. Licensing requirements vary widely. Some States have very liberal requirements, or none at all, while others have stringent regulations. For example, the California Department of Consumer Affairs Bureau of Security and Investigative Services requires 6,000 hours of investigative experience, a background check, and a qualifying score on a written examination. A growing number of States are enacting mandatory training programs for private detectives and investigators. In most States, convicted felons may not be licensed.

In most investigations firms, the screening process for potential employees includes a background check, to confirm education and work experience, to inquire about criminal history, and to interview references and others who know the applicant.

For private detective and investigator jobs, most employers look for individuals with ingenuity who are curious, aggressive, persistent, and assertive. A candidate must not be afraid of being confrontational, should communicate well, and should be able to think on his or her feet. The courts are often the ultimate judge of a properly conducted investigation, so the investigator must be able to present the facts in a manner a jury will believe.

Training in subjects such as criminal justice are helpful to the aspiring private detective and investigator. Most corporate investigators must have a bachelor's degree, preferably in a business-related field. Some corporate investigators have masters of business administration or law degrees, while others are certified public accountants.

Corporate investigators hired by larger companies may receive formal training from their employers on business practices, management structure, and various finance-related topics. Good interviewing and interrogation skills are important and are usually acquired in earlier careers in law enforcement or other fields.

Most investigations firms are small, with little room for advancement. Usually there are no defined ranks or steps, so advancement is in terms of salary and assignment status. Many detectives and investigators work for various investigations firms at the beginning of their careers and after a few years try to start their own firms. Corporate and legal investigators may rise to supervisor or manager of the security or investigations department.

Job Outlook

Employment of private detectives and investigators is expected to grow about as fast as the average for all occupations through the year 2006. In addition, job turnover should create many additional job openings, particularly among wage and salary workers. Nevertheless, competition is expected for the available openings because private detective and investigator careers are attractive to many, and there are many individuals who retire from law enforcement and military careers at a relatively young age who are qualified to enter the field.

Increased demand for private detectives and investigators is expected to be generated by fear of crime, increased litigation, and the need to protect confidential information and property of all kinds. Additional private investigators will be needed by law firms to meet the needs for criminal defense and civil litigation among companies and individuals. Greater corporate financial activity worldwide will increase the demand for investigators to control internal and external financial losses, as well as to find out what competitors are doing and to prevent industrial spying.

Opportunities should be best for entry-level jobs as store detectives or with detective agencies on a part-time basis. Those seeking store detective jobs may find the best opportunities with private guard and security firms since some retail businesses are replacing their own workers with outside contract workers.

Earnings

Earnings of private detectives and investigators vary greatly depending on their employer, specialty, and the geographic area in which they work. According to a study by Abbott, Langer & Associates, security/loss prevention directors and vice presidents earned an average $67,700 a year in 1996, investigators about $37,800 a year, and store detectives about $19,100.

Most private investigators bill their clients between $50 and $150 per hour to conduct investigations. Except for those working for large corporations, most private investigators do not receive paid vacation or sick days, health or life insurance, retirement packages, or other benefits. Investigators are usually reimbursed for expenses and generally receive a car allowance.

Most corporate investigators received health insurance, pension plans, profit-sharing plans, and paid vacation.

Related Occupations

Private detectives and investigators often collect information and protect property and assets of companies. Others with related concerns include security guards, insurance claims examiners, inspectors, collectors, and law enforcement officers. Investigators who specialize in conducting financial profiles and asset searches do work closely related to that of accountants and financial analysts.

Sources of Additional Information

For information on local licensing requirements, contact your State Department of Public Safety, State Division of licensing, or your local or State police headquarters.

Mechanics, Installers, and Repairs

Aircraft Mechanics, Including Engine Specialists

(D.O.T. 621.261-022, 621.281 except -030, .684-014; 806.384-038; 807.261, .381-014, and .684-018)

Significant Points

- The vast majority learn their job in 1 of about 200 trade schools certified by the Federal Aviation Administration.

- Earnings are very high.

- Opportunities should generally be favorable, but competition is likely for the best paying jobs with airlines.

Nature of the Work

To keep aircraft in peak operating condition, aircraft mechanics and engine specialists perform scheduled maintenance, make repairs, and complete inspections required by the Federal Aviation Administration (FAA).

Many aircraft mechanics specialize in preventive maintenance. Following a schedule based on the number of hours the aircraft has flown, calendar days, cycles of operation, or a combination of these factors, mechanics inspect the engines, landing gear, instruments, pressurized sections, accessories—brakes, valves, pumps, and air-conditioning systems, for example—and other parts of the aircraft and do the necessary maintenance and replacement of parts. They may examine an engine through specially designed openings while working from ladders or scaffolds, or use hoists or lifts to remove the entire engine from the craft. After taking the engine apart, mechanics may use precision instruments to measure parts for wear, and use x-ray and magnetic inspection equipment to check for invisible cracks. Worn or defective parts are repaired or replaced. They may also repair sheet-metal or composite surfaces, measure the tension of control cables, or check for corrosion, distortion, and cracks in the fuselage, wings, and tail. After completing all repairs, mechanics must test the equipment to ensure that it works properly.

Mechanics specializing in repair work rely on the pilot's description of a problem to find and fix faulty equipment. For example, during a preflight check, a pilot may discover that the aircraft's fuel gauge does not work. To solve the problem, mechanics may troubleshoot the electrical system using electrical test equipment to make sure no wires are broken or shorted out and then may replace electrical or electronic components. They work as fast as safety permits so the aircraft can be put back into service quickly.

Some of the larger more sophisticated planes have aircraft monitoring systems which consist of electronic boxes and consoles which monitor the aircraft's basic operations and provides valuable diagnostic information to the mechanic.

Mechanics may work on one or many different types of aircraft, such as jets, propeller-driven airplanes, and helicopters; or, for efficiency, they may specialize in one section of a particular type of aircraft, such as the engine, hydraulic, or electrical system. *Powerplant mechanics* are authorized to work on engines and to do limited work on propellers. *Airframe mechanics* are authorized to work on any part of the aircraft except the instruments, powerplants, and propellers. *Combination airframe-and-powerplant mechanics*—called A & P mechanics— work on all parts of the plane, except instruments. The majority of mechanics working on civilian aircraft today are airframe and powerplant mechanics. In small, independent repair shops, mechanics usually inspect and repair many different types of aircraft.

Avionics systems are now an integral part of aircraft design and have vastly increased an aircraft's capability. *Avionics technicians*

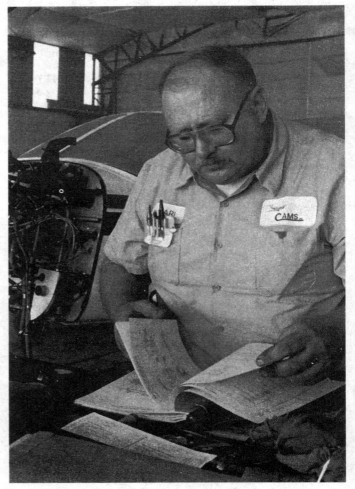

Aircraft mechanics must follow established procedures to meet FAA inspection standards.

repair and maintain components used for aircraft navigation and radio communications, weather radar systems, and other instruments and computers that control flight, engine and other primary functions. These duties may require additional licenses such as a FCC radio telephone licence. As a result of technological advances, an increasing amount of time is spent repairing electronic systems such as computerized controls. Technicians may also be required to analyze and develop solutions to complex electronic problems.

Working Conditions

Mechanics usually work in hangars or in other indoor areas, although they may work outdoors—sometimes in unpleasant weather—when the hangars are full or when repairs must be made quickly. Mechanics often work under time pressure to maintain flight schedules or, in general aviation, to keep from inconveniencing customers. At the same time, mechanics have a tremendous responsibility to maintain safety standards and this can cause the job to be stressful.

Frequently, mechanics must lift or pull objects weighing as much as 70 pounds. They often stand, lie, or kneel in awkward positions and occasionally must work in precarious positions on scaffolds or ladders. Noise and vibration are common when testing engines. Aircraft mechanics generally work 40 hours a week on 8-hour shifts around the clock. Overtime work is frequent.

Employment

Aircraft mechanics held about 137,000 jobs in 1996. Over three-fifths of all salaried mechanics worked for airlines, nearly one-fifth for aircraft assembly firms, and nearly one-sixth for the Federal Government. Most of the rest were general aviation mechanics, the majority of whom worked for independent repair shops or companies that operate their own planes to transport executives and cargo. Very few mechanics were self-employed.

Most airline mechanics work at major airports near large cities. Civilian mechanics employed by the Armed Forces work at military installations. A large proportion of mechanics who work for aircraft assembly firms are located in California or Washington. Others work for the FAA, many at the facilities in Oklahoma City, Atlantic City, or Washington, D.C. Mechanics for independent repair shops work at airports in every part of the country.

Training, Other Qualifications, and Advancement

The majority of mechanics who work on civilian aircraft are certificated by the FAA as "airframe mechanic," "powerplant mechanic," or "avionics repair specialist." Mechanics who also have an inspector's authorization can certify work completed by other mechanics and perform required inspections. Uncertificated mechanics are supervised by those with certificates.

The FAA requires at least 18 months of work experience for an airframe, powerplant, or avionics repairer's certificate. For a combined A & P certificate, at least 30 months of experience working with both engines and airframes are required. Completion of a program at an FAA certificated mechanic school can substitute for the work experience requirement. Applicants for all certificates also must pass written and oral tests, and demonstrate that they can do the work authorized by the certificate. To obtain an inspector's authorization, a mechanic must have held an A & P certificate for at least 3 years. Most airlines require that mechanics have a high school diploma and an A & P certificate.

Although a few people become mechanics through on-the-job training, most learn their job in one of about 200 trade schools certified by the FAA. Student enrollment in these schools varies greatly; some have as few as 50 students while at least one school has about 800 students. About one-third of these schools award two and four-year degrees in avionics, aviation technology, or aviation maintenance management.

FAA standards established by law require that certificated mechanic schools offer students a minimum of 1,900 actual class hours. Courses in these trade schools generally last from 2 years to 30 months, and provide training with the tools and equipment used on the job. Aircraft trade schools are placing more emphasis on newer technologies such as turbine engines, aviation electronics, and composite materials—including graphite, fiberglass, and boron—all of which are increasingly being used in the construction of new aircraft. Less emphasis is being placed on older technologies such as woodworking and welding. Employers prefer mechanics who can perform a wide variety of tasks.

Some aircraft mechanics in the Armed Forces acquire enough general experience to satisfy the work experience requirements for the FAA certificate. With additional study, they may pass the certifying exam. Generally, however, jobs in the military services are too specialized to provide the broad experience required by the FAA. Most mechanics have to complete the entire training program at a trade school, although a few receive some credit for the material they learned in the service. In any case, military experience is a great advantage when seeking employment; employers consider trade school graduates who have this experience to be the most desirable applicants.

Courses in mathematics, physics, chemistry, electronics, computer science, and mechanical drawing are helpful because many of their principles are involved in the operation of an aircraft and knowledge of the principles is often necessary to make repairs. Courses that develop writing skills are also important because mechanics are often required to submit reports.

New FAA regulations require current experience to keep the A&P certificate valid. Applicants must have at least 1,000 hours work experience in the previous 24 months or take a refresher course. As new and more complex aircraft are designed, more employers are requiring mechanics to take on-going training to update their skills. Recent technological advances in aircraft maintenance necessitate a strong background in electronics—both for acquiring and retaining jobs in this field. New FAA certification standards also make ongoing training mandatory. Every 24 months, mechanics are required to take at least 16 hours of training to keep their certificate. Many mechanics take courses offered by manufacturers or employers, usually through outside contractors.

Aircraft mechanics must do careful and thorough work that requires a high degree of mechanical aptitude. Employers seek applicants who are self-motivated, hard-working, enthusiastic, and able to diagnose and solve complex mechanical problems. Agility is important for the reaching and climbing necessary for the job. Because they may work on the top of wings and fuselages on large jet planes, aircraft mechanics must not be afraid of heights.

As aircraft mechanics gain experience, they have the opportunity for advancement. Opportunities are best for those who have an aircraft inspector's authorization. A mechanic may advance to lead mechanic (or crew chief), inspector, lead inspector, and shop supervisor. In the airlines, where promotion is often determined by examination, supervisors may advance to executive positions. Those with broad experience in maintenance and overhaul have become inspectors with the FAA. With additional business and management training, some open their own aircraft maintenance facilities. Mechanics learn many different skills in their training that can be applied to other jobs, and some transfer to other skilled repairer occupations or electronics technician jobs.

Job Outlook

There should be an improved outlook for aircraft mechanics over the next ten years. The smaller numbers of younger workers in the labor force, coupled with fewer entrants from the military, and a larger number of retirements points to more favorable employment conditions for students just beginning training.

Job prospects for aircraft mechanics are expected to vary among types of employers. Opportunities are likely to be the best at the smaller commuter and regional airlines, FAA repair stations, and in general aviation. Because wages in these companies tend to be relatively low, there are fewer applicants for these jobs than for jobs with the major airlines. Also, some jobs will become available as experienced mechanics leave for higher paying jobs with airlines or transfer to another occupation. Mechanics will face more competition for airline jobs because the high wages and travel benefits attract more qualified applicants than there are openings. Prospects will be best for applicants with significant experience. Mechanics who keep abreast of technological advances in electronics, composite materials, and other areas will be in greatest demand. The number of job openings for aircraft mechanics in the Federal Government should decline as the size of the Armed Forces is reduced.

Employment of aircraft mechanics is expected to increase about as fast as the average for all occupations through the year 2006. A growing population and rising incomes are expected to stimulate the demand for airline transportation, and the number of aircraft is expected to grow. However, employment growth will be restricted somewhat by increases in productivity resulting from greater use of automated inventory control and modular systems that speed repairs and parts replacement.

Most job openings for aircraft mechanics through the year 2006 will stem from replacement needs. Each year, as mechanics transfer to other occupations or retire, several thousand job openings will arise. Aircraft mechanics have a comparatively strong attachment to the occupation, reflecting their significant investment in training and a love for aviation. However, because aircraft mechanics' skills are transferable to other occupations, some mechanics leave for work in a related field.

Declines in air travel during recessions force airlines to curtail the number of flights, which results in less aircraft maintenance and, consequently, layoffs for aircraft mechanics.

Earnings

In 1996, the median annual salary of aircraft mechanics was about $35,000. The middle 50 percent earned between $29,000 and $44,000. The top 10 percent of all aircraft mechanics earned over $48,000 a year, and the bottom 10 percent earned less than $23,200. Mechanics who worked on jets generally earned more than those working on other aircraft. Airline mechanics and their immediate families receive reduced fare transportation on their own and most other airlines.

Earnings of airline mechanics are generally higher than mechanics working for other employers. Average hourly pay for beginning aircraft mechanics was estimated to range from $18.00 at the smaller turbo-prop airlines, to $22.00 at the major airlines in 1996. Earnings of experienced mechanics were estimated to ranged from $25.00 to $32.00 an hour.

Almost one-half of all aircraft mechanics, including those employed by some major airlines, are covered by union agreements. The principal unions are the International Association of Machinists and Aerospace Workers and the Transport Workers Union of America. Some mechanics are represented by the International Brotherhood of Teamsters.

Related Occupations

Workers in some other occupations that involve similar mechanical and electrical work are electricians, elevator repairers, and telephone maintenance mechanics.

Sources of Additional Information

Information about jobs in a particular airline may be obtained by writing to the personnel manager of the company. For general information about aircraft mechanics, write to:

☛ Professional Aviation Maintenance Association, 1200 18th St. NW., Suite 401, Washington, DC 20036.

For information on jobs in a particular area, contact employers at local airports or local offices of the State employment service.

frames and sections to alignment machines that use hydraulic pressure to align damaged components. "Unibody" vehicles, designs built without frames, must be restored to precise factory specifications for the vehicle to operate correctly. To do so, repairers use bench systems to make accurate measurements of how much each section is out of alignment and hydraulic machinery to return the vehicle back to its original shape.

Body repairers remove badly damaged sections of body panels with a pneumatic metal-cutting gun or other means and weld in replacement sections. Repairers pull out less serious dents with a hydraulic jack or hand prying bar, or knock them out with handtools or pneumatic hammers. They smooth out small dents and creases in the metal by holding a small anvil against one side of the damaged area while hammering the opposite side. They also remove very small pits and dimples with pick hammers and punches in a process called metal finishing.

Body repairers also repair or replace the plastic body parts used increasingly on newer model vehicles.They remove the damaged panels and identify the family and properties of the plastic. With most types, they can apply heat from a hot-air welding gun or by immersion in hot water, and press the softened panel back into its original shape by hand. They replace plastic parts which are badly damaged or more difficult to repair.

Body repairers use plastic or solder to fill small dents that cannot be worked out of the plastic or metal panel. On metal panels, they file or grind the hardened filler to the original shape and sand it before painting. In many shops, automotive painters do the painting. (These workers are discussed in the *Handbook* statement on painting and coating machine operators.) In smaller shops, workers often do both body repairing and painting. A few body repairers specialize in repairing fiberglass car bodies.

In large shops, body repairers may specialize in one type of repair, such as frame straightening or door and fender repair. Some body repairers specialize in installing glass in automobiles and other vehicles. Glass installers remove broken, cracked, or pitted windshields and window glass. Glass installers apply a moisture-proofing compound along the edges of the glass, place it in the vehicle, and install rubber strips around the sides of the windshield or window to make it secure and weatherproof.

Automotive Body Repairers

(D.O.T. 620.364-010, .684-034, -010; 807.267-010; .281-010; .361-010; .381 -010, -018, -022, and -030; -484; .684-010; and 865.684-010)

Significant Points

- Many still learn this trade on the job as helpers, although employers prefer to hire persons with automotive repair training.

- Good reading and basic mathematics skills are needed to follow instructions and diagrams in technical manuals.

Nature of the Work

Thousands of motor vehicles are damaged in traffic accidents every day. Although some are sold for salvage or scrapped, most can be repaired to look and drive like new. Automotive body repairers straighten bent bodies, remove dents, and replace crumpled parts that are beyond repair. They repair all types of vehicles, but mostly work on cars and small trucks, while a few work on large trucks, buses, or tractor-trailers.

When a damaged vehicle is brought into the shop, body repairers generally receive instructions from a supervisor who determines which parts to restore or replace and how much time the job should take.

Automotive body repairers use special equipment to restore damaged metal frames and body sections. They chain or clamp the

Automotive body repairers replace plastic parts which are badly damaged or more difficult to repair.

Body repair work has variety and challenges—each damaged vehicle presents a different problem. Repairers must develop appropriate methods for each job, using their broad knowledge of automotive construction and repair techniques.

Body repairers usually work alone with only general directions from supervisors. In some shops, helpers or apprentices assist experienced repairers.

Working Conditions

The majority of automotive body repairers work a standard 40 hour week, although the self employed may work 60 or more hours a week. Repairers work indoors in body shops that are noisy because of hammering against metal and the use of power tools. Most shops are well ventilated to partially disperse dust and paint fumes. Body repairers often work in awkward or cramped positions, and much of their work is strenuous and dirty. Hazards include cuts from sharp metal edges, burns from torches and heated metal, injuries from power tools, and fumes from paint. Serious accidents are avoided when the shop is kept clean and orderly and safety practices are observed.

Employment

Automotive body repairers held about 225,000 jobs in 1996. Most repairers worked for automobile and truck dealers who specialize in body repairs and painting. Others worked for organizations that maintain their own motor vehicles, such as trucking companies and automobile rental companies. A few worked for motor vehicle manufacturers. About 1 automotive body repairer out of 5 was self-employed.

Training, Other Qualifications, and Advancement

Most employers prefer to hire persons who have completed formal training programs in automotive body repair, but these programs supply only a portion of employers' needs. Formal training is highly desirable because advances in technology have greatly changed the structure, components, and materials used in automobiles. As a result, these new technologies require proficiency in new repair techniques and skills. For example, the bodies of newer automobiles are increasingly made of a combination of materials—traditional steel, aluminum, and a growing variety of metal alloys and plastics—each requiring the use of somewhat different techniques to reshape and smooth out dents and small pits. Many high schools, vocational schools, private trade schools, and community colleges offer automotive repair training programs. Formal training in automotive body repair can enhance chances for employment and speed promotion.

Employers also hire many persons without formal automotive body repair training. They learn the trade as helpers, picking up skills on the job from experienced body repairers. For helper jobs, most employers prefer to hire high school graduates who know how to use handtools. Good reading and basic mathematics and computer skills are essential to becoming a fully skilled automotive body repairer. Restoring unibody automobiles to their original form requires such precision that body repairers must follow instructions and diagrams in technical manuals to make very precise three-dimensional measurements of the position of one body section relative to another.

Helpers begin by assisting body repairers in tasks such as removing damaged parts and installing repaired parts. They learn to remove small dents and to make other minor repairs. They then progress to more difficult tasks such as straightening body parts and returning them to their correct alignment. Generally, to become skilled in all aspects of body repair requires 3 to 4 years of on-the-job training.

Certification by the National Institute for Automotive Service Excellence (ASE), though voluntary, is the recognized standard of achievement for automotive body repairers. To be certified, a body repairer must pass a written examination and must have at least 2 years of experience in the trade. Completion of a post-secondary program in automotive body repair may be substituted for 1 year of work experience. Automotive body repairers must retake the examination at least every 5 years to retain certification.

Automotive body repairers must buy their own handtools, but employers usually furnish power tools. Trainees generally accumulate tools as they gain experience, and many workers have thousands of dollars invested in tools.

Continuing education throughout a career in automotive body repair is required. Automotive parts, body materials, and electronics continue to change and become more complex and technologically advanced. Gaining new skills, reading technical manuals, and attending seminars and classes is important for keeping up with these technological advances.

An experienced automotive body repairer with supervisory ability may advance to shop supervisor. Some workers open their own body repair shops. Others become automobile damage appraisers for insurance companies.

Job Outlook

Employment of automotive body repairers is expected to increase about as fast as the average for all occupations through the year 2006. Opportunities should be best for persons with formal training in automotive body repair and mechanics.

Demand for qualified body repairers will increase because, as the number of motor vehicles in operation grows with the Nation's population, the number of vehicles damaged in accidents is expected to increase as well. New automobile designs increasingly have body parts made of steel alloys, aluminum, and plastics—materials that are more difficult to work with than the traditional steel body parts. Also, new, lighter weight automotive designs are prone to greater collision damage than older, heavier designs and, consequently, more time is consumed in repair. Nevertheless, the need to replace experienced repairers who transfer to other occupations, retire, or stop working for other reasons will still account for the majority of job openings.

The automotive repair business is not very sensitive to changes in economic conditions, and experienced body repairers are rarely laid off. However, most employers hire fewer new workers during an economic slowdown. Although major body damage must be repaired if a vehicle is to be restored to safe operating condition, repair of minor dents and crumpled fenders can often be deferred.

Earnings

Median weekly earnings of automotive body repairers were $463 in 1996. The middle 50 percent earned between $319 and $686 a week. The lowest-paid 10 percent earned less than $249 a week, while the highest-paid 10 percent earned over $855 a week. Helpers and trainees usually earn from 30 to 60 percent of the earnings of skilled workers.

The majority of body repairers employed by automotive dealers and repair shops are paid on an incentive basis. Under this method, body repairers are paid a predetermined amount for various tasks, and earnings depend on the amount of work assigned to the repairer and how fast it is completed. Employers frequently guarantee workers a minimum weekly salary. Helpers and trainees usually receive an hourly rate until they are skilled enough to be paid on an incentive basis. Body repairers who work for trucking companies, bus lines, and other organizations that maintain their own vehicles usually receive an hourly wage.

Some automotive body repairers are members of unions, including the International Association of Machinists and Aerospace Workers; the International Union, United Automobile, Aerospace and Agricultural Implement Workers of America; the Sheet Metal Workers' International Association; and the International Brotherhood of Teamsters. Most body repairers who are union members work for large automobile dealers, trucking companies, and bus lines.

Related Occupations

Repairing damaged motor vehicles often involves working on their mechanical components as well as their bodies. Automotive body repairers often work closely with several related occupations including automotive and diesel mechanics, automotive repair service estimators, painters, and body customizers.

Sources of Additional Information

More details about work opportunities may be obtained from automotive body repair shops and motor vehicle dealers; locals of the unions previously mentioned; or local offices of the State employment service. The State employment service also is a source of information about training programs.

For general information about automotive body repairer careers, write to:

☛ Automotive Service Association, Inc., 1901 Airport Freeway, Bedford, TX 76021-5732.

☛ Automotive Service Industry Association, 25 Northwest Point, Elk Grove Village, IL 60007-1035.

☛ National Automobile Dealers Association, 8400 Westpark Dr., McLean, VA 22102

For information on how to become a certified automotive body repairer, write to:

☛ ASE, 13505 Dulles Technology Dr., Herndon, VA 22071-3415.

For a directory of certified automotive body repairer programs, contact:

☛ National Automotive Technician Education Foundation, 13505 Dulles Technology Dr., Herndon, VA 22071.

For a directory of accredited private trade and technical schools that offer training programs in automotive body repair, write to:

☛ Accrediting Commission of Career Schools and Colleges of Technology, 2101 Wilson Blvd., Suite 302, Arlington, VA 22201.

For a list of public automotive mechanic training programs, contact:

☛ Vocational Industrial Clubs of America, P.O. Box 3000, 1401 James Monroe Hwy, Leesburg, VA 22075.

Automotive Mechanics

(D.O.T. 620.261-010, -012, -030, and -034; .281-010, -026, -034, -038, -062, -066, and -070; .381-010 and -022; .682; .684-018 and -022; 706.381-046; 806.361-026 and .684-038; 807.664and .684-022; 825.381-014)

Significant Points

● Automotive mechanics will be among the occupations with the most job openings.

● Oportunities are expected to be good for persons who complete formal automotive training programs.

● Knowledge of basic electronics is becoming essential for mechanics because computers are increasingly being used in components throughout the vehicle.

Nature of the Work

Automotive mechanics, often called automotive service technicians, inspect, maintain, or repair automobiles and light trucks with gasoline engines, such as vans and pickups. (Mechanics who work on diesel-powered trucks, buses, and equipment are discussed in the *Handbook* statement on diesel mechanics. Motorcycle mechanics—who repair and service motorcycles, motorscooters, mopeds, and occasionally small all-terrain vehicles—are discussed in the *Handbook* statement on motorcycle, boat, and small-engine mechanics.)

Anyone whose car or light truck has broken down knows the importance of the mechanic's job. The ability to diagnose the source of the problem quickly and accurately, one of the mechanic's most valuable skills, requires good reasoning ability and a thorough knowledge of automobiles. Many mechanics consider diagnosing "hard to find" troubles one of their most challenging and satisfying duties.

When mechanical or electrical troubles occur, mechanics first get a description of the symptoms from the owner or, if they work in a large shop, the repair service estimator who wrote the repair order. To locate the problem, the mechanic may have to test drive the vehicle or use a variety of testing equipment, such as on-board and hand-held diagnostic computers and compression gauges. Mechanics make adjustments or repairs once the cause of the problem is found. If a part is damaged, worn beyond repair, or not repairable at a reasonable cost, it is replaced, usually after consultation with the vehicle's owner.

During routine service, mechanics inspect and lubricate engines and other components. They also repair or replace parts before they cause breakdowns. Mechanics usually follow a checklist to ensure they examine all important parts. Belts, hoses, plugs, brake and fuel systems, and other potentially troublesome items are among those closely watched.

Mechanics use a variety of tools in their work. They use power tools such as pneumatic wrenches to remove bolts quickly, machine tools like lathes and grinding machines to rebuild brakes, welding and flame-cutting equipment to remove and repair exhaust systems, and jacks and hoists to lift cars and engines. They also use common handtools like screwdrivers, pliers, and wrenches to work on small parts and in hard-to-reach places.

In the most modern shops of automobile dealers, service technicians use electronic service equipment, such as infrared engine analyzers and computerized diagnostic devices. These devices diagnose problems and make precision adjustments with precise calculations downloaded from large databases. The computerized systems have the capacity to automatically update technical manuals and allow technicians unlimited access to manufacturers' service information, technical service bulletins, and other computerized information databases to keep current on trouble spots and new procedures

Automotive mechanics in larger shops have increasingly become specialized. For example, *automatic transmission mechanics* work on gear trains, couplings, hydraulic pumps, and other parts of automatic transmissions. Extensive training and experience in electronics is needed for the complex components and technology used in new vehicles. *Tune-up mechanics* adjust the ignition timing and valves, and adjust or replace spark plugs and other parts to ensure efficient engine performance. They often use electronic test equipment to locate and adjust malfunctions in fuel, ignition, and emissions control systems.

Automotive air-conditioning mechanics install and repair air conditioners and service components such as compressors, condensers, and controls. They require special training in Federal and State regulations governing the handling and disposal of refrigerants. *Front-end mechanics* align and balance wheels and repair steering mechanisms and suspension systems. They frequently use special alignment equipment and wheel-balancing machines. *Brake repairers* adjust brakes, replace brake linings and pads, and make other repairs on brake systems. Some mechanics specialize in both brake and front-end work.

Automotive-radiator mechanics clean radiators with caustic solutions, locate and solder leaks, and install new radiator cores or complete replacement radiators. They also may repair heaters and air-conditioners, and solder leaks in gasoline tanks.

Working Conditions

Most automotive mechanics work a standard 40-hour week, but many self-employed mechanics work longer hours. To satisfy customer service needs, many mechanics provide evening and weekend service. Generally, mechanics work indoors in well ventilated and lighted repair shops. However, some shops are drafty and noisy. Mechanics frequently work with dirty and greasy parts, and in awkward positions. They often lift heavy parts and tools. Minor cuts, burns, and bruises are common, but serious accidents are avoided when the shop is kept clean and orderly and safety practices are observed. Some problems can be fixed with simple computerized adjustments avoiding the need to get dirty.

Employment

Automotive mechanics held about 775,000 jobs in 1996. The majority worked for retail and wholesale automotive dealers and independent automotive repair shops, and gasoline service stations. Others found employment in automotive service facilities at department, automotive, and home supply stores. A small number maintained automobile fleets

One of an auto mechanic's most valuable skills is the ability to diagnose the source of a problem quickly and accurately.

for taxicab and automobile leasing companies; Federal, State, and local governments; and other organizations. Motor vehicle manufacturers employed some mechanics to test, adjust, and repair cars at the end of assembly lines. About 20 percent of automotive mechanics were self-employed.

Training, Other Qualifications, and Advancement

Automotive technology is rapidly increasing in sophistication and most training authorities strongly recommend that persons seeking automotive mechanic jobs complete a formal training program after graduating from high school. However, some automotive mechanics still learn the trade solely by assisting and working with experienced mechanics.

Many high schools, community colleges, and public and private vocational and technical schools offer automotive mechanic training programs. Post-secondary programs generally provide more thorough career preparation than high school programs. High school programs, while an asset, vary greatly in quality. Some high school programs offer only an introduction to automotive technology and service for the future consumer or hobbyist, while others aim to equip graduates with enough skills to get a job as a mechanic's helper or trainee mechanic after graduation.

Post-secondary automotive mechanic training programs vary greatly in format, but generally provide intensive career preparation through a combination of classroom instruction and hands-on practice. Some trade and technical school programs provide concentrated training for 6 months to a year, depending on how many hours the student must attend each week. Community college programs normally spread the training out over 2 years, supplement the automotive training with instruction in English, basic mathematics, computers, and other subjects, and award an associate degree or certificate.

The various automobile manufacturers and their participating dealers sponsor 2-year associate degree programs at 213 post-secondary schools across the Nation. The manufacturers provide ASE certified instruction, service equipment and current model cars on which students practice new skills, and learn the latest automotive technology. Curriculums are updated frequently to reflect changing technology and equipment. Students in these programs typically spend alternate 6- to 12-week periods attending classes full time and working full time in the service departments of sponsoring dealers.

While working in the dealerships, they are assigned an experienced mechanic to relate experiences and provide hands-on instruction. Also, some sponsoring dealers provide students with financial assistance for tuition or the purchase of tools.

The National Automotive Technicians Education Foundation (NATEF), an affiliate of the National Institute for Automotive Service Excellence (ASE), certifies automobile mechanic, collision specialist, and diesel and medium/heavy truck mechanic training programs offered by high schools, post-secondary trade schools, technical institutes, and community colleges. While NATEF certification is voluntary, certification does signify that the program meets uniform standards for instructional facilities, equipment, staff credentials, and curriculum. In early 1996, 1,245 high school and post-secondary automotive mechanic training programs had been certified by NATEF, of which 1,033 trained automobile service technicians, 174 collision specialists, and 38 diesel and medium/heavy truck specialists.

There are more computers aboard a car today than aboard the first spaceship. A new car today has from 10 to 15 on-board computers operating everything from the engine to the radio. As a result, knowledge of electronics has grown increasingly important for automotive mechanics. Engine controls and dashboard instruments were among the first components to use electronics, but now electronics are used in brakes, transmissions, steering systems, and a variety of other components. In the past, a specialist usually handled any problems involving electrical systems or electronics. But electronics are now commonplace, so all automotive mechanics must be familiar with at least the basic principles of electronics to recognize when an electronic malfunction may be responsible for a problem. In addition, automotive mechanics must be able to test and replace electronic components.

For trainee mechanic jobs, employers look for people with strong communication and analytical skills. Quality mathematics and computer skills are needed to study technical manuals to keep abreast of new technology. People who have a desire to learn new service and repair procedures and specifications are excellent candidates for trainee mechanic jobs. Trainees also must possess mechanical aptitude and knowledge of how automobiles work. Most employers regard the successful completion of a vocational training program in automotive mechanics at a postsecondary institution as the best preparation for trainee positions. Experience working on motor vehicles in the Armed Forces or as a hobby is also valuable. Because of the complexity of new vehicles, completion of high school is required by a growing number of employers. Courses in automotive repair, electronics, physics, chemistry, English, computers, and mathematics provide a good educational background for a career as an automotive mechanic.

Beginners usually start as trainee mechanics, helpers, lubrication workers, or gasoline service station attendants and gradually acquire and practice their skills by working with experienced mechanics. Beginners perform many routine service tasks and make simple repairs with a few months' experience. It usually takes 2 to 5 years of experience to acquire adequate proficiency to become a journey-level service mechanic and quickly perform the more difficult types of routine service and repairs. However, graduates of the better postsecondary mechanic training programs are often able to earn promotion to the journey level after only a few months on the job. An additional 1 to 2 years experience familiarizes the mechanic with all types of repairs. Difficult specialties, such as transmission repair, require another year or two of training and experience. In contrast, automotive radiator mechanics and brake specialists, who do not need an all-round knowledge of automotive repair, may learn their jobs in considerably less time.

In the past, many persons have become automotive mechanics through 3- or 4-year formal apprenticeship programs. However, more employers now look for persons who have completed formal automotive training programs to reduce the amount of time invested in training a prospective mechanic.

The most important possessions of mechanics are their handtools. Mechanics usually provide their own tools and many experienced mechanics have thousands of dollars invested in them. Employers typically furnish expensive power tools, engine analyzers, and other diagnostic equipment, but handtools are accumulated with experience.

Employers increasingly send experienced automotive mechanics to manufacturer training centers to learn to repair new models or to receive special training in the repair of components such as electronic fuel injection or air-conditioners. Motor vehicle dealers may also send promising beginners to manufacturer sponsored mechanic training programs. Factory representatives come to many shops to conduct short training sessions. This additional training is typically furnished by the employer to maintain or upgrade employee skills and increase their value to the dealership.

The standard achievement for automotive mechanics is voluntary certification by Automotive Service Excellence (ASE). Certification in one or more of eight different service areas, such as electrical systems, engine repair, brake systems, suspension and steering, and heating and air conditioning is awarded to mechanics. To be certified as a master automotive mechanic, mechanics must be certified in all eight areas. For certification in each area, mechanics must have at least 2 years of experience and pass a written examination. Completion of an automotive mechanic program in high school, vocational or trade school, or community or junior college may be substituted for 1 year of experience. Mechanics must retake the examination at least every 5 years to maintain their certification.

Experienced mechanics who have leadership ability may advance to shop supervisor or service manager. Mechanics who work well with customers may become automotive repair service estimators. Some with sufficient funds open independent repair shops.

Job Outlook

Job opportunities in this occupation are expected to be good for persons who complete automotive training programs in high school, vocational and technical schools, or community colleges. Persons whose training includes basic electronics skills should have the best opportunities. Persons without formal mechanic training are likely to face competition for entry level jobs. Mechanic careers are attractive to many because they afford the opportunity for good pay and the satisfaction of highly skilled work with one's hands.

Employment opportunities for automotive mechanics are expected to increase about as fast as the average for all occupations through the year 2006. Employment growth will continue to be concentrated in automobile dealerships, independent automotive repair shops, and specialty car care chains. Employment of automotive mechanics in gasoline service stations will continue to decline as fewer stations offer repair services.

The number of mechanics will increase because expansion of the driving age population will increase the number of motor vehicles on the road. The growing complexity of automotive technology necessitates that cars be serviced by skilled workers, contributing to the growth in demand for highly trained mechanics. With more young people entering the job market not interested in mechanic and repairer careers, automotive mechanics presents an excellent opportunity for bright, motivated people who have a technical background and desire to make a good living.

More job openings for automotive mechanics are expected than for most other occupations as experienced workers transfer to related occupations, retire, or stop working for other reasons. This large occupation needs a substantial number of entrants each year to replace the many mechanics who leave the occupation.

Most persons who enter the occupation can expect steady work because changes in economic conditions have little effect on the automotive repair business. During a downturn, however, some employers may be more reluctant to hire inexperienced workers.

Earnings

Median weekly earnings of automotive mechanics who were wage and salary workers were $478 in 1996. The middle 50 percent earned between $333 and $667 a week. The lowest paid 10 percent earned less than $250 a week, and the top 10 percent earned more than $850 a week.

Many experienced mechanics employed by automotive dealers and independent repair shops receive a commission related to the labor cost charged to the customer. Under this method, weekly earnings depend on the amount of work completed by the mechanic. Employers frequently guarantee commissioned mechanics a minimum weekly salary. Many master mechanics earn from $70,000 to $100,000 annually.

Some mechanics are members of labor unions. The unions include the International Association of Machinists and Aerospace Workers; the International Union, United Automobile, Aerospace and Agricultural Implement Workers of America; the Sheet Metal Workers' International Association; and the International Brotherhood of Teamsters.

Related Occupations

Other workers who repair and service motor vehicles include diesel truck and bus mechanics, motorcycle mechanics, and automotive body repairers, painters, customizers, and repair service estimators.

Sources of Additional Information

For more details about work opportunities, contact local automotive dealers and repair shops, or the local office of the State employment service. The State employment service also may have information about training programs.

A list of certified automotive mechanic training programs may be obtained from:
☛ National Automotive Technicians Education Foundation, 13505 Dulles Technology Dr., Herndon, VA 22071-3415.

Information on automobile manufacturer sponsored 2-year associate degree programs in automotive service technology may be obtained from:
☛ Ford ASSET Program, Ford Customer Service Division, Fairlane Business Park III, 1555 Fairlane Dr., Allen Park, MI 48101 or by calling (800) 272-7218.
☛ Chrysler Dealer Apprenticeship Program, National C.A.P. Coordinator, CIMS 423-21-06, 26001 Lawrence Ave., Center Line, MI 48015, or by calling (800) 626-1523.
☛ General Motors Automotive Service Educational Program, National College Coordinator, General Motors Service Technology Group, MC 480-204-001, 30501 Van Dyke Ave., Warren, MI 48090, or by calling (800) 828-6860.

Information on how to become a certified automotive mechanic is available from:
☛ ASE, 13505 Dulles Technology Dr., Herndon, VA 22071-3415.

For general information about the work of automotive mechanics, write:
☛ Automotive Service Association, Inc., 1901 Airport Freeway, Bedford, TX 76021-5732.
☛ Automotive Service Industry Association, 25 Northwest Point, Elk Grove Village, IL 60007-1035.
☛ National Automobile Dealers Association, 8400 Westpark Dr., McLean, VA 22102

For a directory of accredited private trade and technical schools that offer programs in automotive technician training, write:
☛ Accrediting Commission of Career Schools and Colleges of Technology, 2101 Wilson Blvd., Suite 302, Arlington, VA 22201.

For a list of public automotive mechanic training programs, contact:
☛ Vocational Industrial Clubs of America, P.O. Box 3000, 1401 James Monroe Hwy, Leesburg, VA 22075.

Diesel Mechanics

(D.O.T. 620.281-046, -050, and -058; 625.281-010, -014, -022, and 625.361 -010)

Significant Points

- Careers in diesel mechanics offer relatively high wages and the challenge of skilled repair work.

- Opportunities are expected to be good for persons who complete formal diesel mechanic training programs.

Nature of the Work

The diesel engine is the workhorse powering the Nation's heavy vehicles and equipment, because it delivers more power per unit of fuel, and is more durable, than its gasoline-burning counterpart.

Diesel mechanics, often referred to as diesel technicians, repair and maintain the diesel engines that power transportation equipment, such as heavy trucks, buses, and locomotives. Some mechanics also work on bulldozers, cranes, road graders, and farm tractors and combines, and a small number repair automobiles or boats. (For information on mechanics who work primarily on automobiles or boats, see the *Handbook* statements on automotive mechanics or motorcycle, boat, and small-engine mechanics.) Diesel mechanics also service a variety of diesel-powered electric generators, compressors, and pumps used in oil well drilling and irrigation systems.

Mechanics who work for organizations that maintain their own vehicles spend most of their time doing preventive maintenance to ensure that equipment can be operated safely and to eliminate unnecessary wear and damage to parts that could result in costly breakdowns. During a routine maintenance check on a truck, a diesel mechanic follows a checklist that includes the inspection of brake systems, steering mechanisms, wheel bearings, and other important parts. Following an inspection, a mechanic usually repairs or adjust parts that do not work properly and replaces parts that cannot be fixed.

In many mechanic shops, it is common for workers to do all kinds of repairs. Jobs can vary from working on a vehicle's electrical system one day to doing major engine repairs the next. In some large shops, mechanics specialize in one or two types of work. For example, a shop may have mechanics who specialize in major engine repair, transmission work, electrical systems, or suspension or brake systems. Diesel maintenance is becoming more complex, as electronic components increasingly are used to control engine operation. In modern shops, diesel mechanics use handheld computers to diagnose problems and adjust engine functions.

Diesel mechanics use a variety of tools in their work, including power tools, such as pneumatic wrenches to remove bolts quickly; machine tools, like lathes and grinding machines, to rebuild brakes; welding and flame-cutting equipment to remove and repair exhaust systems; and jacks and hoists to lift and move large parts. Common handtools—screwdrivers, pliers, and wrenches—are used to work on small parts and get at hard-to-reach places. Diesel mechanics also use a variety of computerized testing equipment to pinpoint and analyze malfunctions in electrical systems and engines.

Mechanics generally receive their assignments from shop supervisors or service managers. Most supervisors and managers are experienced mechanics who also assist in diagnosing problems and maintaining quality standards. Mechanics may work as a team or be assisted by an apprentice or helper, when doing heavy work like removing engines and transmissions.

Working Conditions

Diesel mechanics usually work indoors, although they occasionally make repairs to vehicles on the road. Mechanics lift heavy parts and tools; and minor cuts, burns, and bruises are common, although serious accidents can usually be avoided, if the shop is kept clean and orderly, and safety practices are observed. Mechanics handle greasy and dirty parts and may stand or lie in awkward positions to repair vehicles and equipment. They usually work in well lighted, heated, and ventilated areas, however, some shops are drafty and noisy. Many employers provide locker rooms and shower facilities.

Employment

Diesel mechanics held about 266,000 jobs in 1996. Nearly 25 percent serviced trucks and other diesel-powered equipment for customers of vehicle and equipment dealers, leasing companies, or independent automotive repair shops. Over 20 percent worked for local and long-distance trucking companies, and nearly 10 percent maintained the buses and trucks of buslines, public transit companies, school systems, or Federal, State, and local government. The remaining mechanics maintained the fleets of trucks and other equip-

Diesel mechanics handle greasy and dirty parts and may work in awkward positions to repair vehicles and equipment.

ment for manufacturing, construction, or other companies. A relatively small number were self-employed. Nearly every section of the country employs diesel mechanics, though most work in towns and cities where trucking companies, bus lines, and other fleet owners have large operations.

Training, Other Qualifications, and Advancement

Although many persons qualify for diesel mechanic jobs through years of on-the-job training, authorities recommend completion of a formal diesel mechanic training program after graduating from high school. Employers prefer to hire graduates of formal training programs, because of these workers' head start in training and their ability to quickly advance to the journey mechanic level. Many community colleges and trade and vocational schools offer programs in diesel repair. These 1- to 2-year programs lead to a certificate of completion or an associate degree. This training provides a foundation in the latest diesel technology and electronics and instruction in the service and repair of the vehicles and equipment mechanics will encounter on the job. These programs also improve the communication skills needed to interpret technical manuals and communicate with colleagues and customers. Increasingly, employers work closely with training programs, providing instructors with the latest equipment, techniques, and tools, and offer jobs to graduates.

There is a shortage of diesel mechanics who have completed formal training programs. As a result many continue to learn skills on the job. Unskilled beginners usually do tasks, such as cleaning parts, fueling and lubricating vehicles, and driving vehicles in to and out of the shop. Beginners are usually promoted to mechanics' helpers, as they gain experience and as vacancies become available. In some shops, beginners who have automobile service experience start as mechanics' helpers.

Most mechanics' helpers perform routine service tasks and make minor repairs after a few months' experience. These workers advance to increasingly difficult jobs, as they prove their ability and competence. After mechanics master the repair and service of diesel engines, they learn to work on related components, such as brakes, transmissions, and electrical systems. Generally, a mechanic with at least 3 to 4 years of on-the-job experience will qualify as a journeyman diesel truck or bus mechanic. Completion of a formal training program speeds advancement to the journeyman level.

For unskilled entry level jobs, employers generally look for applicants who have mechanical aptitude and strong problem solving skills, and who are at least 18 years of age and in good physical condition. Completion of high school is required by nearly all employers. Courses in automotive repair, electronics, English, mathematics, and physics provide a strong educational background for a career as a diesel mechanic. A State commercial driver's license is needed for test driving trucks or buses on public roads. Practical experience in automobile repair in a gasoline service station, in the Armed Forces, or as a hobby is also valuable.

Employers often send experienced mechanics to special training classes conducted by manufacturers and vendors where the mechanics learn the latest technology and repair techniques. As mechanics constantly receive updated technical manuals and service procedures that outline changes in techniques and standards for repair, it is essential for them to read, interpret, and comprehend service manuals, to keep abreast of engineering changes.

Voluntary certification by the National Institute for Automotive Service Excellence (ASE) is recognized as the standard of achievement for diesel mechanics. Mechanics may be certified as Master Heavy-Duty Truck technicians or in one or more of six different areas of heavy-duty truck repair: Brakes, gasoline engines, diesel engines, drive trains, electrical systems, and suspension and steering. For certification in each area, a mechanic must pass a written examination and have at least 2 years of experience. High school, vocational or trade school, or community or junior college training in gasoline or diesel engine repair may substitute for up to 1 year of experience. To retain certification, mechanics must retake the tests at least every 5 years.

The most important work possessions of mechanics are their handtools. Mechanics usually provide their own tools, and many experienced mechanics have thousands of dollars invested in them. Employers typically furnish expensive power tools, computerized engine analyzers, and other diagnostic equipment, but handtools are ordinarily accumulated with experience.

Experienced mechanics who have leadership ability may advance to shop supervisors or service managers. Mechanics who have sales ability sometimes become sales representatives. A few mechanics open their own repair shops.

Job Outlook

Employment of diesel mechanics is expected to increase slower than average for all occupations through the year 2006. Opportunities will exist for entrants to replace the mechanics who retire or transfer to other occupations.

Employment of diesel mechanics is expected to grow, as freight transportation by truck increases. More trucks will be needed for both local and intercity hauling, due to increased production of goods. Additional diesel mechanics will be needed to repair and maintain growing numbers of buses and heavy construction graders, cranes, earthmovers, and other equipment. Due to the greater durability and economy of the diesel relative to the gasoline engine, it is expected that buses and trucks of all sizes will be increasingly powered by diesels. This will subsequently create new jobs for diesel mechanics.

Careers in diesel mechanics attract many because of the relatively high wages and the challenge of skilled repair work. Opportunities should be good for persons who complete formal training in diesel mechanics at community and junior colleges and vocational and technical schools, but others may face competition for entry-level jobs.

Most persons who enter this occupation can expect steady work, because changes in economic conditions have little effect on the diesel repair business. During a financial downturn, however, some employers may be reluctant to hire inexperienced workers.

Earnings

Median weekly earnings of diesel mechanics who were wage and salary workers were $545 in 1996. The middle 50 percent earned between $405 and $685 a week. The lowest paid 10 percent earned less than $297 a week, and the top 10 percent earned more than $816 a week. Earnings may vary by industry and geographic location.

Beginners usually earn from 50 to 75 percent of the rate of skilled workers and receive increases as they become more skilled, until they reach the rate of skilled mechanics.

The majority of mechanics work a standard 40-hour week, although many work as many as 70 hours per week, particularly if they are self employed. A growing number of shops have expanded their hours to better perform repairs and routine service when needed, or as a convenience to customers. Those employed by truck and bus firms that provide service around the clock may work evenings, nights, and weekends. These mechanics usually receive a higher rate of pay for working non-traditional hours.

Many diesel mechanics are members of labor unions, including the International Association of Machinists and Aerospace Workers; the Amalgamated Transit Union; the International Union, United Automobile, Aerospace and Agricultural Implement Workers of America; the Transport Workers Union of America; the Sheet Metal Workers' International Association; and the International Brotherhood of Teamsters.

Related Occupations

Diesel mechanics repair trucks, buses, and other diesel-powered equipment to keep these mechanics in good working order. Related mechanic occupations include aircraft mechanics, automotive mechanics, boat engine mechanics, farm equipment mechanics, mobile heavy equipment mechanics, and motorcycle mechanics and small-engine specialists.

Sources of Additional Information

More details about work opportunities for diesel mechanics may be obtained from local employers such as trucking companies, truck dealers, or bus lines; locals of the unions previously mentioned; and local offices of the State employment service. Local State employment service offices also may have information about training programs.

For general information about a career as a diesel mechanic, write:

☞ Automotive Service Industry Association, 25 Northwest Point, Elk Grove Village, IL 60007-1035.

☞ American Trucking Associations, Inc., Maintenance Council, 2200 Mill Rd., Alexandria, VA 22314-4677.

☞ Kenworth Truck Company, Service Coordinator, 700 East Gate Dr., Suite 325, Mt. Laurel, N. J 08054.

☞ Detroit Diesel, Personnel Director, MS B39, 13400 West Outer Dr., Detroit, MI 48239.

For a directory of accredited private trade and technical schools with training programs for diesel mechanics, contact:

☞ Accrediting Commission of Career Schools and Colleges of Technology, 2101 Wilson Blvd., Suite 302, Arlington, VA 22201.

☞ National Automotive Technicians Education Foundation, 13505 Dulles Technology Dr., Herndon, VA 22071-3415.

For a directory of public training programs for diesel mechanics, contact:

☞ Vocational Industry Clubs of America, P. O. Box 3000, 1401 James Monroe Hwy, Leesburg, VA 22075.

Information on how to become a certified heavy-duty diesel mechanic is available from:

☞ ASE, 13505 Dulles Technology Dr., Herndon, VA 22071-3415.

Electronic Equipment Repairers

Significant Points

- Most employers prefer to hire persons who have completed 1- or 2-year formal training programs in electronics.

- Although overall employment of electronic equipment repairers is projected to increase slowly, employment of computer and office machine repairers should increase rapidly while electronic home entertainment equipment repairer and telephone installer and repairer jobs should decline.

Nature of the Work
Electronic equipment repairers, also called service technicians or field service representatives, install, maintain, and repair electronic equipment used in offices, factories, homes, hospitals, aircraft, and other places. Equipment includes televisions, radar, industrial equipment controls, computers, telephone systems, and medical diagnosing equipment. Repairers have numerous job titles, which often refer to the kind of equipment with which they work. (Electronics technicians, who use the principles and theories of science, engineering, and mathematics in their work, but may also do some repairs, are discussed in the statement on engineering technicians elsewhere in the *Handbook*. For information on workers who operate and maintain electronic equipment used to record and transmit radio and television programs, see the statement on broadcast technicians. Additional information about electronic equipment repairers is given in the separate statements in this section.)

Electronic repairers install, test, repair, and calibrate equipment to ensure it functions properly. They keep detailed records on each piece of equipment to provide a history of tests, performance problems, and repairs.

When equipment breaks down, repairers first examine work orders, which indicate problems, or talk to equipment operators. Then they check for common causes of trouble, such as loose connections or obviously defective components. If routine checks do not locate the trouble, repairers may refer to schematics and manufacturers' specifications that show connections and provide instruction on how to locate problems. They use voltmeters, ohmmeters, signal generators, ammeters, and oscilloscopes, and run diagnostic programs to pinpoint malfunctions. It may take several hours to locate a problem, but only a few minutes to fix it. However, more equipment now has self-diagnosing features, which greatly simplifies the work. To fix equipment, repairers may replace defective components, circuit boards, or wiring, or adjust and calibrate equipment, using test equipment, small handtools such as pliers, screwdrivers, and soldering irons.

Field repairers visit worksites in their assigned area on a regular basis to do preventive maintenance according to manufacturers' recommended schedules and whenever emergencies arise. During these calls, repairers may also advise customers on how to use equipment more efficiently and how to spot problems in their early stages. They also listen to customers' complaints and answer questions, promoting customer satisfaction and good will. Some field repairers work full time with a lot of equipment at the clients' establishment.

Bench repairers work at repair facilities, in stores, factories, or service centers. They repair portable equipment—such as televisions and personal computers brought in by customers—or defective components and machines requiring extensive repairs that have been sent in by field repairers. They determine the source of a problem in the equipment, and may estimate whether it is wiser to buy a new part or machine, or to fix the broken one.

Working Conditions
Some electronic equipment repairers work shifts, including weekends and holidays, to service equipment in computer centers, manufacturing plants, hospitals, and telephone companies operating round the clock. Shifts are generally assigned on the basis of seniority. Repairers may also be on call at any time to handle equipment failure.

Repairers generally work in clean, well-lighted, air-conditioned surroundings—an electronic repair shop or service center, hospital, military installation, or a telephone company's central office. However, some, such as commercial and industrial electronic equipment repairers, may be exposed to heat, grease, and noise on factory floors. Some may occasionally have to work in cramped spaces. Telephone installers and repairers may work on rooftops, ladders, and telephone poles.

The work of most repairers involves lifting, reaching, stooping, crouching, and crawling. Adherence to safety precautions is essential to guard against work hazards such as minor burns and electrical shock.

Employment
Electronic equipment repairers held about 396,000 jobs in 1996. Many worked for telephone companies. Others worked for electronic and transportation equipment manufacturers, machinery and equipment wholesalers, hospitals, electronic repair shops, and firms that provide maintenance under contract (called third-party maintenance firms). The distribution of employment by occupation was as follows:

Computer and office machine repairers	141,000
Communications equipment mechanics	116,000
Commercial and industrial electronic equipment repairers	60,000
Telephone installers and repairers	37,000
Electronic home entertainment equipment repairers	33,000

Training, Other Qualifications, and Advancement
Most employers prefer applicants with formal training in electronics. Electronic training is offered by public post secondary vocational-technical schools, private vocational schools and technical institutes, junior and community colleges, and some high schools and correspondence schools. Programs take 1 to 2 years. The military services also offer formal training and work experience.

Training includes general courses in mathematics, physics, electricity, electronics, schematic reading, and troubleshooting. Students also choose courses which prepare them for a specialty, such as computers, commercial and industrial equipment, or home entertainment equipment. A few repairers complete formal apprenticeship programs sponsored jointly by employers and local chapters of the International Brotherhood of Electrical Workers.

Applicants for entry-level jobs may have to pass tests measuring mechanical aptitude, knowledge of electricity or electronics, manual dexterity, and general intelligence. Newly hired repairers, even those with formal training, usually receive some training from their employer. They may study electronics and circuit theory and math. They also get hands-on experience with equipment, doing basic maintenance and using diagnostic programs to locate malfunctions. Training may be in a classroom or it may be self-instruction, consisting of videotapes, programmed computer software, or workbooks that allow trainees to learn at their own pace.

Experienced technicians attend training sessions and read manuals to keep up with design changes and revised service procedures. Many technicians also take advanced training in a particular system or type of repair.

Good eyesight and color vision are needed to inspect and work on small, delicate parts and good hearing to detect malfunctions revealed by sound. Because field repairers usually handle jobs alone, they must be able to work without close supervision. For those who have frequent contact with customers, a pleasant personality, neat appearance, and good communications skills are important. Repairers must also be trustworthy, because they may be exposed to money and other valuables in places such as banks and securities offices, and some employers require that they be bonded. A security clearance may be required for technicians who repair equipment or service machines in areas in which people are engaged in activities related to national security.

The International Society of Certified Electronics Technicians and the Electronics Technicians Association each administer a voluntary certification program. In both, an electronics repairer with 4 years of experience may become a Certified Electronics Technician. Certification, which is by examination, is offered in computer, radio-TV, industrial and commercial equipment, audio, avionics, wireless communications, video distribution, satellite, and radar systems repair. An Associate Level Test, covering basic electronics, is offered for students or repairers with less than 4 years of experience. An A+

certification is now desired for computer technicians. This certification is awarded by the Computing Technology Industry Association (CompTIA) and requires knowledge of specific products manufactured by the vendor. The Telecommunications Act of 1996 eliminated the requirement of an FCC license for those who repair radio transmitting equipment.

Experienced repairers with advanced training may become specialists or troubleshooters who help other repairers diagnose difficult problems, or work with engineers in designing equipment and developing maintenance procedures.

Because of their familiarity with equipment, repairers are particularly well qualified to become manufacturers' sales workers. Workers with leadership ability also may become maintenance supervisors or service managers. Some experienced workers open their own repair services or shops, or become wholesalers or retailers of electronic equipment.

Job Outlook

Overall, employment of electronic equipment repairers is expected to grow slower than the average for all occupations through the year 2006. Although the amount of electronic equipment in use will grow very rapidly, improvements in product reliability and ease of service and lower equipment prices will dampen the need for repairers. The following tabulation presents the expected job change, in percent, for the various electronic equipment repairer occupations:

Computer and office machine repairers	37
Commercial and industrial electronic equipment repairers	12
Communications equipment mechanics	4
Electronic home entertainment equipment repairers	-19
Telephone installers and repairers	-74

Employment of computer equipment repairers will grow much the than average for all occupations through the year 2006 as the number of computers in service increases rapidly. Employment of commercial and industrial equipment repairers outside the Federal Government will increase faster than the average as the amount of equipment grows. Mainly because of cuts in the defense budget, their employment in the Federal Government will decline. Employment of those who repair electronic home entertainment equipment will decline as equipment becomes more reliable and easier to service. Telephone installer jobs are expected to decline sharply, and communication equipment mechanics are expected to grow slower than the average because of improvements in the telephone equipment reliability, ease of maintenance, and low equipment replacement cost.

Earnings

In 1996, median weekly earnings of full-time electronic equipment repairers were $619. The middle 50 percent earned between $444 and $802. The bottom 10 percent earned less than $329, while the top 10 percent earned more than $979. Median weekly earnings varied widely by occupation and the type of equipment repaired, as follows:

Telephone installers and repairers	$717
Electronic repairers, communications and industrial equipment	602
Office machine repairers	582
Data processing equipment repairers	573

Central office installers, central office technicians, PBX installers, and telephone installers and repairers employed by AT&T and the Bell Operating Companies and represented by the Communications Workers of America and the International Brotherhood of Electrical Workers, earned between $279 and $962 a week in 1996.

According to a survey of workplaces in 160 metropolitan areas, beginning maintenance electronics technicians had median earnings of $11.50 an hour in 1995, with the middle half earning between $10.50 and $13.25 an hour. The most experienced repairers had median earnings of $20.13 an hour, with the middle half earning between $18.24 and $22.12 an hour.

Related Occupations

Workers in other occupations who repair and maintain the circuits and mechanical parts of electronic equipment include appliance and powertool repairers, automotive electricians, broadcast technicians, electronic organ technicians, and vending machine repairers. Electronics engineering technicians may also repair electronic equipment as part of their duties.

Sources of Additional Information

For career, and certification information, contact:
☛ The International Society of Certified Electronics Technicians, 2708 West Berry St., Fort Worth, TX 76109.

For certification, career, and placement information, contact:
☛ Electronics Technicians Association, 602 North Jackson, Greencastle, IN 46135.

For information on the telephone industry and career opportunities contact:
☛ United States Telephone Association, 1401 H St. NW., Suite 600, Washington, DC 20005-2136.
☛ International Brotherhood of Electrical Workers, Telecommunications Department, 1125 15th. St. NW, Room 807, Washington, DC 20005.

For information on electronic equipment repairers in the telephone industry, write to:
☛ Communications Workers of America, Department of Apprenticeships, Benefits, and Employment, 501 3rd St. NW., Washington, DC 20001.

Commercial and Industrial Electronic Equipment Repairers

(D.O.T. 726.361-022, .381-014, .684-090; 828.251-010, .261-014, -022, -026, and .281-022)

Nature of the Work

Commercial and industrial electronic equipment repairers, also called industrial electronics technicians, install and repair industrial controls, radar and missile control systems, medical diagnostic equipment, and communications equipment.

Those who work for the Defense Department install radar, missile control, and communication systems on aircraft, ships, and tanks, and in buildings and other structures. Some set up and service electronic equipment which controls machines and production processes in factories. They often coordinate their efforts with workers installing mechanical or electromechanical components. (See the statements on industrial machinery repairers and millwrights elsewhere in the *Handbook.*)

Employment

Commercial and industrial electronic equipment repairers held about 60,000 jobs in 1996. About 1 out of 4 repairers was employed by the Federal Government, almost all in the Department of Defense at military installations around the country. Repairers were also employed by electronic and transportation equipment manufacturers, machinery and equipment wholesalers, telephone companies, hospitals, electronic repair shops, and firms that provide maintenance under contract (called third-party maintenance firms).

Job Outlook

Overall employment of commercial and industrial electronic equipment repairers is expected to increase about as fast as the average for all occupations through the year 2006. Job prospects in private industry, however, should differ significantly from those within the Federal Government. Opportunities for employment outside of the Federal Government are expected to be good. Employment in nongovernment industries is expected to grow faster than the average for all occupations, as business and industrial firms install more electronic equipment to boost productivity and improve product

Job opportunities are expected to be good for commercial and industrial electronic equipment repairers outside the Federal Government.

quality. In addition, more electronic equipment will be used in energy conservation and pollution control. Because of cuts in the defense budget, however, employment in the Federal Government is expected to decline significantly.

(See the introductory part of this section for information on working conditions, training requirements, earnings, and sources of additional information.)

Communications Equipment Mechanics

(D.O.T. 722.281; 726.381-014; 822.261-010, .281-010, -014, -022, -026, -030 and -034, .361-014, .381-010, -018, -022, and .684-010; 823.261-010, -018, -022, and -030, .281-014, and -022; 825.261-010; and 829.281-022)

Nature of the Work

Installing, repairing, and maintaining complex and sophisticated telephone communications equipment are the responsibilities of communications equipment mechanics. Most communications equipment mechanics—sometimes referred to as telecommunication technicians—work either in telephone company central offices or on customers' premises installing and repairing telephone switching and transmission systems.

Central office equipment installers, or equipment installation technicians, set up, rearrange, and remove the switching and dialing equipment used in central offices. They install equipment in new central offices, add equipment in expanding offices, or replace outdated equipment. *Central office repairers*, often referred to as central office technicians or switching equipment technicians, test, repair, and maintain all types of local and toll switching equipment that automatically connects lines when customers dial numbers. When customers report trouble with their telephones, *maintenance administrators* find the source of the problem. Their jobs are largely automated; they enter instructions into a computer terminal and analyze the output. Maintenance administrators also update and maintain computerized files of trouble status reports. *Trouble locators* who work for cable television companies ensure that subscribers' television sets receive the proper signal. They may work with cable installers to track down the cause of the interference and make repairs.

PBX installers, also called systems technicians, install complex telephone equipment, often creating customized switching systems.

PBX repairers, with the assistance of maintenance administrators, locate the malfunction in customers' PBX or other telephone systems and make the necessary repairs. They also maintain associated equipment such as batteries, relays, and power supplies. Some PBX repairers maintain and repair equipment for mobile radiophones, microwave transmission equipment, switching equipment, and data processing equipment.

An increasing number of communications equipment repairers in the telephone industry are being trained to perform multiple tasks, ranging from splicing fiber optic cable, to programming switches, to installing telephones. As a result, the specific titles used above are becoming less common.

Radio repairers and mechanics install and repair stationary and mobile radio transmitting and receiving equipment. Some repair microwave and fiber optics installations. *Office electricians* handle submarine cable repeater and terminal circuits and related equipment. When trouble arises, they may rearrange cable connections to ensure that service is not interrupted. *Submarine cable equipment technicians* repair, adjust, and maintain the machines and equipment used in submarine cable offices or stations to control cable traffic.

Other communications equipment mechanics include *instrument repairers*, sometimes referred to as shop repairers or shop technicians, who repair, test, and modify a variety of communications equipment. *Data communications technicians* install and repair data communications lines and equipment for computer systems. They connect microcomputers or terminals to data communication lines.

Most communications equipment mechanics work for telephone companies.

Employment

Communications equipment mechanics held about 116,000 jobs in 1996. Most worked for telephone companies. Others worked for electrical repair shops, cable television firms, railroads, air transportation, and the Federal Government.

Job Outlook

Employment of communications equipment mechanics is expected to grow more slowly than the average through the year 2006 as communications equipment in use increases with population growth, but requires less frequent service. The telephone industry has almost completed a dramatic transformation from an electromechanical system to a completely electronic one. Digital systems, the most recent version of electronic switching, use computers and software to switch calls. Fewer workers are needed for maintenance and repair because the new systems are more reliable and compact, and permit more efficient, centralized maintenance. In addition, the systems have self-diagnosing features which detect the source of problems and direct repairers to the defective part, which usually can simply be replaced. Once the transformation of the system has been completed, some time before 2006, the need for installers will drop.

Decreased labor requirements due to improved technology have already caused some layoffs of communications equipment mechanics. Efficiencies resulting from consolidations and mergers of cable and telephone companies and pressure to reduce costs in the competitive environment following additional deregulation of the industry could cause further decreases in employment. Competition for available openings should intensify, making it much more difficult for other telephone workers to move into these positions without experience or formal training, and virtually impossible for "outsiders" without the necessary skills to compete for jobs.

(See introductory part of this section for information on working conditions, training requirements, earnings, and sources of additional information.)

Computer and Office Machine Repairers

(D.O.T. 633.261-014, .281; 706.381-010 and -030)

Nature of the Work

Computer and office machine repairers install equipment, do preventive maintenance, and correct problems. Computer repairers work on computers (mainframes, minis, and micros), peripheral equipment, and word processing systems, while office machine repairers work on photocopiers, cash registers, mail processing equipment, fax machines, and typewriters. Some repairers service both computer and office equipment. They also make cable and wiring connections when installing equipment, and work closely with electricians who install the wiring. (A description of the work of electricians can be found elsewhere in the *Handbook.*)

Even with preventive maintenance, computers and other machines break down. Repairers run diagnostic programs to locate malfunctions. Although some of the most modern and sophisticated computers have a self-diagnosing capacity that identifies problems, computer repairers must know enough about systems software to determine if the malfunction is in the hardware or in the software.

Employment

Computer and office machine repairers held about 141,000 jobs in 1996. Approximately 80,000 worked mainly on computer equipment, and the other 61,000 repaired mainly office machines. About 3 of every 5 were employed by wholesalers of computers and other office equipment, including the wholesaling divisions of equipment manufacturers, and by firms that provide maintenance services for a fee. Others worked for retail establishments and some with organizations that serviced their own equipment.

Employment of computer and office machine repairers is expected to grow much faster than average.

Repairers work throughout the country, even in relatively small communities. Most repairers, however, work in large cities, where computer and office equipment is concentrated.

Job Outlook

Employment of computer and office machine repairers is expected to grow much faster than the average for all occupations through the year 2006. However, employment of repairers will grow less rapidly than the anticipated increase in the amount of equipment because of the improved reliability of computer and office machines and ease of repair. Applicants for computer repairer positions will have the most favorable job prospects.

Employment of those who repair computers is expected to grow much faster than the average for all occupations. Demand for computer repairers will increase as the amount of computer equipment increases—organizations throughout the economy should continue to automate in search of greater productivity and improved service. The development of new computer applications and lower computer prices will also spur demand. More repairers will be needed to install new equipment coming on the market and upgrade existing systems.

Employment of those who repair office machines is expected to grow about as fast the average for all occupations. Slower growth in the amount of non-computer-based office equipment will somewhat dampen the demand for these repairers.

(See introductory part of this section for information on working conditions, training requirements, earnings, and sources of additional information.)

Electronic Home Entertainment Equipment Repairers

(D.O.T. 720.281, 729.281-010, 730.281-018, 823.361-010, and 828.261-010)

Nature of the Work

Electronic home entertainment equipment repairers, also called service technicians, repair audio systems, televisions, , disc players, recorders, public address systems, video cameras, video games, home security systems, microwave ovens, and electronic organs. Some repairers specialize in one kind of equipment; others repair many types.

They replace faulty parts or make adjustments, such as focusing and converging the picture of a television set, or setting up the balance of a surround sound audio system. They may also make recordings of test patterns to detect problems in an 8mm video camera. Some install and repair automobile sound systems.

Employment

Electronic home entertainment equipment repairers held about 33,000 jobs in 1996. Most repairers work in electronic repair shops and service centers, or in stores that sell and service electronic home entertainment products. Employment is distributed in much the same way as the population. About 1 out of 7 electronic home entertainment equipment repairers was self employed.

Job Outlook

Employment of electronic home entertainment equipment repairers is expected to decline through the year 2006. Improvements in reliability and ease of servicing should reduce service requirements even though the amount of equipment in use is expected to increase. Also, some of the home entertainment equipment is cheap enough to replace rather than repair. Nevertheless, opportunities should be good, due to the need to replace the many electronic home entertainment equipment repairers who transfer to higher paying occupations requiring a knowledge of electronics, such as computer and office machine repairer. (See introductory part of this section for information on working conditions, training requirements, earnings, and sources of additional information.)

About 1 out of 7 electronic home entertainment equipment repairers is self-employed.

Telephone Installers and Repairers

(D.O.T. 822.261-022 and .281-018)

Nature of the Work

Telephone installers and repairers install, service, and repair telephones and other telecommunications systems on customers' property. When customers move or request new types of service, installers relocate telephones or make changes to existing equipment. In buildings under construction, they install wiring and telephone jacks.

Telephone installers—sometimes called station installers, service technicians, or customer system engineers—assemble equipment and install wiring and switches on the customers' premises. They connect telephones to outside service wires and sometimes climb poles or ladders to make these connections. In apartment and office buildings, they connect wires and cables to terminals and test equipment to make sure it works properly. They also resolve maintenance problems by interpreting diagnostic results and system tests, or through the use of maintenance from another location, sometimes with engineering support. When on-site procedures fail to resolve installation or maintenance problems, they request technical support from their technical services center.

Some experienced installers and repairers have multiple skills; they are considered especially valuable by many small companies. Installers and repairers may handle special cases, such as complaints to public service commissions, illegal or unauthorized use of equipment, and electric or acoustic shocks.

Telephone installers may work on rooftops, ladders, and telephone poles.

Employment

Telephone installers and repairers held about 37,000 jobs in 1996. More than 9 out of 10 worked full time for telecommunications companies.

Job Outlook

Employment of telephone installers and repairers is expected to decline sharply through the year 2006. Employment will continue to fall due to technological improvements. For example, prewired buildings that enable customers to buy telephones and plug them into prewired jacks have effectively eliminated the functions of the installer. The modular assembly of telephones, in which components plug in and out, will also reduce the time and skills needed for repair. Also, fewer phones will be worth repairing as unit prices continue to decline. In addition, the use of portable terminals that hook into a central testing system makes repairers more efficient. Increased competition for customers due to consolidations and mergers of cable and telephone companies will further contribute to the decline of telephone installers and repairers.

With employment projected to decline, job openings will result exclusively from the need to replace persons who transfer to other occupations or leave the labor force. Traditionally, most openings for telephone installers and repairers have been filled by workers in other telephone company jobs. As technology continues to displace installers and repairers, it will remain difficult for telephone workers without additional training to get these jobs, and virtually impossible for "outsiders" without the necessary skills. Some telephone installers and repairers are being retrained and moved into positions such as service or systems technicians.

(See introductory part of this section for information on working conditions, training requirements, earnings, and sources of additional information.)

Elevator Installers and Repairers

(D.O.T. 825.261-014, .281-030, -034, and .361-010)

Significant Points

- Elevator installers and repairers learn the trade through years of on-the-job training, usually through a program run by their union.

- Almost 80 percent of elevator installers and repairers are union members, a greater proportion than nearly any other occupation.

- The combination of slow employment growth and the high pay these workers earn should continue to result in low job turnover and relatively few job openings.

Nature of the Work

Elevator installers and repairers—also called *elevator constructors* or *elevator mechanics*—assemble, install, and replace elevators, escalators, dumbwaiters, moving walkways, and similar equipment in new and old buildings. Once the equipment is in service, they maintain and repair it. They are also responsible for modernizing older equipment.

In order to install, repair, and maintain modern elevators, which are almost all electronically controlled, elevator installers and repairers must have a thorough knowledge of electronics, electricity, and hydraulics. Many elevators today are installed with microprocessors, which are programmed to constantly analyze traffic conditions in order to dispatch elevators in the most efficient manner. With these computer controls, it is now possible to get the greatest amount of service with the least number of cars.

When installing a new elevator, installers and repairers begin by studying blueprints to determine the equipment needed to install rails, machines, car enclosures, motors, pumps, cylinders, and plunger foundations. Once this has been determined, they begin equipment

installation. Working on scaffolding or platforms, installers bolt or weld steel rails to the walls of the shaft to guide the elevator.

Elevator installers put in electrical wires and controls by running tubing, called conduit, along the shaft's walls from floor to floor. Once in place, mechanics pull plastic-covered electrical wires through the conduit. They then install electrical components and related devices required at each floor and at the main control panel in the machine room.

Installers bolt or weld together the steel frame of the elevator car at the bottom of the shaft, install the car's platform, walls, and doors, and attach guide shoes and rollers to minimize the lateral motion of the car as it travels through the shaft. They also install the outer doors and door frames at the elevator entrances on each floor.

For cabled elevators, these workers install geared or gearless machines with a traction drive wheel which guides and moves heavy steel cables connected to the elevator car and counterweight. The counterweight moves in the opposite direction from the car and aids in its swift and smooth movement. Elevator installers also install elevators in which a car sits on a hydraulic plunger that is driven by a pump. The plunger pushes the elevator car up from underneath, similar to a lift in an auto service station.

Installers and repairers also install escalators. They put in place the steel framework, the electrically powered stairs, and the tracks, and install associated motors and electrical wiring. In addition to elevators and escalators, they also may install devices such as dumbwaiters and material lifts, which are similar to elevators in design, moving walkways, stair lifts, and wheelchair lifts.

The most highly skilled elevator installers and repairers, called "adjusters," specialize in fine-tuning all of the equipment after installation. Adjusters must make sure that the elevator is working according to specifications, such as stopping correctly at each floor within a specified time period. Once an elevator is operating properly, it must be maintained and serviced regularly to keep it in safe working condition. Elevator maintenance mechanics generally do preventive maintenance—such as oiling and greasing moving parts, replacing worn parts, testing equipment with meters and gauges, and adjusting equipment for optimal performance. They also troubleshoot and may be called in to do emergency repairs.

A service crew usually handles major repairs—for example, replacing cables, elevator doors, or machine bearings. This may require cutting torches or rigging equipment—tools a maintenance mechanic would not normally carry. Service crews also do major modernization and alteration work, such as moving and replacing electrical motors, hydraulic pumps, and control panels.

Elevator installers and repairers usually specialize in installation, maintenance, or repair work. Maintenance and repair workers generally need more knowledge of electricity and electronics than installers because a large part of maintenance and repair work is troubleshooting. Similarly, construction adjusters need a thorough knowledge of electricity, electronics, and computers to ensure that newly installed elevators operate properly.

Working Conditions

Most elevator installers and repairers work a 40-hour week. However, maintenance and service mechanics often work overtime when repairing essential elevator equipment. They are sometimes on 24-hour call. Maintenance mechanics, unlike most elevator installers, are on their own most of the day and typically service the same elevators periodically.

Elevator installers lift and carry heavy equipment and parts and may work in cramped spaces or awkward positions. Hazards include falls, electrical shock, muscle strains, and other injuries related to handling heavy equipment. Because most of their work is performed indoors in buildings under construction or in existing buildings, elevator installers and repairers lose less work time due to inclement weather than other building trades workers.

Employment

Elevator installers and repairers held about 25,000 jobs in 1996. Most were employed by special trade contractors. Others were em-

Most elevator installers and repairers work a 40-hour week.

ployed by field offices of elevator manufacturers; wholesale distributors; small, local elevator maintenance and repair contractors; or by government agencies or businesses that do their own elevator maintenance and repair.

Training, Other Qualifications, and Advancement

Most elevator installers and repairers apply for their jobs through a local of the International Union of Elevator Constructors. Applicants for trainee positions must be at least 18 years old, have a high school diploma or equivalent, and pass an aptitude test. Good physical condition and mechanical aptitude also are important.

Elevator installers and repairers learn their trade in a program administered by local joint educational committees representing the employers and the union. These programs, through which the trainee learns everything from installation to repair, combine on-the-job training with classroom instruction in electrical and electronic theory, mathematics, applications of physics, and safety. In nonunion shops they may complete training programs sponsored by independent contractors.

Generally, trainees or helpers must complete a 6-month probationary period. After successful completion, they work toward becoming fully qualified mechanics within 4 to 5 years. To be classified as a fully qualified mechanic, union trainees must pass a standard mechanics examination administered by the National Elevator Industry Educational Program. Most States and cities also require elevator constructors to pass a licensing examination.

Most trainees or helpers assist experienced elevator installers and repairers. Beginners carry materials and tools, bolt rails to walls, and assemble elevator cars. Eventually, they learn to do more difficult tasks, such as wiring, which requires a knowledge of local and national electrical codes.

High school courses in electricity, mathematics, and physics provide a useful background. As elevators become increasingly sophisticated, workers may find it necessary to acquire more advanced formal education—for example, in postsecondary technical school or junior college—with an emphasis on electronics. Workers with more formal education generally advance more quickly than their counterparts.

Many elevator installers and repairers also receive training from their employers or through manufacturers to become familiar with the company's particular equipment. Retraining is very important to keep abreast of technological developments in elevator repair. In fact, union elevator constructors typically receive continual training throughout their careers, either through correspondence courses, seminars, or formal classes. Although voluntary, this training greatly improves one's chances for promotion.

Some installers may receive further training in specialized areas and advance to mechanic-in-charge, adjuster, supervisor, or elevator inspector. Adjusters, for example, may actually be picked for the position because they possess particular skills or are seen to be more electronically inclined. Other workers may move into management, sales, or product design jobs.

Job Outlook

Employment of elevator installers and repairers is expected to increase slower than the average for all occupations through the year 2006, and relatively few new job opportunities will be generated because the occupation is small. Replacement needs, another source of jobs, also will be relatively low, in part, because a substantial amount of time is invested in specialized training that yields high earnings and workers tend to remain in this field. The job outlook for new workers is largely dependent on activity in the construction industry and opportunities may vary from year to year as conditions within the industry change. Job prospects should be best for those with postsecondary training in electronics or more advanced formal education.

Demand for elevator installers and repairers will increase as equipment ages and needs more repairs and the construction of new buildings with elevators and escalators increases. Growth also should be driven by the need to continually update and modernize older equipment, including improvements in appearance and the installation of more sophisticated equipment and computerized controls. Because equipment must always be kept in working condition, economic downturns will have less of an effect on employment of elevator maintenance and repair mechanics than on other occupations. The need for people to service elevators and escalators should increase as equipment becomes more intricate and complex.

Earnings

Median weekly earnings of elevator installers and repairers who worked full time were $844 in 1996. The middle 50 percent earned between $740 and $1,088. The lowest 10 percent earned less than $633 a week, and the top 10 percent earned more than $1,322 a week.

Average weekly earnings for union elevator installers and repairers were about $865 in 1996, according to data from the International Union of Elevator Constructors. Rates vary with geographic location. Probationary helpers started at about 50 percent of the rate for experienced elevator mechanics, or about $432 a week. Non-probationary helpers earned about 70 percent of this rate, or an average of about $605 a week. Mechanics-in-charge averaged $973 a week.

In addition to free continuing education, elevator installers and repairers receive basic benefits enjoyed by most other workers.

The proportion of elevator installers and repairers who are union members is higher than nearly any other occupation. Almost 80 percent of elevator installers and repairers are members of the International Union of Elevator Constructors, compared to 15 percent in all occupations, and 23 percent for other craft and repair occupations.

Related Occupations

Elevator installers and repairers combine electrical and mechanical skills with construction skills such as welding, rigging, measuring, and blueprint reading. Other occupations that require many of these skills are boilermaker, electrician, industrial machinery repairer, millwright, sheet-metal worker, and structural ironworker.

Sources of Additional Information

For further details about opportunities as an elevator installer and repairer, contact elevator manufacturers, elevator repair and maintenance contractors, a local of the International Union of Elevator Constructors, or the nearest local public employment service office.

Farm Equipment Mechanics

(D.O.T. 624.281-010 and -014, .361-014, .381, and .684; and 629.281-018)

Significant Points

- Skill in using computerized diagnostic equipment is becoming more important.

- Opportunities should be best for persons who complete post secondary programs in farm equipment or diesel mechanics.

- Jobs are concentrated in small towns and rural areas.

Nature of the Work

Today's farms use more sophisticated equipment and advanced business practices than ever before. They have become larger—although fewer in number—allowing the economical use of specialized farm equipment to continually increase crop yields even while employing fewer and fewer workers. Specialized farm machinery has grown in size, complexity, and variety, and does everything from tilling the land to milking the cows. To operate efficiently, many farms have several tractors equipped with 40- to 400-horsepower engines. Planters, tillers, manure spreaders, and spray and irrigation equipment help grow the crops and combines, hay balers, swathers, and crop drying equipment aid in harvesting them.

Farm equipment dealers employ farm equipment mechanics, often called service technicians, to service, maintain, and repair farm equipment as well as smaller lawn and garden tractors sold to suburban homeowners. What was typically a handy-man's job around the farm has evolved into a highly demanded technical career. Farmers have increasingly turned to farm equipment dealers to service and repair their equipment because the machinery has grown in complexity. Modern equipment uses more electronics and hydraulics making it difficult to perform repairs without some advanced training.

Mechanics work mostly on equipment brought into the shop for repair and adjustment. During planting and harvesting seasons, they may travel to farms to make emergency repairs to minimize delays in farm operations.

Mechanics also perform preventive maintenance on older equipment. Periodically, they test, adjust, clean, and tune engines to keep them in proper working order. The level of service is determined by the difficulty of the problem. In large shops, mechanics generally specialize in certain types of work, such as diesel engine overhaul, hydraulic maintenance, or clutch and transmission repair. Others specialize in certain repairs, such as air-conditioning units often included to cool the cabs of combines and large tractors, or the repair of specific types of equipment such as hay balers. In addition, some mechanics assemble new machinery, do body work, and repair dented or torn sheet metal on tractors or other machinery.

Mechanics use many basic handtools, including wrenches, pliers, hammers, and screwdrivers. They also use precision equipment, such as micrometers and torque wrenches, and use welding equipment and power tools to repair broken parts. Increasingly, computerized engine testing equipment, such as dynamometers, engine analysis units, and compression testers are used to measure engine performance and find worn piston rings or leaking cylinder valves. Soon, mechanics

Farm equipment mechanics use many basic handtools, including wrenches, pliers, hammers, and screwdrivers.

will have access to computerized diagnostic equipment to monitor and locate malfunctions without turning a wrench.

New technology allows farmers to achieve record crop yields from small plots of their land by more precisely tailoring their tillage to accommodate the soil conditions of each. This growing use of site-specific technology, or precision farming, as it is known, makes use of the Global Positioning System (GPS), yield monitors, and variable rate applicators. These computerized systems link the farmer to satellites and other advanced devices to better monitor their crops and land use. More often than not, farmers rely on their equipment dealer to be their one stop for all repair needs. To better satisfy customer needs, traditional repair shops have begun to service advanced equipment, requiring the mechanic to acquire new skills.

Working Conditions

Generally, farm equipment mechanics work indoors though some do repairs on the farms. Most modern farm equipment mechanics work in well ventilated, lighted, and heated repair shops, but older shops may not offer these amenities. Farm equipment mechanics handle greasy and dirty parts and may stand or lie in awkward positions to repair vehicles and equipment. They often lift heavy parts and tools and handle various agricultural chemicals and solutions. Minor cuts, burns, and bruises are common, but serious accidents can be avoided when the shop is kept clean and orderly and safety practices observed.

As with most agricultural occupations, the hours of work for farm equipment mechanics vary according to the season of the year. During the busy planting and harvesting seasons, mechanics often work 6 or 7 days a week, 10 to 12 hours daily. In slow winter months, however, mechanics may work fewer than 40 hours a week.

Employment

Farm equipment mechanics held about 44,000 jobs in 1996. Most mechanics work in service departments of farm equipment dealers. Others worked in independent repair shops, and in shops on large farms. Most farm equipment mechanics worked in small repair shops. Nearly 1 out of 10 farm equipment mechanics was self-employed.

Because nearly every area of the United States has some form of farming, it is common to find farm equipment mechanics employed throughout the country. Employment is concentrated in small cities and towns, making this an attractive career choice for people who wish to live away from the big city. However, many mechanics work in the rural fringes of metropolitan areas, so farm equipment mechanics who prefer the conveniences of city life need not live in rural areas.

Training, Other Qualifications, and Advancement

With the development of more complex farm machinery, technical training has become more important. Employers prefer to hire trainee farm equipment mechanics who have completed a 1- or 2-year post-secondary training program in agricultural or farm mechanics at a vocational school or community college. However, if these programs are not offered, study of diesel or gasoline mechanics offers a strong background. Mechanics also need a knowledge of electronics, hydraulics, computers, and must have the aptitude to read circuit diagrams and blueprints in order to make complex repairs to electrical systems.

Most farm equipment mechanics enter the occupation as trainees and become proficient in their trade by assisting experienced mechanics. The length of training varies with the helper's aptitude and prior experience. Usually, 2 years of on-the-job training is necessary for a mechanic to do routine types of repair work efficiently. Highly specialized repair and overhaul jobs usually require additional training.

Many farm equipment mechanics enter this occupation through careers in related occupations. For example, they may have experience working as diesel mechanics, mobile heavy equipment mechanics, or automotive mechanics. Prior experience in farm work will also provide a foundation of the skills and training necessary to become a farm equipment mechanic because farm workers typically make minor equipment repairs to save repair costs. Similarly, people with military backgrounds in mechanics have valuable experience and training. Persons who enter from related occupations may start as trainees or helpers, however, they may require less on-the-job training.

Employers look for skilled individuals with the aptitude needed to handle tools and equipment. Occasionally, strength is required to lift, move, or hold heavy parts in place. Difficult repair jobs require problem-solving skills to diagnose the source of the machine's malfunction and choose the correct course of action to fix the problem. The importance of computer skills will increase as many more dealers gain access to computerized diagnostic equipment on a laptop computer. This technology will allow mechanics to simply plug into the farm equipment and have a complete diagnostic check done by pushing a button. Experienced mechanics should be able to work independently with minimal supervision.

Keeping abreast of changes in farm equipment technology requires careful study of service manuals and analysis of complex diagrams. Many farm equipment mechanics and trainees receive refresher training in short-term programs conducted by farm equipment manufacturers. This is the dealers way of keeping its employees trained in the latest concepts and standards within the industry. A company service representative explains the design, function, and techniques required to repair and maintain new models of farm equipment. In addition, some dealers may send employees to local vocational schools that hold special week-long classes in subjects such as air-conditioning repair or hydraulics. Satellite and video taped training courses have become an increasingly popular way to standardize training techniques and to cut expenses needed to reach individual dealers and repair shops.

Key to the mechanic's livelihood is their personal tools. Farm equipment mechanics usually buy their own handtools, although employers furnish power tools and computerized test equipment. Trainee mechanics are expected to accumulate their own tools as they gain experience. Experienced mechanics have thousands of dollars invested in their tools.

Farm equipment mechanics may advance to shop supervisor, service manager, or manager of a farm equipment dealership. Some mechanics open their own repair shops or invest in franchised dealers. A few farm equipment mechanics with strong customer service backgrounds advance to service representatives for farm equipment manufacturers.

Job Outlook

Because farms use fewer, but more efficient and reliable, pieces of equipment, employment of farm equipment mechanics should decrease through the year 2006. Most job openings will arise from the need to replace experienced mechanics who retire. However, opportunities should be good for persons who have completed formal training in farm equipment repair or diesel mechanics.

The continued consolidation of farmland into fewer and larger farms and the use of new farming practices means farmers will need smaller stock of equipment. They will also be more able to invest in new, efficient and specialized equipment, allowing farmers to till greater acreage more productively and profitably. For example, new planting equipment uses electronics to spread seeds more uniformly, and electronic controls help harvesters reduce waste.

Farm machinery is expensive and usually designed and manufactured to withstand many years of rugged use. Nevertheless, it requires periodic service and repairs. New farm equipment has longer intervals between service but because of its increased complexity, many farmers will continue to rely on mechanics for service and repairs. For example, many newer tractors have large, electronically controlled engines, and air-conditioned cabs, and feature advanced transmissions with many speeds, equipment characteristics that farmers usually cannot repair themselves.

Sales of smaller lawn and garden equipment constitute a growing share of the business of most farm equipment dealers. Most large manufacturers of farm equipment now offer a line of smaller tractors to sell through their established dealerships. However, this equipment is designed for easy home service and only requires a mechanic when major repairs are needed.

The agricultural equipment industry experiences periodic declines—mostly in sales. Layoffs of mechanics, however, are uncommon because farmers often elect to repair old equipment rather than purchase new equipment.

Earnings

Farm equipment mechanics had median weekly earnings of about $418 in 1996. The middle 50 percent earned between $312 and $613 a week. The lowest paid 10 percent earned less than $256 a week, and the top 10 percent earned over $780 a week. Most farm equipment mechanics also have the opportunity to work overtime during the planting and harvesting seasons, which generally pays time and one-half.

Very few farm equipment mechanics belong to labor unions, but those who do are members of the International Association of Machinists and Aerospace Workers; the International Union, United Automobile, Aerospace and Agricultural Implement Workers of America; and the International Brotherhood of Teamsters.

Related Occupations

Other workers who repair large mobile machinery include aircraft mechanics, automotive mechanics, diesel mechanics, and mobile heavy equipment mechanics.

Sources of Additional Information

Details about work opportunities may be obtained from local farm equipment dealers and local offices of the State employment service. For general information about the occupation, write to:

☛ Equipment Manufacturers Institute, 10 South Riverside Plaza, Room 1220, Chicago, IL 60606.

☛ North American Equipment Dealers Association, 10877 Watson Rd., St. Louis, MO 63127.

☛ John Deere and Co., John Deere Rd., Moline, IL 61265.

General Maintenance Mechanics

(D.O.T. 899.261-014 and .381-010)

Significant Points

- Job openings should be plentiful, the result of an expected average growth rate and significant turnover in this large occupation.

- Most workers learn their skills informally on the job; others learn by working as helpers to other repairers or construction workers such as carpenters, electricians, or machinery repairers.

Nature of the Work

Most craft workers specialize in one kind of work such as plumbing or carpentry. General maintenance mechanics, however, have skills in many different crafts. They repair and maintain machines, mechanical equipment, and buildings, and work on plumbing, electrical, and air-conditioning and heating systems. They build partitions, make plaster or drywall repairs, and fix or paint roofs, windows, doors, floors, woodwork, and other parts of building structures. They also maintain and repair specialized equipment and machinery found in cafeterias, laundries, hospitals, stores, offices, and factories. Typical duties include troubleshooting and fixing faulty electrical switches, repairing air-conditioning motors, and unclogging drains. New buildings sometimes have computer-controlled systems, requiring mechanics to acquire basic computer skills. For example,

General maintenance mechanics have skills in many different crafts.

new air conditioning systems often can be controlled from a central computer terminal. Additionally, light sensors can be electronically controlled to automatically turn off lights after a set amount of time.

Those in small establishments, where they are often the only maintenance worker, do all repairs except for very large or difficult jobs. In larger establishments, their duties may be limited to the general maintenance of everything in a workshop or a particular area.

General maintenance mechanics inspect and diagnose problems and determine the best way to correct them, often checking blueprints, repair manuals, and parts catalogs. They obtain supplies and repair parts from distributors or storerooms. They use common hand and power tools such as screwdrivers, saws, drills, wrenches, and hammers, as well as specialized equipment and electronic test devices. They replace or fix worn or broken parts, where necessary, or make adjustments.

These mechanics also do routine preventive maintenance and ensure that machines continue to run smoothly, building systems operate efficiently, and the physical condition of buildings does not deteriorate. Following a checklist, they may inspect drives, motors, and belts, check fluid levels, replace filters, and perform other maintenance actions. Maintenance mechanics keep records of maintenance and repair work.

Working Conditions

General maintenance mechanics often do a variety of tasks in a single day, generally at a number of different locations in a building, or in several buildings. They may have to stand for long periods, lift heavy objects, and work in uncomfortably hot or cold environments, in awkward and cramped positions, or on ladders. They are subject to electrical shock, burns, falls, and cuts and bruises. Most general maintenance workers work a 40-hour week. Some work evening, night, or weekend shifts, or are on call for emergency repairs.

Those employed in small establishments, where they may be the only maintenance worker, often operate with only limited supervision. Those working in larger establishments often work under the direct supervision of an experienced worker.

Employment

General maintenance mechanics held about 1,362,000 jobs in 1996. They were employed in almost every industry in the economy. More than one-third worked in service industries; most of these worked for elementary and secondary schools, colleges and universities, hotels, and hospitals and nursing homes. About 17 percent worked in manufacturing industries. Others worked for real estate firms that operate office and apartment buildings, wholesale and retail firms, or government agencies.

Training, Other Qualifications, and Advancement

Most general maintenance mechanics learn their skills informally on the job. They start as helpers, watching and learning from skilled maintenance workers. Helpers begin by doing simple jobs such as fixing leaky faucets and replacing light bulbs, and progress to more difficult tasks such as overhauling machinery or building walls.

Others learn their skills by working as helpers to other repair or construction workers such as carpenters, electricians, or machinery repairers. Necessary skills can also be learned in high school shop classes and postsecondary trade or vocational schools. It generally takes from 1 to 4 years of on-the-job training or school, or a combination of both, to become fully qualified, depending on the skill level required. Because a growing proportion of new buildings rely on computers to control building systems, general maintenance mechanics may need basic computer skills such as logging on to a central system and navigating through a series of menus. Usually companies that install computer-controlled equipment provide on-site training for general maintenance mechanics.

Graduation from high school is preferred for entry into this occupation. High school courses in mechanical drawing, electricity, woodworking, blueprint reading, science, and mathematics are useful. Mechanical aptitude, ability to use shop math, and manual dexterity are important. Good health is necessary because the job involves much walking, standing, reaching, and heavy lifting. Difficult jobs require problem-solving ability, and many positions require the ability to work without direct supervision.

Many general maintenance mechanics in large organizations advance to maintenance supervisor or to one of the crafts such as electrician, heating/air-conditioning mechanic, or plumber. In small organizations, promotion opportunities are limited.

Job Outlook

Job openings should be plentiful for general maintenance mechanics. Employment is related to the number of buildings—for example, office and apartment buildings, stores, schools, hospitals, hotels, and factories—and amount of equipment needing maintenance and repair. Although the pace of construction of these facilities is expected to be slower than in the past, employment growth is still expected to be about as fast as the average for all occupations through the year 2006. In addition to growth openings, this is a large occupation with a significant turnover rate, and many replacements are needed for those who transfer to other occupations or stop working for other reasons.

Earnings

Earnings vary widely by industry, geographic area, and skill level. According to a survey of workplaces in 160 metropolitan areas, general maintenance mechanics had median earnings of about $9.88 an hour in 1995, with the middle half earning between $8.36 and $11.86 an hour. Median earnings were about $9.41 an hour in service businesses, and about $9.90 an hour in manufacturing businesses. On average, workers in the Midwest and Northeast earned more than those in the West and South. Mechanics earn overtime pay for work in excess of 40 hours per week.

Some general maintenance mechanics are members of unions, including the American Federation of State, County and Municipal Employees and the United Automobile Workers.

Related Occupations

Some of the work of general maintenance mechanics is similar to that of carpenters, plumbers, industrial machinery mechanics, electricians, and air-conditioning, refrigeration, and heating mechanics.

Sources of Additional Information

Information about job opportunities may be obtained from local employers and local offices of State Employment Services.

Heating, Air-Conditioning, and Refrigeration Technicians

(D.O.T. 637.261-014, -026, -030, and -034, and .381; 827.361-014; 862.281 -018, .361-010; and 869.281-010)

Significant Points

- Opportunities should be very good for technicians with technical school or formal apprenticeship training.

- Technicians need a basic understanding of microelectronics because they increasingly install and service equipment with electronic controls.

Nature of the Work

What would those living in Chicago do without heating, those in Miami do without air-conditioning, or blood banks in all parts of the country do without refrigeration? Heating and air-conditioning systems control the temperature, humidity, and the total air quality in residential, commercial, industrial, and other buildings. Refrigeration systems make it possible to store and transport food, medicine, and other perishable items. Heating, air-conditioning, and refrigeration technicians install, maintain, and repair such systems.

Heating, air-conditioning, and refrigeration technicians follow blueprints, design specifications, and manufacturers' instructions to install motors, compressors, condensing units and other components.

Heating, air-conditioning, and refrigeration systems consist of many mechanical, electrical, and electronic components, including motors, compressors, pumps, fans, ducts, pipes, thermostats, and switches. In central heating systems, for example, a furnace heats air that is distributed throughout the building via a system of metal or fiberglass ducts. Technicians must be able to maintain, diagnose, and correct problems throughout the entire system. To do this, they may adjust system controls to recommended settings and test the performance of the entire system using special tools and test equipment.

Although they are trained to do both, technicians often specialize in either installation or maintenance and repair. Some specialize in one type of equipment—for example, oil burners, solar panels, or commercial refrigerators. Technicians may work for large or small contracting companies or directly for a manufacturer or wholesaler. Those working for smaller operations tend to do both installation and servicing, and work with heating, cooling, and refrigeration equipment.

Furnace installers, also called *heating equipment technicians*, follow blueprints or other specifications to install oil, gas, electric, solid-fuel, and multiple-fuel heating systems. After putting the equipment in place, they install fuel and water supply lines, air ducts and vents, pumps, and other components. They may connect electrical wiring and controls and check the unit for proper operation. To ensure the proper functioning of the system, furnace installers often use combustion test equipment such as carbon dioxide and oxygen testers.

After a furnace has been installed, technicians often perform routine maintenance and repair work in order to keep the system operating efficiently. During the fall and winter, for example, when the system is used most, they service and adjust burners and blowers. If the system is not operating properly, they check the thermostat, burner nozzles, controls, or other parts in order to diagnose and then correct the problem. During the summer, when the heating system is not being used, technicians do maintenance work, such as replacing filters and vacuum-cleaning vents, ducts, and other parts of the system that may accumulate dust and impurities during the operating season.

Air-conditioning and *refrigeration technicians* install and service central air-conditioning systems and a variety of refrigeration equipment. Technicians follow blueprints, design specifications, and manufacturers' instructions to install motors, compressors, condensing units, evaporators, piping, and other components. They connect this equipment to the duct work, refrigerant lines, and electrical power source. After making the connections, they charge the system with refrigerant, check it for proper operation, and program control systems.

When air-conditioning and refrigeration equipment breaks down, technicians diagnose the problem and make repairs. To do this, they test parts such as compressors, relays, and thermostats. During the winter, air-conditioning technicians inspect the systems and do required maintenance, such as overhauling compressors.

When servicing equipment, heating, air-conditioning, and refrigeration technicians must use care to conserve, recover, and recycle chlorofluorocarbon (CFC) and hydrochlorofluorocarbon (HCFC) refrigerants used in air-conditioning and refrigeration systems. The release of CFC's and HCFC's contributes to the depletion of the stratospheric ozone layer, which protects plant and animal life from ultraviolet radiation. Technicians conserve the refrigerant by making sure that there are no leaks in the system; they recover it by venting the refrigerant into proper cylinders; and they recycle it for reuse with special filter-dryers.

Heating, air-conditioning, and refrigeration technicians use a variety of tools, including hammers, wrenches, metal snips, electric drills, pipe cutters and benders, measurement gauges, and acetylene torches, to work with refrigerant lines and air ducts. They use voltmeters, thermometers, pressure gauges, manometers, and other testing devices to check air flow, refrigerant pressure, electrical circuits, burners, and other components.

Cooling and heating systems sometimes are installed or repaired by other craft workers. For example, on a large air-conditioning installation job, especially where workers are covered by union contracts, duct work might be done by sheet-metal workers; electrical work by electricians; and installation of piping, condensers, and other components by plumbers and pipefitters. Room air-conditioners and household refrigerators usually are serviced by home appliance repairers. (Additional information about each of these occupations appears elsewhere in the *Handbook*.)

Working Conditions

Heating, air-conditioning, and refrigeration technicians work in homes, supermarkets, hospitals, office buildings, and factories—anywhere there is climate control equipment. They may be assigned to specific job sites at the beginning of each day, or if they are making service calls, they may be dispatched to jobs by radio or telephone.

Technicians may work outside in cold or hot weather or in buildings that are uncomfortable because the air-conditioning or heating equipment is broken. In addition, technicians often work in awkward or cramped positions and sometimes are required to work in high places. Hazards include electrical shock, burns, muscle strains, and other injuries from handling heavy equipment. Appropriate safety equipment is necessary when handling refrigerants because contact can cause skin damage, frostbite, or blindness. Inhalation of refrigerants when working in confined spaces is also a possible hazard, and may cause asphyxiation.

Technicians usually work a 40-hour week, but during peak seasons they often work overtime or irregular hours. Maintenance workers, including those who provide maintenance services under contract, often work evening or weekend shifts, and are on call. Most employers try to provide a full workweek the year round by doing both installation and maintenance work and many manufacturers and contractors now provide or even require service contracts. In most shops that service both heating and air-conditioning equipment, employment is very stable throughout the year.

Employment

Heating, air-conditioning, and refrigeration technicians held about 256,000 jobs in 1996, more than half of these worked for cooling and heating contractors. The remainder were employed in a wide variety of industries throughout the country, reflecting a widespread depend-

ence on climate control systems. Some worked for fuel oil dealers, refrigeration and air-conditioning service and repair shops, and schools. Others were employed by the Federal Government, hospitals, office buildings, and other organizations that operate large air-conditioning, refrigeration, or heating systems. Approximately 1 of every 7 technicians was self-employed.

Training, Other Qualifications, and Advancement

Because of the increasing sophistication of heating, air-conditioning, and refrigeration systems, employers prefer to hire those with technical school or apprenticeship training. A sizable number of technicians, however, still learn the trade informally on the job.

Many secondary and postsecondary technical and trade schools, junior and community colleges, and the Armed Forces offer 6 month- to 2-year programs in heating, air-conditioning, and refrigeration. Students study theory, design, and equipment construction, as well as electronics. They also learn the basics of installation, maintenance, and repair.

Apprenticeship programs are frequently run by joint committees representing local chapters of the Air-Conditioning Contractors of America, the Mechanical Contractors Association of America, the National Association of Plumbing-Heating-Cooling Contractors, and locals of the Sheet Metal Workers' International Association or the United Association of Journeymen and Apprentices of the Plumbing and Pipefitting Industry of the United States and Canada. Other apprenticeship programs are sponsored by local chapters of the Associated Builders and Contractors and the National Association of Home Builders. Formal apprenticeship programs generally last 3 or 4 years and combine on-the-job training with classroom instruction. Classes include subjects such as the use and care of tools, safety practices, blueprint reading, and air-conditioning theory. Applicants for these programs must have a high school diploma or equivalent.

Those who acquire their skills on the job usually begin by assisting experienced technicians. They may begin performing simple tasks such as carrying materials, insulating refrigerant lines, or cleaning furnaces. In time, they move on to more difficult tasks, such as cutting and soldering pipes and sheet metal and checking electrical and electronic circuits.

Courses in shop math, mechanical drawing, applied physics and chemistry, electronics, blueprint reading, and computer applications provide a good background for those interested in entering this occupation. Some knowledge of plumbing or electrical work is also helpful. A basic understanding of microelectronics is becoming more important because of the increasing use of this technology in solid-state equipment controls. Because technicians frequently deal directly with the public, they should be courteous and tactful, especially when dealing with an aggravated customer. They also should be in good physical condition because they sometimes have to lift and move heavy equipment.

All technicians who purchase or work with refrigerants must be certified in their proper handling. To become certified to purchase and handle refrigerants, a technician must pass a written examination specific to the type of work in which they specialize. The three possible areas of certification are: Type I—servicing small appliances, Type II—high pressure refrigerants, and Type III—low pressure refrigerants. Exams are administered by organizations approved by the Environmental Protection Agency, such as trade schools, unions, contractor associations, or building groups. Though no formal training is required for certification, training programs designed to prepare workers for the certification examination, as well as for general skills improvement training, are provided by heating and air-conditioning equipment manufacturers; the Refrigeration Service Engineers Society (RSES); the Air Conditioning Contractors of America (ACCA); the Mechanical Service Contractors of America; local chapters of the National Association of Plumbing-Heating-Cooling Contractors; and the United Association of Plumbers and Pipefitters. RSES, along with some other organizations, also offer basic self-study courses for individuals with limited experience. In addition to understanding how systems work, technicians must be knowledgeable about refrigerant products, and legislation and regulation that govern their use.

There are also two newly created certification programs for technicians. The North American Technician Excellence Program is sponsored by a coalition of associations representing all segments of the industry. The other is sponsored by the Air Conditioning Contractors of America, and Ferris State University in Big Rapids, Michigan. Both programs are voluntary measures of competency.

Advancement usually takes the form of higher wages. Some technicians, however, may advance to positions as supervisor or service manager. Others may move into areas such as sales and marketing. Those with sufficient money and managerial skill can open their own contracting business.

Job Outlook

Job prospects for highly skilled air-conditioning, heating, and refrigeration technicians are expected to be very good, particularly those with technical school or formal apprenticeship training to install, remodel, and service new and existing systems. In addition to job openings created by employment growth, thousands of openings will result from the need to replace workers who transfer to other occupations or leave the labor force.

Employment of heating, air-conditioning, and refrigeration technicians is expected to increase about as fast as the average for all occupations through the year 2006. As the population and economy grow, so does the demand for new residential, commercial, and industrial climate control systems. Technicians who specialize in installation work may experience periods of unemployment when the level of new construction activity declines, but maintenance and repair work usually remains relatively stable. People and businesses depend on their climate control systems and must keep them in good working order, regardless of economic conditions.

Concern for the environment and energy conservation should continue to prompt the development of new energy-saving heating and air-conditioning systems. An emphasis on better energy management should lead to the replacement of older systems and the installation of newer, more efficient systems in existing homes and buildings. Also, demand for maintenance and service work should increase as businesses and home owners strive to keep systems operating at peak efficiency. Regulations prohibiting the discharge of CFC and HCFC refrigerants and banning CFC production by the year 2000 also should continue to result in demand for technicians to replace many existing systems, or modify them to use new environmentally safe refrigerants. In addition, the continuing focus on improving indoor air quality should contribute to the growth of jobs for heating, air-conditioning, and refrigeration technicians. Also, certain businesses contribute to a growing need for refrigeration. For example, nearly 50 percent of products sold in convenience stores require some sort of refrigeration. Supermarkets and convenience stores have a very large inventory of refrigerated equipment. This huge inventory will also create increasing demand for service technicians in installation, maintenance, and repair.

Earnings

Median weekly earnings of air-conditioning, heating, and refrigeration technicians who worked full time were $536 in 1996. The middle 50 percent earned between $381 and $701. The lowest 10 percent earned less than $287 a week, and the top 10 percent earned more than $887 a week.

Apprentices usually begin at about 50 percent of the wage rate paid to experienced workers. As they gain experience and improve their skills, they receive periodic increases until they reach the wage rate of experienced workers.

Heating, air-conditioning, and refrigeration technicians enjoy a variety of employer-sponsored benefits. In addition to typical benefits like health insurance and pension plans, some employers pay for work-related training and provide uniforms, company vans, and tools.

Nearly 1 out of every 6 heating, air-conditioning, and refrigeration technicians is a member of a union. The unions to which the greatest numbers of technicians belong are the Sheet Metal Workers' International Association and the United Association of Journeymen and Apprentices of the Plumbing and Pipefitting Industry of the United States and Canada.

Related Occupations

Heating, air-conditioning, and refrigeration technicians work with sheet metal and piping, and repair machinery, such as electrical motors, compressors, and burners. Other workers who have similar skills are boilermakers, electrical appliance servicers, electricians, plumbers and pipefitters, sheet-metal workers, and duct installers.

Sources of Additional Information

For more information about employment and training opportunities in this trade, contact local vocational and technical schools; local heating, air-conditioning, and refrigeration contractors; a local of the unions previously mentioned; a local joint union-management apprenticeship committee; a local chapter of the Associated Builders and Contractors; or the nearest office of the State employment service or State apprenticeship agency.

For information on career opportunities, training, and technician certification, contact:
☛ Air Conditioning Contractors of America, 1712 New Hampshire Ave., NW., Washington, DC 20009.

For information on technician certification, contact:
☛ North American Technician Excellence (NATE), P.O. Box 8127, Reston, VA 20195-2025.
☛ Air Conditioning Contractors of America, 1712 New Hampshire Ave., NW., Washington, DC 20009.

For information on career opportunities and training, write to:
☛ Associated Builders and Contractors, 1300 North 17th St., Rosslyn, VA 22209.
☛ Refrigeration Service Engineers Society, 1666 Rand Rd., Des Plaines, IL 60016-3552.
☛ Home Builders Institute, National Association of Home Builders, 1201 15th St. NW., Washington, DC 20005.
☛ National Association of Plumbing-Heating-Cooling Contractors, 180 S. Washington St., P.O. Box 6808, Falls Church, VA 22046.
☛ Mechanical Contractors Association of America, 1385 Piccard Dr., Rockville, MD 20850-4329.
☛ Air Conditioning and Refrigeration Institute, 4301 North Fairfax Dr., Suite 425, Arlington, VA 22203.

Home Appliance and Power Tool Repairers

(D.O.T. 637.261-010 and -018; 723.381 and .584; 729.281-022; and 827.261, and .661)

Significant Points

- Although employment of home appliance and power tool repairers is expected to grow slowly, opportunities should be good for skilled repairers.
- Many repairers are high school graduates who are trained on the job.
- Knowledge of basic electronics is becoming increasingly important.

Nature of the Work

If your air-conditioner or refrigerator has ever broken, you know the importance of a dependable repair person. Appliance and power tool repairers, often called service technicians, fix home appliances such as ovens, washers, dryers, refrigerators, freezers, room air-conditioners, as well as power tools such as saws and drills. Some repairers only service small appliances such as microwaves and vacuum cleaners; others specialize in major appliances such as refrigerators, dishwashers, washers, and dryers; and others only handle power tools or gas appliances.

Repairers visually inspect appliances or power tools and check for unusual noises, excessive vibration, fluid leaks, or loose parts to determine why they fail to operate properly. They consult service manuals and troubleshooting guides to diagnose particularly difficult problems. They disassemble the appliance or tool to examine its internal parts for signs of wear or corrosion. Repairers follow wiring diagrams and use testing devices, such as ammeters, voltmeters, and wattmeters to check electrical systems for shorts and faulty connections.

After identifying problems, they replace or repair defective belts, motors, heating elements, switches, gears, or other items. They tighten, align, clean, and lubricate parts as necessary. Repairers use common handtools, including screwdrivers, wrenches, files, and pliers, as well as soldering guns and special tools designed for particular appliances. When repairing appliances with electronic parts, they may replace circuit boards or other electronic components.

Many manufacturers incorporate "fuzzy logic" technology into their more expensive appliances. Fuzzy logic technology involves sensors, or inputs, strategically placed inside an appliance to transmit information to an on-board computer. The computer processes this information and adjusts variables such as water and electricity, to optimize appliance performance and reduce wasted resources. Fuzzy logic uses 1 input; "neurofuzzy logic" uses up to 5 inputs; and "chaos logic" uses up to 10 inputs. Dishwashers, washers, and dryers commonly use neurofuzzy logic in their components.

When repairing refrigerators and window air-conditioners, repairers must use care to conserve, recover, and recycle chlorofluorocarbon (CFC) and hydrochlorofluorocarbon (HCFC) refrigerants used in

Home appliance and power tool repairers check for unusual noises, excessive vibration, fluid leaks, or loose parts.

their cooling systems. The release of CFC's and HCFC's contributes to the depletion of the stratospheric ozone layer, which protects plant and animal life from ultraviolet radiation. Repairers conserve the refrigerant by making sure there are no leaks in the system; they recover it by venting the refrigerant into proper cylinders; and they recycle it for reuse with special filter-dryers.

Repairers who service gas appliances may check the heating unit and replace tubing, thermocouples, thermostats, valves, and indicator spindles. They also answer emergency calls for gas leaks. To install gas appliances, repairers may have to install pipes in a customer's home to connect the appliances to the gas line. They measure, lay out, cut, and thread pipe and connect it to a feeder line and to the appliance. They may have to saw holes in walls or floors and hang steel supports from beams or joists to hold gas pipes in place. Once the gas line is in place, they turn on the gas and check for leaks.

Repairers also answer customers' questions about the care and use of appliances. For example, they demonstrate how to load automatic washing machines, arrange dishes in dishwashers, or sharpen chain saws.

Repairers write up estimates of the cost of repairs for customers, keep records of parts used and hours worked, prepare bills, and collect payments.

Working Conditions

Home appliance and power tool repairers who handle portable appliances usually work in repair shops that are generally quiet, well lighted, and adequately ventilated. Those who repair major appliances usually make service calls to customers' homes. They carry their tools and a number of commonly used parts with them in a truck or van and may spend several hours a day driving. They may work in clean comfortable rooms such as kitchens, or an area of the home that is damp, dirty, or dusty. Repairers sometimes work in cramped and uncomfortable positions when replacing parts in hard-to-reach areas of appliances.

Repairer jobs generally are not hazardous, but they must exercise care and follow safety precautions to avoid electrical shocks and injuries when lifting and moving large appliances. When repairing gas appliances and microwave ovens, they must be aware of the dangers of gas and radiation leaks.

Many home appliance and power tool repairers work a standard 40-hour week. Some repairers work early morning, evening, and weekend shifts. Many repairers remain on-call in case of emergency. Many repairers work overtime and weekend hours in the summer months, when repairers are in high demand to fix air-conditioners and refrigerators. Repairers of power tools such as saws and drills may also have to work overtime during spring and summer months when use of such tools increases and breakdowns are more frequent.

Home appliance and power tool repairers usually work with little or no direct supervision, a feature of the job that appeals to many people.

Employment

Home appliance and power tool repairers held nearly 71,000 jobs in 1996. Nearly 1 out of 10 repairers was self-employed. Almost 2 out of 3 salaried repairers worked in retail establishments such as department stores, household appliance stores, and fuel dealers. Others worked for gas and electric utility companies, electrical repair shops, and wholesalers.

Almost every community in the country employs appliance and power tool repairers; a high concentration of jobs are found in more populated areas.

Training, Other Qualifications, and Advancement

Employers generally require a high school diploma for home appliance and power tool repairer jobs. Many repairers learn the trade primarily on the job, while some receive their training in a formal trade school or community college. Mechanical aptitude is desirable, and those who work in customers' homes must be courteous and tactful.

Employers prefer to hire people with formal training in appliance repair and electronics. Many repairers complete 1-or 2-year formal training programs in appliance repair and related subjects in high schools, private vocational schools, and community colleges. Courses in basic electricity and electronics are becoming increasingly necessary as more manufacturers install circuit boards and other electronic control systems in home appliances.

Regardless of whether their basic skills are developed through formal training or on the job, trainees usually receive additional training from their employer and manufacturers. In shops that fix portable appliances, they work on a single type of appliance, such as a vacuum cleaner, until they master its repair. Then they move on to others, until they can repair all those handled by the shop. In companies that repair major appliances, beginners assist experienced repairers on service visits; They may also study on their own. They learn to read schematic drawings, analyze problems, determine whether to repair or replace parts, and follow proper safety procedures. Up to 3 years of on-the-job training may be needed for a technician to become skilled in all aspects of repair.

Some appliance and power tool manufacturers and department store chains have formal training programs that include home study and shop classes, in which trainees work with demonstration appliances and other training equipment. Many repairers receive supplemental instruction through 2- or 3- week seminars conducted by appliance and power tool manufacturers. Experienced repairers also often attend training classes and study service manuals. Repairers who are authorized for warranty work by manufacturers are required to attend periodic training sessions.

The Environmental Protection Agency (EPA) has mandated that all repairers who buy or work with refrigerants must be certified in its proper handling; a technician must pass a written examination to become certified to buy and handle refrigerants. Exams are administered by organizations approved by the EPA, such as trade schools, unions, and employer associations. There are even EPA-approved take-home certification exams. Though no formal training is required for certification, many of these organizations offer training programs designed to prepare workers for the certification examination.

To protect consumers and provide recognition to home appliance and power tool repairers who have become highly skilled, the Association of Home Appliance Manufacturers has instituted the National Appliance Service Technician Certification Program (NASTeC). Manufacturers, schools and field experts have cooperated in writing questions that measure the skills of their trade. To become certified, technicians must pass a comprehensive examination testing their competence in the diagnosis, repair and maintenance of major home appliances. The examination is given twice a year at locations throughout the country. While there has not previously been standardized certification, growing numbers of employers now encourage repairers to become certified.

The Professional Service Association (PSA) has a certification program with similar goals to the NASTeC program. To become certified, technicians must pass an examination. The PSA certification is valid for 4 years, and for renewal the technician must complete at least 12 credit hours of instruction every year during the 4 years. If the technician fails to accumulate the 48 hours, they must retake the examination.

Repairers in large shops or service centers may be promoted to supervisor, assistant service manager, or service manager. A few repairers advance to managerial positions such as regional service manager or parts manager for appliance or tool manufacturers. Preference is given to those who demonstrate technical competence and show an ability to get along with coworkers and customers. Experienced repairers who have sufficient funds and knowledge of small business management may open their own repair shop.

Job Outlook

Employment of home appliance and power tool repairers is expected to increase slower than the average for all occupations through the year 2006. The number of home appliances and power tools in use is expected to increase as the number of households and businesses grows and new and improved appliances and tools are introduced.

The increased use of electronic parts such as solid-state circuitry, microprocessors, and sensing devices in appliances will reduce the frequency of repairs. Nevertheless, as the current pool of appliance and power tool repairers retires or transfers to other occupations, job openings will arise. Prospects should continue to be good for well-trained repairers, particularly those with a strong background in electronics. Most people with the electronics training needed to repair appliances go into other repairer occupations.

Employment is relatively steady because the demand for appliance repair services continues even during economic downturns. Jobs are expected to be increasingly concentrated in larger companies as the number of smaller shops and family owned businesses decline.

Earnings

Home appliance and power tool repairers who usually worked full time had median earnings of $579 a week in 1996. The middle 50 percent earned between $354 and $760 a week. The lowest paid 10 percent earned $255 a week or less, while the highest paid 10 percent earned $929 a week or more. Earnings of home appliance and power tool repairers vary widely according to the skill level required to fix equipment, geographic location, and the type of equipment repaired. Earnings tend to be highest in large firms and for those servicing gas appliances. Many receive commission along with their hourly wage salary.

Many larger dealers, manufacturers and service stores offer benefits such as health insurance coverage, sick leave, and retirement and pension programs. Some home appliance and power tool repairers belong to the International Brotherhood of Electrical Workers.

Related Occupations

Other workers who repair electrical and electronic equipment include heating, air-conditioning, and refrigeration mechanics; pinsetter mechanics; office machine and cash register servicers; electronic home entertainment equipment repairers; and vending machine servicers and repairers.

Sources of Additional Information

For information about jobs in the home appliance and power tool repair field, contact local appliance repair shops, manufacturers, vocational trade schools, appliance dealers, and utility companies, or the local office of the State employment service.

For general information about the work of home appliance repairers, contact:
☛ Appliance Service News, P.O. Box 789, Lombard, IL 60148.
☛ National Association of Service Dealers, P.O. Box 9680, Denver, CO 80222.
☛ United Servicers Association, Inc., P.O. Box 59707, Dallas, TX 75229.
☛ National Appliance Service Association, 9247 N. Meridian, Suite 216, Indianapolis, In 46260.

For information technician certification, as well as general information about the work of home appliance repairers, contact:
☛ National Appliance Service Technician Certification Program (NASTeC), Suite 1231, 20 N. Wacker Dr., Chicago, IL 60606 or call toll free 1-888-NASTEC1 (627-8321).
☛ Professional Service Association, 71 Columbia St., Cohoes, NY 12047.
☛ National Association of Service Dealers, 10 E. 22nd St., Suite 310, Lombard, IL 60148.

Industrial Machinery Repairers

(D.O.T. codes available on request. See p. 496.)

Significant Points

- More than a third work over 40 hours a week because workers may be called to the plant at night or on weekends for emergency repairs.

- Workers learn their trade through a 4-year apprenticeship program or informal on-the-job training supplemented by classroom instruction.

- While employment of industrial machinery repairers is projected to grow more slowly than average, applicants with broad skills in machine repair should have favorable job prospects.

Nature of the Work

When production workers encounter problems with the machines they operate, they call on industrial machinery repairers. These workers, also called industrial machinery mechanics or maintenance machinists, maintain and repair machinery found in a plant or factory. Their work is not only important because an idle machine will delay production, but also because a machine that is not properly repaired and maintained may damage the final product or injure the operator.

Maintenance mechanics must be able to spot minor problems and correct them before they become major ones. For example, after hearing a vibration from a machine, the mechanic must decide whether it is due to worn belts, weak motor bearings, or some other problem. Computerized maintenance-management, vibration analysis techniques, and self-diagnostic systems are making this task easier. Self-diagnostic features on new industrial machinery can determine the cause of a malfunction and, in some cases, alert the mechanic to potential trouble spots before symptoms develop.

After diagnosing the problem, the mechanic disassembles the equipment and repairs or replaces the necessary parts. The final step is to test the machine to ensure it is running smoothly. When repairing electronically controlled machinery, maintenance mechanics may work closely with electronic repairers or electricians who maintain the machine's electronic parts. However, industrial machinery repairers increasingly need electronic and computer skills to repair sophisticated equipment on their own. (Additional information about commercial and industrial electronic equipment repairers, as well as electricians, appears elsewhere in the *Handbook*.)

A wide range of tools may be used when performing preventive maintenance or making repairs. For example, repairers may use a screwdriver and wrench to adjust a motor, or a hoist to lift a printing press off the ground. When replacements for broken or defective parts are not readily available, or when a machine must be quickly returned to production, repairers may sketch a part that can be fabricated by the plant's machine shop. Repairers use catalogs to order replacement parts and often follow blueprints and engineering specifications to maintain and fix equipment.

Although repairing machines is the most important job of industrial machinery repairers, they also spend much of their time performing preventive maintenance. This includes keeping machines and their parts well oiled, greased, and cleaned. Repairers regularly inspect machinery and check performance. For example, they adjust and calibrate automated manufacturing equipment such as industrial robots, and rebuild components of other industrial machinery. By keeping complete and up-to-date records, mechanics try to anticipate trouble and service equipment before factory production is interrupted.

Installation of new machinery is another responsibility of industrial machinery repairers. As plants retool and invest in new equipment, they increasingly rely on these workers to properly situate and install the machinery. In many plants, this has traditionally been the job of millwrights. (See the statement on millwrights elsewhere in the *Handbook*.) As employers increasingly seek workers who have a variety of skills, industrial machinery repairers are taking on new responsibilities.

Working Conditions

Working conditions for repairers who work in manufacturing are similar to those of production workers. These workers are subject to common shop injuries such as cuts and bruises, and use protective equipment such as hard hats, protective glasses, and safety belts. Industrial machinery repairers may also face additional hazards because they often work on the top of a ladder or underneath or above large machinery in cramped conditions.

Industrial machinery mechanics repair the growing number of machines in the Nation's factories.

Because factories and other facilities cannot afford breakdowns of industrial machinery, repairers may be called to the plant at night or on weekends for emergency repairs. Overtime is common among industrial machinery repairers—more than a third work over 40 hours a week.

Employment

Industrial machinery repairers held about 459,000 jobs in 1996. About 7 of every 10 worked in manufacturing industries, primarily food processing, textile mill products, chemicals, fabricated metal products, and primary metals. Others worked for government agencies, public utilities, mining companies, and other establishments in which industrial machinery is used.

Because industrial machinery repairers work in a wide variety of plants, they are employed in every part of the country. Employment is concentrated, however, in heavily industrialized areas.

Training, Other Qualifications, and Advancement

Many workers learn their trade through a 4-year apprenticeship program combining classroom instruction with on-the-job-training. These programs are usually sponsored by a local trade union. Other workers start as helpers and pick up the skills of the trade informally and by taking courses offered by machinery manufacturers and community colleges.

Repairers learn from experienced repairers how to operate, disassemble, repair, and assemble machinery. Classroom instruction focuses on subjects such as shop mathematics, blueprint reading, welding, electronics, and computer training.

Most employers prefer to hire those who have completed high school. High school courses in mechanical drawing, mathematics, blueprint reading, physics, and electronics are especially useful.

Mechanical aptitude and manual dexterity are important characteristics for workers in this trade. Good physical conditioning and agility are also necessary because repairers sometimes have to lift heavy objects or climb to reach equipment located high above the floor.

Opportunities for advancement are limited. Industrial machinery repairers advance either by working with more complicated equipment or by becoming supervisors. The most highly skilled repairers can be promoted to master mechanic or can become machinists or tool and die makers.

Job Outlook

Employment of industrial machinery repairers is projected to grow more slowly than the average for all occupations through the year 2006. Nevertheless, applicants with broad skills in machine repair should have favorable job prospects. As more firms introduce automated production equipment, industrial machinery mechanics will be needed to ensure these machines are well-maintained and consistently in operation. This growth will be moderated, however, by the self-diagnostic capabilities and growing reliability of many new machines that help to reduce the need for repairs. Most job openings will result from the need to replace repairers who transfer to other occupations or leave the labor force.

Unlike many other manufacturing occupations, industrial machinery repairers are not usually affected by seasonal changes in production. During slack periods, when some plant workers are laid off, repairers often are retained to do major overhaul jobs. Although these workers may face layoff or a reduced workweek when economic conditions are particularly severe, they generally are less affected than other workers because machines have to be maintained regardless of production level.

Earnings

Median weekly earnings of full-time industrial machinery repairers were about $570 in 1996; the middle 50 percent earned between $420 and $750 weekly. The lowest 10 percent earned less than $330, while the top 10 percent earned more than $930. Earnings vary by industry and geographic region.

Labor unions to which some industrial machinery repairers belong include the United Steelworkers of America; the United Automobile, Aerospace and Agricultural Implement Workers of America; the International Association of Machinists and Aerospace Workers; and the International Union of Electronic, Electrical, Salaried, Machine, and Furniture Workers.

Related Occupations

Other occupations that involve repairing machinery include aircraft mechanics and engine specialists; elevator installers and repairers; machinists; millwrights; and automotive, motorcycle, diesel, farm equipment, general maintenance, mobile heavy equipment, and heating, air-conditioning, and refrigeration mechanics.

Sources of Additional Information

Information about employment and apprenticeship opportunities for industrial machinery repairers may be obtained from local offices of the State employment service or from:
☛ United Brotherhood of Carpenters and Joiners of America, 101 Constitution Ave. NW., Washington, DC 20001.
☛ The National Tooling and Machining Association, 9300 Livingston Rd., Fort Washington, MD 20744.

Line Installers and Cable Splicers

(D.O.T. 821.261-010, -014, -022, and -026, .281-010, .361-010, -018, -022, -026, -030, and -038, .684-022, .687-010; 822.381-014; 823.261-014; 829.361-010 and -014; and 959.367-010)

Significant Points

- Line installers and cable splicer jobs do not require education beyond high school, but provide substantial on-the-job training that leads to relatively high earnings.

- Employment is expected to increase moderately, but competition is expected for jobs.

- Line installers and cable splicer work outdoors in all weather; when severe weather damages cables, they may

be called out on short notice and work long hours until service is restored.

Nature of the Work

Vast networks of wires and cables transmit the electric power produced in generating plants to individual customers, connect telephone central offices to customers' telephones and switchboards, and extend cable television to residential and commercial customers. These networks are constructed and maintained by line installers and cable splicers and their helpers.

To install new electric power or telephone lines, line installers or line erectors install poles and terminals, erect towers, and place wires and cables. They usually use power equipment to dig holes and set poles. Line installers climb the poles or use truck-mounted buckets (aerial work platforms) and use handtools to attach the cables. When working with electric power lines, installers bolt or clamp insulators onto the pole before attaching the cable. They may also install transformers, circuit breakers, switches, or other equipment. To bury underground cable, they use trenchers, plows, and other power equipment.

Line installers also lay cable television lines underground or hang them on poles with telephone and utility wires. These lines transmit broadcast signals from microwave towers to customers' homes. Installers place wiring in the house, connect the customers' television sets to it, and check that the television signal is strong.

After telephone line installers place cables in position, cable splicers, also referred to as cable splicing technicians, complete the line connections. (Electric power line workers install and splice the cables simultaneously.) Splicers connect individual wires or fibers within the cable and rearrange wires when lines have to be changed. They first read and interpret service orders and circuit diagrams to determine splicing specifications. Splices are then made by joining wires and cables with small handtools, epoxy, or mechanical equipment. At each splice, they place insulation over the conductor and seal the splice with some type of moisture proof covering. They may fill the cable sheathing on critical transmission routes with compressed air, so leaks in the sheathing can be monitored and repaired. Splicers work on poles, aerial ladders and platforms, in manholes, or in basements of large buildings.

Fiber optic cables are used to replace worn or obsolete copper cables. These tiny hair-thin strands of glass are able to carry more signals per cable because they transmit pulses of light instead of electricity. Splices of fiber optic cables are completed in a van positioned near the splice point. These vans house workshops that contain all the necessary equipment, such as machines that heat the glass fibers so they can be joined.

Line installers and cable splicers also maintain and repair telephone, power, and cable television lines. They periodically make sure lines are clear of tree limbs or other obstructions that could cause problems, and check insulation on cables and other equipment on line poles. When bad weather or earthquakes break wires or cables, knock poles down, or cause underground ducts to collapse, they make emergency repairs.

Working Conditions

Because telephone, electric, and television cables are strung from utility poles or are underground, line installers and cable splicers must climb and lift or work in stooped and cramped positions. They usually work outdoors in all kinds of weather and are subject to 24-hour calls. Most usually work a 40-hour week, but unexpected circumstances may create a need for overtime work. For example, when severe weather damages transmission and distribution lines, they may work long and irregular hours to restore service. At times, they may travel to distant locations, and occasionally stay for a lengthy period to help restore damaged facilities or build new ones.

Line installers and cable splicers face many situations in which safety procedures must be followed. They wear safety equipment when entering manholes and test for the presence of gas before going underground. They may be exposed to hazardous chemicals from the solvents and plugging compounds they use when splicing cables.

Line installers and cable splicers usually work outdoors in all kinds of weather and are subject to 24-hour calls.

Electric power line workers have the most hazardous jobs. They typically work 20 to 40 feet above ground level because electric cable is always strung above telephone and cable television lines.In addition to this danger, the voltages in electric power lines are lethal.

Employment

Line installers and cable splicers held about 309,000 jobs in 1996. More than half were telephone and cable television line installers and repairers. Nearly all worked for telephone, cable television companies, or electric power companies, or for construction companies specializing in power line, telephone, and cable television construction.

Training, Other Qualifications, and Advancement

Line installers are often hired as helpers or ground workers. Most employers prefer high school graduates. Many employers test applicants for basic verbal, arithmetic, and abstract reasoning skills. Some employers test for physical ability such as balance, coordination, and strength and mechanical aptitude. Because the work entails a lot of climbing, applicants should have stamina and must be unafraid of heights. Knowledge of basic electricity and training in installing telephone systems obtained in the Armed Forces or vocational education programs may be helpful. The ability to distinguish colors is necessary because wires and cables are usually coded by color. Motivation, self-discipline, and the ability to work as part of a team are needed to work efficiently and safely.

Line installers and cable splicers in electric companies and construction firms specializing in cable installation generally complete a formal apprenticeship program. These are administered jointly by the employer and the union representing the workers, either the International Brotherhood of Electrical Workers or the Communications Workers of America. These programs last several years and combine formal instruction with on-the-job training. Workers in telephone companies generally receive several years of informal on-the-job training, in some cases learning other skills such as telephone installation and repair. They may also attend training provided by equipment manufacturers.

A growing number of employers are using computer-assisted instruction, video cassettes, movies, or "programmed" workbooks. Some training facilities are equipped with poles, cable-supporting clamps, and other fixtures, to simulate working conditions as closely

as possible. Trainees learn to work on poles while keeping their hands free. In one exercise, for example, they play catch with a basketball while on the poles.

Formal training includes instruction in electrical codes, blueprint reading, and basic electrical theory. Afterwards, trainees learn on the job and work with a crew of experienced line installers under a line supervisor. Line installers and cable splicers receive training throughout their careers to qualify for more difficult assignments, and to keep up with technological changes.

Since deregulation of the telephone industry, many telephone companies have reduced the scope of their training programs in order to reduce their costs and to remain competitive. Increasingly, workers are responsible for their own training, which is provided by community colleges and postsecondary vocational schools.

For installers in the telephone industry, advancement may come about through promotion to splicer. Splicers can advance to engineering assistants or may move into other kinds of work, such as sales. Promotion to a supervisory position also is possible. In the electric industry, promotion is usually to a supervisory position.

Job Outlook

Job seekers are expected to face competition. Because there are few prerequisite skills, training is largely provided on the job, and earnings are above average, applicants should outnumber available job openings. Besides employment growth, many job openings will result from the need to replace the large number of older workers reaching retirement age. Job prospects will be best in telephone companies, particularly for those who combine knowledge of line installation, fiber optic and copper cable splicing, and repair of many types of equipment.

Overall employment of line installers and cable splicers is expected to grow about as fast as the average through the year 2006. Technological advances will result in divergent trends within this occupation. Technological change is expected to have little impact on electrical power line installers, and their employment is expected to grow more slowly than the average for all occupations to meet the growing demand for electricity and the need to maintain existing lines. Employment of telephone and cable television line installers and repairers, however, is projected to grow about as fast as the average, in line with the growth in telephone and cable television usage. If, as expected, telephone companies expand their services to provide cable TV, electronic publishing, and other telecommunication services, they will have to modernize their networks by laying fiber-optic cables that dramatically expand the electronic pipeline that reaches each home. Line installers and cable splicers will be needed to lay the new larger capacity cables.

Earnings

Pay rates for line installers and cable splicers vary greatly across the country and depend on length of service; specific information may be obtained from local telephone, electric power, and cable television companies. It generally takes about 5 years to go from the bottom to the top of the pay scale. In 1996, line installers and repairers who worked full time earned a median weekly wage of $703. The middle 50 percent earned between $498 and $892. The bottom 10 percent earned less than $351; the top 10 percent earned more than $1,072 a week.

Line installers and cable splicers employed by AT&T and the Bell Operating Companies and represented by the Communications Workers of America earned between $279 and $962 a week in 1996. Because of low job turnover in these occupations, many workers earn salaries near the top of the pay scale.

According to the International Brotherhood of Electrical Workers, average hourly wages in 1997 for line installers and cable splicers were between $17.81 and $19.35.

Most line installers and cable splicers belong to unions, principally the Communications Workers of America and the International Brotherhood of Electrical Workers. For these workers, union contracts set wage rates, wage increases, and the time needed to advance from one step to the next. These contracts require extra pay for overtime and all work on Sundays and holidays. Most contracts provide for additional pay for night work. Time in service determines the length of paid vacations. Depending on job locality, there are 9 to 12 holidays a year.

Related Occupations

Workers in other skilled crafts and trades who work with tools and machines include communications equipment mechanics, biomedical equipment technicians, telephone installers and repairers, electricians, and sound technicians.

Sources of Additional Information

For more details about employment opportunities, contact the telephone or electric power company in your community or local offices of the unions that represent these workers. For general information on line installer and cable splicer jobs, write to:

☞ Communications Workers of America, Department of Apprenticeships, Benefits, and Employment, 501 3rd St. NW., Washington, DC 20001.

For additional information on the telephone industry and career opportunities contact:

☞ United States Telephone Association, 1401 H St. NW., Suite 600, Washington, DC 20005-2136.

For information on employment and training contact:

☞ Utility Workers Union of America, 815 16th. St. NW., Washington, DC 20006.

☞ International Brotherhood of Electrical Workers, Telecommunications Department, 1125 15th. St. NW., Room 807, Washington, DC 20005.

Millwrights

(D.O.T. 638.261-010, -014, -018, -026, .281-018, -022)

Significant Points

- Training lasts 4 years—through apprenticeship programs that combine on-the-job training with classroom instruction, or through community college coupled with informal on-the-job training.

- While employment of millwrights is projected to decline slightly, skilled applicants should have good job opportunities.

- About 55 percent belong to labor unions, one of the highest rates of membership in the economy.

Nature of the Work

Millwrights install, repair, replace, and dismantle the machinery and heavy equipment used in almost every industry. These responsibilities require a wide range of skills—from blueprint reading and pouring concrete to diagnosing and solving mechanical problems.

The millwright's responsibilities begin when machinery arrives at the job site. New equipment must be unloaded, inspected, and then moved into position. To lift and move light machinery, millwrights use rigging and hoisting devices such as pulleys and cables. In other cases, they require the assistance of hydraulic lift-truck or crane operators to position the machinery. Because millwrights often decide which device to use for moving machinery, they must know the load-bearing properties of ropes, cables, hoists, and cranes.

Millwrights consult with production managers and others to determine the optimal placement of machines in the plant. In some instances, this placement may require a new foundation to be built. Millwrights either personally prepare the foundation or supervise its construction, so they must know how to read blueprints and work with building materials such as concrete, wood, and steel.

When assembling machinery, millwrights fit bearings, align gears and wheels, attach motors, and connect belts according to the manufacturer's blueprints and drawings. Precision leveling and alignment are important in the assembly process; millwrights must have good mathematical skills so they can measure angles, material thickness, and small distances with tools such as squares, calipers, and micrometers. When a high level of precision is required, devices such as lasers and ultrasonic measuring tools may be used. Millwrights also work with hand and power tools, cutting torches, welding machines, and soldering guns. Some of these workers use metalworking equipment such as lathes or grinders to modify parts to specifications.

Increasingly sophisticated automation means more complicated machines for millwrights to install and maintain. This machinery may require special care and knowledge, so millwrights often work closely with computer or electronic experts, electricians, engineers, and manufacturer's representatives to install it. (Additional information about commercial and industrial electronic equipment repairers, as well as electricians, appears elsewhere in the *Handbook*.)

In addition to installing and dismantling machinery, many millwrights repair and maintain equipment. This includes preventive maintenance, such as lubrication, and fixing or replacing worn parts. (For further information on machinery maintenance, see the statement on industrial machinery repairers elsewhere in the *Handbook*.)

Working Conditions

Working conditions vary by industry. Millwrights employed in manufacturing often work in a typical shop setting and use protective equipment to avoid common hazards. For example, injuries from falling objects or machinery may be prevented by protective devices such as safety belts, protective glasses, and hard hats. Those in construction may work outdoors in uncomfortable weather conditions.

Millwrights may work independently or as part of a team. They must work quickly and precisely, because non-functioning machinery costs a company time and money. Many millwrights work overtime; nearly half report working more than 40 hours during a typical week.

Employment

Millwrights held about 78,000 jobs in 1996. Most worked in manufacturing, primarily in durable goods industries such as motor vehicles and equipment and basic steel products. Millwrights found in other sectors were employed primarily by construction firms and machining and equipment wholesalers; many of these workers are contractors. Although millwrights work in every State, employment is concentrated in heavily industrialized areas.

Millwrights must install machinery in accordance with precise specifications.

Training, Other Qualifications, and Advancement

Millwrights normally train for 4 years—through apprenticeship programs that combine on-the-job training with classroom instruction, or through community college coupled with informal on-the-job training. These programs include training in dismantling, moving, erecting, and repairing machinery. Trainees may also work with concrete and receive instruction in related skills such as carpentry, welding, and sheet-metal work. Classroom instruction is provided in mathematics, blueprint reading, hydraulics, electricity, and increasingly, computers or electronics.

Employers prefer applicants with a high school diploma or equivalency and some vocational training or experience. Courses in science, mathematics, mechanical drawing, and machine shop practice are useful. Millwrights are expected to keep their skills up-to-date, and may need additional training on technological advances such as laser shaft alignment and vibration analysis.

Because millwrights assemble and disassemble complicated machinery, mechanical aptitude is very important. Strength and agility also are necessary, because the work can require a considerable amount of lifting and climbing. Millwrights need good interpersonal and communication abilities in order to work as part of a team and give detailed instructions to others.

Advancement for millwrights usually takes the form of higher wages. Some advance to supervisor, while others may become self-employed contractors.

Job Outlook

Employment of millwrights is projected to decline slightly through the year 2006; nevertheless, skilled applicants should have good job opportunities. Productivity increases resulting from new automation, limited growth in new industrial construction, and the growing utilization of lower-paid workers for installation and maintenance of machinery will contribute to a slight decline in employment. However, millwrights will still be needed to maintain and repair existing machinery, dismantle old machinery, and install new equipment. These highly skilled workers will encounter a number of job openings stemming from the need to replace experienced millwrights who transfer to other occupations or leave the labor force.

Millwrights are becoming more productive through use of technologies like hydraulic torque wrenches, ultrasonic measuring tools, and laser shaft alignment that allow fewer workers to perform more work. In addition, the demand for millwrights will be adversely affected as lower-paid workers, such as electronic technicians and industrial machinery mechanics, increasingly assume some installation and maintenance duties. And, industrial construction is expected to be insufficient to maintain current employment levels. Nevertheless, historical employment of millwrights has been fairly stable, and the growing use of machinery in the Nation's economy should ensure that the employment decline will be small.

Earnings

Median weekly earnings of full-time millwrights were about $670 in 1996, compared to $490 for all workers. The middle 50 percent earned between $510 and $820; the lowest 10 percent earned less than $380, while the top 10 percent earned more than $1,030. Earnings vary by industry and geographic location. About 55 percent of millwrights belong to labor unions, one of the highest rates of membership in the economy.

Related Occupations

To set up machinery for use in a plant, millwrights must know how to use hoisting devices and how to assemble, disassemble, and in some cases repair machinery. Other workers with similar job duties include industrial machinery repairers, aircraft mechanics and engine specialists, ironworkers, machine assemblers, and mobile heavy equipment, diesel, and farm equipment mechanics.

Sources of Additional Information

For further information on apprenticeship programs, write to the Apprenticeship Council of your State's labor department, local offices of your State employment service, or local firms that employ millwrights. In addition, you may contact:

☛ The United Brotherhood of Carpenters and Joiners of America, 101 Constitution Ave. NW., Washington DC 20001.

☛ Associated General Contractors of America, 1957 E St. NW., Washington, DC 20006.

☛ The National Tooling and Machining Association, 9300 Livingston Rd., Fort Washington, MD 20744.

Mobile Heavy Equipment Mechanics

(D.O.T. 620.261-022, .281-042, .381-014)

Significant Points

- Opportunities should be good for persons who complete formal post-secondary training in diesel mechanics or mobile heavy equipment repair.

- This occupation offers the opportunity for relatively high earnings while performing challenging skilled work.

- Mechanics increasingly use computerized diagnostic equipment.

Nature of the Work

Mobile heavy equipment is indispensable to construction, logging, surface mining, and other industrial activities. Various types grade land, lift beams, and dig earth to pave the way for new development. Mobile heavy equipment mechanics repair and maintain the engines, transmissions, hydraulics, and electrical systems that power graders, backhoes, and stripping and loading shovels. (Mechanics who specialize in servicing diesel engines only are discussed in the section on diesel mechanics elsewhere in the *Handbook*.)

Mobile heavy equipment mechanics typically work for large construction companies, local and Federal governments, and other organizations that operate and maintain their own heavy equipment fleets. They perform routine maintenance checks on diesel engines, transmission components, and brake systems to ensure safety and longevity of the equipment. Maintenance checks and feedback from equipment operators usually alert the mechanics to problems. With modern heavy equipment, hand held computers can be plugged in to an on-board computer to diagnose any component that needs adjustment or repair. After the problem has been found, technicians rely on their training and experience to use the best possible technique to solve the problem. If necessary, they may partially dismantle the component to examine parts for damage or excessive wear. Then, using hand-held tools, they repair, replace, clean, and lubricate the parts as necessary. Once the component is reassembled and tested for safety, it is put back into the equipment and sent back to the field.

Many types of mobile heavy equipment use hydraulics to raise and lower movable parts such as scoops, shovels, log forks, and scraper blades. Repairing malfunctioning hydraulic components is an important responsibility of mobile heavy equipment mechanics. When components lose power, mechanics examine them for hydraulic fluid leaks, ruptured hoses, or worn gaskets on fluid reservoirs. Occasionally, the equipment requires more extensive repairs such as replacing a defective hydraulic pump.

In addition to routine maintenance checks, mobile heavy equipment mechanics perform a variety of other repairs. They diagnose electrical problems and adjust or replace defective electronic components. They also disassemble and repair undercarriages and track assemblies. Occasionally, mechanics weld broken equipment frames and structural parts using electric or gas welders.

Many mechanics work in repair shops for construction contractors, local government road maintenance departments, and logging and mining companies. They typically perform the routine maintenance and minor repairs necessary to keep the equipment in operation. Mechanics in larger repair shops—particularly those of mobile

Mobile heavy equipment mechanics rely on their training and experience to use the best possible technique to solve problems.

heavy equipment dealers and the Federal Government—perform more difficult repairs. They include rebuilding or replacing engines, repairing hydraulic fluid pumps, or correcting electrical problems.

It is common for mechanics in some large shops to specialize in one or two types of work. For example, a shop may have individual specialists in major engine repair, transmission work, electrical systems, and suspension or brake systems. The technology used in heavy equipment is becoming more sophisticated with the increased use of electronic components to control a growing variety of functions. Training in electronics is essential for these mechanics in order to make engine adjustments and to diagnose problems. Hand held computers serve as the link from technician to vehicle.

Mobile heavy equipment mechanics use a variety of tools in their work. They use power tools such as pneumatic wrenches to remove bolts quickly, machine tools like lathes and grinding machines to rebuild brakes, welding and flame-cutting equipment to remove and repair exhaust systems, and jacks and hoists to lift and move large parts. They use common handtools like screwdrivers, pliers, and wrenches to work on small parts and hard-to-reach places. Heavy equipment mechanics also use a variety of computerized testing equipment to pinpoint and analyze malfunctions in electrical systems and engines. For example, they use tachometers and dynamometers to locate engine malfunctions. When working on electrical systems, they use ohmmeters, ammeters, and voltmeters.

Working Conditions

Mobil heavy equipment mechanics usually work indoors, although many make repairs at the work site. Mechanics often lift heavy parts and tools. Minor cuts, burns, and bruises are common, but serious accidents can be avoided when the shop is kept clean and orderly and when safety practices observed. Mechanics frequently get dirty—they may handle greasy and dirty parts and may stand or lie in awkward positions to repair vehicles and equipment. While they usually work in well lighted, heated, and ventilated areas, some shops are drafty and noisy. Many employers also provide uniforms, locker rooms and shower facilities.

When mobile heavy equipment breaks down at a construction site, it may be too difficult or expensive to bring it into a repair shop, so a field service mechanic is sent to the job site to make repairs. Field service mechanics work outdoors and spend much of their time away from the shop. Generally, the more experienced mobile heavy equipment mechanics specialize in field service. They usually drive specially equipped trucks and, on occasion, must travel many miles to reach disabled machinery. Because of their experience and travel requirements, field mechanics usually earn a higher wage than their counterparts.

Employment

Mobile heavy equipment mechanics held about 104,000 jobs in 1996. Nearly 50 percent worked for mobile heavy equipment dealers and construction contractors. About 20 percent were employed by Federal, State, and local governments; the Department of Defense is the primary Federal employer. Other mobile heavy equipment mechanics worked for surface mine operators, public utility companies, logging camps and contractors, and heavy equipment rental and leasing companies. Still others repaired equipment for machinery manufacturers, airlines, railroads, steel mills, and oil and gas field companies. Fewer than 1 out of 20 mobile heavy equipment mechanics was self-employed.

Nearly every section of the country employs mobile heavy equipment mechanics in some form, though most work in towns and cities where trucking companies, construction, and other fleet owners have large operations.

Training, Other Qualifications, and Advancement

Although many persons qualify for heavy equipment mechanic jobs through years of on-the-job training, most employers prefer that applicants complete a formal diesel heavy equipment mechanic training program after graduating from high school. They seek persons with mechanical aptitude who are knowledgeable about the fundamentals of diesel engines, transmissions, electrical systems, and hydraulics. The constant change in equipment technology makes it necessary for mechanics to be flexible and have the capacity to learn new skills quickly.

Most community colleges and vocational schools offer programs in diesel mechanics or automotive repair. Some tailor programs to heavy equipment mechanics. These programs educate the student in the basics of analysis and diagnostic techniques, while improving communication skills. The increased use of electronics and computers makes training in the fundamentals of electronics an essential tool for new mobile heavy equipment mechanics. Some 1- to 2-year programs lead to a certificate of completion while others lead to an associate degree in diesel or heavy equipment mechanics. These programs provide a basic foundation in the components of diesel and heavy equipment technology. This also enables trainee mechanics to advance more rapidly to the journey, or experienced worker, level.

A combination of formal and on-the-job training prepares trainee mechanics with the knowledge to efficiently service and repair the equipment handled by the shop. Most beginners perform routine service tasks and make minor repairs after a few months' experience. They advance to increasingly difficult jobs as they prove their ability and competence. After they master the repair and service of diesel engines, they learn to work on related components such as brakes, transmissions, and electrical systems. Generally, a mechanic with at least 3 to 4 years of on-the-job experience is accepted as a fully qualified heavy equipment mechanic.

Many employers send trainee mechanics to training sessions conducted by heavy equipment manufacturers. These sessions, which typically last up to 1 week, provide intensive instruction in the repair of a manufacturer's equipment. Some sessions focus on particular components found in all of the manufacturer's equipment, such as diesel engines, transmissions, axles, and electrical systems. Other sessions focus on particular types of equipment, such as crawler-loaders and crawler-dozers. As they progress, trainees may periodically attend additional training sessions. When appropriate, experienced mechanics attend training sessions to gain familiarity with new technology or with types of equipment they have never repaired.

High school courses in automobile mechanics, physics, chemistry, and mathematics provide a strong foundation for a career as a mechanic. It is also essential for mechanics to be able to read, interpret, and comprehend service manuals to keep abreast of engineering changes. Experience working on diesel engines and heavy equipment acquired in the Armed Forces also is valuable.

Voluntary certification by the National Institute for Automotive Service Excellence (ASE) is recognized as the standard of achievement for mobile heavy equipment mechanics. They may be certified as Master Heavy-Duty Diesel technician or in one or more of six different areas of heavy-duty equipment repair: Brakes, gasoline engines, diesel engines, drive trains, electrical systems, and suspension and steering. For certification in each area, mechanics must pass a written examination and have at least 2 years of experience. High school, vocational or trade school, or community or junior college training in gasoline or diesel engine repair may substitute for up to 1 year of experience. To retain certification, mechanics must retake the tests at least every 5 years.

The most important possessions of mechanics are their handtools. Mobile heavy equipment mechanics typically buy their own handtools and many experienced mechanics have thousands of dollars invested in them. Employers typically furnish expensive power tools, computerized engine analyzers, and other diagnostic equipment, but handtools are accumulated with experience.

Experienced mechanics may advance to field service jobs, where they have a greater opportunity to tackle problems independently and earn additional pay. Mechanics who have leadership ability may become shop supervisors or service managers. Some mechanics open their own repair shops or invest in a franchise.

Job Outlook

Opportunities for heavy equipment mechanics should be good for persons who have completed formal training programs in diesel or heavy equipment mechanics. This is due more to a lack of qualified entrants into the occupation than growth in available jobs. Persons without formal training are expected to encounter growing difficulty entering this occupation.

Employment of mobile heavy equipment mechanics is expected to grow more slowly than the average for all occupations through the year 2006. Increasing numbers of mechanics will be required to support growth in the construction industry, equipment dealers, and rental and leasing companies. As equipment becomes more complex, repairs increasingly must be made by specially trained mechanics. More mechanics will be needed by all levels of government to service construction equipment that build and repair the country's highways and bridges.

Due to the nature of construction activity, demand for mobile heavy equipment mechanics follows the Nation's economic cycle. As the economy expands, construction activity increases, resulting in the use of more mobile heavy equipment. More equipment will be needed to grade construction sites, excavate basements, and lay water and sewer lines, and this would increase the necessity for periodic service and repair. In addition, the construction and repair of highways and bridges also will require more mechanics to service equipment.

Because construction and mining are sensitive to changes in the level of economic activity, mobile heavy equipment may be idled during downturns. In addition, winter is traditionally the slow season for construction activity particularly in colder regions. Fewer mechanics may be needed during periods when equipment is used less, but employers usually try to retain experienced workers. However,

employers may be reluctant to hire inexperienced workers during slow periods.

Earnings

Median weekly earnings of mobile heavy equipment mechanics were about $613 in 1996. The middle 50 percent earned from $501 to $762 a week; the lowest 10 percent earned less than $383 a week, and the top 10 percent earned over $981 a week in 1996.

Some mobile heavy equipment mechanics are members of unions including the International Association of Machinists and Aerospace Workers; the International Union of Operating Engineers; and the International Brotherhood of Teamsters.

Related Occupations

Workers in other occupations who repair and service diesel-powered vehicles and heavy equipment include rail car repairers and diesel, farm equipment, and mine machinery mechanics.

Sources of Additional Information

More details about work opportunities for mobile heavy equipment mechanics may be obtained from local mobile heavy equipment dealers, construction contractors, surface mining companies, and government agencies. Local offices of the State employment service may also have information on work opportunities and training programs.

For general information about a career as a mobile heavy equipment mechanic contact:

☛ The Equipment Maintenance Counsel, 2020 Lake Shore Ct., Sanger, TX 76266.

☛ Associated General Contractors of America, Training and Educational Services, 1957 E St., N.W., Washington, DC 20006.

☛ Specialized Carriers and Rigging Association, 2750 Prosperity Ave., Suite 620, Fairfax, VA 22031-4312

For a directory of public training programs for mobile heavy equipment mechanics contact:

☛ Vocational Industry Clubs of America, P.O. Box 3000, 1401 James Monroe Hwy, Leesburg, VA 22075.

Information on how to become certified as a heavy-duty diesel mechanic is available from:

☛ ASE, 13505 Dulles Technology Dr., Herndon, VA 22071-3415.

☛ National Center for Construction Education and Research, University of Florida, P.O. Box 141104, Gainsville, FL 32614-1104.

Motorcycle, Boat, and Small-Engine Mechanics

(D.O.T. 620.281-054, .684-026; 623.261; .281-038, -042; 625.281-018, -026, -030, -034, .381; 721.281-022)

Significant Points

- Employment is expected to grow slowly, but persons with formal mechanic training should enjoy good job prospects.

- Use of motorcycles, boats, and outdoor power equipment is seasonal in many areas so in winter mechanics may service other types of equipment or work reduced hours.

Nature of the Work

Though smaller in size, engines that power motorcycles, boats, and lawn and garden equipment share many characteristics with their larger counterparts, including breakdowns. Motorcycle, boat, and small-engine mechanics repair and service power equipment ranges from racing motorcycles to chain saws.

Small engines, like larger engines, require periodic service to minimize the chance of breakdowns and to keep them operating at peak efficiency. During routine equipment maintenance, mechanics follow a checklist including the inspection and cleaning of brakes, electrical systems, plugs, carburetors, and other parts. Following inspection, mechanics usually repair or adjust parts that do not work properly, or replace unfixable parts. Routine maintenance is normally a major part of the mechanic's work.

When equipment breakdowns occur, mechanics use various techniques to diagnose the source and extent of the problem. The mark of a skilled mechanic is the ability to diagnose mechanical, fuel, and electrical problems, and to make repairs in a minimal amount of time. Quick and accurate diagnosis requires problem-solving ability and a thorough knowledge of the equipment's operation.

In larger repair shops, mechanics may use special computerized diagnostic testing equipment as a preliminary tool in analyzing situations. These computers provide a systematic performance report of various components, and how they compare to normal ratings. After pinpointing the problem, the mechanic makes the needed adjustments, repairs, or replacements. Some jobs require minor adjustments or the replacement of a single item, such as a carburetor or fuel pump. In contrast, a complete engine overhaul requires a number of hours to disassemble the engine and replace worn valves, pistons, bearings, and other internal parts.

Motorcycle, boat, and small-engine mechanics use common handtools such as wrenches, pliers, and screwdrivers. They also use power tools, such as drills and grinders when customized repairs warrant. Computerized engine analyzers, compression gauges, ammeters and voltmeters, and other testing devices help mechanics locate faulty parts and tune engines. Hoists may be used to lift heavy equipment such as motorcycles, snowmobiles, or boats. Mechanics often refer to service manuals for detailed directions and specifications while performing repairs.

Motorcycle mechanics repair and overhaul motorcycles, motor scooters, mopeds, and all-terrain vehicles. Besides engines, they may work on transmissions, brakes, and ignition systems, and make minor body repairs. Mechanics usually specialize in the service and repair of one type of equipment, although they may work on closely related products. Mechanics may only service a few makes and models of motorcycles because usually the dealers only service the products they sell.

Boat mechanics, or *marine equipment mechanics*, repair and adjust the engines, and electrical and mechanical equipment of inboard and outboard marine engines. Most small boats have portable outboard engines that are removed and brought into the repair shop. Larger craft, such as cabin cruisers and commercial fishing boats, are powered by diesel or gasoline inboard or inboard-outboard engines, which are only removed for major overhauls. Boat mechanics may also work on propellers, steering mechanisms, marine plumbing, and other boat equipment.

Some motorcycle and boat mechanics use the latest techniques and customized components on highly specialized race equipment. This relatively new segment of the industry rewards highly skilled mechanics with creative ability and good mechanical skills.

Small-engine mechanics service and repair outdoor power equipment such as lawnmowers, garden tractors, edge trimmers, and chain saws. They may also occasionally work on portable generators and go-carts. In addition, small engine mechanics in northern parts of the country may work on snowblowers and snowmobiles. It is rare for a mechanic to specialize in this type of repair because certain areas and times of the year strongly affect demand for repairs.

Working Conditions

Motorcycle, boat, and small-engine mechanics usually work in repair shops that are well lighted and ventilated, but are sometimes noisy when testing engines. However, boat mechanics may work outdoors at docks or marinas, and in all weather conditions, when making repairs aboard boats. They may work in cramped, or awkward positions to reach a boat's engine.

During the winter months in the northern United States, mechanics may work fewer than 40 hours a week because the amount of repair and service work declines when lawnmowers, boats and motorcycles are not in use. Many mechanics only work during the busy spring and summer seasons. Scheduling time-consuming engine overhauls and working on snowmobiles and snowblowers eases some winter-time slack. Mechanics may work considerably more than 40 hours a week in the spring, summer, and fall, or in warmer climates.

Employment

Motorcycle, boat, and small-engine mechanics held more than 45,000 jobs in 1996. About 12,000 were motorcycle mechanics, while the remainder specialized in the repair of boats or outdoor power equipment such as lawnmowers, garden tractors, and chain saws. Two-thirds of all motorcycle, boat, and small-engine mechanics worked for retail dealers of boats, motorcycles, and miscellaneous vehicles. Others were employed by independent repair shops, marinas and boat yards, equipment rental companies, and hardware and lawn and garden stores. About one-fourth were self-employed.

Training, Other Qualifications, and Advancement

Due to the increasing complexity of motorcycles and boats, most employers prefer to hire mechanics who graduate from formal training programs for motorcycle, marine, or small-engine mechanics. Because the number of these specialized post-secondary programs is limited, most mechanics learn their skills on the job or while working in related occupations. For trainee jobs, employers hire persons with mechanical aptitude who are knowledgeable about the fundamentals of small 2- and 4-cycle engines. Many trainees develop an interest in mechanics and acquire some basic skills through working on automobiles, motorcycles, boats, or outdoor power equipment as a hobby. Others may be introduced to mechanics through vocational automotive training in high school, or one of many post-secondary institutions.

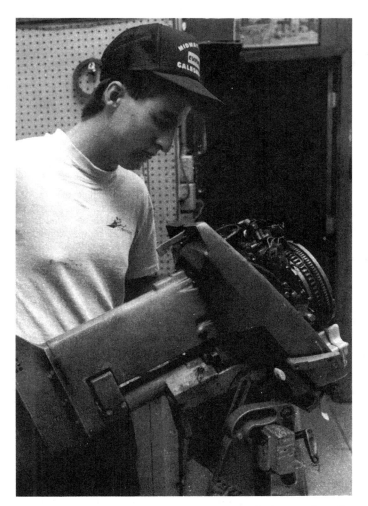

During routine equipment maintenance, motorcycle, boat, and small-engine mechanics often follow a checklist that includes the inspection and cleaning of plugs, carburetors, and other important parts.

Trainees begin by learning routine service tasks under the guidance of experienced mechanics, such as replacing ignition points and spark plugs, or taking apart, assembling, and testing new equipment. As trainees gain experience and proficiency, they progress to more difficult tasks, such as advanced computerized diagnosis and engine overhauls. Up to 3 years of training on the job may be necessary before a novice worker becomes competent in all aspects of the repair of motorcycle and boat engines.

Employers often send mechanics and trainees to special training courses conducted by motorcycle, boat, and outdoor power equipment manufacturers or distributors. These courses, which can last as long as 2 weeks, upgrade the worker's skills and provide information on repairing new models. They are usually a prerequisite for any mechanic who performs warranty work for manufacturers or insurance companies.

Most employers prefer to hire high school graduates for trainee mechanic positions, but will accept applicants with less education if they possess adequate reading, writing, and arithmetic skills. Many equipment dealers employ students part-time and during the summer, to help assemble new equipment and perform minor repairs. Helpful high school courses include small-engine repair, automobile mechanics, science, and business arithmetic.

Knowledge of basic electronics is essential for motorcycle, boat, and small-engine mechanics. Electronics components control engine performance, instrument displays, and a variety of other functions of motorcycles, boats, and outdoor power equipment. Mechanics should be familiar with the basic principles of electronics in order to recognize and fix potential problems.

The most important possessions of mechanics are their handtools. Mechanics usually provide their own tools and many experienced mechanics have invested thousands of dollars in them. Employers typically furnish expensive power tools, computerized engine analyzers, and other diagnostic equipment, but mechanics accumulate handtools with experience.

The skills used as a motorcycle, boat, and small engine mechanic generally transfer to other occupations such as automobile, truck, or heavy equipment mechanics. Experienced mechanics who have leadership ability may advance to shop supervisor or service manager jobs. Mechanics who have sales ability sometimes become sales representatives or open their own repair shop.

Job Outlook

Employment of motorcycle, boat, and small-engine mechanics is expected to grow slower the average for all occupations through the year 2006. The majority of job openings are expected to be replacement jobs because many experienced motorcycle, boat, and small-engine mechanics leave each year to transfer to other occupations, retire, or stop working for other reasons. Job prospects should be especially favorable for persons who complete mechanic training programs.

Growth of personal disposable income over the 1996-2006 period should provide consumers with more discretionary dollars to buy boats, lawn and garden power equipment, and motorcycles. This will require more mechanics to keep the growing amount of equipment in operation. Also, routine service will always be a significant source of work for mechanics. While technology will lengthen the interval between check-ups, the need for qualified mechanics to perform this service will increase.

Employment of motorcycle mechanics should increase slowly as the popularity of motorcycles rebounds. In the late 1990s, the number of persons between the ages of 18 and 24 should begin to grow. Motorcycle usage should continue to be popular with persons in this age group, which historically has had the greatest proportion of motorcycle enthusiasts. Motorcycles are also increasingly popular with persons over the age of 40. Traditionally, this group has more disposable income to spend on recreational equipment such as motorcycles and boats. Over the next decade, more people will be entering the over-40 age group; this group is responsible for the largest segment of marine craft purchases. These potential buyers will help expand the market for boats, while helping to maintain the demand for qualified mechanics. Construction of new single-family houses

will result in an increase in the lawn and garden equipment in operation, increasing the need for mechanics. However, equipment growth will be slowed by trends toward smaller lawns and contracting out their maintenance to lawn service firms.

Earnings

Motorcycle, boat, and small-engine mechanics who usually worked full time had median earnings of about $412 a week in 1996. The middle 50 percent earned between $289 and $549 a week. The lowest paid 10 percent averaged $224 a week, while the highest paid 10 percent averaged $676 a week.

Motorcycle, boat, and small-engine mechanics tend to receive few fringe benefits in small shops, but those employed in larger shops often receive paid vacations, sick leave, and health insurance. Some employers also pay for work related training and provide uniforms.

Related Occupations

Motorcycle, boat, and small-engine mechanics closely relate to mechanics and repairers who work on other types of mobile equipment powered by internal combustion engines. Related occupations include automotive mechanic, diesel mechanic, farm equipment mechanic, and mobile heavy equipment mechanic.

Sources of Additional Information

For more details about work opportunities, contact local motorcycle, boat, and lawn and garden equipment dealers, and boat yards and marinas. Local offices of the State employment service may also have information about employment and training opportunities.

General information about motorcycle mechanic careers may be obtained from:
☛ Motorcycle Mechanics Institute, 2844 West Deer Valley Rd., Phoenix, AZ 85027.
☛ American Motorcycle Institute, 3042 West International Speedway Blvd., Daytona Beach, FL 32124 or 1-800-874-0645.

General information about motorboat mechanic careers may be obtained from:
☛ Marine Mechanics Institute, 2844 West Deer Valley Rd., Phoenix, AZ 85027.
☛ American Marine Institute, 3042 West International Speedway Blvd., Daytona Beach, FL 32124 or 1-800-874-0645.

General information about small engine mechanic careers may be obtained from:
☛ Outdoor Power Equipment Institute, 341 South Patrick St., Alexandria, VA 22314.

For a list of public motorcycle, boat, and small-engine mechanic training programs, contact:
☛ Vocational Industrial Clubs of America, P.O. Box 3000, 1401 James Monroe Hwy, Leesburg, VA 22075.

Musical Instrument Repairers and Tuners

(D.O.T. 730.281-014, -026, -038, -050, -054, .361, .381-010, -026, -034, -038, -042, -058, .681-010, .684-022, -026, and -094)

Significant Points

- Half of all musical instrument repairers and tuners are self employed.

- Opportunities should be excellent for persons with formal training in piano technology or brass, woodwind, string, and electronic musical instrument repair.

- Musical instrument repairers and tuners should be able to play the instruments on which they work.

Nature of the Work

Musical instruments provide entertainment and recreation to millions of people everyday. Those who repair and tune instruments combine their love of music with a highly skilled craft. Musical instrument repairers and tuners, often referred to as technicians, work in four specialties: band instruments, pianos and organs, violins, and guitars. (Repairers and tuners who work on electronic organs are discussed in the *Handbook* statement on electronic home entertainment equipment repairers.)

Band Instrument repairers work on woodwind, brass, reed, and percussion instruments damaged through deterioration or accident. Starting with the customer's description of the problem, they examine instruments and determine what must be done to restore them to proper performance levels and established industry specifications. These technicians also regularly tune and adjust instruments.

Brass and woodwind instruments include trumpets, cornets, french horns, trombones, tubas, clarinets, flutes, saxophones, oboes, and bassoons. *Brass and wind instrument repairers* clean, adjust, and repair these instruments. They move mechanical parts or play scales to find defects. They may unscrew and remove rod pins, keys, and pistons and remove soldered parts using gas torches. They repair dents in metal instruments using mallets or burnishing tools. They fill cracks in wood instruments by inserting pinning wire and covering them with filler. Repairers also inspect instrument keys and replace worn pads and corks.

Percussion instrument repairers work on drums, cymbals, and xylophones. To repair a drum, technicians remove tension rods by hand or by using a drum key. They cut new drumheads from animal skin, stretch the skin over the rimhoops, and tuck the skin under the hoop using hand tools. To prevent a crack from advancing in a cymbal, gong, or similar instrument, repairers may drill holes at the inside edge of the crack; another technique involves cutting out sections around the cracks using shears or grinding wheels. Percussion repairers also replace the bars and wheels of xylophones.

Pianos and organs have thousands of parts made from wood, steel, iron, brass, ivory, felt, and sometimes Teflon that can be plagued by an assortment of problems. It is the task of *piano and organ repairers and tuners* to locate and correct these problems. While the piano and organ are each over 300 years old, the basic engineering of today's piano and organ was done almost 100 years ago and the methodology has changed very little since. To diagnose problems, *piano repairers* talk with customers and examine the piano's parts. Depending on the severity of the problem, they may replace worn parts, recondition usable parts, or completely rebuild pianos. In some cases, they may reconfigure or redesign parts to solve a specific problem. For work such as regulating, repining, and restringing, repairers use common handtools as well as specialty tools. In addition to repair work, piano repairers may also tune pianos.

Piano tuners increase and decrease the tension of piano strings to tune pianos to the proper pitch. A string's pitch is the frequency at which it vibrates, and produces sound, when it is struck by one of the piano's hammer. Pianos are tuned with the aid of either an electric or an acoustic pitch reference. The tuner strikes a key and compares the reference strings' pitch with that of the pitch reference. A tuning hammer (also called a tuning lever) is used to turn a tuning pin to increase or decrease tension on the reference string until its pitch matches that of the pitch reference. The pitch of each of the other strings is set in relation to the reference string. Modern 88-key pianos have over 200 strings and can be tuned in one to two hours, depending on the condition of the piano.

Generally, most piano technicians can tune, repair, and rebuild pianos. Some piano technicians provide additional service for pianos with built-in humidity control devices, recording devices, and automatic player-piano devices. These specialty services and repairs require additional training, yet are still considered part of the technician's duties.

Pipe-organ repairers tune, repair, and install organs that make music by forcing air through flue pipes or reed pipes. The flue pipe sounds when a current of air strikes a metal lip in the side of the pipe. The reed pipe sounds when a current of air vibrates a brass reed inside the pipe.

Pipe-organ repairers locate problems, repair or replace worn parts, and clean pipes. Repairers also assemble organs on site in churches and auditoriums, following manufacturer's blueprints. They use hand and power tools to install and connect the air chest, blowers, air ducts, pipes, and other components. They may work in teams or be assisted by helpers. Depending on the size of the organ, an installation job may take several weeks or even months.

To tune an organ, repairers first match the pitch of the "A" pipes with that of a tuning fork. The pitch of other pipes is set by comparing it to that of the "A" pipes. To tune a flue pipe, repairers move the metal slide that increases or decreases the pipe's "speaking length." To tune a reed pipe, the tuner alters the length of the brass reed. Most organs have hundreds of pipes, so often a day or more is needed to completely tune an organ.

Violin repairers adjust and repair bowed instruments, such as violins, violas, and cellos, using a variety of handtools. They find defects by inspecting and playing instruments. They replace or repair cracked or broken sections and damaged parts. They also restring instruments and repair damage to the instruments' finish.

Guitar repairers inspect and play the instrument to determine defects. They replace levels using handtools, and replace or repair damaged wood or metal parts. They reassemble and string guitars.

Working Conditions

Although they may suffer small cuts and bruises, the work of musical instrument repairers and tuners is relatively safe. Most brass, woodwind, percussion, and string instrument repairers work in repair shops or music stores. Piano and organ repairers and tuners usually work on instruments in homes, schools, colleges and universities, and churches, and may spend several hours a day driving. Salaried repairers and tuners work out of a shop or store; the self-employed generally work out of their homes.

Violin repairers restring instruments and replace or repair cracked or broken sections and damaged parts.

Recently, musical instrument repairers have switched to using non-toxic chemicals to clean, fill, and mold instruments, instead of the traditional sodium cyanide and chromate solutions. These changes have made workplaces cleaner and safer.

Employment

Musical instrument repairers and tuners held about 9,000 jobs in 1996. Most technicians worked on pianos. About half were self-employed. About 8 of 10 wage and salary repairers and tuners worked in music stores, and most of the rest worked in repair shops or for musical instrument manufacturers.

Training, Other Qualifications, and Advancement

For musical instrument repairer and tuner jobs, employers prefer people with post high school training in music repair technology. Some musical instrument repairers and tuners learn their trade on the job as apprentices or assistants, but employers willing to provide on-the-job training are difficult to find. A few music stores, large repair shops, and self-employed repairers and tuners hire inexperienced individuals as trainees to learn how to tune and repair instruments under the supervision of experienced workers. Trainees may sell instruments, clean up, and do other routine work. Usually 2 to 5 years of training and practice are needed to become fully qualified.

A small number of technical schools and colleges offer courses in piano technology or brass, woodwind, string, and electronic musical instrument repair. A few music repair schools offer 1- or 2-year courses. There are also home-study (correspondence school) courses in piano technology. Graduates of these courses generally refine their skills by working with an experienced tuner or technician.

Music courses help develop the student's ear for tonal quality. The ability to play an instrument is helpful. Knowledge of woodworking is useful for repairing instruments made of wood.

Repairers and tuners need good hearing, mechanical aptitude, and manual dexterity. For those dealing directly with customers, a neat appearance and a pleasant, cooperative manner are important.

Musical instrument repairers keep up with developments in their fields by studying trade magazines and manufacturers' service manuals. The Piano Technicians Guild helps its members improve their skills through training conducted at local chapter meetings and at regional, national, and international seminars. Guild members can also take a series of tests, one written and two practical, to earn the title Registered Piano Technician. The National Association of Professional Band Instrument Repair Technicians offers similar programs, scholarships, and a trade publication. Its members specialize in the repair of woodwind, brass, string and percussion instruments. Repairers and technicians who work for large dealers, repair shops, or manufacturers can advance to supervisory positions or go into business for themselves.

Job Outlook

Musical instrument repairer and tuner jobs are expected to increase more slowly than the average for all occupations through the year 2006. Replacement needs will provide the most job opportunities as many repairers and tuners near retirement age. The small number of openings, due to both growth and replacement needs, is very low relative to other occupations. Because training is difficult to receive—there are only a few schools that offer training programs and few experienced workers are willing to take on apprentices—opportunities should be excellent for those who do receive training.

Several factors are expected to influence the demand for musical instrument repairers and tuners. The number of people employed as musicians will increase, mainly due to a slight increase in the number of students of all ages playing musical instruments. Because instruments are quite expensive to purchase, growing numbers of instrument repairers will be needed to work on rental equipment leased to students, schools, and other organizations.

Earnings

Musical instrument repairers and tuners who usually worked full time had median weekly earnings of $559 in 1996. The middle 50 percent earned between $428 and $855 a week. The lowest 10 percent earned less than $300, while the highest 10 percent earned more than $939 a week. Earnings were generally higher in urban areas.

Related Occupations

Musical instrument repairers need mechanical aptitude and good manual dexterity. Electronic home entertainment equipment repairers, vending machine servicers and repairers, home appliance and power tool repairers, and computer and office machine repairers all require similar talents.

Sources of Additional Information

Details about job opportunities may be available from local music instrument dealers and repair shops.

For general information about piano technicians and a list of schools offering courses in piano technology, write to:
☛ Piano Technicians Guild, 3930 Washington St., Kansas City, MO 64111-2963.

For general information on musical instrument repair, write to:
☛ National Association of Professional Band Instrument Repair Technicians (NAPBIRT), P.O. Box 51, Normal, IL 61761.

Vending Machine Servicers and Repairers

(D.O.T. 319.464-014 and 639.281-014)

Significant Points

- Vending machine servicers and repairers learn their skills on the job.

- Although employment is expected to decline, opportunities should be good for persons with some knowledge of electronics.

Nature of the Work

Coin-operated vending machines are a familiar sight. These machines dispense many types of refreshments, from cold soft drinks to hot meals. Vending machine servicers and repairers install, service, and stock these machines and keep them in good working order.

Vending machine servicers, often called "route drivers," visit coin-operated machines that dispense soft drinks, candy and snacks, and other items. They collect money from the machines, restock merchandise, and change labels to indicate new selections. They also keep the machines clean. Because many vending machines dispense food, these workers comply with State and local public health and sanitation standards.

Repairers, often called "mechanics" or "technicians," make sure machines operate correctly. When checking complicated electrical and electronic machines, such as beverage dispensers, they make sure that the machines mix drinks properly and that refrigeration and heating units work correctly. On the relatively simple gravity-operated machines, servicers check handles, springs, plungers, and merchandise chutes. They also test coin and change-making mechanisms. When installing the machines, they make the necessary water and electrical connections and recheck the machines for proper operation. They also make sure installation complies with local plumbing and electrical codes.

Preventive maintenance—avoiding trouble before it starts—is a major job of repairers. For example, they periodically clean refrigeration condensers, lubricate mechanical parts, and adjust machines to perform properly.

If a machine breaks down, *vending machine repairers* inspect it for obvious problems, such as loose electrical wires, malfunctions of the coin mechanism, and leaks. If the problem cannot be readily located, they refer to technical manuals and wiring diagrams and use testing devices such as electrical circuit testers to find defective parts.

Repairers decide the malfunction can be fixed on-site or if it must be replaced and sent back to the repair shop. When servicing electronic machines, repairers test them with hand held diagnostic computers that determine the extent and location of any problems. Repairers may only have to replace a circuit board or other component to fix the problem. They also repair microwave ovens used to heat food dispensed from machines.

In the repair shop, they use power tools, such as grinding wheels, saws, and drills as well as voltmeters, ohmmeters, oscilloscopes, and other testing equipment. They also use ordinary repair tools such as screwdrivers, pliers, and wrenches.

Vending machine servicers and repairers employed by small companies may both fill and fix machines on a regular basis. These combination servicers-repairers stock machines, collect money, fill coin and currency changers, and repair machines when necessary.

Servicers and repairers also do some clerical work, such as filing reports, preparing repair cost estimates, ordering parts, and keeping daily records of merchandise distributed. However, new machines with computerized inventory controls reduce the paperwork a servicer must complete.

Working Conditions
Some vending machine repairers work primarily in company repair shops, but many spend much of their time on the road visiting machines wherever they have been placed. Vending machines operate around the clock, so repairers often work at night and on weekends and holidays.

Vending machine repair shops generally are quiet, well lighted, and have adequate work space. However, when servicing machines on location, the work may be done where pedestrian traffic is heavy, such as in busy supermarkets, industrial complexes, offices, or schools. Repair work is relatively safe, although servicers and repairers must take care to avoid hazards such as electrical shocks and cuts from sharp tools and metal objects. They also must follow safe work procedures, especially when moving heavy vending machines or working with electricity and radiation from microwave ovens.

Employment
Vending machine servicers and repairers held about 21,000 jobs in 1996. Most repairers work for vending companies that sell food and other items through machines. Others work for soft drink bottling

Vending machine servicers and repairers test and clean the electrical parts inside machines.

companies that have their own coin-operated machines. Some work for companies that also own video games, pin-ball machines, juke boxes, and similar types of amusement equipment. Although vending machine servicers and repairers are employed throughout the country, most are located in areas with large populations and many coin and vending machines.

Training, Other Qualifications, and Advancement
Employers generally prefer to hire high school graduates. They are trained to fill and fix machines informally on the job by observing, working with, and receiving instruction from experienced repairers. High school or vocational school courses in electricity, refrigeration, and machine repair are an advantage in qualifying for entry jobs. Employers usually require applicants to demonstrate mechanical ability, either through their work experience or by scoring well on mechanical aptitude tests. Because vending machine servicers and repairers sometimes handle thousands of dollars in merchandise and cash, employers hire persons who have a record of honesty. The ability to deal tactfully with people also is important. A commercial driver's license and a good driving record are essential for most vending machine servicer and repairer jobs. Some employers require their servicers to be bonded.

Electronics have become more prevalent in vending machines, so employers increasingly prefer applicants who have some training in electronics. Technologically advanced machines with features such as multilevel pricing, inventory control, and scrolling messages extensively use electronics and microchip computers. Some vocational high schools and junior colleges offer 1- to 2-year training programs in basic electronics.

Beginners may start their training with simple jobs such as cleaning or painting machines. They then may learn to rebuild machines by removing defective parts, repairing, adjusting, and testing the machines. Next, they accompany an experienced repairer on service calls, and finally make visits on their own. This learning process takes from 6 months to 3 years, depending on the individual's abilities, previous education, types of machines, and the quality of instruction.

The National Automatic Merchandising Association has a self-study mechanics training program for vending machine repairers. Repairers use manuals for instruction in subjects such as customer relations, safety, electronics, and schematic reading. Upon completion of the program, a written test must be passed to become certified as a journey or master mechanic.

To learn about new machines, repairers and servicers sometimes attend training sessions sponsored by manufacturers, which may last from a few days to several weeks. Both trainees and experienced workers sometimes take evening courses in basic electricity, electronics, microwave ovens, refrigeration, and other related subjects. Skilled servicers and repairers may be promoted to supervisory jobs.

Job Outlook
Employment of vending machine servicers and repairers is expected to decline through the year 2006 because improved technology will require servicers and repairers to check on machines less frequently. More vending machines are likely to be installed in industrial plants, hospitals, stores, and other business establishments to meet the public demand for vending machine items. In addition, the range of products dispensed by machine can be expected to increase as vending machines continue to become more automated and more are built with microwave ovens, mini-refrigerators, and freezers. These new machines will need to be repaired and restocked less often, and will contain computers that record sales and inventory data, reducing time-consuming paperwork now done by servicers. Some new machines will use wireless data transmitters to signal the vending machine company when they need to be restocked or repaired. This allows servicers and repairers to be dispatched only when needed, instead of their having to check each machine on a regular schedule.

Although employment is expected to decline, there will be job openings as experienced workers transfer to other occupations or leave the labor force. Persons with some background in electronics should have good job prospects because electronic circuitry is an important component of vending machines. If firms cannot find trained or experienced workers for these jobs, they are likely to train qualified route drivers or hire inexperienced people who have acquired some mechanical, electrical, or electronic training by taking high school or vocational courses.

Earnings

According to a survey conducted by the National Automatic Merchandising Association, the average hourly wage rate for nonunion vending machine servicers was $8.66 in 1996. Rates ranged from just under $5.00 to nearly $17.00 an hour, depending on the size of the firm and the region of the country. Nonunion repairers averaged $10.38 an hour in 1996, but rates also ranged from about $5.00 to $17.00. Servicers and repairers who were members of unions usually earned slightly more.

Most vending machine repairers work 8 hours a day, 5 days a week, and receive premium pay for overtime. Some union contracts stipulate higher pay for night work and for emergency repair jobs on weekends and holidays.

Some vending machine repairers and servicers are members of the International Brotherhood of Teamsters.

Related Occupations

Other workers who repair equipment with electrical and electronic components include home appliance and power tool repairers, electronic equipment repairers, and general maintenance mechanics.

Sources of Additional Information

Further information on job opportunities in this field can be obtained from local vending machine firms and local offices of the State employment service. For general information on vending machine repair, write to:

☛ National Automatic Merchandising Association, 20 N. Wacker Dr., Suite 3500, Chicago, IL 60606-3102.

☛ American Vending Sales, Inc.,750 Morse Ave., Elk Grove Village, IL 60007.

Construction Trades Occupations

Bricklayers and Stonemasons

(D.O.T. 779.684-058; 861.361-010 and -014, .381-010 through -042, except -034, .684-010 and -014; and 899.364-010)

Significant Points

- Opportunities should be very good because job openings are expected to grow faster than the number of workers being trained.

- Work is often outdoors, requires lifting heavy bricks and blocks, and sometimes involves working on scaffolds.

- Nearly one out of every four bricklayers and stonemasons is self employed.

Nature of the Work

Bricklayers and stonemasons work in closely related trades producing attractive, durable surfaces and structures. The work they perform varies in complexity, from laying a simple masonry walkway to installing the ornate exterior of a high-rise building. *Bricklayers* build walls, floors, partitions, fireplaces, chimneys, and other structures with brick, precast masonry panels, concrete block, and other masonry materials. Some specialize in installing firebrick linings in industrial furnaces. *Stonemasons* build stone walls, as well as set stone exteriors and floors. They work with two types of stone—natural cut, such as marble, granite, and limestone, and artificial stone made from concrete, marble chips, or other masonry materials. Stonemasons usually work on structures such as houses of worship, hotels, and office buildings.

In building a wall, bricklayers create the corners of the structure first. Due to the necessary precision, these corner leads are very time consuming to construct erect and require the skills of the most experienced bricklayers on the job. After the corner leads are complete, less experienced bricklayers fill in the wall between the corners, using a line from corner to corner to guide each course or layer of brick. Because of the expense associated with building corner leads, an increasing number of bricklayers are using corner poles, also called masonry guides, that enable them to build the entire wall at the same time. They fasten the corner posts or poles in a plumb position to define the wall line, and stretch a line between them. The line serves as a guide for each course of brick. Bricklayers then spread a bed of mortar (a cement, sand, and water mixture) with a trowel (a flat, bladed metal tool with a handle), place the brick on the mortar bed, and then press and tap it into place. As blueprints specify, they either cut brick with a hammer and chisel, or saw them to fit around windows, doors, and other openings. Mortar joints are finished with jointing tools for a sealed, neat, and uniform appearance. Although bricklayers generally use steel supports, or "lintels", at window and door openings, they sometimes build brick arches that support and enhance the beauty of the brickwork.

Bricklayers are assisted by hod carriers, or helpers, who bring bricks and other materials to them while working, mix mortar, and set up and move the scaffolding.

Stonemasons often work from a set of drawings in which each stone has been numbered for identification. Helpers may locate and bring the prenumbered stones to the masons. A derrick operator using a hoist, may be needed to lift large pieces into place.

When building a stone wall, masons set the first course of stones into a shallow bed of mortar. They align the stones with wedges, plumblines, and levels, and adjust them into position with a hard rubber mallet. Masons build the wall by alternating layers of mortar and courses of stone. As the work progresses, they remove the wedges and fill the joints between stones and use a pointed metal tool, called a "tuck pointer," to smooth the mortar to an attractive finish. To hold

large stones in place, stonemasons attach brackets to the stone and weld or bolt them to anchors in the wall. Finally, masons wash the stone with a cleansing solution to remove stains and dry mortar.

When setting stone floors, which often consist of large and heavy pieces of stone, masons first use a trowel to spread a layer of damp mortar over the surface to be covered. Using crowbars and hard rubber mallets for aligning and leveling, they then set the stone in the mortar bed. To finish, workers fill the joints and wash the stone slabs.

Masons use a special hammer and chisel to cut stone. They cut it along the grain to make various shapes and sizes. Valuable pieces often are cut with a saw that has a diamond blade. Some masons specialize in setting marble which, in many respects, is similar to setting large pieces of stone. Bricklayers and stonemasons also repair imperfections and cracks, or replace broken or missing masonry units in walls and floors.

Most nonresidential buildings are now built with prefabricated panels made of concrete block, brick veneer, stone, granite, marble, tile, or glass. In the past, bricklayers performed mostly interior work, such as block partition walls and elevator shafts. Now they must be more versatile and work with many materials. For example, bricklayers now install lighter-weight insulated panels used in new skyscraper construction.

Refractory masons are bricklayers who specialize in installing firebrick and refractory tile in high-temperature boilers, furnaces, cupolas, ladles, and soaking pits in industrial establishments. Most

Bricklayers spend much of their time standing, kneeling, or bending.

work in steel mills, where molten materials flow on refractory beds from furnaces to rolling machines.

Working Conditions
Bricklayers and stonemasons usually work outdoors. They stand, kneel, and bend for long periods and often have to lift heavy materials. Common hazards include injuries from tools and falls from scaffolds, but these can be avoided when proper safety practices are followed.

Employment
Bricklayers and stonemasons held about 142,00 jobs in 1996. The vast majority were bricklayers. Workers in these crafts are employed primarily by special trade, building, or general contractors. They work throughout the country but, like the general population, are concentrated in metropolitan areas.

Nearly one-fourth of all bricklayers and stonemasons were self-employed. Many of the self-employed specialize in contracting on small jobs such as patios, walkways, and fireplaces.

Training, Other Qualifications, and Advancement
Most bricklayers and stonemasons pick up their skills informally, observing and learning from experienced workers. Many receive training in vocational education schools. The best way to learn these skills, however, is through an apprenticeship program, which generally provides the most thorough training.

Individuals who learn the trade on the job usually start as helpers, laborers, or mason tenders. They carry materials, move scaffolds, and mix mortar. When the opportunity arises, they are taught to spread mortar, lay brick and block, or set stone. As they gain experience, they make the transition to full-fledged craft workers. The learning period generally lasts much longer than an apprenticeship program, however.

Apprenticeships for bricklayers and stonemasons are usually sponsored by local contractors or by local union-management committees. The apprenticeship program requires 3 years of on-the-job training in addition to a minimum 144 hours of classroom instruction each year in subjects such as blueprint reading, mathematics, layout work, and sketching.

Apprentices often start by working with laborers, carrying materials, mixing mortar, and building scaffolds. This period generally lasts about a month and familiarizes them with job routines and materials. Next, they learn to lay, align, and join brick and block. Apprentices also learn to work with stone and concrete. This enables them to be certified to work with more than one masonry material.

Applicants for apprenticeships must be at least 17 years old and in good physical condition. A high school education is preferable, and courses in mathematics, mechanical drawing, and shop are helpful. The International Masonry Institute, a division of the International Union of Bricklayers and Allied Craftsmen, operates training centers in several large cities that help job seekers develop the skills needed to successfully complete the formal apprenticeship program.

Bricklayers who work in nonresidential construction usually work for large contractors and receive well-rounded training in all phases of brick/stone work, usually through apprenticeship. Those who work in residential construction usually work primarily for small contractors and specialize in only one or two aspects of the job.

Experienced workers can advance to supervisory positions or become estimators. They also can open contracting businesses of their own.

Job Outlook
Job opportunities for skilled bricklayers and stonemasons are expected to be good as the growth in demand outpaces the supply of workers trained in this craft. Employment of bricklayers and stone-

masons is expected to grow about as fast as the average for all occupations through the year 2006, and additional openings will result from the need to replace bricklayers and stonemasons who retire, transfer to other occupations, or leave the trades for other reasons. However, the pool of young workers available to enter training programs will also be increasing slowly, and many in that group are reluctant to seek training for jobs that may be strenuous and have uncomfortable working conditions.

Population and business growth will create a need for new factories, schools, hospitals, offices, and other structures, increasing the demand for bricklayers and stonemasons. Also stimulating demand, will be the need to restore a growing stock of old masonry buildings, as well as the increasing use of brick for decorative work on building fronts and in lobbies and foyers. Brick exteriors should continue to be very popular as the trend continues toward more durable exterior materials requiring less maintenance. Employment of bricklayers who specialize in refractory repair will decline, along with employment in other occupations in the primary metal industries.

Employment of bricklayers and stonemasons, like that of many other construction workers, is sensitive to changes in the economy. When the level of construction activity falls, workers in these trades can experience periods of unemployment.

Earnings
Median weekly earnings for bricklayers and stonemasons were about $484 in 1996. The middle 50 percent earned between $345 and $624 weekly. The highest 10 percent earned more than $926 weekly; the lowest 10 percent earned less than $247. Earnings for workers in these trades may be reduced on occasion, because poor weather and downturns in construction activity limit the time they can work.

In each trade, apprentices or helpers usually start at about 50 percent of the wage rate paid to experienced workers. This increases as they gain experience.

Some bricklayers and stonemasons are members of the International Union of Bricklayers and Allied Craftsmen.

Related Occupations
Bricklayers and stonemasons combine a thorough knowledge of brick, concrete block, stone, and marble with manual skill to erect very attractive yet highly durable structures. Workers in other occupations with similar skills include concrete masons, plasterers, terrazzo workers, and tilesetters.

Sources of Additional Information
For details about apprenticeships or other work opportunities in these trades, contact local bricklaying, stonemasonry, or marble setting contractors; a local of the union listed above; a local joint union-management apprenticeship committee; or the nearest office of the State employment service or State apprenticeship agency.

For general information about the work of either bricklayers or stonemasons, contact:
☛ International Union of Bricklayers and Allied Craftsmen, International Masonry Institute Apprenticeship and Training, 823 15th St. NW., Suite 1001, Washington, DC 20005.

Information about the work of bricklayers also may be obtained from:
☛ Associated General Contractors of America, Inc., 1957 E St. NW., Washington, DC 20006.
☛ Brick Institute of America, 11490 Commerce Park Dr., Reston, VA 22091-1525.
☛ Home Builders Institute, National Association of Home Builders, 1201 15th St. NW., Washington, DC 20005.
☛ National Concrete Masonry Association, 2302 Horse Pen Rd., Herndon, VA 22071.

Carpenters

(D.O.T. 806.281-058; 860.281-010 through .664-010 and .684-101 and -014; 863.684-010; 869.361-018, .381-010, -034, .684-018, -034, -042, and -058; and 962.281-010)

Significant Points

- The largest construction trade in 1996 with 996,000 workers, nearly one-third of whom were self employed.

- Although employment is expected to grow slowly, job opportunities should be excellent because high turnover rates create many job openings.

- Carpenters with skills in all aspects of carpentry work the most steadily because they have the versatility to perform whatever types of jobs that may be available.

Nature of the Work

Carpenters are involved in many different kinds of construction activity. They cut, fit, and assemble wood and other materials in the construction of buildings, highways, bridges, docks, industrial plants, boats, and many other structures. Their duties vary by type of employer. A carpenter employed by a special trade contractor, for example, may specialize in one or two activities, such as setting forms for concrete construction or erecting scaffolding. However, a carpenter employed by a general building contractor may perform many tasks, such as framing walls and partitions, putting in doors and windows, hanging kitchen cabinets, and installing paneling and tile ceilings.

Local building codes often dictate where certain materials can be used, and carpenters must know these requirements. Each carpentry task is somewhat different, but most involve the same basic steps. Working from blueprints or instructions from supervisors, carpenters first do the layout—measuring, marking, and arranging materials. They then cut and shape wood, plastic, ceiling tile, fiberglass, or drywall using hand and power tools, such as chisels, planes, saws, drills, and sanders, and then join the materials with nails, screws, staples, or adhesives. In the final step, they check the accuracy of their work with levels, rules, plumb bobs, and framing squares and

Carpenters risk injury from the use of power equipment.

make any necessary adjustments. When working with prefabricated components, such as stairs or wall panels, the carpenter's task is somewhat simpler because it does not require as much layout work or the cutting and assembly of as many pieces. These components are designed for easy and fast installation and generally can be installed in a single operation.

Carpenters employed outside the construction industry perform a variety of installation and maintenance work. They may replace panes of glass, ceiling tiles, and doors, as well as repair desks, cabinets, and other furniture. Depending on the employer, they may install partitions, doors, and windows; change locks; and repair broken furniture. In manufacturing firms, carpenters may assist in moving or installing machinery. (For more information on workers who install this machinery, see the sections on industrial machinery repairers and millwrights elsewhere in the *Handbook*.)

Working Conditions

As in other building trades, carpentry work is sometimes strenuous. Prolonged standing, climbing, bending, and kneeling are often necessary. Carpenters risk injury from slips or falls, working with sharp or rough materials, and using of sharp tools and power equipment. Many carpenters work outdoors.

Some carpenters change employers each time they finish a construction job. Others alternate between working for a contractor and working as contractors themselves on small jobs.

Employment

Carpenters, the largest group of building trades workers, held about 996,000 jobs in 1996. Four of every 5 worked for contractors who build, remodel, or repair buildings and other structures. Most of the remainder worked for manufacturing firms, government agencies, wholesale and retail establishments, and schools. Nearly one-third were self-employed.

Carpenters are employed throughout the country in almost every community.

Training, Other Qualifications, and Advancement

Carpenters learn their trade through on-the-job training and through formal training programs. Some pick up skills informally by working under the supervision of experienced workers. Many acquire skills through vocational education. Others participate in employer training programs or apprenticeships.

Most employers recommend an apprenticeship as the best way to learn carpentry. Because the number of apprenticeship programs is limited, however, only a small proportion of carpenters learn their trade through these programs. Apprenticeship programs are administered by local joint union-management committees of the United Brotherhood of Carpenters and Joiners of America, the Associated General Contractors, Inc., or the National Association of Home Builders. Training programs are administered by local chapters of the Associated Builders and Contractors and by local chapters of the Associated General Contractors, Inc. These programs combine on-the-job training with related classroom instruction. Apprenticeship applicants must generally be at least 17 years old and meet local requirements. For example, some union locals test an applicant's aptitude for carpentry. The length of the program, usually about 3 to 4 years, varies with the apprentice's skill.

On the job, apprentices learn elementary structural design and become familiar with common carpentry jobs such as layout, form building, rough framing, and outside and inside finishing. They also learn to use the tools, machines, equipment, and materials of the trade. Apprentices receive classroom instruction in safety, first aid, blueprint reading, and freehand sketching, basic mathematics, and different carpentry techniques. Both in the classroom and on the job, they learn the relationship between carpentry and the other building trades.

Informal on-the-job training is usually less thorough than an apprenticeship. The degree of training and supervision often depends on the size of the employing firm. A small contractor specializing in home-building may only provide training in rough framing. In contrast, a large general contractor may provide training in several carpentry skills. Although specialization is becoming increasingly common, it is important to try to acquire skills in all aspects of carpentry and to have the flexibility to perform any kind of work. Carpenters with a well-rounded background can switch from residential building to commercial construction to remodeling jobs, depending on demand.

A high school education is desirable, including courses in carpentry, shop, mechanical drawing, and general mathematics. Manual dexterity, eye-hand coordination, physical fitness, and a good sense of balance are important. The ability to solve arithmetic problems quickly and accurately is alsohelpful. Employers and apprenticeship committees generally view favorably, training and work experience obtained in the Armed Services and the job corps.

Carpenters may advance to carpentry supervisors or general construction supervisors. Carpenters usually have greater opportunities than most other construction workers to become general construction supervisors, because they are exposed to the entire construction process. Some carpenters become independent contractors. To advance, carpenters should be able to estimate the nature and quantity of materials needed to properly complete a job. They must also be able to estimate, with accuracy, how long a job should take to complete, and its cost.

Job Outlook

Job opportunities for carpenters are expected to be plentiful through the year 2006, due primarily to extensive replacement needs. Thousands of job openings will become available each year as carpenters transfer to other occupations or leave the labor force. The total number of job openings for carpenters is usually greater than for other craft occupations, because the occupation is large and the turnover rate is high. Because there are no strict training requirements for entry, many people with limited skills take jobs as carpenters but eventually leave the occupation because they dislike the work or cannot find steady employment.

Increased demand for carpenters will create additional job openings. Employment is expected to increase more slowly than the average for all occupations through the year 2006. Construction activity should increase slowly in response to demand for new housing and commercial and industrial plants, and the need to renovate and modernize existing structures. Opportunities for frame carpenters will be particularly good. The demand for carpenters will be offset somewhat by expected productivity gains resulting from the increasing use of prefabricated components, such as prehung doors and windows and prefabricated wall panels and stairs, that can be installed much more quickly. Prefabricated walls, partitions, and stairs can be quickly lifted into place in one operation; beams, and in some cases entire roof assemblies, can be lifted into place using a crane. As prefabricated components become more standardized, their use will increase. In addition, stronger adhesives reducing the time needed to join materials and lightweight cordless pneumatic and combustion tools such as nailers and drills, as well as sanders with electronic speed controls, will make carpenters more efficient and reduce fatigue.

Although employment of carpenters is expected to grow over the long run, people entering the occupation should expect to experience periods of unemployment. This results from the short-term nature of many construction projects, and the cyclical nature of the construction industry. Building activity depends on many factors—interest rates, availability of mortgage funds, government spending, and business investment—that vary with the state of the economy. During economic downturns, the number of job openings for carpenters declines. The introduction of new and improved tools, equipment, techniques, and materials has vastly increased carpenters' versatility. Therefore, carpenters with all-round skills will have better opportunities than those who can only do relatively simple, routine tasks.

Job opportunities for carpenters also vary by geographic area. Construction activity parallels the movement of people and businesses and reflects differences in local economic conditions. Therefore, the number of job opportunities and apprenticeship opportunities in a given year may vary widely from area to area.

Earnings

Median weekly earnings of carpenters, excluding the self-employed, were $476 in 1996. The middle 50 percent earned between $345 and $660 per week. Weekly earnings for the top 10 percent of all carpenters were more than $874; the lowest 10 percent earned less than $267.

Earnings may be reduced on occasion because carpenters lose work time in bad weather and during recessions when jobs are unavailable.

Many carpenters are members of the United Brotherhood of Carpenters and Joiners of America.

Related Occupations

Carpenters are skilled construction workers. Workers in other skilled construction occupations include bricklayers, concrete masons, electricians, pipefitters, plasterers, plumbers, stonemasons, and terrazzo workers.

Sources of Additional Information

For information about carpentry apprenticeships or other work opportunities in this trade, contact local carpentry contractors, locals of the union mentioned above, local joint union-contractor apprenticeship committees, or the nearest office of the State employment service or State apprenticeship agency.

For general information about carpentry, contact:

☛ Associated Builders and Contractors, 1300 North 17th Street, Rosslyn, VA 22209.

☛ Associated General Contractors of America, Inc., 1957 E St. NW., Washington, DC 20006.

☛ Home Builders Institute, National Association of Home Builders, 1201 15th St. NW., Washington, DC 20005.

☛ United Brotherhood of Carpenters and Joiners of America, 101 Constitution Ave. NW., Washington, DC 20001.

Carpet Installers

(D.O.T. 864.381-010)

Significant Points

- The majority of carpet installers are self employed.

- Working conditions are generally more pleasant than those of other construction trades,because carpet is installed in finished, or nearly finished, structures.

- Carpet installers are less likely than other construction trades to be idled by slowdowns in construction or inclement weather.

Nature of the Work

Carpet installers work in many types of buildings—including homes, offices, stores, and restaurants. Before installing the carpet, these craft workers first inspect the surface to be covered to determine its condition and, if necessary, correct any imperfections that could show through the carpet. They must measure the area to be carpeted and plan the layout, keeping in mind expected traffic patterns and placement of seams for best appearance and maximum wear.

When installing wall-to-wall carpet without tacks, installers first fasten a tackless strip to the floor, next to the wall. They then install the padded cushion or underlay. Next, they roll out, measure, mark, and cut the carpet, allowing for 2 to 3 inches of extra carpet for the final fitting. Using a knee kicker, they position the carpet, stretching it to fit evenly on the floor and snugly against each wall and door threshold. They then rough cut the excess carpet. Finally, using a power stretcher, they stretch the carpet, hooking it to the tackless strip to hold it in place. The installer then finishes the edges using a wall trimmer.

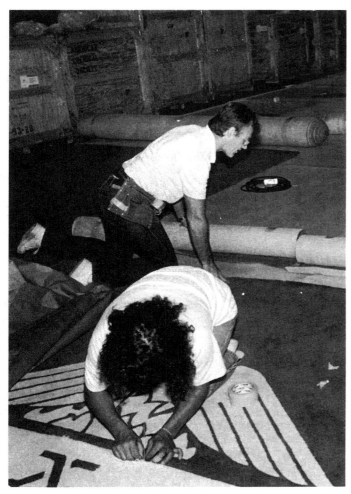

Carpet installers constantly bend and kneel.

Because most carpet comes in 12-foot widths, wall-to-wall installations require installers to tape or sew sections together for large rooms. They join the seams by sewing them with a large needle and special thread or by using heat-taped seams—a special plastic tape made to join seams when activated with heat.

On special upholstery work, such as stairs, carpet may be held in place with staples. Also, in commercial installations, carpet is often glued directly to the floor or to padding which has been glued to the floor.

Carpet installers use handtools such as hammers, drills, staple guns, carpet knives, and rubber mallets. They also may use carpet-laying tools, such as carpet shears, knee kickers, wall trimmers, loop pile cutters, heat irons, and power stretchers.

Working Conditions
Carpet installers generally work regular daytime hours, but when recarpeting stores or offices, they may work evenings and weekends to avoid disturbing customers or employees. Installers usually work under better conditions than most other construction workers, although, the work is very labor intensive. Because carpets are installed in finished or nearly finished structures, work areas usually are clean, well lighted, safe, and comfortable. Installers kneel, reach, bend, stretch, and frequently lift heavy rolls of carpet. They also may move heavy furniture. Safety regulations may require that they wear knee pads or safety goggles when using certain tools.

Employment
Carpet installers held about 64,000 jobs in 1996. Many worked for flooring contractors or floor covering retailers. About 60 percent of all carpet installers were self-employed.

Although installers are employed throughout the Nation, they tend to be concentrated in urban areas where there are high levels of construction activity.

Training, Other Qualifications, and Advancement
The vast majority of carpet installers learn their trade informally, on the job, as helpers to experienced installers. Others learn through formal apprenticeship programs, which include on-the-job training as well as related classroom instruction.

Informal training is often sponsored by individual contractors and generally lasts from about 1 1/2 to 2 years. Helpers begin with simple assignments, such as installing stripping and padding, or helping stretch newly installed carpet. With experience, helpers take on more difficult assignments, such as measuring, cutting, and fitting.

Apprenticeship programs and some contractor-sponsored programs provide comprehensive training in all phases of carpet laying. Most apprenticeship programs are union sponsored and consist of weekly classes and on-the-job training usually lasting 3 to 4 years.

Persons who wish to begin a career in carpet installation as a helper or apprentice should be 18 years old and have good manual dexterity. Because carpet installers frequently deal directly with customers, they should be courteous and tactful. A High school diploma is preferred, though not necessary; courses in general mathematics and shop are helpful. Some employers may require a driver's license and a criminal background check.

Carpet installers may advance to positions as supervisors or installation managers for large installation firms. Some installers become salespersons or estimators. Many installers who begin working for a large contractor or installation firm also eventually go into business for themselves as independent subcontractors.

Job Outlook
Employment of carpet installers is expected to grow about as fast as the average for all occupations through the year 2006. Growth will be due primarily to the continued need to renovate and refurbish existing structures, usually involving laying new carpet. Carpet as a floor covering continues to be popular and its usage is expected to grow in structures such as schools, offices, hospitals, and industrial plants.

Demand for carpet will also be stimulated by new, more durable fibers that are stain and crush resistant, and come in a wider variety of colors. More resilient carpet needs to be replaced less often, but these attractive new products may induce more people to replace their old carpeting, contributing further to the demand for carpet installers.

Job opportunities for carper installers are expected to be excellent as the growth in demand outpaces the supply of workers trained in this craft. This occupation is less sensitive to changes in economic conditions than most other construction occupations, because much of their work involves replacing carpet in existing buildings, and renovation work usually allows employment of carpet installers to remain relatively stable. In the many houses built with plywood, rather than hardwood floors, wall-to-wall carpeting is a necessity. Similarly, offices, hotels, and stores often cover concrete floors with wall-to-wall carpet, which must be periodically replaced.

Earnings
Median weekly earnings of all full-time carpet installers were about $476 in 1996. The middle 50 percent earned between $345 and $660 per week. The top 10 percent earned more than $874 and the lowest 10 percent earned less than $267.

Carpet installers are paid either on an hourly basis, or by the number of yards of carpet installed. The rates vary widely depending on the geographic location and whether the installer is affiliated with a union. Apprentices and other trainees usually start out earning about half of what an experienced worker earns, though their wage rate increases as they advance through the training program. Some installers belong to the United Brotherhood of Carpenters and Joiners of America, or the International Brotherhood of Painters and Allied Trades.

Related Occupations
Carpet installers measure, cut, and fit carpet materials. Workers in other occupations involving similar skills but using different materi-

als, include carpenters, cement masons, drywall installers, floor layers, lathers, painters and paperhangers, roofers, sheet-metal workers, terrazzo workers, and tilesetters.

Sources of Additional Information

For details about apprenticeships or work opportunities, contact local flooring contractors or retailers; locals of the unions previously mentioned; or the nearest office of the State apprenticeship agency or the State employment service.

For general information about the work of carpet installers, contact:
☛ Floor Covering Installation Contractors Association, P.O. Box 948, Dalton, GA 30722-0948.

For information concerning training contact:
☛ United Brotherhood of Carpenters and Joiners of America, 101 Constitution Ave. NW., Washington, DC 20001.
☛ International Brotherhood of Painters and Allied Trades, 1750 New York Ave. NW., Washington, DC 20006.

Concrete Masons and Terrazzo Workers

(D.O.T. 844.364-010, -014, .461-010, .684-010; and 861.381-046, and -050)

Significant Points

- Employment of concrete masons and terrazzo workers will increase slowly as new technology makes these workers more productive.

- Most learn their trade on the job, either through formal 3-year apprenticeship programs or by working as helpers.

- Jobs are often outdoors and require a lot of bending and kneeling.

Nature of the Work

Concrete—a mixture of Portland cement, sand, gravel, and water—is used for many types of construction projects. Whether small jobs, such as patios and floors, huge dams or miles of roadway, *concrete masons* place and finish the concrete. They may also color concrete surfaces, expose aggregate (small stones) in walls and sidewalks, or fabricate concrete beams, columns, and panels.

Terrazzo workers create attractive walkways, floors, patios, and panels by exposing marble chips and other fine aggregates on the surface of finished concrete. Much of the preliminary work of terrazzo workers is similar to that of concrete masons.

In preparing a site for placing concrete, masons set the forms for holding the concrete to the desired pitch and depth and properly align them. They then direct the casting of the concrete and supervise laborers who use shovels or special tools to spread it. Masons then guide a straightedge back and forth across the top of the forms to "screed," or level, the freshly placed concrete. Immediately after leveling the concrete, masons carefully smooth the concrete surface with a "bull float," a long-handled tool about 8 by 48 inches that covers the coarser materials in the concrete and brings a rich mixture of fine cement paste to the surface.

After the concrete has been leveled and floated, finishers press an edger between the forms and the concrete and guide it along the edge and the surface. This produces slightly rounded edges and helps prevent chipping or cracking. They use a special tool called a "groover" to make joints or grooves at specific intervals that help control cracking. Next, finishers trowel the surface using either a powered or a hand trowel, a small, smooth, rectangular metal tool. Troweling removes most imperfections and brings the fine cement paste to the surface.

As the final step, masons retrowel the concrete surface back and forth with powered and hand trowels to create a smooth finish. For a coarse, nonskid finish, masons brush the surface with a broom or stiff-bristled brush. For a pebble finish, they embed small gravel chips into the surface. They then wash any excess cement from the exposed chips with a mild acid solution. For color, they use colored premixed concrete. On concrete surfaces that will remain exposed after forms are stripped, such as columns, ceilings, and wall panels, concrete masons cut away high spots and loose concrete with hammer and chisel, fill any large indentations with a Portland cement paste and smooth the surface with a rubbing carborundum stone. Finally, they coat the exposed area with a rich Portland cement mixture using either a special tool or a coarse cloth to rub the concrete to a uniform finish.

Attractive, marble-chip terrazzo requires three layers of materials. First, concrete masons or terrazzo workers build a solid, level concrete foundation that is 3 to 4 inches deep. After the forms are removed from the foundation, workers place a 1-inch deep mixture of sandy concrete. Before this layer sets, terrazzo workers partially embed metal divider strips into the concrete wherever there is to be a joint or change of color in the terrazzo. These strips separate the different designs and colors of the terrazzo panels and help prevent cracks. For the final layer, terrazzo workers blend and place a fine marble chip mixture that may be color-pigmented into each of the panels, then hand trowel each panel until it is level with the tops of the ferrule strips. While the mixture is still wet, workers toss additional marble chips of various colors into each panel and roll a lightweight roller over the entire surface.

When the terrazzo is thoroughly dry, helpers grind it with a terrazzo grinder, which is somewhat like a floor polisher, only much heavier. Slight depressions left by the grinding are filled with a matching grout material and hand troweled for a smooth, uniform surface. Terrazzo workers then clean, polish, and seal the dry surface for a lustrous finish.

Working Conditions

Concrete or terrazzo work is fast paced and strenuous. Because most finishing is done at floor level, workers must bend and kneel a lot. Many jobs are outdoors, but work is generally halted during rain or freezing weather. To avoid chemical burns from uncured concrete and sore knees from frequent kneeling, many workers wear kneepads. Workers usually wear water-repellent boots while working in wet concrete.

Concrete masons trowel the concrete back and forth to make a smooth surface.

Employment

Concrete masons and terrazzo workers held about 137,000 jobs in 1996; terrazzo workers accounted for a very small proportion of the total. Most concrete masons worked for concrete contractors or for general contractors on projects such as highways, bridges, shopping malls, or large buildings such as factories, schools, and hospitals. A small number were employed by firms that manufacture concrete products. Most terrazzo workers worked for special trade contractors who install decorative floors and wall panels.

Fewer than 1 out of 10 concrete masons and terrazzo workers was self-employed, a smaller proportion than in other building trades. Most self-employed masons specialized in small jobs, such as driveways, sidewalks, and patios.

Training, Other Qualifications, and Advancement

Concrete masons and terrazzo workers learn their trades either through on-the-job training as helpers or through 3-year apprenticeship programs. Many masons first gain experience as construction laborers.

When hiring helpers and apprentices, employers prefer high school graduates who are at least 18 years old, in good physical condition, and have a driver's license to drive. The ability to get along with others also is important because concrete masons frequently work in teams. High school courses in shop mathematics, blueprint reading, or mechanical drawing provide a helpful background.

On-the-job training programs consist of informal instruction from experienced workers in which helpers learn to use the tools, equipment, machines, and materials of the trade. They begin with tasks such as edging and jointing and using a straightedge on freshly placed concrete. As they progress, assignments become more complex, and trainees can usually do finishing work within a short time.

Three-year apprenticeship programs, usually jointly sponsored by local unions and contractors, provide on-the-job training in addition to a recommended minimum of 144 hours of classroom instruction each year. A written test and a physical exam may be required. In the classroom, apprentices learn applied mathematics, blueprint reading, and safety. Apprentices generally receive special instruction in layout work and cost estimating.

Experienced concrete masons or terrazzo workers may advance to become supervisors or contract estimators. Some open their own concrete contracting businesses.

Job Outlook

Employment of concrete masons and terrazzo workers is expected to grow slower than the average for all occupations through the year 2006. In addition to job openings that will stem from the rising demand for the services of these workers, other openings will become available as experienced workers transfer to other occupations or leave the labor force.

The demand for concrete masons and terrazzo workers will rise as the population and the economy grow. More masons will be needed to build highways, bridges, subways, factories, office buildings, hotels, shopping centers, schools, hospitals, and other structures. In addition, the increasing use of concrete as a building material—particularly in nonresidential construction—will add to the demand. More concrete masons also will be needed to repair and renovate existing highways, bridges, and other structures.

Employment growth of concrete masons and terrazzo workers, however, will not keep pace with the growth of these construction projects. Their productivity will increase as a result of the use of improved concrete pumping systems, continuous concrete mixers, quicker setting cement, troweling machines, prefabricated masonry systems, and other improved materials, equipment, and tools.

Employment of concrete masons and terrazzo workers, like that of many other workers, is sensitive to the flucuations of the economy. Workers in these trades may experience periods of unemployment when the level of nonresidential construction falls. On the other hand, shortages of these workers may occur in some areas during peak periods of building activity.

Earnings

Median weekly earnings of full-time concrete masons and terrazzo workers were about $467 in 1997. The middle 50 percent earned between $375 and $650 per week. The top 10 percent earned more than $823, and the lowest 10 percent earned less than $286.

According to the limited information available, average hourly earnings—including benefits—for concrete masons who belonged to a union and worked full time, ranged between $15.10 and $45.84 in 1996. Concrete masons in, New York, Boston, San Francisco, Chicago, Los Angeles, Philadelphia, and other large cities received the highest wages. Nonunion workers generally have lower wage rates than union workers. Apprentices usually start at 50 to 60 percent of the rate paid to experienced workers.

Concrete masons often work overtime, with premium pay, because once concrete has been placed, the job must be completed.

Annual earnings of concrete masons and terrazzo workers may be lower than the hourly rates suggest, because bad weather and downturns in construction activity may limit the time they can work.

Many concrete masons and terrazzo workers belong to the Operative Plasterers' and Cement Masons' International Association of the United States and Canada, or to the International Union of Bricklayers and Allied Craftsmen. Some terrazzo workers belong to the United Brotherhood of Carpenters and Joiners of the United States.

Related Occupations

Concrete masons and terrazzo workers combine skill with knowledge of building materials to construct buildings, highways, and other structures. Other occupations involving similar skills and knowledge include bricklayers, form builders, marble setters, plasterers, stonemasons, and tilesetters.

Sources of Additional Information

For information about apprenticeships and work opportunities, contact local concrete or terrazzo contractors; locals of unions previously mentioned; a local joint union-management apprenticeship committee; or the nearest office of the State employment service or apprenticeship agency.

For general information about concrete masons and terrazzo workers, contact:

☞ Associated General Contractors of America, Inc., 1957 E St. NW., Washington, DC 20006.
☞ International Union of Bricklayers and Allied Craftsmen, International Masonry Institute Apprenticeship and Training, 815 15th St. NW., Suite 1001, Washington, DC 20005.
☞ Operative Plasterers' and Cement Masons' International Association of the United States and Canada, 1125 17th St. NW., Washington, DC 20036.
☞ National Terrazzo and Mosaic Association, 3166 Des Plaines Ave., Suite 132, Des Plaines, IL 60018.
☞ Portland Cement Association, 5420 Old Orchard Rd., Skokie, IL 60077.
☞ United Brotherhood of Carpenters and Joiners of America, 101 Constitution Ave. NW., Washington, DC 20001.

Drywall Workers and Lathers

(D.O.T. 842.361-010, -014, and -030, .664-010, .684-014; and 869.684-050)

Significant Points

● Employment is projected to grow slowly, but thousands of job openings will arise annually because turnover is high.

● Inclement weather seldom interrupts work, but workers may be idled when downturns in the economy slow new construction activity.

● Most drywall workers and lathers learn the trade on the job, either by working as helpers or through a formal apprenticeship.

Nature of the Work

Drywall consists of a thin layer of gypsum between two layers of heavy paper. It is used today for walls and ceilings in most buildings because it is both faster and cheaper to install than plaster.

There are two kinds of drywall workers: installers and finishers. *Installers*, also called *applicators*, fasten drywall panels to the inside framework of residential houses and other buildings. *Finishers*, or *tapers*, prepare these panels for painting by taping and finishing joints and imperfections.

Because drywall panels are manufactured in standard sizes—usually 4 feet by 8 or 12 feet—installers must measure, cut, and fit some pieces around doors and windows. They also saw or cut holes in panels for electrical outlets, air-conditioning units, and plumbing. After making these alterations, installers may glue, nail, or screw the wallboard panels to the wood or metal framework. Because drywall is heavy and cumbersome, a helper generally assists the installer in positioning and securing the panel. A lift is often used when placing ceiling panels.

After the drywall is installed, finishers fill joints between panels with a joint compound. Using the wide, flat tip of a special trowel, they spread the joint compound into and along each side of the joint with brushlike strokes. They immediately use the trowel to press a paper tape—used to reinforce the drywall and to hide imperfections—into the wet compound and to smooth away excess material. Nail and screw depressions also are covered with this compound, as are imperfections caused by the installation of air-conditioning vents and other fixtures. On large commercial projects, finishers may use automatic taping tools that apply the joint compound and tape in one step. Finishers apply second and third coats, sanding the treated areas after each coat to make them as smooth as the rest of the wall surface. This results in a very smooth and almost perfect surface. Some finishers apply textured surfaces to walls and ceilings with trowels, brushes, or spray guns.

Lathers apply metal or gypsum lath to walls, ceilings, or ornamental frameworks to form the support base for plaster coatings. Gypsum lath is similar to a drywall panel, but smaller. Metal lath is used where the plaster application will be exposed to weather or water, or for curved or irregular surfaces for which drywall is not a practical material. Lathers usually nail, screw, staple, or wire-tie the lath directly to the structural framework.

Working Conditions

As in other construction trades, drywall and lathing work sometimes is strenuous. Applicators, tapers, finishers, and lathers spend most of the day on their feet, either standing, bending, or kneeling. Some finishers use stilts to tape and finish ceiling and angle joints. Installers have to lift and maneuver heavy panels. Hazards include falls from ladders and scaffolds, and injuries from power tools. Because sanding joint compound to a smooth finish creates a great deal of dust, some finishers wear masks for protection.

Employment

Drywall workers and lathers held about 133,000 jobs in 1996. Most worked for contractors specializing in drywall or lathing installation; others worked for contractors doing many kinds of construction. Nearly one-third were self employed independent contractors.

Most installers, finishers, and lathers are employed in urban areas. In other areas, where there may not be enough work to keep a drywall worker or lather employed full time, the work is usually done by carpenters and painters.

Training, Other Qualifications, and Advancement

Most drywall and lathing workers start as helpers and learn their skills on the job. Installer and lather helpers start by carrying materials, lifting and holding panels, and cleaning up debris. Within a few weeks, they learn to measure, cut, and install materials. Eventually, they become fully experienced workers. Finisher apprentices begin by taping joints and touching up nail holes, scrapes, and other imperfections. They soon learn to install corner guards and to conceal openings around pipes. At the end of their training, they learn to estimate the cost of installing and finishing drywall and gypsum lath.

Drywall panels are manufactured in standard sizes but installers must measure, cut, and fit some pieces around doors and windows.

Some installers and lathers learn their trade in an apprenticeship program. The United Brotherhood of Carpenters and Joiners of America, in cooperation with local contractors, administers an apprenticeship program in carpentry that includes instruction in drywall and lath installation. In addition, local affiliates of the Associated Builders and Contractors and the National Association of Home Builders conduct training programs for nonunion workers. The International Brotherhood of Painters and Allied Trades conducts a 2-year apprenticeship program for drywall finishers.

Employers prefer high school graduates who are in good physical condition, but they frequently hire applicants with less education. High school or vocational school courses in carpentry provide a helpful background for drywall work. Regardless of educational background, installers must be good at simple arithmetic.

Drywall workers and lathers with a few years' experience and leadership ability may become supervisors. Some workers start their own contracting businesses.

Job Outlook

Replacement needs will account for almost all job openings for drywall workers and lathers through the year 2006. Thousands of jobs will open up each year due to of the need to replace workers who transfer to jobs in other occupations or leave the labor force. Turnover in this occupation is very high, reflecting the lack of formal training requirements and the flucuations of the business cycle, to which the construction industry is very sensitive. Because of their relatively weak attachment to the occupation, many workers with limited skills leave the occupation when they find they dislike the work or because they can't find steady employment.

Additional job openings will be created by the rising demand for drywall work. Employment is expected to grow more slowly than the average for all occupations, reflecting the slow growth of new construction and renovation. In addition to traditional interior work, the growing acceptance of insulated exterior wall systems will provide additional jobs for drywall workers.

Despite the growing use of exterior panels, most drywall installation, finishing, and lathing are usually done indoors. Therefore, these workers lose less work time because of bad weather than some other construction workers. Nevertheless, they may be unemployed between construction projects and during downturns in construction activity.

Earnings

Median weekly earnings for drywall workers and lathers were about $430 in 1996. The middle 50 percent earned between $293 and $630 weekly. The top 10 percent earned over $871 and the bottom 10 percent earned less than $204 a week. Trainees usually started at about half the rate paid to experienced workers and received wage increases as they became more highly skilled.

Some contractors pay these workers according to the number of panels they install or finish per day; others pay an hourly rate. A 40-hour week is standard, but sometimes the workweek may be longer. Those who are paid hourly rates receive premium pay for overtime.

Related Occupations

Drywall workers and lathers combine strength and dexterity with precision and accuracy to make materials fit according to a plan. Other occupations that require similar abilities include carpenters, floor covering installers, form builders, insulation workers, and plasterers.

Sources of Additional Information

For information about work opportunities in drywall application and finishing, contact local drywall installation contractors; a local of the unions previously mentioned; a local joint union-management apprenticeship committee; a State or local chapter of the Associated Builders and Contractors; or the nearest office of the State employment service or State apprenticeship agency.

For details about job qualifications and training programs in drywall application and finishing, write to:

☛ Associated Builders and Contractors, Inc., 1300 North 17th St., Rosslyn, VA 22209.

☛ International Brotherhood of Painters and Allied Trades, 1750 New York Ave. NW., Washington, DC 20006.

For information on training programs in drywall application and lathing, write to:

☛ United Brotherhood of Carpenters and Joiners of America, 101 Constitution Ave. NW., Washington, DC 20001.

☛ Home Builders Institute, National Association of Home Builders, 1201 15th St. NW., Washington, DC 20005.

Electricians

(D.O.T. 729.381-018; 806.381-062; 822.361-018, -022; 824.261, .281-010, -018, .381, .681; 825.381-030, -034; 829.261-018; and 952.364 and .381)

Significant Points

- Job opportunities are expected to be very good for qualified electricians.

- Most people acquire their skills by completing a formal 4- or 5-year apprenticeship program.

- In contrast to other construction trades, about a third of all electricians work in industries other than construction.

Nature of the Work

Electricity is essential for light, power, air-conditioning, and refrigeration. Electricians install, connect, test, and maintain electrical systems for a variety of purposes, including climate control, security, and communications. They also may install and maintain the electronic controls for machines in business and industry. Although most electricians specialize in either construction or maintenance, a growing number do both.

Electricians work with blueprints when they install electrical systems in factories, office buildings, homes, and other structures. Blueprints indicate the location of circuits, outlets, load centers, panel boards, and other equipment. Electricians must follow the National Electric Code and comply with State and local building codes when they install these systems. In factories and offices, they first place conduit (pipe or tubing) inside designated partitions, walls, or other concealed areas. They also fasten to the wall small metal or plastic boxes that will house electrical switches and outlets. They then pull insulated wires or cables through the conduit to complete circuits between these boxes. In lighter construction, such as residential, plastic-covered wire usually is used rather than conduit.

Regardless of the type of wire used, electricians connect it to circuit breakers, transformers, or other components. Wires are joined by twisting ends together with pliers, and covering the ends with special plastic connectors. When stronger connections are required, electricians may use an electric "soldering gun" to melt metal onto the twisted wires, which they then cover with durable electrical tape. When the wiring is finished, they test the circuits for proper connections.

In addition to wiring a building's electrical system, electricians may install coaxial or fiber optic cable for computers and other telecommunications equipment. A growing number of electricians install telephone and computer wiring and equipment. They also may connect motors to electrical power and install electronic controls for industrial equipment.

Maintenance work varies greatly, depending on where the electrician is employed. Electricians who specialize in residential work may rewire a home and replace an old fuse box with a new circuit breaker to accommodate additional appliances. Those who work in large factories may repair motors, transformers, generators, and electronic controllers on machine tools and industrial robots. Those in office buildings and small plants may repair all types of electrical equipment.

Maintenance electricians spend much of their time in preventive maintenance. They periodically inspect equipment, and locate and correct problems before breakdowns occur. Electricians may also advise management on whether continued operation of equipment

Electricians often must work in awkward positions and risk injury from electrical shocks, falls, and cuts.

could be hazardous or not. When needed, they install new electrical equipment. When breakdowns occur, they must make the necessary repairs as quickly as possible in order to minimize inconvenience. Electricians may replace items such as circuit breakers, fuses, switches, electrical and electronic components, or wire. When working with complex electronic devices, they may work with engineers, engineering technicians, or industrial machinery repairers. (For information about each of these occupations, see the statements located elsewhere in the *Handbook*.)

Electricians use handtools such as screwdrivers, pliers, knives, and hacksaws. They also use power tools and testing equipment such as oscilloscopes, ammeters, and test lamps.

Working Conditions

Electricians' work is sometimes strenuous. They may stand for long periods of time and frequently work on ladders and scaffolds. They often work in awkward or cramped positions. Electricians risk injury from electrical shock, falls, and cuts; to avoid injuries, they must follow strict safety procedures. Some electricians may have to travel to job sites, which may be up to 100 miles away.

Most electricians work a standard 40-hour week, although overtime may be required. Those in maintenance work may have to work nights, on weekends, and be on call. Companies that operate 24 hours a day may employ 3 shifts of electricians. Generally, the first shift is primarily responsible for routine maintenance, while the other shifts perform preventive maintenance.

Employment

Electricians held about 575,000 jobs in 1996. More than half were employed in the construction industry. Others worked as maintenance electricians and were employed in virtually every industry. In addition, about 1 out of 10 electricians was self-employed.

Because of the widespread need for electrical services, jobs for electricians are found in all parts of the country.

Training, Other Qualifications, and Advancement

Most people learn the electrical trade by completing a 4- or 5-year apprenticeship program. Apprenticeship gives trainees a thorough knowledge of all aspects of the trade and generally improves their ability to find a job. Although more electricians are trained through apprenticeship than workers in other construction trades, some still learn their skills informally, on the job.

Large apprenticeship programs are usually sponsored by joint training committees made up of local unions of the International Brotherhood of Electrical Workers, and local chapters of the National Electrical Contractors Association. Training may also be provided by company management committees of individual electrical contracting companies and by local chapters of the Associated Builders and Contractors and the Independent Electrical Contractors. Because of the comprehensive training received, those who complete apprenticeship programs qualify to do both maintenance and construction work.

The typical large apprenticeship program provides at least 144 hours of classroom instruction each year, and 8,000 hours of on-the-job training over the course of the apprenticeship. In the classroom, apprentices learn blueprint reading, electrical theory, electronics, mathematics, electrical code requirements, and safety and first aid practices. They also receive specialized training in welding and communications and fire alarm systems. On the job, under the supervision of experienced electricians, apprentices must demonstrate mastery of the electrician's work. At first, they drill holes, set anchors, and set up conduit. Later, they measure, fabricate, and install conduit, as well as install, connect, and test wiring, outlets, and switches. They also learn to set up and draw diagrams for entire electrical systems.

Those who do not enter a formal apprenticeship program can begin to learn the trade informally by working as helpers for experienced electricians. While learning to install conduit, connect wires, and test circuits, helpers are also taught safety practices. Many helpers supplement this training with trade school or correspondence courses.

Regardless of how one learns the trade, previous training is very helpful. High school courses in mathematics, electricity, electronics,

mechanical drawing, science, and shop provide a good background. Special training offered in the Armed Forces and by postsecondary technical schools also is beneficial. All applicants should be in good health and have at least average physical strength. Agility and dexterity also are important. Good color vision is needed because workers must frequently identify electrical wires by color.

Most apprenticeship sponsors require applicants for apprentice positions to be at least 18 years old and have a high school diploma or its equivalent. For those interested in becoming maintenance electricians, a background in electronics is increasingly important because of the growing use of complex electronic controls on manufacturing equipment.

Most localities require electricians to be licensed. Although licensing requirements vary from area to area, electricians generally must pass an examination that tests their knowledge of electrical theory, the National Electrical Code, and local electric and building codes.

Electricians periodically take courses offered by their employer or union to keep abreast of changes in the National Electrical Code, materials, or methods of installation.

Experienced electricians can become supervisors and then superintendents. Those with sufficient capital and management skills may start their own contracting business, although this may require an electrical contractor's license.

Job Outlook

Job opportunities for skilled electricians are expected to be very good as the growth in demand outpaces the supply of workers trained in this craft. There is expected to be a shortage of skilled workers during the next decade because of the anticipated smaller pool of young workers entering training programs.

Employment of electricians is expected to increase more slowly than the average for all occupations through the year 2006. As the population and economy grow, more electricians will be needed to install and maintain electrical devices and wiring in homes, factories, offices, and other structures. New technologies also are expected to continue to stimulate the demand for these workers. Increasingly, buildings will be prewired during construction to accommodate use of computers and telecommunications equipment. More and more factories will be using robots and automated manufacturing systems. Installation of this equipment, which is expected to increase, should also stimulate demand for electricians. Additional jobs will be created by rehabilitation and retrofitting of existing structures.

In addition to jobs created by increased demand for electrical work, many openings will occur each year as electricians transfer to other occupations, retire, or leave the labor force for other reasons. Because of their lengthy training and relatively high earnings, a smaller proportion of electricians than other craft workers leave their occupation each year. The number of retirements is expected to rise, however, as more electricians reach retirement age.

Employment of construction electricians, like that of many other construction workers, is sensitive to changes in the economy. This results from the limited duration of construction projects and the cyclical nature of the construction industry. During economic downturns, job openings for electricians are reduced as the level of construction declines. Apprenticeship opportunities also are less plentiful during these periods.

Although employment of maintenance electricians is steadier than that of construction electricians, those working in the automotive and other manufacturing industries that are sensitive to cyclical swings in the economy may be laid off during recessions. Also, efforts to reduce operating costs and increase productivity through the increased use of contracting out for electrical services may limit opportunities for maintenance electricians in many industries. However, this should be partially offset by increased demand by electrical contracting firms.

Job opportunities for electricians also vary by geographic area. Employment opportunities follow the movement of people and businesses among States and local areas, and reflect differences in local economic conditions. The number of job opportunities in a given year may fluctuate widely from area to area. Some parts of the country may experience an oversupply of electricians, for example, while others may have a shortage.

Earnings

Median weekly earnings for full-time electricians who were not self-employed were $620 in 1996. The middle 50 percent earned between $468 and $8140 weekly. The lowest 10 percent earned less than $339, while the highest 10 percent earned more than $1,018 a week.

According to a survey of workplaces in 160 metropolitan areas, maintenance electricians had median hourly earnings of $18.78 in 1995. The middle half earned between $15.23 and $21.83 an hour. Annual earnings of electricians also tend to be higher than those of other building trades workers because electricians are less affected by the seasonal nature of construction.

Depending on experience, apprentices usually start at between 30 and 50 percent of the rate paid to experienced electricians. As they become more skilled, they receive periodic increases throughout the course of the apprenticeship program. Many employers also provide training opportunities for experienced electricians to improve their skills.

Many construction electricians are members of the International Brotherhood of Electrical Workers. Among unions organizing maintenance electricians are the International Brotherhood of Electrical Workers; the International Union of Electronic, Electrical, Salaried, Machine, and Furniture Workers; the International Association of Machinists and Aerospace Workers; the International Union, United Automobile, Aerospace and Agricultural Implement Workers of America; and the United Steelworkers of America.

Related Occupations

To install and maintain electrical systems, electricians combine manual skill and a knowledge of electrical materials and concepts. Workers in other occupations involving similar skills include air-conditioning mechanics, cable installers and repairers, electronics mechanics, and elevator constructors.

Sources of Additional Information

For details about apprenticeships or other work opportunities in this trade, contact offices of the State employment service, the State apprenticeship agency, local electrical contractors or firms that employ maintenance electricians, or local union-management electrician apprenticeship committees. This information may also be available from local chapters of the Independent Electrical Contractors, Inc.; the National Electrical Contractors Association; the Home Builders Institute; the Associated Builders and Contractors; and the International Brotherhood of Electrical Workers.

For general information about the work of electricians, contact:

☛ Independent Electrical Contractors, Inc., 507 Wythe St., Alexandria, VA 22314.

☛ National Electrical Contractors Association (NECA), 3 Metro Center, Suite 1100, Bethesda, MD 20814.

☛ International Brotherhood of Electrical Workers (IBEW), 1125 15th St. NW., Washington, DC 20005.

☛ Associated Builders and Contractors, 1300 North 17th St., Rosslyn, VA 22209.

☛ Homebuilders Institute, National Association of Home Builders, 1201 15th St. NW., Washington, DC 20005.

Glaziers

(D.O.T. 865.361 and .381)

Significant Points

- Glaziers learn the trade on the job, either through a formal apprenticeship or by working as helpers to glaziers.

- Glazier employment is expected to increase slowly due to the generally slow growth anticipated in construction.

Nature of the Work

Glass serves many uses in modern buildings. Insulated and specially treated glass keeps in warmed or cooled air, and provides good condensation and sound control qualities; tempered and laminated glass makes doors and windows more secure. In large commercial buildings, glass panels give skyscrapers a distinctive look while reducing the need for artificial lighting. The creative use of large windows, glass doors, skylights, and sun room additions make homes bright, airy, and inviting.

Glaziers generally work on four types of projects. Residential glazing involves work such as replacing glass in home windows, installing glass mirrors, shower doors and bathtub enclosures, and glass for table tops and display cases. On commercial interior projects, glaziers install items such as heavy, often etched, decorative room dividers and windows with speak holes and security glazing. Glazing projects may also involve replacement of storefront windows for establishments such as, supermarkets, auto dealerships, and banks. In construction of large commercial buildings, glaziers build metal framework extrusions and install glass panels or curtainwalls.

Glaziers select, cut, install, and remove all types of glass as well as plastics, granite, marble, and similar materials used as glass substitutes. They may mount steel and aluminum sashes or frames and attach locks and hinges to glass doors. For most jobs, the glass is precut and mounted in frames at a factory or a contractor's shop. It arrives at the job site ready for glaziers to position and secure it in place. They may use a crane or hoist with suction cups to lift large, heavy pieces of glass. They then gently guide the glass into position by hand.

Once glaziers have the glass in place, they secure it with mastic, putty, or other pastelike cement, or with bolts, rubber gaskets, glazing compound, metal clips, or metal or wood molding. When they secure glass using a rubber gasket—a thick, molded rubber half-tube with a split running its length—they first secure the gasket around the perimeter within the opening, then set the glass into the split side of the gasket, causing it to clamp to the edges and hold the glass firmly in place.

When they use metal clips and wood molding, glaziers first secure the molding to the opening, place the glass in the molding, and then force spring-like metal clips between the glass and the molding. The clips exert pressure and keep the glass firmly in place.

When a glazing compound is used, glaziers first spread it neatly against and around the edges of the molding on the inside of the opening. Next, they install the glass. Pressing it against the compound on the inside molding, workers screw or nail outside molding that loosely holds the glass in place. To hold it firmly, they pack the space between the molding and the glass with glazing compound and then trim any excess material with a glazing knife.

For some jobs, the glazier must cut the glass manually at the job site. To prepare the glass for cutting, glaziers rest it either on edge on a rack or "A-frame," or flat against a cutting table. They then measure and mark the glass for the cut.

Glaziers cut glass with a special tool that has a very hard metal wheel about 1/6 inch in diameter. Using a straightedge as a guide, the glazier presses the cutter's wheel firmly on the glass, guiding and rolling it carefully to make a score just below the surface. To help the cutting tool move smoothly across the glass, workers brush a thin layer of oil along the line of the intended cut or dip the cutting tool in oil. Immediately after cutting, the glazier presses on the shorter end of the glass to break it cleanly along the cut.

In addition to handtools such as glass cutters, suction cups, and glazing knives, glaziers use power tools such as saws, drills, cutters, and grinders. An increasing number of glaziers use computers in the shop or at the job site to improve their layout work and reduce the amount of glass that is wasted.

Working Conditions

Glaziers often work outdoors, sometimes in inclement weather. At times, they work on scaffolds at great heights. They do a considerable amount of bending, kneeling, lifting, and standing. Glaziers may be injured by broken glass or cutting tools, falls from scaffolds, or from improperly lifting heavy glass panels.

Employment

Glaziers held about 36,000 jobs in 1996. Most worked for glazing contractors engaged in new construction, alteration, and repair. Oth-

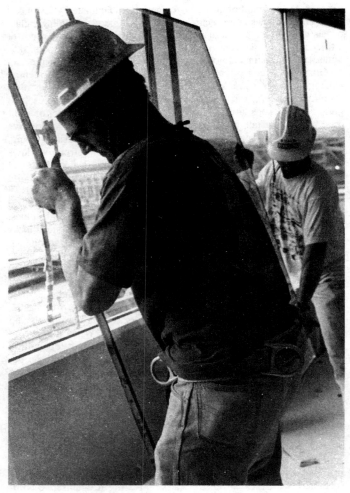

Glaziers often work in pairs.

ers worked for retail glass shops that install or replace glass and for wholesale distributors of products containing glass.

Training, Other Qualifications, and Advancement

Many glaziers learn the trade informally on the job. They usually start as helpers, carrying glass and cleaning up debris in glass shops. They often practice cutting on discarded glass. After a while, they are given an opportunity to cut glass for a job. Eventually, helpers assist experienced workers on simple installation jobs. By working with experienced glaziers, they eventually acquire the skills of a fully qualified glazier.

Employers recommend glaziers learn the trade through a formal apprenticeship program that lasts 3 to 4 years. Apprenticeship programs, which are administered by the National Glass Association and local union-management committees or local contractors' associations, consist of on-the-job training, as well as 144 hours of classroom instruction or home study each year. On the job, apprentices learn to use the tools and equipment of the trade; handle, measure, cut, and install glass and metal framing; cut and fit moldings; and install and balance glass doors. In the classroom, they are taught basic mathematics, blueprint reading and sketching, general construction techniques, safety practices, and first aid. Learning the trade through an apprenticeship program usually takes less time and provides more complete training than acquiring skills informally on the job, but opportunities for apprenticeships are declining.

Local apprenticeship administrators determine how apprentices are recruited and selected. In general, applicants for apprenticeships and for helper positions must be in good physical condition and at least 17 years old. High school or vocational school graduates are preferred.

In some areas, applicants must take mechanical aptitude tests. Courses in general mathematics, blueprint reading or mechanical drawing, general construction, and shop provide a good background.

Standards for acceptance into apprenticeship programs are rising to reflect changing requirements associated with new products and equipment. Glaziers need a basic understanding of electricity and electronics in order to be able to install electrochromatic glass and electronically controlled glass doors. In addition, the growing use of computers in glass layout requires more and more that glaziers be familiar with personal computers.

Because many glaziers do not learn the trade through a formal apprenticeship program, the National Glass Association (NGA) offers a series of written examinations which certify an individual's competency to perform glazier work at three progressively more difficult levels of proficiency. These levels include Level I, Glazier; Level II, Commercial Interior/Residential Glazier or Storefront/ Curtainwall Glazier; and Level III, Master Glazier.

Advancement generally consists of increases in pay for most glaziers; some advance to supervisory jobs or become contractors or estimators.

Job Outlook

Employment of glaziers is expected to increase more slowly than the average for all occupations through the year 2006, as a result of anticipated slow growth in residential and non-residential construction. Demand for glaziers will be spurred by the continuing need to modernize and repair existing structures and the popularity of glass in bathroom and kitchen design. Improved glass performance in insulation, privacy, safety, condensation control, and noise reduction are also expected to contribute to the demand for glaziers. In addition, job openings for glaziers will occur each year due to the need to replace experienced workers who retire or leave the occupation for other reasons.

People wishing to become construction glaziers should expect to experience periods of unemployment resulting from the limited duration of construction projects and the cyclical nature of the construction industry. During bad economic times, job openings for glaziers are reduced as the level of construction declines. Because construction activity varies from area to area, job openings,as well as apprenticeship opportunities,fluctuate with local economic conditions. Consequently, some parts of the country may experience an oversupply of these workers while others may have a shortage. Employment and apprenticeship opportunities should be greatest in metropolitan areas, where most glazing contractors and glass shops are located.

Earnings

The median weekly earnings of glaziers were about $592 a week in 1996. The middle 50 percent earned between $353 and $886 a week. The lowest paid 10 percent earned less than $297 a week, while 10 percent with the highest pay earned $886 or more a week.

According to the *Engineering News Record*, union glaziers received an average hourly wage of $27.81 in 1997, including benefits. Wages ranged from a low of $15.12 in San Antonio to a high of $41.37 in New York City. Glaziers covered by union contracts generally earn more than their non-union counterparts. Apprentice wage rates usually start at 50 to 60 percent of the rate paid to experienced glaziers and increase every 6 months. Because glaziers can lose time due to weather conditions and fluctuations in construction activity, their overall earnings may be lower than their hourly wages suggest.

Many glaziers employed in construction are members of the International Brotherhood of Painters and Allied Trades.

Related Occupations

Glaziers use their knowledge of construction materials and techniques to install glass. Other construction workers whose jobs also involve skilled, custom work are bricklayers, carpenters, floor layers, paperhangers, terrazzo workers, and tilesetters.

Sources of Additional Information

For more information about glazier apprenticeships or work opportunities, contact local glazing or general contractors; a local of the International Brotherhood of Painters and Allied Trades; a local joint union-management apprenticeship agency; or the nearest office of the State employment service or State apprenticeship agency.

For general information about the work of glaziers, contact:
☛ International Brotherhood of Painters and Allied Trades, 1750 New York Ave. NW., Washington, DC 20006.

For information concerning training for glaziers contact:
☛ National Glass Association, Education and Training Department, 8200 Greensboro Dr., 3rd floor, McLean, VA 22102.
☛ Flat Glass Marketing Association, White Lakes Professional Building, 3310 Southwest Harrison St., Topeka, KS 66611-2279.

Insulation Workers

(D.O.T. 863.364-010 and -014, .381-010 and -014, .664-010, and .685-010)

Significant Points

- Insulation worker jobs are projected to increase about as fast as the average for all occupations, but will be one of the fastest growing construction occupations.

- High turnover rate of insulation worker jobs keeps job openings plentiful.

- Workers who remove hazardous asbestos insulation from older buildings are required to be specially trained.

Nature of the Work
Properly insulated buildings reduce energy consumption by keeping heat in during the winter and out in the summer. Refrigerated storage rooms, vats, tanks, vessels, boilers, and steam and hot water pipes also are insulated to prevent the wasteful transfer of heat. Insulation workers install this insulating material.

Insulation workers cement, staple, wire, tape, or spray insulation. When covering a steam pipe, for example, insulation workers measure and cut sections of insulation to the proper length, stretch it open along a cut that runs the length of the material, and slip it over the pipe. They fasten the insulation with adhesive, staples, tape, or wire bands. Sometimes they wrap a cover of aluminum, plastic, or canvas over it and cement or band the cover in place. Insulation workers may screw on sheet metal around insulated pipes to protect the insulation from weather conditions or physical abuse.

When covering a wall or other flat surface, workers may use a hose to spray foam insulation onto a wire mesh. The wire mesh provides a rough surface to which the foam can cling, and adds strength to the finished surface. Workers may then install drywall or apply a final coat of plaster for a finished appearance.

In attics or exterior walls of uninsulated buildings, workers blow in loose-fill insulation. A helper feeds a machine with fiberglass, cellulose, or rock wool insulation while another worker blows the insulation with a compressor hose into the space being filled.

In new construction or major renovations, insulation workers staple fiberglass or rockwool batts to exterior walls and ceilings before drywall, paneling, or plaster walls are put in place. In major renovations of old buildings or when putting new insulation around pipes and industrial machinery, insulation workers often must first remove the old insulation. In the past, asbestos—now known to cause cancer in humans—was used extensively in walls and ceilings and for covering pipes, boilers, and various industrial equipment. Because of this danger, U.S. Environmental Protection Agency regulations require that asbestos be removed before a building undergoes major renovations or is demolished. When removing asbestos, insulation workers must follow carefully prescribed asbestos removal techniques and work practices. First, they seal and depressurize the area containing the asbestos, then they remove it using hand tools and special filtered vacuum cleaners and air-filtration devices.

Insulation workers use common handtools—trowels, brushes, knives, scissors, saws, pliers, and stapling guns. They use power saws to cut insulating materials, welding machines to join sheet metal or secure clamps, and compressors for blowing or spraying insulation.

Working Conditions
Insulation workers generally work indoors. They spend most of the workday on their feet, either standing, bending, or kneeling. Sometimes, they work from ladders or in tight spaces. However, the work is not strenuous; it requires more coordination than strength. Insulation work is often dusty and dirty. The minute particles from insulation materials, especially when blown, can irritate the eyes, skin, and respiratory system. Removing cancer-causing asbestos insulation is a hazardous task and is done by specially trained workers. To protect themselves from the dangers of asbestos and irritants, workers follow strict safety guidelines, take decontamination showers, keep work areas well ventilated, and wear protective suits, masks, and respirators.

Employment
Insulation workers held about 65,000 jobs in 1996; most worked for insulation or other construction contractors. Others worked for the Federal Government, in wholesale and retail trade, in shipbuilding, and in other manufacturing industries that have extensive installations for power, heating, and cooling. Most worked in urban areas. In less populated areas, insulation work may be done by carpenters, heating and air-conditioning installers, or drywall installers.

Training, Other Qualifications, and Advancement
Most insulation workers learn their trade informally on the job, although some workers complete formal apprenticeship programs. For entry jobs, insulation contractors prefer high school graduates who are in good physical condition and are licensed to drive. High school courses in blueprint reading, shop math, sheet-metal layout, and general construction provide a helpful background. Applicants seeking apprenticeship positions must have a high school diploma or its equivalent, and be at least 18 years old.

Trainees are assigned to experienced insulation workers for instruction and supervision. They begin with simple tasks, such as carrying insulation or holding material while it is fastened in place. On-the-job training can take up to 2 years, depending on the work. Learning to install insulation in homes generally requires less training than insulation application in commercial and industrial settings. As

When removing older asbestos insulation, workers wear protective suits and respirators.

they gain experience, trainees receive less supervision, more responsibility, and higher pay.

In contrast, trainees in formal apprenticeship programs receive in-depth instruction in all phases of insulation. Apprenticeship programs may be provided by a joint committee of local insulation contractors and the local union of the International Association of Heat and Frost Insulators and Asbestos Workers, to which many insulation workers belong. Programs normally consist of 4 years of on-the-job training coupled with classroom instruction, and trainees must pass practical and written tests to demonstrate a knowledge of the trade.

Insulation workers who work with asbestos usually have to be licensed. Although licensure requirements vary from area to area, most States require asbestos removal workers to complete a 3-day training program in compliance with the 1986 Asbestos Hazard Emergency Removal Act (AHERA). The National Asbestos Council (NAC) provides this training in over 100 locations. This program emphasizes "hands-on" training. Typically, students build a decontamination unit, handle a respirator and filtered vacuum cleaners, and perform simulated asbestos removal. In addition, they receive classroom instruction on a wide variety of topics, such as government regulations, health effects and worker protection, sampling for asbestos, and work practices. The NAC also offers a 2-day course on compliance with Occupational Safety and Health Administration (OSHA) regulations governing industrial asbestos removal in plants and factories, and an annual AHERA recertification program.

Skilled insulation workers may advance to supervisor, shop superintendent, insulation contract estimator, or set up their own insulation or asbestos abatement business.

Job Outlook

Opportunities for insulation workers are expected to be good because is it one of the fastest growing construction occupations, and replacement needs are usually high due to the many workers who transfer to other occupations. Employment of insulation workers is expected to increase about as fast as the average for all occupations through the year 2006, reflecting the demand for insulation associated with new construction and renovation as well as the demand for asbestos removal in existing structures. Concerns about the efficient use of energy to heat and cool buildings will result in growth in demand for insulation workers in the construction of new residential, industrial, and commercial buildings. In addition, renovation and efforts to improve insulation in existing structures also will increase demand.

Asbestos removal will also provide many jobs for insulation workers, not only because insulation workers often remove asbestos, but because they replace it with another insulating material. The 1986 Asbestos Hazard Emergency Removal Act requires all public and private schools to have an asbestos management plan. Federal regulations also require that asbestos be removed from buildings that are to be demolished or undergo major renovations. In addition, many banks require that buildings be free of asbestos before a real estate loan will be granted. All of these regulatory requirements are expected to stimulate asbestos removal and employment growth. The need to maintain, remove, and replace asbestos insulation on old pipes, boilers, and a variety of equipment in chemical and refrigeration plants and petroleum refineries will also add to employment requirements.

Despite this growth in demand, replacement needs will account for most job openings. This occupation has the highest turnover of all the construction trades. Each year thousands of jobs will become available as insulation workers transfer to other occupations or leave the labor force. However there are no strict training requirements for entry, many people with limited skills work as insulation workers for a short time and then move on to other types of work, creating many job openings.

Insulation workers in the construction industry may experience periods of unemployment because of the short duration of many construction projects and the cyclical nature of construction activity. Workers employed in industrial plants generally have more stable employment because maintenance and repair must be done on a continuing basis. Most insulation is applied after buildings are enclosed.

Earnings

Median weekly earnings for insulation workers who worked full time were $508 in 1996. The middle 50 percent earned between $351 and $758. The lowest 10 percent earned less than $267, and the top 10 percent earned more than $968.

According to the *Engineering News Record*, union insulation workers received an average hourly wage of $31.92 in 1997, including benefits. Wages ranged from a low of $21.68 an hour in New Orleans to a high of $47.77 in New York City. Insulation workers doing commercial and industrial work earn substantially more than those working in residential construction, which does not require as much skill.

Related Occupations

Insulation workers combine a knowledge of insulation materials with the skills of cutting, fitting, and installing materials. Workers in occupations involving similar skills include carpenters, carpet installers, drywall applicators, floor layers, roofers, and sheet-metal workers.

Sources of Additional Information

For information about training programs or other work opportunities in this trade, contact a local insulation contractor; a local chapter of the International Association of Heat and Frost Insulators and Asbestos Workers; the nearest office of the State employment service or State apprenticeship agency, or:

☞ International. Association of Heat and Frost Insulators and Asbestos Workers, 1300 Connecticut Ave., NW., Washington, DC 20005

☞ National Insulation and Abatement Contractors Association, 99 Canal Center Plaza, Suite 222, Alexandria, VA 22314.

☞ Insulation Contractors Association of America, 1321 Duke St., Suite 303, Alexandria, VA 22314.

Painters and Paperhangers

(D.O.T. 840.381, .681, and .684; 841.381)

Significant Points

- Painters and paperhangers are one of the larger construction occupations.

- Most painters and paperhangers learn their craft informally, on the job as helpers to experienced painters.

- Opportunities for jobs should be good due to high job turnover rates in the occupation.

Nature of the Work

Paint and wall coverings make surfaces clean, attractive and bright. In addition, paints and other sealers protect outside walls from wear caused by exposure to the weather. Although some people do both painting and paperhanging, each requires different skills.

Painters apply paint, stain, varnish, and other finishes to buildings and other structures. They choose the right paint or finish for the surface to be covered, taking into account customers' wishes, durability, ease of handling, and method of application. They first prepare the surfaces to be covered so the paint will adhere properly. This may require removing the old coat by stripping, sanding, wire brushing, burning, or water and abrasive blasting. Painters also wash walls and trim to remove dirt and grease, fill nail holes and cracks, sandpaper rough spots, and brush off dust. On new surfaces, they apply a primer or sealer to prepare them for the finish coat. Painters also mix paints and match colors, relying on knowledge of paint composition and color harmony.

There are several ways to apply paint and similar coverings. Painters must be able to choose the right paint applicator for each job, depending on the surface to be covered, the characteristics of the finish, and other factors. Some jobs only need a good bristle brush with a soft, tapered edge; others require a dip or fountain pressure roller; still others can best be done using a paint sprayer. Many jobs need several

Painters fill cracks and smooth surfaces prior to painting.

types of applicators. The right tools for each job not only expedite the painter's work but also produce the most attractive surface.

When working on tall buildings, painters erect scaffolding, including "swing stages," scaffolds suspended by ropes, or cables attached to roof hooks. When painting steeples and other conical structures, they use a "bosun chair," a swinglike device.

Paperhangers cover walls and ceilings with decorative wall coverings made of paper, vinyl, or fabric. They first prepare the surface to be covered by applying "sizing," which seals the surface and makes the covering stick better. When redecorating, they may first remove the old covering by soaking, steaming, or applying solvents. When necessary, they patch holes and take care of other imperfections before hanging the new wall covering.

After the surface has been prepared, paperhangers must prepare the paste or other adhesive. Then they measure the area to be covered, check the covering for flaws, cut the covering into strips of the proper size, and closely examine the pattern to match it when the strips are hung.

The next step is to brush or roll the adhesive onto the back of the covering, then to place the strips on the wall or ceiling, making sure the pattern is matched, the strips are hung straight, and the edges butted together to make tight, closed seams. Finally, paperhangers smooth the strips to remove bubbles and wrinkles, trim the top and bottom with a razor knife, and wipe off any excess adhesive.

Working Conditions
Most painters and paperhangers work 40 hours a week or less; about 1 out of 6 works part time. Painters and paperhangers must stand for long periods. Their jobs also require a considerable amount of climbing and bending. These workers must have stamina because much of the work is done with their arms raised overhead. Painters often work outdoors, but seldom in wet, cold, or inclement weather.

Painters and paperhangers risk injury from slips or falls off ladders and scaffolds. They may sometimes work with materials that can be hazardous if masks are not worn or if ventilation is poor. Some painting jobs can leave a worker covered with paint.

Employment
Painters and paperhangers held about 4449,000 jobs in 1996; most were painters. The majority of painters and paperhangers work for contractors engaged in new construction, repair, restoration, or remodeling work. In addition, organizations that own or manage large buildings, such as apartment complexes, employ maintenance painters, as do some schools, hospitals, and factories.

Self-employed independent painting contractors accounted for over 40 percent of all painters and paperhangers, significantly greater than the proportion of building trades workers in general.

Training, Other Qualifications, and Advancement
Painting and paperhanging are learned through apprenticeship or informal, on-the-job instruction. Although training authorities recommend completion of an apprenticeship program as the best way to become a painter or paperhanger, most painters learn the trade informally on the job as a helper to an experienced painter. Few opportunities for informal training exist for paperhangers because few paperhangers have a need for helpers.

The apprenticeship for painters and paperhangers consists of 3 to 4 years of on-the-job training, in addition to 144 hours of related classroom instruction each year. Apprentices receive instruction in color harmony, use and care of tools and equipment, surface preparation, application techniques, paint mixing and matching, characteristics of different finishes, blueprint reading, wood finishing, and safety.

Whether a painter learns the trade through a formal apprenticeship or informally as a helper, on-the-job instruction covers similar skill areas. Under the direction of experienced workers, trainees carry supplies, erect scaffolds, and do simple painting and surface preparation tasks while they learn about paint and painting equipment. Within 2 or 3 years, trainees learn to prepare surfaces for painting and paperhanging, to mix paints, and to apply paint and wall coverings efficiently and neatly. Near the end of their training, they may learn decorating concepts, color coordination, and cost-estimating techniques. In addition to learning craft skills, painters must become familiar with safety and health regulations so their work is in compliance with the law.

Apprentices or helpers generally must be at least 16 years old and in good physical condition. A high school education or its equivalent that includes courses in mathematics is generally required to enter an apprenticeship program. Applicants should have good manual dexterity and good color sense.

Painters and paperhangers may advance to supervisory or estimating jobs with painting and decorating contractors. Many establish their own painting and decorating businesses.

Job Outlook
Employment of painters and paperhangers is expected to grow about as fast as the average for all occupations through the year 2006, as the level of new construction increases and the stock of buildings and other structures that require maintenance and renovation grows. Painting is very labor intensive and not suitable to technological gains which might make workers more productive and restrict employment growth. In addition to job openings created by rising demand for the services of these workers, thousands of jobs will become available each year as painters and paperhangers transfer to other occupations or leave the labor force. There are no strict training requirements for entry, so many people with limited skills work as painters or paperhangers for a short time and then move on to other types of work, creating many job openings. Many fewer openings will occur for paperhangers because the number of these jobs is comparatively small.

Prospects for jobs as painters or paperhangers should be favorable since there are no strict training requirements and many individuals are able to enter the field. However, job seekers considering these occupations should expect some periods of unemployment, especially until they become fully skilled. Many construction projects are of the short duration and construction activity is cyclical and seasonal in nature. Remodeling, restoration, and maintenance projects, however, often provide many jobs for painters and paperhangers even when new construction activity declines. The most versatile painters and skilled paperhangers generally are most able to keep working steadily during downturns in the economy.

Earnings

Median weekly earnings for painters who were not self-employed were about $381 in 1996. Most earned between $285 and $517 weekly. The top 10 percent earned over $688 and the bottom 10 percent earned less than $2150 a week. In general, paperhangers earn more than painters. Earnings for painters may be reduced on occasion because of bad weather and the short-term nature of many construction jobs.

Hourly wage rates for apprentices usually start at 40 to 50 percent of the rate for experienced workers and increase periodically.

Some painters and paperhangers are members of the International Brotherhood of Painters and Allied Trades. Some maintenance painters are members of other unions.

Related Occupations

Painters and paperhangers apply various coverings to decorate and protect wood, drywall, metal, and other surfaces. Other occupations in which workers apply paints and similar finishes include billboard posterers, metal sprayers, undercoaters, and transportation equipment painters.

Sources of Additional Information

For details about painting and paperhanging apprenticeships or work opportunities, contact local painting and decorating contractors; a local of the International Brotherhood of Painters and Allied Trades; a local joint union-management apprenticeship committee; or an office of the State apprenticeship agency or State employment service.

For general information about the work of painters and paperhangers, contact:

☛ Associated Builders and Contractors, 1300 North 17th St., Rosslyn, VA 22209.
☛ International Brotherhood of Painters and Allied Trades, 1750 New York Ave. NW., Washington, DC 20006.
☛ Home Builders Institute, National Association of Home Builders, 1201 15th St. NW., Washington, DC 20005.

Plasterers

(D.O.T. 842.361-018, -022, and -026, and .381-014)

Significant Points

- Plasterers are projected to be one of the fastest growing occupations in construction trades, increasing about as fast as the average for all occupations.

- As it was one time supplanted by drywall construction, plaster is regaining popularity because of its durability, finish, and fire-retardant qualities.

- Plastering usually is learned on the job, either through a formal apprenticeship program or by working as a helper.

Nature of the Work

Plastering—one of the oldest crafts in the building trades—is enjoying a resurgence in popularity because of the introduction of newer, less costly materials and techniques. Plasterers apply plaster to interior walls and ceilings to form fire-resistant and relatively soundproof surfaces. They also apply plaster veneer over drywall to create smooth or textured abrasion-resistant finishes. They apply durable plasters such as polymer-based acrylic finishes and stucco to exterior surfaces, and install prefabricated exterior insulation systems over existing walls, for good insulation and interesting architectural effects. In addition, they cast ornamental designs in plaster. Drywall workers and lathers, a related occupation, use drywall instead of plaster when erecting interior walls and ceilings. (See the section on drywall workers and lathers elsewhere in the *Handbook*.)

When plasterers work with interior surfaces such as cinder block and concrete, they first apply a brown coat of gypsum plaster that provides a base, followed by a second or finish coat—also called "white coat"—which is a lime-based plaster. When plastering metal lath (supportive wire mesh) foundations, they apply a preparatory, or "scratch coat", with a trowel. They spread this rich plaster mixture into and over the metal lath. Before the plaster sets, they scratch its surface with a rake-like tool to produce ridges so the subsequent brown coat will bond to it tightly.

Laborers prepare a thick, smooth plaster for the brown coat. Plasterers spray or trowel this mixture onto the surface, then finish by smoothing it to an even, level surface.

For the finish coat, plasterers prepare a mixture of lime, plaster of Paris, and water. They quickly apply this onto the brown coat using a "hawk"—a light, metal plate with a handle—trowel, brush, and water. This mixture, which sets very quickly, produces a very smooth, durable finish.

Plasterers also work with a plaster material that can be finished in a single coat. This thin-coat or gypsum veneer plaster is made of lime and plaster of Paris and is mixed with water at the job site. It provides a smooth, durable, abrasion resistant finish on interior masonry surfaces, special gypsum base board, or drywall prepared with a bonding agent.

Plasterers create decorative interior surfaces as well. They do this by pressing a brush or trowel firmly against the wet plaster surface and using a circular hand motion to create decorative swirls.

For exterior work, plasterers usually apply a mixture of Portland cement, lime, and sand (stucco) over cement, concrete, masonry, and

Plasterers can create arches and other ornamental effects that cannot be achieved with drywall.

lath. Stucco is also applied directly to a wire lath with a scratch coat followed by a brown coat and then a finish coat. Plasterers may also embed marble or gravel chips into the finish coat to achieve a pebblelike, decorative finish.

Increasingly, plasterers apply insulation to the exteriors of new and old buildings. They cover the outer wall with rigid foam insulation board and reinforcing mesh and then trowel on a polymer-based or polymer-modified base coat. They apply an additional coat of this material with a decorative finish.

Plasterers sometimes do complex decorative and ornamental work that requires special skill and creativity. For example, they mold intricate wall and ceiling designs. Following an architect's blueprint, they pour or spray a special plaster into a mold and allow it to set. Workers then remove the molded plaster and put it in place according to the plan.

Working Conditions

Most plastering jobs are indoors; however, plasterers work outside when applying stucco or exterior wall insulation and decorative finish systems. Because plaster can freeze, heat is usually necessary to complete plastering jobs in cold weather. Sometimes plasterers work on scaffolds high above the ground.

Plastering is physically demanding, requiring considerable standing, bending, lifting, and reaching overhead. The work can be dusty and dirty; plaster materials also soil shoes and clothing and can irritate the skin and eyes.

Employment

Plasterers held about 32,000 jobs in 1996. Most plasterers work on new construction sites, particularly where special architectural and lighting effects are part of the work. Some repair and renovate older buildings. Many plasterers are employed in Florida, California, and the Southwest, where exterior plasters with decorative finishes are very popular.

Most plasterers work for independent contractors. About 1 out of every 5 plasterers is self-employed.

Training, Other Qualifications, and Advancement

Although most employers recommend apprenticeship as the best way to learn plastering, many people learn the trade by working as helpers to experienced plasterers. Those who learn the trade informally as helpers usually start by carrying materials, setting up scaffolds, and mixing plaster. Later they learn to apply the scratch, brown, and finish coats.

Apprenticeship programs, sponsored by local joint committees of contractors and unions, generally consist of 2 or 3 years of on-the-job training, in addition to at least 144 hours annually of classroom instruction in drafting, blueprint reading, and mathematics for layout work.

In the classroom, apprentices start with a history of the trade and the industry. They also learn about the uses of plaster, estimating materials and costs, and casting ornamental plaster designs. On the job, they learn about lath bases, plaster mixes, methods of plastering, blueprint reading, and safety. They also learn how to use various tools, such as hand and powered trowels, floats, brushes, straightedges, power tools, plaster-mixing machines, and piston-type pumps. Some apprenticeship programs allow individuals to obtain training in related occupations such as cement masonry and bricklaying.

Applicants for apprentice or helper jobs must generally be at least 17 years old, be in good physical condition, and have good manual dexterity. Applicants who have a high school education are preferred. Courses in general mathematics, mechanical drawing, and shop provide a useful background.

Plasterers may advance to supervisors, superintendents, or estimators for plastering contractors, or may become self-employed contractors.

Job Outlook

Employment of plasterers is expected to increase about as fast as the average for all occupations through the year 2006. In addition to job openings due to rising demand for plastering work, additional jobs will open up as plasterers transfer to other occupations or leave the labor force.

In past years, employment of plasterers declined as more builders switched to drywall construction. This decline has halted, however, and employment of plasterers is expected to continue growing as a result of greater appreciation for the durability and attractiveness troweled finishes provide. Thin-coat plastering—or veneering—in particular, is gaining greater acceptance as more builders recognize its ease of application, durability, quality of finish, and fire-retarding qualities. An increasing use of prefabricated wall systems and new polymer-based or polymer-modified acrylic exterior insulating finishes are also gaining popularity, not only because of their durability, attractiveness, and insulating properties, but also because of their lower cost. These wall systems and finishes are growing in popularity particularly in the South and Southwest regions of the country. In addition, plasterers will be needed to renovate plaster work in older structures, and create special architectural effects such as curved surfaces, which are not practical with drywall materials.

Most plasterers work in construction, where prospects fluctuate from year to year due to changing economic conditions. Bad weather affects plastering less than other construction trades because most work is indoors. On exterior surfacing jobs, however, plasterers may lose time because materials cannot be applied under wet or freezing conditions. Best employment opportunities should continue to be in Florida, California, and the Southwest, where exterior plaster and decorative finishes are expected to remain popular.

Earnings

Median weekly earnings for plasterers working full time were about $531 a week in 1996. The middle 50 percent earned between $354 and $760 a week. The top 10 percent earned more than $960and the lowest 10 percent less than $251 a week.

According to the limited information available, average hourly earnings—including benefits—for plasterers who belonged to a union and worked full time ranged between $14.45 and $39.08 in 1997. Plasterers in New York, Boston, Chicago, San Francisco, Los Angeles, and other large cities received the higher hourly earnings. Apprentice wage rates start at about half the rate paid to experienced plasterers. Annual earnings for plasterers and apprentices may be less than the hourly rate would indicate because poor weather and periodic declines in construction activity may limit their work time.

Many plasterers are members of unions. They are represented by the Operative Plasterers' and Cement Masons' International Association of the United States and Canada, or the International Union of Bricklayers and Allied Craftsmen.

Related Occupations

Other construction workers who use a trowel as their primary tool include drywall finishers, bricklayers, concrete masons, marble setters, stonemasons, terrazzo workers, and tilesetters.

Sources of Additional Information

For information about apprenticeships or other work opportunities, contact local plastering contractors; locals of the unions previously mentioned; a local joint union-management apprenticeship committee; or the nearest office of the State apprenticeship agency or the State employment service.

For general information about the work of plasterers, contact:

☛ International Union of Bricklayers and Allied Craftsmen, 815 15th St. NW., Washington, DC 20005.

☛ Operative Plasterers' and Cement Masons' International Association of the United States and Canada, 1125 17th St. NW., Washington, DC 20036.

Plumbers and Pipefitters

(D.O.T. 862.261; .281-010, -014, -022, and -026;.361-014, -018, and -022; .381 except -010 and -038; .681; .682-010; and .684-034)

Significant Points

- Although employment is projected to increase slowly, job opportunities should be excellent because not enough people are seeking training as plumbers and pipefitters.

- Most workers are trained through a formal 4-5 year apprenticeship program.

- Plumbers and pipefitters are one of the larger, as well as higher paid construction occupations.

Nature of the Work

Most people are familiar with plumbers who come to their home to unclog a drain or install an appliance. In addition to these activities, however, plumbers and pipefitters install, maintain, and repair many different types of pipe systems. For example, some systems move water to a municipal water treatment plant, and then to residential, commercial, and public buildings. Others dispose of waste. Some bring in gas for stoves and furnaces. Others supply air-conditioning. Pipe systems in power plants carry the steam that powers huge turbines. Pipes also are used in manufacturing plants to move material through the production process.

Although plumbing and pipefitting are sometimes are considered a single trade, workers generally specialize in one or the other. *Plumbers* install and repair the water, waste disposal, drainage, and gas systems in homes and in commercial and industrial buildings. They also install plumbing fixtures—bathtubs, showers, sinks, and toilets—and appliances such as dishwashers and water heaters. *Pipefitters* install and repair both high and low-pressure pipe systems that are used in manufacturing, in the generation of electricity, and in heating and cooling buildings. They also install automatic controls that are increasingly being used to regulate these systems. Some pipefitters specialize in only one type of system. *Steamfitters*, for example, install pipe systems that move liquids or gases under high pressure. *Sprinklerfitters* install automatic fire sprinkler systems in buildings.

Plumbers and pipefitters use many different materials and construction techniques, depending on the type of project. Residential water systems, for example, use copper, steel, and increasingly plastic pipe that can be handled and installed by one or two workers. Municipal sewerage systems, on the other hand, are made of large cast iron pipes; installation normally requires crews of pipefitters. Despite these differences, all plumbers and pipefitters must be able to follow building plans or blueprints and instructions from supervisors, lay out the job, and work efficiently with the materials and tools of the trade.

When construction plumbers install piping in a house, for example, they work from blueprints or drawings that show the planned location of pipes, plumbing fixtures, and appliances. They lay out the job to fit the piping into the structure of the house with the least waste of material and within the confines of the structure. They measure and mark areas where pipes will be installed and connected. They check for obstructions, such as electrical wiring, and, if necessary, plan the pipe installation around the problem.

Sometimes plumbers have to cut holes in walls, ceilings, and floors of a house. For some systems, they may have to hang steel supports from ceiling joists to hold the pipe in place. To assemble the system, plumbers cut and bend lengths of pipe using saws, pipe cutters, and pipe-bending machines. They connect lengths of pipe with fittings; the method depends on the type of pipe used. For plastic pipe, plumbers connect the sections and fittings with adhesives. For copper pipe, they slide fittings over the end of the pipe and solder the fitting in place with a torch.

After the piping is in place in the house, plumbers install the fixtures and appliances and connect the system to the outside water or

Plumbers connect lengths of pipe with fittings and solder the fittings in place.

sewer lines. Using pressure gauges, they check the system to insure the plumbing works properly.

Working Conditions

Because plumbers and pipefitters frequently must lift heavy pipes, stand for long periods, and sometimes work in uncomfortable or cramped positions, they need physical strength as well as stamina. They may have to work outdoors in inclement weather. They also are subject to possible falls from ladders, cuts from sharp tools, and burns from hot pipes or from soldering equipment.

Plumbers and pipefitters engaged in construction generally work a standard 40-hour week; those involved in maintaining pipe systems, including those who provide maintenance services under contract, may have to work evening or weekend shifts, as well as be on call. These maintenance workers may spend quite a bit of time traveling to and from work sites.

Employment

Plumbers and pipefitters held about 389,000 jobs in 1996. About two-thirds worked for mechanical and plumbing contractors engaged in new construction, repair, modernization, or maintenance work. Others did maintenance work for a variety of industrial, commercial, and government employers. For example, pipefitters were employed as maintenance personnel in the petroleum and chemical industries, where manufacturing operations require the moving of liquids and gases through pipes. Almost one of every 5 plumbers and pipefitters was self-employed.

Jobs for plumbers and pipefitters are distributed across the country in about the same proportion as the general population.

Training, Other Qualifications, and Advancement

Virtually all plumbers undergo some type of apprenticeship training. Many programs are administered by local union-management committees made up of members of the United Association of Journeymen and Apprentices of the Plumbing and Pipefitting Industry of the United States and Canada, and local employers who are members of either the Mechanical Contractors Association of America, Inc., the National Association of Plumbing-Heating-Cooling Contractors, or the National Fire Sprinkler Association, Inc.

Nonunion training and apprenticeship programs are administered by local chapters of the Associated Builders and Contractors, the National Association of Plumbing-Heating-Cooling Contractors, the American Fire Sprinkler Association, and the Home Builders Institute of the National Association of Home Builders.

Apprenticeships—both union and nonunion—consist of 4 to 5 years of on-the-job training, in addition to at least 144 hours annually of related classroom instruction. Classroom subjects include drafting and blueprint reading, mathematics, applied physics and chemistry, safety, and local plumbing codes and regulations. On the job, apprentices first learn basic skills such as identifying grades and types of pipe, the use of the tools of the trade, and the safe unloading of materials. As apprentices gain experience, they learn how to work with various types of pipe and install different piping systems and plumbing fixtures. Apprenticeship gives trainees a thorough knowledge of all aspects of the trade. Although most plumbers are trained through apprenticeship, some still learn their skills informally on the job.

Applicants for union or nonunion apprentice jobs must be 18 years old and in good physical condition. Apprenticeship committees may require applicants to have a high school diploma or its equivalent. Armed Forces training in plumbing and pipefitting is considered very good preparation. In fact, persons with this background may be given credit for previous experience when entering a civilian apprenticeship program. Secondary or post secondary courses in shop, plumbing, general mathematics, drafting, blueprint reading, and physics also are good preparation.

Although there are no uniform national licensing requirements, most communities require plumbers to be licensed. Licensing requirements vary from area to area, but most localities require workers to pass an examination that tests their knowledge of the trade and of local plumbing codes.

Some plumbers and pipefitters may become supervisors for mechanical and plumbing contractors. Others go into business for themselves.

Job Outlook

Job opportunities for skilled plumbers and pipefitters are expected to be excellent as the growth in demand outpaces the supply of workers trained in this craft. Employment of plumbers and pipefitters is expected to grow more slowly than the average for all occupations through the year 2006. However, the pool of young workers available to enter training programs will also be increasing slowly, and many in that group are reluctant to seek training for jobs that may be strenuous and have uncomfortable working conditions.

Construction activity—residential, industrial, and commercial—is expected to grow slowly over the next decade. Demand for plumbers will stem from building renovation, including the increasing installation of sprinkler systems; repair and maintenance of existing residential systems, and maintenance activities for places having extensive systems of pipes, such as power plants, water and wastewater treatment plants, pipelines, office buildings, and factories. However, the growing use of plastic pipe and fittings, which are much easier to use; more efficient sprinkler systems; and other technologies will mean employment will not grow as fast as it has in past years. In addition, several thousand positions will become available each year from the need to replace experienced workers who leave the occupation.

Traditionally, many organizations with extensive pipe systems have employed their own plumbers or pipefitters to maintain their equipment and keep everything running smoothly. But, in order to reduce their labor costs, many of these firms no longer employ a full-time in-house plumber or pipefitter. Instead, when they need one they rely on workers provided, under service contracts, by plumbing and pipefitting contractors.

All construction projects provide only temporary employment, so when a project ends, plumbers and pipefitters working on it may experience short bouts of unemployment. Because construction activity varies from area to area, job openings, as well as apprenticeship opportunities, fluctuate with local economic conditions. However, employment of plumbers and pipefitters is generally less sensitive to changes in economic conditions than some of the other construction trades. Even when construction activity declines, maintenance, rehabilitation, and replacement of existing piping systems, as well as the growing installation of fire sprinkler systems, provide many jobs for plumbers and pipefitters.

Earnings

Median weekly earnings for plumbers and pipefitters who were not self-employed were $591 in 1996. The middle 50 percent earned between $413 and $812 weekly. The lowest 10 percent earned less than $312; the highest 10 percent earned more than $1,047 a week.

In 1995, the median hourly wage rate for maintenance pipefitters in 160 metropolitan areas was about $21.46. The middle 50 percent earned between about $19.20 and $21.65 an hour. In general, wage rates tend to be higher in the Midwest and West than in the Northeast and South.

Apprentices usually begin at about 50 percent of the wage rate paid to experienced plumbers or pipefitters. This increases periodically as they improve their skills. After an initial waiting period, apprentices receive the same benefits as experienced plumbers and pipefitters.

Many plumbers and pipefitters are members of the United Association of Journeymen and Apprentices of the Plumbing and Pipefitting Industry of the United States and Canada.

Related Occupations

Other occupations in which workers install and repair mechanical systems in buildings are boilermakers, stationary engineers, electricians, elevator installers, industrial machinery repairers, millwrights, sheet-metal workers, and heating, air-conditioning, and refrigeration mechanics.

Sources of Additional Information

For information about apprenticeships or work opportunities in plumbing and pipefitting, contact local plumbing, heating, and air-conditioning contractors; a local or State chapter of the National Association of Plumbing, Heating, and Cooling Contractors; a local chapter of the Mechanical Contractors Association; a local chapter of the United Association of Journeymen and Apprentices of the Plumbing and Pipefitting Industry of the United States and Canada; or the nearest office of the State employment service or State apprenticeship agency. This information is also available from:

☛ The Home Builders Institute, National Association of Home Builders, 1201 15th St. NW., Washington, DC 20005.

For general information about the work of plumbers, pipefitters, and sprinklerfitters, contact:

☛ National Association of Plumbing-Heating-Cooling Contractors, P.O. Box 6808, Falls Church, VA 22046.

☛ Associated Builders and Contractors, 1300 North 17th St., Rosslyn, VA 22209.

☛ National Fire Sprinkler Association, Robin Hill Corporate Park, Patterson, NY 12563.

☛ American Fire Sprinkler Association, Inc., 12959 Jupiter Rd., Suite 142, Dallas, TX 75238-3200.

☛ Mechanical Contractors Association of America, 1385 Piccard Dr., Rockville, MD 20850.

Roofers

(D.O.T. 866.381-010, -014, and .684-010)

Significant Points

- Jobs for roofers should be plentiful through the year 2006 because roofing work is hot, strenuous, and dirty, and job turnover is high.

- Demand for roofers is less susceptible to downturns in the economy than some of the other construction trades, because the majority of roofing work is repair and reroofing.

- Roofing has the highest accident rate of all construction occupations.

Nature of the Work

A leaky roof can damage ceilings, walls, and furnishings. To protect buildings and their contents from water damage, roofers repair and install roofs of tar or asphalt and gravel, rubber, thermoplastic, and metal; and shingles made of asphalt, slate, fiberglass, wood, tile, or other material. Repair and reroofing—replacing old roofs on existing buildings—provide many job opportunities for these workers. Roofers also may waterproof foundation walls and floors.

There are two types of roofs, flat and pitched (sloped). Most commercial, industrial, and apartment buildings have flat or slightly sloping roofs. Most houses have pitched roofs. Some roofers work on both types; others specialize.

Most flat roofs are covered with several layers of materials. Roofers first put a layer of insulation on the roof deck. Over the insulation, they then spread a coat of molten bitumen, a tar-like substance. Next, they install partially overlapping layers of roofing felt—a fabric saturated in bitumen—over the insulation surface and use a mop to spread hot bitumen over it and under the next layer. This seals the seams and makes the surface watertight. Roofers repeat these steps to build up the desired number of layers, called "plies". The top layer is either glazed to make a smooth finish, or has gravel embedded in the hot bitumen for a rough surface.

An increasing number of flat roofs are covered with a single-ply membrane of waterproof rubber or thermoplastic compounds. Roofers roll these sheets over the roof's insulation and seal the seams. Adhesive, mechanical fasteners, or stone ballasts hold the sheets in place. The building must be of sufficient strength to hold the ballast.

Most residential roofs are covered with shingles. To apply shingles, roofers first lay, cut, and tack 3-foot strips of roofing felt lengthwise over the entire roof. Then, starting from the bottom edge, they nail overlapping rows of shingles to the roof. Workers measure and cut the felt and shingles to fit intersecting roofs, and to fit around vent pipes and chimneys. Wherever two roof surfaces intersect or shingles reach a vent pipe or chimney, roofers cement or nail "flashing," strips of metal or shingle, over the joints to make them watertight. Finally, roofers cover exposed nailheads with roofing cement or caulking to prevent water leakage.

Some roofers also waterproof and dampproof masonry and concrete walls and floors. To prepare surfaces for waterproofing, they hammer and chisel away rough spots or remove them with a rubbing brick before applying a coat of liquid waterproofing compound. They may also paint or spray surfaces with a waterproofing material or attach waterproofing membrane to surfaces. When dampproofing, they usually spray a bitumen-based coating on interior or exterior surfaces.

Working Conditions

Roofing work is strenuous. It involves heavy lifting, as well as climbing, bending, and kneeling. Roofers risk injuries from slips or falls from scaffolds, ladders, or roofs, and burns from hot bitumen. In fact, of all construction industries, the roofing industry has the highest accident rate. Roofers work outdoors in all types of weather, particularly when making repairs. Roofs are extremely hot during the summer.

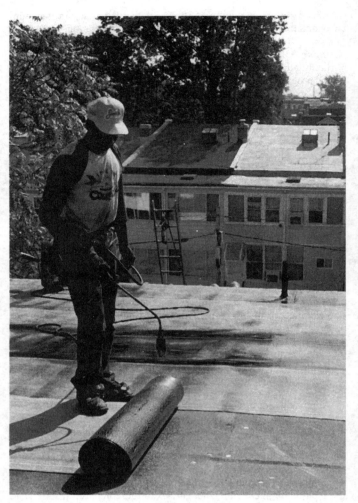

The work of roofers is very strenuous and hazardous.

Employment

Roofers held about 138,000 jobs in 1996. Almost all wage and salary roofers worked for roofing contractors. Nearly 3 out of every 10 roofers were self-employed. Many self-employed roofers specialize in residential work.

Training, Other Qualifications, and Advancement

Most roofers acquire their skills informally by working as helpers for experienced roofers. They start by carrying equipment and material and erecting scaffolds and hoists. Within 2 or 3 months, they are taught to measure, cut, and fit roofing materials, and then to lay asphalt or fiberglass shingles. Because some roofing materials are used infrequently, it can take several years to get experience working on all the various types of roofing applications.

Some roofers train through 3-year apprenticeship programs administered by local union-management committees representing roofing contractors and locals of the United Union of Roofers, Waterproofers, and Allied Workers. The apprenticeship program generally consists of a minimum of 2,000 hours of on-the-job training annually, plus 144 hours of classroom instruction a year in subjects such as tools and their use, arithmetic, and safety. On-the-job training for apprentices is similar to that for helpers, except the apprenticeship program is more structured. Apprentices also learn to dampproof and waterproof walls.

Good physical condition and good balance are essential for roofers. A high school education or its equivalent is helpful, as are courses in mechanical drawing and basic mathematics. Most apprentices are at least 18 years old.

Roofers may advance to supervisor or estimator for a roofing contractor, or become contractors themselves.

Job Outlook

Jobs for roofers should be plentiful through the year 2006, primarily because of the need to replace workers who transfer to other occupations or leave the labor force. Turnover is high; roofing work is hot, strenuous, and dirty, and a significant number of workers treat roofing as a temporary job until something better comes along. Some roofers leave the occupation to go into other construction trades.

Employment of roofers is expected to grow more slowly than the average for all occupations through the year 2006. Roofs deteriorate faster than most other parts of buildings and periodically need to be repaired or replaced. About 75 percent of roofing work is repair and reroofing, a higher proportion than in most other construction work. As a result, demand for roofers is less susceptible to downturns in the economy than some of the other construction trades. In addition to repair and reroofing work on the growing stock of buildings, new construction of industrial, commercial, and residential buildings will add to the demand for roofers. However, many innovations and advances in materials, techniques, and tools have made roofers more productive and will restrict the growth of employment at least to some extent. Jobs should be easiest to find during spring and summer, when most roofing is done.

Earnings

Median weekly earnings for roofers working full time were about $363 a week in 1996. The middle 50 percent earned between $283 and $513 a week. The top 10 percent earned more than $711 weekly and the lowest 10 percent less than $210 a week.

According to the *Engineering News Record*, average hourly earnings—including benefits—for union roofers were $25.75 in 1997. Wages ranged from a low of $14.97 in Nashville, to a high of $40.38 in New York City. Apprentices generally start at about 40 percent of the rate paid to experienced roofers and receive periodic raises as they acquire the skills of the trade. Earnings for roofers are reduced on occasion because poor weather often limits the time they can work.

Some roofers are members of the United Union of Roofers, Waterproofers & Allied Workers.

Related Occupations

Roofers use shingles, bitumen and gravel, single-ply plastic or rubber sheets, or other materials to waterproof building surfaces. Workers in other occupations who cover surfaces with special materials for protection and decoration include carpenters, concrete masons, drywall installers, floor covering installers, plasterers, terrazzo workers, and tilesetters.

Sources of Additional Information

For information about roofing apprenticeships or job opportunities in this trade, contact local roofing contractors; a local chapter of the Roofers union; a local joint union-management apprenticeship committee; or the nearest office of the State employment service or State apprenticeship agency.

For information about the work of roofers, contact:

☞ National Roofing Contractors Association, 10255 W. Higgins Rd., Rosemont, IL 60018.

☞ United Union of Roofers, Waterproofers and Allied Workers, 1125 17th St. NW., Washington, DC 20036.

Sheetmetal Workers

(D.O.T. 804.281-010 and -014)

Significant Points

- Job prospects should be good for persons who complete apprenticeship programs.
- Sheetmetal work tends to be steadier than some other construction crafts because it usually is indoors and is rarely idled by bad weather, work in existing buildings can compensate for slack in new construction.
- Unlike most construction craft occupations, few sheet metal workers are self-employed.

Nature of the Work

Sheetmetal workers make, install, and maintain air-conditioning, heating, ventilation, and pollution control duct systems; roofs; siding; rain gutters,downspouts; skylights; restaurant equipment; outdoor signs; and many other building parts and products made from metal sheets. They may also work with fiberglass and plastic materials. Although some workers specialize in fabrication, installation, or maintenance, most do all three jobs. (Workers employed in the mass production of sheetmetal products in manufacturing are not included in this section.)

Sheetmetal workers usually fabricate their products at a shop away from the construction site. They first study plans and specifications to determine the kind and quantity of materials they will need. They then measure, cut, bend, shape, and fasten pieces of sheet metal to make duct work, counter tops, and other custom products. In an increasing number of shops, sheetmetal workers use computerized metalworking equipment. This enables them to experiment with different layouts and to select the one that results in the least waste of material. They cut or form the parts with computer-controlled saws, lasers, shears, and presses.

In shops without computerized equipment, and for products that cannot be made on such equipment, sheetmetal workers use hand calculators to make the required calculations and use tapes, rulers, and other measuring devices for layout work. They then cut or stamp the parts on machine tools.

Before assembling the pieces, sheetmetal workers check each part for accuracy and, if necessary, finish it by using hand, rotary, or squaring shears and hacksaws. After the parts have been inspected, workers fasten the seams and joints together with welds, bolts, cement, rivets, solder, specially formed sheetmetal drive clips, or other connecting devices. They then take the parts to the construction site where they further assemble the pieces as they install them. These workers install ducts, pipes, and tubes by joining them end to end and hanging them with metal hangers secured to a ceiling or a wall. They also use shears, hammers, punches, and drills to make parts at the work site or to alter parts made in the shop.

Some jobs are done completely at the job site. When installing a metal roof, for example, sheetmetal workers measure and cut the roofing panels that are needed to complete the job. They secure the first panel in place and interlock and fasten the grooved edge of the next panel into the grooved edge of the first. Then they nail or weld the free edge of the panel to the structure. This two-step process is repeated for each additional panel. Finally, they fasten machine-made molding at joints, along corners, and around windows and doors for a neat, finished effect.

In addition to installation, some sheetmetal workers specialize in testing, balancing, adjusting, and servicing existing air-conditioning and ventilation systems to make sure they are functioning properly and to improve their energy efficiency

Working Conditions

Sheetmetal workers usually work a 40-hour week. Those who fabricate sheetmetal products work in shops that are well lighted and well ventilated. They stand for long periods and lift heavy materials and finished pieces. Sheetmetal workers must follow safety practices because working around high-speed machines can be dangerous. They are subject to cuts from sharp metal, burns from soldering and welding, and falls from ladders and scaffolds. They generally wear safety glasses and must not wear jewelry or loose-fitting clothing that could easily get caught in a machine.

Those doing installation work do considerable bending, lifting, standing, climbing, and squatting, sometimes in close quarters or in awkward positions. Although installing duct systems and kitchen equipment is done indoors, the installation of siding, roofs, and gutters involves much outdoor work, requiring sheetmetal workers to work in various kinds of weather.

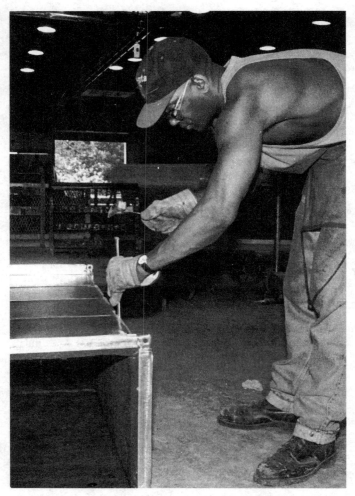

Sheetmetal workers do considerable bending and kneeling, sometimes in close quarters.

Employment

Sheetmetal workers held about 110,000 wage and salary jobs in the construction industry in 1996. About three-fourths worked for plumbing, heating, and air-conditioning contractors; most of the rest worked for roofing and sheetmetal contractors; and a few worked for other special trade contractors and for general contractors engaged in residential and commercial building. Unlike many other construction trades, very few sheetmetal workers are self-employed.

Jobs for sheetmetal workers are distributed throughout the country in about the same proportion as the total population.

Training, Other Qualifications, and Advancement

Sheetmetal contractors consider apprenticeship the best way to learn this trade. The apprenticeship program consists of 4 or 5 years of on-the-job training and a minimum of 144 hours per year of classroom instruction. Apprenticeship programs provide comprehensive instruction in both sheetmetal fabrication and installation. They are administered by local joint committees composed of the Sheet Metal Workers' International Association, local chapters of the Sheet Metal and Air-Conditioning Contractors National Association, or by local chapters of the Associated Builders and Contractors.

On the job, apprentices learn the basics of pattern layout and how to cut, bend, fabricate, and install sheet metal. They begin with basic ductwork and gradually advance to more difficult jobs, such as making more complex ducts, fittings, and decorative pieces. They also use materials such as fiberglass, plastics, and other non-metallic materials.

In the classroom, apprentices learn drafting, plan and specification reading, trigonometry and geometry applicable to layout work, the use of computerized equipment, welding, and the principles of heat-ing, air-conditioning, and ventilating systems. Safety is stressed throughout the program. In addition, apprentices learn the relationship between sheetmetal work and other construction work.

A relatively small number of persons pick up the trade informally, usually by working as helpers to experienced sheetmetal workers. Most begin by carrying metal and cleaning up debris in a metal shop while they learn about materials and tools and their uses. Later, they learn to operate machines that bend or cut metal. In time, helpers go out on the job site to learn installation. Those who acquire their skills this way often take vocational school courses in mathematics or sheetmetal fabrication to supplement their work experience. To be promoted to the journey level, helpers usually must pass the same written examination as apprentices.

Applicants for jobs as apprentices or helpers should be in good physical condition and have mechanical and mathematical aptitude. Good eye-hand coordination, spatial and form perception, and good manual dexterity are also important. Local apprenticeship committees require a high school education or its equivalent. Courses in algebra, trigonometry, geometry, mechanical drawing, and shop provide a helpful background for learning the trade, as does work experience obtained in the Armed Services.

It is important for experienced sheetmetal workers to keep abreast of new technological developments, such as the growing use of computerized layout and laser cutting machines. Workers often take additional training provided by the union or by their employer in order to improve existing skills or to acquire new ones.

Sheetmetal workers may advance to supervisory jobs. Some take additional training in welding and do more specialized work. Others go into the contracting business for themselves. Because a sheetmetal contractor must have a shop with equipment to fabricate products, this type of contracting business is more expensive to start than other types of construction contracting.

Job Outlook

Opportunities should be good for individuals who acquire apprenticeship training. Employment of sheetmetal workers in construction is expected to increase about as fast as the average for all occupations through the year 2006 reflecting growth in the demand for sheetmetal installations as more industrial, commercial, and residential structures are built. Growing demand for more energy-efficient air-conditioning, heating, and ventilation systems in the growing stock of older buildings, as well as other types of renovation and maintenance work, also should boost employment. In addition, the greater use of decorative sheetmetal products and increased architectural restoration are expected to add to the demand for sheetmetal workers. Despite this growth in demand, most job openings will result from the need to replace workers who leave the occupation.

Job prospects are expected to be good for skilled sheetmetal workers over the long run, although workers may experience periods of unemployment when construction projects end and economic conditions reduce the amount of construction activity. Because local economic conditions can vary so widely, there can be shortages of experienced workers in some areas and an oversupply in other parts of the country. The availability of training slots also fluctuates with economic conditions, so the number of openings may vary from year to year and by geographic area. Nevertheless, employment of sheetmetal workers is less sensitive to declines in new construction than employment of some other construction workers, such as carpenters. Maintenance of existing equipment—which is less affected by economic fluctuations than new construction—makes up a large part of the work done by sheetmetal workers. Installation of new air-conditioning and heating systems in existing buildings also continues during construction slumps as individuals and businesses seek more energy-efficient equipment to cut utility bills. In addition, a large proportion of sheetmetal installation and maintenance is done indoors so these workers usually lose less work time due to bad weather than other construction workers.

Earnings

Median weekly earnings for sheetmetal workers working full time were about $498 a week in 1996. The middle 50 percent earned between $388 and $770 a week. The top 10 percent earned more than $1,012 and the lowest 10 percent less than $325 a week.

According to the Engineering News Record, average hourly earnings—including benefits—for union sheetmetal workers were $31.87 in 1997. Wages ranged from a low of $18.83 in Nashville to a high of $48.40 in New York City. Apprentices generally start at about 40 percent of the rate paid to experienced workers. As they acquire more skills of the trade throughout the course of the apprenticeship program, they receive periodic increases until their pay approaches that of experienced workers. In addition, union workers in some areas receive supplemental wages from the union when they are on layoff or shortened workweeks. Many sheetmetal workers are members of the Sheet Metal Workers' International Association.

Related Occupations

To fabricate and install sheetmetal products, sheetmetal workers combine metalworking skills and knowledge of construction materials and techniques. Other occupations in which workers lay out and fabricate metal products include layout workers, machinists, metal fabricators, metal patternmakers, shipfitters, and tool and die makers. Construction occupations requiring similar skills and knowledge include heating, air-conditioning, and refrigeration technicians and glaziers.

Sources of Additional Information

For more information about apprenticeships or other work opportunities, contact local sheetmetal contractors or heating, refrigeration, and air-conditioning contractors; a local of the Sheet Metal Workers; a local of the Sheetmetal and Air Conditioning Contractors Association; a local joint union-management apprenticeship committee; or the nearest office of the State employment service or apprenticeship agency.

For general information about sheetmetal workers, contact:
☛ The Sheet Metal National Training Fund, 601 N. Fairfax St., Suite 240, Alexandria, VA 22314.
☛ Associated Builders and Contractors, 1300 N. 17th St. NW., Rosslyn, VA 22209.
☛ The Sheetmetal and Air Conditioning Contractors Association, 4201 Lafayette Center Dr., Chantilly, VA 22021.
☛ The Sheet Metal Workers International Association, 1750 New York Ave. NW., Washington, DC 20006.

Structural and Reinforcing Ironworkers

(D.O.T. 801.361-014, -018, -022, .381-010, .684-026; and 809.381-022, and -026)

Significant Points

- Structural and reinforcing ironworkers earn high pay but often can't work during inclement weather.

- These workers are among the most likely to be put out of work when downturns in the economy slow new construction.

- Most people enter this occupation through a formal 3-year apprenticeship.

Nature of the Work

Builders use materials made from iron, steel, aluminum, fiberglass, precast concrete, brass, and bronze to construct highways, bridges, office buildings, power transmission towers, and other large buildings. These structures have frames made of steel columns, beams, and girders. In addition, reinforced concrete—concrete containing steel bars or wire fabric—is an important material in buildings, bridges, and other structures. The steel gives the concrete additional

strength. Metal stairways, catwalks, floor gratings, ladders, and window frames, as well as lampposts, railings, fences, and decorative ironwork make these structures more functional and attractive. Structural and reinforcing ironworkers fabricate, assemble, and install these products. They also repair, renovate, and maintain older buildings and structures such as steel mills, utility plants, automobile factories, highways, and bridges.

Before construction can begin, ironworkers must erect the steel frames and assemble the cranes and derricks that move structural steel, reinforcing bars, buckets of concrete, lumber, and other materials and equipment around the construction site. This equipment arrives at the construction site in sections. There it is lifted into position by a mobile crane. Ironworkers then connect the sections and set the cables to do the hoisting.

Once this job has been completed, *structural ironworkers* begin to connect steel columns, beams, and girders according to blueprints and instructions from supervisors and superintendents. Structural steel, reinforcing rods, and ornamental iron generally come to the construction site ready for erection—cut to the proper size with holes drilled for bolts and numbered for assembly. Ironworkers do this work in fabricating shops generally located away from the construction site. In fabrication shops, iron workers lay out the raw steel received from a steel mill and cut, bend, drill, bolt, and weld each piece according to the specifications for that particular job. Ironworkers at the construction site unload and stack the fabricated steel so it can be hoisted easily when needed.

To hoist the steel, ironworkers attach cables from a crane or derrick. One worker directs the hoist operator with hand signals. Another worker holds a rope (tag line) attached to the steel to prevent it from swinging. The crane or derrick hoists steel into place in the framework, where several workers using spud wrenches position it with connecting bars and jacks. Workers using driftpins or the handle of a spud wrench—a long wrench with a pointed handle—align the holes in the steel with the holes in the framework. Then they bolt the piece in place temporarily, check vertical and horizontal alignment with plumb bobs, laser equipment, transits, or levels and then bolt or weld it permanently in place.

Reinforcing ironworkers set the bars in the forms that hold concrete, following blueprints showing the location, size, and number of reinforcing bars. They fasten the bars together by tying wire around

Structural and reinforcing ironworkers usually work outside in all kinds of weather.

them with pliers. When reinforcing floors, workers place blocks under the reinforcing bars to hold them off the deck. Although these materials usually arrive ready to use, ironworkers occasionally must cut the bars with metal shears or acetylene torches, bend them by hand or machine, or weld them with arc-welding equipment. Some concrete is reinforced with welded wire fabric. Using hooked rods, workers cut and fit the fabric and, while a concrete crew places the concrete, ironworkers position it properly in the concrete.

Workers install ornamental ironwork and related pieces after the exterior of the building has been completed. As they hoist pieces into position, ironworkers bring them into position, make sure they fit correctly, and bolt, braze, or weld them for a secure fit. They also erect metal tanks used to store petroleum, water, or other fluids and assemble prefabricated metal buildings according to plans or specifications.

Working Conditions

Structural and reinforcing ironworkers usually work outside in all kinds of weather. However, those who work at great heights do not work when it is wet, icy, or extremely windy. Because the danger of injuries due to falls is so great, ironworkers use safety devices such as safety belts, scaffolding, and nets to reduce the risk.

Employment

Structural and reinforcing ironworkers held about 770,000 jobs in 1996. Almost all of these workers were employed in the construction industry. Nearly 6 of every 10 worked for structural steel erection contractors; most of the remainder worked for a variety of contractors specializing in the construction of homes, factories, commercial buildings, churches, schools, bridges and tunnels, and water, sewer, communications, and power lines.

Ironworkers are employed in all parts of the country, but most work in metropolitan areas, where most commercial and industrial construction takes place.

Training, Other Qualifications, and Advancement

Most employers recommend apprenticeship as the best way to learn this trade. The apprenticeship consists of 3 or 4 years of on-the-job training and a minimum of 144 hours a year of classroom instruction. Apprenticeship programs are usually administered by joint union-management committees made up of representatives of local unions of the International Association of Bridge, Structural, Ornamental and Reinforcing Iron Workers and local chapters of contractors' associations.

Ironworkers must be at least 18 years old. A high school diploma may be preferred by employers and may be required by some local apprenticeship committees. High School courses in general mathematics, mechanical drawing, and shop are helpful. Because materials used in ironworking are heavy and bulky, ironworkers must be in good physical condition. They also need good agility, balance, eyesight, and depth perception in order to work at great heights on narrow beams and girders. Ironworkers should not be afraid of heights or suffer from dizziness.

In the classroom, apprentices study blueprint reading, mathematics for layout work, the basics of structural erecting, rigging, reinforcing, welding and burning, ornamental erection and assembling. They also study the care and safe use of tools and materials. On the job, apprentices work in all aspects of the trade, such as unloading and storing materials at the job site, rigging materials for movement by crane or derrick, connecting structural steel, and welding.

Some ironworkers learn the trade informally on the job without completing an apprenticeship. These workers generally do not receive classroom training, although some large contractors have extensive training programs. On-the-job trainees usually begin by assisting experienced ironworkers by doing simple jobs, like carrying various materials. With experience, they perform more difficult tasks like cutting and fitting different parts. Learning through work experience alone may not provide training as complete as an apprenticeship program, however, and usually takes longer.

Some experienced workers become supervisors. Others may go into the contracting business for themselves.

Job Outlook

Employment of structural and reinforcing ironworkers is expected to increase more slowly than the average for all occupations through the year 2006 largely because of the continued slow growth in industrial and commercial construction. The rehabilitation and maintenance of an increasing number of older buildings, factories, power plants, and highways and bridges is expected to increase, mitigating somewhat slower employment growth. In addition, more ironworkers will be needed to build incinerators and other structures to contain hazardous materials as part of ongoing toxic waste cleanup. Although employment growth will create many new jobs for structural and reinforcing ironworkers, most openings will result from the need to replace experienced ironworkers who transfer to other occupations or leave the labor force.

The number of job openings fluctuates from year to year as economic conditions and the level of construction activity change. During economic downturns, ironworkers can experience high rates of unemployment. Similarly, job opportunities for ironworkers may vary widely by geographic area. Job openings for ironworkers usually are more abundant during the spring and summer months, when the level of construction activity increases.

Earnings

Median weekly earnings of structural and reinforcing ironworkers employed full time were about $598 a week in 1996. The middle 50 percent earned between $445 and $778 a week. The top 10 percent earned more than $958 and the lowest 10 percent less than $306 a week.

According to the *Engineering News Record*, prevailing union wage rates—including benefits—for ironworkers averaged about $30.56 an hour in 1997. Their wages ranged from a low of about $14.56 in Houston to a high of 47.35 in New York City.

Apprentices generally start at about 50 to 60 percent of the rate paid to experienced journey workers. They receive periodic increases throughout the course of the apprenticeship program as they acquire the skills of the trade until their pay approaches that of experienced workers.

Earnings for ironworkers may be reduced on occasion because work can be limited by bad weather, the short-term nature of construction jobs, and economic downturns.

Many workers in this trade are members of the International Association of Bridge, Structural, Ornamental, and Reinforcing Iron Workers.

Related Occupations

Structural and reinforcing ironworkers play an essential role in erecting buildings, bridges, highways, powerlines, and other structures. Others who also work on these construction jobs are operating engineers, concrete masons, and welders.

Sources of Additional Information

For more information on apprenticeships or other work opportunities, contact local general contractors; a local of the International Association of Bridge, Structural, Ornamental, and Reinforcing Iron Workers union; a local joint ironworkers' union-management apprenticeship committee; a local or State chapter of the Associated Builders and Contractors, or the nearest office of the State employment service or apprenticeship agency.

For general information about ironworkers, contact:

☛ Associated General Contractors of America, Inc., 1300 North 17th St., Rosslyn, VA 22209-3883

☛ International Association of Bridge, Structural, Ornamental, and Reinforcing Iron Workers, 1750 New York Ave. NW., Suite 400, Washington, DC 20006.

☛ National Erectors Association, 1501 Lee Hwy., Suite 202, Arlington, VA 22209.

☛ National Association of Reinforcing Steel Contractors, P.O. Box 280, Fairfax, VA 22030.

Tilesetters

(D.O.T. 861.381-054, -058, and .684-018)

Significant Points

- Nearly half of all tilesetters are self-employed.
- Relatively few job openings are expected because it is a small occupation that is growing slowly and has low job turnover.

Nature of the Work

In ancient Egypt and Rome, tile was used for mosaics—an art form using small, decorative ceramic squares. Over the years, tile has been a popular building material because it is durable, impervious to water, and easy to clean. It is used today, for instance, in shopping centers, hospitals, tunnels, lobbies of buildings, bathrooms, and kitchens.

Tilesetters, like the ancient artists, apply tile to floors, walls, and ceilings. To set tile, which generally ranges in size from 1 inch to 12 inches square, they use cement or "mastic," a very sticky paste. When using cement, tilesetters nail a support of metal mesh to the wall or ceiling to be tiled. They use a trowel to apply a cement mortar—called a "scratch coat"—onto the metal screen and scratch the surface of the soft mortar with a small tool, similar to a rake. After the scratch coat has dried, tilesetters apply another coat of mortar to level the surface and then apply mortar to the back of the tile and place it onto the surface.

To set tile in mastic, or a cement adhesive, called "thin set," tilesetters need a flat, solid surface such as drywall, concrete, plaster, or wood. They use a tooth-edged trowel to spread mastic on the surface or apply cement adhesive to the back of the tile and then properly position it.

Because tile varies in color, shape, and size, workers sometimes prearrange tiles on a dry floor according to a specified design. This allows workers to examine the pattern and make changes. In order to cover all exposed areas, including corners and around pipes, tubs, and wash basins, tilesetters cut tiles to fit with a machine saw or a special cutting tool. Once the tile is placed, they gently tap the surface with their trowel handle or a small block of wood to seat the tiles evenly.

When the cement or mastic has set, tilesetters fill the joints with "grout," a very fine cement. They then scrape the surface with a rubber-edged device called a "squeegee" to dress the joints and remove excess grout. Before the grout sets, they finish the joints with a damp sponge for a uniform appearance.

Working Conditions

Tilesetters generally work indoors. Because most of the structure has been completed, the work area is relatively clean and uncluttered. Much of the workday is spent bending, kneeling, and reaching, activities that require endurance but not exceptional strength. To protect their knees, most workers wear kneepads.

Although workers are subject to cuts from tools or materials, falls from ladders, and strained muscles, the occupation is not as hazardous as some other construction occupations.

Employment

Tilesetters held about 29,000 jobs in 1996. Most wage and salary tilesetters were employed by tilesetting contractors who work mainly on nonresidential construction projects, such as schools, hospitals, and office buildings. Nearly half of all tilesetters were self-employed, compared to less than one-quarter of all construction workers. Most self-employed tilesetters work on residential projects.

Tilesetters are employed throughout the country but are found largely in urban areas.

Training, Other Qualifications, and Advancement

Most tilesetters acquire their skills on the job by working as helpers to experienced workers. They begin by learning about the tools of

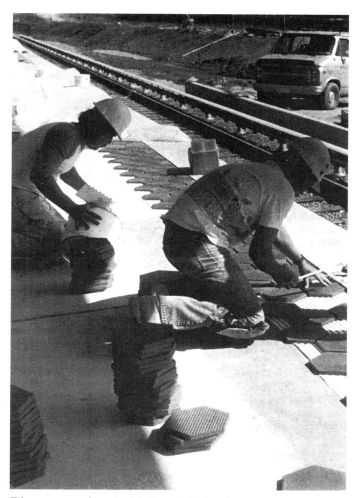

Tilesetters spend much of their workday bending, kneeling, and reaching.

the trade, and then they learn to mix and apply cement and to apply mastic. As they progress, they learn to cut and install tile, apply grout, and do finishing work.

Employers recommend completion of a 3-year apprenticeship program, which consists of on-the-job training and related classroom instruction in subjects such as blueprint reading, layout, and basic mathematics.

When hiring apprentices or helpers, employers usually prefer high school graduates who have had courses in general mathematics, mechanical drawing, and shop. Good physical condition, manual dexterity, and a good sense of color harmony also are important assets.

Skilled tilesetters may start their own contracting businesses or may become supervisors or estimators for other contractors.

Job Outlook

Employment of tilesetters is expected to increase more slowly than the average for all occupations through the year 2006. Increased demand for tilesetters will stem from population and business growth, which should result in more construction of shopping malls, hospitals, schools, restaurants, and other structures where tile is used extensively. Tile is expected to continue to increase in popularity as a building material. In more expensive homes, whose construction is expected to increase, its use should be quite common. In more modestly priced homes, however, the use of tile substitutes, such as plastic or fiberglass tub and shower enclosures, will increase, slowing the growth in demand for tilesetters.

Despite the increased demand for tilesetting, most job openings will result from the need to replace tilesetters who retire or leave the occupation for other reasons. Job opportunities will not be as plentiful as in other construction occupations because the occupation is small and turnover is relatively low.

Earnings

The median weekly earnings for tilesetters were about $492 in 1996. The middle 50 percent earned between $316 and $620 a week; 10 percent earned less than $221 a week; 10 percent earned more than $777 a week.

Apprentices usually start earning 50 to 55 percent of experienced workers' wages. Earnings vary greatly by geographic location. They tend to be highest in the North and West Coast and the lowest in the South.

Some tilesetters belong to the International Union of Bricklayers and Allied Craftsmen or the United Brotherhood of Carpenters and Joiners of America.

Related Occupations

Tilesetters use their knowledge of tools and masonry materials along with skill and dexterity to produce attractive, durable surfaces. Other workers with similar abilities include bricklayers, concrete masons, marblesetters, plasterers, stonemasons, and terrazzo workers.

Sources of Additional Information

For details about apprenticeship or other work opportunities in this trade, contact local tilesetting contractors; locals of the unions previously mentioned; or the nearest office of the State employment service or State apprenticeship agency.

For general information about the work of tilesetters, contact:
☛ International Union of Bricklayers and Allied Craftsmen, International Masonry Institute, Apprenticeship and Training, 823 15th St. NW., Washington, DC 20005.

Production Occupations

Assemblers

Precision Assemblers

(List of D.O.T. codes available on request. See p. 496.)

Significant Points

- Virtually all precision assemblers worked in plants that manufacture durable goods.

- Increasing automation and internationalization of production will offset most increases in employment that would have resulted from industrial growth.

Nature of the Work

Precision assemblers are highly skilled workers who assemble a wide range of finished products from manufactured parts or subassemblies. They produce intricate manufactured products, such as aircraft, automobiles, computers, and small electrical and electronic components. Unlike some assemblers who perform simple, repetitive tasks, precision assemblers generally perform a series of more complex tasks.

Precision assemblers involved in product development must know how to read and interpret engineering specifications from text, drawings, and computer-aided drafting systems. They also must know how to use a variety of tools and precision measuring instruments. Some experienced assemblers work with engineers and technicians, assembling prototypes or test products.

Precision assemblers may work on subassemblies or the final assembly of finished products or components of a vast array of products. For example, precision electrical and electronic equipment assemblers put together or modify prototypes or final assemblies of items such as missile control systems, radio or test equipment, computers, machine-tool numerical controls, radar, sonar, and appliances. Precision electromechanical equipment assemblers prepare and test equipment or devices, such as dynamometers, ejection seat mechanisms, and tape drives. Precision machine builders construct, assemble, or rebuild engines and turbines, and office, agricultural, construction, oil field, rolling mill, textile, woodworking, paper, printing, and food wrapping machinery. Precision aircraft assemblers put together and install parts of airplanes, space vehicles, or missiles, such as wings or landing gear. Precision structural metal fitters align and fit structural metal parts according to detailed specifications prior to welding or riveting.

As technology changes, so too does the manufacturing process. For example, flexible manufacturing systems include the manufacturing applications of robotics, computers, programmable motion control, and various sensing technologies. These systems change the way goods are made, and affect the jobs of those who make them. The concept of cellular manufacturing, for example, places a greater premium on the communication and teamwork of "cells" than it does on the old assembly line process. As the U.S. manufacturing sector continues to evolve in the face of growing international competition, the nature of precision assembly will change along with it.

Working Conditions

The working conditions for precision assemblers varies both from plant to plant and from industry to industry. Electronics assemblers, for example, sit at tables in rooms that are clean, well lit, and free from dust. Assemblers of aircraft and industrial machinery, however, usually come in contact with oil and grease, and their working areas may be quite noisy. They may also have to lift and fit heavy objects. In many cases, the increased use of robots or other pneumatically powered machinery has improved working conditions by lowering the overall noise level of the facility.

Most full-time assemblers work a 40-hour week, although overtime and shift work is fairly common in some industries. Work schedules of assemblers may vary at plants with more than one shift. In some plants, workers can accept or reject a certain job on a given shift, usually in order of seniority.

Employment

Virtually all of the 380,000 precision assembler jobs in 1996 were in plants that manufacture durable goods. One-third of all jobs involved assembly of electronic and electrical machinery, equipment, and supplies, including electrical switches, welding equipment, electric motors, lighting equipment, household appliances, and radios and television sets. Three-tenths of all jobs involved assembly of industrial machinery—diesel engines, steam turbine generators, farm tractors, mining and construction machinery, and office machines. Other industries employing many precision assemblers were transportation equipment (aircraft, autos, trucks, and buses) and instruments manufacturing.

The following list shows the wage and salary employment of precision assemblers in 1996 by industry.

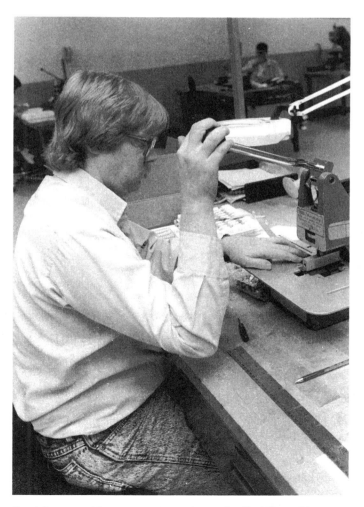

Precision assemblers must pay attention to detail while working quickly.

413

Electronic and other electrical equipment manufacturing	126,000
Industrial machinery and equipment manufacturing	120,000
Transportation equipment manufacturing	61,000
Instruments and related products manufacturing	53,000
Fabricated metal products manufacturing	16,000
All other industries	4,000

Training, Other Qualifications, and Advancement

Promotion to precision assembler often comes from the ranks of workers in lesser skilled jobs in the same establishment. Outside applicants may be hired if they possess suitable experience. The ability to do accurate work at a rapid pace is a key job requirement. A high school diploma is preferred.

Applicants need specialized training for some precision assembly jobs. For example, employers may require that applicants for electrical or electronic assembler jobs be technical school graduates or have equivalent military training.

Good eyesight, with or without glasses, is required for assemblers who work with small parts. Plants that make electrical and electronic products may test applicants for color vision, because many of their products contain many differently colored wires.

As precision assemblers become more experienced, they may progress to jobs that require more skill and be given more responsibility. Experienced assemblers may become product repairers if they have learned the many assembly operations and understand the construction of a product. These workers fix assembled articles that operators or inspectors have identified as defective. Assemblers also can advance to quality control jobs or be promoted to supervisor. Experienced precision assemblers also may become members of research and development teams, working with engineers and other project designers to design, develop, and test new product models. In some companies, assemblers can become trainees for one of the skilled trades. Those with a background in math, science, and computers may advance to programmers or operators of more highly automated production equipment.

Job Outlook

Little growth in employment of precision assemblers is expected through the year 2006. Increasing automation and internationalization of production will offset most increases in employment that would have resulted from industrial growth. As manufacturers strive for greater precision and productivity, work that can be performed more economically or more accurately by automated equipment will be transferred to these machines.

Recent advancements have made robotics more applicable and more affordable in manufacturing. The introduction of robots should continue, raising the productivity of assembly workers and adversely affecting their employment.

The effects of automation will be felt more acutely in some industries than in others. Flexible manufacturing systems are expensive, and a large volume of repetitive work is required to justify their purchase. Also, where the assembly parts involved are irregular in size or location, new technology is only now beginning to make inroads. For example, much precision assembly in the aerospace industry is done in hard-to-reach locations unsuited for robots—inside airplane fuselages or gear boxes, for example—and replacement of these workers by automated processes will be slower and less comprehensive than replacement of other workers such as welders and painters. On the other hand, automation will continue to make more inroads in the precision assembly of electronic goods, where one-third of these workers are employed.

In addition, many producers send their subassembly or component production functions to countries where labor costs are lower. This growing internationalization of production, promoted by more liberal trade and investment policies, results in shifts in the composition of this country's manufacturing workforce. For example, decisions by American corporations to relocate assembly in other nations may lead to employment reductions for precision assemblers in some industries. A freer trade environment will lead to growth in the export of goods assembled in the United States and will result in the creation of additional jobs in other industries. On balance, the changes will restrain precision assemblers' employment growth.

Because of the little employment growth expected, almost all job openings will arise as workers transfer to other occupations or leave the labor force.

Earnings

Earnings information is somewhat limited for precision assemblers. Assemblers of electrical and electronic products had median weekly earnings of $340. Most earned between $268 and $437; the lowest 10 percent earned less than $215 a week while the highest 10 percent earned over $577. In addition to earnings, most precision assemblers receive benefits such as health and life insurance, a pension plan, paid vacation, and sick leave.

Many precision assemblers are members of labor unions. These unions include the International Association of Machinists and Aerospace Workers; the United Electrical, Radio and Machine Workers of America; the United Automobile, Aerospace and Agricultural Implement Workers of America; the International Brotherhood of Electrical Workers; and the United Steelworkers of America.

Related Occupations

Other occupations that involve operating machines and tools and assembling products include welders, ophthalmic laboratory technicians, and machine operators.

Sources of Additional Information

Information about employment opportunities for assemblers is available from local offices of the State employment service and from locals of the unions mentioned earlier.

Blue-Collar Worker Supervisors

(List of D.O.T. codes available on request. See p. 496.)

Significant Points

- Although many workers still rise through the ranks with high school diplomas, employers increasingly seek applicants with postsecondary training.
- Employment in manufacturing is expected to decline, reflecting the increasing use of computers, the implementation of self-directed work teams, and corporate downsizing; employment in construction and most other nonmanufacturing industries is expected to rise along with employment of the workers they supervise.
- Supervisors in the highly cyclical construction industry may be laid off when construction activity declines.

Nature of the Work

For the millions of workers who assemble manufactured goods, service electronics equipment, work in construction, load trucks, or perform thousands of other activities, a blue-collar worker supervisor is the boss. In addition to "the boss," blue-collar worker supervisors go by many other titles. The most common are first-line supervisor or foreman/forewoman, but titles vary according to the industry in which these workers are employed. For example, in the textile industry, these supervisors may be referred to as second hands; on ships, they may be called boatswains. In the construction industry, they can be referred to as superintendents, crew chiefs, or foremen/forewomen, depending upon the type and size of their employer. Toolpushers or gang pushers are common terms used to describe blue-collar supervisors in the oil drilling business.

Although the responsibilities of blue-collar worker supervisors are as varied as the titles they hold, their primary task is to ensure that workers, equipment, and materials are used properly to maximize productivity. To accomplish this, they perform many duties. Supervisors make sure machinery is set up correctly, schedule or perform repairs and maintenance work, create work schedules, keep production and employee records, monitor employees, and ensure that work is done correctly and on time. In addition, they organize workers' activities, make necessary adjustments to ensure that work continues uninterrupted, train new workers, and ensure the existence of a safe working environment.

The means by which supervisors perform these duties have changed dramatically in recent years as companies have restructured their operations for maximum efficiency. Supervisors now use computers to schedule work flow, monitor the quality of workers' output, keep track of materials used, update the inventory control system, and perform other supervisory tasks. In addition, new management philosophies that emphasize fewer levels of management and greater employee power in decisionmaking have altered the role of these supervisors. In the past, supervisors exercised their authority to direct the efforts of blue-collar workers; increasingly, supervisors are assuming the role of a facilitator for groups of workers, aiding in group decisionmaking and conflict resolution.

Because they serve as the main conduit of information between management and blue-collar workers, supervisors have many interpersonal tasks related to their job. They inform workers about company plans and policies; recommend good performers for wage increases, awards, or promotions; and deal with poor performers by outlining expectations, counseling workers in proper methods, issuing warnings, or recommending disciplinary action. They also meet on a regular basis with their managers, reporting any problems and discussing possible solutions. Supervisors may often meet among themselves to discuss goals, company operations, and performance. In companies with labor unions, supervisors must follow all provisions of labor-management contracts.

Working Conditions

Blue-collar worker supervisors work in a wide range of settings based on the industry in which they are employed. Many supervisors work on the shop floor. This can be tiring if they are on their feet most of their shift, working near loud and dangerous machinery. Other supervisors, such as those in construction and oil exploration and production, sometimes work outdoors in severe weather conditions.

Over 270,000 blue-collar worker supervisors are employed in the construction industry.

Supervisors may be on the job before other workers arrive and often stay after others leave. Some supervisors work in plants that operate around the clock, so they may work any one of three shifts, as well as weekends and holidays. In some cases, supervisors work all three shifts on a rotating basis; in others, shift assignments are made on the basis of seniority.

Because organizational restructuring and downsizing have required many blue-collar worker supervisors to oversee more workers and departments in recent years, longer hours and added responsibilities have increased on-the-job stress for many supervisors.

Employment

Blue-collar worker supervisors held about 1.9 million jobs in 1996. Although salaried supervisors are found in almost all industries, 2 of every 5 work in manufacturing. Other industries employing blue-collar worker supervisors include wholesale and retail trade, public utilities, repair shops, transportation, and government. The vast majority of the 188,000 self-employed workers in this occupation are employed in construction.

Training, Other Qualifications, and Advancement

When choosing supervisors, employers generally look for experience, job knowledge, organizational skills, and leadership qualities. Employers also emphasize the ability to motivate employees, maintain high morale, and command respect. In addition, well-rounded applicants who are able to deal with different situations and a diverse work force are desired. Communication and interpersonal skills are also extremely important attributes in this occupation.

Completion of high school is often the minimum educational requirement to become a blue-collar worker supervisor, but workers generally receive training in human resources, computer software, and management before they advance to these positions. Although many workers still rise through the ranks with high school diplomas, employers increasingly seek applicants with postsecondary technical degrees. In high-technology industries, such as aerospace and electronics, employers may require a bachelor's degree or technical school training. Large companies usually offer better opportunities for promotion to blue-collar worker supervisor positions than do smaller companies.

In most manufacturing companies, a degree in business or engineering, combined with in-house training, is needed to advance from supervisor to department head or production manager. In the construction industry, supervisors increasingly need a degree in construction management or engineering if they expect to advance to project manager, operations manager, or general superintendent. Some use their skills and experience to start their own construction contracting firms. Supervisors in repair shops may open their own businesses.

Job Outlook

Employment of blue-collar worker supervisors is expected to grow more slowly than average through the year 2006. As the number of workers in the economy increases, so will the need to supervise these workers. In addition to growth, many openings will arise from the need to replace workers who transfer to other occupations or leave the labor force.

Projected job growth varies by industry. In manufacturing, employment of supervisors is expected to decline slightly as each supervisor is expected to oversee more workers. This trend reflects the increasing use of computers to meet supervisory responsibilities, such as production analysis and scheduling; greater involvement of production workers in decisionmaking and the formation of self-directed work teams; and corporate downsizing. These developments are not as prevalent in construction and most other nonmanufacturing industries, where the employment of blue-collar worker supervisors is expected to rise along with employment of the workers they supervise.

Because of their skill and seniority, blue-collar worker supervisors often are protected from layoffs during a recession. However, some supervisors in the highly cyclical construction industry may be laid off when construction activity declines.

Earnings

Median weekly earnings for blue-collar worker supervisors were about $640 in 1996. The middle 50 percent earned between $480 and $820. The lowest 10 percent earned less than $350, while the highest 10 percent earned over $1,020. Most supervisors earn significantly more than the workers they supervise. While most blue-collar workers are paid by the hour, the majority of supervisors receive an annual salary. Some supervisors receive extra pay when they work overtime.

Related Occupations

Other workers with supervisory duties include those who supervise professional, technical, sales, clerical, and service workers. Some of these are retail store or department managers, sales managers, clerical supervisors, bank officers, head tellers, hotel managers, postmasters, head cooks, head nurses, and surveyors.

Sources of Additional Information

For information on educational programs for blue-collar worker supervisors, contact:

☛ American Management Association, 1601 Broadway, New York, NY 10019.

☛ National Management Association, 2210 Arbor Blvd., Dayton, OH 45439.

☛ American Institute of Constructors, 466 94th Ave. North, St. Petersburg, FL 33702.

Fishing, Hunting, and Forestry Occupations

Fishers, Hunters, and Trappers

(D.O.T. 197.133-010, -018; 441; 442; 443; 447; 449.664, .667; 461)

Significant Points

- The proportion of self-employed workers is among the highest in the economy. Strenuous work, long hours, and seasonal jobs also characterize these occupations.

- Employment is projected to decline because of technological advances and because many fishing, hunting, and trapping operations exceed a sustainable level.

Nature of the Work

Fishers, hunters, and trappers catch and trap animals for human consumption, animal feed, bait, and other uses. They also manage animals for research and control purposes. The range of occupational functions reflects the wide variety of aquatic and animal life and their environments. (Aquaculture—the raising and harvesting of fish and other aquatic life in ponds or artificial bodies of water for commercial purposes—is covered in the *Handbook* statement on farmers and farm managers.)

Fishing hundreds of miles from shore with commercial fishing vessels—large boats capable of hauling a catch of tens of thousands of pounds of fish—requires a crew with specialized skills including a captain, or skipper, a first mate and sometimes a second mate, boatswain, and deckhands.

The *captain* plans and oversees the fishing operation—the fish to be sought, the location of the best fishing grounds, the method of capture, the duration of the trip, and the sale of the catch. The captain ensures the fishing vessel is in suitable condition; oversees the purchase of supplies, gear, and equipment such as fuel, netting, and cables; and hires qualified crew members and assigns their duties. The vessel's course is plotted with navigation aids such as compasses, sextants, and charts; it uses electronic equipment such as autopilots, a loran system, and satellites to navigate. The ships also use radar to avoid obstacles and depth sounders to indicate the water depth and the existence of marine life between the vessel and sea bottom. The captain directs the fishing operation through the officers, and records daily activities in the ship's log. Upon returning to port, the captain arranges for the sale of the catch directly to buyers or through a fish auction, and ensures each crew member receives the prearranged portion of adjusted net proceeds from the sale of the catch.

The *first mate*—the captain's assistant, who must be familiar with navigation requirements and the operation of all electronic equipment—assumes control of the vessel when the captain is off duty. These duty shifts, called "watches," usually last 6 hours. The mate's regular duty, with the help of the boatswain and under the captain's oversight, is to direct the fishing operations and sailing responsibilities of the deckhands. These include the operation, maintenance, and repair of the vessel and the gathering, preservation, stowing, and unloading of the catch.

The *boatswain*, a highly experienced deckhand with supervisory responsibilities, directs the *deckhands* as they carry out the sailing and fishing operations. Prior to departure, the boatswain directs the deckhands to load equipment and supplies, either manually or with hoisting equipment, and untie lines from other boats and the dock. When necessary, boatswains repair fishing gear, equipment, nets, and accessories. They operate the fishing gear, letting out and pulling in nets and lines. They extract the catch, such as pollock, flounder, menhaden, and tuna, from the nets or lines' hooks. Deckhands use dip nets to prevent the escape of small fish, and gaffs to facilitate the landing of large fish. The catch is then washed, salted, iced, and stowed away. Deckhands must also ensure that decks are clear and clean at all times and the vessel's engines and equipment are kept in good working order. Upon return to port, they secure the vessel's lines to and from the docks and other vessels. Unless "lumpers," or laborers, are hired, the deckhands unload the catch.

Large fishing vessels that operate in deep water generally have more technologically advanced equipment, and some may have facilities on board where the fish are processed and prepared for sale. They are equipped for longer stays at sea and can perform the work of several smaller boats. (For information about merchant marine occupations, see the section on water transportation occupations elsewhere in the *Handbook*.)

Some full-time and many part-time fishers work on small boats in relatively shallow waters, often in sight of land. Navigation and communication needs are modest, and there is little need for much electronic equipment or provisions for long stays at sea. Crews are small—usually only one or two people collaborate on all aspects of the fishing operation. This may include placing gill nets across the mouths of rivers or inlets, entrapment nets in bays and lakes, or pots and traps for shellfish such as lobsters and crabs. Dredges and scrapes are sometimes used to gather shellfish such as oysters and scallops. A very small proportion of commercial fishing is conducted as diving operations. Depending upon the water's depth, divers—wearing regulation diving suits with an umbilical (air line) or a scuba outfit and equipment—use spears to catch fish and nets and other equipment to gather shellfish, coral, sea urchins, abalone, and sponges. In very shallow waters, fish are caught from small boats having an outboard motor, or from rowboats, or by wading. Fishers use a wide variety of hand-operated equipment—for example, nets, tongs, rakes, hoes, hooks, and shovels—to gather fish and shellfish, catch amphibians and reptiles such as frogs and turtles, and harvest marine vegetation such as Irish moss and kelp.

Although most fishers are involved with commercial fishing, some captains and deckhands are primarily employed in sport or recreational fishing. Typically a group of people charter a fishing vessel—for periods ranging from several hours to a number of days—for sport fishing, socializing, and relaxation, and employ a captain and possibly several deckhands.

Fishers, hunters, and trappers work outdoors in a physically demanding environment.

Hunters and *trappers* hunt and trap wild animals for human consumption, fur, feed, bait, or other purposes. Hunters may hunt alone or with others and may use dogs to locate the quarry; they use guns and crossbows to hunt most game animals. Occasionally, they use poisons to kill predatory animals such as coyotes. All legal hunting activities are approved and monitored by appropriate Federal, State, or local government agencies. Exceptions are made for Native Americans on their own reservations and Alaskan Natives.

Trappers catch animals or birds using baited, scented, or camouflaged traps, snares, cages, or nets. Many hunters and trappers skin animals and prepare and sell the pelts and skins. Trappers may also be involved with animal damage control, wildlife management, disease control, and research activities. Animal damage control involves the killing of animals that are a nuisance or pose a potential danger to humans or populated areas. Wildlife management involves the relocation of animals to deal with environmental disruption or animal population imbalance. Disease control involves the capture and destruction of rabid animals threatening public or animal health. Research activities include blood sampling for health determination, and the banding of wildfowl to ascertain migratory movements.

Working Conditions

Fishing, hunting, and trapping operations are conducted under various environmental conditions, depending on the region of the country and the kind of species sought. Fishing vessels may be hampered by storms, fog, or wind. Divers are affected by murky water and unexpected shifts in underwater currents. Hunters and trappers are disrupted by storms and rough terrain.

Fishers, hunters, and trappers work under hazardous conditions, and often help is not readily available. Malfunctioning navigation or communication equipment may lead to collisions or even shipwrecks. Malfunctioning fishing gear poses the danger of injury to the crew, who also must guard against entanglement in fishing nets and gear, slippery decks resulting from fish processing operations, ice formation in the winter, or being swept overboard—a fearsome situation. Treatment for serious injuries may have to await transfer to a hospital. Divers must guard against entanglement of air lines, malfunction of scuba equipment, decompression problems, or attacks by predatory fish. Hunters and trappers face numerous hazards such as assault by predators, falling branches and trees, slippery ground, danger of drowning by falling through ice on ponds, accidental self-inflicted gunshot and knife wounds, and snake and insect bites. Danger from incapacitating injuries is especially high, because these individuals often work alone in isolated areas. A disabled individual may die of injuries that could be routinely treated in an urban area.

This occupation entails strenuous outdoor work and long hours. Commercial fishing trips may require a stay of several weeks, or even months, hundreds of miles away from home port. The pace of work varies—intense while netting and hauling the catch aboard and relatively relaxed while traveling between home port and the fishing grounds. However, lookout watches are a regular responsibility and crew members must be prepared to stand watch at prearranged times of the day or night. Although fishing gear has improved and operations have become more mechanized, netting and processing fish are strenuous activities. Even though newer vessels have improved living quarters and amenities such as television and shower stalls, crews still experience the aggravations of confined conditions, continuous close personal contact, and the absence of family. Hunters and trappers generally must travel many miles by car or truck and then carry equipment and supplies on foot through swamps or forests, over rugged terrain. Long hours—dawn to dusk—often are the rule, and many spend lonely nights camped out in sparsely populated, forested, or mountainous areas.

Employment

Fishers, hunters, and trappers held an estimated 47,000 jobs in 1996. About 7 out of 10 were self-employed. About half worked part time, particularly in the summer when demand for these workers peaks. Captains, mates, and deckhands on fishing vessels accounted for the majority of jobs; hunters and trappers accounted for relatively few jobs.

Outside of the fishing, hunting, and trapping industry, some people employed in these occupations are involved in sport fishing activities, while small numbers are employed by museums. Others work for government, or buy and sell fur.

Training, Other Qualifications, and Advancement

Fishers generally acquire their occupational skills on the job, many as members of families involved in fishing activities. No formal academic requirements exist. Operators of large commercial fishing vessels are required to complete a Coast Guard-approved training course. Students can expedite their entrance into these occupations by enrolling in 2-year vocational-technical programs offered by secondary schools. In addition, some community colleges and universities offer fishery technology and related programs that includes courses in seamanship, vessel operations, marine safety, navigation, vessel repair and maintenance, health emergencies, and fishing gear technology; this is accompanied by hands-on experience. Secondary and postsecondary programs are generally offered in or near coastal areas.

Experienced fishers may find short-term workshops offered through various postsecondary institutions especially useful. These programs provide a good working knowledge of electronic equipment used in navigation and communication and the latest improvements in fishing gear.

Captains and mates on larger fishing vessels of at least 200 gross tons must be licensed. Captains of sport fishing boats used for charter, regardless of size, must also be licensed. Crew members on certain fish processing vessels may need a merchant mariner's document. These documents and licenses are issued by the U.S. Coast Guard to individuals who meet the stipulated health, physical, and academic requirements.

Fishers must be in good health and possess physical strength. Coordination and mechanical aptitude are necessary to operate, maintain, and repair equipment and fishing gear. They need perseverance to work long hours at sea, often under difficult conditions. On larger vessels, they must be able to work as members of a team. They must be patient, yet always alert, to overcome the boredom of long watches when not engaged in fishing operations. The ability to assume any deckhand's functions, on short notice, is important. As supervisors, mates must be able to assume all duties, including the captain's, when necessary. The captain must be highly experienced, mature, decisive, and possess the necessary business skills needed to run business operations.

On fishing vessels, most fishers begin as deckhands. Deckhands whose experience and interests are in ship engineering—maintenance and repair of ship engines and equipment—can eventually become licensed chief engineers on large commercial vessels after meeting the Coast Guard's experience, physical, and academic requirements. Divers in fishing operations can enter commercial diving activity— for example, ship repair and pier and marina maintenance—usually after completion of a certified training program sponsored by an educational institution or industry association. Experienced, reliable deckhands who display supervisory qualities may become boatswains. Boatswains may, in turn, become second mates, first mates, and finally captains. Almost all captains become self-employed, and the overwhelming majority eventually own or have an interest in one or more fishing ships. Some may choose to run a sport or recreational fishing operation. When their seagoing days are over, experienced individuals may work in or, with the necessary capital, own stores selling fishing and marine equipment and supplies. Some captains may assume advisory or administrative positions in industry trade associations or government offices such as harbor development commissions, or teaching positions in industry-sponsored workshops or in educational institutions.

Hunters and trappers generally acquire their knowledge of wildlife and hunting and trapping equipment and supplies gradually, through experience. Some are members of rural families for whom hunting and trapping have been a way of life for generations. Formal training for hunters consists of a federally mandated and State-sponsored hunter safety class, covering safety and ethics, which must be passed prior to being issued a hunting license in every State. Inexperienced individuals may join an established sports association to observe professional demonstrations and gain knowledge of hunting weapons and related equipment and tracking and survival techniques. After acquiring the mandatory State hunting license, they should hunt with an experienced hunter as an apprentice. Government hunters who hunt rabid or nuisance animals may be trained in the use of airplanes or helicopters.

Trappers may undergo various forms of training. For those interested in the sale of animals and their skins, pelts, or furs, experience is fundamental. Inexperienced trappers may serve an internship under the supervision of a professional trapper and take trapper education programs. Trapper education programs are offered by State wildlife departments or State trappers associations; in some States, these programs are mandatory. A trapper's license permits the trapping of animals forbidden to unlicensed trappers. Trappers interested in research associated with control and management of wildlife populations and disease may take courses, or even complete a degree program, in wildlife biology, wildlife management, or related fields.

Hunters and trappers must be in good health, possess physical strength and stamina, and have the desire, patience, and ability to work outdoors, sometimes for long periods, under difficult conditions. Maturity and judgment are important to deal with hazards. Good physical coordination and mechanical aptitude are necessary to safely and skillfully use hunting weapons and trapping equipment and to maintain camping and other gear.

Some hunters are employed by the Federal or State governments to work in such areas as predator control. Other hunters who have extensive experience may work as guides for hunting parties. Those with initiative, business skills, and the required capital may become self-employed outfitters, some of who own sites in the wilderness. Outfitters organize hunting parties, select hunting areas, and assume responsibility for the hunting expedition—providing equipment and supplies, instructing the party members in hunting techniques and safety measures, and overseeing leisure activities during the expedition. Most States require a license to work as a hunting guide.

Experienced trappers with the appropriate academic background may enter other occupations, such as wildlife technician, or wildlife refuge manager. Professional trappers with business skills and initiative may become self-employed fur traders.

Job Outlook

Employment of fishers, hunters, and trappers is expected to decline through the year 2006. Hunting, fishing, and trapping occupations depend on the natural ability of stock to replenish itself through growth and reproduction. Many operations are currently at or beyond maximum sustainable yield, and the number of workers who can earn an adequate income from fishing, hunting, and trapping is expected to decline. Most job openings will arise from the need to replace workers who retire or leave the occupation. Some fishers, hunters, and trappers leave the occupation because of the strenuous and hazardous nature of the job, and the lack of steady, year-round income.

In many areas, particularly the North Atlantic, pollution and excessive fishing have adversely affected the stock of fish and, consequently, the demand for fishers. In some areas, States have greatly reduced permits to fishers, allowing stocks of fish and shellfish to replenish themselves, idling many fishers. Other factors contributing to the projected decline in employment of fishers include the use of sophisticated electronic equipment for navigation, communication, and fish location; improvements in fishing gear, which have greatly increased the efficiency of fishing operations; and the use of highly automated "floating processors," where the catch is processed aboard the vessel. Sport fishing boats will continue to provide some job opportunities.

Employment of hunters and trappers is also expected to decline as trapping activities increasingly become ancillary duties of wildlife scientists and technicians and related workers. The U.S. Forest Service, State fish and wildlife agencies, and pest control companies may provide some jobs. Some qualified hunters should be able to obtain positions as hunting guides or outfitters, although work generally is seasonal.

Earnings

Median earnings of full-time fishers, hunters, and trappers were about $390 a week in 1996. The middle 50 percent earned between $280 and $480 a week. The highest paid 10 percent earned over $520, while the lowest paid 10 percent earned less than $230.

Earnings of fishers, hunters, and trappers generally are highest in the summer and fall—when demand for their services peaks and environmental conditions are favorable—and lowest during the winter. Many full-time and most part-time workers supplement their income by working in other activities during the off-season. For example, fishers may work in seafood processing plants, establishments selling fishing and marine equipment, or in construction. Hunters may work as self-employed guides, for an outfitter, or in stores selling guns or hunting and related equipment. Trappers may work in stores selling trapping and related equipment.

Earnings of fishers vary widely depending upon the specific occupational function, the size of the ship, and the amount and value of the catch. The costs of the fishing operation—operating the ship, repair and maintenance of gear and equipment, and the crew's supplies—are deducted from the sale of the catch. The net proceeds are distributed among the crew members in accordance with a prearranged percentage. Generally, the ship's owner—usually its captain—receives half of the net proceeds, which covers any profit as well as the depreciation, maintenance, and replacement costs of the ship.

Related Occupations

Numerous occupations involve outdoor activities similar to those of fishers, hunters, and trappers. Among these are zoo keepers, loggers, animal control officers, forest rangers, fishing and hunting guides, fish hatchery and aquaculture workers, game wardens, harbor pilots, merchant marine officers and seamen, and wildlife management specialists.

Sources of Additional Information

For information on licensing requirements to fish in a particular area, contact:

☛ National Marine Fisheries Service, NMFS Scientific Publications Office, 7600 Sand Point Way NE., Seattle, WA 98115.

Names of postsecondary schools offering fishing and related marine educational programs are available from:

☛ Marine Technology Society, 1828 L St. NW., Suite 906, Washington, DC 20036-5104.

Information on licensing of fishing vessel captains and mates, and requirements for merchant mariner documentation, is available from the U.S. Coast Guard Marine Inspection Office or Marine Safety Office in your State, or:

☛ Licensing and Evaluation Branch, U.S. Coast Guard, 2100 Second St. SW., Washington, DC 20593.

Information on licensing of hunting guides is available from the department of fish and game in your State.

Forestry and Logging Occupations

(D.O.T. 408.664, .667; 451.687; 452.364-010, .687-010, -018; 453; 454 except .134; 455 except .134; 459.387, .687; 669.485; 921.364, .664-014, .667-014, .687-014 -022, -030; 922.687-082; and 929.663-010)

Significant Points

● Workers spend all their time outdoors, sometimes in poor weather and often in isolated areas.

● These jobs are physically demanding and hazardous.

● Little or no change is expected in overall employment of forestry and logging occupations due to increased mechanization and forest conservation efforts that may restrict the volume of public timber available for harvesting, and budgetary constraints in government.

Nature of the Work

The Nation's forests are a rich natural resource, providing beauty and tranquillity, varied recreational areas, and wood for commercial use. Managing forests and woodlands requires many different kinds of workers. Forest and conservation workers help develop, maintain, and protect these forests by growing and planting new tree seedlings, fighting insects and diseases that attack trees, and helping to control soil erosion. Timber cutting and logging workers harvest thousands of acres of forests each year for the timber that provides the raw material for countless consumer and industrial products.

Generally working under the direction of a professional forester, *forestry technicians* compile data on the size, content, and condition of forest land tracts. These workers travel through sections of forest to gather basic information, such as species and population of trees, disease and insect damage, tree seedling mortality, and conditions that may cause fire danger. Forestry technicians also train and lead forest and conservation workers in seasonal activities, such as planting tree seedlings, putting out forest fires, and maintaining recreational facilities.

Forest workers are less skilled workers who perform a variety of tasks to reforest and conserve timberlands and maintain forest facilities, such as roads and campsites. Some forest workers, called tree planters, using digging and planting tools called dibble bars and hoedads, plant tree seedlings to reforest timberland areas. Forest workers also remove diseased or undesirable trees with a powersaw or handsaw and spray trees with insecticides or herbicides to kill insects and to protect against disease. Forest workers in private industry usually work for professional foresters and paint boundary lines, assist with prescribed burning, and aid in tree marking and measuring by keeping a tally of the trees examined and counted. Those who work for Federal and State governments also clear away brush and debris from jurisdictional camp trails, roadsides, and camping areas. Some clean kitchens and rest rooms at recreational facilities and campgrounds.

Other forest and conservation workers work in forest nurseries, sorting out tree seedlings and discarding those that do not meet prescribed standards of root formation, stem development, and foliage condition.

Some forest workers work on tree farms, where they plant, cultivate, and harvest many different kinds of trees. Duties vary depending on the type of tree farm. Those who work on specialty farms, such as those growing Christmas or ornamental trees for nurseries, are responsible for shearing tree tops and limbs to control growth, increase limb density, and improve tree shape. In addition, duties include planting, spraying to control surrounding weed growth and insects, and harvesting.

Other forest workers gather, by hand or using hand tools, products from the woodlands such as decorative greens, tree cones and barks, moss, and other wild plant life. Still others tap trees for sap to make syrup or to produce chemicals.

The timber cutting and logging process is carried out by a variety of workers who make up a logging crew. Fallers cut down trees with axes or hand-held power chain saws. Usually using gas-powered chain saws, buckers trim off the tops and branches and buck (cut) the resulting logs into specified lengths.

Choke setters fasten chokers (steel cables or chains) around logs to be skidded (dragged) by tractors or forwarded by the cable yarding system to the landing or deck area where logs are separated by species and loaded onto trucks. Riggers set up and dismantle the cables and guy wires of the cable yarding system.

Logging tractor operators drive crawler or wheeled tractors called skidders, or forwarders, which drag or transport logs from the felling site in the woods to the log landing area for loading; grapple loaders, which lift and load logs into trucks; tree fellers or shears, which cut the trees; and tree harvesters, which shear the tops off, cut and limb the trees, and then cut the logs into desired lengths. Log handling equipment operators operate tracked or wheeled equipment similar to a fork lift to load logs and pulpwood off trucks or gondola railroad cars, usually in a sawmill or pulpmill woodyard.

Log graders and scalers inspect logs for defects, measure logs to determine their volume, and estimate the marketable content or value of logs or pulpwood. These workers often use hand-held data collection terminals to enter data about individual trees, which can later be downloaded or sent, via modem, from the scaling area to a central computer.

Other timber cutting and logging workers have a variety of responsibilities. Some workers hike through forests to assess logging conditions. Laborers clear areas of brush and other growth to prepare for logging activities or to promote growth of desirable species of trees.

The timber cutting and logging industry is characterized by a large number of small crews of 4 to 8 workers. A typical crew might consist of one or two fallers or one feller machine operator, one bucker, two logging tractor operators to drag cut trees to the loading deck, and one equipment operator to load the logs onto trucks. Most crews work for self-employed logging contractors who possess substantial logging experience, the capital to purchase equipment, and skills needed to run a small business successfully. Most contractors work alongside their crews as working supervisors and often operate one of the logging machines, such as the grapple loader or the tree harvester. Many manage more than one crew and function as owner-supervisors.

Although timber cutting and logging equipment has greatly improved and operations are becoming increasingly mechanized, many logging jobs are still labor intensive. These jobs require various lev-

Most logging operations are concentrated in the Southeast and Northwest.

Forest and conservation workers	40,000
Log handling equipment operators	33,000
Logging tractor operators	21,000
Fallers and buckers	17,000
All other timber cutting and related logging ccupations	11,000

Most salaried logging workers are employed in the logging camps and logging contractors industry. Others work in sawmills and planing mills or for services specializing in the care and maintenance of ornamental trees. Although logging operations are found in most States, the Southeast employs the most, about 40 percent of logging workers, followed by the Northwest, which employs 25 percent.

Self-employed logging workers account for 1 of every 3 logging workers—a much higher proportion of self-employment than for most occupations.

Most forest and conservation workers are employed by government at some level. Of these workers, about 14,000 are employed by the Federal Government, mostly in the U.S. Department of Agriculture's Forest Service; 8,700 work for State governments, and 6,000 work for local governments. Most of the remainder work for companies that operate timber tracts, tree farms, or forest nurseries, or for establishments that supply forestry services. Although forest and conservation workers are located in every State, employment is concentrated in the West and Southeast where many national and private forests and parks are located.

Seasonal demand for forestry and logging workers varies by region. For example, in the northern States, winter work is common because the frozen ground facilitates logging. In the Southeast, logging and related activities occur year round.

els of skill, ranging from the unskilled task of manually moving logs, branches, and equipment to skillfully using chain saws, peavies (hooked poles), and log jacks to cut and position logs for further processing or loading. In order to keep costs down, some timber cutting and logging workers maintain and repair the equipment they use in order to keep costs down. A skillful, experienced logger is expected to handle a variety of logging operations.

Working Conditions

Forestry and logging occupations are physically demanding. These workers spend all their time outdoors, sometimes in poor weather and often in isolated areas. A few lumber camps in Alaska house workers in bunkhouses or company towns. Workers in sparsely populated western States commute long distances between their homes and logging sites. In the more densely populated eastern and southern States, commuting distances are much shorter.

Most logging occupations involve lifting, climbing, and other strenuous activities. Loggers work under unusually hazardous conditions. Falling trees and branches are a constant menace, as are the dangers associated with log handling operations and use of sawing equipment, especially delimbing devices. Strong winds require special care and can even halt operations. Slippery or muddy ground and hidden roots or vines not only reduce efficiency but present a constant danger, especially in the presence of moving vehicles and machinery. Poisonous plants, brambles, insects, snakes, and heat and humidity are minor annoyances. If safety precautions are not taken, hearing may be impaired by the high noise level of sawing and skidding operations over long periods of time. Experience, exercise of caution, and use of proper safety measures and equipment—such as hardhats, eye and ear protection, and safety clothing and boots—are extremely important to avoid injury.

The jobs of forest and conservation workers are generally much less hazardous. It may be necessary for some forestry aides or forest workers to walk long distances through densely wooded areas to do their work.

Employment

Forestry and logging workers held about 122,000 jobs in 1996, distributed among the following occupations:

Training, Other Qualifications, and Advancement

Most forestry and logging workers develop skills through on-the-job training with instruction coming primarily from experienced workers. Logging workers must familiarize themselves with the character and potential dangers of the forest environment and the operation of logging machinery and equipment. However, large logging companies and trade associations, such as the Northeastern Loggers Association and the American Pulpwood Association, offer special programs, particularly for workers training to operate large, expensive machinery and equipment. Often, a representative of the manufacturer or company spends several days in the field explaining and overseeing the operation of newly purchased machinery. Safety training is a vital part of instruction for all logging workers.

Many State forestry or logging associations provide training sessions for fallers, whose job duties require more skill and experience than other positions on the logging team. Sessions may take place in the field, where trainees, under the supervision of an experienced logger, have the opportunity to practice various felling techniques. Fallers learn how to manually cut down extremely large and/or expensive trees safely and with minimal damage to the felled or surrounding trees.

Training programs for loggers are becoming common in many States, in response to a collaborative effort by the American Forest and Paper Association and others in the forestry industry, to encourage the health and productivity of the Nation's forests. Logger training programs vary by State, but generally include some type of classroom and/or field training in a number of areas—best management practices, safety, endangered species, reforestation, and business management. Some programs lead to logger certification.

Experience in other occupations can expedite entry into some logging occupations. For example, equipment operators, such as truckdrivers and bulldozer and crane operators, can assume skidding and yarding functions. Some loggers have worked in sawmills or on family farms with extensive wooded areas. Some logging contractors were formerly crew members of family-owned businesses operated over several generations.

Generally, little formal education is required for most forestry and logging occupations. The minimum requirement for a forestry technician or aide is a high school education. Many secondary schools, including vocational and technical schools, and some community colleges offer courses or a 2-year degree in general forestry, wildlife, conservation, and forest harvesting, which could be helpful in obtaining a job. A curriculum that includes field trips to observe or participate in forestry or logging activities provides a particularly good background. There are no educational requirements for forest worker jobs. Many of these workers are high school or college students who are hired on a part-time or seasonal basis to perform short-term, labor-intensive tasks, such as planting tree seedlings.

Forestry and logging workers must be in good health and able to work outdoors every day. They must also be able to work as part of a team. Many logging occupations require physical strength and stamina. Maturity and good judgment are important in making quick, intelligent decisions in dealing with hazards as they arise. Mechanical aptitude and coordination are necessary qualities for operators of machinery and equipment, who often are responsible for repair and maintenance as well. Initiative and managerial and business skills are necessary for success as a self-employed logging contractor.

Experience working at a nursery or as a laborer can be useful in obtaining a job as a forest worker. Logging workers generally advance from occupations involving primarily manual labor to those involving the operation of expensive, sometimes complicated, machinery and other equipment. Inexperienced entrants generally begin as laborers, who carry tools and equipment, clear brush, and load and unload logs and brush. For some, familiarization with logging operations may lead to jobs such as log handling equipment operator. Further experience may lead to jobs involving the operation of more complicated machinery and yarding towers to transport, load, and unload logs. Those who have the motor skills required for the efficient use of power saws and other equipment may become fallers and buckers.

Job Outlook

Little or no change is expected in overall employment of forestry and logging workers through the year 2006. Most job openings will result from replacement needs. Many logging workers transfer to other jobs that are less physically demanding and dangerous. In addition, many forestry workers are young workers who are not committed to the occupation on a long-term basis. Some take jobs to earn money for school; others only work in this occupation until they find a better-paying job.

Little change is expected in employment of timber cutting and logging occupations. Despite steady demand for lumber and other wood products, increased mechanization of logging operations and improvements in logging equipment will continue to depress demand for workers. In addition, forest conservation efforts may restrict the volume of public timber available for harvesting, particularly in Federal forests in the West and Northwest, further dampening demand for timber cutting and logging workers.

Slow growth is expected in employment of forest and conservation workers. Environmental concerns may spur the demand for workers who maintain and conserve our woodlands, especially at the State and local government levels; however, budgetary constraints within the Federal Government and in many State governments are expected to suppress job growth.

Increasing mechanization will have different effects on timber cutting and logging workers. Employment of fallers, buckers, choke setters, and other workers whose jobs are labor intensive should decline, as safer, labor-saving machinery and other equipment are increasingly used. Employment of machinery and equipment operators, such as logging tractor and log handling equipment operators, should be less adversely affected.

Weather can force curtailment of logging operations during the muddy spring season and cold winter months, depending on the geographic region. Changes in the level of construction, particularly residential construction, also affect logging activities in the short term. In addition, logging operations must be relocated when timber harvesting in a particular area has been completed. During prolonged periods of inactivity, some workers may stay on the job to maintain or repair logging machinery and equipment; others are forced to find jobs in other occupations or be without work.

Earnings

Median weekly earnings for all full-time, wage and salary forestry and logging workers, including supervisors, were $445 in 1996. The middle 50 percent earned between $310 and $525 weekly. The lowest 10 percent earned less than $230, while the highest 10 percent earned more than $640. Generally, earnings of more skilled workers, such as yarder operators, are higher than those of less skilled workers, such as laborers and choke setters.

Earnings of logging workers vary widely by size of establishment and by geographic area. Earnings of workers in the largest establishments are higher than those in the smallest establishments. Workers in Alaska and the Northwest earn more than those in the South, where the cost of living is generally lower.

In 1997, forestry technicians and aides who worked for the Federal Government averaged about $28,300.

Forest and conservation workers who work for Federal, State, and local governments and large private firms generally enjoy more generous benefits than workers in smaller firms. Small logging contractors generally offer timber cutting and logging workers few benefits. However, some employers offer full-time workers basic benefits, such as medical coverage, and provide safety apparel and equipment.

Related Occupations

Other occupations concerned with the care of trees and their environment include arborist, gardener, groundskeeper, landscaper, nursery worker, and soil conservation technician. Logging tractor operators and logging equipment operators have skills similar to material moving equipment operators, such as industrial truck and tractor operators and crane and tower operators.

Sources of Additional Information

For information about forestry jobs with the Federal Government, contact:

☛ Chief, U.S. Forest Service, U.S. Department of Agriculture, 14th St. and Independence Ave. SW., Washington, DC 20013.

For information about timber cutting and logging careers and secondary and postsecondary programs offering training for logging occupations, contact:

☛ Northeastern Loggers Association, P.O. Box 69, Old Forge, NY 13420.

☛ Timber Producers Association of Michigan and Wisconsin, P.O. Box 39, Tomahawk, WI 54487.

☛ American Pulpwood Association, Inc., 600 Jefferson Plaza, Suite 350, Rockville, MD 20852.

The school of forestry at your State land-grant college or university should also be able to provide useful information.

A list of State forestry associations and other forestry-related State associations is available at most public libraries.

Food Processing Occupations

Butchers and Meat, Poultry, and Fish Cutters

(D.O.T. 316.681-010 and .684 except -014; 521.687-058, -106, and -126; 525.361, .381, .664, .684 except -026, -034, and -040, and .687-030, -066, and -074; and 529.686-022.)

Significant Points

- Workers are highly susceptible to injury; those in meatpacking plants had among the highest incidences of injury and illness of all workers.

- Length of training ranges from a few days for some cutters to 1 or 2 years for highly skilled butchers.

- Job growth will be concentrated among lower skilled meat, poultry, and fish cutters, as more meat cutting and processing shifts from retail stores to food processing plants.

Nature of the Work

Butchers and meat, poultry, and fish cutters are employed at different stages in the process that converts animal carcasses into manageable pieces of meat suitable for sale to consumers. Meat, poultry, and fish cutters generally work in meatpacking or fish and poultry processing plants, while butchers are usually employed at the retail level. As a result of this distinction, the nature of these jobs varies significantly.

In meatpacking plants, *meatcutters* slaughter cattle, hogs, goats, and sheep and cut the carcasses into large wholesale cuts, such as rounds, loins, ribs, and chucks to facilitate the handling, distribution, and marketing of meat. In some of these plants, meatcutters also further process these primal parts into cuts that are ready for retail use. These workers also produce hamburger meat and meat trimmings, which are used to prepare sausages, luncheon meats, and other fabricated meat products. Meatcutters usually work on assembly lines, with each individual responsible for only a few of the many cuts needed to process a carcass. Depending on the type of cut, they use knives, cleavers, meat saws, bandsaws, or other equipment.

In grocery stores, wholesale establishments that supply meat to restaurants, and institutional food service facilities, *butchers* separate wholesale cuts of meat into retail cuts or individual size servings. Additionally, they cut meat into steaks and chops, shape and tie roasts, and grind beef for sale as chopped meat. Boneless cuts are prepared using knives, slicers, or power cutters, while bandsaws are required to carve bone-in pieces. Butchers in retail food stores may also weigh, wrap, and label the cuts of meat, arrange them in refrigerated cases for display, and prepare special cuts of meat to fill unique orders.

Poultry cutters slaughter and cut up chickens, turkeys, and other types of poultry. The poultry processing industry is becoming increasingly automated, but many jobs such as trimming, packing, and deboning are still done manually. As in the meatpacking industry, most poultry cutters perform routine cuts on poultry as it moves along production lines.

Unlike the occupations listed above, *fish cutters,* also called *fish cleaners*, are likely to be employed in both manufacturing and retail establishments. These workers primarily cut, scale, and dress fish by removing the head, scales, and other inedible portions and cutting the fish into steaks or boneless fillets. In markets, they may also wait on customers and clean fish to order.

Retail meat, poultry, and fish cutters also prepare ready-to-heat foods. This often entails filleting meat or fish or cutting it into bite-sized pieces, preparing and adding vegetables, or applying sauces or breading.

Working Conditions

Working conditions vary by type and size of establishment. In meatpacking plants and large retail food establishments, butchers and meatcutters work in large meatcutting rooms equipped with power machines and conveyors. In small retail markets, the butcher or fish cleaner may work in a space behind the meat counter. To avoid viral and bacterial infections, work areas must be clean and sanitary.

Meatpacking plants had one of the highest incidences of work-related injury and illness of any industry in 1995. Butchers and meat, poultry, and fish cutters often work in cold, damp rooms, which are refrigerated to prevent meat from spoiling and are damp because meat cutting generates large amounts of blood, condensation, and fat. These cool damp floors increase the likelihood of slips and falls. In addition, the low temperature, combined with the need to stand for long periods of time and perform physical tasks, makes the work tiring. As a result, butchers and meat, poultry, and fish cutters are more susceptible to injury than most other workers. Cuts, and even amputations, occur when knives, cleavers, and power tools are used improperly. Repetitive slicing and lifting often lead to cumulative

Butchers in grocery stores transform wholesale cuts of meat into consumer-ready portions.

trauma injuries, such as carpal tunnel syndrome. To reduce the incidence of cumulative trauma disorders, some employers have reduced work loads, redesigned jobs and tools, and increased awareness of early warning signs. Nevertheless, workers in this occupation still face serious threat of disabling injuries.

Employment
Butchers and meat, poultry, and fish cutters held about 369,000 jobs in 1996. Nearly 60 percent worked in meatpacking or poultry and fish processing plants, while most others in this occupation were employed at the retail level in grocery stores, meat and fish markets, restaurants, or hotels. The majority of the 217,000 skilled butchers and meatcutters worked in retail grocery stores, while nearly all meat, poultry, and fish cutters worked in meatpacking or poultry and fish processing plants. Highly skilled butchers and meatcutters are employed in almost every city and town in the Nation, while lower skilled meat, poultry, and fish cutter jobs are concentrated in communities with food processing plants.

Training, Other Qualifications, and Advancement
Most butchers and meat, poultry, and fish cutters acquire their skills on the job through formal and informal training programs. The length of training varies significantly in this occupation, with simple cutting operations requiring a few days to learn, for example, while more complex tasks, like eviscerating, generally require about a month to learn. The training period for a highly skilled butcher at the retail level may be a year or two.

Generally, on-the-job trainees begin by doing less difficult jobs, such as simple cuts or removing bones. Under the guidance of experienced workers, trainees learn the proper use of tools and equipment and how to prepare various cuts of meat. After demonstrating skill with various meatcutting tools, they learn to divide carcasses into wholesale cuts and wholesale cuts into retail and individual portions. Trainees may also learn to roll and tie roasts, prepare sausage, and cure meat. Those employed in retail food establishments often are taught operations such as inventory control, meat buying, and record keeping. In addition, growing concern about the safety of meats has led employers to offer extensive training in food safety to employees.

Skills important in meat, poultry, and fish cutting are manual dexterity, good depth perception, color discrimination, and good hand-eye coordination. Physical strength is often needed to lift and move heavy pieces of meat. Butchers and fish cleaners who wait on customers should have a pleasant personality, a neat appearance, and the ability to communicate clearly. In some States, a health certificate is required for employment.

Butchers and meat, poultry, and fish cutters in retail or wholesale establishments may progress to supervisory jobs, such as meat or seafood department managers in supermarkets. A few of these workers become meat or seafood buyers for wholesalers or supermarket chains. Some open their own meat or fish markets. In processing plants, meat, poultry, and fish cutters may advance to supervisory positions or become team leaders.

Job Outlook
Overall employment of butchers and meat, poultry, and fish cutters is expected to grow more slowly than the average for all occupations through the year 2006. Job growth will be concentrated among lower skilled meat, poultry, and fish cutters, as more meat cutting and processing shifts from retail stores to food processing plants. Nevertheless, job opportunities should be plentiful at all levels of the occupation due to the need to replace experienced workers who transfer to other occupations or leave the labor force.

As the Nation's population grows, the demand for meat, poultry, and seafood should continue to increase. Successful marketing by the poultry industry is likely to increase demand for rotisserie chicken and ready-to-heat products. Similarly, the development of lower-fat and ready-to-heat products promises to stimulate the consumption of red meat. Although per capita consumption of fish and other seafood has been constant over the previous decade, population growth will push consumption to record levels in coming years.

Employment growth of lower skilled meat, poultry, and fish cutters—who work primarily in meatpacking, poultry, and fish processing plants—is expected to increase faster than the average for all occupations in coming years. Although much of the production of poultry and fabricated poultry products is performed by machines, the growing popularity of labor-intensive, ready-to-heat goods promises to spur demand for poultry workers. Meat and fish cutters also will be in demand, as the task of preparing ready-to-heat meat and fish goods slowly shifts from retail stores to processing plants. Although the supply of edible ocean fish is limited, advances in fish farming, or "aquaculture," should help meet the growing demand for fish and produce ample opportunities for fish cutters.

Employment of more highly skilled butchers and meatcutters, who work primarily in retail stores, is expected to gradually decline. New automation and the consolidation of the meatpacking and poultry processing industries are enabling employers to transfer employment from higher-paid butchers to lower-wage meatcutters in meatpacking plants. At present, most red meat arrives at grocery stores partially cut up, but a growing share of meat is being delivered pre-packaged with additional fat removed to wholesalers and retailers. This trend is resulting in less work for retail butchers and a declining demand for their employment.

Earnings
Butchers and meatcutters had median weekly earnings of $370 in 1996. The middle 50 percent earned between $280 and $520 a week. The highest paid 10 percent earned more than $740 a week. Meatcutters employed by retail grocery stores are generally among the higher-paid workers in this occupation.

Butchers and meat and fish cutters generally received typical benefits, including pension plans for those who were union members or employed by grocery stores. However, poultry workers rarely earned substantial benefits.

Many butchers and meat, poultry, and fish cutters are members of the United Food and Commercial Workers International Union. In 1996, nearly a third of all butchers and meatcutters were union members or covered by a union contract.

Related Occupations
Butchers and meat, poultry, and fish cutters must be skilled at both hand and machine work and must have some knowledge of processes and techniques involved in handling and preparing food. Other occupations in food preparation that require similar skills and knowledge include bakers, chefs and cooks, and food preparation workers.

Sources of Additional Information
Information about work opportunities can be obtained from local employers or local offices of the State employment service. For information on training and other aspects of this trade, contact:
☛ United Food and Commercial Workers International Union, 1775 K St. NW., Washington, DC 20006.

Inspectors, Testers, and Graders

(List of D.O.T. codes available on request. See p. 496.)

Significant Points

- For workers who perform simple "pass/fail" tests of products, a high school diploma is sufficient; more complex precision inspecting positions are filled by experienced production workers.

- Like many other occupations concentrated in manufacturing, employment is expected to decline, reflecting the growth of automated inspection and the redistribution of quality control responsibilities from inspectors to other production workers.

Nature of the Work

Inspectors, testers, and graders ensure that your food won't make you sick, your car will run properly, and your pants won't split the first time you wear them. These workers monitor quality standards for virtually all manufactured products, including foods, textiles, clothing, glassware, motor vehicles, electronic components, computers, and structural steel. As quality has become a more central focus in many production firms, daily duties of inspectors have changed. In some cases, their titles also have changed to "quality control inspector" or a similar name, reflecting the growing importance of quality.

Regardless of title, all inspectors, testers, and graders work to guarantee the quality of the goods their firms produce. Specific job duties vary across the wide range of industries in which these workers are found. For example, they may check products by sight, sound, feel, smell, or even taste to locate imperfections, such as cuts, scratches, bubbles, missing pieces, misweaves, or crooked seams. These workers also may verify dimensions, color, weight, texture, strength, or other physical characteristics of objects. Machinery testers generally verify that parts fit, move correctly, and are properly lubricated; check the pressure of gases and the level of liquids; test the flow of electricity; and do a test run to check for proper operation. Some jobs involve only a quick visual inspection; others require a longer, detailed one.

Inspectors, testers, and graders are involved at every stage of the production process. Some inspectors examine materials received from a supplier before sending them to the production line. Others inspect components, subassemblies, and assemblies or perform a final check on the finished product. Depending on the skill level of the inspectors, they may also set up and test equipment, calibrate precision instruments, or repair defective products.

Inspectors, testers, and graders rely on a number of tools to perform their jobs. Many use micrometers, electronic equipment, calipers, alignment gauges, and other instruments to check and compare the dimensions of parts against the parts' specifications. Those testing electrical devices may use voltmeters, ammeters, and oscilloscopes to test insulation, current flow, and resistance.

Inspectors mark, tag, or note problems. They may reject defective items outright, send them for rework, or, in the case of minor problems, fix them themselves. If the product checks out, they may screw on a nameplate, tag it, stamp a serial number, or certify it in some other way. Inspectors, testers, and graders record the results of their inspections, compute the percentage of defects and other statistical parameters, prepare inspection and test reports, notify supervisors of problems, and help analyze and correct problems in the production process.

Recent emphasis on quality control in manufacturing has meant that inspection is becoming more fully integrated into the production process. Many machines are now self-monitoring to ensure that the product is produced within quality standards. Inspectors still test products to ensure that they meet specifications, but, with the help of self-monitoring machines, inspectors can direct the production line to adjust the machinery before unusable parts are produced. Many firms have completely automated inspection with the help of advanced vision systems, using machinery installed at one or several points in the production process. Inspectors in these firms generally are trained to operate this equipment.

Working Conditions

Working conditions vary by industry and establishment size. As a result, some inspectors examine similar products for an entire shift, while others examine a variety of items. Most inspectors in manufacturing remain at one work station, but some in transportation or construction travel from place to place to do inspections. Inspectors in some industries may be on their feet all day and may have to lift heavy objects, whereas in other industries they sit during most of their shift and do little strenuous work. Workers in heavy manufacturing plants may be exposed to the noise and grime of machinery; in other plants, inspectors work in clean, quiet environments.

Some inspectors work evenings, nights, or weekends. In these cases, shift assignments generally are made on the basis of seniority. Overtime may be required to meet production goals.

Employment

Inspectors, testers, and graders held about 634,000 jobs in 1996. About 3 out of 4 worked in manufacturing establishments that produced such

Inspectors, testers, and graders employ a variety of precision instruments to ensure quality.

products as industrial machinery and equipment, motor vehicles and equipment, primary and fabricated metals industries, electronic components and accessories, textiles, apparel, and aircraft and parts. Inspectors, testers, and graders also were found in temporary help services, communications and utilities, wholesale trade, engineering and management services, and government agencies.

Training, Other Qualifications, and Advancement

Training requirements vary, based on the responsibilities of the inspector, tester, or grader. For workers who perform simple "pass/fail" tests of products, a high school diploma is preferred and may be required for some jobs. Simple jobs are generally filled by beginners with a few days of training. In-house training for new inspectors may cover the use of special meters, gauges, computers, or other instruments; quality control techniques; blueprint reading; and reporting requirements. There are some postsecondary training programs in testing, but many employers prefer to train inspectors themselves.

Complex precision inspecting positions are filled by experienced assemblers, machine operators, or mechanics who already have a thorough knowledge of the products and production processes. To advance to these positions, experienced workers may need training in statistical process control, new automation, or the requirements of quality assurance certification systems.

In general, inspectors, testers, and graders need mechanical aptitude and good hand-eye coordination and vision. Advancement for these workers frequently takes the form of higher pay. They also may advance to inspector of more complex products, supervisor, or quality control technician.

Job Outlook

Like many other occupations concentrated in the manufacturing sector, employment of inspectors, testers, and graders is expected to decline through the year 2006. The primary causes of this decline are the growth of automated inspection and the redistribution of quality control responsibilities from inspectors to other production workers. In spite of declining employment, a large number of job openings will arise due to normal turnover in this large occupation. Many of these jobs, however, will be available only to experienced production workers.

Employment of inspectors, testers, and graders will be significantly affected by the increasing focus on quality in American industry. The emphasis on quality is leading manufacturers to invest in automated inspection equipment and to take a more systematic approach to quality inspection. New technologies, such as spectrophotometers and computer-assisted visual inspection systems, allow firms to effectively automate simple inspection tasks, increasing worker productivity and reducing the demand for inspectors. This automation is expected to improve in coming years. As it does, it will become more cost-effective for firms and will be more widely implemented in a broad range of industries.

Apart from automation, firms are improving quality by building it into the production process. This has led firms to redistribute many inspection duties from inspectors, testers, and graders to other production workers who monitor quality at every stage of the process. In addition, the growing implementation of statistical process control is resulting in "smarter" inspection. Using this system, firms survey the sources and incidence of defects so these firms can better focus their efforts and reduce production of defective products. Inspection has, thus, become more selective, and as sources of defects are eliminated, the need for comprehensive inspection declines.

In many industries, however, automation is not being aggressively pursued as an alternative to manual inspection. When key inspection elements are oriented to size, such as length, width, or thickness, automation may play some role in the future. But when taste, smell, texture, appearance, or product performance are important, inspection will probably continue to be done by humans. Employment of inspectors, testers, and graders is expected to grow along with production in some of these industries, such as wholesale trade. Employment of inspectors is also projected to grow in business services, as more manufacturers and industrial firms hire temporary inspectors to increase the flexibility of their staffing strategies.

Earnings

Inspectors, testers, and graders had median weekly earnings of about $570 in 1996. The middle 50 percent earned between $430 and $760 a week. The lowest 10 percent earned less than $330 a week; the highest 10 percent earned more than $950.

Related Occupations

Other workers who inspect products or services are construction and building inspectors and inspectors and compliance officers, which includes consumer safety, environmental health, agricultural commodity, immigration, customs, postal, and motor vehicle, among other inspectors.

Sources of Additional Information

For general information about this occupation, contact:

☛ The National Tooling and Machining Association, 9300 Livingston Rd., Fort Washington, MD 20744.

☛ The American Society for Quality Control, 611 East Wisconsin Ave., Milwaukee, WI 53202-4606.

Metalworking and Plastics-Working Occupations

Boilermakers

(D.O.T. 805.261; .361; and .381)

Significant Points

- A formal apprenticeship is the best way to learn this trade.
- Due to the limited number of apprenticeships available and relatively good wages, prospective boilermakers may face competition.

Nature of the Work

Boilermakers and boilermaker mechanics make, install, and repair boilers, vats, and other large vessels that hold liquids and gases. Boilers supply steam to drive huge turbines in electric power plants and to provide heat or power in buildings, factories, and ships. Tanks and vats are used to process and store chemicals, oil, beer, and hundreds of other products.

Boilers and other high pressure vessels are usually made in sections by casting each piece out of molten iron or steel. Manufacturers are increasingly automating this process to increase the quality of these vessels. The boiler sections are then welded together, often using automated orbital welding machines, which make more consistent welds than is possible by hand. Small boilers may be assembled in the manufacturing plant; larger boilers are usually assembled on site.

Following blueprints, boilermakers locate and mark reference points on the boiler foundation for installing boilers and other vessels, using straightedges, squares, transits, and tape measures. They attach rigging and signal crane operators to lift heavy frame and plate sections and other parts into place. They align sections, using plumb bobs, levels, wedges, and turnbuckles. Boilermakers use hammers, files, grinders, and cutting torches to remove irregular edges so the edges fit properly. Then they bolt or weld them together. Boilermakers align and attach water tubes, stacks, valves, gauges, and other parts, and test complete vessels for leaks or other defects. Usually they assemble large vessels temporarily in a fabrication shop to insure a proper fit before final assembly on their permanent site.

Because boilers last a long time—35 years or longer—boilermakers regularly maintain them and update components such as burners and boiler tubes to increase efficiency. Boilermaker mechanics maintain and repair boilers and similar vessels. They inspect tubes, fittings, valves, controls, and auxiliary machinery, and clean or supervise the cleaning of boilers. They repair or replace defective parts, using hand and power tools, gas torches, and welding equipment, and may operate metalworking machinery to repair or make parts. They also dismantle leaky boilers, patch weak spots with metal stock, replace defective sections, or strengthen joints.

Working Conditions

Boilermakers often use potentially dangerous equipment such as acetylene torches and power grinders, handle heavy parts, and work on ladders or on top of large vessels. Work may be done in cramped quarters inside boilers, vats, or tanks that are often damp and poorly ventilated. To reduce the chance of injuries, they may wear hardhats, harnesses, respirators, protective clothing, and safety glasses and shoes. Boilermakers usually work a 40-hour week but may experience extended periods of overtime when equipment is shut down for maintenance. Overtime work may also be required to meet construction or production deadlines.

Employment

Boilermakers held about 18,000 jobs in 1996. About 40 percent worked in the construction industry, assembling and erecting boilers and other vessels. One-third worked in manufacturing, primarily in boiler manufacturing shops, iron and steel plants, petroleum refineries, chemical plants, and shipyards. Some also work for boiler repair firms, railroads, and in Navy shipyards and Federal power facilities.

Training, Other Qualifications, and Advancement

Most training authorities recommend a formal apprenticeship to learn this trade. Some people become boilermakers by working as helpers to experienced boilermakers, but generally lack the wide range of skills acquired through an apprenticeship. Apprenticeship programs usually consist of 4 years of on-the-job training, supplemented by about 144 hours of classroom instruction each year in subjects such as set-up and assembly rigging, welding of all types, blueprint reading, and layout. Experienced boilermakers often attend apprenticeship classes to keep their knowledge current.

When an apprenticeship becomes available, the local union will publicize the opportunity by notifying local vocational schools and high school vocational programs. Qualified applicants take an aptitude test administered by the union, specifically designed for boilermaking. The apprenticeship is awarded to the person scoring highest on this test.

When hiring helpers, employers prefer high school or vocational school graduates. Courses in shop, mathematics, blueprint reading, welding, and machine metalworking are useful. Mechanical aptitude and the manual dexterity needed to handle tools also are important.

Some boilermakers advance to supervisory positions. Because of their broader training, apprentices generally have an advantage in promotion.

Job Outlook

Persons who wish to become boilermakers may face some competition, due to the limited number of apprenticeships available and the relatively good wages an experienced boilermaker earns. In addition, employment of boilermakers is expected to decline through the year 2006. However, a limited number of openings will arise from the need to replace experienced workers who leave the occupation.

Growth should be limited by several factors: The trend toward repairing and retrofitting rather than replacing existing boilers; the use of smaller boilers, which require less on-site assembly; and automation of production technologies.

Boilers have a long life and require regular maintenance and updating by boilermakers.

Most of the industries that purchase boilers are sensitive to economic conditions. Therefore, during economic downturns, construction boilermakers may be laid off. However, because boilers are maintained and repaired even during economic downturns, boilermaker mechanics generally have more stable employment.

Earnings

According to the limited data available, boilermakers who usually worked full time had median earnings of about $610 per week in 1996.

According to the International Brotherhood of Boilermakers, journey boilermakers earned approximately $22.00 per hour in 1996. Apprentices started at 60 percent of journey wages, or about $13.00 hourly, with wages gradually increasing to the journey wage as progress is made in the apprenticeship. However, wages vary greatly around the country, with higher wages in Northeastern, Great Lakes, and Far Western cities than in other areas of the country.

Many boilermakers belong to labor unions. The principal union is the International Brotherhood of Boilermakers. Others are members of the International Association of Machinists, the United Automobile Workers, and the United Steelworkers of America.

Related Occupations

Workers in a number of other occupations assemble, install, or repair metal equipment or machines. These include assemblers, blacksmiths, instrument makers, ironworkers, machinists, millwrights, patternmakers, plumbers, sheet-metal workers, tool and die makers, and welders.

Sources of Additional Information

For further information regarding boilermaking apprenticeships or other training opportunities, contact local offices of the unions previously mentioned, local construction companies and boiler manufacturers, or the local office of the State employment service.

For general information regarding boilermaking and opportunities in the boiler manufacturing industry, contact:

☛ American Boiler Manufacturing Association, 950 North Glebe Rd., Suite 160, Arlington, VA 22203-1824.

☛ International Brotherhood of Boilermakers, 753 State Avenue, Suite 570, Kansas City, KS 66101.

Jewelers

(D.O.T. 199.281; 700.281-010, -014, -022, and .381-030, -042, and -046)

Significant Points

- Over one-third of all jewelers were self-employed; many operated their own store or repair shop, and some specialized in designing and creating custom jewelry.

- Slightly over half of all salaried jewelers worked in retail establishments, while 33 percent were employed in manufacturing plants.

- Employment is expected to decline slightly, further limiting the number of available jobs in this small occupation.

Nature of the Work

Jewelers design, make, repair, and adjust rings, necklaces, bracelets, earrings, and other jewelry. Using a variety of common and specialized handtools, and increasingly, computers, they mold and shape metal and set gemstones.

Jewelers usually specialize in one or more areas of the jewelry field—design, gem cutting, repair, sales, or appraisal. In small retail or repair shops, they may be involved in all aspects of the work. Regardless of the type of establishment or work setting, however, their work requires a high degree of skill and attention to detail. Those working in retail jewelry stores, in addition to their primary responsibility to sell jewelry, may spend some time repairing or adjusting it. In other cases, retailers send jewelry to specialized jewelry repair shops. Typical repair work includes enlarging or reducing ring sizes, resetting stones, and replacing broken clasps and mountings. Some jewelers also design or make their own jewelry. Following their own designs or those created by designers or customers, they begin by shaping the metal or carving wax to make a model for casting the metal. The individual parts are then soldered together, and the jeweler may mount a diamond or other gem, or engrave a design into the metal.

Jewelers who own or manage stores or shops hire and train employees; order, market, and sell merchandise; and perform other managerial duties. In manufacturing, jewelers usually specialize in a single operation. Some may make models or tools for the jewelry that is to be produced. Others do finishing work, such as setting stones, polishing, or engraving. A growing number of jewelers use lasers for cutting and improving the quality of stones. In larger manufacturing establishments, jewelers may be required to perform several tasks as new manufacturing processes make their way through the industry.

Technology, in the form of various computerized systems, is beginning to affect the jewelry industry. Some manufacturing firms use CAD/CAM (computer-aided design and manufacturing) to facilitate product design and automate some steps in mold and model making. Use of such systems should increase in the future as they become more affordable for smaller companies. In retail stores, computers are used mainly for inventory control; some jewelers use computers to design and create customized pieces according to their customers' wishes. With the aid of computers, customers visualize different combinations of styles, cuts, shanks, sizes, and stones to create their own pieces.

Working Conditions

While the work of jewelers is not physically strenuous, there is a lot of work with detail and intricate designs that may be tiring to some. In manufacturing and repair shops, caution must be taken because the chemicals, sawing and drilling tools, and torches a jeweler uses can cause serious injury. In addition, doing delicate work on precious stones or metals while trying to satisfy demands for speed and quality from customers and employers can cause stress, and bending over a workbench for long periods can be uncomfortable. In the future, the use of computers may ease some of these conditions because applications such as CAD/CAM greatly increase the speed and accuracy of the design and manufacturing process.

Because many of the materials with which they work are very valuable, jewelers working in retail stores must observe strict security procedures. These may include locked doors that are only opened by a buzzer, barred windows, burglar alarms, and the presence of armed guards.

In repair shops, jewelers generally work alone with little supervision. In retail stores, on the other hand, they may talk with customers about repairs, perform custom design work, and even do some sales work.

Employment

Jewelers held about 32,000 jobs in 1996. Over one-third of all jewelers were self-employed; many operated their own store or repair shop, and some specialized in designing and creating custom jewelry.

Slightly over 50 percent of all salaried jewelers worked in retail establishments, while 33 percent were employed in manufacturing plants. Although jewelry stores and repair shops can be found in every city and many small towns, most job opportunities are in larger metropolitan areas. Many jewelers employed in manufacturing work in Rhode Island and New York.

Training, Other Qualifications, and Advancement

Jewelers' skills usually are learned in technical schools, through correspondence courses, or informally on the job. Colleges and art schools also offer programs that can lead to a bachelor's or master's degree of fine arts in jewelry design. Formal training in the basic skills of the trade enhances one's employment and advancement opportunities. Many employers prefer well-rounded jewelers with design, repair, and sales skills. Some aspiring jewelers begin working as clerks in department stores, and transfer to jobs in jewelry shops or manufacturing firms after gaining experience.

For those interested in working in a jewelry store or repair shop, technical schools or courses offered by local colleges are the best sources of training. In these programs, which vary in length from 6 months to 2 years, students learn the use and care of jewelers' tools and machines and basic jewelry making and repairing skills, such as design, casting, stone setting, and polishing. Technical school courses also cover topics including blueprint reading, math, and shop

Technical schools often provide the best training for those interested in working in jewelry repair shops.

theory. Most employers feel that graduates need several more years of supervised, on-the-job training to refine their repair skills and learn more about the operation of the store or shop. In addition, some employers encourage workers to improve their skills by enrolling in short-term technical school courses such as sample making, wax carving, or gemology. Many employers pay all or part of the cost of this additional training.

The Gemological Institute of America offers programs lasting about 6 months, and self-paced correspondence courses lasting several years, leading to a gemologist diploma and a jeweler diploma. These advanced programs cover a wide range of topics including appraisal, evaluating diamonds and colored stones, identifying gems, and designing jewelry.

In jewelry manufacturing plants, workers traditionally have developed their skills through apprenticeships and informal on-the-job training. This training lasts 3 to 4 years, depending on the difficulty of the specialty. Training usually focuses on casting, stonesetting, modelmaking, or engraving. In recent years, a growing number of technical schools and colleges have begun to offer training designed for jewelers working in manufacturing. Like employers in retail trade, though, those in manufacturing now prefer graduates of these programs because they are familiar with the production process, allowing less in-house training.

To enter most technical school or college programs, a high school diploma or its equivalent is required. Courses in art, math, mechanical drawing, and chemistry are useful. Because computer-aided design is increasingly used in the jewelry field, it is recommended that students—especially those interested in design and manufacturing—obtain training in CAD.

The precise and delicate nature of jewelry work requires finger and hand dexterity, good hand-eye coordination, patience, and concentration. Artistic ability and fashion consciousness are major assets because jewelry must be stylish and attractive. Those who work in jewelry stores have frequent contact with customers and should be neat, personable, and knowledgeable about the merchandise. In addition, employers require someone of good character because jewelers work with very valuable materials.

Advancement opportunities are limited and greatly dependent on an individual's skill and initiative. In manufacturing, some jewelers advance to supervisory jobs, such as master jeweler or head jeweler, but for most, advancement takes the form of higher pay for doing the same job. Jewelers who work in jewelry stores or repair shops may become salaried managers; some open their own businesses.

For those interested in starting their own business, a substantial financial investment is needed to acquire the necessary inventory. Also, because the jewelry business is highly competitive, jewelers who plan to open their own store should have experience in selling, as well as knowledge of marketing and business management. Courses in these areas often are available from technical schools and community colleges.

Job Outlook

Employment of jewelers is expected to decline slightly through the year 2006. Jewelers have a relatively strong attachment to their occupation—reflecting the large proportion of self-employed workers. Nevertheless, job openings will largely result from the need to replace jewelers who transfer to other occupations, retire, or leave the labor force for other reasons.

Traditionally, job opportunities for jewelers depended largely on jewelry sales and on demand for jewelry repair services. Now, however, non-traditional jewelry marketers such as discount stores, mail-order catalogue companies, and television shopping networks have limited the growth of sales made by traditional jewelers, limiting job opportunities because these types of establishments require few if any jewelers.

Opportunities in jewelry stores and repair shops will be best for graduates from jeweler or gemologist training programs. Demand for repair workers will be strong because maintaining and repairing jewelry is an ongoing process, even during economic slowdowns. In fact, demand for jewelry repair may increase during recessions as people repair or restore existing pieces rather than purchase new ones.

Within manufacturing, increasing automation will adversely affect employment of low-skilled occupations, such as assembler and polisher. Automation will have a lesser impact on more creative, highly skilled positions, such as mold and model maker. Furthermore, small manufacturers, which typify the industry, will have an increasingly difficult time competing with the larger manufacturers when it comes to supplying large retailers. Because of recent international trade agreements, exports are steadily increasing as manufacturers become more competitive in foreign markets. However, these same agreements have allowed imports from foreign manufacturers to increase as well.

The demand for jewelry is largely affected by the amount of disposable income people have. Therefore, the increasing number of affluent individuals, working women, double-income households, and fashion conscious men are expected to keep jewelry sales strong.

Earnings

According to the *Jewelers' Circular-Keystone* annual salary survey, the median salary of jewelry repair workers in retail stores was between $30,200 and $32,100 in 1995. Depending on the employer, jewelers may receive commissions on what they sell, or bonuses for outstanding work. According to the Manufacturing Jewelers and Silversmiths of America, the median average hourly wage of jewelers in companies with more than 10 employees was $12.63 in 1996. Beginners in jewelry factories generally start at considerably less than experienced workers; as they become more proficient, they receive periodic raises.

Most jewelers enjoy a variety of fringe benefits including reimbursement from their employers for work-related courses and discounts on jewelry purchases.

Related Occupations

Other skilled workers who do similar jobs include polishers, dental laboratory technicians, gemcutters, hand engravers, and watch makers and repairers.

Sources of Additional Information

Information on job opportunities and training programs for jewelers is available from:

☛ Gemological Institute of America, 5345 Armada Dr., Carlsbad, CA 92008. Homepage: http://www.gia.org

General career information is available from:

☛ Jewelers of America, 1185 Avenue of the Americas, 30th Floor, New York, NY 10036.

☛ Manufacturing Jewelers and Silversmiths of America, 1 State St., 6th Floor, Providence, RI 02908-5035. Homepage: http://mjsa.polygon.net

To receive a list of technical schools accredited by the Accrediting Commission of Career Schools and Colleges of Technology which have programs in jewelry design, contact:

☛ Accrediting Commission of Career Schools and Colleges of Technology, 2101 Wilson Blvd., Suite 302, Arlington, VA 22201.

Machinists and Tool Programmers

(D.O.T. 007.167-018; 600.260-022, .280-022, -026, -030, -034, -042, .281-010, .380-010; 609.262-010; and 714.281-018)

Significant Points

- Formal training in high schools, vocational schools, or community colleges is typical; many entrants to these occupations have previously worked as machine tool operators or setters.

- Increasing automation will contribute to a slight decline in employment; nevertheless, job opportunities will be good as employers continue to report difficulties in finding workers with necessary skills and knowledge.

Nature of the Work

Machinists use machine tools such as lathes, drill presses, and milling machines to produce precision metal parts. Although they may produce large quantities of one part, machinists usually produce small batches or one-of-a-kind items. They use their knowledge of the working properties of metals and their skill with machine tools to plan and carry out the operations needed to make machined products that meet precise specifications.

Before they machine a part, machinists must carefully plan and prepare the operation. These workers first review blueprints or written specifications for a job. Next, they calculate where to cut or bore into the workpiece, how fast to feed the metal into the machine, and how much metal to remove. They then select tools and materials for the job, plan the sequence of cutting and finishing operations, and mark the metal stock to show where these cuts should be made.

After this layout work is completed, machinists perform the necessary machining operations. They position the metal stock on the machine tool—drill presses, lathes, milling machines, or others—set the controls, and make the cuts. During the machining process, they must constantly monitor the feed and speed of the machine. Machinists also ensure that the workpiece is being properly lubricated and cooled because the machining of metal products generates a significant amount of heat.

Some machinists, often called production machinists, may produce large quantities of one part, especially parts requiring complex operations and great precision. For unusually sophisticated procedures, expensive machinery is used. Usually, however, large numbers of parts requiring more routine operations are produced by metalworking and plastics-working machine operators (see the statement on metalworking and plastics-working machine operators elsewhere in the *Handbook*). Other machinists do maintenance work—repairing or making new parts for existing machinery. To repair a broken part, maintenance machinists may refer to blueprints and perform the same machining operations that were needed to create the original part.

Increasingly, the machine tools used to produce metal parts are computer numerically controlled (CNC)—that is, they contain computer controllers that direct the machine's operations. The controller "reads" a program—a coded list of the steps necessary to perform a specific machining job—and runs the machine tool's mechanisms through the steps. The introduction of CNC machine tools has changed the nature of the work of machinists. These machines enable machinists to be more productive and to produce parts with a level of precision that is not possible with traditional machining techniques. Furthermore, because precise movements are recorded in the program, they allow this high level of precision to be consistently repeated. It also allows various functions to be performed with one setup, reducing the need for additional, labor-intensive setups.

The quality of the products these machines produce depends largely on the programs, which may be produced by machinists or by tool programmers. Tool programmers begin as machinists do—by analyzing blueprints, computing the size and position of the cuts, determining the sequence of machine operations, selecting tools, and calculating the machine speed and feed rates. They then write the program in the language of the machine's controller and store it. Skilled machinists may also do programming. In fact, as computer-aided manufacturing (CAM) software becomes more user-friendly and CNC machines are more widely used, machinists are increasingly expected to perform this function.

Machinists may work alone or with tool programmers to check new programs to ensure that machinery will function properly and the output will meet specifications. Because a problem with the program could damage the costly machinery and cutting tools, computer simulations may be used instead of a trial run to check the program. If errors are found, the program must be changed and retested until the problem is resolved. In addition, growing connectivity between computer-aided design software and CNC machine tools is raising productivity by automatically translating designs into instructions which are understood by the computer controller on the machine tool. These new CAM technologies enable programs to be more easily modified for use on other jobs with similar specifications, thereby reducing the time and effort.

Working Conditions

Most machine shops are well lit and ventilated. Nevertheless, working around high-speed machine tools presents certain dangers, and workers must follow safety precautions. Machinists must wear protective equipment such as safety glasses to shield against bits of flying metal and earplugs to protect against machinery noise. They must also exercise caution when handling hazardous coolants and lubricants. The job requires stamina because machinists stand most of the day and may lift moderately heavy workpieces.

Some tool programmers work in offices that are near, but separate from, the shop floor. These work areas are usually clean, well lit, and free of machine noise.

Most machinists and tool programmers work a 40-hour week. Evening and weekend shifts are becoming more common as companies justify investments in more expensive machinery by extending their hours of operation. Overtime is common during peak production periods.

Employment

Machinists and tool programmers held about 393,000 jobs in 1996. Most machinists worked in small machining shops or in manufacturing firms that produce durable goods, such as metalworking and industrial machinery, aircraft, or motor vehicles. Maintenance machinists work in most industries that use production machinery. Although machinists and tool programmers work in all parts of the country, jobs are most plentiful in areas where manufacturing is concentrated.

Training, Other Qualifications, and Advancement

A high school or vocational school education, including mathematics, blueprint reading, metalworking, and drafting, is generally a prerequisite for becoming a machinist or tool programmer. A basic knowledge of computers and electronics is helpful because of the increased use of computer-controlled machine tools. Experience with machine tools also is extremely important. In fact, many entrants to these occupations have previously worked as machine tool operators or

Machinists are among the most highly skilled industrial workers.

setters. Persons interested in becoming machinists or tool programmers should be mechanically inclined, able to work independently, and able to do highly accurate work that requires concentration and physical effort.

Machinist training varies from formal apprenticeship and postsecondary programs to informal on-the-job training. Apprentice programs consist of shop training and related classroom instruction. In shop training, apprentices learn filing, handtapping, and dowel fitting, as well as the operation of various machine tools. Classroom instruction includes math, physics, blueprint reading, mechanical drawing, and shop practices. In addition, as machine shops have increased their use of computer-controlled equipment, training in the operation and programming of CNC machine tools has become essential. Such apprenticeships have become relatively rare, however, as a growing number of machinists and tool programmers receive most of their formal training from community or technical colleges.

Qualifications for tool programmers vary widely depending upon the complexity of the job. Basic requirements parallel those of machinists. Employers often prefer skilled machinists, tool and die makers, or those with technical school training. For some specialized types of programming, such as with complex parts for the aerospace or shipbuilding industries, employers may prefer individuals with a degree in engineering.

For those entering tool programming directly, a basic knowledge of computers and electronics is necessary and experience with machine tools is extremely helpful. Classroom training includes an introduction to numerical control and the basics of programming and then advances to more complex topics such as computer-aided manufacturing. Trainees start writing simple programs under the direction of an experienced programmer. Although machinery manufacturers are trying to standardize programming languages, there are numerous languages in use. Because of this, tool programmers should be able to learn new programming languages.

As new automation is introduced, machinists and tool programmers generally receive additional training to update their skills. This training is usually provided by a representative of the equipment manufacturer or a local technical school. Some employers offer tuition reimbursement for job-related courses.

Workers may advance in several ways. Experienced machinists may become tool programmers; some move into supervisory or administrative positions in their firms; and a few may open their own shops.

Job Outlook

Employment of machinists and tool programmers is expected to decline slightly through the year 2006. Despite this decline, job opportunities will be good for machinists, as employers continue to report difficulties in finding workers with the necessary skills and knowledge to fill machining and tool programming openings. Many job openings will arise each year from the need to replace experienced machinists and programmers who transfer to other occupations or retire. The number of openings for machinists is expected to be far greater than the number of openings for tool programmers, primarily because the occupation is larger.

Automation is contributing to the slight employment decline projected for machinists and tool programmers. The use of computer-controlled machine tools, for example, reduces the time required for machining operations and increases worker productivity. This allows fewer machinists to accomplish the same amount of work previously performed by more workers. The impact of CNC technology on the employment of machinists is limited, however, because many of the unique operations performed by these workers cannot be efficiently automated, and because firms are likely to retain their most skilled workers to operate expensive new machinery.

Although employment of tool programmers was initially made possible by the introduction of new automation in firms, recent technological advancements are reducing demand for these workers. For example, advanced machine tool technology allows some programming and minor adjustments to be performed on the shop floor by

machinists, tool and die makers, and machine operators. In addition, fewer programmers will be needed to translate part and product designs into CNC machine tool instructions due to the increasing use of software that automatically performs this function.

Employment levels in these occupations is also influenced by economic cycles; as the demand for machined goods falls, machinists and tool programmers involved in production may be laid off or forced to work fewer hours. Employment of machinists involved in plant maintenance, however, is often more stable because proper maintenance and repair of costly equipment remain vital concerns even when production levels fall.

Earnings

Earnings of machinists compare favorably with those of other skilled workers. In 1996, median weekly earnings for machinists were about $550. Most earned between $410 and $700. The lowest paid 10 percent of all machinists had median weekly earnings of less than $310; the 10 percent with the highest earnings made more than $870 a week.

Related Occupations

Occupations most closely related to that of machinist and tool programmer are the other machining occupations. These include tool and die maker, metalworking and plastics-working machine operator, tool planner, and instrument maker. Workers in other occupations that require precision and skill in working with metal include blacksmiths, gunsmiths, locksmiths, metal patternmakers, and welders.

Tool programmers apply their knowledge of machining operations, metals, blueprints, and machine programming to write programs that run machine tools. Computer programmers also write detailed instructions for a machine—in this case, a computer.

Sources of Additional Information

For general information about this occupation, contact:
☛ The Precision Machined Products Association, 6700 West Snowville Rd., Brecksville, OH 44141.
☛ The National Tooling and Machining Association, 9300 Livingston Rd., Fort Washington, MD 20744.

Metalworking and Plastics-Working Machine Operators

(List of D.O.T. codes is available on request. See p. 496.)

Significant Points

- A few weeks of on-the-job training is sufficient for most workers to learn basic machine operations, but several years are required to become a skilled operator.

- Projected employment change in the occupation varies. Employment of most manual cutting and forming machine tool operators, and sheet metal workers, is expected to decline. Operators of automated machines will grow.

Nature of the Work

Consider the parts of a toaster, such as the metal or plastic housing or the lever that lowers the toast. These parts, and many other metal and plastic products, are produced by metalworking and plastics-working machine operators. In fact, machine tool operators in the metalworking and plastics industries play a major part in producing most of the consumer products on which we rely daily.

In general, these workers can be separated into two groups—those who set up machines for operation and those who tend the machines during production. Set-up workers prepare the machines prior to production and may adjust the machinery during operation. Operators and tenders, on the other hand, primarily monitor the machinery during operation, sometimes loading or unloading the machine or making minor adjustments to the controls. Many workers do both—set up and operate the equipment. Because the set-up process requires an understanding of the entire production process, setters usually have more training and are more highly skilled than those who simply operate or tend machinery. As new automation simplifies the setup process, however, less skilled workers are also increasingly able to set up machines for operation.

Setters, operators, tenders, and set-up operators are usually identified by the type of machine with which they work. Some examples of specific titles are screw machine operator, plastics-molding machine set-up operator, punch press operator, and lathe tender. Although some workers specialize in one or two types of machinery, many are trained to set up or operate a variety of machines. Job duties usually vary based on the size of the firm and on the type of machine being operated.

Metalworking machine setters and operators set up and tend machines that cut and form all types of metal parts. Traditionally, set-up workers plan and set up the sequence of operations according to blueprints, layouts, or other instructions. They adjust speed, feed, and other controls, choose the proper coolants and lubricants, and select the instruments or tools for each operation. Using micrometers, gauges, and other precision measuring instruments, they may also compare the completed work with the tolerance limits stated in the specifications.

Although there are many different types of metalworking machine tools that require specific knowledge and skills, most operators perform similar tasks. Whether tending grinding machines that remove excess material from the surface of machined products or presses that extrude metal through a die to form wire, operators usually perform simple, repetitive operations that can be learned quickly. Typically, these workers place metal stock in a machine on which the operating specifications have already been set. They may watch one or more machines and make minor adjustments according to their instructions. Regardless of the type of machine they operate, machine tenders usually depend on skilled set-up workers for major adjustments when the machines are not functioning properly.

Plastics-working machine operators set up and tend machines that transform plastic compounds—chemical-based products that can be produced in powder, pellet, or syrup form—into a wide variety of consumer goods such as toys, tubing, and auto parts. These products are produced by various methods, of which injection molding is the most common. The injection molding machine heats a plastic compound and forces it into a mold. After the part has cooled and hardened, the mold opens and the part is released. Many common kitchen products are produced using this method. To produce long parts such as pipes or window frames, an extruding machine is usually employed. These machines force a plastic compound through a die that contains an opening of the desired shape of the final product. Yet another type of plastics working technique is blow molding. Blow-molding machines force hot air into a mold which contains a plastic tube. As the air moves into the mold, the plastic tube is inflated to the shape of the mold and a plastic container is formed. The familiar 2-liter soft drink bottles are produced using this method.

Regardless of the process used, plastics-working machine operators check the materials feed, the temperature and pressure of the machine, and the rate at which the product hardens. Depending on the type of equipment in use, they may also load material into the machine, make minor adjustments to the machinery, or unload and inspect the finished products. Plastics-working machine operators also remove clogged material from molds or dies. Because molds and dies are quite costly, operators must exercise care to avoid damaging them.

Metalworking and plastics-working machine operators are increasingly being called upon to work with numerically controlled (NC) equipment. These machine tools have two major components—an electronic controller and a machine tool. Today, most NC machines are computer numerically controlled (CNC), which means

that the controllers are computers. The controller directs the mechanisms of the machine tool through the positioning and machining described in the program or instructions for the job. A program could contain, for example, commands that cause the controller to move a drill bit to certain spots on a workpiece and drill a hole at each spot.

Each type of CNC machine tool, such as a milling machine, a lathe, or a punch press, performs a specific task. A part may be worked on by several machines before it is finished. CNC machines are often used in computer-integrated manufacturing systems. In these systems, automated material handling equipment moves workpieces through a series of work stations where machining processes are computer numerically controlled. In some cases, the workpiece is stationary and the tools change automatically. Although the machining is done automatically, numerically controlled machine tools must be set up and used properly in order to obtain the maximum benefit from their use. These tasks are the responsibility of NC machine-tool operators or, in some instances, machinists. (See the statement on machinists and tool programmers elsewhere in the *Handbook*.)

Like the duties of manual metal and plastics machine operators, the duties of numerical-control machine-tool operators vary. In some shops, operators tend just one machine. More likely, however, they tend a number of machines or do some programming. As a result, the skill requirements of these workers vary from job to job. Although there are many variations in operators' duties, they generally involve many of the tasks described below.

Working from given instructions, operators load programs that are usually stored on disks into the controller. They also securely position the workpiece, attach the necessary tools, and check the coolants and lubricants. Many NC machines are equipped with automatic tool changers, so operators may also load several tools in the proper sequence. This entire process may require a few minutes or several hours, depending on the size of the workpiece and the complexity of the job.

A new program often must be adjusted to obtain the desired results. If the tool moves to the wrong position or makes a cut that is too deep, the program must be changed so the job is done properly. A machinist or tool programmer usually performs this function, occasionally with the assistance of a computer automated design program that simulates the operation of machine tools. (See the statement on machinists and tool programmers elsewhere in the *Handbook*.) However, a new generation of machine tool technology, known as direct numerical control, allows operators to make changes to the program and enter new specifications using minicomputers on the shop floor.

Because NC machine tools are very expensive, an important duty of operators is to monitor the machinery to prevent situations that could result in costly damage to the cutting tools or other parts. The extent to which the operator performs this function depends on the type of job as well as the type of equipment being used. Some NC machine tools automatically monitor and adjust machining operations. When the job has been properly set up and the program has been checked, the operator may only need to monitor the machine as it operates. These operators often set up and monitor more than one machine. Other jobs require frequent loading and unloading, tool changing, or programming. Operators may check the finished part using micrometers, gauges, or other precision inspection equipment to ensure that it meets specifications. Increasingly, however, this function is being performed by NC machine tools that are able to inspect products as they are produced.

CNC machines are changing the nature of the work that machine setters and operators perform. Computer-controlled machines simplify setups by using formerly tested computer programs for new workpieces. If a workpiece is similar to one previously produced, small adjustments can be made to the old program instead of developing a new program from scratch. Also, operators of this equipment have less physical interaction with the machinery or materials. They primarily act as "troubleshooters," monitoring machines on which the loading, forming, and unloading processes are often controlled by computers.

Machine operators increasingly need to acquire computer skills.

Working Conditions

Most metalworking and plastics-working machine operators work in areas that are clean, well lit, and well ventilated. Regardless of setting, all of these workers operate powerful, high-speed machines that can be dangerous if strict safety rules are not observed. Most operators wear protective equipment, such as safety glasses and earplugs to protect against flying particles of metal or plastic and noise from the machines. Other required equipment varies by work setting and machine. For example, workers in the plastics industry who work near materials that emit dangerous fumes or dust must wear face masks or self-contained breathing apparatuses.

Most metal and plastics-working machine operators work a 40-hour week, but overtime is common during periods of increased production. Because many metalworking and plastics-working shops operate more than one shift daily, some operators work nights and weekends.

The work requires stamina because operators are on their feet much of the day and may do moderately heavy lifting. Approximately one-third of these workers are union members; the metalworking industries have a higher rate of unionization than the plastics industry.

Employment

Metalworking and plastics-working machine operators held about 1,512,000 jobs in 1996. Of these, 1,420,000 were manual machine operators, and 92,000 were NC machine operators. About 8 out of every 10 metalworking and plastics-working machine operators are found in five manufacturing industries—fabricated metal products, industrial machinery and equipment, miscellaneous plastic products, transportation equipment, and primary metals. The following tabulation shows the distribution of employment of metalworking and plastics-working machine operators by detailed occupation.

Cutting and forming machine tool setters and operators	723,000
Molding machine setters and operators	228,000
Sheet metal workers and duct installers	120,000
Combination machine tool setters and operators	96,000
Numerical control machine operators	92,000
Metal fabricators, structural metal products	46,000
Plating machine setters and operators	42,000
Heat treating machine setters and operators	21,000
All other metal and plastics-working machine operators	144,000

Training, Other Qualifications, and Advancement

Metalworking and plastics-working machine operators learn their skills on the job. Trainees begin by observing and assisting experienced workers, often in formal training programs. Under supervision they may supply material, start and stop the machine, or remove finished products from the machine. As part of their training they advance to more difficult tasks like adjusting feed speeds, changing cutting tools, or inspecting a finished product for defects. Eventually they become responsible for their own machines.

The complexity of equipment largely determines the time required to become an operator. Most operators learn the basic machine operations and functions in a few weeks, but they may need several years to become a skilled operator or to advance to the more highly skilled job of set-up operator.

Set-up operators often need a thorough knowledge of the machinery and of the products being produced. They may study blueprints, plan the sequence of work, make the first production run, and determine which adjustments need to be made. Strong analytical abilities are particularly important to perform this job. Some companies have formal training programs for set-up operators that combine classroom instruction with on-the-job training.

CNC machine tool operators undergo similar training. Working under a supervisor or an experienced operator, trainees learn to set up and run one or more types of numerically controlled machine tools. They usually learn the basics of their jobs within a few months. However, the length of the training period varies with the number and complexity of the machine tools the operator will run and with the individual's ability. If the employer expects operators to write programs, trainees may attend programming courses offered by machine tool manufacturers or technical schools.

Although no special education is required for most operating jobs, employers prefer to hire applicants with good basic skills. Many require employees to have a high school education and to read, write, and speak English. This is especially true for NC machine operators, who may need to be retrained often in order to learn to operate new equipment. Because machinery is becoming more complex and shop floor organization is changing, employers increasingly look for persons with good communication and interpersonal skills. Mechanical aptitude, manual dexterity, and experience working with machinery are also helpful. Those interested in becoming metalworking or plastics-working machine operators can improve their employment opportunities by completing high school courses in shop, mathematics, and blueprint reading and by gaining a working knowledge of the properties of metals and plastics.

Advancement for operators usually takes the form of higher pay, although there are some limited opportunities for operators to advance to new positions as well. For example, they can become multiple machine operators, set-up operators, or trainees for the more highly skilled positions of machinist or tool and die maker. Manual machine operators can move on to CNC equipment when it is introduced in their establishments. Some set-up workers and CNC operators may advance to supervisory positions. CNC operators who have substantial training in NC programming may advance to the higher-paying job of tool programmer. (See the statements on machinists and tool programmers, and tool and die makers elsewhere in the *Handbook*.)

Job Outlook

Divergent employment trends are expected over the 1996-2006 period among the various metalworking and plastics-working machine operators. In general, employment of these workers will be affected by the rate of technological implementation, the demand for the goods they produce, the effects of trade, and the reorganization of production processes. These trends are expected to spur employment growth among NC machine operators, combination machine tool operators, plastics molding machine operators, and a number of miscellaneous operating positions. On the other hand, employment is projected to decline in some of the more traditional operator occupations, such as manual cutting and forming machine tool operators, and sheet metal workers. Despite differing rates of employment change, a large number of metalworking and plastics-working machine operator jobs will become available as workers transfer to other occupations or leave the labor force.

One of the most important factors influencing employment change in this occupation is the implementation of labor-saving machinery. In order to remain competitive, many firms are adopting new technologies, such as computer-controlled machine tools, to improve quality and lower production costs. Computer-controlled equipment allows operators to simultaneously tend a greater number of machines and often makes setup easier, thereby reducing the amount of time set-up workers spend on each machine. For these reasons, the lower-skilled positions of manual machine tool operators and tenders are more likely to be eliminated by this new technology because the functions they perform are more easily automated. The spread of new automation will lead to rising employment, however, for NC machine tool operators.

The demand for metalworking and plastics-working machine operators largely mirrors the demand for the parts they produce. Recent growth in the domestic economy, for example, has led to rebounding employment in a number of machine tool operating occupations. In addition, the consumption of plastic products has grown as they have been substituted for metal goods in many consumer and manufacturing products in recent years. Although the rate of substitution may slow in the future, this process is likely to continue and should result in stronger demand for machine operators in plastics than in metalworking. Both industries, however, face stiff foreign competition that is limiting the demand for domestically-produced parts. One way that larger U.S. producers have responded to this competition is by moving production operations to other countries where labor costs are lower. These moves are likely to continue and will further reduce employment opportunities for many metalworking and plastics-working machine tool operators in the United States.

Workers with a thorough background in machine operations, exposure to a variety of machines, and a good working knowledge of the properties of metals and plastics will be best able to adjust to this changing environment. In addition, new shopfloor arrangements will reward workers with good basic mathematics and reading skills, good communication skills, and the ability and willingness to learn new tasks. As workers are called upon to adapt to new production methods and to operate more machines, the number of combination machine tool operators will continue to rise.

Earnings
Median weekly earnings for most metalworking and plastics-working machine operators were about $440 in 1996. The middle 50 percent earned between $320 and $600. The top 10 percent earned over $770 and the bottom 10 percent earned less than $250. Metal and plastics molding, plating, heat-treating, and other processing machine operators earned somewhat less, about $400 a week. NC machine operators had median weekly earnings of about $520, more than either of these groups.

Earnings of production workers vary considerably by industry. The following tabulation shows 1996 average weekly wages for production workers in manufacturing industries where employment of metalworking and plastics-working machine operators is concentrated.

Transportation equipment	$760
Primary metals industries	660
Industrial machinery and equipment	590
Fabricated metal products	530
Rubber and miscellaneous plastics products	470

Related Occupations
Workers in occupations closely related to metalworking and plastics-working machine occupations include machinists, tool and die makers, extruding and forming machine operators producing synthetic fibers, woodworking machine operators, and metal patternmakers. Numerical-control machine-tool operators may program CNC ma-

chines or alter existing programs, which are functions closely related to those performed by NC machine tool programmers.

Sources of Additional Information
For general information about the metalworking trades, contact:
☛ The National Tooling and Machining Association, 9300 Livingston Rd., Fort Washington, MD 20744.
☛ The Precision Machined Products Association, 6700 West Snowville Rd., Brecksville, OH 44141.

Tool and Die Makers

(D.O.T. 601.260-010, -014, .280 except -038 and -054, .281-010, -014, -026, .380, .381 except -018 and -038; 739.381-018, -022)

Significant Points

- Tool and die makers learn their trade through 4 or 5 years of education and training—formal apprenticeship, postsecondary programs, or informal on-the-job training.

- Advancements in automation will contribute to the projected decline in employment; nevertheless, jobseekers with the appropriate skills and background should enjoy excellent opportunities.

Nature of the Work
Tool and die makers are among the most highly-skilled production workers in the economy. These workers produce tools, dies, and special guiding and holding devices that enable machines to manufacture a variety of products we use daily—from clothing and furniture to heavy equipment and parts for aircraft.

Toolmakers craft precision tools which are used to cut, shape, and form metal and other materials. They also produce jigs and fixtures (devices that hold metal while it is bored, stamped, or drilled) and gauges and other measuring devices. Diemakers construct metal forms (dies) that are used to shape metal in stamping and forging operations. They also make metal molds for diecasting and for molding plastics, ceramics, and composite materials. In addition to designing and producing new tools and dies, these workers may also repair worn or damaged tools, dies, gauges, jigs, and fixtures.

To perform these functions, tool and die makers employ many types of machine tools and precision measuring instruments. They must also be familiar with the machining properties, such as hardness and heat tolerance, of a wide variety of common metals and alloys. As a result, tool and die makers usually must have a much broader knowledge of machining operations, mathematics, and blueprint reading than most other machining workers.

Working from blueprints or instructions, tool and die makers first must plan the sequence of operations necessary to manufacture the tool or die. Next, they measure and mark the pieces of metal that will be cut to form parts of the final product. At this point, tool and die makers cut, bore, or drill the part as required, checking the accuracy of what they have done to ensure that the final product meets specifications. Finally, these workers assemble the parts and perform finishing jobs such as filing, grinding, and smoothing surfaces.

Modern technology is helping to change the ways that tool and die makers perform their jobs. For example, these workers increasingly use computer-aided design (CAD) to develop products and parts. Specifications from the computer program can then be used to electronically develop drawings for the required tools and dies. The electronic drawings are then processed by a computer-aided manufacturing program to calculate cutting tool paths and the sequence of operations. Once these instructions are developed, computer numerically controlled (CNC) machines usually are used to produce the die. Programs can also be electronically stored and adapted for future use. This saves time and increases worker productivity.

Many employers report difficulty in finding skilled tool and die makers.

Working Conditions

Tool and die makers usually work in toolrooms. These areas are quieter than the production floor because there are fewer machines in use at one time. Machines have guards and shields that minimize the exposure of workers to moving parts. Tool and die makers must follow safety rules and wear protective equipment, such as safety glasses to shield against bits of flying metal, earplugs to protect against noise, and gloves and masks to reduce exposure to hazardous lubricants and cleaners. These workers also need stamina, as they often spend much of the day on their feet and may do moderately heavy lifting.

Companies employing tool and die makers traditionally operate one shift per day. However, as the cost of new machinery and technology has increased, many employers now have more than one shift. Overtime and weekend work are common, especially during peak production periods.

Employment

Tool and die makers held about 134,000 jobs in 1996. Most worked in industries that manufacture metalworking machinery and equipment, motor vehicles, aircraft, and plastics products. Although they are found throughout the country, jobs are most plentiful in the Midwest and Northeast, where many of the metalworking industries are located.

Training, Other Qualifications, and Advancement

Tool and die makers learn their trade through 4 or 5 years of education and training—formal apprenticeship, postsecondary programs, or informal on-the-job training. The best way to learn all aspects of tool and die making, according to most employers, is a formal apprenticeship program that combines classroom instruction and job experience. These programs are increasingly rare, however. A growing number of tool and die makers receive most of their formal training from community and technical colleges.

Tool and die maker trainees learn to operate milling machines, lathes, grinders, and other machine tools. They also learn to use handtools in fitting and assembling tools, gauges, and other mechanical and metal-forming equipment. In addition, they study metalworking processes such as heat treating and plating. Classroom training usually consists of mathematics, mechanical drawing, tool designing, tool programming, and blueprint reading. Tool and die makers increasingly must learn to use CAD technology and CNC machine tools.

Workers who become tool and die makers without completing formal apprenticeships generally acquire their skills through a combination of informal on-the-job training and classroom instruction at a vocational school or community college. They often begin as machine operators and gradually take on more difficult assignments. Many machinists become tool and die makers. In fact, tool and die makers are often considered highly specialized machinists. (See the statement on machinists and tool programmers elsewhere in the *Handbook*.)

Because tools and dies must meet strict specifications—precision to one ten-thousandth of an inch is common—the work of tool and die makers requires a high degree of patience and attention to detail. Good eyesight is essential. Persons entering this occupation should also be mechanically inclined, able to work independently, and capable of doing work that requires concentration and physical effort.

There are several ways for skilled workers to advance. Some move into supervisory and administrative positions in their firms; others become tool designers or tool programmers; and a few may open their own shops.

Job Outlook

Employment of tool and die makers is expected to decline through the year 2006. Nevertheless, jobseekers with the appropriate skills and background should enjoy excellent opportunities, as employers across the Nation report difficulties in finding skilled workers to fill these positions. Many openings will be created each year by tool and die makers who retire. As more of these highly skilled workers retire, employers in certain parts of the country may face pronounced shortages. The shortage of new entrants in the field may be one of the factors retarding employment growth.

Apart from a shortage of new entrants, the projected decline in employment reflects advancements in automation, including CNC machine tools and computer-aided design. CNC machine tools have made tool and die makers more productive, while CAD and CAM have allowed some functions previously performed by these workers to be carried out by a computer and tool programmer. In addition, because precision metal products are a primary component of manufacturing machinery, increased imports of finished goods and precision metal products may lessen the demand for tool and die makers. These workers, however, are highly skilled and play a key role in the operation of many firms. As firms invest in new equipment and modify production techniques, they will continue to rely heavily on skilled tool and die makers for retooling. This fact, coupled with a growing demand for motor vehicles, aircraft, machinery, and other products that use machined metal parts, should help to moderate the decline in employment.

Earnings

Median weekly earnings for tool and die makers who worked full time were $720 in 1996. Most earned between $600 and $910 a week. Ten percent earned less than $480 a week, and the 10 percent with the highest weekly earnings made more than $1,160.

Related Occupations

The occupations most closely related to the work of tool and die makers are other machining occupations. These include machinist, mold maker, instrument maker, metalworking and plastics-working machine operator, and tool programmer.

Other occupations that require precision and skill in working with metal include blacksmith, gunsmith, locksmith, metal patternmaker, and welder.

Sources of Additional Information

For general information about tool and die makers, contact:

☛ The National Tooling and Machining Association, 9300 Livingston Rd., Ft. Washington, MD 20744.

☛ The Precision Machined Products Association, 6700 West Snowville Rd., Brecksville, OH 44141.

Welders, Cutters, and Welding Machine Operators

(D.O.T. 613.667-010; 614.684-010; 709.684-086; 727.662, .684-022; 810; 811; 812; 814; 815; 816 except .482 and .682; 819.281-010, -014, -022, .361, .381, .384, .684, and .685)

Significant Points

- Training for welders can range from a few weeks of school or on-the-job training for low skilled positions to several years of combined school and on-the-job training for highly skilled jobs.

- Although much of the welding done in manufacturing settings is increasingly being automated, there still will be a significant demand for welders in other areas, making for good employment opportunities.

Nature of the Work

Welding is the most common way of permanently joining metal parts. Heat is applied to the pieces to be joined, melting and fusing them to form a permanent bond. Because of its strength, welding is used to construct and repair ships, automobiles, spacecraft, and thousands of other manufactured products. Welding is used to join beams when constructing buildings, bridges, and other structures, and pipes in pipelines, nuclear power plants and refineries.

Welders use all types of welding equipment in a variety of positions, such as flat, vertical, horizontal, and overhead. They may perform manual welding, in which the work is entirely controlled by the welder, or semi-automatic welding, in which the welder uses machinery, such as a wire feeder, to help perform welding tasks. They generally plan work from drawings or specifications, or by analyzing damaged metal parts, using their knowledge of welding and metals. They select and set up welding equipment and examine welds to insure they meet standards or specifications. Some welders have more limited duties. They perform routine production work that has already been planned and laid out. These jobs do not require knowledge of all welding techniques.

In some production processes—in which the work is repetitive and the items to be welded are relatively uniform—automated welding is used. In this process, a machine performs the welding tasks while monitored by a welding machine operator. Welding machine operators set up and operate welding machines as specified by layouts, work orders, or blueprints. Operators must constantly monitor the machine to ensure that it produces the desired weld.

The work of arc, plasma, and flame cutters is closely related to that of welders. However, instead of joining metals, cutters use the heat from burning gases or an electric arc to cut and trim metal objects to specific dimensions. Cutters also dismantle large objects, such as ships, railroad cars, automobiles or aircraft. Some operate and monitor cutting machines similar to those used by welding machine operators.

Working Conditions

Welders and cutters are often exposed to potential hazards. They wear protective clothing, safety shoes, goggles, hoods with protective lenses, and other devices to prevent burns and eye injuries, and to protect them from falling objects. Automated welding machine operators are not exposed to as many hazards. A face shield or goggles generally provide adequate protection. Because some metals may give off toxic gases and fumes as they melt, Federal regulations require ventilation to meet strict guidelines to minimize these hazards. Occasionally, some workers are in contact with rust, grease, and dirt on metal surfaces. Some welders are isolated for short intervals while they work in booths constructed to contain sparks and glare. Welders often work in a variety of awkward positions, having to make welds while bending, stooping, or working overhead. In some settings, however, working conditions are much better and there are few haz-

Welders wear protective gear for welding metals in various production and repair tasks.

ards or discomforts. Overtime is sometimes necessary to complete special projects.

Employment

Welders, cutters, and welding machine operators held about 453,000 jobs in 1996. About 9 out of 10 welders and cutters were employed in manufacturing, services, construction, or wholesale trade. The majority of those in manufacturing were employed in transportation equipment, industrial machinery and equipment, or fabricated metal products. All welding machine operators were employed in manufacturing industries, primarily fabricated metal products, machinery, and motor vehicles. Almost 2 of 5 welders are employed in six States: Texas, California, Ohio, Pennsylvania, Michigan, and Illinois—States heavily dominated by automobile and fabricated metal products manufacturing, and by the petroleum and chemical industry.

Training, Other Qualifications, and Advancement

Training for welders can range from a few weeks of school or on-the-job training for low skilled positions to several years of combined school and on-the-job training for highly skilled jobs. Formal training is available in high schools, vocational schools, and postsecondary institutions such as vocational-technical institutes, community colleges, and private welding schools. The Armed Forces operate welding schools as well. Some employers provide training to help welders improve their skills. Courses in blueprint reading, shop mathematics, mechanical drawing, physics, chemistry, and metallurgy are helpful. A knowledge of computers is gaining importance, especially for welding machine operators, as some welders are becoming responsible for the programming of computer-controlled welding machines, including robots.

Some welders become certified, a process whereby the employer sends a worker to an institution, such as an independent testing lab or technical school, to weld a test specimen to specific codes and standards required by the employer. The testing procedures are based on the standards and codes set by one of several industry associations with which the employer may be affiliated. If the welding inspector at the examining institution determines that the worker has performed according to the employer's guidelines, he or she then certifies that the welder being tested is able to work with a particular welding procedure.

Welders and cutters need good eyesight, good hand-eye coordination, and manual dexterity. They should be able to concentrate on detailed work for long periods and be able to bend, stoop, and work in awkward positions. In addition, welders need to be adaptable, as it is becoming increasingly common for welders and cutters to receive cross-training for other production jobs.

Welders can advance to more skilled welding jobs with additional training and experience. They may be promoted to welding technicians, supervisors, inspectors, or instructors. Some experienced welders open their own repair shops.

Job Outlook

Opportunities for those who wish to become welders, cutters, and welding machine operators differ by occupational specialty. Employment of welders and cutters is expected to increase slowly, while that of welding machine operators should remain unchanged through the year 2006. Most job openings will result from the need to replace experienced workers who transfer to other occupations or leave the labor force. Certified welders, especially those certified in more than one process, will have much better employment opportunities than non-certified welders.

As research in welding technology expands, an increase in the use of automated and robotic welding techniques in manufacturing will result in the employment of welding machine operators staying about level, despite an expected increase in production. Manual welders, however, especially those with a wide variety of skills, will increasingly be needed for sophisticated fabrication tasks and repair work that do not lend themselves to automation. Also, the aging of the Nation's infrastructure is adding to the number of metal products needing repairs and will provide additional opportunities. Welders can expect to find more jobs in the business services industry as companies increasingly contract out repair and maintenance functions.

Welders, cutters, and welding machine operators in construction and manufacturing are vulnerable to periodic layoffs due to economic downturns.

Earnings

Median earnings for welders and cutters were about $478 a week in 1996. The middle 50 percent earned between $346 and $605. The top 10 percent earned more than $807, and the lowest 10 percent earned less than $278.

More than one-fourth of welders belong to unions. Among these are the International Association of Machinists and Aerospace Workers; the International Brotherhood of Boilermakers, Iron Ship Builders, Blacksmiths, Forgers and Helpers; the International Union, United Automobile, Aerospace and Agricultural Implement Workers of America; the United Association of Journeymen and Apprentices of the Plumbing and Pipe Fitting Industry of the United States and Canada; and the United Electrical, Radio, and Machine Workers of America.

Related Occupations

Welders and cutters are skilled metal workers. Other metal workers include blacksmiths, forge shop workers, all-round machinists, machine-tool operators, tool and die makers, millwrights, sheet-metal workers, boilermakers, and metal sculptors.

Welding machine operators run machines that weld metal parts. Others who run metalworking machines include lathe and turning, milling and planing, punching and stamping press, and rolling machine operators.

Sources of Additional Information

For information on training opportunities and jobs for welders, cutters, and welding machine operators, contact local employers, the local office of the State employment service, or schools providing welding training.

Information on careers in welding is available from:

☛ American Welding Society, 550 N.W. Lejeune Rd., Miami, FL 33126-5699.

For a list of accredited schools that offer training in welding, contact:

☛ Career College Association, 750 1st Street NE., Suite 900, Washington, DC 20002.

Plant and Systems Operators

Electric Power Generating Plant Operators and Power Distributors and Dispatchers

(D.O.T. 820.662-010; 951.685-010; 952.167-014, .362, .367-014, and .382)

Significant Points

- Little increase is expected in the employment of operators, distributors, and dispatchers as the electric utility industry restructures in response to deregulation and increasing competition.

- Construction of new power plants is expected to be curtailed due to the present overcapacity of electric power generators, creating few additional jobs.

- Helpers and laborers will have fewer opportunities to advance to operator positions due to shrinking employment and low turnover.

Nature of the Work

Electricity is vital for most of our everyday activities. From the moment you flip the first switch each morning, you are connecting to a huge network of people, electric lines, and generating equipment. Power plant operators control the machinery that generates electricity. Power distributors and dispatchers control the flow of electricity from the power plant over a network of transmission lines to industrial plants and substations, and finally over distribution lines to residential users.

Electric power generating plant operators who work in plants fueled by coal, oil, or natural gas regulate and monitor boilers, turbines, generators, auxiliary equipment such as coal crushers, ventilation equipment, electrical breakers, and switching gear. Operators distribute power demands among generators, combine the current from several generators, and monitor instruments to maintain voltage and regulate electricity flows from the plant. When power requirements change, they start or stop generators and connect or disconnect them from circuits. They increasingly use computers to keep records of switching operations and loads on generators, lines, and transformers; and prepare reports of unusual incidents, malfunctioning equipment, or maintenance performed during their shift.

Operators in newer plants with automated control systems work mainly in a central control room and usually are called control room operators and control room operator trainees or assistants. In older plants, the controls for the equipment are not centralized, and operators work throughout the plant, operating and monitoring valves, switches, and gauges. Job titles in older plants may be more varied than in newer plants. Auxiliary equipment operators work throughout the plant, while switchboard operators control the flow of electricity from a central point.

Operators of nuclear power plants are licensed by the Nuclear Regulatory Commission (NRC). They are authorized to operate

Keen competition is expected for jobs as power plant operators and power distributors and dispatchers.

equipment that affects the power of the reactor in a nuclear power plant. In addition, an NRC-licensed senior reactor operator acts as the supervisor of the plant for each shift, and supervises operation of all controls in the control room.

Power distributors and dispatchers, also called load dispatchers or systems operators, control the flow of electricity through transmission lines to industrial plants and substations that supply residential electric needs. They operate current converters, voltage transformers, and circuit breakers. Dispatchers monitor equipment and record readings at a pilot board, which is a map of the transmission grid system showing the status of transmission circuits and connections with substations and industrial plants.

Dispatchers also anticipate power needs such as those caused by changes in the weather. They call control room operators to start or stop boilers and generators to bring production into balance with needs. They handle emergencies such as transformer or transmission line failures and route current around affected areas. They also operate and monitor equipment in substations, which step up or step down voltage, and operate switchboard levers to control the flow of electricity in and out of substations.

Working Conditions
Because electricity is provided around the clock, operators, distributors, and dispatchers usually work one of three daily 8-hour shifts on a rotating basis. Shift assignments are changed periodically so that duty on less desirable shifts is shared by all operators. Work on rotating shifts can be stressful and fatiguing because of the constant change in living and sleeping patterns. Operators, distributors, and

dispatchers who work in control rooms generally sit or stand at a control station. This work is not physically strenuous, but requires constant attention. Operators who work outside the control room may be exposed to danger from electric shock, falls, and burns.

Nuclear power plant operators are subject to random drug and alcohol tests, as are most workers at nuclear power plants.

Employment
Electric power generating plant operators and power distributors and dispatchers held about 47,000 jobs in 1996. Jobs are located throughout the country. About 93 percent worked for utility companies and government agencies that produced electricity. Others worked for manufacturing establishments that produce electricity for their own use.

Training, Other Qualifications, and Advancement
Employers seek high school graduates for entry level operator, distributor, and dispatcher positions. Those with strong math and science skills are preferred. College level courses or prior experience in a mechanical or technical job may be helpful. Computer proficiency is increasingly being required by employers, as computers are used to keep records, generate reports, and track maintenance. Most entry level positions are in helper or laborer jobs in power plants or in other areas of the utility such as powerline construction. Depending on the results of aptitude tests, worker preferences, and availability of openings, workers may be assigned to train for any one of many utility positions in operations, maintenance, or other areas.

Workers selected for training as a power distributor or power plant operator at a fossil-fueled power plant undergo extensive on-the-job and classroom training provided by the employer. Several years of training and experience are required to become a fully qualified control room operator or power distributor. With further training and experience, workers may advance to shift supervisor. Because utilities generally promote from within, opportunities to advance by moving to another employer are limited.

Entrants to nuclear power plant operator trainee jobs must have strong math and science skills. Experience in other power plants or with Navy nuclear propulsion plants also is helpful. Extensive training and experience are necessary to pass the Nuclear Regulatory Commission's examinations for licensed reactor operator and senior reactor operator, including on-the-job and simulator training, classroom instruction, and individual study. Licensed reactor operators must pass an annual practical plant operation exam and a biennial written exam administered by their employer to maintain their license. With further training and experience, reactor operators may advance to senior reactor operators, who are qualified to be shift supervisors.

In addition to preliminary training as a power plant operator or power distributor or dispatcher, most workers are given periodic refresher training. Nuclear power plant operators are given frequent refresher training. This training is usually taken on plant simulators designed specifically to replicate the procedures and situations they might expect to encounter working at their plant.

Job Outlook
People who want to become power plant operators and power distributors and dispatchers are expected to encounter keen competition for these high-paying jobs, as slow growth in employment and low turnover in this occupation result in few job opportunities for the large number of eligible candidates.

Little increase in employment of electric power generating plant operators, distributors, and dispatchers is expected through the year 2006 as the industry restructures in response to deregulation and increasing competition. The Energy Policy Act of 1992 has had a tremendous impact on the organization of the utilities industry. This legislation enabled greater competition in power generating utilities by allowing independent power producers to sell their power directly to industrial and other wholesale customers. Utilities, historically operated as regulated local monopolies, are restructuring their operations to reduce costs and compete effectively, resulting in fewer jobs at all levels and reducing job security.

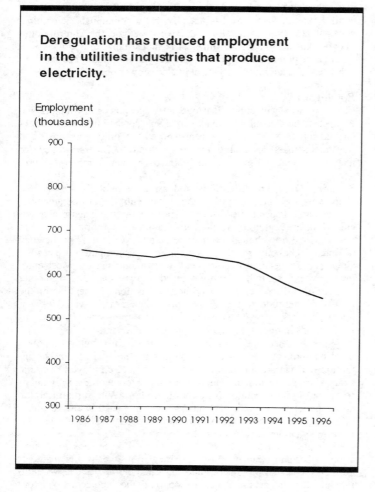

Deregulation has reduced employment in the utilities industries that produce electricity.

Employment
(thousands)

900

800

700

600

500

400

300

1986 1987 1988 1989 1990 1991 1992 1993 1994 1995 1996

Opportunities for those interested in working as power plant operators, distributors, and dispatchers will be affected by the pace of new plant construction and equipment upgrading. The pace of expansion in power generating capacity through the year 2006 is expected to be moderate because capacity was overbuilt in the past and growth in the demand for electricity is expected to continue to slow down. The increasing use of automatic controls and more efficient equipment should further offset the need for new plant construction and operators. Also, few new nuclear power plants are likely to be operational before the year 2006.

Earnings

Earnings in the electric utility industry are relatively high. According to the limited information available, median weekly earnings for conventional power plant operators were about $869 in 1996. According to information from union surveys, wages for fossil fuel power plant operators ranged from $498 to $1,100 weekly, averaging $837 in 1995. Nuclear power plant operators earned from about $862 to $1216 weekly, averaging $1,006 in 1995. Senior or chief operators in both nuclear and conventional power plants earned 10-15 percent more than operators. Over half of these workers are union members.

Related Occupations

Other workers who monitor and operate plant and systems equipment include stationary engineers, water and sewage treatment plant operators, waterworks pumpstation operators, chemical operators, and refinery operators.

Sources of Additional Information

For information about employment opportunities, contact local electric utility companies, locals of unions mentioned below, or an office of the State employment service.

For general information about power plant and nuclear reactor operators and power distributors and dispatchers, contact:
☛ International Brotherhood of Electrical Workers, 1125 15th St. NW., Washington, DC 20005.
☛ Utility Workers Union of America, 815 16th St. NW., Washington, DC 20006.

For a copy of Careers in Electric Power and a catalog of other guidance information, send $5 to:
☛ Edison Electric Institute, P.O. Box 2800, Kearneysville, WV 25430-2800.

Stationary Engineers

(D.O.T. 950.362-014, .382 except -014 and -022; .485, and .585)

Significant Points

• Equipment operated and maintained by stationary engineers is increasingly being controlled and monitored by automated systems.

• A license to operate boilers, ventilation, air conditioning, and other equipment is required in most States and cities.

Nature of the Work

Heating, air-conditioning, and ventilation systems are what keep large buildings comfortable all year long. Industrial plants often have facilities to provide electrical power, steam, or other services as well. Stationary engineers operate and maintain these systems, which can include boilers, air-conditioning and refrigeration equipment, diesel engines, turbines, generators, pumps, condensers, and compressors. These workers are called stationary engineers because the equipment they operate is similar to equipment operated by locomotive or marine engineers, except it is not on a moving vehicle.

Stationary engineers start up, regulate, and shut down equipment. They ensure that it operates safely, economically, and within established limits by monitoring meters, gauges, and other instruments, and computerized controls. They manually control equipment, and if necessary, make adjustments. They use hand and power tools to perform repairs and maintenance ranging from a complete overhaul to replacing defective valves, gaskets, or bearings. They also record relevant events and facts concerning operation and maintenance in an equipment log. On steam boilers, for example, they observe, control, and record steam pressure, temperature, water level and chemistry, power output, fuel consumption, and emissions. They watch and listen to machinery and routinely check safety devices, identifying and correcting any trouble that develops.

The mechanical systems of new buildings and plants are increasingly being run by stationary engineers using computers. Engineers monitor, adjust, and diagnose these systems from a central location or from a laptop computer linked into the buildings' communications network.

Stationary engineers also perform routine maintenance, such as lubricating moving parts, replacing filters, and removing soot and corrosion that can reduce operating efficiency. They test boiler water and add chemicals to prevent corrosion and harmful deposits. They also may check the air quality of the ventilation system and make adjustments to keep within mandated guidelines.

In a large building or industrial plant, a stationary engineer may be in charge of all mechanical systems in the building or an industrial power plant or engine room. Engineers may direct the work of assistant stationary engineers, turbine operators, boiler tenders, and air-conditioning and refrigeration operators and mechanics. In a small building or industrial plant, there may be only one stationary engineer. Some also perform other maintenance duties, such as carpentry, plumbing, and electrical repairs.

Working Conditions

Stationary engineers generally have steady year-round employment. They usually work a 5-day, 40-hour week. Many work one of three daily 8-hour shifts, and weekend and holiday work often is required.

Stationary engineers check boiler plant plans.

and heating plants. The increasing complexity of the equipment with which they work has made a high school diploma or its equivalent necessary. Many stationary engineers have some college education.

Apprenticeship programs are sponsored by the International Union of Operating Engineers, the principal union to which stationary engineers belong. In selecting apprentices, most local labor-management apprenticeship committees prefer applicants who have received instruction in mathematics, computers, mechanical drawing, machine-shop practice, physics, and chemistry. Mechanical aptitude, manual dexterity, and good physical condition also are important.

An apprenticeship usually lasts 4 years. In addition to 8,000 hours of on-the-job training, apprentices receive 600 hours of classroom instruction in boiler design and operation, basic chemistry and water treatment, elementary physics, pneumatics, refrigeration and air conditioning, electricity and electronics, computer systems, and other technical subjects.

Those who acquire their skills on the job usually start as helpers to experienced stationary engineers or as boiler tenders. This practical experience may be supplemented by postsecondary vocational training in computerized controls and instrumentation. However, becoming a stationary engineer without completing a formal apprenticeship program usually requires many years of work experience.

Most large and some small employers encourage and pay for skill-improvement training for their employees. Training is almost always provided when new equipment is introduced, usually by a representative of the machinery manufacturer, or when regulations concerning some aspect of their duties change.

Most States and cities have licensing requirements for stationary engineers. Applicants usually must be at least 18 years of age, reside for a specified period in the State or locality, meet experience requirements, and pass a written examination. Because of regional differences in licensing requirements, a stationary engineer who moves from one State or city to another may have to pass an examination for a new license.

Generally, there are several classes of stationary engineer licenses, each specifying the type of equipment or the steam pressure or horsepower of the equipment the engineer can operate without supervision. A licensed first-class stationary engineer is qualified to run a large facility, supervise others, and operate equipment of all types and capacities. An applicant for this license may be required to have a high school education, apprenticeship or on-the-job training, and several years of experience. Lower class licenses limit the types or capacities of equipment the engineer may operate without the supervision of a higher-rated engineer.

Stationary engineers advance by being placed in charge of larger, more powerful, or more varied equipment. Generally, engineers advance to these jobs as they obtain higher class licenses. Some stationary engineers advance to boiler inspectors, chief plant engineers, building and plant superintendents, or building managers. A few obtain jobs as examining engineers or technical instructors.

Engine rooms, power plants, and boiler rooms usually are clean and well lighted. Even under the most favorable conditions, however, some stationary engineers are exposed to high temperatures, dust, dirt, and high noise levels from the equipment. General maintenance duties may cause contact with oil and grease, as well as fumes or smoke. Workers spend much of their time on their feet. They may also have to crawl inside boilers and work in crouching or kneeling positions to inspect, clean, or repair equipment.

Because stationary engineers work around boilers as well as electrical and mechanical equipment, they must be alert to avoid burns, electric shock, and injury from moving parts. They also must be aware of exposure to hazardous materials such as asbestos and certain chemicals.

Employment

Stationary engineers held about 27,000 jobs in 1996. They worked in a wide variety of places, including factories, hospitals, hotels, office and apartment buildings, schools, and shopping malls. Some are employed as contractors to a building or plant.

Stationary engineers work throughout the country, generally in the more heavily populated areas where large industrial and commercial establishments are located.

Training, Other Qualifications, and Advancement

Most stationary engineers acquire their skills through a formal apprenticeship program or through informal on-the-job training which usually is supplemented by courses at trade or technical schools. In addition, a good background can be obtained in the Navy or the Merchant Marine because marine engineering plants are similar to many stationary power

Job Outlook

Persons wishing to become stationary engineers may face competition for job openings. Employment opportunities will be best for those with apprenticeship training or vocational school courses covering systems operation using computerized controls and instrumentation. Employment is expected to decline through the year 2006. Continuing commercial and industrial development will increase the amount of equipment to be operated and maintained. However, automated systems and computerized controls are making newly-installed equipment more efficient, thus reducing the number of jobs needed for their operation. Although some job openings will arise from the need to replace experienced workers who transfer to other occupations or leave the labor force, turnover in this occupation is low, partly due to its high wages, and relatively few replacement openings are expected.

Earnings

In 1996, the median weekly earnings for stationary engineers who worked full time were about $621. The middle 50 percent earned between $466 and $814 a week; 10 percent earned less than $341 a week; and 10 percent earned more than $1,037.

Related Occupations

Other workers who monitor and operate stationary machinery include nuclear reactor operators, power station operators, water and wastewater treatment plant operators, waterworks pump-station operators, chemical operators, and refinery operators. Often workers who operate and maintain all of the equipment in a building or plant are called general maintenance mechanics.

Sources of Additional Information

Information about apprenticeships and vocational training or work opportunities is available from local offices of State employment services, locals of the International Union of Operating Engineers, vocational schools, and from State and local licensing agencies.

Specific questions about this occupation should be addressed to:
☛ International Union of Operating Engineers, 1125 17th St. NW., Washington, DC 20036.
☛ National Association of Power Engineers, Inc., 1 Springfield St., Chicopee, MA 01013.
☛ Building Owners and Managers Institute International, 1521 Ritchie Hwy., Suite 3A, Arnold, MD 21403.

Water and Wastewater Treatment Plant Operators

(D.O.T. 954.382-010, -014; 955.362-010, .382, and .585)

Significant Points

- Employment is concentrated in local government and private water supply and sanitary services companies.

- In 49 States, operators must pass exams certifying that they are capable of overseeing various treatment processes.

- Educational requirements are increasing as treatment plants become more complex to meet new water pollution control regulations.

Nature of the Work

Clean water is essential for good health, recreation, fish and wildlife, and industry. Water treatment plant operators treat water so that it is safe to drink. Wastewater treatment plant operators remove harmful pollutants from domestic and industrial wastewater so that it is safe to return to the environment.

Water is pumped from wells, rivers, and streams to water treatment plants where it is treated and distributed to customers. Wastewater is collected from customers, traveling through sewer pipes to wastewater treatment plants where it is treated and returned to streams, rivers, and oceans, or reused for irrigation and landscaping. Operators in both types of plants control processes and equipment to remove solid materials, chemical compounds, and micro-organisms from the water or to render them harmless. They also control pumps, valves, and other processing equipment to move the water or wastewater through the various treatment processes, and dispose of the waste materials removed from the water.

Operators read and interpret meters and gauges to make sure plant equipment and processes are working properly and adjust controls as needed. They operate chemical-feeding devices, take samples of the water or wastewater, perform chemical and biological laboratory analyses, and test and adjust the amount of chemicals such as chlorine in the water. Operators also make minor repairs to valves, pumps, and other equipment. They use a variety of instruments to sample and measure water quality, gauges, and common hand and power tools to make repairs.

Water and wastewater treatment plant operators increasingly rely on computers to help monitor equipment, store sampling results, make process control decisions, schedule and record maintenance activities, and produce reports. When problems occur, operators may use their computers to determine the cause of and solution to the malfunction.

Occasionally operators must work under emergency conditions. A heavy rainstorm, for example, may cause large amounts of wastewater to flow into sewers, exceeding a plant's treatment capacity. Emergencies also can be caused by conditions inside a plant, such as chlorine gas leaks or oxygen deficiencies. To handle these conditions, operators are trained in emergency management response using special safety equipment and procedures to protect public health and the facility. During these periods, operators may work under extreme pressure to correct problems as quickly as possible. These periods may create dangerous working conditions and operators must be extremely cautious.

The specific duties of plant operators depend on the type and size of plant. In smaller plants, one operator may control all machinery, perform tests, keep records, handle complaints, and do repairs and maintenance. A few operators may handle both a water treatment and a wastewater treatment plant. In larger plants with many employees, operators may be more specialized and only monitor one process. The staff may also include chemists, engineers, laboratory technicians, mechanics, helpers, supervisors, and a superintendent.

Water pollution standards have become increasingly stringent since adoption of two major Federal environmental statutes: the Clean Water Act of 1972, which implemented a national system of regulation on the discharge of pollutants, and the Safe Drinking Water Act of 1974, which established standards for drinking water. Industrial facilities that send their wastes to municipal treatment plants must meet certain minimum standards and ensure that these wastes have been adequately pretreated so that they do not damage municipal treatment facilities. Municipal water treatment plants also must meet stringent drinking water standards. The list of contaminants regulated by these statutes has grown over time. For example, the 1996 Safe Drinking Water Act Amendments includes standards for the monitoring of cryptosporidium and giardia, two biological organisms that have caused health problems recently. Operators must be familiar with the guidelines established by Federal regulations and how they affect their plant. In addition to Federal regulations, op-

Wastewater treatment plant operators take water samples.

erators also must be aware of any guidelines imposed by the State or locality in which the plant operates.

Working Conditions

Water and wastewater treatment plant operators work both indoors and outdoors and may be exposed to noise from machinery and some unpleasant odors, although chemicals may be used to minimize these. Operators have to stoop, reach, and climb and sometimes get their clothes dirty. They must pay close attention to safety procedures for they may be confronted with hazardous conditions, such as slippery walkways, dangerous gases, and malfunctioning equipment. Because plants operate 24 hours a day, 7 days a week, operators work one of three 8-hour shifts and weekends and holidays on a rotational basis. Whenever emergencies arise, operators may be required to work overtime.

Employment

Water and wastewater treatment plant operators held about 98,000 jobs in 1996. The vast majority worked for local governments. Some worked for private water supply and sanitary services companies, which increasingly provide operation and management services to local governments on a contract basis. About half worked as water treatment plant operators and half worked as wastewater treatment plant operators.

Water and wastewater treatment plant operators are employed throughout the country, with most jobs in larger towns and cities. Although nearly all work full time, those who work in small towns may only work part time at the water or wastewater treatment plant— the remainder of their time may be spent handling other municipal duties.

Training, Other Qualifications, and Advancement

Trainees usually start as attendants or operators-in-training and learn their skills on the job under the direction of an experienced operator. They learn by observing the processes and equipment in operation and by doing routine tasks such as recording meter readings; taking samples of wastewater and sludge; and doing simple maintenance and repair work on pumps, electric motors, valves, and other plant equipment. Larger treatment plants generally combine this on-the-job training with formal classroom or self-paced study programs.

Operators need mechanical aptitude and should be competent in basic mathematics, as they need to apply data to formulas of treatment requirements, flow levels, and concentration levels. Because of the introduction of computer-controlled equipment and more sophisticated instrumentation, a high school diploma generally is required. In addition, employers prefer those who have had high school courses in chemistry, biology, and mathematics.

Some positions, particularly in larger cities and towns, are covered by civil service regulations, and applicants may be required to pass written examinations testing elementary mathematics skills, mechanical aptitude, and general intelligence.

Some 2-year programs leading to an associate degree in water and/or wastewater technology and 1-year programs leading to a certificate are available. These provide a good general knowledge of water and wastewater treatment processes as well as basic preparation for becoming an operator. Because plants are becoming more complex, completion of such courses increases an applicant's chances for employment and promotion.

Most State drinking water and water pollution control agencies offer training courses to improve operators' skills and knowledge. These courses cover principles of treatment processes and process control, laboratory procedures, maintenance, management skills, collection systems, safety, chlorination, sedimentation, biological treatment, sludge treatment and disposal, and flow measurements. Some operators take correspondence courses on subjects related to water and wastewater treatment, and some employers pay part of the tuition for related college courses in science or engineering.

As operators are promoted, they become responsible for more complex treatment processes. Some operators are promoted to plant supervisor or superintendent, while others advance by transferring to a larger facility. Some postsecondary training in water and wastewater treatment coupled with increasingly responsible experience as an operator may be sufficient to qualify for superintendent of a small plant, since at many small plants the superintendent also serves as an operator. However, educational requirements are rising as larger, more complex treatment plants are built to meet new drinking water and water pollution control standards. With each promotion, the operator must have greater knowledge of Federal, State, and local regulations. Superintendents of large plants generally need an engineering or science degree. A few operators get jobs with State drinking water or water pollution control agencies as technicians, who monitor and provide technical assistance to plants throughout the State. Vocational-technical school or community college training generally is preferred for technician jobs. Experienced operators may transfer to related jobs with industrial wastewater treatment plants, companies selling water or wastewater treatment equipment and chemicals, engineering consulting firms, or vocational-technical schools.

In 49 States, operators must pass an examination to certify that they are capable of overseeing wastewater treatment plant operations. A voluntary certification program is in effect in the remaining State. Typically, there are different levels of certification depending on the operator's experience and training. Higher certification levels qualify the operator for a wider variety of treatment processes. Certification requirements vary by State, and by size of treatment plants. While relocation may mean having to become certified in a new location, many States accept other States' certifications.

There is presently no nationally mandated certification program for operators. However, the Safe Drinking Water Act Amendments of 1996 require that within 2 years the Environmental Protection Agency specify minimum standards for drinking water operator certification, and that States implement those standards within another 2 years.

Job Outlook

Those who wish to become water and wastewater treatment plant operators should have good opportunities through the year 2006. Despite job growth that is expected to be faster than average, the number of applicants in this field is normally low, making for good job prospects for qualified applicants.

The increasing population and growth of the economy are expected to increase demand for water and wastewater treatment services. As new plants are constructed to meet this demand, employment of water and wastewater treatment plant operators should increase. In addition, some job openings will occur as experienced operators transfer to other occupations or leave the labor force.

Although local government is the largest employer of water and wastewater treatment plant operators, increased reliance on private firms specializing in the operation and management of water and wastewater treatment facilities should shift some employment demand to these companies. Increased pre-treatment activity by manufacturing firms should also create new job opportunities.

Water and wastewater treatment plant operators generally have steady employment because the services they provide are essential and required by law.

Earnings

Water and wastewater treatment plant operators had median weekly earnings of $551 in 1996; the lowest paid 10 percent of the occupation earned about $313 a week, the middle 50 percent of the occupation earned between $392 and $703 a week, and the top 10 percent earned about $808 a week. According to information from union surveys, wages for water and wastewater treatment plant operators ranged from $335 to $1,034 weekly, averaging $668 in 1995. Salaries depend, among other things, on the size and location of the plant, the complexity of the operator's job, and the operator's level of certification.

In addition to their annual salaries, water and wastewater treatment plant operators generally receive benefits that include health and life insurance, a retirement plan, and educational reimbursement for job-related courses.

Related Occupations

Other workers whose main activity consists of operating a system of machinery to process or produce materials include boiler operators, gas-compressor operators, power plant operators, power reactor operators, stationary engineers, turbine operators, chemical plant operators, and petroleum refinery operators.

Sources of Additional Information

For information on certification, contact:
☛ Association of Boards of Certification, 208 Fifth St., Ames, IA 50010-6259.

For educational information on careers as a water treatment plant operator, contact:
☛ American Water Works Association, 6666 West Quincy Ave., Denver, CO 80235.
☛ Water Environment Federation, 601 Wythe St., Alexandria, VA 22314.

For information on jobs, contact State or local water pollution control agencies, State water and waste water operator associations, State environmental training centers, or local offices of the State employment service.

Printing Occupations

Bindery Workers

(D.O.T. 653.360, .382, .662, .682, .685; 692.685-146; 794.687-026; and 977.381 and .684-026)

Significant Points

- Most learn their jobs through on-the-job training.
- The majority of jobs are in commercial printing plants.
- Opportunities for hand bookbinders are limited by the small number of establishments that do this highly specialized work.

Nature of the Work

The process of combining printed sheets into finished products such as books, magazines, catalogs, folders, directories, or product packaging is known as "binding." Binding involves cutting, folding, gathering, gluing, stapling, stitching, trimming, sewing, wrapping, and other finishing operations. Bindery workers operate and maintain the machines that perform these various tasks.

Job duties depend on the kind of material being bound. In firms that do *edition binding*, for example, workers bind books produced in large numbers, or "runs." *Job binding* workers bind books produced in smaller quantities. In firms specializing in *library binding*, workers repair books and provide other specialized binding services to libraries. *Pamphlet binding* workers produce leaflets and folders, and *manifold binding* workers bind business forms such as ledgers and books of sales receipts. *Blankbook binding* workers bind blank pages to produce notebooks, checkbooks, address books, diaries, calendars, and note pads.

Some binding consists of only one step. Preparing leaflets or newspaper inserts, for example, requires only folding. Binding of books and magazines, on the other hand, requires the steps that follow.

Bookbinders assemble books and magazines from large, flat, printed sheets of paper. Machines are used extensively throughout the process. Skilled bookbinders operate machines that first fold printed sheets into units known as "signatures," which are groups of pages arranged sequentially. Bookbinders then sew, stitch, or glue the assembled signatures together, shape the book bodies with presses and trimming machines, and reinforce them with glued fabric strips. Covers are created separately, and glued, pasted, or stitched onto the book bodies. The books then undergo a variety of finishing operations, often including wrapping in paper jackets.

A small number of bookbinders work in hand binderies. These highly skilled workers design original or special bindings for limited editions, or restore and rebind rare books. The work requires creativity, knowledge of binding materials, and a thorough background in the history of binding. Hand bookbinding gives individuals the opportunity to work at the greatest variety of jobs.

Bindery workers in small shops may perform many binding tasks, while those in large shops are usually assigned only one or a few operations, such as operating complicated paper cutters or folding machines. Others specialize in adjusting and preparing equipment, and may perform minor repairs as needed.

Working Conditions

Binderies are often noisy and jobs can be fairly strenuous, requiring considerable lifting, standing, and carrying. They may also require stooping, kneeling, and crouching. Binding often resembles an assembly line, and workers should not mind performing repetitive tasks.

Employment

In 1996, bindery workers held about 86,000 jobs, including just under 4,400 working as skilled bookbinders and over 81,000 working as lesser skilled bindery machine operators.

Although some bindery workers are employed by large libraries and book publishers, the majority of jobs are in commercial printing plants. Few publishers maintain their own manufacturing facilities, so most contract out the printing and assembly of books to commercial printing plants or bindery trade shops. Bindery trade shops, the second largest employer of bindery workers, specialize in binding for printers without binderies, or whose printing production exceeds their binding capabilities.

Bindery workers are employed in all parts of the country, but jobs are concentrated near large metropolitan areas such as New York, Chicago, Washington, DC, Los Angeles, Philadelphia, and Dallas.

Bindery workers assemble a large variety of printed materials.

Training, Other Qualifications, and Advancement
For bindery jobs, employers prefer high school graduates with basic mathematics and language skills. Accuracy, patience, neatness, and good eyesight are also important. Bindery work requires careful attention to detail. Mistakes at this stage in the printing process may require redoing work from the previous printing stages, and so can be quite costly. Manual dexterity is essential in order to count, insert, paste, and fold. Mechanical aptitude is needed to operate the newer, more automated equipment. Artistic ability and imagination are necessary for hand bookbinding.

Most bindery workers learn the craft through on-the-job training. Inexperienced workers are usually assigned simple tasks such as moving paper from cutting machines to folding machines. They learn basic binding skills, including the characteristics of paper and how to cut large sheets of paper into different sizes with the least amount of waste. As workers gain experience, they advance to more difficult tasks and learn to operate one or more pieces of equipment. Generally, it takes 1 to 3 months to learn to operate the simpler machines but it can take up to 1 year to become completely familiar with more complex equipment, such as computerized binding machines.

Employers prefer to hire and train workers with some basic knowledge of binding operations. High school students interested in bindery careers can gain some exposure to the craft by taking shop courses or attending a vocational-technical high school. Occupational skill centers, usually operated by labor unions, also provide an introduction.

Formal apprenticeships are not as common as they used to be, but are still offered by some employers. They provide a more structured program that enables workers to acquire the high levels of specialization and skill needed for some bindery jobs. For example, a 4-year apprenticeship is usually necessary to teach workers how to restore rare books and to produce valuable collectors' items.

Training in graphic arts is also an asset. Postsecondary programs in the graphic arts are offered by vocational-technical institutes, skill updating or retraining programs, and community and junior colleges. Some updating and retraining programs require students to have bindery experience; other programs are available through unions for members. Four-year colleges also offer programs, but their emphasis is on preparing people for careers as graphic artists or managers in the graphic arts field. To keep pace with ever-changing technology, occasional retraining will become increasingly important for bindery workers.

Without additional training, advancement opportunities outside of bindery work are limited. In large binderies, experienced bookbinders may advance to supervisory positions.

Job Outlook
Employment of bindery workers is expected to grow more slowly than the average for all occupations through the year 2006 as demand for printed material grows, but productivity in bindery operations increases. Most job openings for bindery workers will result from the need to replace experienced workers who change jobs or leave the labor force.

Growth of the printing industry will continue to spur demand for bindery workers by commercial printers. The volume of printed material should grow due to increased marketing of products through catalogs, newspaper inserts, and direct mail advertising. Book publishing is expected to grow slowly. Rising school enrollments and the expanding middle-aged and older population—age groups that do the most leisure reading—will account for most of this growth.

Even though major technological changes are not anticipated, binding is becoming increasingly mechanized as computers are attached to, or associated with binding equipment. New "in-line" equipment performs a number of operations in sequence, beginning with raw stock and ending with a complete finished product. Technological advances such as automatic tabbers, counters, palletizers and joggers reduce labor and improve the appearance of the finished product. These improvements are increasingly inducing printing companies to invest in in-house binding and finishing equipment. Growth in demand for special skills for bindery workers who assist skilled bookbinders will be slowed as binding machinery continues to become more efficient.

The growth of product packaging, such as that required for CD-ROMS, videos, and other business and educational products, is contributing to the relative stability of binding services. The packaging of these items typically involves folding, gluing, finishing and shrink wrapping.

Opportunities for hand bookbinders are limited by the small number of establishments that do this highly specialized work. Experienced bindery workers will have the best opportunities.

Earnings
Bindery workers in 1996 had median weekly earnings of about $408. The middle 50 percent earned about $312 to $627 a week. The lowest paid 10 percent earned less than $215 a week, while the highest paid 10 percent earned $958 a week or more. Workers covered by union contracts generally had higher earnings.

Related Occupations
Other workers who set up and operate production machinery include papermaking machine operators, printing press operators, and various precision machine operators.

Sources of Additional Information
Information about apprenticeships and other training opportunities may be obtained from local printing industry associations, local bookbinding shops, local offices of the Graphic Communications International Union, or local offices of the State employment service.

For general information on bindery occupations, write to:
☛ Graphic Communications International Union, 1900 L St. NW., Washington, DC 20036.

For information on careers and training programs in printing and the graphic arts, contact:
☛ Education Council of the Graphic Arts Industry, 1899 Preston White Dr., Reston, VA 20191.
☛ PIA-Printing Industries of America, Inc. 100 Daingerfield Rd., Alexandria, VA 22314.

Prepress Workers

(A list of D.O.T. codes is available upon request. See page 496.)

Significant Points
- The nature of work has changed greatly due to computers.
- Increased use of computers in typesetting and page layout should eliminate many prepress jobs.
- Some kinds of prepress work are rapidly becoming obsolete.

Nature of the Work
The printing process has three stages—prepress, press, and binding or finishing. Prepress workers prepare material for printing presses. They perform a variety of tasks involved with transforming text and pictures into finished pages and making printing plates of the pages.

As personal computers have come into more widespread use, advances in computer software and printing technology continue to change prepress work. Much of the typesetting and page layout work formerly done by prepress workers is increasingly done by customers on their computers. Customers, as well as prepress workers, are able to use their computers to produce material that looks like the desired finished product. This change, called "desktop publishing," poses new challenges for the printing industry. Instead of receiving simple typed text from customers, prepress workers get the material on a computer disk, and instead of relying on prepress workers to suggest a format, customers are increasingly likely to have already settled on one by experimenting on their personal computers. The printing industry is rapidly moving toward complete "digital imaging," by which customers' material received on computer disks is converted directly into printing plates. Other innovations in prepress work include digital color page makeup systems, electronic page layout systems, and off-press color proofing systems.

Typesetting and page layout have been greatly affected by technological changes. Today, composition work is done with computers and "cold type" technology. The old "hot type" method of text composition—which used molten lead to create individual letters, paragraphs, and full pages of text—is nearly extinct. Cold type, which is any of a variety of methods creating type without molten lead, has traditionally used "phototypesetting" to ready text and pictures for printing. Although this method has many variations, all use photography to create positive images on paper. The images are assembled into page format and rephotographed to create film negatives from which the actual printing plates are made. However, newer cold type methods are becoming more common. These automate the photography or make printing plates directly from material in a computer.

In one common form of phototypesetting, text is entered into a computer programmed to hyphenate, space, and create columns of text. Keyboarding of text may be done by typesetters or data entry clerks at the printing establishment or, increasingly, by the author before the job is sent out for composition. The coded text is then transferred to a typesetting machine which uses photography, a cathode-ray tube, or a laser to create an image on typesetting paper or film. Once it has been developed, the paper or film is sent to a lithographer who makes the actual printing plate.

Desktop publishing specialists use a keyboard to enter and select the size and style of type, the column width, and appropriate spacing, and to store it in the computer. The computer then displays and arranges columns of type on a screen resembling a television screen. An entire newspaper page, complete with artwork and graphics, can be made up on the screen exactly as it will appear in print. Operators transmit the pages for production into film and then into plates, or directly into plates, eliminating the role of paste up artists. *Preflight technicians* edit the work of the desktop publishing specialists and ensure the overall quality of the finished product before it is delivered to the customer. In small shops, *job printers* may be responsible for composition and page layout, reading proofs for errors and clarity, correcting mistakes, and printing.

New technologies are also affecting the roles of other composition workers. Improvements in desktop publishing software allow customers to do more of their own typesetting. Laser printers, or "imagesetters" read text from computer memory and then "beam" it directly onto film, paper, or plates, bypassing the slower photographic process traditionally used.

With traditional photographic processes, the material is arranged and typeset, and then passed on to workers who further prepare it for the presses. *Camera operators* are generally classified as line camera operators, halftone operators, or color separation photographers. Line camera operators start the process of making a lithographic plate by photographing and developing film negatives or positives of the material to be printed. They adjust light and expose film for a specified length of time, and then develop film in a series of chemical baths. They may load unexposed film in machines that automatically develop and fix the image. The use of film in printing will decline as electronic imaging becomes more prevalent. With decreased costs and improved quality, electronic imaging has become the method of choice in the industry.

The printing process requires that images be made up of tiny dots coming together to form a picture. Photographs cannot be reprinted without them. When normal "continuous tone" photographs need to be reproduced, halftone camera operators separate the photograph into pictures containing the dots. Color separation photography is more complex. In this process, camera operators produce four-color separation negatives from a continuous-tone color print or transparency which is being reproduced.

More of this separation work will be done electronically in the future on scanners. *Scanner operators* use computerized equipment to create film negatives or positives of photographs or art. The computer controls the color separation of the scanning process, and with

Technology continues to have a significant effect on prepress work.

the help of the operator, corrects for mistakes, or compensates for deficiencies in the original color print or transparency. Each scan produces a dotted image, or halftone, of the original in one of four primary colors—yellow, magenta, cyan, and black. The images are used to produce printing plates that print each of these colors, with transparent color inks, one at a time. These produce "secondary" color combinations of red, green, blue, and black which can then be combined to produce all the colors and hues of the original photograph.

Scanners which can perform color correction during the color separation procedure are rapidly replacing *lithographic dot etchers,* who retouch film negatives or positives by sharpening or reshaping images. They do the work by hand, using chemicals, dyes, and special tools. Dot etchers must know the characteristics of all types of paper and must produce fine shades of color. Like camera operators, they are usually assigned to only one phase of the work, and may have job titles such as dot etcher, retoucher, or letterer.

New technology is also lessening the need for *film strippers,* who cut the film to required size and arrange and tape the negatives onto "flats"—or layout sheets used by platemakers to make press plates. When completed, flats resemble large film negatives of the text in its final form. In large printing establishments such as newspapers, arrangement is done automatically.

Platemakers use a photographic process to make printing plates. The film assembly or flat is placed on top of a thin metal plate treated with a light-sensitive chemical. Exposure to ultraviolet light activates the chemical in parts not protected by the film's dark areas. The plate is then developed in a special solution that removes the unexposed nonimage area, exposing bare metal. The chemical on areas of the plate exposed to the light hardens and becomes water repellent. The hardened parts of the plate form the text.

A growing number of printing plants use lasers to directly convert electronic data to plates without any use of film. Entering, storing, and retrieving information from computer-aided equipment requires technical skills. In addition to operating and maintaining the equipment, lithographic platemakers must make sure that plates meet quality standards.

During the printing process, the plate is first covered with a thin coat of water. The water adheres only to the bare metal nonimage areas, and is repelled by the hardened areas that were exposed to light. Next, the plate comes in contact with a rubber roller covered with an oil-based ink. Because oil and water do not mix, the ink is repelled by the water-coated area and sticks to the hardened areas. The ink covering the hardened text is transferred to paper.

Technological changes will continue in the prepress area as hand work is automated. Although computers will perform a wider variety of tasks, printing will still involve text composition, page layout, and plate making, so printing will still require prepress workers. Computer skills will be increasingly important to prepress workers. These workers will, however, need to demonstrate a desire and an ability to benefit from the frequent retraining required by rapidly changing technology.

Working Conditions

Prepress workers usually work in clean, air-conditioned areas with little noise. Some workers, such as typesetters and compositors, may develop eyestrain from working in front of a video display terminal, or musculoskeletal problems, such as backaches. Lithographic artists and film strippers may find working with fine detail tiring to the eyes. Platemakers, who may work with toxic chemicals, face the hazard of skin irritations. Stress may be an important factor as workers are often subject to the pressures of shorter deadlines and tighter work schedules.

Prepress employees generally work an 8-hour day. Some workers—particularly those employed by newspapers—work night shifts, weekends, and holidays.

Employment

Prepress workers held about 155,000 jobs in 1996. Employment was distributed as follows:

Prepress precision workers

Desktop publishing specialists	30,000
Film strippers, printing	26,000
Job printers	15,000
Paste-up workers	15,000
Platematers	14,000
Camera operators	11,000
Compositors and typesetters	6,500
Photoengravers	4,800
All other precision printing workers	13,000

Prepress machine operators

Typesetting and composing machine operators	14,000
Photoengraving and lithographic machine operators	5,500

Most prepress jobs were found in firms that handle commercial or business printing, and in newspaper plants. Commercial printing firms print newspaper inserts, catalogs, pamphlets, and advertisements, while business form establishments print material such as sales receipts. Additional jobs are found in printing trade service firms and "in-plant" operations. Establishments in printing trade services typically perform custom compositing, platemaking, and related prepress services.

The printing and publishing industry is one of the most geographically dispersed in the United States, and prepress jobs are found throughout the country. However, job prospects may be best in large printing centers such as New York, Chicago, Los Angeles, Philadelphia, Washington DC, and Dallas.

Training, Other Qualifications, and Advancement

The length of training required for prepress jobs varies by occupation. Some, such as typesetting, can be learned in only a few months, but they are the most likely to be automated. Others, such as stripping, require years of experience to master. Nevertheless, even workers in these occupations should expect to receive intensive retraining. Workers often start as helpers who are selected for on-the-job training programs once they demonstrate their reliability and interest in learning the job. They begin instruction with an experienced craft worker and advance based on their demonstrated mastery of skills at each level of instruction. All workers should expect to be retrained from time to time to handle new, improved equipment.

Apprenticeship is another way to become a skilled prepress worker, although few apprenticeships have been offered in recent years. Apprenticeship programs emphasize a specific craft—such as camera operator, film stripper, lithographic etcher, scanner operator, or platemaker—but apprentices are introduced to all phases of printing.

Generally, most employers prefer to hire high school graduates who possess good communication skills, both oral and written. Prep-

ress workers need to be able to deal courteously with people, because in small shops they may take customer orders. They may also need to add, subtract, multiply, divide, and compute ratios to estimate job costs. Persons interested in working for firms using advanced printing technology need to know the basics of electronics and computers. Mathematical skills are also essential for operating many of the software packages used to run modern, computerized prepress equipment.

Prepress workers need good manual dexterity, and they must be able to pay attention to detail and work independently. Good eyesight, including visual acuity, depth perception, field of view, color vision, and the ability to focus quickly, is an asset. Artistic ability is often a plus. Employers seek persons who are even-tempered and adaptable, important qualities for workers who often must meet deadlines and learn how to operate new equipment.

Formal graphic arts programs, offered by community and junior colleges and some 4-year colleges, also introduce persons to the industry. These programs provide job-related training, and enrolling in one demonstrates an interest in the graphic arts; this may favorably impress an employer. Bachelor's degree programs in graphic arts are generally intended for students who may eventually move into management positions, and 2-year associate degree programs are designed to train skilled workers.

Courses in various aspects of printing are also available at vocational-technical institutes, industry-sponsored update and retraining programs, and private trade and technical schools.

As workers gain experience, they advance to positions with greater responsibility. Some move into supervisory positions.

Job Outlook

Employment of prepress workers is expected to decline through the year 2006. Demand for printed material should grow rapidly, spurred by rising levels of personal income, increasing school enrollments, and higher levels of educational attainment. However, increased use of computers in typesetting and page layout should eliminate many prepress jobs.

New technologies are also expected to spur demand for printed materials by expanding markets, allowing advertising dollars currently allotted to nonprint media, such as television, to be spent on direct mail. Work previously requiring a week or more can now be completed in a few days. Much faster turnaround time will permit printers to compete with nonprint media for time-sensitive business, providing advertisers with specialty advertisements used to target specific market segments, for example.

Technological advances will have a varying effect on employment among the prepress occupations. Employment of desktop publishing specialists is expected to grow much faster than average, reflecting the increasing proportion of page layout and design that will be performed using computers. In contrast, a decline in prepress machine operators is expected as the work these workers perform manually is increasingly automated. Occupations that are expected to experience declines as hand work becomes automated include paste-up workers, compositors and typesetters, photoengravers, platemakers, film strippers and camera operators.

Job prospects also will vary by industry, most notably for compositors and typesetters. Changes in technology have shifted many employment opportunities away from the traditional printing plants into advertising agencies, public relations firms, and large corporations. Many companies are turning to in-house typesetting or desktop publishing as personal computers with elaborate graphic capabilities have become common. Corporations are finding it more profitable to print their own newsletters and other reports than to send them out to trade shops. In addition, press shops themselves have responded to desktop publishers' needs by sending their own staff into the field to help customers prepare a disk that will live up to the customer's expectations.

Compositors and typesetters should find competition extremely keen in the newspaper industry, currently their largest employer. Computerized equipment allowing reporters and editors to specify type and style, and to format pages at a desktop computer terminal, has already eliminated many typesetting and composition jobs. More are certain to disappear in the years ahead.

Many new jobs for prepress workers are expected to emerge in commercial printing establishments. New equipment should reduce the time needed to complete a printing job, and allow commercial printers to make inroads into new markets that require fast turn-around. Because small establishments predominate, commercial printing should provide the best opportunities for inexperienced workers who want to gain a good background in all facets of printing.

Opportunities for prepress workers should also be good in the printing trade services industry. Despite the fact that companies may have their own typesetting and printing capabilities, they usually turn to professionals in printing trade services if quality and time are of the essence.

Most employers prefer to hire experienced prepress workers. Among persons without experience, however, opportunities should be best for those with a computer background who have completed postsecondary programs in printing technology. Many employers prefer graduates of these programs because the comprehensive training they receive helps them learn the printing process and adapt more rapidly to new processes and techniques.

Earnings

Wage rates for prepress workers vary according to occupation, level of experience and training, location and size of the firm, and whether they are union members. According to limited data available, the median earnings of full-time workers were $497 a week in 1996 for lithographers and photoengravers and $421 a week for typesetters and compositors.

Of the unionized prepress workers, scanner operators earned an hourly wage of $22.05 in 1996, and film strippers earned $18.88 per hour, according to the Graphic Communications International Union, the principal union for prepress workers.

Related Occupations

Prepress workers use artistic skills in their work. These skills are also essential for sign painters, jewelers, decorators, engravers, and graphic artists. In addition to typesetters, other workers who operate machines equipped with keyboards include typists and data entry keyers.

Sources of Additional Information

Details about apprenticeship and other training programs may be obtained from local employers such as newspapers and printing shops, or from local offices of the State employment service.

For information on careers and training in printing and the graphic arts, write to:

☛ PIA-Printing Industries of America, Inc., 100 Daingerfield Rd., Alexandria, VA 22314.
☛ Education Council of the Graphic Arts Industry, 1899 Preston White Dr., Reston, VA 20191.
☛ Graphic Communications International Union, 1900 L St. NW., Washington, DC 20036.

The Graphic Arts Technical Foundation, 200 Deer Run Road, Sewickley, PA 15143.

Printing Press Operators

(List of D.O.T. codes available on request. See p. 496.)

Significant Points

- Most are trained informally on the job working as assistants or helpers to experienced operators.

- Basic computer skills are useful for operators of newer presses.

- Employment growth will be slowed by the increasing use of new, more efficient computerized printing presses.

Nature of the Work

Printing press operators prepare, operate, and maintain the printing presses in a pressroom. Duties of press operators vary according to the type of press they operate—offset lithography, gravure, flexography, screen printing, or letterpress. Offset lithography, which transfers an inked impression from a rubber-covered cylinder to paper or other material, is the dominant printing process and is expected to remain so into the next century. With gravure, the recesses on an etched plate or cylinder are inked and pressed to paper. Flexography is a form of rotary printing in which ink is applied to the surface by a flexible rubber printing plate with a raised image area. Gravure and flexography should increase in use, but letterpress, in which an inked, raised surface is pressed against paper, should continue being phased out. In addition to the major printing processes, plateless, or nonimpact processes, are coming into general use. Plateless processes—including electronic, electrostatic, and ink-jet printing—are used for copying, duplicating, and document and specialty printing, generally by quick and in-house printing shops.

To prepare presses for printing, press operators install and adjust the printing plate, adjust pressure, ink the presses, load paper, and adjust the press to the paper size. Press operators ensure that paper and ink meet specifications, and adjust control margins and the flow of ink to the inking rollers accordingly. They then feed paper through the press cylinders and adjust feed and tension controls.

While printing presses are running, press operators monitor their operation and keep the paper feeders well stocked. They make adjustments to correct uneven ink distribution, speed, and temperatures in the drying chamber, if the press has one. If paper jams or tears, and the press stops, which can happen with some offset presses, operators quickly correct the problem to minimize downtime. Similarly, operators working with other high-speed presses constantly look for problems, making quick corrections to avoid expensive losses of paper and ink. Throughout the run, operators also occasionally pull sheets to check for any printing imperfections.

In many shops, press operators perform preventive maintenance. They oil and clean the presses and make minor repairs to keep them running smoothly.

Press operators' jobs differ from one shop to another because of differences in the kinds and sizes of presses. Small commercial

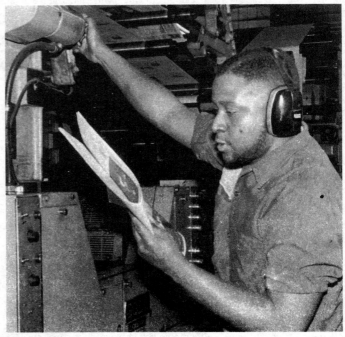

A printing press operator makes adjustments to ensure the quality of the printed product.

shops tend to have relatively small presses, which print only one or two colors at a time and are operated by one person. Operators who work with large presses have assistants and helpers. Large newspaper, magazine, and book printers use giant "in-line web" presses that require a crew of several press operators and press assistants. These presses are fed paper in big rolls, called "webs," up to 50 inches or more in width. Presses print the paper on both sides; trim, assemble, score, and fold the pages; and count the finished sections as they come off the press.

Most plants have, or will soon have installed printing presses that have computers and sophisticated instruments to control press operations, making it possible to set up for jobs in less time. Computers allow press operators to perform many of their tasks electronically. With this equipment, press operators monitor the printing process on a control panel that allows them to adjust the press electronically by pushing buttons.

Working Conditions

Operating a press can be physically and mentally demanding, and sometimes tedious. Press operators are on their feet most of the time. Often, operators work under pressure to meet deadlines. Most printing presses are capable of high printing speeds, and adjustments must be made quickly to avoid waste. Pressrooms are noisy, and workers in certain areas wear ear protectors. Working with press machinery can be hazardous, but accidents can be avoided when safe work practices are observed. The threat of accidents is less with newer computerized presses because operators make most adjustments from a control panel. Many press operators work evening, night, and overtime shifts.

Employment

Press operators held about 244,000 jobs in 1996. Employment was distributed as follows:

Printing press machine setters and operators	119,000
Offset lithographic press operators	76,000
Screen printing machine setters and setup operators	9,000
Letterpress operators	14,000
All other printing press setters and set-up operators	6,300

Most press operator jobs were in newspaper plants or in firms handling commercial or business printing. Commercial printing firms print newspaper inserts, catalogs, pamphlets, and the advertisements found in mailboxes, and business form establishments print items such as sales receipts and paper used in computers. Additional jobs were in the "in-plant" section of organizations and businesses that do their own printing—among them, banks, insurance companies, and government agencies.

The printing and publishing industry is one of the most geographically dispersed in the United States, and press operators can find jobs throughout the country. However, jobs are concentrated in large printing centers such as New York, Los Angeles, Chicago, Philadelphia, Washington, DC, and Dallas.

Training, Other Qualifications, and Advancement

Although completion of a formal apprenticeship or a postsecondary program in printing equipment operation continue to be the best way to learn the trade, most printing press operators are trained informally on the job working as assistants or helpers to experienced operators. Beginning press operators load, unload, and clean presses. With time, they move up to operating one-color sheet-fed presses and eventually advance to multicolor presses. Operators are likely to gain experience on many kinds of printing presses during the course of their career.

Apprenticeship, once the dominant method of preparing for this occupation, is becoming less prevalent with the growing importance of formal postsecondary programs in printing equipment operation offered by technical and trade schools and community and junior colleges. Apprenticeships for press operators in commercial shops take 4 years. In addition to on-the-job instruction, apprenticeships

include related classroom or correspondence school courses. In contrast, some postsecondary school programs require 2 years of study and award an associate degree, but most programs can be completed in 1 year or less. Postsecondary courses in printing are increasingly important because they provide the theoretical knowledge needed to operate advanced equipment.

Persons who wish to become printing press operators need mechanical aptitude to make press adjustments and repairs and an ability to visualize color in order to work on color presses. Oral and writing skills are also required. Operators should be able to compute percentages, weights, and measures, and should possess adequate mathematical skills to calculate the amount of ink and paper needed to do a job. Because of technical developments in the printing industry, courses in chemistry, electronics, color theory, and physics are helpful.

Technological changes have had a tremendous effect on the skills needed by press operators. New presses require basic computer skills. Printing plants that change from sheet-fed offset presses to web-offset presses have to retrain the entire press crew because skill requirements for the two types of presses are different. Web-offset presses, with their faster operating speeds, require faster decisions, monitoring of more variables, and greater physical effort. Even experienced operators periodically receive retraining and skill updating. In the future, workers are expected to need to retrain several times during their career.

Press operators may advance in pay and responsibility by taking a job working on a more complex printing press. For example, a one-color sheet-fed press operator may, through experience and demonstrated ability, become a four-color sheet-fed press operator. Others may advance to pressroom supervisor and become responsible for the work of the entire press crew.

Job Outlook

Persons seeking jobs as printing press operators will face keen competition from experienced operators and prepress workers who have been displaced by new technology, particularly those who have completed retraining programs. Opportunities to become printing press operators are likely to be best for persons who qualify for formal apprenticeship training or who complete postsecondary training programs.

Employment of press operators is expected to grow more slowly than the average for all occupations through the year 2006. Although demand for printed materials will grow, employment growth will be slowed by the increased use of new, more efficient computerized printing presses. However, employment growth will vary among press operator jobs. Employment of offset, gravure, and flexographic operators will increase, while employment of letterpress operators will decline sharply. Most job openings will result from the need to replace operators who retire or leave the occupation.

Most new jobs will result from expansion of the printing industry as demand for printed material increases in response to demographic trends, U.S. expansion into foreign markets, and growing use of direct mail by advertisers. Demand for books and magazines will increase as school enrollments rise, and as substantial growth in the middle-aged and older population spurs adult education and leisure reading. Additional growth should stem from increased foreign demand for domestic trade publications, professional and scientific works, and mass-market books such as paperbacks.

Much of the growth in commercial printing will be spurred by increased expenditures for print advertising materials to be mailed directly to prospective customers. New market research techniques are leading advertisers to increase spending on messages targeted to specific audiences, and should continue to require the printing of a wide variety of newspaper inserts, catalogs, direct mail enclosures, and other kinds of print advertising.

Other printing, such as newspapers, books, and periodicals, will also provide jobs. Experienced press operators will fill most of these jobs because many employers are under severe pressure to meet deadlines and have limited time to train new employees.

Earnings

The basic wage rate for a press operator depends on the type of press being run and the area of the country in which the work is located. Median weekly earnings of press operators who worked full time were about $484 in 1996. The middle 50 percent earned between $376 and $655. The lowest 10 percent earned $267 or less a week, while the highest 10 percent earned over $846 a week.

Related Occupations

Other workers who set up and operate production machinery include papermaking machine operators, shoemaking machine operators, bindery machine operators, and various precision machine operators.

Sources of Additional Information

Details about apprenticeships and other training opportunities may be obtained from local employers such as newspapers and printing shops, local offices of the Graphic Communications International Union, local affiliates of Printing Industries of America, or local offices of the State employment service.

For general information about press operators, write to:

☛ Graphic Communications International Union, 1900 L St. NW., Washington, DC 20036.

For information on careers and training in printing and the graphic arts, write to:

☛ PIA-Printing Industries of America, Inc., 100 Daingerfield Rd., Alexandria, VA 22314.

☛ Education Council of the Graphic Arts Industry, 1899 Preston White Dr., Reston, VA 20191.

☛ The Graphic Arts Technical Foundation, 200 Deer Run Road, Sewickley, PA 15143.

Textile, Apparel, and Furnishings Occupations

Apparel Workers

(A list of D.O.T. codes is available on request. See page 496.)

Significant Points

- Most workers are trained on-the-job; those in firms which use modular manufacturing systems that emphasize teamwork are cross-trained in all operations performed by their team.

- Employment of apparel workers is expected to decline due to increased imports, offshore assembly, and labor-saving machinery.

- Earnings of most apparel workers are very low.

Nature of the Work

Apparel workers help to keep us warm, comfortable, and in style. They play this important role in our lives by transforming cloth, leather, and fur into clothing and other consumer products. Many apparel workers also repair and alter these products. (Some items that we think of as apparel, such as socks or pantyhose, are produced in knitting mills. Workers who are employed in these factories are classified as textile rather than as apparel workers. A separate statement on textile machinery operators is presented in this section of the *Handbook*.)

Apparel production begins with a designer's creation that has been made into a sample product. (A separate statement on designers is presented elsewhere in the *Handbook*.) Because many of these goods are to be mass produced, a pattern of the product must be developed. This is usually done with the aid of a computer. After a design is made, sample makers produce the sample garment for the designer.

Once the pattern has been created, the fabric must be spread and cut. Many layers of material may be spread on the cutting table, depending on the quantity being produced and the type of material. Workers known as markers must determine the best arrangement or layout of the pattern pieces to minimize waste. In many plants, this step depends on the judgment of the worker, but computers increasingly are used to determine the optimum arrangement of the pattern pieces.

Using an electric knife or other cutting tool, other workers cut out the various pieces of material following the outline of the pattern. On especially delicate or valuable items, this may be done by hand. Workers must pay close attention to detail because a mistake in the cutting process can ruin many yards of material. In more automated firms, electronic copies of layouts are sent to computer-controlled cutting machines that are monitored by cutting machine operators.

Once the material has been cut, it is ready to be sewn together into a shirt, knapsack, dress, or other product. Most sewing is done by sewing machine operators, who are classified by the type of machine and product on which they work. The most basic division is between sewing machine operators who produce clothing and those who produce nongarment items such as towels, sheets, and curtains. Both garment and nongarment machine operators usually specialize in a single operation, such as bindings, collars, or hems. Because each product requires a variety of sewing operations that cannot be done on the same machine, companies producing apparel have many types of specialized sewing machines.

Some materials may be sewn by hand rather than by machine due to their value and delicacy. Hand sewers may specialize in a particular operation, such as sewing buttonholes or adding lace or other trimming. They also work with the designer to make a sample of a new product.

When sewing operations have been completed, workers remove loose threads, basting stitching, and lint from the finished product. Although final inspection of the product is usually done at this time, inspectors are found in all stages of the production process. They mark defects in uncut fabric so that layout workers can position the pattern to avoid them, or they mark defects in semi-finished garments, which they may repair themselves or send back to be mended. (For a more detailed discussion, see the statement on inspectors, testers, and graders elsewhere in the *Handbook*.)

Pressers ensure that finished products are free of wrinkles. Some pressers specialize in a particular garment part; others do the final pressing before the product is shipped to the store. Pressing may be done by hand, but it is more likely to be performed by specially-designed, steam pressing machines that are much more productive than hand pressing.

A large number of apparel workers are employed by small firms that lack the capital resources to invest in new, more efficient equipment. Because of this and the difficulty of automating the assembly process, the nature of the work for many apparel workers has remained relatively unchanged. Nevertheless, in larger firms with modern facilities, some operations are computerized, and some of the product-moving operations are performed by automated material handling systems.

In addition, many firms use another workplace innovation—the modular manufacturing system—to increase product quality while reducing production time. In this system, operators work together in a module or team; in the older bundle system, each work performed a specific operation on a piece of fabric as it moved through the factory in a bundle. Although each worker in the modular system usually specializes in one operation, most are cross-trained in the various operations performed by their team so that they can fill in for other workers. Not only do operators communicate more with other work-

Apparel workers use a variety of tools and materials.

ers in the new system, they are given added responsibilities, including correcting problems, scheduling, and monitoring standards.

Not all apparel goods are mass produced, however. Some people prefer clothing made especially for them. Custom tailors make garments from start to finish by taking measurements and helping the customer select the right fabric and design. These workers are highly skilled and must be knowledgeable in all phases of clothing production. Many work in retail outlets, including laundries and dry-cleaning establishments, where they make alterations and adjustments to ready-to-wear clothing.

Working Conditions
Working conditions in apparel production vary by establishment and by occupation. Older factories tend to be congested and poorly lit and ventilated, but more modern facilities are usually better planned, have more work space, and are well-lit and ventilated. Due to the nature of the work and the machinery being used, sewing and pressing areas are usually noisy, whereas patternmaking and spreading areas are quieter. Laundries and dry-cleaning establishments are often hot and noisy; retail stores, on the other hand, tend to be relatively quiet and comfortable.

Most persons in apparel occupations work a standard 5-day, 35- to 40-hour week. Some apparel manufacturers add second shifts to justify the expense of new machinery. Also, those employed in retail stores and in laundry and dry-cleaning establishments may work evenings and weekends.

Apparel production work can be physically demanding. Some workers sit for long periods, and others spend many hours on their feet, leaning over tables and operating machinery. In some instances, new machinery and production techniques have decreased the physical demands upon workers. For example, newer pressing machines are now operated by foot pedals or computer controls and do not require much strength to operate. Along with new ergonomically-designed equipment, these developments have helped to reduce the significant problem of repetitive strain injuries among apparel workers. Although there are no life-threatening dangers or health hazards associated with apparel occupations, operators must be attentive while running equipment such as sewing machines, pressers, and automated cutters. A few workers wear protective devices such as gloves.

In some areas of apparel production, the emphasis on individual performance is shifting to an emphasis on teamwork and cooperation. Incentive programs may also be based on a team's performance. The team or module often has managerial authority over itself, increasing the overall responsibility of each operator and allowing more interpersonal contact.

Employment
Apparel workers held 835,000 jobs in 1996. The following tabulation shows that about 7 out of 10 were sewing machine operators.

Garment sewing machine operators	453,000
Nongarment sewing machine operators	130,000
Custom tailors	87,000
Pressing machine operators	78,000
Hand cutters and trimmers	46,000
Patternmakers and layout workers	14,000
Hand pressers	14,000
Hand sewers	13,000

Production jobs are concentrated in California, New York, North Carolina, Pennsylvania, Tennessee, and Georgia. Most of these jobs are in the apparel and textile industries, except for pressers and custom tailors. Although pressing operations are an integral part of the apparel production process, more than one-half of all pressers are employed in the laundry and dry-cleaning industry. In addition, more than one-half of all custom tailors work in retail clothing establishments; many others are self-employed. For both of these occupations, jobs are found in every part of the country.

Training, Other Qualifications, and Advancement
Training requirements vary by industry. In the apparel industry, for example, few employers require production workers to have a high school diploma or previous work experience. Nevertheless, entrants with secondary or postsecondary vocational training or previous work experience in apparel production usually have a better chance of getting a job and advancing to a supervisory position.

Retailers prefer to hire custom tailors and sewers with previous experience in apparel manufacture, design, or alterations. Knowledge of fabrics, design, and construction is very important. Although laundries and dry cleaners prefer entrants with previous work experience, they routinely hire inexperienced workers.

In general, apparel workers need good hand-eye coordination and the ability to perform repetitive tasks for long periods. Knowledge of fabrics and their characteristics is sometimes required.

Regardless of setting, workers usually begin by performing simple tasks. As they gain experience, they are assigned more difficult operations. Further advancement is limited, however. Some production workers may become first-line supervisors, but the majority remain on the production line. Occasionally, a patternmaker may advance to designer, but usually only after additional training at a design school. Some experienced custom tailors open their own tailoring shop. Custom tailoring is a very competitive field, however, and training in small business operations can mean the difference between success and failure.

Machine operators are usually trained on the job by more experienced employees or by machinery manufacturers' representatives. As machinery in the industry continues to become more complex, some apparel workers will need training in the basics of computers and electronics. In addition, the trend toward cross-training of operators will increase the time needed to learn different machines, and the rise of modular manufacturing will require workers to learn the interpersonal skills necessary to work effectively as part of a team.

Job Outlook
Employment of apparel workers is expected to decline through the year 2006. The job outlook of these workers depends largely on conditions in the apparel industry, where most apparel workers are employed. Increased imports, use of offshore assembly, and greater productivity through the introduction of labor-saving machinery will reduce the demand for these workers. Because of the large size of this occupation, however, many thousands of job openings will arise each year from the need to replace persons who transfer to other occupations, retire, or leave the occupation for other reasons.

Employment in the domestic apparel industry has declined in recent years as foreign producers have gained a greater share of the U.S. market. Imports now account for roughly half of domestic apparel consumption, and this share is expected to increase as the U.S. market is opened further by the North American Free Trade Agreement (NAFTA) and the Agreement on Textiles and Clothing (ATC) of the World Trade Organization (WTO). NAFTA allows apparel produced in Mexico and Canada to be imported, duty-free, to the United States. Some apparel companies are expected to move their production facilities to Mexico to reduce costs. In addition, the ATC will result in the elimination of quotas and a reduction in tariffs for many apparel products. As this agreement is phased in through the year 2005, domestic production will continue to move abroad and imports into the U.S. market will increase, causing further employment decline for apparel workers in the United States.

To avoid losing more of the market, domestic manufacturers are developing the ability to take advantage of their proximity to the U.S. market by responding more quickly to changes in market demand. This is especially important in high-fashion items with rapidly-changing demand. U.S. producers are able to use computers and electronic data interchange to closely monitor the sales of the items that they produce and to respond quickly to diminishing inventories. They are, therefore, able to keep retailers stocked with the most popular items and to reduce production of apparel that is not selling well.

Despite these advances in technology, it has been difficult to use automated equipment extensively in the apparel industry due to the soft properties of textile products. In addition, it is time consuming and expensive to adapt existing technology to the wide variety of items produced and the frequent style and seasonal changes. However, some of the larger firms and those that produce standardized items have automated pre-sewing functions, material handling, and some very simple sewing procedures. Technological developments, such as computer-aided marking and grading, computer-controlled cutters, semiautomatic sewing and pressing machines, and automated material handling systems, have increased output while reducing the need for some workers in larger firms. As the apparel industry continues to restructure and consolidate, more of the smaller, less efficient producers will lose market share to larger firms.

Another practice that will influence employment levels is the use of offshore assembly. A provision in U.S. tariff regulations reduces tariffs on apparel imports from Caribbean nations that are assembled from pieces of fabric which were cut in the United States. This enables the most labor-intensive step in the production process—assembly—to be performed at much lower wage rates. This trend is expected to continue, and will curtail job opportunities for sewing machine operators in the United States. Because many pre-sewing functions will continue to be done domestically, however, workers who perform these functions will not be as adversely affected.

Custom tailors and sewers, the most skilled apparel workers, are also expected to experience declining employment. Demand for their services will continue to dampen as consumers are increasingly likely to buy new, mass-produced apparel instead of purchasing custom-made apparel or having clothes altered or repaired.

Earnings

Earnings of apparel workers vary by industry and by occupation. Average weekly earnings of production workers in the apparel industry were $290 in 1996, compared to about $410 for production workers in all manufacturing industries. Earnings vary significantly, depending on the product being manufactured. Average weekly earnings ranged from a low of $230 in firms producing women's blouses and shirts to a high of $470 in establishments making automotive and apparel trimmings.

Sewing machine operators—accounting for 7 of every 10 apparel workers—had median weekly earnings of $250 in 1996. Because many production workers in apparel manufacturing are paid according to the number of acceptable pieces they or their group produce, their total earnings depend on skill, speed, and accuracy.

Benefits also vary. Large employers increasingly include child care in their benefits package. Those employed in retail trade also may receive a discount on their purchases. In addition, some of the larger manufacturers operate company stores, where employees can purchase apparel products at significant discounts. Some small firms, however, offer only limited benefits. In addition to employer-sponsored benefits, the principal union—the Union of Needletrades,

Industrial, and Textile Employees (UNITE)—provides benefits to its members.

Related Occupations

The work of apparel workers varies from that requiring very little skill and training to that which is highly complex, requiring several years of training. Those operating machinery and equipment, such as pressing or sewing machine operators, perform duties similar to metalworking and plastics-working machine operators, textile operatives, and shoe sewing machine operators. Other workers who perform handwork are precision woodworkers, precision assemblers, upholsterers, and shoe and leather workers.

Sources of Additional Information

Information regarding careers in apparel is available from numerous technical institutes that have specialized textile and apparel programs. A list of these can be found in college guides. In addition, the local office of the State employment service or an apparel manufacturer can provide information on job opportunities in a specific area.

For general information on the apparel industry, write to:
☛ American Apparel Manufacturers Association, 2500 Wilson Blvd., Suite 301, Arlington, VA 22201.

Shoe and Leather Workers and Repairers

(D.O.T. 365.361; 780.381-030; 781.381-018; 783.361-010, .381-018 through -026; 788.261-010, .381)

Significant Points

- Workers generally learn their craft on the job; trainees become fully skilled in 6 months to 2 years.

- Employment is expected to decline, reflecting increases in imports, labor-saving machinery, and business costs; workers employed in the manufacture and modification of custom-made molded or orthopedic shoes may enjoy the best job prospects.

Nature of the Work

Creating stylish and durable leather products is the job of precision shoe and leather workers; keeping them in good condition is the work of repairers. These workers produce and repair a variety of goods ranging from therapeutic shoes to saddles and luggage. Although they produce different goods, shoe and leather workers share many tasks. For example, they must first check the texture, color, and strength of the leather. They then place a pattern of the item being produced on the leather, trace the pattern onto the leather, cut along the outline, and sew the pieces together. Other steps may vary according to the type of good being produced.

Orthopedic and therapeutic shoemakers, for instance, make or modify footwear according to a doctor's prescription. These workers attach the insoles to shoe lasts (a wooden form shaped like a foot), affix the shoe uppers, and apply heels and outsoles. They shape the heels with a knife and then sand them on a buffing wheel for smoothness. Finally, they dye and polish the shoes. Custom shoe workers also may modify existing footwear for people with foot problems and special needs. This can involve preparing inserts, heel pads, and lifts from casts of customers' feet.

Saddlemakers often apply leather dyes and liquid top coats to produce a gloss finish on a saddle. They may also decorate the saddle surface by hand stitching or by stamping the leather with decorative patterns and designs. *Luggage makers* fasten leather to a frame and attach handles and other hardware. They also cut and secure linings inside the frames and sew or stamp designs onto the luggage exterior.

Shoe and leather repairers use their knowledge of leatherworking to give worn leather goods extended wearability. The most common

Shoe and leather workers perform a variety of intricate operations to make and repair shoes.

type of shoe repair is replacing soles and heels. Repairers place the shoe on a last and remove the old sole and heel with a knife or pliers or both. They attach new soles and heels to shoes either by stitching them in place or by using cement or nails. Other leather goods, suitcases or handbags, for example, may need seams to be re-sewn or handles and linings replaced.

All leather workers and repairers use handtools and machines. The most commonly used handtools are knives, hammers, awls (used to poke holes in leather to make sewing possible), and skivers (for splitting leather). Power-operated equipment includes sewing machines, heel nailing machines, sanding machines, hole punching machines, sole stitchers, and computerized machinery to analyze foot needs and conditions.

Depending on the size of the factory or shop, a leather worker may perform one or more of the steps required to complete or repair a product. In smaller factories or shops, workers generally perform several tasks, while those in larger facilities tend to specialize. However, most leather workers eventually learn the different skills involved in producing leather goods as they move from one task to another.

Self-employed shoe repairers and owners of custom-made shoe and leather shops have managerial responsibilities in addition to their regular duties. They must maintain good relations with their customers, make business decisions, and keep accurate records.

Working Conditions
Working conditions of leather workers vary according to the type of work performed, the size of the factory or business, and the practices of each shop. Workers employed in custom leather goods manufacturing establishments generally work a regular 40-hour week. Those in repair shops work nights and weekends and often work irregular hours. For those who own repair shops, long hours are common.

Shoe and leather workers and repairers need to pay close attention when working with machines to avoid punctures, lacerations, and abrasions. Although there are few health hazards if precautions are followed, work areas can be noisy and odors from leather dyes and stains are often present.

Employment
Shoe and leather workers and repairers held about 21,000 jobs in 1996. Salaried workers held about 15,000 jobs. About half were employed in the manufacture of footwear products; one-fifth were employed in the production of leather goods such as luggage, handbags, and apparel; and another fifth worked in shoe repair and shoeshine shops. Self-employed individuals, who typically own and operate small shoe repair shops or specialty leather manufacturing firms, held about 6,000 jobs.

Training, Other Qualifications, and Advancement
Precision shoe and leather workers and repairers generally learn their craft on the job, either through in-house training programs or working as helpers to experienced workers. Helpers usually begin by performing simple tasks and then progress to more difficult projects like cutting or stitching leather. Trainees generally become fully skilled in 6 months to 2 years; the length of training varies according to the nature of the work and the aptitude and dedication of the individual.

A limited number of schools and national shoe repair chains offer training in shoe repair and leather work. These programs may last from a few weeks to 1 year and impart basic skills including leather cutting, stitching, and dyeing. Students learn shoe construction, practice shoe repair, and study the fundamentals of running a small business. Graduates are encouraged to gain additional training by working with an experienced leather worker or repairer.

Shoe repairers need to keep their skills up-to-date to work with rapidly changing footwear styles. Some repairers do this by attending trade shows and receiving training from product manufacturers. Others attend specialized training seminars and workshops in custom shoe making, shoe repair, and other leather work sponsored by national and regional associations.

Pedorthists—who produce or modify prescription footwear—may receive certification from the Pedorthic Footwear Association. These workers become certified after completing 120 hours of training and passing an exam.

Manual dexterity and the mechanical aptitude to work with handtools and machines are important in the shoe repair and leatherworking occupations. Shoe and leather workers who produce custom goods should have artistic ability as well. These workers must have self-discipline to work alone under little supervision. In addition, leather workers and repairers who own shops must have knowledge of business practices and management, as well as a pleasant manner when dealing with customers.

Many individuals who begin as workers or repairers advance to salaried supervisory and managerial positions. Some may open their own shop or business.

Job Outlook
Employment of shoe and leather workers is expected to decline through the year 2006, primarily because of the growing number of imported shoes and other leather goods which have displaced domestic production. In addition, inexpensive imports have made the cost of replacing shoes and leather goods cheaper or more convenient than repairing them, thus reducing the demand for shoe and leather repairers.

These workers are also adversely affected by other factors, such as the rising cost of leather and higher rents in the high-traffic areas in which more shoe repairers are relocating. Moreover, shoe repair shops that offer "while-you-wait" service are investing in new machinery which is making repairers more productive and helping to reduce the demand for these workers. Some of the more expensive, fine leather products will continue to be repaired, however, and this demand will moderate the employment decline of shoe repairers. Consumers are also buying more comfort-soled leather shoes, which should increase demand for the services provided by shoe repairers. In the future, though, most job openings in this occupation will arise from the need to replace experienced workers who transfer to other occupations or leave the work force.

Prospects for workers employed in the manufacture and modification of custom-made molded or orthopedic shoes are better than those for most other leather workers. This reflects rapid growth in the elderly population and an increasing emphasis on preventive foot care. The employment effects of these trends may be limited, however, since the demand for orthopedic footwear is increasingly fulfilled by manufactured shoes that are modified to specification instead of completely custom made.

Earnings
Data on earnings of shoe and leather workers are very limited. Their earnings vary greatly depending upon the place of employment. Beginning workers often start near the minimum wage ($5.15 an hour) and can advance in just a few months. Owners of shoe repair and custom shoe manufacturing shops can earn substantially more.

Related Occupations
Other workers who make or repair items using handtools and machinery include dressmakers, custom tailors and sewers, designers and patternmakers, and furriers.

Sources of Additional Information
For information about the custom-made prescription shoe business, and about training opportunities in this field, contact:
☛ Pedorthic Footwear Association, 9861 Broken Land Pkwy., Suite 255, Columbia, MD 21046-1151.

For information about opportunities in shoe repair, contact:
☛ Shoe Service Institute of America, Educational Library, 5024-R Campbell Blvd., Baltimore, MD 21236-5974.

Textile Machinery Operators

(List of D.O.T. codes is available on request. See page 496.)

Significant Points
- Night and weekend shifts are common, as many textile and fiber mills operate 24 hours a day.
- Employment is expected to decline primarily due to labor-saving machinery and a less restrictive foreign trade environment.
- Earnings are very low.

Nature of the Work
Textile machinery operators tend machines that manufacture a wide range of textile products. Most people know that hosiery, towels, and socks are textiles, but many are surprised to learn that textile products are used in such things as roofs, tires, and roads. Textile machinery operators play an important part in producing all of these goods by controlling equipment that cleans, cards, combs, and draws the fiber; spins the fiber into yarn; and weaves, knits, or tufts the yarn into textile products. They are responsible for numerous machines that they start, stop, clean, and monitor for proper functioning.

There are many phases in the textile production process, and operators' duties and responsibilities depend on the product and the type of machinery in use. The process begins with the preparation of synthetic or natural fibers for spinning. Fibers are cleaned and aligned through carding and combing. To prepare the fiber for the spinning process, very short fibers and any foreign matter are removed and the fibers are drawn into a substance called sliver. During this process, different types of fibers may be combined to give products the desired textures, durability, or other characteristics. This is how "50-percent cotton, 50-percent polyester" blends, for example, are created. Operators constantly monitor their machines during this stage, checking the movement of the fiber, removing and replacing cans of sliver, repairing breaks in the sliver, and making minor repairs to the machinery.

The full cans of sliver are then taken to the spinning area. Spinning draws and twists the sliver to produce yarn which is then wound onto conical structures called bobbins or cones. This is an automated version of the old fashion spinning wheel.

Some workers oversee machinery that makes manufactured fibers. These fibers are created from materials that, unlike cotton, wool, and flax, are not fibrous in their natural form. To make this fiber, wood pulp or chemical compounds are dissolved or melted in a liquid which is then extruded, or forced, through holes in a metal plate, called a spinneret. The sizes and shapes of the holes in the spinneret determine the shape and the uses of the fiber. Workers adjust the flow of fiber base through the spinneret, repair breaks in the fiber, and make minor adjustments to the machinery. Because this fiber is created by a chemical process, the majority of these workers are employed by chemical companies, not textile mills.

When the yarn is ready, it is taken to be woven, knitted, tufted, or bonded with heat or chemicals. Each of these processes creates a different type of textile product and requires a different type of machine. Woven fabrics are made on looms that interlace the yarn. Knit products, such as socks or women's hosiery, are produced by intermeshing loops of yarn. Carpeting is made through the tufting process, in which the loops of yarn are pushed through a backing material. Although the processes are now highly automated, these concepts have been used for many centuries to produce textile products.

Once the yarn has been woven, knitted, or tufted, the resulting fabric is ready to be dyed and finished either at the textile mill or at a plant specializing in textile finishing. Depending upon the end use of the yarn, it may be dyed before or after it is woven, knitted, or tufted. Some fabric is treated before it is dyed to remove other chemical additives that could affect the quality of the finished product.

In addition to dyeing and printing, products are often finished by treating them to prevent excessive shrinkage, provide strength, make them stain-resistant, or give them a silky luster. In the production of hosiery and socks, for example, the stocking or sock is placed on a form and then exposed to steam and heat to give it shape.

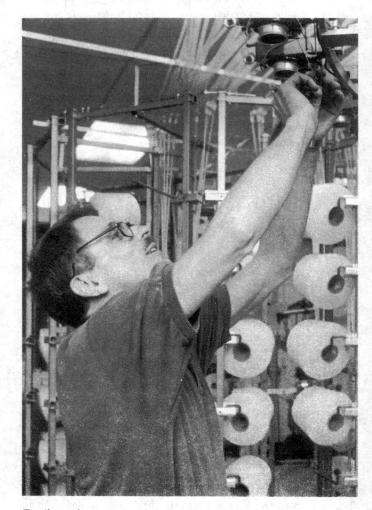

Textile workers monitor the operation of various machines.

Textile machinery operators play a vital role in all of the various processes described above. In spite of the wide range of machines with which they work, machine operators share many responsibilities. Most prepare their machinery prior to a production run and help maintain the equipment by adjusting the timing on a machine, threading the harnesses that create patterns in textile goods, and repairing machinery. Each operator oversees numerous machines, performing such duties as repairing breaks in the yarn and monitoring its supply. Because more automated machinery is used in textile mills, a greater number of processes are controlled by computers, making it possible for each operator to monitor a larger area or number of machines. The complexity of many machines often requires operators to specialize in a particular type of machine.

Working Conditions

Most textile machine operators work in textile mills or chemical plants. Working conditions depend upon the age and degree of modernization of the factory. Newer facilities usually offer better ventilation and climate control that reduce potential problems caused by airborne fibers and fumes. In a few older facilities, workers in areas with high levels of these airborne materials often use protective glasses and masks that cover their nose and mouth.

Although some of the newer machinery has reduced the level of noise, workers in some areas still wear ear protection. Many machines operate at high speeds, and workers must be careful not to wear clothing or jewelry that could get caught in moving parts. In addition, extruding and forming machine operators wear protective shoes and clothing when working with certain chemical compounds.

Most textile machinery operators work a standard 40-hour week. Night and weekend shifts are common, as many textile and fiber mills operate 24 hours a day. However, many employers use a rotating schedule of shifts so that operators don't consistently work nights or weekends.

Although workers have traditionally worked under close supervision, new management philosophies are placing an increasing emphasis on teamwork, which will allow operators greater interpersonal contact and more initiative.

Employment

Textile machinery operators held about 272,000 jobs in 1996. Most of these workers were employed in weaving, finishing, yarn, and thread mills. Knitting mills and manufactured fiber producers also employed a large number of these workers. Most extruding and forming machine operators were employed in chemical plants.

North Carolina was the leading State in the employment of textile workers, accounting for about 30 percent of the total. Georgia and Carolina combined accounted for another 30 percent. Most of the remaining workers were employed in other southern States and in the Northeast.

Training, Other Qualifications, and Advancement

A high school diploma or its equivalency—while not required for all machine operating positions—is becoming more common for entry-level positions in many mills. Some mills prefer applicants to possess a high school diploma and additional technical training. This training may be obtained, in part, at a formal training institution, such as a technical school. In addition, extensive on-the-job training may be offered by more experienced workers or representatives of machinery manufacturers.

As the textile industry becomes more highly automated, some operators will need to understand complex machinery and be able to diagnose problems. Because textile machinery is increasingly controlled electronically, prospective employees will benefit from a basic knowledge of computers and electronics.

Physical stamina and manual dexterity are important attributes for these jobs. In addition, self-direction and interpersonal skills are becoming more important for textile machinery operators, as organizational changes that promote teamwork and encourage fewer levels of management are leading operators to assume greater responsibility and to take more initiative.

Textile machinery operators can advance in several ways. Some workers become instructors and train new employees. Others advance by taking positions requiring higher skills and greater responsibility. First-line supervisory positions usually are filled from the ranks of skilled operators.

Job Outlook

Employment of textile machinery operators is expected to decline over the 1996-2006 period. The most important factors influencing the employment outlook will be greater worker productivity through the introduction of labor-saving machinery and a more open trading environment. In spite of the projected decline, thousands of openings will be created annually as workers change occupations or leave the labor force.

Textile firms will respond to growing competition in coming years by investing in new equipment, reorganizing their work practices, and consolidating. New machinery, such as faster air jet looms and computer-integrated manufacturing technology, will increase productivity and allow each operator to monitor a larger number of machines. Many factories are also reorganizing production floors to further increase productivity and to give workers more responsibility. In addition, textile firms are merging to benefit from economies of scale and pool their resources to invest in new equipment. Although each of the above practices should make the textile industry more competitive, they are likely to adversely affect the outlook for many machine operators.

Another major uncertainty for textile workers is the future of trade. Recent trade initiatives, like the North American Free Trade Agreement and the Agreement on Textiles and Clothing of the World Trade Organization, will help to open export markets for textiles produced in the United States. At the same time, they will dismantle much of the protection that has been provided to the industry for decades. While the textile industry is highly efficient and will be able to compete in many product lines, the labor-intensive U.S. apparel industry will be more adversely affected by these trade initiatives. This, in turn, will negatively affect the demand for textile machinery operators because the apparel industry is the largest consumer of American-made textiles.

Because the textile industry is highly automated, persons with technical skills and some computer training will have the best opportunities. Textile machinery operators who are expected to fare the best are bleaching and dyeing machine operators and extruding machine operators who produce synthetic fibers.

Earnings

Average weekly earnings for production workers in the textile mill products industry industries were about $390 in 1996, compared to $530 for production workers in all manufacturing industries and $410 for production workers throughout private industry. Earnings vary significantly, depending upon the type of mill, job specialty, shift, and seniority. Average weekly earnings for production workers in the chemical industry, where most extruding machine operators are found, were around $700 in 1996.

In addition to typical benefits, some firms provide on-site daycare facilities and offer employees discounts in company-owned outlet stores.

Related Occupations

Metalworking and plastics-working machine operators perform similar duties and have many of the same entry and training requirements as extruding and forming machine operators and tenders, textile machine operators and tenders, and textile bleaching and dyeing machine operators. Setters and setup operators in other industries—metal fabrication and plastics manufacturing, for example—perform duties comparable to those of textile machine setters and setup operators.

Sources of Additional Information

Information about job opportunities in textile and synthetic fiber production is available from local employers or local offices of the State employment service.

For general information on careers, technology, or trade regulations in the textile industry, write to:

☛ American Textile Manufacturers Institute, Inc., 1130 Connecticut Ave. NW., Suite 1200, Washington, DC 20036-3954.

☛ Institute of Textile Technology, 2551 Ivy Rd., Charlottesville, NC 22903-4614.

Upholsterers

(D.O.T. 780.381 except -030 and -034, .384, .684-034, -118, and -122)

Significant Points

- About 30 percent are self-employed, three times the average for all craft workers.

- Most upholsterers are trained on the job as a helper to become an experienced worker.

- Opportunities for experienced upholsterers should be good because few young people want to enter the occupation and because few shops are willing to train people.

Nature of the Work

Employing an intimate knowledge of fabrics and materials, upholsterers make our lives more comfortable and aesthetically pleasing by making new upholstered furniture and renewing existing upholstered furniture (reupholstery). In addition to this, some upholsterers repair or replace automobile upholstery and convertible and vinyl tops.

Upholsterers who produce new furniture work in factories and typically perform a limited range of skilled, often repetitive tasks. Upholsterers doing reupholstery or custom work, however, perform a broader range of highly skilled upholstery tasks.

Although the many fabrics and other materials used in an upholstered product have changed considerably over time, the basic process of constructing and assembling a piece of furniture has changed very little. The process of upholstering, or reupholstering, a piece of furniture always starts with the frame. For both new and reconditioned pieces of upholstered furniture, the upholsterer examines the base for wood defects, loose sections, and finish. Upholsterers may make minor repairs, such as regluing or refinishing, but major repairs, such as repairs to etched or intricate items, may be referred to a general furniture repairer or to a highly skilled craftsperson.

When restoring an old piece to new life, upholsterers first discard the old, worn coverings using a hammer or tack puller to remove staples, tacks, or other fasteners. The padding is removed and as much of it as possible is reused in order to preserve the shape of the item. After removing all material to expose the bare frame, the upholsterer examines the frame for bent and broken springs, repairing or replacing old ones as necessary. The webbing is checked for wear. If it is too weak to hold the springs properly and support the upholstered sections, then new webbing is installed.

The upholsterer stretches the webbing, a strong cloth mat that holds the springs, from one side of the frame to the other. Typically, the webbing is made of nylon, jute, or cotton and is stretched tightly and tacked securely on both ends. Additional webbing is layered onto the first and attached to the frame, forming a new mat. The upholsterer positions the springs, either sinuous-wire or hand-tied coils, on the mat so they conform with it and compress evenly. The coils are then sewn or stapled to the mat or frame and tied to each other. Burlap or a pad of compressed fiber is stretched over the springs to hold their shape, then cut, smoothed, and tacked to the frame. The frame is prepared with cardboard to fill in open areas or give curve to the frame. Upholsterers then cover the springs with filler, such as foam or a polyester batt or similar fibrous batting material, to form a smooth, rounded surface.

Upholsterers also measure and cut fabric for arms, backs, and other furniture sections, leaving as little waste as possible. Using a basting stitch, the fabric pieces are sewn together to ensure a tight, smooth fit. The cover is removed and any necessary adjustments are made. The final upholstered item is sewn together then tacked, stapled, or glued to the frame. Finally, upholsterers attach any ornaments, such as fringes, buttons, or rivets.

Upholsterers use common hand tools: tack hammers, staple guns, tack and staple removers, pliers, and shears for example. They also employ such specialty equipment as webbing stretchers and upholstery needles; they may use sewing machines.

Upholsterers who work in upholstery shops may pick up and deliver furniture, or help customers select new coverings. Those who manage shops also order supplies and equipment and keep business records.

Working Conditions

Most upholsterers work inside a shop or factory. Working conditions in these facilities vary, typically according to size. Although many shops and factories are spacious, have adequate lighting, and are well ventilated and heated, some may be cramped and dusty.

Upholstery work is not dangerous, but upholsterers typically wear protective gloves and clothing when using sharp tools and lifting and handling furniture or springs. Upholsterers stand most of the workday, doing a lot of bending and heavy lifting. Also, they have to work in awkward positions for short periods of time.

Upholsterers typically spend long periods of time on their feet, often bending to do their work.

Employment

Furniture upholsterers held about 57,000 jobs in 1996; about 1 out of 3 was self-employed. Companies that manufacture household and office furniture employed 62 percent of the wage and salary upholsterers, and shops that reupholster and repair furniture employed another 17 percent. Over 10 percent worked in shops specializing in reupholstering the seats of automobiles and other motor vehicles, and a few worked in furniture stores.

Training, Other Qualifications, and Advancement

Most upholsterers are trained on the job as a helper to become an experienced worker. On-the-job training in a furniture factory, usually about six-weeks, may be supplemented by an additional 3 years of training in order to become a fully qualified upholsterer doing skilled production work. It may take as many as 8 to 10 years of experience and progressively more difficult work, however, for an upholsterer to reach the top of the trade. Generally, these upholsterers work on custom-made and reupholstered pieces at the high end of the market. Others learn upholstery through apprenticeship or formal training.

When hiring helpers, employers generally prefer people with some knowledge of the trade. Inexperienced persons may get basic training in upholstery in high school, vocational and technical schools, and some community colleges. Programs include sewing machine operation, measuring, cutting, springing, frame repair, tufting, and channeling, as well as business and interior design courses. However, additional training and experience are usually required before graduates can perform as quickly and efficiently as experienced upholsterers.

Upholsterers should have manual dexterity, good coordination, and, in some cases, the strength needed to lift heavy furniture. An eye for detail, a flair for color, and a creative use of fabrics are helpful.

The major forms of advancement for upholsterers are opening their own shop or moving into management. It is relatively easy to open a shop because a small investment in hand tools and a sewing machine are all that is needed. The upholstery business is extremely competitive, however, so operating a shop successfully is difficult. In large shops and factories, experienced or highly skilled upholsterers may become supervisors or sample makers.

Job Outlook

Little or no growth in employment of upholsterers is expected through the year 2006. Although automation is expected to reduce employment opportunities in many production occupations, this is not expected to occur with upholsterers in the furniture industry. Upholstery work is unique, and does not lend itself well to automation. Furthermore, the increased manufacture of new, relatively inexpensive upholstered furniture is expected to solidify employment at the current level. There still will continue to be a steady demand for upholsterers to restore more valuable furniture. Employment of upholsterers in automobile upholstery repair has been declining for some time although the rate of decline should slow. The widespread use of more durable fabrics for automobile seat covers, soft-tops, and convertibles is responsible, in part, for the loss of workers in this industry segment. However, this is offset, in part, by the reemergence of the luxury automobile, especially those with leather upholstery and convertible tops.

Despite the little or no growth in employment expected, there will still be many job openings created by the need to replace experienced workers who transfer to other occupations or leave the labor force. Therefore, opportunities for experienced upholsterers should be good. The number of upholsterers with experience is limited because few young people want to enter the occupation and few shops are willing to train people.

Earnings

Median weekly earnings of upholsterers were $366 in 1996; the middle 50 percent earned between $291 and $550 per week. The lowest 10 percent earned less than $250, and the top 10 percent earned more than $660.

Earnings of self-employed upholsterers depend not only on the size and location of the shop, but also on the number of hours worked.

Related Occupations

Other workers who combine manual skills and knowledge of materials such as fabrics and wood are fur cutters, furniture finishers, pattern and model makers, and casket coverers.

Sources of Additional Information

For details about work opportunities for upholsterers in your area, contact local upholstery shops or the local office of the State employment service.

To receive a list of technical schools accredited by the Accrediting Commission of Career Schools and Colleges of Technology that have programs in upholstery, contact:

☞ Accrediting Commission of Career Schools and Colleges of Technology, 2101 Wilson Blvd., Suite 302, Arlington, VA 22201.

Woodworking Occupations

(A list of D.O.T. codes is available on request. See page 496.)

Significant Points

- Most woodworkers are trained on the job; basic machine operations may be learned in a few months, but becoming a skilled woodworker often requires 2 years or more.

- Overall employment is projected to grow more slowly than average; demand for customized wood products will spur growth among precision woodworkers, while increasing automation and imports will result in a decline among woodworking machine operators.

- Job prospects will be best for highly skilled workers and those with knowledge of computer-controlled machine tool operation.

Nature of the Work

In spite of the development of sophisticated composites and alloys, the demand for wood products continues unabated. Helping to meet this demand are production and precision woodworkers. Production woodworkers can be found in primary industries, such as sawmills and plywood mills, as well as in secondary industries that manufacture furniture, kitchen cabinets, musical instruments, and other fabricated wood products. Precision woodworkers, on the other hand, usually work in small shops that make architectural woodwork, furniture, and many other specialty items.

All woodworkers are employed at some stage of the process through which logs of wood are transformed into finished products. Some of these workers produce the structural elements of buildings; others mill hardwood and softwood lumber; still others assemble finished wood products. They operate machines that cut, shape, assemble, and finish raw wood to make the doors, windows, cabinets, trusses, plywood, flooring, paneling, molding, and trim that are components of most homes. Others may fashion home accessories such as beds, sofas, tables, dressers, and chairs. In addition to these household goods, they also make sporting goods, including baseball bats, racquets, and oars, as well as musical instruments, toys, caskets, tool handles, and thousands of other wooden items.

Production workers usually set up, operate, and tend woodworking machines—such as power saws, planers, sanders, lathes, jointers, and routers—to cut and shape components from lumber, plywood, and other wood panel products. Working from blueprints, instructions from supervisors, or shop drawings that they produce, woodworkers first determine the best method of shaping and assembling parts. Before cutting, they must often measure and mark the materials. They also verify dimensions to adhere to specifications and may trim parts to insure a tight fit, using handtools such as planes, chisels, wood files, or sandpaper.

Most production woodworkers operate a specific woodworking machine, but others are responsible for a variety of machines. Lower skilled operators may merely press a switch on a woodworking machine and monitor the automatic operation, while more highly skilled operators set up equipment, cut and shape wooden parts, and verify dimensions using a template, caliper, or rule. In sawmills, machine operators cut logs into planks, timbers, or boards. In veneer mills, they cut veneer sheets from logs for making plywood. And in furniture plants, they make furniture components such as table legs, drawers, rails, and spindles.

The next step in the manufacturing process is the production of subassemblies using fasteners and adhesives. These pieces are then brought together to form a complete unit. The product is then finish sanded, stained, and if necessary, coated with a sealer such as lacquer or varnish. Woodworkers may perform this work in teams or be assisted by a helper.

Woodworkers have been greatly affected by the introduction of computer-controlled machinery. This technology raises worker productivity by allowing one operator to simultaneously tend a greater number of machines. With computerized numerical controls, an operator can program a machine to perform a sequence of operations automatically, resulting in greater precision and reliability. The integration of computers with equipment has improved production speeds and capabilities, simplified setup and maintenance requirements, and increased the demand for workers with some computer skills.

While this costly equipment has had a great impact on workers in the largest, most efficient firms, precision or custom woodworkers—who generally work in smaller firms—have continued to employ the same production techniques they have used for many years. These workers, such as cabinetmakers, model makers, wood machinists, and furniture and wood finishers, work on a customized basis, often building one-of-a-kind items. Precision woodworkers generally perform a complete cycle of cutting, shaping, surface preparation, and assembling prepared parts of complex wood components into a finished wood product. For this reason, they normally need substantial training and an ability to work from detailed instructions and specifications. In addition, they often are required to exercise independent judgment when undertaking an assignment.

Working Conditions

Working conditions vary by industry and specific job duties. In primary industries, such as logging and sawmilling, working conditions are physically demanding due to the handling of heavy, bulky material. Workers in this area may also encounter excessive noise and dust and other air pollutants. However, these factors may be controlled by using earplugs and respirators. Rigid adherence to safety precautions minimizes risk of injury from contact with rough woodstock, sharp tools, and power equipment. The risk of injury is also lowered by the installation of computer-controlled equipment that reduces the physical labor and hands-on contact with the machine.

In secondary industries, such as furniture and kitchen cabinet manufacturing, working conditions also depend on the industry and the particular job. Employees who operate machinery must often wear ear and eye protection, follow operating safety instructions, and use safety shields or guards. Those who work in the finishing area must either be provided with an appropriate dust or vapor mask, a complete protective safety suit, or be in a finishing environment that removes all vapors and particle matter from the atmosphere. Prolonged standing, lifting, and fitting heavy objects are also common characteristics of the job.

Hearing protection is required in some woodworking factories due to loud machinery.

Employment

Woodworkers held about 359,000 jobs in 1996. Self-employed woodworkers, mostly cabinetmakers and furniture finishers, accounted for 35,000 of these jobs. Employment was distributed as follows:

Woodworkers, precision	229,000
Woodworking machine setters and operators	130,000
Head sawyers	66,000
Woodworking machine operators	64,000

About 80 percent of salaried woodworkers were employed in manufacturing industries. Among these woodworkers, 27 percent were found in establishments fabricating household and office furniture and fixtures; another 27 percent were in establishments making millwork, plywood, and structural wood members, used primarily in construction; and 12 percent worked in sawmills and planing mills manufacturing a variety of raw, intermediate, and finished woodstock. Woodworkers also were employed by wholesale and retail lumber dealers, furniture stores, reupholstery and furniture repair shops, and construction firms.

Woodworking jobs are found throughout the country. However, production jobs are concentrated in the South and Northwest, close to the supply of wood, while furniture makers are more prevalent in the East. Custom shops can be found everywhere, but are generally concentrated in or near highly populated areas.

Training, Other Qualifications, and Advancement

Most woodworkers are trained on the job, picking up skills informally from experienced workers. Some acquire skills through vocational education or by working as carpenters on construction jobs. Others may attend colleges or universities that offer training in areas including wood technology, furniture manufacturing, wood engineering, and production management. These programs prepare students for positions in production, supervision, engineering, or management.

Beginners usually observe and help experienced machine operators. They may supply material or remove fabricated products from the machine. Trainees do simple machine operating jobs and are at first closely supervised by experienced workers. As they gain experience, they perform more complex jobs with less supervision. Some may learn to read blueprints, set up machines, and plan the sequence of their work. Most woodworkers learn the basic machine operations or job tasks in a few months, but becoming a skilled woodworker often requires 2 years or more.

Employers increasingly seek applicants with a high school diploma or the equivalent because of the growing sophistication of machinery and the constant need for retraining. Persons seeking woodworking jobs can enhance their employment and advancement prospects by completing high school and receiving training in mathematics, science, and computer applications. Other important qualities for entrants in this occupation include mechanical ability, manual dexterity, and the ability to pay attention to detail.

Advancement opportunities are often limited and depend upon availability, seniority, and a worker's skills and initiative. Experienced woodworkers may become inspectors or supervisors responsible for the work of a group of woodworkers. Production workers can advance into these positions by assuming additional responsibilities and by attending workshops, seminars, or college programs. Those who are highly skilled may set up their own woodworking shops.

Job Outlook
Employment of woodworkers is expected to grow more slowly than the average for all occupations through the year 2006, as job growth among precision woodworkers will be partially offset by the decline in employment of woodworking machine operators. Demand for woodworkers will be generated by increases in population, personal income, and business expenditures, in addition to the continuing need for repair and renovation of residential and commercial properties. Therefore, opportunities should be particularly good for woodworkers who specialize in such items as moldings, cabinets, stairs, and windows. Prospects will also be good for other highly skilled woodworkers and those with knowledge of computer-controlled machine tool operation.

Several factors may limit the growth of woodworking occupations in coming years. Technological advances like robots and computerized numerical control machinery will prevent employment from rising as fast as the demand for wood products, particularly in the mills and manufacturing plants where many of the processes can be automated. In addition, some jobs will be lost in the United States as imports continue to grow and as U.S. firms move production to other countries. Environmental measures designed to control various pollutants used in or generated by woodworking processes may also impact employment, especially in secondary industries such as household furniture. Finally, the demand for wood may be reduced somewhat as materials such as metal, plastic, and fiberglass continue to be used as alternatives to wood in many products. As a result of these trends, employment opportunities in the primary wood industries may be more limited than those in the secondary industries.

Employment in all woodworking occupations is highly sensitive to economic cycles, so job growth will be primarily affected by the overall state of the economy. Although this growth will be modest, thousands of openings will arise each year because of the need to replace experienced woodworkers who transfer to other occupations or leave the labor force.

Earnings
Median weekly earnings for salaried full-time precision woodworkers were about $400 in 1996. The middle 50 percent earned between $290 and $520. The lowest 10 percent earned less than $240, while the highest 10 percent earned over $690. Median weekly earnings for full-time woodworking machine operators were around $370 in 1996. The middle 50 percent earned between $290 and $500. The lowest 10 percent earned less than $220, while the highest 10 percent earned over $620. Earnings vary by industry, geographic region, skill, educational level, and complexity of the machinery operated.

Some woodworkers, such as those in logging or sawmills, who are engaged in processing primary wood and building materials, are members of the International Association of Machinists. Others may belong to the United Furniture Workers of America or the United Brotherhood of Carpenters and Joiners of America.

Related Occupations
Many woodworkers follow blueprints and drawings and use machines to shape and form raw wood into a final product. Workers who perform similar functions working with other materials include precision metalworkers, metalworking and plastics-working machine operators, metal fabricators, molders and shapers, and leather workers.

Sources of Additional Information
For information about woodworking occupations, contact local furniture manufacturers, sawmills and planing mills, cabinetmaking or millwork firms, lumber dealers, a local of one of the unions mentioned above, or the nearest office of the State employment service.

For general information about furniture woodworking occupations, contact:

☛ American Furniture Manufacturers Association, Manufacturing Services Division, P.O. Box HP-7, High Point, NC 27261.

Miscellaneous Production Occupations

Dental Laboratory Technicians

(D.O.T. 712.381-014, -018, -022, -026, -030, -042, -046, and -050, .664-010)

Significant points
- Employment should increase slowly as the public's improving dental health requires fewer dentures, but more bridges and crowns.

- Technicians' salaries usually start at a little over the minimum wage, but earnings tend to rise dramatically as skills and experience are acquired.

- Dental laboratory technicians require an artistic aptitude for detailed and precise work, a high degree of manual dexterity, and good vision.

Nature of the Work
Dental laboratory technicians fill prescriptions from dentists for crowns, bridges, dentures, and other dental prosthetics. Dentists send a specification of the item to be fabricated, along with an impression (mold) of the patient's mouth or teeth, to the technicians. Then dental laboratory technicians, also called dental technicians, create a model of the patient's mouth by pouring plaster into the impression and allowing

it to set. They place the model on an apparatus that mimics the bite and movement of the patient's jaw. The model serves as the basis of the prosthetic device. Technicians examine the model, noting the size and shape of the adjacent teeth or gaps within the gumline. Based upon these observations and the dentist's specifications, technicians build and shape a wax tooth or teeth using small hand instruments called wax spatulas and wax carvers. They use this wax model to cast the metal framework for the prosthetic device.

Once the wax tooth has been formed, dental technicians pour the cast and form the metal. Using small hand-held tools, they prepare the surface of the metal to allow the metal and porcelain to bond. They apply porcelain in layers to arrive at the precise shape and color of a tooth. Technicians place the tooth in a porcelain furnace to bake the porcelain onto the metal framework, then adjust the shape and color with subsequent grinding and addition of porcelain to achieve a sealed finish. The final product is an exact replica of the lost tooth or teeth.

In some laboratories, technicians perform all stages of the work, while in others, each does only a few. Dental laboratory technicians also may specialize in one of five areas: Orthodontic appliances, crowns and bridges, complete dentures, partial dentures, or ceramics. Job titles may reflect specialization in these areas. For example, technicians who make porcelain and acrylic restorations are called *dental ceramists*.

Salaried dental laboratory technicians usually work 40 hours a week, while self-employed technicians frequently work longer hours.

Working Conditions
Dental laboratory technicians generally work in clean, well-lighted, and well-ventilated areas. Technicians usually have their own workbenches, which may be equipped with Bunsen burners, grinding and polishing equipment, and hand instruments, such as wax spatulas and wax carvers.

The work is extremely delicate and quite time consuming. Salaried technicians usually work 40 hours a week, but self-employed technicians frequently work longer hours.

Employment
Dental laboratory technicians held about 47,000 jobs in 1996. Most jobs were in commercial dental laboratories, which usually are small, privately owned businesses with fewer than five employees. However, some laboratories are larger; a few employ over 50 technicians.

Some dental laboratory technicians worked in dentists' offices. Others worked for hospitals providing dental services, including Department of Veterans Affairs hospitals. Some technicians work in dental laboratories in their homes, in addition to their regular job. Approximately 1 technician in 7 is self-employed, a higher proportion than in most other occupations.

Training, Other Qualifications, and Advancement
Most dental laboratory technicians learn their craft on the job. They begin with simple tasks, such as pouring plaster into an impression, and progress to more complex procedures, such as making porcelain crowns and bridges. Becoming a fully trained technician requires an average of 3 to 4 years depending upon the individual's aptitude and ambition, but it may take a few more years to become an accomplished technician.

Training in dental laboratory technology is also available through community and junior colleges, vocational-technical institutes, and the Armed Forces. Formal training programs vary greatly both in length and the level of skill they impart.

In 1997, 35 programs in dental laboratory technology were approved (accredited) by the Commission on Dental Accreditation in conjunction with the American Dental Association (ADA). These programs provide classroom instruction in dental materials science, oral anatomy, fabrication procedures, ethics, and related subjects. In addition, each student is given supervised practical experience in the school or an associated dental laboratory. Accredited programs generally take 2 years to complete and lead to an associate degree.

Graduates of 2-year training programs need additional hands-on experience to become fully qualified. Each dental laboratory owner operates in a different way, and classroom instruction does not necessarily expose students to techniques and procedures favored by individual laboratory owners. Students who have taken enough courses to learn the basics of the craft are generally considered good candidates for training, regardless of whether they have completed the formal program. Many employers will train someone without any classroom experience.

Certification, which is voluntary, is offered by the National Board for Certification in five specialty areas: Crowns and bridges, ceramics, partial dentures, complete dentures, and orthodontic appliances.

In larger dental laboratories, technicians may become supervisors or managers. Experienced technicians may teach or take jobs with dental suppliers in such areas as product development, marketing, or sales. Still, for most technicians, opening one's own laboratory is the way toward advancement and higher earnings.

A high degree of manual dexterity, good vision, and the ability to recognize very fine color shadings and variations in shape are necessary. An artistic aptitude for detailed and precise work is also important. Useful high school courses are art, metal and wood shop, drafting, and sciences. Courses in management and business may help those wishing to operate their own laboratories.

Job Outlook
Job opportunities for dental laboratory technicians should be favorable despite very slow growth in the occupation. Employers have difficulty filling trainee positions, probably because of relatively low entry-level salaries and lack of familiarity with the occupation. Also, experienced technicians who have built up a favorable reputation with dentists should have good opportunities for establishing laboratories of their own.

Although job opportunities are favorable, employment of dental laboratory technicians is expected to grow more slowly than average through the year 2006, due to changes in dental care. The fluoridation of drinking water, which has reduced the incidence of dental cavities, and greater emphasis on preventive dental care since the early-1960s have improved the overall dental health of the population. As a result, fewer people are turning to full dentures. Most people will need only a bridge or crown. During the last few years, demand has arisen from an aging public that is growing increasingly interested in cosmetic prosthesis. For example, many dental laboratories are filling orders for composite fillings that are white and look like a natural tooth to replace older less attractive fillings.

Earnings
The average annual wage for all workers in dental laboratories was $23,723 in 1995. According to limited data, trainees in dental laboratories average only a little over minimum wage. However, earnings rise sharply with experience. Technicians who are particularly productive or have an artistic ability to carve exact replicas of lost teeth may make $50,000 a year or more. In general, earnings of self-employed technicians exceed those of salaried workers. Technicians in large laboratories tend to specialize in a few procedures, and therefore tend to be paid a lower wage than those employed in small laboratories who perform a variety of tasks.

Related Occupations
Dental laboratory technicians fabricate artificial teeth, crowns and bridges, and orthodontic appliances following the specifications and instructions provided by dentists. Other workers who make medical devices include arch-support technicians, orthotics technicians (braces and surgical supports), prosthetics technicians (artificial limbs and appliances), opticians, and ophthalmic laboratory technicians.

Sources of Additional Information
For a list of accredited programs in dental laboratory technology, contact:

☛ Commission on Dental Accreditation, American Dental Association, 211 E. Chicago Ave., Chicago, IL 60611. Homepage: http://www.ada.org

General information on grants and scholarships is available from dental technology schools.

For information on career opportunities in commercial laboratories, contact:

☛ National Association of Dental Laboratories, 555 E. Braddock Rd., Alexandria, VA 22314.

For information on requirements for certification, contact:

☛ National Board for Certification in Dental Technology, 555 E. Braddock Rd., Alexandria, VA 22314.

Ophthalmic Laboratory Technicians

(D.O.T. 711.381-010; 713.381-010, .681-010; 716.280-010, -014, and -018, .381-014, .382-010, -014, -018, and -022, .462-010, .681-010, -014, and -018, .682-014, and -018)

Significant points

- Nearly all ophthalmic laboratory technicians learn their skills on the job.

- The number of job openings will be low because the occupation is small and little growth in employment is expected.

Nature of the Work

Ophthalmic laboratory technicians—also known as manufacturing opticians, optical mechanics, or optical goods workers—make prescription eyeglass lenses. Prescription lenses are curved in such a way that light is correctly focused onto the retina of the patient's eye, improving vision. Some ophthalmic laboratory technicians manufacture lenses for other optical instruments, such as telescopes and binoculars. Ophthalmic laboratory technicians cut, grind, edge, and finish lenses according to specifications provided by dispensing opticians, optometrists, or ophthalmologists, and may insert lenses into frames to produce finished glasses.

Ophthalmic laboratory technicians should not be confused with workers in other vision care occupations. Ophthalmologists and optometrists are "eye doctors" who examine eyes, diagnose and treat vision problems, and prescribe corrective lenses. Ophthalmologists also perform eye surgery. Dispensing opticians, who may also do work described here, help patients select frames and lenses, and adjust finished eyeglasses. (See the section on physicians, which includes ophthalmologists, and the sections on optometrists and dispensing opticians elsewhere in the *Handbook*.)

Ophthalmic laboratory technicians read prescription specifications, then select standard glass or plastic lens blanks and mark them to indicate where the curves specified on the prescription should be ground. They place the lens into the lens grinder, set the dials for the prescribed curvature, and start the machine. After a minute or so, the lens is ready to be "finished" by a machine which rotates it against a fine abrasive to grind it and smooth out rough edges. The lens is then placed in a polishing machine with an even finer abrasive, to polish it to a smooth, bright finish.

Next, the technician examines the lens through a lensometer, an instrument similar in shape to a microscope, to make sure the degree and placement of the curve is correct. The technician then cuts the lenses and bevels the edges to fit the frame, dips each lens into dye if the prescription calls for tinted or coated lenses, polishes the edges, and assembles the lenses and frame parts into a finished pair of glasses.

In small laboratories, technicians usually handle every phase of the operation. In large ones, technicians may specialize in one or more steps, assembly-line style.

Working Conditions

Ophthalmic laboratory technicians work in relatively clean and well-lighted laboratories and have limited contact with the public. Surroundings are relatively quiet despite the humming of machines. At times, technicians wear goggles to protect their eyes, and may spend a great deal of time standing.

Most ophthalmic laboratory technicians work a 5-day, 40-hour week, which may include weekends, evenings, or occasionally, some overtime. Some work part time.

Ophthalmic laboratory technicians need to take precautions against the hazards associated with cutting glass, handling chemicals, and working near machinery.

Employment

Ophthalmic laboratory technicians held about 19,000 jobs in 1996. Forty percent were in retail optical stores that manufacture and sell prescription glasses. A little over thirty percent were in optical laboratories. These laboratories manufacture eyewear for sale by retail stores that fabricate prescription glasses, and by ophthalmologists and optometrists. Most of the rest were in optical laboratories that manufacture lenses for other optical instruments, such as telescopes and binoculars.

Training, Other Qualifications, and Advancement

Nearly all ophthalmic laboratory technicians learn their skills on the job. Employers filling trainee jobs prefer applicants who are high school graduates. Courses in science and mathematics are valuable; manual dexterity and the ability to do precision work is essential.

Technician trainees start on simple tasks such as marking or blocking lenses for grinding, then progress to lens grinding, lens cutting, edging, beveling, and eyeglass assembly. Depending on the individual's aptitude, it may take up to 6 months to become proficient in all phases of the work.

Ophthalmic laboratory technicians grind lenses for prescription eyeglasses.

Some ophthalmic laboratory technicians learn their trade in the Armed Forces. Others attend the few programs in optical technology offered by vocational-technical institutes or trade schools. These programs have classes in optical theory, surfacing and lens finishing, and the reading and applying of prescriptions. Programs vary in length from 6 months to 1 year, and award certificates or diplomas.

Ophthalmic laboratory technicians can become supervisors and managers. Some technicians become dispensing opticians, although further education or training may be required.

Job Outlook

Overall employment of ophthalmic laboratory technicians is expected to show little growth through the year 2006. Employment is expected to fall in manufacturing as firms invest in more efficient machinery. On the other hand, employment in retail trade will grow as fast as the average due to rising demand for corrective lenses from retail optical stores that manufacture prescription glasses on the premises and provide fast service.

Demographic trends make it likely that many more Americans will wear glasses in the years ahead. Not only will the population grow, but the number of middle-aged and older adults is projected to increase rapidly. Middle age is a time when many people use corrective lenses for the first time, and elderly persons require more vision care, on the whole, than others.

Fashion, too, influences demand. Frames come in a growing variety of styles and colors—encouraging people to buy more than one pair. Demand is also expected to grow in response to the availability of new technologies that improve the quality and look of corrective lenses, such as anti-reflective coatings and bifocal lenses without the line visible in more traditional bifocals.

Most job openings will arise from the need to replace technicians who transfer to other occupations or leave the labor force. Only a small number of job openings will occur in any year because the occupation is small.

Earnings

Data on earnings of ophthalmic laboratory technicians are very limited. Earnings vary greatly according to geographical region. Beginning workers often start near the minimum wage and can advance in just a few months. Supervisors and managers can earn substantially more.

Related Occupations

Workers in other precision production occupations include biomedical equipment technicians, dental laboratory technicians, orthodontic technicians, orthotics technicians, prosthetics technicians, and instrument repairers.

Sources of Additional Information

For general information about a career as an ophthalmic laboratory technician and a list of accredited programs in ophthalmic laboratory technology, contact:

☛ Commission on Opticianry Accreditation, 10111 Martin Luther King, Jr. Hwy., Suite 100, Bowie, MD 20720-4299.

Painting and Coating Machine Operators

(List of D.O.T. codes available on request. See p. 496.)

Significant Points

- Most workers acquire their skills on the job; for most operators, training lasts from a few days to several months, but becoming skilled in all aspects of automotive painting usually requires 1 to 2 years.

- Average employment growth is projected for skilled automotive painters, while expanding automation will re-

sult in slower-than-average growth for lesser skilled workers; job prospects should be favorable.

Nature of the Work

Millions of items ranging from cars to candy are covered by paint, plastic, varnish, chocolate, or some other type of coating solution. Often, the paints and coatings are merely intended to enhance the products' appeal to consumers, as with the chocolate coating on candy. More often, however, the protection provided by the paint or coating is essential to the product, as with the coating of insulating material covering wires and other electrical and electronic components. Many paints and coatings have dual purposes, such as the paint finish on an automobile, which heightens the visual appearance of the vehicle while providing protection from corrosion.

Painting and coating machine operators control the machinery that applies these paints and coatings to a wide range of manufactured products. Perhaps the most straightforward technique is simply dipping an item in a large vat of paint or other coating. This is the technique used by dippers, who immerse racks or baskets of articles in vats of paint, liquid plastic, or other solutions using a power hoist. Similarly, tumbling barrel painters deposit articles made of porous materials in a barrel of paint, varnish, or other coating, which is then rotated to insure thorough coverage.

Another familiar technique is spraying products with a solution of paint or other coating. Spray-machine operators use spray guns to coat metal, wood, ceramic, fabric, paper, and food products with paint and other coating solutions. Following a formula, operators fill the equipment's tanks with a mixture of paints or chemicals, adding prescribed amounts of solution. They also adjust nozzles on the spray guns to obtain the proper dispersion of the spray and hold or position the guns to direct the spray onto the article. Operators also check the flow and viscosity of the paint or solution and visually inspect the quality of the coating. When products are drying, these workers must often regulate the temperature and air circulation in drying ovens.

Painting and coating machine operators use various types of spray machines to coat a wide range of products. Often, their job title reflects the specialized nature of the machine or the coating being applied. For example, enrobing machine operators coat, or "enrobe," confectionery, bakery, and other food products with melted chocolate, cheese, oils, sugar, or other substances. Paper coating machine operators spray "size" on rolls of paper to give it its gloss or finish. And silvering applicators spray silver, tin, and copper solutions on glass in the manufacture of mirrors.

In response to concerns about air pollution and worker safety, manufacturers are increasingly using new types of paints and coatings on their products instead of high-solvent paints. Water-based paints and powder coatings are two of the most common. These compounds do not emit as many volatile organic compounds into the air and can be applied to a wide variety of products. Powder coatings are sprayed much like liquid paints and then heated to melt and cure the coating.

The adoption of new types of paints is often accompanied by a conversion to more automated painting equipment that the operator sets and monitors. When using these machines, operators position the automatic spray guns, set the nozzles, and synchronize the action of the guns with the speed of the conveyor carrying articles through the machine and drying ovens. The operator may also add solvents or water to the paint vessel that prepares the paint for application. During operation, these workers tend painting machines, observe gauges on the control panel, and randomly check articles for evidence of any variation from specifications. The operator then uses a spray gun to "touch up" spots where necessary.

Although the majority of painting and coating machine operators are employed in manufacturing, the best known group of these workers refinish old and damaged cars, trucks, and buses in automotive body repair and paint shops. Automotive painters are among the most highly skilled manual spray operators because they perform intricate, detailed work and mix paints to match the original color, a task which is especially difficult if the color has faded.

Painting and coating machine operators apply coatings to a variety of materials.

To prepare a vehicle for painting, automotive painters or their helpers use power sanders and sandpaper to remove the original paint or rust, and then fill small dents and scratches with body filler. They also remove or mask parts they do not want to paint, such as chrome trim, headlights, windows, and mirrors. Automotive painters use a spray gun to apply several coats of paint. They apply lacquer, enamel, or water-based primers to vehicles with metal bodies, and flexible primers to newer vehicles with plastic body parts. Controlling the spray gun by hand, they apply successive coats until the finish of the repaired sections of the vehicle matches that of the original undamaged portions. To speed drying between coats, they may place the freshly painted vehicle under heat lamps or in a special infrared oven. After each coat of primer dries, they sand the surface to remove any irregularities and to improve the adhesion of the next coat. Final sanding of the primers may be done by hand with a fine grade of sandpaper. A sealer is then applied and allowed to dry, followed by the final topcoat. When lacquer is used, painters or their helpers usually polish the finished surface after the final coat has dried.

Painting and coating machine operators work indoors and may be exposed to dangerous fumes from paint and coating solutions. Although painting is usually done in special ventilated booths, many operators wear masks or respirators that cover their noses and mouths. In addition, the Clean Air Act of 1990 has led to a decrease in workers' exposure to hazardous chemicals by regulating emissions of volatile organic compounds from paints and other chemicals. This legislation has also led to increasing use of more sophisticated paint booths and fresh air systems which provide a safer work environment.

Operators have to stand for long periods of time and, when using a spray gun, they may have to bend, stoop, or crouch in uncomfortable positions to reach different parts of the article. Most operators work a normal 40-hour week, but self-employed automotive painters sometimes work more than 50 hours a week, depending on the number of vehicles customers want repainted.

Employment

Painting and coating machine operators held about 171,000 jobs in 1996. Lesser skilled operators accounted for 7 out of 10 jobs, while more skilled transportation equipment painters accounted for 3 out of 10. About 85 percent of salaried workers were found in manufacturing establishments, where they applied coatings to items such as fabri-

cated metal products, motor vehicles and related equipment, industrial machines, household and office furniture, and plastics, wood, and paper products. Other workers included automotive painters employed by independent automotive repair shops and body repair and paint shops operated by retail automotive dealers. About 6 percent of painting and coating machine operators were self-employed; most of these were automotive painters.

Training, Other Qualifications, and Advancement

Most painting and coating machine operators acquire their skills on the job, usually by watching and helping experienced operators. For most operators, training lasts from a few days to several months. Coating and painting machine operators who modify the operation of computer-controlled equipment during operation may require additional training in computer operations and minor programming.

Similar to painting and coating machine operators, most automotive painters start as helpers and gain their skills informally on the job. Becoming skilled in all aspects of automotive painting usually requires 1 to 2 years of on-the-job training. Beginning helpers usually remove trim, clean and sand surfaces to be painted, mask surfaces that they do not want painted, and polish finished work. As helpers gain experience, they progress to more complicated tasks, such as mixing paint to achieve a good match and using spray guns to apply primer coats or final coats to small areas.

Painters should have keen eyesight and a good sense of color. Completion of high school is generally not required but is advantageous. Additional instruction is offered at many community colleges and vocational or technical schools. Such programs enhance one's employment prospects and can speed promotion to the next level.

Some employers sponsor training programs to help their workers become more productive. This training is available from manufacturers of chemicals, paints, or equipment or from other private sources. It may include safety and quality tips and knowledge of products, equipment, and general business practices. Some automotive painters are sent to technical schools to learn the intricacies of mixing and applying different types of paint.

Voluntary certification by the National Institute for Automotive Service Excellence (ASE) is recognized as the standard of achievement for automotive painters. For certification, painters must pass a written examination and have at least 2 years of experience in the field. High school, trade or vocational school, or community or junior college training in automotive painting and refinishing may substitute for up to 1 year of experience. To retain certification, painters must retake the examination at least every 5 years.

Experienced painting and coating machine operators with leadership ability may become team leaders or supervisors. Those who acquire practical experience or college or other formal training may become sales or technical representatives for chemical or paint companies. Some automotive painters open their own shops.

Job Outlook

Job prospects should be favorable for skilled automotive painters and new entrants with vocational school training in this specialty, as numerous employers have reported difficulties in locating qualified applicants. Overall employment of painting and coating machine operators is expected to grow more slowly than the average for all occupations through the year 2006. Average growth is projected for highly skilled transportation painters and automotive refinishers, compared to slower-than-average growth for lesser skilled painting and coating machine operators. In addition to job growth, several thousand jobs will become available each year as employers replace experienced operators who transfer to other occupations or leave the labor force.

An increasing population demanding more manufactured goods will spur employment growth among painting and coating machine operators. Employment growth will be limited, however, by improvements in the automation of paint and coating applications that will raise worker productivity. For example, operators will be able to coat goods more rapidly as they use increasingly sophisticated industrial robots that move and aim spray guns more like humans; as the cost of robots continues to fall, they will be more widely used. The Clean Air Act of 1990, which sets limits on the emissions of ozone-forming volatile organic compounds, also is expected to retard the employment growth of operators in manufacturing because firms tend to introduce more efficient automation as they switch to water-based and powder coatings to comply with the law.

Because the detailed work of refinishing automobiles in collision repair shops and motor vehicle dealerships does not lend itself to automation, painters employed in these establishments are projected to experience more rapid growth. As the demand for refinishing continues to grow, slower productivity growth among these workers will lead to employment increases more in line with the growing demand for their services.

The number of job openings for painting and coating machine operators may fluctuate from year to year due to cyclical changes in economic conditions. When demand for manufactured goods lessens, production may be suspended or reduced, and workers may be laid off or face a shortened workweek. Automotive painters, on the other hand, can expect relatively steady work because automobiles damaged in accidents require repair and refinishing regardless of the state of the economy.

Earnings

Painting and coating machine operators who usually worked full time had median weekly earnings of $420 in 1996. The middle 50 percent had usual weekly earnings between $330 and $630, while the highest 10 percent earned more than $760 weekly. Beginning automotive painter trainees earn considerably less than fully qualified painters.

Many automotive painters employed by automobile dealers and independent repair shops receive a commission based on the labor cost charged to the customer. Under this method, earnings depend largely on the amount of work a painter does and how fast it is completed. Employers frequently guarantee commissioned painters a minimum weekly salary. Helpers and trainees usually receive an hourly rate until they become sufficiently skilled to work on commission. Trucking companies, bus lines, and other organizations that repair their own vehicles usually pay by the hour.

Many painting and coating machine operators belong to unions, including the International Association of Machinists and Aerospace Workers; the International Brotherhood of Painters and Allied Trades; the International Union, United Automobile, Aerospace and Agricultural Implement Workers of America; the Sheet Metal Workers' International Association; and the International Brotherhood of Teamsters. Most union operators work for manufacturers and the larger automobile dealers.

Related Occupations

Other occupations in which workers apply paints and coatings include construction and maintenance painters, electrolytic metal platers, and hand painting, coating, and decorating occupations.

Sources of Additional Information

For more details about work opportunities, contact local manufacturers, automotive-body repair shops, automotive dealers, and vocational schools; locals of the unions previously mentioned; or the local office of the State employment service. The State employment service also may be a source of information about training programs.

For general information about a career as an automotive painter, write to:

☛ Automotive Service Association, Inc., P.O. Box 929, Bedford, TX 76021-0929.

Information on how to become a certified automotive painter is available from:

☛ National Institute for Automotive Service Excellence (ASE), 13505 Dulles Technology Dr., Herndon, VA 22071-3415.

Photographic Process Workers

(D.O.T. 962.361; 970.281-010 and -018, .381-010 and -034; 976.361, .380 -010, .381-010, -018, and -022, .382-010, -014, -018, -022, and -038, .384 -010, .385, .665, .681, .682-010, -014, -018, and -022, .684-014, and -030, .685-014, -018, -022, -026, -030, -034, and -038; 979.384)

Significant points

- Employment opportunities for photographic process workers are expected to decline as digital cameras become cheaper and more widely used.

- Most photographic process workers receive on-the-job training from their companies, manufacturers' representatives, and more experienced workers.

Nature of the Work

Both amateur and professional photographers rely heavily on photo processing workers to develop their film, make prints or slides, and do related tasks such as enlarging or retouching photographs. Photographic processing machine operators and tenders operate various machines, such as motion picture film printing machines, photographic printing machines, film developing machines, and mounting presses. Precision photographic process workers perform more delicate tasks, such as retouching photographic negatives and prints to emphasize or correct specific features. They may restore damaged and faded photographs, and may color or shade drawings to create photographic likenesses using an airbrush. They also may color photographs, using oil colors to produce natural, lifelike appearances.

The following jobs are examples of the work that machine operators perform. *Film process technicians* operate machines that develop exposed photographic film or sensitized paper in a series of chemical and water baths to produce negative or positive images. They first mix the developing and fixing solutions, following a formula. They then load the film in the machine, which immerses the

Photographic process workers must take certain precautions when working with harmful chemicals and fumes.

exposed film in a developer solution to bring out the latent image, immerses the negative in stop-bath to halt the developer action, immerses it in hyposolution to fix the image, and finally immerses it in water to remove chemicals. The worker then dries the films. In some cases, these steps may be performed by hand.

Color printer operators control equipment which produces color prints from the negatives. They read customer instructions to determine processing requirements. They load the rolls into color printing equipment, examine the negatives to determine equipment control settings, set the controls, and produce a specified number of prints. They inspect the finished prints for defects, remove any that are found, and finally insert the processed negatives and prints into an envelope for return to the customer.

Paper process technicians develop strips of exposed photographic paper; *takedown sorters* sort processed film; and *automatic mounters* operate equipment that cuts and mounts slide film into individual transparencies.

Precision photographic process workers, also known as digital imaging technicians, use computer images of conventional negative and use specialized computer software to vary the contrast of images, remove a unwanted background, or even combine features from several different photographs. Precision photographic process workers who work in portrait studios, on the other hand, deal in very high volume, and tend to work directly on the photo negative, rather than on a computer. These workers include *airbrush artists,* who restore damaged and faded photographs; *photographic retouchers*, who alter photographic negatives and prints to accentuate the subject; *colorists*, who apply oil colors to portrait photographs to create natural, lifelike appearances; and *photographic spotters*, who spot out imperfections on photographic prints.

Working Conditions

Work generally is performed in clean, appropriately lighted, well-ventilated, and air-conditioned offices, photofinishing laboratories, or 1-hour minilabs. In recent years, more commercial photographic processing has been done on computers than in darkrooms, and this trend is expected to continue. At peak times, portrait studios hire individuals who work at home retouching negatives.

Photographic process machine operators must do repetitive work at a rapid pace without any loss of accuracy. Precision process workers do detailed tasks, such as airbrushing and spotting, which may contribute to eye fatigue.

Some photographic process workers are continuously exposed to the chemicals and fumes associated with developing and printing. These workers must wear rubber gloves and aprons and take precautions against chemical hazards.

Many photo laboratory employees work a 40-hour week, including weekends, and may work overtime during peak seasons.

Employment

Photographic process workers held about 63,000 jobs in 1996; less than one quarter of the jobs were for precision workers. Photofinishing laboratories and 1-hour minilabs employed almost 70 percent. About 1 out of 4 worked for portrait studios and commercial laboratories that specialize in processing the work of professional photographers for advertising and other industries.

Employment fluctuates over the course of the year; peak periods include school graduation, summer vacation, and the December and January holiday season.

Training, Other Qualifications, and Advancement

Most photographic process workers receive on-the-job training from their companies, manufacturers' representatives, and more experienced workers. New employees gradually learn to use the machines and chemicals that develop and print film.

Employers prefer applicants who are high school graduates or those who have some experience or knowledge in the field. As preparation for precision work, proficiency in mathematics, art, chemistry, and computer science, as well as photography courses that

include instruction in film processing are valuable. Such courses are available through high schools, vocational-technical institutes, private trade schools, and colleges and universities.

On-the-job training in photographic processing occupations can range from just a few hours for print machine operators to several months for precision workers like airbrush artists, spotters, and negative retouchers. Some workers attend periodic training seminars to maintain a high level of skill. Manual dexterity, good hand-eye coordination, and good vision, including normal color perception, are important qualifications for precision photographic process workers. They must be comfortable with computers and able to adapt to technological advances.

Photographic process machine workers can advance from jobs as machine operators to supervisory positions in laboratories, or to management positions within retail stores.

Job Outlook

Employment of photographic process workers is expected to increase more slowly than the average for all occupations through the year 2006. Most openings will result from replacement needs, which tend to be higher for machine operators than for precision process workers.

Digital cameras, which use electronic memory rather than a film negative to record the image, are now available. Due to their expense, however, these cameras are typically used by advanced amateurs and professionals, and are popular in certain industries such as real estate and newspaper publishing. Therefore, conventional cameras, which use film to record images, are expected to continue to be the camera of choice among most amateur photographers. The film from these cameras is usually handled by photographic process machine operators and tenders who work in 1-hour mini-labs or off-site labs. Thus, traditional photo development will coexist, rather than compete directly, with electronic photography.

Once digital cameras and imaging become cheaper and more widely used by average consumers, the demand for photographic process workers is expected to be reduced. With this technology, consumers who have a personal computer and the proper software installed will not only be able to download and view their pictures on their computer, they will be able to manipulate, correct, and retouch their own picture, doing away with the need for photographic process workers. No matter what improvements occur in camera technology, though, there always will be some images which require precise manipulation and processing.

Earnings

Earnings of photographic process workers vary greatly depending on skill level, experience, and geographic location. Median earnings for full-time photographic process workers in 1996 were about $314 a week. The middle 50 percent earned between $251 and $412 a week. The lowest 10 percent earned less than $203 a week while the highest 10 percent earned more than $611.

Precision photographic process workers generally earn more as their skill level and the complexity of tasks they can perform increases.

Related Occupations

Precision photographic process workers need a specialized knowledge of the photodeveloping process. Other workers who apply specialized technical knowledge include chemical laboratory technicians, crime laboratory analysts, food testers, medical laboratory assistants, metallurgical technicians, quality control technicians, engravers, and some of the printing occupations, such as photolithographer.

Photographic process machine operators perform work similar to that of other machine operators, such as computer and peripheral equipment operators and printing press operators.

Sources of Additional Information

For information about employment opportunities in photographic laboratories and schools that offer degrees in photographic technology, write to:

☛ Photo Marketing Association International, 3000 Picture Place, Jackson, MI 49201.

Transportation and Material Moving Occupations

Busdrivers

(D.O.T. 913.363, .463-010, and .663-014 and -018)

Significant Points

- Opportunities should be good, particularly for school busdriver jobs.

- Many full-time transit, intercity, and motorcoach busdriver jobs offer relatively high earnings but have few prerequisite training requirements.

Nature of the Work

Busdrivers provide transportation for millions of Americans every day. *Intercity busdrivers* transport people between regions of a State or of the country; *local transit busdrivers*, within a metropolitan area or county; *motorcoach drivers*, on charter excursions and tours; and *school busdrivers*, to and from schools and related events. All drivers follow time schedules and routes over highways and city and suburban streets, to provide passengers with an alternative to the automobile and other forms of transportation.

Intercity busdrivers and local transit busdrivers report to their assigned terminal or garage, where they receive tickets or transfers and prepare trip report forms. School busdrivers do not always have to report to an assigned terminal or garage. In some cases, school busdrivers often have the choice of taking their bus home, or parking it in a more convenient area. Before beginning their routes, drivers check their vehicle's tires, brakes, windshield wipers, lights, oil, fuel, and water supply. Drivers also verify that the bus has safety equipment, such as fire extinguishers, first aid kits, and emergency reflectors in case of an emergency.

Drivers pick up and drop off passengers at bus stops, stations, or, in the case of students, at regularly scheduled neighborhood locations. Intercity and local transit busdrivers collect fares; answer questions about schedules, routes, and transfer points; and sometimes announce stops. School busdrivers do not collect fares. Instead, they prepare weekly reports with the number of students, trips or runs, work hours, miles, and the amount of fuel consumption. Their supervisors set time schedules and routes for the day or week. School busdrivers also must maintain order on their bus and enforce school safety standards by allowing only students to board.

Busdrivers' days are run by the clock, as they must adhere to strict time schedules. Drivers must operate vehicles safely, especially when traffic is heavier than normal. However, they cannot let light traffic put them ahead of schedule so that they miss passengers.

Busdrivers must be alert to prevent accidents, especially in heavy traffic or in bad weather, and to avoid sudden stops or swerves which jar passengers. School busdrivers must exercise particular caution when children are getting on or off the bus. They must know and reinforce the same set of rules used elsewhere in the school system.

Bus routes vary. Local transit busdrivers may make several trips each day over the same city and suburban streets, stopping as frequently as every few blocks. School busdrivers also drive the same routes each day, stopping to pick up pupils in the morning and return them to their homes in the afternoon. School busdrivers may also transport students and teachers on field trips or to sporting events. Intercity busdrivers may make only a single one-way trip to a distant city or a round trip each day, stopping at towns just a few miles apart or only at large cities hundreds of miles apart.

Motorcoach drivers transport passengers on charter trips and sightseeing tours. Drivers routinely interact with customers and tour

Busdrivers must be alert to prevent accidents, especially in heavy traffic or bad weather, and to avoid sudden stops or swerves which jar passengers.

guides to make the trip as comfortable and informative as possible. They are directly responsible for keeping to strict schedules, adhering to the guidelines of the tours' itinerary, and the overall success of the trip. Trips frequently last more than one day, and if they are assigned to an extended tour, they may be away for a week or more.

Local transit busdrivers submit daily trip reports with a record of tickets and fares received, trips made, and significant delays in schedule, and report mechanical problems. All busdrivers must be able to fill out accident reports when necessary. Intercity drivers who drive across State or national boundaries must comply with U.S. Department of Transportation regulations. These include completing vehicle inspection reports and recording distances traveled and the periods of time they spend driving, performing other duties, and off duty.

Working Conditions

Driving a bus through heavy traffic while dealing with passengers is not physically strenuous, but it can be stressful and fatiguing. On the other hand, many drivers enjoy the opportunity to work without direct supervision, with full responsibility for the bus and passengers.

Intercity busdrivers may work nights, weekends, and holidays and often spend nights away from home, where they stay at hotels at company expense. Senior drivers with regular routes have regular weekly work schedules, but others do not have regular schedules and must be prepared to report for work on short notice. They report for work only when called for a charter assignment or to drive extra buses on a regular route. Intercity bus travel and charter work tend to be seasonal. From May through August, drivers may work the maximum number of hours per week that regulations allow. During winter, junior drivers may work infrequently, except for busy holiday travel periods, and may be furloughed for periods of time.

School busdrivers work only when school is in session. Many work 20 hours a week or less, driving one or two routes in the morning and afternoon. Drivers taking field or athletic trips or who also have midday kindergarten routes may work more hours a week.

Regular local transit busdrivers usually have a 5-day workweek; Saturdays and Sundays are considered regular workdays. Some drivers work evenings and after midnight. To accommodate commuters, many work "split shifts," for example, 6 a.m. to 10 a.m. and 3 p.m. to 7 p.m., with time off in between.

Most busdrivers operate school buses.

Distribution of wage and salary employment, 1996

School busdrivers

Local busdrivers

Intercity busdrivers

Other busdrivers

Tour and charter bus drivers may work any day and all hours of the day, including weekends and holidays. Their hours are dictated by the charter trips booked and the schedule and the prearranged itinerary of tours. However, like all busdrivers, their weekly hours must be consistent with the Department of Transportation's rules and regulations concerning hours of service. For example, a long-distance driver cannot work more than 60 hours in any 7-day period and drivers must rest eight hours for every 10 hours of driving.

Employment
Busdrivers held about 592,000 jobs in 1996. More than a third worked part time. Nearly 3 out of 4 drivers worked for school systems or companies providing school bus services under contract, as shown in the accompanying chart. Most of the remainder worked for private and local government transit systems; some also worked for intercity and charter buslines.

Training, Other Qualifications, and Advancement
Busdriver qualifications and standards are established by State and Federal regulations. All drivers must comply with Federal regulations and any state regulations that exceed Federal requirements. Federal regulations require drivers who operate vehicles designed to transport 16 or more passengers to hold a commercial driver's license (CDL) from the State in which they live.

To qualify for a commercial driver's license, applicants must pass a written test on rules and regulations and then demonstrate they can operate a bus safely. A national data bank permanently records all driving violations incurred by persons who hold commercial licenses. A State may not issue a commercial driver's license to a driver who already has a license suspended or revoked in another State. Trainees must be accompanied by a driver with a CDL until they get their own CDL. Information on how to apply for a commercial driver's license may be obtained from State motor vehicle administrations.

While many States allow those who are 18 years and older to drive buses within state borders, the U.S. Department of Transportation establishes minimum qualifications for busdrivers engaged in interstate commerce. Federal Motor Carrier Safety Regulations require that drivers must be at least 21 years old and pass a physical examination once every two years. The main physical requirements include good hearing, 20/40 vision with or without glasses or corrective lenses, and a 70 degree field of vision in each eye. Drivers must not be color blind. Drivers must be able to hear a forced whisper in one ear at not less than 5 feet, with or without a hearing aide. Drivers must have normal use of arms and legs and normal blood pressure. Drivers may not use any controlled substances, unless prescribed by a licensed physician. Persons with epilepsy or diabetes controlled by insulin are not permitted to be interstate busdrivers. Federal regulations also require employers to test their drivers for alcohol and drug use as a condition of employment, and require periodic random tests while on duty. In addition, a driver must not have been convicted of

a felony involving the use of a motor vehicle; a crime involving drugs; driving under the influence of drugs or alcohol; or hit-and-run driving which resulted in injury or death. All drivers must be able to read and speak English well enough to read road signs, prepare reports, and communicate with law enforcement officers and the public. In addition, drivers must take a written examination on the Motor Carrier Safety Regulations of the U.S. Department of Transportation.

Many employers prefer high school graduates and require a written test of ability to follow complex bus schedules. Many intercity and public transit bus companies prefer applicants who are at least 24 years of age; some require several years of bus or truck driving experience. In some States, school busdrivers must pass a background investigation to uncover any criminal record or history of mental problems.

Because busdrivers deal with passengers, they must be courteous. They need an even temperament and emotional stability because driving in heavy, fast-moving, or stop-and-go traffic and dealing with passengers can be stressful. Drivers must have strong communication skills and be able to coordinate and manage large groups of people.

Most intercity bus companies and local transit systems give driver trainees 2 to 8 weeks of classroom and "behind-the-wheel" instruction. In the classroom, trainees learn U.S. Department of Transportation and company work rules, safety regulations, State and municipal driving regulations, and safe driving practices. They also learn to read schedules, determine fares, keep records, and deal courteously with passengers.

School busdrivers are also required to obtain a commercial driver's license from the State in which they live. Many persons who enter school busdriving have never driven any vehicle larger than an automobile. They receive between 1 and 4 weeks of driving instruction plus classroom training on State and local laws, regulations, and policies of operating school buses; safe driving practices; driver-pupil relations; first aid; disabled student special needs; and emergency evacuation procedures. School busdrivers must also be aware of school systems rules for discipline and conduct for busdrivers and the students they transport.

During training, busdrivers practice driving on set courses. They practice turns and zigzag maneuvers, backing up, and driving in narrow lanes. Then they drive in light traffic and, eventually, on congested highways and city streets. They also make trial runs, without passengers, to improve their driving skills and learn the routes. Local transit trainees memorize and drive each of the runs operating out of their assigned garage. New drivers begin with a "break-in" period. They make regularly scheduled trips with passengers, accompanied by an experienced driver who gives helpful tips, answers questions, and evaluates the new driver's performance.

New intercity and local transit drivers are usually placed on an "extra" list to drive charter runs, extra buses on regular runs, and special runs (for example, during morning and evening rush hours and to sports events). They also substitute for regular drivers who are ill or on vacation. New drivers remain on the extra list, and may work only part time, perhaps for several years, until they have enough seniority to receive a regular run.

Senior drivers may bid for runs they prefer, such as those with more work hours, lighter traffic, weekends off, or, in the case of intercity busdrivers, higher earnings or fewer workdays per week.

Opportunities for promotion are generally limited. However, experienced drivers may become supervisors or dispatchers, assigning buses to drivers, checking whether drivers are on schedule, rerouting buses to avoid blocked streets or other problems, and dispatching extra vehicles and service crews to scenes of accidents and breakdowns. In transit agencies with rail systems, drivers may become train operators or station attendants. A few drivers become managers. Promotion in publicly owned bus systems is often by competitive civil service examination. Some motorcoach drivers purchase their own equipment and go in to business for themselves.

Job Outlook
Persons seeking jobs as busdrivers over the 1996-2006 period should encounter good opportunities. Many employers are having difficulty

finding qualified candidates to fill vacancies left by departing employees. Opportunities should be best for individuals with good driving records who are willing to start on a part-time or irregular schedule, as well as for those seeking jobs as school busdrivers in metropolitan areas that are growing rapidly. Those seeking higher paying intercity and public transit busdriver positions may encounter competition.

Employment of busdrivers is expected to increase about as fast as average for all occupations through the year 2006, primarily to meet the transportation needs of a growing school-age population. Thousands of additional job openings are expected to occur each year because of the need to replace workers who take jobs in other occupations, retire, or leave the occupation for other reasons.

School busdriving jobs should be easiest to acquire because most of these positions are part time and often have a high turnover rate. The number of school busdrivers is expected to increase as a result of growth in elementary and secondary school enrollments. In addition, as more of the Nation's population is concentrated in suburban areas—where students generally ride school buses—and less in the central cities—where transportation is not provided for most pupils—more school busdrivers will be needed.

Employment of local transit and intercity drivers will grow as bus ridership increases. Local and intercity bus travel is expected to increase as the population and labor force grow and incomes rise, but more individual travelers will opt to travel by airplane or automobile rather than by bus. Most growth in intercity drivers will probably be in group charter travel, rather than scheduled intercity bus services. There may continue to be competition for local transit and intercity busdriver jobs in some areas because many of these positions offer relatively high wages and attractive benefits. The most competitive positions will be those offering regular hours and steady driving routes.

Full-time busdrivers are rarely laid off during recessions. However, hours of part-time local transit and intercity busdrivers may be reduced if bus ridership decreases, because fewer extra buses would be needed. Seasonal layoffs are common. Many intercity busdrivers with little seniority, for example, are furloughed during the winter when regular schedule and charter business falls off; school busdrivers seldom work during the summer or school holidays.

Earnings
Median weekly earnings of busdrivers who worked full time were $400 in 1996. The middle 50 percent earned between about $293 and $588 a week. The lowest 10 percent earned less than $233 a week, while the highest 10 percent earned more than $760 a week.

According to the American Public Transit Association, in early 1997 local transit busdrivers in metropolitan areas with more than 2 million inhabitants were paid an average hourly wage rate of $17.06 by companies with over 1,000 employees, and $15.43 by those with fewer than 1,000 employees. In smaller metropolitan areas, they had an average hourly wage rate of $14.04 in areas with between 250,000 and 500,000 residents, and $11.76 in areas with populations below 50,000. Generally, drivers can reach the top rate in 3 or 4 years.

According to a survey by the Educational Research Service, the average rate for school busdrivers employed by public school systems was $11.50 an hour during the 1996-97 school year. Lowest hourly rates averaged $9.93 while highest hourly rate averaged $13.06.

The fringe benefits busdrivers receive from their employers vary greatly. Most intercity and local transit busdrivers receive paid health and life insurance, sick leave, and free bus rides on any of the regular routes of their line or system. Drivers who work full time also get as much as 4 weeks of vacation annually. Most local transit busdrivers are also covered by dental insurance and pension plans. School busdrivers receive sick leave, and many are covered by health and life insurance and pension plans. Because they generally do not work when school is not in session, they do not get vacation leave. In a number of States, local transit and school busdrivers who are employed by local governments are covered by a State-wide public employee pension system.

Most intercity and many local transit busdrivers are members of the Amalgamated Transit Union. Local transit busdrivers in New York and several other large cities belong to the Transport Workers Union of America. Some drivers belong to the United Transportation Union and the International Brotherhood of Teamsters.

Related Occupations
Other workers who drive vehicles on highways and city streets are taxi drivers, truckdrivers, and chauffeurs.

Sources of Additional Information
For further information on employment opportunities, contact local transit systems, intercity buslines, school systems, or the local offices of the State employment service.

General information on busdriving is available from:
☛ American Bus Association, 1100 New York Avenue, N.W., Suite 1050, Washington, DC 20005.

General information on school busdriving is available from:
☛ National School Transportation Association, P.O. Box 2639, Springfield, VA 22152.

General information on local transit busdriving is available from:
☛ American Public Transit Association, 1201 New York Ave. NW., Suite 400, Washington, DC 20005.

General information on motorcoach driving is available from:
☛ United Motorcoach Association, 113 S. West St., 4th Floor, Alexandria, VA 22314 Telephone (toll free) 1-800-424-8262.

Material Moving Equipment Operators

(List of D.O.T. codes available on request. See p. 496.)

Significant Points
- Most acquire their skills on the job, but some construction equipment operators complete formal apprenticeship programs.

- Employment is expected to grow slowly because jobs are concentrated in the manufacturing and construction industries.

- Workers in these occupations often have high pay rates, but many cannot work in inclement weather, thus reducing earnings.

Nature of the Work
Material moving equipment operators use machinery to move construction materials, earth, petroleum products, coal, grain, manufactured goods, and other heavy materials. Generally, they move materials over short distances—around a construction site; factory; warehouse; or on, or off trucks and ships. Operators control equipment by moving levers or foot pedals, operating switches, or turning dials. They may also set up and inspect equipment, make adjustments, and perform minor repairs.

Material moving equipment operators are classified by the type of equipment they operate. Each piece of equipment requires different skills to move the different types of loads.

Crane and tower operators lift materials, machinery, or other heavy objects from the ground. They extend or retract a horizontally mounted boom to lower, or raise a hook attached to the loadline, often in response to hand signals and radioed instructions. Operators position the loads from the on-board console or from a remote console at the site. While crane and tower operators are conspicuous at office building and other construction sites, the biggest group works in primary metal, metal fabrication, and transportation equipment manufacturing industries that use heavy, bulky materials as inputs.

Excavation and loading machine operators dig and load sand, gravel, earth, or similar materials into trucks or onto conveyors using machinery equipped with scoops, shovels, or buckets. Construction and mining industries employ virtually all *excavation and loading machine operators.*

Grader, dozer, and scraper operators gouge out, distribute, level, and grade earth with vehicles equipped with a concave blade attached across the front. In addition to the familiar bulldozers, they operate trench excavators, road graders, and similar equipment. Operators maneuver the equipment in successive passes to raise or lower terrain to a specific grade. They may uproot trees and move large rocks while preparing the surface. Although most work in the mining and construction industries, a significant number of grader, dozer, and scraper operators work for state and local governments.

Hoist and winch operators control movement of cables, cages and platforms to move workers and materials for construction, manufacturing, logging and other industrial operations. They also lube and maintain the drum and cables and make other minor repairs.

Industrial truck and tractor operators drive and control industrial trucks or tractors equipped with lifting devices, such as a forklift or boom, and trailer hitches. A typical industrial truck, often called a forklift or lift truck, has a hydraulic lifting mechanism and forks. Industrial truck operators use these to carry loads on a skid, or pallet, around a factory or warehouse. They also pull trailers loaded with materials, goods, or equipment within factories and warehouses, or around outdoor storage areas.

Operating engineers are unique in that they use several types of moving equipment discussed above. They also may operate and maintain compressors, pumps, and other power equipment at the work site.

Other material moving equipment operators only tend air compressors or pumps at construction sites, or operate oil or natural gas pumps and compressors at wells and on pipelines. Still, some others operate ship loading and unloading equipment, conveyors, hoists, and other kinds of various specialized material handling equipment such as mine or railroad tank car unloading equipment.

Material moving equipment operators may keep records of materials moved, and do some manual loading and unloading. They also may clean, fuel, and service their equipment.

Working Conditions

Many material moving equipment operators work outdoors, in nearly every type of climate and weather condition. Industrial truck and tractor operators work mainly indoors, in warehouses or manufacturing plants. Some machines, particularly bulldozers and scrapers, are noisy and shake or jolt the operator. These jobs have become much safer with the adoption of overhead guards on forklift trucks and roll bars on construction machinery. As with most machinery,

most accidents can be avoided when observing proper operating procedures and safety practices.

Employment

Material moving equipment operators held about 1,097,000 jobs in 1996. They were distributed among the detailed occupation groups as follows:

Industrial truck and tractor operators	479,000
Operating engineers	157,000
Grader, dozer, and scraper operators	107,000
Excavation and loading machine operators	97,000
Crane and tower operators	45,000
Hoist and winch operators	9,000
All other material moving equipment operators	202,000

The largest proportion—30 percent—of material moving equipment operators worked in manufacturing. Most of these were industrial truck and tractor operators or crane and tower operators; a little over 50 percent of both worked for manufacturing companies. Over 25 percent of all material moving equipment operators worked in mining and construction; these operators were mostly in the remaining occupations, nearly half of whom worked in these two industries. Significant numbers of industrial truck and tractor operators also worked in State and local governments and in the trucking and warehousing, and wholesale trade industries. State and local governments also employed a large proportion of grader, dozer, and scraper operators, and operating engineers. A few material moving equipment operators were self-employed.

Material moving equipment operators work in every section of the country. Some work in remote locations on large construction projects, such as highways and dams, or in factory or mining operations.

Training, Other Qualifications, and Advancement

Material moving equipment operators usually learn their skills on the job. Operators need a good sense of balance, the ability to judge distance, and good eye-hand-foot coordination. Employers of material moving equipment operators prefer high school graduates, although, some equipment may require less education to operate. Mechanical aptitude and high school training in automobile mechanics are helpful because workers may perform some maintenance on their machines. Experience operating mobile equipment, such as farm tractors or heavy equipment in the Armed Forces, is an asset.

Beginning material moving equipment operators handle light equipment under the guidance of an experienced operator. Later, they may operate heavier equipment such as bulldozers and cranes. Some construction equipment operators, however, train in formal 3-year apprenticeship programs administered by union-management committees of the International Union of Operating Engineers and the Associated General Contractors of America. Because apprentices learn to operate a wider variety of machines than other beginners, they usually have better job opportunities. Apprenticeship programs consist of at least 3 years, or 6,000 hours of on-the-job training and 144 hours a year of related classroom instruction.

Private vocational schools offer instruction in the operation of certain types of construction equipment. Completion of such a program may help a person get a job as a trainee or apprentice. However, persons considering such training should check the reputation of the school among employers in the area.

Job Outlook

Employment of material moving equipment operators will increase about as fast as the average for all occupations through the year 2006. The expected growth stems from increased spending on improving the Nation's infrastructure of highways, bridges, and dams. However, equipment improvements, including the growing automation of material handling in factories and warehouses, continue to raise productivity and moderate for demand skilled operators. In addition to employment growth in this large occupation, many jobs will open up

The addition of overhead guards and roll bars to industrial trucks have made the work of material moving equipment operators safer.

because of the need to replace experienced workers who transfer to other occupations or leave the labor force.

Growth of employment among material moving equipment operators largely depends on the growth of the various industries that employ them. Construction and manufacturing employ the majority of these workers. Total employment in construction will grow more slowly than the average for all occupations, but employment of construction material moving equipment operators will grow as fast as the average. Employment of operators in manufacturing should decline in tandem with overall industry employment. However, very rapid employment growth of material moving operators is expected in temporary help organizations and companies that lease equipment

Growth of industrial truck and tractor operators, the largest occupation in this group, will be about as fast as the average for all occupations due to increased demand for operators who can manuever multiple pieces of equipment. In addition, more operator jobs will result as large factories and warehouses consolidate material handling systems and require more operators. However, growth of industrial truck and tractor operators will be constrained by technological improvements. Some systems use computerized dispatching or onboard data communication devices to enable industrial truck and tractor operators to move goods more efficiently. In other handling systems, industrial trucks and tractors may be replaced by computer-controlled conveyor systems, overhead handling systems, or automated vehicles that do not require operators.

Precision computerized controls and robotics will automate crane and tower operator and hoist and winch operator positions, slowing employment growth. Slow employment growth in construction and declines in manufacturing should cause all other material moving equipment operating occupations to grow more slowly than the average for all occupations. In addition, both construction and manufacturing are very sensitive to changes in economic conditions, so the number of job openings for operators in these industries may fluctuate from year to year.

Earnings
Earnings for material moving equipment operators vary considerably. In 1996, median earnings of all material moving equipment operators were $456 a week; the middle 50 percent earned between $329 and $606. The lowest ten percent earn an average $264 a week and the highest ten percent averaged $806 a week. The following shows 1996 median weekly earnings among the detailed occupation groups:

Crane and tower operators	$551.00
Operating engineers	508.00
Grader, dozer, and scraper operators	490.00
Hoist and winch operators	490.00
Excavation and loading machine operators	485.00
Industrial truck and tractor operators	415.00
All other material moving equipment operators	451.00

Pay scales generally are higher in metropolitan areas. Annual earnings of some workers may be lower than weekly rates would indicate, because the amount of time they work may be limited by bad weather.

Related Occupations
Other workers who operate mechanical equipment include truck and bus drivers, manufacturing equipment operators, and farmers.

Sources of Additional Information
For further information about apprenticeships or work opportunities for construction equipment operators, contact a local of the International Union of Operating Engineers; a local apprenticeship committee; or the nearest office of the State apprenticeship agency. In addition, the local office of the State employment service may provide information about apprenticeship and other training programs.

For general information about the work of construction equipment operators, contact:

☛ National Center for Construction Education and Research, University of Florida, P.O. Box 141104, Gainsville, FL 32614-1104.
☛ Associated General Contractors of America, Inc., 1957 E St. NW., Washington, DC 20006.
☛ International Union of Operating Engineers, 1125 17th St. NW, Washington, DC 20036.
☛ Specialized Carriers and Rigging Association, 2750 Prosperity Ave., Suite 620, Fairfax, VA 22301.

Information on industrial truck and tractor operators is available from:
☛ Industrial Truck Association, 1750 K St. NW, Suite 460, Washington, DC 20006.

Rail Transportation Workers

(D.O.T. 184.167-278; 198; 850.663-018; 910.362, .363, .364, .367-010, -022, .382, .583, .664, .667-026, .683-010, -014, -022; 913.463-014; 919.663-014, .683-018, -026; 932.664-010)

Significant Points

- The increasing efficiency of railroads should allow more goods to be shipped by rail with less employment of rail transportation workers, resulting in few job openings.

- Employment of locomotive engineers and subway and streetcar operators is projected to grow slowly.

- Many rail transportation workers have very high earnings.

Nature of the Work
Rail transportation is one of the centerpieces of the Nation's transportation network. Railroads deliver thousands of travelers and millions of tons of freight to destinations throughout the nation, while subways and streetcars provide passenger service within a single metropolitan area. Rail transportation workers make sure the goods and passengers arrive safely and on time.

Railroad transportation workers. *Locomotive engineers* and *rail yard engineers* are among the most experienced and skilled workers on the railroad. Locomotive engineers operate large trains, carrying cargo and passengers between stations, while rail yard engineers move cars within the yard to assemble or disassemble trains. In addition, some operators called *dinkey operators* run smaller engines that pull cars loaded with coal, rock, or supplies around industrial plants or mines.

The majority of engineers run diesel locomotives, but a few run electrically powered locomotives. Before and after each run, engineers check their locomotives for mechanical problems. Minor adjustments are made on the spot, while the engine shop supervisor handles any major problems.

Engineers use a throttle to start and accelerate the locomotive and air brakes or electric brakes to slow and stop the train. They monitor gauges and meters that measure speed, amperage, battery charge, and air pressure both in the brake lines and in the main reservoir. Both on the open road and in the yard, engineers watch for signals indicating track obstructions, other train movements, and speed limits. They must have a thorough knowledge of the signaling systems, yards, and terminals in addition to their routes. Engineers must be constantly aware of the condition and makeup of their train. This is extremely important because trains react differently to acceleration, braking, and curves, depending on the number of cars, the ratio of empty to loaded cars, and the amount of slack in the train.

Traditionally, freight train crews included either one or two brake operators—one in the locomotive with the engineer and another who rode with the conductor in the rear car. In an effort to reduce costs and take advantage of new technology, most railroads are phasing out *assistant engineers* and *brake operators*. Assistant engineers help monitor locomotive instruments and signals and observe the track for obstructions. Brake operators work under the direction of conductors

Engineers use a throttle to start and accelerate the locomotive and air brakes or electric brakes to slow and stop trains.

and did the physical work involved in adding and removing cars at railroad stations and assembling and disassembling trains in railroad yards. Now, most freight trains only use an engineer and a conductor, now stationed with the engineer, because new visual instrumentation and monitoring devices have eliminated the need for crew members located on the rear of the train.

Road conductors and *yard conductors* are in charge of the train and yard crews. Road conductors assigned to freight trains record each car's contents and destination, and add and remove cars at the proper points along the route. Conductors assigned to passenger trains collect tickets and fares and monitor passengers. At stops, conductors signal engineers when to pull out of the station. Most passenger trains also employ *assistant conductors* to help collect tickets and assist passengers.

Before a train leaves the terminal, the road conductor and engineer discuss instructions received from the dispatcher concerning the train's route, timetable, and cargo. While underway, conductors receive additional information by radio. This may include information about track conditions or instructions to pull off at the next available stop and let another train pass. During the run, conductors use two-way radios to communicate with engineers and conductors of other trains. They pass on instructions received from dispatchers and remind engineers of stops, reported track conditions, and the presence of other trains.

Conductors receive information from the crew regarding any equipment problems on the train. They may arrange for defective cars to be removed from the train for repairs at the nearest station or stop. They inform dispatchers of any problems using a radio or way-side telephone.

Yard conductors supervise the crews that assemble and disassemble trains. Some cars are sent to unload their cargo on special tracks, while other cars are moved to other tracks to await assemblage into new trains destined for different cities. Conductors tell engineers the make-up of trains and where to move the cars. Computerized switches divert the locomotive or cars to the proper track for coupling and uncoupling.

Before departure, the train is inspected to make sure all couplers and air-hoses are fastened, all hand brakes on the cars have been released, and the air brakes work properly. While underway, the crew regularly looks for smoke, sparks, and other signs of sticking brakes, overheated axle bearings, and other potentially faulty equipment. They may make minor repairs to air-hoses and couplers. In case of unexpected stops, the crew sets up signals to protect both ends of the train.

Subway and streetcar operators. *Subway operators* control trains that transport passengers throughout a city and its suburbs. The trains run on tracks in underground tunnels, on the surface or elevated above streets. Operators start, slow, or stop the train. They make announcements to riders, open and close the doors, and ensure that passengers get on and off the subway safely. Operators should have a basic understanding of the operating system and be able to recognize common equipment problems and the signaling systems used by the trains. When breakdowns or emergencies occur, operators contact their dispatcher or supervisor and may have to evacuate cars. To meet predetermined schedules, operators must control the train's speed and the amount of time spent at each station. Increasingly, however, these functions are controlled by computers and not by the operator.

Streetcar operators drive electric-powered streetcars or trolleys that transport passengers in metropolitan areas. Some tracks may be recessed in city streets or have grade crossings, so operators must observe traffic signals and cope with car and truck traffic. Operators start, slow, and stop their cars so passengers may get on or off with ease. They collect fares, and issue change and transfers. They also answer questions from passengers concerning fares, schedules, and routes.

Working Conditions

Because trains operate 24 hours a day, 7 days a week, many rail transportation employees often work nights, weekends, and holidays. On some days, operators work multiple shifts. Typically, seniority dictates who receives the more desirable shifts.

Most freight trains are unscheduled, and few workers on these trains have scheduled assignments. Instead, their names are placed on a list and they must await their turn to work. Jobs are usually handed out on short notice and often at odd hours. Because road service personnel often work on trains operating between stations that are hundreds of miles apart, they may spend several nights at a time away from home.

Freight and yard conductors spend most of their time outdoors in varying weather. The work of operators on local runs, where trains frequently stop at stations to pick up and deliver cars, is physically demanding. Climbing up and down and getting off moving cars is strenuous and can be dangerous.

Employment

Rail transportation workers held 83,000 jobs in 1996—including 25,000 conductors; 21,000 locomotive engineers; 18,000 brake, signal, and switch operators; and 5,000 rail yard engineers and dinkey operators. Subway and streetcar operators accounted for nearly 13,000 jobs. Railroads employ about 82 percent of all rail transportation workers. The rest work for state and local governments as subway and streetcar operators, and for mining and manufacturing establishments operating their own locomotives and rail cars to move ore, coal, and other bulk materials.

Training, Other Qualifications, and Advancement

Most railroad transportation workers begin as yard laborers, and later may have the opportunity to be trained for engineer or conductor jobs. Railroads require that applicants have a minimum of a high school diploma or equivalent. Applicants must have good hearing, eyesight, and color vision, as well as good hand-eye coordination, manual dexterity, and mechanical aptitude. Physical stamina is required for brake operator jobs. Employers require applicants for railroad transportation jobs to pass a physical examination and tests that screen for drug and alcohol use. In addition, under Federal law all members of train crews are subject to random drug and alcohol testing while on duty.

On most railroads, brake operators begin by helping assemble and disassemble trains in the yard. After these operators gain experience, they may have the opportunity for road assignments, although trains now carry brake operators only when they pick up, and drop off a lot of cars en route. On most railroads, new brake operators undergo extensive on-the-job training and classroom instruction, including instruction in signaling, coupling and uncoupling cars, throwing switches, and boarding moving trains.

Railroads require that applicants for locomotive engineer jobs be at least 21 years old. Frequently, employers fill engineer positions with workers who have experience in other railroad operating occupations. Federal regulations require that beginning engineers complete a formal engineer training program, including classroom and hands-on instruction in locomotive operation. The instruction is usually administered by the rail company. At the end of the training period, they must pass qualifying tests covering locomotive equipment, air brake systems, fuel economy, train handling techniques, and operating rules and regulations. The company issues the engineer a license once the applicant successfully passes the examinations. Other conditions and rules may apply to entry-level engineers, and these rules usually vary between railroads.

Engineers undergo periodic physical examinations and drug and alcohol testing to determine their fitness to operate locomotives. Unannounced safety and efficiency tests are also given to judge their overall conduct of operations. In some cases, engineers who fail to meet these physical and conduct standards are restricted to yard service; in other instances, they may be disciplined, trained to perform other work, or discharged.

Conductor jobs are generally filled from the ranks of experienced brake operators who have passed tests covering signals, timetables, operating rules, and related subjects. Some companies require these tests to be passed within the first 2 years of employment. New conductors are put on the extra board where they substitute for experienced conductors who are absent, because of vacation, illness, or other personal reasons, until permanent positions become available. On most railroads, conductors on the extra board may work as brake operators if there are not enough conductor runs available that month. Seniority usually is the main factor in determining promotion from brake operator to conductor and from extra board to a permanent position. There is a great deal of competition for conductor positions because they are fewer in number than entry-level occupations.

Most railroads maintain separate seniority lists for road service and yard service conductors. On some railroads, conductors start in the yards, then move to freight service, and finally to passenger service. Some conductors advance to managerial or administrative positions.

Newly trained workers, including brake operators, engineers, and conductors, are placed on the "extra board." Extra board designees work only when the railroad needs substitutes for regular workers who are absent. Extra board workers frequently must wait years until they accumulate enough seniority to get a regular assignment. Seniority rules may also allow workers with greater seniority to select their type of assignment. For example, an engineer may move from an initial regular assignment in yard service to road service.

For subway and streetcar operator jobs, subway transit systems prefer applicants to have a high school education. Applicants must be in good health, have good communication skills, and able to make quick, responsible judgments.

New operators are generally placed in training programs that last from a few weeks to 6 months. At the end of the period of classroom and on-the-job training, operators usually must pass qualifying examinations covering the operating system, troubleshooting, and evacuation and emergency procedures. Some operators with sufficient seniority can advance to station managers or other supervisory positions.

Job Outlook

Competition for available opportunities is expected to be keen. Many persons qualify for rail transportation occupations because education beyond high school is generally not required. Many more desire employment than can be hired because the pay is good and the work steady.

Employment for a majority of railroad transportation workers is expected to decline through the year 2006, with only locomotive engineers and subway and streetcar operators expected to grow. The total number of new jobs, however, will not be large. Also, relatively few opportunities resulting from replacement needs will occur because the attractive pay, tenure, and job security results in relatively few rail transportation workers leaving their jobs. In addition, the industry continues to reduce the workforce by eliminating positions left vacant by employees who retire from the rail industry or leave for other reasons. Mergers and divestiture-related cutbacks are also responsible for the reduction of rail occupation employment.

Demand for railroad freight service will grow as the economy and the intermodal transportation of goods expand and railroads become more efficient. Intermodal systems use trucks to pick-up and deliver the shippers' sealed trailers or containers, and trains to transport them long distance. This saves customers time and money by efficiently carrying goods across country. Intermodalism is the fastest growing type of railroad transportation. For railroads, the benefit has been the increased efficiency of equipment use, allowing increases in the number of runs each train makes in a year. In order to compete with other modes of transportation such as trucks, ships and barges, and aircraft, railroads are improving delivery times and on-time service while reducing shipping rates. As a result, businesses are expected to increasingly use railroads to carry their goods.

However, growth in the number of railroad transportation workers will generally be adversely affected by innovations such as larger, faster, more fuel-efficient trains and computerized classification yards that make it possible to move freight more economically. Computers are used to keep track of freight cars, match empty cars with the closest loads, and dispatch trains. Computer-assisted devices alert engineers to train malfunctions and new work rules have become widespread allowing trains to operate with two- or three-person crews instead of the traditional five-person crews. Employment of locomotive and yard engineers should grow as the industry expands and more trains are in operation, and because they will be less affected by technological changes and reductions in crew size.

Subway and streetcar operator employment is expected to grow as metropolitan areas build new rail systems and add new lines to existing systems. State and local governments support new construction because population growth in metropolitan areas has increased automobile traffic, making streets and highways more congested. Improved rail systems offer an alternative to automobile transportation that can reduce road congestion and, by reducing automobile use, contribute to government mandated improvements in air quality.

Earnings

According to the National Railroad Labor Conference in early 1997, the annual earnings for engineers ranged from an average of $52,903 for yard-freight engineers, to $65,374 for passenger engineers. For conductors, earnings ranged from an average of $48,991 for yard-freight conductors, up to $62,169 for local-freight conductors. The NRLC reports that brake operators averaged from $41,968 for yard-freight operators, up to $54,448 for local-freight operators.

According to mid 1997 American Public Transit Association data, hourly earnings of operators for commuter rail averaged $21.44; operators for heavy rail $18.70; and operators for light rail, $17.04. Wages generally varied about $5.00 to $7.00 per hour in either direction on the high and low end.

Most rail transportation employees in yards work 40 hours a week and receive extra pay for overtime. Most railroad workers in road service are paid according to miles traveled or hours worked, whichever leads to higher earnings. Full-time employees have steadier work, more regular hours, and higher earnings than those assigned to the extra board.

Most railroad transportation workers are members of unions. Many different railroad unions represent various crafts on the railroads. Most railroad engineers are members of the Brotherhood of Locomotive Engineers, while most other railroad transportation workers are members of the United Transportation Union. Many subway operators are members of the Amalgamated Transit Union, while others belong to the Transport Workers Union of North America.

Sources of Additional Information

To obtain information on employment opportunities for railroad transportation workers, contact the employment offices of the various railroads and rail transit systems, or State employment service offices.

For general information about career opportunities in passenger transportation, contact:
☛ American Public Transit Association, 1201 New York Ave. NW., Suite 400, Washington, D.C. 20005.

General information on rail transportation occupations and career opportunities as a locomotive engineer is available from:
☛ Brotherhood of Locomotive Engineers, 1370 Ontario Ave., Cleveland, OH 44113-1702.
☛ Association of American Railroads, 50 F Street, N.W., Washington, D.C. 20001.

For information on certification and training programs, contact:
☛ Johnson County Community College, National Association of Railroad Sciences, 12345 College Blvd., Overland Park, KS 66210.

Taxi Drivers and Chauffeurs

(D.O.T. 359.673-010 and -014; 913.463-018, .663-010; 919.663-010, and .683-014)

Significant Points

- There are taxi driver and chauffeur jobs to accommodate all work schedules, including full-time, part-time, night and evening, and weekend work.

- Opportunities should be good because replacement needs are high.

- The work of taxi drivers is unstructured and free from supervision, but the work of chauffeurs is dictated by the needs of the client or employer.

Nature of the Work

Anyone who has been in a large city knows the importance of taxi cab and limousine service. Drivers pick up passengers from street corners, airports, bus terminals, and train stations and drive them to their destinations. Their service helps residents, commuters, and visitors get from one place to another in a timely fashion.

Taxi drivers, also known as cab drivers, drive taxicabs, which most frequently are large, conventional automobiles modified for commercial passenger transport. Drivers collect fares from passengers at standardized rates based on zone areas, miles traveled, or time spent to reach the destination. They record the length of each trip and the point of origin and destination on a log, or trip sheet. These logs help check the drivers activity and efficiency.

At the start of their driving shift, cab drivers usually report to a cab service or garage where they are assigned a cab. They are given a trip sheet to record their name, work date, and cab identification number. Drivers check the cab's fuel and oil levels, and make sure the lights, brakes, and windshield wipers are in good working order. Drivers adjust rear and side mirrors and their seat for comfort. Any equipment or part not in good working order is reported to the dispatcher or company mechanic.

Taxi drivers pick up their passengers in one of three ways. Customers requesting transportation may call the cab company and give a location, an approximate pick up time, and their destination. The cab company dispatcher then relays the information to a driver by two-way radio, cellular telephone, or on-board computer. In urban areas, drivers may cruise streets and pick up passengers who hail or "wave" them down. Drivers also may get passengers by waiting at cab stands or in taxi lines at airports, train stations, hotels, and other places where people frequently seek taxis.

Drivers should be familiar with streets in the areas they serve so they can use the most efficient route to destinations. They should also know the locations of frequently requested destinations, such as airports, bus and railroad terminals, convention centers, hotels, and other points of interest. In case of emergency, the driver should know the location of fire and police stations and hospitals.

Upon reaching the destination, drivers determine the fare and announce it to the rider. Fares often consist of many parts. In many taxicabs, a taximeter measures the fare based on the length of the trip and the amount of time the trip took. Drivers turn the taximeter on when passengers enter the cab and turn it off when the they reach the final destination. The fare may also include a surcharge for additional passengers or for handling luggage, or an additional "drop charge" or flat fee added for the use the cab. Along with paying the fare, most passengers will give the driver a tip. The amount of the gratuity depends on the passengers' satisfaction with the quality and efficiency of the ride and courtesy of the driver. A driver will issue a receipt upon request from the passenger. Drivers enter onto the trip sheet all information regarding the trip, including the place and time of pick-up and drop-off and the total fee. They also must fill out accident reports when necessary.

Chauffeurs operate limousines, vans, and private cars for limousine companies, private businesses, government agencies, and wealthy individuals. Many chauffeurs transport customers in large vans between hotels and airports, bus, or train terminals. Others drive luxury automobiles, such as limousines, to popular entertainment and social events. Still others provide full time personal transportation for wealthy families and private companies.

At the start of the work day, chauffeurs ready their automobiles or vans for use. They inspect the vehicle for cleanliness and, when needed, vacuum the interior and wash the exterior body, windows, and mirrors. They check fuel and oil levels and make sure the lights, tires, brakes, and windshield wipers work. Chauffeurs may perform routine maintenance and make minor repairs, such as changing tires or adding oil and other fluids when needed. The chauffeur will take the vehicle to a professional mechanic if the vehicle requires more complicated repairs.

Chauffeurs cater to their passengers with attentive customer service and a special regard for detail. They help riders into the car by holding open doors, holding umbrellas when raining, and loading packages and luggage into the trunk of the car. They may perform errands for their employers such as delivering packages or picking up items. Drivers are also hired to meet clients who arrive at airports. Many chauffeurs offer conveniences and luxuries in their limousines to insure a pleasurable ride, such as newspapers, music, drinks, televisions, and telephones.

Working Conditions

Taxi drivers and chauffeurs occasionally have to load and unload heavy luggage and packages. Driving for long periods of time can be tiring, especially in densely populated urban areas, and driving in bad weather, heavy traffic, or mountainous and hilly areas can be nerve racking. Sitting for long periods of time can be uncomfortable. Drivers must be alert to conditions on the road, especially in heavy and congested traffic or in bad weather. They must also take precau-

Taxi drivers record the length of each trip, the point of origin, and the destination on a log or trip sheet.

tion to prevent accidents and avoid sudden stops, turns, and other driving maneuvers that would jar the passenger.

Work hours of taxi drivers and chauffeurs vary greatly. Some jobs offer full-time or part-time employment with work hours that can change from day to day or remain the same every day. It is often necessary for drivers to report to work on short notice. Chauffeurs who work for a single employer may be on call much of the time. Evening and weekend work are common for limousine and taxicab services.

The needs of the client or employer dictate the work schedule for chauffeurs. The work of taxi drivers is much less structured. Working free from supervision, they may break for a meal or a rest whenever their vehicle is unoccupied. However, taxi drivers risk robbery because they work alone and often carry large amounts of cash.

Full-time taxi drivers usually work one shift a day, which may last from 8 to 12 hours. Part-time drivers may work half a shift each day, or work a full shift once or twice a week. Drivers must be on duty at all times of the day and night, because most taxi companies offer services 24 hours a day. Early morning and late night shifts are common. Drivers work long hours during holidays, weekends, and other special events to support heavier demand for their services. Independent drivers, however, often set their own hours and schedules.

Design improvements in newer cabs have reduced stress and increased the efficiency of drivers. Many are equipped with tracking devices, fare meters, and dispatching equipment. Satellites and tracking systems link many of these state-of-the-art vehicles with company headquarters. Directions, traffic advisories, weather reports, and other important communications can be delivered to the driver anywhere in the transporting area in a matter of seconds. The satellite link-up also allows the dispatcher to track the vehicle's location, fuel consumption, and engine performance. Drivers can easily communicate with the dispatcher to discuss delivery schedules and courses of action should there be mechanical problems. When threatened with crime or violence, drivers may be able to alert authorities of emergency situations and have help arrive quickly.

Taxi drivers and chauffeurs meet many different types of people. Dealing with rude customers and waiting for passengers requires patience. Many municipalities and taxicab and chauffeur companies require dress codes. Typically, cities require taxicab drivers to wear clean and neat clothes. Many chauffeurs wear more formal attire, such as a tuxedo, a coat and tie, a dress, or a uniform and cap.

Employment

Taxi drivers and chauffeurs held about 106,000 jobs in 1996. About two-thirds were wage and salary workers employed by a company or business. Of these, about 33 percent worked for local and suburban transportation companies and about 20 percent worked for taxicab companies. Others worked for automotive rental dealerships, private households, and funeral homes. About a third were self-employed.

Training, Other Qualifications, and Advancement

Local governments set license standards and requirements for taxi drivers and chauffeurs. Although requirements vary, most municipalities have minimum qualifications for driving experience and training. Many taxi and limousine companies set higher standards than the ones required by law. It is common for an applicant's medical, credit, criminal, and drivers record to be reviewed. In addition, many companies require a higher minimum age and prefer that drivers be high school graduates.

Persons interested in driving a limousine or taxicab must first have a regular automobile driver's license. They also must acquire a chauffeur or taxi driver's license, commonly called a "hack" license. Local authorities generally require applicants for a hack license to pass a written exam or complete a training program. To qualify either through an exam or a training program, applicants must know local geography, motor vehicle laws, safe driving practices, regulations governing taxicabs, and display some aptitude for being able to deal courteously with the public. Training programs usually include a test on English proficiency, usually in the form of listening comprehension; applicants who do not pass the English exam must take an English course along with the formal driving program. Many taxicab or limousine companies sponsor applicants and give them a temporary permit that allows them to drive, even though they may not yet have finished the training program or passed the test.

Some taxi and limousine companies give new drivers on-the-job training. They show drivers how to operate the taximeter and communications equipment, and how to complete paperwork. Other topics covered may include driver safety and popular sightseeing and entertainment destinations. Many companies have contracts with social service agencies and transportation services to transport elderly and disabled citizens in non-emergency situations. To support these services, new drivers may get special training on how to handle wheelchair lifts and other mechanical devices.

Taxi drivers and chauffeurs should be able to get along with many different types of people. They must be patient when waiting for passengers or when dealing with rude customers, and driving in heavy and congested traffic requires tolerance and a mild temperament. Drivers should also be dependable because passengers rely on them to be picked up at prearranged times and taken to the correct destination. To be successful, drivers must be responsible and self-motivated because they work with little supervision.

The majority of taxi drivers and chauffeurs are called "lease drivers." Lease drivers pay a monthly or weekly fee to the company allowing them to lease their vehicle and have access to the company dispatch system. The fee may also include a charge for vehicle maintenance, insurance, and a deposit on the vehicle. Lease drivers may take their cars home with them when they are not on duty.

Opportunities for advancement are limited for taxi drivers and chauffeurs. Experienced drivers may obtain preferred routes or shifts. Some advance to dispatcher or manager jobs; others may start their own limousine company. On the other hand, many drivers like the independent, unsupervised work of driving their automobile.

In many small and medium size communities, drivers are able to buy their taxi, limousine, or other type of automobile and go into business for themselves. These independent owner-drivers require an additional permit that allows them to operate their vehicle as a company. Some big cities limit the number of operating permits and one may only become an owner-driver by buying a permit from an owner-driver who is leaving the business. Although many owner-drivers are successful, some fail to cover expenses and eventually lose their permit and automobile. Good business sense and courses in accounting, business, and business arithmetic can help an owner-driver become successful. Knowledge of mechanics can enable owner-driver to perform their routine maintenance and minor repairs to cut expenses.

Job Outlook

Persons seeking jobs as taxi drivers and chauffeurs should encounter good opportunities. Thousands of job openings will occur each year as drivers transfer to other occupations or leave the labor force. However, driving jobs vary greatly in terms of earnings, work hours, and working conditions. Because driving does not require education beyond high school, competition is expected for jobs offering regular hours and attractive earnings and working conditions. Opportunities should be best for persons with good driving records who are able to work flexible schedules.

Employment of taxi drivers and chauffeurs is expected to grow slower than the average for all occupations through the year 2006 as local and intercity travel increases with population growth. Opportunities should be best in metropolitan areas that are growing rapidly.

Job opportunities can fluctuate from season to season and from month to month. Extra drivers may be hired during holiday seasons and peak travel and tourist times. During economic slowdowns, drivers are seldom laid off but they may have to increase their working hours, and earnings may decline somewhat. Independent owner-operators are particularly vulnerable to economic slowdowns.

Earnings

Earnings of taxi drivers and chauffeurs vary greatly, depending on the number of hours worked, customers' tips, and other factors. Those who usually worked full time had median weekly earnings of $387 in 1996. The middle 50 percent earned between $258 and $653 a week. The lowest 10 percent earned less than $192, while the highest 10 percent earned more than $850 a week. Earnings were generally higher in more urban areas.

According to limited information available, the majority of independent taxi owner-drivers earned from about $20,000 to $30,000, including tips. However, professional drivers with a regular clientele often earn more. Many chauffeurs who worked full time earned from about $25,000 to $50,000, including tips.

Related Occupations

Other workers who drive vehicles on highways and city streets are ambulance drivers, busdrivers, and truckdrivers.

Sources of Additional Information

Information on licensing and registration of taxi drivers and chauffeurs is available from offices of local governments that regulate taxicabs. For information about work opportunities as a taxi driver or chauffeur, contact local taxi or limousine services or State employment service offices.

For general information about the work of taxi drivers, contact:

☛ International Taxicab and Livery Association, 3849 Farragut Ave., Kensington, MD 20895.

For general information about the work of limousine drivers, contact:

☛ National Limousine Association, 900 North Pitt Street, Suite 220, Alexandria, VA 22314, or call 1-800-652-7007.

Truckdrivers

(D.O.T. 292.353, .363, .463, .483, and .667; 900 through 904; 905.483, .663, and .683; 906; 909.663; 919.663-018, -022, -026 and .683-022 and -030; and 953.583)

Significant Points

- Opportunities in truck driving should be good because this occupation has among the greatest number of job openings each year.

- Competition is expected for jobs offering the highest earnings or most favorable work schedules.

- A commercial drivers' license is required to operate most larger trucks.

Nature of the Work

Throughout the day and night, trucks transport everything from milk to automobiles. Due to a trucks ability to link with rail, sea, or air transportation facilities, truckdrivers usually make the initial pickup from factories, consolidate cargo at terminals for intercity shipment, and deliver goods from terminals to stores and homes. Indeed, trucks move nearly all goods at some point in their journey from producers to consumers

Before leaving the terminal or warehouse, truckdrivers check their trucks for fuel and oil. They also inspect the trucks to make sure the brakes, windshield wipers, and lights are working and that a fire extinguisher, flares, and other safety equipment are aboard and in working order. Drivers adjust mirrors so that both sides of the truck are visible from the driver's seat, and make sure cargo will not shift during the trip. Drivers report to the dispatcher any equipment that does not work or is missing, or cargo that is not loaded properly.

Once underway, drivers must be alert to prevent accidents. Because drivers of large tractor-trailers sit higher than cars, pickups, and vans, they can see farther down the road. They seek traffic lanes that allow them to move at a steady speed, while keeping sight of varying road conditions.

The length of deliveries varies according to the merchandise being transported and the goods final destination. Local drivers provide daily service for a specific route while other drivers provide inter-city and interstate services that may vary from job to job. The drivers responsibilities and assignments reflect the time spent on the road and the type of payloads they transport.

On short "turnarounds," truckdrivers deliver a shipment to a nearby city, pick up another loaded trailer, and drive it back to their home base the same day; other runs take an entire day and keep drivers on the road overnight. On longer runs, drivers may haul loads from city to city for a week or more before returning home. Some companies use two drivers on very long runs. One drives while the other sleeps in a berth behind the cab. "Sleeper" runs may last for days, or even weeks, usually with the truck stopping only for fuel, food, loading, and unloading.

Some long-distance drivers who have regular runs transport freight to the same city on a regular basis. Many drivers perform unscheduled runs because shippers request varying service to different cities every day. Dispatchers tell these drivers when to report for work and where to haul the freight.

After long-distance truckdrivers reach their destination or complete their operating shift, the U.S. Department of Transportation requires they complete reports detailing the trip, the condition of the truck, and the circumstances of any accidents. In addition, federal regulations require employers to subject drivers to random alcohol and drug tests while on duty.

Long-distance truckdrivers spend most of their working time behind the wheel but may load or unload their cargo after arriving at the final destination. This is especially common when drivers haul specialty cargo, because they may be the only one at the destination familiar with this procedure or certified to handle the materials. Auto-transport drivers, for example, drive and position cars on the trailers and head ramps and remove them at the dealerships. When picking up or delivering furniture, drivers of long-distance moving vans hire local workers to help them load or unload.

When local truckdrivers receive assignments from the dispatcher to make deliveries, pickups, or both, they also get delivery forms. Before the drivers arrive for work, material handlers generally have loaded the trucks and arranged the items in order of delivery to minimize handling of the merchandise.

Local truckdrivers usually load or unload the merchandise at the customer's place of business. Drivers may have helpers if there are many deliveries to make during the day or if the load requires heavy

Even when goods are transported in containers by train or ship, they still must be delivered to their final destination by truck.

moving. Customers must sign receipts for goods and pay the drivers the balance due on the merchandise if there is a cash-on-delivery arrangement. At the end of the day, drivers turn in receipts, money, records of deliveries made, and report any mechanical problems on their trucks.

The work of local truckdrivers varies depending on the product they transport. Produce truckers usually pick up a loaded truck early in the morning and spend the rest of the day delivering produce to many different grocery stores. Lumber truckdrivers, on the other hand, make several trips from the lumber yard to one or more construction sites. Gasoline tank truckdrivers attach the hoses and operate the pumps on their trucks to transfer the gasoline to gas stations' storage tanks.

Some local truckdrivers have sales and customer relations responsibilities. The primary responsibility of "driver-sales workers," or "route drivers," is to deliver their firm's products and represent the company in a positive manner. Their reaction to customer complaints and requests for special services makes the difference between a large order and a lost customer. Route drivers also use their selling ability to increase sales and gain additional customers.

The duties of driver-sales workers vary according to their industry, the policies of their particular company, and the emphasis placed on their sales responsibility. Most have wholesale routes that deliver to businesses and stores rather than homes. For example, wholesale bakery driver-sales workers deliver and arrange bread, cakes, rolls, and other baked goods on display racks in grocery stores. They estimate the amount and variety of baked goods to stock by paying close attention to the items that sell well, and those sitting on the shelves. They may recommend changes in a store's order or may encourage the manager to stock new bakery products. Driver-sales workers employed by laundries that rent linens, towels, work clothes, and other items visit businesses regularly to replace soiled laundry. From time to time, they solicit new orders from businesses along their route.

Vending machine driver-sales workers service machines in factories, schools, and other buildings. They check items remaining in the machines, replace stock, and remove money deposited in the cash boxes. They also examine each vending machine to make minor repairs, clean machines, and to see merchandise and change are dispensed properly.

After completing their route, driver-sales workers order items for the next delivery based on what products have been selling well, the weather, time of year, and any customer feedback.

Working Conditions

Truckdriving has become less physically demanding because most trucks now have more comfortable seats, better ventilation, and im-

proved ergonomically designed cabs. However, driving for many hours at a stretch, unloading cargo, and making many deliveries can be tiring. Local truckdrivers, unlike long-distance drivers, usually return home in the evening. Some self-employed long distance truckdrivers who own and operate their trucks spend over 240 days a year away from home.

Design improvements in newer trucks are reducing stress and increasing the efficiency of long-distance drivers. Many are a virtual mini-apartment on wheels, equipped with refrigerators, televisions, and bunks. Satellites and tracking systems link many of these state-of-the-art vehicles with company headquarters. Troubleshooting, directions, weather reports, and other important communications can be delivered to the truck anywhere in the country in a matter of seconds. Drivers can easily communicate with the dispatcher to discuss delivery schedules and courses of action, should there be mechanical problems. The satellite link-up also allows the dispatcher to track the truck's location, fuel consumption, and engine performance.

Local truckdrivers frequently work 48 or more hours a week. Many who handle food for chain grocery stores, produce markets, or bakeries drive at night or early morning. Although most drivers have a regular route, some have different routes each day. Many local truckdrivers, particularly driver-sales workers, load and unload their own trucks. This requires considerable lifting, carrying, and walking each day.

The U.S. Department of Transportation governs work hours and other matters of trucking companies engaged in interstate commerce. For example, a long-distance driver cannot work more than 60 hours in any 7-day period. Federal regulations also require that truckers rest 8 hours for every 10 hours of driving. Many drivers, particularly on long runs, work close to the maximum time permitted because they are typically compensated by the number of miles or hours they drive. Drivers on long runs may face boredom, loneliness, and fatigue. Drivers frequently travel at night, on holidays, and weekends to avoid traffic delays and deliver cargo on time.

Employment

Truckdrivers held about 3,050,000 jobs in 1996. Most truckdrivers find employment in large metropolitan areas where major trucking, retail, and wholesale companies have their distribution outlets. Some drivers work in rural areas where they provide specialized services, such as delivering milk to dairies or coal to a railhead.

Trucking companies employed about a third of all truckdrivers in the U.S. Another 30 percent worked for companies engaged in wholesale or retail trade, such as auto parts stores, oil companies, lumber yards, or distributors of food and grocery products. The remaining truckdrivers were distributed across many industries including, construction, manufacturing, and services.

Fewer than 1 out of 10 truckdrivers are self-employed. Of these, a significant number are owner-operators who either serve a variety of businesses independently or lease their services and trucks to a trucking company.

Training, Other Qualifications, and Advancement

State and Federal regulations govern the qualifications and standards for truckdrivers. All drivers must comply with Federal regulations and any state regulations exceeding Federal requirements. Truckdrivers must have a driver's license issued by the State in which they live, and most employers require a clean driving record. Drivers of trucks designed to carry at least 26,000 pounds—including most tractor-trailers as well as bigger straight trucks—must obtain a commercial driver's license (CDL) from the State in which they live. All truckdrivers who operate trucks transporting hazardous materials must obtain a CDL regardless of truck size. Federal regulations governing the CDL exempt certain groups including farmers, emergency medical technicians, firefighters, some military drivers, and snow and ice removers. In many States, a regular driver's license is sufficient for driving light trucks and vans.

To qualify for a commercial driver's license, applicants must pass a written test on rules and regulations, and then demonstrate they can operate a commercial truck safely. A national data bank permanently records all driving violations incurred by persons who hold commercial licenses. A State will check these records and not issue a commercial driver's license to a driver who already has a license suspended or revoked in another State. Licensed drivers must accompany trainees until they get their own CDL. Information on how to apply for a commercial driver's license may be obtained from State motor vehicle administrations.

While many States allow those who are 18 years and older to drive trucks within state borders, the U.S. Department of Transportation establishes minimum qualifications for truckdrivers engaged in interstate commerce. Federal Motor Carrier Safety Regulations require that drivers must be at least 21 years old and pass a physical examination once every two years. The main physical requirements include good hearing, 20/40 vision with or without glasses or corrective lenses, and a 70 degree field of vision in each eye. Drivers can not be color blind. Drivers must be able to hear a forced whisper in one ear at not less than 5 feet, with or without a hearing aide. Drivers must have normal use of arms and legs and normal blood pressure. Drivers can not use any controlled substances, unless prescribed by a licensed physician. Persons with epilepsy or diabetes controlled by insulin are not permitted to be interstate truckdrivers. Federal regulations also require employers to test their drivers for alcohol and drug use as a condition of employment, and require periodic random tests while on duty. In addition, a driver must not have been convicted of a felony involving the use of a motor vehicle; a crime using drugs; driving under the influence of drugs or alcohol; or hit-and-run driving which resulted in injury or death. All drivers must be able to read and speak English well enough to read road signs, prepare reports, and communicate with law enforcement officers and the public. Also, drivers must take a written examination on the Motor Carrier Safety Regulations of the U.S. Department of Transportation.

Many trucking operations have higher standards than those described. Many firms require that drivers be at least 25 years old, be able to lift heavy objects, and have driven trucks for 3 to 5 years. Many prefer to hire high school graduates and require annual physical examinations.

Because drivers often deal directly with the company's customers, they must get along well with people. For jobs as driver-sales workers, employers emphasize the ability to speak well, a neat appearance, self-confidence, initiative, and tact. Employers also look for responsible, self-motivated individuals able to work with little supervision.

Driver-training courses are a desirable method of preparing for truckdriving jobs and for obtaining a commercial driver's license. High school courses in driver-training and automotive mechanics may also be helpful. Many private and public technical-vocational schools offer tractor-trailer driver training programs. Students learn to inspect the trucks and freight for compliance with Federal, State, and local regulations. They also learn to maneuver large vehicles on crowded streets and in highway traffic. Some programs provide only a limited amount of actual driving experience, and completion of a program does not assure a job. Persons interested in attending one of these schools should check with local trucking companies to make sure the school's training is acceptable. It is also a good idea to seek a school certified by the Professional Truck Driver Institute of America as providing training that meets Federal Highway Administration guidelines for training tractor-trailer drivers.

Training given to new drivers by employers is usually informal, and may consist of only a few hours of instruction from an experienced driver, sometimes on the new employee's own time. New drivers may also ride with, and observe experienced drivers before assignment of their own runs. Drivers receive additional training for driving a special type of truck or for handling hazardous materials. Some companies give 1 to 2 days of classroom instruction covering general duties, the operation and loading of a truck, company policies, and the preparation of delivery forms and company records. Driver-sales workers also receive training on the various types of products they carry so they will be more effective sales workers and better able to handle customer requests.

Very few people enter truckdriving professions directly out of school; most truckdrivers previously held jobs in other occupations. Driving experience in the Armed Forces can be an asset. In some instances, a person may also start as a truckdriver's helper, driving part of the day and helping to load and unload freight. Senior helpers receive promotion when driving vacancies occur.

New drivers sometimes start on panel, or other small "straight" trucks. As they gain experience and show competent driving skills, they may advance to larger and heavier trucks, and finally to tractor-trailers.

Although most new truckdrivers are assigned immediately to regular driving jobs, some start as extra drivers, substituting for regular drivers who are ill or on vacation. They receive a regular assignment when an opening occurs.

Advancement of truckdrivers is generally limited to driving runs that provide increased earnings or preferred schedules and working conditions. For the most part, a local truckdriver may advance to driving heavy or special types of trucks, or transfer to long-distance truckdriving. Working for companies that also employ long-distance drivers is the best way to advance to these positions. A few truckdrivers may advance to dispatcher, manager, or traffic work—for example, planning delivery schedules.

Some long-distance truckdrivers purchase a truck and go into business for themselves. Although many of these owner-operators are successful, some fail to cover expenses and eventually go out of business. Owner-operators should have good business sense as well as truckdriving experience. Courses in accounting, business, and business arithmetic are helpful, and knowledge of truck mechanics can enable owner-operators to perform their own routine maintenance and minor repairs.

Job Outlook

Opportunities should be favorable for persons interested in truckdriving. This occupation has among the largest number of job openings each year. Although growth in demand for truckdrivers will create thousands of openings, the majority will occur as experienced drivers transfer to other fields of work, retire, or leave the labor force for other reasons. Jobs vary greatly in terms of earnings, weekly work hours, number of nights spent on the road, and in the quality of equipment operated. Because truckdriving does not require education beyond high school, competition is expected for jobs with the most attractive earnings and working conditions.

Employment of truckdrivers is expected to increase about as fast as the average for all occupations through the year 2006 as the economy grows and the amount of freight carried by trucks increases. The increased use of rail, air, and ship transportation requires truck drivers to pick up and deliver shipments. Growth of long-distance drivers may slow as rail cars increasingly ship loaded trailers across country, but long-distance truckdrivers will continue to haul perishable goods.

Average growth of local and long-distance truckdriver employment should outweigh the slow growth in driver-sales worker jobs. The number of truckdrivers with sales responsibilities is expected to increase slowly because companies are increasingly splitting their responsibilities among other workers. They will shift sales, ordering, and customer service tasks to sales and office staffs, and use regular truckdrivers to make deliveries to customers.

Job opportunities may vary from year to year, because the strength of the economy dictates the amount of freight moved by trucks. Companies tend to hire more drivers when the economy is strong and deliveries are in high demand. Consequently, when the economy slows, employers hire fewer drivers or even lay off drivers. Independent owner-operators are particularly vulnerable to slowdowns. Industries least likely to be affected by economic fluctuation tend to be the most stable places for employment.

Earnings

As a general rule, local truckdrivers receive an hourly wage and extra pay for working overtime, usually after 40 hours. Employers pay long-distance drivers primarily by the mile. Their rate per mile can vary greatly from employer to employer and may even depend on type of the cargo. Typically, earnings increase with mileage driven, seniority, and the size and type of truck driven. Most driver-sales workers receive a commission, based on their sales in addition to an hourly wage.

In 1995, truckdrivers had average straight-time hourly earnings of $13.39. Depending on the size of the truck, average hourly earnings were as follows:

Medium trucks	$14.64
Tractor-trailers	14.07
Heavy straight trucks	13.17
Light trucks	8.56

Typically, the size of the trucking establishment influenced the relative size of drivers' earnings. Drivers employed by large establishments—those with 2,500 or more employees––had the highest earnings, averaging about $11.17 to $19.23 an hour in 1995. Smaller establishments—those with fewer than 500 employees—had average earnings that ranged from $8.31 to $16.11an hour in 1995. Truckdrivers in the Northeast and West had the highest earnings; those in the South had the lowest.

Most long-distance truckdrivers operate tractor-trailers, and their earnings vary widely, from as little as $20,000 to over $40,000 annually. Most self-employed truckdrivers are primarily engaged in long-distance hauling. After deducting their living expenses and the costs associated with operating their trucks, earnings of $20,000 to $25,000 a year are common.

Many truckdrivers are members of the International Brotherhood of Teamsters. Some truckdrivers employed by companies outside the trucking industry are members of unions representing the plant workers of the companies for which they work.

Related Occupations
Other driving occupations include ambulance driver, busdriver, chauffeur, and taxi driver.

Sources of Additional Information
Information on truckdriver employment opportunities is available from local trucking companies and local offices of the State employment service.

Information on career opportunities in truckdriving may be obtained from:
☛ American Trucking Associations, Inc., 2200 Mill Rd., Alexandria, VA 22314.
☛ American Trucking Association Foundation, 660 Roosevelt Ave., Pawtucket, RI 02860.

The Professional Truck Driver Institute of America, a nonprofit organization established by the trucking industry, manufacturers, and others, certifies truckdriver training programs meeting industry standards. A free list of certified tractor-trailer driver training programs may be obtained from:
☛ Professional Truck Driver Institute of America, 2200 Mill Rd., Alexandria, VA 22314, or by calling (703) 838-8842.

Water Transportation Occupations

(D.O.T 197.130-010, .133 except -010 and -018, .137-010, .161-010, .163 -010, -014, -018, .167-010; 911.131-010, .133-010, .137-010, -014, .263-010, .363-010, -014, .364-010, .584-010, .664-010, -014, .687-022 and -030, 951.685-018)

Significant Points
- Many jobs in water transportation occupations require a mariner's document or a license from the U.S. Coast Guard.

- Merchant mariners on ocean going ships are hired for various periods ranging from a single voyage to several continuous voyages and may be away from home continuously for months.

- Due to a declining ocean going fleet, there is keen competition for jobs aboard ocean going vessels and merchant mariners usually have to wait many months to find work.

Nature of the Work
Movement of huge amounts of cargo, as well as passengers, between nations and within our nation depends on workers in water transportation occupations. They operate and maintain deep sea merchant ships, tugboats, towboats, ferries, dredges, excursion vessels, and other waterborne craft on the oceans, the Great Lakes, in harbors, on rivers and canals, and on other waterways. (Workers who operate water craft used in commercial fishing are described in the section on fishers, hunters, and trappers elsewhere in the *Handbook*.)

Captains or *masters* are in overall command of the operation of a vessel and they supervise the work of any other officers and crew. They determine the course and speed, maneuver to avoid hazards, and continuously monitor the vessels position using charts and navigation aides. They either direct or oversee crew members who steer the vessel, determine its location, operate engines, communicate to other vessels, perform maintenance, handle lines, or operate vessel equipment. Captains and their department heads insure that proper procedures and safety practices are followed, check that machinery and equipment are in good working order, and oversee the loading and unloading of cargo or passengers. They also maintain logs and other records tracking the ships' movements and cargo/passenger carrying history.

Deck officers or *mates* perform the work for captains on vessels when they are on duty. Mates also supervise and coordinate activities for the crew aboard the ship. They inspect the cargo holds during loading to ensure the load is stowed according to specifications. Mates supervise crew members engaged in maintenance and the primary up-keep of the vessel. All mates stand watch for specified periods, usually 4 hours on and 8 hours off. However, on smaller vessels, there may be only one mate (called a pilot on some inland vessels) who alternates watches with the captain. The mate would assume command of the ship if the captain becomes incapacitated. When more than one mate is necessary aboard a ship, they are typically designated Chief Mate or First Mate, Second Mate, and Third Mate.

Engineers or *marine engineers* operate, maintain, and repair propulsion engines, boilers, generators, pumps, and other machinery.

Captains set course and speed, maneuver to avoid hazards, and periodically monitor position using charts and navigation aides.

Merchant marine vessels usually have four engineering officers: A chief engineer, and a first, second, and third assistant engineer. Assistant engineers stand periodic watches, overseeing the safe operation of engines and machinery.

Seamen, also called *deckhands*, particularly on inland waters, operate the vessel and its deck equipment under the direction of the ship's officers, and keep the non-engineering areas in good condition. They stand watch, looking out for other vessels and obstructions in the ship's path, and aids to navigation. They also steer the ship, measure water depth in shallow water, and maintain and operate deck equipment such as life boats, anchors, and cargo-handling gear. When docking or departing, they handle lines. They also perform routine maintenance chores such as repairing lines, chipping rust, and painting and cleaning decks or other areas. Seamen may also load and unload cargo, if necessary. On vessels handling liquid cargo, they hook up hoses, operate pumps, and clean tanks. Deckhands on tugboats or tow vessels tie barges together into tow units, inspect them periodically, and disconnect them when the destination is reached. Larger vessels usually have a *boatswain* or head seaman.

Qualified members of the engine department, or QMED's, work in the engine spaces below decks under the direction of the ship's engineers. They lubricate gears, shafts, bearings, and other moving parts of engines and motors, read pressure and temperature gauges and record data, and may assist with repair and adjust machinery.

A typical deep sea merchant ship has a captain, three deck officers or mates, a chief engineer and three assistant engineers, plus six or more seamen and QMED's. The size and service of the ship determines the number of crew for a particular voyage. Small vessels operating in harbors, rivers, or along the coast may have a crew comprised only of a captain and one deckhand. The cooking responsibilities usually fall under the deckhands duties. On larger ships, the crew may be as large as a captain, a mate or pilot, an engineer, and seven or eight seamen. Non-licensed positions on a large ship may include a full-time cook, an electrician, machinery mechanics, and a radio officer.

Pilots guide ships in and out of harbors, through straits, and on rivers and other confined waterways where a familiarity with local water depths, winds, tides, currents, and hazards such as reefs and shoals are of prime importance. Pilots on river and canal vessels are usually regular crew members, like mates. Harbor pilots are generally independent contractors, who accompany vessels while they enter or leave port. They may pilot many ships in a single day.

Working Conditions
Merchant mariners spend extended periods at sea, and earn leaves. Most are hired for one or more voyages that last for several months, although there is no job security after that voyage. Merchant marine officers and seamen, both experienced and beginners, are hired for voyages through union hiring halls or directly by shipping companies. These hiring halls prioritize the candidates by the length of time the person has been out of work, and fill open slots accordingly. Hiring halls are typically found in major sea ports.

At sea, these workers usually stand watch for 4 hours and are off for 8 hours, 7 days a week. Those employed on Great Lakes ships work 60 days and have 30 days off, but do not work in the winter when the lakes are frozen. Workers on rivers, canals, and in harbors are more likely to have year-round work. Some work 8- or 12-hour shifts and go home every day. Others work steadily for a week or month and then have an extended period off. When working, they are usually on duty for 6 or 12 hours and are off for 6 or 12 hours.

People in water transportation occupations work in all weather conditions. Although merchant mariners try to avoid severe storms while at sea, working in damp and cold conditions is often necessary. It is uncommon for vessels to sink, but workers face the possibility that they may have to abandon their craft on short notice if it collides with other vessels or runs aground. They also risk injury or death from falling overboard, and hazards associated with working with machinery, heavy loads, and dangerous cargo.

Most newer vessels are air-conditioned, soundproofed from noisy machinery, and have comfortable living quarters. Nevertheless, some mariners do not prefer the long periods away from home and the confinement aboard ship and leave the industry.

Employment
Water transportation workers held about 51,000 jobs in 1996. The total number who worked at during some point in the year was somewhat higher because many merchant marine officers and seamen worked only part of the year. The following tabulation shows employment in the occupations that make up this group:

Ship captains and mates 21,000
Sailors and deckhands 22,000
Marine engineers.. 9,000

Over 1,400 of the captains and pilots were self-employed, operating their own vessel, or were pilots who were independent contractors.

About 40 percent of all water transportation workers were employed on board merchant marine ships or U.S. Navy Military Sealift ships operating on the oceans or Great Lakes. Another 40 percent were employed in transportation services, working on tugs, towboats, ferries, dredges, and other watercraft in harbors, on rivers and canals, and other waterways. Others worked in water transportation services such as piloting vessels in and out of harbors, operating lighters and chartered boats, and in marine construction, salvaging, and surveying. The remaining water transportation workers were employed on vessels that carry passengers, such as cruise ships, casino boats, sightseeing and excursion boats, and ferries.

Training and Other Qualifications
Entry, training, and educational requirements for most water transportation occupations are established and regulated by the U.S. Coast Guard, part of the U.S. Department of Transportation. All officers and operators of watercraft must be licensed by the U.S. Coast Guard, which offers various different licenses, depending on the position and type of craft.

To qualify for a deck or engineering officers license, applicants must have graduated from the U.S. Merchant Marine Academy, or one of the six State academies, and pass a written examination. Federal regulations also require an applicant pass a physical examination and a drug screening before being considered. For example, persons without formal training can be licensed if they pass the written exam and posses at least 3 years of appropriate sea experience. However, it is difficult to pass the examination without substantial formal schooling or independent study. Also, because seamen may work 6 months a year or less, it can take 5 to 8 years to accumulate the necessary experience. The academies offer a 4-year academic program leading to a bachelor of science degree, a license as a third mate (deck officer) or third assistant engineer (engineering officer) issued by the U.S. Coast Guard, and a commission as ensign in the U.S. Naval or Coast Guard Reserve. With experience and passing of additional exams, third officers may qualify for higher rank. Because of keen competition, however, officers may have to take jobs below the grade for which they are licensed.

For employment in the merchant marine as an unlicensed seaman, a merchant mariner's document is needed. Applicants for merchant marine documents do not need to be U.S. citizens, but must be a registered alien. A medical certificate of excellent health, and a certificate attesting to vision, color perception, and general physical condition may be required for higher-level deckhands. While no experience or formal schooling is required, training at a union-operated school is the best source. Beginners are classified as ordinary seaman and may be assigned to the deck or engineering department. With experience at sea, and perhaps union-sponsored training, an ordinary seaman can pass the able seaman exam and move up with 3 years of service.

No special training or experience is needed to become a seaman or deckhand on vessels operating in harbors or on rivers or other waterways. Newly hired workers are generally given a short introductory course and then learn skills on the job. With experience, they are eligible to take a Coast Guard exam to qualify as a mate, pilot, or captain. Substantial knowledge gained through experience, courses taught at approved schools, and independent study are needed to pass the exam.

Harbor pilot training is usually an extended apprenticeship with a towing company or a pilot association. Entrants may be able seamen or licensed officers.

Job Outlook

Keen competition is expected to continue for jobs in water transportation occupations. Overall, employment in water transportation occupations is projected to decline through the year 2006. Opportunities will vary by sector.

Employment in deep sea shipping is expected to continue its long-term sharp decline as U.S.-staffed ships carry an even smaller proportion of international cargo. Stringent Federal regulations require larger crews on U.S.-flagged ships, which allow vessels that fly foreign flags—and have smaller crew sizes—to operate at lower cost and make a larger profit. A fleet of deep sea U.S.-flagged ships is considered to be vital to the Nation's defense, so some receive Federal support through a maritime security subsidy and other provisions in laws limit certain Federal cargoes to ships that fly the U.S. flag.

Newer ships are designed to be operated safely by much smaller crews. Innovations include automated controls and computerized monitoring systems in navigation, engine control, watchkeeping, ship management, and cargo handling. As older vessels are replaced, crew responsibilities will change. Seamen will need to learn new skills to be able to handle these varied duties.

Vessels on rivers and canals and on the Great Lakes carry mostly bulk products such as coal, iron ore, petroleum, sand and gravel, grain, and chemicals. Shipments of these products are expected to grow through the year 2006, but productivity increases should cause employment to decline. Employment in water transportation services is likely to show little or no change.

The decline in new opportunities has created competition for existing jobs, with many experienced merchant mariners going for long periods without work. As a result, unions generally accept few new members. Also, many merchant marine academy graduates have not found licensed shipboard jobs in the U.S. merchant marine, although most do find industry related jobs. Most are commissioned as ensigns in the U.S. Naval Reserve, and some may be selected for active duty in the Navy. Some find jobs as seamen on U.S. flagged or foreign-flagged vessels, tugboats, other watercraft, or civilian jobs with the U.S. Navy. Some take land-based jobs with shipping companies, marine insurance companies, manufacturers of boilers or related machinery, or other related jobs. Unless the number of people seeking merchant marine jobs declines sharply, the present intense competition is likely to continue.

Earnings

Water transportation workers who usually worked full time had median weekly earnings of $579 in 1996. The middle 50 percent earned between $402 and $860 a week. The lowest 10 percent earned less than $287, while the highest 10 percent earned more than $1,157 a week.

Captains and mates had median weekly earnings of $653 a week in 1996. The middle 50 percent earned between $394 and $904 a week. The lowest paid 10 percent earned less than $275, while the highest more than $1,203 a week.

Seamen had median weekly earnings of $520 a week in 1996. The middle 50 percent earned between $395 and $695 a week. The lowest 10 percent earned less than $288 a week, while the highest 10 percent earned more than $983 a week.

Related Occupations

Workers in occupations having duties and responsibilities similar to these occupations include fishing vessel captains, ferryboat operators, and long shoremen.

Sources of Additional Information

Information on merchant marine careers, training, and licensing requirements is available from:

☛ Maritime Administration, U.S. Department of Transportation, 400 7th St. SW., Room 302, Washington, DC 20590.

☛ U.S. Coast Guard, Licensing and Manning Compliance Division (C-MOC-1), 2100 2nd St. SW., Washington, DC 20593-0001.

Individuals interested in attending a merchant marine academy should contact:

☛ Admissions Office, U.S. Merchant Marine Academy, Steamboat Rd., Kings Point, NY 11024.

Handlers, Equipment Cleaners, Helpers, and Laborers

A list of D.O.T. codes is available on request. See page 496.)

Significant Points

- Job openings should be numerous because the occupation is very large and turnover is relatively high.

- Most jobs require no work experience or specific training, but earnings are low.

Nature of the Work

Employers in almost all industries hire entry-level workers to do tasks requiring little training, or to assist more skilled production, construction, operating, and maintenance workers. These workers perform a broad array of material mover, helper, or laborer jobs, ranging from moving boxes and feeding machines, to cleaning equipment and work areas. Many do tasks that are needed to make the work of more skilled employees flow smoothly. Handlers, equipment cleaners, helpers, and laborers often do routine physical work under close supervision. They generally follow oral or written instructions from supervisors or more experienced workers, and have little opportunity to make decisions. In order to perform their jobs effectively, helpers and laborers must be familiar with the duties of workers they help, as well as with the materials, tools, and machinery they use.

Freight, stock, and material hand movers move materials to and from storage and production areas, loading docks, delivery vehicles, ships' holds, and containers. They move materials either manually, or with forklifts, dollies, handtrucks, or carts. Their specific duties vary by industry and work setting. Specialized workers within this group include stevedores, who load and unload ships; baggage and cargo handlers, who work in transportation industries; and furniture movers. In factories, they may move raw materials, components, and finished goods between loading docks, storage areas, and work areas. They receive and sort materials and supplies and prepare them according to work orders for delivery to work or storage areas.

Hand packers and *packagers* manually pack, package or wrap a wide variety of materials. They may inspect items for defects, label cartons, stamp information on products, keep records of items packed, and stack packages on loading docks. This group also includes order fillers, who pack materials for shipment, as well as grocery store courtesy clerks. In grocery stores, they may bag groceries, carry packages to customers' cars, and return shopping carts to designated areas.

Machine feeders and *offbearers* feed materials into or remove materials from automatic equipment or machines tended by other workers.

Service station attendants fill fuel tanks and wash windshields on automobiles, buses, trucks, and other vehicles. They may perform simple service and repair tasks under the direction of a mechanic, such as change oil, repair tires, and replace belts, lights, windshield wipers, and other accessories. They may also collect payment for services and supplies.

Refuse and *recyclable material collectors* gather trash, garbage, and recyclables from homes and businesses along a regularly scheduled route, and deposit the refuse in their truck for transport to a dump, landfill, or recycling center. They lift and empty garbage cans or recycling bins by hand, or operate a hydraulic lift truck that picks up and empties dumpsters.

Vehicle washers and *equipment cleaners* clean machinery, vehicles, storage tanks, pipelines, and similar equipment using water and other cleaning agents, vacuums, hoses, brushes, cloths, and other cleaning equipment.

Parking lot attendants assist customers in parking their cars in lots or storage areas and collect fees from customers.

Helpers assist skilled construction trades workers, mechanics and repairers, and workers in production and extractive occupations. (Information on these occupations appears elsewhere in the *Handbook.*) They aid machine operators and tenders by moving materials, supplies, and tools to and from work areas. Some may tend machines if an operator is not available. Helpers may sort finished products, keep records of machine processes, report malfunctions to operators, and clean machinery after use. Mechanics' helpers assist mechanics and service technicians who repair motor vehicles, industrial machinery, and electrical, electronic, and other equipment. They may fetch tools, materials, and supplies; hold materials or tools; take apart defective equipment; remove rivets; prepare replacement parts; or clean work areas. Construction trades' helpers carry tools, materials, and equipment to carpenters, electricians, plasterers, masons, painters, plumbers, roofers, and other construction trades workers.

Construction craft laborers, on the other hand, are skilled workers who provide much of the physically demanding labor at building, highway, and heavy construction projects, tunnel and shaft excavations, and demolition sites. In addition to assisting other

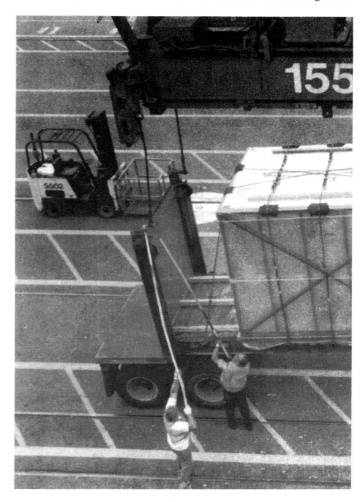

Freight, stock, and material movers move cargo onto a truck bed for transport.

trades workers, construction craft laborers clean and prepare sites, dig trenches, set braces to support the sides of excavations, and clean up rubble and debris. They perform a variety of excavation, tunneling, and pipe work, and work on their own on highly specialized tasks. The installation of utility pipe, for example, requires the set up and operation of laser guidance equipment for precise pipe elevation and placement. Tunnel and shaft projects require workers to be trained and experienced in the use of drilling equipment and explosives. Construction craft laborers operate jackhammers, earth tampers, cement mixers, buggies, skid steer loaders, "walk-behind" ditchdiggers, small mechanical hoists, laser beam equipment, and surveying and measuring equipment.

In addition to working on building and transportation projects, construction craft laborers work on other projects, such as hazardous waste cleanup and asbestos and lead abatement. In hazardous waste removal, they may operate, maintain, and read monitoring devices; perform material and atmospheric sampling; build, clean, or maintain facilities for hazardous material removal and decontamination; and package and transport hazardous or radioactive materials.

Working Conditions
Most handlers, equipment cleaners, helpers, and laborers do repetitive, physically demanding work. They may lift and carry heavy objects, and stoop, kneel, crouch, or crawl in awkward positions. Some work at great heights, or outdoors in all weather conditions. Some jobs expose workers to harmful materials or chemicals, fumes, odors, loud noise, or dangerous machinery. In order to avoid injury, these employees may need to wear safety clothing, such as gloves and hard hats, and devices to protect their eyes, mouth, or hearing.

Handlers, equipment cleaners, helpers, and laborers generally work 8 hour shifts, though 12 hour shifts are also common. In many industries, handlers, equipment cleaners, helpers, and laborers may have to work evening or "graveyard" shifts. Service station and parking lot attendants may work at night because these establishments may be open at all hours; handlers in grocery stores may stock shelves at night when stores are closed. Refuse and recyclable material collectors often work early morning shifts, starting at 5:00 or 6:00.

Employment
Handlers, equipment cleaners, helpers, and laborers held about 5 million jobs in 1996. Their employment was distributed among the following detailed occupations:

Hand packers and packagers	986,000
Freight, stock, and material movers, hand	808,000
Helpers, construction trades	546,000
Vehicle washers and equipment cleaners	274,000
Machine feeders and offbearers	265,000
Service station attendants	174,000
Refuse collectors	116,000
Parking lot attendants	68,000
All other helpers, laborers, and material movers, hand	1,737,000

Handlers, equipment cleaners, helpers, and laborers are employed throughout the country in virtually all industries, with the greatest numbers concentrated in manufacturing, construction, wholesale and retail trade, and certain services industries. Nearly 1 out of 4 works part time. A growing number are employed on a temporary or contract basis, many through firms providing personnel supply services. For example, companies that only need a laborer for a few days to move materials or clean up a site, contract with temporary help agencies specializing in providing this type of worker on a short term basis.

Training, Other Qualifications, and Advancement
For most handler, equipment cleaner, helper, and laborer jobs, employers will hire people without work experience or specific training. Some require a high school diploma, others do not. Most employers, however, require workers to be at least 18 years old and physically able to perform the work. For those jobs requiring physical exertion,

employers may require that applicants pass a physical exam. Some employers also require mandatory drug testing prior to employment. These workers are often younger than workers in other occupations—reflecting the limited training but significant physical requirements of many of these jobs.

For all of these jobs, employers look for people who are reliable and hard working. For those jobs that involve dealing with the public, such as grocery store helpers and service station or parking lot attendants, workers should be pleasant and courteous. Most jobs require reading and basic mathematics skills to read safety procedures and operating manuals, or billing and other records, and collect payment for services from customers.

Handlers, equipment cleaners, helpers, and laborers generally learn skills informally, on the job from more experienced workers or supervisors. However, workers who use dangerous equipment or handle toxic chemicals, for example, usually receive specialized training in safety awareness and procedures.

Formal apprenticeship programs provide more thorough preparation for jobs as construction craft laborers. Local apprenticeship programs are operated under guidelines established by the Laborers-Associated General Contractors of America (AGC) Education and Training Fund. Programs include at least 4,000 hours of on-the job training, including 144 hours of classroom training. Most union contractors and laborer unions require some training before an apprentice is placed on the job. Apprentices are instructed in the correct use of numerous tools and equipment that must be mastered before they complete the program.

Experience in many of these jobs may allow workers to qualify for, or become trainees for other skilled positions as construction trades workers, machine operators, assemblers, or other production workers; transportation, material moving equipment, or vehicle operators, or mechanics or repairers. In fact, many employers prefer to promote qualified handlers, equipment cleaners, helpers, and laborers as openings arise. Some may eventually advance to become supervisors.

Job Outlook
Employment of handlers, equipment cleaners, helpers, and laborers is expected to grow about as fast as the average for all occupations through the year 2006. Job openings should be numerous because the occupation is very large and turnover is relatively high—characteristic of occupations requiring little formal training. Many openings will arise from the need to replace workers who retire, transfer to other occupations, or who leave the labor force for other reasons.

Projected employment growth varies by detailed occupation. Among machine feeders and offbearers, for example, employment is expected to decline slightly, while employment of service station attendants is expected to experience little change. Employment of refuse collectors and other fright, stock, and material movers, on the other hand, should increase more slowly than the average, as should employment of construction trades helpers. Finally, driven largely by rapid growth in the industries in which they are most concentrated, faster than average growth is expected for vehicle washers and equipment cleaners, hand packers and packagers, and parking lot attendants.

Overall, demand for handlers, equipment cleaners, helpers, and laborers depends not only on growth in the industries employing these workers, but also on growth among the skilled workers whom they assist. Slower than average growth among helpers in construction, for example, is directly related to construction activity and the overall demand for construction trades workers. However, growth of helper and construction craft laborer employment will continue to be spurred by the Nation's emphasis on hazardous waste cleanup and other environmental projects, and on rebuilding infrastructure—roads, bridges, tunnels, and communications facilities, for example.

Employment growth will also be affected by automation. Some of these jobs are repetitive and, therefore, easily replaced by new machines and equipment that improve productivity and quality control. Some helper, handler, and hand packer and packaging jobs will be eliminated by automated material handling equipment, such as conveyor belts and computer-controlled lift mechanisms, and machines that automatically load, unload, and package materials. As more skilled jobs, such as those of assemblers, become automated, demand for these types of employees who assist them will decline.

Many employers have also begun consolidating or combining job responsibilities or contracting out labor. Job combinations may lead to displacement of handlers, equipment cleaners, helpers, and laborers because the tasks they perform may be assumed by more highly skilled workers, or they may be required to assist more than one type of worker. In addition, these types of occupations may increasingly be staffed by contingent workers as more employers turn to hiring temporary handlers, equipment cleaners, helpers, and laborers.

Earnings

Median weekly earnings for handlers, equipment cleaners, helpers, and laborers in 1996 were about $330. The middle 50 percent earned from $252 to $478 weekly. The top 10 percent earned over $648 weekly, and the bottom 10 percent earned less than $196 weekly. Median weekly earnings for the detailed occupations that comprise this group of workers are shown in the following tabulation.

Construction laborers	$372
Freight, stock, and material movers, hand	327
Helpers, construction and extractive occupations	311
Hand packers and packagers	310
Vehicle washers and equipment cleaners	292
Helpers, mechanics and repairers	283
Garage and service station related occupations	276
Parking lot attendants	272

Construction craft laborers generally have higher weekly earnings than other workers in this group. However, they may be more likely to lose work time because of bad weather and the cyclical nature of construction work. Mechanics and repairers' helpers, garage and service station related occupations, and parking lot attendants have the lowest weekly earnings among workers in this group.

About 20 percent of all handlers, equipment cleaners, helpers, construction craft, and other laborers are members of a union. Many belong to the Laborers' International Union of North America.

Related Occupations

Other entry-level workers who perform mostly physical work are roustabouts in the oil industry, certain timber cutting and logging occupations, and groundskeepers. The jobs of handlers, equipment cleaners, helpers, and laborers are often similar to those of the more experienced workers they assist, including machine operators, construction craft workers, assemblers, mechanics, and repairers.

Sources of Additional Information

For information about jobs as handlers, equipment cleaners, helpers, and laborers, contact local building or construction contractors, manufacturers, and wholesale and retail establishments, or the local office of the State employment service.

For general information about the work of construction craft laborers, contact:

☛ Laborers' International Union of North America, 905 16th St. NW., Washington, DC 20006.

Job Opportunities in the Armed Forces

Significant Points

- Opportunities should be good in all branches of the Armed Forces through the year 2006 for applicants meeting the desired standards.

- The needs of the military always come first, so hours and working conditions can vary substantially.

- Some training or duty assignments may be hazardous, even in peacetime.

Nature of the Work

Maintaining a strong National defense encompasses such diverse activities as running a hospital, commanding a tank crew, programming computers, operating a nuclear reactor, and repairing and maintaining a helicopter. The military's occupational diversity provides educational opportunities and work experience in literally hundreds of occupations. Military personnel hold managerial and administrative jobs; professional, technical, and clerical jobs; construction jobs; electrical and electronics jobs; mechanical and repair jobs; and many others. The military provides training and work experience for people who serve a single enlistment of 3 to 6 years of active duty, those who embark on a career that lasts 20 years or more, and those who serve in the Army, Navy, Marine, Air Force, and Coast Guard Reserves and Army and Air National Guard.

There are more than 360 basic and advanced military occupational specialties for enlisted personnel and almost as many for officers. Over 75 percent of these occupational specialties have civilian counterparts. A brief discussion of the major military occupational groups follows.

Infantry, gun crews, and seamanship specialists are the front line of the Armed Forces. Officers plan and direct military operations, oversee security activities, and serve as combat leaders and pilots. Enlisted personnel serve as infantry or weapons specialists, aircraft crew members, armored and amphibious vehicle crew, artillery, gunnery, or rocket specialists, and combat engineers. Some of these specialties involve skills that can be applied to a number of civilian occupations such as police officers, commercial pilots, and heavy equipment operators. In addition, people in this category learn how to work as team members and develop leadership, managerial, and supervisory skills.

Military personnel assigned to *electronic equipment repair occupations* are responsible for maintaining and repairing many different types of equipment. Officers oversee the regular maintenance and repair of avionics, communications, radar, and air traffic control equipment. Enlisted personnel repair radio, navigation, missile guidance, and flight control equipment as well as telephone and data processing equipment. Many of these skills are directly transferable to jobs in the civilian sector.

Communications and intelligence specialists in the military have civilian scientific, engineering, and investigative counterparts. Officers serve as intelligence gatherers and interpreters, cryptologists, information analysts, translators, and in related intelligence occupations. Enlisted personnel work as computer programmers, air traffic controllers, interpreters and translators, radio, radar, and sonar operators, and interrogation and investigative specialists.

Military *medical and dental occupations* all have civilian counterparts. Holding the rank of health care officer are physicians, dentists, optometrists, nurses, therapists, veterinarians, pharmacists, and others in health diagnosing and treating occupations. Enlisted personnel are trained to work as medical laboratory technologists and technicians, radiological technologists, emergency medical technicians, dental assistants, optical assistants, pharmaceutical assistants, sanitation specialists, and veterinary assistants. Health professions training obtained in the military is usually recognized in the civilian sector and service-trained health professionals are eligible to apply for certi-

Marines undergo rigorous training.

fication or registration in the civilian sector, which is often a hiring prerequisite.

Military experience in *other technical and allied specialty occupations* is often directly transferable to civilian life. Officers in this field work as meteorologists, mapping directors, television and motion picture directors, and band directors. Enlisted personnel are trained to work as photographers, motion picture camera operators, mapping and surveying specialists, illustrators, weather data collectors, explosives disposal specialists, divers, and musicians.

Functional support and administrative occupations in military service require the same skills as similar jobs in private businesses and government agencies. Officers in this category work as directors, executives, adjutants, administrative officers, personnel managers, training administrators, budget officers, finance officers, public affairs officers, accountants, hospital administrators, inspectors, computer systems managers, and lawyers. Enlisted personnel in this category work as accounting, payroll, personnel, and postal clerks; computer programmers and operators; chaplain assistants; counseling aides; typists; and storekeepers.

Those in *electrical and mechanical equipment repair occupations* maintain aircraft, motor vehicles, and ships. Officers oversee the maintenance of aircraft, missiles, conventional and nuclear-powered ships, trucks, earth-moving equipment, and other vehicles. Enlisted personnel serve as mechanics, engine specialists, and boiler technicians. They also install and maintain wire communications systems such as telephones. Skills obtained in these jobs are readily transferable to those in the civilian sector.

Military personnel assigned to *craft occupations* are skilled craft workers. Officers serve as civil engineers and architects and manage the work of enlisted personnel who work as carpenters, construction equipment operators, metalworkers, machinists, plumbers, welders, electricians, and heating and air-conditioning specialists.

Military personnel in *service and supply occupations* handle food service, security, and personal services and supply. Officers work as logistics officers, supply managers, transportation and traffic managers, and procurement officers. Enlisted personnel include military police, correctional specialists, criminal investigators, firefighters, and food preparation and other service workers. They operate or service transportation equipment such as trucks, ships, boats, airplanes, and helicopters, and act as quartermasters, supply specialists, and cargo specialists. Many of these skills can be transferred to civilian occupations.

Working Conditions

Military life is much more regimented than civilian life, and one must be willing to accept the discipline. It is important to remember that signing an enlistment contract obligates you to serve for a specified period of time.

Dress and grooming requirements are stringent, and rigid formalities govern many aspects of everyday life. For instance, officers and enlisted personnel do not socialize together, and commissioned officers are saluted and addressed as "sir" or "ma'am." These and other rules encourage respect for superiors whose commands must be obeyed immediately and without question.

The needs of the military always come first. As a result, hours and working conditions can vary substantially. However, most military personnel not deployed on a mission usually work 8 hours a day, 5 days a week. While off duty, military personnel usually do not wear their uniforms and are free to participate in family and recreational activities like most civilians. Some assignments, however, require night and weekend work, or require people to be on call at all hours. All may require substantial travel. Depending on the service, assignments may require long periods at sea, sometimes in cramped quarters or lengthy overseas assignments in countries offering few amenities. Some serve tours in isolated parts of the world, where they are subject to extreme cold or heat and the possibility of hostilities breaking out at any time. Others, such as sailors on carrier flight deck duty, have jobs that are hazardous even in noncombat situations.

During wartime, many military personnel engage in combat, and find themselves in life or death situations. They rely on countless hours of training to produce teamwork that is critical to the success or failure of an operation, and to protecting the lives of the individuals in their unit. Rapidly advancing military technology has made warfare more precise and lethal, further increasing the need for teamwork. Noncombatants may also face danger if their duties bring them close to a combat zone. Even in peacetime, most members of the combat arms branches of the military participate in hazardous training activities.

Ship and air crews travel extensively, while others in the military are stationed at bases throughout the country or overseas. Military personnel are usually transferred to a new duty station every few years.

Military personnel enjoy more job security than their civilian counterparts. Satisfactory job performance generally assures one of steady employment and earnings, and many of their requirements such as meals, clothing, and living quarters are provided for them.

Employment

In 1997, about 1.48 million individuals were on active duty in the Armed Forces—about 483,000 in the Army; 405,000 in the Navy; 383,000 in the Air Force; 172,000 in the Marine Corps; and 35,000 in the Coast Guard.

Military personnel are stationed throughout the United States and in many countries around the world. California, Texas, North Carolina, and Virginia accounted for more than 1 in 3 military jobs. About 249,000 were stationed outside the United States in 1997. Over 100,000 of these were stationed in Europe (mainly in Germany) and in the Western Pacific area.

Table 1 shows the occupational composition of enlisted personnel in 1997. Nearly 4 out of 10 held jobs that involved communications, electronic, mechanical, or related equipment, a reflection of the highly technical nature of the fighting forces today. Table 2 shows the occupational composition of officer personnel in 1997. Officers—who accounted for about 20 percent of all military personnel—are concentrated in activities in which they serve as ships' officers, aircraft pilots and crew members, and infantry or artillery officers. Officers also serve in administrative, support, engineering and maintenance, and medical and dental positions.

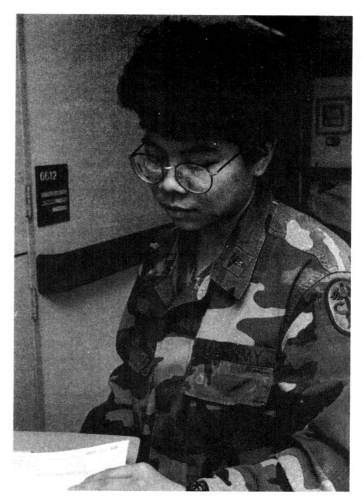

Army nurse studies patient records.

Qualifications, Training, and Advancement

General enlistment qualifications. As it has since 1973, the military expects to meet its personnel requirements through volunteers. Enlisted members must enter a legal agreement called an enlistment contract, which usually involves a commitment to 8 years of service. Depending on the terms of the contract, 2 to 6 years are spent on active duty, the balance in the reserves. The enlistment contract obligates the service to provide the agreed-upon options—job, rating, pay, cash bonuses for enlistment in certain occupations, medical and other benefits, occupational training, and continuing education. In return, enlisted personnel must serve satisfactorily for the specified period of time.

Requirements for each service vary, but certain qualifications for enlistment are common to all branches. Enlistees must be between the ages of 17 and 35, must be a U.S. citizen or immigrant alien holding permanent resident status, must not have a felony record, and must possess a birth certificate. Applicants who are 17 must have the consent of a parent or legal guardian before entering the service. Air Force enlisted personnel must enter active duty before their 28th birthday. Applicants must pass both a written examination—the Armed Services Vocational Aptitude Battery—and meet certain minimum physical standards such as height, weight, vision, and overall health. All branches prefer high school graduation or its equivalent and require it for certain enlistment options. In 1997, over 9 out of 10 enlistees were high school graduates. Single parents are generally not eligible to enlist.

Table 1. Military enlisted personnel by broad occupational category and branch of military service, 1997

Occupational Group	Total	Army	Navy	Marine Corps	Air Force
Total	1,195,745	397,583	340,537	153,943	303,682
Infantry, gun crews, and seamanship specialists	211,312	115,287	40,273	36,318	19,436
Electronic equipment repairers	108,963	25,949	42,098	8,829	32,087
Communications and intelligence specialists	104,627	38,312	33,961	11,074	21,280
Health care specialists	83,089	30,893	27,199	(¹)	24,870
Other technical and allied specialists	33,712	11,464	6,820	3,670	11,538
Functional support and administration	195,114	65,888	37,456	25,152	66,614
Electrical/mechanical equipment repairers	236,245	53,519	87,847	23,943	70,936
Craftworkers	47,566	7,621	19,838	4,075	14,038
Service and supply handlers	108,346	46,759	17,608	21,144	22,837
Non-occupational	68,991	1,893	27,314	19,738	20,046

[1] The Marine Corps employs no medical personnel. Their medical services are provided by the Navy.

SOURCE: U.S. Department of Defense

Table 2. Military officer personnel by broad occupational category and branch of service, 1997

Occupational Group	Total	Army	Navy	Marine Corps	Air Force
Total	226,398	77,810	56,069	17,968	74,551
General officers and executives	2,072	310	220	698[1]	844[3]
Tactical operations officers	86,653	31,611	21,548	8,434	25,060
Intelligence officers	11,774	5,351	2,271	720	3,434
Engineering and maintenance officers	29,313	9,269	6,277	1,744	12,023
Scientists and professionals	10,595	2,834	2,214	457	5,090
Medical officers	39,754	15,049	11,070	(²)	13,635
Administrators	14,185	4,603	2,949	1,665	4,968
Supply, procurement, and allied officers	19,651	7,844	3,157	2,171	6,479
Non-occupational	9,866	180	5,555	2,020	2,111

[1] The Marine Corps includes colonels as general officers. There were 79 generals in the Marine Corps in 1997.

[2] The Marine Corps employs no medical personnel. Their medical services are provided by the Navy.

[3] There were 274 general officers and 570 executives, not elsewhere classified, in the Air Force in 1997.

SOURCE: U.S. Department of Defense

People thinking about enlisting in the military should learn as much as they can about military life before making a decision. This is especially important if you are thinking about making the military a career. Speaking to friends and relatives with military experience is a good idea. Determine what the military can offer you and what it will expect in return. Then talk to a recruiter, who can determine if you qualify for enlistment; explain the various enlistment options; and tell you which military occupational specialties currently have openings for trainees. Bear in mind that the recruiter's job is to recruit promising applicants into the military, so the information he or she gives you is likely to stress the positive aspects of military life.

Ask the recruiter to assess your chances of being accepted for training in the occupation or occupations of your choice, or, better still, take the aptitude exam to see how well you score. The military uses the aptitude exam as a placement exam, and test scores largely determine an individual's chances of being accepted into a particular training program. Selection for a particular type of training depends on the needs of the service, general and technical aptitudes, and personal preference. Because all prospective recruits are required to take the exam, those who do so before committing themselves to enlist have the advantage of knowing in advance whether they stand a good chance of being accepted for training in a particular specialty. The recruiter can schedule you for the Armed Services Vocational Aptitude Battery without any obligation. Many high schools offer the exam as an easy way for students to explore the possibility of a military career, and the test also provides insight into career areas where the student has demonstrated aptitudes and interests.

Enlistment contract. If you decide to join the military, the next step is to pass the physical examination and then enter into the enlistment contract. This involves choosing, qualifying, and agreeing on a number of enlistment options such as length of active duty time, which may vary according to the enlistment option. (Most active duty programs have enlistment options ranging from 3 to 6 years, although there are some 2-year programs.) The contract will also state the date of enlistment and other options such as bonuses and types of training to be received. If the service is unable to fulfill its part of the contract (such as providing a certain kind of training) the contract may become null and void.

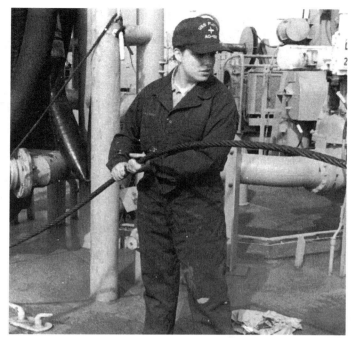

Military personnel in all branches receive the same pay and benefits according to grade.

All services offer a "delayed entry program" by which an enlistee can delay entry into active duty for up to 1 year. High school students can enlist during their senior year and enter a service after graduation. Others choose this program because the job training they desire is not currently available but will be within the coming year, or because they need time to arrange personal affairs.

Women are eligible to enter almost all military specialties. Although many women serve in medical and administrative support positions, women also work as mechanics, missile maintenance technicians, heavy equipment operators, fighter pilots, and intelligence officers. Only occupations involving a high probability of direct exposure to combat are excluded—for example, the artillery and infantry branches of the Army.

People planning to apply the skills gained through military training to a civilian career should look into several things before selecting their military occupation. First, they should determine how good the prospects are for civilian employment in jobs related to the military specialty which interests them. Second, they should know the prerequisites for the related civilian job. Many occupations require a license, certification, or a minimum level of education. In such cases, it is important to determine whether military training is sufficient to enter the civilian equivalent or, if not, what additional training will be required.

Other *Handbook* statements discuss the job outlook for civilian occupations for which military training is helpful. Additional information often can be obtained from school counselors.

Training programs for enlisted personnel. Following enlistment, new members of the Armed Forces undergo recruit training. Better known as "basic" training, recruit training provides a 6- to 11-week introduction to military life with courses in health, first aid, and military skills and protocol. Days and nights are carefully structured and include rigorous physical exercises designed to improve strength and endurance.

Following basic training, most recruits take additional training at technical schools that prepare them for a particular military occupational specialty. The formal training period generally lasts from 10 to 20 weeks, although training for certain occupations—nuclear power plant operator for example—may take as much as 1 year. Recruits not assigned to classroom instruction receive on-the-job training at their first duty assignment.

Many service people get college credit for the technical training they receive on duty, which, combined with off-duty courses, can lead to an Associates degree through community college programs such as the Community College of the Air Force.

In addition to on-duty training, military personnel may choose from a variety of educational programs. Most military installations have tuition assistance programs for people wishing to take courses during off-duty hours. These may be correspondence courses or degree programs offered by local colleges or universities. Tuition assistance pays up to 75 percent of college costs. Also available are courses designed to help service personnel earn high school equivalency diplomas. Each service branch provides opportunities for full-time study to a limited number of exceptional applicants. Military personnel accepted into these highly competitive programs receive full pay, allowances, tuition, and related fees. In return, they must agree to serve an additional amount of time in the service. Other very selective programs enable enlisted personnel to qualify as commissioned officers through additional military training.

Officer training. Officer training in the Armed Forces is provided through the Federal service academies (Military, Naval, Air Force, and Coast Guard); the Reserve Officers Training Corps (ROTC); Officer Candidate School (OCS) or Officer Training School (OTS); the National Guard (State Officer Candidate School programs); the Uniformed Services University of Health Sciences; and other programs. All are very selective and are good options for those wishing to make the military a career.

Federal service academies provide a 4-year college program leading to a bachelor of science degree. The midshipman or cadet is provided free room and board, tuition, medical care, and a monthly allowance. Graduates receive regular or reserve commissions and have a 5-year active duty obligation, or longer if entering flight training.

To become a candidate for appointment as a cadet or midshipman in one of the service academies, most applicants obtain a nomination from an authorized source (usually a Member of Congress). Candidates do not need to know a Member of Congress personally to request a nomination. Nominees must have an academic record of the requisite quality, college aptitude test scores above an established minimum, and recommendations from teachers or school officials; they must also pass a medical examination. Appointments are made from the list of eligible nominees.

Appointments to the Coast Guard Academy are made strictly on a competitive basis. A nomination is not required.

ROTC programs train students in about 950 Army, 60 Navy and Marine Corps, and 550 Air Force units at participating colleges and universities. Trainees take 2 to 5 hours of military instruction a week in addition to regular college courses. After graduation, they may serve as officers on active duty for a stipulated period of time, at the convenience of the service. Some may serve their obligation in the Reserves or Guard. In the last 2 years of an ROTC program, students receive a monthly allowance while attending school and additional pay for summer training. ROTC scholarships for 2, 3, and 4 years are available on a competitive basis. All scholarships pay for tuition and have allowances for subsistence, textbooks, supplies, and other fees.

College graduates can earn a commission in the Armed Forces through OCS or OTS programs in the Army, Navy, Air Force, Marine Corps, Coast Guard, and National Guard. These officers must serve their obligation on active duty.

Persons with training in certain health professions may qualify for direct appointment as officers. In the case of health professions students, financial assistance and internship opportunities are available from the military in return for specified periods of military service. Prospective medical students can apply to the Uniformed Services University of Health Sciences, which offers free tuition in a program leading to an M. D. degree. In return, graduates must serve for 7 years in either the military or the Public Health Service. Direct appointments also are available for those qualified to serve in other special duties, such as the judge advocate general (legal) or chaplain corps.

Aircraft require constant care and maintenance by highly trained specialists.

The Coast Guard enforces laws and rescues ships and aircraft in distress.

Flight training is available to commissioned officers in each branch of the Armed Forces. In addition, the Army has a direct enlistment option to become a warrant officer aviator.

Advancement opportunities. Each service has different criteria for promoting personnel. Generally, the first few promotions for both enlisted and officer personnel come easily; subsequent promotions are much more competitive. Criteria for promotion may include time in service and grade, job performance, a fitness report (supervisor's recommendation), and written examinations. People who are passed over for promotion several times generally must leave the military.

Job Outlook

Opportunities should be good in all branches of the Armed Forces through the year 2006 because many qualified youth prefer civilian employment. About 190,000 enlisted personnel and 15,000 officers must be recruited each year to replace those who complete their commitment or retire. Educational requirements will continue to rise as military jobs become more technical and complex; high school graduates and applicants with a college background will be sought to fill the ranks of enlisted personnel.

America's strategic position is stronger than it has been in decades. Although there have been reductions in personnel due to the reduction in the threat from Eastern Europe and Russia, the number of active duty personnel is now expected to remain about constant through 2006. The Armed Forces' goal is to maintain a sufficient force to fight and win two major regional conflicts occurring at the same time. However, political events could cause these plans to change.

Earnings, Allowances, and Benefits

Starting salaries. Annual salaries by rank and years of service of military personnel are shown in table 3. Most enlisted personnel started as recruits at Grade E-1 in 1997; however, those with special skills or above-average education started as high as Grade E-4. Most warrant officers started at Grade W-1 or W-2, depending upon their occupational and academic qualifications and the branch of service. Most commissioned officers started at Grade O-1; highly trained officers—for example, physicians, engineers, and scientists—started as high as Grade O-3 or 0-4.

Table 3. Military basic pay by grade for active duty personnel with fewer than 2 years service at grade, 1997

Rank and title				Basic monthly pay
Army	**Navy and Coast Guard**	**Air Force**	**Marine Corps**	
Commissioned officers:				
O-6 Colonel	Captain	Colonel	Colonel	$3,638.40
O-5 Lieutenant Colonel	Commander	Lieutenant Colonel	Lieutenant Colonel	2,910.30
O-4 Major	Lieutenant Commander	Major	Major	2,452.80
O-3 Captain	Lieutenant	Captain	Captain	2,279.40
O-2 1st Lieutenant	Lieutenant (JG)	1st Lieutenant	1st Lieutenant	1,987.80
O-1 2nd Lieutenant	Ensign	2nd Lieutenant	2nd Lieutenant	1,725.90
Warrant officers:				
W-2 Chief Warrant Officer	Chief Warrant Officer		Chief Warrant Officer	1,848.60
W-1 Warrant Officer	Warrant Officer	NONE	Warrant Officer	1,540.20
Enlisted personnel:				
E-6 Staff Sergeant	Petty Officer 1st Class	Technical Sergeant	Staff Sergeant	1,360.80
E-5 Sergeant	Petty Officer 2nd Class	Staff Sergeant	Sergeant	1,194.30
E-4 Corporal / Specialist	Petty Officer 3rd Class	Senior Airman	Corporal	1,113.60
E-3 Private First Class	Seaman	Airman 1st Class	Lance Corporal	1049.70
E-2 Private	Seaman Apprentice	Airman	Private 1st Class	1010.10
E-1 Private	Seaman Recruit	Airman Basic	Private	900.90
E-1[1]				833.40

[1] Fewer than 4 months active duty.

SOURCE: U.S. Department of Defense

Allowances. In addition to basic pay, military personnel receive free room and board (or a tax-free housing and subsistence allowance), medical and dental care, a military clothing allowance, military supermarket and department store shopping privileges, 30 days of paid vacation a year (referred to as leave), and travel opportunities. Other allowances are paid for foreign duty, hazardous duty, submarine and flight duty, and employment as a medical officer.

Athletic and other recreational facilities—such as libraries, gymnasiums, tennis courts, golf courses, bowling centers, and movies—are available on many military installations.

Military personnel are eligible for retirement benefits after 20 years of service.

Veterans' benefits. The Veterans Administration (VA) provides numerous benefits to those who have served at least 2 years in the Armed Forces. Veterans are eligible for free care in VA hospitals for all service-connected disabilities regardless of time served; those with other medical problems are eligible for free VA care if they are unable to pay the cost of hospitalization elsewhere. Admission to a VA medical center depends on the availability of beds, however. Veterans are also eligible for certain loans, including home loans. Veterans, regardless of health, can convert a military life insurance policy to an individual policy with any participating company in the veteran's State of residence. In addition, job counseling, testing, and placement services are available.

Veterans who participate in the New Montgomery GI Bill Program receive educational benefits. Under this program, Armed Forces personnel may elect to deduct from their pay up to $100 a month to put toward their future education for the first 12 months of active duty. Veterans who serve on active duty for three years or more, or two years active duty plus four years in the Selected Reserve or National Guard, will receive $427.87 a month in basic benefits for 36 months. Those who enlist and serve for less than 3 years will receive $347.65 a month. In addition, each service provides its own additional contributions to put toward future education. This sum becomes the service member's educational fund. Upon separation from active duty, the fund can be used to finance an education at any VA-approved institution. VA-approved schools include many vocational, correspondence, business, technical, and flight training schools; community and junior colleges; and colleges and universities.

Information on educational and other veterans' benefits is available from VA offices located throughout the country.

Sources of Additional Information
Each of the military services publishes handbooks, fact sheets, and pamphlets describing entrance requirements, training and advancement opportunities, and other aspects of military careers. These publications are widely available at all recruiting stations, most State employment service offices, and in high schools, colleges, and public libraries.

Data for Occupations Not Studied in Detail

Employment in the approximately 250 occupations covered in detail in the main body of the *Handbook* accounts for about 114 million or 86 percent of all jobs in the economy. Although occupations covering the full spectrum of work are included, those requiring lengthy education or training are generally given the most attention.

This chapter presents summary data on 73 additional occupations, for which employment projections are prepared, but for which detailed occupational information is not developed. These occupations account for about 5 percent of all jobs. For each occupation, a brief description of the nature of work, the number of jobs in 1996, a phrase describing the projected employment change from 1996 to 2006, and the most significant source of training are presented. For guidelines to interpreting the description of projected employment change, refer to an earlier chapter, Occupational Information Included in the *Handbook*.

The approximately 9 percent of all jobs not covered either in the detailed occupational descriptions in the main body of the *Handbook* or in the summary data presented in this chapter are mainly residual categories, such as "all other management support workers," for which little meaningful information could be developed.

Executive, Administrative, and Managerial Occupations

Communications, transportation, and utilities operations managers

Plan, organize, direct, control, or coordinate management activities related to: Communications by telephone, telegraph, radio, or television; transporting people or goods by air, highway, railway, water, or pipeline; transportation facilities, such as airports, harbors, or terminals; warehouse and storage facilities; and electricity, gas, water, steam, or sanitation services.

1996 employment: 156,000
Projected 1996-2006 employment change: About as fast as average
Most significant source of training: Work experience plus bachelor's degree

Credit analysts

Analyze current data and financial statements of individuals or firms to determine the degree of risk involved in extending credit or lending money. Prepare reports with this credit information for use in making decisions.

1996 employment: 40,000
Projected 1996-2006 employment change: About as fast as average
Most significant source of training: Bachelor's degree

Tax examiners, collectors, and revenue agents

Determine tax liability or collect taxes from individuals or business firms according to prescribed laws and regulations.

1996 employment: 64,000
Projected 1996-2006 employment change: Little change
Most significant source of training: Bachelor's degree

Professional and Technical Occupations

Athletes, coaches, umpires, and referees

Participate in competitive professional athletic events as a player, coach, manager, umpire, or judge.

1996 employment: 42,000
Projected 1996-2006 employment change: About as fast as average
Most significant source of training: More than 12 months of on-the-job training

Directors, religious activities and education

Direct and coordinate activities of a denominational group to meet religious needs of students. Plan, organize, and direct religious school programs designed to promote religious education. Provide counseling and guidance on marital, health, financial, and religious problems.

1996 employment: 85,000
Projected 1996-2006 employment change: Faster than average
Most significant source of training: Bachelor's degree

Farm and home management advisors

Advise, instruct, and assist individuals and families engaged in agriculture and related processes or home economics activities. Apply research findings and procedures to solve problems and provide instruction and training in the development of products, sales, and the use of machinery and equipment.

1996 employment: 16,000
Projected 1996-2006 employment change: A decline
Most significant source of training: Bachelor's degree

Instructors and coaches, sports and physical training

Instruct or coach groups in the fundamentals of sports, and demonstrate techniques and methods of participation. Observe and inform participants of corrective measures to improve their skills. Includes those who are not required to hold teaching degrees.

1996 employment: 303,000
Projected 1996-2006 employment change: Much faster than average
Most significant source of training: 1 to 12 months of on-the-job training

Residential counselors

Coordinate activities for residents of care and treatment institutions, boarding schools, college fraternities or sororities, children's homes, or similar establishments. Work includes developing or assisting in the development of program plans for individuals, maintaining household records, and assigning rooms. Counsel residents in identifying and resolving social or other problems. Order supplies and determine need for maintenance, repairs, and furnishings.

1996 employment: 180,000
Projected 1996-2006 employment change: Much faster than average
Most significant source of training: Bachelor's degree

Pharmacy technicians

Fill orders for unit doses and prepackaged pharmaceuticals and perform other related duties under the supervision and direction of a pharmacy supervisor or staff pharmacist. Duties include keeping records of drugs delivered to the pharmacy, storing incoming merchandise in proper locations, and informing supervisor or stock needs and shortages. May clean equipment used in the performance of duties and assist in the care and maintenance of equipment and supplies.

1996 employment: 83,000
Projected 1996-2006 employment change: About as fast as average
Most significant source of training: 1 to 12 months of on-the-job training

Psychiatric technicians

Provide nursing care to mentally ill, emotionally disturbed, or mentally retarded patients, and participate in rehabilitation and treatment programs. Help with personal hygiene. Administer oral medications and hypodermic injections, following physician's prescriptions and hospital procedures. Monitor patients and their emotional well-being and report to medical staff.

1996 employment: 66,000
Projected 1996-2006 employment change: Slower than average
Most significant source of training: Associate degree

Title examiners and searchers

Title examiners: Search public records and examine titles to determine legal status of property titles. Copy or summarize (abstract) recorded documents, such as mortgages, trust deeds, and contracts, affecting title to property. May prepare and issue policy that guarantees legality of title. *Abstractors*: Summarize pertinent legal or insurance details, or sections of statutes or case law from reference books for examination, proof, or ready reference. Search out titles to determine if title deed is correct. *Searchers*: Compile lists of mortgages, deeds, contracts, judgments, and other instruments pertaining to titles by searching public and private records for real estate or title insurance company.

1996 employment: 26,000
Projected 1996-2006 employment change: About as fast as average
Most significant source of training: 1 to 12 months of on-the-job training

Veterinary technicians and technologists

Perform medical tests in a laboratory environment for use in the treatment and diagnosis of diseases in animals. Prepare vaccines and serums for prevention of diseases. Prepare tissue samples, take blood samples, and execute laboratory tests such as urinalysis and blood counts. Clean and sterilize instruments and materials and maintain equipment and machines.

1996 employment: 27,000
Projected 1996-2006 employment change: Faster than average
Most significant source of training: Associate degree

Administrative Support Occupations, Including Clerical

Court clerks

Perform clerical duties in courts of law; prepare docket of cases to be called; secure information for judges; and contact witnesses, attorneys, and litigants to obtain information for court.

1996 employment: 53,000
Projected 1996-2006 employment change: Slower than average
Most significant source of training: Up to 1 month of on-the-job training

Customer service representatives, utilities

Interview applicants for water, gas, electric, or telephone service. Talk with customers by phone or in person and receive orders for installation, turn-on, discontinuance, or change in service.

1996 employment: 151,000
Projected 1996-2006 employment change: Faster than average
Most significant source of training: Up to 1 month of on-the-job training

Duplicating, mail, and other office machine operators

Duplicating machine operators: Operate one or a variety of duplicating machines to make copies of printed and other information. *Mail machine operators*: Operate machines to emboss names, addresses, and other

matter onto metal plates for use in addressing machines; to print names, addresses and other similar information onto items, such as envelopes, accounting forms, and advertising literature; to address, fold, stuff, seal, and stamp mail; and to open envelopes. *Transit clerks*: Sort, record, proof, and prepare transit items for mailing to or from out-of-city banks to insure correct routing and prompt collection.

1996 employment: 196,000
Projected 1996-2006 employment change: A decline
Most significant source of training: Up to 1 month of on-the-job training

Municipal clerks

Draft agendas for town or city councils, record minutes of council meetings, answer official correspondence, keep fiscal records and accounts, and prepare reports on civic needs.

1996 employment: 22,000
Projected 1996-2006 employment change: Slower than average
Most significant source of training: Up to 1 month of on-the-job training

Proofreaders and copy markers

Read transcript or proof of type setup to detect and mark for correction any grammatical, typographical, or compositional errors.

1996 employment: 26,000
Projected 1996-2006 employment change: A decline
Most significant source of training: Up to 1 month of on-the-job training

Real estate clerks

Perform duties concerned with rental, sale, and management of real estate, such as typing copies of listings, computing interest owed or penalty payments, holding collateral in escrow, and checking due notices on taxes and renewal dates of insurance and mortgage loans.

1996 employment: 24,000
Projected 1996-2006 employment change: Slower than average
Most significant source of training: Up to 1 month of on-the-job training

Statistical clerks

Compile and compute data according to statistical formulas for use in statistical studies. May also perform actuarial computations, using algebra and trigonometry, and compile charts and graphs for use by actuaries.

1996 employment: 78,000
Projected 1996-2006 employment change: A decline
Most significant source of training: 1 to 12 months of on-the-job training

Service Occupations

Ambulance drivers and attendants, except emergency medical technicians

Drive ambulance or assist ambulance driver in transporting sick, injured, or convalescent persons. Assist in lifting patients and rendering first aid. May be required to have Red Cross first-aid training certificate.

1996 employment: 18,000
Projected 1996-2006 employment change: Much faster than average
Most significant source of training: Up to 1 month of on-the-job training

Amusement and recreation attendants

Perform one or more of the following duties at amusement or recreation facilities: Schedule use of recreation facilities, allocate equipment to participants in sporting events or recreational pursuits, collect fees, set pins, prepare billiard tables, provide caddying and other services for golfers, or operate carnival rides and amusement concessions.

1996 employment: 288,000
Projected 1996-2006 employment change: Much faster than average
Most significant source of training: Up to 1 month of on-the-job training

Baggage porters and bellhops

Carry baggage for travelers at transportation terminals or for guests at hotels or similar establishments. Perform additional duties, such as assisting handicapped persons, running errands, delivering ice, and directing people to their desired destinations.

1996 employment: 38,000
Projected 1996-2006 employment change: Slower than average
Most significant source of training: Up to 1 month of on-the-job training

Crossing guards

Guide or control vehicular or pedestrian traffic at such places as street and railroad crossings and construction sites.

1996 employment: 61,000
Projected 1996-2006 employment change: A decline
Most significant source of training: Up to 1 month of on-the-job training

Pest controllers and assistants

Spray or release chemical solutions or toxic gases and set mechanical traps to kill pests and vermin, such as mice, termites, and roaches, that infest buildings and surrounding areas.

1996 employment: 60,000
Projected 1996-2006 employment change: Faster than average
Most significant source of training: 1 to 12 months of on-the-job training

Pharmacy assistants

Mix pharmaceutical preparations under direction of pharmacist. Duties include issuing medicine, labeling and storing supplies, and cleaning equipment and work areas.

1996 employment: 47,000
Projected 1996-2006 employment change: About as fast as average
Most significant source of training: Up to 1 month of on-the-job training

Ushers, lobby attendants, and ticket takers

Assist patrons at entertainment events, such as sporting events and motion picture performances. May assist in finding seats, searching for lost articles, and locating rest rooms and telephones. Collect admission tickets and passes from patrons.

1996 employment: 64,000
Projected 1996-2006 employment change: Faster than average
Most significant source of training: Up to 1 month of on-the-job training

Mechanics, Installers, and Repairers

Bicycle repairers

Repair and service bicycles using hand tools.

1996 employment: 13,000
Projected 1996-2006 employment change: Faster than average
Most significant source of training: 1 to 12 months of on-the-job training

Camera and photographic equipment repairers

Repair and adjust cameras and photographic equipment, including motion picture cameras and equipment, using specialized tools and testing devices.

1996 employment: 14,000
Projected 1996-2006 employment change: Faster than average
Most significant source of training: 1 to 12 months of on-the-job training

Electric meter installers and repairers

Install electric meters on pole or customer's premises, test meters, make necessary repairs, and turn current on/off by connecting or disconnecting service drop.

1996 employment: 12,000
Projected 1996-2006 employment change: A decline
Most significant source of training: More than 12 months of on-the-job training

Electromedical and biomedical equipment repairers

Test, adjust, and repair electromedical equipment using hand tools and meters.

1996 employment: 9,700
Projected 1996-2006 employment change: About as fast as average
Most significant source of training: More than 12 months of on-the-job training

Locksmiths and safe repairers

Repair and open locks, make keys, change locks and safe combinations, and install and repair safes.

1996 employment: 25,000
Projected 1996-2006 employment change: About as fast as average
Most significant source of training: 1 to 12 months of on-the-job training

Precision instrument repairers

Install, test, repair, maintain, and adjust indicating, recording, telemetering, and controlling instruments used to measure and control variables such as pressure, flow, temperature, motion, force, and chemical composition.

1996 employment: 38,000
Projected 1996-2006 employment change: A decline
Most significant source of training: More than 12 months of on-the-job training

Riggers

Set up or repair rigging for ships and shipyards, manufacturing plants, logging yards, construction projects, and for the entertainment industry—for example, motion picture production. Select cables, ropes, pulleys, winches, blocks, and sheaves according to weight and size of load to be moved. Coordinate and direct other workers and the movement of equipment to accomplish the task.

1996 employment: 9,300
Projected 1996-2006 employment change: A decline
Most significant source of training: More than 12 months of on-the-job training

Tire repairers and changers

Repair and replace tires, tubes, treads, and related products on automobiles, buses, trucks, and other vehicles. Mount tires on wheels, balance tires and wheels, and test and repair damaged tires and inner tubes.

1996 employment: 94,000
Projected 1996-2006 employment change: Slower than average
Most significant source of training: Up to 1 month of on-the-job training

Watchmakers
Repair, clean, and adjust mechanisms of instruments such as watches, time clocks, and timing switches using hand tools and measuring instruments.

1996 employment: 7,400
Projected 1996-2006 employment change: A decline
Most significant source of training: More than 12 months of on-the-job training

Construction Trades Occupations

Highway maintenance workers
Maintain highways, municipal and rural roads, airport runways, and rights-of-way in safe condition by patching broken or eroded pavement or erecting and repairing guard rails, highway markers, and snow fences. May also clear brush or plant trees along rights-of-way.

1996 employment: 171,000
Projected 1996-2006 employment change: A decline
Most significant source of training: Up to 1 month of on-the-job training

Mining, quarrying, and tunneling occupations
Rock splitters, quarry: Separate blocks of rough dimension stone from quarry mass using jackhammer, wedges, and feathers. *Roof bolters*: Operate self-propelled machine to install roof support bolts in underground mines. *Mining machine operators*: Operate mining machines, such as self-propelled or truck-mounted drilling machines, continuous mining machines, channeling machines, and cutting machines to extract coal, metal and nonmetal ores, rock, stone, or sand from underground or surface excavation. *Continuous mining machine operators*: Operate self-propelled mining machine that rips coal from the face and loads it onto conveyors or into shuttle cars in a continuous operation. *Mine cutting and channeling machine operators*: Cut or channel along the face or seams of coal, quarry stone, or other mining surfaces to facilitate blasting, separating, or removing minerals or materials from mines or from the earth's surface.

1996 employment: 16,000
Projected 1996-2006 employment change: A decline
Most significant source of training: More than 12 months of on-the-job training

Paving, surfacing, and tamping equipment operators
Operate equipment used for applying concrete, asphalt, or other materials to roadbeds, parking lots, or airport runways and taxiways; or equipment used for tamping gravel, dirt, or other materials.

1996 employment: 79,000
Projected 1996-2006 employment change: Faster than average
Most significant source of training: 1 to 12 months of on-the-job training

Pipelayers and pipelaying fitters
Pipelayers: Lay glazed or unglazed clay, concrete, plastic, or cast-iron pipe for storm or sanitation sewers, drains, water mains, and oil or gas lines. May grade trenches or culverts, position pipe, or seal joints. *Pipelaying fitters*: Align pipeline section preparatory to welding. Signal tractor driver in placing pipeline sections in proper alignment and insert steel spacers.

1996 employment: 62,000
Projected 1996-2006 employment change: Slower than average
Most significant source of training: 1 to 12 months of on-the-job training

Roustabouts
Assemble or repair oil field equipment using hand and power tools. Perform other tasks as needed.

1996 employment: 28,000
Projected 1996-2006 employment change: A decline
Most significant source of training: Up to 1 month of on-the-job training

Production Occupations

Bakers, manufacturing
Mix and bake ingredients according to recipes to produce breads, pastries, and other baked goods. Goods are produced in large quantities for sale through establishments such as grocery stores. Generally, high-volume production equipment is used.

1996 employment: 44,000
Projected 1996-2006 employment change: Slower than average
Most significant source of training: 1 to 12 months of on-the-job training

Boiler operators and tenders, low pressure
Operate or tend low-pressure stationary steam boilers and auxiliary steam equipment, such as pumps, compressors, and air-conditioning equipment, to supply steam heat for office buildings, apartment houses, or industrial establishments; to maintain steam at specified pressure aboard marine vessels; or to generate and supply compressed air for operation of pneumatic tools, hoists, and air lances.

1996 employment: 17,000
Projected 1996-2006 employment change: A decline
Most significant source of training: 1 to 12 months of on-the-job training

Cannery workers
Perform a variety of routine tasks in canning, freezing, preserving, or packing food products. May sort, grade, wash, peel, trim, or slice agricultural produce.

1996 employment: 66,000
Projected 1996-2006 employment change: A decline
Most significant source of training: Up to 1 month of on-the-job training

Cementing and gluing machine operators and tenders
Operate or tend cementing and gluing machines to join together items, such as veneer sheets and plywood; paper and glass wool, cardboard, or paper; rubber and rubberized fabric parts; plastic; and simulated leather or other materials, to form completed product or to form product for further processing.

1996 employment: 35,000
Projected 1996-2006 employment change: A decline
Most significant source of training: 1 to 12 months of on-the-job training

Chemical equipment controllers, operators, and tenders

Controllers and operators: Control or operate equipment to control chemical changes or reactions in the processing of industrial or consumer products. Common types of equipment are reaction kettles, catalytic converters, continuous or batch treating equipment, saturator tanks, electrolytic cells, reactor vessels, recovery units, and fermentation chambers. *Tenders*: Tend equipment in which a chemical change or reaction takes place to process chemical substances into industrial or consumer products. Common types of equipment are devulcanizers, batch stills, fermenting tanks, steam-jacketed kettles, and reactor vessels.

1996 employment: 79,000
Projected 1996-2006 employment change: Slower than average
Most significant source of training: 1 to 12 months of on-the-job training

Chemical plant and system operators

Control and operate an entire chemical process or system of machines, such as reduction pots and heated air towers, using panel boards, control boards, or semiautomatic equipment.

1996 employment: 36,000
Projected 1996-2006 employment change: A decline
Most significant source of training: More than 12 months of on-the-job training

Coil winders, tapers, and finishers

Using coil winding machines, wind wire coils used in the manufacturing of electrical components, such as resistors and transformers, and electrical equipment, such as field cores, bobbins, and armature cores; and using coil making machines, form coils for electrical motors, generators, and control equipment.

1996 employment: 22,000
Projected 1996-2006 employment change: A decline
Most significant source of training: Up to 1 month of on-the-job training

Cooking and roasting machine operators and tenders

Cooking machine operators and tenders: Operate or tend cooking equipment, such as steam cooking vats, deep fry cookers, pressure cookers, kettles, and boilers, to prepare food products, such as meats, sugar, cheese, and grain. *Roasting, baking, and drying machine operators and tenders*: Operate or tend roasting, baking, or drying equipment, such as hearth ovens, kiln dryers, roasters, char kilns, steam ovens, and vacuum drying equipment, to reduce moisture content of food or tobacco products such as tobacco, cocoa and coffee beans, macaroni, and grain; to roast grain, nuts, or coffee beans; to bake bread or other bakery products; or to process food preparatory to canning.

1996 employment: 30,000
Projected 1996-2006 employment change: Slower than average
Most significant source of training: 1 to 12 months of on-the-job training

Crushing and mixing machine operators and tenders

Crushing, grinding, and polishing machine operators and tenders: Operate or tend machines to crush or grind materials such as coal, glass, plastic, dried fruit, grain, stone, chemicals, food, or rubber; or operate or tend machines to buff and polish materials such as stone, glass, slate, plastic or metal trim, bowling balls, or eyeglasses. *Mixing and blending machine operators and tenders*: Operate or tend machines to mix or blend materials such as spices, dough batter, tobacco, fruit juices, chemicals, livestock feed, food products, color pigments, or explosive ingredients.

1996 employment: 145,000
Projected 1996-2006 employment change: A decline

Most significant source of training: 1 to 12 months of on-the-job training

Cutting and slicing machine setters, operators, and tenders

Operators and tenders: Operate or tend machines to cut or slice materials such as tobacco, food, paper, roofing slate, glass, stone rubber, cork, and insulating material. *Setters and setup operators*: Set up and operate machines to cut or slice materials such as glass, stone, cork, rubber, crepe, wallboard, and fibrous insulating board, to specified dimensions for further processing.

1996 employment: 95,000
Projected 1996-2006 employment change: Slower than average
Most significant source of training: 1 to 12 months of on-the-job training

Dairy processing equipment operators, including setters

Set up, operate, or tend continuous flow or vat-type equipment to process milk, cream, or other dairy products following specified methods and formulas.

1996 employment: 13,000
Projected 1996-2006 employment change: A decline
Most significant source of training: 1 to 12 months of on-the-job training

Electrical and electronic assemblers

Perform work at a level less than that required of the precision level. Includes occupations such as electronic wirers, armature connectors, electric motor winders, skein winders, carbon brush assemblers, battery parts assemblers, electric sign assemblers, and electronic assemblers.

1996 employment: 229,000
Projected 1996-2006 employment change: A decline
Most significant source of training: Up to 1 month of on-the-job training

Electronic semiconductor processors

Process materials used in the manufacture of electronic semiconductors; load semiconductor material into furnace; saw formed ingots into segments; load individual segment into crystal-growing chamber and monitor controls; locate crystal axis in ingot using x-ray equipment and saw ingots into wafers; clean, polish, and load wafers into series of special-purpose furnaces, chemical baths, and equipment used to form circuitry and change conductive properties. May scribe or separate wafer into dice.

1996 employment: 58,000
Projected 1996-2006 employment change: About as fast as average
Most significant source of training: 1 to 12 months of on-the-job training

Extruding and forming machine setters, operators, and tenders

Operators and tenders: Operate or tend machines to shape and form manufactured products such as glass bulbs, molded food and candy, rubber goods, clay products, wax products, tobacco plugs, cosmetics, or paper products, by means of extruding, compressing, or compacting. *Setters and setup operators*: Set up and operate machines such as glass forming machines, plodder machines, and tuber machines, to manufacture products such as soap bars, formed rubber, glassware, soft candy, brick, and tile, by means of extruding, compressing, or compacting.

1996 employment: 107,000
Projected 1996-2006 employment change: A decline
Most significant source of training: 1 to 12 months of on-the-job training

Farm workers

Plant, cultivate, harvest, and store crops; tend livestock and poultry; operate and maintain farm machinery; and maintain structures. May haul livestock and produce to market or terminal shipping point.

1996 employment: 873,000
Projected 1996-2006 employment change: A decline
Most significant source of training: Up to 1 month of on-the-job training

Foundry mold assembly and shakeout workers

Prepare molds, such as cleaning and assembling foundry molds, for pouring. Assemble cores in fixture of automatic core-sorting machine, and bond cope and drags together to form completed shell mold.

1996 employment: 10,000
Projected 1996-2006 employment change: A decline
Most significant source of training: 1 to 12 months of on-the-job training

Furnace operators and tenders

Operate or tend furnaces, such as gas, oil, coal, electric-arc or electric induction, open-hearth, or oxygen furnaces, to melt and refine metal prior to casting or to produce specified types of steel.

1996 employment: 21,000
Projected 1996-2006 employment change: A decline
Most significant source of training: 1 to 12 months of on-the-job training

Furnace, kiln, or kettle operators and tenders

Operate or tend heating equipment other than basic metal or plastic processing equipment. *Furnace operators and tenders*: May anneal glass, roast sulfur, convert chemicals, or process petroleum. *Kiln operators and tenders*: May heat minerals, dry lumber, fire greenware, anneal glassware, or bake clay products. *Oven operators and tenders*: May bake fiberglass or painted products, fuse glass or enamel to metal products, carbonize coal, or cure rubber or other products. *Drier operators and tenders*: May remove moisture from paper, chemicals, ore, clay products, or slurry. *Kettle operators and tenders*: May melt antimony or asphalt materials, or boil soap.

1996 employment: 28,000
Projected 1996-2006 employment change: A decline
Most significant source of training: 1 to 12 months of on-the-job training

Gas and petroleum plant and systems occupations

Gaugers: Gauge and test oil in storage tanks and regulate flow of oil into pipelines at wells, tank farms, refineries, and marine and rail terminals following prescribed standards and regulations. *Petroleum refinery and control panel operators*: Analyze specifications or follow process schedules to operate and control panelboards and continuous petroleum refining and processing units. *Gas plant operators*: Distribute or process gas for utility companies and others. Distribute the gas for an entire plant or process, often using panel boards, control boards, or semiautomatic equipment. *Petroleum pump systems operators*: Operate and control manifold and pumping systems to circulate liquids through petroleum refinery.

1996 employment: 33,000
Projected 1996-2006 employment change: A decline
Most significant source of training: More than 12 months of on-the-job training

Grinders and polishers, hand

Perform work at a level less than that required of the precision level. Grind and polish a wide variety of metal, stone, clay, plastic, and glass objects or parts, using hand tools or hand-held power tools.

1996 employment: 74,000
Projected 1996-2006 employment change: A decline
Most significant source of training: Up to 1 month of on-the-job training

Laundry and drycleaning machine operators and tenders, except pressing

Operate and tend washing or drycleaning machines to clean or dry-clean commercial, industrial, or household articles, such as suede, leather, and cloth garments, furs, blankets, draperies, fine linens, rugs, and carpets.

1996 employment: 180,000
Projected 1996-2006 employment change: Faster than average
Most significant source of training: 1 to 12 months of on-the-job training

Machine assemblers

Perform work at a level less than that required of the precision level. Includes occupations such as air-conditioning coil assemblers, ball bearing ring assemblers, fuel injection assemblers, and subassemblers.

1996 employment: 59,000
Projected 1996-2006 employment change: A decline
Most significant source of training: Up to 1 month of on-the-job training

Motion picture projectionists

Set up and operate motion picture projection and sound-reproducing equipment to produce coordinated effects on screen.

1996 employment: 8,400
Projected 1996-2006 employment change: A decline
Most significant source of training: Up to 1 month of on-the-job training

Packaging and filling machine operators and tenders

Operate or tend machines, such as filling, casing-running, ham rolling, preservative filling, baling, wrapping, and stuffing machines, to prepare industrial or consumer products, such as gas cylinders, meat and other food products, tobacco, insulation, ammunition, stuffed toys and athletic equipment, and upholstered pads, as end products or for storage and shipment.

1996 employment: 354,000
Projected 1996-2006 employment change: About as fast as average
Most significant source of training: 1 to 12 months of on-the-job training

Painting, coating, and decorating workers, hand

Paint, coat, and decorate, using handtools or hand-held power tools, a wide variety of manufactured items, such as furniture, glass and flatware, lamps, jewelry, books, or leather products.

1996 employment: 31,000
Projected 1996-2006 employment change: About as fast as average
Most significant source of training: Up to 1 month of on-the-job training

Paper goods machine setters and setup operators

Set up and operate paper goods machines to convert, saw, corrugate, band, wrap, box, stitch, form, or seal paper or paperboard sheets into products such as toilet tissue, towels, napkins, bags, envelopes, tubing, cartons, wax rolls, and containers.

1996 employment: 51,000
Projected 1996-2006 employment change: A decline
Most significant source of training: 1 to 12 months of on-the-job training

Separating and still machine operators and tenders
Operate or tend machines, such as filter presses, shaker screens, centrifuges, condenser tubes, precipitator tanks, fermenting tanks, evaporating tanks, scrubbing towers, and batch stills, to extract, sort, or separate liquids, gases, or solid materials from other materials in order to recover a refined product or material.

1996 employment: 16,000
Projected 1996-2006 employment change: A decline
Most significant source of training: 1 to 12 months of on-the-job training

Shipfitters
Lay out and fabricate metal structural parts, such as plates, bulk heads, and frames, and brace them in position within hull or ship for riveting or welding. May prepare molds and templates for fabrication of nonstandard parts.

1996 employment: 9,400
Projected 1996-2006 employment change: A decline
Most significant source of training: More than 12 months of on-the-job training

Shoe sewing machine operators and tenders
Operate or tend single, double, or multiple-needle stitching machines to join or decorate shoe parts, reinforce shoe parts, or attach buckles.

1996 employment: 11,000
Projected 1996-2006 employment change: A decline
Most significant source of training: 1 to 12 months of on-the-job training

Solderers and brazers
Join together metal parts or components of metal products, and fill holes, indentations, and seams of fabricated metal products using hand soldering and brazing equipment as specified by job orders, work layouts, or blueprints.

1996 employment: 26,000
Projected 1996-2006 employment change: Faster than average
Most significant source of training: Up to 1 month of on-the-job training

Soldering and brazing machine operators and setters
Operators and tenders: Operate or tend soldering and brazing machines to braze, solder, or spot-weld fabricated metal products or components as specified by job orders, work layouts, or blueprints. *Setters and setup operators*: Set up and operate soldering and brazing machines to bronze, solder, heat-treat, or spot-weld fabricated metal products or components as specified by job orders, work layouts, or blueprints.

1996 employment: 11,000
Projected 1996-2006 employment change: Little change
Most significant source of training: 1 to 12 months of on-the-job training

Supervisors, farming, forestry, and agricultural-related occupations
Directly supervise and coordinate the activities of agricultural, forestry, fishing, and related workers. May supervise helpers assigned to these workers.

1996 employment: 88,000
Projected 1996-2006 employment change: Slower than average
Most significant source of training: Work experience

Tire building machine operators
Operate machines, such as collapsible drum devices, to build pneumatic tires from rubber components, such as beads, ply stock, tread, and sidewalls.

1996 employment: 14,000
Projected 1996-2006 employment change: A decline
Most significant source of training: 1 to 12 months of on-the-job training

Assumptions and Methods Used in Preparing Employment Projections

Occupational statements in the *Handbook* use one of five adjectives to describe projected change in employment. (See page 20.) The adjectives are based on numerical projections developed using the Bureau's employment projections model system. The employment projections are the final output of the system, which also projects the size and composition of the labor force, the level of gross domestic product (GDP)—sales to all final consuming sectors in the economy—the total output of goods and services by industry, and employment by industry. A full description, including numerical projections of employment, appears in the November 1997 *Monthly Labor Review*, and in *Employment Outlook: 1996-2006,* BLS Bulletin 2502. The Winter 1997-98 *Occupational Outlook Quarterly* presents the projections in a series of charts.

The projections reflect the knowledge and judgment of staff in the Bureau's Office of Employment Projections and of knowledgeable people from other offices in the Bureau, other government agencies, colleges and universities, industries, unions, professional societies, and trade associations, who furnished data and information, prepared reports, or reviewed the projections. The Bureau takes full responsibility for them.

Assumptions. The information in the *Handbook* is based on an economic projection, which is characterized by faster productivity growth than in the past, slower labor force growth, a constant unemployment rate, and decreasing trade and Federal budget deficits. Other assumptions include real cuts in Federal defense and nondefense spending, a slight decline in consumer spending on new automobiles, and an increase in consumer spending on other durable goods, such as computers and household goods. Spending on food and beverages will grow more slowly than the average for all consumer expenditures, while spending on health care and other services, such as entertainment, recreation, and financial services, will grow faster. Investment in production equipment—including factory automation, communication, and computer items—will grow rapidly. Residential construction will be relatively flat while nonresidential construction will make something of a comeback from depressed levels over the previous decade.

While the Bureau considers these assumptions reasonable, the economy may follow a different course, resulting in a different pattern of occupational growth. Real growth could also be different because most occupations are sensitive to a much wider variety of factors than those considered in the various models. Unforeseen changes in consumer, business, or government spending patterns and in the way goods and services are produced could greatly alter the growth of individual occupations.

Methods. This section summarizes the steps by which the Bureau arrives at projections of employment by occupation. BLS uses Bureau of the Census projections of the population by age, gender, and race, combined with projections of labor force participation rates, to arrive at estimates of the civilian labor force.

The projections of the labor force and assumptions about other demographic variables, fiscal policy, foreign economic activity, and energy prices and availability form the input to the macroeconomic model. This model projects GDP and the distribution of GDP by its major demand components—consumer expenditures, investment, government purchases, and net exports. The resulting estimates of demand for goods and services are used to project industry output of final products as well as total output by industry.

Industry output of goods and services is then converted to industry employment. Studies of trends in productivity and technology are used to estimate future output per worker hour, and regression analysis is used to estimate worker hours. These estimates, along with output projections, are used to develop the final industry employment projections.

An industry-occupation matrix is used to project employment for wage and salary workers. The matrix shows occupational staffing patterns—each occupation as a percent of the work force in every industry. The matrix covering the 1996-2006 period includes 261 detailed industries and 510 detailed occupations. Data for current staffing patterns in the matrix come from the Bureau's Occupational Employment Statistics surveys, which collect data from employers on a 3-year cycle.

The occupational staffing patterns for each industry were projected based on anticipated changes in the way goods and services are produced, then applied to projected industry employment, and the resulting employment was summed across industries to get total wage and salary employment by occupation. Using this method, rapid employment growth is projected for health care workers while employment of railroad transportation workers is expected to decline, reflecting the projected change in the health care and railroad transportation industries, respectively.

Employment in an occupation also may grow or decline as a result of many other factors. For example, rapid growth is expected among teacher aides and educational assistants as increasing attention to the quality of education leads schools to hire more support staff. Rapid growth is also expected among computer systems analysts as technology advances and organizations place more emphasis on network applications and maximizing the efficiency of their computer systems. On the other hand, automation, the expanding use of computers, and developments in computer software will result in limited growth or declining employment among many clerical workers, machine operators, and assemblers The projected-year matrix incorporates these expected changes.

Data on self-employed workers in each occupation come from the Current Population Survey. Self-employed workers were projected separately.

Replacement needs. In most occupations, replacement needs provide more job openings than growth. Replacement openings occur as people leave occupations. Some individuals transfer to other occupations as a step up the career ladder or to change careers. Some stop working temporarily, perhaps to return to school or care for a family. Other workers—retirees for example—leave the labor force permanently. A discussion of replacements, including separation rates for selected occupations, is presented in *Occupational Projections and Training Data, 1998 Edition,* BLS Bulletin 2501.

Dictionary of Occupational Titles Coverage

The *Dictionary of Occupational Titles (D.O.T.)* was designed to provide standardized occupational titles to help public employment service offices classify and place job seekers. Its coding structure also is used to help bridge or relate to other occupational classification systems used in the collection of employment data.

Nearly all occupational statements in the *Handbook* list the *D.O.T.* numbers that relate to or match the definitions used in the Bureau's Occupational Employment Statistics Survey (OES)—the source of occupational employment data in the *Handbook*. All numbers so listed are also listed below in numeric order, with the associated D.O.T. title and the page on which the corresponding occupational statement begins. However, the *D.O.T.* numbers associated with the following occupations are too numerous to list:

Apparel workers
Blue-collar worker supervisors
Clerical supervisors and managers
General managers and top executives
Handlers, equipment cleaners, helpers, and laborers
Industrial machinery repairers

Inspectors and compliance officers, except construction
Inspectors, testers, and graders
Manufacturers' and wholesale sales representatives
Material moving equipment operators
Material recording, scheduling, dispatching, and distributing occupations (except for dispatchers, stock clerks, and traffic, shipping, and receiving clerks)
Metalworking and plastics-working machine operators
Painting and coating machine operators
Precision assemblers
Prepress workers
Printing press operators
Retail sales workers
Science technicians
Textile machinery operators
Woodworking occupations

These, nevertheless, are available on request from the Chief, Division of Occupational Outlook, Bureau of Labor Statistics, U.S. Department of Labor, Washington, DC 20212.

Note: The U.S. Department of Labor is replacing the D.O.T. with O*NET, the Occupational Information Network. O*NET is an automated system for collecting, classifying, and disseminating data on jobs. O*NET will have about 1,200 occupational codes and titles, compared to nearly13,000 in the D.O.T. Because of the close link between O*NET and OES, definitions of O*NET and *Handbook* occupations will be comparable. O*NET codes and titles are not included because they were not final at press time. More information is available from the O*NET Program Director, DOL Office of Policy and Research/ETA/O*NET, 200 Constitution Ave., NW, MS N5637, Washington, DC 20210. Phone (202) 219-7161, or on the O*NET homepage: http://www.doleta.gov/programs/onet/

Also, this *Handbook* does not list 1980 Standard Occupational Classification (S.O.C.) codes, as earlier editions did. The S.O.C. is being revised. Codes from the 1998 S.O.C. revision were not final at press time. In fact, because the new S.O.C. system will serve as the framework for O*NET information, S.O.C. and O*NET codes should be the same. More information on the 1998 S.O.C. revision is available on the BLS web site: http://stats.bls.gov/soc/soc_home.htm

Reprints

All the occupational statements in the 1998-99 *Occupational Outlook Handbook* are available in reprint form. Reprints are especially useful for jobseekers who want to know about a single field and for counselors who need to stretch the contents of a single *Handbook* among many students.

The bulletin numbers and titles of all 20 reprints along with an index to the reprints are listed below. Prices for individual reprints or for a complete set of reprints as well as an order form appear on page 532.

Index

Q

R

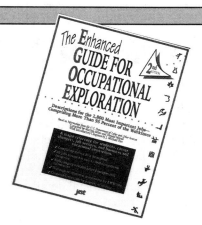

Dictionary of Occupational Titles (DOT), 4th Edition

By U.S. Department of Labor, Employment and Training Administration

This is *the* definitive career reference book because the DOT's classification system is *the* standard for describing jobs. Each job code includes detailed occupational information and reveals the level of skills required to work with people, data, and things. It's organized by major job categories and cross-referenced by industry and job title.

★ Features 12,741 occupational descriptions

★ Descriptions are appended with four occupational analysis codes

★ Indexed by occupational title and industry designations

ISBN: 1-56370-000-X
$39.00 Softcover
Order Code: J000X

ISBN: 1-56370-006-9
$48.00 Hardcover
Order Code: J0069

Young Person's Occupational Outlook Handbook

Based on the U.S. Department of Labor's Occupational Outlook Handbook

An important resource for teachers, students, counselors, and parents. The *Young Person's Occupational Outlook Handbook* is a must for school libraries and career centers. And it is an excellent first reference for anyone exploring career opportunities. Each entry includes:

★ Details on working conditions

★ School subjects related to the job

★ Suggested activities for "trying out" the job

★ Information on earnings, education or training required, and employment outlook

ISBN: 1-56370-201-0
$19.95
Order Code: J2010

The Worker Traits Data Book

By Donald Mayall

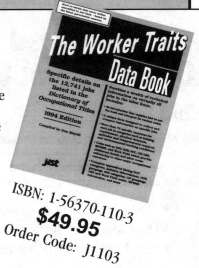

This book provides coded information on more than 70 specific measures for all the jobs in the *DOT*. It is based on the latest government sources and includes hard-to-find data never before available in one source. Includes coded information on more than 70 specific measures for all 12,741 jobs in the *Dictionary of Occupational Titles*! Other codes included are: GOE, SOC, CIP, OES, M<PSMS, and Work Field, which provide additional details and allow cross-referencing to other major occupational resources. The most comprehensive listing of worker traits ever assembled in one book!

ISBN: 1-56370-110-3
$49.95
Order Code: J1103

Career Interest Test Set

Includes:

- The Career Exploration Inventory

- The Leisure/Work Search Inventory

- The GOE Inventory

- The GOE Crosswalks Book (64 pages)

Use one or all of these self-scoring, self-interpreting tests to help clarify your career interests.

$12.95 · Order Code: CC · TestsetA

Dream Catchers Student Activity Book

Developing Career and Educational Awareness in the Intermediate Grades

By Norene Lindsay

- Introduces basic career concepts

- Develops awareness of the world of work

- Relates school to the world of work

- Helps planning to improve academic achievement

- Meets National Career Development Guidelines

$4.95 · Order Code: J515X

Pathfinder Student Workbook

Exploring Career and Educational Paths—Career and Educational Planning for Junior High and High School Students

By Norene Lindsay

Pathfinder is a high-interest workbook written specifically to help students plan their career and educational paths through high school and into post-secondary training. It is now used across the country as the text for students to develop individual career plans.

$6.95 · Order Code: J1200

Hire Learning Series

Your Guide to Successful School-to-Work Transition
By Patricia Duffy and T. Walter Wannie

This three-book series was field tested by thousands of students, incorporates the newest career education guidelines, and prepares students for successful transition from school to work.

Setting Your Career and Life Direction	Landing a Job	Succeeding in Your Work & Community
ISBN: 1-56370-188-X	ISBN: 1-56370-189-8	ISBN: 1-56370-190-1
$6.95	**$6.95**	**$6.95**
Order Code: J188X	Order Code: J1898	Order Code: J1901

Instructor's Guide	Hire Learning Set
ISBN: 1-56370-191-X	ISBN: 1-56370-192-8
$14.95	**$17.95**
Order Code: J191X	Order Code: J1928

Know-How Is the Key

Job Smarts for Students with Learning and Other Disabilities
By Dixie Lee Wright
Job Retention Specialist

Teach your students the 12 steps to finding, getting and keeping a job. This instructional manual *and* accompanying activity book are filled with enlightening exercises, case studies, homework assignments, and even advanced activities for those students who can accept greater challenges.

ISBN: 1-56370-285-1
$39.95
Order Code: J2851

Job Savvy, 2nd Edition

How to Be a Success at Work
By LaVerne L. Ludden, Ed.D.

Job Savvy is a well-researched, step-by-step workbook for job survival and success. A practical guide to workplace readiness. It was written in response to requests from many employers, employment and training programs instructors, and educators. The student workbook and the instructor's guide provide an excellent curriculum to teach basic workplace skills.

ISBN: 1-56370-304-1	ISBN: 1-56370-435-8
$10.95 Workbook	**$19.95** Instructor's Guide
Order Code: J3041	Order Code: J4358

Mind Your Own Business

Getting Started as an Entrepreneur
By LaVerne L. Ludden, Ed.D., & Bonnie Maitlen, Ed.D.

Today, millions of people consider going into business for themselves. This book can help them decide—and get off to a great start with a business best-suited to their needs and strengths. Written by two successful entrepreneurs, it's loaded with sound advice and proven, business-creating strategies.

ISBN: 1-56370-083-2

$9.95

Order Code: J0832

The Resume Solution, 2nd Edition

How to Write (and Use) a Resume That Gets Results
By David Swanson

The Resume Solution is written in a powerful style with tips that make great looking—and reading—resumes.

This book offers a step-by-step approach on how to use a resume to secure more interviews and job offers. Includes information on electronic job seeking and provides numerous examples and worksheets.

ISBN: 1-56370-180-4

$12.95

Order Code: J1804

Dare to Change Your Job and Your Life

By Carole Kanchier, Ph.D.

"Career is a path you carve out for yourself. It also involves a continuing quest for a better fit between who you are and what you do." With these words, Carole Kanchier summarizes what she's learned from thousands of interviews and then provides numerous examples of "Questers," people seeking that better fit.

ISBN: 1-56370-224-X

$14.95

Order Code: J224X

Using the Internet and the World Wide Web in Your Job Search

By Fred E. Jandt & Mary B. Nemnich

Nearly 80% of all college students expect to use the World Wide Web to find jobs!

There are thousands of job opportunities online, and this book shows how to find them, with expert advice on everything from getting connected to getting the job.

ISBN: 1-56370-292-4

$16.95

Order Code: J2924

The Pie Method for Career Success

A Unique Way to Find Your Ideal Job
By Daniel Porot;
Foreword by Richard Bolles

Porot's method combines elements of pleasure, information, and employment into a uniquely useful and motivating career planning and job search approach. The previous edition of this book sold more than 90,000 copies, and this new revision presents Porot's new concepts in a graphic and memorable way.

ISBN: 1-56370-182-0

$14.95

Order Code: J1820

Be Your Own Business

The Definitive Guide to Entrepreneurial Success
From the Editors of JIST Works, Inc.

Millions of Americans dream about starting their own businesses, but don't know where to begin. The information in this book can help readers make all the right choices on their road to becoming successful entrepreneurs. A "must" for everyone considering starting a business.

ISBN: 1-57112-082-3

$16.95

Order Code: P0823

JIST Customer Information

JIST specializes in publishing the very best results-oriented career and self-directed job search material. For sixteen years we have been a leading publisher in career assessment devices, books, videos, and software. We continue to strive to make our materials the best there are so that people can stay abreast of what's happening in the labor market, and so they can clarify and articulate their skills and experiences for themselves as well as for prospective employers. **Our products are widely available through your local bookstores, wholesalers, and distributors.**

The World Wide Web

For more occupational or book information, get on-line and see our web site at **www.jist.com**. Advance information about new products, services, and training events is continually updated.

Quantity Discounts Available!

Quantity discounts are available for businesses, schools and other organizations.

The JIST Guarantee

We want you to be happy with everything you buy from JIST. If you aren't satisfied with a product, return it to us within 30 days of purchase along with the reason for the return. Please include a copy of the packing list or invoice to guarantee quick credit to your order.

How to Order

For your convenience, the last page of this book contains an order form.

24-Hour Consumer Order Line:
Call toll free 1-800-547-8872
Please have your credit card (VISA, MC or AMEX) information ready!

Mail: Mail your order to the address listed on the order form: JIST Works, Inc.
720 North Park Avenue
Indianapolis, IN 46202-3490
Fax: Toll free 1-800-547-8329

JIST Order Form

Please copy this form if you need more lines for your order.

Purchase Order #: _____

Billing Information

Organization Name: _____

Accounting Contact: _____

Street Address: _____

_____

_____

City, State, Zip: _____

Phone Number: ( ) _____

Shipping Information (if different from above)

Organization Name: _____

Contact: _____

Street Address: (we *cannot* ship to P.O. boxes) _____

_____

City, State, Zip: _____

Phone Number: ( ) _____

**Phone:
1-800-JIST-USA
Fax: 1-800-547-8329**

Credit Card Purchases: VISA_____   MC_____   AMEX_____

Card Number: _____

Exp. date: _____

Name as on card: _____

Signature: _____

Quantity	Order Code	Product Title	Unit Price	Total

Subtotal	
+Sales Tax *Indiana Residents add 5% sales tax.*	
+Shipping / Handling *Add $3.00 for the first item and an additional $.50 for each item thereafter.*	
TOTAL	

JIST Works, Inc.
720 North Park Avenue
Indianapolis, IN 46202

JIST thanks you for your order!